Mac OS® X Lion™ Bible

Mac OS® X Lion™ Bible

Galen Gruman

WILEY

John Wiley & Sons, Inc.

Mac OS® X Lion™ Bible

Published by
John Wiley & Sons, Inc.
10475 Crosspoint Boulevard
Indianapolis, IN 46256
www.wiley.com

Copyright © 2011 by John Wiley & Sons, Inc., Hoboken, New Jersey

Published by John Wiley & Sons, Inc., Indianapolis, Indiana

Published simultaneously in Canada

ISBN: 978-1-118-02376-1

Manufactured in the United States of America

10 9 8 7 6 5 4 3 2 1

For general information on our other products and services or to obtain technical support, please contact our Customer Care Department within the U.S. at (877) 762-2974, outside the U.S. at (317) 572-3993 or fax (317) 572-4002.

Library of Congress Control Number: 2011934629

John Wiley & Sons, Inc. also publishes its books in a variety of electronic formats and by print-on-demand. Some content that appears in standard print versions of this book may not be available in other formats. For more information about John Wiley & Sons, Inc., products, visit us at www.wiley.com.

To my partner Ingall and my mother Leah.

To my two felines, Henry and Ghost, who've forlornly watched each evening as I played with a lion instead of with them.

And a toast to everyone at Apple past and present who has made Mac OS X the wonderful example of how technology that actual people use should work.

—Galen Gruman

About the Author

Galen Gruman is the principal at The Zango Group, an editorial development and book production firm. As such, he has produced books for Wiley. He also is author or coauthor of 28 books on desktop publishing, as well as coauthor of the *Mac OS X Snow Leopard Bible* and *Exploring iPad 2 For Dummies*. Gruman has covered Macintosh technology for several publications, including the trade weekly *InfoWorld,* for which he began writing in 1986 and of which he is now executive editor, and *Macworld,* whose staff he was a member of from 1991 to 1998.

Credits

Acquisitions Editor
Aaron Black

Project Editor
Martin V. Minner

Technical Editor
Paul Sihvonen-Binder

Copy Editor
Gwenette Gaddis

Editorial Director
Robyn Siesky

Business Manager
Amy Knies

Senior Marketing Manager
Sandy Smith

Vice President and Executive Group Publisher
Richard Swadley

Vice President and Executive Publisher
Barry Pruett

Project Coordinator
Katie Crocker

Graphics and Production Specialists
Carrie A. Cesavice
Samantha K. Cherolis

Quality Control Technician
Melissa Cossell

Proofreading and Indexing
Evelyn Wellborn
BIM Indexing & Proofreading Services

Contents at a Glance

Part I: Getting Started with Mac OS X 10.7 Lion 1
Chapter 1: Getting Your Mac Up and Running...3
Chapter 2: Discovering the Finder...13
Chapter 3: Using the Finder...51
Chapter 4: Working with Windows, Folders, and Files...81
Chapter 5: Searching with Spotlight..109
Chapter 6: Working with Disks...121
Chapter 7: Getting Help within Mac OS X...137
Chapter 8: Using Mac OS X's Universal Access for the Disabled 147

Part II: Using Applications and Documents 185
Chapter 9: Working with Applications...187
Chapter 10: Working with Documents...211
Chapter 11: Backing Up Files...231
Chapter 12: Working with Services...245
Chapter 13: Using AppleScript and Automator...253

Part III: Working with Mac OS X's Applications 281
Chapter 14: Working with Mac OS X Applications, Utilities, and Widgets 283
Chapter 15: Enhancing Mac OS X with Utilities..323
Chapter 16: Playing Music and Videos..331
Chapter 17: Syncing Macs and iOS Devices..357
Chapter 18: Integrating with Windows...371

Part IV: Using the Internet and Collaboration Services 393
Chapter 19: Using Safari to Surf the Web...395
Chapter 20: Using Mail, iChat, and FaceTime...423
Chapter 21: Using Address Book and iCal...471
Chapter 22: Working with Microsoft Exchange...489

Part V: Setting Up and Using Networks 501
Chapter 23: Setting Up a Network and the Internet...503
Chapter 24: Sharing Files and Other Resources...525
Chapter 25: Using Mac OS X as a Server..539

Part VI: Securing Your Mac and Your Users **563**

Chapter 26: Securing Your Mac...565
Chapter 27: Managing User Accounts 587

Part VII: Configuring Mac Preferences and Services **607**

Chapter 28: Setting System Preferences..609
Chapter 29: Managing Fonts...653
Chapter 30: Printing, Faxing, and Scanning..673

Part VIII: Appendixes **687**

Appendix A: Installing Mac OS X 10.7 Lion 689
Appendix B: What's New in Mac OS X Lion 703
Appendix C: Mac OS X Lion's Key Technologies...727
Appendix D: Commanding Unix..735

Glossary 749

Index 783

Contents

Part I: Getting Started with Mac OS X 10.7 Lion   1

Chapter 1: Getting Your Mac Up and Running 3

Starting up your Mac 3
   Choosing a startup disk.. 4
   Logging in to Mac OS X 5
      Login window options.. 6
      Password entry 6
      The login window's icon buttons 7
Turning Off and Logging Out.. 7
   Logging out of Mac OS X 8
   Putting your Mac to sleep (and waking it up) 8
   Shutting down the Mac.. 9
   Restarting the Mac 10
Resuming Where You Left Off 11
Summary.. 11

Chapter 2: Discovering the Finder 13

Using Input Devices 15
   Working with the keyboard 15
   Working with the mouse 17
   Working with the touchpad 18
Understanding the Desktop.. 21
Working with Menus 22
   Working with drop-down menus 23
   Recognizing menu symbols 25
   Touring the menu bar items 25
      The (Apple) menu.. 25
      The application menu 27
      The File menu 28
      The Edit menu.. 29
      The View menu.. 29
      The Window menu... 29
      The Help menu 30
      The Script menu 30
   Touring the menu bar icons... 30
      AppleScript... 30
      Fax... 31

Contents

Universal Access 31

VPN 31

Modem and WWAN 31

Time Machine 31

Wi-Fi 31

Displays 32

Volume 32

Battery Status 32

Time 32

Input Language 32

Keyboard & Character Viewer 32

Bluetooth 32

User 33

Spotlight 33

Using pop-up menus 33

Using contextual menus 34

Working with the Dock 35

Adding icons to the Dock 37

Removing icons from the Dock 37

Moving icons around the Dock 38

Working with the application side of the Dock 39

Working with the files and windows side of the Dock 40

Customizing the Dock 43

Adjusting the Dock's size 43

Setting the Dock magnification 43

Positioning and automatically hiding the Dock 44

Animating open applications in the Dock 45

Minimizing windows in the Dock 45

Using Exposé, Spaces, and Mission Control 46

Summary 49

Chapter 3: Using the Finder **51**

Using the Finder's Menus 51

The Finder menu 51

The File menu 52

The Edit menu 54

The View menu 54

The Go menu 56

The Window menu 58

The Help menu 58

Opening and Using Finder Windows 58

Working with the title bar 60

Investigating the toolbar 61

Working with the Sidebar 64

Contents

Working with Finder view modes..66

   Choosing a different view mode 66

   Working in icon view..66

   Working in list view...67

   Working in column view 69

   Working in Cover Flow view 70

Changing Finder Behavior for Files and Folders...................................72

   Using Get Info to change disk, folder, and file permissions.....72

   Using Get Info to change files' application owners 74

Adjusting Finder Preferences 74

Adjusting Finder View Options 76

   Desktop view settings...76

   Folder and disk view settings..77

Summary..79

Chapter 4: Working with Windows, Folders, and Files 81

Working with Windows 82

   Understanding windows controls 82

      Title bar 82

      Scroll bar 83

      Status bar 85

   Understanding active and inactive windows 85

Recognizing Folder, File, and Disk Icons...86

Interacting with Items 88

   Selecting single items...88

   Selecting multiple items 89

   Moving and copying items..90

   Deleting items 92

   Creating aliases for items..93

   Renaming items...93

   Compressing items...96

   Locking items 96

Getting Item Information..97

   Using the Info window 97

      Icon and summary 97

      Spotlight comments..98

      General 98

      More Info...99

      Name & Extension..99

      Preview..99

   Using Quick Look to view file contents 99

      Live preview icons 99

      The Quick Look window...100

      Column view mode preview 101

      The slideshow viewer..101

Contents

Working with Folders' Unique Operations 101

  Using smart folders 101

  Using folder actions 103

    Attaching actions to folders 103

    Using actions 105

    Editing actions 105

  Touring Mac OS X's special folders 105

    The system folders 105

    Working with the Home folder 106

Working with Files' Unique Operations 107

Summary 107

Chapter 5: Searching with Spotlight 109

How Spotlight Works Behind the Scenes 110

Using Spotlight 112

  Spotlight searches from the menu bar 112

  Spotlight searches from a Finder window 115

  Working with Finder search results 118

  Using Spotlight with applications 119

    Using the Spotlight contextual menu 119

    Using Spotlight with supported applications 120

Summary 120

Chapter 6: Working with Disks 121

Working with Disks and Other Storage Medias 121

  Accessing disks and volumes 122

  Ejecting disks and disconnecting from volumes 123

Recording to Optical Discs 124

  Creating a burn folder 124

  Using Finder burn 125

  Finishing the burn 125

Using Disk Utility 126

  Checking and fixing disks 127

  Restoring and copying disks 128

  Adding, partitioning, and formatting disks 129

Using RAID Redundancy 131

  Understanding RAID 131

  Setting up a RAID in Mac OS X 133

    Setting up a Mac Mini Server for RAID 133

    Installing internal hard disks on a Mac Pro 134

    Installing external hard disks for other Macs 135

    Configuring RAID in Disk Utility 135

Summary 136

Chapter 7: Getting Help within Mac OS X 137

Touring the Help Center 138
    Browsing the Help Center...139
    Searching the Help Center 140
    Navigating the Help Center 141
Using Applications' Help...142
Understanding Help Tags 144
Working with Command-Line Help 144
Exploring Other Avenues of Help..145
Summary..146

Chapter 8: Using Mac OS X's Universal Access for the Disabled 147

Setting Up Mac OS X with Universal Access 147
Enabling Visual Assistance 148
    Hearing your Mac with VoiceOver 148
    Understanding the VoiceOver keys...150
        VoiceOver keyboard commands 150
        Using keyboard help 150
    Navigating with VoiceOver...151
        Using the Dock 151
        Using the menu bar...151
        Selecting buttons, check boxes, and sliders 151
        Entering text into text fields 152
        Navigating rows and columns...152
        Using smart groups in web pages 152
    VoiceOver help...152
    Zooming in on the screen 153
    Adjusting zoom options 153
        Maximum Zoom and Minimum Zoom sliders 153
        Show Preview Rectangle When Zoomed Out option 154
        Smooth Images option 154
        Zoom Follows the Keyboard Focus option................................155
        When Zoomed In, the Screen Image Moves options 155
        Use Scroll Wheel with Modifier Keys to Zoom option............155
    Adjusting display options...156
Enabling Hearing Assistance..156
Enabling Keyboard Assistance...157
    Pressing more than one key at a time..157
    Pressing keys accidentally..159
Enabling Mouse Assistance..159
    Getting help with using the mouse or touchpad 160
    Getting help with seeing the pointer...161
    Adjusting touchpad and mouse behavior 161
    Using hot spots 162

Contents

Setting Up Speech Recognition 162
   Using a microphone 163
   Configuring speech recognition 163
   Adjusting speech recognition settings... 164
      Microphone pop-up menu 164
      Calibrate button 164
      Change Key button 165
      Listening Method options 165
      Upon Recognition options 165
   Using the Speech Feedback window 166
      Getting to know the Speech Feedback window 166
      Using Speech Feedback window controls 166
      Minimizing the Speech Feedback window 167
   Investigating the Speech Commands window 167
   Specifying active commands... 168
   Setting up the Text to Speech option 168
   Selecting text-to-speech options 169
      Announce When Alerts Are Displayed option 170
      Announce When an Application Requires Your Attention option 170
      Speak Selected Text When the Key Is Pressed option 170
      Open Date & Time Preferences button 171
      Open Universal Access Preferences button 171
Setting Up the VoiceOver Utility 171
   Adjusting the General settings... 171
      Greeting options 171
      Portable Preferences... 172
      Allow VoiceOver to Be Controlled with AppleScript option 172
   Adjusting the Verbosity settings.. 172
      Speech subpane.. 172
      Braille subpane... 173
      Text subpane 173
      Announcements subpane 173
      Hints pane.. 174
   Adjusting the Speech settings 174
      Voices subpane... 174
      Pronunciation subpane... 174
   Adjusting Navigation settings.. 175
   Adjusting Web settings 176
      Navigation subpane... 176
      Page Loading subpane.. 176
      Web Rotor subpane... 176
   Adjusting Sound settings... 177
   Adjusting the Visuals settings.. 177
      VoiceOver Cursor subpane.. 177
      Caption Panel subpane... 178

Braille Panel subpane 178

Touch subpane 178

Menus subpane..178

Adjusting the Commanders settings 179

Trackpad subpane...179

NumPad subpane 180

Keyboard subpane 180

Quick Nav subpane 181

Setting up Braille..181

Layout subpane 182

Displays subpane 182

Setting up Activities 183

Summary...184

Part II: Using Applications and Documents 185

Chapter 9: Working with Applications 187

Installing Applications in Mac OS X...188

Installing applications from the Mac App Store 188

Installing downloaded applications 190

Installing applications from disc..190

Updating applications..191

Removing applications..191

Opening Applications...192

Using and Managing the Launchpad..193

Managing Multiple Open Applications...196

Switching among applications 197

Using Hide to reduce application clutter..198

Knowing when an application wants your attention.....................................198

Surveying Applications' Controls...199

Function containers...199

Controls..202

Using Full-Screen Applications 204

Quitting Applications..205

Quitting from within an application 206

Quitting an application from the Dock..206

Quitting by logging out, shutting down, or restarting 206

Using the Force Quit command 207

Using the Force Quit dialog box 207

Using the Dock..207

Using the Activity Monitor 207

Summary..208

Contents

Chapter 10: Working with Documents **211**

Opening Documents...212

Opening documents from the Finder...212

Opening documents within an application.....................................213

The Open dialog box..214

Creating Documents..216

Creating a copy of a document...216

Creating documents with stationery pads (templates) 217

Working with a Document's Content 217

Using Cut, Copy, and Paste..218

Using drag and drop to move data around..................................219

Using drag and drop in a document......................................219

Using drag and drop between documents..............................220

Using clippings...221

Saving Documents..222

Using the Save As dialog box 223

Saving versions and copies...225

Working with Versions 225

Working with older documents...227

Closing Documents...228

Moving Documents...229

Sharing Documents with Other Users...229

Summary..230

Chapter 11: Backing Up Files **231**

Setting Up for Backup...231

Choosing a backup medium 232

Selecting backup software 233

Using Time Machine to Back Up Files 234

Using external disks for backup 235

Setting up Time Machine..236

Configuring Time Machine for backups.................................236

Choosing a backup disk 237

Choosing backup exclusions and options 238

Setting up Time Machine with a Time Capsule............................240

Using Time Machine to Restore Files 241

Using the Time Machine browser..242

Restoring files with Time Machine 243

Searching for changes...243

Exiting the Time Machine browser...243

Summary..244

Contents

Chapter 12: Working with Services. **245**

Understanding Service Availability..245

A Tour of the Common Services 246

    Development services...247

    Files and Folders services 247

    Internet services 248

    Messaging services 248

    Pictures services 248

    Searching services 249

    Text services 249

Changing Services Preferences 250

Summary...251

Chapter 13: Using AppleScript and Automator. **253**

Understanding Messages and Events...254

Introducing AppleScript...255

    The AppleScript language 255

    Scripting additions 256

Introducing AppleScript Editor 256

    Scriptable applications and environments...257

    Looking at a script window 257

Creating a Simple Script..258

Analyzing a Script 260

    Learning application commands and objects...260

    Inspecting a dictionary..261

        Displaying a dictionary window 261

        Looking at a dictionary window 262

Saving a Script 263

Creating a More Complex Script...264

    Making a Finder utility 264

    Beginning the script...264

    Seeing the script's results 265

    Using variables...265

    Capitalizing script statements..266

    Getting file information...266

    Using parentheses 266

    Working with an application 267

    Performing script statements conditionally...267

    Breaking long statements 268

    Ending the use of an application 269

    Trying out your script..270

Creating a Drag-and-Drop Script Application...271

    Retrieving dropped files 271

    Processing dropped files 272

Contents

Using a repeat loop 273
Extending the script 273
Enabling the Script Menu 274
Linking Programs across the Network 274
Allowing remote Apple events 274
Scripting across a network 275
Automating with Automator 276
Recording Actions 279
Summary 279

Part III: Working with Mac OS X's Applications   281

Chapter 14: Working with Mac OS X Applications, Utilities, and Widgets 283

Touring the Applications Folder 284
Address Book 285
App Store 286
Automator 286
Calculator 286
Chess 286
Dashboard 287
Dictionary 287
DVD Player 288
FaceTime 290
Font Book 290
iCal 290
iChat 290
Image Capture 291
iTunes 292
Launchpad 293
Mail 293
Mission Control 293
Photo Booth 293
Preview 295
Opening files 295
Capturing images 296
Adjusting images 297
Working with PDF files 297
Managing display options 298
QuickTime Player 299
Safari 299
Stickies 299
System Preferences 299

TextEdit..299

Time Machine...302

Touring the Utilities Folder 302

Activity Monitor 302

AirPort Utility 302

AppleScript Editor 303

Audio MIDI Setup...303

Bluetooth File Exchange 304

Boot Camp Assistant..305

ColorSync Utility 305

Console...306

DigitalColor Meter...306

Disk Utility 307

Grab 307

Grapher 308

Java Preferences...308

Keychain Access 309

Migration Assistant..310

Network Utility 311

Podcast Capture and Podcast Publisher 311

RAID Utility..311

System Information 311

Terminal..313

VoiceOver Utility..313

X11 313

Touring the Widgets 313

Managing widgets...314

Using the widgets that come with Mac OS X...315

Address Book 315

Calculator...315

Dictionary...315

ESPN...316

Flight Tracker..316

iCal...316

Movies...316

Ski Resort..316

Stickies..317

Stocks..317

Tile Game...318

Translation...318

Unit Converter..318

Weather..318

Web Clip 319

Contents

Widgets 319
World Clock 320
Adding widgets from other sources 320
Summary 321

Chapter 15: Enhancing Mac OS X with Utilities 323

Extending Mac OS X 324
Audio management 324
Battery monitoring 324
Conferencing 325
Disk management 325
File synchronization 325
Font management 326
Media playback and delivery 327
Remote access 327
Screen capture 327
Wi-Fi monitoring 328
Adding New Capabilities 328
Application access 329
Communications 329
File transfer 329
Security 329
Text entry 330
Summary 330

Chapter 16: Playing Music and Videos 331

Using iTunes as Your Music Library 332
Setting music preferences 333
Import settings 333
Playback settings 333
Sharing settings 334
Parental settings 335
Importing music files 335
Buying music online 336
Managing your music 339
Controlling music display 339
Syncing with iPods, iPads, and iPhones 339
Working with playlists 340
Working with Genius 341
Rating music 342
Playing your music 342
Using iTunes for Podcasts 343
Listening to Internet Radio 345
Using iTunes for TV Shows and Movies 345
Setting video preferences 345
Importing and buying videos 346

Contents

Managing your videos...346
Playing your videos..347
Using Home Sharing and AirPlay 347
Using Home Sharing 348
Using AirPlay and Apple TV 348
Watching Videos with DVD Player 348
Working with QuickTime Player 351
Playing media files 351
Editing media files 353
Creating media files 354
Exporting video and screencast files..355
Exporting audio files 356
Summary...356

Chapter 17: Syncing Macs and iOS Devices 357

Syncing via iTunes on a Mac..357
The Info pane..358
The Apps pane..359
The Books pane 361
Preferences for iOS devices 361
Syncing via iCloud...361
Syncing content and apps purchased from Apple's online stores............362
Syncing documents and other information via iCloud.............................364
Setting up iCloud..364
Using iCloud services...366
Managing iCloud storage..367
Using iCloud on Windows PCs..367
Using Cloud Storage Services...369
Summary...370

Chapter 18: Integrating with Windows 371

Working with Windows Files 372
Dealing with filenames and file extensions..373
Using disks and storage media 374
Sharing through servers 375
Connecting to PCs directly for file sharing 376
Letting Windows users connect directly to your Mac.............................378
Sharing via e-mail, FTP, and web services...380
Running Windows on Your Mac 381
Setting up Boot Camp...382
Using Windows via Boot Camp..385
Using Windows virtual machines 387
Summary...391

Contents

Part IV: Using the Internet and Collaboration Services   393

Chapter 19: Using Safari to Surf the Web 395
Navigating the Web..397
  Using hyperlinks 397
  Using bookmarks 398
  Using the Reading List...403
  Using history..404
Working with Safari's Controls...405
  Using navigation buttons 406
  Using window and tab controls..406
  Using view controls 408
  Using sharing controls...409
  Using interface controls...409
  Using specialty controls...409
Setting Safari Preferences 411
Using RSS in Safari...417
Using Other Browsers...419
Summary..421

Chapter 20: Using Mail, iChat, and FaceTime 423
Setting Up Apple's Mail..424
  Setting up new e-mail accounts..424
  Importing existing e-mail accounts 427
  Setting Mail's preferences..427
    General preferences 430
    Accounts preferences 431
    Junk Mail preferences..435
    Fonts & Colors preferences..436
    Viewing preferences 436
    Composing preferences..438
    Signatures preferences...440
    Rules preferences...441
Managing E-Mail Accounts and Mailboxes.......................................442
  Understanding mailbox folders 443
  Turning accounts on and off 446
  Using smart mailboxes...446
  Maintaining mailboxes...448
  Monitoring mail activity 450
Working with E-Mails 450
  Reading messages 451
  Writing messages 455
    Addressing the message..457
    Entering the message itself...457

Using other mail composition controls...459
Sending and saving messages...460
Replying, forwarding, and redirecting messages.................................460
Deleting, moving, and junking messages.......................................461
Using RSS Feeds in Mail..462
Working with Notes in Mail...462
Using iChat...463
Setting up iChat...463
Chatting with people...465
Using audio and video...466
Using screen and file sharing...467
Using FaceTime..468
Summary...470

Chapter 21: Using Address Book and iCal **471**
Working with Address Book...471
Adding and editing cards..472
Working with groups..473
Working with distribution lists...475
Managing cards and groups...476
Setting Address Book preferences...476
General preferences..476
Accounts preferences 477
Template...477
Phone..478
vCard..478
Working with iCal...478
Working with iCal accounts...479
Navigating your calendar...480
Creating and editing events..481
Working with invitations...482
Working with to-do items...484
Publishing and subscribing to calendars...485
Setting iCal preferences...486
General preferences..486
Accounts preferences...487
Advanced preferences..487
Summary...488

Chapter 22: Working with Microsoft Exchange. **489**
How Exchange Works..490
Using Mac OS X's Mail with Exchange...491
Setting up Mail for Exchange 2007 or 2010..491
Setting up iCal for Exchange 2000 or 2003...493
Working with an Exchange e-mail account in Mail...................................493

Contents

Using iCal with Exchange...495
    Setting up iCal for Exchange 2007 or 2010......................................495
    Setting up iCal for Exchange 2000 or 2003......................................495
    Using iCal with Exchange 2007 or 2010..496
Using Address Book with Exchange...496
    Setting up Address Book for Exchange 2007 496
    Setting up Address Book for Exchange 2000 and 2003..................497
Using an iPhone, iPad, or iPod Touch with Exchange 497
Summary...499

Part V: Setting Up and Using Networks   501

Chapter 23: Setting Up a Network and the Internet 503

Understanding Network Technologies...504
    Wired connections 506
    Wireless connections 506
Setting Up a Mac for a Local Network...507
    Setting up Ethernet connections..508
    Setting up Wi-Fi connections..512
    Setting up a Bluetooth network...514
    Setting up a VPN..514
Connecting Macs Directly..515
    Ethernet direct connection...515
    FireWire direct connection 515
    Wi-Fi direct connection...516
    Bluetooth direct connection 516
Connecting to the Internet..516
    Using Internet connection devices...517
    Setting up connections manually...518
    Setting up connections with assistance 519
    Disconnecting from the Internet..520
Using Network Utility...521
    Info..521
    Netstat..522
    Ping...522
    Lookup 522
    Traceroute..522
    Whois..523
    Finger..523
    Port Scan 523
Summary...523

Contents

Chapter 24: Sharing Files and Other Resources **525**

   Enabling File and Other Sharing..526

   Accessing Files and Other Resources...531

      Sharing files with other Macs..531

      Sharing files with Bluetooth...533

      Sharing files with AirDrop...533

      Sharing screens...535

      Sharing other resources...537

   Summary..538

Chapter 25: Using Mac OS X as a Server **539**

   Serving Web Pages from Mac OS X..540

   Using Mac OS X Lion Server..541

      Setting Up Mac OS X Lion Server...542

      Using the Server application..543

         Mac server setup...543

         Setting up users and groups...545

         Enabling and configuring services..548

         Monitoring server status...549

      Working with configuration profiles..550

         Creating configuration profiles...551

         Managing users and devices via configuration profiles...........555

         Managing devices directly...556

      Using the Server Admin tool..556

      Using the Workgroup Manager tool...559

      Using the System Image Utility tool..560

   Summary..562

Part VI: Securing Your Mac and Your Users   **563**

Chapter 26: Securing Your Mac **565**

   Identifying the Four Key Vulnerabilities..566

      Securing the Mac itself...566

      Securing your personal data...567

      Securing your files..567

      Securing your Mac environment...568

   Using Password Protection...568

      Setting the user account...568

      Enforcing password use..570

      Preventing startup from other disks...572

      Setting passwords for applications...573

      Using Keychain Access...574

Contents

Using Encryption...577

Protecting your Location Information...579

Plugging Security Holes..580

    Protecting yourself from network attacks..580

    Protecting yourself from malware...583

Summary...585

Chapter 27: Managing User Accounts 587

Setting Up User Accounts..588

    Adjusting personal settings...588

        Name, password, and related settings 589

        Login items..591

        Login options..592

    Managing additional user accounts...594

        Adding accounts...594

        Managing accounts..595

        Deleting accounts..595

        Using guest accounts...596

        Using account groups..596

    Switching among accounts...597

Using Parental Controls..598

    Apps pane..599

    Web pane..601

    People pane..601

    Time Limits pane 602

    Other pane 603

    Getting activity logs..604

    Settings management...604

Summary...605

Part VII: Configuring Mac Preferences and Services   607

Chapter 28: Setting System Preferences 609

Adjusting System Preferences...609

    Personal preferences 611

        Desktop & Screen Saver...611

        Dock..614

        General...614

        Language & Text 616

        Mission Control..620

        Security & Privacy...621

        Spotlight..621

        Universal Access 622

Hardware preferences..622
    CDs & DVDs..622
    Displays 623
    Energy Saver...625
    FibreChannel 628
    Ink 628
    Keyboard...629
    Mouse 631
    Print & Scan 634
    Sound...636
    Trackpad 637
    Xsan 640
Internet and wireless preferences 640
    Bluetooth...640
    Mail, Contacts & Calendars...644
    Network...645
    Sharing..645
System preferences..646
    Date & Time..646
    Parental Controls...647
    Profiles..647
    Software Update 647
    Speech 648
    Startup Disk..651
    Time Machine...652
    Users & Groups..652
Summary...652

Chapter 29: Managing Fonts. 653
Exactly What Is a Font? 653
Font Formats..654
    PostScript Type 1...655
    TrueType..655
    PostScript Multiple Master...656
    OpenType..656
    dfont..656
Where Fonts Reside...657
Managing Fonts in Font Book..657
    Automatic font monitoring...658
    Adding fonts...659
    Previewing fonts 659
    Working with font collections......................................660
    Managing fonts 663
    Finding fonts..665

Contents

Accessing Special Characters 665

    Using keyboard shortcuts 665

    Using other tools 668

Summary 671

Chapter 30: Printing, Faxing, and Scanning 673

Setting Up Printers, Fax Modems, and Scanners 673

    Adding devices 674

    Configuring printers 677

    Configuring fax modems 678

    Configuring scanners 679

Printing 680

    Using the Print dialog box 680

    Managing the print queue 682

Faxing 683

Scanning 684

Summary 685

Part VIII: Appendixes   687

Appendix A: Installing Mac OS X 10.7 Lion 689

Preparing for Installation 690

    Setting up a Mac for installation 691

    Making a note of system settings 691

    Backing up your data 692

Running the Mac OS X Installer 692

    License agreement window 693

    Disk selector window 693

    Preparing to Install window 693

    Installation progress window 694

Setting Up Your Mac 694

    Welcome window 695

    Select Your Keyboard window 695

    Server settings window 695

    Transfer Information to This Mac window 695

        Transferring information from another computer 696

        Transferring information from another disk 697

    Enter Your Apple ID window 698

    Registration Information window 698

    Create Your Computer Account window 698

    Select a Picture for This Account window 699

    Select Time Zone window 699

    Secure My Mac window 699

Contents

Don't Forget to Register window..700
Thank You window 700
Installing the Java Runtime...700
Reinstalling or Recovering Mac OS X...700
Launching the Recovery System 701
Getting help online...701
Reinstalling Mac OS X...702
Restoring from Time Machine 702
Using Disk Utility 702

Appendix B: What's New in Mac OS X Lion 703

Installing and Setting Up Mac OS X..703
Starting Up and Logging In 704
Using the Finder 705
Application and window navigation 705
Gestures..705
Finder menus..705
Shortcuts 706
The Dock 706
Finder, application, and document windows 706
The Sidebar 706
Finder windows 707
All windows 708
Icons, files, and folders 708
Spotlight...708
Using System Preferences 709
Desktop & Screen Saver 709
Displays..710
Dock..710
Energy Saver 710
General 710
Language & Text..710
Mail, Contacts & Calendar 710
Mission Control...711
Mouse and Trackpad 711
Profiles 711
Sound 711
Time Machine 712
Using the Help System 712
Working with Applications and Documents 712
Application core capabilities 712
Application document controls 713
Application helper services...714
Mac OS X's general-purpose applications 714

Contents

Preview 715
Safari web browser.. 715
Media playback applications 716
Mail application 717
Address Book application 718
iCal application 719
Working with Disks and Backups 720
Working with User Accounts and Parental Controls................................. 720
Securing Your Mac.. 721
Working with Networks... 722
Working with Fonts 723
Printing, Faxing, and Scanning.. 723
Using Speech and the VoiceOver Utility.. 724
Working with Unix 725
Using Mac OS X Server... 725

Appendix C: Mac OS X Lion's Key Technologies 727

Core Processing Technologies... 728
Darwin.. 728
XNU kernel... 728
64-bit kernel 729
Grand Central Dispatch 729
Symmetric multi-processing... 730
Preemptive multi-tasking 730
OpenCL 730
Protected memory and advanced memory management.................... 731
Graphics and Media Technologies.. 731
Quartz... 731
OpenGL... 731
QuickTime.. 732
Aqua.. 732
Mac OS X Application Environments.. 732
Cocoa.. 732
Carbon.. 733
Frameworks.. 733
Java... 734
Core Location... 734
BSD and X11... 734

Appendix D: Commanding Unix 735

Working with Terminal.. 736
Multiple sessions... 737
The command prompt.. 738
Remote access 739

Contents

The shell's special characters 739

Scripting the shell 740

Using Basic Unix Commands 741

Reading man pages 741

Managing files and directories 742

Moving about folders 742

Viewing a folder's contents 743

Copying, moving, renaming, and deleting files and folders 743

Changing file and folder permissions 744

Getting disk and file system statistics 744

Logging in as a different user or as a superuser 745

Using standard input, standard output, and pipes 746

Using X11 747

Glossary 749

Index 783

Introduction

For those who've used the Mac since the mid-1980s as I have, it's hard to believe that it's been 10 years since the first desktop version of Mac OS X (10.0 Cheetah) was released, in March 2001, at a period when Apple's very survival seemed uncertain after years of chaotic management. Returned CEO Steve Jobs changed that chaos into focus and innovation, and a steady stream of improved Mac OS X "big cats" have followed: Mac OS X 10.1 Puma in September 2001, Mac OS X 10.2 Jaguar in August 2002, Mac OS X 10.3 Panther in October 2003, Mac OS X 10.4 Tiger in April 2005, Mac OS X 10.5 Leopard in October 2007, and Mac OS X 10.6 Snow Leopard in August 2009. Now it's time for the biggest cat of all in Apple's feline menagerie: Mac OS X 10.7 Lion. (What's next? Mac OS X Sabertooth? Cougar? Lynx? Tabby?)

Mac OS X Lion moves Mac OS X (pronounced "Mac Oh Ess Ten," by the way) into a new direction, adopting many of the user interface innovations in iOS, the mobile operating system used in iPhones, iPads, and iPod Touches. There's expanded support for gestures, which are easier than ever to use on Macs given that touchpads are standard in MacBooks and add-on touchpads like the Apple Magic Trackpad and Apple Magic Mouse (a touchpad-on-a-mouse) are widely available. Several features are directly lifted from iOS:

- The new full-screen view for applications designed to use it gets rid of the menu bar—something iOS did without from the very beginning.

- The Auto Save feature for applications designed to use it ensures that what you do is saved as you do it—just as on an iOS device.

- The resume feature pays attention when you log out, restart, or shut down, and it has Mac OS X load whatever applications and documents you were working the next time it starts up (or you log back in) to simulate the instant-on capabilities of iOS. It's not instant-on, but at least it brings you back to where you left off.

- The pop-over user interface element—sort of a pop-up menu–like small dialog box— has been adopted from iOS.

- The new Launchpad is a copy of the iOS home screens, where the screen is one big set of application icons. (I have to say I think this feature is unnecessary, because the Dock does a better job of providing application access. Of all the iOS derivations, it has the least natural fit in Mac OS X. Maybe I'll grow to like it over time. And Mac OS X doesn't make you use it.)

- The iCal and Address Book applications have adopted much of the look and feel of their iPad versions, and Mail has adopted the columnar layout of its iPad version.

But don't think for a minute that Mac OS X Lion is Mac OS X with some slapped-on iOS interface elements, or that Apple has run out of steam on the Mac and can only bring iOS features to it. Mac OS X has many enhancements that have nothing to do with iOS:

- AirDrop is one of those incredibly simple ideas that you wonder why it hadn't been done before. Mac OS X Lion users on your network automatically show up in the Finder window's Sidebar; click a user to be able to drag files into that user's Documents folder (with their permission). It's instant file sharing. But note that it works only with Macs that have the right Wi-Fi hardware, which restricts it mostly to Macs made in 2010 and later.

- Mission Control makes Exposé very powerful. Exposé is a nice feature that lets you see all windows open when you click and hold an application icon in the Dock. But it's a pain to go from icon to icon to see what document windows are open. Mission Control shows all open applications with their windows so you now see everything open in Mac OS X and can easily navigate among them. Plus Mission Control lets you switch spaces, those application groups that I think are underused by most people; maybe being available via Mission Control will expose more people to Mac OS X's Spaces capability.

- The new Versions capability keeps a copy of each version of a file *within that file* as you save it, so you can go back in time to a previous version as necessary. The idea of internal version histories is hardly new, but I've never seen it done as elegantly and simply as in Mac OS X Lion. And the use of the Time Machine interface to navigate previous versions was genius.

- A nice accompaniment to Versions is file locking, where after a document has been unchanged for a specific period (two weeks is the default), you can't accidentally save it. You also can lock a document immediately using a new icon menu in compatible applications. Many of us have trained ourselves to press ⌘+S periodically just to be safe, and when we open an old file and do that without thinking, we sometimes save stray changes we didn't intend to. With this feature, Mac OS X makes you confirm that you want save a file that's been unopened for that period, just to be sure.

- The message-threading capability in Mail has been enhanced so that in the revised Message Viewer mode, you see all messages—not just their subject lines—in the thread. Now you really can follow the whole thread (which Mac OS X calls a *conversation*).

- You can now encrypt your entire startup disk in Mac OS X Lion using the FileVault capability, as well as your Time Machine backups and any disks you format with Disk Utility. Encryption is not new to Mac OS X, but before it was restricted to each user's Home folder using the FileVault feature—which frankly left too many holes in Mac OS X's data security. That's no longer an issue, and in Apple style, the encryption process is easy and stays out of your way (like it is and does in iOS).

- Mac OS X Lion Server is now an optional $50 add-on to Lion; it's no longer a separate operating system product. Lion Server has some great features for a workplace, including the ability to let iPads sync wirelessly to it and to create configuration profiles for Mac OS X and iOS users. Some home users may find Lion Server useful, but it's not a media/mobile server. Still, it's easier to use and does everything regular Lion does, so you can try it out and ignore the server applications if they end up being too complex or not useful for you.

- Then you'll find lots of subtle changes in the Finder, such as crisper icons in the Sidebar to an indicator of how many files will be copied when you drag-copy them. Well, mostly subtle. Mac OS X Lion by default gets rid of the scroll bars in windows if you use a gesture-based input device such as the Magic Trackpad, relying on your actions to clue it in when you need them so it can display them as temporary overlays. It's a shocking change that I still haven't gotten used to, and am not sure I will. Fortunately, you can turn that behavior off and leave scroll bars always on.

As you can see, Mac OS X Lion is coming in with a roar. (Appendix B describes all the changes.) And I think that roar will only get louder a people move up to it and spend more time with it. Apple never ceases to amaze me in how it pushes Mac OS X forward, without making changes for change's sake or messing up what came before. If you've watched Microsoft's bumpy journey from Windows 95 to 98 to 2000 to XP to Vista to 7, and how it's foundered in the mobile market, you've seen how a company can really mess up what it has and how hard it is to repair the damage.

Not only has Apple avoided that sad fate, it's expanded from Mac OS X to iOS and kept cross-pollinating the two to make both stronger. Mac OS X Lion is a very visible example of that, but that cross-pollination has been there since the first iPhone was released in 2007 (iOS, after all, is based on the core of Mac OS X, not some totally separate technology). Apple CEO Steve Jobs has said that this cross-pollination is intentional, part of Apple's vision of making easy computing accessible to everyone across the spectrum of devices. Mac OS X Lion delivers on that.

What This Book Offers

So, given Mac OS X's reputation for being intuitive, why do you need this book? For one, because Mac OS X packs lots of capabilities that you may never realize exist unless you go looking for them. This book does the looking for you, so you can take advantage of Mac OS X's many capabilities.

I should note that the Lion edition of the *Mac OS X Bible* is significantly reorganized and rewritten to focus more on *using* Mac OS X. Also, I've found that many people, even longtime Mac users, aren't familiar with some of Mac OS X's capabilities. So I expanded the first part of the book significantly and broke it into more manageable chunks (chapters) to really show you the power of the Finder, and not assume you knew its ins and outs.

In addition to pointing out and explaining how to take advantage of Mac OS X's many strengths, I also identify any weaknesses or ambiguities in Mac OS X's interface and tools and explain how to overcome them—these situations are rare, but they do exist.

Macintosh users fall into several classes, and this book is designed to address them all:

- Users new to the Mac but familiar with other computer operating systems (namely, Windows)
- Users new to computers, period (though there are fewer of those these days!)
- Mac users who know the basics of Mac OS X but have decided to get a deeper understanding of what Mac OS X can do for them so they can take better advantage of it
- Experienced Mac users looking to see what's new and different in the latest version of Mac OS X

No matter which class you're in, this book addresses your needs. Regardless of your level of experience with Macs, this book can help you use Mac OS X efficiently and guide you to discovering more of the operating system's potential.

How to Read This Book

Mac OS X Lion Bible is made up of 30 chapters divided into seven parts, plus five appendixes. The parts cover different aspects of Mac OS X, so you're likely to read parts in the order of interest to you. Still, I suggest that everyone read Part I first to get the basic lay of the land in how Mac OS X operates, so you have the fundamentals in place for the rest of the book.

The following sections provide a brief description of the parts in *Mac OS X Lion Bible*.

Part I: Getting Started with Mac OS X 10.7 Lion

This part walks you through the basic Finder user interface and navigation tools in Mac OS X. After a brief chapter on how to turn on and start up your Mac, and how to shut it down, this part gets deep into the Finder, starting with a chapter in the Finder's basic interface: the Finder's menu bar, Dock, and desktop, plus the Mission Control, Exposé, and Spaces functions that let you switch among applications and windows. That chapter also explains the Mac's special keys, how to use the mouse, and how to use gestures on a touchpad. The next two chapters explain the other two fundamental aspects of the Finder: how to use it and its Finder windows, and how to use the Finder to manipulate files, folders, and disks. The rest of this part investigates specialty aspects of the Finder, including the Spotlight search capability, the help system, Disk Utility to format and repair disks, and the Universal Access extensions to the Finder that help people with disabilities use Mac OS X.

Part II: Using Applications and Documents

The Finder is critical to using Mac OS X, but the whole point of a computer is to do stuff. Mac OS X does stuff by working with applications and documents (from text reports to movies). Mac OS X provides a common set of capabilities for working with applications and documents—how to run them, how to work within them, how to save them, and how to safeguard them via backup. The chapters in this part explain each of these aspects of using any standard application or document. They also show how to work with the special application helpers that come with Mac OS X (called *services*) and how to use scripting and the Automator to create your own applications.

Part III: Working with Mac OS X's Applications

In addition to enabling applications, Mac OS X comes with a whole bunch of applications to do the basics that we all need done. Chapter 14 tours all these applications and utilities, and Chapter 16 delves into the media applications that come with Mac OS X: iTunes and QuickTime Player. Other chapters look at third-party utilities you might want to consider using in addition to what Mac OS X provides, how to run Windows applications on your Mac and connect to Windows users elsewhere, and how to use Apple's iCloud and other cloud services.

Part IV: Using the Internet and Collaboration Services

Everyone is online these days, using the Internet for communicating, collaborating, accessing services, and getting information. This part looks at Mac OS X's applications that help you do all that: the Safari web browser, the Mail e-mail client, the iChat messaging tool, the FaceTime videoconferencing utility, the Address Book contacts manager, and the iCal calendar manager. It also explains how to use Mac OS X with Microsoft's popular corporate e-mail server, Exchange.

Part V: Setting Up and Using Networks

Many Mac users connect to each other via networks, not just via the Internet—even at home, where it's common to have multiple computers and other devices (printers, TiVos, and Apple TVs, for example) connected via a wired (Ethernet) and/or wireless (Wi-Fi) network. Or they connect to the Internet via a network, using a shared DSL modem or cable modem—or a network at the office. This part explains how to connect to various networks, as well as how to share files over the network and even control and observe other users' Macs from your Mac (a great way to help your retiree parents remotely, or for your college-age kids to help you).

Part VI: Securing Your Mac and Your Users

Because Macs are usually connected to the Internet, share files, and/or have multiple users, there's a strong chance that your confidential or personal information will get exposed. There's also the threat of getting a computer virus on your Mac. This part explains how to protect your data and your Mac, how to manage multiple user accounts on a Mac, and how to manage the information the Mac collects on your current location. It also shows how parents can set and manage their kids' Macs to keep them safe from the outside world—and be sure they don't spend all night on their Macs.

Part VII: Configuring Mac Preferences and Services

Because everyone's different, Mac OS X must accommodate different preferences and working styles. It does so using the System Preferences application, which lets you set controls for as many as 31 sets of aspects of Mac OS X, from the background of your desktop to how your data is secured. Mac OS X also provides tools to manage the fonts used on the Mac (for all those fancy documents you create) and to connect to printers, fax modems, and scanners. This part explains how to use those tools.

Part VIII: Appendixes

The five appendixes cover a range of items: how to install (or recover) Mac OS X, what's new in Mac OS X Lion, the key technologies under the hood of Mac OS X, how to use Unix on a Mac, and a glossary of all the special Mac and computer terms that you may not be 100-percent clear on their meaning.

Conventions Used in This Book

Before I begin showing you the ins and outs of Mac OS X Lion, I need to spend a few minutes reviewing the terms and conventions used in this book.

Menu commands

The Mac OS X commands that you select using the program menus appear in this book in normal typeface. When you choose some menu commands, a related pop-up menu appears. If this book describes a situation in which you need to select one menu and then choose a command from a secondary menu or list box, it uses an arrow symbol. For example, "Choose File ➪ Open" means that you should choose the Open command from the File menu.

Shortcuts

Many functions in Mac OS X are accomplished by pressing one or more keys. If more than one key is involved, you press all but the last in the shortcut sequence I provide, then press the last key, and finally release them all. For example, ⌘+K means to press and hold ⌘, then press K, and finally release both keys. Likewise, Control+Option+Shift+U means to press and hold Control, Option, and Shift and—when all three are being held down—press U, then release all four keys. Note that you do *not* press the + key in such shortcuts; I use that symbol so you know these keys are pressed together.

Note that Mac OS X's menus and dialog boxes typically don't show the + symbol when they display keyboard shortcuts—but some applications' help systems do.

Cross-Reference

Macs have several keyboard characters you won't find on a PC or typewriter (remember those?), plus it supports the use of mouse movements and finger gestures on a touchpad to work with onscreen objects. Chapter 2 explains these keys, mouse actions, and gestures. ∎

Literal text

This book uses boldface to indicate literal text; that is, text that you should type exactly as is. I use boldface to indicate text that I instruct you to type. For example, "Type **localhost**, and press Return to see local services."

This book also uses typewriter font to indicate URLs (web addresses), AppleScript and other code, and pathnames for Mac OS X folders—computerese text, basically. For example, "Go to `www.apple.com` and search for the Migration Assistant for Windows Utility" and "The fonts are stored in the `\`*`username`*`\Library\Fonts` folder." (By the way, the italicized text means "fill in the actual user name here.")

When I use both boldface and typewriter font, I'm saying type that computerese into some field or other location.

Windows, dialog boxes, and panes

Mac OS X has a mechanism called a *window* that opens in an application for its contents, such as text or movies. Some applications have an *application window* that contains all its controls and contents; most applications have *document windows* that contain the contents of whatever you're working on within the application. The Finder—the application that you use to work with disks, folders, and files—has its own type of window called the Finder window. And there are other windows you may see—such as informational and status windows—that show the progress of a disk copy or the details on a disk's contents and settings.

Within applications, Mac OS X uses dialog boxes to offer up a bunch of related features in one place. Dialog boxes may have options that open a subsidiary group of options, called a *settings sheet*. Dialog boxes are the most common way to access options in programs; when a dialog box is open, you can't use other features in that application.

In many dialog boxes and in some windows, you may see a feature that has proved to be quite popular called *tabbed panes*. This is a method of stuffing several dialog boxes into one dialog box or window. You see tabs, somewhat like those in file folders, and when you click a tab, the pane of options for that tab comes to the front of the dialog box or window. This book tells you to go to the pane, which you do by clicking the tab where the name of the pane is to display the pane. For example, "Go to the General pane" means click the General tab in the current dialog box or window. But some panes don't have tabs; instead, they are accessed via a button. And some panes are essentially subdivisions of a dialog box or window, a defined space in the existing dialog box or window, rather than something you switch to via a button or tab.

Cross-Reference

Chapter 9 shows all the kinds of user interface elements—including the new pop-over element borrowed from iOS—you can expect to work with in applications, and Chapter 4 explains how windows and their controls work. ■

Labels

I've used big, bold labels throughout this book to call your attention to points that are particularly important or worth noting.

New Feature

The New Feature label indicates a technique or action that is new to or revised in Mac OS X Lion. ■

Tip

The Tip label indicates a technique or action in Mac OS X that will save you time or effort. ■

Note

The Note label indicates information that you should remember for future use—something that may seem minor or inconsequential but will, in reality, resurface. ■

Caution

The Caution label is used to warn you of potential hang-ups or pitfalls you may encounter while using Mac OS X (and how to avoid them). ■

Cross-Reference

The Cross-Reference label points you to different parts of the book that contain related or expanded information on a particular topic. ■

Part I

Getting Started with Mac OS X 10.7 Lion

IN THIS PART

Chapter 1
Getting Your Mac Up and Running

Chapter 2
Discovering the Finder

Chapter 3
Using the Finder

Chapter 4
Working with Windows, Folders, and Files

Chapter 5
Searching with Spotlight

Chapter 6
Working with Disks

Chapter 7
Getting Help within Mac OS X

Chapter 8
Using Mac OS X's Universal Access for the Disabled

Getting Your Mac Up and Running

IN THIS CHAPTER

Starting up and logging in

Logging off and turning off your Mac

Putting your Mac to sleep

Resuming where you left off

There's something about the Mac's startup chime. Most computers today play a sound as they start up, but the Mac started the whole idea decades ago. And even today, its sound has the right length and warmth—not too long, not too loud, and comfortably familiar.

That chime tells you that the Mac has in fact started and that basic hardware elements inside your Mac (hard disk, processor, memory, and so on) are all operational. After this chime sounds, Mac OS X tests the Mac's hardware (that's when you see the gray screen with the Apple logo and the spinning-wheel indicator), and then actually loads Mac OS X itself (that's when the screen turns blue). When you see the menu bar at the top of the screen and your desktop background has loaded, you know Mac OS X is ready to go.

The entire startup—also called *boot*—process takes about 30 to 45 seconds, depending on the speed of your Mac. Note that on faster Macs, some of the events may pass too quickly for you to notice.

Starting up your Mac

You start a Mac running Mac OS X 10.7 Lion in the following ways:

- **Press the power button on the Mac.**
- **Press the power button on some Apple Cinema Display LCD monitors.** Note that on some older models, the power button may simply switch the display off; the Apple LED Cinema Display does not have a power button.

Dealing with Startup Problems

If your Mac does not start up correctly or at all, try booting up from another boot disk (if you have one; it can even be the installation DVD of the previous [Snow Leopard] version of Mac OS X) and make sure the startup disk still contains its folders and files (in case it was accidentally wiped out or corrupted, such as during a power failure). You also can run utilities such as Disk Utility from a Snow Leopard installation DVD to try to repair any disk issues, as Chapter 6 explains. Third-party fix-it tools such as TechTool Pro ($100; www.micromat.com) enable you to create a bootable partition on your hard disk from which you can run its repair utilities.

If you're an advanced user (or a brave one), the Mac has three special startup modes you can use to troubleshoot a Mac that is not starting up correctly. One is single-user mode (press and hold ⌘+S during startup), which boots you into the Mac's Unix core, where you can type Unix commands to explore and troubleshoot the system. Appendix D has more information on working with Unix.

The second special startup mode is verbose mode (press and hold ⌘+V during startup), which displays a list of all startup activities and any error messages. This may help you identify the problem (such as a login item that is corrupt and needs to be deleted); you'll have to boot from a different disk to delete or modify any such files if the Mac won't boot from its normal startup disk. Note that neither single-user or verbose mode works if you've used Firmware Password Utility to protect the Mac from unauthorized use, as Chapter 26 explains.

The third special startup mode is the new Recovery System (press and hold ⌘+R during startup), from which you can run diagnostic utilities such as Disk Utility (see Chapter 6) and reinstall Mac OS X if necessary, as Appendix A explains.

Note

Check whether the Mac has already been turned on and is in sleep mode. In this case, the screen is dark, so it's easy to believe the Mac is turned off. You can tell if the Mac is in sleep mode if a light is pulsating on its case. This is a visual cue that the Mac is asleep; the pulsing light is meant to evoke snoring. If the Mac is asleep, tapping the mouse, touchpad, or keyboard wakes it up. But don't panic if the Mac is asleep and you press its power button: That wakes it up as well, though usually you'll get a dialog box asking if you want to shut it down, put it to sleep, or restart it; just click Cancel to keep it on. ■

Choosing a startup disk

By default, Mac OS X starts up from your primary disk—the hard disk inside your Mac. But it can start from other disks as well, such as DVDs and external hard disks. It can even start up from a disk image on the network. You might start from a DVD—such as the previous Mac OS X Snow Leopard's installation DVD—to run Disk Utility on a non-starting primary disk. You might start up from a bootable external disk that contains applications (including the Mac OS X Lion installer) or setup configurations you are testing (something developers and IT staff might do, but not regular users).

To choose your startup disk, you have several choices:

- Press and hold Option as the Mac's startup chime begins; a screen appears showing icons for each disk available to boot from (you can release Option then). Select the desired disk by using the mouse or touchpad or by pressing ← or → until the desired disk is highlighted (an ↑ icon button appears below it). Then press Return or click the ↑ icon button to boot into the selected disk.

- Press and hold the C key as the Mac's startup chime begins to start up from a CD or DVD. Note that this method is guaranteed to work with Apple's SuperDrives, which come with every Mac but the MacBook Air (and you can buy an external one for that laptop). If you have another manufacturer's DVD drive in or attached to your Mac, it may or may not be bootable.

- Press and hold the D key as the Mac's startup chime begins to start up from the first internal disk in a Mac that has multiple internal disks (meaning a Mac Pro).

- Press and hold the N key as the Mac's startup chime begins to start up from the network. (A network startup disk image must be properly configured and enabled, and the Mac must be connected to the network server that hosts the disk image.)

- Press and hold the T key as the Mac's startup chime begins to boot the Mac into Target Disk mode, which lets another Mac connected to it via a FireWire cable see it as an external disk.

- Boot your Mac from its default disk, and then choose ➪ System Preferences. Go to the Startup Disk system preference (by clicking its icon or choosing View ➪ Startup Disk), choose a startup disk from the list, and click Restart. Note that this startup-disk choice remains in effect each time you start the Mac until you change the Startup Disk system preference again. (By contrast, pressing and holding one of the keys during startup changes the default startup disk for just that one time.)

Note

A system preference is the method that Mac OS X uses to store user preferences on how Mac OS X operates. Some third-party services that work across applications also install system preferences. They're all presented in the Systems Preferences application, which is available at all times from the menu. Chapter 28 surveys the system preferences. ∎

Logging in to Mac OS X

After the Mac has finished its startup process, the login procedure begins. The login procedure essentially identifies you to the computer, as a security measure, to ensure that only people authorized to use your Mac can access it; it also serves a second purpose of activating your personal workspace (called a *user account*, explained in Chapter 27), which contains your applications, preferences, and documents.

The login process is mandatory when you start (or restart) the Mac, but you may never see it occur. That's because by default Mac OS X automatically logs into the primary user account that was created when you first installed Mac OS X. Thus, whenever a user turns on the Mac, he or she is taken directly to the desktop and can begin using the computer.

Login window options

It is possible to disable the automatic login (Chapter 27 explains how to set up user accounts and login options). If you disable automatic login, the Mac asks for your username and password before logging in to your user account and taking you to the desktop.

New Feature

The login window in Mac OS X Lion has been redesigned for a slicker look. But it works the same way as in previous versions of Mac OS X. ■

You might disable automatic login for a Mac used at an office or other public space, so no one but you can use your computer after it is shut down. If automatic login is disabled, you might see one of two login windows when you start the Mac:

- **List of users:** One login window option presents a list of users, where you click your name or the icon representing you from the list of users (for Macs that have multiple accounts set up, such as for a family computer), and then enter your password in the field that appears. A check mark appears to the left of the currently logged-in user name. (If you accidentally selected the wrong user from the list, you can click the ← icon button to the left of the username to return to the list of users.)

- **Name and password:** The other login window option presents a Name text field and a Password text field, and you must type both to log in. This is meant to be more secure, so a visitor must know or guess both the username and password.

The login window also appears after you log out of Mac OS X (a process explained later in this chapter) or when you switch users by using Mac OS X's Fast User Switching feature to let people switch from one user account without restarting or logging out; Chapter 27 explains how to set up and switch accounts.

Password entry

If you enter your username or password incorrectly, the login window shakes sideways. The Password text field also clears so you can reenter the password. Note that the Name text field does not automatically clear; for security reasons, Mac OS X does not inform users if they have entered a wrong username. If you incorrectly entered the username, press the Tab key to highlight the text in the Name text field, so you can reenter it.

Note

Passwords are case-sensitive, so capitalization must match that of the password as originally set up. ■

If you enter the password incorrectly three times in a row, a password hint appears at the bottom of the screen. Clicking the Forgot Password button also reveals the password hint. (You enter password hints when creating a user account.)

New Feature

Clicking the ? icon button on the right side of the password field when logging in opens a pop-over that has an option for resetting the password using your Apple ID, if you enabled that capability during installation (see Appendix A). That pop-over also shows your password hint, should you want to see if before it's automatically displayed after three failed login attempts. ■

The login window's icon buttons

In the login window, three icon buttons appear at the bottom of the window: Sleep, Restart, and Shut Down. You can use these immediately, instead of having to log in to the Mac first. They come in handy when you accidentally turn on the Mac and want to put it back to sleep or shut it down.

You can configure Mac OS X so that the Sleep, Restart, and Shut Down buttons do not appear in the login window. To do so, choose ➪ System Preferences and go to the Users & Groups system preference, click the Login Options button, and then deselect the Show Sleep and Shut Down Buttons option. By coupling this setting with the use of the Firmware Password utility explained in Chapter 26, you can make it all but impossible for someone to circumvent the requirement to log in.

Turning Off and Logging Out

When you've finished using your Mac, you have several options:

- Put the Mac to sleep.

- Leave the Mac on until the screen saver engages and then, later, the Energy Saver system preference settings put the computer to sleep automatically. (See Chapter 28 for details about the Desktop & Screen Saver and Energy Saver system preferences.)

- Log out of your account so people cannot access your Mac without first entering your (or their) login password.

- Shut down the Mac, which logs out of your account and closes the operating system, before switching off the power. This option saves energy and provides greater safety in case of power failure.

- Restart the Mac. This isn't really a way to finish working with your Mac; rather, it's an option typically used to complete the installation of certain system updates or to change startup disks.

Caution

If you cut the power to a Mac without first switching it off (either by pulling the plug or by removing the battery from a MacBook), you risk damaging the files on your Mac. Although this damage may not be immediately noticeable, an accumulation of damage could eventually cause problems, such as applications no longer working correctly or files missing data. Always shut down before disconnecting the power source. ■

Logging out of Mac OS X

You can log out of Mac OS X when you have finished using your computer. This provides an additional level of security over putting the Mac to sleep because it requires people to enter a password before they can begin using the computer. Logging out of Mac OS X is also a way to switch from one user account to another.

You can log out of Mac OS X by choosing ⬥⇨ Log Out *username* or by pressing Shift+⌘+Q. Either way, a dialog box appears that provides two buttons: Log Out and Cancel. Click Log Out or press Return to immediately log out, or wait 60 seconds for the Mac to do it for you. Click Cancel to resume working on the Mac, using your current user account.

You also log out when switching to another user account, as Chapter 27 explains.

When you log out, Mac OS X quits all running applications and then displays the login window. From there, select a user account and enter the corresponding password to log in as that user. You also can click the Sleep, Restart, or Shut Down icon buttons if you meant to do one of those actions instead of logging out.

Putting your Mac to sleep (and waking it up)

When you're not going to use your Mac for a while, you can save energy by putting it to sleep. When you want to start using your Mac again, you can quickly wake it up. Waking up the Mac is much quicker than starting it up from being powered off.

It's usually good to let the Mac sleep during the day when you're not using it, because Mac OS X does some background maintenance when asleep that helps keep it operating smoothly.

You can put your Mac to sleep in any of the following ways:

- If you have a MacBook, simply close the screen lid.
- Choose ⬥⇨ Sleep.
- If you are using a keyboard with an Eject key, press Control+Shift+Eject or Option+⌘+Eject to immediately put the Mac to sleep. Or press Control+Eject, and either click the Sleep option from the dialog box that appears or press the S key.
- Press the power button on your computer (or on your Apple display, if it has a power button). Then click the Sleep button in the dialog box that appears or press the S key.

- Log out of your Mac, and click the Sleep icon button in the login window that appears.
- Choose ⌘⇨ System Preferences, go the Energy Saver system preference (see Chapter 28), and set the automatic "go to sleep" time by using the Computer Sleep slider. That makes the Mac go to sleep automatically after it's been inactive for the specified time (meaning you haven't touched the mouse, touchpad, or keyboard and that no applications are running that are reading from or writing to a disk).

You can wake up your Mac in any of the following ways:

- If you have a MacBook, simply open the lid.
- Press any key on the keyboard. (To prevent the keypress from inserting text into an active document or text field, it's wise to get into the habit of using the Shift key as your wake-up key.)
- Click or move the mouse or touchpad.

Note that when you awaken a sleeping Mac, you may get a login window in which you have to enter your password. The login window also has two icon buttons: Cancel, which puts the Mac back to sleep, and Switch User, which lets you log into a different user account. (The login window appears if you configured the Security & Privacy system preference to require a password to reawaken a Mac, as Chapter 26 explains.)

Shutting down the Mac

While you can leave your Mac permanently running or let it go to sleep, you may want to completely switch it off at the end of the day. That reduces energy usage and makes it less likely the Mac could be damaged due to heat buildup or an electrical surge.

You can shut down a Mac several ways, including:

- Press the power button on your Mac (or your keyboard if it has one), and click Shut Down or press Return when the confirmation dialog box appears onscreen.
- If you are using a keyboard with an Eject key, press Control+Eject and click Shut Down or press Return in the dialog box that appears.
- Choose ⌘⇨ Shut Down. Click Shut Down or press Return when the confirmation dialog box appears, or you can wait 60 seconds and the Mac shuts down automatically.
- Log out and click the Shut Down icon button in the login window.

When you go through the shut-down process, Mac OS X tells all open applications to quit and proceeds to shut down. If any applications have unsaved data, you are prompted with a Save dialog box before shutting down.

Tip

When shutting down, watch the desktop until the screen goes blank, which lets you know the Mac has actually shut down. When you shut down Mac OS X, it first tries to quit all active applications, but applications may not quit if they have unsaved documents. In this case, the applications present a dialog box asking if you want to save the unsaved documents, and the shutdown is delayed. If you walk away, you'll come back only to find that the shutdown didn't complete, and then you have to address the unsaved documents, wait for the Mac to shut down, and start it again to be able to use the Mac—a process that can be quite frustrating. ■

Note

You can use one other method to shut down the Mac: a forced shutdown. This can be handy in the event of a system crash, when there is no other way to shut down or restart the Mac. To use this method, simply hold down the power button for at least five seconds. However, you should avoid a forced shutdown if at all possible: Any unsaved document data is lost, and it is possible to cause damage to the system. ■

Restarting the Mac

You need to restart Mac OS X far less than many other operating systems such as Windows. That's because Mac OS X is very stable and doesn't require a restart to clear its memory as Windows does. Plus, many applications can be installed in Mac OS X without requiring a restart to activate their features. Still, sometimes you need to restart the computer after installing some software updates (such as Apple's Mac OS X software updates) or when installing some applications.

You can use the following methods to restart the Mac:

- Press the power button on your Mac (or on certain Apple-branded monitors). When the confirmation dialog box appears, click Restart.
- If your keyboard has the Eject key, press Control+Eject. In the dialog box that appears, click Restart.
- If your keyboard has the Eject key, press Control+⌘+Eject; the Mac begins to restart immediately.
- Log out and click the Restart icon button.
- Choose ⇨ Restart. When the confirmation dialog box appears, click Restart or press Return—or simply wait 60 seconds and let the Mac restart automatically.

During the restart process, Mac OS X tells all open applications running in the system to quit. If an application has an open document with unsaved changes, it asks you if you want to save the changes before quitting. Only when all the applications have quit does the Mac shut down and then start back up again.

Resuming Where You Left Off

A feature that iPhone, iPod Touch, and iPad users love is that when they turn off their device or put it to sleep, they pick up where they left off when they turn on or reawaken their device. Mac OS X Lion can do the same.

When you shut down, log out of, or restart your Mac, the confirmation dialog box has the Reopen Windows When Logging Back In option, as Figure 1.1 shows. If you want Mac OS X to reopen the currently open applications, documents, folders, and disk windows the next time it starts up or logs in to the same user account, make sure that option is checked before you confirm the shutdown, logout, or restart.

New Feature

The option to have applications and windows reopen upon startup or login is new to Mac OS X Lion. ■

FIGURE 1.1

The logout, restart, and shutdown confirmation dialog boxes all present an option to reopen the current windows when you log into or start the Mac.

Summary

Starting up the Mac is as easy as pressing the power button, but more sophisticated capabilities exist when you need them, such as the ability to start up from different disks and to require login so only authorized users can access the Mac. This combination of simplicity and rich capabilities extends to the Mac's option to go to sleep, restart, and shut down, as well as to switch among authorized users.

And new to Mac OS X Lion is the ability to have the Mac remember what windows were open when you log out, restart, or shut down and automatically reopen them when you next log in or start the Mac.

Discovering the Finder

When the Mac has started up and you have been through the login processes, you are taken to the Mac OS X desktop, where you can begin to use your computer. It's the Mac desktop and the associated controls that most people think of when they think of Mac OS X. But what you're really seeing and interacting with is the Finder, the part of Mac OS X that manages your interactions with disks, folders, and files (both documents and applications).

The desktop is the screen with icons, folders, and windows. By default, the desktop has no icons on it. But most people configure the Finder to display the startup disk and other connected disks along the right side of the desktop, using the Finder's Preferences dialog box, as explained in the "Adjusting Finder Preferences" section in Chapter 3.

At the bottom of the desktop, you see the Dock. This horizontal bar contains icons that represent quick shortcuts to applications and files. At the top of the screen is a menu bar that changes depending on the application in use, but by default is the Finder's menu bar. (The Finder is the application that you use to manage the Mac itself, letting you work with files and folders.)

The Finder has several major components that you interact with routinely, as Figure 2.1 shows:

- **Menu bar:** The menu bar is permanently available at the top of the Mac OS X screen, providing universal functions in the menu, application-specific menus to its right, and icon shortcuts to various Mac OS X and third-party applications on the far right.
- **Desktop:** The canvas on which windows and other icons appear is called the desktop.

- **Dock:** The Dock is a tray of applications that by default is positioned at the bottom of the screen; you can configure what appears in the Dock and use it for quick access to applications and some special Mac OS X folders.

- **Finder windows:** When you open a disk or folder, the Finder shows its contents in a Finder window, which also provides quick access to other disks, folders, and special Mac OS X locations. Chapter 3 explains how to work with Finder windows.

- **Icons:** Disks, folders, documents, and applications are all represented as icons in Mac OS X windows, the Dock, the desktop, and other locations. These icons are selectable using a mouse or touchpad, so you can open them, move them, delete them, and otherwise work with them. You also can navigate them and edit them using the keyboard. Chapter 3 explains how to work with icons and disks, and Chapter 4 explains how to work with files and folders.

FIGURE 2.1

The basic Finder elements are the menu bar (top), disk, folder, and file icons (at right and below the menu bar), and the Dock (bottom). The canvas on which they rest is called the desktop.

The rest of this chapter explains how to use the Finder's major user interface capabilities. Chapter 3 explains how to use the Finder itself as an application and how its Finder windows work. Chapter 4 explains how to work with the disks, folders, and files you access via the

Finder. And Chapter 5 explains how to search for files and information on your Mac via the Finder's Spotlight search tool.

Using Input Devices

To work with the Finder, you need to use input devices—the Finder can't read your mind, after all. The primary input devices are a keyboard, which is used both for text entry and to issue commands, and a mouse or touchpad, which is used to select items and then open, move, delete, or perform other manipulations on them. Some functions use multiple input devices at the same time. Mac OS X also can use speech commands, as described in Chapter 8, for text entry, issuing commands, and item manipulations.

Working with the keyboard

The Mac keyboard is very much like any typewriter's or computer's keyboard: It provides the keys for letters, numerals, and punctuation, as well as special keys to manipulate the text, such as Shift to capitalize letters and access some symbols, Caps Lock to capitalize all letters typed, Delete and Forward Delete to remove text, and Return to add paragraph breaks.

But the keyboard also has keys that never existed in a typewriter. There are *modifier keys* that are used in combination with each other and other keys to access special characters and to issue commands—Command (⌘), Option, Control, Esc, and Fn, as well as Shift—and there are shortcut keys called F keys (because they are labeled F1 through F12 on most Mac keyboards and F1 through F16 on others) to access special functions. Most Macs also have an Eject key to eject any DVD or CD inserted into the Mac. And some Mac keyboards have a Help key.

Note

If you're a Windows user, note that the ⌘ key is equivalent to the PC's Ctrl key, Option is equivalent to Alt, Delete is equivalent to Backspace, and Forward Delete is equivalent to Del. The Mac's Control key has no PC equivalent. Also, recent Macs don't have a Num Lock key; some keyboards assigned F6 to that function, but the Num Lock key is all but disappearing from Macs now. ■

You use the cursor keys (commonly called the *arrow keys*) to move up, down, left, and right. Some keyboards, called *extended keyboards*, have additional navigation keys such as Home, End, Page Up, and Page Down, as well as a numeric keypad.

Here's what the special keys do:

- The ⌘ **key (Command)** is the most-used modifier key for issuing commands. This key has had several labels over the years on various keyboards: Command, Cmd, ⌘, and ⌘.

- The **Shift** key is used both to capitalize text and as a modifier key in keyboard shortcuts. In Mac OS X and in many Mac program menus, Shift is displayed by the symbol ⇧.

- The **Option** key is used in keyboard shortcuts. In Mac OS X and in many Mac program menus, you see the symbol ⌥ used. Note that Mac keyboards often add the label Alt to the Option key; this is for the convenience of Windows users, because the Option key functions as the Windows Alt key when you are running Windows on a Mac.

- The **Control** key is used infrequently for shortcuts; its main use is to open contextual menus when combined with a mouse click. In Mac OS X and in many Mac programs, you see the symbol ⌃ used.

- The **Tab** key is used both to move within fields in panes and dialog boxes and to insert the tab character in text. Mac OS X and many Mac programs indicate it in menus with the symbol ⇥.

- The **Esc** key is typically used to close a dialog box or pane and cancel any settings you entered in it. It's also used in a few keyboard shortcuts. Mac OS X and many Mac programs use the symbol ⎋ in their menus to indicate it.

- The **Return** key is used to apply a dialog box's settings and close the dialog box (equivalent to clicking OK or Done), as well as to insert a hard paragraph return in text. In Mac OS X and many Mac programs, it is indicated in menus by the symbol ↩.

- The **Delete** key deletes text, one character at a time, to the *left* of the text-insertion point. In Mac OS X and many Mac programs, the Delete key is indicated in menus by the symbol ⌫.

- The **Eject** key ejects a CD or DVD from your Mac's optical drive. In Mac OS X and many Mac programs, it is indicated in menus by the symbol ⏏.

- Macs with an extended keyboard—one with a numeric keypad—have a second Delete key (below Help or Fn and next to End) that deletes text to the right of the text-insertion pointer. Called **Forward Delete**, newer Mac keys label it Delete ⌦. In Mac OS X and many Mac programs, the Forward Delete key is indicated in menus by the symbol ⌦. On a regular Mac keyboard, use Fn+Delete to get the Forward Delete action.

- On some MacBook keyboards and on extended keyboards' numeric keypad is a key labeled **Enter** that sometimes works like the regular Return, but not always. (I refer to Enter as *keypad Enter* in this book.) In Mac OS X and many Mac programs, it is indicated in menus by the symbol ⌤. On regular Mac keyboards, Fn+Return acts as Enter.

- Also on extended keyboards, **Home** either moves to the beginning of the line or the beginning of the document, depending on how the application interprets it, **End** moves either to the end of a line or end of the document, **Page Up** moves up one screen, **Page Down** moves down one screen, **Help** opens the Mac OS X help system (see Chapter 7), and **Clear** clears the entries in a calculator-style application and sometimes acts as Num Lock in other applications. Note that not all extended keyboards have all these keys.

- The **Fn** key is used as a modifier key, where you hold it down while pressing one or more other keys to access a specific function. For example, Fn+← acts as an extended keyboard's Home key, Fn+→ as the End key, Fn+↑ as the Page Up key, and Fn+↓ as the Page Down key.

- The **F keys** are rarely used in Mac OS X for their original function: compatibility with Unix and mainframe special functions. Instead, most are now used as shortcuts for controlling the Mac hardware, such as to increase screen brightness (F2) or pause a video (F8), and some are used to invoke Mac OS X interface items (such as F3 to launch Exposé and F4 to launch the Dashboard). Note that newer Macs have icons above the F keys that indicate what hardware and Mac OS X interface items they invoke—and note that what specific F keys do varies across different Mac models. Also note that you may need to press Fn when using such F keys, depending on the settings in the Keyboard system preference (see Chapter 28).

If you're supposed to press several keys at the same time, I indicate that by placing plus signs (+) between them. Thus, Shift+⌘+A means press and hold the Shift and ⌘ keys, and then press A. After you've pressed A, let go of all three keys. (You don't need to hold down the last character in the sequence.)

I also use the plus sign (+) to join keys to mouse movements. For example, Option+drag means to press and hold the Option key while dragging the mouse on the Mac.

Working with the mouse

Apple was the first company to use the mouse in a commercially available computer, and it fundamentally changed how people interacted with computers. The mouse is a pointing device, so it becomes an extension of your hand and lets you virtually grab, move, and press on objects.

On the Mac OS X screen, you see the mouse's current position via the pointer icon, which is usually a black arrowhead but whose shape can change based on the current activity (to help you understand what activity is occurring). For example, when working in text, it appears as the I-beam text cursor icon.

To "grab" an item with the mouse, you click (press) and hold the mouse button and then move the mouse to move the item. Let go of the button to "drop" the item in its new location. (An item could be an icon or a scroll bar, for example.)

Some items need to be selected before they can be moved: For example, for text, you click and hold the mouse button, then drag to the end of your text selection, and finally let go of the mouse button. The text remains selected, and you hover the mouse over it, then click and hold, and then drag (I call that whole operation simply *dragging*) to move the text block. The same principle applies to selecting multiple icons, except that you draw a rectangle (called a *marquee*) around the items you want to select using the same click, hold, drag, and release action.

When using the mouse, you should know these conventions for click actions:

- **Click:** Most Mac mice have only one button, but some have two or more; the Mighty Mouse and Magic Mouse that Apple has included with some Macs for the last several years appear to have one button but can in fact detect which side of the mouse you are pressing, so in effect they have two buttons. If you have a multi-button mouse, quickly press and release the leftmost mouse button (or the left side of the Mighty Mouse or Magic Mouse) once when I say to click the mouse. (If your mouse has only one button—you guessed it—just press and release the button you have.)

- **Double-click:** When I say to double-click, quickly press and release the leftmost mouse button twice; if your mouse has only one button, just press and release twice the button you have. On some multi-button mice, one of the buttons can function as a double-click (you click it once, the mouse clicks twice); if your mouse has this feature, use it because it saves strain on your hand.

- **Right-click:** If your mouse has at least two buttons, right-clicking means clicking the right mouse button. On a one-button mouse, hold the Control key when clicking the mouse button to achieve the right-click effect. (Right-clicking is usually used to open contextual menus, as explained later in this chapter.)

Working with the touchpad

Laptops—both Apple's and Windows-based ones—have long had a device called a trackpad that replaces the mouse, converting finger movements on its surface to the equivalent mouse movements. These trackpads also have buttons that equate to mouse buttons.

But in 2007, Apple released the first iPhone, a device that took touch technology to a whole new level, adding support for more complex gestures than just moving a pointer across the screen. And in 2008, it brought that touch technology to the MacBook laptop line in the form of a *touchpad*, a more sophisticated version of a trackpad. Since then, Apple has increased the sophistication of touch gestures—movements and taps—that the touchpads support in each successive generation of MacBook, as well as introducing the Magic Trackpad and Magic Mouse, two wireless input devices that provide touchpad surfaces to all Macs, not just MacBooks (and they let MacBook users whose MacBook cases are closed—such as when docked—use the touch capabilities).

With sophisticated touch devices now available for all Macs, Mac OS X Lion has made the use of touch a fundamental part of some Finder operations, not just an alternative to the traditional use of a mouse. It's especially used in the new Launchpad (see Chapter 14) and with the new Mission Control feature (covered later in this chapter).

Note

Throughout this book, if I describe a mouse action, you also can use the equivalent touchpad action, unless I say otherwise. ■

Mac OS X Lion supports a large number of gestures, but not all touchpads support them all. All MacBooks before 2008, as well as the Magic Mouse, support only one- and two-finger gestures, while MacBooks produced in 2008 and later, as well as the Magic Trackpad, support one-, two-, three-, and four-finger gestures. The Trackpad system preference (see Chapter 28), shown in Figure 2.2, shows only the gestures supported by your specific touchpad. The figure also shows the gesture preferences in the Mouse system preference (also see Chapter 28) for the Magic Mouse.

FIGURE 2.2

Left: The Trackpad system preference is a great way to become familiar with the gesture options available on your Mac. Right: The Mouse system preference also lets you manage gesture settings on the touch-enabled Magic Mouse.

These gestures are supported:

- **Tap:** This is the equivalent of mouse-clicking, using your finger to lightly tap the touchpad.

- **Double-tap:** Double-tap on the touchpad with one finger for the equivalent a mouse's double-click.

- **Click:** This is also a form of mouse-clicking, though it's intended for actions where a regular tap could have a different meaning. For example, you click when starting to drag-select via a touchpad rather than tap when starting. On a Magic Trackpad and on newer MacBooks, a click differs from a tap in that the touchpad surface actually depresses in a click. On touch surfaces that don't physically depress, there's usually a trackpad button that you click (essentially, a separate mouse button for the touchpad).

- **Right-click (secondary click):** Tap and hold two fingers on the touchpad, and then tap with a second finger. You also can set the touchpad to translate a single tap in a specific location (by default, the lower-right corner) as a right-click if you change the Secondary Click pop-up menu's option in the Trackpad system preference.

- **Drag:** Click the trackpad button (or the touchpad itself if it can depress), hold with one finger, and then drag the item with a second finger. You also can enable a gesture whereby dragging three fingers moves the objects (no clicking required).

- **Drag-select:** Click outside an item on the desktop or Finder window, hold with one finger, and then drag the second finger to create a selection marquee (a rectangle whose first corner is where you tapped and whose diagonally opposite corner is your second finger's location).

- **Scroll:** Drag two fingers simultaneously in the direction you want to scroll the screen or window.

Note

The direction of the swipe may not be intuitive to you: By default, Mac OS X Lion moves the content (such as the text in a text editor, so swiping down moves the text down in the current window, in effect moving you to the top of the text) in the direction you swipe—just like on an iPhone or iPad. But with a mouse's scroll wheel, we've been trained that scrolling moves the scroll bar (so moving the scroll bar down moves the text up as you move toward the bottom of the screen). Mac OS X Lion lets you have touchpad scrolling work like a mouse's scroll wheel rather than like on an iPhone or iPad. In the Scroll & Zoom pane of the Trackpad system preference (and in the Mouse system preference for a Magic Mouse), select the option labeled Scroll with Finger Direction, to have the scroll mimic the behavior of a mouse's scroll wheel instead of the behavior of an iPad or iPhone. ∎

- **Swipe:** This means to move one finger across the touchpad in one direction, such as for scrolling.

- **Pinch:** This means to put two fingers apart on the touchpad and then move them together, to zoom out the view (include more of the content on the screen).

- **Expand:** This means to put two fingers together on the touchpad and then move them apart to zoom in the view (magnify part of the content on the screen).

- **Rotate:** Place two fingers (or your index finger and thumb) on the touchpad and rotate clockwise or counterclockwise to rotate the active object.

- **Two-finger double-tap:** Double-tap two fingers on an object or screen area to "smart zoom" into that area.

- **Zoom screen:** Press and hold Control, and then place two fingers on the touchpad and scroll up to zoom in or down to zoom out. If you move the mouse around the screen at the same time, the zoom's center follows the mouse. (You can change the modifier key used from Control to Option or ⌘ in the Trackpad system preference by clicking the Options button next to the Screen Zoom option to open a settings sheet and select the desired key via the Zoom While Holding pop-up menu.)

- **Three-finger double-tap:** Double-tap three fingers on text or a text selection to have Mac OS X Lion look up the text in its dictionary (the same dictionary terms that you can access as the Dictionary application, as described in Chapter 14).

- **Two-finger scroll:** This gesture by default moves you through pages as you swipe to the left (back or up) or to the right (forward or down). You also can set this action to the two-finger left and right swipe gestures or to the two- or three-finger swipe (any direction) gesture.

- **Four-finger swipe up:** This gesture by default toggles the Mission Control view (explained later in this chapter) and the normal Finder view. It is configurable to use three fingers instead.

- **Four-finger swipe down:** This gesture by default toggles the App Exposé view (explained later in this chapter) and the normal Finder view. It is configurable to use three fingers instead.

- **Four-finger pinch and spread:** These gestures (you move three fingers in one direction and the thumb in the other) switch between showing the Launchpad and the desktop, respectively.

As with mouse commands, some gestures require or behave differently when paired with holding down modifier keys on the keyboard. For example, Control+tapping on a touchpad has the same effect as Control+clicking on a mouse: right-clicking.

New Feature

Mac OS X Lion adds the four-finger pinch and spread gestures for viewing the Launchpad and desktop, the three-finger double-tap gesture for looking up text, and the two-finger double-tap for smart zooming, and Lion redefines the four-finger and three-finger swipe gestures to support the new Mission Control feature. ■

Understanding the Desktop

Apple popularized a graphical user interface (GUI) with a desktop metaphor with its famous Macintosh line, introduced in 1984. As Microsoft followed suit with Windows, it made the desktop metaphor common parlance throughout the world.

The desktop metaphor is the concept of the screen on the monitor acting as a visual representation of your physical desk. In this sense, the desktop contains folders (which are virtual representations of cardboard folders or drawers), documents (which are virtual pieces of paper), a trash can to dispose of items, and other visual icons designed to imitate real-life objects.

Despite being based on a commonplace metaphor, the desktop used in Mac OS X has many features and functions that may not be immediately apparent.

In essence, the desktop is the background on the screen—the expanse of space that sits behind the Dock and below the menu bar, or its canvas. By default, every version of Mac OS X has featured a different background image signifying which version of Mac OS X is running.

New Feature

Mac OS X Lion uses a photo of a galaxy as its default desktop background image, not the stellar auroras of Mac OS X Leopard and Snow Leopard. The selection of background images included with Mac OS X Lion (in the Desktop & Screen Saver system preference, described in Chapter 28) differs from previous versions of Mac OS X, with several new African animal scenes (including one of a lion) and several new nature scenes. Among the removed images are the emblematic space images of Mac OS X Leopard and Snow Leopard. ■

But the arrangement of the default disk icons has not changed: The startup disk appears at the upper right of the desktop, and any additional disks' icons appear below the startup disk's icon. (If you don't see the disk icons, choose Finder⇨Preferences or press ⌘+, [comma] to open the Preferences dialog box. Select the Hard Disks option and the External Disks option in the General pane; click or tap the General icon if that pane is not displayed.)

You must understand that although the desktop is the space on the screen, it is also a folder inside your Home folder, located in /Users/*username*/Desktop. Whatever is in that folder appears on the desktop when that user is logged in. And whatever that user puts on the desktop is actually placed in that folder. Because different users have different Home folders, the desktop is individual to each user. (I explain the folder structure of Mac OS X in Chapter 4.)

Note

Although the icons of disks appear on the desktop, they do not appear inside the `/Users/`**username**`/` `Desktop` **folder, not even as aliases. These icons appear on the desktop purely because it is convenient for Mac OS X to place them there. (They are also accessible via the Finder's Sidebar, as explained in Chapter 3.) The fact that disk icons appear on the desktop, but are not in the** `/Users/`**username**`/Desktop` **folder, is an exception to Mac OS X's rule that all folders display the items they contain. ∎**

The arrangement of icons for disks, folders, and files—all of which can be placed on the desktop by saving them there from applications or dragging them there from other locations—is arbitrary. You can drag icons anywhere you want on the desktop, arranging it as you prefer (even as a mess of items!).

You also can customize the appearance of the desktop using the Desktop & Screen Saver system preference to change the desktop's background image (see Chapter 28) and by using the Finder's View Options controls over how icons display in Finder windows and on the desktop (see Chapter 3).

Working with Menus

Like most operating systems, Mac OS X uses menus to give you lists of commands and functions that can be used by programs and the operating system as a whole. Menus take up considerable space on the screen, so they tend to be hidden except for a single label (a word, such as File or Edit, or an icon); clicking this label (which Apple calls a *title*) brings up a menu of commands, such as New Document, Open, and Save.

In Mac OS X, a single menu appears at the top of the screen called the *menu bar*. Some of the titles for the items in the menu bar change, based on which application is active at the time. Some menu labels, such as , File, Edit, Window, and Help, almost always appear because Apple insists that applications use a consistent interface so users can easily move among them.

Note

Apple uses the **term drop-down menu to refer to the menus in the menu bar and the term pop-up menu to** refer to menus **available within applications and windows. ∎**

Applications and windows also can have menus, called *pop-up menus*, which are accessed by clicking titles, icons, or buttons (both text and icon). Pop-up menus can appear in a variety of areas within an application or window, including in sub-windows, side panes, dialog boxes, and control panels. Most applications make their main menus available in the menu bar, but they may make additional menu options available through a control ribbon at the top or side of the application window. Finder windows also display their window-specific menus at the top of the window, leaving the universal Finder menu controls in the menu bar.

A third type of menu in Mac OS X is the contextual menu. You don't see contextual menus until you hover over an item and then either right-click it with a multi-button mouse or hold down the Control key and click the primary (or only) mouse button (called *Control+click*).

Contextual menus also may be accessed via touchpads using the taps and gestures that equate to the mouse buttons (described later in this chapter). Contextual menus are so named because their contents change according to the context (area or item) that you right-click or Control+click.

Note

Apple's recent mice have one physical button that detects which side you press, interpreting a press on the right side as a right-click and a tap on the left side as a regular (primary) mouse click. ■

Working with drop-down menus

To access an option in a drop-down menu, you typically use the mouse or touchpad to control the pointer and choose one of the options. You can choose menu options one of two ways:

- **Click, move, and click:** Move the pointer over the menu title, and click the mouse button or tap the touchpad to reveal the list of menu options. Then move the pointer down the list to highlight the menu option you are interested in. Click the menu option to activate it. The highlighted option flashes to indicate that it has been chosen, and Mac OS X executes whatever the menu option is designed to do in the application or window, such as execute a task or open a dialog box. (If you click a menu title and decide that you do not want to select any option, simply click anywhere on the screen other than on a menu option to close the menu and continue working.)

- **Click and hold, move, and release:** Move the pointer over the menu title, and click and hold the mouse button or tap and hold the touchpad. While holding the mouse button or your finger down, move to the menu option you want to select and, with the item highlighted, release the mouse button or your finger. The menu option flashes, and the menu option executes whatever it is designed to do. (Note that when you navigate submenus, the pointer must stay within the bounds of the submenu; if it leaves its area, the submenu closes automatically.)

The method you use is largely a case of personal preference.

Some menu options also may expand to reveal further options, as Figure 2.3 shows. These are called *submenus*; a submenu is indicated by a small black triangle to the right of the menu option. Moving the pointer to one of these menu options makes the submenu expand to the right and present further options. (In some applications and windows, the submenu may expand to the left.) Moving the pointer into the submenu enables you to select these further options. It is rare for a submenu to contain further submenu options, known as *nested submenus,* although some complex programs do have nested submenus. (Adobe Dreamweaver CS5 is an example.)

In this book, I indicate a menu sequence using the ⇨ symbol between each option, such as Edit ⇨ Copy to indicate that you open the Edit menu and choose Copy, and Table ⇨ Insert ⇨ Row to indicate that you open the Table menu, choose the Insert option, and then choose the Row option from its submenu.

Using keyboard shortcuts for menu options

As you explore menu options, you'll see that certain ones have symbols and letters next to them. These are keyboard shortcuts, and they represent key combinations you can use instead of the mouse or touchpad to select menu options. Pressing ⌘+O, for example, is commonly used to access the Open option from the File menu.

When you press a keyboard shortcut, the item on the menu bar flashes briefly to indicate that a menu option has been selected, although the menu itself does not expand to show the exact option being invoked.

Keyboard shortcuts can massively increase the speed at which you work and are well worth learning. You can discover many keyboard shortcuts by looking at the Keyboard Shortcuts pane of the Keyboard system preference. Here, you not only learn keyboard shortcuts, but you also can create your own, as Chapter 28 explains. Apple also has a comprehensive list of common keyboard shortcuts on its website (http://support.apple.com/kb/HT1343).

FIGURE 2.3

The Edit drop-down menu for the Pages application, showing a submenu for its Find menu option

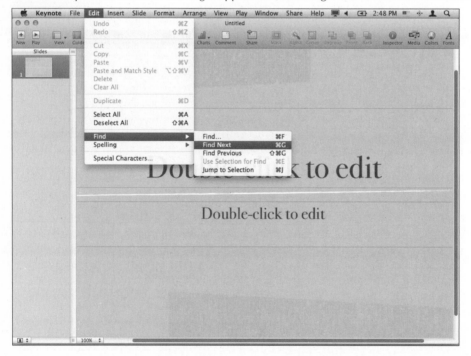

Some menu options may appear in a light gray text (a visual effect often referred to as *grayed out*), which indicates that the menu item is not available at the moment. Common examples are the Save and Print menu options that are grayed out in most applications if no document is open (because there is no document being worked on to save or print).

Recognizing menu symbols

Several symbols accompany menu items. Table 2.1 is a guide to the various symbols and their meanings.

TABLE 2.1

Menu Symbols

Symbol	Description
✓	A check mark next to a menu option indicates that it is currently selected. These menu options act as toggles: If you select the item from the menu, it usually deselects the item; select it again to select the item.
–	A short dash designates an attribute that applies only to some things that are currently selected (and not all of them).
•	The bullet designates a document with unsaved changes. Note that some applications use it instead of the check mark symbol to refer to an attribute that applies to everything that is currently selected.
◆	A diamond that appears before options in the Window menu signifies that the window is minimized in the Dock.
▶	This right-facing triangle indicates that a menu leads to a submenu offering further options.
…	The ellipsis signifies that a menu option will open a dialog box and require further information before the option can take effect.

Touring the menu bar items

Although the menu bar changes according to which application is currently active, several menu options on the left side of the menu bar are common to all applications: , File, Edit, Window, and Help. On the right side of the menu bar sit several icon menus that remain the same no matter which application is highlighted. The other menu options vary, based on what application is active.

The   (Apple) menu

At the far-left side of the menu bar sits the   menu (called the *Apple menu*). The options in this menu typically relate to the Mac as a whole and to system-wide options and commands. You can use the menu options here to get information about your Mac, perform software updates, and change system preferences; you also can log out, put your computer to sleep, or shut it down completely.

Because these menu options remain the same no matter what application is open, let's look at them in depth. These options are available:

- **About This Mac:** Choosing this menu option brings up a window displaying information about your Mac. It informs you which version of Mac OS X you are running, what your processor speed is, the amount of memory (random access memory, or RAM) in your Mac, and what your startup disk is. There are also two buttons in this window. One is labeled More Info; clicking it opens the System Information utility that provides detailed information on all aspects of your computer. The other is labeled Software Update; clicking it opens the Software Update application and automatically connects to the Internet to look for updates to Mac OS X and the various Apple programs installed on your Mac.

Tip

Press and hold Option when the menu displays to change the About This Mac menu option to System Information, which jumps straight to the System Information utility. ∎

- **Software Update:** Choosing this menu option brings up the Software Update application.

- **App Store:** Choosing this menu option launches the Mac App Store, from which you can buy and download software for your Mac. You can sign in using your existing iTunes account and charge your purchases to the same credit card, or you can create a separate account.

- **System Preferences:** Choosing this menu option opens the System Preferences application, where you can adjust various aspects of the Mac OS X environment. The system preferences are explained in depth in Chapter 28.

- **Dock:** Choosing this menu option opens a submenu that provides controls for the Dock (explained later in this chapter). You can quickly adjust the magnification and position of the Dock from this menu option.

- **Location:** This menu option works with the Network system preference (which enables you to set different networking preferences for different environments). Typically, a laptop owner may connect a MacBook to his or her home network, as well as to a work network, and may have different settings depending on the environment. (Networking is explained in depth in Chapter 23.) The Location menu option offers a submenu for selecting different locations, so the appropriate network settings are activated for your current location. This menu option is present only if you have set multiple network locations using the Network system preference.

- **Recent Items:** This particularly handy menu option takes you to a submenu with three separate areas: Applications, Documents, and Servers. Each area contains the last 10 respective items that you have used on the Mac. So you get a list of the 10 recently used applications, documents you have opened, and server locations you have visited.

- **Force Quit:** This menu option brings up the Force Quit Applications dialog box, which shows all running applications on the Mac, and is where you force unruly applications to quit. It is rare that you will need to use the Force Quit menu option, but it can prevent you from having to restart your computer. The Force Quit Applications dialog box is explained in more depth in Chapter 9. (You also can press Option+⌘+Esc to open the Force Quit Applications dialog box.)

- **Sleep**, **Restart**, and **Shut Down:** You use these three menu options when you want to break from what you are doing. Sleep turns off your monitor and puts your Mac into a low-power mode; tapping the mouse, touchpad, or keyboard wakes it back up. Shut Down switches off your Mac. Restart switches off the Mac and begins the boot process automatically. (Chapter 1 explains them in more detail.)

- **Log Out:** The final option is marked Log Out *username*, such as Log Out Galen Gruman. This is used to log off your session; you need to log back in (as described in Chapter 1) to begin working again on your Mac. This logoff option is often used in a work environment when a computer holds sensitive information and should not be accessible without an authorized user present. (In that case, you would log out when taking a break from your computer.) It's also used to switch among user accounts on the same Mac, as Chapter 27 explains.

New Feature
The App Store menu option is new to Mac OS X Lion, though it was available to Snow Leopard users as part of a system update in late 2010. Gone from the menu is the Mac OS X Downloads menu option, which has been essentially replaced with the App Store menu. ■

The application menu
To the immediate right of the menu sits the application menu, the title of which typically signifies the application that is currently running. Because the menu item is limited in space (usually to just one or two words), it doesn't always match exactly the application's name. For example, the application menu for Adobe InDesign CS5 is listed simply as "InDesign." This menu serves as a handy indication of what application is currently active, and it contains a list of items that apply to the application as a whole.

The options in the application menu vary according to the application in question, although some options are common across most applications. They include the following:

- **About:** This is typically labeled with the name of the program, such as About Safari; choosing this menu option brings up information about the application you are running. Typically, this information is limited to the name of the program, its icon, the version number, and some copyright information.

- **Preferences:** Most applications have preferences that enable you to set up and customize the program. You access the preferences in each application through the Preferences menu option. (You also can press ⌘+, [comma] to open the preferences for the current application.)

- **Services:** The Services menu option leads to a submenu of all the services offered by Mac OS X that are available to the current application. Services are explained in depth in Chapter 12.

- **Hide and Show:** These menu options let you hide and show applications. There are two Hide menu options and one Show menu option:

  - Hide *applicationname* (such as Hide Mail): This usually has the shortcut ⌘+H; it hides the application and all its windows.

  - Hide Others: This usually has the shortcut Option+⌘+H; it hides all applications except the active one.

  - Show All: This menu option brings back all running applications and their windows.

- **Quit:** The Quit menu option (again, usually written as Quit followed by the application name, such as Quit Mail) closes the program. You also can press ⌘+Q.

The File menu

The File menu contains options that pertain to documents (or files) used by the active program. It is common across most programs used in the Mac OS X environment, although a few applications and games, such as the Chess game included in Mac OS X, may forgo a File menu because they do not work with documents. The menu options include the following:

- **New:** Typically the File menu begins with one or more New menu options that let you create a new file or document. Sometimes, such as in the Finder, they are used to create new folders and windows. In Mail, for example, they are used to create new e-mail messages. Typically, the shortcut for choosing File⇨New is ⌘+N.

- **Open:** The Open menu options are used to load documents that were previously created and saved by the application. Often, there is also an Open Recent command with a submenu that contains a list of documents recently saved by that application. Occasionally, there are other types of Open commands: In Safari, for example, you can find commands to open URLs (web addresses). Typically, the shortcut for choosing File⇨Open is ⌘+O.

- **Save:** Following the Open menu options are typically options to save documents. There are often both Save and Save As menu options. If the document has not been saved, the Save command is grayed out and only the Save As command is available (signifying that you need to select Save As and give the document a name). Typically, the shortcut for choosing File⇨Save is ⌘+S; for choosing File⇨Save As, it is Shift+⌘+S. Note that applications that take advantage of Mac OS X Lion's new Versions capability (see Chapter 10) do not have a Save As menu option; they also change the name of the Save menu to Save a Version after the first time you save a document.

- **Print:** Typically, near the bottom of the File menu is the Print menu option. It opens the Print dialog box that enables you to output the document onto a sheet of paper, to export it to a PDF (Portable Document Format) file, which is an electronic "printout" that can be retained or shared with other users, or to fax it. Choosing this option opens the Print dialog box, which offers the controls for printing, PDF file creation, and faxing (as Chapter 30 details). Typically, the shortcut for choosing File⇨Print is ⌘+P.

Tip

In some applications, you can press and hold Option when the File menu displays to change some of the options. In many such applications, Close changes to Close All when you press and hold Option. ∎

The Edit menu

The Edit menu contains menu options used to manipulate the contents of a document. As with the File menu, the nature of these options varies greatly, depending on the document in question. Some, such as Undo and Redo, are common across many applications, as are the universal options of Cut, Copy, and Paste:

- **Cut:** This option cuts the selected items (including text or graphics), putting them in the Pasteboard so they can be pasted elsewhere. You also can press ⌘+X.

- **Copy:** This option copies the selected items into the Pasteboard so they can be pasted elsewhere. You also can press ⌘+C.

- **Paste:** This option pastes the last-copied or last-cut items into the current Finder window (or into the desktop if no Finder window is open). You also can press ⌘+V.

Note

The Pasteboard is the name for Mac OS X's temporary holding bin. The last item or set of items that you cut or copied are stored in the Pasteboard so they can be pasted elsewhere. They are automatically removed from the Pasteboard the next time you cut or copy items (including text or graphics) or until you restart, log out of, or shut down your Mac. ∎

Along with the cut and copy menu options is the related Select All option (press ⌘+A), which selects all content in the current window.

Another commonly found option in the Edit menu is the Find command, which you use to search through documents for specific items (usually words or phrases).

Tip

In some applications, you can press and hold Option when the Edit menu displays to change its options. Often, Select All changes to Deselect All. ∎

The View menu

Another commonly found menu is View, which controls how documents are displayed. The menu options themselves vary by application: In iCal, for example, you use them to view and navigate the calendars using the By Day, By Week, and By Month menu options. In many applications, the View menu contains options to control the zoom level for the document display.

The Window menu

This menu enables you to control the application's windows. Two common menu options at the top are Zoom (which usually toggles the application window's size between filling the entire desktop and returning to its original size) and Minimize (which hides the window in the Dock, as explained later in this chapter). Note that the Minimize menu option usually has the keyboard shortcut ⌘+M.

Another common option is Bring All to Front, which brings all windows relating to the application to the front of other windows in use by Mac OS X. The Window menu also usually lists any open application windows and may list other types of windows and panels (which typically are floating windows that hold controls) used by the application.

Tip
In some applications, you can press and hold Option when the Window menu displays to change its options. As common examples, the Zoom menu option changes to Zoom All, and Minimize changes to Minimize All. ■

The Help menu

This menu gives you access to on-screen help. Typically, at the top is the Search box, and typing into it displays menu-option explanations and help topics. The explanations relate to corresponding commands throughout the menu bar, and you can use them to quickly locate items. The help topics open the Help Center, which offers a range of advice on every area of Mac OS X. (Chapter 7 explains Mac OS X's built-in help system.) Below the Search field is usually a set of dedicated help options and often an option to check for program updates. These correspond to either the application as a whole or to particular areas of interest relating to the application.

The Script menu

This menu, represented by the symbol ⑂, appears in the menu bar of many (but not all) applications that support AppleScript, Apple's facility for letting users control applications with mini-programs they write. Chapter 13 explains scripting.

Touring the menu bar icons

On the right side of the menu bar sit various icons that let you access system-wide functions, both those provided by Apple in Mac OS X and those that third-party software may provide. Examples of such third-party functions include scanning controls in an antivirus program such as Intego, connection controls for a 3G USB modem such as an Ovation, or printer management controls for a networked printer such as a Brother multi-function printer.

For those functions that come with Mac OS X, many display only if you enable the menu bar display from their corresponding system preference. The Apple-provided functions include the items described in the following sections, listed in the order they appear in the menu bar if all were enabled.

AppleScript

If you enable display of the AppleScript icon menu (the styled S icon) in the AppleScript Editor's Preferences dialog box (see Chapter 13), you can use it to edit and run scripts.

Fax

If you have a fax set up on your Mac, the Fax icon menu displays (the phone-on-paper icon). You can answer incoming calls and manage fax status. Chapter 30 has more information on setting up faxing services on your Mac.

Universal Access

This icon menu (the icon is a person inside a circle) lets you access Apple's controls to help the visually and hearing-impaired use their Macs, such as to speak aloud screen contents or zoom into the screen. It also lets you open the Universal Access system preference. Chapter 8 explains the Universal Access capabilities.

VPN

This icon menu (a horizontal black rounded rectangle meant to depict a keycard) lets you connect to a virtual private network (VPN) as well as to see the status of such connections and open the Network system preference. Chapter 23 explains such networks.

Modem and WWAN

If you are using a dial-up modem, you can display the Modem icon menu (the phone icon) to control dial-up services. You can connect and disconnect to the Internet over a phone connection via the options in the icon menu. More information on accessing the Internet via a dial-up modem is in Chapter 23.

Likewise, the WWAN icon menu (also the phone icon) appears if you have installed a wide-area wireless network (WWAN) device—a 3G or 4G cellular modem card or USB device, for example. Note that if you have both a modem and a WWAN device installed, only one icon menu appears, with options for both types of devices.

Time Machine

This icon menu (a small counter-clockwise circular arrow icon) represents the status of the Time Machine backup utility; Time Machine is explained in depth in Chapter 11. This menu offers options to perform a backup, restore files, and adjust the preferences.

Wi-Fi

This icon menu appears if you have a wireless networking card installed in your Mac; all current Macs have an Apple AirPort Wi-Fi card installed by default. The icon is composed of four arcs, reminiscent of a radar display, and the number of arcs that display corresponds to the strength of the signal from a corresponding wireless router. If Wi-Fi is switched off, or there is no signal, the symbol is an empty outline (similar in style to the shape of a baseball field). You can use the Wi-Fi icon menu to join a local wireless network, create a wireless network, or open the Network system preference.

Displays

This icon menu (which looks like a monitor) lets you switch screen resolutions, switch the primary screen to a different display (if you have multiple monitors connected), and access the Displays system preference.

Volume

Clicking this icon menu (the speaker icon) brings up a vertical slider you use to adjust how loudly your Mac's speakers emit sound. The icon changes, showing more "sound waves" emanating from the speaker, as you increase the volume. You also can adjust sound levels using the Sound system preference (described in Chapter 28).

Battery Status

Available only on Apple's MacBook line of laptops, this indicator shows how much battery power is left or, if the laptop is plugged into a power source, its charging status. If your battery has a problem, an alert appears in the menu. You also can also use this icon menu to open the Energy Saver system preference, where you control the Mac's power-saving options.

Time

By default, this menu title displays as the current time (in AM/PM format or in 24-hour format, based on the display standard for your current language). Clicking the time shows the full date, as well as options to view the time as analog (via a clock face). You also can access the Date & Time system preference from this menu; Chapter 28 explains the available preferences.

Input Language

This menu displays as an icon of the flag representing the country whose language settings are in use. If you have multiple languages set up on the Mac, you can use this icon menu to switch among them, which changes the language used throughout Mac OS X, as well as related presentation of date formats and keyboard layouts. This menu also has an option to open the Language & Text system preference.

Keyboard & Character Viewer

This icon menu lets you access special characters by opening Mac OS X's Character Viewer and Keyboard Viewer mini-applications. You also can use it to open the Keyboards system preference, where you can change the keyboard's sensitivity and how some keys are interpreted when pressed, as Chapter 28 explains. Note this menu displays only if the Keyboard & Character Viewer option is checked in the Language & Text system preference's Input pane *and* if only one language is active on the Mac. If the Keyboard & Character Viewer icon menu appears, it replaces the Input Language icon menu.

Bluetooth

If you have Bluetooth activated on your Mac, the Bluetooth icon menu (a stylized B icon) appears in the menu bar. You can use it to set up devices such as headsets and keyboards, make your Mac discoverable by other Bluetooth devices, browse devices, and open the Bluetooth system preference (see Chapters 24 and 28).

User

If you have Fast User Switching enabled, this icon displays as one of three variations: the head-and-shoulders icon, your full username, or Mac OS X's short name for your account. (You set the icon menu's display using the Fast User Switching option set in the Users & Groups system preference, as Chapter 27 explains.) Clicking this icon menu enables you to select a different user account. You also can access the login window from here to switch to another user account while keeping the current user account running. (This differs from the Log Out option found in the menu, which logs out the current user before switching to another one.) Finally, this icon menu also offers quick access to the Users & Groups system preference.

Spotlight

At the far right of the screen is the Spotlight icon menu (a magnifying glass icon). Clicking it brings up a search box where you can type a term to be searched throughout your Mac's disks. Spotlight is a powerful technology that permeates the Mac OS X environment, and the terms you enter here search applications, documents, folders, e-mail messages, and even your music and video collections. Spotlight is explained in depth in Chapter 5.

New Feature

In Mac OS X Lion, there's no longer an icon menu for Spaces; instead, use keyboard shortcuts or gestures to switch among them. (The Spaces feature is explained in more detail later in this chapter, along with the related Mission Control feature.) ∎

Tip

Although menu items on the left side of the menu bar are fixed by the application in question, you can move and rearrange those on the right (with the exception of the Spotlight icon menu) that are provided by Mac OS X. Simply ⌘+click an icon and drag it left or right to rearrange it. Note that icon menus added to the menu bar by individual applications typically cannot be moved this way. You also can remove some icon menus by ⌘+dragging them off the menu bar; to redisplay them, use their corresponding system preferences to turn on menu bar display. ∎

Using pop-up menus

Pop-up menus are the menus that appear within a dialog box or panel. Pop-up menus come in several styles. Common types include horizontal bars with text labels or icons, both of which are shown in Figure 2.4. Notice in the figure the downward-pointing triangle on the right side of some menus and double-triangle icons on others. The single-triangle icon indicates the menu list will drop below the menu title when clicked, while the double-triangle icon indicates the list will likely obscure the menu title, starting above it and continuing below it.

FIGURE 2.4

Pop-up menus are signified by triangle icons. Here, an icon pop-up menu is open in a pane that has multiple icon and textual pop-up menus.

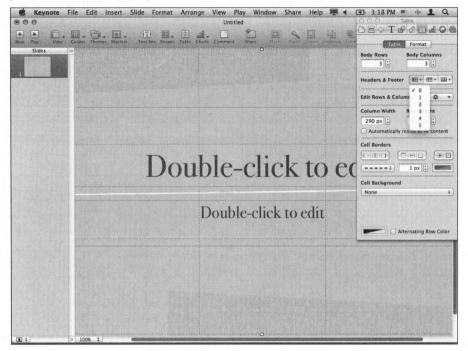

Using contextual menus

As the name suggests, a contextual menu is one that changes based upon its context. This ensures that you see only those menu options that are relevant to a particular file, document, or situation. You display a contextual menu by right-clicking or Control+clicking virtually anywhere in the Mac OS X environment, such as an icon, window, or other selection.

The options that appear are infinitely varied; right-clicking or Control+clicking a file on the desktop, for example, brings up options to open the file, move it to the Trash, get information, compress the file, duplicate it, create an alias, take a quick look at its contents, clean it up, change the color of its label, and send it to somebody as an e-mail attachment. Figure 2.5 shows the contextual menu for a network volume.

It also is possible to highlight multiple items and right-click or Control+click to bring up a contextual menu that applies to several items; in that case, only options that apply to all the selected items appear in the menu.

FIGURE 2.5

A contextual menu for a network volume

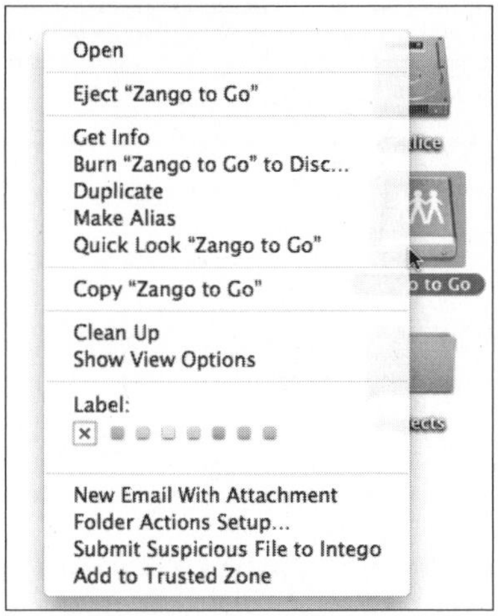

Tip

You can often press and hold Option when a contextual menu displays to change its options. For example, in the Finder, the Open With menu option changes to Always Open With for a document, and Clean Up Selection changes to Clean Up for any icon displaying in icon view, and Quick Look changes to Slide Show for any icon. ■

Working with the Dock

Now that you are familiar with the menu bar, it is time to look at Mac OS X's second stalwart interface mechanism, the Dock, shown in Figure 2.6.

Located at the bottom of the screen, the Dock is a tray for commonly used applications, files, and Mac OS X functions. The Dock uses many visual effects, including see-through transparency, reflections, and magnification and, as such, demonstrates much of Apple's legendary visual flair. But don't be fooled into thinking of it as a mere visual gimmick. The Dock is a powerful organizational tool that keeps your most important items in front of you for immediate access.

The Dock is used to launch your commonly used applications and to access commonly used files and folders. The Dock is divided into two halves: An easy-to-overlook gray dividing line of 3-D dashes marks the separation, like a lane divider stripe on a road. The left side is devoted to applications, whereas the right side is used for documents, folders, and minimized windows. You can adjust the position and appearance of the Dock, as explained later in this chapter.

FIGURE 2.6

The Dock is a tray used to quickly open and switch between applications, and it offers access to files and folders.

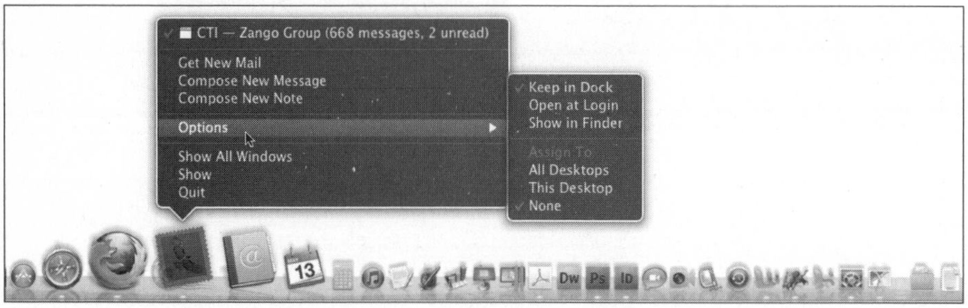

By default, icons for the following items appear on the Dock:

- **Finder:** This main application is used by Mac OS X to manage files, folders, and disks on your computer. The Finder remains active at all times and is a permanent fixture on the left side of the Dock.

- **Launchpad:** This provides control for accessing all your applications through a series of home screens, as on an iPhone or iPad. Chapter 14 explains how to use Launchpad.

- **App Store:** Apple's application for buying apps over the Internet is its Mac App Store.

- **Mail:** This is Apple's program for sending and receiving e-mail. Chapter 20 explains how to use Mail.

- **Safari:** Apple's web browser is included with Mac OS X. Chapter 19 explains how to use Safari.

- **FaceTime:** This is Apple's video conferencing application for Macs and iOS mobile devices—the iPad, iPhone, and iPod Touch.

- **Address Book:** This application is for storing information on contacts (people and companies). Multiple Mac OS X applications such as Mail can use the information stored in Address Book. Chapter 21 explains how to use Address Book.

- **iCal:** Apple's calendar application is for making note of important dates and events, and it's also a to-do task manager. Chapter 21 explains how to use iCal.

- **Preview:** This application is for quickly examining the contents of files.

- **iTunes:** This application is for storing and playing audio and video files, plus managing and synchronizing media and applications with other Apple devices such as the iPods and iPhones. Chapter 15 explains how to use iTunes.

- **Photo Booth:** This application lets you take a picture with the Mac's built-in iSight camera and then apply silly effects to it.

- **System Preferences:** This enables you to adjust various aspects of Mac OS X, as Chapter 28 details.
- **Documents:** This is an alias to the Documents folder (see Chapter 3).
- **Downloads:** This is an alias to the Downloads folder (see Chapter 3).
- **Trash:** This folder contains files that you have discarded. Emptying the Trash permanently deletes the files from the Mac. Along with the Finder, the Trash icon is a permanent fixture on the Dock. Note that the Trash changes to the Eject icon if you drag a disk onto it.

New Feature

In Mac OS X Lion's Dock, the Launchpad, App Store, and FaceTime icons are new. And you can no longer find icons for the Dashboard, iChat, Spaces, or Time Machine. The Dashboard, iChat, and Time Machine applications still exist; they're just no longer loaded into the Dock by default. Likewise, the Applications folder is no longer placed in the Dock by default. (Apple would prefer you use Launchpad.) The Spaces feature no longer exists as its own application but remains as part of the Mac OS X navigation capabilities described later in this chapter. ∎

Hovering the mouse over the icons in the Dock brings up a text description of the application, window, or document.

Icons are temporarily added to the Dock as you use applications, open files, and minimize windows. This can be confusing to the newcomer, although it quickly becomes second nature.

Adding icons to the Dock

You can keep icons already displayed in the Dock—that is, those of running applications and open folders and files—by right-clicking or Control+clicking them and then choosing Options ⇨ Keep in Dock from the contextual menu.

To add new items to the Dock, just drag application, folder, or file icons into the Dock to permanently place them there. But note that applications can go only on the left side of the Dock, and files and folders can go only on the right side. When dragging files and folders into the Dock, be sure to release them between existing files and folders (the existing icons on either side should part ways slightly); if you drag an item over a folder, you end up placing the item inside that folder.

Removing icons from the Dock

To remove an icon from the Dock, simply click it with the mouse, or tap and hold it on the touchpad, and then drag it away from the Dock. The icon appears with a small smoke cloud beneath it; release the mouse button or your finger from the touchpad, and the icon vanishes into a cloud of smoke (replete with a satisfying whooshing sound effect). You also can right-click or Control+click an icon in the Dock and choose Options ⇨ Remove from Dock to remove its icon.

Retrieving Items from the Trash

When you throw items in the Trash—whether by dragging them there or deleting them with a menu option or a keyboard shortcut—you're actually putting them in a folder. So you can move items out of the Trash if you deleted them accidentally—as long as you do so before you empty the Trash, of course. There are two ways to get items out of the Trash. Both start with double-clicking the Trash in the Dock to open it as a folder. (You also can select it and choose File↷Open, press ⌘+O, or right-click or Control+click it and choose Open from the contextual menu.) With the Trash folder open, you have these options:

- Drag the item from the Trash to the desktop or another location on your Mac. This lets you put the item anywhere you want.
- Right-click or Control+click an item, or use the touchpad's equivalent gesture, and choose Put Back from the contextual menu. This saves you from having to remember the item's original location; Mac OS X remembers and places the item there.

Because it is so easy to remove icons from the Dock, you should be careful not to remove items accidentally. If you drag an icon up and the smoke cloud appears, and you don't want to delete an icon, simply drag it back down to the right side of the Dock before releasing the mouse button or your finger from the touchpad.

Moving icons around the Dock

You can rearrange items on the Dock by clicking them with the mouse or by tapping and holding them with the touchpad and then dragging them left and right. Timing is fairly critical, because if you hold the mouse button down or tap and hold on the touchpad for too long without moving the mouse or your finger, a contextual menu appears instead.

As you move the icon around, the other icons move to make space for it. Remember that you cannot move applications and documents and folders beyond their respective sides. (If you try to do so, the icon slides back to its original position.) Because icons are not the documents themselves, you cannot move a document icon inside a folder icon.

Caution

Be careful when moving files to keep an eye out for the cloud-of-smoke image appearing on the icon. The appearance of this cloud-of-smoke image means you are about to remove the icon from the Dock, which is easy to do accidentally. If you don't intend to remove the icon from the Dock, keep the mouse button pressed or your finger held to the touchpad and move the icon back onto the Dock; then you can release the mouse button or your finger. (Releasing the mouse button or your finger when the cloud-of-smoke image appears removes the icon from the Dock.) ∎

Tip

To quickly access options for Dock items, right-click or Control+click them to open a contextual menu. Or click and hold the mouse or touchpad button on a Dock item for a few seconds to open a contextual menu. ∎

Working with the application side of the Dock

Any application that is being used by your Mac has an icon in the left side of the Dock. When you open the application, the icon bounces up and down in the Dock signifying that it is loading. It then sits in the Dock. When you quit the application, the icon disappears from the Dock (unless it has been added to the Dock, as described earlier).

There are exceptions to the bouncing effect at launch: the Launchpad and Time Machine icons. Clicking either of these icons takes you straight to the corresponding function.

Tip

It can be hard to tell what Dock applications are actually running, unless you enable the Show Indicator Lights for Open Applications option in the Dock system preference. If you do so, each running application displays a small blue-and-white sphere beneath it, as Figure 2.6 shows. ■

Note

Icons that remain in the Dock are actually aliases, or quick links, to applications and folders; the applications themselves remain in the Applications or Utilities folder (see Chapter 14), and the folders remain in their normal location (see Chapter 4). ■

The application icons can sometimes provide information relating to the program. Mail, for example, checks for new messages periodically and a numeral in a small red ellipse (called a *badge*) appears next to the icon in the Dock, signifying the number of unread e-mail messages.

As with most items in Mac OS X, you can access a contextual menu for each application in the Dock by right-clicking or Control+clicking its icon in the Dock. Note that the contextual menu changes, depending on whether the application is open. If the application is not running, the contextual menu displays the Open option to launch the application and the Options option whose submenu has the following options:

- **Remove from Dock:** Choosing this option removes the icon from the Dock; it has the same result as dragging the icon out of the Dock.

- **Open at Login:** Choosing this option ensures that the program starts when you boot up and log in to your Mac. This can be useful if there is a program that you always use as soon as you start your Mac. Login items are set in the Users & Groups system preference, as explained in Chapter 27.

- **Show in Finder:** Because icons are aliases to items that exist in the Finder's folder hierarchy, you can quickly open a Finder window and show the original item by choosing this option.

In the Dock, open applications may have additional options depending on the application. Mail, for example, has options to get new e-mail and compose new messages; Safari has options for moving between open browser windows; System Preferences has a complete list of all the available system preferences.

As well as their own custom options, open applications always have the following two menu options:

- **Hide:** Choosing this option removes the application's windows from the desktop. When you choose this option, its name in the contextual menu changes to Show, which you use to bring back the application's windows.
- **Quit:** Choosing this option quits the application.

Tip

Pressing and holding the Option key when accessing an application's contextual menu in the Dock changes some of the options. The Hide option becomes Hide Others, which is used to hide windows from all other applications besides the one selected; Quit turns into Force Quit, which you can use to close down applications that have frozen. (Force Quit is explained in Chapter 9.) ■

Given that the Finder is permanently running, it always displays additional options:

- **New Finder Window:** This option opens a new window that can be used to explore files on your Mac. Finder windows are explained in Chapter 3. You also can press ⌘+N.
- **New Smart Folder:** Smart folders are "intelligent" folders that collect aliases to files based on predefined criteria. The creation of smart folders is explained in Chapter 4. You also can press Option+⌘+N.
- **Find:** The Find option opens a Finder window and takes you directly to the Spotlight search area (see Chapter 5). You also can press ⌘+F.
- **Go to Folder:** The Go to Folder command is used to navigate directly to a folder using its pathname. The pathname is the name of all the folders surrounded by a slash (/) character; for example, `/Library/Documentation`. You also can press Shift+⌘+G.
- **Connect to Server:** This command is used to connect to local and remote servers. You also can press ⌘+K.

The Finder's contextual menu in the Dock also lists any open Finder windows.

Tip

If you press and hold Option when right-clicking or Control+clicking the Finder icon in the Dock, the contextual menu adds an option: Relaunch. This option force-quits the Finder and relaunches it, which you may need to do if the Finder freezes, though this is a very rare occurrence. ■

Working with the files and windows side of the Dock

The right side of the Dock is where you place documents, folders, and disks. When you place a document into the Dock, clicking it opens the document using its default application. (It opens the application as well, if necessary.)

Folders that are added to the Dock expand to reveal their contents when selected with the mouse. They expand in one of three ways, depending on the number of items contained within and on your own personal preferences. As with applications and documents, it is important to remember that the folders are not themselves contained in the Dock, but instead the Dock acts as an alias to the folder stored elsewhere on the Mac.

Dragging documents to and from folders on the Dock moves the files to and from the folder that the Dock item points to. As well as folders, you can add aliases for entire disks to the Dock, which can make accessing multiple disks (both those located on your Mac and on networked volumes) a quick and easy process.

Adding a document, folder, or disk to the Dock is relatively simple. Click and drag the item from its location (either on the desktop or in the Finder) to the right side of the Dock. Be careful to drag it between other items on the Dock and not on top of a folder (or it will be moved *into* that folder). Surrounding items should move out of the way to enable a space for you to drop in the document. Note that the Dock treats a disk as if it were a folder and uses a folder icon for it.

Much of the power of the Dock is apparent when you begin to add folders or disks to the Dock and use it to quickly examine and access their contents.

When you add a folder to the Dock, it is known as a *stack*. This is because the icon is formed from small images from the items in the folder stacked on top of each other—a pile of applications for the Applications folder, for example, or a pile of files and folders for other folders and disks.

Clicking the icon in the Dock reveals the stacked contents in one of three ways:

- As a fan, which shows the contained items in a slightly curved vertical line
- As a grid, which shows the items in a pop-up square grid against a gray translucent background
- As a list, which shows them in a standard linear menu arrangement

By default, items in a stack appear in either fan or grid view automatically, depending on the number of items. If a stack contains nine items or fewer, it appears as a fan; if it contains 10 items or more, it appears as a grid. (You can override these defaults and choose the desired view for individual folders using the Fan, Grid, and List options in the contextual menu rather than the default Automatic option.)

When a stack is opened and the contents are on display, you can click an item to open it or drag items to move them out of the stack (including dragging them to the Trash to delete them).

There are, however, several things that you cannot do with items in a stack:

- You cannot click and drag to rearrange items in the stack. (Clicking an item immediately closes the stack and leaves the item under your pointer.)

- You cannot drag the mouse or your finger to select multiple items; they must be dealt with individually.

- You cannot right-click or Control+click to open a contextual menu for items in a stack.

The stack is designed to provide quick, simple access to items contained within. If you want to do anything more complex with items in the stack, you need to open the original folder that the stack is an alias of. There are three ways to do so:

- Right-click or Control+click the stack, and choose the Open menu option.

- Click the Open in Finder icon button (a menu item in list view) at the bottom of the open stack.

- Even easier: ⌘+click a folder in the Dock.

Tip

When using stacks in grid view, you can scroll through the files and folders: If there are more items than can be displayed on the screen, a scroll bar appears that you can use to navigate through the items using the mouse (including the scroll bar or the mouse's scroll ball or wheel) or touchpad. Also, you can navigate through folders: Clicking a folder in a stack opens the contents of that folder in a new stack, and at the top-left of the stack, you see a Back icon button (the ← icon) containing the name of the previous folder. Clicking this Back icon button takes you to the contents of the previous folder. ∎

Note

If you press and hold Shift when opening a stack (or Shift+click an item in a stack), the list opens (or closes), very slowly, using a slow-motion effect. This seems to be an Easter egg, one of those useless or humorous gems that developers sometimes insert in applications just for fun. ∎

If you right-click or Control+click a folder or stack on the Dock, you get a contextual menu with several sections of options that affect how the folder and its contents are displayed:

- **Sort By:** Items in the folder are sorted automatically, and you cannot manually rearrange them. By default, they are sorted alphabetically by name, but you can change that to Date Added, Date Modified, Date Created, or Kind.

- **Display As:** This option relates to the Dock icon itself, not the stack that expands. Choose Stacks to display the icon as a pile of icons representing its contents, and choose Folder to use the standard Mac OS X folder icon.

- **View Content As:** This option controls how the stack's items are displayed, as noted earlier, as a list, fan, or grid. If you choose Automatic (the default), Mac OS X uses a grid if there are more than nine items and a fan if not.

Below these options, you find the usual contextual menu items covered earlier: Options and Open.

Customizing the Dock

The Dock contains a set of icons that you can rearrange or remove at will. The only two icons that must stay on the Dock are the Finder on the left side and the Trash icon on the right. By default, the Dock is located at the bottom of the screen and is fairly large. You may want to change its location, change its size, or otherwise customize its appearance.

All the options for adjusting the Dock are located in the Dock system preference. You also can adjust many aspects of the Dock via its own contextual menu, which you access by right-clicking the area on the Dock that has the dividing line.

Tip

A fast way to change several Dock preferences is to choose ⌘⇨Dock and then choose one of the submenu options: Turn Hiding On/Off, Turn Magnification On/Off, Position on Left, Position on Right, Position on Bottom, or Dock Preferences. ∎

Adjusting the Dock's size

As you add and remove items from the Dock, it expands left and right to accommodate the extra items. The Dock system preference's Size slider lets you adjust the overall size of the icons in the Dock. The overall size of the icons depends largely on how many you have in the Dock, but the slider, in effect, sets the maximize size.

You can adjust the Dock's size in two ways:

- Drag the Size slider in the Dock system preference from left to right to find the desired size (left is smaller; right is larger). If you have numerous icons in the Dock, you are limited in how large you can resize the Dock. In this case, the slider still moves all the way to the right position, but the Dock itself does not get any larger.

- Hold the mouse over the vertical dividing line until a Dock resizing icon appears. (The icon is a white horizontal line with arrows above and below it.) Click and drag the mouse up or left to make the Dock larger; click and drag the mouse down or right to make the Dock smaller.

Setting the Dock magnification

If you have set the Dock to less than its maximum size, you can use the visual effect called *magnification*. This makes the icons on the Dock that your mouse is hovering over larger than the rest of the Dock, as if you were moving a magnifying glass over it. (Refer to Figure 2.6 to see this effect in action.)

To enable magnification quickly, choose ⌘⇨Dock⇨Turn Magnification On, or right-click or Control+click the white, dashed dividing line in the Dock and choose Turn Magnification On from the contextual menu. (If magnification is already on, the menu option is labeled Turn Magnification Off.) Alternatively, check the Magnification option in the Dock system preference. You can adjust the size of Dock magnification using the Magnification slider.

Dock magnification is very much a personal choice, and many users prefer to keep it switched off. Magnification is a great visual effect and can enable you to focus on the icon under the mouse. However, it also can make clicking desired icons more difficult because they move slightly when expanding. Experiment with both styles to discover which one works for you.

Positioning and automatically hiding the Dock

By default, the Dock appears at the bottom of the screen. However, you can position it at either the left or right side of the screen.

The advantage of having the Dock at the bottom of the screen is that you can fit more icons in the Dock (or have a slightly larger Dock) because the bottom of the screen is wider than the sides of the screen.

The flip side to this is that the Dock's positioning at the bottom of the screen limits the maximum vertical size of windows on the screen. Given that widescreen displays have limited the vertical space in favor of horizontal space, positioning the Dock on the side of the screen can reclaim vertical space, which in turn can make scanning long documents or websites easier.

One way to deal with this is to move the Dock from its default position to either the left or right side of the screen. To do so, choose ⬤⇨Dock⇨Position on Left or ⬤⇨Dock⇨Position on Right, or right-click or Control+click the Dock's dividing line and choose Position on Screen⇨Left or Position on Screen⇨Right from the contextual menu.

A side effect of positioning the Dock on either the left or right side of the screen is that the Dock has a slightly different visual effect. When the Dock is positioned on the bottom of the screen, it displays a reflection of the Dock icons and of any nearby windows and icons on the desktop; when it is on either side of the window, it has no reflection effect and thus has slightly more contrast. Many people find the reflective effect of the Dock distracting and prefer the higher contrast appearance when it is on the side of the screen.

An alternative to moving the Dock is to have it out of the way when it's not required. You can set it to do this using one of the following methods:

- Choose ⬤⇨Dock⇨Turn Hiding On.
- Right-click or Control+click the white divider line in the Dock and choose Turn Hiding on from the contextual menu.
- Press Option+⌘+D.
- Select the Automatically Hide and Show the Dock option in the Dock system preference.

When this hiding option is selected, the Dock automatically slides off the screen when not in use. When you slide the mouse to the edge where the dock is hiding, it automatically slides back onto the screen, enabling you to make selections as normal. This automatic Dock hiding feature is the best way to get the most out of your screen space, although some people prefer the Dock to be on display at all times.

Animating open applications in the Dock

The final visual option in the Dock system preference is Animate Opening Applications. This is selected by default, which means that clicking an application in the Dock causes it to bounce up and down as it launches. Although this is a good visual indicator of an application's status, many users find the bouncing effect distracting. You can switch it off by deselecting the Animate Opening Applications option in the Dock system preference.

Minimizing windows in the Dock

The other feature that the Dock is used for is as a placeholder for minimized windows (both application and Finder windows). You can minimize windows into the Dock by clicking the window's Minimize icon button (the – icon), choosing Window ⇨ Minimize, or pressing ⌘+M. Using an option in the General system preference, you also can have Mac OS X minimize a window when its title bar is double-clicked.

By default, minimized windows disappear into their application icons (folders disappear into the Finder icon). You can see the names of minimized windows in the currently open application's Windows menu. But to see the windows (minimized or not) in another running application, right-click or Control+click, or click and hold (or tap and hold), that application's icon in the Dock. By default, you see a list of all open windows for that application; click a window's title to open it.

But to see live previews of the windows' contents—what's called Exposé view—choose Show All Windows from the contextual menu in the Dock. As Figure 2.7 shows, your screen changes to show miniature versions of each window and its content in Exposé view. At the top are open windows, and at the bottom are minimized windows. You select the desired window to open by moving the pointer to it and clicking it; a blue outline appears around the window the pointer is currently over.

New Feature

Mac OS X Lion no longer shows the Exposé view of open application windows when you click and hold a Dock application icon; you now must choose Show All Windows from the contextual menu. This makes the behavior identical whether you use the right-click or Control+click technique or the click-and-hold technique to display the contextual menu. By contrast, Mac OS X Snow Leopard used click and hold to present the Exposé view and the right-click and Control+click technique to present the menu list.

If you prefer to have windows minimize into their own icons on the right side of the Dock, go to the Dock system preference and deselect the Minimize Windows into Application option. (Choose ⇨ System Preferences and then click the Dock icon or choose ⇨ Dock ⇨ Dock Preferences to open the Dock system preference.)

When you minimize a window into the Dock, Mac OS X uses a nifty animation called the Genie effect, with that genie-in-a-bottle style. You can change the minimize effect in the Dock system preference: Choose Genie Effect or Scale Effect in the Minimize Using pop-up menu. The Genie effect is the default. The Scale effect is a more straightforward shrinking in a quick series of steps.

FIGURE 2.7

The Exposé view of an application's windows, as opened from the Dock

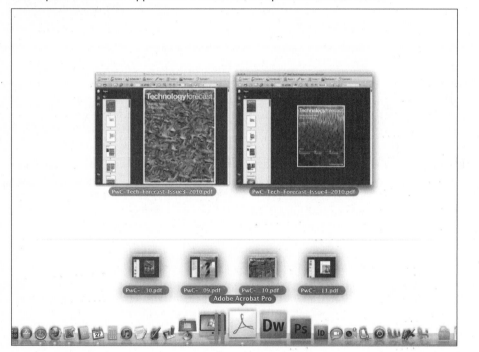

Using Exposé, Spaces, and Mission Control

The Exposé capability in the Dock is just the tip of the iceberg in terms of Mac OS X's abilities to maneuver through application and Finder windows. Mac OS X also has a capability called Spaces and one called Mission Control that work together with Exposé to give you quick access to all your running applications, open windows, and available applications.

New Feature

Mission Control is new to Mac OS X Lion. In Mac OS X Lion, Exposé and Spaces are now components of Mission Control; the Exposé component also now also lets you switch to the Dashboard (see Chapter 14) when using gestures (in addition to the previous keyboard shortcuts). ■

Here's a quick overview of what these three navigation features do:

- **Exposé:** This feature gives you quick access to various windows through shortcuts as well as by clicking or tapping corners of the screen. In what is called App Exposé view, you can use it to show all miniature versions of all windows or all of the active application's windows (including the Finder) so you can navigate among them, as well as jump to the Launchpad, desktop, or Dashboard views. (You set the shortcuts in the Mission Control system preference, explained in Chapter 28.)

- **Spaces:** This feature in essence lets you set up multiple desktops (each called a *space*), each showing the windows of just the applications you specify. It's a handy way to organize your open windows by task, if you're someone who often has lots of applications running simultaneously. Figure 2.8 shows the Mac screen as I switch from one space to another via a gesture. You also can switch via keyboard shortcuts and via Mission Control.

- **Mission Control:** This feature lets you see everything going on in one view, as Figure 2.9 shows: Each space is displayed at the top, and each application's set of open windows displays as a group of windows below. In addition to using the keyboard shortcuts, you can get the Mission Control view by using whatever gesture you set up for it in the Trackpad system preference (described earlier in this chapter) or, if you use a Magic Mouse, in the Mouse system preference.

Tip

The default shortcut for App Exposé view for the current application is Control+↓; press Control+↓ again to go back to the regular desktop view. You also can use the default four-finger swipe-down gesture. If you're in the regular desktop view, press Control+↑ to go to the Mission Control view, and press Control+↑ again to go back to the regular desktop view. You also can use the default four-finger swipe-up gesture. The shortcut to open the Dashboard is Control+← (F12 also works), or you can use the four-finger left swipe; press Control+→ to go back to the regular desktop view (F11 also works), or you can use the four-finger right swipe. You also use Control+→ and Control+← or the horizontal four-finger swipe gestures to move among spaces, if any are defined.

You can change these shortcuts in the Mission Control system preference (see Chapter 28), and note that they may differ on your Mac if you upgraded from Mac OS X Snow Leopard and had different shortcuts set in its Exposé & Spaces system preference. ■

Tip

In Mission Control, you can drag windows around to reduce overlap; you also can use the four-finger expand gesture to open a cluster of windows and the four-finger pinch gesture to bring them closer to each other. ■

To add spaces, go to Mission Control and move the pointer to the upper left of the screen. The + icon button appears. Or you can drag an application or its windows in Mission Control next to a space or between existing spaces to create a space that the application is assigned to. Either way, you'll see a new window in the Mission Control screen called Desktop *x*, where *x* is the space's number.

To add an application to a space, go to that space and then, in the Dock, right-click, Control+ click, or click and hold the desired application to open its contextual menu. Then do one of the following:

- To have the application open only in the current space, choose Options ⇨ This Desktop. You also can drag an application or its windows in Mission Control into a space to add that application to the space.

- To have the application open in every space, choose Options ⇨ All Desktops.

- To have the application open in the whichever space you are currently using (that is, not be assigned to a specific space, choose Options ⇨ None.

To delete a space, go to the Mission Control view and hover the pointer over the top-left corner of the space you want to delete. The Close icon button appears; click it to delete the space.

FIGURE 2.8

Switching from one space to another via gestures

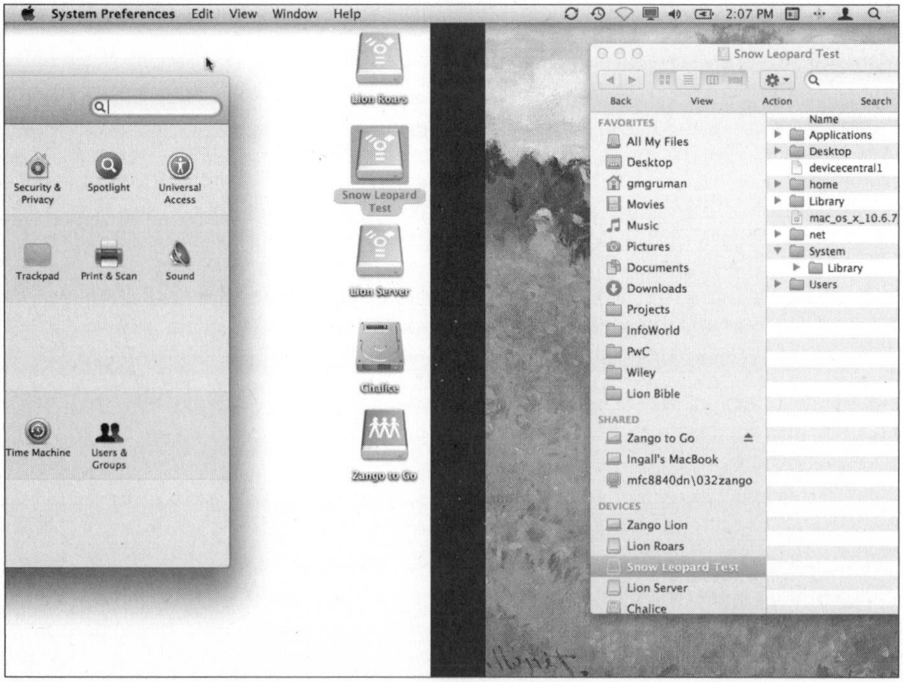

FIGURE 2.9

The Mission Control view shows all spaces and clusters of application windows so you can navigate to any of them.

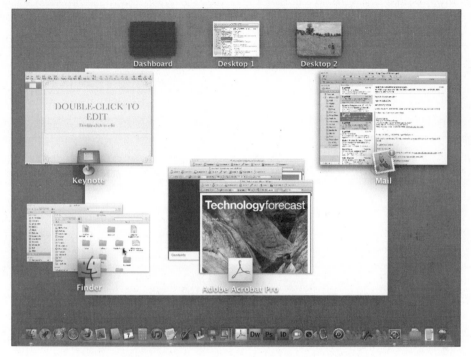

Summary

A key distinguishing feature of Mac OS X is its graphical user interface (GUI), which sets the standard for ease of use even 27 years after Apple delivered the first Macintosh using it. Mac OS X's Finder is your portal to the Mac and uses three main GUI components to interact with its applications and files: the desktop, the menu bar, and the Dock. The desktop is the canvas that holds the icons representing your files, folders, and disks. The menu bar provides access to both applications' and Mac OS X's commands via the mouse or touchpad. The Dock provides quick access to applications, document windows, and files and folders.

You use a keyboard and either or both a mouse and touchpad to manipulate the items on the desktop, in the Dock, and in the menu bar. The extensive use of keyboard shortcuts and contextual menus makes it easy to initiate actions at times when navigating the menu bar can be inefficient. And the increased use of gestures provides new efficiencies in handling complex interactions with Mac OS X and its items.

Apple has more fully integrated gesture controls into Mac OS X Lion, offering the gesture-driven Mission Control as a single view of everything running on your Mac so you can navigate to any active item. The Exposé and Spaces navigation features, which you can use independently or within Mission Control, also provide ways to navigate through the active applications and windows in the Finder.

Using the Finder

A s its name suggests, the Finder is the Mac OS X facility for finding items in your Mac. It's also the mechanism through which you interact with them—opening them, deleting them, renaming them, moving them, copying them, setting permissions for them, and so on.

Chapter 2 explains the major user interface elements the Finder uses to present its contents—the desktop, menus, and the Dock—as well as how to use the keyboard, mouse, and touchpad to interact with those items.

The Finder is an application, one that has its own preferences you can adjust, its own menu bar, and techniques for accessing and working with items in its windows. The Finder runs automatically when your Mac starts up, and you can't really use the Mac for much if it's not running. This chapter explains how to use the Finder.

IN THIS CHAPTER

Learning the Finder-specific menu options

Addressing a frozen Finder

Working with Finder windows

Changing Finder behavior for folders and files

Modifying Finder preferences and view options

Using the Finder's Menus

Like any application, the Finder has a set of menus, with menu options specific to the Finder's operations. The Finder's menu options appear on the menu bar—to the right of the symbol—when the Finder is the active application; click the desktop or the Finder icon in the Dock to make Finder the active application. Let's look at the Finder-specific menus. (Menu options such as About, Preferences, Services, Hide, Show, Cut, Copy, Paste, Minimize, Zoom, Bring All to Front, and Help that are universal to all applications are covered in Chapter 2.)

The Finder menu

The application menu for the Finder is, not surprisingly, called the Finder menu.

- **Empty Trash:** The Trash's trash can icon is located on the far right of the Dock and contains files and folders you've deleted from the Mac. These files stay in the Trash (so they can be recovered) until you choose this menu option. Emptying the Trash permanently removes these items from the Mac. You also can press Shift+⌘+Delete to empty the Trash.

- **Secure Empty Trash:** The Secure Empty Trash option not only empties the Trash but also completely overwrites the files with meaningless numbers, preventing anybody from recovering the data even with an undelete or recovery utility.

The File menu

The File menu offers the following menu options:

- **New Finder Window:** Choosing this option opens a new Finder window. The Finder window enables you to browse through volumes, folders, and files, as described later in this chapter. You also can simply press ⌘+N to open a new Finder window.

- **New Folder:** Choosing this option creates a new folder within the active Finder window or, if no Finder window is open, on the desktop. (You also can simply press Shift+⌘+N.)

- **New Folder with Selection:** Choosing this option puts selected items into a new folder. You also can press Control+⌘+N. Note that at least two items (files and/or folders) must be selected for this option to be active.

New Feature

The New Folder with Selection capability is new to Mac OS X Lion. ■

- **New Smart Folder:** Choosing this option creates a smart folder. Smart folders are "intelligent" folders that collect aliases to files based on predefined criteria. (Smart folders are explained in Chapter 4.) You also can simply press Option+⌘+N.

- **New Burn Folder:** Choosing this option creates a folder where you can place aliases to files and folders that you want to put on a recordable CD or DVD. After you've placed all the aliases to files you want recorded or "burned" to disc, insert a recordable disc into the Mac's SuperDrive and follow the prompts. This is how you create discs without needing special disc-recording software.

- **Open:** This option opens the selected file or application. If a file is selected, the Finder launches an application that its database says can open the file. You also can press ⌘+O.

- **Open With:** This option requires you to select an application from its submenu with which you want to open the selected file. Use it when the regular Open menu option can't find an appropriate application.

- **Print:** This option prints whatever files are selected. You also can press ⌘+P.

- **Close Window:** This option closes the active Finder window. You also can press ⌘+W. Or press Option+⌘+W to close all open Finder windows at once.

- **Get Info:** This option gets information on a highlighted item in the Finder and lets you set access permissions for it, as outlined later in this chapter. You also can press ⌘+I.

- **Compress:** The option creates a Zip-compressed copy of the selected items. These compressed files usually take less space and can more easily be provided to other Mac and Windows users.

- **Duplicate:** This command creates a duplicate of the file, as outlined later in the chapter. You also can press ⌘+D.

- **Make Alias:** This command creates a quick-access link, called an *alias* (Windows users know this as a *shortcut*), to a highlighted item in the Finder. The alias can be used to quickly locate and open files buried deep in the Finder's file structure. You also can press ⌘+L.

Tip

To create the alias in a different location from the original file, press and hold Option+⌘ while dragging an item to a new location in the Finder. (You also can press and hold the Option+⌘ keys after clicking and dragging the item, but you must be sure to hold them until after you release the mouse button.) This method is useful because you typically want an alias to be in a different location than the item it points to. ■

- **Quick Look:** The Quick Look option reveals the contents of most files, as described later in this chapter. You also can press ⌘+Y or simply press the space bar. (Chapter 4 covers this feature in detail.)

- **Show Original:** This option is active only when an alias is highlighted in the Finder. It opens a Finder window displaying the item that the alias points to. You also can press ⌘+R. If a search window is open (see Chapter 5), this option becomes Open Enclosing Folder.

- **Add to Sidebar:** The Sidebar is located on the left side of Finder windows and provides quick access to disks, folders, and files. This option adds the selected items to the Sidebar for such quick access, as explained later in this chapter. You also can press ⌘+T.

- **Move to Trash:** This option moves any item highlighted in the Finder to the Trash (in effect deleting it). You also can press ⌘+Delete.

- **Eject:** Before you can remove CDs, DVDs, external disks, thumb drives, server volumes, and the like from the Mac, you must eject them. Failure to do so can corrupt their data. When the icon has disappeared from the desktop, it is safe to disconnect, shut off, or remove the disk. You also can press ⌘+E. For a CD or DVD, you can press the Eject key if your keyboard has this key.

- **Burn Items to Disc:** This option is used to record selected items to recordable CDs and DVDs. You will be asked to insert a recordable disc if none is present in your Mac's SuperDrive. (If nothing is selected, the option becomes Burn "Desktop" to Disc.)

- **Find:** The Find option opens a search window and places the cursor in the Search box at the top right side of that window so you can type in a search term. If a Finder window is active, this menu option changes it to a search window. Chapter 5 explains the Spotlight search technology this menu option invokes. You also can press ⌘+F.

- **Label:** You can color any item in the Finder by choosing one of the swatches here. If the item's icon doesn't use a generic icon, only the color behind the item's name gets the label color; otherwise, both the icon and the name are colored. You might color items to visually categorize them, such as by making urgent items orange or personal items purple.

Tip

Press and hold Option when the File menu displays to change its options. The Open With menu option changes to Always Open With, Open changes to Open in New Window and Close, Close changes to Close All, Get Info changes to Show Inspector, and Quick Look changes to Slide Show. ■

The Edit menu

The Edit menu offers lots of options you can use to manipulate items in the Finder:

- **Undo:** This menu option reverses, or undoes, the last task performed in the Finder. (As an aid, the menu option specifies the undo action, such as Undo Move of "2009 budget.xls".) You also can press ⌘+Z.

- **Redo:** This option lets you in effect cancel the undo. You also can press Shift+⌘+Z. Note that not all actions can be undone; the menu option becomes Can't Undo and is grayed out in such cases. And if you haven't undone anything, the Redo option is grayed out until you do.

- **Show Clipboard:** When you use the Cut or Copy commands, the item you are cutting or copying is sent to the Clipboard. Choosing the Show Clipboard option opens a window in the Finder to reveal what is currently held in the Clipboard. If the last item copied or cut was text or a graphic, the window shows the text or graphic. If the last item copied or cut was a file, folder, or disk, the item's name is displayed in the Clipboard window.

- **Special Characters:** This option opens the Character Palette, from which you can choose special characters, as Chapter 29 explains.

Tip

Press and hold Option when the Edit menu displays to change its options. The Paste menu option changes to Move Items Here, and Select All changes to Deselect All. ■

The View menu

The View menu provides a number of commands you can use to control how the information inside windows is displayed. Some of the commands offered include these:

- **As Icons, As List, As Columns,** and **As Cover Flow:** These menu options change how information is displayed in the Finder window, as explained later in this chapter. They have the keyboard shortcuts ⌘+1, ⌘+2, ⌘+3, and ⌘+4, respectively.

- **Clean Up:** This option tidies up the icons inside a Finder window (when in icon view mode), arranging them into a neat grid as specified by the Finder's View Options settings (explained later in this chapter). If the menu option is Clean Up Selection, that means one or more items are selected, and only they will be snapped to the grid, rather than all of the folder's contents. If no window is active, it tidies up the icons on the desktop. (You can switch between Clean Up and Clean Up Selection by pressing and holding the Option key, such as to clean up all icons even if some are selected.)

- **Clean Up By:** This option lets you specify how to tidy up the icons inside a Finder window (when in icon view mode) through its submenu options: Name, Date Modified, Date Created, Last Opened, Date Added, Size, Kind, and Label. The icons are reordered based on your selection. Note that this option affects all icons in the Finder window (or desktop), regardless of whether you've selected individual items.

- **Arrange By:** The Arrange By option enables you to sort the items in a window (or on the desktop) via submenu option according to their name (Control+⌘+1), date modified (Control+⌘+2), date created (Control+⌘+3), date last opened (Control+⌘+4), date added (Control+⌘+5), size (Control+⌘+6), kind (Control+⌘+7), or label (Control+⌘+8).

- **Sort By:** If you press and hold Option while the View menu is visible, it provides the Sort By menu option. Sort by lets you sort the items in a window within whatever sort you chose in the Arrange By menu option (or toolbar icon pop-up menu), For example, if you arrange a window by Kind (file type) and want the list of items within each file type's group to be in alphabetical order, you choose Name as the Sort By option. You can think of Sort By as a subsorting tool for Arrange By.

Note

If the desktop is active, the View menu shows the Sort By menu option, not the Arrange By menu option. Press and hold Option to display Arrange By instead. ∎

- **Show/Hide Path Bar:** The path bar appears at the bottom of the Finder window and shows where the current location is in relation to the rest of the Finder. This option shows or hides it, depending on whether it is already visible.

- **Show/Hide Status Bar:** The status bar gives information about the files inside a Finder window. It is available only if the toolbar (explained later in this chapter) is not visible. This option shows or hides the status bar, depending on whether it is already visible. You also can press ⌘+/.

- **Show/Hide Sidebar:** The Sidebar appears on the left side of a Finder window, as explained later in this chapter, and provides shortcuts to a variety of volumes, places, and commonly used folders. You also can press Option+⌘+S.

- **Show/Hide Toolbar:** The toolbar appears at the top of a Finder window and provides buttons for forward and backward navigation, different view options, and a text box for searching through text. You also can press Option+⌘+T.

- **Customize Toolbar:** Choose this option to change the items that appear in the tool-bar, as described later in this chapter.

- **Show View Options:** This option opens the View Options dialog box that lets you fine-tune the appearance of individual Finder windows and the items inside them. You also can press ⌘+J.

New Feature
The ⌘+/ shortcut for Show Status Bar is new to Mac OS X Lion. The Clean Up By menu option is new to Mac OS X Lion. Also new are the Date Last Opened and Date Added options in the View menu's Arrange By submenu. ■

Tip
Press and hold Option when the View menu displays to change its options. The Clean Up menu option changes to Clean Up Selection, and Arrange By changes to Sort By. ■

The Go menu
The Go menu gives you a range of options for navigating through the Finder, including these options:

- **Back** and **Forward:** As you navigate through windows, you may find it useful to go back to previous locations, and then later forward to the locations where you were—similar to how you navigate in a web browser. You also can press ⌘+[to go back and ⌘+] to go forward, or you can use the icon buttons in the Finder window's toolbar.

- **Enclosing folder:** When you are in icon view, you can quickly move into folders by double-clicking them. This command does the reverse, taking you out of the current folder and into the folder above it in the file structure. You also can press ⌘+↑.

- **Locations:** The Go menu has menu options that let you quickly move to standard Finder locations (they're also usually in the Finder window's Sidebar). The first is All My Files (Shift+⌘+F), which shows all files on your Mac. Another is Computer (Shift+⌘+C), which shows you all disks connected to the Mac. Another is Network (Shift+⌘+K), which shows you all network-accessible computers and volumes. Two are system folders for the current user account: Home (Shift+⌘+H) and Desktop (Shift+⌘+D). Four are folders common to all user accounts: Applications (Shift+⌘+A), Documents (Shift+⌘+O), Downloads (Option+⌘+L), and Utilities (Shift+⌘+U). If your Mac supports AirDrop (see Chapter 24), you'll also see the AirDrop menu option, which has the shortcut Shift+⌘+R

New Feature
The AirDrop, All My Files, and Downloads options in the Go menu are new to Mac OS X Lion. ■

Tip
Press and hold Option when the Go menu displays to have another option appear: Library. It opens the current user's Library folder, explained in Chapter 4. ■

Relaunching the Finder

The Finder is an application, and like other applications, it runs in a protected memory area. This helps to ensure that if the Finder has a problem, you don't need to restart the entire computer.

If an application becomes unresponsive in Mac OS X, you can use the Force Quit command to ensure that Mac OS X closes it. (It can then be reopened.). However, because the Finder should be running at all times, the usual Force Quit command used to close unresponsive applications is replaced with one called Relaunch Finder, which forces the Finder to close and then reopens it.

When the Finder becomes unresponsive (typically both the Finder windows and the desktop will cease to respond to mouse clicks or touchpad taps, and the pointer may turn into a spinning wheel), you may need to invoke the Relaunch Finder command. You can relaunch the Finder in several ways:

- Press and hold Option when right-clicking or Control+clicking the Finder icon in the Dock. Choose the Relaunch option from the contextual menu that appears.

- Choose ➪ Force Quit from the menu bar. Select the Finder option from the Force Quit Applications dialog box, and click the Relaunch button.

- Press Control+Option+Esc on the keyboard. This opens the Force Quit Applications dialog box; select the Finder option, and click Relaunch.

- In the Terminal, enter the command **killall Finder**. (The Terminal application is explained in Appendix D.)

- Launch the Activity Monitor application (located in the Utilities folder, which is inside the Applications folder). Scroll down the list, find the Finder application, and click the red Quit Process button. Now click the Quit button; if this fails to quit the Finder, use the Force Quit command. This completely quits the Finder; click the Finder icon in the Dock to relaunch the Finder and continue.

When you invoke the Relaunch Finder command, the Finder's menu bar plus all the icons on the desktop disappear and then reappear. All the Finder windows close and do not reappear.

Because the Finder is treated as an application, when the Finder is unresponsive, other applications are still active. You can switch between applications, continue working, and even save files. This is one of the key strengths of Mac OS X. It is extremely rare that you ever need to restart Mac OS X, and you can continue working and save files even when a key part of the operating system is unresponsive. If the system becomes totally unresponsive, and none of these relaunch solutions works, you can completely restart your Mac by holding down the power button for 10 seconds.

- **Recent Folders:** The Recent Folders option's submenu shows the 10 most recently visited folders. This is useful for quickly going back to a folder you were looking at. The Clear Menu submenu option, which removes all the items in the list, appears at the bottom of the submenu.

- **Go to Folder:** The Go to Folder option opens a dialog box in which you type the exact path of the folder you want to navigate to. For example, the Documents folder is found in /Users/*username*/Documents. (Note that you don't have to match the destination folder's capitalization.) Press Return after entering the pathname, and a Finder window opens for it. Users familiar with Unix and MS-DOS environments will have experience with this form of folder navigation, but most people will prefer to stick with the Finder windows for navigation. You also can use the keyboard shortcut Shift+⌘+G to open the Go to Folder dialog box.

- **Connect to Server:** This option opens the Connect to Server dialog box, which enables you to connect to another computer or server by entering the server address. You also can click Browse to search for available servers, click the + icon button to add a server to the Favorites list for easy access later, or click the clock-shaped icon menu to get a list of recently visited servers. You also can use the shortcut ⌘+K to open the Connect to Server dialog box.

The Window menu

The Window menu has only one option unique to the Finder:

- **Cycle through Windows:** This option opens the next open Finder window. Each time you choose it, the menu option advances down the list of open widows and then goes back through the list from the top if you keep choosing it. You also can press ⌘+`.

Although it's not unique to the Finder's Windows menu, remember that the Window menu lists all open Finder windows. You also can use the Mission Control and Exposé features described in Chapter 2 to navigate among open Finder windows.

The Help menu

As with all other applications, the Help menu includes a search box you can use to look for information about the Finder and to quickly locate items in the Finder's menu structure. The Mac Help option opens a window with help topics you can browse or search. (Chapter 7 covers the Mac's Help Center help system.)

Opening and Using Finder Windows

You typically navigate the myriad of files and folders in Mac OS X via a Finder window. It is a visual representation of the files and folders contained within the various disks on your computer. It presents the information in a variety of different ways, some straightforward, others more abstract. A standard Finder window, shown in Figure 3.1, is a good place to start.

You can open a new Finder Window quite a few ways if the Finder is active: Choose File ⇨ New Finder Window, press ⌘+N, or right-click or Control+click the Finder icon in the Dock and choose New Finder Window from the contextual menu. (To make the Finder the active application, click the desktop or click the Finder icon in the Dock.) The new Finder window opens to your All My Files smart folder, shown in Figure 3.1, unless you change the default location in the Finder's Preferences dialog box, as explained later in this chapter.

New Feature

Mac OS X Lion has updated the look of Finder windows and its icons. The Sidebar icons, for example, have that precision-cut-aluminum feel that Apple's recent Macs favor, muting the colors of previous Mac OS X versions. Likewise, folders' corners are a tad sharper than before. ■

If you double-click a disk's or folder's icon on the desktop or from another Finder window, or you click an item in the Sidebar, its Finder windows opens. (And if you have several disks and/or folders selected, double-clicking any of them opens them all.) If you ⌘+double-click a folder in an open Finder window, that internal folder is opened in its own Finder window. Likewise, ⌘+clicking a disk or folder in the Sidebar also opens the item in its own Finder window.

You also can see open Finder windows simply by clicking them on the desktop or, if they are minimized to the Dock, by using the App Exposé feature explained in Chapter 2 for the Finder icon. Using an option in the General system preference, you also can have Mac OS X minimize a window when its title bar is double-clicked.

Tip

Pressing and holding the Option key while clicking a disk or folder in the Sidebar or double-clicking a disk or folder on the desktop closes the current Finder window and opens a new one with the new item's contents. ■

When you open a Finder window, you are presented with several areas you can use to navigate the files, folders, and volumes on your Mac. Figure 3.1 shows a Finder window. These are its main elements:

- **Title bar:** This band at the top lists the name of the disk or folder whose contents are displayed in the Finder window, along with the standard Close, Zoom, and Minimize window controls (see Chapter 4).

- **Toolbar:** This band below the title bar displays the navigation, view, and other Finder control buttons and the Spotlight search box.

- **Sidebar:** This strip at the left lists connected servers (the Shared section), connected disks (the Devices section), and commonly used folders (the Favorites section) for quick access.

- **The contents pane:** The main area of the Finder window displays the folders and files inside the open disk or folder.

- **The path bar:** This strip at the bottom of the contents pane shows the folder hierarchy leading to the selected item in the Finder window. The file path displays, from left to right, the path from the root of the hard disk to the file that is currently highlighted in the Finder search window (in other words, the folder hierarchy). Double-clicking any of the folders in the file path causes it to open in a new Finder window. The path bar is turned off by default.

Note

Even if you have turned off display of the path bar, it automatically appears if you've used the Spotlight search and selected one of the search results. ■

- **The status bar:** This strip at the bottom of the Finder window provides information on the selected items, such as how many are selected and the available disk space. In icon view, a slider also appears that lets you change the size of the folder and file icons. The status bar is turned off by default.

The Finder window is used to view and manage the files and folders on your Mac. Here, its All My Files view is shown.

Working with the title bar

At the very top of the Finder window is the title bar. It displays a folder, disk, or other icon (depending on what is open) and the name of the folder whose contents appear in the Finder window. You can move the window on the desktop by dragging its title bar.

If you ⌘+click, Control+click, or right-click the icon or the folder or disk name in the title bar, a pop-up menu displays the folder hierarchy, as Figure 3.2 shows in the Finder window on the right. (The folder hierarchy is the list of "parent" folders that traces the path from the current folder to the folder that contains it, and all the way to the topmost level, the root of the volume.) Click one of the folders in the hierarchy to have its contents displayed in the Finder window; it replaces the currently displayed Finder window contents.

Tip

If you Shift+click or Option+click the folder or disk icon, it should be selected; you can then drag the icon elsewhere to copy the folder's, or disk's, contents to wherever you drag the icon. Note that sometimes Shift+ click or Option+click doesn't select the icon; if that occurs, release the key and the mouse and try again. ∎

New Feature

Mac OS X Lion no longer displays the pill-shaped icon at the far right of the title bar, which hid and showed the Toolbar and Sidebar. You can now hide these just by using the View menu controls or corresponding short-cuts described earlier. ∎

FIGURE 3.2

Note the different views of items in the two Finder windows shown.

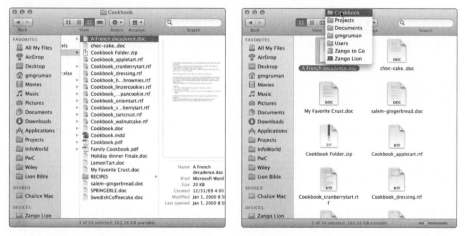

Investigating the toolbar

The toolbar contains several useful icon buttons that enable you to navigate the Finder and access Finder options without having to go through the Finder's menus. You can change some of the icon buttons on the toolbar to suit your own purposes, although other icon buttons are a permanent fixture.

The standard icon buttons are Back, Forward, View as Icons, View as List, View as Columns, View as Cover Flow, and Arrange. There's also the Spotlight-powered Search box. Here's what these icon controls do:

- **Back:** Pressing the Back icon button (the left-facing triangle icon) takes the Finder window to the previous folder or other item that was open or to the previous viewing mode for that item.

- **Forward:** If you have pressed the Back icon button, pressing the Forward icon button (the right-facing arrow icon) returns you to the item or viewing mode that you were originally looking at.

- **View mode selectors:** These four icon buttons change how the Finder presents its contents, in what are called *view modes* or *list views*: Icons, List, Columns, and Cover Flow. Each icon has a small graphic that depicts how the contents will display in the Finder window. Working in these different view modes is outlined later in this chapter.

- **Action:** This icon pop-up menu gives you a variety of controls: Open, Get Info, Quick Look, Arrange By, and Show View Options. Other options and applicable services (see Chapter 16) for the current selection may also appear in the menu options.

- **Arrange:** This icon pop-up menu lets you control how items are sorted in the Finder window: by kind, application, date modified, date created, date last opened, date added, size, and label. The default is None, which lists them in whatever order they were viewed previously.

- **Search box:** Typing into the search box marked with the magnifying glass icon enables you to search for files by using Mac OS X's Spotlight technology, which Chapter 5 explains.

You can change the contents and arrangement of the toolbar by choosing View ➪ Customize Toolbar or by right-clicking or Control+clicking the toolbar and choosing Customize Toolbar from the contextual menu. The Customize Toolbar settings sheet, shown in Figure 3.3, appears. (A *settings sheet* is a set of options that pulls down from a dialog box while the dialog box remains open.)

FIGURE 3.3

You can add, remove, and rearrange buttons in the Finder window by using the Customize Toolbar settings sheet.

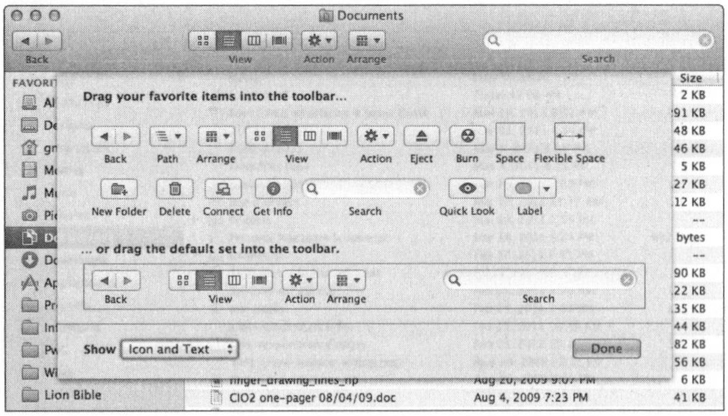

You can perform the following options with the Customize Toolbar settings sheet:

- **Drag your favorite items into the toolbar.** Click and drag any of the icon buttons from the Customize Toolbar dialog box to the toolbar of the active window to add it as a favorite. The following items are available: Back, Path, Arrange, View, Action, Eject, Burn, Space, Flexible Space, New Folder, Delete, Connect, Get Info, Search, Quick Look, and Label. You can add new items to any point on the toolbar, and the other items spread apart to make room for the new button. If you drag more icon buttons to the toolbar than can physically fit, then an icon button displaying two arrows pointing right appears on the right side of the toolbar. Clicking this icon button displays a pop-up menu with the hidden icon buttons. Click Done when you are happy with the selection.

- **Drag the default set into the toolbar.** The default set of icon buttons offers a good selection of tools without cluttering up the toolbar. If you decide that you want to restore the default icon set, you can drag the complete set from the bottom of the Customize Toolbar settings sheet to the toolbar. All the icons currently in the toolbar are replaced with the default set.

- **Arrange the icon buttons.** You can drag the icon buttons to the left and right to rearrange their positions in the toolbar. As you move an icon button, the other icon buttons move to accommodate it.

- **Removing icon buttons.** To remove icon buttons from the toolbar, click and drag them away from the Finder window. As you drag them away, the button's icons have small dust cloud images added to them, indicating that they are about to be trashed. Release the mouse button or move your finger from the touchpad, and the icon buttons disappear into a cloud of dust.

- **Change the buttons' display.** At the bottom of the Customize Toolbar settings sheet is the Show pop-up menu that you can use to adjust the appearance of the buttons. The options are Icon and Text, Icon Only, and Text Only. Next to the pop-up menu is the Use Small Size option; selecting it slightly reduces the size of the icons and text descriptions.

When you're finished, click Done to apply your changes to all Finder windows.

Tip
You can add, remove, and arrange items on the toolbar without opening the Customize Toolbar settings sheet. To do this, press and hold the ⌘ key, and drag icon buttons to remove and rearrange them in any active Finder window. Likewise, ⌘+drag items such as folders, files, and even volumes into the toolbar. When dragging items to the toolbar, a green circle with a + icon appears to indicate that it is an addition. (You may have to hold the ⌘ key for a second or two before dragging the item.) When you've dragged the item to the desired location in the toolbar, release the mouse button or move your finger from the touchpad. ■

You can add these non-default controls to the toolbar from the Customize Toolbar settings sheet:

- **Path:** This icon pop-up menu shows the file hierarchy. Choosing any of the folders in the pop-up menu opens that folder's contents in the current Finder window. (This function is identical to ⌘+clicking the item's icon or name in the title bar.)

- **Action:** The Action icon pop-up menu (the gear icon) provides a set of options extremely similar to the contextual menu, and its options change depending on what is highlighted in the Finder.

- **Eject:** This icon button disconnects any selected attached servers, network-connected computers, optical discs, or external disks. It also physically ejects any CD or DVDs inserted into the computer.

- **Burn:** This icon button opens the Burn Disc dialog box, which walks you through the steps of copying ("burning") the selected items to a recordable CD or DVD. If no CD or DVD is inserted, you are asked to insert an optical disc.

- **Space** and **Flexible Space:** Using the Space and Flexible Space controls, you can move icon buttons apart. The Space control creates a square block of space that is about the same size as most toolbar icons. The Flexible Space control expands and contracts depending on the width of the Finder window.

- **New Folder:** This icon button opens a new Finder window.

- **Delete:** This icon button moves any highlighted items in the Finder to the Trash.

- **Connect:** This icon button opens the Connect to Server dialog box. Connecting to servers is outlined in Chapter 24.

- **Get Info:** This icon button opens the Info window, as outlined later in this chapter.

- **Quick Look:** Clicking the Quick Look icon button (the eye icon) enables you to quickly examine the contents of many files and folders. Its function is identical to highlighting an item in the Finder and pressing the spacebar or right-clicking or Control+clicking an item and choosing Quick Look from the contextual menu. (Chapter 4 covers Quick Look.)

- **Label:** This icon button opens a pop-up menu of the color labels that you can apply to folders and files to help visually mark them, such as using red for files and folders relating to urgent matters.

New Feature

The Customize Toolbar settings sheet adds the New Folder button and the Labels button. Gone from the Customize Toolbar settings sheet in Mac OS X Lion are the Customize and Separator icons. And the default toolbar icon lineup has changed: In Mac OS X Leopard and Snow Leopard, the toolbar by default included the Quick Look icon but not the Arrange icon. Mac OS X Lion does not include by default Quick Look in its toolbar but does include Arrange. The Finder windows' toolbar uses new icons for many of the buttons, and the Customize Toolbar settings sheet arranges the buttons in two rows rather than three. (If you upgrade Snow Leopard to Lion, the toolbar retains whatever icons you had in Snow Leopard but uses their new designs.) ■

Working with the Sidebar

On the left side of the window is the Sidebar. It contains aliases to common areas on the Mac. The aliases are divided into three sections, each of which can expand or collapse the area's options: Favorites, Shared, and Devices. (The Shared section appears only if your Mac detects other computers or devices on the network.)

New Feature

Mac OS X Lion has changed how you show and hide the Sidebar's sections. Previous versions used disclosure triangles to reveal and hide the sections' contents. Lion uses a subtler technique: Hover the pointer over the section name (its header), and a button appears to its right. If the section's list is visible, the button is labeled Hide; if the section's list is hidden, the button says Show. ■

To use an item in the Sidebar, simply click its icon. For example, in the Favorites section, icons for the Music and Movies folders appear; clicking these icons takes you immediately to those specific folders in the Finder window.

You can add aliases to your own items from a Finder window or from the desktop to the Sidebar. To do so, simply drag the items to the Sidebar, or select them and then choose File ⇨ Add to Sidebar, or press ⌘+T; to remove aliases from the Sidebar, simply drag them out of the Sidebar, or right-click or Control+click them and choose Remove from Sidebar from the contextual menu.

Note

If you remove all items under the Devices or Shared header in the Sidebar, the header disappears, too. If you drag an item into the Sidebar that belongs to one of those headers, the header automatically reappears. ■

You cannot add new sections to the Sidebar, but you can specify what disks, shared items, places, and searches appear in the Sidebar's sections via the Finder's Preferences dialog box, as explained later in this chapter. First, let's look at the areas that make up the Sidebar:

- **Favorites:** This section organizes the shortcuts to popular destinations on your hard disk. The default areas include the desktop, Documents, Applications, and your Home folder, as well as the new All My Files smart folder.

- **Shared:** Computers, shared volumes, and other network devices (such as printers) on the same local area network are listed here. If you have multiple Macs connected to the network, you can remotely search through hard disks and even control the screen on one Mac while working on another. (Creating networks and sharing files and screens are covered in detail in Chapters 23 and 24.)

- **Devices:** This section lists hard disks (both internal and external), inserted CDs and DVDs, and other storage media such as thumb drives. If you own a Mac without a built-in DVD drive (such as a MacBook Air), you also see a Remote Disc option, which enables you to "borrow" an optical drive over a network connection from another computer so you can read data and install programs from an optical disc. (The other Mac must have enabled CD or DVD sharing in the Sharing system preference, as Chapter 24 explains.)

If clicked, the All My Files item in the Favorites section shows all the files on your Mac, organizing them by category (like the iPad's and iPhone's Spotlight function). You can change the categorization from the default of Kind to any of the categories available in the View menu's

Arrange By submenu options or in the toolbar's Arrange icon pop-up menu. So, for example, if you choose Date Modified, you see all the files modified today grouped together followed by those modified yesterday, followed by those modified in the previous 30 days, and followed by those modified previously. As is always the case in Finder windows, you can refine what is displayed using the Spotlight search feature explained in Chapter 5.

New Feature

The All My Files item in the Sidebar is new to Mac OS X Lion, as is the AirDrop item (see Chapter 24). The Favorites section in the Mac OS X Lion Sidebar had been called Places in Mac OS X Snow Leopard and Leopard. Gone in Mac OS X Lion is the All item in the Shared section of the Finder window's Sidebar. That item let you quickly browse your network connections. In Lion, you must use the Connect to Server dialog box's Browse button to find network connections not shown in the Sidebar. Also gone from the Mac OS X Lion Sidebar is the Search For section, which had common Spotlight searches presented as links. Search For sections are Today, Yesterday, Past Week, All Images, All Movies, and All Documents. Saved searches, called smart folders (see Chapter 4), now appear in the Favorites section. ■

Working with Finder view modes

You can view the Finder window in one of four view modes. Each offers a different approach to interacting with the files on your Mac, and each has its own advantages in different circumstances. The method you use is largely a case of personal preference. The four view modes are Icon, List, Column, and Cover Flow.

Note

All view modes except icon view provide disclosure triangles for expanding and collapsing folders to make their contents visible from the current folder. Click a right-facing triangle to expand the folder to show its contents; click a down-pointing triangle to collapse the folder to hide its contents. The left side of Figure 3.4 later in this chapter shows the disclosure triangle for the InfoWorld_logo folder, in Cover Flow view. ■

Choosing a different view mode

You can choose a different Finder view mode in several different ways:

- **Via the Finder menu:** Choose View from the menu bar, and then choose from the following menu options: As Icons, As List, As Columns, and As Cover Flow.
- **Using keyboard shortcuts:** Press ⌘+1, ⌘+2, ⌘+3, or ⌘+4 to access the Icons, List, Columns, and Cover Flow view modes, respectively.
- **Using the toolbar icon buttons:** You can use the four icon buttons on the toolbar to change the view mode. From left to right, the icon buttons enable the Icon, List, Column, and Cover Flow views. Each icon has a small graphic showing what the view mode looks like in the Finder.

Working in icon view

Icon view is the oldest view mode used by Mac operating systems, dating all the way back to the original Macintosh computer that shipped in 1984. Over the years, the icon view has been updated and improved, and today the icons provide lots of visual detail about the item they represent, as Chapter 4 explains. But they provide very little additional information beyond the item's name and—if you enable it via the Finder view options explained later in this chapter—basic item information such as file size and number of items in a folder.

Tip

The big advantage of the icon view is the size of the preview, which enables you to get an idea of the contents of icons without opening them. You can increase or decrease their size using the slider that appears at the right side of the status bar (if it's enabled) at the bottom of the Finder window when in icon view. ■

If you use icon view, it is easy to end up with various icons in disarray. It is also a simple task to get the Finder to tidy up icons by choosing View ⇨ Clean Up. Alternatively, you can press and hold the ⌘ key while dragging icons around; this automatically lines them up to the grid you set with the View Options controls explained later in this chapter. You can also reorder icons by name, date, or other criteria by choosing View ⇨ Clean Up By and then choosing the desired sort criterion from the submenu.

Note

Icon view is the only view mode available to the desktop. ■

Working in list view

List view emphasizes textual information about the items in the Finder window, relegating the icon to a small element no taller than the text. The background has alternate blue and white rows, which make it easier to visually distinguish between different items.

Folders are presented with disclosure triangles that enable you to display or hide the files or folders they contain. A right-facing disclosure triangle to the left of a folder's name means it has contents not being shown; a down-facing disclosure triangle means its contents are being displayed (notice how they also are indented to give you an outline-like, *nested* organization.)

Note

When you expand a folder by clicking the disclosure triangle, the next time you open that Finder window, the Finder remembers whether the folders contained within were previously expanded or collapsed. ■

Tip

If you press and hold the Option key while clicking a folder's disclosure triangle to reveal its items, the Finder automatically also expands the first level of subfolders within that folder. ■

Tip

You can expand selected folders in list view (as well as in Cover Flow view) by pressing ⌘+→; press ⌘+← to collapse expanded folders. ■

One key advantage of working in list view is that you can drill down through folder structures and select multiple items from different folders within the same Finder window (by using the disclosure triangles to show the contents of all subfolders so everything is visible in the Finder window).

The other key advantage of working in list view is the ability to sort information quickly. List view has by default four columns of information (though all may not be visible if the window is narrow): Name, Date Modified, Size, and Kind (file type). You can click these column headers to sort the contents; by default they sort alphabetically (A to Z) for Names and Kind, newest to oldest for Date, largest to smallest for Size. If you click the active column again, it reverses the sort; note how the triangle to the right of the active column header's name flips between up-facing and down-facing as you click the column header. (The column header highlighted in blue is the one currently sorting the window's contents.)

Tip

You can add columns to list view for all folders by using the view options described later in this chapter. To add them for the current folder, right-click or Control+click the column titles in the contents pane and choose the additional categories you want to display. A check mark appears to the left of all visible columns titles, Likewise, hide any unwanted categories by selecting them, removing the check mark to their left. For example, you might add the Label column to a Finder window so you can sort files based on the color labels you assigned them. ■

As well as sorting by columns in list view, you can adjust the columns themselves. One adjustment is the ability to change the width of columns, which is useful because many items' labels are too long to fit within the Name or Kind column, as indicated by text truncated with an ellipsis (...).

Follow these steps to change a column's size:

1. **Highlight the column edge.** Position the pointer over the line that divides one column from another. You can tell when the position is correct because the pointer changes from a pointer icon to an icon of a vertical line with two arrows on either side.

2. **Click and hold the mouse button, or click and hold your finger on the touch-pad, on that vertical line.**

3. **Drag the mouse, or your finger, left or right to narrow or widen the column.**

Tip

If you hover the mouse over a filename, Mac OS X shows a light yellow box in list, column, and Cover Flow views displaying the full name of an item whose column's narrow width truncates the name's display. You also can press the spacebar for the select item to get the Quick Look preview window (see Chapter 4) that shows the full details, including a preview of the file's contents in some cases; press the spacebar again to close that preview window. ■

You also can change the order in which the Date Modified, Size, and Kind columns appear. To do this, click the column title and drag the column left or right. As you drag the column header, the pointer transforms into a hand tool and a grayed-out preview of the column appears where it will move. Release the mouse button, and the column moves to its new position, rearranging the other columns as it slides into place. Unfortunately, you cannot move the Name column.

Working in column view

Column view is one the fastest ways to navigate through the Finder. It's also the default view presented in dialog boxes when you are asked to open or save an item by an application.

The real advantage of column view is the ease with which you can review your path through the folder structure on a volume; it also presents a comprehensive preview and substantial file information in the final column when you have selected an item other than a folder. Thus, it is many Mac OS X users' preferred view mode. The disadvantage is that it lacks the sorting options offered by list view, and it does not let you view and manage the contents of multiple folders that are not nested within each other that list view provides.

When you select a folder in column view, the column to the right immediately displays the contents of that folder (including any folders). Column view shows the contents of that folder in the first column and then displays the contents of a selected subfolder in the next column and then the contents of a selected subfolder in the next column, until there are no more subfolders to select. In this manner, you can delve down through the contents of a volume to find the file or folder you are looking for, as the left Finder window in Figure 3.2 shows. This makes it possible to drill down through a menu structure and to return at any point to a previous file or folder found in earlier columns.

If the number of columns exceeds the width of the Finder window, new columns continue to appear on the right side of the Finder window, with the columns to the left scrolling out of sight. A scroll bar appears at the bottom of the Finder window so you can navigate back and forth through the menu structure.

If you select an alias of a folder, the Finder displays the contents of the folder that the alias points to, while keeping the folder structure leading to the alias intact. When you select a file, the column to the right displays basic information for that file, as well as a large preview of the item (refer to Figure 3.2). As in icon view, whether you see a preview of the file's contents or an icon of the application associated with that file depends on the nature of the file itself. And although the preview icon is fairly large, you may want to get a larger look by using the Quick Look feature described in Chapter 4.

For an application, you always see a large picture of the icon used by the application, plus the name, kind (in this case, "application"), size, date the application was created (or installed), and date the application was modified and last opened; you also see the version number of the application. You can show and hide the preview by using the disclosure triangle next to the text labeled Preview.

Note

Opening and closing the preview in column view applies to all items you select in the Finder, not just the currently selected item. ■

For some text or graphic items, the preview shows the contents of the file rather than the application associated with it. For most documents, you also see all the information that you see for an application (with the exception of the version number). If you have selected an image, the final column also displays information on the dimensions of the picture, which is measured in pixels horizontally and then vertically. If the dimensions are listed as 400×200, the image is 400 pixels high and 200 pixels wide. If you have selected an audio or video file, you also get duration information. When you have a movie or sound file selected, hovering the mouse over the preview in the final column reveals a small white circle with a play triangle inside. Clicking this icon button plays the movie or sound file.

The width of the columns in column view is adjustable. You can adjust the width of individual columns or all columns uniformly. To adjust the column width, perform one of the following actions:

- To resize a single column, drag its boundary (the vertical line between columns) to the left or right.
- To resize all columns to a uniform size, hold down the Option key while dragging a boundary left and right. All the columns snap to the size of the one you are adjusting.

New Feature

Gone in Mac OS X Lion is the handle at the bottom of each column for resizing column widths. You now just drag the column boundary at any location. ∎

Working in Cover Flow view

Cover Flow is an Apple technology that first appeared in iTunes. It has slowly permeated many Apple applications. Cover Flow is by far the most visually stimulating of all the view modes, offering a highly graphical way of interacting with the Finder. Cover Flow splits the Finder window in half, with the bottom half using the list view to present files and folders, and the top half providing a horizontal presentation of the items as large icons that you can "thumb through." The currently selected item faces straight out in the middle of the other items, which are arranged in a fan- or carousel-like view, as Figure 3.4 shows.

Tip

You can adjust the size of the Cover Flow part of the window to get a larger (or smaller) visual display. Below the Cover Flow scroll bar is a handle marked by three small horizontal white lines. If you hover the mouse over this handle, the pointer turns into a hand. Click and drag the white lines up for a smaller Cover Flow display or down for a larger Cover Flow display. ∎

You can navigate and sort the bottom half of the window in the same manner as using list view (described earlier). The key difference is that when you highlight an item, the top half flips to a large preview of it.

However, you also can use the top half of the Cover Flow window to flip through the files. You can interact with the Cover Flow window in five ways:

- **Using the scroll bar:** Click and drag the scroll bar directly beneath the images to scroll through the current windows. (As Chapter 2 explains, the scroll bars may not appear if you are using a gesture-savvy touchpad; Apple assumes you are use gestures instead of mouse movements. But you can force scroll bars to always appear in the General system preference, as Chapter 28 explains.)

- **Clicking images:** You can directly click any visual image in the Cover Flow to go directly to that image. By repeatedly clicking an image to the left or right of the current one, you can scroll through all the images in Cover Flow view.

- **Using the arrow keys:** If you press the ← and → keys, you move the Cover Flow images left and right, respectively. You also can use the ↑ and ↓ keys to move up and down the list of items in the bottom half of the Finder window; this has the same effect as using ← and →, respectively.

- **Using the touchpad:** If you have a touchpad or an Apple Magic Mouse, you can scroll through the files using the two-finger scroll gesture.

- **Using the scroll wheel:** If you have an Apple Mighty Mouse or other scroll-wheel mouse attached to your Mac, you can move the scroll wheel on the top of the mouse to move through the items represented in the Cover Flow window. If the scroll wheel moves just up and down, it works like the ↑ and ↓ keys. If the scroll wheel is actually a ball, as on the Mighty Mouse, that can move in several directions, scrolling down or to the right moves through the Cover Flow images to the right, while moving the ball up or to the left moves through the Cover Flow images to the left.

FIGURE 3.4

The Finder window in Cover Flow view splits the window in half, with the bottom showing a list of items and the top half providing a scrollable 3-D fanlike or carousel-like view that you can "thumb through."

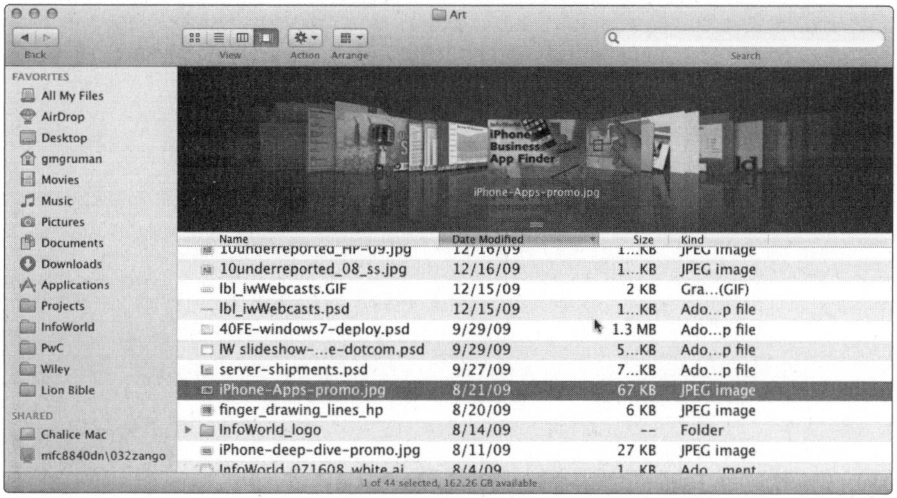

Tip

Cover Flow works exceptionally well in tandem with Apple's Quick Look technology (see Chapter 4). As you scan the items in the Cover Flow window, pressing the spacebar makes the highlighted item zoom out to show a larger preview. Using Cover Flow and Quick Look together is a great way to scan through your files. ■

Changing Finder Behavior for Files and Folders

The Finder has controls to change its behavior for specific folders and files, using the Info window. Most people use the Info window to get details about a file or folder, as Chapter 4 explains, but it has much more capability than that.

To access the Info window and its controls, select an item in the Finder and choose File ➡ Get Info, or press ⌘+I. You also can Control+click or right-click the item and choose Get Info from the contextual menu. Figure 3.5 shows the Info window for both a disk and a file (folders show the same information as disk).

Note

If you press and hold Option, the Get Info menu option is replaced with Show Inspector in the File menu. It opens the Inspector window, which is identical to the Info window except for the title bar, which is not as tall as in the Info window. ■

Using Get Info to change disk, folder, and file permissions

You can share files, folders, and disks with other users, both those with user accounts on your Mac (see Chapter 27) and those who have been given file-sharing access to your Mac (see Chapter 24). For such shared disks, folders, and files, you can quickly enable and change sharing privileges for individual folders and disks by using the Info window. Most of what displays is information on the disk, folder, or file, but you can change some sharing settings:

- **Shared Folder:** You can share a folder or disk by selecting the Shared Folder option (in the General section of the Info window) or stop sharing by deselecting it. (Files are shared if their folders are shared.)

- **Sharing & Permissions:** You can change who has access permissions in the Sharing & Permissions section at the bottom of the Info window. Select Name, and then choose a Privilege for that name; your options are Read & Write, Read Only, and Write Only (Drop Box). You can add and delete users by using the + and – icon buttons, and you can apply your changes to all folders within the selected disk or folder by choosing Apply to Enclosed Items from the Action icon pop-up menu (the gear icon). (This can take several minutes to complete, so be warned.) And you can undo your changes by choosing Action ➡ Revert Changes.

FIGURE 3.5

The Info window has several sections of both information about and control over an item. (Use the disclosure triangles to collapse and expand those sections.) At left is the Info window for a disk, at center for a folder, and at right for a file.

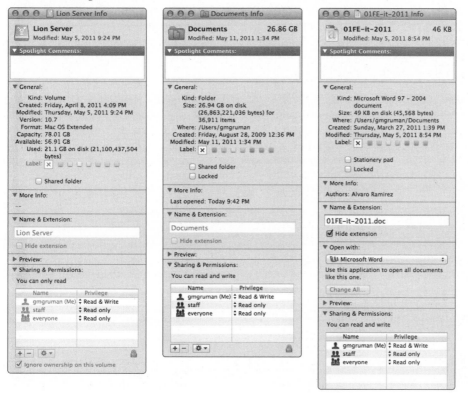

Finally, for non-startup disks only, you can select the Ignore Ownership on This Volume option at the bottom of the Sharing & Permissions section. If selected, any user account is considered to be the disk's owner and thus has all the privileges assigned to an owner. In the Name list, look for the user account that has "(Me)" following its name; that's the current owner, and those are the permissions everyone gets when this option is selected—handy for a shared disk of, say, family photos you pass around. If the Ignore Ownership on This Volume option is deselected, then people who access the disk from their user accounts have the access permissions set for their specific user account in the Info window.

Note
If the Sharing & Permissions settings are grayed out, click the Lock button (the bronze-colored lock icon) and enter your user account password (if your account has permissions to change sharing options) or an administrator's password. ■

Using Get Info to change files' application owners

When you open an Info window for a file, you can change which application opens when you double-click that specific file or that type of file. In the Open With section of the Info window is a pop-up menu from which you choose the new owner application. This change affects only the current file, unless you click the Change All button as well, in which case all files of this type are opened with the new application specified in the pop-up menu. (To permanently change which application opens a file, you also can press and hold Option when opening the File menu in the Finder, choose Always Open With, and then choose the application you want to open it in from now on.)

Note that Mac OS X tries to limit the options in the pop-up menu to those that are compatible with the file type, but it may include incompatible options as well. If you select an incompatible option, you get an error message when you open the file by double-clicking it, letting you know the file is not compatible with the application.

And note that changing the file's application owner changes its icon and its kind in Finder window sorts and search results.

Note

You can open a file using an application other than its application owner at any time by right-clicking or Control+clicking the file and choosing Open With from the contextual menu and then choosing the application you want to open it in. You would change the application owner only when you want to permanently change the application owner. ■

Adjusting Finder Preferences

Most of the Finder preferences reside in the Finder Preferences dialog box, which you access by choosing Finder ➪ Preferences or by pressing ⌘+, (comma). This dialog box has four panes, as Figure 3.6 shows.

FIGURE 3.6

The Finder Preferences dialog box and its four panes: General, Labels, Sidebar, and Advanced

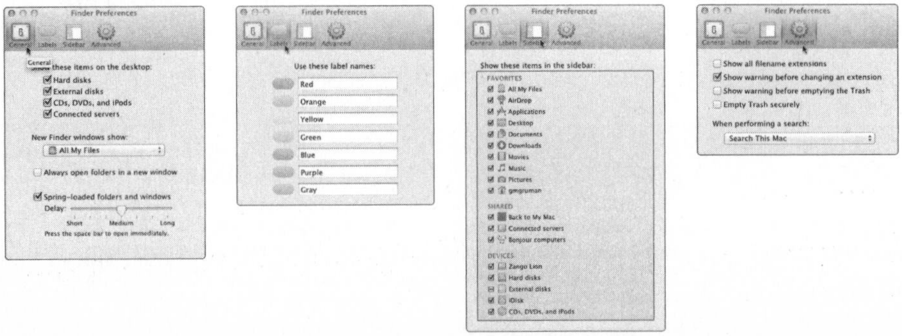

The General pane provides several controls:

- **Show These Items on the Desktop:** Select and deselect the options in this area to control what always displays on the desktop when available: Hard Disks; External Disks (which includes USB thumb drives, floppy disks, and memory cards); CDs, DVDs, and iPods; and Connected Servers. (Note that iPhones, iPod Touches, and iPads won't appear as disk icons. Only non-Touch iPods set to disk mode are available as disks.)

- **New Finder Windows Open:** Use this pop-up menu to choose which folder should open when you open a new Finder Window. (Choose File ➪ Open New Finder Window or press ⌘+N when in the Finder to open a new Finder window.) By default, this option is set to the All My Files smart folder.

- **Always Open Folders in a New Window:** Select this option have folders open in a new window rather than in place of the current window (the default behavior, when this option is deselected).

- **Spring-Loaded Folders and Windows:** When you drag files or folders to put them in other ones, you often aren't sure where the destination folder actually is. If the Spring-Loaded Folders and Windows option is selected, when you drag a file or a folder over another folder or disk and then hover, the folder or disk opens automatically so you can drop the file or folder into it—or hover over a subfolder to open it. (Move the hovering file or folder out of the window to close it.) You can thus explore multiple folders and disks before deciding where to drop the selected folder or file. Adjust the hovering time by using the Delay slider.

The Labels pane is very simple: It shows the seven colors you can apply to folders and enables you to change the labels for each. (You can apply a color to a folder by selecting the folder and then choosing File and the desired color square at the bottom of the File menu.)

You use the Sidebar pane to configure which standard disks and folders appear in the Sidebar of all Finder windows (such as when you open a disk or folder). Select the ones you want to appear, and deselect those you don't want to appear.

Note that when a Finder window is open, you can drag any disk or folder into it so that disk or folder is permanently available in the Sidebar; you're not restricted to the options in the Sidebar pane of the Preferences dialog box. To delete them, just drag them out of a Finder window one at a time, or right-click or Control+click them one at a time and choose Remove from Sidebar in the contextual menu.

The Advanced pane controls the behavior for file extensions and the Trash:

- **Show All Filename Extensions:** A file extension is the typically three- or four-character code that follows a period at the end of the filename to identify what kind of file it is. For example, a `.tiff` file is a TIFF image file, while a `.doc` or `.docx` file is a Microsoft Word document file. Mac OS X uses icons to tell you what type a file is, so by default it hides the file extensions as unneeded. But if you prefer to see them, select the Show All File Extensions option.

- **Show Warning Before Changing an Extension:** If you edit a filename in a way that changes its file extension, Mac OS X asks if you are sure. Deselect this option to tell Mac OS X not to ask. (Typically, you should not change the file extension, because that could confuse Mac OS X and applications as to what the file is, perhaps making applications "believe" that they can no longer open the file. But you may need to do so if a file has no file extension, for example.)

- **Show Warning Before Emptying the Trash:** When you delete files and folders from the Trash (by choosing Finder⇨Empty Trash, pressing Shift+⌘+Delete, or right-clicking or Control+clicking the Trash icon in the Dock and choosing Empty Trash from the contextual menu), Mac OS X displays an alert asking if you are sure because after they are deleted, the files cannot be recovered. To turn off this alert, deselect the Show Warning Before Emptying the Trash option.

- **Empty Trash Securely:** Although it's not easy to recover deleted Trash items, there is software that can do so in some circumstances. If you deal with sensitive data, you may not want anyone to recover your deleted files. To empty the Trash items in a way they can't be recovered, select the Empty Trash Securely option.

- **When Performing a Search:** This pop-up menu lets you control what is searched by default in the Finder, using Mac OS X's Spotlight capability. You have three options: Search This Macintosh (the default option), Search the Enclosing Folder, and Use the Previous Search Scope (which uses whatever search criteria you last set in a Finder search window, as explained in Chapter 5).

Adjusting Finder View Options

Another place to configure the Finder windows' display is in the Finder's View menu.

Choose View⇨Show View Options or press ⌘+J to control how Finder windows display their contents. If no disk, folder, or file is selected, you get a limited set of options that apply to the desktop compared to the options that display when a disk, folder, or file is selected. (If a file is selected, the view options apply to its folder.)

Note that these settings apply only to the desktop (if no disk or file is selected) or just to the selected disk or folder.

The settings for disks and folders also vary based on what the Finder window's current view mode is: icon, list, column, or Cover Flow. Figure 3.7 shows the settings available.

Desktop view settings

For the desktop, you can set the icon size using the Icon Size slider, and you can set the space between icons using the Grid Spacing slider. You can choose the text label's size for the items that display within the desktop, folder, or disk using the Text Size pop-up menu, and you can determine where that label appears by selecting either the Bottom or Right radio button.

FIGURE 3.7

At far left are the View Options settings for the desktop. The other dialog boxes show the settings for disks and folders when viewed in (from left to right) icon, list, column, and Cover Flow view.

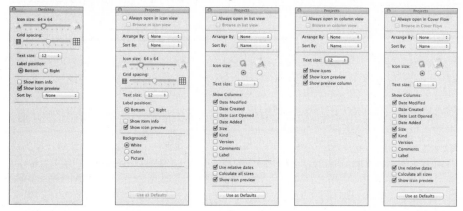

Select the Show Item Info option to have details about the disk or folder—such as its size and number of items—display under the item's name. Deselect the Show Icon Preview option so the Mac no longer creates a thumbnail of the image or document as its icon; instead, the Mac uses the icon for the application that created it.

Finally, you can control how items are arranged in the window by using the Sort By pop-up menu. Your options are None (leave the items where they were placed), Snap to Grid (shift them to the settings specified in the Grid Spacing slider; this setting affects only items you move or add, leaving items in their original location otherwise), Name, Date Modified, Date Created, Date Last Opened, Date Added, Size, Kind, and Label. These last eight options sort the items automatically.

New Feature

The Date Last Opened and Date Added options in the View Options dialog box's Sort By menu are new to Mac OS X Lion. ■

Folder and disk view settings

When you open a folder or disk and open the view options, the options vary based on what view you have set for the folder or disk window—icon, list, column, and Cover Flow—using the View icon buttons at the top of the window or by choosing an option in the Finder's View menu (refer to Figure 3.7).

Note

If you click Use as Defaults, the settings you apply to the current Finder window become the default background for all Finder windows, except those previously customized. ■

New Feature

New to Mac OS X Lion's View Options settings is the Sort By menu. Arrange By groups items in Finder windows, where as Sort By sorts them; for example, you might group items by Kind and sort them within each Kind group by date opened. Also new is the Browse In option for the View Options settings. It uses the current folder's settings to all the folders within the current folder as you browse through them, saving you lots of effort if you want consistent view options within a folder hierarchy. ■

In icon view, you get many of the same options as for the desktop: Icon Size, Grid Spacing, Text Size, Label Position, Show Item Info, Show Icon Preview, and Sort By. But you also get the Arrange By menu, the Always Open in Icon View option, and the Browse in Icon View option, as well as the capability to set a background color or image for the window. (If you select Color, tap the color swatch to open a color wheel from which you can select a color. If you select Picture, drag an image into the box labeled Drag Image Here.)

In list view, you get Always Open in List View option, Browse in List View option, Arrange By menu, Sort By menu, and Show Icon Preview option. But the rest of the options differ from the icon view's options. For example, in list view, you get a choice of two icon sizes, as well as the capability to select which columns you want to display in the list: Date Modified, Date Created, Date Last Opened, Date Added, Size, Kind, Version, Comments, and Label. Select those columns you want to display, and deselect those you don't. The Use Relative Dates option, if selected, replaces today's date with Today and yesterday's date with Yesterday in the date-oriented columns. The Calculate All Sizes option, if selected, shows the size for folders, not just for files. (Note that this option can slow down the display of window information.)

Column view has just a few options, several of which are familiar: Always Open in Column View, Browse in Column View, Text Size, Show Icon Preview, Sort By, and Arrange By. The two unique options are Show Icons (if deselected, only the text label appears for each item) and Show Preview Column (if deselected, no preview of the selected file appears in the rightmost column).

In Cover Flow view, the options are identical to those in list view, except that the Always Open in Cover Flow View option replaces the Always Open in List View option, and Browse in Cover Flow View replaces the Browse in List View option.

Tip

If you want all Finder windows to open in one of the view modes with the view options you've set for the current Finder, be sure to select the Always Open in mode View option. This option makes that view mode and its view options the default view mode (until you change it again). But note that any Finder windows to which you applied custom view settings do not use these new defaults; you must change them by choosing View ➪ View Options for each such window. ■

Summary

The Finder is an application in its own right, so it has specific menu options in its menu bar, including options to create several types of folders, to open files and servers, get item information, make aliases, control the display of Finder windows' elements, and eject discs. Because the Finder is an application, it can occasionally freeze or crash, so Mac OS X provides the relaunch capability to get the Finder back up and running.

Finder windows are the portal to your Mac's contents, displaying files, folders, and disks and providing information about their contents. The Sidebar in a Finder window also provides quick access to disks, servers, commonly used folders, and smart windows. You can add and remove the items that display in the Sidebar to make it more attuned to the resources you want to access quickly. Likewise, you can customize the Finder window's toolbar to make the icon buttons that provide quick access to a variety of functions the ones that are always shown.

You can view Finder windows' contents in four ways: icon, list, column, and Cover Flow. You can easily switch among them, as well as control how they sort their contents and what details they display using the Finder Preferences dialog box, View Options settings, and View menu options. Some aspects, such as column width, column order, and columns displayed, can be customized as you work in a Finder window.

You can customize the Finder for the following actions: how it empties the Trash, how it displays and handles changes to file extensions, what applications it opens specific file types with, and permissions for access to your folders and disks by other users.

Working with Windows, Folders, and Files

IN THIS CHAPTER

Understanding types of windows

Touring disk, folder, and file icons

Manipulating items via common controls: select, move, copy, alias, rename, compress, and lock

Getting information about items

Using smart folders and folder actions

Understanding Mac OS X's special folders

Ever since the graphical user interface became prevalent in desktop computing, first with Mac OS and then with Microsoft Windows, the window metaphor has been used to describe the rectangular panels of information that appear onscreen. A *window* is a container for information—a mini-desktop, essentially. There are many different kinds of windows used by Mac OS X, and each serves a particular function.

But the metaphor doesn't stop at windows. Windows are places to present the actual data you are working on. That data is fundamentally stored in a file, which is represented in Mac OS X as a document icon. Carrying on the paper metaphor, groups of files are kept in what appears as folders on screen. (You may hear them referred to as *directories*, which is the non-graphical metaphor used in the pre-Mac era. Unix users tend to use the term, and because Unix is under the hood of Mac OS X, the term surfaces periodically.)

The one metaphor not taken from the world of paper is the disk. (Otherwise, we'd be calling it a filing cabinet.) A disk is a storage device, typically in a rectangular box, so you'll see various types of disks represented as various types of boxes.

Knowing the onscreen representations of windows, files, folders, and disks is all well and good, but the whole point of having a Mac is to work with them. That's what this chapter explains how to do via the Finder, whose user interface was described in Chapter 2 and whose specific controls were described in Chapter 3. Note that Chapter 6 covers the mechanics of using, formatting, and managing disks; this chapter focuses on their use as Finder items.

Working with Windows

Mac OS X has several kinds of windows. Some windows contain folders and files that the Finder presents to you; these are called *Finder windows* (see Chapter 3). Some windows contain complete applications, such as iTunes; these are called *application windows*. Others display documents within applications, such as Microsoft Word; these are called *document windows*. And some windows display images and movies or play audio files; these are called *playback windows*.

Cross-Reference

Additional elements used within applications often are erroneously called windows, such as dialog boxes and panels. Chapter 9 explains these window-like elements. ■

Most windows in Mac OS X are rectangular and follow guidelines set by Apple that ensure a unified look and feel. There are also common buttons and elements that you can use to resize, maximize, and minimize windows, enabling you to make the most of your desktop real estate.

Understanding windows controls

Windows have few controls, but the ones that do exist are used very frequently.

Title bar

The title bar appears at the top of the window and typically displays the name of the application or document that the window contains. Clicking and dragging the title bar is the common way to move windows around the screen.

New Feature

The pill-shaped icon button at the right side of the title bar in previous versions of Mac OS X no longer exists in Lion. It hid the toolbar on windows that had them. But you can still hide the toolbar portion of the title bar in Finder windows and in some application and document windows by right-clicking or Control+clicking the title bar and choosing Hide Toolbar from the contextual menu. Repeat the action to show the toolbar. Windows often have other controls in that contextual menu, such as Customize Toolbar. ■

A cluster of spherical icon buttons appears on the left side of the title bar of almost every window in Mac OS X. They are useful to know:

- **Close:** When you hover the pointer over this button, an X appears in its center. If you click it, the window disappears (and if there is any data yet to be saved, a dialog box appears, asking if you would like to do so). In some applications, pressing and holding down the Option key while clicking the Close icon button forces all windows attached to that window to close. Note that you also can press ⌘+W to close the active window, and in many programs, pressing Option+⌘+W closes all windows in the active application.

- **Minimize:** When you hover the pointer over this button, a minus symbol (–) appears inside the button. Clicking it shrinks the window down into the Dock, as described in Chapter 2, or in some cases into a floating title bar that appears at the bottom of the application window. In many programs, you also can press ⌘+M to minimize the window. If you've enabled the Double-click a Window's Title Bar to Minimize option in the General system preference (see Chapter 28), you can double-click a title bar to minimize its window. Some applications use the shortcut Option+⌘+M to minimize all their open windows simultaneously.

- **Zoom:** When you hover the pointer over this button, a small plus sign (+) appears inside the button. Clicking the Zoom icon button adjusts the size of the window according to its contents. A zoomed window takes up as much space as required by the window's contents, up to the size of the entire desktop (leaving space for the Dock if it is visible). Clicking the Zoom icon button a second time causes it to return to its previous size. (Some windows have their size determined by the application and cannot be resized; in this case, the Zoom icon button is dimmed and no plus sign appears when you hover the pointer over it. A few applications use the Zoom icon button differently: Clicking the Zoom icon button in iTunes, for example, causes the application to switch between a full window and a small window that displays only shuttle controls and the currently playing track.)

Tip

The color of the Close, Minimize, and Zoom buttons in an active window depends on the setting of the Appearance pop-up menu in the General system preference (see Chapter 28). If the Appearance pop-up menu is set to Graphite, the buttons are all a medium gray. If the Appearance pop-up menu is set to Blue, the Close button is red, the Minimize button is yellow, and the Zoom button is green. ■

Tip

A window doesn't have to be active for you to be able to click its Close, Minimize, or Zoom buttons. Although these buttons appear light gray in inactive windows, as soon as you hover the pointer over them, they return to their active color, meaning you can then click them. Your active window remains active if you click Close or Minimize on another window; if you click Zoom on an inactive window, it becomes the active window. ■

Note

Users migrating from Microsoft Windows will find that these buttons offer much the same functionality as the Close, Minimize, and Maximize buttons found in the top right of a window in Windows. But it is incorrect to think of the Zoom icon button as a Maximize button, and therefore the polar opposite of the Minimize icon button (as it is in Microsoft Windows). Although Zoom often makes the window full size (like Maximize), it also can make the window smaller because it resizes it to the optimum size for the current contents (unlike Maximize). ■

Scroll bar

Scroll bars sit on the right and bottom of a window, as Figure 4.1 shows. They also can appear at the bottom or sides of panes, such as on the right side of a Finder window's Sidebar, if those panes' contents scroll.

By default, Mac OS X Lion determines when scroll bars appear, as follows:

- If you have a Magic Mouse, Magic Trackpad, or a MacBook whose touchpad supports three- and four-finger gestures, they appear only if the contents do not fit in the window *and* Mac OS X Lion detects you are trying to move through the window's contents, such as when you hover the pointer over the right or bottom edges of the window. That detection doesn't always work, but if you begin scrolling through the window through some other means—such as by using the arrow keys, the touchpad's scrolling gesture, or the mouse's scroll wheel—the scroll bars appear, and you can drag them to quickly scroll the window as you would in previous versions of Mac OS X. (If you miss your scroll bars, you can force them to stay on by selecting the Always radio button in the Show Scroll Bars section of the General system preference instead of the default Automatically Based on Input Device option.)

- If your Mac doesn't use such a gesture-savvy input device, then by default Mac OS X Lion always displays the scroll bars if the window's or pane's contents exceed the available room.

Note

Some applications, such as Microsoft Office, show the traditional scroll bar, not the new Mac OS X Lion version. They also always show the scroll bar, despite how the General system preference is set. That's because they don't use Mac OS X's standard set of user-interface controls, which is what the General system preference's settings apply to. ∎

Scroll bars in Mac OS X have two components:

- **Scroll track:** The scroll track is the blank area through which you move the slide. Clicking an area of the scroll track that does not contain the slider makes the slider move in that direction.

- **Slider:** The slider has two functions: One is that you drag it to scroll through the window. The other is to indicate how much of the contents you're currently seeing; the proportion of the slider to the scroll track shows the proportion of visible content to total content in the window. A document, for example, that is twice the size of the window has a slider half the size of the scroll track. Note that the horizontal and vertical sliders may show different proportions, based on how much vertical content there is relative to the window's depth and how much horizontal content there is relative to its width.

New Feature

Mac OS X Lion changes how you scroll within a window when you use a gesture-savvy input device. By default, scroll bars no longer automatically appear in windows, displaying instead only when Lion detects you're navigating the window. Also, the color of the scroll track and slider now depends on the color of the window: If the surrounding background is light, the track is light gray and the slider is dark gray. If the surrounding background is dark, the track is dark gray and the slider is light gray. ∎

New Feature

No matter what types of input devices you use, Mac OS X Lion also gets rid of the scroll arrow icons on the scroll tracks that you could click in previous Mac OS X versions to scroll through a window. There's no system preference option to bring these arrow icons back. ■

When your Mac is using gesture-savvy input devices, the scroll bars in Mac OS X Lion appear as overlays when Mac OS X detects you are trying to move within a window.

New Feature

Mac OS X Lion lets you resize windows by dragging on any corner or side; you're no longer limited to dragging the bottom-right corner as in previous versions. (This also means the three-line icon that previous versions of Mac OS X had on the bottom-right corner to indicate the drag handle is gone in Lion.) If a window is resizable by dragging a corner or side, the pointer changes from the standard arrowhead icon to a double-arrow icon as you hover on the corner or side. ■

Status bar

Along the bottom of most windows is the status bar, which provides information relevant to the window's contents. For example, an iTunes window might show how many songs you have or videos you have, while Safari displays page-load status and shows the URL for any link you are hovering over.

Understanding active and inactive windows

Although Mac OS X can have multiple windows operating at once, only one is considered active at any one time. This is the window you are currently working in.

Mac OS X indicates the active window in several ways simultaneously:

• The active window's title bar is front most, obscuring the parts of any windows it overlaps.

- The active window casts a larger shadow over the other windows it overlaps than the inactive windows do over the windows they overlap.

- The active window's window control buttons—Close, Minimize, and Zoom—are dark gray, whereas the controls of inactive windows are all light gray.

- The active window's title bar (including its toolbar, if it has one) is darker gray than the inactive windows' title bars.

You can switch to other windows easily using any of several methods:

- Click in any part of an inactive window to make it the active window. It moves in front of the other windows, and its buttons are no longer grayed out.

- Use the current application's Window menu to select one of its document windows; all open windows display in this menu.

- In the Finder and most applications, press ⌘+` to move from one window to the next.

- In the Finder and some applications, choose Window ➪ Cycle Through Windows.

- Use the App Exposé or Mission Control navigation features explained in Chapter 2.

- Click the application's icon in the Dock. Its windows come to the fore, with the last active window for that application becoming the currently active window.

- Press ⌘+Tab to open the application switcher (see Chapter 9) and cycle through the active applications; hold ⌘ and press Tab repeatedly to move through the applications. When you release ⌘, the selected application's most recently active window comes to the fore.

Note that if an application has a document window with a dialog box open, you typically cannot access other document windows in that application until you have closed the dialog box (usually by clicking OK in the dialog box to accept any new settings or Cancel to ignore those changes).

Note
In recent years, a new style of document window has become popular: the tabbed window. Pioneered by browsers such as Firefox, a tabbed window doesn't overlap other windows. Instead, it disappears when inactive, leaving just a tab with its name under the application window's title bar. You click the tabs to move among the document windows. The tabbed windows have a Close button (though often it's not visible until you hover over the tab) but not Minimize or Zoom buttons. ∎

Recognizing Folder, File, and Disk Icons

As I noted in this chapter's introduction, Mac OS X uses icons to indicate what an item is, such as a folder, file, or disk. But there's not simply one icon for each type of item; Mac OS X uses a variety of icons to help you know more specifically what type of item a specific item is.

Figure 4.2 shows a sampling of icons to show the details that Mac OS X provides on disks, folders, and files. Here's what the icons show:

- **Disks** (top-left group): From left to right are the icons for an internal disk, an external disk, a removable disk (including USB thumb drives and SD cards), a DVD, and a network-attached volume (a volume can be a computer, disk, or folder connected via the network).

- **Folders** (top-center group): From left to right are the icons for a regular folder, a Mac OS X special folder (in this case, the Applications folder, as indicated by the icon stamped on the folder), a folder alias (note the arrow icon at the lower left), a folder you do not have permission to open (note the red icon at the lower right), and the Home folder for the current user account.

- **Applications** (top-right group): Applications display as unique icons; shown here are the icons for Pages and iCal.

- **Files** (bottom group): Also called *documents*, files' icons all have a curled upper-right corner. Files typically include an icon representing their applications and also show the file extension associated to their file type, as shown in the Zip file icon at the far left. But for many file types, Mac OS X displays a preview of the file's contents instead. In this row, you see pairs of icons for Microsoft Word, Microsoft Excel, text files, and JPEG files showing first the regular icons and then the preview for the specific file. (If you don't want Mac OS X to display the icon previews, you can turn them off for specified folders using the View Options settings described in Chapter 3.) At the far right of this row are four versions of icons for Portable Document Format (PDF) files: the regular icon, an alias icon, a preview icon, and a locked file (notice the lock icon at the lower left) with a preview.

FIGURE 4.2

Examples of disk icons (top-left group), folder icons (top-center group), application icons (top-right group), and file icons (bottom group)

As shown for folders and the PDF files in Figure 4.2, Mac OS X superimposes status icons on disk, folder, and file icons to indicate if the icon is an alias to an item (an arrow icon appears at the lower left), if the item is locked from being edited (a lock icon appears at the lower left), or if the item is not accessible to you because you do not have access permissions (a red circle icon appears at the lower right). Note that I explain how to create aliases later in this chapter and how to set access permissions. Also note that an alias icon always shows the regular icon for the file being aliased, even if you have icon previews enabled (the actual file still displays the icon preview).

How file extensions work

How does Mac OS X know what a file's file type is? It uses the file extension, the (usually) three- or four-letter code at the end of a filename, such as `.zip` for Zip files or `.indd` for Adobe InDesign files. Most applications add that file extension automatically when they save file, but some require you to enable the inclusion of the file extension in their Save As dialog box.

When you install an application in Mac OS X, the application tells Mac OS X what file extensions relate to its files, creating the map Mac OS X uses to associate that application's icon to its file types. You can change those associations using the Info window as described in Chapter 3. If a file has no file extension, or if its file extension is unknown to Mac OS X, a blank file icon appears.

Chances are your Mac doesn't show the file extensions in its filenames. That's because by default it hides them from you. If you want to always see them, choose Finder⇨Preferences or press ⌘+, (comma) and go to the Advanced pane. Then select the Show All Filename Extensions option. (Chapter 3 covers Finder preferences in more detail.)

Note that you can edit a file's file extension, if Mac OS X displays these extensions, by editing the filename in the usual way, as described later in this chapter. Just change the extension, but note that doing so may cause Mac OS X to be unable to open it via double-clicking or cause compatible applications to see the file as one they cannot open. The valid reasons to change a file extension are to add a missing file extension, to fix an extension that got mangled in transit to you, and to standardize file extensions for file types that have several legitimate variations of extensions (such as `.tif` and `.tiff` for TIFF files, `.jpg` and `.jpeg` for JPEG files, and `.htm` and `.html` for HTML files).

Interacting with Items

Whether you are working with disks, folders, or files, the Finder provides a consistent set of operations you can use with them. (Later in this chapter, I detail some additional operations available for each type of item.)

Selecting single items

To select an item in a Finder window or the desktop, you simply click the icon with the mouse or tap it via the touchpad. In Mac OS X, an item that you have selected is highlighted. On the desktop and in icon view, the item's icon is surrounded with an opaque box that often appears as gray against a white background. The text label that accompanies the icon is highlighted. (The default color is blue, although you can change this in the General system preference, as Chapter 28 explains. You also can hide the icon label via the Finder's View Options dialog box, as Chapter 3 explains.) In other views, the selected item's name appears in white with a background color (again, as set in the General system preference).

To deselect an item, ⌘+click it. Or simply click an empty area in a Finder window or on the desktop.

You also can use the keyboard's arrow keys to move from one icon to another; each item you move to is selected in turn. (If no item is selected, the Finder starts from the top left of the window.) Alternatively, you can start typing the name of an item in a folder, and the appropriate item is selected as you type. You do not need to type in the entire name of the desired item; the selection jumps from item to item alphabetically and according to the letters you type. This method is particularly useful if you have a folder with lots of items in it and know a specific item you are looking for.

You also can move through items via the keyboard alphabetically by pressing the Tab key (and reverse-alphabetically by pressing Shift+Tab). This method is particularly helpful if your window's contents are not arranged in alphabetical order. Note that pressing Tab does not work when you are in column view. (Chapter 3 explains the Finder windows' view modes.)

Table 4.1 provides a handy reference for different ways to select items via keyboard commands.

TABLE 4.1

Selecting Items with Keyboard Commands

Key	Result
↑ or ↓	Selects the item above or below the currently highlighted item.
← or →	On the desktop or in icon view, selects the item to the left or right of the current item. In list view, using the left and right arrow keys expands and contracts folders. In column view, these keys move up or down the folder hierarchy based on the selected folder. In Cover Flow view, these keys act as the ↑ and ↓ keys, respectively.
Tab	Selects the next alphabetical item in the list. (This key has no effect in column view.)
Shift+Tab	Selects the previous alphabetical item in the list. (This key has no effect in column view.)

Selecting multiple items

You often want to work with multiple items at once, such as to move or copy them. Mac OS X provides several methods to do so. Note that the Finder window's current view mode affects some of the methods you can use, as noted in the descriptions here. These methods are available:

- **Command+click:** Press and hold the ⌘ key, and click each of the multiple items you want to select. (⌘+click a selected item to deselect it, such as if you mistakenly add an item to your selection group.)

- **Click+drag:** You can select multiple items by holding down the mouse or touchpad button (or depressing a buttonless touchpad such as a Magic Trackpad or a newer MacBook's touchpad) and dragging the pointer across several items. This method works differently depending on where you are:

  - On the desktop, or in a Finder window displaying in icon view, you click an area that does not contain an item and drag the pointer diagonally while holding down the mouse button, touchpad button, or touchpad. This creates an opaque rectangle (known as a *marquee*) around any items within the selection area when you release the mouse or touchpad.

- When you are in column view, list view, or Cover Flow view, you click a location near an icon or its accompanying text label and then drag the pointer over the items you want to select in the group. Note: If you click the icon or the text label itself, you won't be able to drag-select other items in the window.

- **Shift+clicking:** Another method of highlighting a range of files is to click the first item in the group and then hold down the Shift key when clicking the last item in a range. This highlights all the items between the two points. This method is useful for highlighting lots of items in a list without having to individually select them all or having to click+drag across a large area to select all the desired items. Note that Shift+clicking works only when you are in list, column, or Cover Flow view. When you are in icon view or working on the desktop, Shift+clicking selects individual items in the same way as ⌘+clicking does.

Caution

Selecting multiple items in list view can be confusing because you can highlight individual items and the folders that they are contained within. If you have selected two items and the containing folder above them in the list, then copying the items copies the entire folder and all the items inside. ∎

Moving and copying items

After you've selected a few items, you likely want to move them around (or move them to the Trash to delete them). After you've selected the items you want to move, click and hold and then drag them to their new location, releasing the mouse button, touchpad button, or touchpad when finished. The new location can be any open Finder window, any folder icon, any disk icon, or any volume icon. (These folder, disk, and volume icons can be on your desktop, in the Sidebar, or in a Finder window.)

Tip

If you are working in list or icon view, hover a selected item over a folder for a few seconds and that folder opens to expose its contents. (Apple calls this capability spring-loaded folders.) This lets you drill down through folders while items are selected so you can move those items several levels deep in the folder hierarchy. Drag the item outside the folder window if you've drilled down too far or to the wrong location, so you can start over again. ∎

In icon view or on the desktop, you can drag an item by clicking either its icon or the text label below the icon. In list view, you can click and drag any part of the file information on the horizontal line. In column view, you can click and drag any part of the filename. In Cover Flow view, you can either drag the item or any part of the horizontal bar or drag the large preview of the item in the Cover Flow area.

When you drag an item over a folder icon or name, Mac OS X highlights the folder so you know that if you release the mouse or touchpad button, the item is placed in that folder.

Likewise, when you drag an item over an empty area in a Finder window, the window's inside border is highlighted with a blue line so you know this folder is the destination if you release the mouse or touchpad button.

New Feature

Mac OS X Lion adds a visual clue as you move or copy multiple items: A badge (a red ellipse displaying the number of items selected) now appears below the pointer as you drag them. ∎

When you drag items within locations on the same disk or volume, you move the items from one location to the other. But when you drag items to a location on another disk or volume, Mac OS X automatically copies the items to the new location, leaving the original items in their original location.

If you want to copy items within the same disk or volume, press and hold the Option key while dragging them—and be sure Option is still held when you release the mouse or touch-pad button; otherwise, the items aren't copied. And if you want to move an item across volumes, rather than copy them, press and hold ⌘ while dragging and releasing the item; doing so removes the item from the original location.

When copying items, Mac OS X displays an indicator (a green circle with a + symbol) at the bottom of the item's icon. (If multiple items are selected, the indicator appears on the bottommost icon, next to the badge showing how many items are selected.) You see this indicator appear when you press and hold Option or when your pointer moves over an icon or Finder window on another disk or volume.

Note

If you copy a disk or volume into another disk or volume, the original disk or volume is copied as a folder onto the new location. ∎

Another way to copy items is to select them, choose Edit ➪ Copy or press ⌘+C, go to the new destination Finder window, and then choose Edit ➪ Paste or press ⌘+V. To copy an item in its current Finder window, you can use Copy and Paste, or use the simpler File ➪ Duplicate or ⌘+D method. To move items instead of copying them, you can also hold Option and then choose Edit ➪ Move Items Here, or press Option+⌘+V.

Tip

When copying large items, the Copy dialog box appears, showing a progress bar so you know the copy operation is in progress but not yet complete. (The Copy dialog box closes itself automatically after the copying is complete.) You can abort the copy operation by clicking the X icon button at the right side of the progress bar, as well as hide the Copy dialog box by clicking its Minimize icon in the title bar. ∎

What happens if you move or copy an item into a location that contains an item with the same name? It depends:

- If you're copying an item via the Copy and Paste commands or via the Duplicate command, the copied item gets the word `Copy` added to its name, so both versions are in the destination location. (If you copy the same file again, the next copy has `Copy 1` added to its name, and the numeral is incremented for each additional copy.)

- If you move or copy an item in the same disk or volume, Mac OS X appends a numeral to the end of its name: 1 for the first copy, 2 for the second, and so on. Thus, the multiple versions are in the destination location.

- If you move or copy an item across disks or volumes, the Copy dialog box appears with three buttons: Keep Both Files, Stop, and Replace. If you click Keep Both Files, Mac OS X appends a numeral to the end of its name: 1 for the first copy, 2 for the second, and so on. If you click Stop, the item is not moved or copied. If you click Replace, the item at the destination location is replaced with the one you are moving or copying. Note that if multiple items would be replaced, you are asked what to do for each item, but you can select the Apply to All option to have the same action applied to all remaining replacements. And further note that regardless of whether you've selected Apply to All, if you click Stop when copying multiple items, no further items are copied.

New Feature

The Keep Both Files button in the Copy dialog box when moving or copying items across disks or volumes is new to Mac OS X Lion. ∎

Caution

It's not possible to recover a replaced item. The item is not sent to the Trash where you can recover it, as is the case with deleted items. ∎

Deleting items

To delete items, just move them to the Trash using any of the options described previously for moving items. The items remain in the Trash (so you can retrieve them later) until you empty the Trash, which you do by choosing Finder ➪ Empty Trash or pressing Option+⌘+ Delete. Chapter 3 explains the options for emptying the Trash.

Using Undo to move an item back

Sometimes, when moving a folder or a file, you decide that it would be better off where it was. In this case, you can restore the item to its original location by choosing Edit ➪ Undo in the Finder or pressing ⌘+Z. But note that if the moved items replaced items at the new location, the Undo command does not recover the item that was replaced; it is gone for good. (The Undo command just moves the other item back to its original location.)

Note that the Undo command works only on the last action in the Finder—so you have to undo an action pretty much immediately—and you cannot perform multiple Undo commands in the Finder as you can in some applications.

Note

If you delete an item on a disk that belongs to a different user account or from a network volume, you get an alert dialog box letting you know the file will be deleted immediately rather than placed in the Trash. Once you confirm the deletion, the file cannot be recovered from the Trash. ∎

Creating aliases for items

An *alias* is a shortcut to a file, folder, disk, or volume—or even another alias. Aliases exist to enable quick access to items that may be buried deep within Mac OS X's folder hierarchy. By using aliases, you can jump to an item without having to drill down through the folders or disks containing it. An alias uses the same icon as the original item but has a small black curved arrow in its bottom-left corner. And as mentioned previously, aliases of files don't show the icon preview of the file's contents.

Creating an alias is easy: Select the item and choose File ⇨ Make Alias or press ⌘+L in the Finder. You also can choose Make Alias from an item's contextual menu. And you can create an alias by holding both Option and ⌘ when dragging and releasing an item.

Although double-clicking an alias opens it in the appropriate application, sometimes you want to go to the original item, such as to move, copy, or rename it. To do so, select an alias and choose File ⇨ Show Original or press ⌘+R. Or choose Show Original from the contextual menu. This opens a Finder window that contains the original item.

Mac OS X tracks aliases as they and their original files are moved around, so they're kept up to date automatically. However, if the original item has been deleted or moved to a disk that has been ejected, the Finder shows an alert dialog box informing you that the original item can't be found when you try to open the alias. This dialog box offers you three options. You can click OK to accept the warning and continue working without using the alias, you can click the Delete Alias button to move the alias to the Trash, and you can click the Fix Alias button to locate the missing item (or select one you want the alias to point to from now on instead) via the Select New Original dialog box that appears.

You also can reassign an alias to a different item using the Info window. Select the alias, choose File ⇨ Get Info or press ⌘+I, and click the Select New Original button in the Info window's General section. In the settings sheet that appears, navigate to the new file you want the alias to point to, select it, and click Open.

Renaming items

You can rename items in the Finder, whether to make the names more meaningful to you or to correct them. For example, you may want to add `version 2` to the end of a filename to identify that it is an updated version of something, or you may simply want to rename a file so it is more readily identifiable; for example, changing `Picture 2` to `Henry's Birthday Cake`.

However, some filenames are best left unchanged: Application files and system folders should be left alone. Some important files and folders cannot be changed; for example, most folders sitting in the root level of boot disk resist any attempts to change them.

You can rename files, folders, disks, and volumes with complete impunity, but note that renaming disks and volumes may interfere with aliases to their contents, causing error messages saying the original item cannot be found.

Tip

In Mac OS X, you can rename only one file at a time. If you find that you regularly have to rename lots of files (for example, those created by a digital camera), use the Automator utility that comes with Mac OS X to create a rename workflow so you can batch-rename files easily. Chapter 13 covers the Automator. If you're not afraid to use Unix, you can use command lines in the Terminal to batch-rename items as well, as Appendix D explains. ∎

Users migrating from Microsoft Windows undoubtedly will look for a contextual menu option called Rename. However, Mac OS X has no equivalent contextual menu option. To rename an item, you must highlight its current name using one of the following methods:

- **Click the name twice.** This method requires a pause between clicks; do *not* double-click the item, as that opens it. You first click an item's name, pause for a fraction of a second, and then click the name again.

- **Select the item and press the Return key.** But be careful: A slip of the finger on the keyboard and whatever else you type replaces the current name.

- **Select the item's icon, and then click the item name.**

If the filename has an extension, such as .txt, only the file part of the filename is highlighted, not the extension. That's so you don't change the file type accidentally. (See the sidebar "How file extensions work" earlier in this chapter for more details on file extensions.)

After you've highlighted the filename, either type new text (which replaces the existing text) or edit the existing filename. To edit the existing text, click in the text where you want to begin editing, or navigate to that location using the → and ← keys. When the text cursor is at the desired location, delete unwanted characters with the Delete and Forward Delete keys and type in new text—just as you would in a word processor.

Tip

You can even paste text, as well as copy and cut text, using the standard shortcuts: ⌘+V, ⌘+C, and ⌘+X, respectively. Or you can use the standard menu options: Edit ⇨ Paste, Edit ⇨ Copy, and Edit ⇨ Cut. You also can delete selected text using the Delete and Forward Delete keys; such deleted text is not saved on the Clipboard, so it cannot be pasted elsewhere. ∎

Understanding file-naming conventions

Mac OS X is very versatile when it comes to naming files. A filename can be as many as 255 characters long and contain most characters and symbols imaginable. One common character you cannot use in Mac OS X filename is the colon (:), because Mac OS X uses that symbol behind the scenes to indicate folder hierarchies for files. For example, the Documents folder is located in `Macintosh HD:Users:username:Documents`. (In an actual path, *username* is replaced by the name of your user account.) Using colons in your filenames would interfere with this path structure, so Mac OS X prohibits it.

If you ever plan to share, or access, your files on other types of computers, you should stick to a few conventions to accommodate their own file-naming limitations:

- **Avoid special characters.** Avoid using bullet points (•) and currency symbols, such as the euro (€). Also avoid any odd characters such as the infinity symbol (∞). Other operating systems may not be able to render these symbols correctly, so the file may not open.

- **Don't use colons.** Do not use colons (:) in filenames. Even if the other computers' operating systems support colons in their filenames, Mac OS X does not.

- **Don't use slashes.** Although Mac OS X forbids you from using colons in filenames, it permits you to use the forward slash (/) and backslash (\) characters. However, Windows uses the slash character to indicate the file structure, in the same way that the colon character is used by Mac OS X, so Mac files whose names include slashes do not work on a Windows PC. Other operating systems use the backslash for the same purpose.

- **Avoid using periods.** Although Mac OS X (and Windows) lets you use periods (.) in filenames, don't. The period is what's used to separate the filename from its file extension, and the use of periods elsewhere in the filename can confuse some e-mail and file-transfer applications, causing them to chop off the filename after the first period they encounter. Why risk it?

- **Do use common characters.** Except for :, /, and \, it's fine to use the characters on a keyboard that you access by pressing the keys or by holding and pressing Shift with the keys. All alphabetical characters, whether uppercase or lowercase, are acceptable, as are numerical (0 through 9) characters and any symbols in the numbers row. Also acceptable are blank spaces, hyphens (–), underscores (_) and commas (,).

When you're finished replacing or editing the text, either press Return or simply click elsewhere in the Finder to complete the renaming.

If you decide that you do not want to rename the item after you have selected the text, press Esc to restore the original name. If you have changed the name and want to return to the original name, use the Undo command (choose Edit ➪ Undo or press ⌘+Z). See Table 4.2 for a list of keyboard commands you can use when renaming files.

TABLE 4.2

Keyboard Navigation When Editing Items' Names

Key	Action
↑	Moves the insertion point to the beginning of the name when it is first selected and up one line thereafter
↓	Moves the insertion point to the end of the name when it is first selected and down one line thereafter
←	Moves the insertion point to the beginning of the name when it is first selected and to the left one character thereafter
→	Moves the insertion point to the end of the name when it is first selected and to the right one character thereafter
Option+←, Option+→	Moves the insertion point one word to the right or left
Shift+←, Shift+→	Selects more (or less) of the name to the right or left

Compressing items

Mac OS X has a neat ability to compress selected items into a Zip file, a standard format for compressed files. After selecting the items you want to compress, choose File ⇨ Compress Items or choose Compress Items from the contextual menu. If you selected multiple items, the compressed archive is named `Archive.zip`; otherwise, it retains the filename of the original file but has the file extension `.zip` instead.

If the compressed items include folders and disks, their folder hierarchies are preserved, so all files in their subfolders are retained. And the original files are untouched when you compress them.

To extract the contents of a Zip file, just double-click the file. The files are decompressed at the current location, and if the Zip file contained folders, those folders and their original folder hierarchy are reconstituted.

Locking items

Sometimes, you don't want items to be accessible or editable. Mac OS X provides several mechanisms to accomplish this goal, most of which are available via the Info window explained in the next section of this chapter and in Chapter 3.

- **Stationery Pad option:** Available only for files, the Info window has the Stationery Pad option that, if selected, makes the file into a template, so if you open it and save it, a copy is saved instead, leaving the original file untouched. Some applications have a similar option in their Save As dialog box. Note that there is no visual indicator denoting that an item is a Stationery Pad item.

- **Locked option:** Available for disks and folders only, the Info window also has the Locked option; if this option is selected, items cannot be added, renamed, or deleted unless you either enter an administrator password or deselect Locked in the Info window. (A lock icon appears on the folder or disk icon if Locked is selected.) Note that the Locked option is not that strong: You can open locked items in the folder or disk, edit them, and save them. And you can add, rename, or delete items in the folder's or disk's subfolders.

- **Read-only status:** Using the Info window's Sharing & Permissions controls, as explained in Chapter 3, you can make items read-only. That means you can't copy items to a read-only folder, disk, or volume, nor can you save content in it. Note that there is no visual indicator denoting that an item is read-only.

- **Unavailable status:** Using the access permissions set up in user accounts via the Users & Groups system preference (see Chapter 27), you can block other users of your Mac from accessing specific folders and their contents. The inaccessible folders's icons are marked with a red circle icon on their lower right.

Getting Item Information

Mac OS X stores lots of information about items that aren't available from their icons. Some of that information, such as date modified and file size, is visible in several Finder view modes, as Chapter 3 describes.

Using the Info window

But the Info window provides a handy one-stop shop for all the information—technically called *metadata*—that Mac OS X has on items. To open the Info window, select an item and choose File ⇨ Get Info or press ⌘+I in the Finder. (You can also press and hold Option and choose File ⇨ Show Inspector or press Option+⌘+I to open the identical Inspector window.)

Figure 4.3 shows three Info windows: one for a folder, one for an image file, and one for a disk. The window is divided into sections, each with different classes of information: the icon and summary, Spotlight Comments (not available for folders), General, More Info (specific to that item type), Name and Extension (not available for folders), and Preview. (The Open With option for files, the Shared Folder option for folders, and the Sharing & Permissions section for all items are all covered in Chapter 3.)

Icon and summary

At the top of the Info window is an icon for the item, as well as its filename, its size, and the date it was last modified. You can copy and paste icons from one Info window to another, as well as copy icons from almost any graphic into an Info window, to give favorite files and folders custom icons.

FIGURE 4.3

The Info window for, from left to right, the Desktop folder, an image file, and an external hard disk

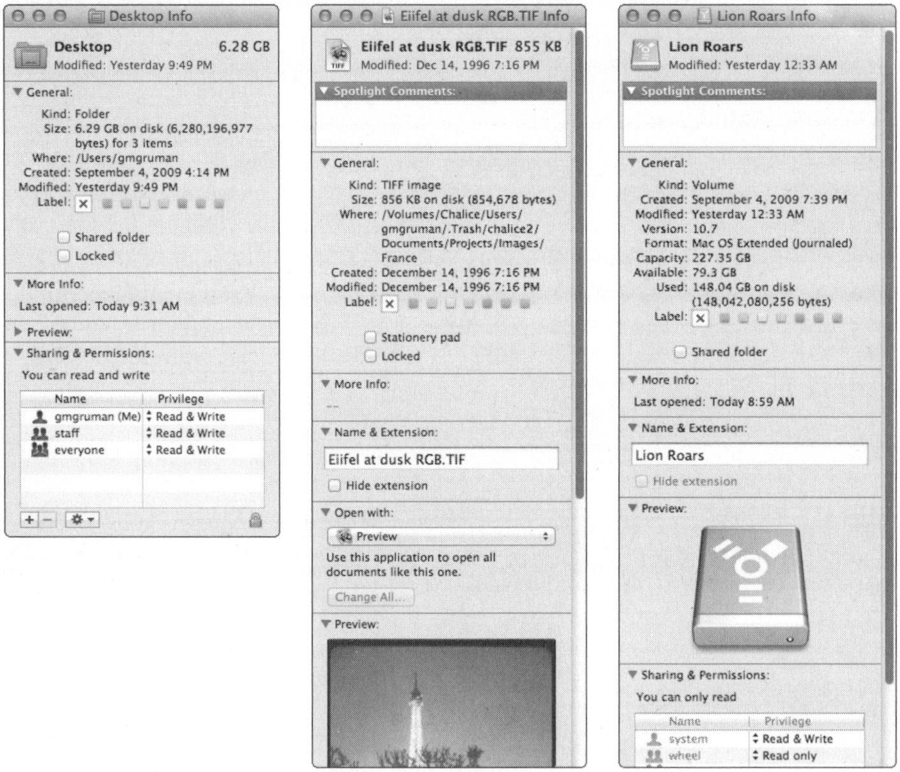

Spotlight comments

Spotlight is Mac OS X's technology for searching throughout files, folders, and application data in Mac OS X. You can populate this field in the Info window with any information that you want, and Spotlight associates this information to the file. For example, you can add the names of people to images of them using this field; then when you search for them by name using Spotlight, it returns these images in its results. Spotlight is covered in depth in Chapter 5.

General

The General section contains the bulk of the information about an item. The information presented changes based on the nature of the item. But files, folders, and disks all have the following information: kind, creation date, last-modified date, and label. Files and folders also have location (Where) information, while disks also have total capacity, available capacity, and used capacity information.

More Info

The More Info section of the Info window presents detailed information about the item. This information varies based on the nature of the item selected. Image files, for example, can have information relating to the dimensions of the image, its color space, profile name, alpha channel, and when it was last opened. Microsoft Word documents may have information on when they were created and modified. HTML documents may have the `<title>` tag information displayed. Music files may have artist, genre, and track information displayed. Folders, disks, and volumes show when they were last opened.

Name & Extension

The name of the current file appears in the Name & Extensions section, and you can select the name and change it. (An exception is the set of special folders such as System and Desktop; these names can be changed, so they have no Name & Extension section in their Info window.) For files, you also can hide or show the file extension by selecting or deselecting the Hide Extension option.

Preview

The Preview area of the Info window shows a small graphic displaying the contents of the item, if available. For folders and disks, the preview is simply a larger version of the icon at the top of the Info window. For graphics, you usually see the actual graphic. For movies and audio files, you see the movie poster or album cover if available and a generic icon if not. If you move the mouse pointer over the preview image, a play button appears. Click it to play the file; the button then turns into a stop button you can click to stop playing the file.

Using Quick Look to view file contents

As mentioned earlier, an icon can display a preview snapshot of the actual document's contents, such as a photo or movie clip. The technology that enables these previews is called Quick Look. Mac OS X makes Quick Look accessible in several ways: through live icon previews in Finder windows, via the Quick Look window, and in column view mode. Figure 4.4 shows all three Quick Look preview methods.

After you start working with Quick Look, you'll wonder how you ever lived without it.

Live preview icons

As noted earlier in this chapter, Mac OS X by default shows a preview of a file's contents in icon and Cover Flow views, at least for those files whose formats it can work with. If that preview is of a multi-page document, video, or audio file, playback controls appear when you hover the pointer over the icon. For videos and audio, click the Play icon button (the icon with a right-facing triangle) to play the contents; the button turns to a Pause button (the icon with two parallel vertical lines) after the contents begin to play. For multi-page documents, two arrow icon buttons appear—one to move forward (→) and one to move backward (←), as shown in the left side of Figure 4.4.

FIGURE 4.4

The three Quick Look preview methods (from left to right): live preview icons, the Quick Look window, and the column view mode's preview

New Feature

The live icon previews have been enhanced in Mac OS X Lion to let you navigate through multi-page documents, not just videos and audio files. ■

The Quick Look window

In any view mode, if you select a file and press the spacebar, the Quick Look window opens and shows you the file contents. (You also can Control+click or right-click an item and choose Quick Look from the contextual menu, or choose File➪Quick Look or press ⌘+Y in the Finder.) Press Shift+spacebar if you want to open the Quick Look window in slow motion. You also can go directly to the full-screen Quick Look window by pressing Option+spacebar when an item is selected.

As with the live preview icons, you can play and navigate file contents.

If you select another item, you get its Quick Look preview; to stop seeing previews, click the Close button in the Quick Look window or press Esc.

The Quick Look window has a title bar with Close and Zoom buttons on the left side and a full-screen button on the far-right side. If you open the full screen, you see two or three large buttons on the bottom, at least for a few seconds: Add to iPhoto, Close, and Exit Full Screen. (Add to iPhoto appears only if an image file is being previewed.) These buttons fade away until you move the pointer. You can switch back to the regular Quick Look window by pressing Esc.

The title bar also has an Open button that lets you open the file in the default application for the file type.

New Feature

Mac OS X Lion has enhanced the Quick Look window. The Zoom button and Open button are both new in the regular Quick Look window, which also now has an appearance more like regular windows than in previous versions of Mac OS X. And the full-screen view adds the Add to iPhoto button when image files are being previewed, so you can have compatible files added to your albums and sync to your iPhone, iPad, or iPod Touch more easily. ∎

Column view mode preview

As mentioned in Chapter 3, the column view mode displays a preview of the file in its right-most column, as well as some metadata about the item. The preview in the column view mode has the same playback controls as the live preview icons do in the icon and Cover Flow view modes.

The slideshow viewer

Mac OS X has a cool slideshow viewer available that uses the Quick Look technology to play a series of selected documents on screen as a slideshow. It's particularly handy for showing multiple images. After selecting the documents whose previews you want to play in the Finder, press and hold Option and choose File⇨Slideshow Items or simply press Option+⌘+Y.

You get a full-screen preview of the first item plus the playback controls at bottom, as shown in Figure 4.5. Those controls are, from left to right, Previous, Play/Pause, Next, View All Slides, Exit Full Screen, and Close. If you click Exit Full Screen, the playback window shrinks into a Quick Look window, which just offers the Close, Previous, Next, View All Slides, and Show in Full Screen controls (at top). You can also move through the "slides" in this Quick Look window using the ← and → keys.

Working with Folders' Unique Operations

In addition to the common controls described in the preceding sections, special operations are available just for folders.

Using smart folders

Mac OS X uses the "smart" concept in several areas: iTunes playlists, Mail folders, and Finder windows. The concept is simple: Create a set of search rules, and save them so they are applied live all the time. For the Finder, that means you can create smart folders that stay updated with the appropriate contents at all times.

FIGURE 4.5

The Finder's slideshow viewer lets you play the preview images of selected documents.

For example, you can create a rule that says the smart folder should display all files that are of the kind documents, have the word "Lion" in their contents, and were modified in the last 30 days. As new files that meet these criteria are discovered, they're automatically shown in that smart folder—and any files that no longer satisfy all these criteria disappear from it.

Creating smart folders is easy: Open a Finder window (a new or existing one), and enter a search term in the Spotlight search box. Refine where the search occurs using the buttons that appear in the search bar at the top of the contents pane: One set lists This Mac and one or more folders based on where you were when you began the search. The other set has two options, Contents and Filename, that tell Spotlight where to search for the text. You can add more search criteria by clicking the + icon button and choosing the desired criteria. The contents of the Finder window reflect the results live as you modify the criteria. Figure 4.6 shows an example.

If you've ever used Spotlight, you'll recognize that this is the same process you use to conduct searches from the Finder. (Chapter 5 explains Spotlight in detail.)

When you're satisfied with your criteria, click the Save button at the upper right of the search bar, give the smart folder a name, and click Save. Before you save, you can click the Add to

Sidebar option to have this smart folder appear in the Sidebar's Favorites section. But you can always drag the folder from wherever you saved them to the Sidebar later to add it there; the default location is the Saved Searches folder in the current user account's Library folder. Note that a smart folder has a gear icon when listed in the Sidebar.

So a smart folder is simply a saved Spotlight search whose current, live results are displayed in a Finder window.

To edit a smart folder's criteria later, select the smart folder in a Finder window or in the Sidebar, choose Show Search Criteria from the contextual menu to display the search bar with the current criteria, modify them as desired, and click Save to save the changes. (You can't save the changes as a separate copy this way, but you can copy the original smart folder and then edit that copy.)

FIGURE 4.6

A smart folder is a Finder window whose search criteria have been saved.

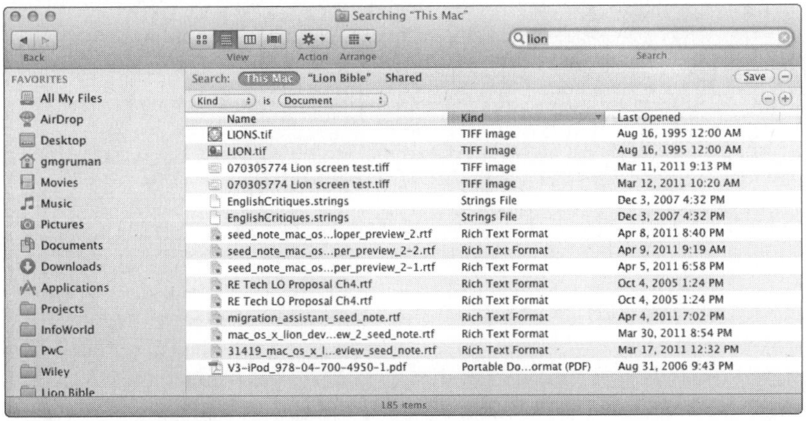

Using folder actions

Mac OS X comes with a collection of AppleScripts known as *folder actions* that enable folders to not just store items but also to act on any items placed in them. (AppleScript is the scripting language used by Mac OS X; Chapter 13 explains how to create such scripts.) Some folder actions change the way information is displayed inside the folders, while others perform basic editing actions (such as rotating all images by 90 degrees). The actions can do whatever the accompanying AppleScript demands.

Attaching actions to folders

You can create your own AppleScripts to attach to folders, as well as use the several scripts that Apple provides with Mac OS X. If you create scripts, they must reside in the Folder Action Scripts folder, whose path is `Library/Scripts/Folder Action Scripts`.

To attach an action to a folder, do the following:

1. **Right-click or Control+click a disk or a folder to open the contextual menu, and choose Services ➪ Folder Actions Setup.** You can also select a folder, then choose Finder ➪ Services ➪ Folder Actions Setup. Either way, this opens the Folder Actions Setup dialog box, shown in Figure 4.7.

2. **Choose a script to attach to the folder from the list that appears, and click the Attach button.** Alternatively, press the Cancel button and use the + icon button explained in Step 4 to select scripts. The selected script appears in the Script pane on the left side of the dialog box.

3. **Select the Enable Folder Actions option in the upper-left side of the Folder Actions Setup dialog box.**

4. **If desired, click the + icon button in the bottom right of the Folder Actions Setup dialog box to attach further scripts.** Select the desired script, and click Attach. Repeat this step for each additional script you want to add.

5. **If desired, click the + icon button in the bottom left of the Folder Actions Setup dialog box to select additional folders to which to attach the scripts.** After you've selected a folder, click Open. Repeat this step for each additional folder you want to have use the attached scripts. Note that the name of the folder selected when you first opened the Folder Actions Setup dialog box should already be listed and checked in the Folders with Actions pane on the left side of the dialog box.

6. **Click the Close icon button to complete the folder action assignment.** The selected actions are now active for the folder.

FIGURE 4.7

The Folder Actions Setup dialog box enables you to attach action scripts to folders. Left: Select a script from the settings sheet. Right: This is the dialog box with a script and folder selected.

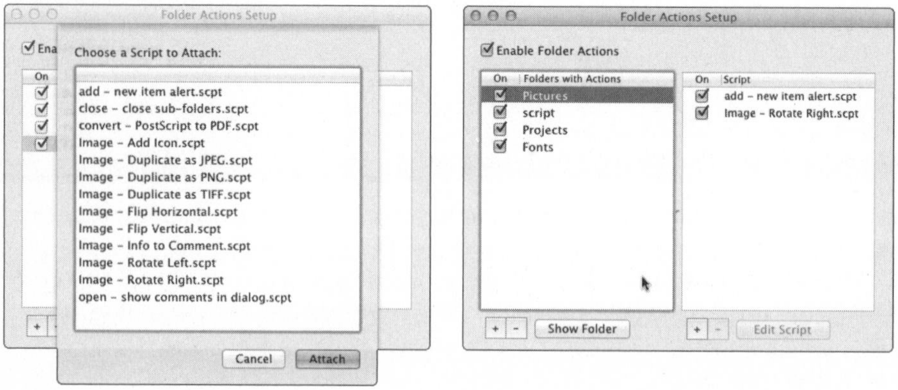

Using actions

When an action script is attached to a folder, the standard method of using a folder action is to drag an item (or items) to the folder. As the item is placed into the folder, the action's AppleScripts are run and perform their action on the items selected. (If a script doesn't apply to the items, nothing happens.) An action creates a subfolder for the results inside the folder with a name determined by the script; for example, if you use the Image – Rotate Right script, the new subfolder is named Rotated Images.

Editing actions

To edit an action, open the Folder Actions Setup dialog box, and select the folder whose actions you want to edit. Deselect the On check box to the left of a script name to stop it from running. Select a script, and click the – icon button under the Script list to completely remove the script from the folder action. Click the + icon button under the Script list to add a script to the folder action.

Click the Edit Script button under the Script list to launch the AppleScript Editor and open the script so you can edit it. This is also a great way to simply look at the code that underlies the script to understand what it does.

Click the + icon button under the Folders with Actions list to add additional folders to which you can apply scripts. Select a folder, and click the – icon button to remove folder actions from that folder. Click the Show Folder button to open the selected folder in a new Finder window.

Touring Mac OS X's special folders

As mentioned previously, Mac OS X has many folders for handling special kinds of items. Some are contained within your Home folder, and some are contained in the root of your main volume and are used by Mac OS X.

The system folders

On your desktop is an icon in the top right for your startup disk, usually named Macintosh HD. (You can rename it as you would any folder or disk: Select it, click its name, and change the text that becomes selected.) Double-clicking the disk's icon opens the first level (called the *root level*) of folders on the startup disk. By default, it contains just four folders:

- **Applications:** As the name suggests, this folder contains programs used for a variety of purposes.
- **Library:** The Library folder contains a set of system-wide settings, as well as some additional files that are used to help the Mac operate. The settings inside this Library folder apply to all users of the Mac, although each user also has his or her own Library folder within his or her Home folder.
- **System:** This folder contains the actual files that represent the heart of Mac OS X. Most of the items stored here are used to make your Mac work, so interfering with

this folder is usually a bad idea. To prevent unintentional changes, this folder isn't easily editable, and you are asked to provide an administrator password before moving, deleting, or editing any files in it.

- **Users:** Each user account set up in Mac OS X has its own Home folder inside the Users folder. Each Home folder acts as a central storage area for all the files and Mac OS X settings for each user, including the Desktop, Documents, Downloads, Library, Movies, Music, Pictures, Public, and Sites folder, as Table 4.3 details. A Home folder may also contain the Applications folder for applications available only to that user.

Working with the Home folder

Mac OS X is designed to be a multi-user operating system that different people can use, with their own personal files, preferences, and even applications. Mac OS X segregates each user account's files in what is called the Home folder, one of which exists for each user in the Users folder. Each user's Home folder is protected from the prying eyes of other users, unless the user gives others permission to access their files, as Chapters 27 explains. When you customize any aspect of Mac OS X, those settings are saved in your Home folder's Library folder—and they don't apply to other user accounts.

When you create or save documents, the documents are stored by default within your Home folder's Documents folder; of course, you can choose a different location in the Save As dialog box of the applications you are saving from.

Because a Mac can have multiple Home folders, one for each user account, the Home folder is not actually named Home. Instead, each Home folder uses the short name set up for its corresponding user account when first installing Mac OS X (see Appendix A) or when creating a user account (see Chapter 27).

Note

The Home folder for the active user account has a house icon (reflecting that it is the current Home folder), while those of inactive users use standard folder icons. ■

You can access the active Home folder in several ways:

- Click the Home folder in the Finder's Sidebar, in the Favorites section. (The Home folder's name is your short name, not "Home.")
- Choose Go ➪ Home in the Finder, or press Shift+⌘+H in the Finder.
- Open the startup disk, open the Users folder, and then open the Home folder. (Again, the Home folder's name is your short name, not "Home.")

Note

Only the currently logged-in user can access his or her Home folder. This security measure ensures that user's system settings and personal documents remain private. But people with administrator passwords can access anyone's Home folder, as Chapter 27 explains. ■

TABLE 4.3

Folders Contained in the Home Folder

Name	Contents
Applications	Contains any applications that are unique to that user.
Desktop	Contains all the files and folders shown on the desktop. Note that volume icons are not displayed here.
Documents	Stores miscellaneous documents created by the user.
Downloads	Temporarily stores files downloaded from the web by Safari and other applications.
Library	Contains applications preferences and other system settings that are unique to the user.
Movies	Is the default location for any files created by Apple's movie-making software. It is also a good place to store any movie files.
Music	Is the default location for the iTunes library, and is a good place to keep any audio files. Note that it also contains videos, ringtones, and apps for your iPhone, iPad, or iPod Touch.
Pictures	Is the default location for the iPhoto picture library, and is a good place to store any pictures.
Public	Is used to share files with other users across the network. The Public folder is outlined in more depth in Chapter 24.
Sites	Is the default location for websites that you want to make available over the network or Internet from your Mac. Chapter 25 explains such personal web hosting.

Working with Files' Unique Operations

In addition to the common controls such as selecting, copying, and renaming, files have a few special controls available only to them:

- Files can be made into Stationery Pad items, so that when opened, only a copy of the original can be saved, preserving the original version. The "Locking items" section earlier in this chapter explains this capability.

- File contents can be previewed using the Quick Look facility in Mac OS X, as described in the section "Using Quick Look to view file contents" earlier in this chapter.

Summary

Windows are the onscreen containers for the folders and files stored on your Mac and on devices connected to it. The desktop is a special type of window that also displays the attached disks and network volumes. All these items—files, disks, and volumes—are represented as icons in the Finder windows and desktop, with the detail varying based on the specifics of the file, folder, disk, or volume.

Windows have standard elements you use to manage the windows themselves and get information on the files, folders, and disk contents they display: the title bar, scroll bar, resize handle, and status bar. When you have several windows open, the Finder differentiates the active window—the one in which any actions you take are applied—through several visual clues.

To work on items in the Finder, you first have to select them, and you can do so singly or in groups using a variety of techniques. After you've selected items, you can move, copy, delete, create an alias for, rename, compress, and lock items.

The Finder also lets you get the details on files, folders, and disks through the Info window and see the contents of many files via the Quick Look feature.

Folders have several unique controls, including the ability to update their contents based on criteria you define via the Spotlight search feature, run specified scripts when files are added to them (called *folder actions*), and collect aliases of items you want to record to optical media such as DVDs. Several special folders in Mac OS X contain users' applications, media, documents, downloads, settings, and Mac OS X itself.

Searching with Spotlight

IN THIS CHAPTER

Understanding how Spotlight works

Conducting simple, fast Spotlight searches

Conducting criteria-based Spotlight searches

Working with Spotlight's search results

Using Spotlight within applications

Most people have far too many files on their Macs to remember where to find all the information they need at any given moment. That's why Mac OS X has the Spotlight search tool: to help you find the files you need when you need them. You can think of it as Googling your Mac.

Searching with Spotlight can be either extremely simple or very sophisticated. Spotlight can search for files and folders by name, in much the same way that traditional search tools have operated on computers for countless years. It also can search for combinations of attributes, such as a file's size, creator, modification date, and label color.

Where Spotlight starts to get particularly clever is when it's searching through files themselves. Spotlight can look through the contents of Word documents, PDF (Portable Document Format) files, and even the metadata attached to music and image files. Spotlight also searches through the information in Mac OS X's built-in applications, such as your e-mail messages, contacts, and calendar events. You'll quickly find yourself turning to Spotlight not just to find information you've lost, but also to quickly access e-mails, contacts, and documents without diving through the Finder. You can even open applications by just typing the first part of an application name and pressing Return.

More recent additions to the Spotlight search scope include definitions from Mac OS X's built-in dictionary and recent web locations visited in Safari. You also can perform basic math equations by typing them into Spotlight. And, if you're logically inclined, you can search with Boolean logic, so you can search with terms such as AND, NOT, and OR. All these capabilities can be used to create smarter searches.

The only possible down side of relying on Spotlight is that it can lead to laziness: You may find yourself no longer as careful at managing files with the Finder as you used to be, knowing that Spotlight will help you find whatever you are looking for no matter how disorganized your hard disk structure has become. Let's hope you don't let that happen! After all, organizing your files has an advantage Spotlight can't always duplicate: Finding related files, which may not have the exact terms you're searching for.

How Spotlight Works Behind the Scenes

Spotlight can search for a file by its name, or it can search for information inside the file, such as text embedded in PDF documents or inside text documents; it can even search through what is called *metadata* attached to images, so you can search for the exposure setting of a picture imported from a digital camera.

Spotlight gets access to information through several means:

- It reads the Mac OS X file system's entries and monitors the file system as you work with files to see the names and locations of all files stored on your Mac and accessible via attached devices.

- It reads the contents of files as you would, by opening them behind the scenes.

- It reads metadata stored with the files, as well as any metadata you or Spotlight-savvy applications add as Spotlight comments. Apple's applications are very Spotlight-savvy, which is why contacts, e-mail, calendars, browser histories, and other such information are easy to access via Spotlight. Adobe's Creative Suite applications also add lots of metadata to their files; likewise Microsoft Office applications also add some metadata to their files. And you can add your own information to files by modifying the Spotlight Comments field in the Info window, as the sidebar "Just what is metadata?" explains.

Spotlight builds an index of these files behind the scenes as you're working, so it doesn't have to actually search through your entire Mac when you perform a search. Instead, it searches its index and then anything new that it hadn't yet indexed. Actually, Spotlight builds three indexes: Every time a file is created, copied, moved, saved, or deleted, it updates the Spotlight Store with new information about the file. Spotlight keeps information on all the metadata associated with a file in a file known as the Metadata Store. And it keeps an index to the contents of your files in its Content Store.

Note

Be aware that Spotlight maintains a single Spotlight Store per file system. This store is a folder called `.Spotlight-V100` that is hidden in the root folder of each disk, such as your startup disk. If you attach another storage device, say an external USB disk, Mac OS X creates a Spotlight Store in its root folder to store information related to that disk. Spotlight data always stays with the devices it indexes; this is crucial when working with networked volumes, because Spotlight has no access to their indexes unless they are visible to your Mac. ∎

Just what is metadata?

All files contain data of some type, such as the text inside Word, PDF, InDesign, and other text-containing documents. Image files include the series of bits that make up their pictures.

But all files also contain metadata. The word *metadata* literally means *data about data*. One type of metadata that all files have is their filename. That's not part of the actual file, but is part of the file's attributes stored by the Finder. File size is another such universal type of metadata, as are the file's location in the Mac's folder hierarchy and its file type.

Some files have metadata specific to their type. For example, an image file's metadata may include information from the camera that took the image, such as the bit depth, color mode (RGB or CMYK), dimensions in pixels, and even the location data of where the photo was taken (such as if you used an iPhone).

The Info window offers lots of information about a file's metadata, though files may contain even more metadata than the Info window displays. (To open an Info window for an item, select it and press ⌘+I or choose File⇨Get Info, or Control+click or right-click the item and choose Get Info from the contextual menu.

There's one area of the Info window where you can add your own metadata for Spotlight to search: the Spotlight Comments box. Any comments you type in it are attached to the file, and Spotlight searches them automatically.

Note

Because Spotlight must index your disk's contents to find them, when you first attach a disk to your Mac, Spotlight is at a disadvantage. Give it some time—several hours for a large hard disk—to index the disk the first time you attach it. A good idea when you first set up your Mac is to connect all your common disks and network volumes to the Mac and let Spotlight index them all overnight or during the day while you're working. ∎

Spotlight natively supports the following file types, meaning it can read their metadata and contents:

- plain text
- RTF (Rich Text Format) documents
- PDF documents
- Mail messages
- Address Book contacts
- Microsoft Word, Excel, and PowerPoint documents
- Apple Pages, Numbers, and Keynote documents
- Adobe Photoshop images
- applications
- folders
- web pages (HTML and associated formats)

- video and audio files: AAC (Apple audio files), MOV (QuickTime movie), MP3, and MP4
- image files: EXIF (used by digital cameras), GIF, JPEG, PNG, and TIFF

This list doesn't mean that other file types are left out of the loop: Apple has made Spotlight extensible so that non-Apple applications can take advantage of the technology. Microsoft, for example, has created a Spotlight extension for its Entourage and Outlook e-mail programs so its users can search their mail messages in Spotlight. Likewise, Wolfram Research has a Spotlight plug-in for its Mathematica software.

Using Spotlight

Now that you're aware of what Spotlight is and have a rough understanding of how it works, it's time to put it into action. Searching in Spotlight couldn't be easier (at least not when you do a simple text search). In its most basic form, a Spotlight search is a single word, such as the name of an application, a contact, or a file you know the name of but not its immediate location.

You can perform a Spotlight search in one of three ways:

- **By clicking the Spotlight icon menu in the menu bar:** This opens the Spotlight search window at the upper right of your screen, in which you can type a search term, as Figure 5.1 shows.

- **From the Search field in a Finder window, as Figure 5.2 shows:** This option gives you more flexibility and control for your search, as I explain shortly.

- **By pressing Shift+⌘+spacebar to get the Spotlight search menu or Option+⌘+ spacebar to get a Finder window to search from:** These shortcuts aren't on by default; you turn them on in the Spotlight system preference (see Chapter 28), where you also can assign other keyboard shortcuts instead of these defaults.

Spotlight searches from the menu bar

Running Spotlight from the menu bar is the easiest and typically the most common method of searching—especially if you are looking to perform a straightforward, no-nonsense search. Typically, more complex searches take place from a Finder window, as described in the next section.

As soon as you start typing letters into the search field, results appear in a drop-down sheet, shown in Figure 5.1. The results are divided into categories of information. Top Hit is at the top; this is the file Mac OS X thinks you are most likely looking for. The remaining information is divided into the following categories (categories that don't apply to the results don't appear):

FIGURE 5.1

Enter search terms into the menu bar's Spotlight search box to find items on your Mac based on keywords. The results appear below, sorted by category.

Spotlight	Lion
	Show All in Finder
Top Hit	Mac OS X **Lion** Developer Preview 2 — Li...
Applications	Mac OS X **Lion** Developer Preview 2 — Z...
	Mac OS X **Lion** Developer Preview 2 — Li...
Documents	9781118023761 ch03_ar.doc
	...is new to Mac OS X **Lion**. [b]° New Folder.. Choosin...
	9781118023761 Ch19.doc
	...New Feature Mac OS X **Lion** uses the name Wi-Fi inst...
	9781118023761 Ch23.doc
	...to Wi-Fi. So Mac OS X **Lion** now refers to Wi-Fi to m...
Messages	update on **Lion** beta changes
	Re: update on **Lion** beta changes
	Re: **Lion** Bible AR
Webpages	Microsoft looks to lure iPhone app devel...
	...Web browsers Kodiak to **Lion**: 10 years of Mac OS X...
	IT news and top technology headlines –...
	...Web browsers Kodiak to **Lion**: 10 years of Mac OS X...
	How to be a modern CIO	Technology b...
	...of Office 365 Kodiak to **Lion**: 10 years of Mac OS X S...
Look Up	**lion** |ˈlīən|
	noun — 1 a large tawny–colored cat that lives in pride...
Web Searches	Search Web for "Lion"
	Search Wikipedia for "Lion"
	Spotlight Preferences...

- **Top Hit:** The item that Spotlight thinks you are most likely looking for
- **Definition:** Articles from Mac OS X's built-in dictionary and thesaurus
- **Applications:** Programs you can run
- **System Preferences:** Items from the System Preferences application
- **Folders & Disks:** Folders on the Mac and attached disks
- **Messages:** E-mail messages contained in Mail
- **Contacts:** People and companies stored in Address Book
- **Events & To-Dos:** Any events or tasks stored in iCal
- **Images:** Graphic files stored on your Mac and its attached devices, as well as within iPhoto
- **PDF Documents:** PDF files stored on the Mac and attached volumes
- **Webpages:** Any recent web pages you have visited from this Mac
- **Music:** Audio tracks on the Mac and attached disks, plus those found in iTunes
- **Movies:** Video tracks on the Mac and attached disks, plus those found in iTunes
- **Fonts:** Any fonts installed on your Mac

- **Text documents:** Files in text, Word, Pages, and similar formats on the Mac and attached disks

- **Spreadsheets:** Files in Excel, Numbers, and similar formats on the Mac and attached disks

- **Presentations:** Files in PowerPoint, Keynote, and similar formats on the Mac and attached disks

Other categories may appear in the results sheet; these are created by applications that have Spotlight extensions.

Tip

Notice that Spotlight starts searching as soon as you begin typing, and if you make a mistake, or decide to search for something else, simply press the Delete key to delete any or all of the search text. You also can clear the text inside the Spotlight search field by pressing the Clear icon button (the X-in-a-gray-circle icon). ■

New Feature

If you want to get more details on a Spotlight menu bar result, hover the pointer over it for a few seconds. Using the Quick Look facility in Mac OS X (see Chapter 4), Spotlight displays a preview of the item in a pop-over to the left of the results sheet. (In some cases, it can't provide such previews, such as for applications and web searches.) ■

Selecting an item couldn't be easier. Simply click the item you want. Alternatively, you can use the arrow keys to move up and down the items and press Return to select the one you want. By default, the Top Hit is highlighted, and pressing Return takes you straight to it.

When you select an item, Spotlight opens a folder with it, if it's a file or folder, or opens the item in the application needed to view it.

Tip

Spotlight is a fantastic alternative to the Dock or Applications folder for launching applications. If you know the name of the application you want to launch, Spotlight invariably places it as the Top Hit. By accessing Spotlight via the Shift+⌘+spacebar shortcut, any application is just a few keystrokes away. ■

The Spotlight results sheet has one option above the results: Show All in Finder. Click this option to open the search results, and the search query, in a Finder window so you can refine the search further. There's also one option below the results: Spotlight Preferences, which opens the Spotlight system preference.

New Feature

In Mac OS X Lion, the Show All in Finder option in the Spotlight results sheet is the new name for what had been called Show All in previous versions of Mac OS X. ■

Spotlight searches from a Finder window

Each Finder window also contains its own Spotlight search field on the right side of the tool-bar. As soon as you begin to enter text into this field, the Finder window's contents of the dis-played folder are replaced with those relating to the Spotlight search. The window also changes to a Finder search window, displayed in whatever view mode the folder is set to, with extra search options appearing below the toolbar in the search bar, as Figure 5.2 shows.

When you use Spotlight in a Finder window, Spotlight searches files and folders, as well as recent web pages—just like the menu bar's Spotlight search does. But it doesn't search the Dictionary like the menu bar's Spotlight search does. As with the menu bar's Spotlight search, the Finder search windows' results are aliases to the files and folders, which remain in their existing locations. You have the same capabilities for these files and folders as for any files and folders (see Chapter 4).

New Feature

Spotlight results in the Finder window can now be displayed in column view mode in Mac OS X Lion, unlike in previous versions of Mac OS X, as well as in the previously supported icon, list, and Cover Flow view modes. ■

FIGURE 5.2

In a Finder window, a search bar appears after you begin a search; from there, you can add multiple crite-ria to refine the search results, and you can save the results for later use as a smart folder.

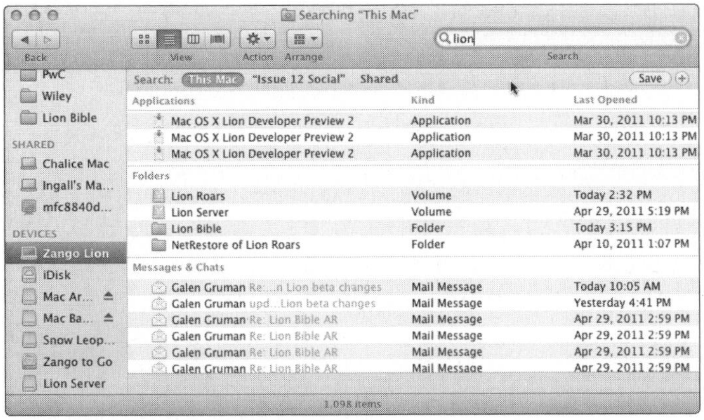

New Feature

Finder windows in which you are conducting a search no longer display the Contents and Filename buttons to determine what Spotlight searches. Instead, you choose the search scope using the menu that appears below your search term. The scope varies based on the results detected by Spotlight, but can include Filename, Kind, and Sent By. ■

If you want to restrict the search to filenames, rather than search files' contents, use the menu that appears below the search phrase to choose Filename Contains *searchtext*, as Figure 5.3 shows. Once you select that, or any of the criteria displayed, a pop-up menu appears on the left side of the Search box, as also shown in Figure 5.3, from which you can change the search scope. Notice that the list of items automatically appears in alphabetical order if you are in column view mode, in last-opened order if you are in list or Cover Flow view mode, and in no particular order if you are in icon view mode. As with other Finder windows, you can change the sort order by using the Arrange icon pop-up menu in the toolbar (if it's there) or by choosing View ⇨ Arrange By. Your sorting options are limited in search-results windows to Name, Kind, and Last Opened.

FIGURE 5.3

Top: The menu that appears with scope options as you enter a search term in a Finder window. Bottom: After you select a scope, a pop-up menu appears in the Search box that lets you change that scope.

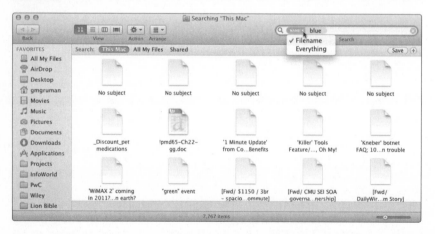

Note

If you enter text into the Search box and press Return, you don't get the pop-up menu that lets you change the search criteria. You must pick the search term from the menu that appears below the text you enter in the Search box to get the ability to use search criteria. ■

The number of results provided by Spotlight in the Finder window can be huge, so Spotlight caps the results at 10,000 items and places a gray More icon button or link (depending on your view mode) at the bottom of the list. Clicking this link opens up the remaining results.

Using Spotlight in the Finder search window also provides several options you can use to narrow the search results. These options appear in the search bar that appears at the top of the contents window, below the toolbar.

At the top-left side of the search bar is where you specify the location for the search:

- **This Mac:** If you began the search from the desktop, this is the default option, and with this option selected, Spotlight returns results from the Mac's startup disk and any disks physically connected to it.

- *current folder:* This option is marked with the name of the current folder or disk that the Finder window was displaying when you entered text in Spotlight. Selecting it narrows the Spotlight search to that specific folder or disk. If you use the keyboard shortcut (by default, Option+⌘+spacebar) to open a Finder search window, you'll see All My Files instead of the name of the current folder.

- **Shared:** This option lets you extend your search to network file shares. Note that it does not appear unless your Mac is already connected to a networked computer or volume.

To the right of these buttons are two other buttons:

- **Save:** This lets you save your search as a smart folder for access later, as Chapter 4 describes.

- **+:** This lets you add criteria for your search. (If All My Files is selected in the Sidebar, then the + button shows as a – button, meaning you can't add criteria. Searches of All My Files are restricted to text searches.)

You can add these criteria:

- **Kind:** This is the type of item you are looking for, as defined in the Kind column in the Finder. Its companion pop-up options are Any, Application, Document, Executable (applications and widgets), Folder, Image, Movie, Music, PDF, Presentation, Text, and Other. (Selecting Other brings up a text field enabling you to enter a specific Kind attribute, such as `tiff` or `font`.)

- **Last Opened Date:** This enables you to select the date, or range of dates, that the file was last opened by an application. Its companion pop-up menus are Within Last, Exactly, Before, After, Today, Yesterday, This Week, This Month, and This Year. Some of these open additional fields and pop-up menus to refine their settings; for example,

Within Last provides a text field to enter a numeric value and a pop-up menu to choose Days, Weeks, Months, or Years.

- **Last Modified Date:** This offers the same options as the Last Opened Date filter, but it checks when an item was last changed rather than merely opened.

- **Created Date:** This checks for items that were created in the date range you specify. Its options are the same as for Last Opened Date.

- **Name:** This looks for items by name. Its companion pop-up menu lets you choose the criteria for filtering items—Matches, Contains, Begins With, Ends With, and Is— based on the text you enter in the adjacent text field. (The text you enter in the Search box is searched as Contains, so this filter exists to narrow down those text results.)

- **Contents:** This searches through the contents of a file for the text entered in the adjacent text field.

- **Other:** This opens a settings sheet with a list of more than 100 other metadata options. Select the In Menu option for each option you want to appear in the search bar's criteria pop-up menu from now on, and then click OK. Examples of the options include Album, Attachment Types, Email Addresses, File Extension, Fonts (for fonts used in items), Languages, Pixel Width, Red Eye (to determine if red-eye correction was applied to a photo), Spotlight Comment, and URL.

To add additional criteria, click the + icon to the right of any search criteria row and choose the search criterion in the row that appears.

Tip

If you want to search for files that meet various criteria, no matter what text may be in their contents or file-names, you have to play a little game with Spotlight. To start a Spotlight search, you must enter text in the Search box. So enter some random text, and then add at least one criterion. Now delete the text in the Search box. This makes Spotlight search based on just the criteria you defined, regardless of what text a file or its file-name may contain. ■

Working with Finder search results

You can work with items that appear in the Finder search window much like any other items in the Finder. You can drag them from the Spotlight window to a new location, double-click them to open them in their default application, and drag them to the Dock to create aliases.

If you right-click or Control+click items, you get a contextual menu that lets you open them, copy them, label them with a color, open their enclosing folder, perform a Quick Look on them, open an Info window, move them to the Trash, send them to a Bluetooth device, and rename the files (although if you rename them, they may disappear from the results list if the new name doesn't fit the search criteria).

Boolean Spotlight searching

Boolean searching (named after English mathematician George Boole) is a method of searching for items via algebraic logic. Boolean logic is familiar to anybody who has created computer code, and its terms are familiar to many users who haven't. Regardless, you can use Boolean logic in Spotlight. Note that the Boolean operators must be entered in all uppercase letters. Spotlight uses these common Boolean operators:

- **AND:** This looks for items containing both terms. Normally, you don't have to type this because when you enter two or more terms, Spotlight looks for items that contain both the terms by default. For example, if you search for *apple mac*, Spotlight looks for items that contain both the term *apple* and *mac*. You also can search for *apple AND mac* to get the same results. Where AND is useful is when you are using other Boolean operators as well.

- **OR:** If you want to look for items that contain either search term, you can place an OR between the two terms. For example, the Spotlight search *apple OR mac* looks for items containing either term on its own (or items with both Apple and Mac included).

- **NOT:** Suppose you want to look for things that have *apple* and *mac* but not *fruit* (if you have any files containing references to the edible kind of apple). Typing *apple AND mac NOT fruit* gives you the desired result.

At the bottom of the Finder search window is the path bar, which shows the folder hierarchy for the selected item in relation to your Home folder. If the Finder search window is too narrow to display the title of each folder, the bar is truncated and just the folder icons appear; hovering the mouse over these icons causes their titles to appear. Double-clicking any of the folder icons in the path bar opens a separate Finder window revealing that folder's contents.

Another way to open the folder that an item is contained within is to select it and choose File ➪ Open Containing Folder or press ⌘+R, or right-click or Control+click the item and choose Open Containing Folder from the contextual menu.

Using Spotlight with applications

As mentioned previously, Spotlight is a system-wide service that is integrated throughout Mac OS X. As such, Spotlight services are available in a wide variety of Mac OS X applications. Some of these offer unique functions that enable you to search through the data contained in that particular application; others enable you to take the data in the application and perform Spotlight searches on it.

Using the Spotlight contextual menu

Many Apple applications have a Spotlight area in a contextual menu. If you use Apple's Safari web browser, for example, you can highlight text and right-click or Control+click it to get a contextual menu that includes the Search in Spotlight option. Choosing that option opens a Finder search window with the search term entered into the search field. Other applications such as Mail and TextEdit also sport this function.

Note

Many applications also have a Search in Google contextual menu option. It enables you to enter the term into the Google search engine and look for it online, if you are connected to the Internet. ■

Using Spotlight with supported applications

Several applications built by Apple have their own Spotlight search fields in the upper right of their windows. These search fields enable you to search through the data contained within the application without having to go through the Finder. It also ensures that you search only through the data applying to that application instead of having to sift through other results. Examples of applications that include Spotlight search fields are Mail, Address Book, iCal, and Automator.

Tip

A great use of Spotlight is found in the System Preferences application. Typing the name of a function in the search field in the System Preferences application window darkens the whole window and highlights the system preference that offers that function. ■

Summary

A key technology in Mac OS X is Spotlight, which indexes all the information on your Mac to make it quickly accessible in searches. You can use Spotlight to quickly search for various types of information, from applications to the content within documents, as well as attributes of files, such as image size and last modification date.

The quick way to access Spotlight is via the Search box at the upper right of the menu bar. But if you want to define criteria for your search, you need to use the options in the Finder window that appear when you begin a search in the window's own Search box.

Some applications integrate Spotlight to search their own contents, such as System Preferences and Mail.

Working with Disks

You can't use a Mac without a disk somewhere—in your Mac, attached to your Mac, or on a network to which your Mac is connected. Disks are what hold your data and applications, so they are fundamental to operating a Mac.

Mac OS X, of course, is what makes a disk attached to a Mac actually run Mac applications and access data. Much of that operation happens behind the scenes, so you don't need to really think much about your disks after they have the data on them you need.

Where you do need to pay attention to your disks after that initial setup is if something goes wrong, which can happen occasionally. And you may find yourself setting up new disks over time, such as to add storage, to set up a disk for backup (Chapter 11 covers backups), to use high-speed disk clusters optimized for disk-intensive tasks such as website serving and video editing (called *RAID drives*), or if you're a developer or other form of geek to have multiple boot disks.

IN THIS CHAPTER

Connecting and disconnecting disks

Using optical discs

Formatting and fixing disks with Disk Utility

Using RAID drives

Working with Disks and Other Storage Medias

The terms *volume*, *drive*, and *disk* are often used interchangeably to describe storage media, but you should know the differences:

- Volumes can be any storage container that a Mac sees as a distinct container (meaning an icon displayed in Finder windows' Sidebar), including disks, partitions, and network file shares. In this book, I use *volume* to mean network file shares, which can be of other computers, disks, or folders on other computers or drives—basically, any storage resource available via the network.

- Drives are the physical mechanisms that contain one or more disks.

- Disks are the media—composed of one or more circular recording platters—that actually store data. They can be magnetic, such as hard disks and floppy disks, or optical, such as CDs and DVDs.

- Partitions are sections of a disk that are presented to Mac OS X as if they were separate disks. (You create such partitions when formatting the disk using Mac OS X's Disk Utility, as explained later in this chapter.)

Note

There's also a form of storage called solid-state media, such as the MacBook Air's SSD drives, those ubiquitous flash-memory-based "thumb" drives, and digital cameras' flash-memory-based SD cards. Solid-state media don't actually have disks (instead, they're basically memory cards, like the RAM in a Mac, that retain their contents even when there's no power), but because the term "disk" has stuck as a generic term of storage, they are often called solid-state disks or solid-state drives. ∎

Note

When it comes to optical media, the spelling of the word becomes disc, with a c rather than a k. Also, Apple brands the optical drive in its Macs a SuperDrive. It can read from and write to a variety of CD and DVD formats. ∎

Files known as *disk images* (with the file extension .dmg) can be mounted on your desktop and in the Sidebar as virtual volumes. (Software updates are often delivered as such files.) Double-clicking a .dmg file or using Disk Utility to mount these files turns them into volumes that operate identically as other volumes.

Accessing disks and volumes

For you to work with a disk, it must be connected to your Mac. The internal startup disk that comes with your Mac is already connected, of course. Most Macs have a slot in which you insert optical media such as DVDs and CDs; the MacBook Air requires an external optical drive, as do some Mac Mini models. And some MacBook models have slots that accept SD cards, a type of flash-memory storage popularly used in digital cameras.

For other disks and storage media, you need to either physically connect the device via a cable or virtually connect it over a network (wired or wireless). (Chapter 23 explains how to connect via networks.)

For physical connections for external devices, you have two choices in most Macs: USB and FireWire ports. But beginning in spring 2011, Apple began using a third connector, called Thunderbolt, in new Mac models. USB is the most common mechanism for attaching disks and other storage media, such as thumb drives. FireWire provides faster connections and is less likely to result in slowdown when you're backing up or transferring large files. Thunderbolt is even faster but costlier, and few devices support it as this book went to press. But USB drives are both ubiquitous and cheap, so they are what most people use.

No matter how you connect a storage device to your Mac, if it's powered on and connected, it shows up in your Mac's Finder windows in the Sidebar's Devices section and likely on your desktop. (If they don't show up on your desktop, be sure your Finder preferences have the Hard Disks, External Disks, and Connected Servers options selected in the General pane, as explained in Chapter 3. Choose Finder ➪ Preferences or press ⌘+, [comma] to open the Finder preferences.)

Of course, if the disk uses a format not compatible with the Mac, it may not appear, or it may prompt Mac OS X to ask you if you want to wipe out its contents by reformatting it for use on the Mac. Mac OS X supports Apple's own HFS disk format, the FAT32 and ExFAT formats used by PCs, the ISO 9600 format used by CDs, the UDF format used by DVDs, and the formats used by flash media such as SD cards and thumb drives. That pretty much covers all the bases except for Windows' NTFS format, for which companies such as Paragon Software and Tuxera offer utilities to let Mac OS X read from and write to such disks.

Also in a Finder window, you see all the network volumes available to your Mac in the Sidebar's Shared section. If you're not on a network, you won't see any, and even if you are, you may see no volumes if you haven't connected to one previously (as Chapter 24 explains) or if sharable devices aren't broadcasting their availability on the network.

Note

Your Mac—indicated with a computer icon—also shows in the Sidebar's Devices section. By default, its name is usually Computer, though Mac OS X may have named it something along the lines of "your name's Macintosh model." You can rename it: Go to the Sharing system preference, and change the name in the Computer Name field. ∎

Cross-Reference

Chapter 4 explains how the Finder works with disks to access and manipulate files. Chapter 11 explains how to back up disks. Chapter 24 has more information on file servers, while Chapter 17 has more information on using Internet-based cloud storage services. ∎

Ejecting disks and disconnecting from volumes

When a Mac is running, disks attached to the Mac should be ejected before the physical device is removed from the computer. (Mac OS X sometimes refers to this action as *putting away* the item.) Thus, before disconnecting external hard disks and USB flash drives, you should first eject the device from the Mac. For optical discs and old-fashioned floppy disks (remember those?), ejecting them sends a signal to the drive to physically pop out the disc/disk.

You don't need to eject a disk/disc before shutting down or restarting your Mac, and you can disconnect a disk with no worries at any time after the Mac is powered off. I do recommend that you eject a disc before shutting down, though, because the discs don't always automatically eject at shutdown, so you could find yourself with a disc stuck inside your powered-off Mac. (The solution is simple: Start your Mac back up and hold the Eject key until the disc ejects. If it doesn't eject during startup, try ejecting the disc when the Finder appears.)

To eject a disk/disc from the Finder, use one of these techniques:

- For optical discs only, press the Eject button on your keyboard, if it has one. If your Mac has two optical drives attached, you can eject the second drive's disc by pressing Option+Eject (this method works only with an optical drive designed to work with Mac OS X).

- Select the disk/disc, and choose File ⇨ Eject or press ⌘+E.

- Select the disk/disc, and drag it to the Trash. The Trash icon changes to the Eject icon, so you know you're not deleting the contents.

- Right-click or Control+click the disk/disc, and choose Eject from the contextual menu.

If you do not eject a non-optical disk before unplugging the physical device from your Mac, a warning appears that says the device was not properly put away (ejected), so data may have been lost or damaged. It's not likely that you'll cause physical damage to the disk, but you may lose data because of a technique called *write-behind caching.* Mac OS X uses this technique to store changes to the disk in a temporary file called a cache. This is transferred to the disk later. (This process speeds up the operation of Mac OS X.) When you eject a disk, the data in the cache is transferred to it first. So if you physically remove the disk before that cache has been transferred, the cached data is lost.

When shutting down a Mac, you may get a message informing you that network volumes need to be disconnected; if so, confirm the disconnection.

Recording to Optical Discs

Most modern Macs can write data to optical media. This process is commonly known as *burning* (or recording) to disc. Many types of recordable media are available, including CD-R, CD-RW, DVD-R, DVD+R, DVD-RW, DVD-RAM, and DVD+-R. Mac OS X supports all these formats, so you don't have to worry about them. (One exception is the Blu-ray DVD format, which Mac OS X can't read or write to, but third-party programs such as Roxio's Toast can write to it—if you have a recordable Blu-ray drive, of course.)

Creating a burn folder

Burn folders are an easy way of organizing content that you want to take from your Mac to an optical disc. The great thing about burn folders is that after you've recorded the contents to the optical disc, you still have the burn folder so you make new copies easily later, and you can update it and make copies of the changed version, without starting from scratch. This is handy if you want to back up a changing set of documents, such as project files or family photo albums.

To create a burn folder, choose File ⇨ New Burn Folder. The burn folder is created in the active Finder window or on the desktop (if no Finder window is open). By default, the name of the folder is Burn Folder, instead of a regular folder's default name of Untitled; but like other newly created folders, the name is highlighted so you can change it.

Now you can drag items from the Finder into the burn folder. As you drag items into the burn folder, aliases from the original items are placed inside it. (Unlike normal folders, items dragged to burn folders remain in their original position.) You can open the burn folder to examine its contents, and you can remove or reorganize these files at will—just as with any folder.

Tip

If you think you'll work with a burn folder repeatedly, you might drag it in the Sidebar for one-click access at any time. ■

When you are happy with the contents, you can burn the disc by selecting the burn folder and choosing File ➪ Burn to Disc, or by right-clicking or Control+clicking the folder and choosing Burn to Disc from the contextual menu. If you don't have a blank disc inserted into the computer, Mac OS X requests that you insert one before continuing.

Tip

If you burn lots of discs, you might want to modify the toolbar, as explained in Chapter 3, to add the Burn icon button. Then you just need to select a burn folder and click the Burn icon button in the toolbar to burn the contents to disc. ■

Using Finder burn

An alternative to using burn folders is called *Finder burn*. This is where you drag items from the Finder directly to a recordable optical disc mounted in the Finder.

First, insert a blank optical disc into the drive. A dialog box appears asking what action you want to perform: Open Finder, Open iTunes, or Open Disk Utility. In the Action pop-up menu, choose Open Finder to inform the Finder that it is responsible for recording the disc. Then click OK. This creates a folder on the desktop called Untitled CD or Untitled DVD, which for all intents and purposes is a burn folder.

Note

The dialog box has an Eject button so you can eject the disc immediately; this is handy if you inserted a blank disc by mistake. It also has an Ignore button, which tells the Finder to do nothing with the disc. That can be dangerous, because no icon appears in the Finder, so you may forget you have a disc in your SuperDrive, which might lead someone to jam in a new disc later, not knowing there's already a disc in it, and damage the SuperDrive. ■

If you double-click the burn folder, it opens to reveal its contents (empty to begin with). Drag files to this folder and when you are ready to commit the files to the optical disc, click the Burn icon button in the Sidebar (the icon appears to the right of the disc's name) or use one of the burn commands described in the section on using burn folders.

Finishing the burn

Whether you created your own burn folder or used a Finder burn, when you tell Mac OS X to burn the disc, an alert dialog box appears requesting confirmation that you are ready to burn.

Some discs can be recorded on only once, so this request helps keep you from ruining discs by burning to them before you are ready. This dialog box also contains the Burn Speed pop-up menu, which is set to Maximum by default. You can choose a slower speed, which is useful if you find the discs aren't burning correctly; using a slower speed can help with lower quality discs that can't accept data as fast as the Mac can provide it.

After clicking Burn in the confirmation dialog box, the burn process begins and a progress bar tells you how it is going. The Finder follows this process: It prepares the data, writes the data, and finally verifies the condition of the optical disc. When the burn is complete, the disc is ejected.

At any time you can halt the burn process by clicking the Stop button. However, doing so usually makes the optical disc useless.

Using Disk Utility

When you're setting up or troubleshooting disks, you use Mac OS X's Disk Utility, shown in Figure 6.1. Among its capabilities are formatting disks, checking (verifying) and repairing disks, mounting and unmounting disks, converting disks into disk images, and recording ("burning") disk images to CDs and DVDs.

To run Disk Utility, launch it from the Utilities folder, which you can get to quickly by choosing Go ➪ Utilities or pressing Shift+⌘+U.

FIGURE 6.1

Disk Utility is where you manage disks, repair them, and burn their images to CDs and DVDs.

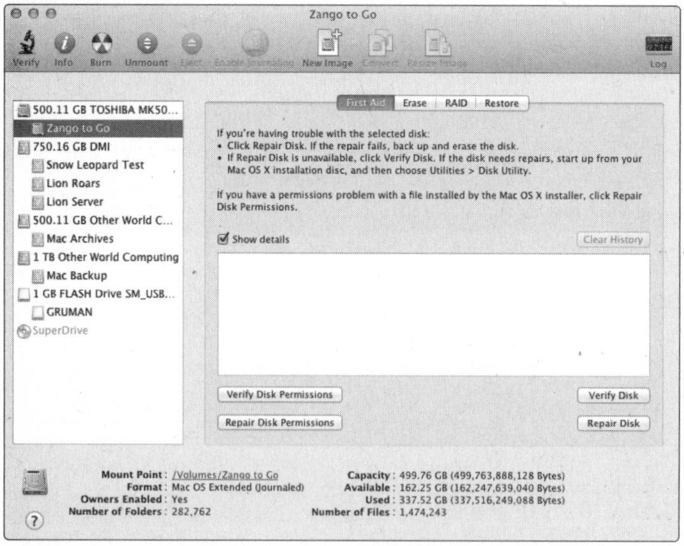

Creating additional startup disks

A really cool capability of Mac OS X is that you can have multiple boot disks and even share them among multiple Macs. This is great for developers and IT support staff who want to have multiple versions of Mac OS X available for testing, without needing a separate Mac. It also can be helpful for IT and other people who move from Mac to Mac to bring their own environment with them, no matter what Mac they are using.

You can create a startup disk for the Mac in two ways:

- Use the installation disk image downloaded from the Mac App Store, and follow the instructions in Appendix A, making sure to choose the external disk you want to use as your startup disk as where Mac OS X is installed.

- Copy an existing startup disk to another using Disk Utility, as described in this chapter.

Note that not all Mac models can start from other Mac models' startup disks, because essential driver differences may exist among them. So you may not get a universal startup disk, just one that works with many Macs. And note that Intel-based Macs cannot start up from disks formatted by a PowerPC-based Mac, and vice versa. (Although Apple discontinued use of the PowerPC chip in 2006, many Power Macs are still in use.) If a Mac cannot start up from a Mac OS X startup disk, the international "no" symbol (the slash in a circle) appears instead of the Apple logo when you try to start up.

To boot up from a disk other than the internal one, press and hold Option as you start the Mac to get a list of available startup disks, and choose one via the mouse, touchpad, or keyboard (press Return to use the keyboard to select the disk).

Note
Mounting means making the disk appear in the Finder; unmounting means making it invisible but still connected. (Compare that to ejecting, which both unmounts and disconnects the disk so you can unplug it.) A disk image is a file that contains all the contents of a disk, so you can move it to another disk or to a removable medium such as a recordable DVD. ∎

Note
In the Sidebar at the left of Disk Utility, the drives are shown aligned to the far left, while the disks (for a multiple-disk drive) and partitions for each disk are listed indented below the drive name. ∎

Checking and fixing disks

The most-used part of Disk Utility is the First Aid pane, where you can check a disk's health and try to repair it. Select the drive, disk, or partition from Disk Utility's Sidebar, and click Verify Disk to check it or Repair Disk to both check and repair it. You also have the options on some disks to verify and repair the disk permissions, which are used by Mac OS X to determine who can access what files: the operating system, the Mac's administrator, and/or individual users if the Mac is set up for multiple owners, as described in Chapter 27.

Caution

You cannot repair the disk you started Mac OS X from. So if you have a problem with the Mac's built-in disk (the one nearly everyone starts up from), you need to instead start up via the new Mac OS X Recovery System covered in Appendix A and run Disk Utility from it, or boot from a separate disk. I recommend that you always have a backup disk for your files and that the disk have Mac OS X installed on it so you can boot from it when repairs are necessary to your standard boot disk—even with Mac OS X Lion's new Recovery System, as it won't work if the startup disk itself is damaged. Apple has no problem in letting you create multiple boot disks, because they can run only on its computers. ■

Disk Utility can access S.M.A.R.T. (Self-Monitoring Analysis and Reporting Technology) information supplied by hard disks installed in your Mac. S.M.A.R.T. was developed to provide information on predicted disk failures and diagnose the media and mechanics of a hard disk. The S.M.A.R.T. status of a disk is displayed at the bottom of the Disk Utility window when a disk is selected in the Sidebar list. When a disk is functioning correctly, Disk Utility reports a status of "Verified." If the words "About to Fail" appear in red text, you should immediately make a backup of your disk and replace the defective disk.

Restoring and copying disks

Disk Utility comes with a handy set of features to create and restore disk images. This means you can make a copy of an entire disk and store it as a single file on another disk or on a recordable DVD. This is a handy way to store disk backups and then reinstall them later or transfer them to another Mac. To create an image, select the disk, partition, or drive, and click the New Image icon button at the top of the Disk Utility window. (You also can open the disk image by choosing File ⇨ Open Disk Image or pressing Option+⌘+O.) To put the contents of a disk image on a disk, go to the Restore pane and click Image to select the source disk image. Drag the disk you want to write the disk image onto from the list at the left into the Destination field. If you want to erase the target disk's contents, enable the Erase Destination option. Click Restore to begin the restoration process.

Tip

You can copy a disk using the Restore pane without first creating a disk image for it. Simply drag the source disk into the Source field of the Restore pane, drag the target disk into the Destination field, and follow the restoration instructions previously described. ■

Tip

You can burn a disk or a disk image to CD or DVD by selecting it in the disk list and then clicking the Burn icon button. ■

Sometimes, you need to convert disk images for their destination. To do so, open the disk image by choosing File ⇨ Open Disk Image or pressing Option+⌘+O, and click the Convert icon button. In the settings sheet that appears, you can choose the disk image's new location, its image format (compressed, read-only, read/write, or CD/DVD master), and its encryption level (none, 128-bit, or 256-bit).

Adding, partitioning, and formatting disks

When you add a new hard disk or SSD to your Mac, you have to format it, which you do in Disk Utility. (You usually do not have to format thumb drives or flash-memory cards, and you do not have to format recordable discs.)

But you also may want to partition to disk, which means to divide it into several sections, each of which appears in the Finder as if it were a separate disk. Disk Utility enables you to do this as well. Figure 6.2 shows Disk Utility partitioning an external disk into a Mac disk and a Windows disk. A disk must have at least one partition.

When you add a disk, it displays in Disk Utility's Sidebar. Select it—note that you need to choose its drive icon, not its disk icons (disk icons are the indented icons in Disk Utility's Sidebar)—and then go to the Partition pane to set up the partitions. Use the + and – icon buttons to add and delete partitions. If an existing partition is selected, clicking + splits that partition to make room for the new one.

Note

If a disk's partition already has data on it, Disk Utility indicates that by shading part of that partition in light blue. The amount of blue indicates how much data is stored on that partition, and the white area indicates how much space is available for a new partition if you choose to split the existing partition to make room for the new one. ∎

You can enter the size for each in the Size field or simply drag the bottom of each partition up or down to change the size. It's also a good idea to give the partition a name in the Name field, though you can always rename the partition from the desktop or Sidebar later, using the same method for renaming a folder or file (see Chapter 4).

A key decision is how to format the partition. You have four variations of Mac OS Extended (called *HFS+* on some older versions of Mac OS X) to choose from: journaled, encrypted journaled, case-sensitive journaled, and case-sensitive encrypted journaled. Usually, you should pick Mac OS Extended (Journaled). The case-sensitive option is best suited if you are running Linux or Unix on the disk, because those operating systems treat words that are capitalized differently in different instances as separate words. Use one of the encryption options to save the step and time of encrypting the partition later.

Note

You don't have to partition a disk to format it. If you select a disk and go to the Erase pane, you also can format the disk. In this case, one partition is created for the whole disk. You can use the Erase pane at any time—not just when first setting up a disk—to wipe out all the data and applications on it, such as to clear off old disks you're getting rid of or giving to others. ∎

New Feature

The two encrypted options for formatting a Mac OS X partition are new to Lion. ∎

New Feature

If you erase an encrypted disk (see Chapter 26), the disk remains encrypted even after you erase it. Disk Utility does let you set a new encryption password, though: choose File⇨Change Password. You'll need to know the encryption password to install Mac OS X on it. If you don't want the erased disk to be encrypted, select the disk in Disk Utility, then choose File⇨Turn Off File Encryption. Then erase the disk. ■

FIGURE 6.2

Disk Utility's Partition pane, set to separate a disk into two partitions

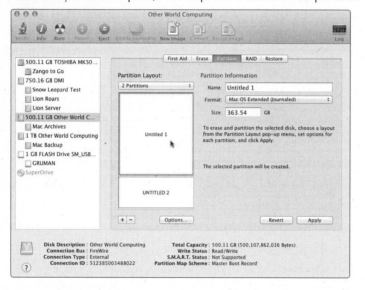

The MS-DOS (FAT) formatting option creates a Windows-compatible disk, which the Mac can read as well. (Note that FAT means File Access Table, the name of the Windows directory structure used to locate files.) If you install Windows on a separate partition using the Boot Camp utility, that partition is formatted as MS-DOS. You might create an MS-DOS disk for use as an external disk that you want accessible to a Boot Camp partition or to a Parallels or VMware Fusion virtual machine. (See Chapter 18 for more on using Windows with Mac OS X.)

The ExFAT format, also called FAT64, is used for solid-state drives (SSDs) formatted for use on Windows PCs; it's Microsoft's version of FAT for SSDs.

The Free Space format basically means "don't format," such as to wall off space on a disk for later use, so the user doesn't put anything in that space in the interim.

New Feature

Mac OS X Lion's Disk Utility drops two HFS+ format variants—the two non-journaled regular and case-sensitive formats. Journaling slows down disk access a bit to allow the indexing for recovery purposes, so

previous Mac OS X versions offered non-journaled formatting to help users with older, slower disks. But these days, all disks are fast enough to support journaling. ■

Tip
If you have a non-journaled disk or partition, you can convert it to be journaled by selecting it in the Sidebar and then choosing File⇨Enable Journaling or pressing ⌘+J. ■

Once you've set up your partitions, click Apply to create them, or Revert to cancel the partitioning and keep the current settings.

Using RAID Redundancy

For servers and other critical uses where you need information available all the time, a major enemy is disk failure. If something goes wrong in the disk itself, you can lose all the data stored on it. Using a backup utility such as Mac OS X's Time Machine (see Chapter 11) can help you get back up and running, but you lose any data saved after the last backup.

RAID, which stands for *redundant array of independent disks*, is a technology meant to better protect your data in case of failure. Basically, RAID writes the data to multiple disks, so if one fails, the information is still available on the other disks. That also means there's no downtime, because the data remains accessible. (You would repair or replace the broken disk, but you can usually do so without taking the Mac offline.)

Understanding RAID

RAID is a technology with two distinct uses. First, it can use multiple disks to create a single volume. For example, you can install four 512GB hard disks to create a single volume providing 2TB of space. This is particularly useful for server space and for users who use large files. (For example, high-definition video editing takes up a significant amount of space.)

You have two ways to use RAID to create shared disks. One is called a *concatenated disk set*, which stores the files on whatever disk is available but presents the array of disks to the Finder as if it were one disk so the Mac can put the file on the most accessible disk at the moment. The other is called *striping,* which saves files in pieces across multiple disks so data can be pulled simultaneously from multiple locations to get it to the Mac faster, which is very useful for video. But the risk is this: If one disk in the array fails, any file with a piece of itself on that failed disk is now corrupted because it is incomplete.

The second use of RAID is to keep an ongoing copy of all data in a mirrored set in case one disk fails—a key issue for Macs used as servers or for other heavy production uses. A failed disk can be replaced without the loss of any data (because a complete set of data still exists on the other disk). When a replacement disk is installed, the data is copied from the remaining hard disk to the new hard disk, and you can continue working as before.

The next thing to understand is that RAID can be controlled via hardware or software configurations. By default, a Mac Pro controls RAID via software contained within Mac OS X.

However, a RAID card can be installed to control the RAID via hardware instead. A hardware approach offers numerous benefits: It opens a wider range of RAID configurations, it contains a 512MB or greater cache of memory for increased performance and stability, and it enables faster hard disks (up to 15,000 rpm) to be installed.

There are many types of RAID configurations, each with different requirements and offering different benefits. Table 6.1 explains the different types of RAID configurations available and what each configuration offers.

TABLE 6.1

Different Types of RAID Configurations

RAID Level	Disk Requirements	Description and Benefits
RAID 0 (striped)	One to four identical hard disks	Up to four identical hard disks can be used to create a single volume. The size of the volume is the sum of all the hard disks' space. When data is written to the striped array, it is sent in pieces to all disks in parallel; therefore, a striped array offers faster performance. It also provides a volume larger than the physical size of a single hard disk. However, if any of the hard disks fail, the whole volume is lost, because the files on the surviving disks are incomplete. Therefore, a separate backup system is critical.
RAID 1 (mirrored)	Two identical hard disks	Two identical hard disks are used to create a single volume. The volume size is identical to one of the hard disks. The data on each disk is kept identical at all times, so if one of the hard disks suffers a mechanical problem, the other can replace it immediately without any data loss.
Concatenated RAID (also called JBOD, or "just a bunch of disks")	One to four hard disks	This is a RAID array similar to RAID 0 (striped). However, it does not split (stripe) data across multiple disks; instead, it keeps files intact wherever they are stored. Thus, there is no performance advantage as with striped disks, but there's also less risk of data loss, because only the files on a failed disk are lost.
Enhanced JBOD	One to four hard disks	This format isn't technically an array; however, it is a format whereby individual disks can be turned into a RAID without requiring them to be reformatted. If you order a Mac Pro with multiple disks, they are supplied as individual disks using the JBOD format. This means that you have multiple individual disks, with Mac OS X installed on the first disk, but the JBOD format enables you to turn the disks into a single RAID array without reinstalling Mac OS X.

RAID Level	Disk Requirements	Description and Benefits
RAID 0+1	Four identical hard disks	This format uses four hard disks and combines both features of RAID 0 and RAID 1. The first two disks are striped to create a single volume, which is the sum of both disks. The second two disks are striped and used to mirror the first set.
RAID 5	Three or four hard disks	RAID 5 uses block-level striping and redundancy to create a hard disk that has some of the advantages of RAID 0, while implementing redundancy features of RAID 1. In this sense, it is similar to RAID 0+1, but its technology creates a larger disk space. For example, if you have four 1TB disks, you can create a 4TB array in RAID 0 or a 2TB redundant array with RAID 0+1. In RAID 5, you can create a 3TB disk with redundancy features. If any of the disks fails, you can replace them.

Tip

Hot swapping is a term often associated with RAID. It is a process where you can remove a mirrored hard disk while a computer is still running and insert a replacement disk without having to turn off the computer (or without even interrupting your work). Obviously, a hard-disk failure is a rare occurrence, so the hot-swappable feature is required only in time-critical work environments. The hard disks in Apple's discontinued Xserve servers are hot-swappable, whereas the disks in its Mac Pros are not. ■

Setting up a RAID in Mac OS X

To create a RAID system in Mac OS X, you need two disks of equal capacity, which means RAID is pretty much limited to use on Mac Pros, Mac Mini Servers, and Apple's discontinued line of Xserve servers, all three of which support multiple internal disks. You could use RAID on other Macs by booting from an external RAID drive that contains the multiple disks, but then you risk slowdown due to the communication over the cable between the Mac and the drive.

If you do go the external RAID route with a MacBook, iMac, or non-Server Mac Mini, you should use FireWire 800 cables—the fastest cable type on most Macs. Drives using the Thunderbolt technology introduced in 2011's Mac models can provide an external RAID nearly as fast as an internal RAID, letting Thunderbolt-equipped Macs offer almost the same RAID performance as a Mac Pro, Mac Mini Server, or Xserve.

Setting up a Mac Mini Server for RAID

The Mac Mini Server model comes with two 2.5-inch 500GB hard disks already installed, though the first disk is set as the startup disk and the second as a data disk. To convert the disks to a RAID 0 or RAID 1 system, start the Mac Mini Server using its Recovery System (see Appendix A) or from another Mac using Target Disk Mode (see Chapter 1), then run Disk Utility from that installer or from the other Mac to set up the desired RAID configuration, as described later in this chapter.

Installing internal hard disks on a Mac Pro

If you own a Mac Pro with a single hard disk, you need to install additional hard disks to create a RAID volume. Installing additional hard disks into the Mac Pro is a relatively easy process (at least, when compared to many other computers). The Mac Pro contains SATA (Serial Advanced Technology Attachment) 3Gbps, 3.5-inch, single-height (1U) hard disks—that is, the commonly sold 3.5-inch desktop SATA disks.

The only tool you need is a Phillips #1 screwdriver. (It's the one with a cross head; be sure to use a #1 size one so you don't damage the screwheads.) Follow these steps to install the hard disk into your Mac Pro:

1. **Shut down your Mac Pro.**

2. **Wait 5 to 10 minutes.** Apple recommends this to allow the internal systems to cool.

3. **Unplug all external cables except for the power cord.**

4. **Discharge any static electricity from your body.** You can do this by touching the metal PCI (Peripheral Component Interconnect) slots' access covers. Another common technique is to touch a heat radiator. Professionals also invest in wearing anti-static wristbands.

5. **Unplug the power cord.**

6. **Lift the latch on the rear of the Mac Pro.**

7. **Remove the side panel from the Mac Pro.**

8. **Locate the hard disk bays.** These are four metal rectangular openings, arranged in a horizontal row, located near the top half of the computer.

9. **Remove the metal carrier.** The first hard disk bay (the one to the left) typically contains the boot disk. This disk can be replaced, but if you are adding an additional disk, you should install it in the adjacent disk bay to the right. Installation is easy: Pull the metal carrier out of the bay. Note: The latch on the rear of the computer (used in Step 6) must be open still, or the disk is locked in place.

10. **Insert the hard disk.** The disk is attached to the carrier via four metal screws. Each carrier has four screws on the bottom. You can remove these by hand, or you can use the Phillips screwdriver. All hard disks have four matching screw sockets. Place the hard disk into the carrier, and use the screws to attach the hard disk to the carrier.

11. **Slide the carrier back into the hard disk bay.** Push it firmly in so the connections in the Mac Pro insert into the hard disk. The carrier should slide smoothly back in to the Mac Pro. Do not force it in.

12. **Replace the metal access panel to the side of the Mac Pro.**

13. **Close the latch on the rear of the Mac Pro to lock the access panel and disks in place.**

14. **Reattach all the cables, and power up your Mac Pro.**

Note that you also can buy external RAID drives with hardware RAID cards designed for the Mac Pro. These typically connect via an eSATA connection. (Refer to their documentation for their specific setup and operation.)

Installing external hard disks for other Macs

If you don't have a Mac Pro, you should use an external RAID drive containing multiple disks; you'll find these at many Mac-oriented e-commerce sites such as Other World Computing (www.macsales.com), LaCie.com, MacMall.com, and MacConnection.com, with models for both FireWire and USB 2.0 connections. They're the places you're likely to find Thunderbolt-compatible drives as well as those become available.

Tip

Data Robotics has created an interesting device called the Drobo, which offers functionality similar to an external RAID drive, but with an interesting twist. Rather than requiring you to install identical disks, the Drobo accepts up to four disks that can be any size. The built-in hardware controller uses the disks to create a single volume that is approximately three-quarters of the total space of all the disks installed. The advantage is that any single disk can be removed without any loss of data. You also can pull out a single disk and insert a larger one, and the device automatically increases the total amount of storage available on a volume. The technology has attracted lots of attention, and it could point to a future of RAID-style storage that is more user-friendly and accessible to the general public, while offering both striped and mirrored functionality. You can find more information at www.drobo.com. ■

Configuring RAID in Disk Utility

After you've connected the disks to your Mac, follow these steps to configure it:

1. **Go to Disk Utility's RAID pane, and drag the disks into its central area.** This creates a RAID set—a group of disks in the RAID.

2. **Give the RAID set a name in the RAID Set Name field.**

3. **Specify the RAID set's formatting type using the Format pop-up menu.**

4. **Choose Mirrored RAID Set from the RAID Type pop-up menu.**

Caution

You have two other options in the RAID Type pop-up menu: Striped RAID and Concatenated RAID Set. Neither stores your data redundantly, so if one disk fails, you lose all your data. These two options are meant to combine several physical disks as if they were one big "logical" disk; you're essentially fooling the Mac to think the multiple disks are just one big one. (The striped and concatenated options use different technical approaches to accomplish the same result.) It's fine to use these RAID options to pool together several disks, but don't think it makes your data safer. ■

5. **Choose RAID Spare or RAID Slice.** Select any of the disks (not the RAID sets) in the window; the RAID Type pop-up menu becomes the Disk Type pop-up menu, which offers two options for each disk: RAID Slice and RAID Spare. By default, the option is set to RAID Slice, which ensures that the disk is used as part of the RAID array. Choosing RAID Spare designates that the disk is not to be used as part of the main RAID volume but instead is to be used automatically in the event of a failure of one of the other disks. When you are creating a Mirrored RAID Set, you can use this option with a third disk. Set it as a RAID Spare to have it automatically substitute for one of the other disks in the event of a disk failure.

6. **Select your options.** Click the Options button to open a settings sheet in which you choose the block size using the RAID Block Size pop-up menu. (A block is a contiguous area on the hard disk in which data is stored. You can think of them as the equivalent bricks that make up your files. Larger blocks are accessed faster but store data less efficiently.) By default, the block size is 32K; your options are 16K, 32K, 64K, 128K, and 256K. You are advised by Mac OS X to select a block size that matches the kind of data you will be accessing. For example, video may access large blocks of data, but databases access smaller blocks.

7. **Decide whether to enable automatic rebuilding.** If you are creating a RAID mirrored set, select the Automatically Rebuild RAID Mirrored Sets option. Click OK to close the sheet.

8. **Create the RAID.** Now that you are ready to set up your disks, click Create to begin building the RAID array. Mac OS X gives you a dialog box warning that you will destroy all the information contained on the disks (which it lists for you) used in the RAID array. Click Create again to confirm that you are happy to wipe the disks and create the RAID array.

You can add more RAID sets by clicking the + icon button and following these steps to configure each added RAID set.

Note

Disk Utility cannot create a RAID array using a disk that is currently running Mac OS X. If you want to create a RAID array with Disk Utility using one of your startup disks, you must boot Mac OS X from the Recovery System and run Disk Utility during the installation process (see Appendix A for more information). Creating a RAID during the installation erases all information on the target disk, so you need to install Mac OS X from scratch if you're using an existing startup disk. Combining Time Machine with the Migration Assistant (as explained in Chapter 11) enables you to copy all your information back to the disk. ■

Summary

Mac OS X works with a variety of disks and storage media, which are accessible from a Finder window's Sidebar and can be visible on the desktop. Because of how Mac OS X writes data to disks, it's important to eject them before you physically disconnect them from your Mac, so you have several methods for ejecting external disks. You also can use them to eject optical discs.

Disk Utility is where you repair, format, partition, copy, and restore disks, as well as where you mount disks that aren't already mounted and where you create disk images.

In some cases, you'll want to take advantage of RAID drives to increase disk speed and reliability for high-performance tasks such as video editing, database serving, and web serving; Disk Utility lets you do that as well.

Getting Help within Mac OS X

As you explore Mac OS X, you will increasingly come across new and exciting areas of the operating system. Mac OS X is a huge, and complex, operating system and—despite its intuitive nature—sooner or later everybody needs help. When you come across unfamiliar territory, Mac OS X offers several methods of built-in assistance.

The main method of reading help files is through Mac OS X's built-in Help Center. The Help Center provides explanations for most basic tasks, as well as documentation relating to Mac OS X. You can use it to learn basic features about Mac OS X and discover how to use basic hardware, and it acts as a showcase for new features found in Mac OS X 10.7 Lion.

Another type of assistance offered by Mac OS X is help tags. These yellow labels appear when the pointer is positioned over various onscreen elements and offer further explanation as to what function the element provides. You may know them better by the name popularized in Microsoft Office: Tool Tips.

A further help service is available via man (short for *manual*) pages in Terminal. These pages outline the Unix command-line tasks used in the Terminal application.

In addition to the Mac OS X help system, many applications provide their own help sections. Furthermore, you can use the Internet as a resource. Apple provides help through its website, and many product manufacturers provide online support. User groups are also a great place to turn for advice. And, of course, there's this book! The index can help you find specific information, and the chapter organization can help you explore broader activities. One thing is certain: You'll rarely be short of help if you know where to look.

IN THIS CHAPTER

Understanding the Help Center

Navigating the Help Center

Getting help inside an application

Understanding help tags

Working with command-line help

Exploring other avenues of help

Touring the Help Center

The Help Center is your main source of information on Mac OS X, as well as for features found within various Apple applications and Apple technologies (such as QuickTime X). In addition to the standard help included with Mac OS X, many applications include sections of specialized help, which in combination with the Help Viewer provides a more complete system that accurately represents the contents of your operating system.

The Help Center, shown in Figure 7.1, is reminiscent of a web browser and has a table of contents that can take you through common items. Links taking you to more detailed information on the item specified are highlighted in blue, and hovering the pointer over them makes an underline appear. As in a web browser, clicking the links navigates you to an area that expands on the information outlined in the link.

FIGURE 7.1

Left: The main Help Center screen shows links to groups of common Mac OS X capabilities. Right: The Help Center's index page for application-specific help.

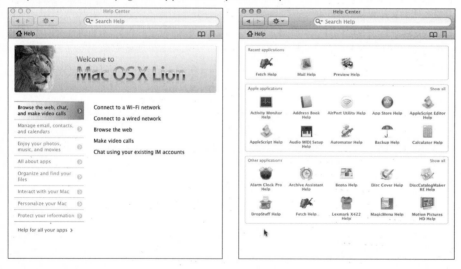

Other links in the Help Center can take you to specific areas within the Mac OS X environment, such as system preference panes, while giving you information on the changes you need to make. Links in the Help Center also can take you to associated websites, such as the Apple Support pages.

New Feature

Mac OS X Lion has significantly reworked the organization of the Help Center's contents. It's also given the help system a new name: Help Center. ■

New Feature

At the bottom of the main Help Center window is the Help for All Your Apps link that, if clicked, opens a window with icon buttons for the help pages for the applications installed on your Mac, as Figure 7.1 shows. That application's help page even has a handy Recent Applications section at the top, assuming that any questions you have are likely about the applications you recently used. ■

You can access the Help Center in different ways, but typically you do so using the Help menu in the menu bar or by clicking the Help icon button—often shown as a circle with a question mark (?) inside—in applications, system preferences, and widgets.

Whatever application you are running determines what the Help menu options are. If you're in the Finder, you have two options: Search and Help Center. Choosing Help Center displays the dialog box shown in Figure 7.1, which provides links to Mac OS X-specific help. You also can enter a term in the Search field to search all the help pages, both Mac OS X's and your applications' help pages. If you're in another application, you get its help pages.

Browsing the Help Center

These options are available in the Mac Help Center's home page:

- **Browse the Web, Chat, and Make Video Calls:** Selecting this option opens a submenu that includes items such as Connect to a Wi-Fi Network, Browse the Web, and Chat Using Your Existing IM Accounts.

- **Manage Email, Contacts, and Calendars:** Selecting this option opens a submenu that includes items such as Set Up Email with Your Existing Accounts, and Keep Track of Meetings, Appointments, and More.

- **Enjoy Your Photos, Music, and Movies:** Selecting this option opens a submenu that includes items such as Organize, Edit, and Share Photos, and Make Music.

- **All about Apps:** Selecting this option opens a submenu that includes items such as Get Apps at the Mac App Store, Easily View and Open All Your Apps, and Take Apps Full Screen.

- **Organize and Find Your Files:** Selecting this option opens a submenu that includes items such as Find Anything on Your Mac, and Print Your Documents.

- **Interact with Your Mac:** Selecting this option opens a submenu that includes items such as Drag and Drop, Your Mac's Desktop, and Window Basics.

- **Personalize Your Mac:** Selecting this option opens a submenu that includes items such as Customize the Dock, Create User Accounts for Others, and Save Energy.

- **Protect Your Information:** Selecting this option opens a submenu that includes items such as Back Up Your Mac and Privacy.

Note

Unlike other applications, the Help Center application window stays above all other windows on your screen, even if another application is active. (In fact, the Help Center ends up being an additional active application; switching to it does not make the previous application inactive.) To get it out of the way without closing it, click its Minimize button to hide the Help Center in the Dock. Note that you cannot use the standard shortcut ⌘+M to minimize the Help Center; that minimizes whatever window is open in the other application that is active. ■

Note

Because the Help Center acts to support other applications, many shortcuts—such as ⌘+P to print—do not work inside the Help Center. Instead, pressing ⌘+P instructs the active application to print. Therefore, to print an article from the Help Center, you must use its Action icon pop-up menu's Print command. ■

Searching the Help Center

You can search the Help Center from the Finder in two ways:

- Choose Help in the menu bar or press Shift+⌘+/ (which you can likely remember more easily as ⌘+?), and enter a search term in the Search box that appears. A list of matching help topics appears below your search term; choose the appropriate one, or choose Show All Help Topics to get to open the Help Center to a results page that includes links to all help pages that contain the text typed so far in the Search box. (Note that your search term is *not* retained in the Help Center's Search box.)

- Choose Help ⇨ Help Center to open the Help Center's home page, where you enter your search term in its Search box. A list of possible terms appears as you begin typing; select one if you want, or continue typing your own term and press Return. A list of possible matches displays, along with terms at the bottom that you might want to search instead; just click one of them to do so. The returned matches are grouped into categories; to see the actual entries, click Show to the right of the category name.

Tip

When searching the Help Center, you can choose to include product support results (information from Apple's online knowledge base) or not by using the unnamed pop-up menu to the right of the magnifying-glass icon in the Search box. Click the small downward-facing triangle icon to open the pop-up menu in which you can select or deselect the Include Product Support Results option. ■

For more complex searches that involve Boolean logic expressions, you can use special characters when searching; Table 7.1 describes these special characters.

TABLE 7.1

Special Characters for Boolean Searching in Help

Character	Meaning	Search Example	Search Results
+	AND	desktop + Finder	This example finds articles that include both "desktop" and "Finder."
|	OR	desktop | Finder	This example finds articles that include either "desktop" or "Finder."
!	NOT	desktop ! Finder	This example finds articles that include "desktop" but exclude "Finder."
()	grouping	picture + (Finder | desktop)	This example finds articles that include "picture" and either "Finder" or "desktop."

Navigating the Help Center

The Help Center works in much the same way as a web browser, and you navigate it via a system of links. Unlike in a web browser, the Help Center's links are rarely blue and underlined; instead, almost every text element is a link to a page with details.

To navigate among the Help Center's pages, you click the desired links, you click the Back and Forward buttons to traverse the path of links you've followed, and you click the Home button to go back to the Help Center's home page—all just like a web browser. You can use the Search box at any time as well.

Note
In Mac OS X's Help Center, some links perform actions for you, such as opening the relevant system preference. ■

Next to the Back and Forward buttons is the Action icon pop-up menu (the gear icon), which has four options:

- **Make Text Smaller.** You also can use the keyboard shortcut ⌘+–.
- **Make Text Bigger.** You also can use the keyboard shortcut ⌘+= (the menu option shows it as ⌘+, but you do not have to hold the Shift key as you would to type an actual + symbol).
- **Find.** You also can use the keyboard shortcut ⌘+F. This opens a search bar above the search results in which you can type additional text to search within the displayed search results. Click Done to close that search bar.
- **Print.** This prints the current help page to your printer. (Chapter 30 explains printing.)

The Help Center has another great navigation feature: the ability to bookmark help entries. At the upper-right side of each help page are two bookmark icons. One, called Add Bookmark, looks like a ribbon and is the one you click to add the current page to the bookmarks list. (The bookmarks are organized based on application.) The other, called Bookmarks, looks like an open book and is the one you click to open the pop-over containing the bookmarks list, shown in Figure 7.2. In the Bookmarks pop-over, double-click the bookmarked help page you want to open, or select a bookmark and click either Remove to delete the bookmark or Email to mail it to someone. (The e-mail message contains a link to the help page, so the recipient needs to open it on a Mac running Mac OS X Lion to access the page.) Click outside the Bookmarks pop-over to close it.

FIGURE 7.2

Left: The expanded search results for a Help Center query. Right: A bookmarks list in the Help Center.

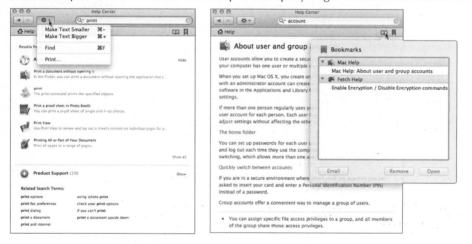

Using Applications' Help

Most applications running in Mac OS X provide their own help, from the Help menu, a Help icon button, or the shortcut Shift+⌘+/. Figure 7.3 shows the Help Center home pages for Apple Mail and Parallels Desktop as examples. As you can see, they use the same Help Center system as Mac OS X does, so you navigate these applications' help systems as described in the preceding section.

Note

Unlike the Mac OS X Help Center, when you're perusing help pages in many applications' Help Centers, note the Index link on many; clicking it gives you an alphabetically organized index page to all help topics. Also note applications' Help Centers often have two home links: The button with the house graphic opens the Mac OS X Help Center's home page, while the text link Home or applicationname's Help goes to the application's Help Center home page. ■

Even if they support the Help Center browser for help pages, many applications come with extra help options in their Help menus. Apple Keynote, for example, offers video tutorials on your Mac and a function and shortcuts guide downloadable from the web.

Retrieving help from the Internet

At times, the Help Center accesses the Internet to retrieve help articles. An application may have only the most commonly accessed help topics stored on your Mac, so it offers a search index that links to the Internet for more details. If you click a help article that is located on the Internet, the Help Center automatically caches the information inside Mac OS X for later use. If you want to read the same article at a later point, the Help Center automatically displays the document from the cache. However, the Help Center also checks the Internet to see if the article has been updated; if a newer version is available, it is displayed instead.

Note that the Help Center does not add, index, or let you bookmark web pages that you visit either from the Help Center's links or from an application's other options in its Help menu. It only adds information from Help Center-formatted databases accessed via the Internet.

The Help Center also adds articles to your Mac's help topics from the Internet as they become available, so your help system continually is expanded and updated. Of course, the Help Center can access online articles only if your Mac is connected to the Internet.

Note that some applications, such as Microsoft Office, use their own help system, not the Help Center, and some—notably Adobe's Creative Suite and Mozilla Firefox—use web-based help systems that require you to be online to open their help pages.

FIGURE 7.3

Left: The Help Center for Apple Mail showing its index page. Right: Parallels Desktop showing its home page.

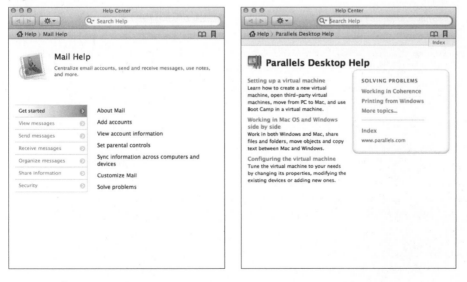

Understanding Help Tags

Help tags are a quick form of help that can offer expanded information on items found throughout Mac OS X and in many applications. Many applications enable you to get immediate information about Finder items (buttons and icons, for example) via expanded information shown in the help tags.

If an object in Mac OS X has a help tag description, when you hover the pointer over it for a few seconds, a yellow box appears. Inside the box is a description of what action the item performs, as shown in Figure 7.4. If no such box appears, the object has no help tag associated with it.

Note
Some applications call these help tags ToolTips. ■

FIGURE 7.4

Help tags are enabled throughout Mac OS X and provide quick information regarding various items. Here, a help tag displays at the bottom of the toolbar.

Not all objects have help tags. Common menu items—such as scroll arrows and menus—do not have help tags because they are considered self-explanatory. And not all applications offer the same level of help tag functionality as those created by Apple. Help tags are primarily used by custom buttons and icons to describe what the image used by the icon represents.

Working with Command-Line Help

Most of the help offered by Mac OS X is displayed in the Finder's graphical interface. However, Mac OS X has a comprehensive command-line interface that you can access through the Terminal application, which runs the Unix operating system that underlies Mac OS X.

Mac OS X's command-line interface has an integrated help system referred to as the *man pages* (*man* is short for *manual*). The man pages, shown in Figure 7.5, provide an online user manual that contains information on just about every command used in Terminal. Appendix D covers Terminal in detail and provides more detailed information regarding the man command.

FIGURE 7.5

The man command, used in Terminal, provides user-manual entries relating to various command-line functions.

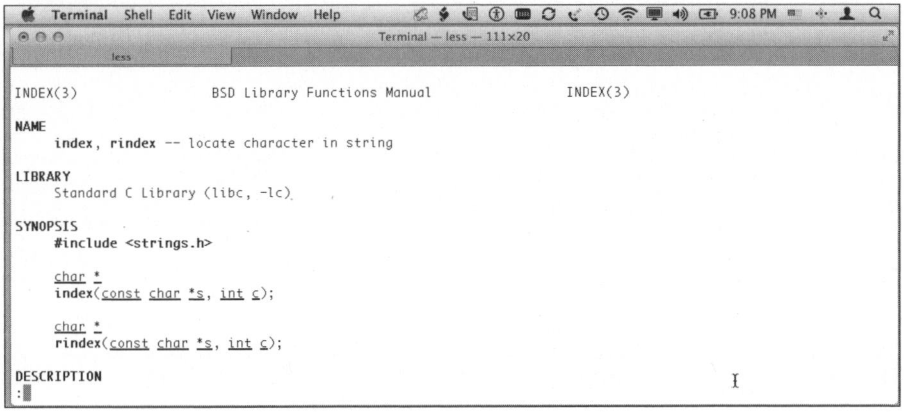

Exploring Other Avenues of Help

Beyond the Help Center and the help that comes with your applications, many other resources can help Mac users with questions. This book is one, but plenty of resources are available on the web:

- **AppleCare Service and Support:** www.apple.com/support
- **AppleCare Knowledge Base:** http://kbase.info.apple.com
- **Apple Manuals:** www.apple.com/support/manuals
- **Apple Mac OS X Support:** www.apple.com/macosx/lion
- **Mac user groups:** www.apple.com/usergroups
- **Mac User Group (MUG) Center:** www.mugcenter.com
- **MacTalk user forum:** www.macusers.org

- **MacFixIt:** www.macfixit.com

- *Macworld* **magazine and website:** www.macworld.com

- *Mac Life* **magazine and website:** www.maclife.com

- **MacFixIt:** www.macfixit.com

- **The websites of the application developers and hardware makers whose products you use**

Summary

In the Help Center, you can search for help articles relating to Mac OS X and applications, and you can narrow down your choices using Boolean logic. The Help Center's browser interface enables you to navigate through help pages using the familiar concept of links, Back, Forward, and Home. Plus you can bookmark, print, and e-mail links to help pages for easy referral later. You also can do a quick text search directly from the Help menu's Search box.

Pop-up labels called *help tags* provide a quick reminder of some Finder and application elements' functions, while the man commands in the Terminal let you access help articles in the Mac's Unix environment.

Many manufacturers offer a range of support through online support pages. And several key websites are a great place to start for help for Mac computers, hardware, software, and Mac OS X itself.

Using Mac OS X's Universal Access for the Disabled

Mac OS X is designed from the ground up to work effectively for everybody, including people with disabilities or special needs. People with limited hearing, sight, or ability to control a keyboard or mouse will find Mac OS X is an extremely effective operating system.

These features are mostly located in Mac OS X via the Universal Access system preference, but Mac OS X's sound input and speech capabilities (found in the Sound and Speech system preferences, respectively) also are extremely useful.

A key support application for the visually impaired, VoiceOver Utility enables Mac OS X to read aloud information displayed on the screen. In many ways, VoiceOver Utility is an extension of Universal Access. The application can be configured to provide the voice a user understands best when the app speaks the text onscreen. A nice touch is that VoiceOver Utility can be used to speak chat combinations such as smiley face :) or lol (which stands for "laughing out loud'). You can customize VoiceOver Utility so it reads aloud an appropriate command for your personalized text chats.

You'll find Mac OS X is a great operating system for everyone, regardless of what abilities they possess.

IN THIS CHAPTER

Setting up Mac OS X with Universal Access

Setting up access for assistive devices

Enabling visual assistance

Enabling hearing assistance

Enabling keyboard assistance

Enabling mouse assistance

Setting up speech recognition

Setting up the VoiceOver Utility

Setting Up Mac OS X with Universal Access

If you have a special requirement for Mac OS X, you should start by investigating the Universal Access system preference. Open the System

Preferences application (choose ⇨ System Preferences), and click the Universal Access icon.

The Universal Access system preference has four panes: Seeing, Hearing, Keyboard, and Mouse & Trackpad. Each enables you to set up a different array of assistive options for a variety of access needs. These are the options:

- **Seeing:** In this section, you can turn on VoiceOver technology and set custom zoom and display contrast levels.

- **Hearing:** In this section, you can adjust the volume and set up screen flash alerts to complement the usual audio alerts.

- **Keyboard:** In this section, you can use the keyboard options to activate sticky keys, which enable you to type key combinations (such as ⌘+O) one letter at a time; additional options assist with key repeat options.

- **Mouse & Trackpad:** In this section, the options enable you to activate *mouse keys*. These enable you to use the keyboard as a replacement for the mouse or touchpad. Additional options control the speed, delay, and size of the pointer.

Note that the bottom of the Universal Access system preference—regardless of what pane you are in—is the Enable Access for Assistive Devices option. Selecting it enables third-party devices to harness the capabilities of Universal Access. This option must be selected for AppleScripts to run that use the Finder's graphical interface. Also, many applications designed to assist people require that this option be selected. Thus, it is a mistake to think that the Enable Access for Assistive Devices option relates only to applications that improve access for people with disabilities. Because many applications use it, this option should be on for everyone (which it is by default).

Also at the bottom of the Universal Access system preference is the Show Universal Access Status in the Menu Bar option to get quick access to various Universal Access settings.

Enabling Visual Assistance

The first pane in the Universal Access system preference is Seeing, and its options improve the visual display of Mac OS X or substitute visual information with audio equivalents. The technologies available are designed to enable people with limited visual abilities to use the full Mac OS X. Figure 8.1 shows the Seeing pane.

Hearing your Mac with VoiceOver

The first section in the Seeing pane in the Universal Access preference is VoiceOver. You can turn on VoiceOver in two ways:

- **Select the On option in the Seeing pane's VoiceOver section.** Select On to switch on VoiceOver; select Off to disable it.

- **Press ⌘+F5.** Use this keyboard shortcut to toggle VoiceOver on and off. (If your keyboard has an Fn key *and* you selected the Use All F1, F2, etc. Keys as Standard Function Keys in the Keyboard pane of the Keyboard system preference, you use the shortcut Fn+⌘+F5.

FIGURE 8.1

The Seeing pane of the Universal Access system preference

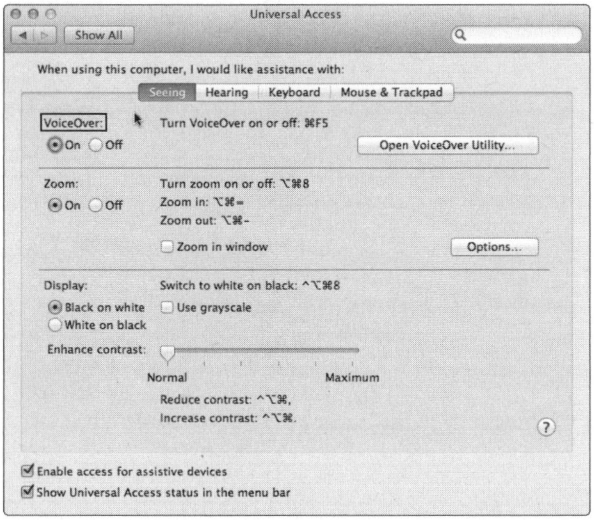

As soon as you turn on VoiceOver, a message window called the *caption panel* appears at the bottom of the screen, as Figure 8.2 shows, displaying whatever text VoiceOver is reading aloud. It starts with a welcome message, which you can edit in the General pane of the VoiceOver Options dialog box, covered later in this section. (If the caption panel does not display, turn it on in the Visuals pane of the VoiceOver Utility, as described later in this chapter.)

The VoiceOver caption panel provides other information as well. For example, it tells you when the screen saver has been activated. It provides guidance on what navigation options are available. When you are in a dialog box, window, or panel with multiple options, it informs you to click down to select options. As you move through the options, VoiceOver reads them aloud.

You can control in great detail how VoiceOver works using the VoiceOver Utility, described at the end of this chapter—including turning it off.

FIGURE 8.2

The caption panel displays whatever VoiceOver is speaking.

Understanding the VoiceOver keys

You use the VoiceOver keys (known as the *VO keys*) to enter VoiceOver commands. By default, the VO keys are Control+Option. Typically, you press and hold both keys while pressing another key to issue a VoiceOver command—just like any other keyboard shortcut. Thus, if a VO command is shown in Mac OS X menus, dialog boxes, and help systems as VO-F8, you press Control+Option+F8 to access it.

Many VO key commands are available, and they do everything from read a currently selected item to interact with Mac OS X interface elements. You also can use them to navigate the screen.

VoiceOver keyboard commands

Many of the available VO keys are outlined in the Help Center; choose Help ➪ VoiceOver Commands from the VoiceOver Utility to get lists of the various VO keys. The commands are split into nine sections: General, Orientation, Navigation, Web, Text, Interaction, Search, Standard Gestures, and New and Changed Commands. (To open the VoiceOver Utility, go to the Utilities folder on your Mac and double-click the VoiceOver Utility application icon.)

New Feature

Mac OS X Lion has expanded the number of sections for VoiceOver command help from six to nine; new ones are Web, Standard Gestures, and New and Changed Commands. ■

Using keyboard help

Pressing Control+Option+K brings up the keyboard help function. In keyboard help mode, you hear the name of each key as it is pressed. Someone who cannot clearly see the keys to find his or her way around can use this function to learn the keyboard. When you press the VO keys (Control+Option) and press a key, the function speaks the associated command along with a brief description of what the command does.

Tip

A standard feature on most keyboards (including all Apple keyboards) is a slight protruding line on the F and J keys. These are designed for touch typists, enabling users to quickly locate their positions on the keyboard without having to look at the keys. The F and J keys also serve as a great navigation tool for the visually impaired. The two keys are located where you place your index fingers, and your other fingers are on the adjacent keys. (The keys your left hand rests on are A, S, D, and F; the keys your right hand rests on are J, K, L, and the semicolon [;] key.) From this position, your fingers can move up and down to reach any key on the keyboard, and you naturally return to the position. Consequently, you can navigate the entire keyboard without needing to look at it. ■

Navigating with VoiceOver

To move the VoiceOver cursor (the black rectangle that surrounds items being spoken), press Control+Option and the arrow keys. The VoiceOver cursor moves in that direction to the next item on the horizontal, or vertical, line. You hear a description of each item as the cursor highlights it. You select items by pressing Control+Option+spacebar, which is the equivalent of pressing the mouse or touchpad button.

Note

You move around items within a list by pressing the arrow keys as normal, but holding down the VoiceOver keys (Control+Option) while pressing the arrow keys takes you to the next section. ■

When navigating the screen via mouse or touchpad, VoiceOver describes the elements the pointer passes over.

Using the Dock

To move to the Dock, press Control+Option+D. By default, the VoiceOver cursor is placed around the Finder item in the Dock. To move to the next item in the Dock, press Control+Option+→; to move to the previous item, press Control+Option+←. You select an item in the Dock by pressing Control+Option+spacebar.

Using the menu bar

Another quick command to help you get started is Control+Option+M. This takes you to the menu bar, and you can use the arrow keys to move through menu items and press Control+⌘+spacebar (or press Return) to choose a menu item.

Selecting buttons, check boxes, and sliders

To click a button, you typically press Control+Option+spacebar (although you also can press the Return key, as you can when VoiceOver is switched off). This works for selection buttons, check boxes, and radio buttons.

To open a pop-up menu, navigate to it with VoiceOver and press Control+Option+spacebar, and then use the arrow keys (↑ and ↓) to move through the options; press Control+Option+spacebar to select the appropriate option.

To move a slider, highlight it with the VoiceOver cursor, and press Control+Option+Shift+↓ to begin interacting with it. Use the arrow keys (↑ and ↓ for vertical slider; ← and → for a horizontal slider) to move the slider. As you move the slider, you hear verbal feedback regarding the amount (such as a percentage, or number, relating to the slider's current position).

Entering text into text fields

When you move the VoiceOver cursor to a text field, any text inside the field is read aloud. As you type letters into the field, VoiceOver speaks each letter as you type. The exception is when you are typing text into a secure field (such as a password entry point); at this point, no text is read aloud.

Navigating rows and columns

When you are navigating a table, these additional commands enable you to move among rows and columns:

- **Control+Option+R:** Read a row.
- **Control+Option+C:** Read the column header.
- **Control+Option+C then C:** Read a table column. Upon the first press of the C key, it reads the column header (as above), and on the second press of C, it reads the content of the table column.

Using smart groups in web pages

One more unique feature in VoiceOver is worth mentioning: smart groups. They are a unique way to browse web pages based upon their visual layout. Web pages are designed to group information together in boxes, which may not be visible onscreen, but internally they hold related content together. The smart groups capability uses this information to determine what related information should be handled by VoiceOver. The following commands work with smart groups:

- **Control+Option+⌘+N:** Move to the next smart group.
- **Control+Option+Shift+⌘+N:** Move to the previous smart group.
- **Control+Option+→:** Move to the next item in a smart group.
- **Control+Option+←:** Move to the previous item in a smart group.

VoiceOver help

To get help with VoiceOver, press Control+Option+H. This brings up the VoiceOver help menu with the following options:

- Online Help (Control+Shift+Option+/)
- Commands Help (Control+Option+ H, and then press H again)
- Keyboard Help (Control+Option+K)

- Sounds Help
- Quick Start Tutorial (Control+Option+⌘+F8)
- Getting Started Guide

Zooming in on the screen

Another way to provide access to the Mac OS X environment for visually impaired people is to enable the zoom option. As the name suggests, zoom homes in on a part of the screen (around the cursor) and magnifies everything, making it clear and easy to see. As you move the cursor to the edge of the screen, the zoomed area scrolls over to that part of the screen.

To activate the zoom in Mac OS X, select the On option under the Zoom section in the Universal Access system preference's Seeing pane, or simply press Option+⌘+8 in the Finder. (That same shortcut turns off the zoom.)

You can increase or decrease the zoom level in two ways:

- **Using keyboard commands:** Press Option+⌘+= to zoom in and Option+⌘+− to zoom out.
- **Using the mouse scroll wheel or touch surface:** Mouse users can press ⌘ and move the mouse's scroll wheel (it may be a ball on your mouse) up to zoom in and down to zoom out. Touchpad users can press ⌘ and push two fingers up on the touchpad to zoom in and down to zoom out.

Adjusting zoom options

You can personalize the zoom settings in several ways. First, select the Zoom in Window option if you want the zoom-in action to focus on the active window; otherwise, it zooms in at the mouse location.

The other zoom options reside in the settings sheet that appears when you click the Options button.

Maximum Zoom and Minimum Zoom sliders

By default, the Maximum Zoom and Minimum Zoom sliders are both set to 0, and you zoom in one increment at a time (1×, 2×, and so on). However, each slider can be moved up to a maximum of 20. What these sliders do is set a point at which zooming in (maximum) and out (minimum) automatically moves to. So, if you set the maximum slider at 20, and the minimum at 10, clicking Option+⌘+= to zoom in automatically takes you straight to a 20× level of magnification; zooming out takes you to a 10× level of magnification.

Tip

You can zoom in or out past the minimum and maximum settings by holding down the Option+⌘+= and Option+⌘+− shortcuts. ∎

Show Preview Rectangle When Zoomed Out option

Selecting the Show Preview Rectangle When Zoomed Out option places a thick rectangular outline around the pointer, if you've set the Maximum Zoom to more than 0. This outline displays the area of the screen that will be zoomed in to when you press Control+⌘+=, as shown in Figure 8.3. By default, the zoom area is set to 0 magnification, and no outline appears at that setting.

FIGURE 8.3

The preview rectangle (at the upper right) displays exactly which part of the screen will be shown when you zoom in.

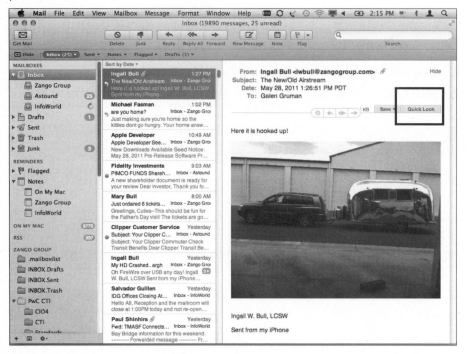

Tip

Zoom isn't just for people who need visual assistance. It is a very handy tool for anybody who wants to focus on a specific area of a display. The Zoom tool is often used by people wanting to demonstrate a feature or function of an item in Mac OS X (such as an application). By zooming in on a specific part of the screen, you can focus on the feature close up, without any of the distractions of other elements. ■

Smooth Images option

The images on the screen are made up of pixels, which are small squares. By default, these are so small that the items that make up the Mac OS X interface appear smooth and rounded.

However, when you zoom in, you quickly see the jagged edges that make up most interface items. With the Smooth Images option selected (the default), items appear less jagged when highly magnified—though the trade-off is that items can appear slightly blurry.

Zoom Follows the Keyboard Focus option

When you zoom in, the zoom area automatically follows the pointer. If you zoom in on a text area (a large text box or word-processing document, for example), the text you type may go off the edge of the screen. Selecting the Zoom Follows the Keyboard Focus option ensures that the zoom follows the text cursor, not the pointer, as you type.

When Zoomed In, the Screen Image Moves options

Because a zoomed screen no longer displays the desktop in its entirety, you must scroll around a zoomed-in screen view to see different parts of the interface. There are three options to control this screen movement:

- **Continuously with Pointer:** When this option is selected, the zoomed screen moves in time with the pointer. As you move the pointer, it initially moves on its own, and then the screen starts to move with it. This is one of the most natural zoom modes you can use.

- **Only When the Pointer Reaches an Edge:** When this option is selected, the screen zooms in around the pointer, and you can move the pointer around the zoomed portion of the screen without changing the view at all. But if you move the pointer to the edge of the screen, the zoomed area moves in that direction. This option is great when you want to work within a zoomed area without the zoom level or focus changing.

- **So the Pointer Is At or Near the Center of the Image:** When this option is selected, the screen zooms in with the pointer in the center. As you move the pointer, it stays in the center of the screen and the zoomed background moves around it. The exception is when you move to the edge of the screen, at which point the pointer moves instead of the background.

Use Scroll Wheel with Modifier Keys to Zoom option

The Use Scroll Wheel with Modifier Keys to Zoom option enables you to zoom in and out using the scroll wheel (or ball) on a mouse or using the two-finger scroll gesture on a touchpad. If you want to zoom in and out with the scroll ball or wheel, select this option. (Note that it is selected by default.)

Beside the option is a text field that enables you to determine which modifier key must be pressed along with the movement of the scroll (or the touchpad gesture) for the zoom to occur. By default, this is the Control key; however, you can change this to any combination of the modifier keys (⌘, Shift, Control, and Option). To change the option, click in the text field or press Tab until it is highlighted; then press the modifier key or keys you want to assign.

Click Done to save your changes in the settings sheet.

Adjusting display options

The next settings in the Seeing pane of the Universal Access system preference appears in the Display section. These settings enable you to adjust the color scheme for the Mac OS X screen and the level of contrast. Adjusting these settings can make the display easier to read for some visually impaired individuals. These options are available:

- **Black on White.** This is the default setting, and it provides a standard display, where black is black, white is white, and all other colors are unchanged.

- **White on Black:** This is the polar opposite of the Black on White settings, and clicking this option reverses the whole color spectrum. Areas that were black now become white, and white areas become black. In this sense, it is like viewing an old-fashioned negative photograph. It's applied to all colors, so purple becomes green, red becomes cyan, and yellow becomes blue (and vice versa for all). The shortcut Control+Option+⌘+8 lets you invert the colors quickly.

- **Use Grayscale:** Selecting this option removes all the color from the screen; instead, everything displays as shades of gray.

- **Enhance Contrast:** As the name suggests, the Enhance Contrast slider makes the contrast of the screen more pronounced. The greater the contrast, the more that the normally gentle fades between colors are replaced with light hues and dark hues, and the medium hues are gone. You also can use the keyboard shortcuts instead of this pane to adjust contrast incrementally: Control+Option+⌘+, (comma) to reduce it and Control+Option+⌘+. (period) to increase it.

It is important to note that you can use these settings in concert to great effect. You can, for example, create a white-on-black background with a grayscale setting and high level of contrast to produce a highly readable display for text.

Tip
If you inadvertently make the screen display as white-on-black, just press Control+Option+⌘+8 to switch back to the regular black-on-white mode. The shortcut toggles between the two modes. ■

Enabling Hearing Assistance

The second pane on the Universal Access system preference is Hearing, shown in Figure 8.4. The pane has just three options.

The first option is to flash the screen while sounding an alert. If you select the Flash the Screen When an Alert Sound Occurs option, any sound alerts (as specified in the Sound system preference) are accompanied with a flash of the screen. The screen quickly flashes white, and then returns to normal, drawing your attention to whatever the alert may be. (You can test the flashing alert by clicking Flash Screen.)

The second option is the Play Stereo Audio as Mono option. If selected, this option combines the left and right speakers' audio into one signal sent to all connected speakers and headsets. This helps people who may hear poorly in one ear and thus miss sounds that come out of, say, just the speaker on the right.

The final setting in the Hearing pane is the Adjust Volume button, which if clicked opens the Sound system preference. There, you can adjust both the Alert volume and the Output volume for all sounds issued by your Mac. (Chapter 28 details the Sound system preference.)

FIGURE 8.4

The Hearing pane of the Universal Access system preference

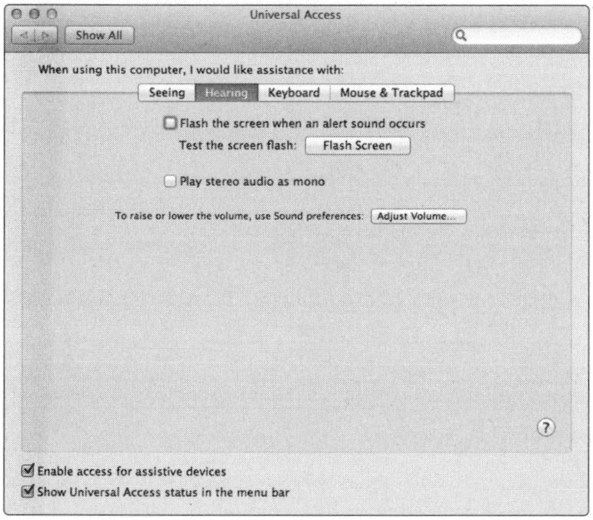

Enabling Keyboard Assistance

The third pane in the Universal Access system preference is Keyboard, shown in Figure 8.5. Its options include help for people who have difficulty pressing more than one key at the same time, people who have difficulty with initial key presses, and people who have difficulty with repeated keystrokes.

Pressing more than one key at a time

Mac OS X offers several options designed to help people overcome difficulties in pressing multiple keys simultaneously, which most shortcuts require you do.

The first option in the Keyboard pane controls sticky keys. If On is selected, this setting enables you to press modifier keys (Control, Option, Shift, and ⌘) one at a time—rather than all at the same time as normal—and use them to create keyboard combinations. With Sticky Keys set to On, you can press ⌘ and then N, for example, to open a new Finder window, rather than use the standard method of holding ⌘ and then pressing N.

Tip

When the Sticky Keys option is set to On and you press a modifier key a second time, you lock it. This means that you can use it repeatedly for multiple keyboard commands. Modifier keys pressed accidentally can be cancelled by pressing the key a third time. Alternatively, pressing the Esc key cancels the whole modifier key sequence, unless you have locked down the key (in which case, you must press the same key again to unlock it). ■

Three options appear beneath the Sticky Keys option:

- **Press the Shift Key Five Times to Turn Sticky Keys On or Off:** As the name suggests, this enables you to activate or deactivate the sticky keys function through multiple presses of the Shift key.

- **Beep When a Modifier Key Is Set:** By default, Mac OS X makes a small clicking sound when a modifier key is set and a slightly firmer sound when you press it a second time to lock it. (No sound is made for canceling a modifier key.) By default, this sound is active. Deselecting this option cancels the audio feedback.

- **Display Pressed Keys On Screen:** When you press a modifier key, a small symbol of the key appears onscreen. The symbol fades slightly for a single press, but it remains bold when locked with a second key press. This option is selected by default.

FIGURE 8.5

The Keyboard pane of the Universal Access system preference

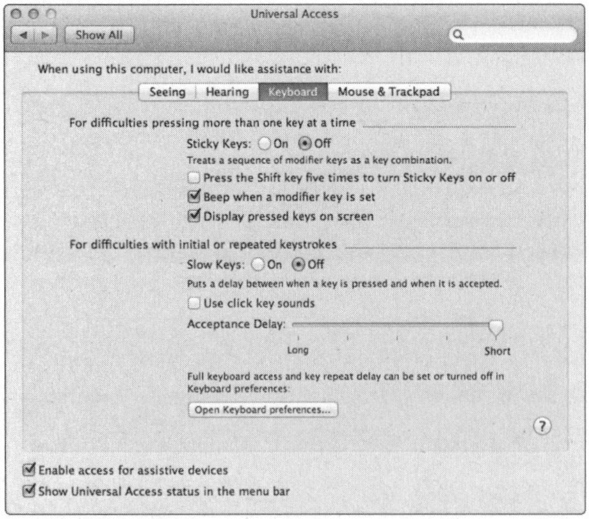

Pressing keys accidentally

Some people may find accidental key presses make it difficult for them to accurately enter text. Mac OS X's solution for this is *slow keys*. With this feature activated, a key must be pressed and held for a short period before it is registered by Mac OS X as an actual keystroke. If the key is released before the required period, the keystroke is ignored.

This feature can be extremely useful for people who find themselves accidentally brushing the wrong key.

Select the On option next to Slow Keys to turn on the feature. Now, when you press a key, you must wait until a noise (similar to a camera click) sounds before the keystroke is registered. The delay is less than a second, but it does prevent you from typing quickly.

Below the Slow Keys option are three control configurations:

- **Use Click Key Sounds:** When the Slow Keys option is set to On, a sound notifies you that the keystroke has been registered.

- **Acceptance Delay:** This slider determines how long you must wait when using slow keys before a key press is registered. Moving the slider to the left (marked Long) increases the delay between pressing the key and registering it; moving the slider to the right (marked Short) decreases the delay between the key press and registering it.

- **Open Keyboard Preferences:** Click Open Keyboard Preferences to be taken to the Keyboard preference (see Chapter 28), which has keyboard access controls. In the Full Keyboard Access section at the bottom of the Keyboard system preference's Keyboard Shortcuts pane, you have two options:

  - **Text Boxes and Lists Only:** This is the default option. When it is selected, pressing the Tab key moves the keyboard focus between text fields (text boxes) and lists, but ignores other options, such as check boxes.

  - **All Controls:** When this option is selected, pressing the Tab key moves the focus between all elements in a list, including check boxes, radio buttons, and push buttons.

  You can use the shortcut Control+F7 in the Finder to toggle between the two settings.

  In the Keyboard system preference's Keyboard pane, you also can address an area that can cause problems for users who have difficulty pressing and releasing keys quickly. Use the Delay Until Repeat slider to increase the delay (by moving the slider to the left). You also can move the slider all they way to the Off position to cancel the repeat-key function entirely. In the Keyboard system preference, you also can use the Key Repeat Rate to control how many key presses occur as you hold down a key.

Enabling Mouse Assistance

The fourth pane of the Universal Access system preference is Mouse & Trackpad, shown in Figure 8.6. As the name suggests, it offers several functions to help people who have difficulty using either a mouse or a touchpad.

FIGURE 8.6

The Mouse & Trackpad pane of the Universal Access system preference

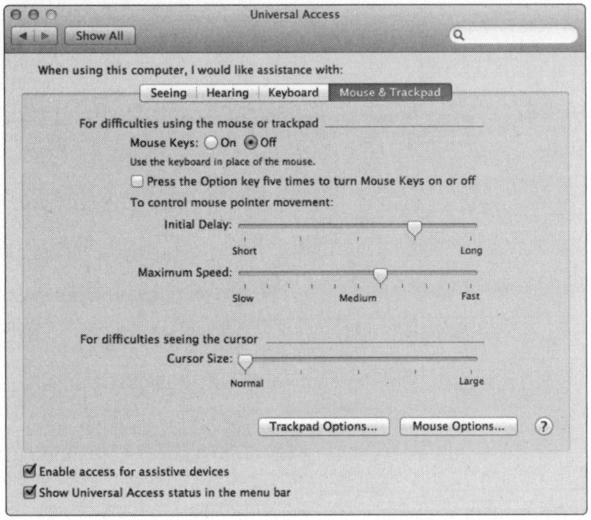

Getting help with using the mouse or touchpad

Users who have difficulty using the mouse or touchpad can use the keyboard to control the pointer instead. This feature is known as *mouse keys*.

To enable mouse keys, select the On option in the Mouse Keys section. The mouse keys feature uses the numeric keypad in an extended keyboard to control the pointer. The 8 key moves the pointer up, 4 moves it left, 6 moves it right, and 2 moves it down; the 5 key (in the middle) indicates a mouse or touchpad press. Note that the 1, 3, 7, and 9 keys move the pointer diagonally.

If you have a regular Mac keyboard (without a keypad), you use the 8, K, U, and O keys for up, down, left, and right, respectively, the I key as a click, and the 7, 9, J, and L keys for diagonal movement.

Note

On some older laptops, you also can use the keys surrounding K as a numeric keypad (these keys have smaller numerals printed alongside the letters). On such keyboards, press F6 to activate Num Lock so you can use these keys as a replacement for the numeric keypad. ■

The Mouse Keys section has the following options:

- **Press the Option Key Five Times to Turn Mouse Keys On or Off:** This option enables you to activate and deactivate mouse keys without entering the Universal

Access system preference. This is especially useful for MacBook owners who need to switch between use of mouse keys and regular keyboard input.

- **Initial Delay:** This slider controls how long you must hold down a mouse key before the pointer or text cursor begins to move. Move the slider to the left for a short delay and to the right for a long delay.

- **Maximum Speed:** As you hold down a mouse key, the pointer speeds up from an initial slow speed to a fairly rapid movement. This technique enables you to perform small pointer movements and move around the interface reasonably quickly. The slider enables you to set the speed at which the pointer moves when you hold down a mouse key. Move the slider to the left (the Slow setting) to limit the pointer speed, and move it farther to the right (the Fast setting) to enable the pointer to move rapidly around the screen.

Tip

Although the mouse is ubiquitous in the computer world, it is not the only device for controlling pointer motion in Mac OS X. You have many alternatives to using a mouse. People with limited hand movement but accurate control may find touchpads a more suitable alternative. If you have difficulty holding a mouse, a trackball may be more suitable; special joysticks (not to be confused with gaming joysticks, incidentally) can be used as effective mouse replacements. Disabled Online (www.disabledonline.com) has lots of alternative input devices worth looking at. ■

Getting help with seeing the pointer

The third slider in the Mouse & Trackpad pane is Cursor Size. You can use it to increase the size of the pointer, making it easier to see. By default, the slider is set all the way to the left; dragging it to the right increases the size. Note that this option affects the size of both the text cursor and the pointer.

Adjusting touchpad and mouse behavior

The final options in the Mouse & Trackpad pane in the Universal Access system preference are the Trackpad Options and Mouse Options buttons. Each opens a settings sheet with controls over how each input device behaves.

The settings sheet for touchpads lets you adjust the double-click and scrolling speeds via sliders and offers four other options you can enable or disable:

- **Scrolling:** Enabled by default, this option controls whether the touchpad can be used to scroll. (Those with motor-coordination difficulties may prefer to disable scrolling to prevent accidental movement of the pointer and objects onscreen.) The adjacent pop-up menu lets you enable scrolling with or without inertia. If you choose With Inertia, the scrolling continues a little bit after you let your finger off the touchpad.

- **Dragging:** Disabled by default, this option controls whether you can use the touchpad to drag options. If enabled, the adjacent pop-up menu controls whether drag lock is enabled. If you choose the With Drag Lock option, you must tap the touchpad to stop dragging the object; otherwise, you just have to lift your finger off the touchpad. You would consider choosing With Drag Lock if you have to drag items far beyond where your finger can move on the touchpad. In such a case, you would lift your finger off the touchpad and then put it down and drag more.

- **Ignore Built-in Trackpad when Mouse Keys Is On:** Users of MacBooks may want to enable this setting. Selecting it ensures that accidental touches of the touchpad do not interfere with movement of the pointer. Note that this setting has no effect on an external touchpad such as the Magic Trackpad.

- **Ignore Built-in Trackpad when Mouse or Wireless Trackpad Is Present:** This setting disables a MacBook's built-in touchpad if a mouse (USB or Bluetooth) or external touchpad (Bluetooth-only) is connected to the laptop. If you're typing on the MacBook's built-in keyboard, you might use this option so accidental brushes against the built-in touchpad don't result in unwanted pointer movements.

New Feature

The controls over speed, scrolling, and dragging have been moved in Mac OS X Lion from the Mouse and Trackpad system preferences to the Universal Access system preference. ∎

The options in the settings sheet for mouse behavior depend on whether your mouse supports gestures (as the Magic Mouse does). Regardless of the mouse's capabilities, the settings sheet has sliders to control double-click speed and scrolling speed. It may provide options to control scrolling and dragging if the mouse supports these gestures. (For example, if you are using a Magic Mouse, the Scrolling option appears.) The settings sheet's options for these gestures are the same as for a touchpad.

Using hot spots

VoiceOver has a handy feature called *hot spots*: These are markers you insert in text by pressing Control+Option+Shift+n, where n is a numeral from 0 to 9. You jump to a hot spot by pressing Control+Option+n. It's that simple.

Setting Up Speech Recognition

The idea of being able to talk to a computer has been a staple of science fiction for decades, but recently the idea has started to make serious movement from science fiction to science fact.

At the introduction of the Macintosh in 1984, the computer introduced itself by speaking aloud to an audience. Over time, Macs have become increasingly verbose.

Listening is, of course, a slightly more complex matter than speaking. The wide range of human languages, regional dialects, semantic variations, and, of course, personal pronunciation differences all pose a real challenge for any speech recognition system.

But Apple has, over time, chipped away at the concept of speech recognition, and every version of Mac OS X has increased the capability of the Mac to understand what people are saying.

Mac OS X has a built-in English speech recognition program that can be activated in the Speech system preference. Speech recognition in Mac OS X is designed to recognize hundreds of commonly spoken commands. You can use it to control the interface, switch between applications, and even start iChat conversations.

Tip

What you can't use Mac OS X's speech recognition for is general dictation. If you want to take full control of your Mac verbally, you need to invest in a separate program. A good one to look at is MacSpeech Scribe ($150; www.nuance.com). ■

Tip

It's not just people with limited movement who need to consider speech-based input. Voice recognition technology is especially useful to people suffering, or worried about developing, RSI (repetitive strain injury). Repeated small movements caused by typing on a keyboard or moving a mouse can lead to RSI-related problems. Voice recognition technology can be a great boon to preventing or adjusting to RSIs. ■

Using a microphone

Speech recognition requires a microphone. Fortunately, most Mac users are in luck because most Macs have a built-in microphone. (It accompanies the built-in iSight camera, usually located just above the screen.)

The built-in microphones in MacBooks, MacBook Pros, iMacs, and Mac Minis, as well as in some of the recent Cinema Display flat-panel monitors made by Apple, are all high-quality affairs, and most of them work just fine for speech recognition.

Using a built-in microphone is fine for Mac OS X's speech recognition, but if you find that you have difficulty with the built-in microphone, you might consider upgrading to a dedicated external microphone. Some speech recognition systems, such as Dragon Dictate ($200; www.nuance.com), often come supplied with high-quality microphones. If you use speech recognition permanently, you might consider a dedicated noise-canceling microphone and earphone headset. Many makes and models are available.

Configuring speech recognition

Open the System Preferences application (choose ⌘ ➪ System Preferences), and click the Speech icon to open the Speech system preference and go to the Speech Recognition pane. To activate speech recognition, select the On option next to Speakable Items. When you do this, a circular window known as the Speech Feedback window appears, indicating that speech recognition is up and running. (Figure 8.7 shows this window). You can now turn speech recognition on and off, and the feedback window lets you know when Mac OS X is listening.

FIGURE 8.7

The Speech system preference's Speech Recognition pane, with the Speech Feedback circular window to its right side

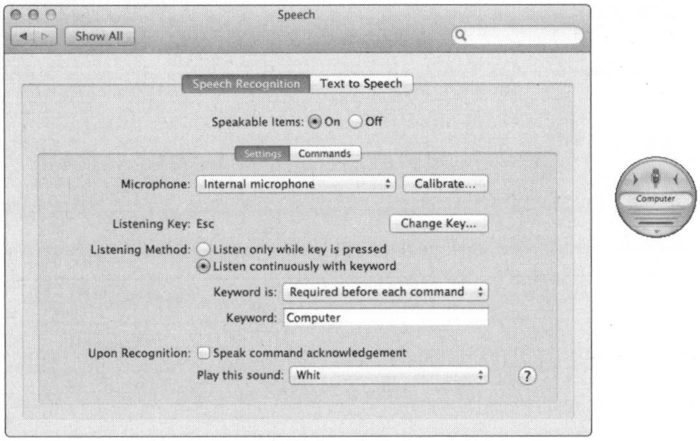

Turning on speech recognition is very simple. Getting it to work, however, takes a little more practice. The first step is to adjust the speech recognition settings.

Adjusting speech recognition settings

The Speech Recognition pane has two subpanes: Settings and Commands. The Settings subpane enables you to adjust various options related to activating the speech input. They are described next.

Microphone pop-up menu

This pop-up menu has Internal Microphone selected by default. If you have multiple microphones attached to your Mac, you can choose which one to use with this menu. Note that the Line In option takes the signal from the Mac's line-in jack (also called the microphone jack). If you have a USB microphone attached, it shows up as a separate option in this menu.

Calibrate button

To the right of the Microphone pop-up menu is the Calibrate button; click it to open the Microphone Calibration dialog box.

To calibrate the microphone, you need to speak naturally (as you will when speaking to your Mac) and watch the meter. The meter lights up as you speak, through the blue and green areas and into the red area. As you speak, move the slider between Low and High until the meter stays in the green area as you speak. You may find it easier to read something aloud while calibrating the meter.

When you have the meter calibrated (so it's in the green area when you speak), start saying the various items listed on the left side of the window. As each command is recognized, its text blinks. If Mac OS X is having difficulty recognizing any of the commands, you may need to adjust the slider again until all the listed commands are recognized.

Change Key button

By default, speech recognition on Mac OS X works by listening when you are holding down a key. (The Esc key is used by default.) Click Change Key to change this key to your own choice.

Listening Method options

If you do not want to hold down a key while speaking to enable speech recognition, you can opt to use a keyword instead. The way this works is that the speech recognition function continuously listens for you to say a specific word. When it hears that word, it treats whatever you say next as a command. By default, the keyword is "computer": Saying the word "computer" out loud activates the speech recognition. So to open iTunes, you would say, "Computer, open iTunes."

Select the Listen Continuously with Keyword option to switch to this mode.

Tip

Even when the Mac is continuously listening, you can stop it from doing so without going to the Speech system preference. Just press Esc or whatever key you set via the Change Key button. Press that key again to resume continuous listening. ■

Under that option is the Keyword Is pop-up menu with the following options: Optional before Commands, Required before Each Command, Required 15 Seconds after Last Command, and Required 30 Seconds after Last Command. Changing these settings adjusts when the keyword needs to be said in relation to the command.

Under the Keyword Is pop-up menu is a text field containing the keyword. You can change the keyword from its default of "computer" to something else by typing it in this field.

To turn off continuous listening, select the Listen Only While Key Is Pressed option.

Upon Recognition options

By default, when a command has been recognized, Mac OS X plays a sound called Whit. (It sounds like an extremely short whistle.) The Speak Command Acknowledgement option enables you to set up Mac OS X to speak aloud the action you have just commanded, so if you say, "Open iTunes," your Mac responds with "opening iTunes." This is a cool way to interact with your computer, although it can become tiresome.

The Play This Sound pop-up menu enables you choose from a range of sound effects to replace Whit. Aside from Whit and Single Click, all are the same as the system alerts found in the Sound system preference. Be careful not to choose the same sound effect as your system alert, which can lead to confusion. You also have the option of None, which turns off the audible feedback that a command is recognized.

Using the Speech Feedback window

When you turn on speech recognition, a small round window appears, as shown in Figure 8.7. This is the Speech Feedback window. This is an unusual window in many respects: It has no associated menu bar; it has no Minimize, Close, or Zoom icon buttons; and it floats above all other windows.

Getting to know the Speech Feedback window

The Speech Feedback window provides several visual clues regarding speech recognition:

- **Attention mode:** The top half of the feedback window contains an icon of an old-fashioned microphone. This icon indicates whether the Mac is standing by, actively listening to, or recognizing commands. The microphone icon has the following states: not listening, listening, and hearing.

  - **Not listening:** If the small microphone icon is grayed out, speech recognition is not currently listening for commands.

  - **Listening (but not hearing):** If the small microphone icon turns solid black, it is actively listening, but not currently hearing a command.

  - **Hearing a command:** If you see small arrowheads moving toward the microphone icon, speech recognition is currently hearing a command (usually because you are talking).

- **Listening method:** The middle section of the Speech Feedback window indicates how you can make the computer switch from not listening to listening mode. By default, it shows Esc, which indicates that you must press Esc before or while speaking. You also may see the name of the word you must speak to activate listening mode.

- **Loudness:** The four colored bars at the bottom of the Speech Feedback window measure the loudness of your voice. In use, there seems to be little relationship between loudness and successful speech recognition (assuming, of course, that your voice is loud enough to be heard at all). One bar indicates that you're speaking quietly; a blue bar and one or two green bars means you're speaking at a moderate volume; these three bars plus a red bar indicate that you're speaking very loudly (probably shouting). Apple recommends that you speak loudly enough to have green bars appear, but not so loud that the red bar appears.

- **Recognition:** When speech recognizes a command that you speak, it displays the corresponding command in a yellow tag above the Speech Feedback window. The displayed command may not completely match the command you uttered, because speech recognition offers a degree of flexibility when understanding what you speak. For example, if you say, "Close window," the feedback window displays "Close This Window." If speech recognition has a response to your command, it displays it in a help tag below the feedback window. (Chapter 7 explains help tags.)

Using Speech Feedback window controls

At the bottom of the Speech Feedback window is an icon pop-up menu, indicated by a small downward-facing triangle. Clicking this icon pop-up menu reveals two menu options:

- **Open Speech Commands Window:** Choosing this option opens a palette displaying all the available speech commands, arranged by category.

- **Speech Preferences:** Choosing this option takes you to the Speech system preference.

Minimizing the Speech Feedback window

As noted earlier, the Speech Feedback window is slightly odd in that it does not have a Minimize icon button. However, you can minimize it to the Dock by double-clicking the window or by speaking the command "Minimize Speech Feedback window."

While sitting in the Dock, the Speech Feedback window continues to offer much the same functionality as before. You continue to press Esc (or press the appropriate key or speak the appropriate command) to activate speech recognition, and the minimized feedback window displays the same symbols for speech recognition as does its regular version. Two notable differences are that it no longer displays help tags containing recognized commands, and because it is minimized, you can no longer access its pop-up menu. It's also worth noting that because it is smaller when minimized, you may no longer be able to as clearly identify the different feedback states.

Opening the feedback window from the Dock and returning it to the main part of the interface is easy: Simply click it in the Dock, or right-click or Control+click it and choose Open Speech Feedback from the contextual menu. Alternatively you can speak the command "Open Speech Feedback window."

Investigating the Speech Commands window

The Speech Commands window provides a list of all your recently spoken commands and the responses to them; it also displays a list of the commands you can speak in the current context. You access this window by clicking the icon pop-up menu (the arrow icon) at the bottom of the Speech Feedback window and choosing Open Speech Commands Window. Fittingly, you also can open the Speech Commands window by saying the command "Open Speech Commands window."

The tools offered by the Speech Commands window make it a great tool for learning what you can do with the speech function of your Mac.

The commands you have recently spoken appear in bold at the top of the Speech Commands window, and any responses appear below in plain text. The bottom part of the window displays the commands available in the current context. The list is organized into these categories:

- **Current application:** This category appears only if the active application has its own speakable commands. For example, if Mail is the active application, the first menu option in Commands is Mail.

- **Address Book:** In this category, you find commands relating to your contacts. As well as with Address Book, these commands interact with Mail and iChat.

- **Speakable Items:** The items in this category are available no matter which application is currently active.

- **Application Switching:** The commands in this category enable you to move between applications. This also contains commands for opening and quitting applications used by Mac OS X.

Each category has a disclosure triangle that can be used to hide or show the various commands contained within each category. You can resize the two parts of the Speech Commands window by dragging the drag handle located between the two windows (identified as a horizontal gray bar with a small gray thumb in the middle.) You also can add extra speakable commands to this window, as I explain shortly.

Specifying active commands

The Speech Commands window organizes commands into groups (known as *command sets*). You can choose which groups of commands Mac OS X listens for by going to the Commands subpane in the Speech system preference's Speech Recognition pane. The default command sets are Address Book, Global Speakable Items, Application Specific Items, Application Switching, Front Window, and Menu Bar. By default, Front Window and Menu Bar are turned off; the others are turned on.

To choose commands by group from this subpane, follow these steps:

1. **Use the On option for each command set in the Select a Command Set list to select or deselect command sets.** Selecting an option activates a particular command set. Note that if you want to activate the Front Window and Menu Bar command sets, the Enable Access for Assistive Devices option in the Universal Access system preference must be enabled.

2. **Configure global speakable items.** Select the Global Speakable Items command set in the list, and click Configure. This brings up a dialog box with the Speak Command Names Exactly as Written option. If selected, this option requires the speaker to use the exact name of the command. This option is selected by default, which improves accuracy and system speed. Deselecting this option requires Mac OS X to try to understand variations of the command so you can speak more naturally.

3. **Click OK to continue.**

Note that you also can configure the Address Book command set. Select that command set, and click Configure. A list of all the names in your Address Book appears. Deselect any names that you don't want to be recognized when you speak as names in the Address Book for use in Address Book, iCal, iChat, and Mail.

Setting up the Text to Speech option

Text to Speech is the other half of the conversation, where the Mac talks to you. Computer speech has come along in leaps and bounds in recent years, and if your last memory of computer speech is a monotone robotic voice droning on, you're in for a pleasant surprise.

You can investigate the different vocal options for Mac OS X by going to the Text to Speech pane in the Speech system preference. Here, you can specify what voice to use, choose the speed at which Mac OS X speaks, and define what, when, and how things are spoken. You can determine alert options, choose from a built-in list of alerts, and even add your own phrases. There's plenty of room for customization: You can set different voices for alerts than normal speech and specify a time delay. There are even options for speaking text, as well as the date and time.

More than a dozen voices are included with Mac OS X. But note that some are more advanced than others. Each one is given a name, and Alex is the most advanced so far for American English. This is the default voice and by far the clearest and most adept at speaking. Still, you have several voices to choose from, both male and female.

But, as the game show host liked to say, "Wait! There's more!" Click Customize to get a settings sheet with a longer list of voices, including a set of comic-effect novelty voices such as Trinoids and Zarvox. You can play any selected voice by clicking the Play button in the settings sheet. Select the check boxes to the left of the voice names to include them in the pane's list, and deselect the voices' check boxes to remove them from the pane's list. Then press OK to add them to the System Voice pop-up menu.

New Feature

Mac OS X Lion's list of voices has expanded considerably, to several dozen. Plus, voices are available for more than a dozen languages, so they speak more correctly for those languages than the previous English-oriented voices did. (Note that these foreign-language voices are often hard to understand when speaking English.) Most of these new voices are not automatically installed with Mac OS X Lion, so if you select any of them, you will get a prompt asking if you want to download the voices over an Internet connection. ∎

You also can adjust the rate at which each voice speaks, changing how it sounds. Follow these steps to change the voice and adjust the rate at which Mac OS X talks to you in the Text to Speech pane:

1. **Select a voice from the System Voice pop-up menu.**

2. **Click Play to hear what the voice sounds like.** Mac OS X speaks a single sentence randomly picked from a selection. If you choose another voice before the sentence has finished, Mac OS X starts another random sentence in the desired voice. Click Stop or wait for the sentence to end.

3. **Adjust the speaking rate.** You can speed up the rate at which a voice talks by moving the Speaking Rate slider to the right; moving it to the left slows the rate at which a voice talks.

Selecting text-to-speech options

Below the System Voice pop-up menu are several options that you can use to customize how speech is used by Mac OS X.

Announce When Alerts Are Displayed option

Selecting the Announce When Alerts Are Displayed option has Mac OS X read aloud system alerts. Click Set Alert Options to bring up a settings sheet where you can select a separate voice from the system voice to speak alerts.

The Phrase pop-up menu enables you to choose how the alert is phrased. You have these choices:

- **Application Name:** This option has Mac OS X inform you which application has an alert.
- **Next in the Phrase List:** This option moves through a set of phrases.
- **Random in the Phrase List:** This option picks random phrases from the phrase list.
- **Phrase List:** This option enables you to set a particular phrase from the phrase list. The options are Alert!, Attention!, Excuse Me!, and Pardon Me!.
- **Edit Phrase List:** This option brings up the Alert Phrases dialog box. Click Add and type a phrase that you want Mac OS X to speak during an alert. You can remove alerts from the list by selecting them and clicking Remove.

You can use the Delay slider to set a delay between 0 and 60 seconds between when the alert appears onscreen and when Mac OS X speaks it.

In the settings sheet, click Play to test your options. Click Cancel to undo your changes or OK to confirm them and return to the Text to Speech pane.

Announce When an Application Requires Your Attention option

Selecting the Announce When an Application Requires Your Attention option causes Mac OS X to speak when an application requires your attention. This verbal alert supplements Mac OS X's usual alert method: an application icon in the Dock bouncing up and down.

Speak Selected Text When the Key Is Pressed option

Select the Speak Selected Text When the Key Is Pressed option to enable a key combination that, when pressed, causes Mac OS X to speak whatever text is currently highlighted. (The default shortcut is Shift+Option+⌘+V.) Click the Change Key button to open a settings sheet asking you to enter a key combination. Hold down one or more modifier keys (Control, Option, Shift, and ⌘) and press the desired key to set the command. For example, you might choose Control+Option+S. Now, when you highlight a piece of text in Mac OS X, pressing this key combination causes Mac OS X to read the text aloud.

Note

You also can have Mac OS X read text by using Mac OS X services that some applications support. In TextEdit, for example, you can right-click or Control+click a highlighted piece of text and choose Speech ➪ Start Speaking from the contextual menu to have Mac OS X read aloud the highlighted text. (Chapter 12 covers services.) ■

Open Date & Time Preferences button

You can click the Open Date & Time Preferences button next to the To Have Clock Announce the Time label to make Mac OS X speak the date and time. Clicking it takes you to the Date & Time system preference (see Chapter 28). Go to its Clock pane, and select the Announce the Time option. A pop-up menu enables you to choose between On the Hour, On the Half Hour, and On the Quarter Hour. Click Customize Voice to choose the audio style with which you would like the time announced. (The options are the same as for system alerts, described earlier.)

Open Universal Access Preferences button

The final option in the Text to Speech pane in the Speech system preference—the Open Universal Access Preferences button—takes you to the Universal Access system preference. From there, you can enable VoiceOver (as explained earlier in the chapter) or—from the Seeing pane—click the Open VoiceOver Utility button to further customize voice settings of Mac OS X.

Setting Up the VoiceOver Utility

The VoiceOver Utility is something of an oddity in Mac OS X. In many ways, it is an extension of the Universal Access system preference (described in the beginning of this chapter), although in other ways it is clearly an application in its own right.

VoiceOver, as explained earlier, is a technology that enables Mac OS X to read aloud whatever is on the screen, under the pointer, or under the VoiceOver window (a rectangular window that appears over items onscreen).

The VoiceOver Utility enables you to fine-tune almost every aspect of VoiceOver, including the amount of punctuation it interacts with, how it navigates applications and web pages, the visual effects that accompany it, and even how it interacts with a Braille display (if one is attached to your Mac).

The VoiceOver Utility application is in the Utilities folder; go there quickly by pressing Shift+⌘+U and then double-clocking the application's icon. You also can open it from the Seeing pane of the Universal Access system preference.

Adjusting the General settings

Click General in the list to the left to access the General pane.

Greeting options

Here you can change the VoiceOver message that greets you when you log in. By default, this welcomes you to Mac OS X and informs you that VoiceOver is running; it also may tell you that you can access help by pressing Control+Option+H. You can change this message to anything you want by editing the Speak the Following Greeting after Login text field.

You also can have this message appear when VoiceOver starts by selecting the Display Welcome Dialog Box when VoiceOver Starts option.

Portable Preferences

The portable preferences capability lets you take your VoiceOver settings with you via an external disk. This could be an external hard disk or, more commonly, a USB flash drive. To set up portable preferences, attach an external storage device and click Set Up, choose File ➪ Set Up Portable Preferences, or press Shift+⌘+V. Select the desired storage device in the settings sheet, and click OK.

Now the settings you made in the VoiceOver Utility are saved to the external storage device as well. When you plug this device into another Mac, that Mac automatically asks if you would like to use portable preferences. Click Yes so you can use all your settings on that computer, without having to set everything up from scratch. Note that those preferences are available to the other Mac as long as that storage device is attached to it.

Allow VoiceOver to Be Controlled with AppleScript option

Selecting the Allow VoiceOver to Be Controlled with AppleScript option enables AppleScript to control VoiceOver. Chapter 13 has more information on how you can use AppleScript to interact with Mac OS X.

Adjusting the Verbosity settings

VoiceOver is, by nature, quite verbose. Put simply, it likes to talk. The VoiceOver Utility enables you to fine-tune, almost to a granular level, how much VoiceOver talks and the kind of things it talks about. Clicking the Verbosity option in the list brings up five subpanes: Speech, Braille, Text, Announcements, and Hints.

New Feature

The Speech subpane was named General in previous versions of Mac OS X, and the Braille subpane is new to Mac OS X Lion. ∎

Speech subpane

In the General subpane of the Verbosity pane is the Default Speech Verbosity pop-up menu. It is set to High by default, but it also has Medium and Low settings.

Clicking the disclosure triangle to the pop-up menu's right reveals exactly what each of the settings has for every part of Mac OS X. You also can set different levels of verbosity for different Mac OS X controls by choosing an option for a specific control in its Verbosity pop-up menu, as shown in Figure 8.8; the options are Default, Low, Medium, High, and Custom. Choosing Default has the control's verbosity match that in the Default Speech Verbosity pop-up menu. Choosing Custom brings up a settings sheet with options for each individual item spoken by that control.

You can fine-tune the verbosity of Mac OS X. You can do this across the board or to an extremely granular level.

Braille subpane

In the Braille subpane of the Verbosity pane is the Default Braille Verbosity pop-up menu, which works just like Default Speech Verbosity in the Speech pane, except it affects the feedback presented via Braille readers attached to the Mac.

Text subpane

In the Text subpane of the Verbosity pane is a series of pop-up menus that enable you to adjust various aspects of VoiceOver when you are working with text. You can change the way text-to-speech handles punctuation, typing, text cursor location, text attributes, misspelled words, links, numbers, capital letters, deleting text, and word separation. Each pop-up menu has several options.

Announcements subpane

VoiceOver announces various aspects of Mac OS X. The Announcements subpane in the Verbosity pane contains a set of options that can increase the number of announcements. These are the options:

- Announce When Mouse Cursor Enters a Window (*mouse cursor* means the pointer)
- Announce When a Modifier Key Is Pressed
- Announce When the Caps Lock Key Is Pressed
- Speak Header When Navigating Across a Table Row
- Automatically Speak Text in Dialog Boxes
- Use Phonetics

New Feature

The Use Phonetics option is new to Mac OS X Lion. It has Mac OS X speak words when it encounters individual letters, such as "a alpha" or "t tango" when, for example, it sees *a* or *t* alone. ∎

This subpane has several other controls:

- **When Status Text Changes Under VoiceOver Cursor pop-up menu:** The options are Play Tone, Speak Text (the default), and Do Nothing.

- **When Progress Indicator Changes Under VoiceOver Cursor pop-up menu:** The options are Play Tone (the default), Speak Update, and Do Nothing.

- **Speak Size and Position In pop-up menu:** The options are Inches (the default), Millimeters, and Pixels.

- **Speak Text under Mouse After Delay slider:** Use the slider to set how long VoiceOver waits to speak the text under the mouse or touchpad pointer's current location.

Hints pane

VoiceOver gives several hints relating to items under the VoiceOver cursor. The Speak Instructions for Using the Item in the VoiceOver Cursor option (selected by default) activates these instructions. The When an Item Has a Help Tag pop-up menu enables you to choose from the following options: Do Nothing, Speak Notification, and Speak Help Tag (the default). The final option is a slider marked Speak Hints After Delay, with options from Short to Long.

Adjusting the Speech settings

The Speech pane in the VoiceOver Utility dialog box enables you to fine-tune the voices used by Mac OS X. Click the Speech item in the list on the left to access the settings; it has two subpanes: Voices and Pronunciation.

Voices subpane

The Voices subpane has several options:

- **Mute Speech:** This option enables you to silence the speech.

- **Default:** Here, you set the default options for how Mac OS X speaks. The Voice pop-up menu lets you choose the default voice, and the fields in the same row enable you to choose the rate, pitch, volume, and intonation values; if you change the voice, these other settings stick, rather than reset for the new voice. If you click the disclosure triangle next to Default, you get the same options for several other categories of speaking: Content, Status, Type, Attributes, and VoiceOver Menu.

Pronunciation subpane

The Pronunciation subpane enables you to substitute spoken terms for specific text, such as acronyms (to pronounce NATO as "nay-toh," not "en-ay-tee-oh," for example) and messaging symbology (called *emoticons*) such as ;) ("wink").

You can change the text spoken for any of the items in the list by clicking the text in the Substitution column. You can add new substitutions by clicking the + icon button and entering the details in the appropriate columns. Clicking the – icon button enables you to remove a selected substitution from the list.

Adjusting Navigation settings

The Navigation pane of the VoiceOver Utility enables you to adjust how the VoiceOver cursor moves around the screen. The following controls are available:

- **Initial Position of VoiceOver Cursor pop-up menu:** Two options are available in this pop-up menu. The default is Keyboard Focused Item (meaning where the text cursor is), or you can choose First Item in Window.

- **Keyboard Focus Follows VoiceOver Cursor option.**

- **VoiceOver Cursor Follows Keyboard option.**

- **Insertion Point Follows VoiceOver Cursor option.**

- **VoiceOver Cursor Follows Insertion Point option.**

- **Mouse Pointer pop-up menu:** This pop-up menu lets you specify how the mouse or touchpad pointer interacts with the VoiceOver cursor: The options are Ignores VoiceOver Cursor, Follows VoiceOver Cursor, and Moves VoiceOver Cursor.

- **Allow Cursor Wrapping option:** If selected, this option specifies that the pointer should be able to move off the side of the screen and appear on the other side. The pointer can wrap horizontally, and vertically, in a continuous loop.

- **Skip Redundant Labels option.** This option has the VoiceOver cursor skip duplicate labels in dialog boxes and so on.

- **Automatically Interact When Using Tab Key option:** This means to automatically follow the screen's area of focus as it changes as the user presses the Tab key to move from control to control; you don't have to press Control+Option+↓ to manually shift the VoiceOver cursor focus as is the default.

- **Enable Fast Searching option:** This option lets you move more quickly to other elements onscreen. In the adjacent pop-up menu, choose Left Command Key or Right Command Key to set which ⌘ key is used to invoke fast search. Then use that ⌘ key with the first letter of the desired control name to jump to it. For example, to jump to the URL field, with Left Command Key enabled, press ⌘+U to jump to that field (or at least the next field whose name begins with *U*.) Note that the left ⌘ key is the one to the left of the spacebar, and the right ⌘ key is the one to the right of the spacebar.

New Feature
The Enable Fast Searching option is new to Mac OS X Lion. ∎

Adjusting Web settings

You can adjust how VoiceOver interacts with web pages (spelled by Apple as "webpages" in the VoiceOver Utility) several ways, using the Web pane's three subpanes: Navigation, Page Loading, and Web Rotor.

New Feature

The Web pane in Mac OS X Lion has been divided into three subpanes, the Enable Live Regions option is new, the option to have a verbal cue when a web page loads is new, and the list of Web Rotor options has been expanded. ∎

Navigation subpane

The options in this subpane are as follows:

- **Navigate Webpages By option:** You have two options: You can either navigate by DOM Order (DOM means Document Object Model, a technical standard for web pages' internal organization), which uses the layout of a web page to determine what objects are grouped together; or you can use Grouping Items, which moves the VoiceOver cursor from one group of information to the next, such as from paragraph to paragraph.

- **When Navigating Web Tables option:** You have two options: The first is to group items within the table; the second is to speak column and row numbers.

- **Navigate Images pop-up menu:** This pop-up menu offers the choices of Never, With Descriptions (the default option), and Always.

- **Enable Live Regions option:** If selected, this option has VoiceOver speak any live region it encounters on web pages, rather than the specific regions set up in the Web Rotor subpane. (A live region is a dynamically updated part of a web page, such as for stock prices or sports scores.)

Page Loading subpane

The options in this subpane are as follows:

- **When Loading a New Webpage option:** Three options are available here: Speak Webpage Summary, Move the VoiceOver Cursor to It, and Automatically Speak the Webpage. The third option is available only if the Move the VoiceOver Cursor to It option is selected.

- **When a Webpage Loads pop-up menu:** Here you choose what sound plays as a web page is loading to give you an audible clue that a page is in fact loading: Speak Progress, Play Tone, and Do Nothing.

Web Rotor subpane

This subpane lists various types of live regions—automatically updated parts of web pages—that you can then enable to have VoiceOver read and disable to have VoiceOver skip. (If you enable the Enable Live Regions option in the Navigation subpane, they are all read aloud by VoiceOver.)

The options are Links, Headings, Form Controls, Web Spots, Tables, Landmarks, Auto Web Spots, Frames, Buttons, Text Fields, Images, Lines, Lists, Live Regions, Non-Visited Links, Visited Links, Static Text, Radio Groups, and Checkboxes. You can reorder these options, which determines the reading order by VoiceOver, by selecting an item and pressing ⌘+↑ to move it up the list and ⌘+↓ to move it down the list.

Adjusting Sound settings

You can choose from three options in the Sound Settings pane of the VoiceOver Utility:

- **Mute Sound Effects option:** Selecting this option turns off all sound effects other than VoiceOver.

- **Enable Positional Audio option:** This option (selected by default) enables you to use dual speakers, or headphones, to hear audio positioned in different locations.

- **Output Device pop-up menu:** This pop-up menu lets you select the audio device that VoiceOver's speech is played by, if you have more than one device. By default, it is set to Built-in Output, using the audio device selected in the Sound system preference (see Chapter 28).

New Feature
The ability to choose a separate output device for VoiceOver audio is new to Mac OS X Lion. ■

Adjusting the Visuals settings

The Visuals pane has five subpanes, each offering different ways that VoiceOver displays information on the screen. Customizing these sections can be extremely useful for those with limited sight abilities.

VoiceOver Cursor subpane

The controls here enable you to adjust how the VoiceOver cursor appears on the screen:

- **Show VoiceOver Cursor option:** This option enables you to turn on or off the VoiceOver cursor (the rectangular outline that surrounds onscreen items being read aloud).

- **VoiceOver Cursor Magnification slider:** This slider enables you to magnify the VoiceOver cursor and the contents displayed within it. Moving the slider to the right sets it to the Large setting, which can make the VoiceOver cursor extremely useful for people who see partially.

- **When Reading Text, Move VoiceOver Cursor By pop-up menu:** This pop-up menu has two options: Sentence and Word. By default, the VoiceOver cursor moves by each sentence that is read, but here you can tell VoiceOver to move by each individual word.

Caption Panel subpane

The caption panel is a dark gray rounded rectangle (normally positioned on the bottom left of the screen) that provides information regarding the VoiceOver caption, such as a description of the current action. (Figure 8.2, near the beginning of this chapter, shows an example of the caption panel.) Several settings here control the caption panel:

- **Show Caption Panel option:** This option shows or hides the caption panel. It is selected by default.
- **Caption Panel Font Size slider:** Moving this slider to the right increases the size of the text in the caption panel.
- **Rows in Caption Panel:** By default, the caption panel has two rows of text, with overflow text indicated with ellipses (...). Moving this slider to the right enables you to expand the caption panel to accommodate up to 10 rows of text.
- **Caption Panel Transparency slider:** Moving this slider farther to the right makes the caption panel more opaque and thus less obtrusive.

Braille Panel subpane

A refreshable Braille display can be attached to a Mac, and VoiceOver automatically sends information from the screen to that display. The Braille panel also displays this information on the screen. Several options here relate to the Braille panel:

- **Show Braille Panel pop-up menu:** The options here are Automatic, On, and Off.
- **Braille Font Color pop-up menu:** The color is yellow by default, but this pop-up menu enables you to select from six colors.
- **Braille Panel Font Size slider:** This slider enables you to adjust the size of the Braille panel's font. Move the slider to the right to make the font larger, and move it to the left to make the font smaller.
- **Braille Panel Transparency slider:** Moving this slide to the right decreases the opacity of the Braille panel, making it more transparent.

Touch subpane

This subpane appears only if you have a gesture-savvy touchpad connected to your Mac. It has just one option, the Background Transparency slider, which you use to decrease or increase the opacity of the dimmed area around your touchpad pointer. The more transparent, the easier it is to see the area surrounding the pointer location, and the less transparent, the easier it is to see where your finger is on the touchpad relative to the screen.

New Feature

The Touch subpane is new to Mac OS X Lion. ■

Menus subpane

The options in this subpane adjust the display of the VoiceOver Help menu (accessed by clicking Control+Option+H when VoiceOver is running):

- **VoiceOver Menus Font Size slider:** Moving this slider to the right makes the VoiceOver menu larger.

- **VoiceOver Menus Transparency slider:** Moving this slider to the right increases the transparency of the VoiceOver Menu, making it less obtrusive.

Adjusting the Commanders settings

The Commanders pane lets you map commands to the touchpad, numeric keypad, and keyboard. Use it to attach commonly used commands (such as Go To Desktop, Open Item Chooser, and open specific applications) to specific keys. This is a useful feature that simplifies complex commands by assigning them to single keys or key combinations.

There are four subpanes: Trackpad, NumPad, Keyboard, and Quick Nav.

New Feature
The Trackpad and Quick Nav subpanes are new to Mac OS X Lion. ■

Trackpad subpane

The new Trackpad subpane appears only if you have a gesture-savvy touchpad connected to your Mac. It controls how VoiceOver works with your touchpad. Note that it works only with newer touchpads in recent MacBoooks and the Apple Magic Trackpad, not on two-finger-only touchpads in 2007 and earlier MacBooks. These are its options:

- **Enable Trackpad Commander:** If selected, this option enables the use of gestures to control VoiceOver. Press Control+Option to enable the use of gestures, and rotate two fingers to switch among the types of VoiceOver actions. The options vary based on what type of user interface element you are over and thus what options are available. For example, if you select the Navigation action, your touchpad gestures move among elements, but if you select Words or Characters, the gestures invokes editing and selection functions for textual elements. Figure 8.9 shows the gesture-based VoiceOver action selection that rotating the two fingers displays onscreen.

- **Automatically Select Items in Lists and Tables:** If selected, VoiceOver automatically selects the last item in a table or list when you navigate to it.

- **Pause Speech When Not Touching the Trackpad:** If selected, moving your finger off the touchpad stops VoiceOver from speaking until you touch the touchpad again.

- **Scroll Gesture Moves Content Instead of Scroll Bar:** Selected by default, this option has the scroll gesture move the content within the current area of focus, rather than move it out of view, as is normally the case when you scroll with a mouse's scroll wheel or drag a window's scroll bars.

- **Assign Commands button:** This opens a settings sheet where you can add a modifier key (Control, Option, Shift, or ⌘) to be held when you use various touchpad gestures. Doing so makes it harder to accidentally navigate or act on the screen through inadvertent gestures.

FIGURE 8.9

The Commanders pane's Trackpad subpane in the VoiceOver Utility with the gesture-based VoiceOver action selector displayed

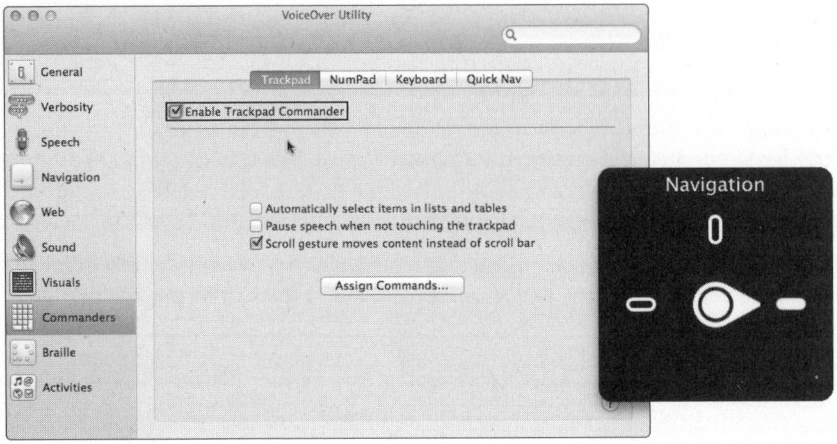

NumPad subpane

The NumPad subpane contains a list of commands that are mapped to the numeric keypad (the numeric keys found to the right of Apple extended keyboards; these keys are not present on Apple MacBooks nor on many Mac keyboards). You must select the Enable NumPad Commander option to enable the mapping capability.

The list of commands in the subpane shows what command VoiceOver performs when you press the appropriate key. VoiceOver commands are available for more than just the regular keyboard keys. You can see the assignments for specific modifier combinations using the unnamed pop-up menu to the right of the Enable NumPad Commander option to choose from these modifier options: Command (the⌘ key), Option, Control, Shift, and NumPad Zero (the numeric keypad's 0 key). When you choose an option, the list of VoiceOver command assignments changes to those using that particular modifier key.

You also can replace any of the default commands used by the NumPad Commander with your own. Each command listed is actually a pop-up menu (indicated by the small down-pointing arrow to the right of each command). Then navigate through the pop-up menu to find the desired replacement command.

Note

You cannot use mouse keys (a feature described earlier in this chapter) while using the NumPad Commander. ∎

Keyboard subpane

The Keyboard Commander works in much the same way as the NumPad Commander. Selecting the Enable Keyboard Command option at the top of the subpane enables the Keyboard Commander.

One key difference is that the keyboard commands must be used with a modifier key. This is because you are likely to need the keyboard's letters for general tasks. Because you also are likely to require regular keyboard commands, complete with modifier keys, the Keyboard Commander distinguishes between the Mac keyboard's two Option keys, on either side of the spacebar. (Normally, Mac OS X doesn't care which Option key you press; it treats them as if they were the same key.) You select which Option key the Keyboard Commander uses by selecting one of the options from Use options: Left Option Key, Right Option Key, and Both Option Keys. If you select Right Option Key, pressing the right Option key invokes a VoiceOver keyboard shortcut, while pressing the left Option key invokes Mac OS X's or the application's normal keyboard shortcut using Option.

New Feature

In Mac OS X Lion, you can choose Both Option Keys, which means both Option keys must be pressed to invoke the VoiceOver keyboard shortcut. ■

The number of keyboard commands in the Keyboard Commander is much more limited than in the NumPad Commander. However, you can add new keyboard commands using the + icon button in the bottom left of the subpane.

Quick Nav subpane

The new Quick Nav Commander works in much the same way as the NumPad Commander and Keyboard Commander, except it lets you assign commands to single characters as well as use the arrow and other navigation-oriented keys. Selecting the Enable Quick Nav option at the top of the subpane enables the Quick Nav Commander.

These options are available:

- **Allow Toggling of Quick Nav Using Left and Right Arrow Keys:** If selected, pressing both ← and → simultaneously toggles Quick Nav on and off, rather than needing to use the VoiceOver Utility.

- **Enable Single-Key Webpage Navigation when Using Quick Nav:** If selected, you can press a single letter to invoke a VoiceOver shortcut.

- **Assign Commands button:** Clicking this button opens a settings sheet that displays the VoiceOver commands associated with arrow keys and individual characters. You can't change the arrow key assignments, but you can change those for letters and other characters by choosing Letters from the pop-up menu at the upper right. Select a letter whose VocieOver action you want to change, and click the reveal icon to its right to get a hierarchical list of actions to select for that character.

Setting up Braille

Braille converts text shown in VoiceOver into a form readable by touch—human touch, that is. Many Braille readers are available for Mac OS X. If you attach a compatible Braille display to the Mac, it is detected automatically, and you can adjust its settings in the VoiceOver Utility's Braille pane. The Braille pane has two subpanes: Layout and Displays.

Layout subpane

These settings are available in the Layout subpane of the Braille pane:

- **Braille Display indicator:** The model of your connected display appears here.
- **Braille Translation section:** This section has three options on how certain items are converted to Braille:
  - **Braille Translation pop-up menu:** The default option is English (the American version). This pop-up menu shows additional languages installed in Mac OS X.
  - **Show Contracted Braille option:** Contracted Braille is a set of about two dozen words represented by a single symbol each, for faster communication.
  - **Show Eight-Dot Braille:** If selected, characters use the extended form of Braille rather than the traditional six-dot cell matrix. The eight-dot method allows for single-cell display of extended characters, whereas the six-dot method does not.
  - **Use Dots 7 and 8 to Indicate Cursor option:** This raises dots 7 and 8 in the Braille reader to indicate where the VoiceOver cursor is.
- **Status Cells section:** This section has three options that control how status cells are used: Show General Display Status, Show Text Style, and Show Extended Text Style.
- **Show Status On The option:** Two options are available: Left and Right.
- **Display Alert Messages:** This slider controls how long alerts display on the Braille reader. Slide all the way to the left to turn off the display of alerts.

New Feature

The Show Eight-Dot Braille option and Display Alert Messages slider are new to Mac OS X Lion. ■

Displays subpane

Any Braille displays attached to your Mac are listed here. If a display is connected via USB, it is automatically connected and listed. However, if your Braille display operates via Bluetooth, you can connect it by using the following method:

1. **Make sure the Braille display is discoverable.** Consult the instructions with the display to discover how to put it in discoverable mode.
2. **Click the + icon button.**
3. **Find the device.** A dialog box appears that searches for all available Bluetooth devices. When the Braille display appears in the list, click it.
4. **Select the Remember This Device option.** If you want Mac OS X to remember the device so it automatically reconnects in the future, make sure you select this option.
5. **Click Select.**

Note

You can connect multiple USB Braille readers to a Mac but just one Bluetooth reader. (Chapter 28 explains Bluetooth device setup in more detail; the process is the same for Braille displays as for other devices.) ■

Setting up Activities

The Activities pane lets you choose distinct VoiceOver settings for different activities. For example, you may have one activity set for browsing the web and another for working on business documents. Click the + icon button to add an activity (and double-click its name to edit it). Select an activity and click the − icon button to delete it.

As Figure 8.10 shows, the Activities pane has two clusters of controls. One control lets you change the verbosity and voice for the specific activity, which provides handy context as to what you are doing at the moment, and it adjusts the level of feedback for the activity at hand. You can also enable hot spots (covered earlier in this chapter).

The Activities pane of the VoiceOver Utility lets you set up different VoiceOver settings for different activities.

The other control gives you most of the fine-grained controls available in the various VocieOver Utility panes that you can apply to each activity individually. Click the disclosure triangle to the right of the Hot Spots option to reveal the 10 controls, as shown in Figure 8.10. Select the controls you want to customize, and click Set for each in turn. Doing so opens the appropriate VoiceOver Utility panes for that option.

The final Activities pane control is the Automatically Use This Activity For pop-up menu. It lets you have the current activity automatically enabled when the application selected in this pop-up menu is launched.

New Feature
The ability to set up separate activity settings is new to Mac OS X Lion. ∎

Summary

Universal Access lets you interact with Mac OS X in a variety of ways. Although primarily designed to help those with impaired sight, hearing, or hand usage, some of these interaction controls can benefit anyone.

For example, for those with visual impairment, the VoiceOver technology enables users to hear what is displayed on the screen, as well as to control output to Braille devices. But it also can give everyone more awareness of alerts. Similarly, options for the hearing impaired provide extra visual feedback for anyone. And controls over keyboard and mouse interactions help not only those with difficulty using keyboards and mice, but also poor typists.

Apple's speech technology lets the Mac both listen to and execute your spoken commands and speaks aloud alerts and user interface elements.

The VoiceOver Utility enables you to fine-tune the VoiceOver text-to-speech technology to your exact needs, with separate groups of settings assignable to specific activities and applications.

Part II

Using Applications and Documents

IN THIS PART

Chapter 9
Working with Applications

Chapter 10
Working with Documents

Chapter 11
Backing Up Files

Chapter 12
Working with Services

Chapter 13
Using AppleScript and Automator

Working with Applications

IN THIS CHAPTER

Installing and removing applications

Opening applications

Using the Launchpad

Understanding applications' user interface elements

Managing multiple open applications

Working with full-screen applications

Quitting applications

Now that you've set up your Mac and become familiar with the Finder, it's time to get down to the business of working with applications and the day-to-day activity of creating, saving, and working with documents.

Most of the time you spend working on your Mac is in the traditional manner: opening applications, creating documents, printing and sharing them, and saving them for future posterity. In this sense, applications are the tools; documents (covered in Chapter 10) are the things you create and share with them.

Although chances are good that you're familiar with the basics of using applications from using a Mac or Windows PC before, Mac OS X Lion does bring a few new approaches to the table that make it worth reviewing how applications work.

Mac OS X includes a huge range of applications, as Chapter 14 covers, but the beauty of computers is that you can install and run programs built by other people. Most applications work the same way in Mac OS X, following Apple's human interface guidelines, but some programs—notably Adobe's Creative Suite and Microsoft's Office—add their own approaches on top of Apple's. But even these applications have the basic Mac OS X application foundation in place.

Mac OS X is a multi-tasking environment, which means you can run several applications at once (both in the foreground and background), switch among them, and share data among them through copy and paste and other mechanisms.

Note

Several terms are used interchangeably by those who produce applications and use them: software, application (and its nickname app), program, utility, tool, and solution. Software is the general term for code that runs on a computer to perform a task, whether in the form of its own application, a plug-in to another application, or a component of the operating system. Application, app, and program all refer to the same thing: software that you think of as collection of related functions, such as iTunes or Photoshop. Utility usually means a specialized program with a small set of functions, often designed to help you prepare for other tasks; examples are Disk Utility and QuickTime Player. Tool is more of a marketing term to describe software, though sometimes people use it to mean software that people use to produce a result (such as making a movie or indexing a book). Solution is purely marketing-speak for software, hardware, and combinations of the two. Note that none of these terms' definitions is exact, so don't worry about trying to differentiate them. ∎

Installing Applications in Mac OS X

Straight out of the box, your Mac has a compelling suite of core applications already installed, including the Safari web browser, Mail e-mail client, Address Book contacts manager, iCal calendar, iChat instant messenger, TextEdit word processor, Time Machine backup tool, and iTunes media manager and player.

Note

New Macs also include Apple's iLife suite (which includes the iPhoto photo management and editing tool, iMovie video-editing tool, and GarageBand music creation and editing tool), although when you upgrade Mac OS X, the iLife versions on your Mac aren't updated along with the operating system. ∎

But chances are good that you'll want other applications to handle other tasks. And you may prefer to use an application other than Apple's, or in addition to Apple's; for example, you may want to use the Mozilla Firefox or Google Chrome browser instead of or in addition to Apple's Safari. So you're likely to buy additional applications.

The applications in Mac OS X are typically stored in one of two folders: Applications or Utilities. You can jump to the Applications folder by choosing Go ➪ Applications or pressing Shift+⌘+A, and you can jump to the Utilities folder by choosing Go ➪ Utilities or pressing Shift+⌘+U. The Utilities folder resides in the Applications folder, so you also can double-click its folder from there. No law says that applications must be in one of these folders, but putting them there does make it easy to find them later.

Installing these other applications is fairly easy, although a few different methods are available.

Installing applications from the Mac App Store

You probably know the iTunes Store for buying music and buying or renting videos. If you have an iPhone, iPad, or iPod Touch, you probably know the Apple App Store for buying iOS apps. Mac OS X has its own Mac App Store, where you can buy applications directly over the Internet. It comes with Mac OS X Lion, but was also added to Mac OS X Snow Leopard via a system update in early 2011, so you likely have seen it already.

The Mac App Store is easily accessible in Mac OS X: Choose ⇨ App Store, or click the App Store icon in the Dock. When the Mac App Store loads, you can search or browse for applications as you would in the iTunes Store or iOS App Store.

To use the App Store, you need an active Internet connection and an account with Apple; if you have an iTunes account (which you likely do for using the iTunes Store or iOS App Store), you can use the same account in the Mac App Store. That charges the purchases to the same credit card as in the iTunes or iOS App Store. If you want to use a separate account, you can do that, too.

Sign in by choosing Store ⇨ Sign In. You also can set up a separate account with different billing information if you prefer; choose Store ⇨ Create Account. (You can't be signed into an account when creating a new one; to sign out of an account, choose Store ⇨ Sign Out.)

When you find an application you want to buy, click its Buy link—which shows the price or the word "Free"—and then confirm your account password when requested. During installation, the Buy link changes to "Installing," as Figure 9.1 shows, and after it's installed, it changes to "Installed." The application is downloaded and installed for you in the Mac OS X Applications folder. That's it!

FIGURE 9.1

Installing an app from the Mac App Store

If you received a redemption code for an application—perhaps from an coupon that came with something you bought elsewhere—or a gift card whose credit you want to use to buy an application, click the Redeem link in the Quick Links pane at the right side of the Mac App Store's main window, then type or paste that code in the Enter Your Gift Card or Other iTunes Code field, then click Redeem. If the code is for a specific application, it begins downloading to your Mac; if the code is for a gift card or other credit, the credit's value is transferred to the App Store account for future purchases.

Note
You can use an application purchased via the App Store on as many as five Macs that are signed in to the same App Store account. (Most applications purchased in other venues limit you to one or two installations.) Go to the Purchases pane (click the Purchases icon button at the top of the App Store window) to see the application you've bought, then click Install on the ones you want to install on a Mac linked to your App Store account. ∎

Installing downloaded applications

Many applications today are available as downloads from the Internet, usually from the developer's website. You purchase the application there, and then you're provided a link to download the installer file onto your Mac. Sometimes, the download happens automatically. The files typically are downloaded to your Downloads folder (choose Go ⇨ Downloads, press Option+⌘+L, or open the folder in the Dock), but sometimes they're placed on the desktop or in another location.

Typically, most applications are delivered as a *disk image* (with a file extension of .dmg, so some people call them *DMG files*) or as a compressed archive (with a file extension of .zip, so most people call them *Zip files*).

Either way, double-click the file to open its contents. You get one of two scenarios:

- Most commonly, you get a draggable application installer file. You drag that file into your Applications folder (or to an alias of that folder that displays in the Finder window containing the draggable installer), and you're done. There's likely a text file called Read Me or Installation Instructions in the window as well, which you should peruse.

- You get an installation package (with the file extension of .pkg), which you double-click to launch. You're then guided through various options in a series of windows. This method is typically used by applications that have configurable options or that make you enter a serial number to use them. In many instances, you're asked to restart the Mac after installing such packaged applications, because they put support files in Mac OS X's various system folders and thus need Mac OS X restarted to have those made active.

Installing applications from disc

Installing an application you buy from a store in a physical package follows essentially the same process as installing a downloaded installer. The only real difference is that the installer file comes on a CD or DVD, which you need to insert on your Mac and open from the desktop or a Finder window's Sidebar. After you've opened the installation window, you choose one of the two options described in the previous section for downloaded installers.

Updating applications

It's a rare application that never changes. Most are upgraded over time, which means buying an upgrade and installing it as you would a new application. But between these paid upgrades are often program *updates*, which fix minor issues or add smaller capabilities than warrant a new payment.

If you bought an application via the Mac App Store, go to the store's Updates pane (click the Updates icon button at the top of the App Store window) to see if any applications have updates and then choose to update any individual one or all of them. If you use an iPhone, iPad, or iPod Touch, this will be a very familiar experience.

Many applications automatically check for updates on their own and then provide an alert when one is available, with a link for you to click to install or download it. Other applications leave the checking to you, usually through a menu option in either the Help menu or in the application's menu (and sometimes in its About window). There's no one standard method for accessing updates, but the ideal is for applications that have automatic updates or let you turn on automatic updates. When you install a new program, hunt around for its update methods so you can be sure to have the latest version at all times for as many applications as possible.

Removing applications

Sooner or later you may decide that you no longer want an application on your Mac. It may have been only a trial application that you have decided not to purchase, or you may have realized that you no longer use the program and want to reclaim the space it takes up on the hard disk.

Removing applications from Mac OS X couldn't be easier. Simply locate the program in the Applications folder and drag it straight to the Trash in the Dock. After emptying the Trash (choose ⇨ Empty Trash), the application is gone for good. As with deleting any item you don't want, be sure that you no longer want to use it before emptying the Trash.

Some programs, such as Microsoft Office and Adobe Creative Suite, come with uninstaller programs that remove all the files associated with an application. If a program has a dedicated uninstaller, run that instead of dragging the files directly to the Trash.

If you are uninstalling your software to reinstall it on another Mac (or on a clean copy of Mac OS X) and that software uses activation to discourage use of pirated copies (such as Adobe Creative Suite, Zevrix LinkOptimizer, and QuarkXPress), be sure to deactivate the software before uninstalling it; otherwise, the software may not run when you reinstall it.

Most applications place other small files in various places on the Mac. Typically, they place files in the Library folder. Subfolders such as Application Support and Preferences are good places to look for support files to delete after you've removed the main application files. These support files are typically small and used only by the application, so leaving them on your Mac isn't typically considered a bad thing (at least not by Apple). You can hunt down these files and move them to the Trash, although you should be careful not to empty the Trash until you're sure that all your other programs run correctly.

Tip

There's a good reason for leaving the support files for a deleted application in the Library folder: If you ever decide to reinstall the program, all your preferences are retained. ∎

Tip

If you install lots of programs and like to keep a clean system, you should invest in a program that specializes in removing the associated clutter created by program installation. Programs like AppZapper (www.appzapper. com) track the files installed by applications and remove them when you delete a program. ∎

Opening Applications

When you want to work with an application, you start, or open, the program. This process also is known as *launching* an application. When you open an application, you can view or edit compatible contents, or you can create new content from scratch.

Often, the content you create in an application can be saved as a document. For example, you can open an application like TextEdit and use it to write a letter; then you can save that letter as a document. You can close the application, shut down the Mac, and then come back another day and reopen the document to continue working on it. (Chapter 10 explains how to work with documents.)

You can launch an application via many different methods:

- **(Apple) menu:** Choose ⌘⇨ Recent Items, and choose an item from the Applications section of the menu. Applications you've opened recently appear, but not others, so this option is limited. Likewise, you can choose a document from the Recent Items submenu to launch its application and then open the document in it.

- **Applications folder:** Locate the program's icon in the Applications folder. Double-click it to launch the application. Alternatively, right-click or Control+click the icon and choose Open from the contextual menu, or you can select the icon and choose File⇨Open or press ⌘+O. You also can drag a compatible document onto the application's icon to open the application and then load the document into it.

- **Dock:** Many applications have a shortcut to them placed in the Dock (and you can add application shortcuts to the Dock, as Chapter 2 explains). Click the Dock icon to launch the application, or right-click or Control+click it and choose Open from the contextual menu. You also can drag a compatible document onto the application's icon to open the application and then load the document into it. Plus, you can click a document from any of the folders in the Dock to launch its application and open the document in it.

- **Finder window:** Go to a document that is associated with the application, double-click the document to launch its application, and then open the document in it. You also can select the document and choose File ➪ Open, press ⌘+O, or right-click or Control+click it and choose Open in its contextual menu.

Tip
To open a document in another application than it is associated with, choose Open With in the contextual menu and choose a different compatible application from the list that appears. To make the change permanent, change the Open With settings in the document's Info window, as Chapter 3 explains. ∎

- **Launchpad:** Open the Launchpad as explained later in this chapter, and then click the application from whatever screen it is in.

- **Spotlight:** Type the name of the application in the Spotlight search (see Chapter 5), and choose the corresponding application from the list of results.

Most people use the Dock and Finder window approaches most often.

When an application launches, its icon usually bounces in the Dock, indicating that the application is launching. After it has launched, the icon stops bouncing. (If the application's icon was already in the Dock, that icon usually begins to bounce when you launch the application.) The application icon can show a glowing blue-and-white sphere underneath to signify that it is an open application and not a shortcut. (You can turn off the bouncing-icon effect for program launch and turn on the indicator sphere, as Chapter 2 explains.)

If you downloaded the application from the Internet, a warning appears. Click Open to run the program. You see this warning only the first time you launch the application. This warning is a security measure designed to confirm that you downloaded the program and are comfortable that the application's origin is one you trust. (See Part IV for more information on Mac OS X security.)

Using and Managing the Launchpad

The Launchpad provides a one-stop shop for all the applications on your Mac, using the concept of home screens popularized on the iPhone, iPod Touch, and iPad. To open the Launchpad, just click its icon in the Dock or use the four-finger pinch gesture on a compatible touchpad (using your thumb and three fingers). Your screen is taken over by a blank background with application icons on it, as Figure 9.2 shows. Click an icon to launch the app.

If you decide not to launch an app, press Esc to close the Launchpad, click an icon in the Dock, or use the four-finger expand gesture (using your thumb and three fingers).

FIGURE 9.2

The Launchpad, with the first home screen showing the Apple-provided Mac OS X applications

New Feature
The Launchpad is new to Mac OS X Lion. ∎

Tip
You also can set up Exposé to open the Launchpad through clicks on corners of the screen. Chapter 2 explains the Exposé feature, and Chapter 28 explains the Mission Control system preference. ∎

The first home screen lists the applications that Apple installs along with Mac OS X. Note that this home screen also has an icon for the Utilities folder; click it to open the folder's contents so you can select one of its apps, as Figure 9.3 shows. (Click outside the folder or press Esc to close it.)

The other home screens list the rest of your applications from the Applications folder, Utilities folder, and folders contained in them (including aliases to folders) in essentially random order. Note that you may see Windows applications listed in addition to Mac OS X applications if you're using a program such as Parallels Desktop or VMware Fusion that lets you run Windows simultaneously with Mac OS X, as Chapter 18 explains.

FIGURE 9.3

Clicking a group in the Launchpad opens it, revealing its application icons.

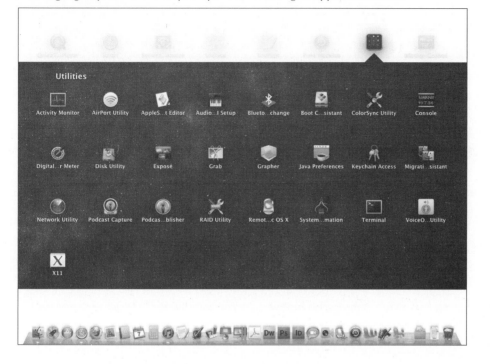

To move to these other home screens, press the → and ← buttons, use your mouse's scroll wheel or scroll ball, or use a touchpad's scroll gesture. (Screens are arranged horizontally, but vertically scrolling the mouse or touchpad is interpreted as a horizontal scroll within the Launchpad. However, the keyboard's ↑ and ↓ keys are ignored.)

You can rearrange applications within and across home screens the same way you do on an iPhone, iPad, or iPod Touch: Drag them to a new location, as shown in Figure 9.4. They insert themselves between two existing applications, causing the affected icons to rearrange themselves so all remain in the invisible grid. When dragging across screens, move the pointer all the way to the edge and wait a second for the screen to slide to reveal the next screen. You can create new screens after the rightmost screen by dragging an application past the current rightmost screen.

To create groups, simply drag an icon over another. A new group appears containing both application icons. You can edit the group name by clicking it and typing a new name. To remove an item from a group, open the group by clicking it and drag the item out of the group. If no application remains in a group, the group is automatically deleted.

FIGURE 9.4

Drag an application icon and move it to a new location to customize the Launchpad's layout.

Tip

If you decide not to open an application, you can quickly close the Launchpad by pressing Esc. ■

Managing Multiple Open Applications

Mac OS X has *preemptive multi-tasking*, which means the operating system can run more than one process (such as an application or various functions within an application) at a time, in a way in which Mac OS X dynamically parcels out chunks of time to the various open application processes so no one process can hog all the resources.

In practice, this means you can have multiple applications running and switch among them easily. But the ability to run multiple programs at once can be disorientating. A stray mouse click can take you from one program to another, bringing its windows to the front and putting the application you were working on to the back. To a complete newcomer, it may appear as if a program has disappeared completely, leaving you confused. Of course, most computer users these days are familiar with the concept of using multiple programs at once, and Mac OS X makes the process as straightforward as possible. Even so, you must get used to having multiple layers of programs and documents open at once; these can lie on top of each other on the desktop, like different paper documents lying on top of each other on your desk.

Fortunately, Mac OS X provides many methods to switch among documents and applications. And Mac OS X features such as Mission Control, App Exposé, and Spaces (covered in Chapter 2) offer you a quick means to organize and access documents and applications on your Mac. Mission Control, for example, lets you see all open applications with their windows and move among them from a common screen. Plus, you can quickly hide open documents and bring them back in an instant using the Dock and Mac OS X's Hide menu option, as described later in this chapter.

Although several programs can run simultaneously (and indeed the Finder is always running), only one application in Mac OS X can control the menu bar at any one time. The application currently in control is called the *active application*, and you can tell which one it is by looking at the menu bar—the menu option next to the menu is the name of the active application. If you click the desktop, the active application is the Finder; when you switch to any other application, the name Finder in the menu bar changes to the name of that application.

Switching among applications

As Chapter 2 explains, all open applications display an icon in the Dock. When you have an application open, you can switch to that application by clicking its icon in the Dock, making it the active application. This is the most straightforward and commonly used method of switching among open applications.

But using the Dock isn't the only method of moving among applications. You also can move from one application to another by clicking in any visible window belonging to that other application. Of course, opening up a new document switches to the application associated with that document (launching it, if necessary, as described earlier in the chapter).

Another way to switch among applications is to use the application switcher, shown in Figure 9.5. This appears over the desktop as a translucent gray window with icons for each running application. Here's how to use the application switcher:

1. **Press ⌘+Tab.** The application switcher opens, with the current application's icon at the far left and the other open applications' icons shown to its right.

2. **Continue holding ⌘.** Now, with each additional press of Tab, the selection moves to the right. You also can use the → and ← keys or the mouse to move through the applications instead of pressing Tab (but keep holding ⌘).

3. **Release ⌘.** When the application you want to switch to is selected, release the ⌘ key. The selected icon's application becomes the active application.

If you decide not to switch to a different application, simply release ⌘.

New Feature

There is no touchpad gesture that opens the application switcher in Mac OS X Lion. The four-finger horizontal swipe that had been used in Mac OS X Snow Leopard now moves you through spaces, as Chapter 2 explains. ∎

FIGURE 9.5

The application switcher appears enabling you to switch from one application to another.

When you switch from one application to another using the application icon in the Dock or the application switcher, all the windows associated with that application come forward as a group, with one window active (meaning you can work in it). The exception is for document windows that are minimized to the Dock; they remain in the Dock. But if all document windows for an application are minimized in the Dock, one of the windows opens as the application comes forward.

If you switch to an application by clicking one of its windows in the desktop or in the Dock, that window becomes active, along with the application.

Using Hide to reduce application clutter

A fast way to get an application out of the way if your screen is too cluttered is to use Mac OS X's Hide capability, which makes the application and its windows disappear. You can access it in several ways:

- Choose Hide from the application menu (for example, iTunes ⇨ Hide).
- Press ⌘+H.
- Right-click or Control+click the icon in the Dock, and choose Hide from the contextual menu.
- Option+click anywhere on the desktop.

If you want to hide everything except the current application, choose Hide Others from the application menu, press Option+⌘+H, or Option+⌘+click the desktop.

To get back a specific hidden application, click its icon in the Dock or use the application switcher. To get back *all* the hidden applications in one fell swoop, choose Show All from the application menu.

Knowing when an application wants your attention

Sometimes, an application running in the background needs your attention. It might be to notify you that it has finished its task, or there may be a dialog box that needs your attention; either way you need to switch to the application, find out what it wants, and deal with it. It may be that a program is quitting and Mac OS X is asking you if you want to save a document first.

Mac OS X has a particular way of attracting your attention (one that has as many fans as detractors): When an application wants your attention, it bounces up and down in the Dock, like an excitable kid in class. It bounces, then sits in the Dock for a moment, and then bounces again. Even if the Dock is minimized, the icon bounces fairly high so it's hard to miss. Ignoring this bouncing Dock icon requires a Herculean effort, and you're better off just dealing with the precocious application, because usually it has a good reason to interrupt you.

Some applications display alerts on the screen instead of using the bounce-icon method, such as reminding you of an appointment. Usually, programs that provide alerts but don't need you to act on them use the alert box method.

Surveying Applications' Controls

Most Mac OS X applications have the same kinds of user interface elements after you've opened them. Apple provides these elements with Mac OS X, so all developers can use them and users get a consistent experience—one of the Mac's hallmarks.

Not all applications use the standard Mac OS X elements; Microsoft insists on bringing over Windows-style controls in its Office, and Adobe Systems has developed two separate visual approaches of its own (one in Creative Suite and one in its Elements series) that it imposes on both Mac OS X and Windows users. Typically, the "foreign" approaches favor cramped, cluttered presentation, obscure icons, and lots and lots of toolbars. But even these variations follow the same basic approaches that Mac OS X offers, so most differences are cosmetic.

Function containers

Of course, every Mac OS X application has its menu bar. And almost every application uses windows for its documents. Chapter 3 explains the common menu options in the menu bar for all applications, and Chapter 4 explains the basic controls in windows. These elements contain functions in a clear location that operate in a consistent manner.

But there are other major containers for functions in applications:

- **Toolbars:** Usually, one or more toolbars contain icon buttons and/or text buttons for quick access to major features. Figure 9.6 shows the Firefox 4 toolbar as an example.

FIGURE 9.6

A toolbar (from Firefox)

- **Dialog boxes:** One of the original Apple user interface inventions, dialog boxes contain controls specific to a task, usually a mix of sliders, fields, pop-up menus, and buttons, as you can see on the left side of Figure 9.7 (the Exposure dialog box in Adobe

Photoshop CS4). When a dialog box is open, you can't do anything else in the application until you close the dialog box by clicking OK (sometimes Done) or Cancel. You can drag dialog boxes out of the way if they cover what you're working on; you can just reposition them appropriately for the task at hand.

- **Panels:** A more recent invention from Adobe, panels are like dialog boxes in that they contain multiple related controls. But unlike dialog boxes, you can enter and leave them whenever you want to work elsewhere in the application, which means that any changes in their settings take effect immediately. Programs can have multiple panels open simultaneously as well. The right side of Figure 9.7 also shows a panel (Paragraphs) in Photoshop. Panels can be independent or grouped like panes in a panel group, as is the case in the figure.

FIGURE 9.7

A dialog box (Exposure) at left and a panel (Paragraph) at right (both from Photoshop)

- **Pop-overs:** A new element introduced in the iPhone's iOS, a pop-over is a cross between a dialog box and a pop-up menu. It opens from a button like a pop-up menu, but like a dialog box it contains one or more controls. Like a pop-up menu, you don't have to close them; simply going elsewhere closes them. Figure 9.8 shows an example from iCal.

New Feature

Pop-overs are new to Mac OS X Lion. ∎

- **Settings sheet:** Similar to a dialog box, a settings sheet won't let you work on anything else while it is open, and it must be explicitly closed. A settings sheet is accessible only from within a dialog box or application window, and "pulls down" from the title bar or toolbar. Unlike a dialog box, a settings sheet can't be moved, though if you move the parent dialog box or window, its settings sheet moves with it. Figure 9.9 shows an example from Pages.

FIGURE 9.8

A pop-over (Create Quick Event) from iCal

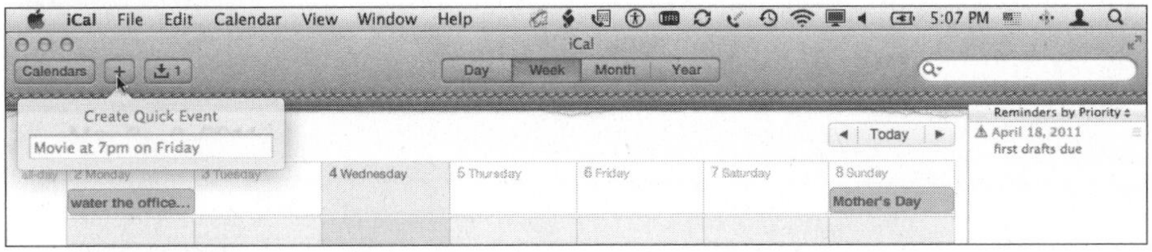

FIGURE 9.9

A settings sheet at left and a panel (Layout) at right (both from Pages)

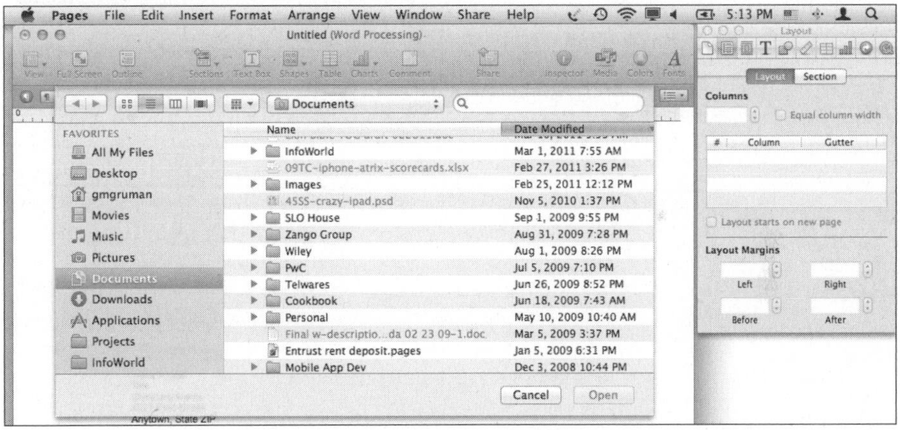

- **Panes:** Panes are groups of functions within a dialog box, window, or panel. You move among the panes by clicking their tabs, which can be icons or text-based; the tabs are usually at the top of the dialog box or panel but can be on the left side as well. Figure 9.10 shows the Accounts pane in Mail's Preferences dialog box. Panes can have their own panes, called *subpanes*: for example, note the subpanes within the Accounts pane: Account Information, Mailbox Behaviors (the active one), and Advanced. A pane also is called a *tabbed pane* (and thus often erroneously called a *tab*).

FIGURE 9.10

A pane (Accounts) with three subpanes (at left, from Mail); the Mailbox Behaviors subpane is active.

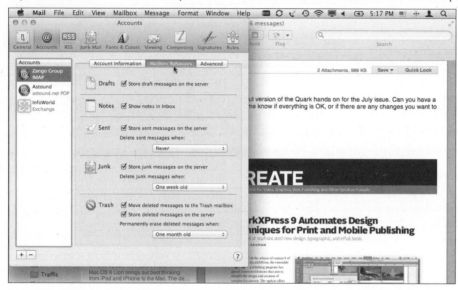

Controls

Within dialog boxes, settings sheets and the like are the various specific controls. Mac OS X provides many types; Figure 9.11 shows a sampling. These are the most common:

- **Button:** A button is a control that causes an action to take place when you click it with the mouse. (Apple's formal term is *push button*, but everyone simply calls them *buttons*.) Buttons come in a variety of shapes and sizes, and they can be marked with either text or a graphic. Buttons with text are generally horizontal with rounded edges; icon (graphic) buttons can be any shape, and sometimes they are accompanied by text descriptions.

- **OK and Cancel buttons:** These standard buttons appear in most dialog boxes. Clicking the OK button accepts the settings in the corresponding window, whereas clicking Cancel rejects any changes you made to the settings; both buttons close the dialog box. Occasionally, you may find the buttons marked differently: Deleting a file from a connected server, for example, displays Delete and Cancel buttons instead of OK and Cancel buttons. Some applications use Done instead of OK. Note that if a button is glowing or colored, pressing Return is the same as clicking that button. Also, in most cases, pressing Esc is the same as clicking Cancel.

- **Radio button:** When an action has multiple predefined settings to choose from, you may find radio button options used. They are named after the physical buttons that used to appear on car radios, where pushing one button caused the others to pop out.

Only one button can be used at a time. In Mac OS X, radio buttons are small gray circles that turn blue with a black dot in the center when an option is selected. Radio buttons can be displayed either horizontally or vertically.

FIGURE 9.11

Here's a sampling of controls. Upper left: Photoshop's Exposure dialog box has a textual and icon pop-up menu at upper left, with two textual buttons and three icon buttons at upper right. The Preview option at the right side of the dialog box uses a check box control, while the Exposure, Offset, and Gamma Correction controls are all sliders. At upper right: Pages' Layout panel uses radio buttons in the Page Numbers section, as well as stepper controls to the right of the Start At text field. At lower left: Disclosure triangles in InDesign's Scripts panel. At lower right: A sortable ordered list in the Language & Text system preference.

- **Check boxes:** Another group of settings might be displayed with check box options. A check box is similar to a radio button, except that it is square, and when an option is selected, the check box becomes blue with a small black check mark inside. The key difference between check boxes and radio buttons is that multiple options can be selected with check boxes (whereas radio buttons allow for only a single selection). Click a check box to select it, and click it again to deselect it. Some check boxes also have a third, intermediate state, marked as a horizontal line. This usually indicates that it has a sub-selection of check boxes and that some, but not all, of the items are selected.

- **Sliders:** A slider is a track (normally horizontal) that displays a range of values. On the track is a square with a triangular edge known as the *thumb*. You move the thumb along the track to select a value between the two ends of the slider.

Sometimes, you use sliders to select a numerical range, and the number appears nearby. At other times, you use them to choose from a non-numerical condition (a range between Slow and Fast, for example).

- **Stepper controls:** Also known as *little arrows*, these small arrows are used to raise or lower a value incrementally. Clicking an arrow adjusts the value by one predefined increment. Clicking and holding one of the arrows continuously increases the value until it reaches the end of its range.

- **Disclosure triangles:** One of these devices is a small black triangle that is used to control how much detail is displayed by an item in a window. Typically, a disclosure triangle points to the right, which indicates that its detail is *collapsed* (hidden); clicking it rotates the triangle by 90 degrees to point downward, and the remaining information is *expanded* (revealed).

- **Ordered lists:** This is a less commonly used control, where a list of items is displayed. Typically, you can click and drag the items to arrange them in a different order. In the Language & Text system preference's Language pane, for example, it lets you determine in what order languages are displayed in options. Sometimes, an ordered list also uses check boxes that enable you to switch items in the list on or off.

Using Full-Screen Applications

One of Apple's goals in Mac OS X Lion was to bring in some of the innovations and user interface approaches of iOS, especially from the iPad. One such feature is the introduction of full-screen applications. Developers can make their software take over the entire screen, obscuring the Mac OS X menu bar. (The Dock is unaffected.)

Applications that have such full-screen modes provide the Enter Full Screen button in their upper right corner, as shown at the top of Figure 9.12. The software Apple includes with Mac OS X Lion, such as Mail and iTunes, supports full-screen mode. If you don't see the Enter Full Screen icon button in an application, it doesn't support full-screen mode.

New Feature
Full-screen applications are new to Mac OS X Lion. ■

Note
Some applications that predate Mac OS X Lion—notably Apple's iWork '09 suite, which has Pages, Numbers, and Keynote—have their own version of full-screen mode. They typically provide an icon button In their toolbar to enter full-screen mode; if you hover the pointer at the top of the screen, the menu bar and toolbar reappear, so you can exit full-screen mode using a menu command or button (the Exit button, in iWork toolbars). ■

When an application is in full-screen mode (see the center image in Figure 9.12), you're not limited to using the capabilities that are onscreen; you can still use menus by hovering the mouse at the top of the screen until the menu bar reappears. Choose the desired menu item;

the application then returns to full-screen mode. Still, full-screen applications tend to bring more of their functionality into the main window, such as through toolbars and panels, so you don't have to unhide the menu bar often.

You can, of course, get back to the non-full-screen view of an application. Hover the pointer to show the menu bar, and then click the Exit Full Screen button in the upper right corner, as shown at the bottom of Figure 9.12.

FIGURE 9.12

Top: Full-screen applications such as Mail have the Enter Full Screen icon button in their upper-right corner. Center: The Mail application in full-screen mode. Bottom: Hover at the top of the screen to display the menu bar, which includes the Exit Full Screen icon button at upper right.

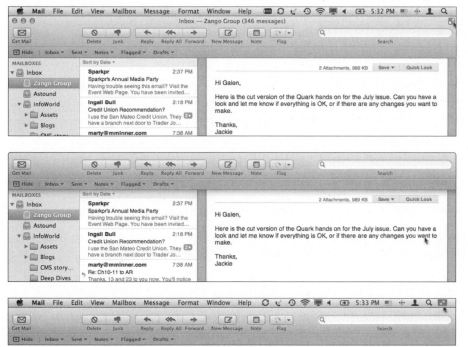

Quitting Applications

When you've finished working with an application, you can quit it, which stops Mac OS X from running it. This frees up some system resources, enabling Mac OS X to run other programs more efficiently. Mac OS X offers several methods for quitting an application. Some are for typical situations, whereas others are for when a program stops responding.

Quitting from within an application

Mac OS X provides a uniform way to quit applications: Choose Quit from the application menu (such as Word⇨Quit), or press ⌘+Q in the active application.

If you have any documents with unsaved data, Mac OS X displays an alert dialog box for each unsaved document. This is the same dialog box that appears if you try to close a document before saving its content. You can click one of three buttons:

- **Don't Save:** This option quits the application without saving your document. Any changes that you have made to the document are discarded.
- **Cancel:** This option cancels the quit process, returning you to the document window.
- **Save:** This option saves the document and then quits the application.

Quitting an application from the Dock

You also can quit an application via its Dock icon. Right-click or Control+click the application icon in the Dock, and choose Quit from the contextual menu. This method is useful for quitting applications that are running in the background, because you don't have to switch to it first to choose Quit from its application menu or press ⌘+Q.

If you quit an application while it is in the background, it may cause the icon in the Dock to bounce up and down. This is to alert you that it has an unsaved document that requires your attention. Switch to the application to deal with the unsaved document.

Tip

A quick way to quit multiple applications is to use the application switcher (described earlier in this chapter). Press ⌘+Tab to bring up the application switcher. As described earlier, select the desired application, but press Q instead of releasing the mouse button. Pressing Q quits that application. You can now repeat this process for other applications, quitting them one at a time. Release the ⌘ key when you're finished. ∎

Quitting by logging out, shutting down, or restarting

One method of quitting all open applications is to end your computer session. Logging out, shutting down, or restarting your Mac (see Chapter 1) causes all open applications to quit. A dialog box asks if you are sure that you want to quit all applications and log out, restart, or shut down (as the case may be).

Any applications with unsaved data interrupt the logout, restart, or shutdown process and display alert dialog boxes where you can decide whether to save the unsaved documents. (Applications that support Mac OS X Lion's Auto Save capability, described in Chapter 10, save the files for you when you quit.) Mac OS X quits the applications when you have dealt with all the unsaved documents, and then it proceeds to log out, restart, or shut down.

Note

When you shut down, restart, or log out of Mac OS X and select the Reopen Open Windows When Logging Back In (a new option in Mac OS X Lion described in Chapter 1), Mac OS X quits your applications. But when you boot, restart, or log into the Mac later, Mac OS X Lion relaunches the applications that had been open, which reloads any windows that had been open. This may appear as if the applications never quit, but they in fact did. ■

Using the Force Quit command

Although it's increasingly rare, your application may freeze or become unresponsive to any input commands. You may see the spinning colored ball when you try to use the application, and the Quit command is no longer accessible from the menu (or the application does not respond to any command to quit).

In these situations, you need to use a Force Quit command, which will almost certainly quit the application and enable you to carry on with your computing session. You can force an application to quit in several ways.

Using the Force Quit dialog box

Choose ⬛ ➪ Force Quit or press Option+⌘+Esc to bring up the Force Quit Applications dialog box, as shown Figure 9.13. It displays a list of all currently running applications. If the applications are running normally, you can select one and click Relaunch to shut it down and relaunch it. If an application is not responding, its name appears in red and the button becomes Force Quit when you select that application; click Force Quit to shut it down.

Using the Dock

You can force applications to quit from the Dock. Option+⌘+click the application icon in the Dock, and then choose Force Quit from the contextual menu.

Using the Activity Monitor

Another option for forcing an application to quit is to use a utility called Activity Monitor. It is located in the Utilities folder. (In the Finder, choose Go ➪ Utilities or press Shift+⌘+U to open or go to the Utilities folder quickly.) Activity Monitor lists all the active processes, which includes the currently active applications, again shown in Figure 9.13. Select an application in the list and click Quit Process, choose View ➪ Quit Process, or press Option+⌘+Q.

Caution

Forcing an application to quit skips any alerts to save unsaved documents, so any unsaved changes you have made are lost. Sometimes, this is unavoidable, but if you can save a document first, and quit it the standard way, that's the best course of action. ■

FIGURE 9.13

Left: The Force Quit Applications dialog box makes applications quit, even when they are unresponsive. Right: The Activity Monitor lists all the processes currently active in Mac OS X. This includes all the applications.

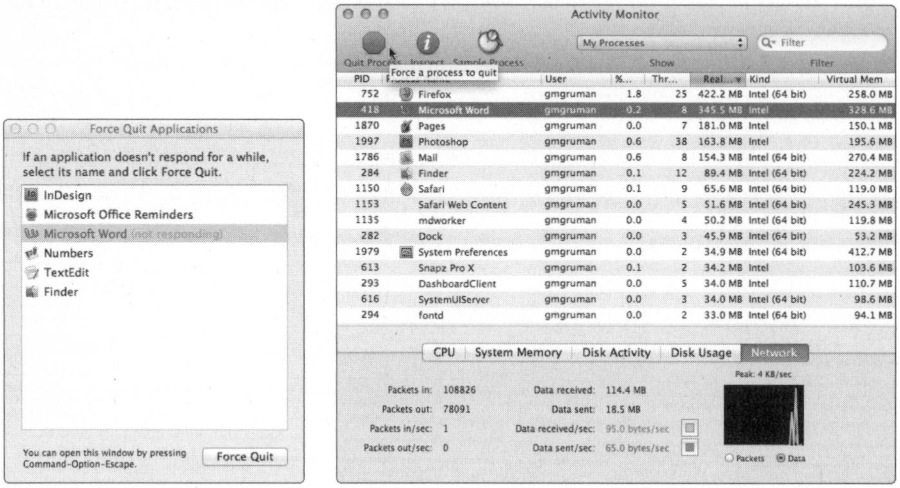

Summary

Mac OS X comes with dozens of applications and utilities, but you also can install applications from other companies to do even more things with your Mac.

Mac OS X provides many ways to open applications, though double-clicking them from the Applications folder or Utilities folder is the one way to access all your applications. The Dock and recent Items menu option in the menu are handy ways to launch frequently used applications. And the new Launchpad lets you see all your applications in home screens reminiscent of an iPhone, iPad, or iPod Touch.

Uninstalling applications is usually as simple as dragging them to the Trash or running their uninstaller applications.

You can easily switch among running applications using the Dock or application switcher or by clicking a window from an open application. When you get overwhelmed by having too many open windows, use the Hide commands to move applications out of the way without quitting them.

Most Mac OS X applications use a common set of controls presented in a common set of function containers such as dialog boxes and panels. Even applications that use their own interface approaches work essentially the same way as applications that follow Apple's standards, even if they have visual differences.

Mac OS X Lion introduces the concept of full-screen applications. Applications that support this mode provide a button to hide the menu bar, which can be redisplayed as needed.

Quitting an application is usually a simple matter of pressing ⌘+Q or choosing Quit from the application menu, but you also can quit applications from the Dock or the application switcher. (If the application has any unsaved documents, you are given a chance to save them before quitting.) Applications also are quit automatically when you log out, restart, or shut down the Mac. And if you do have trouble with an unresponsive application, you can force it to quit from the Force Quit Applications dialog box or the Activity Monitor utility.

Working with Documents

IN THIS CHAPTER

Opening documents

Creating documents

Working with a document's content

Saving documents

Working with document versions and locking

Closing documents

Moving and sharing documents with other users

What you typically use a Mac for is to work with documents, whether text, spreadsheets, photos, music, or web pages. Documents—basically, those files that people work with on a computer—are what you work in, and the Finder and applications are basically the tools designed to let you open, read or play, modify, and save.

Most of the time you spend working on documents is in the traditional manner: creating and modifying documents, printing and sharing them, and saving them for future use.

Documents can reside in all sorts of places: On your Mac's startup disk, on other disks connected to your Mac via a USB, Thunderbolt, or FireWire cable or over the network (see Chapter 6), or on storage servers accessible via the Internet.

That last type of storage, known as "cloud storage," is increasingly popular, because it makes your documents accessible from any Mac, any PC, and many mobile devices (including Apple's) over an Internet connection. In an era when most of us use several computers and also smartphones or iPads, the ability to store documents in a central, easily accessible location is increasingly important. Box.net (www.box.net), Dropbox (www.dropbox.net), Google Docs (www.docs.google.com), and Apple's soon-to-be-discontinued MobileMe web applications (www.me.com) are typical examples of this sort of service. (Chapter 17 explains how to use cloud services.)

Mac OS X provides the core mechanisms that applications use to work with documents, so most applications work the same way. That helps make it easier for users, because the techniques you learn for one application apply to most other applications. But application developers can and do implement their own methods, so you'll see differences in the basics of working with documents in some applications. Still, you'll find the basic principles are usually the same, even if there are additional methods or differences in the user interface to access those core methods.

Opening Documents

You can open documents in Mac OS X in two basic ways: from the Finder and within an application.

Tip
To preview a document's contents before opening it, select it and press the spacebar to open the Quick Look preview window. You also can page through Quick Look previews in many documents directly from its Finder icon. Chapter 4 explains both Quick Look methods. ■

Opening documents from the Finder

To open a document from the Finder, several routes are available:

- **(Apple) menu:** Choose ➪ Recent Items, and choose an item from the Documents section of the menu.

- **Dock:** Drag a document onto a compatible application icon in the Dock. Or click a document icon residing inside a stacks folder in the Dock (see Chapter 2).

- **Finder window:** Double-click the document icon, press ⌘+O, choose File ➪ Open, or right-click or Control+click the document and choose Open from the contextual menu. (To open the document in an application other than the default one assigned to this document type, choose Open With instead from either the File menu or the contextual menu and then choose the application to open the document in.) You also can drag a document onto a compatible application icon in the Applications folder.

- **Spotlight:** Type the name of the application in the Spotlight search box (see Chapter 5), and choose the corresponding application from the results sheet.

The most commonly used method is the simple double-clicking of a document icon. But no matter which method you use, the document opens in the default application for that document (or in the application you choose if you use the Open With option), and the document window comes to the foreground so you can begin working with it. If that application is not running, it launches first.

If there is no corresponding application for a file (because the file type is unknown to Mac OS X), you get an error message. You can use the Open With menu option to open the file in the desired application. To make that association permanent, so you no longer get the error message, you have two options:

Using the Recent Items menu option

You can access both documents and applications by choosing ➪ Recent Items, which displays a submenu with three sections: Applications, Documents, and Servers. The Recent Items submenu enables you to quickly reopen an application or document you recently used, as well as access again a server that you recently accessed.

Although it's useful for applications, the Recent Items menu is even more important for recently accessed documents. This is because your documents are less likely to be stored in a single location; instead, they are distributed throughout your disks and folders. (Also, people tend to add their favorite applications to the Dock instead of using the Recent Items submenu.)

The Recent Items submenu in Mac OS X keeps track of the 10 most recent items by default. But you can set the number of items displayed to any amount between 0 and 50 items. Use the General system preference to set the number of items that appear in the Recent Items submenu, as explained in Chapter 28.

The Clear Menu option appears at the bottom of the Recent Items submenu. Choosing it removes all the items from the Recent Items submenu, leaving it a blank slate. This doesn't affect the actual items on your disks; it merely removes them from the Recent Items submenu.

- Set the default application for this file type using the Info window, as Chapter 3 explains.

- Right-click or Control+click the document, and choose Open With ➪ Other from the contextual menu. This opens a dialog box listing the applications in the Applications folder (you also can navigate to other folders from it, such as the Utilities folder). Compatible applications are displayed in black; incompatible applications are displayed in gray and cannot be selected. Select the desired application, and then select the Always Open With check box—this is the key step—before clicking Open.

Tip
Opening multiple file types is easy, even if they are different file types. Simply select the documents and double-click, or use one of the Open commands. If the documents are handled by different applications, those applications launch and open the documents. ∎

Opening documents within an application

As you work with documents, you're very likely to find yourself inside an application looking to open a previously created document. These are standard methods for opening a document within an application:

- **Open dialog box:** Choose File ➪ Open, or press ⌘+O, and use the Open dialog box to navigate to the desired file. Highlight the document, and click Open.

- **Open Recent menu:** Choose File ➪ Open Recent, and choose a document recently used by the application. (Note that not all applications have this menu option.)

Some applications offer further options for opening documents. Adobe applications, for example, have a menu option called Browse (choose File ⇨ Browse) that opens a dedicated application called Bridge to browse and open documents used by various Adobe applications. Microsoft Office applications can have the optional menu item Open from Document Connection, which is similar to Adobe's Browse option for access to network-based documents, such as those available through Microsoft's SharePoint server.

Note

When you open documents from within an application, you aren't restricted to documents created by that application. You can open any file type supported by that application, no matter what application was used to create it. The document's file extension, explained in Chapter 4, tells Mac OS X—and thus the application—what the document's file type is. ■

The Open dialog box

When you choose File ⇨ Open in a Mac OS X application, you get the Open dialog box, as shown in Figure 10.1. (Most applications also let you press ⌘+O to open the Open dialog box.) The Open dialog box has the same navigation controls as a Finder window and by default shows the Columns view mode. You can switch the view among column, icon, Cover Flow, and list view modes using the icon buttons in the top left of the dialog box.

Note

Some applications don't use the standard Mac OS X Open dialog box, and thus may not have the same appearance or controls described in this section. ■

The Open dialog box has the same navigation options as a Finder window. You use it within applications to locate and open documents.

You navigate in the Open dialog box just as you do in a Finder window through the folder structure of your hard disks and other volumes. In the default column view, each column shows the contents of a folder, and clicking a folder opens the contents of that folder in the column to the right. You scroll left to see folders higher up the folder hierarchy and scroll right to move to the currently selected folder. In icon view, double-clicking folders takes you inside that folder, and you use the navigation buttons or pop-up menu to navigate back up the folder structure. In list view, you use the disclosure triangles to reveal the contents of folders.

To the left of the Open dialog box is the Sidebar, which includes the same items as a Finder window. You use it to access different volumes and common areas on the Mac (such as the desktop and Documents folder). You can quickly navigate to any volume or folder displayed in the Finder by dragging it into the Open dialog box.

Initially, the Open dialog box displays two columns. You can resize the columns by dragging the handle at the bottom of each column divider. You also can click and drag the handle on the bottom right of the Open dialog box to resize it. Although the Open dialog box lacks Close and Minimize icon buttons (non-functional placeholders appear in their place), it has a Zoom icon button that you can click to maximize the size of the Open dialog box. You can move the dialog box around by clicking and dragging its title bar.

As you move around the Open dialog box, notice that some files are in black text, while others are grayed out. The black text indicates that the application can be opened; files with grayed-out text cannot be opened by the current application.

Tip

You also can use Spotlight within the Open dialog box. Type a search term in the search box at the top right of the dialog box to use Spotlight technology to search Mac OS X for that term. (Chapter 5 covers Spotlight in detail.) ■

Two buttons appear at the bottom of the Open dialog box:

- **Open:** Click this button, and the application opens any selected files in the Open dialog box.
- **Cancel:** Click this button to close the Open dialog box without opening any file.

Many applications also offer a selection of customized options at the bottom of the Open dialog box. Microsoft Office, for example, has two pop-up menus: The Enable pop-up menu lets you narrow down the file choices based on file type as well as select any file; the reason for this Any File option is that the desired file may be lacking a file extension or have an incorrect one but is otherwise compatible, so letting users explicitly choose such files is a convenience. If the file truly cannot be opened, a message appears indicating that after you try to open the file. The Open pop-up menu in Office provides three options—Original, Copy, and Read-Only—that enable you to open the file in any of these modes. Adobe's Creative Suite applications have similar controls.

Creating Documents

Although you'll certainly be working with documents that someone else created, sooner or later, you need to create something from scratch, and when this time comes, you need to create a new document.

Many applications save you the trouble by creating a new document whenever you open the program; Microsoft Word and TextEdit are examples of such programs. However, some applications do not automatically open a new document; Adobe Photoshop is one such example. Even if an application opens a new document by default when you launch the program, sometimes you want to create a new document when the program is already running. Some applications may have their own unique way of doing things, but most Mac OS X applications enable you to create a new document using one of the following methods:

- Choose File ⇨ New.
- Press ⌘+N.

For some applications, you also can right-click or Control+click the application icon in the Dock and choose New Document from the contextual menu.

Creating a copy of a document

You also can create a new document by copying an existing file in the Finder. This method is especially useful if the document has content that you want to use, such as a letterhead or some stock text. The easiest way to make a copy of a document is to select it in the Finder and choose File ⇨ Duplicate or press ⌘+D. Alternatively, you can press and hold Option and drag a document from the desktop or a Finder window to another location (release Option when your mouse is in the new location). Chapter 3 has more information on duplicating documents.

In Mac OS X, you also can use the Copy and Paste commands to duplicate files. Select an item in the Finder and choose Edit ⇨ Copy or press ⌘+C, and then navigate to another part of the Finder and choose Edit ⇨ Paste Item or press ⌘+V.

Tip

Although you cannot use the Cut command rather than Copy to move the document to a new location; you can still move the item in the new location rather than duplicate. The trick is to hold Option before using the Finder menu; with Option held, choose Edit ⇨ Move Item Here at the new location. You also can press Option+⌘+V. ∎

The Cut, Copy, and Paste commands as used for documents are explained in Chapter 2; I cover how to use the Cut, Copy, and Paste commands within documents later in this chapter.

Creating documents with stationery pads (templates)

If you have a document that often serves as a base for creating other documents, you can create a *stationery pad*. Most applications call these *templates*, but Apple still refers to these in its own applications as stationery pads. When you open a stationery pad, the preformatted content and settings appear. For example, you could have a text document with a company logo, address, phone number, e-mail, and basic text, all of which you preformatted. It's like tearing a sheet off an endless pad of preprinted stationery, which is where the name comes from.

You create stationery pads using the Info window (see Chapter 4). Follow these steps to turn an ordinary document into a stationery pad:

1. **Select the file you want to use as a stationery pad in the Finder.**
2. **Choose File ⇨ Get Info, press ⌘+I, or right-click or Control+click it, and choose Get Info from the contextual menu.** This opens the Info window, as described earlier in the chapter.
3. **Select the Stationery Pad option so it is checked.** This turns the document into a stationery pad.

Using stationery pads is almost the same as using a regular document. You open the document, as outlined earlier in the chapter. Doing so usually has the application create a duplicate of the file in the same location in the Finder (with the same filename plus "copy" appended to the end). If the application does not understand stationery pads, it simply opens the document as if it were a regular file. In some cases, the stationery pad document opens in a document window and is named Untitled, and when you save the file you are prompted to give it a name; this prevents the original stationery pad from being overwritten.

Some applications enable you to save documents as stationery pads, or templates, as explained later in the chapter.

If you create a stationery pad and then decide at a later point that you want to go back and make changes, you need to revisit the Info window for the document and deselect the Stationery Pad check box. This returns the stationery pad to a regular document. You can now open it, edit it, and save it as you would a normal document. When you have finished making your changes, use the Info window to convert it back to a stationery pad.

Working with a Document's Content

When an application is active and a document window is on the screen, you can generally adjust its content.

Whether you are creating a new document or editing an existing one, you can add content to a document, move existing content around, and even move content from one document to another document.

Each application works with at least one content type, and many use their own content type. For example, Microsoft Word works with text, RTF, and Word document file types; Adobe Photoshop works with Photoshop, TIFF, JPEG, PNG, GIF, and many more file types; iMovie works with MPEG-4 video and iMovie project file types; and so on. For in-depth details on working with just about every major application that runs on Mac OS X, consult Wiley's excellent books on them.

Although applications work on a great range of documents and have many specific controls for them, there are standard techniques that work commonly across many applications, regardless of the type of data created and how it is managed by the application. Good examples are the Cut, Copy, and Paste commands. They are universal concepts used to shuffle content around in a document. For example, in Word, you use them to move blocks of text around a document (or to another document), and in Adobe Photoshop, you use them to move around parts of images. Additionally, many programs enable you to drag content from one part of a document to another—or by holding down the Option key, copy content from one spot and duplicate it in another.

Using Cut, Copy, and Paste

One of the first things any computer user learns is how to perform cut, copy, and paste operations. This is a universal computer technique that works identically in many operating systems. Indeed, it's hard to imagine any part of the computer world that is more universally recognized. Essentially, you select a part of a document and either remove it (cut) or duplicate it (copy) and then insert it elsewhere (paste).

Select part of a document, and Choose Edit ⇨ Cut or press ⌘+X (if you want to move the data) or Edit ⇨ Copy or press ⌘+C (if you want to duplicate the data in another location). Either of these actions places the data on the Clipboard, which is a temporary storage area in Mac OS X's memory for data being moved or copied.

Now that you have the content in the Clipboard, you can place it somewhere else. Typically, items are pasted at the point where the cursor is, although the paste location can differ depending on the application. Select where you want the data to be placed, and choose Edit ⇨ Paste or press ⌘+V.

Pasting does not remove data from the Clipboard, so you can paste the same data multiple times in different locations. The data remains in the Clipboard until it is overwritten with new data (typically when you next use the Cut or Copy commands). This means that you can paste one set of data at a time, and when you cut or copy another set of data, the original data is removed from the Clipboard. So if you want to go back and paste the first set of data again, you locate it and use Cut or Copy to place it in the Clipboard again.

Tip

Although Mac OS X enables users to cut or copy only one item at a time, plenty of applications extend the Clipboard and enable users to paste multiple different sets of data without having to repeatedly use the Cut or Copy commands. One popular choice is a free program called PTHPasteboard (http://pth.com/products/pthpasteboard/). **Some applications, such as Microsoft Office, also allow multiple items to be stored in the Clipboard—but only for use within those applications.** ∎

You can cut, copy, and paste within a single document, among multiple documents in use by a single application or among the documents of different applications. These applications include the Finder, so you can cut, copy, and paste text to and from filenames, for example. Using the Cut, Copy, and Paste commands rapidly becomes second nature—especially if you use the keyboard shortcuts:

- **Cut: ⌘+X**
- **Copy: ⌘+C**
- **Paste: ⌘+V**

Unlike most keyboard shortcuts, these are not all named logically after letters they begin with (although Copy is based upon C). Instead, they are in a line on the bottom row of the keyboard. (It can help to think of X as "X out," as a synonym for cut, and to think of V as an insertion wedge, such as is common in copyediting.) The X, C, and V shortcut keys used for the Cut, Copy, and Paste shortcuts are a standard found on most operating systems.

Using drag and drop to move data around

Mac OS X provides another quick way to move around text, graphics, and other material: *drag-and-drop editing*. This technique works only with applications designed to take advantage of it, but fortunately this includes most applications in Mac OS X.

Using drag and drop in a document

To use drag and drop in a document, first open it and select the text, graphics, or other data you want to move. Next, position the pointer inside the selected area, and press and hold the mouse or touchpad button down. Drag the pointer; as Figure 10.2 shows, you see a lightened image of whatever data you are dragging appear under it, so you know the intended selection is being dragged. Typically, an insertion point appears in the document as you drag the pointer around, indicating the exact position where the data will be copied. Release the mouse or touchpad button to move the data from its original position to the new one.

As you can see, drag and drop is the functional equivalent of cut and paste. If you want to copy the data and leave the original rather than move it, press and hold down the Option key before, or while, dragging the data from one part of the document to another. This copies the data and leaves the original source material in place. (A small green + icon appears near the pointer, so you know you're copying the data instead of moving it.)

FIGURE 10.2

With drag-and-drop editing, you can move data around a document (see the text being moved toward the bottom left).

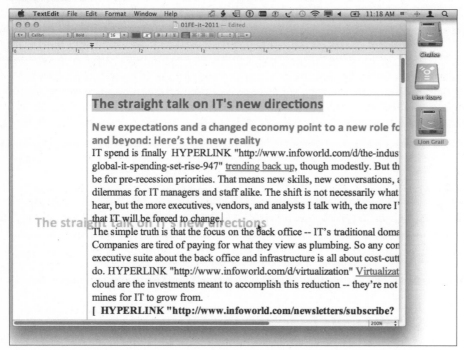

Tip

Drag and drop can be a surprisingly tricky maneuver to master at first. If you find yourself continuously selecting new data instead of dragging data, you are probably clicking and moving too quickly. Try holding down the mouse or touchpad button, without moving the pointer, for a moment before moving the pointer. This pause signifies to Mac OS X that you are performing a drag-and-drop operation. ∎

Using drag and drop between documents

You also can use drag and drop to move material from one document to another. To do this, first open both documents and make sure both are visible on the screen. Also make sure that the destination to which you want to drag material is visible, because it is difficult to navigate to a document while performing a drag-and-drop procedure. Now select the text, graphic, or other source material, and click it to start the drag-and-drop procedure. Drag the selected material from the first document to the desired insertion point in the second document.

As you drag, a lightened image of the selected material follows the pointer. When you drag the pointer into a new window, a small green + icon appears and an insertion point shows you where the item will be inserted when you release the mouse or touchpad button. Unlike the regular drag-and-drop procedure within a document, the data isn't moved from one document to another, but copied. This is the same as if you had held down the Option key when moving material within a document. The only requirement is that the destination document be capable of handling the type of material you're dragging.

Whether you prefer drag-and-drop editing or cut-and-paste commands is largely a question of personal taste. Most people find themselves using whichever technique is at hand: If you're using the mouse or touchpad, drag and drop lets you keep using the mouse or touchpad, while if you're using the keyboard, cut and paste lets you keep using the keyboard.

Tip
Drag-and-drop editing does not wipe the content of the Clipboard, as copy and paste does. So it's a good method to use when you have a Clipboard containing important data that you want to leave in the Clipboard but still want to move something else around. You can use the drag-and-drop method for that something else and continue pasting whatever is in the Clipboard. ■

Using clippings

Another technique related to drag and drop is called *clip editing*. This is where you use the drag-and-drop technique described previously, except instead of dragging an item to another location within a document, you drag it directly to the desktop or another location within the Finder. This creates a clipping of the file with an icon similar to that of a regular document, except that it has the curl on the bottom-left corner rather than the usual top-right corner. Clipping files can contain text, pictures, QuickTime movies, or sound, but a single clipping file can contain only one kind of data.

When you open a clipping file in the Finder, it appears in its own window. This window offers a preview of the contents; you can select all or some of its contents but not modify them. To copy the contents of a clipping window into a document, you drag the clipping file itself from the Finder into a document. As with drag-and-drop copying from a document, an insertion point shows where the contents will be inserted. Releasing the mouse or touchpad inserts the contents of a clipping document. Figure 10.3 shows a clipping being inserted into a document; the clipping file is to the right of the document window and has a curled bottom-right corner to indicate it is a clipping file.

The great thing about clipping files is that they can be stored on Mac OS X and used again and again. For example, you could keep a clipping document of your address and drag it to a document every time you wanted to insert it. Clipping files make great repositories of frequently used content snippets, such as your address, company logo, and signature.

FIGURE 10.3

You can drag a clipping file (to the right of the document window) into a compatible document to copy its contents where you release the pointer.

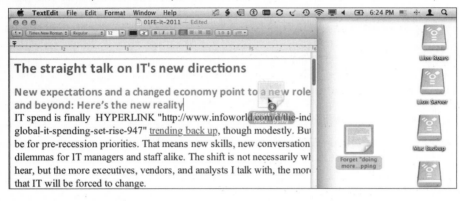

Saving Documents

After creating a new document, or while editing a document, you need to save your progress. Saving is an essential part of working with documents, committing the document you are working on—in its current state—to the disk. If you didn't save your progress while working on a document, you would need to create the document from scratch every time you worked on it. When you are working on documents for a length of time, I strongly advise you to save at periodical intervals to protect your work in case of any problems.

Make sure that the document you are working on is in the currently active window, and save your progress by choosing File ➪ Save or pressing ⌘+S. The Save command automatically updates the file on the disk with the contents of the new one.

New Feature

Mac OS X Lion adds a new capability called Versions that lets documents keep track of all the changes you make to them, so you can revert to an earlier version easily, even in files that get moved or sent to other people. If an application supports this capability, the Save menu option is named Save a Version. ■

New Feature

Mac OS X Lion also adds a new capability called Auto Save that saves changes to your document as you make them (in applications that implement this capability). That way, should your Mac freeze or lose its power, you haven't lost the changes you made since the last explicit save (when you chose File ➪ Save a Version or pressed ⌘+S). Note that the incremental changes saved since the last explicit save aren't available through the Versions feature's revert capability (covered later in this chapter) until you explicitly save the file. ■

If you are working on a new document that has not already been saved, choosing the Save command instead performs a Save As command. This opens a dialog box, shown in Figure 10.4, that enables you to name and select a location for the new document. The document and its contents are then stored in a file on that location.

Left: The simple version of the Save As dialog box enables you to enter a name and location for a new document to be saved on your computer. Right: The expanded Save As dialog box offers a wider range of options for saving files.

Using the Save As dialog box

The Save As dialog box comes in two flavors: simple and expanded, both shown in Figure 10.4. The simple version enables you to give a name to your document and choose from a preset list of destinations in the Where pop-up menu. You also may get some options regarding the file type to save. In TextEdit, for example, you can choose from Rich Text Format, Rich Text Format with Attachments, Web Page (.html), Web Archive, OpenDocument Text (.odt), Word 2007 Format (.docx), Word 2003 Format (.xml), and Word 97 Format (.doc).

This simple version of the Save As dialog box is fine for most purposes, although there may come a point where you want to select a more detailed location for your file. When this happens, you need to use the expanded Save As dialog box. To access the expanded Save As dialog box, click the down-pointing arrow icon button to the right of the Save As text field, shown in Figure 10.4. Note that the button's icon changes to an up-pointing arrow; click it again to access the simple Save As dialog box.

Note

In some applications—notably Apple's AppleScript Editor, TextEdit, Pages, Numbers, and Keynote—the Save As dialog box displays as a settings sheet instead of as a dialog box. But they work the same way as their equivalent dialog boxes. ■

Saving a stationery pad

In some applications, you can use the Save As dialog box to specify that the document is a stationery pad (or template). Depending on the application, the capability to save a document as a template can vary. Some applications offer this choice via radio buttons or a check box in the Save As dialog box; others, such as Microsoft Word and Adobe Creative Suite, offer it via a pop-up menu usually named Format. The file type in the pop-up menu usually has the word *template* in it; for example, in the case of Microsoft Word, the menu option is Word Template (.dotx).

The expanded Save As dialog box has a location browser similar to that in the Finder window for navigating the Mac's folder structure. This enables you to select a specific disk and save your document in it. As with the Open dialog box, the Save As dialog box displays the folder hierarchy in column view mode by default; you choose from column, icon, list, and Cover Flow view modes using the icon buttons in the top left of the window.

The unnamed pop-up menu offers the list of standard documents, plus a list of recent places to choose from. The Sidebar to the left of the Save As dialog box enables you to navigate to the devices, volumes, folders, and smart folders found in a Finder window (see Chapter 3).

The Save As dialog box includes the Spotlight search function. Although it makes little sense to search for items while saving a document, you can use the Spotlight search box to search for folders you know the name of but not their exact locations. Enter a term into the Spotlight search box, and folders matching the search term appear in the Save As dialog box. Double-click a desired folder to make it the save location.

Another option you have in the expanded Save As dialog box is the ability to create a new folder while saving a document. Click New Folder, and a dialog box appears asking for a name for the folder. Enter the desired name, and click Create. The new folder appears as the save location in the Save As dialog box.

Another way of choosing a location for the file is to drag a folder from the Finder to the Save As dialog box. This changes the save location to that area.

Either before or after choosing the file's location, you need to give it a name. Do so in the Save As text field at the top of the dialog box.

Tip
You can use the Cut, Copy, and Paste commands while using the Save As dialog box. This method enables you to copy (or cut) a part of the document for use as the new filename before using the Save As option and then paste it into the Save As text field at the top of the dialog box. You can use the Edit menu, or any of the keyboard shortcuts outlined earlier, to cut and paste text into the dialog box. ■

When you have selected a name and location for the document, click Save.

Saving versions and copies

With Mac OS X Lion's new Versions capability, you're likely to encounter two different methods for saving copies of your documents from within applications: The Save As method and the Duplicate method.

The Save As method has been the Mac OS's primary way to save a copy of a document from within an application for more than two decades: Simply choose File ➪ Save As or, in many applications, press Shift+⌘+S. This enables you to save the changes you have made to a document as a new document, without replacing the original file you were working on, such as to have different versions of the document.

But applications that implement the new Versions capability usually do not have a Save As menu option in their File menu. The assumption is that people were using Save As to create separate versions of their documents, so they no longer need it with Mac OS X Lion adding that capability within files. But for many people, creating a copy via Save As remains a useful capability, even with the Versions feature; for example, you may want different versions of the same file, each modified for a different recipient. The Versions capability can't accomplish that diversity of documents from a common source.

Applications that no longer have the Save As menu option—such as the TextEdit lightweight word processor that comes with Mac OS X Lion—offer a new menu option to replace the Save As menu option: Duplicate. Choose File ➪ Duplicate to create a copy of the current document in a new document window, and then save that copy using the Save As dialog box (choose File ➪ Save or press ⌘+S).

Note
The first time you save a version-enabled document, the File menu shows the Save menu option; after that initial save, the menu option is renamed Save a Version. ■

Note
Some programs have their own versioning function. For example, Adobe Creative Suite CS2 through CS4 had a versioning capability called Version Cue that worked only with those applications. ■

Working with Versions

Before Mac OS X Lion, many applications used a primitive form of versioning: You could choose File ➪ Revert to Saved to close the current document, not save any of its changes, and reopen the last version saved. It was a handy way to handle a document gone horribly wrong but not yet saved. But as soon as you saved a document, those previous changes were saved and could not be undone except by you manually changing them back (if you could remember all the changes you had made!).

The new Versions capability lets applications that implement it track each set of changes so you can roll back to a previous version whenever you want. Each time you save the file (choosing File ⇨ Save a Version or pressing ⌘+S), a new version is created, even though you can't see it onscreen. When you have unsaved changes in a document, the text "—Edited" appears in gray to the right of the filename in the title bar, as you can see in Figures 10.2 and 10.3 earlier in this chapter.

You can get all the controls in one place for a Versions-enabled document, once you've saved at least one set of changes: If you hover the pointer over the filename, a pop-up menu icon appears to the right of the filename in the title bar; click it to open the menu with the following options:

- **Lock:** This immediately locks the document. If the document is already locked, the menu becomes Unlock.

- **Revert to Last Opened Version:** This restores the version of the document that existed when you opened it—that is, the last-saved version.

- **Browse All Versions:** This opens the Time Machine-like screen shown in Figure 10.5, from which you can choose which version to revert to.

FIGURE 10.5

The Time Machine-like screen appears when you revert a document to a previous version in an application that supports Versions.

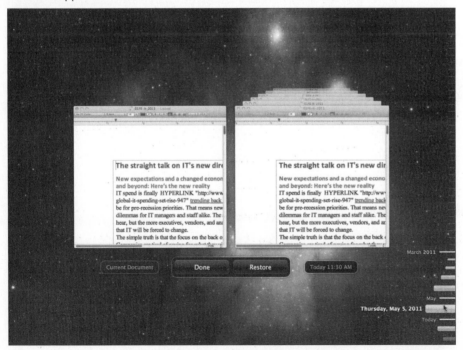

Note

If you duplicate (using the File ➪ Duplicate command or the Finder's copy capability), e-mail, or otherwise share a Versions-enabled document, Mac OS X Lion is smart enough not to send all the versions of the file, which would reveal earlier drafts that you may not want the recipient to access. All the recipient gets is the final version. But this also means you need to keep a document in its original location to retain its versions. ■

Note

Versioning is similar to the tracked-changes feature common in word processors such as Microsoft Word and Apple Pages, but they are not the same. The tracked changes capability lets you view and reject (undo) every single change you make to a document, whether they had been saved or not. The Versions capability isn't that detailed; it simply rolls back to a previously saved version of the file. Thus, if you roll back to a version from three days ago, you lose all changes made since then. You can't pick and choose what changes to undo, as you can with tracked changes. ■

Applications that support Versions have a Revert to Saved option in their File menu, but it works differently than in applications that don't support versions. When you choose File ➪ Revert to Saved in a Versions-compatible application, you get the screen shown in Figure 10.5 (complete with that starry background image). At left is the current document; at right is a stack of previous versions, with the most recent on top. The slider at the far right lets you roll back in time; you also can click the title bar of a previous version from the stack. (This screen will look familiar to anyone who's used the Time Machine backup utility covered in Chapter 11; it's the same interface and works essentially the same way.)

You can navigate through the previous versions to refresh your memory as to their contents, but you can't modify them. As you navigate through the stack, note that date and time for the version being displayed is listed below its window.

Click Restore to roll back to the version being displayed; doing so wipes out all changes since that version. Or click Done to leave the current version alone.

Tip

You also can copy text or images from a previous version and paste it into your current version. That's a really handy way to recover a deletion or undo a change you made along the way without losing all the other changes you made since then. ■

Working with older documents

It's happened to me, and I'm sure it's happened to you: You opened an old document to check something, inadvertently and perhaps unknowingly made a change, and saved the document without thinking (after hearing for years how you should press ⌘+S periodically to reduce the chance of losing data if the Mac crashes).

New Feature

Mac OS X Lion now automatically protects documents from being saved accidentally as part of the new Auto Save capability. ■

Mac OS X Lion changes that scenario—at least for documents from applications that support the Auto Save capability. If you edit or save a document that hasn't been opened in a while, you get a confirmation dialog box, as shown in Figure 10.6, that lets you decide to unlock the document so you can edit and/or save it, duplicate the document to work on a copy, or cancel the edits or save.

FIGURE 10.6

The alert you get when you try to save a document that Mac OS X Lion has locked because you haven't opened it in a while

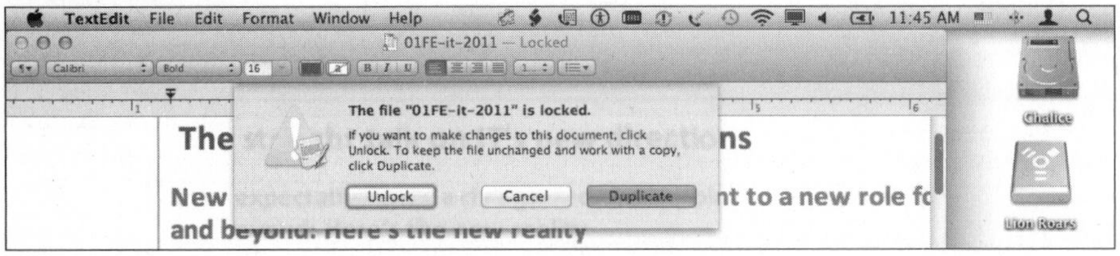

This document-locking feature is enabled by default in Mac OS X Lion. You can turn it on or off, as well as set how long it's been since a document was last edited before the document is automatically locked. Do so in the Time Machine system preference (see Chapter 28): Select the Lock Documents option in the settings sheet that appears when you click Options to turn this on; deselect it to turn document locking off. Set the lock period in the adjacent pop-up menu; your options are 1 Day, 1 Week, 2 Weeks (the default), 1 Month, and 1 Year. (Chapter 11 covers Time Machine.)

You also can immediately lock a document in a compatible application using the new icon pop-up menu that appears if you hover the pointer over the filename in the title bar (the pop-up menu appears to the right of the filename); click it to get a menu with three options: Lock (or Unlock, if the document is already locked), Duplicate, Revert to Last Saved Version, and Browse All Versions.

When a document is locked, you see the "—Locked" gray text to theright of the filename in the title bar, as shown in Figure 10.6.

Closing Documents

When you've saved a document and no longer want to work on it, you can close the document but leave the application running. The easiest way is to click the Close icon button in the upper left of the document window. You also can choose File ⇨ Close or press ⌘+W. Some applications have a Close All command, accessed by choosing File ⇨ Close All or pressing Option+⌘+W.

If you quit an application (as described in Chapter 9), its document windows are closed as well.

If you close a document window whose document has unsaved content, an alert dialog box appears, giving you a chance to save the changes.

Moving Documents

After you have created and saved a document, you may well decide to move it from its original location. Moving documents in Mac OS X is straightforward: Simply locate the file in the Finder, and click and drag it to a new location. You can drag a document to any folder or volume displayed in the Finder; you also can drag it to the Sidebar of any Finder window, to any folder displayed in the Dock, to the desktop, or to the root level of your hard disk. Chapter 4 explains moving files around in more detail.

Sharing Documents with Other Users

Mac OS X is a multi-user operating system, so it is possible that the account you are working in is running alongside many other user accounts on the same Mac. While different users share the Mac OS X disks and many of the system files, the elements of each user account (including the personal documents) are available only to the user who is currently logged in. The process of setting up and managing different accounts is covered in detail in Chapter 20.

While you are logged in to your account, you cannot access the files stored on another user's portion of Mac OS X on your Mac, unless they've given you file-sharing access to their folders, as explained in Chapter 27. To get at the files on another user's account, you need to log out and then log back in as that user. Of course, this means that you won't be able to access the documents in your account (or copy any files from that user's account to your own).

However, you can share files with other users—both those with accounts on your Mac and those whose computers are available on the network—by means of the Drop Box or the new AirDrop feature, as Chapter 24 explains.

Picking up a file that has been placed in the Drop Box is easy. Go to the Drop Box in the Public Folder in your Home folder. Any files that other users have placed in your Drop Box are located here. You can copy the files from the Drop Box to any location in your disks or other volumes. Files shared via AirDrop appear in the recipient's Downloads folder.

Summary

Documents can be opened from the Finder using a variety of methods (double-clicking the file icon is the simplest) or from within compatible applications (pressing ⌘+O is the simplest method). The Open dialog box in applications resembles a Finder window, with similar views and access to the Sidebar. You also can use the Open With option to open a document from the Finder in an application that's not the default application for that document's file type.

Creating documents is accomplished with the File ⇨ New command or ⌘+N shortcut. To copy documents, you can use the Finder's copy and duplicate commands, or you can save a copy of the document from within an application. When working within documents, you can move or copy contents within and across documents using the standard Cut, Copy, and Paste commands. You also can drag and drop contents within and across documents. And you can create clipping files by dragging contents from a document to the desktop or to a Finder window and then dragging that clipping file into other documents.

The new Versions feature in Mac OS X Lion saves within your document a copy of each set of changes, so you can revert to any previously saved version by selecting the older version you want from a Time Machine-like interface, or you can copy contents from a previous version into your current version—assuming the application uses this new capability.

The new Auto Save feature also saves changes you make in the document as you make them, in case your Mac freezes or loses power while you are working—again only if your application uses this new capability. Auto Save also locks files after a default of two weeks of nonuse so when you open them later (presumably just to read their contents), you can't accidentally save inadvertent changes; you're asked to unlock the file to save changes after those two weeks or to save them in a new copy. A new unnamed pop-up menu in Auto Save–compatible applications lets you immediately lock or unlock a document.

Mac OS X has the Stationery Pad feature in a document's Info window to convert the document into a template that can't be saved over itself; instead, when you try to save it, you create a copy. Some applications give you this option from within their Save As dialog boxes.

Macs offer several methods for saving documents, though the most common is to choose File ⇨ Save or press ⌘+S in the active application. The first time you save a document, you get the Save As dialog box, in which you specify the filename and its location.

Applications that use the new Versions feature no longer have the Save As menu option to let you do so; they instead use the Duplicate menu option to create a copy of the document in a new window, from which you then save it with a new name using the Save menu option.

You close document windows using the Close button in the document window, the shortcut ⌘+W, or the menu command File ⇨ Close. When you quit an application, its documents windows are closed automatically. If you close a document with unsaved changes, Mac OS X gives you a chance to save those changes.

Backing Up Files

Backing up files, as well as restoring them, is fundamentally important but often ignored. That's too bad, because not backing up risks losing all your key information—family photos, business records, music, and more. And backing up is so very easy to do on the Mac, thanks to the built-in Time Machine utility. So there's really no excuse not to back up your Mac.

Time Machine makes the backup process quick and simple to set up, virtually unnoticeable in operation, and reliable for restoring files. It even comes with an attractive 3-D interface that adds a touch of life to the otherwise insipidly dull process of file restoration.

Cross-Reference

Although Time Machine does a great job backing up files from your Mac, chances are that you also have an iOS device such as an iPhone, iPad, or iPod Touch that also should be backed up. You can do so in iTunes (see Chapter 16) or via the free iCloud service (see Chapter 17). ∎

Setting Up for Backup

A backup is—as the name suggests—a reserve force that comes into play when something has gone wrong, typically when something has been lost from your Mac. Usually, you use a backup in two different circumstances. The first is when a file is lost, either because it was accidentally deleted or it became corrupted and is no longer usable. The second—a more serious use—is for disaster recovery. In that case, your

IN THIS CHAPTER

Preparing for backup

Using Time Machine to back up files

Using Time Machine to restore files

Mac is essentially unusable. It may be because of a physical failure of the hard disk or because something critical has happened to the file structure of Mac OS X. Either way, you'll be glad to have a backup on hand.

A backup enables to you to roll back part of your Mac's data to an earlier point—a point where you still had a file that has now been deleted or where the data on your hard disk wasn't corrupted. Fittingly then, Apple offers a comprehensive backup tool called Time Machine, which automatically records changes made to your hard disk and enables you to move back in time to recover files and data on your Mac. Furthermore, Time Machine can work directly in many of Apple's key applications.

New Feature

On MacBooks, Mac OS X Lion automatically saves a copy of recent changes to the startup, which helps Mac OS X recover files if your files hadn't yet been backed up (which could be days or weeks for a MacBook-toting traveler). No user action is required. ■

Choosing a backup medium

Because the data on your Mac is stored on its hard disk, it makes sense to ensure that your backup is stored elsewhere. And the most obvious place is on removable media. At one time, personal computer users stored pretty much everything on floppy disks (first the 5.25-inch variety and then the smaller 3.5-inch versions).

Today, floppy disks are no longer a practical option. Not only did Apple remove the floppy disk from its computer range with the introduction of the iMac a decade ago, but the limited capacity of the disks themselves is dwarfed by the data held on modern computers. Even the Zip disks that provided data storage of up to 750MB are no longer practical. (However, the Zip's maker, Iomega, has a similar product called the Rev that provides up to 120GB of storage on a single removable disk, but the disks are expensive.)

Businesses working in the enterprise environment often use tape drives to back up large amounts of data. Tape drives work on the same principle as video recording (or early audio recording) equipment, and modern tapes can contain up to a terabyte (1,024GB) of data. These solutions tend to be overkill for the home environment, and with the cost of setting up and maintaining them (not to mention the time involved with retrieving data), tape-based backups are losing popularity even in the enterprise environment.

For many years, using CD and DVD drives was the backup solution of choice for many people, and even these days it is an option worth considering. However, the relative size of DVDs (4.7GB for a single-layer [SL] disc; 8.5GB for a dual-layer [DL] disc) is quite small, especially compared to modern hard disks. Having said that, the ease with which optical discs can be recorded, the prevalence of optical drives on Macs, and the relative price and availability of optical media make this backup method one that many people still choose—especially when they want a permanent store of a specific kind of data (such as photographs from a wedding).

However, the external hard disk has become the de facto backup system of choice. These hard disks are cheap and readily available. They are essentially based on the same hard-disk technology used in your Mac's startup disk, except they are encased in a separate plastic shell and are connected to the Mac typically via FireWire or USB (Universal Serial Bus), but it can also be via a third option called Thunderbolt that Apple began providing in new Mac models in 2011.

Tip

If you use a USB disk for backup, be sure that it is the USB 2.0 standard rather than the USB 1.0 variant. USB 1.0's slower transfer speeds can make backups interminably slow. ∎

Of course, if you own a Mac Pro, you can install up to four separate hard disks internally and use one for backup storage.

Caution

You can also partition a single hard disk, such as your startup disk, and use the second partition to store a backup. But this is not particularly wise. A second partition may provide a backup for retrieving files that have been accidentally deleted or corrupted, but it provides no disaster recovery protection from a total hard-disk failure. That's why, if you try to use Time Machine on a partition existing on the same disk you are backing up, Time Machine repeatedly warns you against doing so. ∎

Finally, it is becoming more common to back up your data to an online (or *cloud*) storage space. Such dedicated services include Mozy (http://mozy.com), iDrive (www.idrive.com), and Carbonite (www.carbonite.com). Many of these services come with dedicated backup software.

Selecting backup software

If you decide to create backups to an external hard disk, several applications are available:

- **Time Machine:** Ever since Apple introduced Time Machine with Mac OS X 10.5 Leopard, Mac users interested in quickly setting up a backup solution have opted for this straightforward application, which comes with Mac OS X at no additional cost. Most of this chapter explains setting up and using Time Machine. (Mac OS X Server, covered in Chapter 25, lets you have a central Time Machine backup disk for all the Macs on your network. Apple's Time Capsule device also provides Time Machine backup to a common disk over Wi-Fi for multiple Macs in a home or small office.)

- **Retrospect:** If you are looking for a more high-end solution than Time Machine, or are looking for a solution for a small- or medium-size business with multiple computers, then Roxio's Retrospect (www.roxio.com) is a popular choice with a long history on the Mac under several owners. This program offers a wide array of customization options and supports a wide range of backup media. It also is cross-platform, which makes it useful for network environments with both Mac OS X and Windows computers.

- **SuperDuper:** Before Apple released Time Machine, SuperDuper (`www.shirt-pocket. com`) had been a popular choice among Mac OS X users. Although it lacks the highly integrated restore functions of Time Machine, SuperDuper is a simple backup tool, and its capability to back up to network volumes and optical discs make it an option still worth considering.

- **Carbon Copy Cloner:** Another popular solution among Mac OS X users is a program called Carbon Copy Cloner (`www.bombich.com`). Rather than creating incremental backups (those that save just the changes to your disk since the last backup), this program clones your entire hard disk onto an external source (usually another hard disk). The target hard disk has to be larger than your original hard disk, and the cloning process can be time-consuming; however, it is a good way to create a complete backup of your hard disk. In the event of a disaster, you can even boot your Mac from the cloned hard disk and use Carbon Copy Cloner to restore your regular boot disk from the backup.

Of course, you do not have to use software to create a backup. You can manually copy files that you want to back up. You can copy important files to an external hard disk, and you can burn files you want to back up to an optical disc. (The process of recording files to a recordable CD or DVD is explained in Chapter 6.) You also can use Mac OS X's Automator feature to create actions that add a layer of intelligence to the process of backing up files in the Finder. Using Automator, you can schedule the process of copying files and copy only the files that have changed. (Automator is described in Chapter 13.)

Tip

You can find a useful Automator function for backing up files at `www.apple.com/downloads/macosx/automator/backupfolder.html.` ∎

The problems inherent with any backup solution are largely related to setting up and maintaining a regular backup process. You need to determine which files to back up and then regularly transfer these files to another storage location for the backup to be effective. Performing regular backups is a time-consuming and largely unrewarding process (until, of course, a disaster strikes and you need to restore vital data).

Using Time Machine to Back Up Files

Time Machine has revolutionized how the backup process works. Time Machine was designed to be incredibly easy to set up; virtually invisible in operation; and, thanks to some flashy eye candy (its space-themed background), it even makes the normally tedious process of restoring files fun.

Time Machine boasts some great features that cement its status as the top backup app for Mac OS X users. The most important of these is automatic stop and resume functionality. If you remove an external disk or unplug your Mac (or disconnect from a network volume),

Time Machine just stops where it is, with no fuss, not even a notification; when you reconnect, Time Machine quietly resumes the backup as if nothing had ever happened. This is great: It means you don't have to wait for backups to complete, and therefore, don't have to schedule backups.

Time Machine is a permanent, always-on solution. You don't have to take time out to perform backups.

Because Time Machine is constantly tracking changes on your Mac, you can use it to recover files and data that have been accidentally deleted. It also is a superb disaster recovery tool; if your Mac is so badly damaged that you can't even use it, simply plug the Time Machine disk into another Mac and you can restore your entire computer from it.

You can even restore your version of Mac OS X to a completely different Mac and carry on working. This is because Time Machine works in tandem with a Mac OS X technology called Migration Assistant (described in Appendix A). So if you set up a new Mac, you can plug in your Time Machine disk and use Migration Assistant to copy all your files, programs, and settings, and set up the new Mac just like your original Mac.

Using external disks for backup

The main requirement of Time Machine is that you have a second hard disk on which to store the backup. Typically, this is an external hard disk, although those of you with Mac Pros can use a second internal hard disk. The advantage to using an external hard disk is that you can take the disk with you and connect it to another Mac with relative ease. This enables you to use it to migrate data from one Mac to another.

Tip

When installing a second hard disk for Time Machine, it's wise to make sure the disk is larger than the total of all the disks that you are backing up. (I recommend you use a disk of at least double the capacity of the disks you are backing up.) Time Machine uses compression technology to save space, but each incremental backup increases the size of the file stored on the backup disk, so the backups keep growing. A smart move is to buy the largest external hard disk you can afford; 2TB external disks are readily available at reasonable prices. Time Machine saves backups until it runs out of room and then starts deleting the older versions of files, so the larger your backup disk, the farther back you can go to retrieve files. ∎

With today's high-capacity hard disks, you can use a single disk to back up multiple Macs. Just partition the disk so each Mac has its own dedicated volume to keep the backups separate. Of course, this technique means that you have to remember to plug the disk into each Mac long enough for Time Machine to back each one up, and you don't get automatic backup on the Macs not currently connected to the disk, so there is danger of data loss in between backup rotations. Consider one of the options described in the sidebar "Backing up wirelessly" instead.

When Apple first released Time Machine, it stated that you would have to use a disk that wasn't bootable and that you wouldn't be able to copy files to a hard disk being used by Time

Machine. In fact, you can back up to a bootable disk, and you can write files to a Time Machine backup disk. Having the Time Machine be bootable is a nice safety precaution should your startup disk fail. But I don't advise that you use the backup disk for storing other files, because these files are not backed up elsewhere and could be permanently lost should the Time Machine backup disk get damaged (the whole point of backup is to have duplicates of your files on a separate disk that is unaffected if the main disk is damaged).

Setting up Time Machine

Setting up Time Machine really couldn't be simpler. You set it up in the Time Machine system preference, which you can access in any of the following ways.

- **Plug in a new disk:** If Time Machine is not already configured on your Mac, then connecting an external hard disk prompts Mac OS X to open a dialog box that asks if you want to use that disk to back up with Time Machine. Click Use as Backup Disk to open the Time Machine system preference.

- **Via the System Preferences application:** Open System Preferences by choosing ⌘⇨ System Preferences, and click the Time Machine icon.

- **Via the menu bar:** If the Time Machine icon menu is available in the menu bar, choose Open Time Machine Preferences from it.

Configuring Time Machine for backups

The Time Machine system preference has a large Off/On icon toggle, the Select Disk and the Options buttons, and the Show Time Machine Status in the Menu Bar option, as shown in Figure 11.1.

FIGURE 11.1

The Time Machine system preference enables you to switch the backup on and off, and it offers basic options for adjusting the nature of the backup.

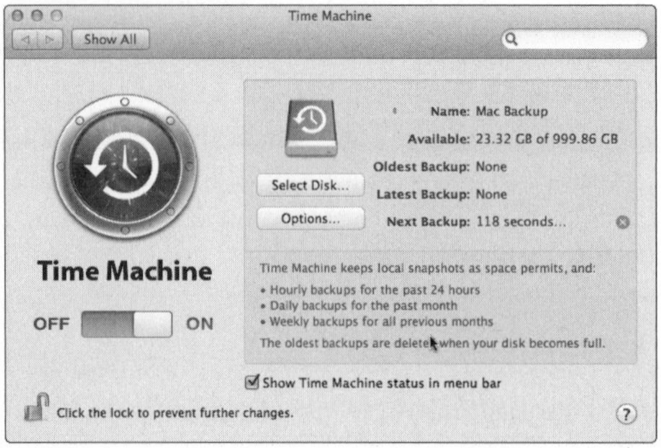

Backing up wirelessly

Those of you with a MacBook or other Mac who want to back up wirelessly have two options (both of which involve additional Apple hardware).

The first option is to buy an Apple-branded AirPort Extreme router and connect an external USB 2.0 hard disk to the router. Time Machine can use this hard disk to store the backup files. Note that Mac OS X supports this feature only on its AirPort Extreme router; those of you with other Wi-Fi routers that let you connect a hard disk to them cannot use this feature.

The second option for wireless backups is to buy an Apple device called Time Capsule. It is essentially an AirPort Extreme router with a built-in hard disk. Time Capsule acts as a dedicated hub for creating a wireless network and backing up files. Although investing in a Time Capsule device isn't as cost-effective as using a USB 2.0 hard disk tethered to your Mac, it is an incredibly simple way to create backups for one or more Macs without worrying about cables. Best of all, setting up a Time Capsule is as simple as setting up Time Machine. Together they make a great backup combination.

Note that wireless connections are much slower than the local USB, FireWire, or Thunderbolt connections, so your backups take longer. You trade the advantage of sharing a backup disk and worrying about cabling each Mac to a disk for the disadvantages of lower speed and higher cost.

If you clicked Use as Backup Disk when you plugged in a new disk, the Off/On switch is set to On and the attached disk is automatically selected as the Time Machine backup disk. In this case, you really are good to go: Time Machine automatically begins backing up the contents of your main hard disk to the backup disk. Kick back and relax; you're done.

When you first create a backup with Time Machine, a status window opens to show you the progress of the backup. The initial backup may take a couple of hours (or longer if you are backing up over a network). Subsequent backups are incremental, so they copy over only files that have changed since the last backup; consequently, all backups after the first are much quicker.

Like all Time Machine activity, the initial backup is designed not to interfere with the operation of Mac OS X, so you can minimize the Time Machine status window (by clicking the Minimize icon button) and close the Time Machine system preference (by clicking the Close icon button); now just continue with your work. If you notice a slight slowdown, don't worry; it will pass.

Tip

Time Machine is designed to work seamlessly, regardless of interruptions. However, I advise that you let the initial backup take place uninterrupted. You can carry on using your Mac, but it's best not to remove the hard disk, disconnect from a network volume, or turn off your Mac until the first Time Machine backup is complete. ■

Choosing a backup disk

If you have more than two disks attached to your Mac, you need to tell Mac OS X which disk to use. Click Select Disk in the Time Machine system preference to open a settings sheet listing all the disks accessible to Mac OS X. Select the disk you want to use, and click Use for Backup.

237

New Feature

Mac OS X Lion can encrypt your backups, so if someone steals your backup disk, they can't access its data. In the Select Disk settings sheet, select the Encrypt Backup Disk option to enable encryption. You're asked for a password that you need to remember to be able to access the backup's contents in the future. ■

If the hard disk you have selected does not contain enough free space to store the backup, the Time Machine Error dialog box appears that informs you of the size that the current backup requires and the amount of space free on the hard disk you have selected. This dialog box has two options: You can click OK, which cancels the backup and turns off Time Machine, or you can click Preferences; from here you can click Select Disk and either choose another disk with more free space or use the Time Machine options to reduce the amount of data backed up on your hard disk.

Choosing backup exclusions and options

When you click the Options button in the Time Machine system preference, a settings sheet appears with options to control the backup.

The main area of the Time Machine options sheet enables you to set areas from the Finder that you do *not* want Time Machine to back up. Not all parts of your Mac OS X disk are vital, and cutting back the backup offers two advantages: It reduces the size of the backup, and it reduces the amount of time required to make a backup. You may consider some types of files less important than others; many users consider movies and music to be less important than photographs and documents, although your own priorities may differ.

If you decide not to include some disks or folders in the Time Machine backup, you add them to the main pane labeled Exclude These Items from Backups. The list includes all disks connected to your Mac via USB, FireWire, or Thunderbolt cable (network volumes are not backed up via Time Machine), but you can add items to this window from other volumes in one of two ways:

- **Drag and drop:** Open a new Finder window, and locate a file or folder that you do not want Time Machine to include in the backup. Drag it to the Exclude These Items from Backups pane. As you hover over the window, a horizontal blue line appears; let go of the mouse to add the item to the window.

- **Click the + icon button below the list of disks:** A dialog box appears from which you navigate to the disk, folder, or file you want; select it and click Exclude. Note the Show Invisible Items option; selecting it reveals the files and folders that are usually hidden on your hard disk, such as internal Mac OS X system files.

Note

Folders and files displayed in the Exclude These Items from Backups list include the path structure to the item, so when you come back to this settings sheet, you can see exactly where these excluded files and folders reside. Next to the + and – icon buttons is a display showing the amount of space that the current backup will require. ■

Moving your backup to a bigger disk

As your Time Machine backup disk gets full—whether from backing up additional external disks onto it or from backing up the ever-increasing number of files on your Mac—you may decide you want a bigger disk to back up to. The process is not quite as straightforward as you might expect.

First, if you simply connect a new backup disk and set it up in Time Machine, that new backup disk will not have all the previous backups; instead, it starts from scratch by copying all your current files and then doing the incremental backup after that.

You might think that all you have to do is connect your new disk, copy or move the old files to the new disk, and then set it up as the new Time Machine backup disk. But if you do so, Time Machine ignores those previous backup files and starts the backup process from scratch, so again your old backups aren't available via Time Machine.

What you have to do is clone the old disk's contents to the new disk, so Time Machine sees it as the same disk. To do so, first turn off Time Machine, and then connect the old and new backup disks. Now open Mac OS X's Disk Utility, and go to the Restore pane. At the left of the Disk Utility window is a list of connected disks. Drag the old disk's icon into the Source field, and drag the new disk's icon into the Destination field. Then click Restore.

After Disk Utility has cloned the old disk to the new disk, close Disk Utility and rename the old disk something else so Time Machine doesn't get confused. (I suggest you not delete the old disk's contents or reformat it until you are sure that the new backup disk is working correctly.) Turn Time Machine back on, and you should be set.

To remove items from the Exclude These Items from Backup list, select them and press the Delete key or click the – icon button.

Four Time Machine options appear below the Exclude These Items from Backups pane:

- **Back Up while on Battery Power:** This option appears for owners of Mac laptops and is selected by default. Deselecting the option prevents Time Machine from backing up a Mac laptop unless it is powered via its cord.

- **Notify after Old Backups Are Deleted:** Time Machine backs up data daily, weekly, and monthly. When the hard disk begins to fill up, the program consolidates older backups (days into weeks, and weeks into months). By default, Time Machine warns you when it is going to delete older backups; deselecting this option prevents Time Machine from warning you when it is going to delete older backups.

- **Lock Documents:** If selected, this option locks documents from accidental saves after a document hasn't been changed for the period specified in the adjacent pop-up menu. This option is part of the Auto Save feature covered in Chapter 10.

New Feature

The Lock Documents option is new to Mac OS X Lion. ∎

Setting up Time Machine with a Time Capsule

If you have an Apple Time Capsule device, you can set it up to work with Time Machine. The process of setting up a Time Capsule is identical to that of setting up an Apple AirPort Extreme Wi-Fi router. When you first attach a Time Capsule to your home network, the AirPort Utility automatically opens, enabling you to set up the Time Capsule. You also can access the AirPort Utility by opening the Time Machine system preference, clicking Select Disk, and clicking Set Up Time Capsule.

You set up a Time Capsule as follows:

1. **Turn on Wi-Fi.** If Wi-Fi is not already switched on, you need to activate it. You can do this by clicking the Wi-Fi icon menu in the menu bar and choosing Turn Wi-Fi On, or by choosing ➪ System Preferences, clicking the Network icon, selecting Wi-Fi from the list on the left of the Network system preference, and clicking Turn Wi-Fi On.

2. **Connect to the network.** By default, the Time Capsule is called Apple Network followed by a six-digit alphanumeric identifier (for example, *Apple Network a8a4d8*). Choose this name from the Wi-Fi icon menu in the menu bar, or in the Network system preference, choose the name in the Network Name pop-up menu.

3. **Open AirPort Utility.** The AirPort Utility should open automatically if a new Time Capsule is attached to your network. If not, you can locate the AirPort Utility inside the Utilities folder (inside the Applications folder in the Finder).

4. **Highlight Time Machine.** An icon for Time Machine appears in the list on the left side of the AirPort Utility. Select it, and click Continue.

5. **Enter a name and password.** You can personalize your Time Capsule by giving it a name (by default, it uses your username). You also must enter a password (and then reenter the same password in the Verify Password text field) to protect the settings of your Time Capsule. By default, the password is saved to your Keychain, so you do not need to enter it every time you make changes to the Time Capsule (the Keychain is explained in Chapter 26). If you deselect the Remember This Password in My Keychain option, you are prompted to enter the password whenever you want to make changes to the Time Capsule. By default, the same password also gives you access to the Time Capsule disk through the Finder. If you select the Use a Different Password to Secure Disks option, you can set a different password for disk access. When you've entered your name and password, click Continue.

6. **Select what you want to do with Time Capsule.** Your Time Capsule may be attached to your current router or to your DSL or cable modem. In that case, you need to tell it how to interact with the network. You have three options to choose from:

   - I Want to Create a New Network.
   - I Want to Replace an Existing Base Station or Wireless Router with Time Capsule.
   - I Want Time Capsule to Join My Current Network.

   Select the appropriate option and click Continue.

7. **Update the Time Capsule.** When you have selected the appropriate settings for attaching the Time Capsule to your network, click the Update button. A dialog box appears warning you that the Time Capsule will be unavailable during the update. The update shouldn't take longer than a couple of minutes, after which the AirPort Utility shows a congratulations message. Click Quit to finish setting up your Time Capsule.

When the Time Capsule is set up, Time Machine can back up to it. Open the Time Machine system preference, click Select Disk, select the Time Capsule volume, and click Use for Backup. You are prompted to enter the password you entered during the Time Capsule setup; enter it, and click Connect. Time Machine begins backing up your volume wirelessly.

Using Time Machine to Restore Files

The point of having a backup is to be able to restore files—a process that Time Machine makes so visually spectacular that you'll find yourself looking forward to it. When you restore files, the Time Machine browser replaces your desktop with a starry background and a row of Finder windows zooming off into infinity, each window representing the Mac's files at a different point in time, as Figure 11.2 shows.

There are typically three reasons for wanting to retrieve a file from an earlier point in time:

- **Accidental deletion:** You may have moved a file to the Trash and then emptied the Trash. If you decide at a later point that you need the file, Time Machine can help you retrieve it.

- **File corruption:** Even though Mac OS X is a stable operating system, it is possible for a file to become corrupted and unworkable. In this case, you can use Time Machine to retrieve an earlier instance of the file when it was in full working order.

- **Version rollback:** Suppose you have made substantial changes to a file and then saved it, but decide at a later point that you want to revert to the earlier version of the file. Although it's usually wiser to track changes in documents and undo the ones you don't want, not all applications have this capability, so Time Machine can come in very handy in those cases.

You can access the Time Machine browser using any of the following methods:

- **Use the Dock icon.** By default, a Time Machine icon is present in the Mac OS X dock. Click it to open Time Machine.

- **Use the menu bar's Time Machine icon menu.** In the Time Machine icon menu in the menu bar (if one is present), choose Enter Time Machine.

- **Open the application.** Time Machine is an application and, as such, is located in the Applications folder. Double-click the Time Machine icon to access the program.

FIGURE 11.2

The Time Machine interface depicts a star field with windows stretching out back in time. You use controls to the right to move back through different instances.

Using the Time Machine browser

By default, accessing Time Machine replaces the desktop with a star field window and a Finder window. Behind the Finder window is a cascade of other Finder windows, each one representing an earlier instance in time. The initial Finder window represents the current state of all the files on the Mac. You can navigate the Finder window in the same manner as a Finder window opened in Mac OS X (as explained in Chapter 3). You also can use Spotlight search to locate files in the Finder window displayed in the Time Machine browser. (Spotlight search is covered in Chapter 5.)

Where the Time Machine browser differs from the regular desktop is the vertical time bar and arrows on the right side. Move the pointer over the time bar, and it expands with a visual effect similar to the dock in magnification mode. Each horizontal line on the time bar represents a different instance in time. Click to select a time instance.

Time Machine backs up files according to the following schedule:

- Hourly backups for the last 24 hours
- Daily backups for the last month
- Weekly backups for all previous months

The lowest line on the vertical time bar represents the present; each horizontal line moving upward represents the next instance back in time (moving through hourly, weekly, and monthly backups). To the left of each bar is the time and date that the line represents. Clicking any of these lines takes the Finder window to that point in time (complete with a swooshing display as the windows in the Time Machine browser flip through to the appropriate one). The Finder window then displays all the files that were present on the Mac and its attached disks at that point in time.

Restoring files with Time Machine

If you see a file that you want to restore, highlight the file in the Finder window in the Time Machine browser and click Restore. That Finder window flips forward to the foremost instance (the one that represents the present), and the file is deposited into it, in its original location.

If the restored file exists in the present Finder window, a dialog box opens with three options:

- **Keep Original:** Choosing this option cancels the retrieval and keeps the file that is in the present Finder window.
- **Keep Both:** Choosing this option retains the original file into the past Finder window and copies it into the present Finder window. (A number is added to the copied, past filename to differentiate the two files.)
- **Replace:** Choosing this option deletes the file in the present Finder window and replaces it with the past version being retrieved from Time Machine.

Searching for changes

Just as you can use the vertical timeline to search through folders, you also can skim through Finder windows and look for changes. Clicking the ↑ icon button in the Time Machine browser flips back in time, moving through the various save points, until one of the files in the Finder's location changes. This is useful for when you know the location of a file, but not the point at which it was changed or deleted. Clicking the ↓ icon button moves forward through time, again stopping at the point at which the location displayed in the Finder window changes.

Exiting the Time Machine browser

When you have decided to finish restoring files from the Time Machine browser, you can return to the main Mac OS X in three ways:

Using the Time Machine with applications

Because Time Machine works to back up and restore files on your Mac, you can use it within the Finder to restore anything used by Mac OS X. However, you also can use it to restore some Mac OS X applications to a previous state, such as to restore Address Book contacts if they get corrupted in a file sync or to roll back to old e-mail lists in Mail. These applications are supported by the Time Machine browser:

- Mail
- Address Book
- iPhoto
- GarageBand

To use Time Machine with these applications, first open the application and then open the Time Machine browser. You see the same series of windows stretching into the past as you do for files, and you move through the browser and restore past application states the same way as you do for files.

- By clicking the Cancel button
- By pressing the Esc key
- By clicking the Close icon button in the foremost window in the Time Machine browser

Summary

It is critical to have a backup plan in place in case files are accidentally deleted or corrupted. Mac OS X's Time Machine utility is an easy-to-use, powerful backup-and-restore tool that everyone should use.

Time Machine backs up data automatically to external hard disks, and it provides options as to what disks on your Mac to back up, whether to encrypt those backups, and what disks, folders, and files to not back up. Apple's Time Capsule combines a wireless router and a hard disk to allow wireless backup for one or more Macs.

If you need to restore old files and folders, the Time Machine browser enables you to navigate through Finder windows that contain those old items; you can then tell Time Machine to restore those old files into the current Finder window, thus bringing back a missing file or replacing a damaged one. Time Machine can restore past settings in some applications, such as Mail and Address Book. Time Machine also enables you to restore an entire volume, such as in the case of disk failure, to another disk. It also can restore one Mac's contents to another Mac when used with the Migration Assistant.

Working with Services

I t's amazing just how much software comes with Mac OS X Lion. Chapter 14 details the several dozen applications, utilities, and widgets. But there's another kind of software in Mac OS X beyond these: helper applications called *services*.

A service can be specific to an application or general purpose (meaning it's available for several applications). The services available at any moment depend on which application (including the Finder) is running. Apple includes a bunch of services in Mac OS X, and individual applications can add their own (Opera and Skype both do, for example), some of which other applications can use as well (depending on how they are designed).

To find out what services are available, choose Services from your application's menu. For example, choose Finder ➪ Services, Pages ➪ Services, or Excel ➪ Services.

IN THIS CHAPTER

Understanding what services are

The contextual nature of services

The common services available

Options for services preferences

Understanding Service Availability

The services are displayed contextually based—not only based on the application that is running but also based on what is selected. For example, Pages shows the Look Up in Dictionary, Make New Sticky Note, Send Selection, and Search in Google menu options only when text is selected. And both Numbers and Keynote show Look Up in Dictionary, Make New Sticky Note, Capture Full Screen, Capture Screen Region, Capture Timed Screen, Send Selection, and Search in Google when text is highlighted.

Figure 12.1 shows the services available in the Finder when a folder is selected: Folder Actions Setup, New Email with Attachment, and Services Preferences. It also shows the services available for Firefox when a URL is selected. Remember that the services displayed depend not just on the application in use but what content is selected or active in that application.

Note

Mac OS X categorizes the available services based on the applications they are designed to work with, as Figure 12.1 shows. This keeps the services list uncluttered with irrelevant options. ∎

Note

The Services Preferences menu option lets you control which services appear in the Services menu, as explained later in this chapter. ∎

FIGURE 12.1

The services available in the Finder (at left) and Firefox (at right)

A Tour of the Common Services

Although the services are contextual, you may not come across them all, so Mac OS X Lion supplies 42 services that are commonly available, organized in seven groups.

Applications may add their own services, so you may see services not listed here available on your Mac. If you're not sure what application a service is from, go to the Keyboard system preference's Keyboard Shortcuts pane, select Services from its Sidebar, right-click or Control+ click the service name in the list at right, and choose Show in Finder from the contextual menu. The folder containing that service's parent application opens, with the application's name highlighted.

Tip

Some services are available if you right-click or Control+click a text selection or other element in an application. These services display at the bottom of the contextual menu that appears. ∎

Development services

Five services may appear in the Development group in the Services submenu. They do the following:

- **Create Service:** This option lets you create a service from a series of actions via Automator.
- **Create Workflow:** This option lets you create an Automator workflow. (See Chapter 13 for more details on Automator.)
- **Get Result of AppleScript:** This option runs the select text as an AppleScript and presents any results as text. (See Chapter 13 for more details on AppleScript.)
- **Make New AppleScript:** This option launches the AppleScript Editor and places the selected text in it.
- **Run as AppleScript:** This option runs the selected text in the AppleScript Editor.

Files and Folders services

Eight services may appear in the Files and Folders group in the Services submenu. They do the following:

- **Open Selected File in TextEdit:** This option opens the selected file in TextEdit.
- **New Terminal at Folder:** This option opens a Terminal window (see Appendix D) to the current folder location.
- **New Terminal Tab at Folder:** This option opens a Terminal tab (see Appendix D) to the current folder location.
- **Encode Selected Video Files:** This option converts the selected video files in the H.264/AAC format for use on iPhones, iPods, iPads, Apple TVs, Macs, and PCs.
- **Folder Actions Setup:** This option lets you set up a series of folder actions (see Chapter 4).
- **Open:** This option opens the Open dialog box.
- **Reveal:** This option opens the folder in which the selected files reside (handy if you've selected an alias).
- **Show Info:** This option displays the Info window. (Chapters 3 and 4 cover the Info window in detail.)
- **Send File to Bluetooth Device:** This option sends the selected file to a Bluetooth device, if any is available, that you select.

New Feature

New to Mac OS X Lion are the New Terminal at Folder, New Terminal Tab at Folder, and Encode Selected Video Files services in the Files and Folders group. ■

Internet services

The Internet group has only one option:

- **Open URL:** If you select a web address (a URL, or Uniform Resource Locator), the Open URL service opens it in your default web browser.

Messaging services

The message-oriented services includes four default options. They do the following:

- **New Email To Address:** If you select an e-mail address, this service opens Apple's Mail program (see Chapter 20) and addresses an e-mail to that address.
- **New Email with Attachment:** This service sends a file to the destination of your choice via Apple's Mail program.
- **New Email with Selection:** This service opens Mail and places the text selection in the message body. If no text is selected, the service simply opens Mail. Note that the Send Selection service does *not* attach to the message any files you may have selected, as you might expect.
- **New Note with Selection:** This service creates a note in Mail from the selected text.

New Feature

In the Messaging group, Mac OS X Lion has renamed the Send File service to New Email with Attachment, the Send Selection service to New Email with Selection, and the Send To service to New Email To Address. ■

Pictures services

Five options are in the Pictures group. The options do the following:

- **Capture Full Screen:** As you would expect, this option takes an image of the entire screen.
- **Capture Screen Using Timer:** This option gives you a ten-second delay before the entire screen is captured, so you can move the mouse, start a process, or do any other last-minute activity you want captured.
- **Capture Selection from Screen:** This option enables you to use your mouse to draw a rectangular area that you want captured.
- **Import Images:** This option lets you import images into the current application.
- **Set Desktop Picture:** This option sets the currently selected image as the desktop's background image.

Note

The Capture Full Screen, Capture Screen Using Timer, and Capture Selection from Screen options all run the Grab utility covered in Chapter 14, which saves an image of your screen as a .PNG file. ■

Tip

You can always press Shift+⌘+3 to capture the full screen at any time and Shift+⌘+4 to capture a screen region at any time. Press Shift+⌘+4 and then click and hold the mouse or touchpad button when dragging the pointer to create a selection marquee of what you want to capture; release the button to complete the section and capture its image. Or press Shift+⌘+4 and then press the spacebar to get a camera icon that you click in a window, dialog box, menu, or other element to capture just that element. ∎

Searching services

The Searching group has three options. Here's what they do:

- **Look Up in Dictionary:** This option opens the Dictionary application (see Chapter 14) and looks up the first word in the selected text, displaying any results found.

- **Search with *searchengine*:** As you would expect, choosing Search in *searchengine* opens the Safari web browser to the search page for whatever search engine you've specified in Safari's preferences (Yahoo, Google, or Bing) and searches for that selected text, so you see the results instantly. (Chapter 19 covers Safari.)

- **Spotlight:** This option searches for the selected text on your Mac and in Spotlight-compatible applications such as Address Book and Mail; Chapter 5 covers Spotlight in detail.

Text services

The greatest number of built-in services is in the Text grouping. Here's what the 13 services do:

- **Add to iTunes as a Spoken Track:** This option converts the text to an audio file and adds it to your iTunes library.

- **Convert Selected Simplified Chinese File** and **Convert Selected Traditional Chinese File:** The two Chinese-text options convert the selected text file not to English but between the two forms of Chinese: simplified and traditional. If the selected file's text is in traditional Chinese script, you get the option to convert it to simplified script. If the selected file's text is in simplified Chinese script, you get the option to convert it to traditional script.

- **Convert Selected Simplified Chinese Text** and **Convert Selected Traditional Chinese Text:** The two Chinese-text options convert the text selection not to English but between the two forms of Chinese: simplified and traditional. If the selected text is in traditional Chinese script, you get the option to convert it to simplified script. If the selected text is in simplified Chinese script, you get the option to convert it to traditional script.

- **Create Collection from Text:** This option creates a font collection based on the fonts used in the selected text.

- **Create Font Library from Text:** This option creates a font library based on the fonts used in the selected text.

- **Make New Sticky Note:** This option creates a new onscreen note containing the selected text. Chapter 14 covers the Stickies application in detail. (If you use the Make New Sticky Note service in the Finder, such as when highlighting part of a filename, it creates a new note but does not include the selected text.)

- **New TextEdit Window Containing Selection:** This option opens a new document window in TextEdit containing the selected text.

- **Open Man Page in Terminal:** This option opens the Unix help page (a man—short for *manual*—page) in the Terminal (see Appendix D).

- **Search Man Pages in Terminal:** This option enables you to search the Unix help page system (composed of man pages) in the Terminal (see Appendix D).

- **Show Address in Google Maps:** This option opens Google Maps in Safari and shows the selected location.

- **Summarize:** This option summarizes the text selection into a more concise version.

New Feature

New to Mac OS X Lion are the Open Man Page in Terminal and Search Man Pages in Terminal services in the Text group. ∎

Changing Services Preferences

If you choose Services Preferences from the Services submenu, the Keyboard Shortcuts pane of the Keyboard system preference opens, as shown in Figure 12.2. Although the pane is named Keyboard Shortcuts, if you click the Services option in the list at the left, you gain control over which services appear in the Services submenu.

In the Services subpane, the available services from both Mac OS X and individual applications display, grouped by the categories that display in the Services submenu. Click a disclosure triangle to expand the list of options for a category. Select any options you want to appear in the Services submenu, and deselect any options you don't want to appear.

Note

Even if you select a Services submenu option to enable it, remember that it displays only in applications for which that service is compatible. ∎

FIGURE 12.2

The Services subpane of the Keyboard Shortcuts pane in the Keyboard system preference is where you determine which services are available in the Services submenu.

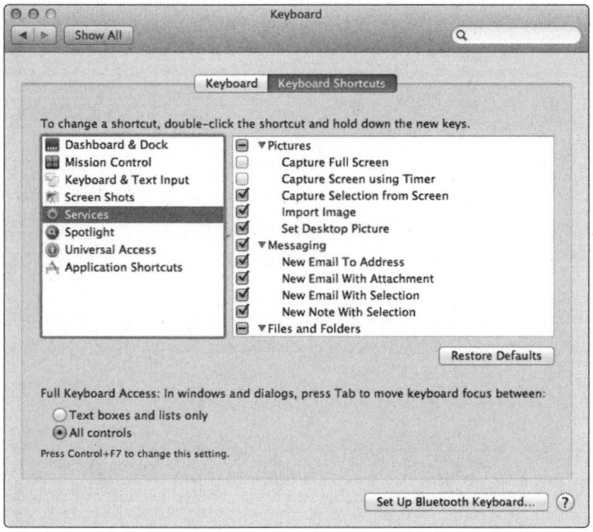

Summary

Mac OS X Lion comes with 42 services that are available contextually in the Services menu option in the Finder's and in applications' menus. The default services fall into seven groupings: Development, Files and Folders, Internet, Messaging, Pictures, Searching, and Text. Services display contextually, based on what application they were chosen from and what is selected. Most work with text, so they require that text be selected to become available.

Some services also are available when you right-click or Control+click text within an application.

You can control which services are available in the Services subpane of the Keyboard Shortcuts pane in the Keyboard system preference.

Using AppleScript and Automator

IN THIS CHAPTER

Understanding how Mac OS X messages and events let scripts work

Understanding the AppleScript language

Using the AppleScript Editor application to create scripts

Creating, analyzing, and saving basic scripts

Developing drag-and-drop script applications

Accessing scripts via the Scripts menu

Using AppleScript to run programs on other Macs

Using Automator to create programming-free workflows

Although you may be impressed by components in all the technologies that come with Mac OS X, individually, the components don't do much by themselves—they tend to require user input. Scripting has long been a way to coordinate the different components of a task by enabling you to compose a script that plays back a set of commands in order.

Mac OS X's AppleScript scripting language is a simplified programming language that enables you to control your applications and perform tasks automatically. Scripts range from the simplest to the highly complex, depending on your skill at scripting, your knowledge of AppleScript's nuances, and the requirements of your task. This chapter contains enough information about AppleScript that even a scripting novice can get scripts up and running.

I begin by showing the underlying technologies that make AppleScript possible: messages and events. Then it's on to an introduction of AppleScript and a look at the tools that enable you to run, modify, and create scripts of your own. Finally, I run through a few basic scripts, to show the AppleScript language in practice.

AppleScript is great for programmers, even casual ones, but for many people, AppleScript is too scary. That's why Mac OS X includes the Automator application, which enables you to assemble script-like actions without programming skills and save them for reuse later.

Understanding Messages and Events

Macintosh applications perform tasks in response to events. Users originate events with the keyboard and mouse or touchpad, and applications respond to the events by performing tasks. Similarly, an application can make other applications perform tasks by sending messages about events.

The events that applications send to each other in messages are called *Apple events*. AppleScript makes applications perform tasks by sending them Apple events.

When an application receives a message about an Apple event, the application takes a particular action based on the specific event. This action can be anything from performing a menu command to taking some data, manipulating it, and returning the result to the source of the Apple event message.

For example, when you choose ➪ Shut Down or ➪ Restart, Mac OS X sends an Apple event message to every open application saying a Quit event occurred. For this reason, applications quit automatically when you choose ➪ Shut Down or ➪ Restart.

When you drop document icons on an application icon, the Finder sends a message to Mac OS X saying this event happened, and the system sends the application an Apple event message that says an Open Documents event occurred. The Open Documents message includes a list of all the documents whose icons you dragged and dropped. When you double-click an application icon, the Finder sends Mac OS X a message that says this event happened, and Mac OS X sends the application an Open Application message. When you double-click a document, the application that created the document gets an Open Documents message with the name of the document you double-clicked.

Virtually all Mac applications respond to at least three Apple events: Open Application, Open Documents, and Quit Application. Applications that print also respond to the Apple event Print Documents. Only very old, very specialized, or poorly engineered Mac applications don't respond to these basic Apple events.

Applications that go beyond the three basic Apple events understand another two dozen core Apple events. These Apple events encompass actions and objects that almost all applications have in common, such as the Close, Save, Undo, Redo, Cut, Copy, and Paste commands. Applications with related capabilities recognize still more sets of Apple events. For example, word-processing applications understand Apple events about text manipulation, and drawing applications understand Apple events about graphics manipulation. Application developers can even define private Apple events that only their applications know.

Mac OS X provides the means of communicating Apple event messages between applications. The applications can be on the same computer or on different computers connected to the same network. To understand how Apple event messages work, think of them as a telephone system. Mac OS X furnishes a telephone for each application, as well as the wires that connect them. Applications call each other with messages about Apple events.

Apple events offer many intriguing possibilities for the world of personal computing. No longer does one application need to handle every possible function; instead, it can send Apple event messages to helper applications.

Introducing AppleScript

Apple event messages aren't just for professional software engineers. Macintosh enthusiasts with little technical training can use Apple event messages to control applications by writing statements in the AppleScript language. For example, suppose that you want to quit all open applications. Mac OS X doesn't have a Quit All command, but you can create one with AppleScript. You can use AppleScript commands to automate simple tasks, as well as to automate a more complicated series of tasks, as the rest of this chapter demonstrates.

The AppleScript language

With AppleScript, you tell applications what to do, using natural language. This means simply that AppleScript is a programming language designed especially to make it easy for computer users, not computer engineers, to build their own solutions. (Actually, engineers use it, too.)

You tell applications what to do by writing statements in the AppleScript language. Although AppleScript is an artificial language, its statements are similar to sentences in a natural language such as English. You can look at many AppleScript statements and easily figure out what they're supposed to do.

The words and phrases in AppleScript statements resemble English, but they are terms that have special meanings in the context of AppleScript. Some terms are commands, and some terms are objects that the commands act on. Other terms control how AppleScript performs the statements.

A single AppleScript statement can perform a simple task, but most tasks require a series of statements that are performed one after the other. A set of AppleScript statements that accomplishes a task (or several tasks) is called a *script*. The term *script* is used because the computer follows the statements you put in order, much like an actor follows the script of a movie. A script can rename a batch of files, change an application's preference settings, copy data from a database to another application, or automate a sequence of tasks that you previously performed one at a time by hand. You can develop your own script tools to accomplish exactly what you need.

As an added boon, AppleScript can actually watch you as you work with an application and write a script for you behind the scenes. This process is called *script recording*.

Although AppleScript is designed to be a simple-to-understand language, it offers all the capabilities of a traditional programming language and won't frustrate programmers and advanced users. You can store information in variables for later use, write `if ... then` statements to perform commands selectively according to a condition that you specify, or repeat a set of commands as many times as you want. AppleScript also offers error checking and object-oriented programming.

Scripting additions

AppleScript has an expandable lexicon of terms. It knows meanings of basic terms, and it augments this knowledge with terms from other sources. Many additional AppleScript terms come from the very applications that AppleScript controls. I explore this source of AppleScript terms in greater detail later in this chapter.

Additional AppleScript terms also come from special files called *scripting additions.* AppleScript looks for scripting addition files in the following folders:

- **ScriptingAdditions:** Located in the Library folder of the System folder (path `/System/Library/ScriptingAdditions/`), it contains standard scripting additions from Apple that are available to all users of your computer. (This folder also may contain other files that are not scripting additions.) There's also a `Scripting Additions` folder located in the main Library folder (path `/Library/Scripting Additions/`) that applications place scripts in, also available to all users.

- **Scripts:** Located in the main Library folder (path `/Library/Scripts/`), it contains more scripting additions that are available to all users of your computer.

Tip
If the `ScriptingAdditions` folder doesn't exist in a Library folder where you want to put a scripting addition file, create a new folder and name it `ScriptingAdditions` (put no spaces in the name). Put your scripting addition file in this new folder. ■

Introducing AppleScript Editor

For creating and editing AppleScript scripts, you can use the AppleScript Editor utility included with Mac OS X. AppleScript Editor also can run scripts and make scripts into self-contained applications that run when you double-click them in the Finder. AppleScript Editor normally is located in the Utilities folder in the Applications folder.

Tip
If you end up doing lots of scripting, you may want to replace AppleScript Editor with a more capable script development application, such as Script Debugger from Late Night Software ($199; www.latenightsw.com). Make sure you get the version made for Mac OS X. ■

Scriptable applications and environments

The scripts you create with AppleScript Editor can control any *scriptable application*. A prime example of a scriptable application is the Finder. Other scriptable applications that come with Mac OS X include ColorSync Scripting, iCal, iChat, iTunes, Safari, Mail, QuickTime Player, Safari, Spotlight, System Information, Terminal, and TextEdit. Interestingly enough, even AppleScript Editor is scriptable. In addition, many Mac OS X applications—both those from Apple and from other companies—are scriptable.

Looking at a script window

When you open AppleScript Editor, an empty script window appears. Each script window can contain one script. The top part of the script window is the script editing area, where you type and edit the text of the script just as you type and edit in any text-editing application. The bottom part of the window is the script description area. You use this area to type a description of what the script does. Figure 13.1 shows an empty script window.

FIGURE 13.1

A new script window appears when AppleScript Editor opens.

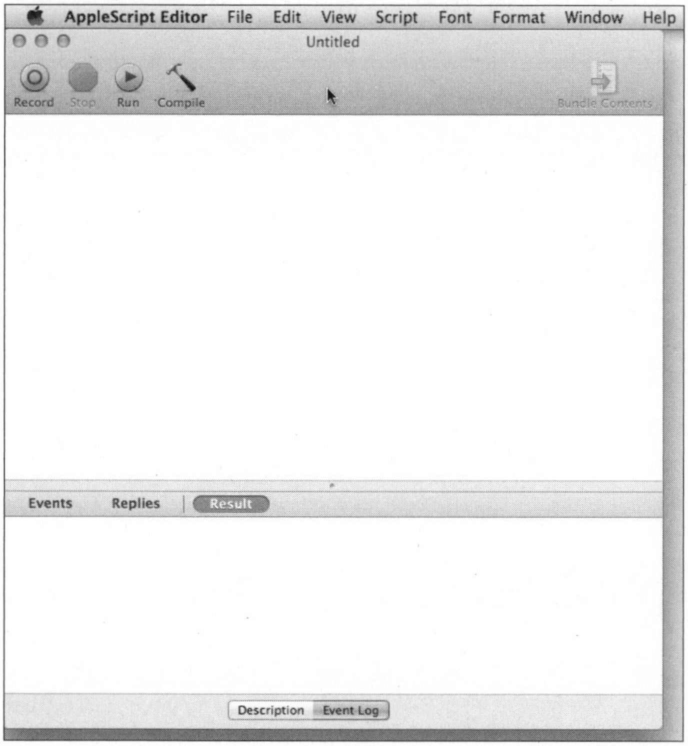

Tip

You can change the default size of a new script window. Make the script window the size you want, and choose Window ⇨ Save as Default. ∎

The toolbar of a script window has five buttons. You find out more about each of them in later sections, but the following list summarizes their functions:

- **Record:** AppleScript goes into recording mode and creates script statements corresponding to your actions in applications that support script recording. You also can press Shift+⌘+R or choose Script ⇨ Record to start recording. You cannot record scripts for every scriptable application because software developers must do more work to make an application recordable than to make it scriptable. You can find out whether an application is recordable by trying to record some actions in it.

- **Stop:** This button takes AppleScript out of recording mode or stops a script that is running, depending on which action is relevant at the time. Pressing ⌘+. (period) on the keyboard or choosing Script ⇨ Stop is the same as clicking Stop.

- **Run:** This button starts running the script that is displayed in the script-editing area. You also can press ⌘+R or choose Script ⇨ Run to run the script. Before running the script, AppleScript Editor scans the script to see if you changed any part of it since you last ran it or checked its syntax (as described next). If the script has changed, AppleScript Editor checks the script's syntax.

- **Compile:** This button checks for errors in the script, such as incorrect punctuation or missing parts of commands. (You also can press ⌘+K or choose Script ⇨ Compile to compile the current script.) If any errors turn up, AppleScript Editor highlights the error and displays a dialog box explaining the problem. AppleScript Editor also formats the text to make keywords stand out and the structure of the script more apparent. AppleScript Editor may even change the text, but the changes do not affect the meaning of the script.

  If the script's syntax is correct, AppleScript Editor tells AppleScript to *compile* the script, which means it converts the text of the script into codes. These codes are what Apple event messages actually contain and what applications understand. You don't usually see these codes in AppleScript Editor because AppleScript translates them into words for the enlightenment of human beings.

- **Bundle Contents:** I explain bundles later in the chapter. However, if you are editing a script that is saved as a bundle, this button shows you the contents.

Creating a Simple Script

An easy way to see how a script looks and works is to type a simple script into a new script window. If AppleScript Editor is not already the active application, open it or switch to it. If you need to create a new script window, choose File ⇨ New or press ⌘+N. In the script-editing area at the bottom of the new script window, type the following statements:

```
tell application "Finder"
activate
set the bounds of the first Finder window to {128, 74, 671, 479}
set the current view of the first Finder window to icon view
set the icon size of the icon view options of the first Finder window
    to 32
select the first item of the first Finder window
end tell
```

Check your script for typographical errors by clicking the Compile button in the script window. If AppleScript Editor reports an error, carefully compare the statement you typed in the script window to the same statement in the book. Pay particular attention to spelling, punctuation, omitted words, and omitted spaces.

When you click Compile, AppleScript Editor formats your script, changing the text formatting as it compiles the script using different type styles to show different kinds of terms. The statements that you typed probably changed from Courier font to Verdana font after you clicked Compile. AppleScript Editor normally formats text that hasn't been compiled as 10-point Courier. Most other words, including commands from scripting additions and application dictionaries, are normally formatted in plain 10-point Verdana. Verdana 10-point Bold normally indicates native words in the AppleScript language. Figure 13.2 shows how AppleScript Editor formats the script that you typed.

FIGURE 13.2

Check your script for errors and format it for readability by clicking the Compile button.

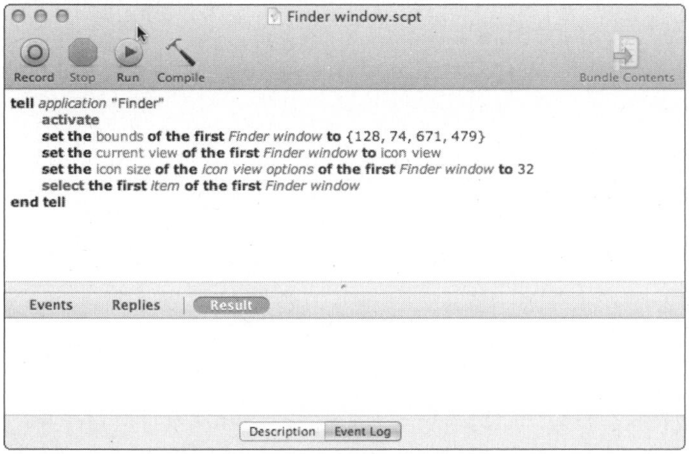

Before running this script, return to the Finder and make sure that a Finder window is displayed. If you really want to see the script in action, set the front Finder window to list view and resize the window so it is very small.

After setting the stage for the script, switch back to AppleScript Editor and click Run in your script's window. AppleScript executes each script statement in turn. When the script finishes running, the Finder window should be a standard size and set to icon view. The item that comes first alphabetically in the window should be selected.

Switch to AppleScript Editor again, and examine the script. You find that the script is fairly understandable. It may not be fluent English, but many of the commands should make sense as you read them.

Analyzing a Script

Looking through the script that you wrote in the previous example, you may be surprised to learn that AppleScript doesn't know anything about the Finder's operations. Although your recorded script contains commands that set the position, size, and view of a Finder window and selects an item in it, AppleScript doesn't know anything about these or other Finder operations. In fact, AppleScript knows how to perform only the five following commands:

- `copy`
- `count`
- `get`
- `run`
- `set`

AppleScript learns about moving and resizing Finder windows from the Finder; even the `tell` command that's ubiquitous in AppleScripts is a command it learns from the Finder. More generally, AppleScript learns about commands in a script from the application that the script controls. The application has a dictionary of AppleScript commands that work with the application. The dictionary defines the syntax of each command. AppleScript learns about more commands from scripting addition files on your computer. Each scripting addition file contains a dictionary of supplemental AppleScript commands.

Learning application commands and objects

Look at the sample script you created. The first statement says:

```
tell application "Finder"
```

To AppleScript, this statement means "start working with the application named Finder." When AppleScript sees a `tell application` statement, it looks at the dictionary for the specified application and figures out what commands the application understands. For example, by looking at the Finder's dictionary, AppleScript learns that the Finder understands the `select` command. The dictionary also tells AppleScript which objects the application knows how to work with, such as files and windows. In addition, an application's dictionary tells

AppleScript how to compile the words and phrases that you write in scripts into Apple event codes that the application understands.

After learning from the `tell application` statement which application it will send event messages to, AppleScript compiles the remaining statements to determine what Apple event messages to send. One by one, AppleScript translates every statement it encounters in your script into an Apple event message based on the application's dictionary. When the script runs, the Apple event messages are sent to the application named in the `tell` statement. The application receives the messages and takes the appropriate action in response to the Apple events.

AppleScript stops using the application dictionary when it encounters the `end tell` statement at the end of your script.

A complex script may have several `tell application` statements that name different scriptable applications. In each case, AppleScript starts using the dictionary of the application named by the `tell application` statement, compiles subsequent statements using this dictionary, and stops using this dictionary when it encounters the next `end tell` statement. Because AppleScript gets all the information about an application's commands and objects from the application itself, you never have to worry about controlling a new application. As long as the application has a dictionary, AppleScript can work with it.

Inspecting a dictionary

Just as AppleScript can get information about an application's commands and objects from its dictionary, so can you. Using AppleScript Editor, you can display the AppleScript dictionary of an application to see which commands the application understands and which objects the commands work with. You also can look at the dictionaries of scripting addition files.

Displaying a dictionary window

In AppleScript Editor, choose File ➪ Open Dictionary or press Shift+⌘+O. A dialog box appears, listing scriptable applications and scripting additions. Select an application or scripting addition file in the list, and click Open. AppleScript Editor displays a dictionary window for the application or scripting addition you selected, as shown in Figure 13.3 for Firefox.

Tip

In the Open Dictionary dialog box, you can select several applications and scripting additions whose dictionaries you want to display (each in a separate window). To select adjacent items in the list, drag across or Shift+click the items. To select non-adjacent items, ⌘+click each item that you want to select. ∎

FIGURE 13.3

An AppleScript dictionary defines suites of commands and objects for a scriptable application or a scripting addition file.

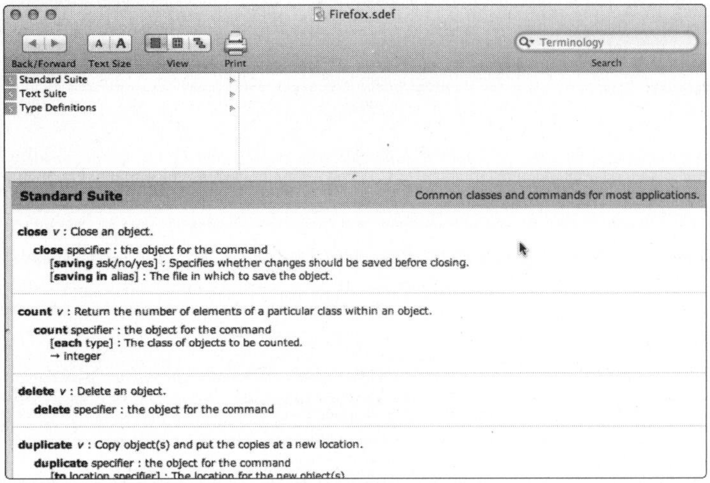

Looking at a dictionary window

The top of the window shows hierarchically the commands that are available to you. In the left pane is a list of groups of related commands called *suites*. They appear with a box with an *S* in it next to them. When you click a suite, its constituent commands appear in the middle pane. Commands are depicted with a square with the letter *c* inside. Clicking a command displays its constituent elements and properties (depicted with an *e* and a *p*, respectively). Verbs are shown with a blue square, and nouns have a purple square; elements have orange squares, and properties have purple. Below the triple-paned view, you see the full explanation of the commands. The commands appear in bold, and objects appear in italic. AppleScript Editor groups related commands and objects into suites and displays the names of suites in bold. You don't have to worry about suites when you're scripting.

The description of a command briefly explains what the command does and defines its syntax. In the syntax definition, bold words are command words that you must type exactly as written. Words in plain text represent information that you provide, such as a value or an object for the command to work on. Any parts of a syntax definition enclosed in brackets are optional.

The description of an object very briefly describes the object and may list the following:

- **Plural Form:** States how to refer to multiple objects collectively. For example, you can refer to a specific window or to all windows.
- **Elements:** Enumerates items that can belong to the object. In a script, you would refer to `item` of `object`. For example, you could refer to a file named `index.html` in the Sites folder as `file "index.html" of folder "Sites"`.

- **Properties:** Lists the attributes of an object. Each property has a name, which is displayed in bold, and a value, which is described in plain text. Scripts can get and set property values, except that properties designated [r/o] (means read-only) can't be changed.

Saving a Script

In AppleScript Editor, you save a script by choosing File ⇨ Save or pressing ⌘+S, or by choosing File ⇨ Save As or pressing Shift+⌘+S. When you choose one of these commands, AppleScript Editor displays the Save dialog box. (The dialog box does not appear when you choose Save for a script that is open and has previously been saved.) In the dialog box, you can choose any of several different file formats for the saved script. The five options are Script, Application, Script Bundle, Application Bundle, and Text.

When you save a new script or a copy of a script, you specify a file format by choosing the format from the Format pop-up menu in the Save dialog box. AppleScript Editor can save in the following file formats:

- **Script** or **Script Bundle:** This saves the script as Apple event codes rather than plain text. You can open it with AppleScript Editor and then run or change it. In versions of Mac OS X prior to 10.4 Tiger, you run compiled scripts by using the Script Runner application and applications that have a script menu, such as Apple's iWork suite. In Mac OS X 10.4 Tiger and later, Mac OS X manages the running of the scripts. You can save scripts as Run Only so they cannot be edited, only run.

- **Application:** This saves the script as an application, complete with an icon. Opening the icon (by double-clicking it, for example) runs the script. When you choose the application format, the following three options appear at the bottom of the Save dialog box:

  - **Run Only:** Allows the script application to be run only, but not edited.

  - **Stay Open:** Causes the application to stay open after its script finishes running. If this option is turned off, the application quits automatically after running its script.

  - **Startup Screen:** Displays an identifying window that appears when the application is opened. The Startup screen confirms that the user wants to run the script.

- **Text:** This saves the script as a plain text document. You can open it in AppleScript Editor, in a word-processing application, and in many other applications. Although a more portable file, this format is not as efficient as the others because the script must be compiled in AppleScript Editor before it can be run.

A handy capability is being able to save scripts as Mac OS X bundles. Mac OS X's applications are bundles (another name for *packages*) that, though they appear as a single item or application, are actually a collection of the files and resources that the application needs to run. (Apple calls this style of application packaging *Cocoa applications*.)

If you right-click or Control+click a Cocoa application, you can see inside of an application's bundle by choosing Show Package Contents from the contextual menu. You see all the necessary files and folders that make up an application's contents. The application bundle enables developers to make their applications installable via drag-and-drop instead of using an installer that places files all over your computer. When you save a script as either a Script Bundle or an Application Bundle, it creates a similar package from your script, and you can right-click or Control+click your saved document and see the package contents just like any Cocoa application.

Cross-Reference

You can get the AppleScript documentation for developers online at the Apple Developer Connection website (go to `http://developer.apple.com/devcenter/mac/index.action` and search for AppleScript) if you are interested in more information about bundles and how they can be used. Access to this documentation requires registration with the Apple Developer Connection; you can find information about the ADC and sign up for $100 per year at `http://developer.apple.com/index.html`. ■

Creating a More Complex Script

You now know how to use AppleScript Editor to create a simple AppleScript script. This type of script, however, has limited value. A simple script that doesn't take advantage of the full AppleScript language is not very intelligent.

More frequently, you'll use AppleScript to create more complex scripts. This section explains how to create a full-blown script quickly and use the resulting custom utility to augment an application's capabilities.

Making a Finder utility

Your Mac OS X disk is full of special folders, but when someone sends you a file, it's up to you to figure out where the file belongs. For example, you have to sort TIFF and JPEG files into your Pictures folder, QuickTime files into your Movies folder, and MP3 files into your Music folder. You also have to classify and put away fonts, sounds, and so on. The Finder doesn't help you sort out any of this.

You can, however, write a simple script that recognizes certain types of files and uses the Finder to move files to the folders where you want the files to go. The destination folders can be any folders that you have permission to change. These include all the folders in your home folder. If you log in as a user with administrator privileges, the destination folders also can include folders in the main Library folder.

Beginning the script

To begin writing a new script in AppleScript Editor, choose File ⇨ New or press ⌘+N, and then type the following statement in the script editing area of the new script window:

```
choose file
```

This command gives the script user a way to specify the file to be moved. The `choose file` command displays a dialog box for choosing a file. This command is part of a scripting addition that is preinstalled in Mac OS X. The name of this scripting addition is Standard Additions.

Tip

You can change how AppleScript Editor formats text by choosing AppleScript Editor ⇨ Preferences or pressing ⌘+, (comma) and then going to the Formatting pane. A dialog box appears listing various components of AppleScript commands and the text format of each component. You can change the format of any component by selecting it in the dialog box and choosing different formatting from the Font and Style menus. ■

Seeing the script's results

The script isn't finished, but you can run it now to see the results of the one statement you have entered thus far. Click Run to run the script in its current condition. When AppleScript performs the `choose file` statement, it displays a dialog box for choosing a file. Select any file, and click Choose. Because there are no more script statements, AppleScript stops the script.

AppleScript shows you the result of the last script action in the result window. If this window isn't open, choose View ⇨ Show Result or press ⌘+3. The result window contains the word *alias* and the path through your folders to the file you selected. This wording does not mean that the file is an alias file. In the context of a script, *alias* means the same thing as *file path*.

Using variables

The result of the `choose file` statement is called a file specification, or *file spec*. A file spec tells Mac OS X exactly where to find a file or folder. You need the file spec later in the script, so you must put it in a *variable*, which is a container for information. You can place data in a variable and retrieve it whenever you want to before the script finishes running. The data in a variable is called the variable's *value*. You can change a variable's value by placing new data in it during the course of the script.

On the next line of the script, type the following statement:

```
copy the result to thisFile
```

This statement places the result of the `choose file` statement in a variable named `this-File`. You can include the `thisFile` variable in any subsequent script statements that need to know the file spec of the chosen file. When AppleScript sees a variable name, it uses the current value of the variable. In this case, the value of variable `thisFile` is the file spec you got from the first statement.

When you run the script, you see that the `copy` command doesn't change the result of the script (as displayed in the result window). Because the result is just being copied to a variable, the result doesn't change.

Capitalizing script statements

You may notice the capital *F* in the `thisFile` variable and wonder whether capitalization is important when entering AppleScript statements. In general, you can capitalize any way that makes statements easier to read. Many AppleScript authors adopt the convention of capitalizing each word in a variable name except the first word, hence `thisFile`. This practice helps you distinguish variables from other terms in statements, which are generally all lowercase.

Getting file information

Ultimately, the script you are creating decides where to move a selected file based on the type of file it is. In Mac OS X, a file's type may be indicated by a file extension (suffix) at the end of the filename known as the *file type*, such as `.pdf` for Portable Document files and `.xlsx` for Excel 2008 files. (By default, Mac OS X does not display the file extension; Chapter 4 explains how to turn its display on and off.) Therefore, the script needs to determine the name and the file type of the selected file. You can use another command from the Standard Additions scripting addition to get this information. (Standard Additions is preinstalled in Mac OS X.) Enter the following statements beginning on the third line of the script:

```
copy the info for thisFile to fileInfo
copy the name extension of the fileInfo to nameExtension
copy the file type of the fileInfo to fileType
```

The first of these statements uses the `info for` command to get an information record about the selected file that is now identified by the variable `thisFile`. The first statement also copies the entire information record into a variable named `fileInfo`.

A record in AppleScript is a structured collection of data. Each data item in a record has a name and a value. AppleScript statements can refer to a particular item of a record by name, using a phrase similar to `item of record`. This is the phrasing used in the second two statements listed earlier.

Each of the second two statements gets an item of a record and copies it into a variable. The item names in these statements, `name extension` and `file type`, are taken from the AppleScript dictionary definition of the record. In this script, the record was obtained by the `info for` command in a previous statement.

To test the script so far, run it, choose a file, and look at the result. The result window should contain the four-letter file type of the file you chose, displayed as a piece of text.

Using parentheses

You may notice that when AppleScript compiles the example script, which happens when you run the script or check its syntax, AppleScript adds parentheses around `info for thisFile` but does not add parentheses in other statements. AppleScript adds parentheses around a command that returns a value, which any `info for` command does. However, AppleScript does not add parentheses around a command at the end of a statement, such as the `choose file` command in the first statement of the example script. Nor does AppleScript add parentheses around elements that refer to a property, such as `the name extension of the fileInfo` in the example script.

Parentheses group elements of a command together. You can type your own parentheses around elements that you want to group in a statement. Parentheses make a complex AppleScript statement easier to read. They also may affect the result of a statement because AppleScript evaluates elements within parentheses before evaluating other elements of a statement.

Working with an application

For the next part of the script, you need to add statements that move the chosen file to the folder where it belongs. The script can use an application—the Finder—to move the file. Add the following statement to have AppleScript start using the Finder:

```
tell application "Finder"
```

After AppleScript encounters this statement, it knows all the commands and objects from the Finder's AppleScript dictionary. This means that subsequent statements use commands and objects that the Finder understands. AppleScript sends these commands and objects to the Finder in Apple event messages. The script doesn't yet include any statements for the Finder, but I add some next. Later I add an `end tell` statement to have AppleScript stop using the Finder.

Performing script statements conditionally

When creating complex scripts, you may want to give your script the ability to decide what to do based on the factors you specify. AppleScript, like all programming languages, lets you include a series of conditional statements, or *conditionals* for short. Each conditional begins with an `if` statement, which defines the condition to be evaluated. The `if` statement is followed by one or more other statements to be performed only if the condition is true. The conditional ends with an `end if` statement. In AppleScript, a simple conditional looks like this:

```
if the fileType is "MooV" or the nameExtension is "mov" then
move thisFile to folder "Movies" of home
end if
```

In this example, the `if` statement contains a two-part condition. The first part of the condition determines whether the current value of the `fileType` variable is `MooV`, which is the four-letter file type of QuickTime movie files. The second part of the condition determines whether the filename ends with `mov`, which is the file extension for a QuickTime movie file. If either part of the condition is true, AppleScript performs the included `move` statement. If both parts are false, AppleScript skips the included `move` statement and goes on to the statement that follows the `end if` statement. Remember that AppleScript sends the `move` command to the Finder because of the `tell application` statement earlier in the script.

Finding a folder path

If you don't know the full path of a folder, you can use a script to get this information. Open a new window in AppleScript Editor and type the following command in the script-editing area:

```
choose folder
```

Run the script, and select a folder. The result is a file spec for the folder you selected. You can copy the text from the result window and paste it in any script.

You may notice that the file spec has a colon after each folder name. AppleScript uses colons in file specs to maintain compatibility with Mac OS 9 and earlier. Outside of AppleScript, Mac OS X generally follows the Unix and Internet convention of putting a slash after each folder name.

Note

AppleScript considers the dot, or period, between the filename and the extension to be a separator. The dot is not part of the extension or the filename as far as AppleScript is concerned. ■

Include as many conditionals in the example script as you want. In each conditional, use the four-character file type and corresponding file extension for a different type of file, and specify the path of the folder to which you want AppleScript to move files of that type. A quick way to enter several conditionals is to select one conditional (from the if statement through the end if statement), copy it, paste it at the end of the script, and change the relevant pieces of information. You can repeat this for each conditional you want to include.

You can make the previous script a bit more interesting by using the choose folder command in the second line in place of a hard-coded folder path:

```
if the fileType is "MooV" or the nameExtension is "mov" then
move thisFile to choose folder
end if
```

This asks the user where to place the file after it is moved.

Breaking long statements

When you type a long statement, AppleScript Editor never breaks it automatically (as a word processor does). Long sentences wrap to the width of your window. Remember that each *line* is a statement and a *return* delimits a line, whereas a *break* only *visually* ends the line and doesn't change the *statement*. You can break a long statement manually, for better readability, by pressing Option+Return. (Do not break a statement in the middle of a quoted text string, however.) AppleScript displays a special symbol (¬) to indicate a manual break. Here's an example:

Finding a file's type

You may not know the file type of the files that you want to move. For example, you may know that you want to put font files in your Fonts folder, but you may not know that the four-letter file type of a font file is FFIL. To make a script that reports the file type, copy the following three-line script to a new AppleScript Editor window:

```
choose file
copy the result to thisFile
copy the file type of the info for thisFile to fileType
```

Run this three-line script, and select a file whose four-character file type you need to learn. If the result window is not visible, choose View➪Show Result or press ⌘+3. The result of the script is the file type of the selected file. You can copy and paste the result from the result window into a conditional statement in any script window.

If you choose a file that has no file type, one of two things happens: The result window displays an empty value (indicated by quotation marks with nothing between them) or AppleScript reports an error, saying that it can't get the file type.

```
if the fileType is "JPEG" or ¬
the nameExtension is "jpg" or ¬
the nameExtension is "jpeg" then
move thisFile to folder "Pictures" of home
end if
```

In this example, the first statement, which goes from `if` through `then`, takes three lines because it has two manual line breaks.

Ending the use of an application

After the last statement that is directed at the Finder, the script needs a statement that makes AppleScript stop using the application. Type the following statement at the end of the script:

```
end tell
```

This statement doesn't include the name of the application to stop using because AppleScript automatically pairs an `end tell` statement with the most recent `tell` statement. Subsequent statements in the script can't use the commands and objects of that application.

Now is a good time to recheck the script's syntax. If you tried to compile recently, you got an error message about a missing `end tell` statement. Click Compile now, and after AppleScript compiles the script, you see AppleScript Editor neatly indent statements to make the structure of the script more apparent. If AppleScript encounters any errors while compiling your script, AppleScript Editor advises you of them one by one.

Trying out your script

After creating a new script, you must run it and test it thoroughly. To test the script that moves files according to their type, follow these steps:

1. **Run your script.**

2. **When the dialog box appears, select a file that is of a type your script should recognize but that is not in the destination folder, and then click Choose.**

3. **Switch to the Finder, and make sure that the file you selected actually moved from the source folder to the destination folder.**

4. **Repeat the test, selecting a different file type that your script should recognize.**

Figure 13.4 shows an example of a script with four conditional statements that move a selected file depending on its file type or file extension.

FIGURE 13.4

This script uses conditional statements to determine where to put a file.

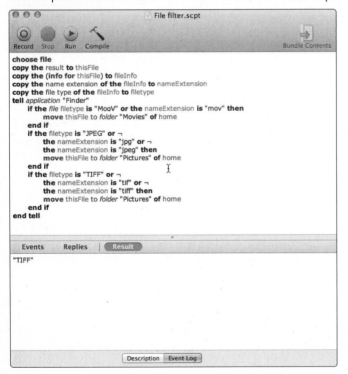

Creating a Drag-and-Drop Script Application

Although the sample script you created is useful, it would be more useful as an application with an icon on your desktop. Then you could drag files that you wanted to sort into folders and drop them on the application's icon. This would cause the application to run and move the files to their appropriate folders. You wouldn't have to open AppleScript Editor every time you wanted to sort files into folders, and you could sort more than one file at a time. Applications respond to this type of drag-and-drop Apple event, and so can AppleScripts.

You already know that AppleScript can save a script as an application. With a little extra work, you can make an application with drag-and-drop capability, so you can simply drag files to it to choose them.

Retrieving dropped files

Remember that when you drop a set of icons on an application in a Finder window, the Finder sends that application an Open Documents message that includes a list of the files you dropped on the icon. This message is sent to all applications, even to applications that you create yourself with AppleScript.

You need to tell your script to intercept that event message and retrieve the list of items that were dropped onto the application icon. Place the following statement at the beginning of your script, and delete the `choose file` line I added earlier:

```
on open itemList
```

Now enter the following statement at the end of your script:

```
end open
```

This `on open` statement enables the script to intercept an Open Documents event message and puts the message's list of files in a variable named `itemList`. The `end open` statement helps AppleScript know which statements to perform when the open message is received. Any statements between the `on open` and `end open` statements are performed when the script receives an Open Documents event message.

Save this script by choosing File ⇨ Save As. From the File Format pop-up menu in the Save As dialog box, choose the Application option. (You may want to save the script on the desktop, at least for experimental purposes.) If you switch to the Finder and look at the icon of the application you just created, you can see that the icon includes an arrow, which indicates that the icon represents a drag-and-drop application. The application has this kind of icon because its script includes an `on open` statement.

Processing dropped files

The script won't be fully operational until you make a few more changes. As the script stands, it places the list of files in a variable, but it doesn't do anything with that information. If you dropped several files on the application now, the script would still display a dialog box asking you to pick a file and then quit, having accomplished nothing.

First, you need to eliminate the script statements that obtain the file to be processed from a dialog box. Delete what now are the second and third lines of the script (the ones beginning with the words `choose` and `copy`) and replace them with the following:

```
repeat with x from 1 to the number of items in the itemList
copy item x of the itemList to thisFile
```

Between the `end tell` and `end open` statements, which are the last two lines of the script, enter the following statement:

```
end repeat
```

Figure 13.5 shows the complete sample script modified for drag-and-drop operation.

FIGURE 13.5

This script application processes items dropped on its icon.

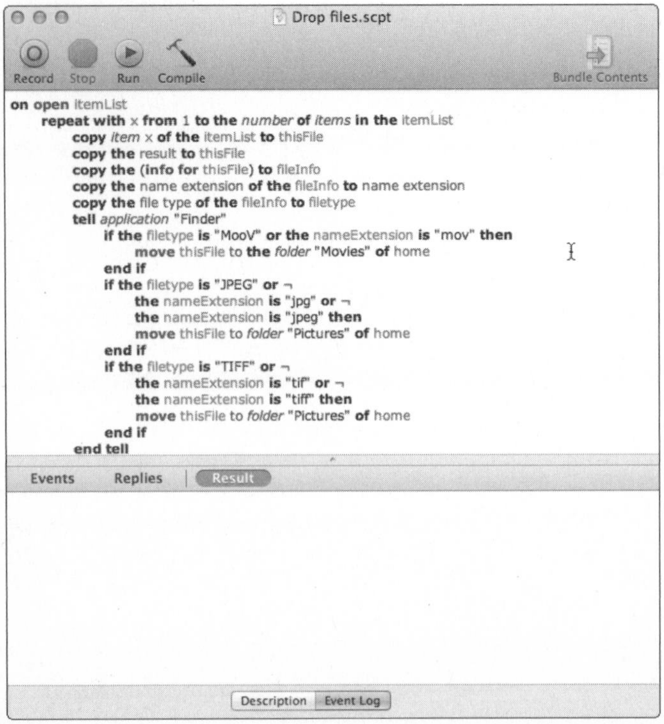

Borrowing scripts

An easy way to make a script is to modify an existing script that does something close to what you want. You simply duplicate the script file in the Finder, open the duplicate copy, and make changes. You can do this with scripts that have been saved as applications, compiled scripts, or text files. (You can't open a script that has been saved as a run-only script.)

Apple has developed a number of scripts that you can use as starting points or models for your own scripts. You can find some scripts in the Example Scripts folder, which is in the AppleScript folder in the Applications folder. Another place to look is the Scripts folder, which is in the Library folder. The unofficial AppleScript site has some (`http://www.macosxautomation.com/applescript/`). Check out the Learn and Explore areas of this site. You'll find snippets of code, links to third-party resources, and even some scripts to download directly.

Save the script so your changes take effect, and then switch back to the Finder. You now have a drag-and-drop application that you can use to move certain types of files to specific folders.

Using a repeat loop

In the modified script, AppleScript repeatedly performs the statements between the `repeat` and `end repeat` statements for the number of times specified in the `repeat` statement. This arrangement is called a *repeat loop*. The first time AppleScript performs the `repeat` statement, it sets variable x to 1, as specified by `from 1`. Then AppleScript performs statements sequentially until it encounters the `end repeat` statement.

In the first statement of the repeat loop, variable x determines which file spec to copy from variable `itemList` to variable `thisFile`. The rest of the statements in the repeat loop are carried over from the previous version of the script.

When AppleScript encounters the `end repeat` statement, it loops back to the `repeat` statement, adds 1 to variable x, and compares the new value of x with the number of items that were dragged to the icon (as specified by the phrase `the number of items in the item-List`). If the two values are not equal, AppleScript performs the statements in the repeat loop again. If the two values are equal, these statements are performed one last time, and AppleScript goes to the statement immediately following `end repeat`. This is the `end open` statement, which ends the script.

Extending the script

Anytime you want the application to handle another type of file, open the script application in AppleScript Editor, add a conditional that covers that type of file, and save the script.

The script in its drag-and-drop form now no longer functions if you double-click it. You can modify the script to restore this functionality by placing a copy of the original script at the end of the `end open` statement.

Tip

You can't open a script application to edit it by double-clicking it because doing so causes the application to run. To open a script application in AppleScript Editor, choose File ⇨ Open, press ⌘+O, or drop the script application on the AppleScript Editor icon in the Finder. ∎

Enabling the Script Menu

After you've built up a collection of scripts that you run frequently, you're not going to want to switch to AppleScript Editor every time you want to run one. This reason is precisely why Mac OS X includes the Script menu (which displays as a stylized *S* icon).

The Script menu sits in the toolbar at the top of the Mac OS X screen. You can run any of the listed scripts by choosing the script from the Script menu. To activate the Script menu, run the AppleScript Editor application from the /Applications/Utilities folder, open the Preferences dialog box by choosing AppleScript Editor ⇨ Preferences or pressing ⌘+, (comma), going to the General pane, selecting the Show Script Menu in Menu bar option, and closing the Preferences dialog box. (You also can change the default script editor, if you find a third-party editor you prefer, in the AppleScript Editor Preference dialog box's General pane.)

Linking Programs across the Network

You have seen how AppleScript can automate tasks on your own computer. AppleScript can send Apple events messages to open applications on other Macs in a network. As a result, you can use AppleScript to control applications on other people's computers. Of course, the reverse is also true: Other people can use AppleScript to control applications on your computer.

Sharing programs by sending and receiving Apple events messages across a network is called *program linking*. For security reasons, program linking is normally disabled. Computers that you want to control with AppleScript must be set to allow remote Apple events. Likewise, you must set your computer to allow remote Apple events.

Mac OS X uses the TCP/IP (Transmission Control Protocol/Internet Protocol) standard to send and receive Apple events messages over a network. Therefore, Mac OS X can send and receive Apple events messages over the Internet as well as over a local network.

Allowing remote Apple events

If you want a Mac OS X computer to receive Apple events from remote computers, you must set it to allow remote Apple events. First, open the Sharing system preference and go to the Remote Apple Events pane. Select the check box to the left of the Remote Apple Events label in the Sidebar to turn on Apple events. You can restrict the execution of Apple events to specific users by selecting Only These Users and clicking the + icon button to add the permitted users.

Caution

The All Users option can compromise your Mac's security by providing an entry point for hackers to control your Mac. If you must use this option, use it sparingly, being sure to turn it off when not needed. Preferably, you use the Only These Users option to restrict access to your Mac to people you trust. ∎

Scripting across a network

Using AppleScript to run a program across the network doesn't take much more work than writing a script to use a program on the same computer. For example, the following script sends commands to the Finder on the computer at IP address 192.168.1.203:

```
set remoteMachine to machine "eppc://192.168.1.203"
tell application "Finder" of remoteMachine
   using terms from application "Finder"
         activate
         open the trash
   end using terms from
end tell
```

The example script begins by setting the value of variable `remoteMachine` to the URL of a remote computer. A URL for remote Apple events begins with `eppc://` and is followed by the remote computer's IP address or DNS (Domain Name Service) name. (The prefix `eppc` stands for *event program-to-program communication*.) Macs also can be called by their Bonjour name (the name you see in a Finder window's Shared list when connected to another Mac) in scripts, so no URL is required.

The second statement of the example script names the application, in this case Finder, and uses the variable `remoteMachine` to identify the remote computer.

Inside the `tell application...end tell` block is another block that is bracketed by the statements `using terms from` and `end using terms from`. When AppleScript encounters the statement `using terms from`, it compiles subsequent statements by using the named application's scripting dictionary but does not send the resulting Apple events to this application. The Apple events from a `using terms from` block are sent to the application named in the enclosing `tell application` block. In the example script, AppleScript compiles the `activate` and `open the trash` statements using terms from the Finder's scripting dictionary on the local computer (your computer) but sends the resulting Apple events to the Finder on the remote computer.

When you run a script that sends remote Apple events, AppleScript has to connect to the remote application. Before doing this, AppleScript displays a dialog box in which you must enter a name and password of a user account on the remote computer. If you connect successfully, the script continues. At this point, the example script should cause the remote computer's Finder to become the active application and open the Trash in a Finder window.

If you run the script again, you don't have to go through the authentication process. After AppleScript is connected to an application on a particular remote computer, you don't have to go through the authentication dialog box each time you want to send an Apple event.

Automating with Automator

You have seen that using AppleScript is an extremely powerful tool to create your own applications and make your life easier by scripting repetitive tasks simply and cleanly. Mac OS X has an even easier tool to automate your life: Automator, which lets you build AppleScripts by dragging and dropping commands into what Apple calls a *workflow* to tell programs what to do.

Automator has a very basic windowed interface, as shown in Figure 13.6. It has three basic sections: a paned section similar to a Finder window where you can choose from a list of applications, a description pane on the right, and the workflow pane on the bottom. The top-left frame contains three panes; one that groups actions by application or name, one that holds your application "library," and one that holds the actions available for each application. To the right of these three panes is a frame that provides descriptions for actively selected actions. The pane on the bottom is your workspace; you drag actions from the left to build your workflow here.

The Library pane contains available actions and workflows that you can drag to the right frame in order to create new workflows to automate your life. In this example, you begin by making a PDF. You first have Automator help you choose your files. Click the Files and Folders library in the Library pane to show the available actions for the Finder. Click and drag the list—Find Finder Items—action to the workspace pane. You can use this action to predefine a specific search in the same way that you would use the find function in the Finder. Type .png in the name field.

Note
You can leave the text fields blank, click the Options button in the upper-bottom portion of the action, and select Show this action when the workflow runs. Then when you run your workflow, you are prompted to specify the parameters for the search. Alternatively, you can use one of the other file-choosing actions in the Finder library to get files, such as Get Selected Items From Finder, which enables you to select whichever files you want manually and then run your workflow. ■

Next, drag the Open Files action to the workspace. The action pops into place right below the action you already placed: Find Finder Items. Notice a little white triangle at the bottom of the Find Files In Finder action, which is dovetailed with the gray portion of the action just below it, Open Files. This is a graphical representation of the idea that the output of the previous action is passed to the action just below it, which in this case is a string of found files. The workflow you have just created searches your computer for PNG files and when found, opens them in the default application for JPEG files on your system, usually Preview. This is not particularly useful for your purposes, so remove the Open Files action from your workflow.

The Automator interface has a paned application selector, a description pane, and a workspace on the bottom.

You can remove an action from your workflow in several ways that should be familiar to you by now. First, you can click the gray X in the upper right of each action; alternatively, you can click and drag an action out of the workspace. You also can select an action and press Delete on your keyboard. Because you probably don't want to create a PDF contact sheet out of PNG files that have the word *John* in them, you should use one of these methods to clear your workspace of actions and begin again.

Begin again by dragging the Ask for Finder Items action from the Finder Library, and then select Desktop in the Start At pop-up menu and Folders in the Type pop-up menu. If you want to select multiple folders at a time, make sure that you specify multiple selections can be made by using the Allow Multiple Selections option, as shown in Figure 13.6; otherwise, you can select only one folder in the dialog box during runtime.

Next, you can make things interesting by using CoreImage to do some image processing. From the Photo actions, drag Apply Quartz Composition Filter to Images. Apple has made it as easy as possible to prevent accidents from happening. Because the Quartz Composition Filter makes changes to the original files, the act of dragging the action over to the workflow triggers Automator to ask you if you want to add an action that it's been programmed to "suspect" you want; in this case, make a copy of your files before applying the filter action.

Choose to add the copy action, and specify in the resulting action that you want to choose where to put the duplicated files when the workflow runs. In Figure 13.7, you can see the runtime option is checked for the copy action, but not for the filter. Choose Sepia from the pop-up menu in the Apply Quartz Composition Filter pane to make an old-style contact sheet.

FIGURE 13.7

You can use the Apply Quartz Composition Filter action to make your pictures look like old-time photos.

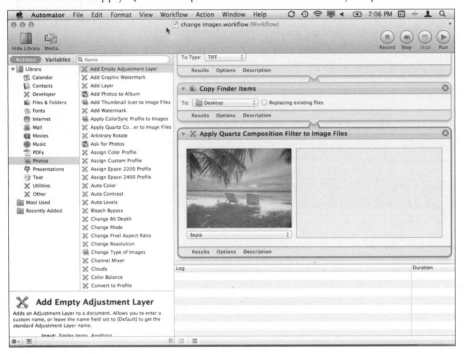

Still in the Photo actions library, choose New PDF Contact Sheet and drag it into your work-flow after the Filter action. Configure the options such as paper size and number of columns.

You have just created a contact sheet-making workflow that you can use over and over. To reuse the workflow, however, you need to save the workspace. Similar to AppleScript scripts, you can save a workspace in two forms: as an application or as a workflow document. Like AppleScript applications, Automator applications can't be edited without directly opening them from within Automator, and workflows can't be run outside of Automator.

Another neat way to use Automator workflows is to create a plug-in for other programs out of your workflow. By choosing File ⇨ Save As Plug-in, you can add the workflow as a contextual menu item in supported applications such as the Finder.

Recording Actions

Mac OS X enables you to record your actions to build workflows and create Automator actions. This addition makes Automator even easier to use to automate your life. Be aware that Automator records pointer movements and keystrokes, and plays them back in sequence, so its recording capability is not as elegant a solution as using an application's built-in workflow actions. However, if an application developer has not provided the interface that you need to build a workflow, or you want to do something more complex, this can be an easy way to accomplish your goal.

Note

To use this recording feature, you must have Assistive Devices enabled in the Universal Access system preference (see Chapter 8). If you do not have Assistive Devices enabled and try to record an action, Automator prompts you to enable it. ■

To begin recording an action, click the Record button in the main Automator window. Begin the procedure you want to record. When you are finished recording the set of keystrokes, return to Automator and click the Stop button. Your recorded keystrokes and mouse movements are grouped together in a single new workflow action that you can see and edit.

Summary

AppleScript makes applications perform tasks by sending Apple event messages to the applications. AppleScript is a programming language designed with everyday users in mind, but it has enough power for advanced users and programmers.

Use the AppleScript Editor application to create, edit, and run AppleScript scripts. AppleScript Editor also can make scripts into applications. Apple has developed a number of scripts that you can use as starting points or models for your own scripts.

Many AppleScript terms come from the applications the script is controlling. AppleScript terms also come from files called scripting additions. AppleScript Editor can display the AppleScript dictionary of an application to see which commands an application or scripting addition understands and which objects the commands work with.

You can save a script in any of three formats: text, compiled script, or application.

You type AppleScript statements into a new AppleScript Editor window, check the syntax for errors using the Compile button, and run the script to test it. Your script can use a `copy` statement to set the value of a variable. To start controlling an application, you use a `tell application` statement. A matching `end tell` statement stops controlling the application. With `if` statements, you can have AppleScript perform some operations only when specified conditions are met. Repeat loops execute a group of statements over and over. To make a drag-and-drop script application, you include an on open statement and a matching end open statement.

You can use the Script menu to run compiled scripts, no matter which application is currently active. AppleScript can control applications over a network or the Internet on computers that are set to allow remote Apple events.

Automator is a graphical interface to AppleScript that doesn't give you the same fine control as AppleScript does, but it's much easier for the average person to use. You can save Automator documents as plug-ins to extend the usefulness of other programs that support Automator or as stand-alone applications you can provide for other people to use.

Part III

Working with Mac OS X's Applications

IN THIS PART

Chapter 14
Working with Mac OS X Applications, Utilities, and Widgets

Chapter 15
Enhancing Mac OS X with Utilities

Chapter 16
Playing Music and Videos

Chapter 17
Syncing Macs and iOS Devices

Chapter 18
Integrating with Windows

Working with Mac OS X Applications, Utilities, and Widgets

M ac OS X Lion is much more than an operating system. It's chock-full of tools that enable you to do all sorts of things, from managing your address book to taking photographic snapshots. These tools come in three forms: applications, utilities, and widgets.

What distinguishes the three types of tools from each other comes down essentially to complexity. Technically, all three types are software programs. However, an *application* (which Apple is fond of calling an *app*) usually is software that you use to perform a task unrelated to managing your computer, such as surfing the web or playing DVDs. A *utility* usually is a tool to manage the computer itself, such as one that manages color profiles or formats disks. And a *widget* usually is a very simple program that gives you quick access to a feature, such as translating text or accessing weather information.

But these are arbitrary distinctions, and Apple may have classified some tools differently in Mac OS X than you might have. In the end, what really matters about the labels *application*, *utility*, and *widget* is where you find the tools on your Mac. Mac OS X stores them, respectively, in the Applications folder, the Utilities folder, and the Dashboard (for widgets). All three locations have tools that Apple includes with Mac OS X Lion; you also can add your own.

Note
You can move applications from the Applications folder to the Utilities folder, or vice versa, if you want. You might do so to organize your applications in a configuration that's more logical to you. Just drag them to the desired folder. However, you cannot move widgets into these folders, nor can you move applications into the Dashboard. Do note that moving applications or utilities can cause issues such as Software Update not being able to update them. ■

IN THIS CHAPTER

How applications, utilities, and widgets differ

Mac OS X's built-in applications

The utilities that come with Mac OS X

The widgets included with Mac OS X

Cross-Reference

The fourth kind of built-in program in Mac OS X is a service. Services are functions that you can use within your applications, such as converting text between the two forms of Chinese, Googling text, or taking a screen shot. Chapter 12 explains how to use them. ∎

Touring the Applications Folder

The Applications folder has the most preinstalled tools, and it is where software you download or buy is typically installed, as Chapter 9 explains in more detail. Figure 14.1 shows the Applications folder.

FIGURE 14.1

The Applications folder in icon view mode, showing a sampling of Apple and third-party applications

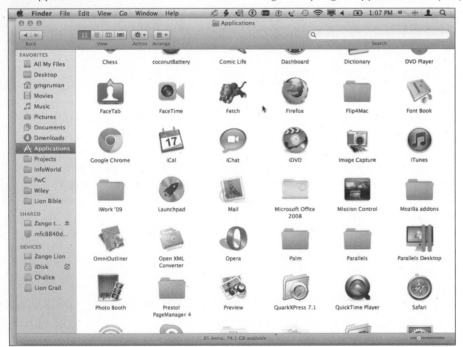

The easiest way to get to the Applications folder is to open a Finder window (just double-click any disk or folder icon in the Finder) and press Shift+⌘+A. You also can choose Go ⇨ Applications, or navigate to the folder by double-clicking your startup disk to open a Finder window and then double-clicking the Applications folder. But note that a second Applications folder may exist on your Mac, inside your Home folder; this Applications folder contains applications available only to that user account. (Chapter 27 explains user accounts.)

Tip

Should you delete your Mac's included applications, such as when recovering your system from a crash, you can reinstall them from the Recovery System by reinstalling Mac OS X Lion, as Appendix A explains. Any applications purchased from the Mac App Store can simply be re-downloaded from there. And the iLife applications that come with a new Mac can be reinstalled using the applications DVD that came with the Mac. ■

Note

New Macs include a copy of Apple's iLife software, which includes GarageBand, iMovie, iPhoto, iDVD, and iWeb. (The newest version, iLife '11, costs $49 if you have an older version on your Mac or no version on your Mac at all.) You also can buy GarageBand, iMovie, and iPhoto for $15 each from the Mac App Store. For details on the iLife applications, check out *iLife '11 Portable Genius* by Guy Hart-Davis, published by this book's publisher, Wiley. ■

New Feature

Mac OS X Lion has replaced the Spaces utility with the Mission Control application, and has added the Dashboard and Launchpad applications. Also included with Mac OS X Lion is FaceTime, which Apple began including in new Macs sold in 2011 and charged $1 to download from the Mac App Store for older Macs. Lion no longer includes the iSync application that had synced contact and other data from some pre-iPhone-era cell phones, nor the Front Row playback app meant to make a Mac display video like a TV; iTunes' and QuickTime Player's full-screen mode handles that need now. ■

Address Book

The Address Book holds information on your contacts, such as names, mailing addresses, phone numbers, and e-mail addresses. It's easy to add contacts; just click the + button under the Names list, and fill in the fields in the contact's "card." Use the Preferences dialog box (choose Address Book ⇨ Preferences or press ⌘+, [comma]) to customize how your Address Book displays contact information, as well as determine other preferences.

Tip

To change the picture associated with a person, double-click the square to the left of the person's name. You get a dialog box that enables you to choose an image from your Mac, as well as resize it and apply special effects to it. ■

But that's just the beginning. The Address Book works with other Mac OS X tools. For example, it synchronizes with the Mail e-mail application's contacts, so as you add contacts to either program, they are available to both. It also syncs with the iCal calendar application, so you can choose attendees to calendar events from your address book and even e-mail calendar invitations to people in your address book.

In the Preferences dialog box's Accounts pane, you also can set Address Book to synchronize contacts with Google's Gmail (via the CardDAV option) and Yahoo's Yahoo Mail services, as well as with Microsoft Exchange servers commonly used for corporate e-mail, calendaring, and contacts. (CardDAV is the Distributed Authoring and Versioning protocol for contact "cards.") You also can import contacts from a variety of sources by choosing File ➪ Import or pressing ⌘+O. Finally, Address Book can export contacts to the vCard format, which many other mail applications can import, as well as export a backup copy of your address book.

Chapter 21 covers Address Book in more detail, and Chapter 22 covers how to use Address Book with a Microsoft Exchange server.

App Store

Modeled on the iTunes Store for music and videos and the iOS App Store for iPhone, iPad, and iPod Touch, the Mac App Store lets you buy and download Mac OS X applications over the Internet. Chapter 9 explains how to use the App Store.

Automator

Another way to automate work in Mac OS X is to use Automator. Automator differs from the AppleScript script editor in that it takes advantage of *workflows*, series of steps that are pre-defined within various applications. Automator enables you to combine these predefined workflows however you want to accomplish a repetitive task, without having to write script code. (By contrast, the commands available in AppleScript are each one step, so it takes more work to combine them.) Chapter 13 covers Automator in detail.

Calculator

The Calculator application is actually three calculators—Basic, Scientific, and Programmer—as Figure 14.2 shows. Choose the one you prefer using the View menu. Other View menu options include using reverse Polish notation (RPN), setting the preferred number of decimal places, and showing separators after thousands. The Paper Tape option (choose Window ➪ Show Paper Tape or press ⌘+T) keeps a recording of all the calculations you've made in a separate window; you can print this record by choosing File ➪ Print Tape or pressing ⌘+P. Note that you don't need to display the paper tape to be able to print it.

The Calculator application also has a set of handy conversions, which you access from the Convert menu. For example, you can convert a result from acres to hectares or from dollars to euros by choosing the desired "from" and "to" measurements.

Chess

If you need a break and like to play chess, use the Chess application to match your skills against those of Mac OS X. Among the options in this man-versus-machine game is the capability to have the Mac speak its moves to you (and yours to it), as well as to change the appearance of the chess board and pieces.

FIGURE 14.2

The three faces of the Calculator: Basic (upper left), Scientific (upper right), and Programmer (lower left), as well as the basic calculator in reverse Polish notation node (lower right)

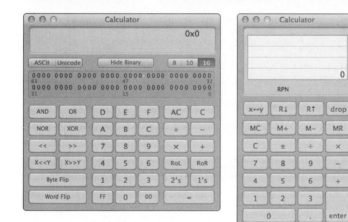

Dashboard

The Dashboard (also available via the default four-finger left-swipe gesture or by pressing the default Control+← keyboard shortcut) is where you access widgets, the set of quick-access tools that come with Mac OS X. When you open the Dashboard, a special space appears instead of the desktop in which any running widgets appear; to get back to what you were doing, use the four-finger right-swipe gesture or press Control+→.

I cover the Dashboard interface and the included widgets later in this chapter, in the section "Touring the Widgets."

Dictionary

The Dictionary application combines the New Oxford American English dictionary, the Apple dictionary of computer terms, the Oxford American Writers thesaurus, and the Wikipedia online encyclopedia, as well as the Oxford Dictionary of (British) English, the Oxford Thesaurus of (British) English, the Shogakukan Japanese dictionary, the Shogakukan Japanese-to-English translation dictionary, and the Shogakukan dictionary of Japanese synonyms. The two British dictionaries and the three Japanese dictionaries don't display by default; turn them on in the Dictionary's Preferences dialog box (choose Dictionary ⇨ Preferences or press ⌘+, [comma]), where you can further customize dictionary settings, such as pronunciation for the American and British English dictionaries and the character presentation order for the Japanese dictionaries.

To use the Dictionary, select which dictionary you want to look in (or click All to search them all), and enter a search term in the Search box. Figure 14.3 shows an example.

New Feature

The inclusion of the Oxford British English dictionary and thesaurus is new to Mac OS X Lion. ■

FIGURE 14.3

The Dictionary application and sample results

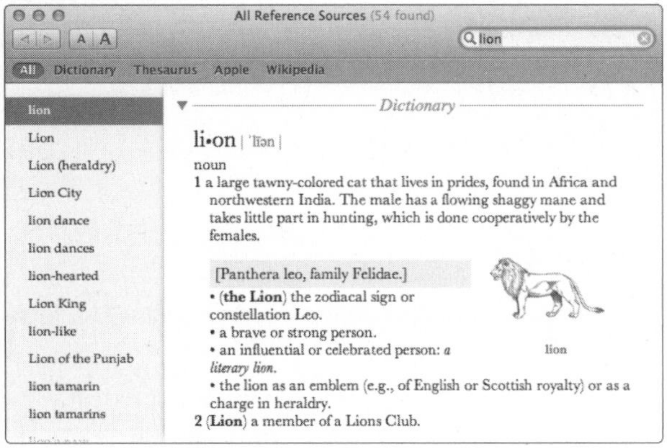

DVD Player

The DVD Player application does exactly what you would expect it to do: play DVDs on your Mac. Mac OS X sets DVD Player as the default player for video DVDs, so when you insert a DVD into your Mac's SuperDrive, DVD Player launches automatically. Its controls include setting the screen size for video playback, navigating to specific chapters, and enabling closed captions. The familiar icon controls are here as well—play, rewind, fast-forward, and pause—plus a slider that enables you to move to any point in the video, as Figure 14.4 shows.

FIGURE 14.4

DVD Player has controls resembling a handheld remote.

You can set DVD Player to not play a DVD automatically by deselecting Start Playing Disc in the Preferences dialog box (choose DVD Player ➪ Preferences or press ⌘+, [comma]). And you can set a different program as the default player using the CDs and DVDs system preference (covered in Chapter 28). Chapter 16 explains the DVD Player's various settings.

Tip

Your Mac can play DVDs on an HDTV monitor or TV set, not just on a computer monitor, at resolutions as great as 1280 × 1024 dpi—that is, if your HDTV unit has a computer input jack and you have the right connector cables for your Mac. ■

Note that DVD Player does not play Blu-ray DVDs, even if you connect a compatible drive to your Mac. If you run Windows on your Mac (see Chapter 18), you can play such discs on a compatible external drive with Windows' DVD player. Or you can use a third-party program such as Roxio's Toast 11 Pro ($150; www.roxio.com) to write Blu-ray DVDs from your Mac (but not play them), if you have a Blu-ray drive, of course.

FaceTime

First introduced in the iPhone 4, FaceTime is Apple's videoconferencing application, which works over Wi-Fi networks, including those connected to each other via the Internet. With FaceTime, you can have videoconferences between any camera-enabled Mac (running Mac OS X 10.6 Snow Leopard or Mac OS X 10.7 Lion), iPhone 4 or later, 2010-or-later model of iPod Touch, and iPad 2 or later. Chapter 20 explains how to use FaceTime.

Font Book

From its very first version in 1984, the Mac OS has supported high-quality type fonts. The Font Book application enables you to manage these fonts, so you can selectively enable and disable them, as well as group them into sets. The more fonts that are enabled, the more memory is used, so if you have lots of fonts, managing which ones are enabled can help you keep your performance fast. Chapter 29 explains how to use Font Book in more detail.

iCal

Managing your schedule is easy with iCal, the Mac's built-in calendar application. You get all the calendar functions you expect, such as recurring events, configurable alarms, to-do lists, multiple calendars (to keep work and personal events separate, for example), and multiple calendar views (such as daily, weekly, and monthly), plus a few cool additions, such as the capability to set the time zone for the meeting (handy if you work across time zones) and attach documents to a calendar event.

iCal also integrates with other applications, such as Address Book and Mail, so you can invite people in your Address Book to a meeting and send reminders and invites via Mail. iCal also checks Mail automatically to see if you've gotten any new meeting invitations. In a group setting, you can connect to other calendars over the web using a technology called WebDAV (Web-based Distributed Authoring and Versioning) running on Mac OS X Server or other server to enable a calendar server that multiple people can access. The Availability Panel (choose Window⇨Availability Panel or press Shift+⌘+A) helps find when multiple people are available for a meeting—if you are using a shared calendar.

Chapter 21 details how to use iCal, while Chapter 22 covers how it works with Microsoft Exchange.

iChat

With the built-in instant messaging (IM) iChat application, you can chat with almost anyone. That's because iChat supports AIM (AOL Instant Messenger), Google Talk, Jabber, Mac.com/Me.com accounts (formerly MobileMe and now part of iCloud), and Yahoo Messenger accounts. (Sorry, Microsoft's Windows Live Messenger IM system is not supported.) You log into whichever account you have; you can configure multiple accounts in the Accounts pane of the Preferences dialog box (choose iChat⇨Preferences or press ⌘+, [comma]). You also can chat with people on your local network using Mac OS X's Bonjour technology, even if they don't have IM accounts.

New Feature

Support for Yahoo Messenger in iChat is new to Mac OS X Lion. ∎

iChat's capabilities include videoconferencing, saving chat transcripts, sending SMS messages to mobile users, support for Bluetooth headsets, and sharing documents with chat participants.

Chapter 20 explains how to use iChat in more detail.

Image Capture

Many people use Apple's iPhoto software (part of the iLife suite) to work on their images, and they transfer images from digital cameras, iPods, iPhones, iPads, and scanners directly to iPhoto. So they tend not to know about Image Capture, an application that comes with Mac OS X. Image Capture enables you to bring in images from almost any camera or scanner, as well as from iOS devices such as iPhones, iPads, and iPod Touches.

Image Capture can connect to devices connected via USB cables; it also can connect to network-accessible scanners. (To see network-connected devices, move the pointer to the right of the Shared label in the Sidebar and click Show.)

Image Capture is easy to use. Any supported device shows up in the Sidebar when connected. Select the desired device, and Image Capture shows the images available to transfer to your Mac. Figure 14.5 shows an example for a connected iPad that has some photos on it, and Figure 14.6 shows an example for a connected scanner, after clicking the Show Details button.

For a camera or iOS device, just select the images to transfer and click Download, or click Download All to bring them all into your Mac. (You can determine where the images are saved using the Import To pop-up menu beneath the file list, as well as change the view mode for the images.) You can delete images from the source device by selecting them and clicking the Delete icon button (the circle-with-backslash icon).

For a scanner, click the Show Details button to get a preview of whatever is in the scanner along with scanning controls shown in Figure 14.6. After adjusting the settings, click Scan to begin the scan. (You can determine where the images are saved using the Scan To pop-up menu in the third group of controls.)

You can tell Image Capture whether to load automatically when a supported device is connected to your Mac by clicking the arrow-in-a-box icon button at the bottom left of the Image Capture window. When a digital camera or iOS device is connected, you get a list of applications such as iPhoto and Image Capture, as well as No Application. Choose the one you want to launch for the selected device, or choose No Application if you want to manually choose what application to use each time.

FIGURE 14.5

Image Capture showing images available for transfer from a connected iPad

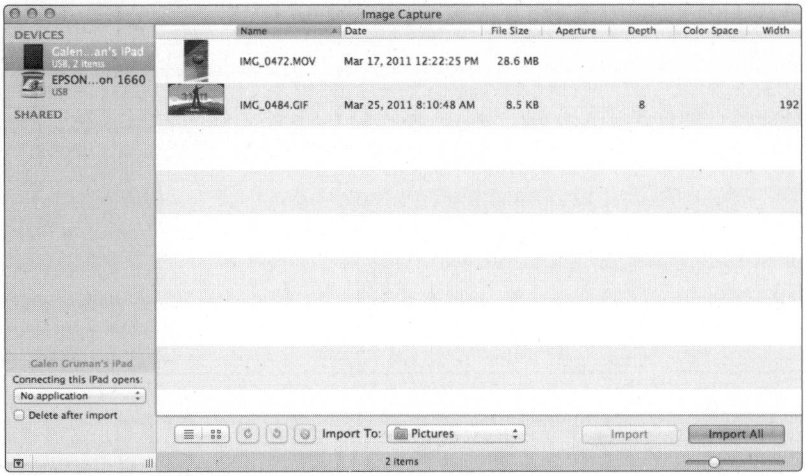

FIGURE 14.6

Image Capture showing the controls to operate a connected scanner

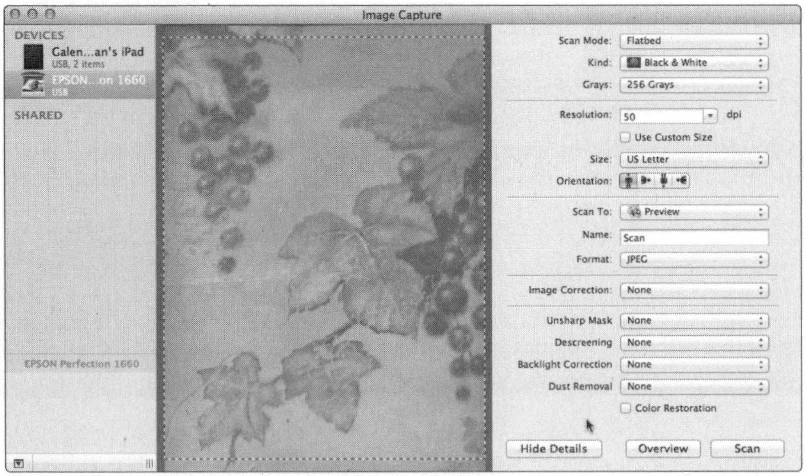

iTunes

iTunes has evolved from a music repository and playback application to a central command and repository for buying, backing up, and sharing music, videos, iOS device apps, and e-books (for use on iOS devices such as the iPad, iPhone, and iPod Touch). Chapter 16 explains how to use iTunes.

Launchpad

This application makes all applications in the Applications and Utilities folders available to be opened from a set of screens similar to the iPad's home screens, as described in Chapter 9.

Mail

Apple's Mail application does much more than let you read your mail, though it does that too. It reads RSS (Really Simple Syndication) feeds and enables you to set up reminder notices and to-do lists, synchronizing any items to iCal. Chapter 20 details how to use Mail to read, send, and manage e-mail. Sure, you can use e-mail applications like Microsoft Outlook and Mozilla Thunderbird, but Mail works just as well (or better) and automatically integrates with other Apple applications such as iCal and Address Book.

Mission Control

This application replaces the Spaces application from earlier versions of Mac OS X and displays all open applications and their open windows so you can navigate among them, as described in Chapter 2.

Photo Booth

The Mac comes with a built-in camera, called an iSight, that is quite handy for videoconferencing and for taking pictures. You can use Photo Booth to take those pictures, whether you use the built-in iSight or other digital camera attached to your Mac. The application is simple: Launch Photo Booth, choose an effect from the five windows of options in the Effects view (see Figure 14.7), double-click the desired effect, and in the Photo view window that appears choose from the three photo options using the icon buttons at the bottom left of the screen: a rapid-succession ("burst") series of four photos, single photo (the default), and a movie clip.

New Feature

Photo Booth now opens by default in full-screen mode, from which you can navigate the various effects using the navigation icons at the bottom of the screen. If you switch to regular view, the effects grid remains but the background changes. The Mac OS X Lion version of Photo Booth has a dozen or so fancy new distortion effects, which follow your face as you move within the picture frame. If you like an effect, double-click the photo to get a larger window, also shown in Figure 14.7, where you can adjust your pose and take the picture using the Camera icon. (You can switch back to the effects view by choosing View ⇨ Show Effects or pressing ⌘+2.) ∎

To take a picture, click the camera icon button, press ⌘+T, or choose File ⇨ Take Picture (or if you selected the movie clip option, File ⇨ Record Movie). The photos you take display in the "roll" at the bottom of the window.

FIGURE 14.7

Top: The Photo Booth application, shown here in regular view, enables you to take photos or movie clips using an iSight camera and then apply effects to them in its Effects view (one of the five panes of effects is shown here). Bottom: Once you select a desired effect, you can take the picture in the Photo view; shown here is the full-screen view.

The still photos are stored in the web-friendly JPEG format, whereas the movie clip is stored in Apple's QuickTime Movie format. You find the images stored in the Photo Booth folder inside your Mac's Pictures folder. And you see them in a "roll" at the bottom of the Photo Booth application when in Photo view (choose View ⇨ Show Photo or press ⌘+1).

In normal view, click a thumbnail image to display it at a large size and get four icon buttons: Email, iPhoto, Account Picture, and Buddy Picture. In full-screen view, click a thumbnail to open a pop-over with the same options. Click Email to send someone the image, click the iPhoto button to send the image to the iPhoto application (part of Apple's iLife suite), click the Account Picture button to make the current image the one that displays for your account (such as when choosing who to log in as and in your personal card in the Address Book), and click the Buddy Picture button to make the current image the one that displays when you use iChat.

In either case, you can click the Close button that appears in the photo's upper left corner to delete it, and you can choose File ⇨ Export to export the photo or movie to a file. Also, the camera button turns the camera back on so you can take more pictures.

Preview

Few applications are as useful as Preview, a tool you'll use all the time—often without even thinking about it. Preview enables you to open a variety of image files, so you can see what an image is without waiting for a slow-loading application like Adobe Photoshop to open. Even better, Preview launches automatically for any image formats that another program hasn't "claimed" as its own. (Remember, applications associate various file formats to them, so when you double-click the file, the associated application launches automatically.)

Opening files

What does Preview open? Quite a bit:

- **EPS:** This is the Encapsulated PostScript format that helped launch the desktop publishing revolution in the mid-1980s. Although Adobe PDF (Portable Document Format) has largely supplanted it, EPS files exist by the millions on people's hard disks and servers.

- **GIF:** The Graphics Interchange Format is widely used on the web.

- **ICNS:** This is the Apple icon format used to display the icons on your Mac, such as for applications in the Dock and files in the Finder.

- **iWork:** These are the Pages text document, Numbers spreadsheet, and Keynote slideshow formats.

- **JPEG:** The Joint Photographers Expert Group format is widely used on the web and in digital cameras; the JPEG-2000 variant is less used.

- **Microsoft BMP:** This is the native image format on Windows PCs.

- **Microsoft Icon:** This icon format is used by Windows to display application and file icons in the Explorer and Start menu.

- **Microsoft Office:** These are the Word text document, Excel spreadsheet, and PowerPoint slideshow formats.
- **Open EXR:** This high-definition video-image format was created recently by Industrial Light & Magic (which does special effects for tons of movies, starting with the original *Star Wars* effects) for use in its special effects work. It's also used in digital cameras.
- **PDF:** Adobe's Portable Document Format has become a nearly universally used file format to distribute documents of all sorts.
- **Photoshop (.psd):** Adobe's native format for bitmap images is widely used by artists and publishers.
- **PNG:** The Portable Network Graphics format is supported by most web browsers.
- **TIFF:** The Tagged Image File Format, a longtime standard image format, is still widely used by publishing and photo-editing applications.

Tip

Many Adobe Illustrator native files are actually EPS or PDF files, so you can usually open the Illustrator `.ai` files in Preview as well. ■

Capturing images

Shown in Figure 14.8, Preview does much more than just let you open images for preview. It enables you to capture your computer screen as an image (choose File ⇨ Take Screen Shot), e-mail the image being previewed (choose File ⇨ Mail Selected Image), bookmark images for easy access later (in the Bookmarks menu), and import images from a connected iPod, iPad, iPhone, or digital camera (choose File ⇨ Import From) or from a connected scanner (choose File ⇨ Import from Scanner).

Plus, Preview can convert opened images to another supported format (choose File ⇨ Export or press Shift+⌘+S). Note that it can save images in the JPEG, JPEG-2000, Open EXR, PDF, PNG, and TIFF formats, and it can save documents in both their native format and PDF format. If you export from a PDF file, the current page is exported as the image.

New Feature

In Mac OS X Lion, Preview's Go menu has renamed the Previous and Next options to the Up and Down options and added the Next Item and Previous Item options. Next Item and Previous Item move among pages, whereas Up and Down move among screens. Gone from the Preview toolbar are the Next Item and Previous Item icon buttons. The toolbar icons have also been redesigned. ■

New Feature

Also new is support for Lion's new full-screen mode (see Chapter 9) and the new Versions and locking features (see Chapter 10). ■

FIGURE 14.8

The Preview application does much more than let you quickly open images to see what they look like. It also enables you to bookmark pages, convert images and documents into other formats, and make annotations.

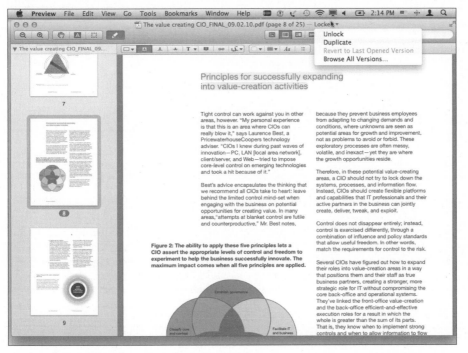

Adjusting images

Preview lets you make all sorts of adjustments to images, using the controls in the Tools menu: Adjust Color, Adjust Size, Rotate Left, Rotate Right, Flip Horizontal, Flip Vertical, Crop (you must first select part of the image before you can crop it), and Assign Profile (to apply a color profile to the image for proper color conversion when printing).

When you adjust the color, a dialog box appears with sliders for various color adjustments, including Exposure, Contrast, Temperature, Saturation, Tint, and Sharpness. This dialog box shows a histogram of the image, which many people familiar with professional editing tools such as Adobe Photoshop use to understand the effects of their color adjustments.

Working with PDF files

If you work with lots of PDF files, you can annotate them in Preview. (Click the Annotate button in the toolbar, choose View ➪ Show Annotations Toolbar or press Shift+⌘+A, and then use the annotation tools that appear at the top of the pane containing the page or image.) You also can choose Tools ➪ Annotate and choose the desired annotation from the submenu. This annotation capability means you don't have to use Adobe's own free Reader application to do such work with PDF files. (Note that people who use Reader or Acrobat Professional can see the annotations you make in Preview.)

Other PDF capabilities include the ability to rearrange pages in a PDF document, to add and edit bookmarks, and to open multiple PDF files in the same Preview window (as long as you open them all at the same time).

Managing display options

Preview has several controls to manage the display of images. For example, by choosing View ⇨ Page Display, you get several sub-options for how multi-page files display, such as in a continuous scroll or as two-page spreads.

Choose View ⇨ Slideshow or press Shift+⌘+F to have Preview create and play all open images as a slideshow.

You also can display or hide the Sidebar in the Preview window by choosing View ⇨ Sidebar ⇨ Show/Hide Sidebar, clicking the Sidebar icon button in the View section at the top of the window, or pressing Shift+⌘+D. The Sidebar contains thumbnail images of whatever is open in that Preview window. If you have opened a PDF, Office, or iWork file, the Sidebar shows thumbnails of each page. You can switch among content-only, thumbnail, table-of-contents, and contact-sheet views by using the first four options in the View menu. The same views are available via the View row of icon buttons at the right side of the toolbar.

New Feature

In Mac OS X Lion, Preview moves several controls from the View ⇨ Sidebar submenu to the main View menu. Four—Content Only, Thumbnails, Tablet of Contents, and Contact Sheet—give you different ways to view multiple images or pages in files, such as in PDF files, for easier navigation. The PDF Display menu option and its submenu options have changed to the Page Display menu option and its submenu options; the new version extends ability to display PDF files as single pages, a continuous roll of pages, or as facing pages to other document types. Gone from the View menu is the Automatically Resize menu option. The toolbar design also has changed, though its buttons' functions remain the same. ∎

If you are working with images or PDF files that you plan to print or display on another device, you can preview how they will look at the destination printer or other device by choosing View ⇨ Soft Proof with Profile and then choosing the output device's color profile from the submenu.

The View menu has the standard controls to zoom in and out, and to display the image or document at actual size. Preview also lets you toggle the background display of images and PDF files by choosing View ⇨ Show Image Background or pressing Option+⌘+B. (Some images have transparent or other backgrounds that Preview normally converts to white to improve the onscreen display; this command lets you turn off that display conversion; the actual image is unaffected.)

QuickTime Player

The QuickTime Player application does just what it says: plays QuickTime movies. Like Preview, QuickTime Player launches automatically if no other program is associated with the QuickTime movie format (.mov files). QuickTime Player can open both movie files from your computer or connected network server and movie files on the web. (Chapter 16 covers QuickTime Player.)

Safari

The Safari browser is perhaps the most-used application that comes with Mac OS X. It's your gateway to the web, and it is just as capable as its principal competitors, Mozilla Firefox and Google Chrome. (People who pick something other than Safari typically do so because they like another application's user interface better; for example, Safari is not so great at keeping bookmarks accessible, while Firefox is. And there's no reason you can't run multiple browsers on your Mac.) Chapter 19 covers Safari in detail.

Stickies

Many people are addicted to using Post-It notes as reminders, covering their workspaces with them. You can do the same on your virtual desktop with the Stickies application. After launching Stickies, choose File ➪ New Note or press ⌘+N to create a note. You can type, paste, or import text, format it using the controls in the Stickies menu bar, and even drag or paste in graphics. To add hyperlinks to web content, choose Edit ➪ Add Link or press ⌘+K. The Window menu enables you to control the display of notes, as well as navigate through them. You also can have Stickies spell-check your notes and speak them to you.

System Preferences

The System Preferences application is where you set up much of Mac OS X's behavior, such as the desktop background, security settings, and time zone. Chapter 28 covers the various system preferences in detail.

TextEdit

The TextEdit application is a lightweight word processor in which you can write, edit, format, and even spell-check text. Although you'll likely use a full-fledged word processor such as Microsoft Word or Apple Pages for reports, flyers, and the like, you'll find that you can do lots of editing work in TextEdit, from instruction sheets to letters. It's also a handy tool to edit the web's HTML pages when you don't need the WYSIWYG and specialty features of a program such as Adobe Dreamweaver.

TextEdit can open text-only (ASCII), Microsoft Word, and Rich Text Format (RTF) files, as well as save files in the text-only, PDF, RTF, Word 97, Word 2003 XML, and Word 2007 formats. (HTML files are really text-only files, but TextEdit is smart enough not to replace the

.htm or .html file extension on web pages with the text-only format's .txt file extension when it saves them.)

Note

To get the option to save in file formats such as PDF or Word 97, your TextEdit document must be a rich-text document. Choose Format⇨Make Rich Text or press Shift+⌘+T. In a rich-text document, you can apply formatting such as boldface, italics, specific fonts, and text sizes. ∎

So just how much can you use TextEdit as a word processor, rather than just a quick-and-dirty text editor? The short answer is "quite a bit." Figure 14.9 shows an example document in TextEdit.

FIGURE 14.9

The TextEdit application provides basic—but not unsophisticated—word-processing capabilities.

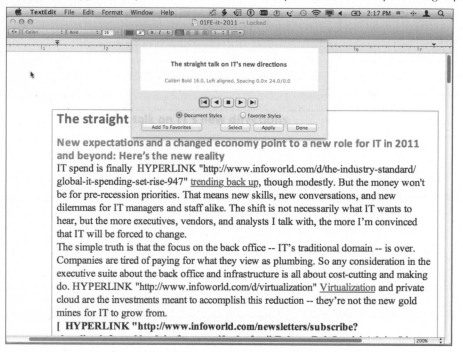

In the Format menu, you find controls to add tables and lists (both bulleted and numbered), enable automatic hyphenation, and set basic text attributes such as font and size. There's also a control to save the file as plain text, stripping out all the fancy formatting (saving the file as a text-only file has the same effect). You also can apply styles, which are collections of text attributes such as font and size, that you can apply all at once to selected text. At the top of the TextEdit window are controls to apply paragraph alignment, lists, styles, and line and paragraph spacing. You also can set tabs and indents using the tab bar right above the document window.

These formatting controls provide the basics that most documents need, though TextEdit doesn't do paragraph styles where the style is applied to the entire paragraph; TextEdit's styles apply only to selected text (as character styles). Plus, unlike the style function in traditional word-processing programs such as Microsoft Word, TextEdit's styles don't update the text that uses them when you edit the styles. But you can save character styles via the ¶ pop-up menu's Other option, which opens a settings sheet in which you add the formatting of the currently selected text as a "favorite" style, which adds it to the ¶ pop-up menu's options.

The Edit menu provides the other editing features that most people use routinely, such as features for inserting page breaks and other special characters; spell-checking and grammar-checking the document; inserting hyperlinks; automatically formatting dates, phone numbers, and other types of data formats (this technology is called *data detectors*); turning on and off typographic dashes and "curly" quotes; changing the text case; and even changing the text order between right-to-left (as in European languages) and left-to-right (as in Middle Eastern languages). There's even a control to have the Mac speak your document's text.

New Feature

The Mac OS X Lion version of TextEdit uses the new Versions capability in Lion (see Chapter 10), so the File ➪ Save menu option becomes File ➪ Save a Version after the first time you save a document, and the File ➪ Save As menu option has been replaced with the File ➪ Duplicate menu option. The File ➪ Revert to Saved menu option now lets you choose which version to revert to, rather than reverting to the last-saved version as in Mac OS X Snow Leopard and earlier. You also can lock or unlock a document using the pop-up menu that appears if you hover the pointer over the filename in the title bar. ■

New Feature

The toolbar has changed in Lion's TextEdit. The Styles pop-up menu has changed to the ¶ pop-up menu, and the Spacing and List pop-up menus have been replaced with icon pop-up menus (their menu options remain unchanged). And there are now new pop-up menus for the font family, text style, and text size, as well as new icon buttons for formatting (boldface, italics, and underline). ■

What TextEdit can't do is generate tables of contents and footnotes, track changes, add comments, insert mailing addresses, insert and create embedded graphics and text boxes, or other such professional features found in Pages and Word.

Among the options you can set in TextEdit's Preferences dialog box (choose Text ➪ Preferences or press ⌘+, [comma]) are enabling spell-checking, enabling the data detectors capability in Mac OS X (see Chapter 20), enabling smart quotes, displaying rulers, adding the .txt file extension automatically to files, enabling rich text in RTF and HTML files, and controlling how files are formatted when saved to the web's HTML format.

Time Machine

Backing up files and applications is something that everyone should do, but few people actually do it with any regularity. Part of the problem is that backup software has been clunky for years. Apple's Time Machine application revolutionized backup software when it was introduced in Mac OS X 10.5 Leopard by making backing up easy and powerful at the same time. Chapter 11 covers in detail how to use Time Machine.

Touring the Utilities Folder

Utilities are small apps that you use infrequently, usually to adjust the behavior of Mac OS X or to do very specific functions such as using the Grapher utility to generate and print graphs. The quick way to open the Utilities folder is to press Shift+⌘+U or choose Go ➪ Utilities in the Finder; you also can open the Utilities folder from the Applications folder. Let's look at the ones that come with Mac OS X Lion.

New Feature

The Exposé and Spaces utilities no longer appear in Mac OS X Lion's Utilities folder. They've been replaced with the Mission Control application in the Applications folder. The Remote Install Mac OS X utility has been removed from Lion; the delivery of the Lion installer from the Mac App Store makes it unnecessary. ■

Activity Monitor

If you're having performance slowdowns or you're simply curious about how your Mac resources are being used, use the Activity Monitor utility to see what is running on your Mac, as well as the CPU, memory, disk, network, and other resources used to run them. You'll get a list of processes—both applications and operating system tasks—that are running. You can filter the list using the pop-up menu at the top of the screen, as well as stop a process or get more information on it using the buttons at the top. Figure 14.10 shows the Activity Monitor.

Tip

Note that stopping an operating system process can make Mac OS X unstable, so do this with care. It's more common to stop applications that may have frozen or are stealing the Mac's resources from everything else, though it's easier to do so by pressing Option+⌘+Esc to open the Force Quit Applications dialog box, selecting the unresponsive or troublesome application, and clicking Force Quit. ■

AirPort Utility

AirPort is Apple's brand of Wi-Fi wireless routers. And the AirPort Utility enables you to manage any AirPort that you have on your network, such as setting access permissions, security levels, and the AirPort's public ID. But this utility does not work with other companies' wireless routers, even though your Mac can connect to them.

FIGURE 14.10

The Activity Monitor utility enables you to see what is running on your Mac and what resources are being consumed.

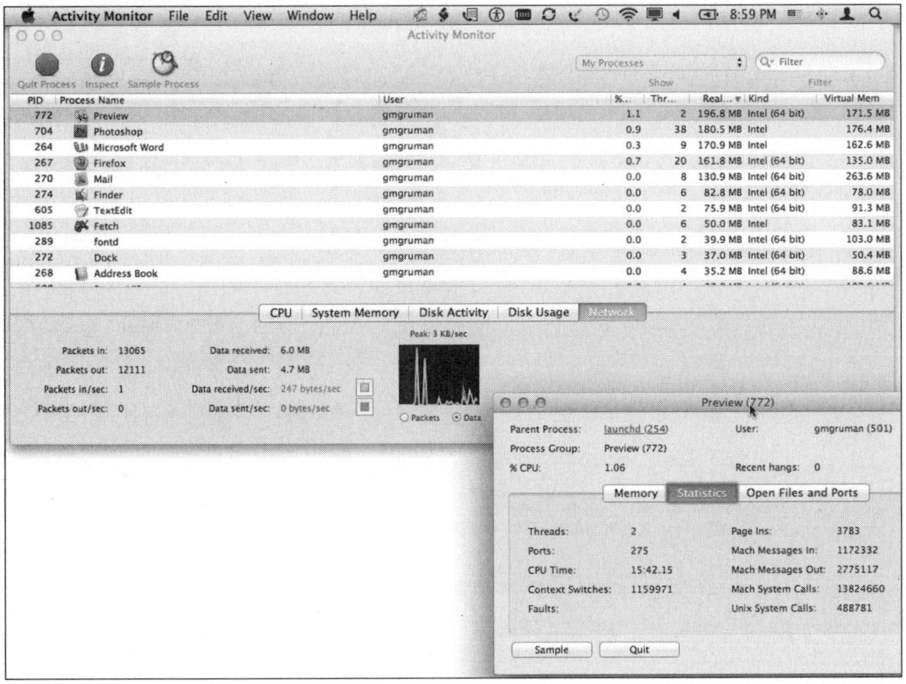

AppleScript Editor

The AppleScript Editor enables you to create and edit scripts, which are a powerful way to automate tasks. You can write your own scripts or record actions and have the sequence stored as a script. Chapter 13 covers AppleScript in detail.

Audio MIDI Setup

The Mac has long supported music, long before the iPod existed. It did so with high-quality input and playback of sound and support for the MIDI (Musical Instrument Digital Interface) standard that enables you to bring sound in from musical instruments and use the Mac as a sound-mixing studio-in-a-box. The Audio MIDI Setup utility enables you to manage how the Mac handles incoming and outgoing audio connections. Figure 14.11 shows the utility controls for microphone input.

The utility has built-in controls for microphone, line in, and headphone connections—something that all Macs support. You can adjust the volume, sound quality (the Format options), and loudness settings. If you have other sound equipment to bring audio into the Mac or to receive audio from the Mac, plug it in to the Mac, and click the + icon button at the bottom right of the Audio MIDI Utility dialog box. (Most devices plug in to the line in and headphone jacks, but some use USB, FireWire, Bluetooth, or other connections, so check with the device's manual. You may need to run an installation utility that adds the device's setup options to the Audio MIDI Utility's controls.) If the Mac recognizes the device, it adds it to the list at the left, and when you select that added item, you see the available controls for it in the main window of the dialog box. Use the – icon button to remove a selected device. Use the Action icon pop-up menu (the gear icon) for additional controls, such as setting up a device as the default input or output channel for the Mac.

FIGURE 14.11

The Audio MIDI Setup utility enables you to control the settings for your audio inputs (microphone, line in, and musical instruments) and output (headphones, speakers, and recording devices).

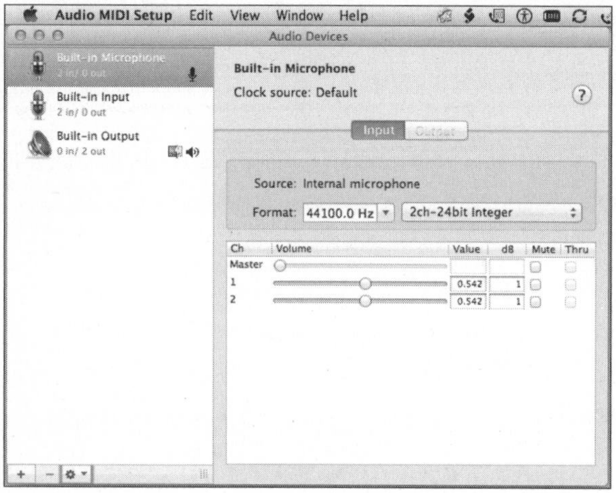

Bluetooth File Exchange

If you have set up a Bluetooth device, use the Bluetooth File Exchange utility to send or receive files on such devices. When you launch Bluetooth File Exchange, you're asked to select a file and then to choose which Bluetooth device to send it to. If you want to download a file from a Bluetooth device instead, click Cancel, choose File ➪ Browse Device, select the desired Bluetooth device, and click Browse. You get a list of files, from which you can select the ones to copy to the Mac.

Cross-Reference
Chapter 23 covers the basics of Bluetooth networking, Chapter 24 covers Bluetooth file sharing in detail, and Chapter 28 covers Bluetooth setup in detail. ∎

Tip

You can send and receive files without launching this utility. Instead, click the Bluetooth icon in the Apple menu bar, and choose Send File or Browse Device instead. Doing so runs the Bluetooth File Exchange utility. These same controls exist in the utility's File menu. ■

Boot Camp Assistant

When Apple began using Intel's processor chips in 2006, it opened the possibility that Macs could run Microsoft Windows, not just Mac OS X. Shortly after making the switch, Apple provided a utility called Boot Camp that enables you to format part of your Mac's internal disk as a Windows disk, install Windows on it, and then install the drivers that enable Windows to take advantage of the Mac's hardware. The result is a Mac that can switch between Mac OS X and Windows, with users choosing which one they want when they start the Mac.

The Boot Camp Assistant utility does the setup work for your Mac. (You need to supply your own copy of Windows.) Chapter 18 covers working with Windows in more detail.

Tip

Boot Camp works well if you want to run either Mac OS X or Windows, but it doesn't let you run both at the same time. To do so, you can use either the Parallels Desktop or the EMC VMware Fusion application. Both create a virtual disk for Windows that you can run from Mac OS X, and both let both Mac and Windows applications run simultaneously and share files, hardware, and other Mac resources. ■

ColorSync Utility

A hallmark of the Mac has been its support for graphics and publishing, which is why the Mac remains the dominant computer used for publishing, photography, and film production. A key issue in dealing with visual media is ensuring correct color as images pass from one device to another, such as from camera to scanner to Mac to printer. Each device handles color differently, so color profiles are used to map devices against each other, and color is adjusted appropriately as it passes among the devices. You use ColorSync Utility to adjust those mappings for the various devices you use.

ColorSync Utility starts with a profile (an ICC, or International Color Consortium, file) assigned to each device. Mac OS X comes with ICC profiles for common devices, and various devices' installation programs typically add any special ICC profiles they need. That means you usually don't have to do anything special with ICC profiles other than make sure that your image-editing and layout applications (such as Adobe Photoshop, Adobe InDesign, and QuarkXPress) are set up to know which profiles to apply to which images so they have the right color source defined. You can see a list of installed profiles in the Profiles pane of the utility.

But if you want to adjust these color profiles, you can do so with ColorSync Utility, shown in Figure 14.12. Do be careful, because these changes require a highly technical set of skills to avoid screwing up the color your Mac presents. The simplest adjustments are to assign different profiles to your devices, or to assign profiles to those that don't have them installed. To assign a profile, go to the Devices pane, click the triangle-icon pop-up menu to the right of

Current Profile, and choose Other to navigate to the new profile. (If you click Open to the right of the profile name, you can see the specific technical settings.)

If you're really advanced, use the Filters pane to adjust and add color adjustments for the selected profile, and use the Calculator pane to calculate the various color values in different color models. (A color model describes the physical capabilities of different color production techniques, such as a monitor's light-based pixels versus printed inks.)

FIGURE 14.12

Use ColorSync Utility to adjust how colors are adjusted by various devices. At left is the Profiles pane and at right is the Devices pane.

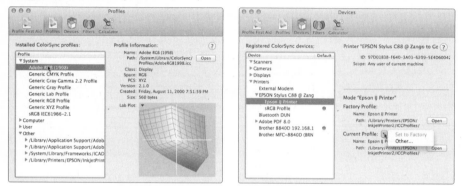

Console

Behind the scenes, applications, utilities, and Mac OS X send messages to each other to communicate instructions, changes, and status. The Console utility enables you to monitor and filter these messages. Hardly anyone uses Console; it's really designed for support technicians to troubleshoot a malfunctioning Mac and for software developers to diagnose issues in the programs they are creating.

DigitalColor Meter

The DigitalColor Meter utility measures the color being sent to your monitor. You can select the color model you want the measurements in and then move the mouse pointer across your screen. The measurements for wherever your pointer happens to be are displayed; you also can save them as text or as an image. The DigitalColor Meter utility calibrates your monitor's color accuracy. You can compare these values of what the Mac "thinks" it is producing to the values that an external color-measuring device, called a *colorimeter*, registers. If the values don't match, you know you need to run the Calibrate feature in the Color pane of the Displays system preference (see Chapter 28) or third-party software to adjust the Mac's color settings.

Disk Utility

Disk Utility does several things, all related to managing your disks. Among its capabilities are formatting disks, checking (verifying) and repairing disks, mounting and unmounting disks, converting disks into disk images, and recording ("burning") disk images to CDs and DVDs. Chapter 6 explains how to use Disk Utility.

Grab

The Grab utility captures whatever is displayed on your monitor, saving it as an image file. Use the Capture menu to determine what to capture: the entire screen, a selection of the screen (you draw a rectangle using the mouse or touchpad), or the selected window. These are the Screen, Selection, and Window options, respectively, in the Capture menu. An option called Timed Screen gives you ten seconds to arrange what's displayed before the display is captured.

A window appears with your screen grab. You can save it by choosing File ⇨ Save or pressing ⌘+S. You're asked to supply a filename and choose the folder to store the file in. Note that screen grabs are saved as TIFF files. You can copy the image to the clipboard for pasting in other applications by choosing Edit ⇨ Copy or pressing ⌘+C. Likewise, you can print a screen grab by choosing File ⇨ Print or pressing ⌘+P.

Tip
You can get information about a screen grab's size and color bit depth by choosing Edit ⇨ Image Inspector or pressing ⌘+1. ∎

Note
The Grab utility may sound familiar to you. That may be because you've seen it as an option in the Preview application: Choose File ⇨ Grab there to launch Grab, saving you a trip to the Utilities folder. ∎

A fast way to use Grab is via keyboard shortcuts (which you can change and turn on or off in the Keyboard Shortcuts pane of the Keyboard system preference, as Chapter 28 explains). The Grab application does not have to be running for these shortcuts to work:

- Press Shift+⌘+3 to grab the whole screen.
- Press Shift+⌘+4 hold down the mouse or touchpad button, and drag the pointer to create a selection area (a *marquee*) of what you want to grab. If you press and hold Option when moving the pointer, the initial pointer location becomes the center of the marquee. Release the mouse or touchpad button to grab the selected area. (Press Esc to cancel the grab.)
- Press Shift+⌘+4 and then press the spacebar. Then click a window, dialog box, menu, or other interface element to select it. (Press Esc to cancel the grab.)

When you use these shortcuts, the files are saved to the desktop in PNG format, not TIFF.

Grapher

If you're a scientist, engineer, or mathematician, you'll find the Grapher utility quite handy. It enables you to create 2-D and 3-D graphs based on mathematical formulas. The key is to understand the math to be able to create the formulas that generate the graphs. Grapher helps by including many examples of common equations. After you create your graph, you can save it and its underlying equations, and you can export the graphic itself in your choice of EPS, JPEG, PDF, and TIFF formats. Figure 14.13 shows an example graph.

FIGURE 14.13

The Grapher utility enables you to display scientific equations as graphs.

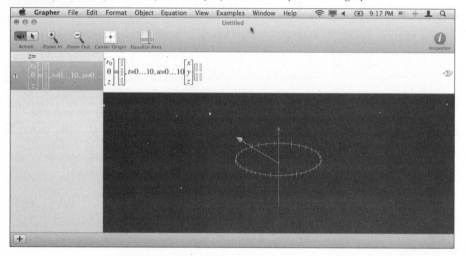

Java Preferences

The Java Preferences utility enables you to configure how the Mac handles Java applications, which are a common way to deliver functionality over the web or through a browser (though Java applications can run directly on the Mac as well).

The default settings work for most people, but if you want to change them, use this utility to do so. The General pane lists the versions of Java installed and lets you determine the version you want to run by default, both for applications (which run in Mac OS X) and applets (which run in your browser). Java Standard Edition, Version 6 for both 64-bit and 32-bit applications (Java SE 6) is the default in Mac OS X Lion, though Apple likely will update that as new Java versions are released over time. You also can change that version preference if you install a newer version of Oracle's Java on your Mac.

Use the Security pane to determine whether Java applets are kept after they are used (faster but less secure), to delete unwanted files, and to set the Keychain settings (described later in this section) to store passwords used by Java applications. You also can set the level of compression for Java resource (.jar) files, though that's about saving disk space more than about enhancing security.

Use the Network pane to have Java applications access the network differently than what is set up in the Network system preference, such as to force Java to use a proxy server or allow it to make direct connections to other networks. You also can configure Java to save temporary files on your Mac to reduce future download times, as well as set the compression level for Java runtime (.jar) files.

Use the Advanced pane to set default behaviors, such as when to prompt the user to let a new Java applet run, whether to display the Java console, and what type of security certificates to accept. These settings should look familiar, because most browsers offer the same controls over Java applets that they run.

Note
Beginning in 2011, Apple stopped including Java with its Mac OS X installer and in the Mac OS X preinstalled on new Macs. Instead, it's downloaded via the Internet after you install Mac OS X (see Appendix A). ■

Keychain Access

When you tell an application or a web browser to store your password or login information, where is it stored? Often, it is stored in the Mac's Keychain, a system for managing passwords and related security settings. (That's why you're often asked if you want to save the password or access settings, such as digital certificates, in the Mac Keychain.) You use Keychain Access to manage those saved passwords and related security settings.

Within Keychain Access, you can specify how you want passwords to be handled, as Figure 14.14 shows. Double-click the item you want to manage from the list in the center of the screen, and go to the Access Control pane to set the options. The options include letting any application access the password, requiring confirmation to use the stored password, and requiring the user to type your Keychain master password first.

Caution
The beauty of the Mac Keychain is that you have to remember just one password (to open Keychain), and Keychain remembers the specific password needed for the current application or password. The ugly side of Keychain is that if someone else knows that master password, he or she has access to all your passwords, such as those you use for online banking and purchasing goods at, say, Amazon.com. So when you set up Keychain (see Chapter 26), pick a hard-to-guess password. ■

FIGURE 14.14

Use Keychain Access to manage your stored passwords, digital certificates, and other stored access controls.

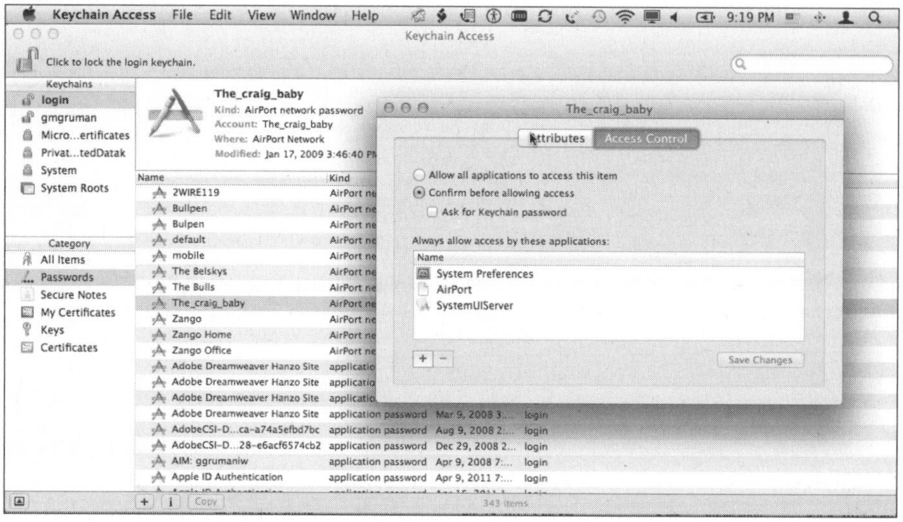

Migration Assistant

The Migration Assistant utility moves the applications, data, security settings, and preferences from one Mac to another. You typically use it when you get a new Mac and want to transfer everything from your old Mac to it or to transfer data such as contacts and e-mail settings from a Windows PC, as Appendix A explains. To use this utility, you need to have both Macs up and running, connected to each other via a FireWire cable or via Ethernet connections through a local area network (LAN). (A MacBook Air requires the use of a USB-to-Ethernet adapter to connect to a LAN.) If the old system has an older Mac OS X version such as Snow Leopard, don't worry: The utility is smart enough to keep Mac OS X Lion on the new system.

After you select the source computer (the old one whose information you want transferred), the utility walks you through the necessary steps, which includes restarting the Macs, so be sure that no other applications are running.

Caution

After you transfer your old Mac, some applications need to be re-enabled by entering a license key as a way to reduce software piracy, so be sure you have those handy. (They're usually on the install disk or in the accompanying manual.) Others (such as those from Adobe Systems, Quark, and Zevrix) need to be deactivated on the original computer and reactivated on the new one; it's best to deactivate them on the old system before you migrate them to the new Mac, so if something goes wrong, you aren't stuck with an activated license you can't actually use. And in some cases, you may need to reinstall an application; that's typically due to the application using a copy-protection scheme that Migration Assistant doesn't recognize. ∎

New Feature

The Migration Assistant in Mac OS X Lion can now transfer files and preferences from Windows PCs to Macs, such as to copy e-mail messages and login information and to copy web browser bookmarks. ■

Network Utility

Network Utility provides a whole suite of tools to monitor your network. Most users won't need to use it, but it's a great utility for a network administrator or support technician. Chapter 23 covers Network Utility in detail.

Podcast Capture and Podcast Publisher

Mac OS X Lion comes with a pair of applications called Podcast Capture and Podcast Publisher that enable you to record audio and video into podcasts for distribution over the Internet and via iTunes. Both tools enable you to use the built-in microphone and iSight camera (and/or FireWire- or USB-connected devices) to record audio and video.

With Podcast Capture, you specify a Podcast Producer Server to upload the files for conversion into podcasts. The Podcast Capture utility does not work unless you have Podcast Producer running on a computer with Mac OS X Server; you also need to connect your Mac to that server using the Podcast Capture utility before you can capture any audio or video for use by Podcast Producer.

If you don't want to use Podcast Producer on Mac OS X Server to distribute your podcasts, use Podcast Publisher instead. After you record your audio or video and import other media files for your current podcast episode, you can edit it with the onscreen controls and, using the Share menu, send the episode to iTunes, send it to someone via Mail, place it on the desktop, or upload it to a Mac OS X Server or other server.

New Feature

Podcast Publisher is a new application in Mac OS X Lion. ■

RAID Utility

The RAID Utility works only if you have an Apple RAID card installed in an Intel-based Apple Xserve (discontinued in early 2011) or Mac Pro system. You use the utility to configure the RAID settings, much as you would for a non-Apple RAID in Disk Utility, as described in Chapter 6.

System Information

You can check the configuration of your Mac easily, using the System Information utility. It gives you detailed information on every aspect of your hardware, network, software, and system settings. After opening the utility, select the aspect of your Mac that you want information on from the list at left, and the utility shows the results in the main window. Figure 14.15

shows an example. Note that you also can access this utility by choosing ⌘ ⇨ About This Mac and clicking System Report.

FIGURE 14.15

Left: The System Information utility displays an incredible amount of information on every aspect of your Mac's settings and configuration. Right: The About This Mac window provides quick access to key system information.

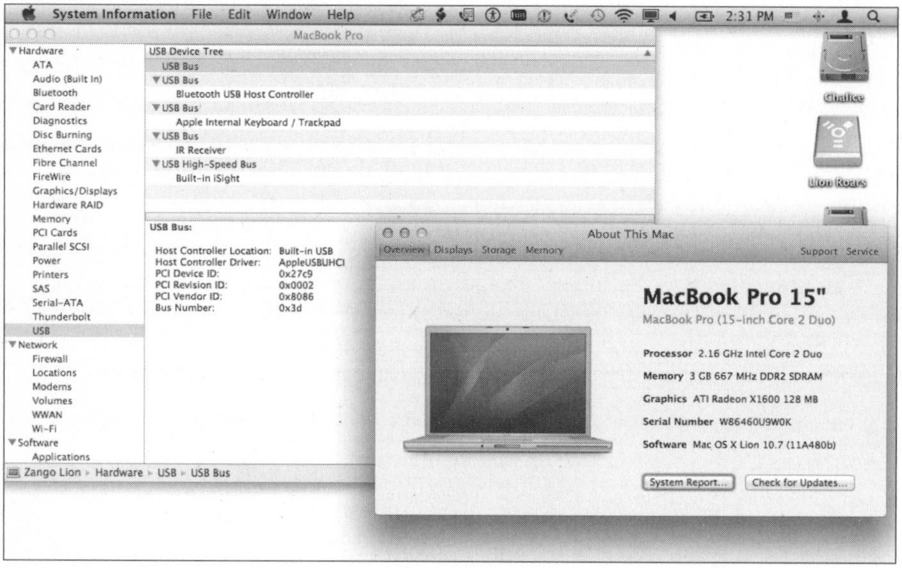

New Feature

System Information had been called System Profiler in previous versions of Mac OS X. The About This Mac window in Mac OS X Lion, shown in Figure 14.15, has been enhanced to show more information about both Mac OS X and the Mac model you have, plus its new Overview, Display, Storage, Memory, Support, and Service panes give you quick access to key information on your Mac, such as hard disk usage and memory configuration. ∎

Tip

Choose File ⇨ Refresh Information or press ⌘+R to have System Information update the information to the current state; this is especially handy for network and application information that can change while you have System Information open. ∎

If the information presented is overwhelming, choose File ⇨ Show Less Information for those panes that show optional details. (Choose File ⇨ Show More Information to get all the detail.)

Terminal

It's easy to forget that Mac OS X is a version of the Unix operating system best known for cryptic commands that must be entered precisely to work. But Unix runs under the graphical interface that makes Mac OS X so easy to use, and the Terminal utility is your way into that part of the operating system.

When you run Terminal, you get a plain window where you type your commands and see the responses. Appendix D explains how to use Unix and the Terminal.

VoiceOver Utility

VoiceOver Utility is where you set the conditions for when and how the Mac speaks what is onscreen. It is intended for visually impaired users. With the utility, you can specify dozens of conditions, such as whether content in web pages is spoken, whether captions are displayed, how punctuation symbols are spoken, and whether other sounds are muted. Chapter 7 covers the VoiceOver functionality in detail.

Note

VoiceOver must be turned on via the Universal Access system preference, as described in Chapter 7. You can access this utility from the Universal Access system preference as well as from the Utilities folder. ■

X11

Mac OS X is built on Unix and supports the Unix X11 Window System interface. You use the X11 utility to run such applications. Appendix D covers X11 in more detail.

Touring the Widgets

Since Mac OS X 10.4 Tiger, Macintosh users have been able to run lightweight applications called widgets. As described in the "Touring the Applications Folder" section of this chapter, these widgets are available through the Dashboard application, which you can easily open by pressing Control+← in Mac OS X Lion or using the four-finger left-swipe gesture. (To go back to the Finder, press Control+→ or use the four-finger right-swipe gesture.) Figure 14.16 shows the Dashboard window, which overlays your entire screen when open. By default, four widgets show up in the Dashboard: Calculator, iCal, Weather, and World Clock.

New Feature

The shortcut to open the Dashboard has changed to Control+← in Mac OS X Lion; it had been F4 on most Macs in earlier versions of Mac OS X. ■

Note

You can change the keyboard shortcut for opening and closing the Dashboard, as well as set up a "hot corner" on your Mac's screen to open and close it by using the Mission Control system preference, as described in Chapter 28. ∎

Managing widgets

To add other widgets to the Dashboard, click the large + icon at the bottom left of the Dashboard window to get a scrolling bar of the other available widgets, shown in Figure 14.16. Just drag into the Dashboard window those widgets you want to display when you open the Dashboard. Or simply open the widget by clicking it in the scrolling widget bar. Either way, the widgets appear in the window each time you open the Dashboard until you explicitly remove them. And you can drag any widget anywhere you want in the Dashboard window to arrange the widgets to your taste.

FIGURE 14.16

The Dashboard is where you access widgets. Shown here are the four default widgets, plus the Widgets widget to manage widgets (at the lower right) and the scrolling widget bar (at the bottom).

Tip

You can add a widget to the Dashboard multiple times by clicking it repeatedly from the widget bar. ∎

You can remove any of these widgets from the Dashboard window by clicking the Close icon button (the X icon) in the widget's upper-left corner. But these X icons appear only if the scrolling widget bar is visible, which means you need to have clicked the large + icon at the bottom left of the Dashboard window. Because any widget you open stays in the Dashboard window, that window can get cluttered very easily. So you occasionally have to open the scrolling widget bar so you can clean up the Dashboard window.

Note
To close the scrolling bar and display just the Dashboard window, click the large X that appears at the bottom left of the screen. ∎

You also can use the Widgets widget to remove and add widgets, as described later in this chapter. To access it, click the Widgets icon button in the scrolling widget bar or click the Manage Widgets button.

Widgets themselves often come with preference controls. Look for the **i** icon (the international symbol for information), usually in one corner of the widget's window, to open its preferences.

Using the widgets that come with Mac OS X

Mac OS X Lion comes with 16 preinstalled widgets from Apple and other providers, covering a variety of functions, from information display to calculators.

New Feature
Widgets that are no longer included with Mac OS X Lion are Business, Google, iTunes, and People. ∎

Address Book

The Address Book widget enables you to quickly search the Address Book application. Type all or part of the name, and the widget displays the contact information for that person. You also can scroll through Address Book entries using the arrow buttons that appear at the bottom of the widget, but only after you have found one entry through the search function.

Calculator

The Calculator widget is a simple arithmetic calculator—not nearly as powerful as the Calculator application. If you need to use a calculator often, you'd do better to add the Calculator application to your Dock for easy access. (Chapter 2 explains how to manage the items in the Dock.)

Dictionary

The Dictionary widget works like the Dictionary application, except that it provides less information than the application does. It's great for a quick lookup, but no more. Note that you can use the pop-up menu or arrow icons at the top of the Dictionary widget to move among the Oxford New American dictionary, Apple dictionary, and thesaurus results for your search term; the Oxford dictionary results are displayed by default. (The Wikipedia, Oxford

British English, and Shogakukan Japanese dictionaries available in the Dictionary application are not available in the widget.) This widget requires an active Internet connection to get the data it displays.

ESPN

Use the ESPN widget to get the latest news and scores for the sport of your choice. The widget has a News tab and a Scores tab, which you switch between using the News and Scores buttons. Clicking a headline opens the related story at the ESPN website in your browser. To choose which sport's information appears in the ESPN widget, use the widget's preferences. This widget requires an active Internet connection to get the data it displays.

Flight Tracker

The Flight Tracker widget is a handy way to find out what flights are scheduled today between the cities of your choice and to track a specific flight's status. First enter the origin and destination, plus the specific airline if you want, in the widget, and then click Find Flights. A list appears at the right; click the desired flight, and then click Track Flights to see its status. This widget requires an active Internet connection to get the data it displays.

iCal

The iCal widget offers a very simple view of the information in the iCal application. It displays the current date and month, and it enables you to move among months using the arrow buttons at the top of the widget window. If you click the name of the month at the top of the widget, the widget displays the current month instead—a quick way to return to the current month.

If you click the big numeral at the left for the current date (or the name of the day above it), a pane slides out listing calendar events for that date. If you click the date number again, the widget collapses so only the date is shown; one more click, and the month view slides back out. You cannot see the events for any day other than the current date.

Movies

If you're looking for a theatrical movie to watch, this widget can help. Based on your city or ZIP code (which you enter in its preferences), it shows a list of all current movies playing, as well as at what theaters and at what times, as Figure 14.17 shows. If tickets can be bought online via Fandango, a button to buy them becomes available. You can watch the film's trailer, if available, by clicking Trailer. Note that when you first open the Movies widget, you get what appear to be poster-style ads for current movies. Click any poster to enter the widget and look up listings. This widget requires an active Internet connection to get the data it displays.

Ski Resort

If you like to ski and want to know the conditions at your favorite resort, this is the widget for you. Enter a ski resort name in the preferences, and the widget displays the snow and other conditions for that resort. Note that the widget displays major resorts but may not have details for smaller ski areas available. This widget requires an active Internet connection to get the data it displays.

FIGURE 14.17

The Movies widget enables you to see what movies are playing nearby, as well as at which theaters and at what times. You also can view a trailer and buy tickets in some cases.

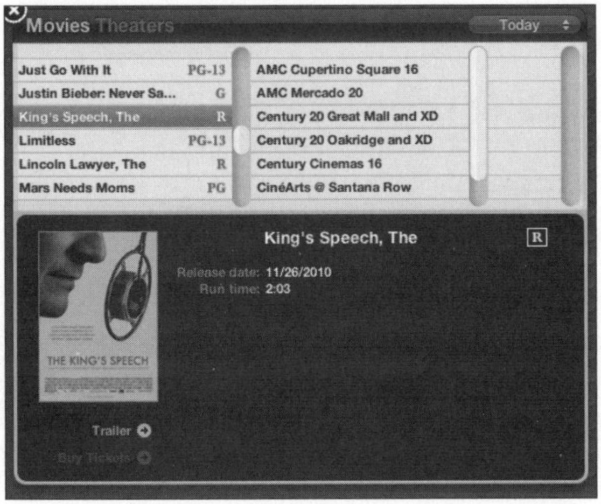

Stickies

The Stickies widget works very much like the Stickies application, though all you can do is add text, choose the sticky note's color, and choose the note's font and size; none of the fancy options from the Stickies application are available here. The one potential caveat to the Stickies widget is that the notes appear only when the Dashboard window is open, so it's really useful only when you have widgets open.

Stocks

The Stocks widget enables you to quickly see how your favorite stocks, mutual funds, and stock indexes are doing, with the latest closing prices and a configurable graph for past performance for the selected stock, fund, or index. You can add and remove entries using the widget's preferences, and you can set the stock price-change display to show as percentages rather than as dollars. (If you have an iPhone or iPod Touch, you'll instantly recognize this widget, which is almost identical on those devices as on the Mac.) This widget requires an active Internet connection to get the data it displays.

Tile Game

The Tile Game widget displays a leopard image as a series of adjacent squares, or tiles, that it then scrambles. The game's objective is to figure out how to restore the image to the unscrambled version. Click inside the game to start the random scrambling, and click it again to stop the scrambling. Then double-click a tile adjacent to the blank tile to move it into that blank tile's location. Keep moving tiles until you figure out the solution—or close the widget and reopen it to start again. (If you close the Dashboard but don't remove the Tile Game widget from the Dashboard screen, you can pick up the game where you left off.)

Translation

The Translation widget does what you'd expect: It translates words and phrases between the two languages you select using the pop-up menus. The languages available for translation are Simplified Han Chinese, Traditional Han Chinese, Dutch, English, French, German, Greek, Italian, Japanese, Korean, Portuguese, Russian, and Spanish. This widget requires an active Internet connection to get the data it displays.

Enter the term to translate and press Enter; the result appears. If you change the destination language, the new translation appears automatically. The icon button to the left of the destination language swaps the source and destination languages; this makes it easy to switch from, say, translating English to French to translating French to English.

Unit Converter

All sorts of measurement systems vary from country to country or discipline to discipline. The Unit Converter widget makes it easy to convert among such measurement systems. In this simple widget, you choose the type of measurement you want to convert: Area, Currency, Energy, Length, Power, Pressure, Speed, Temperature, Time, Volume, and Weight. You get a pop-up menu for the "from" and "to" values within each of those categories, such as the currencies you want to convert if you choose Currency or the types of measurements such as inches, feet, and meters if you choose Length. Enter the "from" value, and press Enter; the widget displays the result. Change the "to" value's measurement from its pop-up menu, and the new value appears automatically. Figure 14.18 shows an example. For the currency conversions, this widget requires an active Internet connection to get the data it displays.

Weather

You can get a quick look at a six-day weather forecast using the Weather widget. It shows the basic predictions (snow, rain, cloudy skies, and so on) using graphics and the predicted high temperatures for each day. Through the widget's preferences, you can change the city for which weather you want predictions, as well as set the widget to also display the predicted low temperatures for each day. This widget requires an active Internet connection to get the data it displays.

Web Clip

A web clip is a widget created from part of a web page. Launching this widget simply opens the Safari web browser, where you can select and save the web clip. (For more details, see the section in this chapter on adding widgets from other sources.)

FIGURE 14.18

The Unit Converter widget converts measurements in 11 categories. Shown here is an area conversion from acres to hectares.

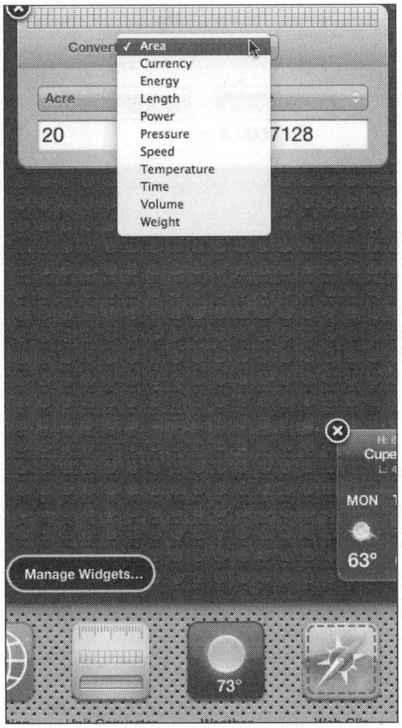

Widgets

The Widgets widget enables you to manage what widgets display in the scrolling widgets bar. Simply deselect the widgets you don't want to display or reselect them to make them visible again. If you added non-Apple widgets (described in the "Adding widgets from other sources" section of this chapter), you'll notice the Delete icon button (a white – in a red circle) to the right of their names; clicking that icon deletes the widget not only from the Dashboard window but also from your Mac.

You also can use the Widgets widget to sort the widgets by name or date. And you can use it to go to the Apple website, where you can download additional widgets via your browser: Just click More Widgets.

World Clock

The World Clock widget simply displays the current time at whatever location you choose in its preferences.

Adding widgets from other sources

You can have more widgets than those Apple provides with Mac OS X. There are three ways to get additional widgets:

- **Download widgets from the web.** An easy way to do so is to click More Widgets in the Widgets widget to open a page at the Apple website in your browser that lists third-party widgets you can download to your Mac. You also can get there by going to `www.apple.com/downloads/dashboard`. You can find such downloadable widgets at other websites as well, such as `www.widgets.yahoo.com/download`. Do a web search for "Mac widgets" to find other sources. (If you download a widget with Apple's Safari browser, Safari asks if you want it to install the widget for you. If you use a different browser, double-click the downloaded file to begin installation.)

- **Install widgets automatically.** Some applications install widgets—either automatically or as an option—for quick access to some of their features. Intego's security software, for example, installs a dashboard widget so you can monitor the security of your system, such as antivirus status. And the Fetch FTP utility's installation gives you the option of installing a widget, as another example.

- **Create a web clip.** In Safari, go to a web page that has a component you want to use as a widget, and choose File ▷ Open in Dashboard. You see a marquee that you can move over the part of the page you want to turn into a widget, as Figure 14.19 shows. Click Add when you're finished (the button appears near the top right of the Safari window). The Safari-based widget—called a *web clip*—now appears in your Dashboard window and can be managed like any other widget.

FIGURE 14.19

To create a web clip in Safari, you choose File ⇨ Open in Dashboard, move the marquee over the part you want to turn into a widget, and then click Add.

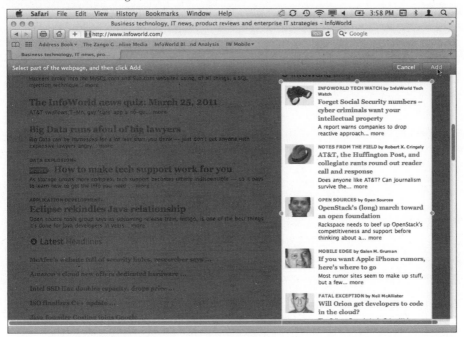

Summary

Mac OS X comes with dozens of applications, utilities, and widgets, all stored in different places. The distinction between applications and utilities is somewhat artificial; applications tend to be more complex and used for purposes beyond managing the Mac itself.

Widgets have very specific functionality, so they are less capable than applications and utilities; furthermore, they are available only from the Dashboard. When you are using widgets, you cannot also use applications and utilities at the same time; instead, you must close the Dashboard to use applications and utilities. A special type of widget, called a web clip, is a snippet from a web page that you can create by using the Safari browser.

In addition to the applications, utilities, and widgets that come with Mac OS X, you can add your own, typically by buying them (though some are free).

Enhancing Mac OS X with Utilities

A lthough Mac OS X Lion comes with an amazing number of utilities, as Chapter 14 explains, there are a few things Mac OS X
doesn't do and a few things that benefit from enhancements.
That's where third-party utilities come in. They fill the gaps and extend
Mac OS X's native capabilities in cool ways.

This chapter surveys utilities you may want to bring into your Mac to
either extend its current capabilities or add new ones. And by "utilities," I
don't mean full-fledged applications like Adobe Creative Suite, Microsoft
Office, FileMaker, or Apple iWork that are used to do major work. Instead,
I mean those little tools that make your life a little bit easier.

Of course, I don't mean to imply that everyone should get all of these
utilities or only these utilities. Everyone's needs are different, so there
may be utilities not listed here that are perfect for you and ones listed
here that you don't need. My selections are meant to be utilities that
many people should consider.

Utilities come from all sorts of sources, from major software providers
to individuals who do it for the sheer joy of solving a problem. Many are
free, and most of the rest are low cost (typically less than $25, though
commercial wares tend to cost between $50 and $100). Some are sold in
stores, but many more are available as downloads on the Internet and
via the Mac App Store.

Because of the volume and variety, it can be hard to know what's available and how to get it. Two good sources for tracking utilities are
Macworld magazine (you can see its utility reviews at `www.macworld.
com/browse.html?type=3&cat=213`) and Cnet's Version Tracker
website (`www.versiontracker.com/macosx`). For both utilities and

applications a business Mac user should consider, I recommend you get a copy of David Sparks' excellent *Mac at Work* book, published by Wiley.

Extending Mac OS X

Consider these utilities to extend Mac OS X's own capabilities or provide better versions of what comes with Mac OS X.

Audio management

Rogue Amoeba (www.rogueamoeba.com) makes a variety of utilities that enhance how the Mac manages audio. Audio Hijack Pro ($32) enables you to capture sounds from any application or audio source on your Mac. Radioshift ($32) enables you to schedule recordings of Internet radio "stations" so you don't miss your favorite programs.

Battery monitoring

Although Mac OS X shows you the state of your MacBook's battery's charge, it doesn't provide much information on how much charge your battery can hold (each time you recharge, you lose some storage capacity). CoconutBattery (free; www.coconut-flavour.com) gives you that precious information so you can see if your battery is working as it should. Figure 15.1 shows the utility.

FIGURE 15.1

The CoconutBattery utility

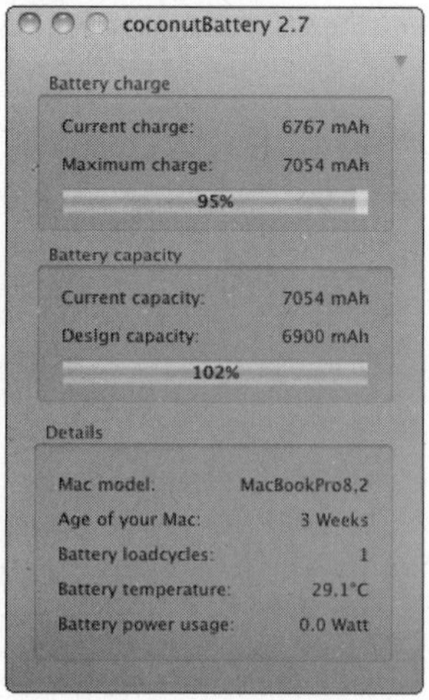

Conferencing

You can hold audio and videoconferences with other Mac users by using iChat, as Chapter 20 explains, but iChat isn't up to the job of business-level conferencing, in which you can have multiple participants. The Yuuguu service and application (free for five simultaneous users, $9 per month for up to 30 simultaneous users; www.yuuguu.com) is easier to use, more flexible, and works—unlike many competing services—with Mac OS X, Windows, and Linux users equally well.

Disk management

Mac OS X's capability to search all attached disks quickly by name, attribute, and content (see Chapter 5) makes it very easy to find files when you need them. But they have to be on a disk attached to your Mac. What if your files are on CD or DVD, such as client archives or deliverables? DiskTracker ($30; www.disktracker.com) solves that problem, maintaining a catalog of offline disks' contents so you can still search for them and know what disk, CD, or DVD the actual files are on.

File synchronization

A couple of really useful applications are great for Mac users on the move.

One called Dropbox (www.dropbox.com) provides 2GB of free online storage and pushes files to all your Macs with Dropbox installed. It also adds a virtual disk to your Mac's Sidebar for easy file access, as well as controls via a menu bar item, shown in Figure 15.2. You can pay $10 per month to get 50GB of storage. A similar service called Box (www.box.net) has both basic versions for individuals and enterprise versions that allow IT to manage access by employees to shared online folders.

FIGURE 15.2

The menu bar controls installed by Dropbox

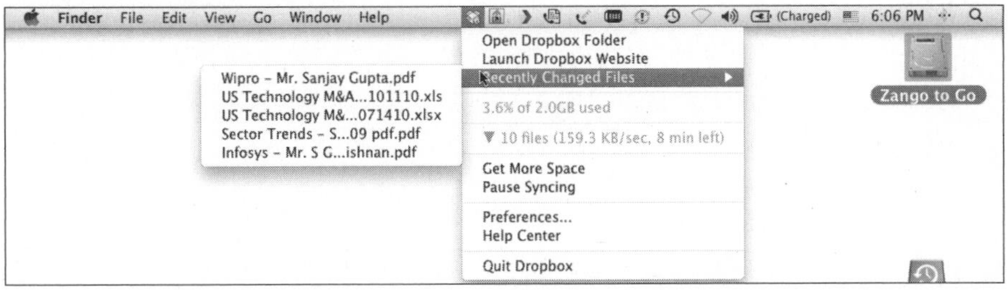

Utilities You May No Longer Need

Peruse any utilities directory on the web, and you're sure to see lots of utilities. Many are specialized and of interest to some people. But some appear to be broadly useful, yet in practice are rarely necessary, mainly because Mac OS X now provides the utility features well enough on its own.

Perhaps the best example of this is file compression. There are dozens, perhaps hundreds, of utilities that compress and decompress files. But Mac OS X does this natively, creating Zip files (right-click or Control+click the files to be compressed, and choose Compress Items from the contextual menu) and opening Zip files (just double-click the file). For years, Aladdin Systems (now Smith Micro) offered StuffIt ($80; www.smithmicro.com), the flagship Mac compression utility that created a Mac-specific compression format (.sit) because there were no Zip utilities on the Mac. (Later, StuffIt added Zip support.) But now that Zip is native to the Mac, there's no need for StuffIt's .sit format. And although StuffIt gives you more control over zipping and unzipping (you can extract and add individual files, for example), it's not worth $80 to most people.

Another formerly popular class of Mac utility was the font manager, which enables you to collect all your fonts in one place and selectively turn them on and off as needed. The Mac's Font Book (see Chapter 29) has handled this task well since Mac OS X 10.5 Leopard for most users, so only professional users really benefit from the commercial utilities such as Suitcase Fusion ($100; www.extensis.com), FontAgent Pro ($100; www.insidersoftware.com), and FontExplorer X ($79; www.fontexplorerx.com).

The third class of utilities you probably don't need are disk utilities. The Mac's Disk Utility (see Chapter 6) enables you to format and repair disks, as well as create disk images and burn them to disc, while Time Machine (see Chapter 11) makes backup and file recovery a snap. So the need for disk-optimization and recovery utilities such as TechTool Pro ($100; www.micromat.com) isn't what it used to be. Such tools are essential for IT support in a workgroup or business, and if you have a serious home-based business or sole proprietorship, you may feel better having TechTool's capabilities in case they're needed.

Tip

To use Dropbox and Box with Apple's iPad versions of Pages, Numbers, and Keynote, you need to use their WebDAV add-on services, available at www.dropdav.com and www.box.net/dav, respectively. ■

A utility called SugarSync ($5 to $25 per month; www.sugarsync.com) provides up to 250GB of storage and can sync any file or folder on your Mac to all your other Macs.

Font management

Although Mac OS X has the Character Palette to provide access to special characters (see Chapter 29), Ergonis's PopChar X (€30; www.ergonis.com) does a better job more simply. It adds a menu to the menu bar that makes it easy to find and insert the characters not on your keyboard.

Media playback and delivery

Every Mac should have the basic media players installed to supplement QuickTime Player, iTunes, and Safari: Adobe Reader to read PDF files and Adobe Flash Player to play Flash animations and videos. You also may want to install the Adobe Shockwave Player to play 3-D games and presentations. All three utilities are free downloads at www.adobe.com.

If you deal with lots of Windows video (WMV) files, you know Mac OS X can't play them. But the Flip4Mac utility enables QuickTime Player, iMovie, and Final Cut Pro to work with WMV files. There's a free basic version at www.telestream.net, as well as a series of professional player and editor versions priced from $29 to $179.

Although Mac OS X can burn CDs and DVDs, anyone who records or copies lots of data and/or media discs will want Roxio's Toast 11 Titanium ($100; www.roxio.com). It enables you to do all sorts of things with media files, such as send files from your Mac to TiVo digital video recorders, capture Internet audio and video streams, and stream your videos and music to your iPod, iPad, or iPhone over the Internet, in addition to creating a variety of CD and DVD formats. The $150 Toast 11 Pro lets you create (but not play) Blu-ray discs and includes Adobe Photoshop Elements 9 for image touchup.

The Plex utility (free; www.plexapp.com), shown in Figure 15.3, is similar to the Front Row application (included in previous versions of Mac OS X, but not in Lion) in its playback capabilities (it even can access your iTunes library), but it plays a wider range of media formats than Front Row did, and it can send movies and music to HDTVs and other devices.

Remote access

Although Mac OS X allows screen sharing and remote control (see Chapter 24), it often does not work well across the Internet and even business networks. For two decades, Timbuktu Pro ($90 per computer; www.netopia.com/software/products/tb2) has provided reliable screen-sharing remote control, not only among Macs but also between Macs and Windows PCs (Windows XP, Vista, and 7). Timbuktu is expensive, but it does a great job.

A less sophisticated, but cheaper, option is RealVNC ($50; www.realvnc.com). It lets Macs take over other Macs and Windows PCs for technical support and screen sharing.

Screen capture

Although you can take screen shots of your Mac by using the Grab utility (see Chapter 14), it's much easier to take screen images for books, manuals, and so on by using Snapz Pro X ($69; www.ambrosiasw.com). With Snapz Pro X, you can be more selective about what you capture, and you can control the filenames as you take the screen captures, turn the pointer on and off, and adjust image transparency and backgrounds. Plus, you can record sequences of actions as videos, so you can show people how to accomplish a series of steps.

FIGURE 15.3

The Plex media player for HDTVs and other devices

Wi-Fi monitoring

The guy behind CoconutBattery also developed CoconutWiFi (free; `www.coconut-flavour.com`), which makes it easier to find Wi-Fi access points nearby. Mac OS X shows available Wi-Fi networks if you click the AirPort menu bar icon, but CoconutWiFi does that one better by showing you a green icon in the menu bar if there are unsecured (and thus easily accessed) Wi-Fi access points nearby and a yellow icon if there are secured ones available, as well as the number of access points available. That way you know immediately if there's a freely accessible access point you can connect to, or if only ones that require a login are available (chances are you won't have the passwords to these if you're casually looking for Wi-Fi access while on the road).

Adding New Capabilities

Consider these utilities to add capabilities that most people should have but that Apple doesn't provide.

Application access

Although they could just as easily be considered applications instead of utilities, Parallels' Desktop ($80; www.parallels.com) or EMC VMware's Fusion ($80; www.vmware.com/products/fusion) is a must-have for anyone who deals with Windows so you can run Windows applications on your Mac. (Both of these are equally good; Chapter 18 covers these tools in more depth.)

I recommend you install Adobe AIR (free; www.adobe.com), which enables you to run desktop widgets that get data from the Internet. AIR widgets run like regular applications, so you don't have to switch to the Widgets window as you do with Apple's built-in widgets (see Chapter 14). Plus, AIR widgets can run in Windows, Linux, and Mac OS X, so they're great for companies, schools, clubs, and other groups whose people use different kinds of computers.

Communications

You can turn your Mac into a phone by using the Skype service and its Mac client (www.skype.com); pricing depends on where you are calling but is typically much cheaper than traditional phone services (there is a $10 minimum initial deposit). If you don't have a landline anymore, it's a great way to make calls overseas without paying the ridiculously high international long-distance rates charged by cellular carriers. You also can make free computer-to-computer audio and video calls to other Skype users. Although theoretically you can use the Mac's built-in microphone and speakers, you'll want to get a USB headset for your audio calls. Your Mac's built-in iSight camera (if it has one) typically works well enough for the video calls. Just note that digital voice services like Skype don't support emergency-services numbers such as 911.

File transfer

If you manage a website—for your business, club, church, or family—or provide design or other services involving creating and distributing files, you'll benefit from a File Transfer Protocol (FTP) utility to make it easy to upload and download files to a web-based server. There are two good ones to choose from: Fetch ($25; www.fetchsoftworks.com) and Transmit ($30; www.panic.com/transmit). The free, open source FileZilla (http://filezilla-project.org) utility is quite capable but not as user-friendly.

If you use a smartphone or tablet that doesn't come from Apple, you'll want a sync utility for it, to transfer contacts, music, and more. Research in Motion and Microsoft have free utilities for their BlackBerry (http://us.blackberry.com/apps-software/desktop/desktop_mac.jsp) and Windows Phone 7 (www.microsoft.com/windowsphone/en-us/apps/mac-connector.aspx) devices, respectively, but for Android devices, you'll want Salling Media Sync ($22; www.salling.com/mediasync/mac). For other devices, Mark/Space likely makes compatible versions of its Missing Sync utility ($40; www.markspace.com).

Security

The Mac is currently not a main target of hackers—unlike Windows PCs—so there aren't many viruses and similar malware threats for it. But as it gains popularity, the chances of getting infected with malware will only increase. In fact, the MacDefender Trojan horse in spring

2011 was the first major such attack, causing Apple to update Mac OS X to detect and remove such fake antivirus programs that actually send your personal information such as credit card numbers to thieves.

Still, today Mac users are at a fraction of the risk of malware attacks as their Windows counterparts, making it hard to justify the cost of products such as VirusBarrier ($50, plus $30 for annual renewal; www.intego.com). But should you get infected, it'll cost you more in time and money to fix your Mac. On the other hand, I've gone a decade with no infections. You have to decide what level of risk you're comfortable with. If you get and click lots of links to funny videos and the likes from people you know, or if you download music and videos from file-sharing sites, you definitely should consider protecting yourself, as these activities are the prime conduits for malware.

You may be tempted to get PC Tools' iAntivirus (www.iantivirus.com; free for home users, $30 for business users), which protects just against viruses, but note that users are charged $30 per year for the required virus definitions (so it's not really free), and many users complain it is difficult to stop the automatic renewal (and thus the credit card charges).

One of the best password tools on the Mac is 1Password ($40; www.1password.com). This application, which also has Windows, iPhone, and iPad versions, installs as a standalone application in Mac OS X and creates shortcuts in your browsers. When you sign up for a new website, 1Password creates a password with a random string of characters extremely difficult to crack. You can even set parameters to the password such as length and avoidance of confusingly similar characters. This software lets you protect each website you visit with a unique password that 1Password remembers for you, so there's no personal password for someone to guess to gain access to all the websites you visit or the sensitive data such as credit card information you have stored on them.

Text entry

When you type the same text repeatedly, wouldn't it be nice if the Mac let you use an abbreviation and automatically replaced it with the full phrase? Well, TextExpander ($35, www.smilesoftware.com) does just that. It'll save you lots of typing—at least when you're on your own Mac.

Summary

Although Mac OS X comes with many applications and utilities, you may find some features are missing and others could be more capable or easier to use. That's where utilities come in, filling in the gaps and improving some of what Apple has created. Hundreds of such utilities are available online in both commercial and hobbyist-created software for prices that range from free to more than $100.

Playing Music and Videos

W ho needs a CD player, radio, DVD player, or TV when you have a Mac? Mac OS X's capability to become an entertainment center is simply amazing, thanks to its support of audio and video formats and to the iTunes, QuickTime Player, and DVD Player software that come with Mac OS X. Sure, you'll likely still have a traditional home entertainment center in your living room, but your Mac can handle the job in the other rooms of your house—and in dorm rooms, small apartments, and other quarters, it can be your home entertainment center if you attach a large-enough monitor and good speakers to it.

Everyone knows that Apple revolutionized the music industry with its iPod. But it's actually iTunes that makes the iPod revolution possible. iTunes is not just the Mac's built-in music player but also its built-in radio and podcast player. It's also your direct connection to buying music, TV shows, and movies that you play back on your Mac or through an Apple TV to your TV or through an AirPort Express to your speakers.

Plus it enables you to manage all your media for both your Mac and your iPod. Oh, and if you have an iOS device such as an iPad, iPhone, or iPod Touch, it also acts as the gateway for keeping your calendars, e-mail, e-books, and mobile applications in order.

Cross-Reference

Apple's free iCloud service lets you synchronize your music automatically across all Macs and iOS devices (iPhones, iPads, and iPod Touches) connected to the same account. You also can sync applications (Mac and iOS) and books, as well as photos, e-mail, contacts, and calendars. Chapter 17 explains how to set this sharing up in the Mac's iTunes and your iOS devices. ■

IN THIS CHAPTER

Understanding what music and video formats iTunes can play

Setting preferences for music import, sharing, and parental controls

Bringing music into iTunes

Managing music display, synchronization, and playlists

Listening to music

Subscribing to and playing podcasts

Accessing Internet radio

Bringing video into iTunes and playing it

Working with Home Sharing and Apple TV

Working with DVD Player and QuickTime Player

Before I get into the details of music and video on your Mac, here are a few things you need to remember:

- **The MP3 format is the most common format for music on computers, and many programs can play this format, including iTunes and the Safari browser.** Other music formats that iTunes supports include AAC (Advanced Audio Coding; also called MP4 audio), AIFF (Audio Interchange File Format), Apple Lossless, Audible audio-book, and WAV (the name comes from the .wav file extension Microsoft uses for its Windows audio format). The AAC format gives you the highest quality, so it's the best to use for music you import from your music CDs into iTunes.

- **The MPEG-4 (MP4) format is the most common format for video on computers, and iTunes, Safari, and other applications that come with Mac OS X can handle it.** But there are many other formats you may encounter, including Silverlight, Flash (.flv), Windows Movie (.wma and .wmv), and QuickTime Movie (.mov). iTunes can play MPEG-4 and QuickTime Movie formats. To play the other formats, you need a separate playback utility or a plug-in for your browser. When you try to play such files in your browser, you usually get a prompt asking if you want to download the associated helper file, which you should do. For Windows Movie files, you need the free Flip4Mac (www.telestream.net).

- **Apple updates iTunes on a different schedule than it updates Mac OS X, so the version of iTunes running on your Mac when you read this may be newer than the 10.3 version that Mac OS X Lion initially included.** You may see new capabilities or interface changes in your version of iTunes compared to what this chapter describes.

- **Don't steal music or videos.** It's perfectly legal to import the CDs and DVDs you've bought into iTunes for playback on your own TVs, Macs, PCs, and iOS devices. It's perfectly legal to buy or rent music and videos from the iTunes Store and other licensed online music and video sites. It's *not* legal to copy music, videos, or other media from your friends' CDs, unlicensed sharing sites such as BitTorrent, or from rented DVDs—when you get such "free" media, you're taking money away from the people who make this stuff, which makes it harder for them to make more. (Extracting the videos from the DVDs you bought by using extraction software such as Mac the Ripper or HandBrake is a weird gray area: It is legal to copy the DVDs you bought as long as the copies are for personal use, but it is not legal for companies to create the software used to remove the copy protection that blocks that legal copying.)

Using iTunes as Your Music Library

iTunes is your Mac's music hub, the application that you use to manage and play your music. You'll spend lots of time in iTunes, which works best if you also have an Internet connection so you can buy music and get album covers that display in your iTunes music library.

Setting music preferences

The first thing to do on a new Mac is set up iTunes' music preferences. (If you're upgrading your Mac OS X to Lion, your previous iTunes settings are retained.)

Import settings

Start by choosing iTunes ⇨ Preferences or pressing ⌘+, (comma) and then going to the General pane. Here you tell iTunes how to import music files from your music CDs. Use the When You Insert a CD pop-up menu to control iTunes' behavior when you insert a music CD into your Mac. The options are Show CD, Begin Playing, Ask to Import CD (the default), Import CD, and Import CD and Eject. Show CD simply displays the CD in the left pane of iTunes but does nothing with it. Begin Playing plays the CD automatically, which can be handy if you want to listen to a friend's CD without making an illegal copy.

Tip

If you're loading your music collection into your Mac, choose the Import CD and Eject option from the When You Insert a CD pop-up menu to make the import process simple and fast: As you insert a CD, iTunes automatically imports the songs and then ejects the CD when done so you know it's time to pop in another. After you have your music collection on your Mac, change the option to either Ask to Import CD (so if you insert a new CD, you're asked whether to add its music to the library or just to make it available for play in iTunes as long as it is inserted in your Mac) or Show CD (so nothing happens, under the assumption you don't want to import it or play it, because you already have the music on your Mac). ■

Before you begin importing music files, it's critical to set your desired audio conversion settings, which you do by clicking Import Settings in the General pane of the Preferences dialog box. The default settings are the best for music CDs: AAC Encoder as the Import Using option and iTunes Plus as its Setting option. This option imports your music in the high-quality AAC file format, which both iTunes and the iPod, iPad, and iPhone devices can handle, but AAC-format music files won't play on many MP3 players or on the web. So if your music is destined for the web or non-Apple music players, choose MP3 in the Import Using pop-up menu and 192 Kbps in the Setting menu (to get the highest quality available to MP3). The other options are useful only in special circumstances, such as choosing the WAV format for use in a Windows music player (though most can also handle MP3).

Playback settings

In the Playback pane (shown in Figure 16.1), you can control how iTunes plays music:

- **Select Crossfade Songs, and choose a crossfade duration from the slider to get that deejay effect of overlapping music, with a new song fading in as another ends and fades out.**

- **Select Sound Enhancer, and adjust the slider to boost the volume of both the treble and bass (or lower them) across all songs.** Use this setting to compensate for weak or overly strong speakers.

- **Select Sound Check to have iTunes control the volume of songs so they all play at the same level of loudness.** This helps get rid of variations in the recordings, but note that it can make intentionally quiet songs play too loudly and intentionally noisy songs play too softly.

FIGURE 16.1

The Playback pane of iTunes' Preferences dialog box

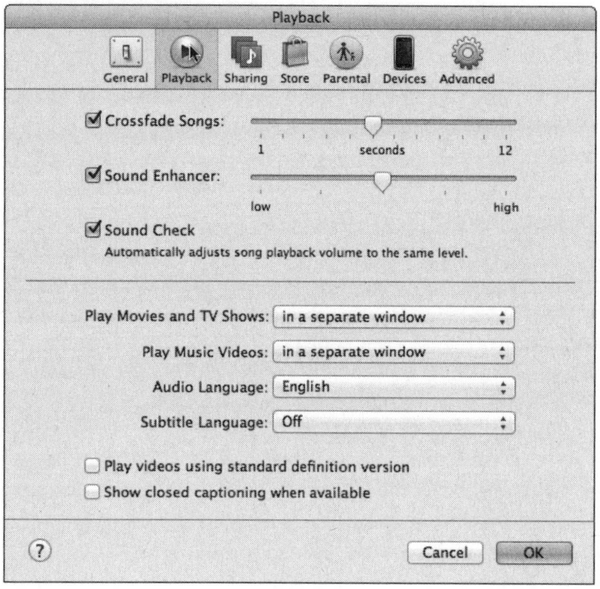

Tip

To make iTunes the default audio player for audio you open in your web browser, go to the Advanced pane of the Preferences dialog box and click the Set button that appears to the left of Use iTunes for Internet Playback. ∎

Sharing settings

iTunes can access music and other media on other Macs and Windows PCs, as well as make your Mac's music accessible to others, as long as all the computers are on the same network and using iTunes. Use the Sharing pane to control what is shared. Selected by default, the Look for Shared Libraries option scans the network for other iTunes libraries. Any detected appear in the Library list in the Sidebar at the left side of the iTunes window.

If you want to share your music and other media, select the Share My Library on My Local Network option, and choose either Share Entire Library or Share Selected Playlists (and then select from the list the types of Media—Music, Podcasts, Movies, and/or TV Shows—plus any specific music playlists you want to share). You can require a password for someone to access your library by selecting Require Password and entering the password in the adjacent text field. (This is handy if you use a wireless network and don't want outsiders tapping into it to access your library, or if visitors are connected to your wired network.)

The Home Sharing Computers and Devices Update Play Counts option, if selected, tells iTunes to track each time someone has played music or other media from your Mac. This can affect the rankings of songs and other media in your smart playlists (covered later, as is the Home Sharing feature).

Parental settings

You may not want your kids to access certain media content, perhaps because of obscene language or sexual content. iTunes enables you to apply parental controls to the media it presents; go to the Parental pane in the Preferences dialog box.

In the Disable section, choose which media sources you want to block access to. Choices include Podcasts, Radio, iTunes Store, Ping (Apple's social music service), and Shared Libraries.

After choosing your country's ratings system in the Ratings For pop-up menu, in the Content Restrictions section, select what kind of ratings you want to limit iTunes Store purchases to. Choices include movies, TV shows, and apps (including games). The Restrict Explicit Content option applies to all media types.

To keep your kids from overriding your iTunes parental controls, click the lock icon button at the lower left of the Parental pane and enter your password. (See Chapter 27 for more details on setting up user accounts, passwords, and parental controls.)

Importing music files

For iTunes to be your music hub, it needs to have music. You can get music files into iTunes in two ways, in addition to getting them from an online music store:

- **If you already have music files on your Mac or in a computer-friendly format such as MP3 on a disk, choose File ⇨ Add to Library or press ⌘+O, and select the disk or folder that contains the music files.** iTunes copies them to its music library folder. (Music in any subfolders is copied as well, as are any iTunes-supported media such as images and video files.)

- **If your music is on a music CD (or DVD), insert the disc into your Mac.** Depending on the option you chose in the When You Insert a CD pop-up menu in the General pane of the iTunes Preferences dialog box, iTunes may automatically import the disc's music, ask you if you want to import the music, play the disc, or just display its contents. If iTunes simply plays the disc or displays its contents, you can import the music by clicking Import CD at the bottom right of the iTunes window, as Figure 16.2 shows. (Note how iTunes displays the disc's contents; if it does not, click the disc's name in iTunes Sidebar, in the Devices list.)

That's all there is to it!

The contents of a CD I am about to import the music from

Buying music online

Apple was the first independent company to get the recording industry to agree to legal online sales, and its iTunes Store has become one of the world's biggest sellers of music online. It's easy to get music from iTunes Store: Click iTunes Store in the Sidebar at the iTunes Sidebar, and browse the store's offerings by genre or artist, or search by artist, album, or song. As Figure 16.3 shows, you can buy whole albums or individual songs.

Tip

To listen to a song in the iTunes Store before you buy it or the album, just double-click the song. ■

If you're not signed in to the iTunes Store, you are asked to do so before you can actually buy the music. You also can sign in by clicking Sign In at the iTunes Store or choosing Store ➪ Sign In in the iTunes application. (If you don't have an account, you can create one in the sign-in window that appears.) After you sign into the iTunes Store, iTunes remembers your sign-in information and signs in automatically each time you use it. To sign out (perhaps you're using a friend's computer or don't want your kids charging music against your credit card), choose Store ➪ Sign Out.

Note that the music you buy from the iTunes Store can be kept on as many computers as you like. (Before late 2008, you were limited to keeping copies of music files on up to five computers for playback. Any music files bought when Apple restricted playback to five computers remains limited to five computers unless you paid in iTunes to upgrade them to unlimited usage.) For videos and apps, you're restricted to using them on no more than five authorized computers. (An iPod, iPad, or iPhone doesn't count as a computer, because an iPod's, iPad's, or iPhone's music library is "tied" to a specific computer's library and can sync only to that one library.)

To access music, videos, and apps downloaded from the iTunes Store, you need to authorize each computer to your iTunes Store account by choosing Store ⇨ Authorize Computer and entering the sign-in information. To disable a computer for the playback of music and for the access to apps with your iTunes sign-in, choose Store ⇨ Deauthorize Computer.

FIGURE 16.3

Searching for music on the iTunes Store

Of course, iTunes Store is not the only source of online music. You can buy music from other venues, such as Amazon.com. These online stores typically download an MP3 file to your Mac, perhaps even into your iTunes library. As far as iTunes is concerned, the music you bought from them is the same as if you imported it from a CD.

iTunes' icon controls

Many of iTunes' controls are available as icon buttons. The figure below shows what they do.

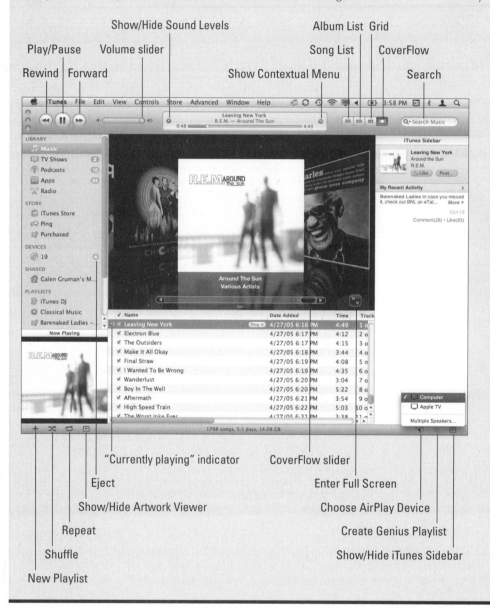

Show/Hide Sound Levels

Album List Grid

Play/Pause   Volume slider

Song List   CoverFlow

Rewind   Forward

Show Contextual Menu

Search

"Currently playing" indicator   CoverFlow slider

Eject

Enter Full Screen

Show/Hide Artwork Viewer

Choose AirPlay Device

Repeat

Create Genius Playlist

Shuffle

Show/Hide iTunes Sidebar

New Playlist

Managing your music

When you import or buy music, iTunes automatically organizes it by the artist and album; if you have an Internet connection, it can look up the related information. If you have an iTunes Store account, it also downloads the album artwork automatically for music you import from disc. (Choose Advanced ⇨ Get Album Artwork to retrieve the album covers for music you've imported from CDs or other sources outside the iTunes Store if you see that some album covers are blank.)

Controlling music display

You can easily peruse your music using iTunes' four view modes: song list, album list, grid, and Cover Flow; using the View icon buttons near the top of the iTunes window; or by choosing View ⇨ As List (alphabetical by song), View ⇨ As Album List (as shown in the "iTunes' icon controls" sidebar), View ⇨ As Grid, or View ⇨ As Cover Flow.

Tip

In grid view, you can switch between album, artist, genre, and composer views by using the buttons at the top of the iTunes window. If more than one album matches an artist, genre, or composer, slide your mouse sideways within the icon to see the various albums that match. To get a detailed view of the results in grid view, just double-click an album cover for album, composer, and artist views, and double-click the genre icon for the genre view to get all the matching songs, arranged by album. Also, you can adjust the size of album covers in grid view using the slider at the upper right of the window. ■

Note in the various views that display songs the check boxes to the left of each song title. Any song that is selected plays if you play that album, and any selected song is synchronized to your iPod, iPad, or iPhone if you select Sync Only Checked Songs and Videos in the Summary pane for a selected device.

Syncing with iPods, iPads, and iPhones

The new iCloud service can automatically sync music, apps, and books purchased through one of Apple's online stores to all your iOS devices, as Chapter 17 explains. Music and other content you obtained from other sources are synced via iTunes after you connect the iOS device to your Mac via a USB cable.

Note

Apple offers a $25-per-year service called iTunes Match that scans all the music imported in your Mac's iTunes (that is, music not bought through the iTunes Store) and lets you use the same music from the iTunes Store on your other devices, rather than upload the music files from your Mac into the free iCloud service. The iCloud service has a 5GB limit for storage of content not purchased through Apple, so if you have lots of ripped music you want to keep available online (such as in case your hard disk crashes and can't be recovered), the iTunes Match subscription may be worthwhile. ■

When you connect an iPod, iPad, or iPhone to your Mac via a USB cable and open iTunes, the device shows in the Devices list in the iTunes Sidebar. If you select a device and click Sync, iTunes copies all music and other iTunes media supported by that device to the device, and it removes from that device any media files that had been removed from iTunes. This is how you keep your iPod, iPad, or iPhone updated on your music and other media files. But a device can be associated to only one copy of iTunes (to prevent media piracy). So if iTunes doesn't recognize an iPod, iPad, or iPhone, it asks if you want to replace all its contents with the contents of the iTunes library—thus, if you connect your iPod, for example, to a friend's Mac and say yes, you lose all the contents of your iPod and have it replaced with your friend's iTunes library.

Note

To prevent music (and videos) from syncing to your iPod, iPad, or iPhone, select Manually Manage Music and Videos in the Summary pane for the selected device. When you sync the device, no music, podcasts, apps, e-books, or video files are copied or removed to reflect the current state of the iTunes library. You might use this when updating your iPod, for example, on a friend's computer to get, say, an iPod software update but not have your music and videos replaced. This can be handy if you are on vacation or otherwise away from your Mac for a long time. You also might use it to sync your iPhone, iPad, or iPod Touch to a work computer to keep your calendar and other data (in the Info pane) synced without losing your music and video in the process. But note that any applications for an iPhone, iPad, or iPod Touch are deleted from the device when synced via a "foreign" iTunes; there is no manual management option for applications in the version of iTunes that initially shipped with Mac OS X. ■

The Summary pane is not the only pane that controls what is synced to your iPod, iPad, or iPhone. Other panes appear based on your device's capabilities, with options to determine what exactly is synced. (Your settings are retained until you change them.) The panes can include any of the following: Music, Movies, TV Shows, Books, Podcasts, Photos, Info, and Apps. When connected, all iPods show the Music and Podcasts panes in iTunes. When connected, video-capable iPods show the Movies, TV Shows, and Photos panes. The Info, Books, and Apps panes display only if an iPhone, iPad, or iPod Touch is connected.

Tip

If you bought music via the iTunes Store on your iPhone, iPad, or iPod and want to transfer it to an authorized computer, do so by choosing File ➪ Transfer Purchases. ■

Working with playlists

A *playlist* is simply a collection of songs—like a mix tape. iTunes has two kinds of playlists: regular playlists and smart playlists.

A regular playlist contains whatever songs you add to it. To create the playlist, click the + icon button at the bottom left of the iTunes window, choose File ➪ New Playlist, or press ⌘+N. The center part of the iTunes window shows an empty list, and an untitled playlist name appears at the bottom of the Playlist group at the left of the iTunes window. Click the untitled playlist name so you can name it something meaningful. Then click Music from the iTunes Sidebar to display your music. Drag the songs you want added to your playlist to the playlist's name. If you click the playlist name, you see all the songs in it. You can drag them within the list to control the order in which they play.

A smart playlist is built on rules, so its contents change automatically based on those rules. For example, you might create a rule that says to include only music not played to iTunes in the last 30 days that is not part of a compilation album, and that is rated at least three stars. Thus, you get a playlist of your favorites that you haven't heard lately that stays automatically updated as you add music and as you rate the music you have.

To create such a smart playlist, choose File ⇨ New Smart Playlist or press Option+⌘+N. You get the dialog box shown in Figure 16.4, in which you add the rules and their parameters. (The rules in Figure 16.4 create the "missed favorites" playlist described previously.) After you click OK to save the playlist, it appears in the Playlist group; click its name to rename it if desired.

Note

Smart playlists are indicated by a purple page icon with a gear in it, while regular playlists are indicated with a blue page icon with a musical note in it. ■

Tip

You can create a CD of a selected playlist by choosing File ⇨ Burn Playlist to Disc or by right-clicking or Control+clicking the playlist name and choosing Burn Playlist to Disc. You need to insert a blank recordable disc when prompted. ■

FIGURE 16.4

Creating a smart playlist

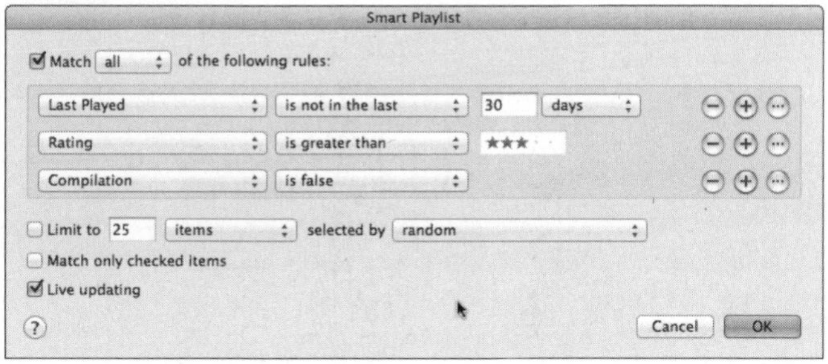

Working with Genius

The Genius feature categorizes music by how it sounds and then can group music accordingly. Primarily meant as a way for Apple to recommend additional music you may want to buy, Genius also can be used to select music for playback—think of it as a playlist based on how the music actually sounds. For example, if you are throwing a dance party, you would select one or more dance songs in your library and then turn on Genius so iTunes plays only similar dance songs, regardless of their genre, album, or artist. Of course, this feature can lead to a monotonous selection (because it's designed to find music that sounds similar to your selection), so you probably won't want to leave it on as your regular listening mode.

To turn on Genius, choose Store ⇨ Turn on Genius. You need to sign in to your iTunes Store account or create one. Genius then goes through all your music and builds "sounds like" profiles for each song, and then it matches those profiles against the music in the iTunes Store—a process than can take quite some time when you first turn on Genius. (The iTunes Sidebar displays Genius recommendations; turn it on and off by choosing View ⇨ Show/Hide iTunes Sidebar or by pressing Shift+⌘+G. It displays the songs that iTunes recommends you buy that are similar to your currently selected song.)

After Genius has processed all your music, you can tell Genius to automatically create smart playlists. Just select the song you want to use as the "sounds like" master, and click the Genius icon button (the atom icon) at the bottom right of the iTunes window. If you click the Genius smart playlist in the iTunes Sidebar, you can hear the songs Genius has decided are good acoustical matches.

Rating music

If you look at your songs in list view, you see a Rating column. By default, songs have no ratings, but you can assign your own ratings to them on a scale of zero to five stars. Click a song choose File ⇨ Rating, and choose the number of stars to assign. You can now sort your songs in list view by rating, which enables you to play music based on your rating—chances are good that you'll use this to easily select and play just your top-rated music.

Playing your music

Playing music is easy in iTunes. Select Music from the Library list in the iTunes Sidebar, and select the album, artist, composer, genre, or composer using the View controls described earlier in this section to choose what you want to play.

Tip

You can select multiple albums, composers, genres, or songs for playback by ⌘+clicking individual selections or Shift+selecting a range. ■

You can narrow down your musical selections using the iTunes browser; choose View ⇨ Column Browser, and select the columns you want to display. You can then scroll each column to make selections that narrow down the results in your songs list. Press ⌘+B to turn the column browser view on and off.

Tip

To quickly find music in iTunes, you can enter a term in the Search box at the upper right of the iTunes window and press Return or click the Search icon button (the magnifying glass icon). ■

Music plays in the order displayed, so if you use list view, you can control the order of play by title, artist, album, genre, or rating.

Or you can choose a playlist from the Playlists list at the bottom-left side of the iTunes window.

Note

If you select no music, iTunes plays your entire library. ■

After you've selected your music, click the Play icon button at the upper left of the iTunes window to play the music. (Or, for a single song, just double-click it.) You can use the Rewind and Forward icon buttons to move back and forth among your song selections. Information about the currently playing song appears at the top of the iTunes window.

Note

There's a volume slider near the Play icon button that controls how loudly iTunes plays the music. But this control does not change the Mac's overall volume; you control that with the volume slider in the menu bar or the Sound system preference (see Chapter 28). So, if the Mac's volume is set to halfway, putting iTunes' volume slider to maximum means that iTunes plays songs at that halfway point (that is, at the maximum level set for the Mac). The reason iTunes has a separate volume control is so you can adjust the volume based on the music you're playing relative to the Mac's overall sound volume. ■

Just like a stereo, iTunes also has controls that enable you to mix it up a bit. Click the Shuffle icon button (it looks like two crossed arrows) at the bottom left of the iTunes window to play the selected music in random order. Click it again to play music in the order of the tracks in the original album. (If the button's icon is black, shuffling is off; if it is blue, shuffling is on.) You also can choose Controls ⇨ Shuffle to more precisely control how the shuffling occurs using the submenu options By Songs, By Albums, and By Groupings.

You also can click the Repeat icon button (its icon is made of two arrows forming a loop) to play the selected items over and over in a loop. (If the button's icon is black, Repeat is not on; if it is blue, Repeat is on. If it is blue and the numeral 1 appears in the lower-left corner, Repeat plays your selection twice—that is, repeats it once—and then stops playing.) The same controls are available by choosing Controls ⇨ Repeat and choosing Off, All, or One in the submenu.

Note

You also can play music in a variety of file formats by using the QuickTime Player application that comes with Mac OS X; choose File ⇨ Open or press ⌘+O to select the desired music file. However, you can open and play only one song at a time. Also, you can listen to MP3 files in your web browser from a web page that provides a link to the file—a handy way to listen to music or podcasts provided on the website. (You can't open an MP3 file on your Mac for playback in your browser.) ■

If you want the computer screen to show images as your music plays, press ⌘+T or choose View ⇨ Show Visualizer to turn on the Visualizer, which creates images based on the music's tempo and tones. You can change the Visualizer style by choosing options from the submenu when you choose View ⇨ Visualizer. Press ⌘+T or choose View ⇨ Hide Visualizer to turn it off.

Using iTunes for Podcasts

At its core, a podcast is simply an audio file. Typically, a podcast is like an episode of a radio program—a newscast, an interview, advice, a deejay's current faves, a comedy routine, and so on—that you listen to on your iPod, iPad, iPhone, or Mac. Typically, a podcast is part of a series that you subscribe to. Lots of radio programs, for example, are now available as podcasts, so you can listen to them at your convenience. And many websites offer their own podcasts, often the equivalent of audiobooks for their textual content.

iTunes enables you to access and play podcasts, as well as synchronize them to your iPod, iPad, or iPhone. To access podcasts, click the Podcasts option in the iTunes Sidebar. A window with any podcast subscriptions appears. To add podcast subscriptions, click Podcast Directory to open the iTunes Store and peruse its list of podcasts. (They are usually free.) You also can add podcasts to iTunes directly at many websites. Look for a Subscribe or iTunes button; clicking these buttons typically adds the podcasts to your iTunes podcast list with no further ado.

After you have a subscription set up, an icon for it appears in the main part of the iTunes window whenever you click Podcasts. If you're in icon view mode, double-click the icon to see all the individual podcast episodes available. The other view modes show the podcast icon and the currently downloaded episodes, as Figure 16.5 shows for the album list view. As with songs, you can select and deselect them, play them, and delete them. (If you downloaded an individual podcast to iTunes and want to subscribe to the whole series, just click the Subscribe button.)

FIGURE 16.5

The episodes available for subscribed podcasts, plus (at the bottom of the window) the subscription management controls

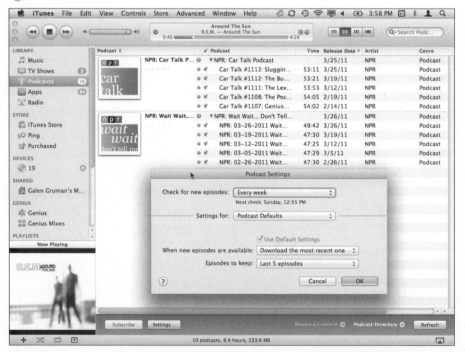

You also can manage the subscription by clicking Settings, which opens the dialog box shown at the bottom of Figure 16.5. Here, you can set how many episodes are kept, how often iTunes checks for new episodes, and which episodes iTunes should download.

Tip

If you have the URL for a podcast subscription, a quick way to subscribe to the podcast is to choose Advanced ⇨ Subscribe to Podcast, paste the URL into the Subscribe to Podcast dialog box that appears, and click OK. ■

Listening to Internet Radio

The web and iOS devices may well kill radio—who needs to listen to the endless blather and commercials on most stations, anyhow?—but it also may reinvent radio. That's because radio itself is moving to the web. Podcasts are one example of how radio is adapting to the web and to the iPod. But radio also is available in its "live" form as streaming audio—instead of its signal coming to you over the radio, it comes to you over the Internet.

In the iTunes Sidebar, click Radio to get a list of genres. Click the disclosure triangle to the left of a genre to get a list of available streams. Now double-click the desired stream to hear what is currently playing. (Just like radio!)

Tip

If you have the URL for an Internet radio "station," a quick way to listen to it in iTunes is to choose Advanced ⇨ Open Stream or press ⌘+U, paste the URL into the Open Audio Stream dialog box that appears, and click OK. ■

Using iTunes for TV Shows and Movies

iTunes plays much more than audio. It can display video as well, such as TV shows and movies in the MPEG-4 format that you download to your Mac or create on it using tools such as Apple's iMovie. The process for managing and watching video in iTunes is very much like that for music files, as covered earlier in this chapter.

Setting video preferences

There's very little in the way of preferences that you need to set for playing back video. In the Preferences dialog box's Playback pane (refer to Figure 16.1), you can control video playback:

- **Use the Play Movies and TV Shows pop-up menu to determine where TV and movie videos play.** The options are in Artwork Viewer, in the iTunes Window, in a Separate Window, Full Screen, and Full Screen (with Visuals). Note that the artwork viewer is the small preview box at the bottom of the iTunes Sidebar; you need to click the Show Artwork Preview icon button—the up-facing-triangle-in-a-box icon— to see the preview box. Also note that the Full Screen (With Visuals) option displays animated graphics when you're playing music; it can be fun at a party where your Mac is being used as your stereo.

- **Use the Play Music Videos pop-up menu to determine where music videos play.** The options are the same as for the Play Movies and TV Shows pop-up menu.

- **Use the Audio Language pop-up menu to choose the default language for your videos.** Note that this option has an effect only if the videos support multiple language audio tracks and if the video has the audio track in the language chosen here. (If it does not, iTunes plays the audio in the language that matches Mac OS X's default language, as set in the Language & Text system preference covered in Chapter 21.)

- **Use the Subtitle Language to choose the default language for the subtitles in your videos (typically available in foreign-language videos).** As with the Audio Language pop-up menu, iTunes uses Mac OS X's default language if the video's subtitles are not available in the language chosen here.

- **Select the Play Videos Using Standard Definition Version if you want iTunes to play the standard (SD) video instead of the high-definition (HD) video in a file that has both formats.** You might choose this if your Mac has a small screen that can't benefit from the extra detail of HD video.

- **Select the Show Closed Captioning When Available option to have iTunes display closed captions.** Closed captions are the subtitles meant to help the hearing impaired—for videos that have them (not many do).

Importing and buying videos

If you have MPEG-4 (.mp4) video files available—perhaps home movies you created in iMovie or videos downloaded from the web—choose File ⇨ Add to Library or press ⌘+O, and select the disk or folder that contains the video files. iTunes copies them to its video library folder.

You also can buy movies and TV shows from the iTunes Store; it works the same way as buying music and podcasts, as described earlier in this chapter. Note that the video files purchased from iTunes have the file extension .m4v.

In both cases, the videos appear in the central iTunes window if you click TV Shows or Movies (as appropriate) from the Library list in the iTunes Sidebar.

Note
Apple restricts playback of videos bought or rented through the iTunes Store to five computers: the one you downloaded it to plus four others of your choice. To choose other computers, you need to authorize each computer to your iTunes Store account by choosing Store ⇨ Authorize Computer and entering the sign-in information. To disable a computer, choose Store ⇨ Deauthorize Computer. (An iPod, iPad, or iPhone doesn't count as a computer, because an iPod's or iPhone's video library is "tied" to a specific computer's library and can sync only to that one library.) ■

Managing your videos

iTunes provides few management controls for videos. Just as with music files, you can change the view to help you peruse them via the four view modes—list, album list, grid, and Cover

Flow—using the View icon buttons near the top of the iTunes window or by Choosing View ⇨ As List, View ⇨ As Album List, View ⇨ As Grid, or View ⇨ As Cover Flow.

You also can use the iTunes browser (choose View ⇨ Column Browser and the desired options from its submenu) to select your videos based on genre, show, and season. Press ⌘+B to toggle the column browser on and off.

You also can control whether videos are synced to a connected iPad, iPhone, or video-capable iPod by selecting Manually Manage Music and Videos in the Summary pane for the selected device. As with music, videos are synced to iPads, iPhones, and video-capable iPods when you sync unless the Manually Manage Music and Videos option is selected.

But iTunes' other management capabilities for music—playlists, ratings, and Genius—are not available for videos.

Playing your videos

As with songs and podcasts, the easiest way to play an individual video in iTunes is to double-click it. Or select the videos to watch and click the Play icon button in the iTunes toolbar. The other playback controls such as Rewind and Forward also are available there via icon buttons. However, you cannot set videos to shuffle or repeat, as you can for music.

You get a full suite of controls in the onscreen controls, which appears at the bottom of the playback window. If the onscreen controls don't appear, move the pointer to have them appear—they disappear after a few seconds so as not to get in the way of the video. The onscreen controls include Volume, Previous Video ("previous" is defined as the previous item in the current list), Rewind, Play/Pause, Forward, Next Video, Closed Captions (visible only if the video supports them), AirPlay, and Enter Full Screen.

New Feature

Mac OS X Lion does not come with the Front Row application for watching videos in full-screen mode. The application was meant to make a computer monitor display movies like a TV. In Mac OS X Lion, you use the full-screen mode in iTunes or DVD Player for the same purpose. Choose View ⇨ Enter Full Screen, press ⌘+F, or click the Enter Full Screen icon button in the playback window's onscreen controls (the icon of two arrows pointing in opposite directions). Move the pointer while a video is playing in full-screen mode to display the onscreen controls, and click the icon button again or press ⌘+F to return to the regular window size. ■

Using Home Sharing and AirPlay

Apple has been working to make the Mac and iOS devices—tied together via iTunes—the new entertainment library. So it's added several technologies that let you stream music and videos from Macs and iOS devices to TVs and speakers, as well as to rent videos via its iTunes Store for playback on TVs.

Those technologies are Home Sharing, AirPlay, and Apple TV.

Using Home Sharing

The Home Sharing capability in iTunes on a Mac and built into iOS 4.3 and later on iPhones, iPads, and iPod Touches, lets each device share its music with anyone else in wireless range. The key is that everyone needs to use the same Home Sharing account.

On any Mac (or PC) running iTunes, choose Advanced ⇨ Turn On Home Sharing, and enter a username and password. It does not have to be the same as your iTunes account username and password; in fact, it shouldn't be, so guests can sign into Home Sharing when visiting without then having your iTunes Store account sign-in information. (On an iOS device, go to the Settings app, select iPod from its Sidebar, and enter the username and password in the Home Sharing section of the main window.)

Everyone on the same Wi-Fi network who signs in with the same username and password can share their music; their libraries will display in the Shared section of the iTunes Sidebar on the Mac, in the Sidebar of the Remote and iPod apps, and in the Shared pane of the Videos app on an iPhone, iPad, or iPod Touch. (The Remote app is a free download from the App Store and is meant to control an Apple TV or other iTunes device.)

Using AirPlay and Apple TV

The AirPlay feature introduced in iOS 4.3 has made it to iTunes 10.2 and later. AirPlay is the technology that lets an iPhone, iPad, iPod Touch, or Mac stream audio or video wirelessly to other devices. Those other devices include Apple's second-generation Apple TV and AirPlay-enabled stereos and speakers from a variety of manufacturers.

When a Mac or iOS device detects an AirPlay device on the Wi-Fi network, it displays the AirPlay icon—an up-pointing triangle in a screen, as you can see at the bottom right of the figure in the "iTunes' icon controls" sidebar earlier in this chapter. (On iOS devices' apps, it usually appears near the Play button.) Click it to get a menu of compatible AirPlay devices, as well as the device you are currently using, so you can choose where to send the audio or video.

By combining Home Sharing and AirPlay, you can stream audio and video from a Mac or iOS device's iTunes library through your Apple TV to a TV set, as well as play audio and video you download from iTunes or Netflix to the Apple TV.

Watching Videos with DVD Player

iTunes can't play video DVDs as it can music CDs. But DVD Player can play DVDs. If you insert a DVD into your Mac, DVD Player automatically begins playing it full screen. Press Esc to get to the menu bar and other controls. (You can set DVD Player to *not* play a DVD automatically by deselecting Start Playing Disc in the Preferences dialog box: Choose DVD Player ⇨ Preferences or press ⌘+, [comma].)

The player offers icon controls over playback (such as Rewind, Forward, Play, Pause, and Stop, plus volume settings, DVD menu navigation, chapter navigation, slow-motion playback, frame-stepping, viewing angle (for DVDs that provide that option), and subtitles/closed captioning) in a controller designed to look like the kind of remote control that came with your physical DVD player, as shown in Figure 16.6. The Control, Features, and Go menus in the menu bar also give you access to these capabilities.

FIGURE 16.6

Top: The DVD Player's controls when the video is played in a window (the default). Bottom: DVD Player in full-screen mode

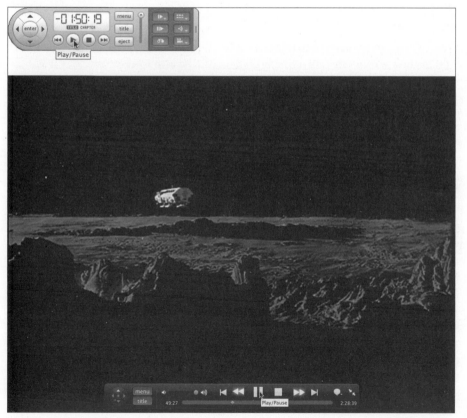

The menu bar offers some capabilities not available in the onscreen controls. For example, you can choose Features ⇨ Enable Parental Control to have Mac OS X require the administrator password to play any DVD. (When enabling or disabling parental control, you also need to

provide the administrator password, which presumably you don't share with your children). The View menu lets you control the size of the playback window (you can also resize the window using the pointer, like any other standard window) and show or hide the onscreen controller.

Choose View ⇨ Enter Full Screen or press ⌘+F to switch to full-screen mode, shown in Figure 16.6. When in full-screen mode, controls appear onscreen when you move the pointer. One of those controls is the Exit Full Screen icon button (the icon composed two arrows), which lets you see the menu bar and the rest of the Finder.

Note

DVD Player does not play Blu-ray or HD DVDs, even if you connect a compatible drive to your Mac. DVD Player can play high-definition (HD) video on conventional DVDs. ∎

In the Preferences dialog box (choose DVD Player ⇨ Preferences or press ⌘+, [comma]), you have six panes of options:

- **Player:** Here, you set whether DVDs play automatically when a disc is inserted and whether they play in full-screen mode by default. You also can set DVD Player not to run when the Mac is operating on battery power, to pause the video if you minimize the viewer, to show closed captions automatically when the sound is muted, and whether to mute the audio or pause playback if you receive an iChat message while watching a DVD.

- **Disc Setup:** Here, you set the default languages for audio, subtitles, and DVD menus; the defaults for all three are Use Disc Default, but if you watch lots of foreign-language DVDs, you can use these settings to force them to, say, English when you insert DVDs. You can also select which devices the audio plays back through and enable access to web links presented by the DVD.

- **Full Screen:** Here, you set how long the controller remains visible after you stop moving the pointer, as well as control whether other displays connected to your Mac are dimmed when playing a DVD in full-screen mode, whether the full-screen display remains when DVD Player is not playing a DVD, and whether the menu bar displays when the pointer is moved in full-screen mode.

- **Previously Viewed:** Here, you set where discs play from (such as always the beginning or at the last position played), as well as whether the DVD's own settings should be used for the audio equalizer, video color, and video zoom.

- **High Definition:** Here, you set the default sizes for standard definition (SD) and high-definition (HD) video. For SD video, your options are Actual Video Size and Disc Default; for HD video, your options are Actual Video Size, 720 Height, and 1080 Height.

- **Windows:** Here, you determine whether status information displays in the upper-left corner of the playback window for a few seconds after you click a button such as Play or Fast Forward. You can also set the color and size of caption text.

Working with QuickTime Player

The QuickTime Player does more than play media files; it lets you record your own and convert media files for use in iTunes and YouTube. But QuickTime Player does not substitute for DVD Player and iTunes (both covered earlier in this chapter); you cannot play DVDs with it, for example.

Playing media files

QuickTime Player's most basic capability is to play supported audio and video formats, which include Apple's QuickTime movie (.mov) format, the MPEG-4 (.m4v and .mp4) video format, the MP3 audio format, and Apple's AAC audio format. To play a supported file on your Mac or on an attached disk, choose File ➪ Open File or press ⌘+O, select the file from the Open dialog box, and click Open. You also can open media files from the web by choosing File ➪ Open URL or pressing ⌘+U; enter the URL in the dialog box that appears or choose a previously opened URL from the Movie URL pop-up menu.

In either case, you get a playback dialog box with the filename in its title bar, as the bottom side of Figure 16.7 shows. (If you open a protected media file, you are prompted to open it in QuickTime Player 7 instead of Mac OS X Lion's QuickTime Player 10; QuickTime Player 7 has just playback controls similar to those in DVD Player, as seen in the top of Figure 16.7.)

Click the Play icon button to play the file (it turns into the Pause icon button), and click and hold the Rewind and Fast Forward icon buttons to navigate through the file—much like any onscreen player. You also can drag the time bar's thumb to move to a desired point in the video or audio file. For audio, and for video that has audio, you also get a volume slider to the left of the playback window.

The playback dialog box for video files has two additional options:

- The Options icon pop-up menu (the arrow-coming-out-of-a-box icon) opens a menu that has options to prepare the file for iTunes and YouTube, as well as to trim the file (both capabilities are covered later in this chapter).

- The Screen Toggle icon button (the opposing-arrows icon) toggles the playback display between full-screen view and the dialog box. You also can resize the dialog box to any size you want by dragging its lower-left corner.

Tip
To see details about an open media file, choose Window ➪ Show/Hide Media Inspector or press ⌘+I. The Media Inspector dialog box displays information such as the file location, format, frames-per-second (fps) rate, data rate, and size. ∎

FIGURE 16.7

Top: QuickTime 7 Player is meant just for playback of protected media. Center: QuickTime 10 Player playing a video. Bottom: QuickTime Player 10 also lets you edit unprotected video (left) and audio (right).

QuickTime Player also has controls for the video playback in its View menu:

- Choose View➪Enter Full Screen or press ⌘+F to toggle to full-screen view.
- Choose View➪Actual Size or press ⌘+1 to see the video at actual size.
- Choose View➪Fit to Screen or press ⌘+3 to fit the video to screen proportionally.
- If you are viewing a video in full-screen mode, you can choose View➪Fill Screen or press ⌘+4 to fill the screen with the video (this may distort or crop the video if the video's ratio is different from the screen's), or choose View➪Panoramic or press ⌘+5 to make the video fill the screen height and compress the sides if they won't otherwise fit; you can then pan (scroll) the video to decompress one side (which compresses the other side even more) to change the area of focus. You would use the Panoramic option if you want to watch a widescreen (16:9 ratio) video at full height on a standard-width (4:3 ratio) monitor and still be able to pan to the cut-off portions (which you could not do with the Fill Screen option).
- Choose View➪Increase Size or press ⌘+= to zoom in the video, or choose View➪Decrease Size or press ⌘+– to zoom out the video.
- For videos that have language options, you can choose View➪Show Closed Captioning or press Option+⌘+T, choose View➪Languages, and then choose an available language from the submenu, and/or choose View➪Subtitles➪On/Off.
- For videos that have chapters, choose View➪Show/Hide Chapters or press ⌘+R to display the chapter-navigation controls in the video playback dialog box.
- Choose View➪Loop or press ⌘+L to have the video playback loop (replay) the video endlessly.

Editing media files

You can edit media files—essentially, cut pieces out or *trim* them—using the controls in QuickTime Player. To do so, choose Edit➪Trim or press ⌘+T. For video files, you also can click the Options icon pop-up menu and choose Trim. The time bar changes to the trim slider, which show a sequence of stills for video and the sound waves for audio (refer to the bottom-right side of Figure 16.8).

Drag the trim slider's thumbs on either the left or right side to trim from the beginning or end, respectively, of the file. You can start with one side and then move onto the other side. For audio files, you also can choose Edit➪Select All But Silence or press Shift+⌘+A to exclude the silent part of the file (this moves the trim sliders to exclude silence at the beginning and/or end of the file, but it leaves silence inside the file). Click Trim to complete the cut. (You can choose Edit➪Undo Trim or press ⌘+Z to cancel the trim.)

When you're finished, choose File➪Save As or press Shift+⌘+S to make the changes permanent in a copy of the original file permanent. (If you want to overwrite the source file, you choose File➪Close or press ⌘+W, and then when the warning dialog box appears asking if you want to discard your changes, click Save to save the original file with the changes.

FIGURE 16.8

Left: The Movie Recording dialog box in QuickTime Player. Right: The Audio Recording dialog box in QuickTime Player.

Creating media files

Although it's called a player, QuickTime Player also can create media files: movies, sound recordings, and screencasts ("movies" of what occurs on your Mac's screen, for how-to guides, for example). The process for all three is similar:

- **Movie recording:** Attach a video camera to your Mac or use its built-in iSight camera. Then choose File ⇨ New Movie Recording or press Option+⌘+N. The Movie Recording dialog box opens. As Figure 16.8 shows, the dialog box has controls for video and audio sources, quality levels, and recording destination; click the Choose icon pop-up menu to select the desired options. The key control is the Record icon button (the big-red-circle-with-a-white-circle-inside icon). Click it to start recording; it changes to the Stop icon button (the big-red-circle-with-a-white-square-inside icon), which you click to end the recording and make the playback dialog box appears so you can see what you just recorded. The dialog box also has the same volume settings and Screen Toggle icon button as the playback dialog boxes. Note that if no camera is attached (or, if you're using an iSight camera on a laptop, but the laptop case is closed), the Movie Recording dialog box displays the message "The camera is off."

- **Audio recording:** Choose File ⇨ New Audio Recording or press Control+Option+⌘+N. The Audio Recording dialog box opens. As Figure 16.8 shows, the dialog box has controls for audio sources, quality levels, and recording destination; click the Choose icon pop-up menu to select the desired options. The key control is the Record icon button (the big-red-circle icon). Click it to start recording; it changes to the Stop icon button, which you click to end the recording and make the playback dialog box appears so you can hear what you just recorded. The dialog box also has the same volume settings as the playback dialog boxes.

- **Screen recording:** Choose File ⇨ New Screen Recording or press Control+⌘+N. The Screen Recording dialog box opens. The dialog box has two controls: the Choose icon pop-up menu for audio sources, quality levels, and recording destination, and the Record icon button (the big-red-circle icon). Click Record to start recording; a settings sheet appears and asks you to confirm that you want to record the screen. The settings sheet notes that you can click the Stop icon button in the menu bar or press Control+⌘+Esc to end the recording and make the playback dialog box appear so you can see what you just recorded. Click Start Recording to begin the screen recording, or click Cancel to not record the screen.

Exporting video and screencast files

QuickTime Player makes it easy to share video and screencast files with others, through applications such as through iTunes, YouTube, Vimeo, Flickr, Facebook, and Mail. Use the Share menu to export the video files at the appropriate size, resolution, frame rate, and format for any of these services.

New Feature
New to QuickTime Player in Mac OS X Lion is the ability to export video to Vimeo, Flickr, Facebook, and Mail. Its iTunes export options also have been renamed to reflect Apple's current iOS device line-up. ■

If you select iTunes, you get three options in the dialog box that appears: iPod & iPhone, iPad, iPhone 4 & Apple TV, and Mac & PC (some may not be available based on the format of the video file being converted). Note that each option shows the file size of the current video if exported with that option. Select one and click to Share to export the video for the desired playback service. QuickTime Player adds the video file to your iTunes library when it's finished.

If you select YouTube, Vimeo, Flickr, or Facebook, a dialog box appears in which you enter your username and password for the selected video-sharing service; enter that information and click Sign In to begin the export and upload process. (If you want your Mac to remember these settings, select the Remember This Password in My Keychain option before clicking Sign In.) Note that these services typically have file-size and limits for uploaded videos. (You need an Internet connection for the file to be uploaded as well.)

If you select Mail, a copy of the movie is attached to a mail message. You can choose to send the movie at its actual size or adjusted to 480p resolution.

Note
Some video exports can take many minutes to complete. To monitor the progress of your video exports, choose Window ⇨ Show Export Progress or press Option+⌘+P. ■

Exporting audio files

When exporting audio files, you get just one option in the Share menu: iTunes. Your file is exported to MP3 format and added to the iTunes library. That's it!

Summary

iTunes is your Mac's central tool for managing and playing music and videos. It not only maintains your library of media files, but it also manages file synchronization with devices such as iPods, iPads, and iPhones. Plus, it enables you to share music and videos with other computers, iOS devices, Apple TVs, and even stereos and speakers, and to access the music and videos from other Macs and iOS devices using the Home Sharing and AirPlay capabilities.

You can import music from your CDs, converting them into digital files that work in iTunes and iPods—even on the web. iTunes also can import MPEG-4 video files that you may have created in a program such as iMovie or downloaded from the web. You also can buy music, TV shows, and movies from the iTunes Store, as well as from other online stores.

iTunes enables you to sort and search your music and to create playlists—collections of music you put together or create the rules for—telling iTunes what to put together. The Genius feature tells iTunes to create a playlist of songs that sound like the currently selected song. For videos, iTunes enables you to sort and search them only.

When playing music, you have all the controls you'd expect from a stereo, including shuffle and repeat. iTunes offers just the basic playback controls for video, such as Play, Pause, Rewind, and Forward, but when you play DVDs in the separate DVD Player application, you get the full set of controls you'd expect from any physical DVD player's remote control.

You also can subscribe to podcasts for playback in iTunes and for synchronization to iPhones, iPads, and iPods so you can listen to them on the go. iTunes' support for Internet radio gives you access to a wealth of programming from hundreds of traditional radio stations and online-only Internet radio "stations."

The QuickTime Player utility does much more than play several video and audio formats. It lets you record your own movies, audio, and screencasts. It also lets you trim video and audio files, such as to take out silence in audio files, as well as export unprotected video for use in iTunes, Vimeo, Flickr, Facebook, and YouTube.

Syncing Macs and iOS Devices

W hen you work with multiple computers, it's easy to get inconsistent information in your calendars and address books. And it's easy to forget to copy a file from one to the other, such as from your iMac to your MacBook. Windows PCs can be part of the mix as well. Add the iPhone, iPad, or iPod Touch to the mix, and it can get impossible to keep everything synchronized and accessible.

With iTunes on your Mac, you can handle a lot of this syncing by connecting each device via a USB cable to your Mac, but that can be frustrating, and if you forget or are away from your Mac a lot, your devices and Mac can quickly get out of sync with each other.

If that's a frustration you experience, Apple offers the free iCloud service for use with Mac OS X Lion computers and iOS 5 devices (iPads, iPod Touches, and iPhones), as well as with limited use with Windows PCs. It replaces the MobileMe service, which offered additional capabilities such as an Internet-based ("cloud") virtual disk drive, public calendars, and photo-sharing capability.

iCloud is a simpler service, intended to help you manage the synchronization of music, apps, e-books, contacts, calendars, e-mail, and photos among your computing devices. You'll need other services to share with others.

IN THIS CHAPTER

Syncing between your Mac and iOS devices using iTunes

Syncing content and apps via iCloud

Syncing documents and photos via iCloud

Backing up iOS devices via iCloud

Working with other cloud services

Syncing via iTunes on a Mac

Although iTunes is generally designed for managing and playing music and videos (see Chapter 16), it also acts as the central manager for other information in the iPhone, iPad, and iPod Touch: e-mail accounts, calendars, contacts, and Safari bookmarks, as well as for any mobile applications on your iPhone, iPad, or iPod Touch. Of course, iTunes' controls for music, podcast, video, and photo syncing available to other iPods work the same way with the iPhone, iPad, and iPod Touch, as Chapter 16 explains.

When you connect an iPhone, iPad, or iPod Touch to your Mac (or Windows PC) and select the device from the Devices list in the iTunes Sidebar, the Summary pane appears. You also see a list of tabs for other panes. The Info pane controls how iTunes manages information on your iPhone, iPad, or iPod Touch when you sync.

The Info pane

The Info pane contains controls for syncing items between your Mac and your iOS device. Note that if you use iCloud, Exchange, Gmail, or other service that syncs over the Internet directly to your iOS device, these options do not affect those syncs. The local sync is mainly meant as a backup for your iOS device. The Info pane offers these sets of controls:

- **Contacts:** Select the Sync Address Book Contacts option, and then select either All Contacts or Selected Groups so the contacts in your Mac's Address Book and in the iPhone's, iPad's, or iPod Touch's Address Book remain synchronized. The Add Contacts Created Outside of Groups on this iPod [or iPad or iPhone] To option, if selected, puts any contacts added on the iPhone, iPad, or iPod Touch into the group you specify in the adjacent pop-up menu. You might use this option to separately track contacts you enter when using your mobile device. Also, you can have iTunes sync Yahoo and Google contacts to your iPhone, iPad, or iPod Touch by selecting the desired service and clicking Configure to set up the specific mappings.

- **Calendars:** Select the Sync iCal Calendars option, and then select either All Calendars or Selected Calendars so the appointments in your Mac's iCal and in the iPhone's, iPad's, or iPod Touch's Calendar are kept synchronized. (Note that if you use Microsoft Exchange's calendar and want it to be synchronized to your iPhone, iPad, or iPod Touch, you need to create a calendar in iCal called Entourage.) You also have the option of limiting calendar syncing to appointments by selecting Do Not Sync Events Older Than __ Days and entering the number of past days to which you want to limit syncing.

- **Mail Accounts:** To sync your mailboxes' account information in Apple's Mail application—not the e-mails themselves but the connection and other settings—with the iPhone's, iPad's, or iPod Touch's Mail application, select the Sync Selected Mail Accounts and then select the accounts you want to keep synchronized (if you have more than one account set up in Mail).

Caution

I advise against syncing Mail via iTunes. After all, your e-mail comes from a server, and if you have each Mac and iOS device access the e-mail directly from that server, they're all kept up to date. The trick, as Chapter 20 explains, is to have each computer and device leave the messages on the server so they're available for the next device that checks in. If you set up your computers and devices this way, selecting Sync Select Mail Accounts can cause your devices to get two copies of all messages. Similarly, if you use a network calendar or contacts list such as the Google Calendar/Gmail combination or Microsoft Exchange, it's better to set up your devices to sync directly with the calendar and contacts than to route them through iTunes. ∎

- **Other:** This section contains two options: Sync Safari Bookmarks and Sync Notes. If you select Sync Safari Bookmarks, the bookmarks in your Mac's Safari browser remain synced with those in your iPhone's, iPad's, or iPod Touch's Safari browser. (To sync Firefox bookmarks, you need to use the Firefox Home app on your iOS device.) If you select Sync Notes, any notes on your Mac or iOS device are synced, such as notes associated to a Gmail or Exchange account. Chances are good that you are syncing these directly via the Internet, so syncing them to your computer may result in duplicates.

- **Advanced:** If you want to clear information from your iPhone, iPad, or iPod Touch and replace it with the information from your Mac, select the desired option in this section: Contacts, Calendars, Mail Accounts, Bookmarks, and/or Notes. The next time you sync, iTunes deletes the specified information from your iPhone, iPad, or iPod Touch and replaces it with the information on your Mac, rather than synchronizes the two. Note that these options are automatically deselected after you sync, so regular syncing resumes for later syncs.

Cross-Reference

For more on using iCal and Address Book, see Chapter 21; for more information on Mail, see Chapter 20. See Chapter 22 for details on using them with Microsoft Exchange. ■

Caution

If your iPhone, iPad, or iPod Touch has applications previously synced to another copy of iTunes—on a different Mac, for example—all the applications on your iPhone, iPad, or iPod Touch are deleted and replaced with just the ones in the current copy of iTunes, just as when you sync music and videos from a "foreign" iTunes. ■

The Apps pane

The second iTunes pane specific to iPhones, iPads, and iPod Touches is the Apps pane, shown in Figure 17.1. This keeps a list of the mobile applications you've downloaded or synced to iTunes. If you select the Sync Apps option, iTunes updates your iPhone, iPad, or iPod Touch with the ones stored on your Mac and transfers any purchases made on your iOS device to your Mac, so you have a local backup. (The iOS App Store and Mac App Store also keep a record of the apps you have downloaded, so you can download them again at no cost to any computer or device using the same Apple ID as you use for the stores.) You can sync all applications or selected ones; if you select specific applications to sync, only those are kept up to date on both your Mac and the mobile device.

By default, apps are synced to all iOS devices attached to your iTunes account. (iPad-only apps of course are not synced to iPhones or iPod Touches.) To control specifically what apps are synced to each device, select it from the iTunes Sidebar's Devices list, go to the Apps pane, and deselect the apps you do not want to sync to that specific device. You also can rearrange the iOS device's home screen by dragging icons within and across the home panes that display in the Apps pane—just as you would on the iPhone, iPad, or iPod Touch.

FIGURE 17.1

The Apps pane for a specific iOS device (here, an iPad)

You can manage your mobile applications in iTunes by clicking Apps in the Library list in the iTunes Sidebar. (List view and Cover Flow view are not available for mobile applications.) You can check to see if any of the applications have updates available by clicking Check for Updates; if iTunes has detected available updates, the option changes to *x* Updates Available. Either way, clicking it opens the iTunes Store, where you can choose which applications to update. The next tine you sync the iPhone, iPad, or iPod Touch, the updated application is transferred to it.

Note

An iPhone, iPad, or iPod Touch also can detect application updates when connected to the Internet via a 3G or Wi-Fi wireless connection, and you can install the updates wirelessly from the device. If you do, the next time you sync the device to iTunes, the update is copied over to iTunes so it remains updated as well. ∎

If you scroll down through the Apps pane, you see the File Sharing section, which lists all apps that can store documents and transfer them between the iOS device and your Mac. Select an app, and drag compatible files into the pane at right to have them synced to the device. Likewise, when you sync, any documents on the iOS device appear here as well, for you to drag out to use on your Mac. You also can use the Add button to add files from your Mac and the Save To button to save them to your Mac.

The Books pane

If you have the iBooks app on your iPhone, iPad, or iPod Touch, any books you purchased appear in the Books pane. Any books you bought from the iBookstore via iTunes on your Mac also appear. Select the Sync Books option to sync books between the iOS device and the Mac, and then select either All Books or Selected Books. If you select Selected Books, you check the books you want synced. You can sort the display of books using the two pop-up menus: Books and PDF Files (its options are Books and PDF Files, Only Books, and Only PDF Files) and Sort by Title (or Sort by Author).

To add PDF files to your iOS device's iBooks library, just drag the PDF file onto the Books icon in the iTunes Sidebar's Library section or into the window of books that appears if you click the Books option. You can copy PDF files from the library by dragging them out of the Books pane onto the desktop or Finder window.

New Feature

The ability to buy e-books from the Mac's iTunes is new to iTunes 10.3, which was released in conjunction with Mac OS X Lion. ■

Note

Books purchased through other bookstores, such as Amazon.com for use in its Kindle app, do not appear in the Books pane. They can't be synced via iTunes' Apps pane either. You manage these files at the website or through the app you used to purchase them, or use a utility such as iPhone Explorer (free; www.macroplant. com) that gives you access to the inner workings of an iPhone's, iPad's, or iPod Touch's hidden file system. ■

Preferences for iOS devices

The Preferences dialog box's Devices pane has one iPhone-, iPad-, and iPod Touch-specific control: Prevent iPods, iPhones, and iPads from Syncing Automatically. Normally, when you sync an iPhone or iPod Touch to your Mac, iTunes backs up any applications, calendar entries, and other data on the device as a safety measure. But this can slow down your syncing considerably. Select this option to disable the automatic backups.

A list of the most recent backup for each device you sync appears in above this option. You can select a backup and click Delete to get rid of it. If you do disable automatic backup, right-click or Control+click your iOS device in iTunes's Sidebar and choose Backup from the contextual menu to manually back it up; I recommend you do so occasionally as a safety measure.

Syncing via iCloud

Apple's new iCloud service provides a central syncing facility for all devices that share an Apple ID (or sign-in account for Apple's various online stores). Macs running Mac OS X Lion with iTunes 10.5 or later plus the iCloud update, mobile devices running iOS 5, and Windows PCs running iTunes 10.5 or later plus the iCloud control panel can all use iCloud. (Mac OS X's Software Update Utility will detect and install iTunes 10.5 and iCloud if it is not already installed on your Mac.

Also, mobile devices running the iOS 4.3.3 beta that Apple released in June 2011 can use iCloud to sync music, apps, and books, but no other iCloud services.

New Feature

iCloud debuted shortly before Mac OS X Lion was released, but most of its capabilities are oriented to syncing with iPads, iPhones, and iPod Touches running the iOS 5 operating system—which was not available until several months after Lion shipped and this book went to press. You can expect updates to iTunes and perhaps other components of Mac OS X Lion as a result; check out `www.wiley.com/go/lionbible` **for an updated version of this chapter detailing the final iCloud service when it becomes fully operational in fall 2011. ■**

Syncing content and apps purchased from Apple's online stores

The basic iCloud services are related to Apple's various online stores (iTunes Store, iBookstore, Newsstand, Mac App Store, and iOS App Store), which track the music, apps, and books you bought and thus can check with each device linked to your account whether it has all the purchases installed on it. Apple calls this iCloud component Automatic Downloads.

Note

As this book went to press, Apple planned to expand iCloud syncing of content bought via Apple's online stores to include online magazine subscriptions from its Newsstand store once iOS 5 became available. ■

On a Mac or Windows PC, you enable iCloud syncing of music, books, and apps in the Store pane of the iTunes Preferences dialog box, show in Figure 17.2. Here, in the Automatic Downloads section, you select the contents you want to have synced via iCloud: Music, Apps, and Books.

FIGURE 17.2

The Store pane in the iTunes Preferences dialog box sets up iCloud syncing for media.

On your iOS devices, you also need to enable iCloud syncing. Go to the Settings app and tap Store from the Sidebar. In the Automatic Downlaods section, slide the switches to On for the content you want to have synced automatically via iCloud, as shown in Figure 17.3. If you want the syncing to occur when you are connected via a 3G cellular connection, also slide Cellular to On—but note that such syncing may quickly eat up the transfer allowances in your data plan. (Whatever you select for the Cellular option, syncing occurs any time you are connected to a Wi-Fi network.)

Any music you have in iTunes or books you have in iBooks that you did not purchase through Apple are also synced to other devices via iCloud (apps from outside the iOS App Store and Mac App Store are not synced). But the iCloud service has a 5GB storage limit per account, excluding apps and media bought from an Apple online store, so the more content you purchased outside of Apple, the more likely you are to run against that limit.

Note

iOS apps are synced only among a maximum of five iOS devices, though they are backed up to your Mac or Windows PCs as well. Mac apps bought via the Mac App Store are synced only among a maximum of five Macs. Music, photos, magazine subscriptions, and books are synced among a maximum of 10 devices and computers. ∎

FIGURE 17.3

The Store pane in the Settings app on an iOS device (an iPad is shown here) also sets up iCloud syncing for media.

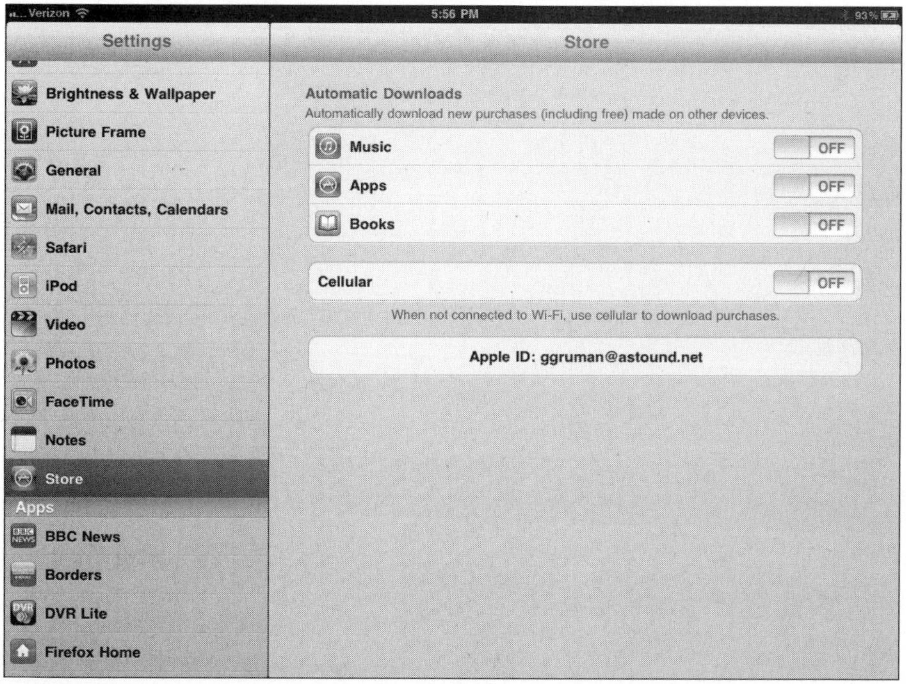

Once iCloud syncing is set up, compatible iOS apps—iTunes and iBooks, for example—display a Purchased pane that shows all purchases and those not downloaded to the current device, as Figure 17.4 shows. Tap the cloud icon button to download the desired content. Likewise, iTunes on the Mac shows the same information if you select iTunes Store from the Sidebar.

Syncing documents and other information via iCloud

Beyond syncing purchases from Apple's online stores, iCloud also provides users a syncing service for various documents across their Macs and iOS devices, include iWork documents (from the Pages, Numbers, and Keynote applications) and images managed in iPhoto. Developers also can implement iCloud syncing directly in their own apps, to allow iCloud synchronization of their files. iCloud also syncs mail, notes, calendars, and contacts, plus provides remote control over the Internet and a utility to find a lost or stolen Mac.

Setting up iCloud

To enable these iCloud services, open the Mail, Contacts & Calendars system preference (choose ⇨ System Preferences, then click the Mail, Contacts & Calendars icon). Click the iCloud button in the right pane, and sign in via your Apple ID and password, as Figure 17.5 shows.

In the settings sheet that appears, you have two options: Manual Setup and Automatic Setup. Clicking Automatic Setup enabled iCloud syncing for Mail, Address Book, iCal, Safari bookmarks (across the Mac OS X, iOS, and Windows versions), Photo Stream (for syncing photos managed by iPhoto, if you have version 9.2 or later of that application), remote control over the Internet (called Back to My Mac), and Find My Mac (a service that lets you track a lost or stolen Mac, based on the similar Find My iPhone feature in iOS). If you click Manual Setup, you can choose which of these applications and services to iCloud-enable.

Note

During setup, iCloud asks you to set up a me.com e-mail address. If you have a me.com address from a MobileMe account, you can use that. Otherwise, create a new address. Note that the address you use cannot be changed; it becomes your permanent iCloud e-mail address. Your me.com address displays as a secondary iCloud account in the Mail, Contacts & Calendars system preference. Click it to open its settings pane, where you can activate that account for e-mail, contacts, and/or calendars. That iCloud account also appears in the accounts list in Mail, Address Book, and/or iCal, respectively. ∎

You can change iCloud sync settings in the Mail, Contacts & Calendars system preference by select the iCloud account in the left pane, shown in Figure 17.5. A list of iCloud services then appears in the right pane. Deselect those you don't want to sync.

You also can add iCloud accounts; click the + icon button below the accounts list. Note that these additional iCloud accounts only sync e-mail, calendars, and contacts associated to the Apple ID provided for those accounts.

FIGURE 17.4

Top, from left to right: The Purchased pane for iTunes showing a list of music not downloaded to this iPhone, the iTunes subpane showing details of undownloaded purchased music from one artist with buttons to download them, and the iBooks pane showing that there are no purchased books that haven't already been synced to this device. Bottom: The similar controls in iTunes in Mac OS X.

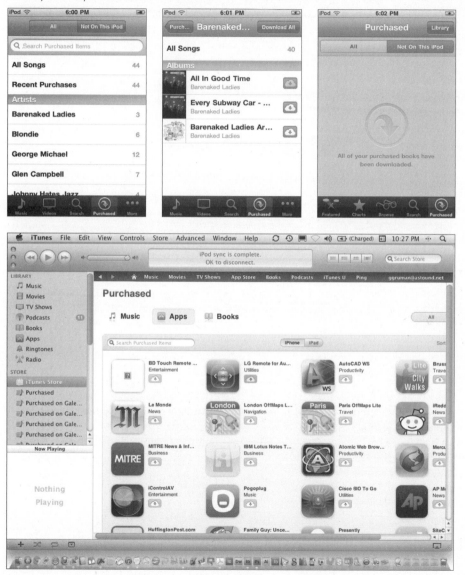

FIGURE 17.5

At left: The settings sheet in the Mail, Contacts & Calendars system preference where you enter your Apple ID and password to activate iCloud. At right: The account pane where you can change your iCloud settings.

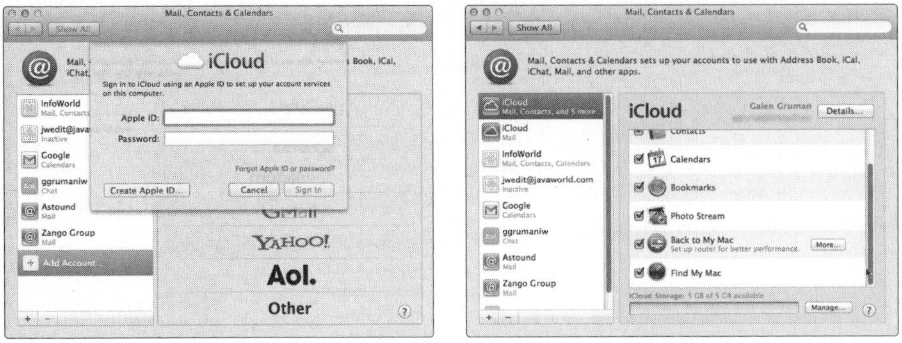

Note

For iOS 5 devices, you set up and manage iCloud using the similar controls in the Settings app's Mail, Contacts, Calendars pane. ■

Using iCloud services

iCloud's syncing of e-mail, contacts, and calendars via iCloud doesn't apply to third-party services such as Microsoft Exchange, IMAP-based e-mail accounts, and Google Calendar, as these services sync all devices logged into them. iCloud's syncing services are meant for local calendars and contacts and for POP-based e-mail accounts, none of which support multiple-device syncing. (Chapters 20 through 22 cover how to use various e-mail, contacts, and calendar services with Mail, Address Book, and iCal.)

Back to My Mac works like file sharing on a local network (see Chapter 24), except it allows you to control a Mac from another Mac connected over the Internet to the same iCloud account. Note that Back to My Mac often doesn't work. It's very picky about the types of connections you have between the two Macs, requiring the routers involved to let the initiating Mac's control request pass through, rather than block it as a potentially dangerous intruder. (If you can adjust your routers' settings, enable UPnP and NAT-PMP, if available—doing so can both establish a more reliable connect and speed up Back to My Mac.) If Back to My Mac can't work over your Internet connection, you get an error message after a few minutes of connection attempts.

Find My Mac lets you find a lost or stolen Mac from another computer or mobile device. From an iOS device, use the Find iPhone app, sign in to your iCloud account using your Apple ID and password, and wait a few seconds for the Mac's last known location (based on its last Wi-Fi connection) to be displayed. You then can tap the Mac's icon to open a pane in which you can lock or wipe the Mac or send a message to whoever is using it. For computers and other devices, log in to iCloud.com, sign in with your iCloud username and password, and use the tools that appear to locate and manage your missing Mac.

To enable the Photo Stream service in iPhoto, open the Preferences dialog box (choose iPhoto ⇨ Preferences or press ⌘+, [comma]), go to the Photo Stream pane, and select the Enable Photo Stream option. Two other options—Automatic Import and Automatic Upload—are automatically selected. Automatic Import adds photos from other devices Photo Stream–enabled apps (such as the Photos app in iOS devices) to iPhoto; Automatic Upload sends all new photos to iCloud for syncing with other Photo Stream–compatible apps on Macs and iOS devices, as well as to the My Picture folder on Windows PCs, connected to your iCloud account. Note that iCloud stores and syncs only photos from the previous 30 days, up to a limit of 1,000; older photos remain on any computer or device storing them but are no longer kept synced via iCloud.

Other iCloud-enabled apps have options in their Preferences dialog box to enable iCloud syncing of their documents.

When this book went to press, Apple planned to update Mac OS X Lion and iTunes to have iOS devices automatically back up over Wi-Fi their contents once a day to a Mac or PC running the iCloud-enabled version of iTunes. When both the computer and iOS device are on the same Wi-Fi network, the iCloud service checks when the last backup of that iOS device occurred, and if it's been more than 24 hours, the iOS device backs up its settings and contents to iCloud, as well as to your computer. (Purchases from Apple's various online stores are not backed up, because they are always available for re-downloading at no cost from the Apple stores.)

Managing iCloud storage

In the iCloud settings pane, you can view how much of the 5GB of the free iCloud storage provided by Apple you have used via the indicator at the bottom of the pane.

Click Manage to open the Storage Details settings sheet to see how much data each application and service is using. Click an application or service to see which of its files are stored in iCloud, then select individual files and click Delete to remove them from the iCloud storage (they remain on your computers and devices).

Using iCloud on Windows PCs

Apple also has made iCloud available for Windows Vista and Windows 7 PCs (sorry, not for Windows XP, though the Automatic Update component of iCloud does work on iTunes for XP). If you have iTunes or Safari on Windows, you also have the Apple Software Update utility. Use it to download the iCloud control panel and iCloud-compatible updated versions of Safari (5.1) and iTunes (10.5).

Windows iTunes provides the same Automatic Update capabilities as in the Mac version, as well as the same ability to wirelessly back up iOS devices. Likewise, Windows Safari syncs bookmarks with Mac OSX's Safari and iOS's mobile Safari via iCloud.

After the iCloud control panel is installed in Windows, launch it from the Start menu. Sign in using your Apple ID and password. After you sign in, you see the configuration options shown in Figure 17.6. Select those applications services you want to enable iCloud syncing with: Mail with Outlook, Calendar with Outlook, Bookmarks with Internet Explorer, and Photo Stream.

The iCloud control panel in Windows

If you use Outlook with an Exchange server, there's no need to sync via iCloud—the Exchange server syncs e-mail, calendars, and contacts to all devices that connected to Exchange. Likewise, an IMAP e-mail account keeps all devices connected to it in sync for mail and a Google Calendar account keeps all devices connected to it in sync for calendars But if you use Outlook for a POP e-mail account, or for locally managed calendars and contacts, you should use iCloud to sync them to other computers and devices.

If you prefer to sync bookmarks with Windows Safari instead of with Internet Explorer, click the Options button to the right of Bookmarks with Internet Explorer, click Safari in the dialog box that opens, and click OK. The option is now called Bookmarks with Safari. (You can change back to Internet Explorer using the same Options button.)

If you enable Photo Stream syncing, click Options to set up the folders in which images are uploaded to and from by iCloud. Any images placed in the selected upload folder are synced to any Macs, PCs, and iOS devices using the same Apple ID as your PC. Likewise, any images synced via Photo Stream from those other devices are placed in the folder you select as the download Folders. Click OK when you've selected the folders.

Toward the bottom of the iCloud control panel is an indicator of how much of the 5GB of the free iCloud storage you have used. Click Details to open the Storage Details dialog box to see how much data each application and service is using. Click an application or service to see which of its files are stored in iCloud, then select individual files and click Delete to remove them from the iCloud storage (they remain on your computers and devices).

The final option is Show iCloud Status in System Tray; if selected any notifications from iCloud display in the system tray to the right of the Start menu. You can also double-click the icon to open the iCloud control panel.

Click Apply to make your settings active. iCloud is now running on your PC.

Note
To open the iCloud control panel in Windows 7, choose Start ⇨ Control Panel, choose either Large Icons or Small Icons from the View By pop-up menu, and click iCloud. In Vista, choose Start ⇨ Control Panel, click the Classic View button at left, and click iCloud in the pane at right. ∎

Using Cloud Storage Services

With the demise of MobileMe's iDisk cloud storage service, Mac users need to look elsewhere for a place to store documents on the Internet, whether to hold documents in applications that don't use iCloud syncing or to share files with others. Fortunately, many companies offer similar services, often with free storage under 1GB or 2GB of usage. Some also offer additional features, such as allowing you to create shared folders for workgroups or providing administrative controls for IT to use to ensure data security.

The two best-known cloud storage services are Dropbox (www.dropbox.com) and Box (www.box.net); Soonr (www.soonr.com) and SugarSync (www.sugarsync.com) also have a following. They work on Macs, Windows PCs, and iOS devices, plus they work on other devices such as Google Android tablets and smartphones. And they give you easy access through desktop disk icons and through web pages.

In mobile productivity apps such as Quickoffice Pro and Documents to Go, you add access to these services via the accounts list. But to use them with Apple's iWork suite of iOS productivity apps (Pages, Keynote, and Numbers), you have to access them through a WebDAV account (WebDAV is one of the options you get when downloading or uploading files from the iWork apps). If you're using Dropbox, set up a $5-per-month WebDAV account at www.dropdav.com; if you're using Box.net, set up a free WebDAV account at www.box.net/dav. After it's set up, you sign in to your cloud storage service using its WebDAV account; all files transferred go in your regular folders on Dropbox or Box.net, so they are available to you from other devices with no special setup or need to navigate to a separate location.

The Soonr and SugarSync services work a little differently. They provide an app for your iOS device through which you sync photos and other files for automatic wireless backup. They also connect with Quickoffice and Documents to Go the same way that Dropbox and Box do. For the iWork suite, you have to use Soonr or SugarSync as an intermediary between iWork app and the cloud storage; you can't directly transfer files between iWork apps and the cloud storage service.

Summary

iTunes acts as the central manager for iPhones', iPads', and iPod Touches' non-media content, such as contacts, appointments, Safari bookmarks, e-books and PDF files, and mobile apps. Individual apps also can transfer docs between the Mac and an iOS device via iTunes. You can sync each iOS device you have to your Mac by connecting it via a USB cable, selecting the device in iTunes, and then clicking iTunes' Sync button.

iCloud's Automatic Updates capability allows Macs, Windows PCs, and iOS devices to keep music, books, magazine subscriptions, photos, and apps wirelessly synchronized across all devices that are tied to the same Apple ID or online store account.

iCloud also lets you sync photos among iOS devices' Photos app, Mac OS X Lion's iPhoto application, and designated folders in Windows Vista and 7 (but not XP). iCloud can also sync bookmarks in Safari across Mac OS X Lion, iOS 5, and Windows Vista and 7 (it also can sync bookmarks with Internet Explorer on Windows), as well as e-mail, calendars, and contacts across these three environments.

The iCloud service also enabled automatic Wi-Fi backup of iOS 5 devices to a Mac running Lion or a PC running Windows Vista or 7. And Apple is allowing software developers to use iCloud to sync among their iOS and Mac OS X applications; Apple's own iWork applications implement iCloud document syncing.

Several companies offer cloud storage services that, like the discontinued MobileMe service's iDisk virtual drive, let you store files on an Internet-connected server for access from any computer and from many mobile devices, including Apple's iPhone, iPad, and iPod Touch. Some allow you to share these files with other users, such as for a workgroup or club.

Integrating with Windows

There's no question that the Mac is special. Many people believe it to be the best personal computer ever developed, thanks mainly to Mac OS X. But although the Mac is indeed special and brilliant, it is also a minority choice in the world of computing. Most people use Microsoft Windows—Windows XP, Windows Vista, or Windows 7. Dealing with Windows is a reality for Mac users. And Mac OS X helps make it easy to work with the wider Windows world while staying firmly on the luxury Mac island.

Mac OS X integrates with Windows at many levels. It supports Windows disk formats, such as for CDs and hard disks. It works with Windows networks. And it can even run Windows and, therefore, Windows programs that have no Mac version available.

So the question for a Mac user is not "Can I integrate with Windows?" but "How should I integrate with Windows?" There's no one right answer to this question because it depends on your circumstances. But two basic levels of integration usually determine how you integrate with Windows:

- If you mainly need to share files with Windows users, you'll find that most common Windows file formats are supported on the Mac. Plus, many standard Windows applications, such as Microsoft Office, are available on the Mac, and most Mac-only applications can usually export to a Windows-friendly format. So you can usually open files you get from Windows users as is, and they can open the files you give them. Usually, you can exchange files via e-mail or a server, but because your Mac reads from and writes to Windows disks, you can exchange files this way as well.

IN THIS CHAPTER

Working with Windows files and media

Using fonts with Mac OS X and Windows

Setting up network-based file sharing

Using Internet-based file-sharing methods

Installing Windows on your Mac using Boot Camp

Running Windows on your Mac using Parallels Desktop and VMware Fusion

- If you need to run Windows programs that are not available on the Mac because you're part of a Windows-based company or workgroup, you're in luck. Any Intel-based Mac can actually run Windows XP, Vista, or 7. Mac OS X comes with the software that enables it to run Windows (you need to buy Windows yourself, though), so you can boot between Windows and Mac OS X as needed, while being able to access all the files on your Mac no matter which operating system is running. And two inexpensive programs (EMC VMware's Fusion and Parallels' Desktop) let you run Windows and Mac OS X at the same time, so you don't have to reboot the Mac to switch from one operating system to another.

Tip

Microsoft's Mac version of Office runs very slow compared to the Windows version, especially on Macs that have many fonts installed, so many users who need Windows on their Macs anyhow find it better to run Office on their Macs via Windows than natively on Mac OS X. Sad but true. ■

Now I show you exactly how this all works.

Working with Windows Files

The most basic way to integrate with Windows is by sharing files. Mac OS X makes it easy to do so via disks, networks, and e-mail.

Software that has versions on both Windows and Mac OS X almost always uses the same file format for both systems, so exchanging files is a snap. Microsoft Office, Adobe Creative Suite, and FileMaker Pro are just a few examples. And many media formats are the same across platforms, such as MP3 files, QuickTime movies, and MPEG-4 videos, as well as the EPS, GIF, JPEG, PNG, and TIFF graphics formats. So are the web formats of HTML, XML, and JavaScript.

For file formats that aren't cross-platform, you could be stuck if the applications you use can't export into a format readable by an application on the other platform. That's because the pair of utilities you could usually rely on to convert file formats—DataViz's MacLinkPlus for Mac and Conversions Plus for Windows—are no longer available.

But there are options for some specialty format conversion needs. For example, if you want to play Windows Media Files on your Mac, the free Flip4Mac Player from Telestream (www.telestream.net) nicely does the job; for editing and otherwise working with WMV files beyond playback, Telestream also offers the $30 WMV Player Pro.

Before you begin sharing files with Windows users, though, you need to be aware of a few issues.

Dealing with filenames and file extensions

The most noticeable difference between Windows and Mac is the file-naming convention, but with the advent of Mac OS X a decade ago, that difference is no longer as great. To be cross-platform–compatible, restrict your filenames to 250 characters (including the file extension), always use a file extension, and do not use the following characters as part of the filename: : / | . * " < > ? / \. These restrictions conform to the Mac OS X standards but Windows users need to make a couple of compromises:

- They can't use the full Windows filename size of 255 characters. (250 is the maximum on the Mac.)

- They can't use the : / | . * " < > ? / \ characters in their filenames because Mac OS doesn't support them, even though Windows supports all of them except :.

Although Mac OS X supports filenames as long as 250 characters, in some cases you may have trouble copying Windows files to the Mac if the Windows filenames exceed 31 characters. That's because of limits in some of the programs to make these cross-platform connections, which enforce pre–Mac OS X filename conventions on all files. It's easy enough to test whether your software is limiting you to 31 characters: Just transfer a file, and see if the software shortens the name or refuses to transfer the file.

Both Windows and Mac OS X use file extensions to identify the file type. For example, a Microsoft Word file has the file extension .doc or .docx (depending on the version), a TIFF file has the extension .tif or .tiff (some applications prefer one over the other but can "see" both), an Apple Pages file has the extension .pages, and an MP3 music file has the extension .mp3.

But file extensions are typically not displayed to the user in the Finder, so you may not know what kind of file you're dealing with. Here's how to make file extensions visible:

- **Mac OS X:** Choose Finder ⇨ Preferences or press ⌘+, (comma). (You have to be using the Finder, not be in an application, to see the Finder menu.) In the Preferences dialog box that appears, go to the Advanced pane, select the Show All Filename Extensions option, and close the dialog box.

- **Windows XP:** Open any folder, and choose Tools ⇨ Folder Options. (You must have a disk or folder open to see the View menu.) In the Folder Options dialog box that appears, go to the View pane. Deselect the Hide Extensions for Known File Types option, and click OK.

- **Windows Vista or Windows 7:** Choose Start ⇨ Computer, and then choose Organize ⇨ Folder and Search Options in the dialog box that appears. Go to the View pane, select the Show Hidden Files and Folders option, and click OK.

Using fonts across platforms

Three types of font formats are in common use today: TrueType (file extension `.ttf`), PostScript Type 1 (these usually have two files for each font, a `.pfb` file and a `.pfm` file), and OpenType (`.otf`). Mac OS X natively supports all three, as do Windows XP, Vista, and 7.

If you use the same font file on both Windows and Mac OS X, you get the same characters, even though Windows and Mac applications may not be able to show you all the same characters in the font. So the files transferred across platforms displays correctly on both.

But if you install a Mac version of a font on the Mac and a Windows version on the PC (a common scenario for PostScript fonts, but an occasional issue as well for TrueType and OpenType fonts, especially those that come with applications), you likely will discover that their special characters (accented letters, foreign characters, math symbols, and so on) don't always match. Some characters may not appear in Windows that appear on the Mac (or vice versa). Even when the characters are the same, their size and spacing might differ slightly, causing text to take more or less room as it moves from one platform to another.

Note that the developer of PostScript Type 1 fonts, Adobe Systems, began phasing out that format in 1999, so it's harder today to buy new PostScript Type 1 fonts. However, users tend not to replace their old PostScript fonts with the OpenType format that Apple, Adobe, and Microsoft all settled on as a joint standard, so chances are very high that you deal with PostScript Type 1 fonts. After all, it can cost thousands of dollars to upgrade your font collection. And some other font makers still create PostScript versions of their fonts.

The TrueType font format was developed by Apple, and Microsoft quickly signed on to use it, which is why it is also very commonly used. It's the standard, for example, for fonts used in web browsers.

So favor TrueType and OpenType fonts where possible, and use the same actual font files on both your Macs and PCs, not just files whose font names are the same.

Using disks and storage media

Mac OS X reads Windows CDs, DVDs, and hard disks without any effort on your part. These disks show up in the Finder like any other disk, and you can work with them as if they were Mac disks: copying, deleting, renaming, and creating files as desired. If you use another kind of external disk, such as a floppy disk, memory card, or thumb drive, it almost always is supported by the Mac directly; sometimes, you may need to install a Mac OS X driver that the hardware maker provides.

When you format a hard disk using Mac OS X's included Disk Utility (see Chapter 6), you can choose to format it as an MS-DOS (FAT) disk, which makes it work on any Windows PC. (FAT stands for File Access Table, a method for tracking a disk's files.)

Likewise, Disk Utility has an option to format disks in the ExFAT format used by solid-state drives (SSDs) in Windows, and Mac OS X Lion can read ExFAT-formatted drives.

What Mac OS X cannot do on its own is write or copy to hard disks formatted as NTFS, the Windows NT File System that Windows NT, 2000, XP, Vista, and 7 all support. (Mac OS X can read and copy *from* NTFS disks.) NTFS is a better disk format than MS-DOS because it stores data more efficiently. To write to NTFS disks from the Mac means buying a driver, such as Paragon Software's NTFS for Mac OS X ($20; www.paragon-software.com).

On the Windows side, it's not so easy to use Mac media. Windows and Mac OS X use the same formats for DVDs and memory cards, so you can pass these back and forth as is. But you need Mac drivers installed in Windows for other kinds of media and disks. Two companies have long offered such software, which not only let Windows PCs read Mac media but also write to them: MediaFour's MacDrive ($50; www.mediafour.com) and Acute Systems' TransMac ($48; www.acutesystems.com). Paragon Software also offers the HFS+ for Windows software that lets PCs open Macs' HFS+-formatted disks ($40; www.paragon-software.com).

Sharing through servers

If your Mac is on a network, it's very easy for it to access files on servers through which Windows users also access files. Your IT department must set up the servers so they are accessible to both Mac and Windows users, of course.

When the servers are ready for use, you need to connect to the server, which mounts it as a disk in the Finder. To connect a file server, use one of the following techniques:

- Choose it from the Sharing section in a Finder window's Sidebar.
- Choose Go ⇨ Connect to Server or press ⌘+K from the Finder, and then click Browse to find the desired file server.
- Use your browser to enter a web or IP address for the file share. Whoever set up the file share must provide you with that address.

When connected, simply drag files between it and your Mac to copy them. Chapter 24 explains in detail how to connect to networks and their file shares.

Another option is to use Microsoft SharePoint, a collaboration server that enables Microsoft Office users to work together on project files and share contacts, calendars, and so on. However, SharePoint uses a proprietary technology called ActiveX that Microsoft has not made available to Mac OS X, so Mac users have limited capabilities as part of a SharePoint environment, even when using it via Microsoft's Internet ("cloud") services called Business Productivity Online Services (BPOS) and Office 365.

For example, when using SharePoint from a Mac, you can't edit files directly in Microsoft Office for Mac versions 2008 and earlier; instead you must download them to your Mac, edit them there, and upload the changed versions. You can edit documents stored on SharePoint in Mac Office 2011, but you can't track the changes you make, as you can in Windows Office 2010. (Microsoft routinely withholds capabilities in its Mac software that it provides in its Windows versions.)

You also can't connect to shared Outlook calendars from Entourage or Mac Outlook. Furthermore, the Windows SharePoint servers must implement a communication protocol called WebDAV for the Macs to be able to see them on the network.

Connecting to PCs directly for file sharing

You can share files directly with a Windows user over a network using the Windows equivalent of file sharing. The key is to have the PC user set up file sharing for whichever folders he or she wants to make accessible to you.

If the server doesn't appear automatically in the Sidebar's Shared section in a Finder window, choose Go⇨Connect to Server or press ⌘+K in the Finder. Then click Browse to detect connected servers, as shown in Figure 18.1.

If the server doesn't appear automatically, try entering the server's IP address in the Server Address field. With the IP address, you simply enter **smb://** followed by the IP address—such as smb://172.18.12.136. If prompted, enter the username and password provided by the Windows user.

FIGURE 18.1

Top: Enter the Windows PC's address that has the desired share folder in the Connect to Server dialog box. Bottom: Browse for available servers by clicking Browse to open the Network Finder window. Connected servers also should display in a Finder window's Sidebar.

Note

The `smb://` tells the Mac to use Microsoft's Server Message Block protocol as opposed to Apple's own Apple Filing Protocol (`afp://`), the File Transfer Protocol (`ftp://`), or the web's Hypertext Transfer Protocol (`http://`). A protocol essentially is a "language" that defines how devices and computers connect through networks. ∎

You can get the PC's IP address in two ways:

- The Windows XP user chooses Start ➪ Run.
- The Windows Vista or 7 user chooses Start ➪ All Programs ➪ Accessories ➪ Run.

Then no matter the version of Windows, the user types **cmd** and presses Enter; in the Command Prompt window that appears, he or she types **ipconfig** and presses Enter. The IP address (called IPv4 in Windows Vista and 7) is presented. (The Windows user types **exit** and presses Enter to close the Command Prompt window.)

To set up the file share, the Windows user first displays the folder to be shared in the Windows Explorer (the Windows equivalent of the Finder) and right-clicks it to display the contextual menu. The next step depends on which version of Windows the user has:

- **Windows XP:** Choose Sharing and Security to open the Sharing pane shown in Figure 18.2. Select the Share This Folder option, and click Permissions to open the Share Permissions dialog box in which you add users and set their permissions (Full Control, Change, and Read). Click OK to save the Share Permissions settings, and click OK again to save the Sharing settings.

- **Windows Vista:** Choose Share to open the File Sharing dialog box, and then choose Share With ➪ Specific People. Choose the Mac user to be allowed to share the folder, or choose Create a New User from the unnamed pop-up menu to add a user through the User Accounts control panel that appears. (Here's how the User Accounts control panel works: Click Manage Other Users to open the Manage Accounts dialog box, click Add a User, give the user a name, close the dialog boxes, navigate back to the folder to share, and select the new user from the unnamed pop-up menu.) Now click Add to give that user permission to share the folder, and choose the level of access, using the Permission Level pop-up menu to the right of the user's name. (The Reader permission level grants read-only access, Contributor grants read and write privileges, and Co-owner grants full control of the folder.) Click Share to turn on sharing for the folder.

- **Windows 7:** Choose Sharing ➪ Advanced Sharing. Click Advanced Sharing, and select the Share This Folder option in the Advanced Sharing dialog box that appears. Click Permissions to add users and groups and set their permissions. In the Permissions dialog box, click Add to add users and groups; select a user or group, and select the Allow or Deny option for the permissions you want to grant: Full Control, Change, and Read.

Figure 18.2 shows the three sharing dialog boxes.

FIGURE 18.2

The Windows XP Sharing dialog box (left), the File Sharing dialog box used by Windows Vista (center), and the Advanced Sharing dialog box used in Windows 7 (right)

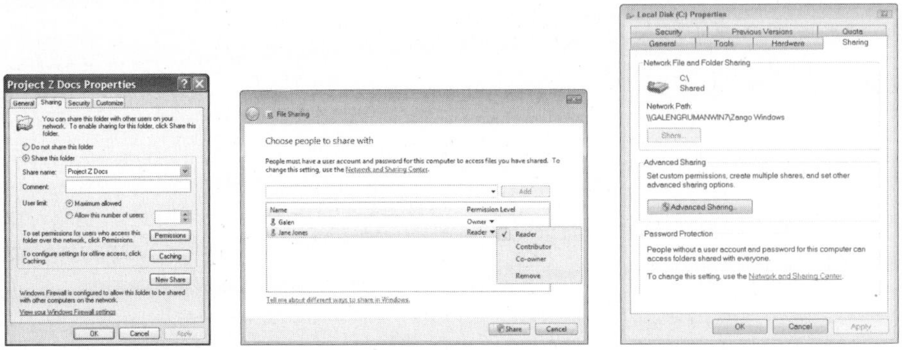

Letting Windows users connect directly to your Mac

Mac OS X comes with its own version of the Windows SMB network protocol built in, but it is available only for those users you specify. For a Windows user to access your Mac's shared files over a network, you first must set up an account with file-sharing privileges for that user in the File Sharing section of the Sharing system preference (see Chapter 28), as Figure 18.3 shows.

FIGURE 18.3

Enabling file sharing for a user

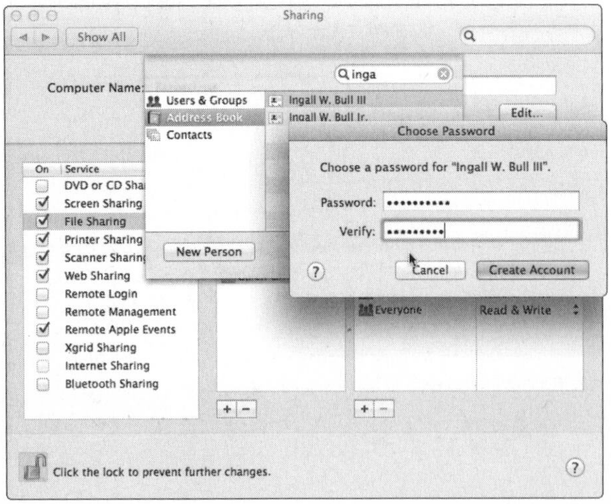

If the user's account doesn't already appear in the Users list, click the + icon button to add the user. Select the user from any of the lists that appear in the settings sheet, and click Select. If the user is not listed, click New Person, enter a username and password, click Done, and then click Select.

Next, enable file sharing for the folders you want Windows users to share, as explained in Chapter 24. (Any folders you've already enabled file sharing for also can be shared with Windows users.)

Then enable SMB sharing. To do so, click Option on the right side of the Sharing system preference. A settings sheet appears with two options. Select the Share Files and Folders Using SMB (Windows), and make sure that every user of this Mac who should have SMB access also is selected in the user list below. (You need to know their Mac OS X passwords to enable SMB access; their Windows passwords may differ.)

Caution

The password protection in the SMB protocol is less secure than in other protocols, so enable SMB sharing only for Windows users. ■

The final step is to make sure all the computers use the same Windows domain; otherwise, they see only those with the same name. By default, PCs are set with the Windows domain Workgroup, as are Macs. To change the domain in Windows, the Windows user should follow these steps:

1. **Choose Start ⇨ Control Panel, and click Switch to Classic View if it is not already enabled.** Double-click the System icon to open the System Properties dialog box.

2a. **In Windows XP, go to the Computer Name pane and click Change.**

2b. **In Windows Vista and 7, click Change Settings and then click Change in the Computer Name pane that appears.**

3. **In all three versions of Windows, select Workgroup, enter the workgroup name in the field below, and click OK.** Click OK again to save the settings and close System Properties.

4. **Restart Windows for the changes to take effect.**

On the Mac, go to the Network system preference and click Advanced. In the settings sheet that appears, go to the WINS pane, enter the correct domain name in the Domain field, and press Return. (WINS stands for Windows Internet Name Service.) Click OK, and then click Apply to save the changes.

The Windows user now has access to any folder to which you provided that specific user access. To access that shared folder, the Windows user does the following:

- **Windows XP:** Choose Start ⇨ My Network Places, and click View Workgroup Computers.
- **Windows Vista:** Choose Start ⇨ Network.
- **Windows 7:** Choose Start ⇨ Computer, and click Network in the sidebar.

In all three cases, the Windows user double-clicks the Mac whose folder is shared to open it.

Alternatively, the Windows user can map the shared folder itself as a network disk:

- **Windows XP:** Choose Start ⇨ My Computer, and choose Tools ⇨ Map Network Drive.
- **Windows Vista and 7:** Choose Start ⇨ Computer, and click Map Network Drive at the top of the window.

The Windows user then enters the full address for the folder, in this form: **\\192.168.1.100\ Users\name\folder\folder**. Make sure backslashes, not forward slashes, are used. The address starts with \\ and is followed with your Mac's IP address. The full path to the folder follows, separated by \ characters. As an example, if you had the folder Working Files on your Mac's desktop, the address might be \\122.18.12.140\Users*yourname*\Desktop\ Working Files. (Your Mac's name is what appears to the right of the house icon in the Favorites list in a Finder window's Sidebar.)

Note
The Windows user may need to click Different User Name in Windows XP or select Connect Using Different Credentials in Windows Vista or 7 to be able to enter the username and password you provided. ∎

Note
If the folder-sharing Mac does not show up in the Windows network, there are many potential causes, all of which need a network administrator to figure out. ∎

Sharing via e-mail, FTP, and web services

If you're not on a network (or not on one that enables Windows PCs and Macs to exchange files) and aren't physically close enough to share disks, you can use the Internet as a big server to exchange files with almost anyone, no matter what kind of computer that person uses.

The easiest way is to attach files to an e-mail that you send to another person. The person saves the files on his computer and open them with his or her applications, assuming his or her applications can work with the file format you're using. The reverse also holds: He or she can send you files via e-mail that you then save on your Mac and open with your compatible applications.

Tip

When sharing files across platforms via e-mail, it's a good idea to first compress the files into a Zip archive. This not only reduces the size of your attachment—so it takes less time to upload, transmit, and download—but also eliminates the possibility that the recipient cannot open the files. Most e-mail programs are smart enough to recognize Mac files and deliver them properly to Windows users, but some are not. Those badly behaved (usually Windows-based) e-mail programs end up stripping out a key part of the Mac file in transmission, making them unusable by a Windows user. Sometimes, they strip out this information when they receive the file, and sometimes they do so only when they forward the file to someone else. Some of these applications offer an option in their preferences to send files in the AppleDouble format; if so, use that option to eliminate the problem. ∎

Another way to create a network file share via the Internet is to set up an FTP folder on a web server and provide everyone with the FTP address, a username, and a password to access that folder. (FTP stands for File Transfer Protocol, a standard for uploading and downloading files via the Internet.) You can upload and download files from it in a way that's very similar to using file sharing on a local network. You need a web server, or a web host that offers FTP capabilities, to set up this kind of Internet-based shared folder and an FTP client such as Fetch Softworks' excellent Fetch application ($29; www.fetchsoftworks.com) to handle the uploading and downloading on the Mac. Windows users might consider an FTP program such as SmartSoft's Smart FTP Home ($37; www.smartftp.com), Ipswitch's WS_FTP Pro ($55; www.ipswitch.com), or FileZilla (free; www.filezilla-project.org).

You also can use Internet file-sharing services Box.net, Dropbox, Soonr, or SugarSync (see Chapter 17) to exchange files with both Mac and Windows users.

Running Windows on Your Mac

One of the most remarkable capabilities of the Mac is that it can double as a Windows PC, thanks to the use of Intel's processor chips beginning in 2006. Any Intel Mac—but not the earlier PowerPC-based Macs—can run Windows XP, Vista, or 7. (Some users also have been able to run Windows 2000, though it is not officially supported.) Mac OS X comes with the Boot Camp tools to set up Windows on your Mac as a separate environment, so you can choose to boot into Mac OS X or Windows when you start up your Mac.

Two other companies, Parallels and EMC's VMware subsidiary, provide inexpensive virtualization software ($80 each) that lets you run Windows and Mac OS X at the same time. (They also let you run the Linux and Unix operating systems, as well as Mac OS X Server.) If you use Windows applications routinely, I recommend you use one of the virtualization options instead of Boot Camp because they make it so much more convenient to use Windows without making you stop using your Mac applications. They install Windows in what is called a *virtual machine*, a disk file that Windows (or other operating system) "thinks" is a computer.

Boot Camp used to have a big advantage over these virtualization options when running PC games or video-editing software, which run more slowly and can have degraded display and video quality when running through a virtualization application. So, many users would set up a

Boot Camp partition and install Parallels Desktop or VMware Fusion. When they needed the full Windows speed, they booted into Windows via Boot Camp. When they didn't, they would run Windows via Parallels or Fusion and kept Mac OS X running at the same time. But as Macs have gotten faster and as Parallels and Fusion have improved, the speed difference is negligible in most cases, so the need to have both a Boot Camp partition and a Paralells or Fusion virtual machine is pretty much gone; you can just use the virtual machine for everything.

Note

No matter which option you choose to run Windows, you need to supply your own licensed copy of Windows. And it must be a full version, not an upgrade version. ■

Caution

Because of its popularity, hackers and other ne'er-do-wells target Windows with viruses, Trojan horses, spyware, scams, and other malware. Although such Windows malware (so far) doesn't cross over to Mac OS X, your Windows partition or virtual machine is just as vulnerable as a Windows PC, so be sure to get security software for it as you would for a "real" PC. ■

Setting up Boot Camp

In the Application folder's Utilities folder, you find the Boot Camp Assistant, which sets up a partition on your Mac's hard disk to hold Windows.

Caution

If you are installing Windows XP, you must install the Service Pack 2 (SP2) or Service Pack 3 (SP3) version. You cannot install a pre-SP2 version and later update it to SP2 or SP3.

Also, you must have a USB keyboard and mouse connected to your Mac (or use a MacBook's built-in keyboard and touchpad) when installing Windows. That's because Windows loads Bluetooth late in its startup sequence, so your wireless keyboard and mouse won't be available to enter the necessary settings when you install Windows. ■

Make sure you have enough hard disk space to hold Windows; 25GB is my minimum recommended size for Windows XP and 32GB is my recommended minimum for Windows Vista or 7 if you plan on running a few Windows applications. If you plan on doing video-to-DVD work with programs like Roxio Creator or Adobe Premiere Elements on your Windows partition, you need at least 15GB more for the DVD source image, cache, and target image.

Also note that you must install the Boot Camp partition on your Mac's startup disk; you cannot install it on an external disk. That startup disk must be formatted with one of the journaled options, which is typically how startup disks are formatted. You can enable journaling for the startup disk in Disk Utility by selecting the disk from the Sidebar and choosing File ➪ Enable Journaling or pressing ⌘+J. (Chapter 6 explains Disk Utility, disk formatting, and journaling.)

Then double-click the Boot Camp Assistant to launch it.

The first thing Boot Camp Assistant does is provide a dialog box with the Print Installation & Setup Guide button. Be sure to print (or save as a PDF file) the 12-page guide for guidance on the various options. Then click Continue to begin the setup.

You're first asked whether to download the Windows drivers and support software for your Mac or to use the drivers that you previously downloaded for this same Mac. Select your preferred option, and click Continue. Note that you need to have these drivers available on a recordable disk or external storage device such as a thumb drive so you can make them available to Windows after Boot Camp has set it up. So be sure to copy the files to a disc or other storage medium before continuing the Boot Camp process.

You're then asked how to *partition* your Mac's startup disk, which means to divide it into separate areas for Mac OS X and Windows. (If you have more than one internal disk, you can select any of them for the Windows partition.) Boot Camp starts with 5GB for Windows; click the dot between the Mac partition and the Windows partition and slide it to the left to increase the Windows partition size. When the maximum free disk space has been used, you can't slide the dot any farther to the left. Slide the dot to the right to decrease the Windows partition size. Figure 18.4 shows the dialog box.

You also can click Use 32GB to set the Windows partition to 32GB. And you can click Divide Equally to divide your hard disk space equally between Mac OS X and Windows. But if Mac OS X uses more than half your disk space already, clicking Divide Equally makes the remainder available for Windows. When you're satisfied with your partition size, click Partition. Then go get a cup of coffee or tea; it can take many minutes to partition the disk, and your Mac is essentially unusable while the partitioning occurs.

FIGURE 18.4

Boot Camp Assistant enables you to select how much hard disk space to allocate to Windows.

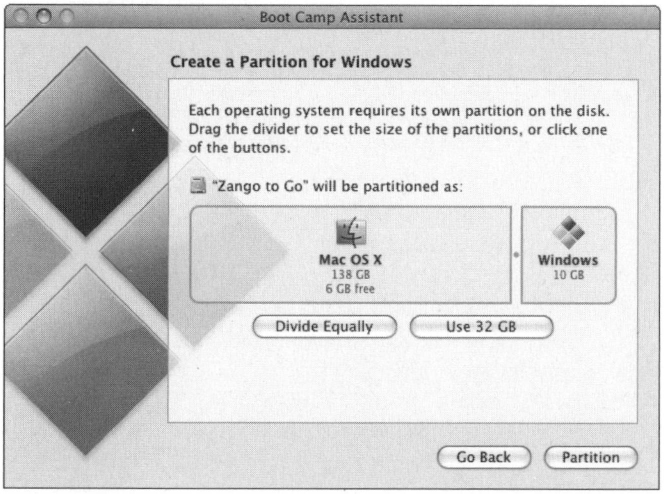

Caution

After you partition the internal disk, you can't resize the Boot Camp Windows partition if you didn't give it enough space or if you gave it too much. You must delete the partition and start over. To delete the Boot Camp partition, run the Boot Camp Setup Assistant, click Continue, select the disk that has Boot Camp on it, select the Restore to a Single Mac OS Partition option, and click Continue. ■

Tip

Well, there is an alternative to deleting a wrong-sized partition and creating a new one: Coriolis Systems' iPartition software enables you to resize the Boot Camp partition easily ($45; www.coriolis-systems.com). And Paragon Software's CampTune ($20; www.paragon-software.com) does the same. ■

After the partitioning is complete, you get a screen with two options: Quit & Install Later and Start Installation. If you're ready now, click Start Installation. If not, click Quit & Install Later; run the Boot Camp Assistant when you are ready to install Windows, select Start the Windows Installer, and click Continue. Either way, you need to insert your Windows installation CD or DVD. Your Mac restarts and runs the Windows installation disc.

The first choice to make when installing Windows is a critical one. The wrong answer can wipe out your Mac's data. You're presented a list of disk partitions on which to install Windows. Choose the one whose name includes Bootcamp. (The other partitions contain your Mac's data, and you do *not* want to install Windows over that.) In Windows XP, use the ↑ or ↓ key to move among them; then press Return (called Enter in Windows). In Windows Vista or 7, use your choice of the mouse or keyboard to choose the Bootcamp partition, and click Next.

You are then asked to format the partition:

- **In Windows XP:** You see a list of options. First, decide what kind of formatting you want for your partition: FAT or NTFS. Note that the FAT option appears only if your Boot Camp partition is 32GB or smaller. I believe that NTFS is a better formatting choice because it is more stable and provides faster file access than FAT. When you've decided which format to use, choose one of the Format options for your chosen format type (the "quick" ones are fine) using the ↑ or ↓ key to move among them, and press Return (called Enter in Windows).
- **In Windows Vista and 7:** Click Drive Options (Advanced), click Format, and then click OK. Your Windows partition is formatted as NTFS.

Note

Mac OS X can read and copy from NTFS-formatted disks, including the Boot Camp partition. But it can't write or copy to such disks unless you buy software such as Paragon Software's NTFS for Mac OS X ($20; www.paragon-software.com). Without such software, you must boot into Windows and copy files from the Mac OS X partition onto the Boot Camp partition to transfer files from Mac OS X. ■

After Windows is finished formatting the partition, it begins installing Windows, which can take 30 to 45 minutes. You are asked a series of questions on your preferred Windows settings, just as if you were installing Windows on a PC.

When Windows is finished installing itself, you need to install the drivers that tell Windows how to work with your Mac's hardware. To do so, first eject the Windows installation disc: Choose My Computer, right-click or Control+click the optical disc (D:), and choose Eject This Disk. Now insert the storage device containing the Windows drives for your Mac. After a few seconds, it should automatically begin installing the necessary drivers; if not, double-click the optical disc (D:)—or whatever drive contains the storage medium with the drivers—in My Computer, and double-click setup.exe in the Boot Camp folder. Either way, if you get an error message saying that the software has not passed Windows testing, click Continue Anyway. Also, do not click any Cancel buttons that appear in the sequence of dialog boxes that open and close. Windows restarts and may display some wizards for updating your software drivers (follow their prompts if so).

Install any Windows software you want.

You're finished!

Using Windows via Boot Camp

With Windows installed, you can boot into it anytime you want. When you start (or restart) your Mac, press and hold Option until a set of disk icons appears. Use your mouse or the ← and → keys to move among them, selecting the Windows disk (really the Boot Camp partition) when you want to boot into Windows and the Mac OS X disk (partition) when you want to boot into Mac OS X.

To set which partition to boot into by default, in Mac OS X choose ⇨ System Preferences and click Startup Disk. Select the startup disk (partition) you want the Mac to boot into by default. The next time you start the Mac, it boots into that disk unless you press and hold Option to choose which disk (or partition) to start from.

You also can make this default startup choice in Windows. Click the Boot Camp icon in the system tray, and choose Boot Camp Control Panel from the menu. Select the startup disk you want to use by default, and click OK. You also can access the Boot Camp control panel by choosing Start ⇨ Control Panel, selecting Classic View (if it's not already selected), and double-clicking the Boot Camp icon.

Tip
A quick way to boot back into the Mac from Windows is to click the system tray's Boot Camp icon and choose Restart in Mac OS X, but note that this option changes the default start disk to the Mac OS X partition as well. ▪

Keep these tips in mind when using Windows in a Boot Camp partition:

- **You can't get Windows' special startup options, such as Safe Mode, by pressing F8 if you use a Bluetooth keyboard.** That's because Windows doesn't load the Bluetooth drivers until long after these options are no longer available. Use a USB keyboard or, if you have a MacBook, a built-in keyboard when you need these options.

- **Be patient when using a Bluetooth keyboard or mouse.** Windows doesn't load the Bluetooth drivers until the very end of the startup process, after your Windows desktop, system tray, and so on have appeared. It may seem that Windows is frozen because it does not respond to your wireless input, but give it a bit more time before giving up.

- **If you have a MacBook that supports gestures on the touchpad, you can use the standard Mac gestures for Window-supported features.** These include holding two fingers on the touchpad and clicking the touchpad button to right-click, as well as dragging two fingers to scroll. (See Chapter 28 for more details on setting touchpad gesture preferences via the Trackpad system preference and Chapter 2 for details on Mac OS X's supported gestures.)

- **The Mac's Control key acts as the Windows Ctrl key, the Option key as the Alt key, and the ⌘ (Command) key as the ⊞ (Windows) key.** Table 18.1 shows other key mappings.

TABLE 18.1

Boot Camp's Key Assignments for Windows and Mac Keyboards

Windows Key	Apple USB Extended Keyboard	MacBook Built-in Keyboard and Apple Bluetooth Keyboard
Alt	Option	Option
AltGr	Control+Option	Control+Option
Backspace	Delete	Delete
Ctrl	Control	Control
Ctrl+Alt+Delete	Control+Option+Forward Delete	Control+Option+Delete
Delete	Forward Delete	Fn+Delete
End	End	Fn+→
Enter	Return	Return
Home	Home	Fn+←
keypad Enter	Enter	Enter*
Insert	Fn+Enter *or* Help	Fn+Enter
Num Lock	Clear	Fn+F6*
Pause/Break	F16	Fn+Esc
Page Down (PgDn)	Page Down	Fn+↓
Page Up (PgUp)	Page Up	Fn+↑
Print Screen (PrtScr)	F14	Fn+Shift+F11
Print Active Window	Option+F14	Fn+Shift+Option+F11
Scroll Lock (ScrLock)	F15	Fn+F12
⊞ (Windows)	⌘ (Command)	⌘ (Command)

*Not available on all MacBooks' built-in keyboards or in Apple Bluetooth wireless keyboards

Using Windows virtual machines

When Parallels first released its Parallels Desktop virtualization software for the Mac ($80; www.parallels.com), it changed the rules about letting Macs fit into Windows-dominated environments. Now that a Mac could run Windows simultaneously with Mac OS X, people quickly began adopting Macs, knowing that it was both a safe and convenient choice given the Windows support. EMC's VMware subsidiary followed up with its similar product, Fusion ($80; www.vmware.com), so Mac users now have a choice. The capabilities are nearly identical, so either is a good choice.

Unlike Boot Camp, Parallels Desktop and VMware Fusion don't need a fixed amount of space for Windows. Each can grow its virtual machine's file size as needed, so you're not stuck with a partition that's too small. Each also enables you to save your virtual machines on any disk accessible to the Mac, such as to an external FireWire or USB disk or even to a network volume. You can even move these virtual machines by moving their folder to a new location.

Tip
It's best to use a FireWire or Thunderbolt disk rather than a USB disk for running a virtual machine. Most Macs have several USB devices connected to them, so the Windows disk must compete for the connection's bandwidth, which can really slow it down. This is particularly an issue if you also are running Time Machine and backing up to a USB disk—performance slows to a crawl when that occurs. FireWire and Thunderbolt are much faster and devices connected through it are much less likely to be competing with so many other devices. ∎

Both Parallels Desktop and VMware Fusion automatically install their own drivers in Windows to make sure the Mac's capabilities are available to Windows, much as Boot Camp's Windows drivers do. But they offer more capabilities, such as the capability to drag and drop files between Windows and Mac OS X and the capability for Mac OS X and Windows to see each other's disks as network file shares.

Both programs also enable you to set up how networking works: You can have the Windows virtual machine use the same network address as the Mac (called *shared networking* in Parallels and *NAT,* short for *network address translation,* in Fusion) or appear on the network as if it were a separate PC (called *bridge networking* by both programs). The use of bridge networking can be handy if you use a Mac at work, where the Windows virtual machine is the "official" system supported by the company, and the Mac is tolerated as long as it is not on the network.

Note
Parallels Desktop sometimes behaves badly when it comes to file shares. You may get a message asking you to provide a username and password for \\.psf. That's the Home folder on your Mac (the .psf file extension indicates a Parallels shared folder, which is its connection to an actual Mac folder or disk), which Parallels needs to access if you want to drag files back and forth or cut and paste information across the two operating systems. It shouldn't ask you for that password, so if it does, try choosing Devices ⇨ Shared Folders ⇨ Disconnect All, letting Windows log out and back in, choosing Devices ⇨ Shared Folders ⇨ Connect All, and letting Windows log out and log in again. This often clears out the issue. ∎

They both give you the option of having the My Pictures, My Documents, Desktop, and My Music folders in Windows be mapped to your Pictures, Documents, Desktop, and Music folders in Mac OS X, so any files placed in these folders are automatically available to both operating systems in their familiar locations. That also means you don't need to duplicate the files in these folders across the operating systems.

You can run both Parallels Desktop and VMware Fusion so that Windows appears in a separate window (as shown in Figures 18.5 and 18.6), in window mode (where Windows runs in its own window), or so your active Mac OS X and Windows programs appear at the same time in what Parallels calls *Coherence mode* and what Fusion calls *Unity mode*. Figures 18.7 and 18.8 show these "melded" Mac OS X/Windows modes that make Windows applications appear to be Mac applications. Both programs also have an option where Mac OS X and Windows run in full-screen mode, and you use a keyboard shortcut to switch between them.

FIGURE 18.5

Parallels Desktop with Windows 7 in a window

FIGURE 18.6

VMware Fusion with Windows XP in a window

Both Parallels Desktop and VMware Fusion have an array of menu options, like any Mac application does, where you can enable and disable various features, such as associating the DVD drive to Windows (or disassociating it so the Mac can use it) and choosing the network type. Both also have icon pop-up menus at the bottom of the screen when you run Windows in a window; those pop-up menus let you enable and disable various aspects such as attached disks, networking, and attached USB devices. You can see these icon pop-up menus at the lower right of the Windows windows (refer to Figures 18.5 and 18.6).

Both programs also let you have multiple virtual machines set up, and both provide a list of them to choose from. You can even run multiple virtual machines simultaneously, though that quickly eats up your Mac's processing capabilities.

Finally, both can import Windows, its settings, and its applications from actual PCs, so you can move your PC onto your Mac and get rid of that PC box.

FIGURE 18.7

Parallels Desktop with Windows 7 in Coherence mode

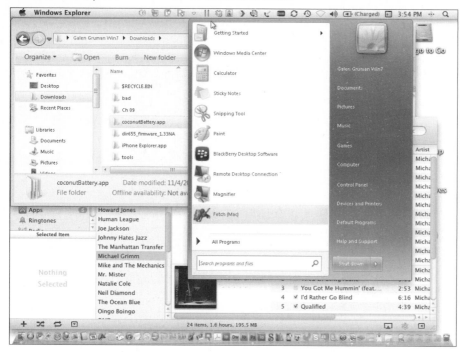

You can use both a Boot Camp Windows partition and either a Parallels Desktop or VMware Fusion virtual machine. This is helpful if you started with a dedicated Boot Camp partition and later decided you don't like having to boot between Windows and Mac OS X and so bought Parallels or Fusion to run Mac OS X and Windows simultaneously. Here's what you need to know to have Parallels or Fusion work with Boot Camp:

- In Parallels, when you create a new virtual machine, be sure to select Custom as the installation type. When asked for the virtual hard-disk option, choose Boot Camp, click Continue, and follow the rest of the prompts.

- In Fusion, there's no special setup step: You see your Boot Camp partition listed as an available virtual machine in the list that appears when you start Fusion—as long as your Mac OS X account has administrator privileges.

FIGURE 18.8

VMware Fusion with Windows XP in Unity mode

Summary

Mac OS X is built to integrate with Windows environments though file exchange, network compatibility, and even the capability to run Windows.

For file exchange, it can read and write to many PC-formatted disks, including CDs, DVDs, flash drives, FAT-formatted hard disks, and ExFAT-formatted solid-state drives. It can read NTFS-formatted disks but not write to them unless you buy extra software to do so. Windows is not so fluent, requiring extra-cost software to read Mac hard disks and older media such as floppy disks.

Because both PCs and Macs use file extensions to identify what type a file is, it's a good idea to have both Windows and Mac OS X display these extensions. That way, you can figure out what the file type is in case you receive a file format that Windows or the Mac does not recognize.

Modern professionally produced fonts are identical on Mac and Windows, so you can be sure they have the same characters and identical output, but older fonts—especially PostScript Type 1 ones—can vary even if their names are the same.

File servers and Internet-based file-exchange methods such as FTP and e-mail make it very easy to exchange files between Mac and Windows users. You also can have Macs and Windows PCs directly share files through a network connection, though significant setup must be done on both ends, and Windows can't always see the Macs' shared folders.

Mac OS X comes with a utility that enables you to reserve (partition) part of your Mac's startup disk so you can install Windows on it. Then you can boot between Mac OS X and Windows based on which operating system you need at the moment. You can use various file-sharing techniques to exchange files between them.

If you use Windows applications frequently, you should buy either Parallels Desktop or EMC VMware's Fusion. They enable you to run Windows and its applications simultaneously with Mac OS X and its applications, so you don't have to switch back and forth. Plus you can share your disks and files—even copy and paste across operating systems—as if everything were on the same operating system.

For those times you need a separate partition for Windows, such as to get the necessary performance or video support for some applications, both programs let you keep your Boot Camp partition and boot into it. When you don't need such dedicated Windows usage, they make your Boot Camp partition available from Mac OS X so you can run Windows programs from it while using Mac OS X.

Part IV

Using the Internet and Collaboration Services

IN THIS PART

Chapter 19
Using Safari to Surf the Web

Chapter 20
Using Mail, iChat, and FaceTime

Chapter 21
Using Address Book and iCal

Chapter 22
Working with Microsoft Exchange

Using Safari to Surf the Web

The World Wide Web—known as the *web* for short—has transformed society. The web was created in the 1990s as a way to use the Internet—a global network originally created so military commands and other government entities could communicate in the aftermath of a nuclear war—for researchers and others to communicate more richly than just via the exchange of text messages. Quickly, the web became widely used for other purposes, such as transmitting e-mail, transferring files, and providing real-time chat. Scientists at the European Center for Nuclear Research (known by its French acronym CERN) created a language that let people create pages with text, images, and hyperlinks to other pages and resources. The Hypertext Markup Language (HTML) language to create these pages and the Hypertext Transfer Protocol (HTTP) to connect users to these pages became the basis for the web we know today.

To access web pages, you use something called a *web browser*, the first popular version of which was invented at the University of Illinois at Champaign and called Mosaic. It evolved into the popular Netscape Navigator browser, which later became the foundation for the Mozilla Firefox browser that is popular on both Macs and Windows PCs. The Microsoft Internet Explorer browser is also a popular way to access the web from Windows PCs because it comes preinstalled on these computers. Apple soon came up with its own browser, Safari. It is preinstalled on Mac OS X, making it the predominant web browser for Mac users. Another popular browser is Google's Chrome.

Regardless of the browser you use, the web has become much more sophisticated than what CERN and Mosaic first delivered. You can use the web as a computer, running applications in it, storing data in it, and doing so much more. And browsers like Safari have more than kept up, becoming sophisticated applications that for many users are the most-used software on their Macs.

IN THIS CHAPTER

Accessing web pages in Safari through URLs, bookmarks, and navigation controls

Managing the Safari user interface

Using Safari's specialty features

Understanding search options

Adjusting Safari preferences

Working with RSS feeds

Exploring browser alternatives to Safari

Apple provides its Safari 5 browser with Mac OS X Lion. After you launch Safari, you can go to any web page simply by entering its URL (Uniform Resource Locator, the technical name for a web address) in the field at the top of the browser window. Figure 19.1 shows the result for the URL `http://www.infoworld.com`.

Top: The Apple Safari browser and its main controls. Bottom: The Safari controls in full-screen mode.

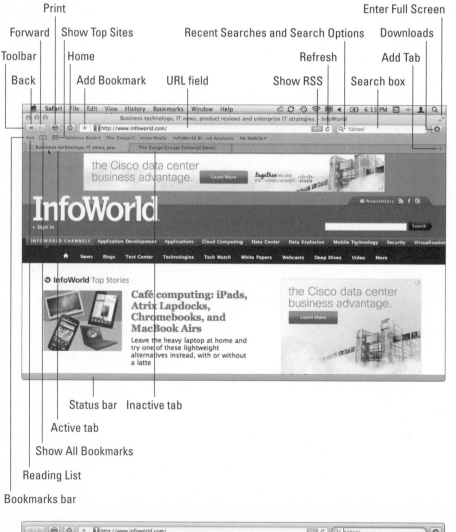

The figure also shows the navigation buttons that help you move among web pages, plus the menu commands at the very top and the row of bookmarks below the navigation buttons.

New Feature

Mac OS X Lion includes the newest version of Safari: Safari 5.1. (Mac OS X Snow Leopard came with Safari 4 but later was updated to Safari 5.0.) Among the new version's new capabilities is support for full-screen mode. ■

Navigating the Web

Entering the URL for every page you want to visit is lots of work, plus it requires you to know the URL of every page you want to visit—a highly unlikely situation. That's why the web has multiple navigation mechanisms. Entering the URL is just the basic way, and it's a fast way to go some place new. For example, if you hear about a new Apple product, typing **apple.com** in the URL field is easy to do.

Using hyperlinks

When you're at a site such as Apple's, you'll notice *hyperlinks*, or highlighted text and images that when clicked open a different web page. Hyperlinked text is usually displayed in blue and underlined, while hyperlinked pictures usually have a blue border around them. But the highlighting of a hyperlink can be different from page to page and site to site—and they don't even have to be highlighted. What you can count on is that the pointer changes when it's over a hyperlink, as Figure 19.2 shows.

When Safari detects a website that uses a security certificate, it displays the Security icon button (the lock icon) at the far right of the title bar, as Figure 19.3 shows. Click that button to see the security certificate information. It also may display the name of the website or its company in bold green within the URL field to indicate that the website is a trusted one; you can click that bold green text to see the security certificate as well.

Most sites that use security certificates have URLs that begin `https://` rather than `http://` (the *s* stands for "secure"). If you go to a URL that you're not familiar with, checking the certificate is one way to make sure you're not at a hacker's site designed to look like a legitimate site and steal your personal information (see Chapter 26). When Safari encounters a site it suspects is such as phishing site, it may display the website or company name in bold red in the URL field as a warning to you.

New Feature

The Security icon button is new to Safari in Mac OS X Lion. ■

FIGURE 19.2

The regular pointer (left, near the upper-right corner) and the pointer when you hover over a hyperlink (right, at the upper-right corner)

FIGURE 19.3

The Security icon button (the lock icon) appears at the far right of the title bar when Safari detects a site using a security certificate. Safari may also, as in this figure, show the site's name in bold green to indicate a trusted site.

Using bookmarks

If you find yourself repeatedly going to a web page, you can *bookmark* it; you save the page in a list that you can go back to and click desired pages from anytime you want. To save a page as a bookmark in Safari, choose Bookmark ⇨ Add Bookmark or press ⌘+D.

Tip
The fastest way to bookmark a page is to click the + icon button to the left of the URL. ∎

As Figure 19.4 shows, you get a settings sheet with an unnamed pop-up menu in which you select where to place the bookmark: in the Reading List, in Top Sites in the bookmarks bar or any of its folders, or in the bookmarks menu or any of its folders. After you select the bookmark's location, the settings sheet adds an unnamed field in which you name the bookmark (by default, the bookmark's name is the same as the web page's title). Click Add to save the bookmark in the selected location. (You also can add currently opened tabbed panes to the Reading List by choosing Bookmarks ⇨ Add These Tabs to Reading List.)

FIGURE 19.4

When you add a bookmark in Safari, you can store it in any of several locations. On the left is the full bookmarks list that you've built over time. To the right is the settings sheet where you decide the location to which to add the bookmark.

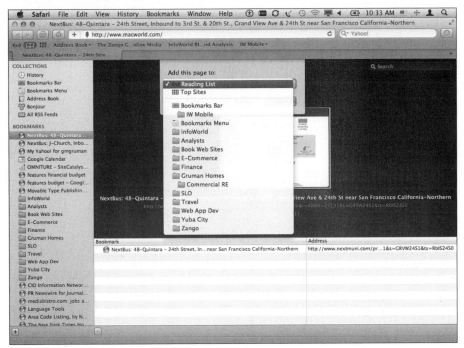

Viewing web pages in Reader mode

Safari has a display option called Reader mode that presents a simplified version of a web page, stripping out most of the page's contents (such as navigation menus, ads, and graphics). If a website supports this mode, you can choose View ➪ Show Reader or press Shift+⌘+R. Click outside the Reader window, choose View ➪ Hide Reader, or press Shift+⌘+R to exit Reader mode and see the original web page. If a website doesn't support this mode, the menu option is grayed out. (Note that the menu options for Reader had been called Enter Reader and Exit Reader in previous versions of Mac OS X.)

The label "Reader" also appears in the URL field when a web page supports Reader mode; you can simply click that Label to toggle between Reader and regular modes. The label is blue when you are in regular mode and violet when you are in Reader mode.

The figure below shows a Macworld.com article in regular mode (at top) and Reader mode (at bottom).

continued

continued

When in Reader mode, you can get a set of onscreen controls—Zoom Out, Zoom In, Print, Mail, and Close Reader—to appear by moving the pointer to the control area at the bottom center of the screen, as the figure shows.

Note that if you click a hyperlink when in Reader mode, the new page opens in regular mode, not Reader mode.

New Feature

Safari 5.1 changes the bookmarking process slightly. You now must choose the destination before you can enter the bookmark's name; in previous versions of Safari, both the location pop-up menu and name field were immediately available. Also new is the addition of the Reading List and Top Sites options in the location pop-up menu. ■

In Safari, the bookmarks bar displays under the URL field. If you see a down-pointing triangle next to a bookmark, that means it's a bookmarks bar folder, and clicking the arrow displays a pop-up menu of all the bookmarked links in that folder.

You also can see all bookmarks saved, including those saved folders outside the bookmarks bar's folders, by clicking the bookmarks bar's Show All Bookmarks icon button (the open-book icon), shown in Figure 19.4. Or choose Bookmarks ➪ Show All Bookmarks, or press Option+⌘+B.

Tip

You can toggle between the Bookmarks list and your web page by clicking the bookmark icon. It switches between the two views each time you click it. ■

In the Sidebar on the left of the Show All Bookmarks window is the Bookmarks list of bookmarks added and imported. The Collections list gives you access to the entries stored in the bookmarks bar and Bookmarks menu, as well as to the browser history (the previously viewed pages), any RSS feeds you subscribe to (covered in the "Using RSS in Safari" section of this chapter), any URLs in your Address Book, and any URLs saved in the Mac's Bonjour network list, such as printers (Chapter 23 explains Bonjour networking).

Note in Figure 19.4 how Safari shows a preview in the Cover Flow presentation style for any selected bookmarks. Over time, Safari fills in the website images, so when you first use Safari, the Cover Flow previews all start out as dark folder icons emblazoned with the Safari logo. (The preview images of websites that require sign-in, such as online banking sites, usually remain displayed as dark folder icons.)

And you can see a slide-show–like preview of your favorite web pages—determined by what you visit the most—by clicking the Top Sites icon button (the grid icon) in the bookmarks bar. You get a set of web page previews, such as those shown in Figure 19.5, in what Safari calls the Top Sites window.

Note

When you are in the Top Sites window, the search field at the bottom right is labeled Search History. Entering a term and pressing Return or clicking the magnifying glass icon doesn't search the web but displays your history of web pages visited. You also can switch to the History view by clicking the History button at the top of the web page previews; note that the History view accessed this way lacks the Sidebar containing the Bookmarks and Collections lists and the list of bookmarks that the normal History view shows (refer to Figure 19.7 later in this chapter). ■

Click Edit to change the Top Sites window's selections (and note that the Search History field disappears). These are your options:

- Click the Close icon button (the X icon) that appears over a preview to remove that preview.

- Click the Retain icon button (the thumbtack icon) to keep that preview in place, rather than replace it later with a more-visited site. (The thumbtack icon turns blue if you've clicked it to keep the preview in place.)

- Drag previews within the Top Sites window to rearrange them.

When you're finished, click Done to go back to the regular view, where you can click a preview to open the web page.

You can export your Safari bookmarks to an HTML file by choosing File ⇨ Export Bookmarks. You can import that bookmark in another browser (not just in Safari, and not just on the Mac), which is a handy way to keep your home and work computer in sync when it comes to bookmarks. You also can import bookmark lists generated by other browsers by choosing File ⇨ Import Bookmarks.

FIGURE 19.5

In the Top Sites view, Safari builds a slide show of web page previews based on the sites you visit most often; clicking the grid icon in the bookmarks bar displays the clickable previews.

Using the Reading List

Bookmarks are great for items you return to regularly, but they're not so good for web pages you want to flag for reading later and then won't likely read again. So Apple has added the Reading List to Safari 5.1. Click the Reading List icon button in the bookmarks bar, press Shift+⌘+L, or choose View ➪ Show Reading List to open a pane in the left side of the Safari window that contains these flagged pages.

The Reading List pane, shown in Figure 19.6, is very simple to use:

- Click any item to open its Web page.
- When you're on a page you want to add to the Reading List, click Add Page in the Reading List pane.
- To remove a page from the Reading List, hover the mouse to the right of its name and click the Close icon button that appears.
- To remove all pages from the Reading List, Click Clear All.
- To see all saved pages, click All; to see just pages you've not yet opened, click Unread.
- Click the Reading List icon button in the bookmarks bar, press Shift+⌘+L, or choose View ➪ Hide Reading List to close the pane.

New Feature
The Reading List is new to Safari 5.1, which comes with Mac OS X Lion. ∎

FIGURE 19.6

The Reading List pane (at left)

Using history

Safari keeps track of the pages you visit, saving them in what it calls History. You can see the pages you visited on specific dates by choosing History and then the specific date from the menu. Choosing History ⇨ Show All History, pressing Option+⌘+2, or clicking the Show History icon button in the bookmarks bar opens the History window, shown in Figure 19.7, of what you've recently visited. In the History window, you can thumb through the recently visited pages using the Cover Flow view mode.

Tip

You can quickly switch to the History window from the bookmarks window by clicking History in the bookmarks window's Collections list. ∎

FIGURE 19.7

In the History view, Safari presents the web pages you've visited as a Cover Flow stack you can thumb through.

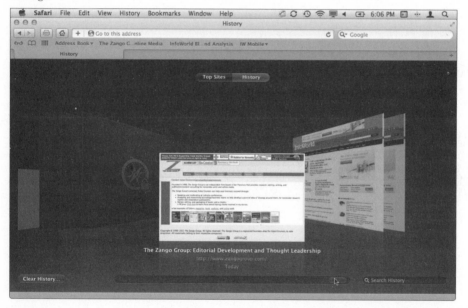

Note

When you are in the Top Sites window—not in the History window as you would expect—you can search for web pages previously visited by entering a term in the Search History field and then pressing Return or clicking the Search icon button (the magnifying glass icon). ∎

Using search engines

The Safari 5.1 browser uses the Yahoo search engine by default to find content on the web (it had been Google in previous versions). If you want to use the Google or Microsoft Bing search engine instead as the default in Safari, you can change the default browser in Safari's Preferences dialog box.

You also can change the search engine directly in the Search box at any time by clicking the unnamed icon pop-up menu (the downward-facing triangle icon) next to the magnifying-glass icon in the Search box. A list of recent searches appears, followed by a list of the three available search engines; choose the search engine you want to use. The search engine chosen remains in place until you change it again or relaunch Safari.

Google offers a range of specialty search tools not available through the Google search box in Safari. You get them from Google's search page on the web. You can explore these tools at `www.google.com/advanced_search`, including tools for news, code, and books, as well as options for narrowing your search based on various criteria.

These other History menu options are available:

- **Search Results SnapBack:** The option reloads your last search results page so you can see those results again. It's handy if you did a search, got sidetracked into browsing various pages, and want to go back to the original results. You also can press Option+⌘+S.

- **Reopen Last Closed Window:** This option is handy when you accidentally close a window and want to get back to it quickly.

- **Reopen All Windows from Last Session:** This option opens the windows that were open when you last quit Safari.

- **Clear History:** This option removes all the history bookmarks, so no one can see what you were browsing (a favorite of teenagers).

Tip
If you don't want Safari to track the web pages you visit, choose Safari ⇨ Private Browsing. This also disables the auto-completion of information on web forms. ■

Working with Safari's Controls

Safari uses several types of controls for access content on the web and managing the Safari user interface when doing so, including navigation buttons, windows and tab controls, sharing capabilities, and user interface controls.

Using navigation buttons

As Figure 19.1 earlier in this chapter shows, the Safari toolbar has icon navigation buttons. These help you move across pages accessed in your current browser session for the current tabbed pane or window:

- **The Home icon button:** Opens your home page (which you set in the Home Page field of the General pane of the Preferences dialog box for Safari); this page opens automatically whenever you launch Safari. You also can choose History ➪ Home or press Shift+⌘+H to go to your home page.

- **The Show the Previous Page icon button (usually called simply Back):** Moves to the previous page you visited, letting you retrace the sequence of pages you've visited. You also can choose History ➪ Back or press ⌘+[.

- **The Show the Next Page icon button (usually called simply Forward):** Moves to the next page you've visited, letting you retrace the sequence of pages you've visited. (Forward has an effect only if you first moved back to a previous page you visited.) You also can choose History ➪ Forward or press ⌘+].

- **The Show RSS icon button:** Opens the current web page's RSS feed. If no RSS feed is attached to this page, the Show RSS icon button does not appear.

- **The Reload the Current Page icon button (usually called simply Reload or Refresh):** Reloads the current page to ensure its contents are current, something you might do for pages with information that changes frequently, such as pages containing the latest news and stock prices. You also can press View ➪ Reload Page or press ⌘+R.

- **The Search box:** Enables you to search for web pages using the search engine specified in the Preferences dialog box; simply type your term and press Return or click the Search icon button (the magnifying glass icon). You also can choose Edit ➪ Find ➪ *searchenginename* Search or press Option+⌘+F.

Using window and tab controls

Normally, when you open Safari and load a web page, it replaces any web page previously loaded. But what if you want to look at several web pages at once? You can, using either or both of two approaches.

The first method is to open a new window for the new web page to display in. Choose File ➪ New Window or press ⌘+N. Then use the Window menu to switch among windows; the open windows are listed at the bottom of the Window menu.

To close the current window, choose File ➪ Close Window, press Shift+⌘+W, or click the Close icon button in the upper left of the window.

Configuring the Safari toolbar

Safari's toolbar is fairly sparse, with no controls for features such as printing and zooming. Unless you add them, that is. Safari lets you customize the toolbar to add or remove any of more than a dozen icon buttons. To do so, right-click or Control+click in the toolbar and choose Customize Toolbar from the contextual menu, or choose View ⇨ Customize Toolbar.

The Customize Toolbar settings sheet appears, as shown in the figure. Drag the desired buttons from the settings sheet into the toolbar at your desired location. (To remove an item, drag it out of the toolbar into the settings sheet. You also can right-click or Control+click it in the toolbar and choose Remove Item from the contextual menu when the Customize Toolbar settings sheet is not open.) To reset the toolbar to the defaults, drag the default set into the toolbar. Click Done when you're finished.

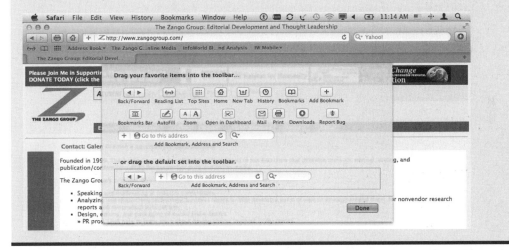

The second method is to open a new tabbed pane (called just *tabs* by most people) in the current window for the new web page to display in. Initially, Safari shows one tabbed pane in the window, displaying the default home page, a blank page, or the Top Sites page, depending on how Safari's preferences are set. To open a new tabbed pane, choose File ⇨ New Tab, press ⌘+T, or double-click in the blank area to the right of the rightmost tab. Doing so opens a new tabbed pane, indicated by a row of file folder-like tabs that appears below the toolbar (refer to Figure 19.1). Adding a tabbed pane also adds the Add Tab icon button (the + icon) to the far right of the tabs row. You can now click the Add Tab icon button to add new tabbed panes (choosing File ⇨ New Tab or pressing ⌘+T works as well). Click a tab to switch to its pane.

To close a tabbed pane, hover the mouse over its tab until the Close icon button (the X icon) appears; click the Close icon button in the tab. (You also can choose File ⇨ Close Tab or press ⌘+W.) If you press and hold Option when clicking the Close icon button, all tabbed panes *except* the one with the Close icon button are closed.

You can have multiple windows open, and each can contain tabbed panes or not, depending on how you want to move among the various web pages. Safari also provides a series of controls over tabbed panes, all of which appear in the Window menu:

- Choose Window ⇨ Select Next Tab or press Control+Tab to move to the next tabbed pane in the current window.
- Choose Window ⇨ Select Previous Tab or press Control+Shift+Tab to move to the previous tabbed pane in the current window.
- Choose Window ⇨ Move Tab to New Window to convert a tabbed pane into a separate window.
- Choose Window ⇨ Merge All Windows to convert all open windows into individual tabbed panes into a single window.

You also can use shortcuts to quickly open new windows and tabbed panes from hyperlinks on a web page:

- **⌘+click** opens a link in a new tabbed pane, leaving the current pane visible.
- **Shift+⌘+click** opens a link in a new tabbed pane and switches to that new pane.
- **Option+⌘+click** opens a link in a new window, leaving the current window visible.
- **Option+Shift+⌘+click** opens a link in a new window and switches to that new window.

As explained in the "Setting Safari preferences" section, you can change these shortcuts so ⌘+click and Shift+⌘+click open new windows instead of tabbed panes and so Option+⌘+click and Option+Shift+⌘+click open new tabbed panes instead of windows.

Using view controls

To help see text and images more clearly, Safari offers two zoom controls:

- **Zoom In:** This makes the web page bigger (useful when the text is small), enlarging the view. Of course, less of the page can fit in the window when you zoom in, so you likely have to scroll more to see the rest of the contents. Choose View ⇨ Zoom In, press ⌘+=, or click the Zoom In icon button (the large letter *A*) in the toolbar (if you customized your toolbar to include it). You also can use the expand gesture on a touchpad.
- **Zoom Out:** This makes the web page smaller, reducing the view and making more of the page fit in the window. Of course, the text gets smaller and may become hard to read. Choose View ⇨ Zoom Out, press ⌘+–, or click the Zoom Out icon button (the small letter *A*) in the toolbar (if you customized your toolbar to include it). You also can use the pinch gesture on a touchpad.

Tip

If you choose View ⇨ Zoom Text Only, the Zoom In and Zoom Out controls affect only the web page's text. This can result in some awkward displays for web pages, but it also keeps the layout more in line with the creator's intent and requires less scrolling than zooming in for everything does. You also can choose View ⇨ Actual Size or press ⌘+0 (zero) to see the web page at its normal, default size. ∎

Using sharing controls

When you visit a web page, you often want to tell someone else about it or make a printout so you can refer to it later or show others. Safari has several controls to help you do so:

- Press ⌘+P to print the current page to the printer of your choice. You also can click the Print This Page icon button (known simply as Print) in the toolbar (if you customized your toolbar to include it) to print the current page.

- Choose File ⇨ Mail Contents of This Page or press ⌘+I to send the web page as an HTML attachment to other people via Apple Mail.

- Choose File ⇨ Mail Link to This Page or press Shift+⌘+I to send the URL for the current page to other people via Apple Mail.

Using interface controls

Safari gives you some controls over what displays onscreen:

- You can hide or show the bookmarks bar by choosing Show/Hide Bookmarks Bar or pressing Shift+⌘+B.

- You can hide or show the toolbar by choosing Show/Hide Toolbar or pressing Shift+⌘+\.

- You can hide or show the status bar by choosing Show/Hide Status Bar or pressing ⌘+/. (It's hidden by default.)The status bar shows the names of page destinations as you hover your mouse over the hyperlinks to them.

- You can change what appears in the Safari toolbar, such as the navigation buttons and other controls—by choosing View ⇨ Customize Toolbar, as the sidebar "Configuring the Safari toolbar" explains.

Using specialty controls

Safari has several other controls that defy easy categorization but are often useful:

- Safari's pop-up blocker can eliminate many of the annoying windows that pop up from ads trying to intrude into your view while you're viewing a web page. Choose Safari ⇨ Block Pop-Up Windows or press Shift+⌘+K to toggle pop-up blocking. (If the menu item has a check mark to its left, pop-up blocking is turned on.)

- Safari can save the current web page to a file on your Mac; choose File ⇨ Save As or press ⌘+S. You have two save options in the dialog box that appears: Web Archive, which saves the HTML page plus the graphics on the same page to the folder of your choice, and Page Source, which saves just the HTML page to the folder of your choice. Click Save after you've decided what to save and where to save it.

- The Downloads dialog box (choose Window ⇨ Downloads) and the Downloads pop-over (click the Downloads icon button) show all recently downloaded files, so you can find them in Finder (click the Show in Finder icon button [the magnifying glass icon] to the right of a download name to open a Finder window containing that file), resume any downloads that were paused, see the status of those currently being downloaded (and halt any you don't want to keep downloading), and clear the list of recent downloads.

New Feature

The Downloads icon button and its pop-over are new to Mac OS X Lion's Safari 5.1. The Downloads button shows an indicator of the download progress while you are downloading files. The pop-over works just like the Downloads dialog box. (Note that the shortcut Option+⌘+L no longer opens the Downloads dialog box; instead it opens the new Reading List explained earlier in this chapter.) ■

- The page search box (choose Edit ⇨ Find ⇨ Find or press ⌘+F) opens the Find banner right above the web page so you can search for text on that page. Enter the text in the Find banner's search field, and press Return or click the Search icon button (the magnifying glass icon). Use the Back and Forward icon buttons in the Find banner to search for other occurrences of the search term on that page. Click Done to close it, choose Edit ⇨ Find ⇨ Hide Find Banner, or press Shift+⌘+F. You can quickly search for any text selected on the page by choosing Edit ⇨ Find ⇨ Use Selection for Find or pressing ⌘+E.

- If you want to see the HTML code used for the current page, to help you recreate something for one of your own pages, for example, choose View ⇨ View Source or press Option+⌘+U to open a new window that displays the HTML code.

- The Open in Dashboard control (choose File ⇨ Open in Dashboard) enables you to select any part of the web page as a module that is stored in the Mac's Dashboard as a widget (see Chapter 14), so you can open just that piece of the web page in the Dashboard later. For example, you may want to save the sports scores box on a news page and see just that score box in the Dashboard.

- The Auto Fill control (choose Edit ⇨ AutoFill Form or press Shift+⌘+A) looks at any forms on the web page and fills in anything it can find appropriate from your Address Book or from previous forms you've filled out. If you have enabled AutoFill in the Preferences dialog box, Safari prompts you when you click in fields on web pages that it "thinks" it has the relevant information for: A menu of one or more possible entries appears that you can choose from if desired.

- The Report a Bug control (choose Safari ⇨ Report Bugs to Apple) opens a form in which you can report errors on the current web page to Apple.

Setting Safari Preferences

You can set lots of preferences for Safari. The key ones are explained in this section. To go to the Preferences dialog box, choose Safari ⇨ Preferences or press ⌘+, (comma).

New Feature

The version of Safari that comes with Mac OS X Lion rearranges the Preferences dialog box's Security pane to split its options between that pane and the new Privacy pane, which also includes new controls on managing websites' access to your location. Safari now also defaults to Yahoo instead of Google as the default search engine, which you can change in the General pane. ■

The General pane and the Security pane, both shown in Figure 19.8, have many of the critical preferences.

FIGURE 19.8

The General pane (left), Security pane (upper right), and Privacy pane (lower right) of the Safari Preferences dialog box

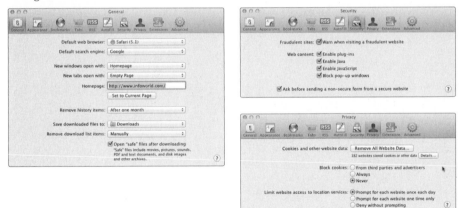

These options are available in the General pane:

- **Default Web Browser:** This pop-up menu determines which browser is opened by default when you click a hyperlink in another program. If you have other browsers installed on your Mac, they display in the pop-up menu's options. Safari is the default choice.

- **Default Search Engine:** This pop-up menu lets you choose Google, Microsoft Bing, or Yahoo as your default search engine; Yahoo is the default.

- **New Windows Open With:** This pop-up menu enables you to choose what appears in new windows: the home page (the default), nothing, the same page as in the current window, the bookmarks window, or a tab folder that you choose (this opens all its tabbed panes).

- **New Tabs Open With:** This pop-up menu enables you to choose what appears in new tabbed panes: the home page, nothing (the default), the same page as in the current tabbed pane (or window if no tabbed pane is open), or the bookmarks window.

- **Homepage:** This field is where you enter the home page for your browser, if you want one. Click Set to Current Page to make it the home page. Delete the entry to have no home page.

- **Remove History Items:** This pop-up menu enables you to specify how long visited items are available in the History menu and list. Your choices are After One Day, After One Week (the default), After Two Weeks, After One Month, After One Year, and Manual (which means they remain until you choose Safari⇨Empty Cache or press Option+⌘+E). To prevent Safari from tracking your web page visits, choose Safari⇨ Private Browsing; if a check mark appears to the left of this menu option, it is enabled.

- **Save Downloaded Files To:** This pop-up menu determines where downloaded files are stored. The default option is the Downloads folder; you can choose Other to select a different folder.

- **Remove Download List Items:** This pop-up menu controls how long downloads stay in the Download dialog box's list: Manually (the default), When Safari Quits, and Upon Successful Download.

- **Open "Safe" Files After Downloading:** This option, if selected, makes Mac OS X open downloaded files automatically. Safari tries to determine which are safe to open, to reduce the chance of a virus or other malware being installed onto your Mac without your being aware (see Chapter 26). But the chance remains, which is why I recommend not selecting this option, so the decision to open a downloaded file is one you consciously make each time.

These options are available in the Security pane:

- **Fraudulent Sites:** This option, if selected, displays a warning when you are visiting a site that appears to be a scam. For example, if a link purports to be to www.apple. com but is to another site, Safari displays a warning. A common trick, called *phishing*, to steal users' identities is to send e-mails allegedly from their banks or credit card agencies asking them to click a link to update information. The link's text may look like a legitimate URL, but the actual hyperlink is to a different site where the thief hopes you enter all your account information so he can go steal your account's funds. This feature tries to detect such phishing expeditions. (See Chapter 26 for more on protecting yourself from identity theft.) This option is selected by default.

- **Web Content:** The four options here determine what actions Safari takes with common web content. If selected, Enable Plug-Ins lets plug-ins such as Adobe Flash and Adobe Reader run in Safari. If selected, Enable Java lets Java-based web applications run in Safari. If selected, Enable JavaScript lets JavaScript run in web pages that are often used to deliver special features in web pages such as recognizing you as a registered user. If selected, Block Pop-Up Windows prevents web pages from opening new windows on their own. (Selecting this option is the same as choosing Safari ⇨ Block Pop-Up Windows or pressing Shift+⌘+K.) All four options are selected by default.

- **Ask Before Sending a Non-Secure Form from a Secure Website:** This option, if selected, provides an alert if the secured website (one with a URL that begins with `https://`) uses a form that is not secured—one that could be an indication of a hacked or fraudulent site.

These options are available in the Privacy pane:

- **Cookies and Other Website Data:** Click Remove All Website Data to remove all data placed onto your Mac to track or reload your personal preferences when you next visit a site. The most common form of such data comes in the form of *cookies*, which are small files placed on your Mac by web pages to store information such as your name or account status. Click Details to see exactly what cookies and similar files are on your Mac; you can individually delete them from the settings sheet that appears.

- **Block Cookies:** The three options here determine how Safari handles cookies. Select the Always option to never have cookies stored. (Many web pages won't work if cookies are blocked.) Select the Never option to allow all cookies to be stored. Select the From Third Parties and Advertisers option to allow cookies from web pages you visit but not from other pages that these pages may link to (such as marketers' and advertisers' sites).

- **Limit Website Access to Location Services:** The three options here let you control to what extent a website can detect your current location. The Prompt Once per Day per Website option displays an alert for each location-tracking website you visit each day asking for permission to provide that location information. The Prompt Once per Website option asks you just once for that permission. The Deny without Prompting option simply refuses to share your location information, without asking you for each website.

As shown in Figure 19.9, the Appearance and Advanced panes control display-oriented preferences.

FIGURE 19.9

The Appearance pane (left) and Advanced pane (right) of the Safari Preferences dialog box

These options are available in the Appearance pane:

- **Standard Font:** This area shows the current font used for regular text. You can change it by clicking Select and choosing a different font and/or size.

- **Fixed-Width Font:** This area shows the current text font used to display code snippets and other such typewriter-like displays. You can change it by clicking Select and choosing a different font and/or size.

- **Display Images When Page Opens:** If selected, this option displays the images on a web page. Deselect this option so images don't display (something that can greatly speed up page load times and is very helpful for dial-up users).

- **Default Encoding:** This pop-up menu sets the language and character set defaults for web pages in case the web page doesn't say what language characters it uses. (Whatever the web page specifies as its language encoding overrides this pop-up menu's settings.) If you open a web page where the language isn't specified and it doesn't match your Default Encoding setting (it looks like gobbledygook), you can choose an encoding for that page by choosing View ⇨ Text Encoding and then the language encoding that you think it is.

These options are available in the Advanced pane:

- **Universal Access:** In this section, select the Never Use Font Sizes Smaller Than option and choose a size in the adjacent pop-up menu to prevent text from being displayed at a smaller size than chosen. This is helpful to keep pages readable even when the designers chose tiny type, but it can make some pages' text wrap incorrectly or even run into other text, especially if you choose larger text sizes as the minimum. If you're over 40 years old, you may want this option selected, though probably at a larger size than the default 9 points.

  Also in the Universal Access section, select Press Tab to Highlight Each Item on a Webpage to be able to press Tab to move among items on a web page. Normally, you would press Option+Tab to do so, but that can be hard for people with arthritis or other physical handicaps.

- **Style Sheet:** If you want to impose your own style sheet (fonts, colors, sizes, and so on) on all web pages, choose Other and then select the CSS (cascading style sheet) file you want to use. Otherwise, leave this set at the default of None Selected.

- **Proxies:** Click Change Settings if you want to open the Proxies pane in the Network system preference to change how your Mac accesses specialized web services such as Gopher. Only an advanced user familiar with networking protocols should adjust these settings.

- **Database Storage:** This pop-up menu determines how much database content from web pages can be stored on your Mac before you are asked to allow more storage. The options are 1MB, 5MB (the default), 10MB, 50MB, 100MB, 500MB, and None. Click Show Databases to show any stored web databases on your Mac; you can delete any unwanted ones from the list that appears.

- **Show Develop Menu in Menu Bar:** This option, if selected, adds the Develop menu to Safari's menu bar. The Develop menu has various options that helps a web page developer find errors in web pages he or she is previewing in Safari, as well as enables the developer to turn various features on or off while testing the pages.

The Bookmarks and Tabs panes, shown in Figure 19.10, provide controls over access to web pages in Safari.

FIGURE 19.10

The Bookmarks pane (left) and Tabs pane (right) of the Safari Preferences dialog box

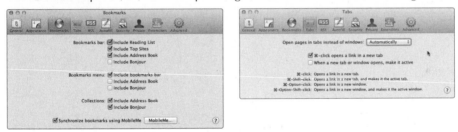

These options are available in the Bookmarks pane:

- **Bookmarks Bar:** Use the four options here to determine whether the Reading List icon button (the glasses icon) and/or the Top Sites icon button (the grid icon) appear in the toolbar, as well as whether Bonjour network links and/or web pages from your Address book display in the bookmarks bar. The Include Reading List and Include Top Sites options are selected by default, whereas the Include Bonjour and Include Address Book options are deselected by default.

- **Bookmarks Menu:** Use the three options here to determine whether the bookmarks bar, Bonjour, and Address Book URLs appear in the Bookmarks menu. By default, the bookmarks bar is selected, which adds the Bookmarks Bar option to the Bookmarks menu; the Bookmarks Bar menu option has a submenu that lists all the URLs book-marked in the bookmarks bar.

- **Collections:** Use the two options here to determine what appears in the Collections list in the bookmarks window. By default, both Address Book and Bonjour are selected and thus listed in the Collections list.

The Tabs pane has these options:

- **Open Pages in Tabs Instead of Windows:** This pop-up menu lets you choose when to open pages in tabbed panes rather than in new windows: Never, Automatically, and Always. The Never option honors the code in a URL that tells the browser to open a new window, the Always option overrides the code and instead opens the page in a new tabbed pane, and the Automatically option honors that code only for pages that specify a particular window size, opening the rest in tabbed panes.

- **⌘+Click Opens Link in a New Tab:** If selected (the default), ⌘+clicking or Shift+⌘+clicking a hyperlink opens it in a new tabbed pane. If deselected, these actions open the hyperlinks in a new window instead. This option also affects the shortcuts for opening hyperlinks in new windows. If selected, Option+⌘+click and Option+Shift+⌘+click open new windows; if deselected, they open new tabbed panes instead.

- **When a New Tab or Window Opens, Make It Active:** This option, if selected, auto-matically switches the browser to a new tabbed pane or window. By default, this option is deselected, so new windows and tabbed panes open in the background, leaving the current window or pane visible.

Two other Preferences dialog box's panes are unrelated, though both are shown in Figure 19.11: AutoFill and RSS.

FIGURE 19.11

The AutoFill pane (left) and RSS pane (right) of the Safari Preferences dialog box

The AutoFill pane has one set of options called AutoFill Web Forms. The three options, if selected, determine where Safari looks for data to fill in web forms automatically: your Address Book card, your username and passwords you've used in Safari for web pages, and other forms you've previously filled out from Safari. If you click Edit next to the Address Book option, the Address Book application launches so you can edit your contact information there (see Chapter 21). In the other two cases, you can remove specific entries by clicking the Edit button next to the option.

The RSS pane has these options (RSS is covered in the next section of this chapter):

- **Default RSS Reader:** This pop-up menu determines what program automatically is used to open and display RSS feeds. Safari is the default option, though you could select Mail or choose another web browser, an RSS-capable mail application, or a stand-alone RSS reader program that you have installed on the Mac.

- **Automatically Update Articles In:** There are two options here: Bookmarks Bar and Bookmarks Menu. Safari automatically updates the RSS feeds for any feeds that are bookmarked in the selected options' locations.

- **Check for Updates:** This pop-up menu determines how often Safari looks to see if an RSS feed has been updated: Every 30 Minutes, Every Hour, Every Day, or Never. If you choose Never, you must open the RSS feed manually, by going to its bookmark, for example.

- **Mark Articles as Read:** This pop-up menu determines how Safari knows you've seen an RSS feed item: After Viewing the RSS Page (the default) or After Clicking Them. The first option assumes that simply seeing the list of entries counts as having read them; the second options makes you actually click the link before the RSS entry is counted as having been read.

- **Highlight Unread Articles:** If selected, articles that have not been read are highlighted in bold. By default this option is deselected.

- **Remove Articles:** This pop-up menu determines how long RSS feed items are retained in the feed list. Safari deletes the entries based on which option you choose: After One Day, After One Week (the default), After Two Weeks, After One Month, or Never. Click Remove Now to delete all RSS feed entries, whether read or not.

The Preferences dialog box has one more pane: Extensions lists any plug-ins you've installed in Safari. These extensions add features to Safari.

Using RSS in Safari

RSS, which stands for Really Simple Syndication, is a way of sending content directly to a browser, e-mail program, or stand-alone RSS reader program. A web browser enables you to go to content, RSS brings the content to you, and as new content is added to a specific RSS feed, it shows up in your list of RSS articles.

Web browsers like Safari can subscribe to RSS feeds, treating them essentially as web pages that you open through bookmarks. When you go to a web page that offers RSS feeds, look for an RSS icon or the word Subscribe. Open the RSS page as you would any web page. Then choose Bookmarks➪Add Bookmark or press ⌘+D to bookmark this RSS feed. Figure 19.12 shows an RSS feed being bookmarked.

FIGURE 19.12

Adding an RSS feed to Safari is no different than bookmarking a web page.

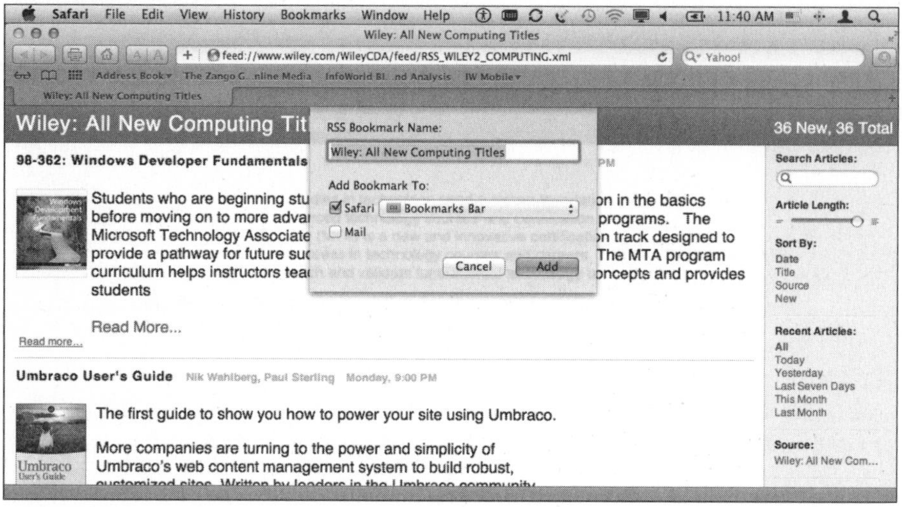

Tip

Safari can detect whether a web page has an RSS feed associated with it. If it finds such an RSS feed, a steel-blue RSS icon appears on the right side of the URL field; click it to open the RSS feed in Safari. ■

As with a web page (see the section "Using bookmarks" earlier in this chapter), you can place the bookmark in the bookmarks bar, in the Bookmarks menu, or in a folder. But, unlike with web page bookmarks, you also get to choose Mail as a bookmarking option, which if selected has Apple Mail subscribe to the RSS feed. (Both Safari and Mail can subscribe to the same feed.)

Cross-Reference

Chapter 20 covers using Mail to read RSS feeds. ■

When you add an RSS feed, the All RSS Feeds option appears in the Collections list in the bookmarks window, plus All RSS Feeds appears in the Bookmarks menu so you have quick access to a list of all your RSS feeds. You can access the RSS feeds from the list of all RSS feeds or from the location you bookmarked it to, such as the bookmarks bar. If you also bookmarked the RSS feed to Mail, you can see the feed entries there as well.

Based on the settings in the RSS pane in Safari's Preferences dialog box (see the previous section), Safari can keep the entries for your bookmarked RSS feed up to date.

Using Other Browsers

Safari comes with Mac OS X Lion, but it's not the only browser available for your Mac. And it may not be the best one for you either. Two other mainstream browsers worth considering are Mozilla Firefox (`www.mozilla.com`) and Google Chrome (`www.google.com/chrome`). You can have multiple browsers on your Mac, and you can run them at the same time, so it's not an either/or proposition. (A third browser option is Opera [`www.opera.com`], but it's never gained many adherents despite its long history.)

Why would you consider a different browser than Safari? These are the two biggest reasons:

- **Security:** Safari is one of the least secure popular browsers available. Firefox and Chrome are more secure, according to security experts, with better protection against phishing and other hacking attacks. Also, Firefox lets you set a password to enable autofill of sensitive data, such as your login information for banking and other sites (in the Security pane of Firefox's Preferences dialog, select Use a Master Password), so someone can't just fire up Firefox and connect to all your accounts for which you have enabled autofill. Safari can't do that, so anything that is set to autofill in Safari can be accessed by anyone who has access to your user account.

- **User interface:** Safari's handling of bookmarks can be awkward: You either need to group bookmarks in a folder accessible from the bookmarks bar, which requires more planning, or open the bookmarks window, which takes over your entire screen. Many people prefer the bookmarks sidebar pane that Firefox uses to keep your bookmarks easily accessible but not in the way. Chrome provides a drop-down menu of bookmarks, which means they're not always taking up room on the screen, as Firefox's bookmarks do, but when displayed Chrome's list is very wide, obscuring more of the window when displayed than Firefox's pane does. Many people like Chrome's highly simplified user interface; it doesn't even have a Home icon unless you turn it on via the Preferences dialog box.

Figure 19.13 shows a web page in Firefox, while Figure 19.14 shows the same web page in Chrome. I suggest you try them both to see if one would be better as your default web browser than Safari or if either would work well as an additional browser on your Mac—after all, there's no law that says you may use only one browser. Don't get me wrong: Safari is a good browser, and it's popular in its own right. But it's not always the best choice, so I hope you'll explore other options as well.

FIGURE 19.13

The Mozilla Firefox 4 browser

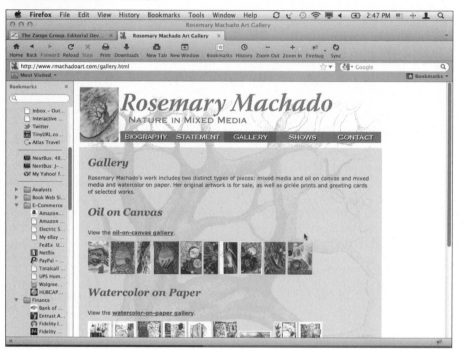

FIGURE 19.14

The Google Chrome 11 browser

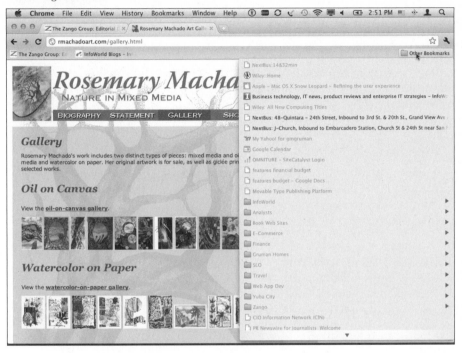

Summary

Mac OS X Lion comes with Apple's Safari browser preinstalled, so it's the default browser for many Mac users. Like all browsers, Safari lets you enter URLs to go to a specific web address, as well as use hyperlinks on those pages to jump to other pages and use bookmarks to save favorite pages in lists that you can later click to go directly to them. Safari also enables you to see the history of your web visits, so you can go back to web pages you've recently visited. The Bookmarks menu, bar, and page all provide access to bookmarked pages and visited-page histories. Toolbar buttons enable you to navigate back and forth among the pages you've visited in the current browser session.

Safari can display web pages in tabbed panes or separate windows or both. It offers a variety of controls to create, delete, and otherwise manage the tabbaed panes and windows. In Safari, you can print and mail web pages to other people, as well as save web pages to your Mac and view the HTML source code used in the web pages you view. If you're a web page developer, the optional Developer menu provides controls to check for coding errors and turn various controls on and off for testing.

The new Reading List pane adds a new form of bookmarking for pages you want to read later and then be done with, as opposed to traditional bookmarks, which are usually used for pages you want to keep permanently accessible.

Safari enables you to search for text on a web page you're visiting, as well as use your choice of the Google, Bing, and Yahoo search engines to find information on the web.

Safari's many preference options enable you to set security, such as blocking pop-ups and preventing some potentially dangerous web technologies from running in your browser. The Preferences dialog box also lets you establish user interface standards such as the default font, font size, and language for web pages, plus how new tabbed panes and windows open by default.

Safari can read RSS feeds and bookmark them for easy access later. It also provides controls on whether RSS feeds' entries are automatically updated and, if so, how often they are updated and their contents retained. You can bookmark RSS feeds not only in Safari but also in Apple Mail, in case you prefer to read RSS feeds there.

Mac users have two main alternatives to Safari: Mozilla Firefox and Google Chrome. Both have better security controls. Many people prefer Firefox's capability to show a list of bookmarks on the side of the screen instead of relying solely on menus or a window of bookmarks that obscures any web page you're viewing. And many people prefer Chrome's highly simplified user interface. With Mac OS X, you can install and run multiple browsers, so you can use any combination of Safari, Firefox, Chrome, and other browsers as you prefer.

Using Mail, iChat, and FaceTime

Just as accessing the web is a major use of the Mac, and a reason that Apple has put so much care into its web applications such as Safari and web-based technologies such as iCloud and the iTunes Store, communicating with other people is a key reason people use a Mac—and again a key area that Apple has focused its applications on.

Communication is a fundamental human activity. People love to talk to each other. All sorts of new technologies have changed how we communicate—e-mail, online chat boards, instant messaging, feeds like Twitter, social network sites like Facebook, and so on—but what's constant is that we are still talking to each other, just over greater distances than ever before possible.

Collaboration—working together—is what enables people to do so many great things, bringing together skills, intuition, and physical labor, along with the energy created by coming together. You can't collaborate if you can't communicate, so the Mac's communication capabilities are key. Other capabilities, such as file sharing, enable you to build on that communication to accomplish actual work.

The two core communications applications that Mac OS X Lion provides are Mail and iChat. Mail is Apple's e-mail client, which enables you to send and receive e-mails. iChat is Apple's instant messaging client, which enables you to send instant messages so you can chat in real time with other people no matter where they are.

And a third application, FaceTime, allows you to have videoconferences with people using an iPad 2, iPhone 4, 2010-edition iPod Touch, or Mac.

IN THIS CHAPTER

Preparing Mail accounts and preferences

Migrating e-mail accounts into Mail

Accessing mail on the road

Handling e-mail accounts and folders

Writing, sending, and reading e-mail messages

Accessing RSS feeds from Mail

Accessing notes in Mail

Engaging in text, audio, video, and screen-sharing iChat sessions

Videoconferencing with FaceTime

Cross-Reference

Chapter 22 explains how to use Mail with Microsoft's Exchange server. Chapter 19 covers Safari, Chapter 17 covers iCloud, and Chapter 16 covers iTunes. Chapter 21 covers the Address Book application that stores contacts used by Mail and other programs, as well as the iCal calendar application. Chapter 24 covers sharing files with other people. ■

Setting Up Apple's Mail

Apple's Mail application is, simply put, world-class. Most people can use it as their regular e-mail client, rather than others such as Microsoft Entourage, Microsoft Outlook, or Mozilla Thunderbird. You can manage multiple e-mail accounts, have your mail automatically sorted, and even access RSS (Really Simple Syndication) feeds in your e-mail list.

New Feature

Mail in Mac OS X Lion supports full-screen mode. Use the Enter Full Screen icon button as described in Chapter 9 to enter this mode. ■

But before you do any of that, you need to set up Mail. If you've upgraded your Mac to Mac OS X Lion, your existing Mail accounts are ready for you in the Lion version of Mail. If you have a new Mac, you need to set up your Mail accounts. Either way, you can import your existing e-mail accounts from other programs so they're all available in Mail.

Setting up new e-mail accounts

If you have no e-mail accounts set up in Mail, the program walks you through a series of steps to set up your e-mail account when you first run it.

If you already had an e-mail account set up (because you upgraded your Mac to Mac OS X Lion, for example) and want to add an additional account, choose File ➪ Add Account. (You don't need to set up previously setup accounts again when you upgrade.)

Whether you are creating your first e-mail account or adding a new one, the process is the same: In the dialog box that appears, enter the name you want people to see in the From field when they receive e-mails from you, as well as your e-mail address and the password for that e-mail account. Click Continue.

Mail tries to connect to the e-mail server automatically. If it cannot, it displays the Incoming Mail Server dialog box where you need to choose the e-mail server type (the Account Type pop-up menu) and server address (the Incoming Mail Server field) and then verify your username and password for the e-mail account. (The Description field is optional; it provides a description in Mail to help you remember the account's purpose, such as Work, Home, or Shopping Address.) There are three types of server types:

- **POP, which stands for Post Office Protocol:** This is the most common type of server account. Note that, by default, POP assumes you have just one computer accessing e-mail, so it downloads the messages to your Mac and then deletes the messages from your e-mail server—which makes those e-mails unavailable if you check e-mail from a different computer later. You can change this default, as I explain in the "Accounts preferences" section later in this chapter. POP is typically the e-mail server type used by free e-mail services such as Gmail and Hotmail, by e-mail accounts you set up with most web hosts, and in the e-mail accounts that come from your Internet service provider (such as your cable company or telephone company).

Tip

Typical POP server addresses take the form pop.domain or mail.domain, such as `pop.apple.com` or `mail.apple.com`. Sometimes, it's just the domain name, such as `apple.com`. If none of these works, check your documentation or ask your IT support staff. ■

- **IMAP, which stands for Internet Mail Access Protocol:** This server type is less common, though it is the protocol that Apple's iCloud service uses. It makes using e-mail from several computers easier because it leaves the messages on the server by default—so they're still available when you access e-mail from a different computer. Typically, businesses set up IMAP e-mail access for their employees. Note that IMAP is the standard for Microsoft Exchange 2003 and earlier, so Mac users can access mail both within a corporate network and over what it calls an Outlook Web Access (OWA) connection for access over the Internet. Note that Mail offers Exchange IMAP as an Account Type option for these users; it's preconfigured for the common Exchange IMAP settings.

Tip

Typical IMAP server addresses take the form `mail.domain`, such as `mail.apple.com`. Sometimes, it's just the domain name, such as `apple.com`. For Exchange 2003 and earlier, the form is often owa.domain, such as `owa.apple.com`. If none of these works, check your documentation or ask your IT support staff. ■

- **Exchange:** This server type provides a direct connection to Microsoft Exchange 2007 and 2010 servers (but not to Exchange 2003 or earlier versions) using Microsoft's ActiveSync technology. If you choose Exchange as the server type, you get two additional options: Address Book Contacts and iCal Calendars. Select either or both to have Exchange synchronize your Mac's contacts and/or schedules with the Exchange address book and calendar you use at work so you have one master set of records. Note that Exchange leaves all messages, calendar entries, and contacts on the server, so they're always accessible from any computer you log in from. (Chapter 22 covers using Mail with Exchange in more detail.)

Click Continue. Mail tries to connect to the server with your new settings. If it cannot, get your tech support to tell you the correct settings and try again. Click Cancel if you want to try again later after you've had a chance to get the correct settings.

When setting up an e-mail account, you may get an error message that asks you to verify the identity of the server you are connecting to. This typically happens when you use a web host, a company that lets you set up a website and e-mail addresses on its servers. In this case, the web host's actual domain isn't the same as for your e-mail server, and Mail notices that difference. Because providing fake domain names is a common trick of identity thieves, Mail asks you to verify that you are connecting to the correct server, as opposed to the server of a scammer who is hoping to get your username and password to access your information elsewhere. You can see the details by clicking Show Certificate, as I did in Figure 20.1. If you're confident that the server is legit, click Connect; otherwise, click Cancel and verify the server information with your tech support or documentation. (And if you're setting up multiple e-mail accounts on this Mac to this server, select the Always Trust option so you're not asked again about this mismatch.)

FIGURE 20.1

If Mail sees a mismatch between your e-mail account's server name and that of the server that claims to host your e-mail, it provides this warning. The mismatch could be harmless, such as when you use a web host to provide your e-mail server, or it could indicate someone is trying to scam you by collecting your username and password.

After Mail has made a connection, it asks you for the setting so it can send out e-mail. Typically, a web host or business uses a different server to send out e-mail than to receive it. Here are the options for outgoing e-mail configuration:

- **Outgoing Mail Server:** This is the server that takes the e-mail from Mail and sends it to the Internet for delivery to your addressees. The typical outgoing server uses a technology called SMTP (Simple Mail Transfer Protocol); therefore, the server's address usually takes the form smtp.*domain*, such as `smtp.apple.com`. Sometimes, it's mail.*domain* or just the domain name, such as `mail.apple.com` or `apple.com`. For Exchange 2003 and earlier, the form is often owa.*domain*, such as `owa.apple.com`. If none of these works, check your documentation or ask your IT support staff.

- **Use Only This Server:** Select this option if you want all outgoing mail to go through the same server. Otherwise, you can specify a separate server for each e-mail account. If you have, for example, your work and personal e-mail accounts on the Mac, you may want your personal e-mail to go through its own server and not pass through your company's server (where it can be monitored). Or your company may insist that all e-mail go through its servers to ensure you're not sending out confidential data.

- **Use Authentication:** Select this option if the outgoing server requires you to authenticate yourself—prove you are who you say you are. Then enter your username and password in the adjacent fields. (Note that the authentication username and password may differ from the one you use to check your e-mail.) More and more web hosts and companies are requiring authentication so spammers can't send e-mails through their servers.

- **Description:** Enter a brief description in this optional field to help you remember what this server is, such as Home, Joe's House, or Office.

Click Continue; Mail tries to make a connection. It may open a new dialog box asking you to enable outgoing mail security. If your Internet service provider (ISP) or web host requires such security, select the Use Secure Sockets Layer (SSL) option and then choose the appropriate option from the Authentication pop-up menu: None, Password, Kerberos Version 5 (GSSAPI, which stands for Generic Security Services Application Programming Interface), NTLM (which stands for Windows NT LAN Manager), or MD5 (Message-Digest algorithm 5) Challenge-Response. Your tech support or documentation should tell you which option to use. Click Continue, and review the settings in the next dialog box. If they're correct, click Create. (If you want to connect immediately, select the Take Account Online option first.) Otherwise, click Go Back to change your settings or Cancel to stop (your settings are not saved if you click Cancel).

Importing existing e-mail accounts

If you have e-mail accounts already set up in another copy of Apple Mail (such as in a different user account on this Mac or in a folder from an old user account) or other e-mail program, you can import the account and its e-mail messages into Mail by choosing File ⇨ Import Mailboxes. In the Import dialog box that appears, choose the e-mail program you want to import from and Click Continue. For most of the options, Mail opens a dialog box asking you to locate the mailbox folder and click Continue to transfer the settings and mail to Mail. For Entourage, it launches Entourage and then imports the settings and e-mail messages. Click Done when the import is completed.

Setting Mail's preferences

You can configure many settings in Apple Mail to manage both overall preferences such as fonts and mailbox layout and mailbox-specific settings such as how to store e-mail, how often to check for e-mail, and the like. To access these preferences, choose Mail ⇨ Preferences or press ⌘+, (comma).

Sending e-mail while traveling

You're at a hotel, a friend's or in-law's home, a café with a Wi-Fi hot spot, or other temporary location. You try to send your e-mails but keep getting "cannot connect" error messages. Yet your e-mails send fine from your home or the office. What's the culprit?

Because spammers send billions of messages each year through other people's e-mail servers to make their scamming messages look like they came from legitimate sources, more and more Internet service providers (ISPs) and web hosts are disallowing use of their servers by strangers. For example, when you use an e-mail address provided by your cable company and you send messages from home over your cable service's broadband connection, your cable company sees that you're sending a message from inside its network and that your outgoing server is on the same network, so it lets your messages through. But when a friend visits and tries to send e-mail, her computer is using, say, her phone company's outgoing e-mail server. The phone company sees her try to send messages through its servers but notes that she's not connected via the phone company's broadband connection, so it blocks her messages from going into its servers.

There's no single answer to addressing this issue for sending your legitimate e-mail. But chances are good that one of the following methods will work. Check with your ISP or web host to see what method they're using to let you send e-mail when traveling.

- **Use authentication to enter your username and password, either in your e-mail account or when prompted by Mail.** Some ISPs accept e-mail coming from foreign networks if there's a valid authentication attached to the message. Try selecting SSL as the authentication method if the username and password aren't accepted. Also, try checking your e-mail before sending, then try to send; some web hosts let you send from a foreign location after you've read your e-mail (and established a legitimate connection) for a set time (such as for 45 minutes after making that initial connection).

- **Set up an outgoing server in Mail using the settings for the location you're in.** (A friend might let you use her settings, but chances are small that a hotel or other business will.) It's also possible that your ISP has a separate outgoing mail server address to use when customers travel, so check with it. To add a server, choose Mail⇨Preferences or press ⌘+, (comma), go to the Accounts pane, and select your account from the list at the left, as shown in the figure. In the Outgoing Mail Server (SMTP) pop-up menu, choose Edit SMTP Server List. Click the + icon button in the settings sheet that appears to add a new outgoing server, as shown on the right side of the figure. Double-click in the Description column to give the new outgoing server setting a name, and double-click in the Server Name column to provide its server address. Go to the Advanced pane, and select the appropriate options for the outgoing server. Click OK when you're finished. You're now back in the Accounts pane. Using the Outgoing Mail Server (SMTP) pop-up menu, choose the new outgoing server to send your e-mails through it. Use the Accounts pane in Mail preferences to switch among outgoing servers as needed.

- **Change the outgoing port to get around blocks set up at some hotels and other facilities.** Sometimes, the issue is not with your ISP but with the ISP serving the location you're working from. Some block the standard SMTP ports (25 and 587). You can try to get around this block by changing the SMTP port to 465. To do so, go to the Accounts pane of the Preferences dialog box, and choose Edit Server List from the Outgoing Mail Server pop-up menu. In the subdialog box that appears, go to the Advanced pane, select Use Custom Port, and enter **465**. Click OK, and close the Preferences dialog box. When you're back at your home or work location, repeat these steps, except select Use Default Ports.

- **Use a VPN if available.** A virtual private network gives you a direct connection to your company's network when outside that network. If you connect via VPN, your e-mail is sent through that network, not through the ISP of wherever you are visiting. You may have a separate VPN program you first need to launch to be able to send e-mail or you may use a VPN set up in the Network system preference, which you then need to activate, as Chapter 23 explains. Note that the VPN approach is unlikely to help you send personal e-mail as it's rare that your ISP or web host offers VPN capability for non-business accounts; if that's the case, you need to try one of the previous options instead.

General preferences

The General pane, shown in Figure 20.2, has a grab bag of settings:

- **Default Email Reader:** Choose the e-mail program that should launch automatically when you click a mail link on the web or other application. The Default is Mail, but if you have other e-mail programs installed, they appear in the pop-up menu as well. No matter what your default e-mail program is, you can use any of them by launching them when desired.

- **Check for New Messages:** Choose how frequently you want Mail to look for new messages. You choices are Manually, Every Minute, Every 5 Minutes (the default), Every 15 Minutes, Every 30 Minutes, and Every Hour. If you choose Manually, you must choose Mailbox ⇨ Get New Mail and then choose the desired mailbox to check, or you can choose Mailbox ⇨ Get All New Mail or press Shift+⌘+N to check all accounts for new messages.

- **New Message Sound:** By default, Mail plays the New Messages sound when it detects new messages. You can change that sound to one of the standard Mac OS X sounds in this pop-up menu, choose your own sound (choose the Add/Remove option), or turn off the audio notification (choose None). Select the Play Sounds for Other Mail Actions options if you want Mail to provide audio feedback, such as when sending messages.

- **Dock Unread Count:** Choose how you want the Mail icon in the Dock to display the number of unread messages available. The Inbox Only option shows the count for messages only in the main inbox, which is where all accounts are placed by default. (You can change their locations, as described in the "Working with e-mails" section later in this chapter.) The All Accounts option shows the count for all accounts, whether or not they are in the main inbox, as well as any messages in the Draft folder and any unread messages in the Trash folder, but not unread messages in the Junk Mail folder. The None option disables the new-message display in the Dock.

- **Add Invitations to iCal:** If you receive an e-mail with an invitation attached (as an .ics file), choosing Automatically in this pop-up menu (the default) adds the item to your iCal calendar automatically. (If you accept the message in your e-mail, it displays in iCal as an appointment; if you don't act on the invitation, the invitation itself appears in iCal, where you can accept or decline it.) If you choose Never, the invitations are not added to iCal. (Chapter 21 covers iCal.)

- **Downloads Folder:** This option determines where attachments in your messages are downloaded to when you save them. The default is the Downloads folder, but you can use an alternative location by choosing Other and navigating to the desired folder.

- **Remove Unedited Downloads:** This option determines when Mail deletes attachments that you have not saved to your Mac or that you have not modified (such as by editing the message in Mail and saving it). The options are When Mail Quits, After Message Is Deleted (the default), and Never.

- **If Outgoing Server Is Unavailable:** The default option is Show a List of Alternate Servers, which has Mail ask you to choose a different outgoing mail sever if available. (See the sidebar, "Sending e-mail while traveling," for details on setting up these alternate servers.) Your other option is Automatically Try Sending Later.

- **When Searching Mailboxes, Include Results From:** This option determines where the search feature in Mail looks when you are searching across all e-mail accounts. You can select any or all of the Trash, Junk, and Encrypted Messages options.

FIGURE 20.2

The General preferences pane in Mail

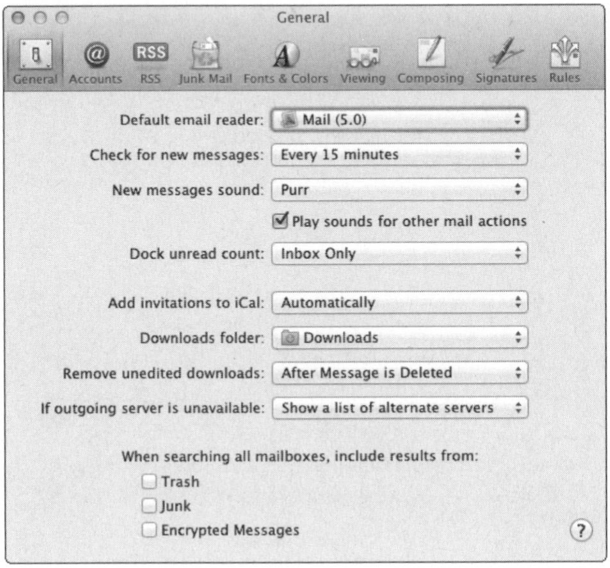

Accounts preferences

In the Accounts pane, shown in Figure 20.3, you can configure your e-mail accounts after you've set them up. At the left is a list of existing accounts; select the one you want to modify. Then go through the three subpanes.

Note

After you make changes in the Accounts pane and close the Preferences dialog box or switch to another pane, Mail asks you to save your changes or cancel them. Changes made to other panes are automatically saved, but not changes to accounts because accidental changes could cause Mail not to access those accounts correctly. ■

The Account Information subpane is where you can modify the basic defaults for the account, such as the e-mail address, the name that appears in messages you send, the Description for this account, the incoming and outgoing mail servers, the username and password for the account (if any), and for IMAP and POP accounts whether the account uses a TLS (Transport Layer Security) certificate. The sidebar "Sending e-mail while traveling" explains how to set up outgoing mail servers.

FIGURE 20.3

The Accounts pane in Mail's Preferences dialog box for an IMAP account. Left: The Mailbox Behaviors subpane. Right: The Advanced subpane.

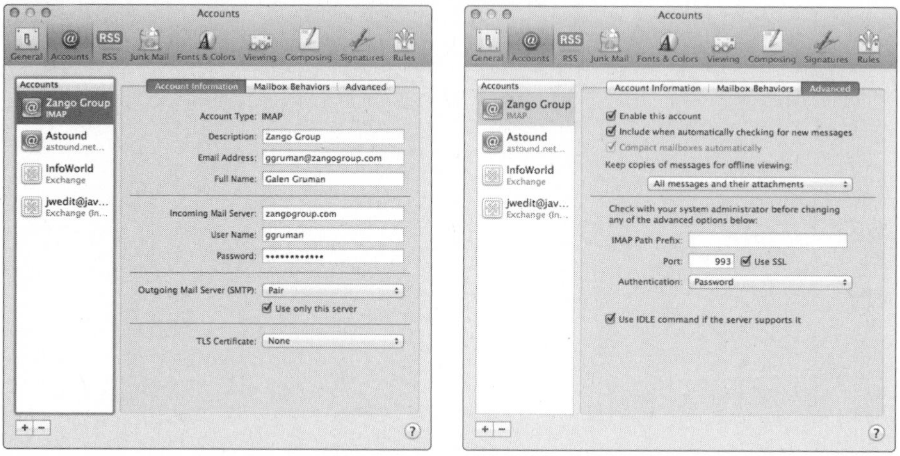

New Feature

The TLS Certificates pop-up menu is new to Mac OS X Lion's Mail application. Use it to choose a Transport Layer Security certificate if required by your web host or ISP; Mac OS X provides a unique TLS certificate for each user account. ∎

The Mailbox Behaviors pane is where you set how mail is retained, as well as how notes are handled, on your Mac. The following settings are available:

- **Drafts:** This option is available only for IMAP and Exchange accounts. Select the Store Draft Messages on the Server option to keep draft messages (those you are composing and have saved but not sent) on the server instead of on your Mac's local folder. But note that IMAP servers sometimes handle this feature unreliably, so messages can be lost because they don't end up being stored on the server as expected.

- **Notes:** Select the Show Notes in Inbox option to have Mail keep track of the notes you've set in services such as Microsoft Exchange.

- **Sent:** In the Delete Sent Messages When pop-up menu, choose when (or if) you want Mail to delete sent messages from your Mac. Your options are Never (the default), One Day Old, One Week Old, One Month Old, and Quitting Mail (immediately after you quit Mail). Deleting messages can save disk space, but it also means you can't find old messages when you want them.

  For IMAP and Exchange accounts, you also get the Store Sent Messages on the Server option; if selected, all e-mails you send are stored on the server and thus are accessible from any computer or mobile device that supports e-mail.

- **Junk:** In the Delete Junk Messages When pop-up menu, choose when (or if) you want Mail to delete sent messages from your Mac. Your options are the same as for Delete Sent Messages. As there's little reason to keep junk mail, the default is One Week Only (so you have a little while to review them in case legitimate mail is inadvertently flagged as junk).

  For IMAP and Exchange accounts, you also get the Store Junk Messages on the Server option; if selected, all e-mails flagged as junk are stored on the server and thus are accessible from any computer or mobile device that supports e-mail .

- **Trash:** If you are working with a POP or IMAP account, select the Move Deleted Messages to the Trash Mailbox if you want to keep deleted messages at least briefly (so you can recover any accidentally deleted ones). If this option is deselected, messages are permanently deleted when you delete them from the inbox.

  For POP and IMAP accounts, if you select the Move Deleted Messages to the Trash Mailbox option, you can choose when they are permanently deleted by using the Permanently Erase Deleted Messages When pop-up menu, which has the same options as the Delete Sent Messages When pop-up menu. (The Permanently Erase Deleted Messages When pop-up menu is available for Exchange accounts as well, even though the Move Deleted Messages to the Trash Mailbox option is not available for them.)

  If you are working with an IMAP or Exchange account, you have the Store Deleted Messages on the Server option, which keeps deleted messages on the server when deleted from your Mac so they are accessible from any computer or mobile device that supports e-mail.

The Advanced pane controls how Mail interacts with your e-mail server:

- **Enable This Account:** Select this option for Mail to connect to the account's server to check for new mail in and send mail from this account. If an account is disabled, it disappears from the list of inboxes, but it is not deleted.

- **Include When Automatically Checking for New Messages:** Select this option for Mail to check for new messages on the schedule you set in the General preferences pane. If deselected, you must manually check for new mail by choosing Mailbox ⇨ Get New Mail and choosing this account from the submenu.

- **Remove Copy from Server After Retrieving a Message:** This option, available for POP accounts only, determines how long messages are retained on the server after you've read them. I recommend you choose After One Week, so if you have multiple computers you check e-mail from, they all get a chance to download the message before it is deleted from the server. Your options in the adjacent pop-up menu are Immediately, After One Day, After One Week, After One Month, and When Moved from Inbox. Click Remove Now to delete all messages stored on your e-mail server, to make space in a server that is running short on storage capacity, for example.

  The When Moved from Inbox menu option can be useful if you have just one Mac you check e-mail from and you create folders in to keep messages sorted; if this option is selected and you move a message, it is deleted from the e-mail server, presumably because you've read it and no longer need to keep a copy. But if you have mail-filtering rules (covered in the "Working with e-mails" section), they typically move mail into specified folders, and that action also deletes the message from the e-mail server even if you haven't actually read it yet.

- **Prompt Me to Skip Messages Over __ KB:** This option, available only for POP accounts, makes Mail ask you whether to download messages (including any attachments) larger than the size you specify here. (Leaving it blank downloads all messages without asking.) That's handy if you are using a slow connection (either at your main location or when traveling).

- **Keep Copies of Messages for Offline Viewing:** This pop-up menu, available for IMAP and Exchange accounts, determines which messages are copied to your local folder so you can read them when not connected to the server. The options are All Messages and Their Attachments (the default), All Messages But Omit Attachments, Only Messages I've Read, and Don't Keep Copies of Any Messages.

- **Compact Mailboxes Automatically:** Available only for IMAP accounts, this option compresses stored e-mails to take less space. It is grayed out for IMAP servers that don't support compacted mailboxes.

- **IMAP Path Prefix:** This field, available only for IMAP accounts, is where you put in a server address as provided by your network administrator to ensure a proper connection to the IMAP server. Leave it blank unless given such an address.

- **Internal Server Path** and **External Server Path:** These fields, available only for Exchange accounts, is where you put in a server address as provided by your network administrator to ensure a proper connection to the Exchange server. Leave these blank unless given such an address. Note that in many cases, you need to fill out just the Internal Server Path. If both are required, the internal path is used by Mail when you are connected to your corporate network and the external path is used when you are connected to the Internet via a different network.

- **Port:** This option should rarely be changed. Mail automatically uses standard ports— addresses at e-mail servers that are used to handle specific requests such as checking e-mail or sending out e-mail. Sometimes, a network administrator uses nonstandard ports to thwart hackers; in that case, enter the correct port number here. Note that for Exchange, there are two port options: Internal Port and External Port.

- **Use SSL:** Select this option to enable SSL authentication for this account. Note that if you select this option for an e-mail server that does not support SSL, you may not be able to connect. Conversely, some servers require that you enable SSL to connect. If SSL is enabled, choose the appropriate authentication method for your server using the Authentication pop-up menu.

- **Authentication:** Use this pop-up menu, available for IMAP accounts only, to choose the authentication method for your IMAP server: Password (the default), MDS Challenge-Response, NTLM, or Kerberos Version 5 (GSSAPI).

- **Use IDLE Command if the Server Supports It:** This option, available for IMAP accounts only, enables what is called *push messaging*. This lets the IMAP server send you new e-mail on its own, rather than wait for you to click the Get Mail button in Mail to retrieve mail or for your scheduled e-mail check interval to occur.

Junk Mail preferences

More than half of all e-mail sent today is junk, unsolicited ads, or scams typically relating to (real or fake) business, drugs, vacations, health insurance, pornography, and more. You can reduce the amount of junk mail that actually makes it into your inbox by selecting the Enable Junk Mail Filtering option in the Junk Mail pane.

If junk mail filtering is enabled, you have the following options, as shown in Figure 20.4:

FIGURE 20.4

The Junk Mail preferences pane in Mail (left) and the settings sheet in which you create your own junk-filtering rules (right)

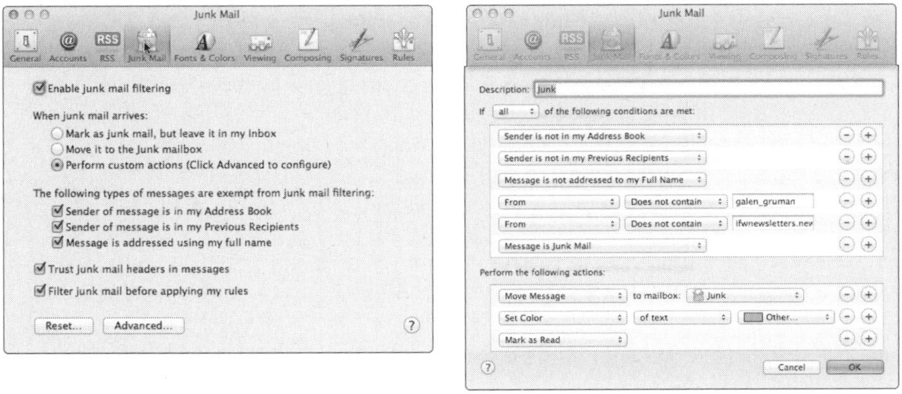

- **When Junk Mail Arrives:** Select how you want Mail to handle mail that it determines to be junk: Mark as Junk Mail but Leave It in My Inbox, Move It to the Junk Mailbox (the default), or Perform Custom Actions (this makes the Advanced button accessible).

- **The Following Types of Messages Are Exempt from Junk Mail Filtering:** Select the kinds of e-mails that are never treated as junk: Sender of Message Is in My Address Book, Sender of Message Is in My Previous Recipients (people you've received e-mail from before and not flagged as junk), and Message Is Addressed Using My Full Name (such e-mail typically comes from a person who has your full name in his or her address book because he or she replied to one of your e-mails, which reduces the chance it's a junk message from a spammer sending to random e-mail addresses).

Tip

To see and edit who's in your Previous Recipients list, choose Window ⇨ Previous Recipients. ■

- **Trust Junk Mail Headers Set by My Internet Service Provider:** Select this option (the default) to treat any messages marked as junk by your ISP or web host as junk. The only reason to deselect this option is if your ISP or web host is so aggressive in flagging messages as junk that many legitimate e-mails are being flagged and thus diverted to the Junk Folder in Mail.

- **Filter Junk Mail Before Applying My Rules:** This option, selected by default, filters out junk mail before applying any message-filtering rules you've set up (see the "Working with e-mails" section in this chapter).

- **Reset:** Click this button to reset the junk mail settings to Mail's recommended defaults.

- **Advanced:** Click this button to specify more rules on how to handle potential junk mail. (For this button to be clickable, you must have selected Perform Custom Actions as the option for When Junk Mail Arrives in this pane.) In the sheet that appears, you set up a series of rules to detect possible junk mail. These rules work just like the message-filtering rules explained in the "Rules preferences" section later in this chapter.

Fonts & Colors preferences

In the Fonts & Colors pane, you can customize the appearance of your mail's text. To change the font and size of messages and other text in Mail, click the Select button that appears to the right of the type of text you want to change: Message List Font (the list of messages for a selected inbox), Message Font (the text within a message itself), Note Font (the font used for text in notes), and Fixed-Width Font (the font used for plain text [unformatted] messages or for HTML [web-formatted] messages that use tags such as `<h1>` and `<code>`). To apply fixed-width font to non-HTML messages, you must select Use Fixed-Width Font for Plain Text Messages option.

New Feature

Mac OS X Lion's version of the Fonts & Colors preferences pane no longer offers the Mailbox Font option to change the appearance of the list of mailboxes in the Sidebar of the Message Viewer. ■

Select the Color Quoted Text option, and choose the desired colors for the three levels of indentation for quoted text in messages. Quoted text is the original message retained in a reply, and the entire thread is available in the message (so you don't have to find the previous messages to remember what was written).

Viewing preferences

The Viewing pane controls how various details are displayed in and for messages:

- **Use Classic Layout:** Select this option to display the Message Viewer in Mail's traditional layout rather than the new layout introduced in Mac OS X Lion.

- **Show To/Cc Label in the Message List:** Select this option to show the To, Cc, and Bcc indicators with the message titles in the message list. (Users of iOS devices such as the iPad, iPhone, and iPod Touch will recognize this new setting.) This option is not available if Use Classic Layout is enabled.

- **Show Contact Photos in the Message List:** Select this option to show a photo of mail senders in the message list. If you have a person's photo in your Address Book (see Chapter 21), the photo appears to the left of the message summary; otherwise, a placeholder graphic appears. This option is not available if Use Classic Layout is enabled.

- **List Preview:** This pop-up menu lets you set how many lines from a message body are shown in the message list's excerpt of each mail message. The options are None, 1 Line, 2 Lines, 3 Lines, 4 Lines, and 5 Lines. (Users of iOS devices will recognize this new setting.) This option is not available if Use Classic Layout is enabled.

New Feature

The Mail application in Mac OS X Lion changes the default view for mail messages, arranging the message preview as a window on the right side of Mail's Message Viewer rather than below the message list. The new Message Viewer layout allows for longer message lists and larger preview window sizes, as you can see from Figure 20.7 later in this chapter. But you can return to the old display by selecting the new Use Classic Layout option in the Viewing preferences pane. Also new are the Show To/Cc Label in the Message List option, the Show Contact Photos in the Message List option, the List Preview pop-up menu, and the set of options in the Viewing Conversations section. ■

- **Show Header Detail:** This pop-up menu enables you to determine what header appears in your e-mail messages received. The default option is Default, which shows the From, Subject, Date, To, Cc, and attachments information for each message. The None option hides all header information. Choose Custom to select which information you want to display in mail headers by selecting options from a list. The All option shows all the detail, including the servers through which the message passed on its way to you. (This can help show a spam message that uses a forged From address.)

- **Show Online Buddy Status:** This option, which is selected by default, adds the Buddy Availability column (labeled with the quote-balloon icon) to your message lists and, if a buddy who sent you an e-mail is online, an icon appears in the Buddy Availability column next to any e-mail from that buddy. A buddy is someone you have added in iChat (covered later in this chapter) *and* for whom you have entered instant messaging (chat) information in Address Book (covered in Chapter 21).

- **Display Unread Messages with Bold Font:** This option, which is selected by default, boldfaces any message in an inbox's message list so you know you haven't read it yet.

- **Display Remote Images in HTML Messages:** This option, which is selected by default, displays any images linked from within the e-mail message. To see the images, you need a live Internet connection.

- **Use Smart Addresses:** This option, which is selected by default, shows only the sender's name in a message's To, From, Cc, or Bcc field if the message contains the name or your Address Book does. (If the name is unknown, the e-mail address appears instead.) If this option is deselected, the message displays both the sender's name (if known) and the e-mail address in these fields. If you're concerned about ensuring that e-mails really come from the people the names indicate, deselect this option.

- **Highlight Messages with Color When Not Grouped:** This option, which is not selected by default, highlights any message related to the currently selected one in an inbox's message list with a colored background—if Organize by Conversation is deselected in the View menu. (Click the color swatch to change that highlight color.) Mail looks at the recipients and message headers to determine related messages, so the accuracy of the results can vary.

- **Include Related Messages:** This option ensures that messages in other mailboxes are displayed in a conversation, not just those in the current mailbox. (In Mail parlance, a mailbox is a folder.)

- **Mark All Messages as Read When Opening a Conversation:** This option marks all messages in a conversation (a message thread) as read if you read the primary message (the one displayed in your message list).

- **Show Most Recent Message at the Top:** This option puts the newest message in a conversation at the top of the conversation's set of messages, rather than at the end.

New Feature

Mail in Mac OS X Lion uses an enhanced version of message threading called conversations; the Viewing preferences add the Mark all Message as Read When Opening a Conversation option and the Show Most Recent Message at Top option as part of the enhanced capabilities. ■

Composing preferences

The Composing pane controls how new and reply messages are formatted, addressed, and routed.

In the Composing section, you have three options:

- **Message Format:** Choose either Rich Text (the default) or Plain Text. The Rich Text option formats the e-mail in the web's HTML format, so formatting such as boldface, indentation, and fonts are transmitted with the text so the recipient sees the same formatting on his or her end (if his or her e-mail application supports such formatting, of course, which most today do). The Plain Text option removes all formatting.

- **Check Spelling:** Your choices are As I Type, When I Send, and Never. If you choose As I Type, Mail indicates possible misspellings by using dotted red underlines; if you choose When I Send, it alerts you to any misspellings and gives you a chance to correct them before sending the message.

- **Automatically _ Myself:** If you select this option, Mail will either Cc (carbon copy) or Bcc (blind carbon copy) you on all messages you send, depending which option you pick in the pop-up menu. Note that recipients won't see any addresses that you Bcc'd on the message in the message header. They do see anyone you Cc'd the message to.

In the Addressing section, you have five options:

- **Automatically Complete Addresses:** If selected, this option tells Mail to look up potential addressees as you type their names in the To, Cc, or Bcc fields in a new or reply message. As you type, it looks for names that contain the characters typed so far in your Address Book, in e-mails you've previously sent or received, and in your LDAP (Lightweight Directory Access Protocol) directory, if you use one. (LDAP is used by some business networks to store employee information such as for a shared company address book. To use LDAP, you must first click the Configure LDAP button and then add each LDAP server you want to check addresses against in the sheet that appears. Click the + icon button to add an LDAP server, and enter the LDAP settings for it in the Server Info dialog box; you need to get those settings from your network administrator. You can have multiple LDAP servers configured to check against.)

- **When Sending to a Group, Show All Member Addresses:** Mail can access groups set up in Address Book, as explained in the "Working with Address Book" section later in this chapter. If this option is selected, when you send a message to a group, each group member's name or address appears in the message's To, Cc, and Bcc fields.

- **Mark Addresses Not Ending With:** This option makes all addressees appear in red unless their e-mail addresses end with the domains specified in the adjacent field. For example, if you enter @apple.com in the field, any addresses in new and reply messages' From, To, Cc, and Bcc fields that don't end in @apple.com are red, while the apple.com addressees are black. To enter multiple domains, separate them with commas, such as @apple.com, @infoworld.com. You use this feature to quickly tell when you are sending e-mails to people outside your organization, for example.

- **Send New Messages From:** This pop-up menu enables you to choose the "from" account for e-mails you send. The default is Account of Selected Mailbox, which means that if you have multiple e-mail boxes, the current one is where messages are sent from (so you end up replying from the same account where you received a message, for example). You also can choose any account set up in Mail, so all messages come from that one e-mail address, no matter which account they were sent to.

- **Create Notes In:** This pop-up menu enables you to define where notes are stored in Mail. The default option is Account of Selected Mailbox, which adds any notes to the current mailbox (if it supports these items; typically Exchange, iCloud, and IMAP accounts do). You also can choose a specific account that supports such items or On My Mac, which stores them in iCal.

The Responding section controls the formatting of reply messages (including those forwarded to others):

- **Use the Same Message Format as the Original Message:** If selected, the reply is in HTML (rich text) if the original message was in that format and in plain text if the original message was in that format. If this option is deselected (the default), the reply is in whatever format you choose in the Message Format pop-up menu.

- **Quote the Text of the Original Message:** This option, which is selected by default, includes the original message in your reply.

- **Increase Quote Level:** This option, which is selected by default, makes the current reply the top level of the quote, meaning the text being replied to is indented one level in from the reply. Each previous reply in the message is indented a further level, with greater indentation for the older portions of the reply to help keep the history of the replies clear. (The original message is thus indented the most.)

- **When Quoting Text in Replies or Forwards:** You have two options: Include All of the Original Message Text and Include Selected Text If Any; Otherwise Include All Text. If you select the latter option and select a portion of the original message when replying, only that selection is included in the reply.

Signatures preferences

In the Signatures pane, shown in Figure 20.5, you can automatically add a signature to the messages you send. This signature typically contains your name and business-card-style information such as your company, address, phone number, and so on. It might also include a saying or other personalized text.

The Signatures pane in Mail's Preferences dialog box

You can have multiple signatures and apply one or more to each mail account you have, though it's typical to have one signature per account.

To start, click the + icon button. A new signature appears in the middle column of the Signatures pane, named Signature #1. (The next new one is named Signature #2 and so on.) Double-click the name to change it. Enter the signature text in the field to the right. You can format text by selecting it and choosing the desired formatting options from the Format menu. Options include fonts, colors, indentation, and alignment. If you select the Always Match My Default Message Font option, your signature ignores any font and size applied here, though the rest of the formatting is retained.

Tip

You can also copy a formatted signature from an e-mail into the signature field; just be sure the Always Match My Default Message Font option is deselected. This is a handy way to use a corporate standard for signature formatting: A company can send all employees a message with the formatted signature and ask them to copy it into their e-mail application and then modify its text. ■

After you've created your signatures, you associate them to e-mail accounts. Select All Signatures in the list at the left of the pane to see all defined signatures in the middle column. Drag each signature onto the account that you want to use that signature, and release the mouse button. (You can associate multiple signatures to one account.)

The next step is to enable the signatures for each account. Select an account; the signatures associated to it display in the middle column. The Choose Signature pop-up menu at the bottom of the Signatures pane also becomes active. By Default, it is set to None, which means no signature is used. Choose the desired signature from the pop-up menu, or choose At Random or In Sequential Order to have Mail choose the signature for you. (If only one signature exists for an account, all options but None use that sole signature.)

Tip

Normally, a signature appears at the very bottom of the message. But if you select the Place Signature Above Quoted Text option, when you reply to or forward a message, the signature appears before any quoted text from the original message. (This assumes you selected the Quote the Text of the Original Message option in the Composing pane.) ■

To delete a signature associated to an account, select that account; only the signatures for that account appear in the middle column. Select the signature to delete, and click the – icon button.

To edit a signature, select it in any account that uses it or from the All Signatures "account," and modify it in the field to the right; all instances of it are updated.

Rules preferences

Mail lets you set up filtering rules that it applies to new messages as it loads them. (You also can apply these rules to existing messages). The typical reason to set up rules is to manage large volumes of e-mail. If you set up folders within your inboxes, such as for individual projects at work, you can set up rules that automatically move messages to specific folders based on their subject or who they came from. Other controls include deleting messages and marking them as read.

Figure 20.6 shows the Rules pane. Any existing rules are listed, and any rules with Active options selected are applied to incoming messages automatically. To delete a rule, select it from the list and click Delete. To duplicate a rule, select it from the list and click Duplicate. To edit a rule, select it from the list and click Edit. To add a rule, click Add Rule.

FIGURE 20.6

Left: The Rules pane. Right: The settings sheet that appears to create and edit rules in.

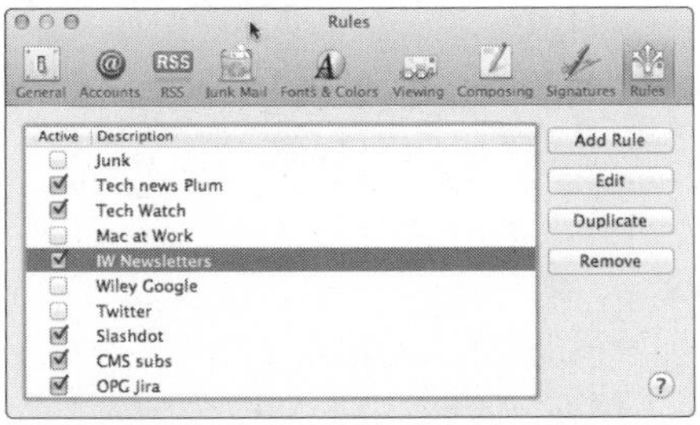

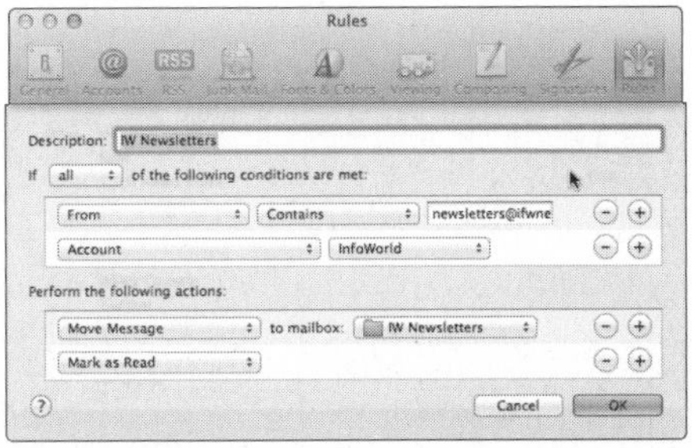

Tip

Drag rules within the list to change the order in which they execute. The topmost rule runs first, followed by the second rule, and so on. ∎

When adding or editing a rule, a settings sheet appears that lets you select the criteria to filter messages with (what Mail calls *conditions*) and the actions you want to apply to those that match the criteria. As Figure 20.6 shows, you can have multiple criteria per rule, as well as multiple actions.

Note

If you do use multiple criteria, be sure to choose either Any or All from the If __ of the Following Conditions Are Met pop-up menu. If you choose Any, only one of the criteria needs to match for the rule to be applied; if you choose All, every one of the criteria you set must match for the rule to be applied. ∎

The first step is to give the Rule a name, which you do in the Description field. Then set up the criteria. Choose the criteria from the rightmost pop-up menu. There are 26 criteria to choose from, such as To, Subject, Date Sent, Sender Is Not in My Address Book, Message Content, and Priority Is High.

If there are options for the selected criterion, choose it from the adjacent pop-up menu that appears. If a criterion is based on text, such as matching part of a sender's name, enter that text in the adjacent field. For each criterion, these adjacent pop-up menus and text fields appear only if needed. For example, if you choose Date Sent, a pop-up menu appears with two options: Is Less Than and Is Greater Than. Choose the appropriate option, and enter a number in the Days Old field that appears. If you choose Is Less Than and enter **10**, the rule finds all messages that were received in the last 10 days.

With the criteria set, you can set the actions to be applied to messages that meet your criteria. There are 13 such actions, including Move Message, Delete, Forward Message, Mark as Read, and Run AppleScript.

Click the + icon button to add a criterion. Select a criterion, and click the – icon button to delete it. If the selected action has additional options, a pop-up menu with them appears next to the action. One action merits special attention: Stop Evaluating Rules. If you choose this action, any rules in the Rules pane that come after this rule do *not* execute.

Click OK to save the rule, or click Cancel to not save it.

Managing E-Mail Accounts and Mailboxes

With your e-mail accounts set up, you're ready to send and receive e-mail messages. But first take a few more minutes to understand how to manage your e-mail accounts and the mailboxes that contain the messages so you don't get overwhelmed with the huge number of messages that are sure to collect in Mail. If you have multiple e-mail accounts set up in Mail, knowing how to manage those accounts is even more crucial to keep everything straight.

Some management controls reside in the Mail Preferences dialog box, those over which accounts are active (the Accounts pane), what accounts messages are sent from by default (the Composing pane), which signature is associated to each account (the Signatures pane), and how messages are filtered (the Rules pane). Refer to the details on those sections in the "Setting Mail's preferences" section in this chapter.

The rest of the account management, as well as your mailbox management, happens in the Message Viewer, which Figures 20.7 and 20.8 show. Figure 20.7 shows the new layout introduced in Mac OS X Lion, and Figure 20.8 shows the "classic" view used in previous versions and still available in Mac OS X Lion, as described earlier in this chapter. In the Sidebar is a list of the active e-mail accounts, with the status of each indicated through a series of icons.

New Feature

The version of Mail included with Mac OS X Lion changes the arrangement of icon buttons in the toolbar. It adds the Flag and Hide/Show Related Messages icon buttons, and removes the To Do icon button. The to-do capability has been dropped from Mail, and the Hide/Show Related Messages icon button is the new name for the former Threads icon button. (Right-click or Control+click the toolbar and choose Customize Toolbar from the contextual menu to add or remove icon buttons from the Mail toolbar.) ■

Note

Apple's Mail uses the terms account and mailbox. Technically, a mailbox is a folder for messages, RSS feeds, and notes. An account is a set of connection settings for an e-mail address and the messages associated to that address. Mail uses the term mailbox to refer to the message, RSS, and notes folders stored locally on your Mac, as well as the messages associated to an account. So deleting an account's mailbox does not delete its account—you have to do that in the Accounts pane of the Preferences dialog box (as explained in the "Accounts preferences" section of this chapter). ■

Understanding mailbox folders

All e-mail accounts appear as folders within the Inbox. The Inbox contains the mailboxes for all e-mail accounts that are active, meaning they connect to the e-mail server to receive and send messages. As I explain later in this section, you can create additional mailboxes that are stored locally on your Mac, not connected to an e-mail server; these appear in the On My Mac list instead.

Tip

The Sidebar in Mail is reorderable, so you can arrange your accounts and inboxes in whatever order you prefer by dragging them to the desired locations. ■

If the account mailboxes have folders, you see a disclosure triangle to the left of the mailbox name; click it to expand the folder list (as you can see was done for the InfoWorld list in Figures 20.7 and 20.8).

An oval to the right of the account mailbox shows the number of unread messages in that account or folder. Note that draft messages—those you haven't sent yet—are considered new messages.

FIGURE 20.7

The new Message Viewer window in Mac OS X Lion shows that each active account's mail is stored in a mailbox folder within the Inbox list in the Sidebar. The center column holds the message list for the current mail account or selected folder. The column on the right shows the selected message.

New message indicator

Sidebar (Mailbox List)

Unread message indicator

Show/Hide Mailbox List

Favorites bar   Message List   Enter Full Screen

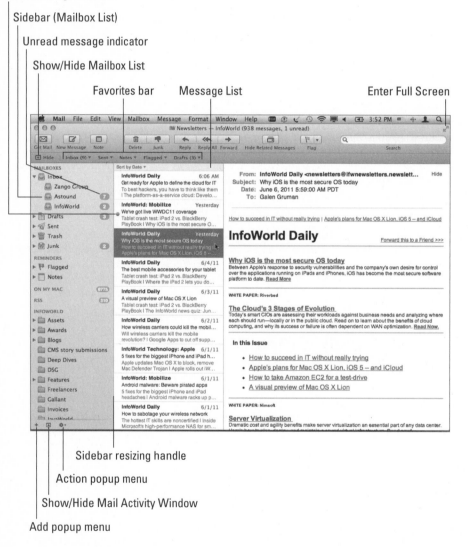

Sidebar resizing handle

Action popup menu

Show/Hide Mail Activity Window

Add popup menu

FIGURE 20.8

The classic Message Viewer window remains available in Mac OS X Lion. The message list appears at the upper right of the Message Viewer and the message preview appears at the lower right.

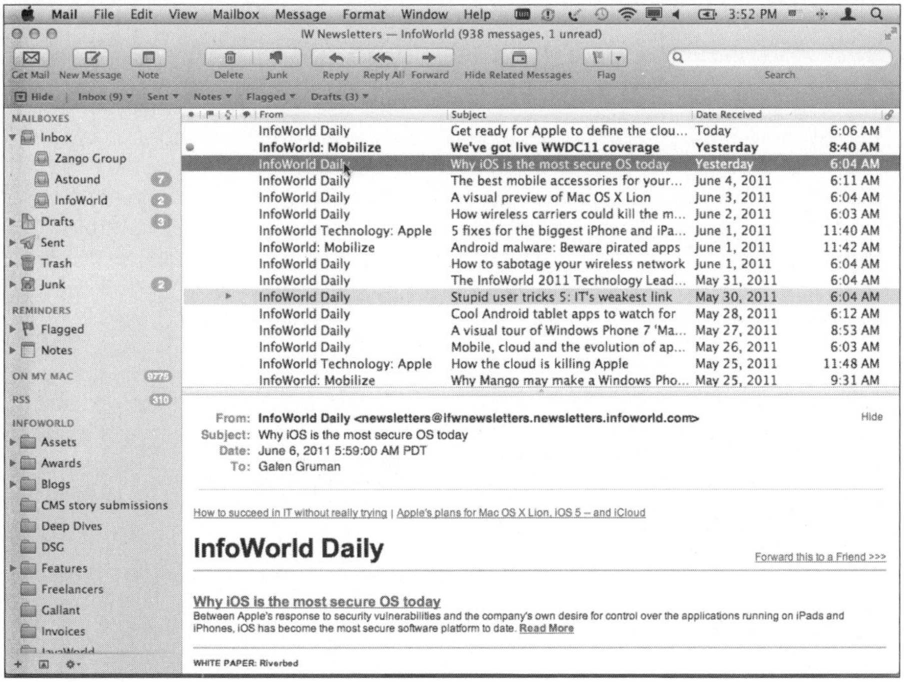

The Mailboxes list includes several standard folders in addition to the Inbox: Drafts, Sent, Trash, and Junk. These four folders contain e-mails from all your accounts. You can switch to these folders by choosing Mailbox⇨Go To and then choosing the desired folder from the submenu.

The Inbox, Draft, Sent, Trash, and Junk folders also collect all mail from all accounts. This means you have one place to see your new messages (the Inbox folder), draft (unsent) messages, junk mail (to see if any legitimate mail got put there), sent messages, and deleted messages (in the Trash folder). If you want to view these folders' messages for a specific account, expand the folder by clicking its disclosure triangle and then choose the specific account whose messages you want to see.

You also can access Inbox, Sent, and Draft folders using the Favorites bar below the toolbar, as well as access notes and flagged messages; Figure 20.7 shows the Favorites bar and its five pop-up menus. Note that the Inbox pop-up menu indicates the number of unread messages in parentheses after its name, as the figure shows.

New Feature

The Favorites bar is new to Mail in Mac OS X. In addition to the default folders placed in it, you can drag any mailbox folders from the Sidebar into it to get quick access to frequently used folders. Drag a folder out to remove it from the Favorites bar. ■

Turning accounts on and off

In the accounts list, a badge containing the ~ character indicates the account is offline, meaning that Mail is not checking messages for it. You might take an account offline when you know the server is down or you are not connected to the Internet (such as when working on an airplane) so you don't get connection error messages. To take an account offline, right-click or Control+click its name in the Inbox list, and choose Take "*accountname*" Offline in the contextual menu. To bring it back online (so it sends and receives messages), right-click or Control+click its name and choose Take "*accountname*" Online.

Tip

To quickly put accounts online or offline, choose Mailbox ⇨ Take All Accounts Online or Mailbox ⇨ Take All Accounts Offline. You also can take any individual account offline or online by choosing Mailbox ⇨ Online Status and choosing the desired account from the submenu. The submenus are toggles, so if an account is currently offline, the menu displays Take "accountname" Online; if an account is currently online, the menu displays Take "accountname" Offline. ■

Note that taking an account online, or offline, is not the same as enabling, or disabling, an account in the Advanced subpane of the Accounts pane in Mail's Preferences dialog box (see the "Accounts preferences" section earlier in this chapter). If an account is enabled, it displays in the Mailboxes list; if it is disabled, it does not.

You also can delete accounts. Select the account in the Inbox, and either choose Mailbox ⇨ Delete Mailbox or right-click or Control+click the account and choose Delete Mailbox from the contextual menu. This deletes the account and all its associated messages from Mail.

Using smart mailboxes

Chances are good that you get lots of e-mails, and you have various folders set up to store messages related to a specific project or task—maybe your volunteer work at the PTA, your vacation planning, or a project at the office. You can use rules (see the "Rules preferences" section earlier in this chapter) to have Mail automatically put mail that matches specific criteria into folders. This lets you put all e-mails with subjects that match keywords related to the project plus all mail from specific people, for example, in one folder. Using rules is a great way to sort your mail for projects.

But there's another way: *smart mailboxes*. A smart mailbox is essentially a special kind of rule. What makes it special? Two things:

- All the messages that match the criteria are put in a folder placed in the mailbox list in the Message Viewer's Sidebar. A new category named Smart Mailboxes then appears in the Sidebar, listing any smart mailboxes you set up.

- A smart mailbox does not remove the messages from their accounts or folders in those accounts. A smart folder is really a view that brings all those messages together no matter where they are stored in Mail. (It's like a playlist in iTunes.) This means that you can use both smart mailboxes and rules, and when you delete a smart mailbox, you don't affect the messages in their account and folders.

To create a smart mailbox, choose Mailbox ⇨ New Smart Mailbox. You get a settings sheet such as the one shown in Figure 20.9. It works very much like the preferences pane you use to create rules (refer to Figure 20.6). You choose a criterion from the pop-up menu, adding any parameters appropriate for that criterion. Click the + icon button to add additional criteria. Also select whether you want the smart mailbox to apply All or Any criteria by using the second pop-up menu in the Contains _ That Match _ of the Following Conditions. But a few controls for smart mailboxes differ from those for creating rules:

- In the first pop-up menu in Contains _ That Match _ of the Following Conditions, you can make the smart mailbox contain either—but not both—e-mail messages or notes.
- To determine whether the smart mailbox contains messages sent to the Trash or Sent folders, you select the Include Messages from Trash and Include Messages from Sent options.

Click OK to save the smart mailbox, which appears in the Message Viewer's Sidebar.

FIGURE 20.9

Setting the criteria for a smart mailbox

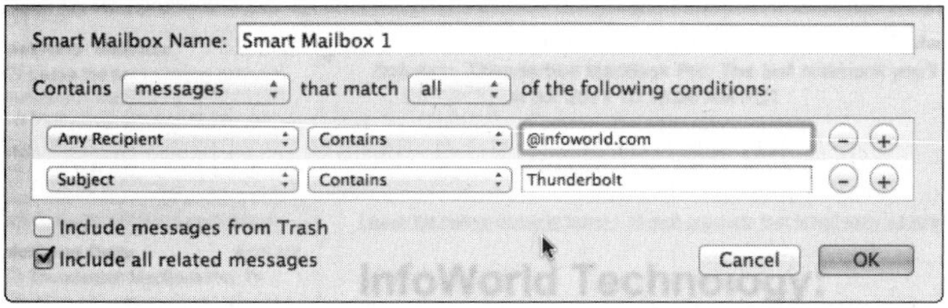

You can edit a smart mailbox by right-clicking or Control+clicking it in the accounts list and choosing Edit Smart Mailbox in the contextual menu; or select the smart mailbox and choose Mailbox ⇨ Edit Smart Mailbox. You can duplicate a smart mailbox (to use it as a template for a new one) by right-clicking or Control+clicking it in the accounts list and choosing Duplicate Smart Mailbox in the contextual menu; or select the smart mailbox and choose Mailbox ⇨ Duplicate Smart Mailbox. You can delete a smart mailbox by choosing Delete Mailbox through either means. (Deleting a smart mailbox does *not* delete the messages or notes items from Mail.)

A related feature is the smart mailbox folder, which you create by choosing Mailbox ⇨ New Smart Mailbox Folder. Give it a name, and click OK. The folder appears under Smart Mailboxes in the left column of the Message Viewer. A smart mailbox folder is just a folder that you can use to contain smart mailboxes (simply drag them into it). For example, if you are a PTA volunteer who works on several committees, you might create a smart mailbox folder called PTA and then have separate smart mailboxes you store in that folder for each committee so you can keep the e-mails or notes items separate for each committee.

Maintaining mailboxes

Mail provides several additional controls that perform maintenance work on your accounts and mailboxes. Unless otherwise indicated, you can access these controls from the Mailbox menu, by right-clicking or Control+clicking an account or mailbox and choosing from the contextual menu, or by clicking the Action icon pop-up menu (the gear icon) at the bottom of the Sidebar. Here's what to do with these controls:

- **You can force Mail to look for new mail by choosing Mailbox ⇨ Get All New Mail, pressing Shift+⌘+N, or clicking Get Mail in the toolbar.** Or get new mail for a specific account by choosing Mailbox ⇨ Get New Mail and then choosing the desired account from the submenu. Note that this command is *not* available via the Action icon pop-up menu or via a contextual menu.

- **If you use Microsoft Exchange or an IMAP server as your e-mail server, you can synchronize what's on your Mac with what's on the server by choosing Synchronize "*accountname*".** (Only Exchange and IMAP accounts display in the menu.) Exchange and IMAP servers synchronize with Mail periodically on their own, so you would choose this option only when you want to synchronize outside of that regular schedule.

- **Choose Erase Deleted Items to force Mail to permanently delete messages from the Trash folder before the time set in the Mailbox Behaviors subpane of the Accounts pane in Mail's Preferences dialog box (see the "Accounts preferences" section earlier in this chapter)—or if you set Mail to not automatically delete messages from the Trash folder at regular intervals**. If you choose this option from the Mailbox menu, you can choose in a submenu to delete all messages in the Trash folder or just those associated to a specific account. If you choose this option through the contextual menu, you delete messages for that account only.

- **Choose Erase Junk Mail to force Mail to permanently delete messages in the Junk folder before the time set in the Mailbox Behaviors subpane of the Accounts pane in Mail's Preferences dialog box—or if you set Mail to not automatically delete messages from the Junk folder at regular intervals**. If you choose this option from the Mailbox menu or press Option+⌘+J, you can choose in a submenu to delete all messages in the Junk folder or just those associated to a specific account. If you choose this option through the contextual menu, you delete messages for that account only.

- **Choose Export Mailbox to save all messages onto your Mac or an attached local or network volume.** This way you can delete the messages from your server and/or your Mac's Mail folders to save on storage space while still having the messages available in an archive should you need to access them later.

New Feature

The Export Mailbox option had been named Archive Mailbox in previous versions of Mac OS X. ∎

- **Choose Edit "*accountname*" to open the Accounts pane of Mail's Preferences dialog box (see the "Accounts preferences" section earlier in this chapter).**

- **Choose Rename Mailbox to change the name of a mailbox.** Note that you cannot change the names of account mailboxes, just local mailboxes (those listed in the On My Mac section of the left column in the Message Viewer) and folders within account mailboxes.

- **Choose Use This Mailbox For (available only from the Mailbox menu) to have Mail use a local folder you created (in the On My Mac section) for Drafts, Sent, Trash, or Junk, as chosen in the submenu, instead of the default folders.**

- **Choose Rebuild (available only from the Mailbox menu) to clean up the mailbox folder stored on your Mac.** Doing so can make the mailbox respond more quickly, for example, when you select messages. But note that if you change the default folders for Junk, Sent, and so on for an Exchange account, those changes are lost and the default folders are used instead.

- **From the contextual menu for an account mailbox, choose Get Account Info to see the server status for the account, as Figure 20.10 shows.** You can switch to another account using the pop-up menu in the Account Info dialog box. The dialog box's display depends on the type of account. The Account Info dialog box has several panes:

  - **Quota Limits:** Available for IMAP and Exchange accounts only, this pane shows what is stored on the server and whether it exceeds the storage limits set by your e-mail administrator.

  - **Messages on Server:** Available for POP accounts only, this pane displays all messages stored on the e-mail server and enables you to delete selected messages from the server. Using the Show Messages pop-up menu, you can view all messages on the POP server, those that have been downloaded to your Mac, and those that have been removed from your Mac but are still on the server.

  - **Out of Office:** Available for Exchange accounts only, this pane lets you have Exchange send automatic replies during the period you specify along with a message you specify. You also can use it to see your current Out of Office settings.

  - **Mailbox Behaviors:** This pane provides access to the Mailbox Behaviors sub-pane in the Accounts pane of the Preferences dialog box.

  - **Subscription List:** Available for Exchange accounts only, this pane shows all RSS and newsgroup feeds subscribed to from the Exchange server and enables you to manage those subscriptions.

  - **Summary:** This pane provides a summary of your account settings.

The Account Info dialog box for an e-mail account, showing the Quota Limits pane

Monitoring mail activity

Mail provides several ways to monitor activity in the application.

If a badge containing a warning icon (the ! character inside a triangle) appears to the right of an account in the Sidebar, Mail is having a problem with that account. Clicking the icon may provide some details as to the issue.

If a badge containing the ~ character appears to the right of an account in the Sidebar, that indicates the account—and very likely your Mac—is offline.

When Mail is checking for new e-mail, a spinning dashed, curved line appears to the right of the account that is being checked in the Sidebar.

If open, the Mail Activity window at the bottom of the Sidebar (refer to Figure 20.7) displays information about current Mail activity, such as a download occurring. You also can open a separate Activity window by choosing Window ⇨ Activity or pressing Option+⌘+0 (zero).

Working with E-Mails

Most of the time you're in Mail, you're working with individual e-mail messages, reading them, responding to them, or writing new ones. Figures 20.7 and 20.8, shown earlier in this chapter, display the Message Viewer, where you can see your mail accounts, mailboxes (mail folders), message list, and individual mail messages.

Reading messages

By default, Mail lists messages in the order they are received, with the most recent message at the bottom, and all unread messages listed in boldface. As noted in the previous section, you can switch among mail accounts and mailbox folders using the Sidebar, to narrow down the messages shown in the message list.

In the new Message Viewer layout, you can change how items in the message list are sorted using the pop-up menu at the top of the message list. Options are Attachments, Buddy Availability, Color, Date Received, Date Sent, Flags, From, Mailbox, Message Status (which puts unread messages together), Number (number of recipients), Size, Subject, and To. By default, messages are shown in reverse-chronological order (newest at top), but you can change that by choosing Ascending Order.

In the classic layout view, you can change the sort order by clicking any of the columns in the message list, such as by sender or subject. When you click a column to sort it, a triangle appears to the left of the column name. If it points down, the column is sorted in reverse alphabetical order (Z to A) or in reverse chronological order (newest first); if it points up, the column is sorted in alphabetical order (A to Z) or in chronological order (oldest first). Note that for the Subject column, Mail ignores the Re: and Fwd: prefixes in subjects that indicate replies and forwarded messages, so all messages with the same subject are kept together (as opposed to having all replies and forwards grouped together regardless of subject).

Also in classic view, you can change the columns displayed by right-clicking or Control+ clicking the column row and selecting the desired columns (and deselecting the undesired ones) from the contextual menu. The Sort By menu option has the same effect as clicking a column to sort it. Or you can choose View ➪ Columns or View ➪ Sort By to change the displayed columns and the default sort order.

In either view, you can search your messages by entering a term in the toolbar's Search field and pressing Return or by clicking the Search icon button (the magnifying glass icon). When you search in Mail, two buttons appear at the top of the message list: All Mailboxes and one showing the current mailbox; click either button to expand the search to all mail or to narrow it to the one mailbox, respectively. You can save the search as a smart mailbox by clicking Save.

New Feature
When you use the toolbar's Search field, Mail 5.1 opens a results sheet that lists likely matches based on its index of your e-mails and contacts, organized by category such as recipient and subject. ∎

Tip
You can open multiple Message Viewer windows by choosing File ➪ New Viewer Window or pressing Option+⌘+N. You might do this so you can switch quickly between different mailboxes. ∎

Tip
To add a message's sender to your Mac's Address Book, choose Message ➪ Add Sender to Address Book or press Shift+⌘+Y. You also can right-click or Control+click a sender's name in the message's From field and choose Add to Address Book. ∎

When you click a message in the message list, you see part of the message in the preview pane below the message list. If you double-click the message, a separate window opens, as shown in Figure 20.11. It displays the sender, subject, send date, recipients, and any attachments included, as well as the actual message text.

You can open messages in their own windows, as shown at the bottom of the screen.

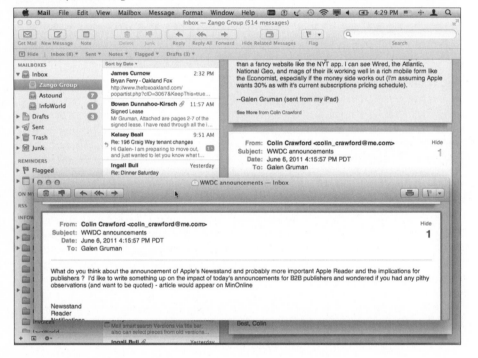

In the message window's toolbar, you can delete the message by clicking Delete, mark it as junk by clicking Junk, print it by clicking Print, or send it to someone else by clicking Reply, Reply All, or Forward (as explained in the "Replying, forwarding, and redirecting messages" section later in this chapter).

Mail provides special controls for file attachments in messages you read, as Figure 20.12 shows. In the message list, a paperclip icon appears to the right of the message title to indicate there is at least one attachment. (In classic layout view, the icon appears in its own column, which you turn on by right-clicking or Control+clicking the column headers and choosing Attachments.)

In the message preview or message window:

- **At the bottom of the message header, Mail shows how many files are attached.**

- **Click the adjacent Save button to save the attachments to your Mac.** If you click and hold the mouse or touchpad button, the Save button acts as a pop-up menu, letting you choose a specific attachment to save.

- **Click Quick Look to see the attachments in a Quick Look window.** If there are multiple attachments, the first attachment is previewed. Hold Option to change the Quick Look button to Slideshow, which then previews the attachments in a single Quick Look window that displays each attachment in turn.

- **At the bottom of the message appear the icons for any file attachments.** You can double-click an icon to open it. For example, double-clicking a calendar invitation (an `.ics` file) adds it to iCal, while double-clicking a PowerPoint file opens it in either Microsoft PowerPoint or Apple Keynote, based on what is set as your default application for this file type. You can right-click or Control+click the icon to open, save, or perform other actions on the attachment. Those other actions depend on the file type; for a calendar invitation, you get the option to add it to iCal, while for image files, you get an option to add them to iPhoto.

FIGURE 20.12

Mail indicates attachments in the message list using a paperclip icon, and may provide controls over attachments in the bottom of message's header, such as the Quick Look for the calendar invitation shown here, depending on the specific attachment.

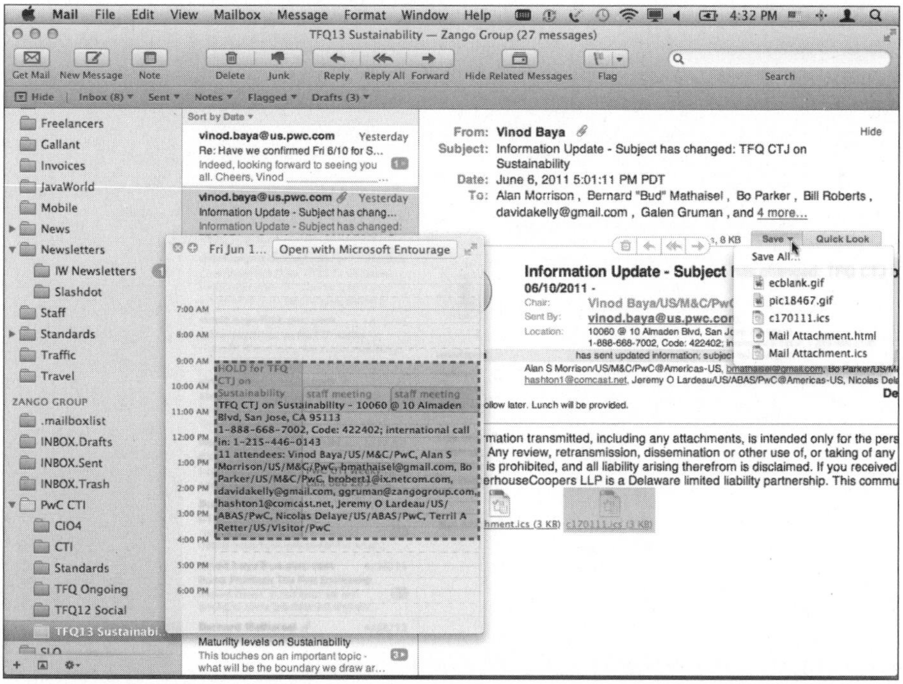

New Feature

Mac OS X Lion's Mail application no longer provides a disclosure triangle for attachments in the message header to let you preview the attachments' icons. Instead, use Quick Look to preview the attachments, use the Save pop-up menu to save them, or go to the bottom of the message to see the attachments' icons. ■

Using a technology called *data detectors*, Mail scans your messages for dates (including relative dates such as "tomorrow"), times, names, phone numbers, and other contact information. If you hover the pointer over such information, it is highlighted as a pop-up menu. Click the pop-up menu to get relevant options, such as Create New Contact, Add to Existing Contact, Create New iCal Event, or Look up Date in iCal. Mail can automatically identify flight numbers and provide a pop-up menu over the flight number to take you directly to the Dashboard's Flight Tracker widget (see Chapter 14) to get current flight information.

New Feature

Mac OS X Lion's Mail application lets you flag messages by assigning one of seven colored flags to them. You decide what those colors mean to you; they simply act as visual labels. You can quickly apply a red flag to a message by pressing Shift+⌘+L. Flagging a message helps you find it later in your message list, plus you can quickly see all flagged messages by clicking the Flagged button below the toolbar (or choosing a specific mailbox from its pop-up menu). To remove a flag from a message, click the Unflag button in the toolbar (it displays only if you have selected a flagged message), or choose Message ➪ Flag ➪ Clear Flag. ■

Mac OS X Lion's Message View by default shows messages as conversations (also called *message threads*), so the set of related messages shows up just once in the message list. When you click the message, all the related messages appear in the message preview window in reverse chronological order (oldest first), so you have the entire conversation available in one place. Figure 20.13 shows an example.

Note the badge to the right of the message summary in the message list for the highlighted message; it shows 7, indicating there are seven messages in that conversation. You can see a list of all the subject lines in a conversation by clicking the disclosure triangle within the badge, as Figure 20.13 shows.

In the message window, each message has a number in the upper-right corner indicating its position in the conversation sequence so you know where you are in the conversation. For longer messages, Mail shows only the beginning of the message in the conversations view; click the See More from *sendername* link at the bottom of the message excerpt to see the rest of that message.

To hide specific messages in a conversation, click Hide at the upper right of the message; click Show to make it visible again.

To turn conversation view off, choose View ➪ Organize by Conversation. Choose it again to enable conversation view again.

FIGURE 20.13

Mail indicates message conversations in the message list displaying the number of related messages to the right of the message summary. In the message window, you can scroll through all the related messages, hiding and showing individual messages if you want.

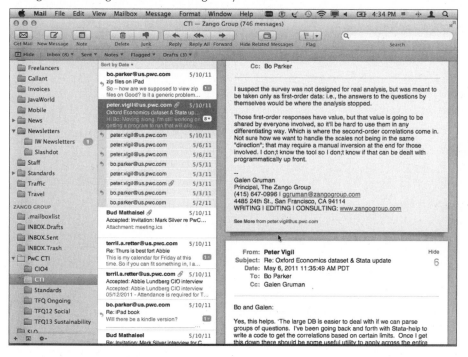

New Feature

The Mail application in Mac OS X Lion adds the conversations display, modeled after the similar capability in iOS devices. Mail in previous versions of Mac OS X had the View ➪ Organize by Thread menu option, which grouped related messages' subject lines under a disclosure triangle, as does View ➪ Organize by Conversation when viewing Mail in the classic layout view in Lion. But previous versions of Mail did not actually group the messages into one window as in Mac OS X Lion's new Mail view. ∎

Writing messages

To send someone a message, click New Message in the toolbar, choose File ➪ New Message, or press ⌘+N. The New Message dialog box appears, as shown in Figure 20.14.

FIGURE 20.14

The New Message dialog box and its default toolbar

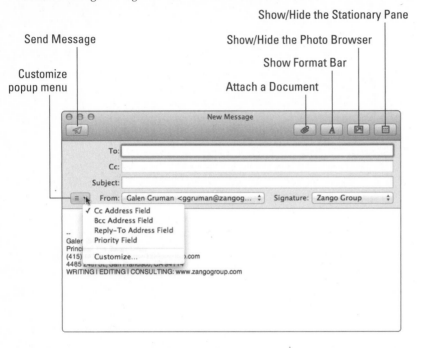

Mail's message indicators

At the very left of the message list, Mail places icons that indicate message status. A blue circle indicates an unread message. A left-pointing circular arrow indicates a message you've replied to, while a right-facing straight arrow indicates a message you've forwarded; click the arrow to open the reply or forwarded message.

Mail also has three priority indicators: !! indicates a high-priority message (as determined by the sender), ! indicates a normal-priority message (as determined by the sender), and – indicates a low-priority message (also as determined by the sender). (In classic view, enable the Flags column to see these icons by right-clicking or Control+clicking the columns and choosing Flags.)

If you flag a message using one of the seven colored flags available in the Flag icon pop-up menu in the toolbar or by choosing Message ➪ Flag, a flag icon appears to the right of the subject in the message list. (In classic view, enable the Flags column to see these icons by right-clicking or Control+clicking the columns and choosing Flags.)

For messages determined to be junk (by your mail server or using Mail's junk filters), a gold mailbag icon appears to the right of the subject in the message list, and the message preview is in gold-colored text. (To see the icon in classic layout view, the Flags column must be enabled.)

Tip

To change the icon buttons in the New Message dialog box's toolbar, right-click or Control+click the toolbar and choose Icon and Text (to show text labels with the icons), Icon Only (the default), Text Only, or Customize Toolbar (to add and remove the icon buttons that appear). The additional buttons available are Print, Append (to add selected messages to this message), Smaller (for text), Larger (for text), Rich Text, Plain Text, Lists, and Link (for hyperlinks). There are also the Space and Flexible Space icons to put spaces between icon buttons. ■

New Feature

The Save as Draft icon button has been removed from the New Message dialog box's toolbar in Mac OS X Lion's version of Mail. It's also not available through the Customize Toolbar settings sheet. ■

Addressing the message

In the To field, type the e-mail address for the person you want to send the message to. As you type, Mail displays a list of people in your Address Book to whom you've previously sent messages or who are in your company's server address book; choose the desired e-mail address rather than continuing to type it. Separate multiple e-mail addresses with commas (,) to send the message to multiple people.

Tip

An easy way to add recipients to the To, Cc, and Bcc fields is to click in the desired field and click Show Addresses (the person icon) in the toolbar. That opens the Addresses panel, from which you can click a person to have his or her e-mail address inserted. (You also can open this panel by choosing Window ➪ Address Panel or pressing Option+⌘+A.) Note that the Addresses panel includes any contacts in the Mac's Address Book for whom you have e-mail addresses. ■

You also can enter addresses in the Cc field, which copies the message to the people in that field. (*Cc* means carbon copy, from the days when secretaries used carbon paper to make copies of memos and indicated in the memo who was sent a carbon copy.) As Figure 20.14 shows, you can use the Customize icon pop-up menu to add a Bcc field which you use to blind-copy (*Bcc* originally meant blind carbon copy) the message to recipients. Anyone who gets the message sees the addresses in the To and Cc fields, but not the recipients (other than themselves) in the Bcc field.

Tip

To delete a recipient, put the text cursor after the name and press Delete. ■

In the Subject field, enter a subject or description for your message. If you leave the Subject blank, Mail asks you when you send the message if you're sure you want to send the message without a subject.

Entering the message itself

Enter your message in the main section of the dialog box. You can format the text by using the options in the Format menu if you've set your account to send Rich Text e-mail, as explained in the "Composing preferences" section earlier in this chapter, or if you enable rich text for this message by choosing Format ➪ Make Rich Text or pressing Shift+⌘+T. Select the text, and choose the desired font, color, alignment, and so on from the Format menu. You also can click the Show Fonts Panel and Show Colors Panels icon buttons in the toolbar to choose fonts and colors, or press ⌘+T and Shift+⌘+C, respectively.

These other formatting options are included in the Format menu:

- **Lists:** This option's submenu lets you insert bulleted or numbered lists and increase or decrease (also called *promote* or *demote*) the selected list items' level.

- **Style:** This option's submenu lets you apply bold, italic, and underline formatting to selected text, change the text size, and apply styles. You also can use shortcuts: ⌘+B for bold, ⌘+I for italic, ⌘+U for underline, ⌘+= for larger text size, and ⌘+– for smaller text size.

- **Alignment:** This option's submenu lets you left-align, center, right-align, or justify text, as well as change its reading order (for example, text that combines left-to-right text such as French with right-to-left text such as Arabic). You also can use shortcuts: ⌘+[for left alignment, ⌘+\ for centering, and ⌘+] for right alignment.

- **Indentation:** This option's submenu lets you increase or decrease the indentation of the selected paragraphs.

- **Quote Level:** This option's submenu lets you increase or decrease the indentation of the quoted text.

Mail also gives you controls over your text, such as spell checking and automatic substitution. Choose Edit ➪ Spelling and Grammar, and then choose the desired submenu option.

Note

To change your spelling and grammar settings, apply capitalization transformations, or adjust text substitutions, you must first create a new message. Otherwise, these options in the Edit menu are grayed out as unavailable. ■

The key submenu option to set is Check Spelling, which has three choices: When Typing, Before Sending, and Never. If you choose When Typing, potential errors are highlighted with red dotted underlines. If you choose Before Sending, the Spelling and Grammar dialog box appears, in which alternative words are suggested for you to choose from, in which you can type in your own corrected text, or in which you can tell Mail to ignore the spelling. (You can see the Spelling and Grammar dialog box at any time when composing a message by choosing Edit ➪ Spelling and Grammar ➪ Show Spelling and Grammar or pressing ⌘+: [colon].)

These three other submenu options are available:

- **Check Document Now (press ⌘+; [semicolon]):** This checks the message's spelling immediately.

- **Check Grammar with Spelling:** This checks your message's grammar along with its spelling. (If a check mark appears to the left of this option, it is enabled.) Note that potential grammatical errors are indicated through green dotted underlines.

- **Correct Spelling Automatically:** This makes Mail correct any misspellings it detects as you type. (If a check mark appears to the left of this option, it is enabled.) Be careful with this option: Mail may "correct" words it does not recognize, even though they are in fact correct.

Mail also has controls to change the capitalization of selected text. Choose Edit ⇨ Transformations and the desired option: Make Upper Case, Make Lower Case, and Capitalize (which capitalizes the first letter of each word).

You also can have Mail automatically replace text with other text as you type. To do so, choose Edit ⇨ Substitutions and select the sub-option for what you want to have automatically substituted: Smart Quotes (which replaces keyboard quotes with their curly, typographic versions), Smart Dashes (which replaces two consecutive hyphens with an em dash), and Smart Links (which converts web and e-mail addresses into clickable hyperlinks). Note that if a sub-option has a check mark to its left, it is enabled.

Three other sub-options are available when you choose Edit ⇨ Substitutions:

- **Smart Copy/Paste:** This ensures that spaces are added and deleted as necessary when you paste text between words.
- **Text Replacement:** This enables any text substitutions you set in the Text pane of the Language & Text system preference (see Chapter 28).
- **Show/Hide Substitutions:** This displays or hides the Substitutions dialog box. This dialog box lets you turn on or off the various substitution settings—dashes, hyperlinks, and quotes—as well as access the Text pane of the Language & Text system preference (by clicking the Text Preferences button). Use the Replace All and Replace in Selection buttons to determine what text in the current message has the substitutions applied: all text or just whatever text is selected.

Using other mail composition controls

To add one or more files as attachments to your message, click Attach (if visible) in the toolbar, choose File ⇨ Attach Files, or press Shift+⌘+A.

If you have multiple e-mail accounts, you can choose which account sends the message by using the From pop-up menu. Likewise, if you have multiple outgoing mail servers set up (see the "Accounts preferences" section earlier in this chapter), you can choose which outgoing mail server to use from the adjacent pop-up menu. You also can choose which signature to use for the message by using the Signature pop-up menu (see the "Signatures preferences" section earlier in this chapter).

Depending on which options you've enabled in the Customize icon pop-up menu, additional controls may appear in the New Message dialog box:

- **The Bcc field enables you to blind-copy recipients, so no other recipients know they received the message.** You also can display this field by choosing View ⇨ Bcc Address Field or pressing Option+⌘+B.

- **The Reply To field enables you to put in an e-mail address to which all replies to this message will be sent, instead of to your e-mail address**. (An assistant might use this field when sending messages on behalf of his or her boss, for example.) You also can display this field by choosing View ⇨ Reply-to Address Field or pressing Option+⌘+R.

- **The Send from Account pop-up menu lets you choose which server to send the message through.** There's rarely a reason not to use the server specified in your mail account settings, but if you're traveling, you may want to use an alternative server, as described in the sidebar "Sending e-mail while traveling."

- **The Priority pop-up menu enables you to choose the messages priority level: low, normal, and high.** Depending on the recipient's e-mail client, the priority may display as an icon in their message list, apply a color to the message, or use some other highlighting. You also can set priority by choosing Message ⇨ Mark and choosing the desired priority level from the submenu.

Mail lets you apply fancy formatting to your messages; click Show Stationery and pick one of the options from the preview area that appears above the area you type the message text. Note that these messages use embedded images and fonts that may not display on recipients' e-mail programs.

The toolbar also has the Photo Browser button. Click it to see photos stored in iPhoto or in Photo Booth. Drag a photo over a person's name in the To, Cc, Bcc, or Reply To fields to attach their photo to the message. Someone with a compatible e-mail program can see the photo in those fields when reading the message.

Sending and saving messages

When you're ready to send your message, click Send Message in the toolbar, choose Message ⇨ Send, or press Shift+⌘+D. If you want to save the message so you can work on it later, click Save This Message to Drafts Mailbox in the toolbar, which stores the message in the Drafts folder. Note that clicking Save This Message to Drafts Mailbox does not close the New Message window, so you can keep working on the message and click Save This Message to Drafts Mailbox again to update what is saved in the Drafts folder. Close the message without sending it by clicking the Close button in the New Message dialog box.

If the sender is in your iChat buddy list (see the "Using iChat" section later in this chapter), you can send an instant-message response via iChat by clicking the Chat with Recipients icon button in the toolbar. (If the button is grayed out, that means you have no recipients in the To field that are available via iChat.)

Replying, forwarding, and redirecting messages

You can use multiple ways to send messages you've received from others, whether you've selected the message in the message list or have the message open. Reply sends a response to the person who sent you the message, Reply All sends the response to anyone who received the message, and Forward sends the message to anyone you choose. In all three cases, you can enter your own message, as well as edit the original message included. You also can change who gets the reply or forwarded message by adding or deleting e-mail addresses in the To, Cc, and Bcc fields.

Cross-Reference

To set what part of the original message is included in your reply or forward, use the options in the Composing pane of Mail's Preferences dialog box, as explained in the "Composing preferences" section earlier in this chapter. ■

You reply to a message by clicking Reply in the toolbar, choosing Message ➪ Reply, or pressing ⌘+R. To reply to all recipients, click Reply All, choose Message ➪ Reply All, or press Shift+⌘+R. If the sender is in your iChat buddy list (see the "Using iChat" section later in this chapter), you can send an instant-message response via iChat by choosing Message ➪ Reply with iChat or pressing Shift+⌘+I.

To forward a message to someone else, click Forward in the toolbar, choose Message ➪ Forward, or press Shift+⌘+F. Choosing Message ➪ Forward as Attachment sends the e-mail as an attachment within an e-mail message; note that not all e-mail programs can open that attachment.

You also can *redirect* a message to another e-mail account by choosing Message ➪ Redirect or pressing Shift+⌘+E. The difference between forwarding and redirecting is that forwarding shows the message as being sent by you, while redirecting shows the message as being sent by the original sender (not you).

Deleting, moving, and junking messages

You can select one or more e-mails (⌘+click each to select multiple e-mails) and delete them all by clicking the Delete button in the toolbar, or send them to the Junk folder by clicking Junk in the toolbar. (If you are in the Junk folder, you can mark messages as not junk by clicking the Not Junk button in the toolbar; the messages are moved back to the Inbox.)

To move a message to a folder, simply drag it into the desired folder in the Message Viewer's Sidebar. Or select it from the message list, choose Message ➪ Move To, and then choose the desired folder from the submenu. You also can copy messages by holding Option when dragging them to a folder or simply by choosing Message ➪ Copy To and then the desired folder from the submenu. To create a folder, select the mailbox or folder that you want to create the folder in, click the + icon pop-up menu under the Message Viewer's Sidebar, and choose New Mailbox from the menu.

Cross-Reference

You can set up rules that automatically move, copy, delete, forward, or mark as junk messages that meet the criteria you set, as explained in the "Rules preferences" section earlier in this chapter. You can apply rules to selected messages by choosing Message ➪ Apply Rules or pressing Option+⌘+L. ■

Using RSS Feeds in Mail

RSS feeds are an easy way to stay up to date on sports scores, news headlines, or other information that is frequently updated. When you subscribe to such a feed, Mail checks periodically to see if there are new entries, which it stores in the RSS list in the Message Viewer. Each RSS feed you subscribe to displays in this list; click the feed name to get a message list that shows all the entries. You read entries just as you would e-mail messages.

You can delete, mark as junk, or print the RSS entries. And you can erase deleted items, mark them as read, archive the feed, delete the feed from the RSS list in Mail, or manually update the feed by right-clicking or Control+clicking the RSS feed name and choosing the desired option from the contextual menu, or by clicking the Action icon pop-up menu (the gear icon) at the bottom of the Message Viewer's left column and choosing the desired options from the menu.

Cross-Reference
You can view RSS entries in Mail and/or Safari. Chapter 19 explains how to subscribe to and view RSS feeds in Safari. ∎

To add feeds to Mail, click the Add icon pop-up menu (the + icon) at the bottom of the Sidebar and choose Add RSS Feeds. Or choose File ➪ Add RSS Feeds. In the dialog box that appears, select RSS feeds previously subscribed to in Safari or enter the feed URL manually.

Feed items appear in the Sidebar, under the RSS label, as their own mailboxes. Click an RSS "mailbox" to see the list of feeds in the message list, and click a specific item, to view its contents in the message window—the same way you view mail messages.

The Preferences dialog box (choose Mail ➪ Preferences or press ⌘+, [comma]) has three sets of RSS options in its RSS pane:

- **Default RSS Reader:** Choose the RSS reader that RSS feeds are automatically added to when you subscribe to an RSS feed. Choose Mail, Safari, or Select to choose an application you've installed to read RSS feeds.

- **Check for Updates:** Choose how often you want Mail to update the RSS feeds it displays: Every 30 Minutes, Every Hour, or Every Day.

- **Remove Articles:** Choose how RSS entries are deleted from Mail: Manually, After One Day, After One Week, After Two Weeks, After One Month, or After One Year.

Working with Notes in Mail

You can add notes in Mail by clicking Note in the toolbar, choosing File ➪ New Note, or pressing Control+⌘+N. Enter your text, format it as desired using the Fonts and Colors buttons or the Format menu, add any attachments using the Attach button, and click Done to save the note. You also can send the note to someone else by clicking Send, which creates a new e-mail message using the Notes stationery and whatever you've entered into the note. Figure 20.15 shows note being created.

FIGURE 20.15

Creating a note

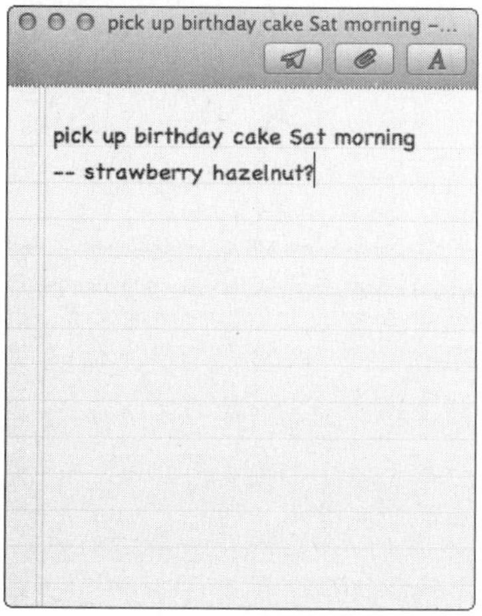

If your IMAP or Exchange server is set up to accept notes (see the "Accounts preferences" section earlier in this chapter), notes appear in the Reminders section of the Message Viewer's Sidebar; click Notes to see all notes or click its disclosure triangle to choose notes associated to a specific account.

New Feature

Mail in Mac OS X Lion has dropped support for to-do items; you must use iCal to create and manage such reminders (see Chapter 21). ∎

Using iChat

E-mail is a great way to send lengthy messages or messages to multiple people, but it can be cumbersome for quick messages between two people. Instant messaging, also called *chat*, is a simpler, faster way to "talk" to someone over computers using text. To help you chat, Mac OS X comes with the iChat application.

Setting up iChat

With iChat, you can chat with people who have Apple Me.com or Mac.com addresses, AOL Instant Messenger (AIM), Google Talk, Yahoo Messenger, and Jabber accounts, as well as with other people on your local network (using what Apple calls its Bonjour technology).

New Feature

Support for Yahoo instant messaging is new to Mac OS X Lion's iChat application. ∎

The first time you launch iChat, it asks what type of chat account you want to set up. Tell iChat what other services you have accounts for in the Preferences dialog box's Accounts pane. (Choose iChat ➪ Preferences or press ⌘+, [comma] to open the Preferences dialog box.) Click the + icon button to select a service, and then provide the login information for that account. If you have multiple accounts, add the login information for each.

Note

You often must have an account on the same service as the people you want to chat with. In that case, iChat cannot connect with users from different chat services. But increasingly, chat services are allowing connections to each other, so you may find that using AIM or Google Talk lets you reach buddies on other networks, reducing the need to maintain several chat accounts in iChat. ∎

For each account, you have three subpanes to set in the Accounts pane:

- **Account Information:** This subpane lets you enable the account, automatically log into this account when iChat launches, have new buddies you chat with automatically added to your buddies list, and—if the chat service permits—allow multiple simultaneous logins so you can have multiple chats at the same time.

- **Security:** This subpane lets you block others from seeing that your account is idle, determine your privacy level (who can see that your account is logged in), and—for services that support this capability—encrypt chat messages.

- **Server Settings:** If your network blocks standard chat sessions, you may be able to get around that by entering proxy server settings in this subpane. Check with your network administrator. For secure chat sessions, you also can enable SSL (Secure Socket Layer) encryption in this subpane, to keep the contents of your chat sessions safe from prying eyes as the session's content is delivered through the public Internet.

For chats over the local network, you can use the Bonjour account. It has just one pane, Account Information, with four options: Enable Bonjour Instant Messaging, Publish My Email and Instant Messaging Addresses, Send Text as I Type, and Block Others from Seeing My Status as Idle (the last option is designed to keep co-workers and bosses from knowing when you're away from your Mac). Anyone who has enabled Bonjour chat and is on the same network you are is available for chatting; there's no sign-in.

In the General pane, you can set the default instant messaging application (if you have others than iChat installed), whether your iChat status is visible in the menu bar, whether separate accounts appear in one window in iChat or each in their own windows, whether a confirmation is required to send file attachments, and how your availability status is affected by activities such as the Mac going to sleep or you switch to another user account.

In the Messages pane, you can set the visual display of chat text, set a keyboard shortcut to switch to iChat if you are working in another application, automatically save chat transcripts, and choose to collect all chats in a single window rather than keep each chat in its own window.

In the Alerts pane, you tell iChat how to alert you to various events, such as logging in, a buddy becoming available, sending a message, receiving a chat invitation, or getting a file transferred to you. Your alert options include choosing a sound, having the iChat icon bounce in the Dock, running an AppleScript, or speaking a message.

The Audio/Video pane lets you choose an external camera (if attached to the Mac) and microphone (including Bluetooth headsets) to use for audio and video chats. You also can limit how much bandwidth the chat can take on your network connection so as not to slow down other network operations, to open iChat when a video camera is attached, and play a ringing sound when invited to a chat conference (a multi-user chat).

Chatting with people

Before you can chat, you must have people to chat with. You can set up *buddies*, people who you can easily chat with by clicking their names in your chat window. Add a buddy by choosing Buddies⇨Add Buddy or pressing Shift+⌘+A. In the dialog box that appears, enter the buddy's account name and what chat service he or she uses (only services for which you have set up in the Accounts pane of the Preferences dialog box appear in this list). You can choose a group to add the buddy to, as well as enter the buddy's first and last names. (Create a group by clicking the + icon pop-up menu at the bottom of the chat window and choosing Add Group.)

In your buddy list, right-click or Control+click a buddy you want to chat with and choose the type of chat you want to initiate, as Figure 20.16 shows. You also can block specific users from chatting with you. Or select a buddy and click one of the chat buttons at the bottom of the window: text, audio, video, or screen share. Or to start a text chat, select a buddy and choose Buddies⇨Send Instant Message or press Shift+⌘+M.

Tip

If you have several chat accounts, or want to use the Bonjour chat with people on your local network, you can open a chat window for any chat account you have in the Window menu By default, all accounts are available within the iChat Buddies window, as Figure 20.16 shows. To get separate windows for each account, deselect the Show All My Accounts in One List option in the General pane of iChat's Preferences dialog box. ■

Tip

If you're not available to chat, you can simply quit iChat so you show as not available in your buddies' chat windows. Or you can choose an away status from the pop-up menu under your name. ■

If you want to chat with someone not in your buddy list, choose File⇨New Chat or press ⌘+N, and enter their chat address. If you have more than one chat account, choose the one you want to chat from. You also can choose the type of chat you are initiating: text, audio, video, or screen sharing. Click OK to send the invitation. If the person accepts your invitation, a chat window opens. People also may initiate a chat with you the same way; click Accept in the alert window that opens to begin the chat session, or click Block to prevent them from chatting with you.

When you've connected to someone else for a chat, the dialog unfolds at the top of the Chat window, shown in Figure 20.16. Enter your text in the window at the bottom, and press Return to send it. If you want to attach various smiley face-type icons—called *emoticons*—select them from the pop-up menu to the right of the text-entry field. You also can choose Edit ⇨ Insert Smiley and choose the desired icon from the submenu.

FIGURE 20.16

Left: The unified buddy list. Right: An active chat session.

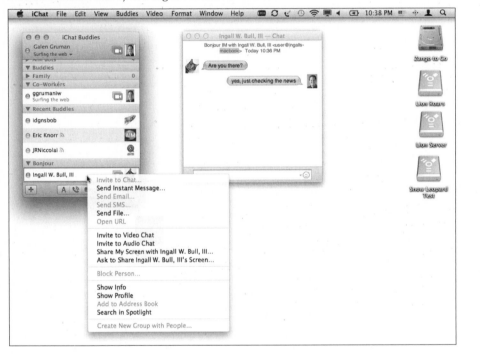

Using audio and video

In addition to chatting via text, you can initiate an audio chat by clicking the Start an Audio Chat icon button (the phone icon) at the bottom of the chat window. Both parties must have a way to hear the conversation (using headphones or speakers) and to be heard (using a microphone) to be able to participate in the chat. (A headset addresses both needs.) Participants also need to configure the Audio/Video pane in iChat's Preferences dialog box to use those devices. After the connection is made, you just start talking. Note that the audio quality may be inferior to a telephone connection.

Similarly, click the Start a Video Chat icon button (the green movie-camera icon) to start a video chat, as shown in Figure 20.17. Both parties must have an external camera or a built-in iSight camera, as well as a microphone and headphones or a speaker, or a headset, set up. A participant without a camera can still join the chat but has access to the audio portion only.

Another form of video chat is what Apple calls iChat Theater. This enables you to share photo albums from iPhoto or files of any sort in a video window.

FIGURE 20.17

A video chat session

One way to initiate a "theater" session is to choose File ➪ Share iPhoto with iChat Theater to share a selected iPhoto album; choose File ➪ Share a File with iChat Theater to share selected files. Either way, click Share to set up the "theater." Then invite a person to a video chat. The person you are chatting with sees a slide show that you control on his or her video chat window.

You also can start by inviting someone to a video chat and, when he or she is connected, click the + icon button at the bottom of the video chat window. Then choose Share iPhoto with iChat Theater or Share a File with iChat Theater, select the desired iPhoto album or files, and click Share.

Using screen and file sharing

You can share screens across iChat. Click the Start Screen Sharing icon button (the two rounded rectangles icon) at the bottom of the chat window to initiate a screen sharing session. The button opens a pop-up menu with two options: one to invite the person to share his or her screen with you and one to accept your shared screen. The other party gets a dialog box asking if he or she agrees to the screen sharing chat. The person can accept the invitation, block you, or send you a text reply. If the screen sharing chat is accepted, the screen sharing window opens on the Mac that is viewing the shared screen. People can initiate a screen sharing chat with you the same way.

You can send someone you're chatting with a file by choosing Buddies ➪ Send File or pressing Option+⌘+F when in the text field of a chat. Choose the desired file and click Send. You also can send a file simply by dragging it into the text box at the bottom of the iChat window. Either way, when you press Return in the text field, the file is sent along with your text message. People can send you files the same way.

Tip
You can use Mac OS X's Quick Look feature to preview the contents of files send to you via iChat before opening them. (Chapter 4 explains Quick Look in detail.) ■

Cross-Reference
Chapter 24 covers file sharing and screen sharing in more depth. ■

Using FaceTime

In 2010, Apple introduced FaceTime on the iPhone 4, a two-way videoconferencing technology that let two people converse with video over a wireless network or via the Internet, as long as they were not using 3G cellular service for the connection. Apple extended FaceTime to its late-2010 iPod Touch models, then to Mac OS X via a $1 download from the Mac App Store in early 2011, and finally to the iPad 2 in March 2011. FaceTime comes free with Mac OS X Lion, so all Mac users can now participate in videoconferences with other FaceTime users. (You need a camera and microphone, both of which are built in to all Macs except the Mac Pro and Mac Mini series.)

The first time you launch FaceTime, you need to sign in with your Apple ID (typically the same as you use to access the iTunes Store) and specify which e-mail address is associated to your FaceTime service. To conference with you, other users double-click that e-mail address in the contacts list that displays in their FaceTime windows, and you would double-click their FaceTime e-mail address or their iPhone phone number to initiate a FaceTime connection.

After you initiate a connection, the other person gets an invite on their Mac, iPhone, iPad, or iPod Touch, with buttons to accept or reject the FaceTime session. If the other person doesn't respond, you can close FaceTime or click the End button. (If someone contacts you, you get the same options.) During the session, the main window shows the other person, while a small window showing what your camera displays appears in a corner. (You can drag that window to any other corner.) Figure 20.18 shows a FaceTime session.

You can mute the microphone by choosing Video ➪ Mute or by clicking the Mute icon button (the microphone icon) in the FaceTime window (move the mouse or flick the touchpad to have the onscreen controls appear). Click End to end the session. If your microphone is muted, an icon labeled Mute appears in the window displaying your camera's image; if the other person's microphone is muted, the icon appears in the main window. Likewise, if the camera is turned off (or, more likely, covered up), a video camera icon labeled Paused appears in the appropriate window.

An iPhone, iPad, or iPod Touch owner can switch between the front and rear cameras, but a Mac user can use just the single iSight camera on the Mac (usually above the screen). But you can rotate the camera during a FaceTime session by choosing Video ➪ Use Landscape if the session is in portrait orientation or by choosing Video ➪ Use Portrait if it is in landscape orientation; or just press ⌘+R to rotate the camera. Choose the Video ➪ Enter Full Screen to display the FaceTime session in full-screen mode, or use the onscreen Full Screen icon button or press Shift+⌘+F to go in and out of full-screen mode.

To end the session, choose Window ➪ Close, press ⌘+W, or click the End button in the onscreen controls.

New Feature

New to FaceTime in Mac OS X Lion is the iOS-style Preferences pane, which appears instead of the previous Preferences dialog box if you choose FaceTime ➪ Preferences or press ⌘+, (comma). In it, you can turn FaceTime on or off, set up or change your accounts, and specify the e-mail addresses where you can be reached for FaceTime sessions. ∎

FIGURE 20.18

Left: Select a contact in the FaceTime application you want to connect to. Right: A FaceTime session.

Summary

Mac OS X has two main collaboration applications focused on communications (Mail and iChat), plus the FaceTime video conferencing that works on Apple's Macs and recent iOS devices. You can import your settings and e-mail messages from other e-mail programs, as well as from previous versions of Mail.

Apple's Mail is a full-featured e-mail application that works with all common e-mail systems, including web-based services such as Google Gmail, POP-based services commonly provided by web hosts, and both IMAP-based and Microsoft Exchange e-mail services common in business.

Mail provides a rich set of controls over how messages are checked, displayed, organized, and filtered. It also lets you access multiple e-mail accounts at the same time. Its new Message Viewer layout allows for longer message lists and larger preview window sizes, which is particularly useful when viewing conversations composed of multiple related messages.

Mail's smart folders feature lets you create playlist-like folders that contain all messages that meet whatever criteria you specify, without moving the original messages from their standard locations in Mail's folders.

When creating and sending e-mails, you can add attachments, apply visual templates, and automatically append a default signature for yourself, as well as control how the original message you are replying to or forwarding is quoted in that reply or forward. When replying to an e-mail, you have the option of replying via iChat instead of Mail if the sender is one of your instant-messaging buddies.

Mail can display RSS feeds as if they were mail messages, as well as let you manage your RSS feeds. You can see and manage your RSS feeds in Safari as well.

For IMAP and Exchange accounts, Mail can also display notes.

The iChat instant messaging service works with several popular IM services, including AOL Instant Messenger, GoogleTalk, Jabber, and Yahoo Messenger, plus any Mac on your local network. You can set up buddy lists that contain the contact information for people you chat with often, for easy chat connections, but strangers also can ask to chat with you (and you can ask to chat with strangers, if you know their instant message addresses).

iChat supports not only text chat, but also audio chat (essentially, Internet-based phone calls), video chat (Internet-based videoconferencing), and screen sharing chat (where you can observe or control the other person's screen or let them control yours). You can enclose files in your text chats to easily exchange files with your chat buddy.

The FaceTime application allows Macs to participate in two-person video conferences with other FaceTime users on other Macs or via an iPad 2, iPhone 4, or 2010-model iPod Touch—as long both parties are connected to each other or to the Internet via a network (rather than over 3G cellular service).

Using Address Book and iCal

pple's Mail is very likely your central tool for communicating on your Mac. Mail takes advantage of two other applications that come with Mac OS X to help facilitate your communications. One is Address Book, which is your central repository for people's contact information. The other is iCal, which is your central calendar for appointments and to-do items.

You can use Address Book and iCal directly, but they also communicate with Mail. For example, Mail searches your Address Book to find a person's e-mail address when you enter the name in a message's To, Cc, or Bcc field. Mail also can intercept calendar invitations sent to you via e-mail and pass them onto iCal. (Chapter 20 covers how to use Mail.)

Like Mail, Address Book and iCal support multiple accounts, so you can access contacts from both your Mac and a server such as Microsoft Exchange or Yahoo, and you can view multiple calendars (such as from your Mac, Exchange, and Google Calendar) in one place.

IN THIS CHAPTER

Setting up and using Address Book

Setting up and using iCal

Coordinating invitations and group calendars in iCal

Working with Address Book

Address Book, shown in Figure 21.1 in its default contacts view, is a simple application that stores your contacts with whatever detail you want to provide.

Adding and editing cards

To add a person, create an address book card by choosing File ⇨ New Card, pressing ⌘+N, or clicking the + icon button at the bottom right of the Name column in the Address Book window. A card form appears in which you enter the person's name, contact information, and any notes, as Figure 21.1 also shows. Leave blank any fields you don't want to complete.

FIGURE 21.1

Upper left: The Address Book with a card displayed. Bottom left: The pane in which you add information for a new contact. Right: The pop-over from which you add a photo to a contact.

New Feature

Mac OS X Lion's Address Book application has undergone a significant overhaul of its appearance, now looking very much like the Address Book app on an iPad. ∎

Note the two icon buttons at the lower right of the contacts view window in Figure 21.1: The Card Only icon button (the square icon) collapses the window to show just a contact's card; you also can choose View ⇨ Card Only or press ⌘+2. The List and Card icon button (the open book icon) expands the window to show both the contacts list pane and the selected contact's card; you also can choose View ⇨ List and Card or press ⌘+1.

To associate a photo or other image with that card, drag the image file onto the square with the person's silhouette in the card. Or select the card and choose Card ⇨ Choose Custom Image or press Option+⌘+I; then in the pop-over that appears, click Choose to select an existing image, click the Camera icon button to take a picture using the Mac's built-in iSight camera, or click the Import face from iPhoto to add a picture from the iPhoto application, if you have that. In this pop-over, you also can apply special effects similar to those available in Photo Booth (see Chapter 14) and crop the photo as you can in Photo Booth. To delete an image from a card, select the card and choose Card ⇨ Clear Custom Image.

To add a field to a selected card, choose Card ⇨ Add Field, and then choose a field from the submenu. Choose Edit Template to add fields to all cards, or use the Preferences dialog box as described later in this chapter.

Tip

Address Book assumes the new contact is a person, but if it is a company, select the Company option; this changes the name fields to the company's name. Or you can change a card from a person to a company by selecting Company when editing the card, or by choosing Card ⇨ Mark as a Company or pressing ⌘+\. If you want to change a company contact to a person, deselect the Company option when editing the card, or choose Card ⇨ Mark as a Person or press ⌘+\. ■

Some fields, such as those for e-mail addresses and phone numbers, are pop-up menus that enable you to choose the type of contact you are providing, such as home fax or work phone. If a green circle with a plus sign appears next to an entry, click it to add an additional contact of the same type, such as a second work e-mail address. Some fields have a minus sign in a red circle next to them; click it to delete that field's contents.

Tip

You can add field options to cards by choosing Card ⇨ Add Field and then choosing the desired field from the submenu. ■

To edit an existing contact, select it in the list of contacts, and click Edit at the bottom of the Address Book window, choose Edit ⇨ Edit Card, or press ⌘+L. Click a field you want to edit, and change the information as desired. When you're finished, click Edit again.

Working with groups

You can group contacts so you can send one e-mail to the group and know everyone in that group will get it. To view groups, choose View ⇨ Groups, press ⌘+3, or click the Groups icon—the red ribbon with two silhouettes—to get the window shown in Figure 21.2.

New Feature

The new look for Mac OS X Lion's Address Book application means it takes more work to get to groups of contacts; instead of being listed at the left side of the Address Book window, in Mac OS X Lion you now must choose View ⇨ Groups, press ⌘+3, or click the Group icon (the red ribbon with two silhouettes) to see your various calendars and groups, as Figure 21.2 shows. ■

Follow these steps to create a group:

1. **Choose File ⇨ New Group, press Shift+⌘+N, or click the + icon button at the bottom left of the window when viewing groups.**

2. **A group named untitled group appears in the left pane; change the name to one that makes sense for the group.**

3. **To add existing contacts to the group, view all your existing contacts by clicking All Contacts.** Drag the contacts from the right column into the group to add them. (If you want to edit a contact, double-click the name from the right pane or single-click it and then click the Card icon button [the single red silhouette].)

4. **To add new contacts, click the group name to open the window shown in Figure 21.2.** Then click the + icon button at the bottom right of the left pane to open a new contact record. Fill in the information, and click Done when you're finished.

5. **When you're finished, click the Groups icon button (the red ribbon with two silhouettes) to get a list of all accounts and groups.** Click All Contacts to see all your contacts, or click another account or group to see its contacts.

You also can select multiple contacts in a contacts list and then choose File ⇨ New Group from Selection.

FIGURE 21.2

The groups view. To add a contact to a group (such as SLO here), just drag the name from the right pane into the desired group in the pane at left.

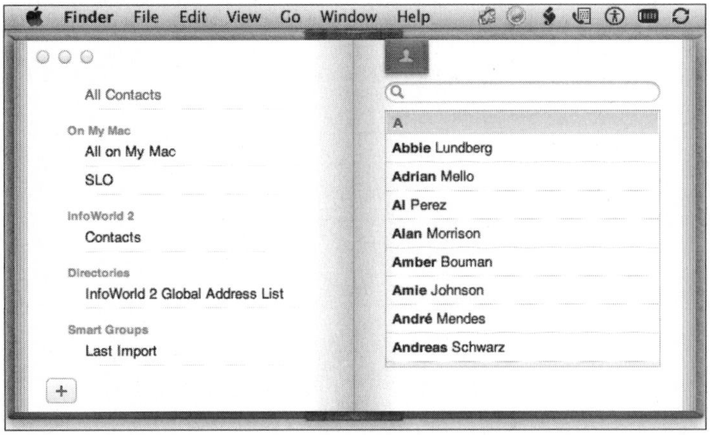

You also can create smart groups, which are kept updated automatically based on the criteria you select. First, create the smart group by choosing File ⇨ New Smart Group or by clicking the + icon pop-up menu at the bottom of the Group list in the Address Book window and choosing New Smart Group. Give the smart group a name, and choose the first criterion from the first pop-up menu, such as Card or Name. In the second pop-up menu, set the condition, such as Contains or Is Set (meaning this field has information in it). In the adjacent text field, add the text for the condition. Add conditions by clicking the + icon button at the end of the condition. Delete them by selecting a condition and clicking the – icon button. Click OK when you're finished.

Working with distribution lists

You can send an e-mail in Mail to a group defined in Address Book; enter or select the group name as you would any individual name in the message's To, Cc, or Bcc field. But sometimes you have groups whose members have multiple e-mail addresses. How do you know which e-mail addresses will be used for such contacts when sending to a group? (For individuals, Mail lets you select the specific address for contacts that have multiple e-mail addresses.) How do you determine which phone number or mailing address is used in, for example, a contacts printout?

The answer is to edit the distribution list associated with that group:

1. **Choose Edit ⇨ Edit Distribution List.**

2. **Select the group from the list at the left side of the Distribution dialog box, shown in Figure 21.3.** For each member, each e-mail address associated to that contact is listed. The bold address is the one that is used by Mail when you send to that group.

FIGURE 21.3

Edit a distribution list to choose primary contact information for members of a group.

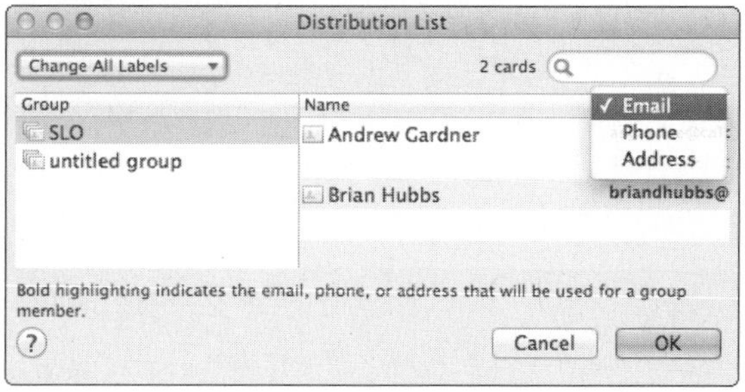

3. **To change the e-mail address, for each contact, select the desired e-mail address; each becomes bold.** You can select just one address per contact.

4. **To change the default phone number, click the Click the Email column header to open the pop-up menu, and choose Phone.** Select the desired phone number for that contact.

5. **To change the default mailing address, click the Click the Email or Phone column header (the label depends on what is currently displayed) to open the pop-up menu, and choose Address.** Select the desired mailing address for that contact.

6. **Click OK when you're finished.**

Managing cards and groups

To delete individual contacts (cards) or groups, select them and choose Edit ⇨ Delete Card or Edit ⇨ Delete Group. You also can simply select a group or contact and press Delete.

To rename a group, just click its name in the Group list; you also can select it and choose Edit ⇨ Rename Group. To rename a contact, you need to edit its card, as explained earlier in this chapter.

Other card management options available include the following; note that one or more cards must be selected:

- To find cards, enter the search text in the Search field and press Return or click the Search icon button (the magnifying glass icon).

- To find messages and documents on your Mac that contain the currently selected contact, choose Edit ⇨ Spotlight "*contactname*" to conduct a Spotlight search. (Chapter 5 explains Spotlight.)

- To import vCard or Address Book archive files, choose File ⇨ Import or press ⌘+O; the export your current address book to either format, choose File ⇨ Export and choose the desired output format from the submenu.

- To send an e-mail to contacts with your updated card, select the groups and/or individuals you want to send the update to and choose File ⇨ Send Updates.

- If you have multiple cards for someone and want to combine them into one card, select them and choose Card ⇨ Merge Selected Cards or press Shift+⌘+\.

- To find duplicate cards, choose Card ⇨ Look for Duplicates.

- To mark a card as your own, select it and choose Card ⇨ Make This My Card.

New Feature

To send someone's contact information as a vCard mail attachment (which they can open in Mail and have automatically added to their Address Book), click the Share button in a person's card. Mail opens with a new, blank message that has the vCard attached. This is a new capability for Address Book in Mac OS X Lion. ∎

Setting Address Book preferences

To set Address Books preferences, choose Address Book ⇨ Preferences or press ⌘+, (comma). The five panes are covered in the following sections.

General preferences

Here you set whether the card displays as *lastname, firstname* or as *firstname lastname*. You also choose how cards are sorted: by first name or last name. In the Address Format pop-up menu, choose the country for which the cards' addresses should be formatted. You also can change the default account in which new cards are added using the Default Account pop-up menu (if you have only one account, the pop-up menu has only the On My Mac option).

New Feature

In Mac OS X Lion, the Default Account pop-up menu has moved from the Accounts pane to the General pane in Address Book's Preferences dialog box. And the Font Size menu that had been in the General pane is gone. ■

Accounts preferences

Address Book can sync with a CardDAV Address Book Server (running on a Mac OS X Server), a Microsoft Exchange 2007 or 2010 server, an LDAP (Lightweight Directory Access Protool) server, a Google account, an iCloud account, or a Yahoo account.

To add a CardDAV, Exchange, iCloud, LDAP, or Yahoo account, click the + icon button at the bottom left of the Accounts pane, choose the supported server, and complete its sign-in information.

To add a Google or Yahoo account, select the On My Mac account from the Accounts pane's Sidebar, go to the Account Information subpane, select Synchronize with Google, and click the adjacent Configure button to set up Google synchronization. Likewise, select Synchronize with Yahoo, and click the adjacent Configure button to set up Yahoo synchronization.

Note

Yes, Yahoo accounts can be configured in two places. ■

All Macs have an On My Mac account, which if selected displays two subpanes: Account Information and Sharing. You also can see the settings for available CardDAV, Exchange, iCloud, LDAP, and Yahoo accounts (if any) by clicking the account name in the Sidebar. For these other accounts, you can enable or disable the account synchronization by selecting or deselecting the Enable This Account option in their Account Information subpane.

Note

You subscribe to an Address Book that someone else has shared by choosing File ➪ Subscribe to Address Book or pressing ⌘+U. ■

If you have an iCloud, LDAP, or CardDAV account, there is only the Account Information subpane in the Accounts pane, in which you specify the account and server access information provided by your network administrator.

If you have an Exchange account, the Accounts pane has two subpanes: Account Information and Server Settings. You can change or specify the account information in the Account Information subpane and the server information in the Server Settings subpane.

Template

If you find yourself adding the same fields over and over to your cards, you can add them permanently to all cards by choosing them in the Add Field pop-up menu in the Template pane.

The pane shows the standard empty card you get when you create a new contact. To delete fields, click the red – symbol to its left. To duplicate a field, click the green + icon to its left;

these icons appear only for fields such as phone numbers and e-mail addresses where multiple entries are allowed. Add fields through the Add Field pop-up menu; they're placed in predetermined locations by Address Book. (In the Add Field pop-up menu, options with a check mark to their left are in the card template, while those unchecked are not in the template.)

Phone

In the Phone pane, select the Automatically Format Phone numbers option to have Address Book convert all phone numbers you enter to a consistent format. (This option is selected by default.) You set your preferred display for phone numbers from a list of six common conventions in the Formats pop-up menu; you also can create your own by choosing the Custom option.

vCard

In the vCard pane, you set the format for vCards generated by Address Book, as well as control whether notes and photos are included. A vCard is a standard for exchanging contact information across applications, and these settings tell Address Book how to exchange card data with vCard-compatible applications.

You select the format—3.0 or 2.1—using the vCard Format radio buttons (3.0 is the default). If you select 2.1, you can set the language encoding for the vCard using the vCard 2.1 Encoding pop-up menu; an encoding determines the settings for character display, such as Western (Mac OS Roman) to use the Roman characters and keyboard mappings common to North America and western Europe. (You typically don't change this option unless you are working with people who use languages with character sets different than yours.)

If you don't want your personal card shared, be sure to select the Enable Private Me card option. The remaining two options in the vCard pane determine whether notes in a card are included in the exported vCard and whether the photo in a card is included in the exported vCard.

Working with iCal

iCal is Mac OS X's calendar application, where you can set and track appointments and to-do items. Figure 21.4 shows its month view. You can change the view to Day, Week, or Month using the View menu, or simply click Day, Week, or Month in the toolbar.

New Feature

Mac OS X Lion changes how iCal appears, making it look and work more like the version of iCal on the iPad. As part of this change, the list of calendars that used to appear on the left side of the window must now be opened in a pop-over by clicking the Calendars button or choosing View ➪ Show Calendar List. Also gone is the Mini Calendar view that let you see your current month in a small window when in other calendar views, though the Week view in iCal now also shows the current month in a miniature calendar. ∎

You can show or hide the To Do Items column at right by clicking the View or Hide To Do Items icon button (the thumbtack icon) at the bottom right of the iCal window, or by choosing View ➪ Show/Hide To Do List or pressing Option+⌘+T.

FIGURE 21.4

The iCal application, displaying the month view and with the Calendars pop-over open and the To Do Items pane open

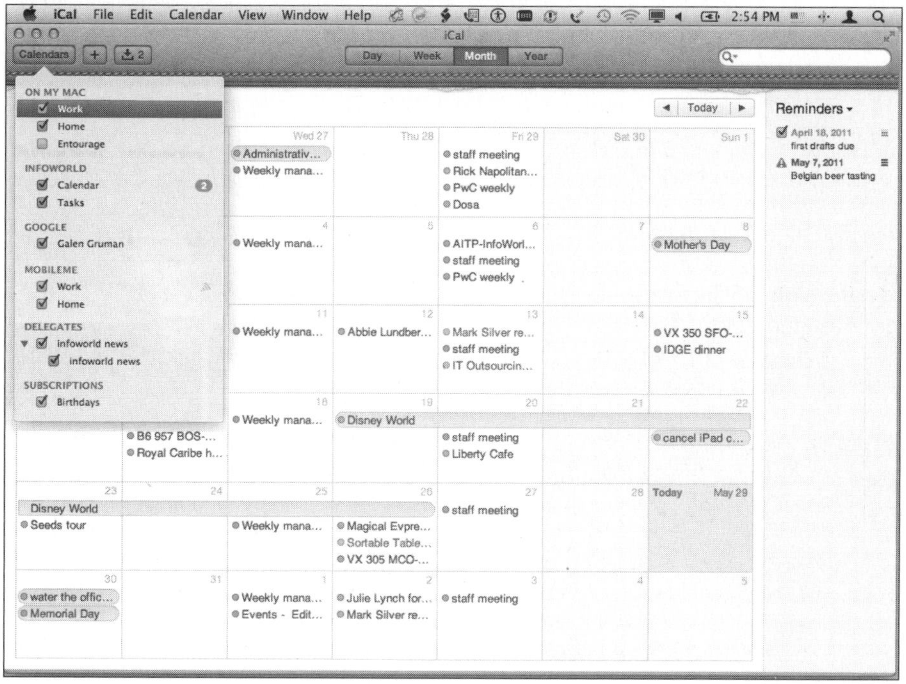

Working with iCal accounts

Although when you use iCal it may appear to be a single calendar, the truth is that iCal can hold multiple calendars. You can create local calendars, as explained in the next section, and you can create accounts that let iCal work with CalDAV (including Google iCloud, and Yahoo) and Microsoft Exchange 2007 and 2010 accounts. (CalDAV is the Distributed Authoring and Versioning protocol for calendars.)

To add an account to iCal, go to the Accounts pane of the Preferences dialog box (choose iCal ➪ Preferences or press ⌘+, [comma]), and click the + icon button at the bottom of the left column. The Add an Account settings sheet appears. Leave the Account Type pop-up menu set to Automatic, and enter the e-mail address and password for the account you want to synchronize iCal to. iCal tries to determine its settings for you automatically. If it can't, choose one of the options from the Account Type pop-up menu—CalDAV (an iCal server), Exchange, Google, iCloud, or Yahoo—and complete the requested account information. Then click Create. The new account displays in the Calendars pop-over.

Accounts can be added to iCal by other programs, not just through the Preferences dialog box. For example, note these things about the Calendars pop-over in Figure 21.4:

- In the On My Mac section, Home and Work are there by default, while Entourage was added in the figure automatically by Microsoft Entourage (2004 or 2008) to support synchronization with that application.

- Apple's Mail application added the InfoWorld calendar to support synchronization with a Microsoft Exchange server set up in Mail (see Chapters 20 and 22).

- I added my Google calendar as well as two delegated Google calendars by setting up an account in iCal's Preferences dialog box.

- I added the Birthdays calendar through the General pane of iCal's Preferences dialog box (covered later in this chapter); it gets its data from the Address Book application.

You can show and hide their appointments in the main calendar window by selecting and deselecting them in the Calendars pop-over.

Note

In your calendar, each account gets its own color, so you can quickly tell what calendar an item is attached to. ■

Cross-Reference

See Chapter 22 for details on using iCal with the Microsoft Exchange server and the Microsoft Entourage e-mail program. ■

You can add new calendars to your accounts by choosing File ➪ New Calendar and choosing the desired account from the submenu. You can subscribe to others' calendars if they've enabled calendar sharing via a CalDAV server by choosing Calendar ➪ Subscribe or pressing Option+⌘+S and entering the calendar's URL in the settings sheet that appears.

Tip

To add calendars created by other people, such as those with federal holidays or phases of the moon, choose Calendar ➪ Find Subscriptions calendars. Your web browser opens, displaying a page of such calendars available for download (some free, some not). ■

You also can add a calendar group by choosing File ➪ New Calendar Group or pressing Shift+⌘+N. The Calendars pop-over opens, with a new Group calendar in the On My Mac section. Drag any from the On My Mac section into that group so you can display or hide them all at once. To name or rename the group, click it and then enter the (new) name. (You cannot group calendars hosted on other servers, such as Exchange, Google, Yahoo, or CalDAV.) To delete a group, right-click or Control+click it in the pop-over and choose delete.

Navigating your calendar

Beyond changing the view as explained in the beginning of the "Working with iCal" section, you can move through the calendar in several ways.

Click the left-facing triangle at the top of the calendar window (to the left of Today), choose View ➪ Previous, or press ⌘+← to move to the previous day, week, or month (depending on the current view). Likewise, click the right-facing triangle (to the right of Today), choose View⇨Next, or press ⌘+→ to move to the next day, week, or month.

Click Today at the top of the calendar, choose View⇨Go to Today, or press ⌘+T to go to the current date's entry. Choose View⇨Go to Date or press Shift+⌘+T to enter a specific date to go to.

Type text in the Search box, and press Return or click the magnifying glass icon to find events or to-do items that contain specific text.

Tip

To get more details on an event, open an Info window for a selected item by pressing ⌘+I, choosing Edit⇨Get Info, or right-clicking or Control+clicking the item and choosing Get Info from the contextual menu. ■

Tip

To get details of whatever item your pointer is hovering over, open the Inspector window by choosing Edit⇨ Show Inspector or pressing Option+⌘+I. ■

Creating and editing events

It's easy to add an event such as an appointment or meeting to your calendar: Double-click in your calendar to add an empty event. (You also can click the + icon button at the upper left of the iCal window, to the right of the Calendars button.) It is associated with whatever calendar is marked as the default in the General pane of the Preferences dialog box (explained later in this chapter), but you can change the calendar it is associated with by double-clicking the new calendar entry to open the details window. In that window, choose a new calendar from the Calendar pop-up menu, as Figure 21.5 shows.

Fill in the relevant fields: event title (labeled New Event by default), Location, URL, and Note. Select All-Day if the event runs the entire day, such as a birthday. Otherwise, choose the start and end days and times using the From and To fields. If Time Zone Support is enabled (explained later in this chapter), the Time Zone pop-up menu is shown, defaulting to your current time zone, but you can choose another time zone here.

Tip

You can set the current time zone in the Time & Date system preference for all applications on your Mac, as Chapter 28 explains. If Time Zone Support is enabled in iCal, to change just iCal's time zone, when you are traveling, for example, click the current time zone's pop-up menu at the upper right of the iCal window, and choose a new time zone. If the desired time zone is not listed, choose Other to open a dialog box where you can click a world map or choose from a list to select a new time zone. (The pop-up menu does not appear if Time Zone Support is disabled.) ■

In the Repeat pop-up menu, you can set the event as a recurring event: Every Day, Every Week, Every Month, Every Year, or Custom, which lets you choose multiple days, such as Tuesday and Thursday every week, or on specific dates, such as the 17th of every month or on every Wednesday of the month. What you can't do is choose a pattern such as the first Monday of the month.

FIGURE 21.5

Adding an event in iCal

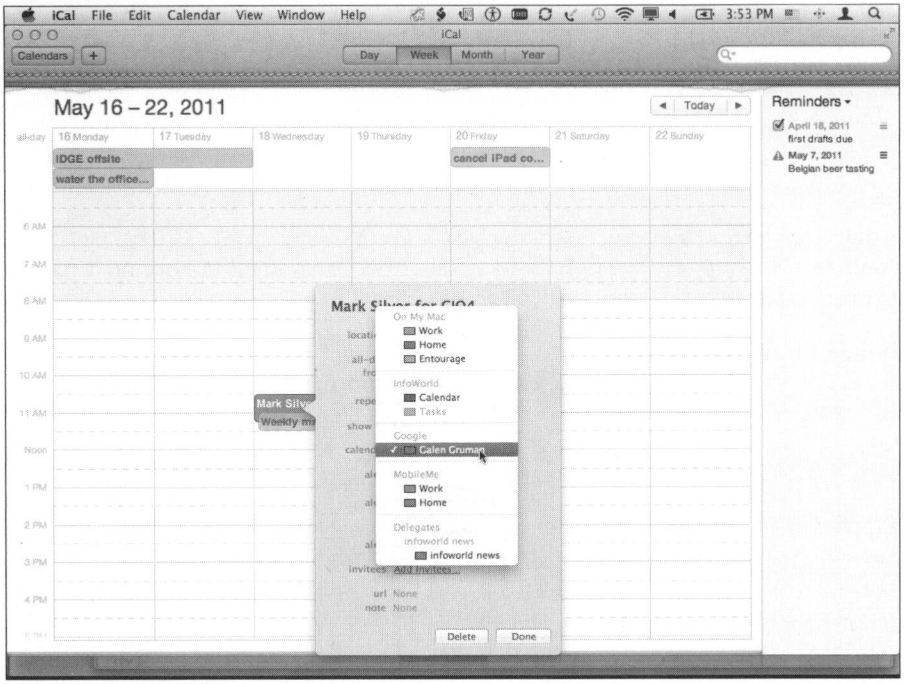

In the Alert pop-up menu, you can set an alert—a sound, e-mail, or pop-up alert—or open a file at a period before the event you specify. Note that some calendar servers (accounts) let you set two alerts; in such cases, a second Alert pop-up menu displays.

Click Add File to attach a file to the event. Note that this field may not display if the calendar server (account) chosen for this event does not support file attachments.

Click Done to save the event. If the event is added to a server-based calendar, it displays on all Macs, PCs, and mobile devices that have access to that calendar the next time they sync.

To edit an event, just double-click it in the calendar, click Edit, change the desired options, and click Done. You can quickly move an event to a new calendar by right-clicking or Control+ clicking it and choosing a new calendar from the Calendar option's submenu in the contextual menu. The contextual menu also has commands to cut, copy, paste, and duplicate the event, see its details (Get Info), and send an e-mail with the event details to someone else (Mail Event).

Working with invitations

When setting up an event, you can invite other people to attend. Do so by clicking the Invitees field; as you begin typing names, a menu of matches from Address Book and Mail appear that you can select from; enter a tab between names. After you add an invitee, you can click it to get a list of options, such as mailing the event to that person, marking the person as an optional invitee, and editing the invitee.

New Feature

In some cases, if the server supports this capability, when you enter a person's name in the Invitees field, a link appears labeled Available Meeting Times. Click it to see when that person's schedule shows him or her to be available. This capability is new to Mac OS X Lion. ∎

If you added invitees, the button at the bottom right is named Send; click it to send each of them an invitation to the event. If you add attendees later, the button is named Update instead, so only the new attendees are invited. If no attendees are added, the button is named Done. In all three cases, clicking the button saves the event.

To invite someone to an event outside of the Invitees field, right-click or Control+click the event in the calendar and choose Mail Event. The Mail application opens with an .ics calendar invitation attached. Add the addresses, type any message you want, and send the invitation via e-mail.

If you have outstanding calendar invitations from Exchange (in the .ics format), either via Entourage or Mail, they appear in your iCal calendar, with gray backgrounds and a thick dashed border around them, to indicate you have not acted on them. Double-click the event to open it, where you can decline, accept, or tentatively accept (the Maybe option) it and assign its calendar using the Calendar pop-up menu.

Pending invitations also display in the upper left of the iCal application, near the Calendars button. The Invitations icon button displays the number of pending invitations (in Figure 21.4, there are two pending invitations indicated). Click the button to open a pop-over listing the invitations; for each new invitation, you have three buttons: Maybe, Decline, and Accept. Some invitations may have the OK button instead, such as those that indicate a change in time for an existing appointment.

Invitation acceptance doesn't always work as expected, so be sure to verify your appointments:

- After you accept an invitation, you can't change it—only the initiator can do that. (Such changes are usually—but not always—updated on your calendar.)

- Sometimes, invitations get accepted on an account you don't want them associated with. You can copy and paste an invitation to another calendar, but that breaks the appointment's connection to the originator's in the new calendar. And if you cut the appointment, the originator usually gets a message saying you declined the invitation.

- Sometimes, invitations get placed at the wrong time. This seems to happen mainly through invitations handled via Google when you have Time Zone Support enabled. In that case, Google seems to assign the item to Eastern time zone, regardless of the time zone specified in the invitation file. (Exchange does not make this error, and the error seems to be on Google's end, as it happens in Mac OS X Snow Leopard, Mac OS X Lion, and in iOS 4 on the iPad, iPhone, and iPod Touch.) So you may need to turn off Time Zone Support if you're syncing via Google Calendar.

New Feature

iCal in Mac OS X Lion no longer has the Notification pane to list all outstanding invitations. You have to look for them in your calendar or in the Invitations icon button. ■

You can accept or decline invitations in Mail, by right-clicking or Control+clicking the `.ics` file at the bottom of the message body and choosing Add to iCal. If you have multiple calendars, you can (usually) choose which calendar to associate it with after you accept it.

Working with to-do items

To create a to-do item (which iCal calls *reminders*), choose File ⇨ New Reminder or press ⌘+K. Or right-click or Control+click the Reminders pane (if it's displayed; turn it on by choosing View ⇨ Show Reminders or pressing Option+⌘+T) and choose New Reminder from the contextual menu. (Click the View or Hide Reminders icon button [the thumbtack icon], choose View ⇨ Show Reminders, or press Option+⌘+T if the To Do Items column is not visible.)

New Feature

iCal in Mac OS X Lion now calls to-do items reminders, and it's changed all its menu and other options to reflect that new nomenclature. ■

Note

Not all calendar servers allow you to create to-do items (which some call tasks). You get an error message when you try to add a to-do item to a calendar that doesn't support them. To change the calendar that a to-do item is being added to, select it in the Calendar pop-up menu. ■

Now type the to-do item's text. To provide more detail, double-click the to-do item to open a pop-over similar to the one shown in Figure 21.6. The options for a to-do item are as follows (not all options display in all calendars, due to differences among calendar servers):

- **Completed:** Select this option when you've finished the task. You also can select the check box to the left of the to-do item in the Reminders pane to mark it completed.
- **Priority:** Set a priority in the Priority pop-up menu. You also can set the priority by clicking the icon pop-up menu to the right of the to-do item in the Reminders pane.
- **Private:** This keeps the item private, so it's not visible to others in a shared calendar.
- **Due Date:** Select this option if the to-do item has a due date, and then set the date.
- **Alert:** Use this pop-up menu to issue an alert at a user-specified interval before the due date.
- **Calendar:** Use this pop-up menu to choose which calendar to associate the to-do item with.
- **URL:** Enter a URL in the URL field, such as a related document on the web.
- **Note:** Add a note in the Note field if desired.

Click Close to save your changes.

FIGURE 21.6

The details of a to-do item

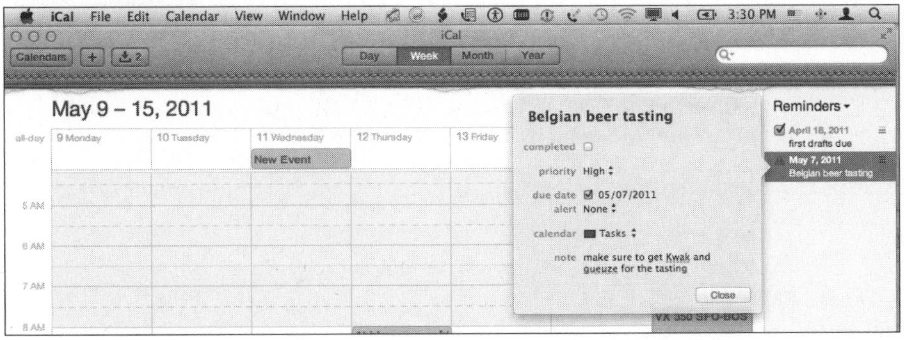

To edit an existing to-do item, simply double-click it. Click Close to save the changes or Revert to undo them.

You can sort the Reminders column by selecting the To Do Items pop-up menu, whose icon is to the right of the Reminders label. The options are Sort by Due Date, Sort by Priority, Sort by Title, Sort by Calendar, and Sort Manually. (This option lets you drag the to-do items in any order you want.) If Hide the Items After the Calendar View is selected (a check mark appears by the option), only to-do items whose calendars are selected in the Calendars pop-over appear; otherwise, all to-do items appear. If the Show All Completed Items is selected, all items appear in the To Do Items column; otherwise, only uncompleted ones appear.

You can work on to-do items by right-clicking or Control+clicking them to get a contextual menu. The options are straightforward: Cut, Copy, Paste (if one or more events was previously cut or copied), Duplicate, Select All, and Get Info. You also can sort them by choosing Sort By, change an item's priority by choosing Priority, change the calendar an item belongs to by choosing Calendar, and mail the item by choosing Mail Reminder.

Note

Any to-do items created on calendar servers that support tasks are automatically added to your iCal calendar. For example, Entourage 2004 and 2008 do not sync to-do items with iCal, but Exchange 2007 and 2010 do. ∎

Publishing and subscribing to calendars

iCal can publish its calendars and subscribe to others people's published calendars.

To publish a calendar to a CalDAV-compatible server, select it in the calendars column and choose Calendar ⇨ Publish. (For iCloud, choose Calendar ⇨ Share Calendar.) Options in the settings sheet that appears include having the published calendar updated automatically as it changes, including to-do items, attachments, and alerts. After publishing the calendar, iCal displays a settings sheet that provides the URL for the calendar, as well as provides the Visit

Page button to open the calendar in your web browser and the Send Mail button to send an e-mail containing the link to other people.

A published calendar has a radio-wave icon to its right in the Calendars pop-over (the icon looks somewhat like the Wi-Fi menu bar icon). You can send e-mails to people and provide its URL by selecting the calendar in the Calendars column and then choosing Calendar ⇨ Send Publish E-Mail, which opens Mail with the calendar's URL entered into the message body. To unpublish a calendar, select it in the Calendars column and choose Calendar ⇨ Unpublish.

You can subscribe to published calendars by choosing Calendar ⇨ Subscribe and entering the calendar's URL.

Setting iCal preferences

iCal has only a few preferences set in its Preferences dialog box, which you access by choosing iCal ⇨ Preferences or pressing ⌘+, (comma). There are three panes: General, Accounts, and Advanced.

General preferences

In the General pane, you have the following options:

- **Days Per Week:** This pop-up menu enables you to choose how many days display per week: 7 or 5.

- **Start Week On:** This pop-up menu enables you to select the first day of the week as displayed in iCal.

- **Scroll in Week View By:** This pop-up menu has two options: Day and Week. If you choose Day, clicking the triangle buttons in the toolbar moves the calendar display one day at a time; if you choose Week, it moves the calendar display one week at a time.

- **Day Starts At:** This pop-up menu enables you to set the time that appears at the top of the iCal week and day views. (Earlier times are grayed in the display.)

- **Day Ends At:** This pop-up menu enables you to set the time that indicates the end of your business day. (Later times are grayed in the display.)

- **Show _ Hours at a Time:** This pop-up menu determines how many hours display onscreen in the day and week views.

- **Default Calendar:** This pop-up menu determines which calendar new events are added to in iCal. (You can change its associated calendar when creating or editing a specific event.)

- **Show Event Times:** If selected, this option shows the event times when you view the calendar in day, week, or month view; note that this considerably shortens the amount of detail visible in the month view.

- **Show Birthdays Calendar:** If selected, this option adds a calendar called Birthdays to the Calendars pop-over.

- **Add a Default Alert to All New Timed Events and Invitations:** If selected, you can enter a number of minutes that will set an alert for every new event at that time interval.

New Feature

The ability to set a default calendar is new to Mac OS X Lion. Also, the Show Event Times option now displays times in day and week views, not just month views. Gone is the Synchronize iCal with Other Computers and Devices Using MobileMe option. ∎

Accounts preferences

The Accounts pane lists the available accounts in a list in the left side of the dialog box. You can add more accounts by clicking the + icon button; you can delete existing accounts by selecting them (one at a time) and clicking the – icon button.

The Accounts pane also lets you see and change the settings for each account. Click an account, and use the Account Information and Server Settings subpanes to view options such as the username and password, how often the calendar is synced (refreshed), and the server configuration. In the Account Information pane, you can disable an account from displaying in iCal and syncing with iCal by deselecting the Enable This Account option. (Select the option to enable the account again.)

The third subpane, Delegation, lets you access other people's calendars, for an assistant managing a boss's calendar or a project team using a shared calendar, for example. Only some servers, such as Exchange and Google, allow such delegation. For Exchange, click the + icon button in the Delegation pane to complete the sign-in information for other accounts (get this information from your IT staff); you can see who has access to your calendar by clicking the Edit button. For Google, a list of calendars you have access to appears in the Delegation pane; select the ones you want to make visible and editable in iCal. Note that some Google calendars display as Read Only, meaning you can see them in iCal but cannot add or modify events in them.

Advanced preferences

The Advanced pane has the following options:

- **Turn On Time Zone Support:** This option, which is selected by default, enables you to set up an independent time zone for iCal, such as when you're traveling, as explained in the section earlier in this chapter on working with events. Note that this option can cause time zone mismatches with invitations sent via Google Calendar.

- **Hide Reminders That Are Due After the Dates Visible in the Calendar:** This option, which is selected by default, shows only to-do items that fall within the current calendar view (day, week, or month).

- **Hide Reminders _ Days After They Have Been Completed:** This option, which is selected by default, hides completed to-do items after the specified number of days have passed; 7 is the default setting.

- **Delete Events _ Days After They Have Passed:** If selected, this option automatically removes events from your calendar after the specified number of days have passed; 30 is the default.

- **Delete Reminders _ Days After They Have Passed:** If selected, this option automatically removes to-do items from your calendar after the specified number of days have passed; 30 is the default.

- **Turn Off All Alerts:** If selected, this option disables all alerts. You might use it in a meeting, so your MacBook doesn't make noises that distract the participants.

- **Open Events in Separate Windows:** If selected, this option opens a new window for each event you open; otherwise, opening an event closes the previously open event.

- **Ask Before Sending Changes to Events:** This option, which is selected by default, displays an alert when changes to events occur, asking you if you want to update the attendees with the new information. If no attendees are selected for an event, this alert does not display.

- **Automatically Retrieve CalDAV Invitations from Mail:** This option, which is selected by default, automatically detects compatible calendar invitations (such as those in most .ics files) in Mail and displays them as gray appointments in iCal, so you can decide whether to accept or decline them.

Summary

The Address Book lets you manage your contacts, and it works with Mail, iChat, and iCal to make it easy to fill in and contact people listed in the Address Book. Address Book can sync with Exchange 2007 and 2010, Google, iCloud, and Yahoo accounts, as well as with LDAP and CardDAV servers.

iCal lets you create and track appointments and to-do items, as well as invite other people to meetings via e-mail notifications. It supports .ics invitations that can be sent via e-mail; the recipient can accept the invitation either in Mail or iCal and have a confirmation sent to the originator.

In addition to syncing invitations with others, you can set up shared calendars in iCal, accessible via the web or the local network. And iCal can sync calendars with your Exchange 2007 and 2010, Google, iCloud, and Yahoo accounts, as well as via CalDAV servers such as Mac OS X Lion Server.

Working with Microsoft Exchange

M ac OS X comes with a great e-mail application (Mail), calendar application (iCal), and contacts manager (Address Book). But many people in the business world use Microsoft's Exchange products to handle all three functions, with Exchange Server on the back end managing everything and Entourage or Outlook on the Mac providing users with access to their e-mail, calendars, and contacts from the Exchange Server.

Microsoft has long made its Entourage application available for the Mac, so users have been able to work with Exchange for more than a decade. Then in 2010, it replaced Exchange with Outlook, an e-mail application more like its Windows version (also called Outlook). But Mac OS X integrates the Microsoft ActiveSync technology used by Exchange Server, making it even easier to work in an Exchange-based business, especially if your business uses the newest versions of that server, Exchange Server 2007 or 2010.

This means you can continue to use Entourage or Outlook as your e-mail, contacts, and calendar applications alongside Address Book and iCal, or you can drop Entourage or Outlook and use Mail, Address Book, and iCal exclusively and still be a "native" participant in your business's Exchange environment.

Cross-Reference

Chapter 20 explains how to set up and use Mail, both for Exchange and other servers. Chapter 21 explains how to set up Address Book and iCal, again both for Exchange and other servers. ∎

How Exchange Works

Microsoft Exchange is a server application that stores and routes several kinds of information to users that connect to it through a *client application* such as Entourage, Outlook, Mail, iCal, or Address Book. Exchange handles e-mail, contacts, calendar entries, to-do items, RSS (Really Simple Syndication) feeds, and newsgroup feeds. By managing these types of information in a central location (the Exchange Server), Exchange makes it easy to share and collaborate, such as being able to check a colleagues' calendar to see if he or she is available, or to send e-mails to people you select from a corporate directory (rather than having to enter their e-mail addresses manually or have them stored in your Mac's Address Book).

Note

Microsoft Exchange is not the only server application you might use for communication and collaboration. IBM's Lotus Notes and Novell's GroupWise also are used by many businesses, and they both come with a Mac client application to allow access to their e-mail, contacts, and calendar information. But Mac OS X does not support their servers natively, so they don't integrate as well with Mail, iCal, or Address Book as Exchange does. ■

Exchange Server has several versions in use: 2000, 2003, 2007, and 2010. Exchange Server 2003 is the most widely deployed, but Exchange Server 2007 is steadily replacing 2000 and 2003 installations. And the most recent version, Exchange 2010, is starting to get adoption. (Businesses tend to upgrade server software more slowly than individuals update applications because doing so affects every user, so it's common for businesses to wait a few years before updating a server application to be sure all the kinks have been worked out.) It's important to know which version of Exchange Server your business uses, because how your Mac works with Exchange Server varies based on the server version your business has.

If your business runs Exchange Server 2000 or 2003, you won't get many of the benefits of Mac OS X's support for Exchange 2007 or 2010. That's because if you're using Mail, it interacts with Exchange Server 2000 or 2003 through an IMAP (Internet Message Access Protocol) connection, which gives it access to just e-mails and the corporate address book. iCal and Address Book won't synchronize to Exchange Server 2000 or 2003 directly; you must use Entourage 2003 as the go-between, as explained later in this chapter. (Chapter 20 explains how to set up Mail through an IMAP connection if you are using Exchange 2000 or 2003, or, for that matter, Lotus Notes or Novell GroupWise.)

Note

Your network administrator must set up Exchange Server 2000 or 2003 to support IMAP connections, such as through a virtual private network (VPN) or Outlook Web Access (OWA), for your Mac to connect outside your corporate network. Inside a corporate network, IMAP or OWA must be enabled for Exchange Server 2000 or 2003 if you want to access Exchange through Mail instead of through Entourage. (By contrast, you can connect natively with Exchange Server 2007 or 2010 from Mail, iCal, and Address Book.) ■

If your business runs Exchange Server 2007 or 2010, you get much better integration with your Mac using Mail, Address Book, and iCal, to the point where you don't need to run Entourage any longer if you don't want to. That's because Mail, Address Book, and iCal can talk directly to the Exchange 2007 or 2010 server, synchronizing e-mail, contacts, and calendar entries (as well as RSS feeds, to-do items, and newsgroup feeds). Plus, with the ActiveSync support, this synchronization happens instantly, not on a scheduled basis as with IMAP. (About the only thing that you can't do with Apple's software is access delegated e-mail accounts, which Entourage and Outlook can do.)

Because Exchange processes and stores all e-mails, contacts, and calendar items centrally, then distributes the relevant items to each user, by default you always have a copy of your e-mail, contacts, and calendar items on the server. So, if you access Exchange from another computer (or from your iPhone, iPad, iPod Touch, or other compatible mobile device), you have access to all the same information as from your "regular" Mac. And if your Mac crashes or you accidentally delete messages, the messages likely are still available on the Exchange server. You can configure for how long these messages are stored on the server in Mail's Preferences dialog box (choose Mail ⇨ Preferences or press ⌘+, [comma]), in the Accounts pane, as Chapter 20 describes.

Note

Typically, Exchange copies your messages, calendar items, and contacts to your Mac as well as keeps copies on the Exchange Server, but sometimes Exchange Server is configured not to allow local copies to be kept. For example, some industries have high standards to safeguard information and thus make employees keep everything only on servers so their data can't get stolen if their Mac is lost or stolen. ■

Using Mac OS X's Mail with Exchange

Mail is the Mac OS X application that you're likely to use the most with Exchange, because people typically spend much more time in e-mail than in their address books or calendars. Plus, you can update Address Book within Mail and accept calendar invitations within Mail. How Mail interacts with Exchange depends on the version of Exchange Server you use.

Cross-Reference

To set up Mail, follow the instructions in Chapter 20. The details here are specific to using Exchange, but most of the setup is the same no matter which e-mail server you use. ■

Setting up Mail for Exchange 2007 or 2010

When setting up an e-mail account in Mail, you have the option of setting up Address Book and iCal at the same time for an Exchange e-mail account (or if you're using Exchange 2010— for the purposes of Mac OS X, Exchange 2010 and 2007 are one and the same). As Figure 22.1 shows, when asked for the incoming mail server information, there are two options not available for other types of e-mail accounts: Address Book Contacts and iCal Calendars. If you select Address Book Contacts, your Exchange contacts list is synchronized automatically with Address Book on your Mac; if you select iCal Calendars, your Exchange calendar and to-do items are synchronized automatically with iCal on your Mac.

New Feature

In Mac OS X Lion's version of Mail, the Exchange mail account replaces what had been labeled Exchange 2007 in Mac OS X Snow Leopard. It's the same feature, but Apple removed the "2007" because it applies to both Exchange 2007 and Exchange 2010 servers. ∎

FIGURE 22.1

When configuring Exchange-based e-mail accounts, you also can synchronize Address Book and iCal with Exchange using the Also Configure options.

When you create an Exchange 2007 or 2010 e-mail account, you can set how long messages are kept on the Exchange server in the Accounts pane of the Preferences dialog box (choose Mail ➪ Preferences or press ⌘+, [comma]), as Chapter 20 describes.

If you are using Exchange 2007 or 2010, you have slightly different options than if you are using an Exchange IMAP connection to Exchange 2000 or 2003.

The differences are in two subpanes of the Accounts pane: Mailbox Behaviors and Advanced:

- **Mailbox Behaviors:** In Trash options, Exchange 2007 and 2010 accounts don't have the Move Deleted Messages to the Trash Mailbox option, given that deleted e-mail is automatically moved to the server's Trash folder.

- **Advanced:** The Internal Server Path and External Server Path fields enable you to put in a server address as provided by your network administrator to ensure a proper connection to the Exchange 2007 or 2010 server. Leave them blank unless given such an address. (These options are not available for Exchange IMAP connections.) The internal path is the connection inside the corporate network, and the external path is the connection from outside the corporate network. Not all organizations use two different paths preferring instead to use a single path no matter where the user is; in that case, you may be given just the Internal Server Path information.

When set up, Mail syncs to Exchange 2007 or 2010 immediately, so both your Mac and the server are always kept up to date. With Exchange 2000 and 2003, Mail syncs periodically as set in the Check for New Messages pop-up menu in the General pane of Mail's Preferences dialog box.

Setting up iCal for Exchange 2000 or 2003

If your company uses Exchange Server 2000 or 2003, set up your e-mail account as standard IMAP connection (called Exchange IMAP in some dialog boxes), as Chapter 20 explains.

Working with an Exchange e-mail account in Mail

Apple's Mail works very well with Exchange 2000, 2003, 2007, and 2010. When you create an account for an Exchange e-mail account, Mail accesses not only its e-mails but also its notes, to-do items, and any RSS and newsgroup feeds set up on that server.

Cross-Reference
For the details on how to use Mail, see Chapter 20. This chapter covers just Exchange-specific functions. ∎

You can force Exchange and Mail to sync by choosing Mailbox ⇨ Synchronize "*accountname*", or by right-clicking or Control+clicking the account in the left column of the Message Viewer window and choosing Synchronize "*accountname*" from the contextual menu. If you're using Exchange 2007 or 2010, you rarely need to force synchronization, because ActiveSync maintains a continuous synchronization; but in earlier versions of Exchange, forcing a sync is a handy way to get new mail before the next scheduled sync takes place (such as when your boss says he or she just sent you a message and needs an immediate answer).

In the Message Viewer's Sidebar, you see your Exchange e-mail account listed in the Mailboxes section at top, as one of the accounts in the Inbox. (Its name matches whatever account name you provided when setting up the account.) Click the disclosure triangle to the left of the Exchange account's name to expand the mailbox and see all the folders set up at your Exchange sever. In addition to the usual Drafts, Junk E-Mail, and Trash, you see any other folders stored in Exchange. In separate sections of the Sidebar, you also find your Exchange account listed where appropriate, such as in the Notes mailbox in the Reminder section.

Right-click or Control+click your Exchange account mailbox anywhere it's listed in the Sidebar, and choose Get Account Info from the contextual menu to see all messages and folders stored for your account on the Exchange server, whether you've exceeded your storage quota limits, and to manage subscriptions to RSS and newsgroup feeds provided through the Exchange server.

Note

To-do items are saved in iCal or, if you choose your Exchange e-mail account or Entourage as the calendar, in Exchange. ■

The version of Mail in Mac OS X Lion supports Exchange's Out of Office feature, so you can set up automatic replies to people who e-mail you that you are not checking your e-mail. To set up an out-of-the-office notice, right-click or Control+click your Exchange account in the Sidebar (in the Inbox list in the Mailboxes section) and choose Out of Office from the contextual menu. The Account Info dialog box appears, set to the Out of Office pane, as Figure 22.2 shows.

FIGURE 22.2

Setting up an out-of-the-office notice for an Exchange account in Mail

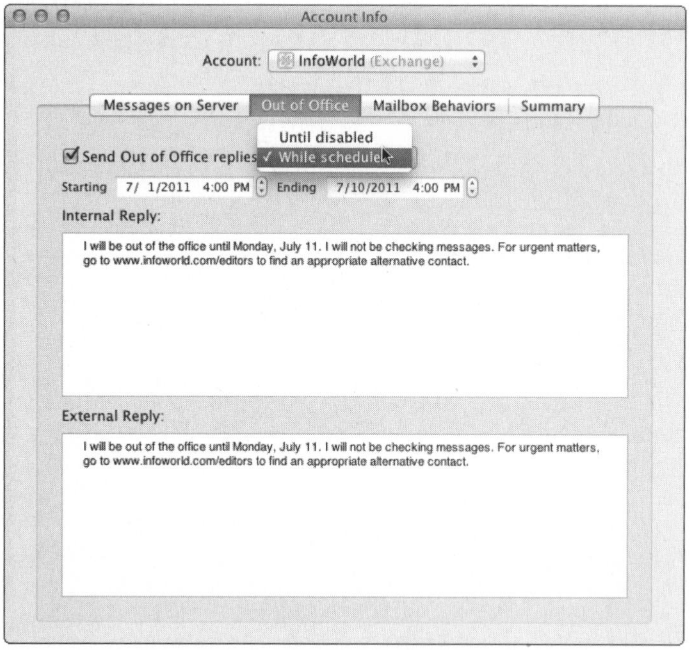

New Feature

The Out of Office feature is new to Mac OS X Lion. Its addition addresses one of the more glaring Exchange deficiencies in previous versions of Mail. ■

One thing you can't do in Mail with an Exchange account is view an account to which you are delegated access, such as for an assistant who checks his or her boss's e-mail. You must use Entourage or Outlook instead of Mail if you need that capability.

Using iCal with Exchange

The process for setting up iCal differs notably, depending on whether you use Exchange 2007 or 2010 or an earlier version of Exchange.

Setting up iCal for Exchange 2007 or 2010

If your business uses Exchange Server 2007 or 2010 and you selected the iCal Calendars option in the Accounts pane of Mail's Preferences dialog box (choose Mail ⇨ Preferences or press ⌘+, [comma]), appointments and to-do items you set in iCal are synced to your Exchange calendar and vice versa.

You also can set up iCal to work with Exchange 2007 or 2010, rather than doing so through Mail. Go to the Accounts pane in iCal's Preferences dialog box by choosing iCal ⇨ Preferences or pressing ⌘+, (comma). Add your account information in the Account Information subpane and the server connection information in the Server Settings subpane. (These should match the Account pane's settings in Mail's Preferences dialog box.)

Cross-Reference

For details on how to use iCal, see Chapter 21. This chapter covers Exchange-specific functions only. ■

Setting up iCal for Exchange 2000 or 2003

If your business uses Exchange 2000 or 2003, you need to use Entourage as the way station between Exchange and iCal. To do so in either Entourage 2004 or Entourage 2008, go to Entourage's Preferences dialog box (choose Entourage ⇨ Preferences or press ⌘+, [comma]), and go to the Sync Services pane. Select the Synchronize Events and Tasks with iCal and .Mac option to set up the Entourage calendar in iCal and have events and to-do items sync automatically.

Note

You must choose either to sync your local Entourage calendar or the Exchange server calendar; you cannot sync both to iCal. ■

In iCal, you now have a calendar called Entourage. Any appointments and to-do items you add to the Entourage calendar in iCal are synchronized to Exchange (the others are not), and any Exchange calendar items are synced to the Entourage calendar in iCal.

Caution

If you use Outlook 2011 on the Mac, note that it cannot sync with iCal through Exchange 2000 or 2003, as Entourage can. Microsoft says it may provide that capability as an update at some point. ∎

Using iCal with Exchange 2007 or 2010

After iCal is set up to sync with Exchange 2007 or 2010, you can do several things you can't do with Exchange 2000 or 2003:

- When you open an event in iCal, click in the Location field to get a list of available meeting rooms to schedule the meeting in (if meeting-room availability is enabled in your Exchange 2007 or 2010 server's Global Address List).
- Likewise, you can check the availability of attendees invited to the event, by choosing individuals in the Invitees field.

Cross-Reference

See Chapter 21 for details on the iCal functions that work with all versions of Exchange, such as sending meeting invites. ∎

Using Address Book with Exchange

The process for setting up Address Book also differs, depending on whether you use Exchange 2007 or an earlier version of Exchange.

Setting up Address Book for Exchange 2007

If your business uses Exchange Server 2007 or 2010 and you selected the Address Book Contacts option in the Accounts pane of Mail's Preferences dialog box (choose Mail ⇨ Preferences or press ⌘+, [comma]), contacts you add and modify in Address Book are synced to your Exchange address book and vice versa.

You also can set up Address Book to work with Exchange 2007 or 2010, rather than doing so through Mail. Go to the Accounts pane in Address Book's Preferences dialog box by choosing Address Book ⇨ Preferences or pressing ⌘+, (comma). Add your account information in the Account Information subpane and the server connection information in the Server Settings subpane. (These should match the Account pane's settings in Mail's Preferences dialog box.)

Cross-Reference

For the details on how to use Address Book, see Chapter 21. This chapter covers just Exchange-specific functions. ∎

Setting up Address Book for Exchange 2000 and 2003

If your business uses Exchange 2000 or 2003, you need to use Entourage as the way station between Exchange and iCal. To do so in either Entourage 2004 or Entourage 2008, go to Entourage's Preferences dialog box (choose Entourage ⇨ Preferences or press ⌘+, [comma]), and go to the Sync Services pane. Select the Synchronize Contacts with Address Book and .Mac option to sync contacts with Address Book automatically.

Note that you cannot use Outlook 2011 in a similar fashion to bridge your Exchange server with Address Book.

Using an iPhone, iPad, or iPod Touch with Exchange

iPhone, iPad, and iPod Touch users have the same ability to directly connect their devices to Exchange servers as Mac OS X users do. If you set up your iOS devices—iPhones, iPads, and iPod Touches—to sync directly with Exchange, and you set up Entourage, Mail, iCal, and/or Address Book to sync to Exchange (directly via Exchange 2007 or 2010 or through Entourage for earlier versions of Exchange), your Mac and your mobile devices stay in sync with each other and with the Exchange server. It really is that simple.

Note

You can use Apple's iCloud service to sync your Mac to your iPhone, iPad, or iPod Touch and to other computers if you don't use Exchange, as Chapter 17 explains. Likewise, if you use IBM's Lotus Notes 8.5, IBM offers the Lotus Notes Traveler application for iPhones, iPads, and iPod Touches to sync e-mail. If you use Novell's GroupWise 8, iOS devices can sync to it directly if your company has installed the Data Synchronizer Mobility Pack on the server as well. ∎

Note

If you use a smartphone or tablet that doesn't come from Apple, you'll want a sync utility for it, to transfer contacts, music, and more. Research in Motion and Microsoft have free utilities for their BlackBerry (http://us.blackberry.com/apps-software/desktop/desktop_mac.jsp) and Windows Phone 7 (www.microsoft.com/windowsphone/en-us/apps/mac-connector.aspx) devices, respectively. If you use an Android device, some smartphone models running the Android 2.2 or 2.3 operating system can sync to Exchange servers, as can most tablets running the Android 3.0 or 3.1 operating system. For other Android devices or to sync with other types of e-mail servers, you'll want Salling Media Sync ($22; www.salling.com/mediasync/mac). For other devices, Mark/Space likely makes compatible versions of its Missing Sync utility ($40; www.markspace.com). ∎

Setting up the iPhone, iPad, or iPod Touch to access Exchange Server 2000, 2003, 2007, or 2010 is easy:

1. **Tap Settings to open the Settings application, and then tap Mail, Contacts, Calendars to set up (or modify) an account.**

2. **Tap Add Account to get a list of supported e-mail servers.** Tap the Microsoft Exchange logo, and follow the prompts to set up your account.

3. **You're asked for your e-mail address and password; if the iPhone, iPad, or iPod Touch can figure out the rest of the settings for you, it does.** Otherwise, it asks you for the server address and any security settings (which your network administrator should provide to you).

4. **You're asked whether you want to sync mail, contacts, and/or calendars.** If you set any of these switches to On, they sync wirelessly to the Exchange server. If you set any of these to Off, you must sync them through iTunes, as explained later. You determine how far back to sync mail by tapping the Mail Days to Sync option and choosing one of its options. You also can set specific folders to automatically stay updated by tapping Mail Folders to Push and tapping each folder (other folders are synced only when you open them on your mobile device).

5. **When set up, Exchange starts loading your messages, calendar items, and/or contacts onto your iPhone, iPad, or iPod Touch. In the device's Mail application, you see a list of your Exchange e-mail folders.** If you tap any folder to open it, Exchange begins loading its messages. (Exchange loads new messages into your inbox automatically, but it loads messages in other folders only when you open them.) Any messages you send are automatically copied to Exchange's Sent Items folder, so they can be synchronized with your Mail's or Entourage's Sent Items folder on your Mac.

To modify your Exchange settings, go to the Settings application, tap Mail, Contacts, Calendars, tap the account to change (you can have multiple e-mail accounts set up, but only one Exchange account), and then change the desired settings. Figure 22.3 shows the series of screens to set up and modify your Exchange settings on an iPhone, iPad, or iPod Touch.

If you don't want to synchronize your contacts or calendar with Exchange—perhaps you want to keep personal items off your company's Exchange server—disable synchronization on the iPhone, iPad, or iPod Touch by sliding the Mail, Contacts, and/or Calendars switches to Off—or deleting the account. You can still sync such items between your Mac and mobile device through iTunes or iCloud. Chapters 16 and 17, respectively, explain how to do so.

FIGURE 22.3

Left: The pane to select the type of e-mail account to set up on an iOS device (an iPhone's screens are shown here). Center: The pane in which you enter your Exchange account settings. Right: The pane in which you enable the Exchange data to sync, as well as set the folder sync preferences.

Summary

Mac OS X comes with Microsoft's ActiveSync technology, which enables direct connections between Microsoft's Exchange Server 2007 or 2010 e-mail, calendar, and contact application and Mac OS X's Mail, iCal, and Address Book applications. If you use an earlier version of Exchange Server, you can still sync Mail to it via an Exchange IMAP connection, and sync iCal and Address Book to it using Microsoft's Entourage client application as a way station.

If you use an iPhone, iPad, or iPod Touch, you can set it to synchronize wirelessly to an Exchange server, rather than synchronize through iTunes to Mail, iCal, and Address Book.

Part V

Setting Up and Using Networks

IN THIS PART

Chapter 23
Setting Up a Network and the Internet

Chapter 24
Sharing Files and Other Resources

Chapter 25
Using Mac OS X as a Server

Setting Up a Network and the Internet

L ongtime Mac users know that Apple practically invented the network. Sure, computer networks existed before the Mac, but the early Macs were the first personal computers that regular human beings could connect to each other. No high priests of IT required. To make this possible, Apple invented a technology called AppleTalk that enabled you to connect Macs to each other over cables so they could communicate, and a technology called Apple Filing Protocol (AFP) that enabled them to exchange files. It was truly revolutionary.

Fast-forward 25 years to today and networking is not so special. Even at home, a network of several computers and a printer or two is not uncommon. The world has caught up to the Mac. Well, mostly. Mac OS X stays a step ahead by connecting to several kinds of networks, not just Apple's own standard. So the Mac can easily fit into all sorts of network situations, while most PCs cannot.

In practice, that means that you can easily set up a Mac-only local network, connect to a Windows network, create a mini-network around your Mac with Bluetooth devices, and—oh, yes—connect to computers of all types that use the ubiquitous Internet Protocol.

This chapter looks at setting up local networks where there is no dedicated server that makes applications, file repositories, and other central resources available to everyone. In this case, each computer acts as both a server and a client, providing information to others and accessing information directly from them in what's known as a *peer-to-peer network*.

It also shows you how to connect to the Internet, the global network that provides access to the web and other online resources most of us use every day.

IN THIS CHAPTER

Understanding what a local network is

Connecting the elements of a network

Configuring wired and wireless network connections

Understanding network addresses

Configuring VPN access

Directly networking two Macs together

Getting your Mac connected to the Internet

Working with Network Utility

Understanding Network Technologies

So what is a local network? Technically, it's a small network of less than a few dozen devices connected to a server, often referred to as a LAN (for *local area network*). But the practical definition, and the one this chapter uses, is a network of a handful or two of computers and devices that have no central server. Instead, each system is set up to "serve" (deliver) its data up to everyone else in more of a collaborative, peer-to-peer setup than the traditional "one server, many clients" client/server approach to networking where everything goes through that central server.

Caution

Being part of a network can expose your Mac to serious dangers, such as data theft and viruses. Be sure to use Mac OS X's security controls, as explained in Chapter 26, to reduce that risk. ■

Note

If you're setting up a network that uses a dedicated server, you are working in what's known as a client/server environment. (The server provides and manages the access to the centrally stored information and other resources used by the clients, meaning your Macs, PCs, and network-attached printers.) This chapter does not cover dedicated server setup because that requires having specialized skills for the specific server you're using (typically, Linux, Mac OS X Server, Unix, or Windows Server). In a client/server environment, Mac OS X uses whatever protocol you specify on that server to connect: Apple's AFP or Windows's SMB (Server Message Block). When setting up the Macs as clients of dedicated servers, just enable networking as explained in this chapter for AFP and in Chapter 18 for SMB, and set up file sharing as explained in Chapter 24, and you're ready to network. Chapter 25 gives you a quick tour of Mac OS X Server, but is not meant to be a complete guide to using it. ■

Before you can have your Mac and other devices communicate, you need first to connect them physically so the communication can happen. There are two ways to do this:

- Connect two Macs directly to each other via a cable (Ethernet or FireWire) or via a wireless connection (Wi-Fi or Bluetooth).
- Connect multiple computers and other devices through a router, switch, or hub by using an Ethernet cable or wireless connection (or both). If you're using a router, it also can connect to the Internet, giving all the devices Internet access as well as access to each other. This is the most common way to network.

Figure 23.1 shows the three most common configurations: a direct connection, a home network, and an office network.

Note

A router can connect multiple networks, both internal ones such as your LAN and external ones such as the Internet. A switch (called an access point on a wireless device) connects devices within a local network, routing traffic just to the intended device. A hub connects devices within a local network and sends all data to all devices, letting each device figure out what data is intended for it. Thus, home networks use routers, while office networks may use a mix of routers and switches. (They rarely use hubs these days because of their inefficient data delivery.) ■

FIGURE 23.1

The three typical network setups: direct connection (top), home (middle), and office (bottom)

Direct connection

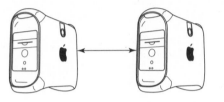

Typical home network

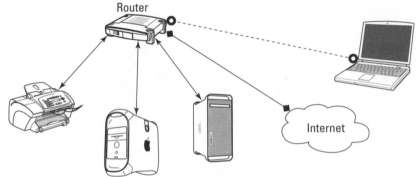

Typical office network

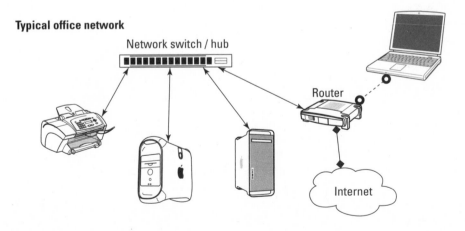

Wired connections

Nearly every Mac comes with an Ethernet (RJ-45) port, which lets you plug in the standard Ethernet cable. An exception is the MacBook Air, which requires a USB-to-Ethernet dongle (a type of adapter) to connect to an Ethernet cable. Every Mac built in the last six years supports the fastest form of Ethernet, called gigabit Ethernet because it can transmit data as fast as 1 gigabit per second (1 Gbps), which is about 125 million characters per second. To get that delivery speed, your network cables and your router, switch, and/or hubs all need to support that speed. Otherwise, you'll get a slower speed, such as the former 100 megabits per second (100 Mbps) standard or the now-ancient 10 Mbps. Don't worry so much about the speed: 100 Mbps and up is fine. And keep in mind that these speed ratings are maximum speeds; typical speeds are about a third to half the maximum.

Note

If you want to connect two Macs directly via Ethernet, you may need a special form of Ethernet cable called a crossover cable. It looks like a regular Ethernet cable, except that the wires inside are ordered differently to provide a direct connection. If your Mac was built before 2002, it likely needs a crossover cable to make a direct Mac-to-Mac connection; if it was built in 2002 or later, it can usually direct-connect by using either a regular cable or a crossover cable. Apple has a list of specific models' requirements at its website (http:// support.apple.com/kb/HT2274). ∎

You also can network two (and only two) Macs together by using a FireWire cable. FireWire cables come in three connector types: 6-pin 400 Mbps, 4-pin 400 Mbps, and 800 Mbps. Each type of connector plugs into a corresponding jack type on a Mac. Most Macs have the 6-pin 400 Mbps jack (called IEEE 1394a or alpha). Newer Macs have the 800 Mbps jack (called IEEE 1394b or beta); many Macs built since 2003 have both, while some Macs built in 2009 and later (such as the MacBooks) have just 800 Mbps jacks. No Macs have the 4-pin 400 Mbps jack, which is typically used in digital camcorders and portable hard disks. Despite the different connector and jack types, you can buy adapters to connect Macs with FireWire jacks. The FireWire 800 jack, for example, supports the older 6-pin and 4-pin FireWire 400 connectors by using an adapter.

Wireless connections

MacBooks and desktop Macs come with wireless networking built in, though in the past some models did not. So if you have an old Mac, you may need to buy a Wi-Fi adapter.

Wi-Fi comes in four types: 802.11b, which runs at up to 11 Mbps; 802.11a, which runs at up to 54 Mbps but uses a different radio band than the other versions of Wi-Fi, so it's less compatible; 802.11g, which runs at up to 54 Mbps; and 802.11n, which runs at up to 100 Mbps. In practice, you'll get a fifth to a third of the maximum speed. A Wi-Fi connection can reach as far as about 300 feet, assuming there are no obstructions—metal and other dense materials can weaken or even block the signal and thus the range.

Note

On most routers, the slowest device on the wireless network makes all other devices run at the same speed. Some recent wireless routers can isolate such slower devices so they don't slow down the rest. ■

Another form of wireless networking is Bluetooth, which most Macs built in the last six years support. Bluetooth is a short-range wireless technology (usually limited to about three feet for headsets and cell phones and 10 feet for other devices such as printers and Macs) and a fairly slow technology as well (1 Mbps to 3 Mbps). Bluetooth is typically used to connect headsets, cellular phones, and input devices (mice, touchpads, keyboards, and Braille readers) to a Mac.

Setting Up a Mac for a Local Network

With the physical (including wireless) connections in place, you need to configure your Mac to communicate across the network. You do so in the Network system preference, as shown in Figure 23.2.

The left side of the Network system preference shows a list of the possible network connections. Active ones have a green dot plus the message "Connected"; inactive ones have a red dot plus either the message "Off," "Not Configured," or "Not Connected," as the case may be; and ones that are set to be active but are not connected have a yellow dot and the message "Not Connected"—in other words, the ones that are having problems or are designed to be manually enabled for specific occasions.

FIGURE 23.2

The Network system preference, with both an Ethernet connection and a Wi-Fi connection active. Also note the two related icons in the menu bar.

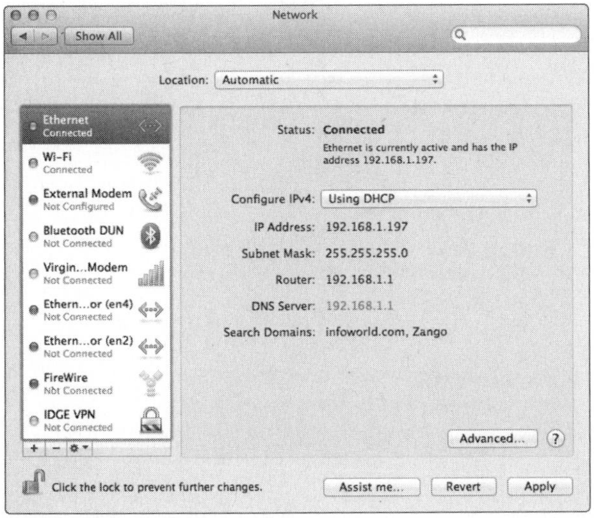

Click one of the connections in the list to see the status details in a settings sheet, as shown for the Ethernet connection in Figure 23.2. You also can change a network connection's settings from the Network system preference's main pane by clicking Advanced, which opens a settings sheet containing multiple panes of configuration options. Figure 23.3 shows the TCP/IP configuration pane for an Ethernet connection.

FIGURE 23.3

The Ethernet settings sheet in the Network system preference, showing the TCP/IP pane

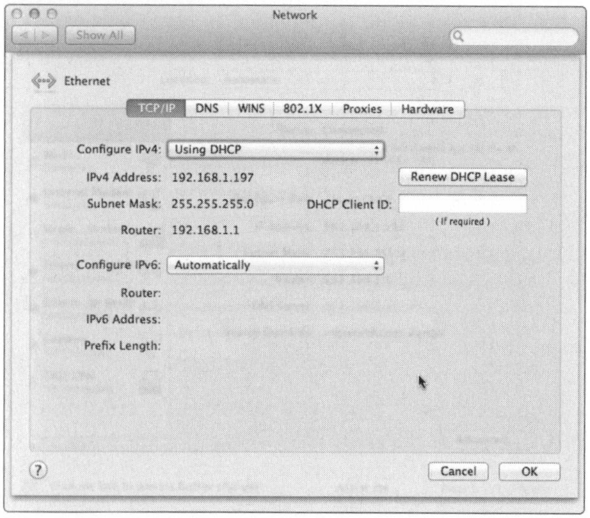

Tip

If you're not very familiar with networking, try clicking Assist Me in the Network system preference to have the Mac walk you through the settings in a friendly Q&A approach. ∎

Tip

If you use your Mac in multiple places, you can store separate settings for each. In the Location pop-up menu in the Network system preference, choose Edit Locations to create a new set, give it a name, and click Done. (Use the Action icon pop-up menu [the gear icon] to rename or duplicate an existing location.) Use the Location pop-up menu to switch to a different set. Most of the time, though, Automatic works just fine figuring out the network settings where possible for you. ∎

Setting up Ethernet connections

For an Ethernet connection to work, your Mac must have an Internet Protocol (IP) address, which is a unique ID for your Mac that enables other Macs and network devices to differentiate it from other devices they're connected to.

If you're using a router or a switch, chances are it uses a technology called Dynamic Host Control Protocol (DHCP) that has issued the IP address for every connected device (so you don't have to worry about it). If not, you will need to give your Mac its own IP address, one that must be unique on your network.

When an Ethernet connection is selected in the Network system preference, the Configure IPv4 pop-up menu is typically set to Using DHCP, which tells the Mac to get its IP address from the router or switch each time it connects. Choosing DHCP automatically fills in the IP Address, Subnet Mask, and Router (the router's IP address, so the Mac knows where to look to get its own IP address) information. And it also usually fills in the DNS (Domain Name Service) Server and Search Domains information used to connect your Mac to the Internet as well. You might choose Using DHCP with Manual Address if you need to give your Mac a permanent address but want the router to manage the rest of the settings.

The other IPv4 menu options are:

- **Using BootP:** Your router may use a different IP-assignment technology than DHCP called Bootstrapping Protocol (BootP). If so, select this option.

- **Manually:** You must type the IP address, subnet mask, router, DNS server, and search domains information yourself. Check with your network administrator for the correct settings.

- **Off:** This turns off the Ethernet connection on your Mac.

- **Create PPPoE Service:** Some DSL-based Internet service providers use a technology called Point-to-Point Protocol over Ethernet (PPPoE) to handle connections to the Internet. If your Mac is directly connected to the DSL service, as opposed to through a router, choose this option and fill in the information provided by the Internet service provider (ISP). Typically, if you set up PPPoE on your Mac, you are not part of a local network. Less frequently, it means that you're on a local network but only your Mac has an Internet connection.

Typically, you just need to choose Using DHCP and you're now on the network. But your network may require other settings, which you access by clicking Advanced to open a settings sheet. For Ethernet, the settings sheet has six panes of settings: TCP/IP, DNS, WINS, 802.1x, Proxies, and Ethernet:

- **TCP/IP:** This pane has the same IPv4 pop-up menu as the main Network system preference does. (TCP stands for Transmission Control Protocol, which handles how IP addresses are managed within a network.) If your Mac can't connect to its IP address, click Renew DHCP Lease; sometimes another device gets assigned the IP address your Mac had and the Mac doesn't realize it's now competing for that old address; clicking Renew DHCP Lease forces the router to assign you a free IP address. Enter a DHCP Client ID only if your network administrator requires it; some networks use these when there are multiple DHCP servers or to block unauthorized users from getting an address. You also can tell the Mac to automatically or manually set an IPv6 address if the router supports it, or to turn off this feature. An IPv6 address is a longer version of an IP address that is slowly replacing the IPv4 addresses we all use today. (Because we're running out of addresses, we need longer addresses; they do to IP addresses what the ZIP+4 addition did to ZIP codes.)

- **DNS:** In this pane, you can add DNS server addresses and search domains. Typically, your router fills them in for you, but if you're not using DHCP or BootP (perhaps when traveling), you can add your own. Click the + icon button at the bottom of the DNS Server column to add a DNS server address, and click the + icon button at the bottom of the Search Domains column to add a search domain. To delete an entry, select it and click the – icon button at the bottom of its column.

- **WINS:** If you're on a Windows-based network, type an ID for your Mac (if there's not one there automatically), choose or enter a Windows network name, and add any Windows servers (click the + icon button). Your network administrator should provide these settings.

- **802.1x:** IEEE 802.1x is a standard for authenticating that users are who they say they are to help keep snoops out of the network. If your network is set up to use 802.1x, click the + icon button to add one or more of the three 802.1x methods—user profile, login window profile, and system profile—and then provide your username and password, select the appropriate authentication options from the list, and if your network uses authentication certificates, click Configure Trust to load the certificates. Your network administrator should provide these settings.

- **Proxies:** Your network may handle certain Internet or network services for you, such as web access and FTP file transfer. If so, select these proxy servers and type their network address (in the long text field) and port number (in the short one after the colon); if a password is required, select Proxy Server Requires Password and fill in the Username and Password fields. Two options are different: Auto Proxy Discovery has the Mac look for proxy servers on its own, and Automatic Proxy Configuration has you type the IP address for a file that will configure all these settings for you. Select the Exclude Simple Hostnames option to bypass proxy servers for services that appear to be local; typically, doing so helps a wireless connection see a resource on your local network that it might otherwise not see. Also, in the Bypass proxy Settings for these Hosts & Domains field, enter any hosts and domains in the same local network as your Mac to reduce network traffic out to and back through a proxy server for something accessible locally. Finally, select the Use Passive FTP Mode (PASV) option to allow File Transfer Protocol connections (see Chapter 24) even if your Mac is protected by a firewall.

- **Hardware:** This pane controls how your Ethernet port functions. Usually, you leave the Configure pop-up menu set to Automatically so Mac OS X can figure out the rest for you. But if you change it to Manually, you can select the network speed in the Speed pop-up menu, the type of flow control in the Duplex pop-up menu, and the delay between "conversations" with other devices in the MTU pop-up menu. (If your Mac "talks" too fast, other devices might not "understand" it. The MTU, or maximum transmission unit, setting controls the "talk" speed.) Your network administrator should provide any such settings.

Understanding IP addresses

An IP address is composed of four sets of numbers, called *segments,* in the form xxx.xxx.xxx.xxx. Within a local network, you use four ranges of addresses, called *private IP addresses:* 10.0.0.0 through 10.255.255.255, 172.16.0.0 through 172.31.255.255, and 192.168.0.0 through 192.168.255.255. Only one device within a network can use any of the numbers, though it's fine if devices on different networks use the same numbers. (Note that the largest permitted number in any IP address segment is 255, not 999.)

Most home-oriented routers are preconfigured to use the address 192.168.0.1, 192.168.1.1, or 192.168.2.1, and thus the devices that connect in the local network are assigned private addresses that start with 192.168.0., 192.168.1., or 192.168.2., respectively. But you can change that router address to anything in those supported ranges.

A subnet mask helps the router manage traffic across several linked networks by indicating what parts of the IP address must be the same for devices to be on the same network: 255.255.255.0 means the first three segments of the IP address must be the same (255 means "must match" and 0 means "don't need to match")—so the devices whose IP addresses are 172.28.5.15 and 172.28.5.75 will be on the same network, but not the device whose address is 172.30.5.16 nor the device whose address is 172.28.74.9, because not all first three segments match as the subnet mask says they must.

The other IP addresses—called *public IP addresses*—are assigned to web and Internet resources, such as websites, and must be unique on the Internet. When you sign up for a domain, such as `apple.com`, the domain registry assigns you a unique public IP address. When a user types **apple.com**, the router looks up its public IP address and routes the request to it. So web addresses are really aliases to public IP addresses.

How does the Mac know where to look up these aliases when it sends e-mail or goes to a website? Through a DNS server. The DNS Server entry in the Network system preference tells your Mac where to find the public IP addresses. Your ISP typically provides its own DNS server and the router looks it up for you, so usually you don't need to tell the Mac what the DNS server is.

New Feature
The Hardware pane had been called the Ethernet pane in previous versions of Mac OS X. ■

Note
Other devices you want to connect to the network will have similar settings as Mac OS X's Network system preference settings for Ethernet, though they may not be as elaborate. Also, in some cases, you configure a device by typing its IP address in your browser to get a configuration screen, while in others you may use settings available through its setup screen, and in still others you may need to connect them to your Mac via a USB cable and run a setup utility for them on your Mac. ■

Setting up Wi-Fi connections

For wireless (Wi-Fi) networking, the main pane of Network system preference is simpler: There's the Network Name pop-up menu where you can select what available wireless network to connect to, where you can turn off wireless networking by clicking Turn Wi-Fi Off, and where you can select the Show Wi-Fi Status in Menu Bar to get an icon menu that lets you select an available network or turn Wi-Fi on or off from the menu bar, so you don't have to first opening the Network system preference. The Ask to Join New Networks option, if selected, displays a window when the Mac detects a new wireless network and asks if you want to join it if you're not already connected to a wireless network.

New Feature

Apple no longer uses the AirPort name to refer to Wi-Fi. So Mac OS X Lion now refers to Wi-Fi to mean the wireless networking technology and to AirPort only to refer to Apple's brand of Wi-Fi routers. ■

Note

A radio-wave icon next to a wireless network's name indicates its signal strength (the more waves, the stronger the signal). Mac OS X shows the signal strengths for all visible wireless networks in the Wi-Fi menu bar icon pop-up menu and in the Network Name pop-up menu in the Network system preference. (A lock signal next to a wireless network's name means that a password is required to connect to that network.) ■

Clicking Advanced displays a settings sheet with seven panes. Six panes are the same as for Ethernet networking: TCP/IP, DNS, WINS, 802.1x, Proxies, and Hardware.

The one special pane (see Figure 23.4) is for wireless configuration, which enables you to save and manage login connections to various wireless networks. (Mac OS X calls these saved connections *preferred networks*.)

Click the + icon button to add a Wi-Fi connection. If you know the wireless network's name, or SSID (Service Set Identifier), type it in the Network Name field, or click Show Networks to have Mac OS X find available networks so you can select one. Using the Security pop-up menu, select the wireless network's security protocol, then type the password in the field that displays. If you select the Show Password option, you can see the password as you type it; otherwise, you see a row of bullets (•). Click Add to add the new Wi-Fi connection. You also have the option Remember This Network; if selected, the Mac automatically connects to the network the next time it sees it and you are not connected to a different Wi-Fi network.

You also can manage your Wi-Fi connections in this pane:

- Select a connection and click the – icon button to delete it.
- Drag Wi-Fi connection names to reorder them; the Mac will connect to the topmost wireless network it sees from the list.
- The Remember Any Network This Computer Has Joined option, which is selected by default, adds Wi-Fi networks to the preferred network list automatically as you log in, including their passwords, so you can connect automatically in the future.

- The Require Administrator Authorization To options let you require that the user type the administrator password to control whichever aspects of the wireless connections you've selected:
  - Create Computer-to-Computer Networks. (This capability allows Macs to see each other's files and use their network connections for Internet and printer access.)
  - Change Networks. You might select this so the kids can't log on to a Wi-Fi hot spot without your okay.
  - Turn Wi-Fi On or Off. Again, you might select this option after turning off Wi-Fi to prevent the kids from accessing the Internet without your knowledge, such as during a trip.

New Feature

Mac OS X Lion does not let you edit Wi-Fi settings such as password and security type for preferred networks, so the Edit icon button (the pencil icon) in previous versions of the Network system preference's Wi-Fi pane does not exist in Mac OS X Lion. To change a preferred network, you need to delete it and add it back. But if the only change needed is to update the password, a prompt appears if the stored password doesn't match the required password that gives you a chance to type it and save it for future use. Also gone from the Wi-Fi pane is the Disconnect from Networks When Logging Out option; Wi-Fi connections are now always disconnected when you log out from the Mac, not just when you shut down or restart the Mac. ■

FIGURE 23.4

The Wi-Fi settings pane in the Network system preference

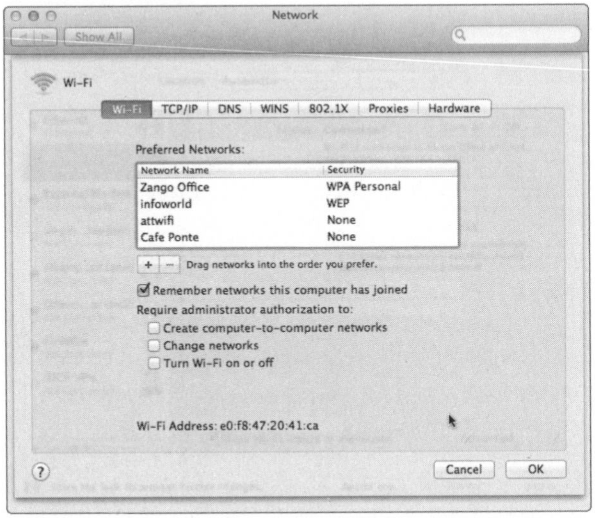

Setting up a Bluetooth network

The principles of setting up Bluetooth networking are the same as for Ethernet and Wi-Fi networking. But the actual process is more complicated because there are many kinds of Bluetooth devices that have different capabilities. (Be sure to read each device's documentation as to its capabilities and how to set it up.) And the Bluetooth technology uses a concept called *pairing,* which means that devices are configured to work with other specific devices. So you have to first pair a Mac and a Bluetooth device for them to communicate. You don't get the same kind of automatic connection that you do with Ethernet and Wi-Fi.

In Mac OS X, you set up Bluetooth networking in two places: the Bluetooth system preference and the Sharing system preference. Chapter 28 covers how to pair Bluetooth devices to the Mac by using the Bluetooth system preference, and Chapter 24 explains how to set up file sharing in Bluetooth.

New Feature

Mac OS X Lion removes the ability to set up a Bluetooth personal area network (PAN) from the Network system preference. This is not handled in the Sharing system preference, as Chapter 24 explains. ■

Setting up a VPN

As people work more and more through Internet connections, such as from a café or home office, lots of sensitive business information is traversing the public Internet. Such information can be intercepted by a hacker, so Apple supports a technology called virtual private networking (VPN) in Mac OS X that creates a secure connection within the Internet between your Mac and the server you are connecting to. It's like having a private, walled lane on the highway between your office and your home.

If your company uses VPN connections to secure access to its file shares, databases, web applications, and/or e-mail, you need to set up and activate a VPN connection from your Mac to be able to connect. To set up a VPN, follow these steps:

1. **Click the + icon button at the bottom left of the Network system preference to open a settings sheet.**

2. **In that settings sheet, choose VPN from the Interface pop-up menu.** Choose the VPN technology your company uses (L2TP over IPSec, PPTP, or Cisco IPSec) in the VPN Type pop-up menu (ask your IT department if you're not sure), and give that VPN connection a name that makes sense to you in the Service Name field. Click Create.

3. **In the VPN settings pane, enter the requested information, which varies based on the type of VPN technology you chose previously.** You're typically asked for the VPN sever address, your account name on that server, and your password for that VPN access. You may also be asked to select the level of encryption desired. Click the Authentication Settings button if it appears to add more sign-in information such as Shared Secret (a group password), hardware token (such as an RSA

SecurID card), or certificate (a file that contains a unique ID for your Mac) that provides a second level of authentication that you are an authorized user. You may need to add further settings required by your IT department by clicking the Advanced button to open the settings panes for the VPN technology selected. Your IT department should provide the necessary information or fill in these settings for you.

4. **Optionally, select the Show VPN Status in Menu Bar option to have the VPN icon menu appear in the menu bar.** (It's a black rectangle with white stripes, meant to look like a security keycard you might use to enter a building with electronic door locks.)

5. **Click Apply to save the configuration.**

When you want to connect to the VPN, be sure you are connected to the Internet via Ethernet, Wi-Fi, or other connection; otherwise, the VPN has no route to your server. Then go to the Network system preference, select the VPN configuration from the list at the left, and click Connect to begin a VPN connection. Or use the VPN icon menu in the menu bar if that is visible. Note that you may be asked for sign-in information, such as for servers set up to disallow users to save their passwords (so if someone steals their Mac, they can't connect to the VPN automatically).

When you're done with the VPN connection, turn it off the same way. (There's no reason to leave the connect active when you're not using it.)

Connecting Macs Directly

Sometimes, you don't need a whole network, just a way to exchange files and other services directly between two Macs in what's called an *ad hoc network*. There are four ways to do that. In all cases, after you establish the network connection, you should be able to share files, as explained in Chapter 24.

Ethernet direct connection

You can connect two Macs directly to each other via an Ethernet connection. (As noted earlier in this chapter, you may need to use a crossover Ethernet cable to do so.) When connected, go to the Network system preference in each, select the Ethernet connection, and assign them a manual IP address. The first three segments should be the same for both, while the final segment should be unique. For example, you might use 192.168.1.101 and 192.168.1.102.

FireWire direct connection

If you have a FireWire cable, connect the two Macs with it. When connected, go to the Network system preference in each, select the FireWire connection, and assign them a manual IP address. The first three segments should be the same for both, while the final segment should be unique. For example, you might use 192.168.1.101 and 192.168.1.102.

Wi-Fi direct connection

You can use Wi-Fi to connect two Macs when there's no wireless router or access point available; instead, you set one of the Macs to act as the access point. Make sure Wi-Fi is enabled on both Macs.

On one Mac, go to the Network system preference and in the Network Name pop-up menu, choose Create Network. In the settings sheet that appears, provide a network name. If you want to require a password, select the Require Password option and then type one. (You also can select a Wi-Fi channel using the Channel pop-up menu, but there's rarely a reason to do so unless you're getting a poor signal.) Click Create to start this ad hoc wireless network.

The other Macs connect to this Mac as they would to any wireless router or access point: Choose it from the wireless list in the Wi-Fi menu bar or in the Network name pop-up menu in the Network system preference.

Caution

The ad hoc Wi-Fi network is listed in the Devices section of the Wi-Fi menu bar menu and of the Network Name pop-up menu in the Network system preference. That gives users a clue they're not connecting to a network router but to another computer. This can help them avoid making connections to computers pretending to be wireless routers, such as in cafés and airport lobbies, as such pretend networks are often used by data thieves to steal passwords. ■

Bluetooth direct connection

If both Macs have Bluetooth, you can use it to establish a direct connection.

First, go to one Mac and enable Bluetooth Discovery Mode in the Bluetooth system preference (see Chapter 28) and turn on Bluetooth File Sharing (see Chapter 24) in the Sharing system preference.

On the second Mac, go to the Bluetooth system preference and click the + icon button to search for a Bluetooth device (if asked, choose Any Device as the device type). When that second Mac finds the first Mac, select the first Mac's name in the device list and click Continue. You will be asked to provide a pairing code; type any number and press Return.

On the first Mac, a dialog box appears asking you to type the same number you typed on the second Mac. Do so, and press Return. You will get a confirmation of the connection and can press Quit to exit the Bluetooth setup.

Connecting to the Internet

Before you can use the web, you must connect to the Internet, because the Internet is the global network through which web pages are accessed. And how you connect to the Internet from your Mac depends on several factors.

Using Internet connection devices

In a home environment, it's very likely that you have a cable modem or a DSL (Digital Subscriber Line) modem that connects your home to the Internet over what is commonly called a *broadband connection.* Your Mac may plug directly into it via an Ethernet cable, or your Mac may connect to a router device, which then connects to the cable modem or DSL modem. Some cable and DSL modems include a router, so multiple computers and other networked devices such as printers all connect to it and thus to each other, as well as to the Internet. (These routers typically have a port labeled WAN, for *wide area network,* used to connect to the Internet and several ports labeled LAN, for *local area network,* used to connect devices within your home or office to each other as well as to the Internet.)

Note
Modem means modulation/demodulation, a fancy way of saying a device that translates the analog sound waves (such as on a phone line or in wireless radios) into a computer's digital signals and back again. Although a cable modem or DSL modem is called a modem, it often nowadays connects to an all-digital network, so it doesn't have to do the analog-digital conversion. But the "modem" name has stuck. ■

Some people use an older technology called a dial-up modem that uses the phone line as the connection to the Internet. In this case, the Mac has a modem either built into it as a card inside the box or attached as a small hardware device, typically to a USB (Universal Serial Bus) port.

It's also possible that your Mac (and other devices) uses a wireless technology called Wi-Fi (technically, the IEEE 802.11a/b/g/n family of standards) to connect to the cable or DSL modem or to a router or wireless access point that is connected to that cable or DSL modem. Some cities have an alternative to DSL and cable modems that uses one of several wireless technologies to connect to the Internet; these wireless devices are typically called *wireless broadband routers,* but yours may have a different name.

You can also establish a connection to the Internet over a 3G or 4G cellular service using any of the following devices: a USB cellular modem, a portable cellular/Wi-Fi interface (the MiFi product is the best known of these), or a smartphone such as an iPhone 4, Droid, or BlackBerry that supports wireless tethering.

In all these cases, the basic setup is that an Internet service provider such as your phone or cable company provides a box or other means to connect to the Internet, and your Mac and other devices connect to that device so they can access the Internet through it.

In a business environment, the basic approach is the same, though a more powerful Internet router that can handle lots of simultaneous user connections is used in place of a cable or DSL modem in larger organizations. There's likely a more complex network between your Mac and the Internet router as well.

For your Mac to connect to the Internet, your cable or DSL modem—or whatever Internet connection device you're using—must be properly set up. The steps to do this vary from device to device and manufacturer to manufacturer, so check your documentation. Most require that you enable something called DHCP (Dynamic Host Configuration Protocol), which assigns your Mac and any other device connected to the network a unique identifier so the network knows how to route traffic to and from each device.

Tip

Having a connection to your DSL modem, cable modem, wireless access point, or router (wired or wireless) does not mean you are connected to the Internet. It just means you are connected locally. If you're not sure you have an Internet connection active, launch Network Utility, go to the Ping pane, type apple.com (or any website's URL) in the Ping field, and click Ping. If you get an error message saying the destination was unavailable (or something similar), you're not connected to the Internet. I explain Network Utility in more detail later in this chapter. ∎

Setting up connections manually

After the Internet connection is set up, you can connect your Mac to that device. Usually, if you plug your Mac into a DSL modem, cable modem, or router by using an Ethernet cable, the Internet access happens automatically, thanks to the magic of DHCP. In the Network system preference, the Ethernet item in the list at the left shows a green dot indicating a connection (refer to Figure 23.2). If you select Ethernet or Wi-Fi, you see a pane that provides details about the connection, as described earlier in this chapter.

If you're using a cellular/Wi-Fi interface such as the MiFi, the device appears in the Network system preference to be a wireless router, and you select it just as you would any Wi-Fi device. The same is true of most smartphones that offer wireless tethering: They usually act as a Wi-Fi router, and you connect your Mac to them as you would any Wi-Fi router. In some cases, such as for the BlackBerry, you may need to install and run a connection application that either comes with the device or is available from the provider's website; typically, such software installs an icon menu in the menu bar to let you initiate the connection from your Mac to that device.

For a dial-up modem connection over a phone line, go to the External Modem pane (click External Modem in the list at the left of the Network system reference) and enter the phone number, your username, and your password in the appropriate fields. You may need to enter additional configuration information by clicking Advanced; check with your dial-up provider's instructions. After your modem is set up, click Connect to make the connection. (Or use the connection software that came with your dial-up service, if such separate software was provided.) If the modem is connected, a green dot appears next to External Modem in the list at the left of the Network system preference.

You also can connect to the Internet via Bluetooth from some smartphones and MiFi-like devices using what's called a Bluetooth DUN (dial-up network). You set up a Bluetooth DUN in the Network system preference by clicking the + icon below the connections list and choosing Bluetooth DUN from the Interface pop-up menu in the settings sheet that appears and then clicking Create. You then complete the information in the main pane (refer to the device's documentation) and in the Modem pane of the settings sheet that appears when you click Advanced.

For a USB cellular modem connection, you have to install a driver using the software that comes with your device (often, you plug the device into your Mac's USB port and an installation disk icon appears on the desktop containing this software). After the driver installation, you typically reboot the Mac. After that, you usually have one of three methods available to manage the connection, depending on your specific device:

- Run a connection application (typically available through an icon menu in the menu bar).

- Connect via the External Modem or WWAN (wireless wide-area network) icon menus in the menu bar. (Make sure you've enabled that icon pop-up menu by selecting the Show Modem Status in Menu Bar option in the External Modem pane or by selecting the Show WWAN Status in Menu Bar option in the main pane that appears when you select the device in the Network system preference.)

- Connect via the Network system preference (refer to Figure 23.2). You may need to first set up the connection, similar to how you would set up a Bluetooth DUN.

Setting up connections with assistance

If you're not comfortable manually setting up a connection, you can use Mac OS X's Network Setup Assistant utility. In the Network system preference, click Assist Me, and then click Assistant in the dialog box that appears. The Network Setup Assistant launches, and its first dialog box asks you to name the connection; enter anything that makes sense to you, such as **Home DSL** or **Wireless Internet**, and click Continue.

Note
You need the connection settings from your Internet service provider (ISP) to complete the setup. ∎

The next dialog box asks you for the type of connection you are trying to set up. You have the following choices:

- **I Use AirPort to Connect to the Internet Wirelessly:** If you choose this item and click Continue, the next dialog box shows a list of available wireless networks; select the one you want to connect to, enter the password (if any) in the password field, and click Continue.

- **I Use a Telephone Modem to Dial My ISP:** If you choose this item and click Continue, the next dialog box asks for the dial-up configuration information: account name, password, ISP's dial-up number, a number to get an outside line (such as 9 or 8 in an office or hotel), and an option to select whether you have call waiting service on the phone line. Click Continue to get the next dialog box, which shows the brand of modem that Mac OS X detects (you can change it by choosing a different model in the unnamed pop-up menu), and then click Continue again to get a dialog box that confirms your setup. Click Continue to try the connection.

- **I Use a DSL Modem to Connect to the Internet:** If you choose this item and click Continue, the next dialog box tells you that it will try to connect you automatically when you click Continue. If it cannot connect you, a new dialog box appears that asks you to enter PPPoE settings (Point-to-Point Protocol over Ethernet, the most common type of DSL connection) and click Continue or to select the More Choices option and click Continue; you are then asked for the DHCP or static IP address provided by your ISP, which you should enter and then click Continue.

- **I Use a Cable Modem to Connect to the Internet:** If you choose this item and click Continue, the next dialog box tells you that it will try to connect you automatically when you click Continue. If it cannot connect you, a new dialog box appears that asks you to enter either PPPoE settings or DHCP settings, as specified by your ISP, and click Continue.

- **I Connect to My Local Area Network (LAN):** If you choose this item and click Continue, the next dialog box tells you that it will try to connect you automatically when you click Continue. If it cannot connect you, a new dialog box appears that asks you to enter the IP address, subnet mask, router address, and DNS host settings, as specified by your ISP or network administrator, and click Continue.

No matter what method you use, if the connection is successful, you get a dialog box saying so; click Done to complete the connection. Otherwise, you get an error message and can either click Diagnose to run the Network Diagnostic Assistant to try to detect the reason for the failed connection, or click OK to close the error message. (You have to edit the connection settings in the Network system preference to try again.)

Disconnecting from the Internet

When you use a broadband connection such as a cable or DSL modem, you tend to stay connected to the Internet as long as your Mac is running. When you're idle with these connections, there's no load on the Internet connection, so there's no harm (unless you're paying by the minute or hour, which is rare for such connections). But because the connection is open, a hacker might try to break into your Mac—though this too is rare unless you use what's called a static IP address to connect your Mac directly to the Internet.

Cross-Reference
Chapter 26 explains how to protect your Mac from hackers. ■

If you use a dial-up connection, you typically pay by the hour or minute, so you don't want to stay connected when you're not using the Internet. Likewise, if you use a cellular device as your connection (a USB cellular modem, a MiFi or similar device, or a smartphone), you typically are restricted to a certain amount of data usage, so you don't want to stay connected when you're not using the Internet—before you know it, your e-mail and chat clients' regular check-ins will have consumed a lot of data.

Here's how to disconnect from the Internet (as well as any local area network you're attached to):

- **Dial-up connection:** If you're using a dial-up modem, click Disconnect from the External Modem pane in the Network system preference, or choose Disconnect from the Modem icon pop-up menu in the menu bar if you've enabled that icon by selecting the Show Modem Status in Menu Bar option in the External Modem pane of the Network system preference.

- **Cellular connection:** If you're using a tethered smartphone or cellular USB modem, select the device in the Network system preference and click Disconnect, choose Disconnect from the External Modem or WWAN icon pop-up menu in the menu bar, or use the disconnect option in the application that came with the device to manage its connections.

- **Wi-Fi connection:** If you're using a Wi-Fi connection, click Turn Wi-Fi Off in the Wi-Fi pane of the Network system preference, or choose Turn Wi-Fi Off from the Wi-Fi icon pop-up menu in the menu bar if you've enabled that icon by selecting Show Wi-Fi Status in Menu Bar option in the Wi-Fi pane of the Network system preference.

- **Wired connection or Bluetooth network:** If you're using a wired connection (DSL modem, cable modem, FireWire, or local area network), or if you're using a Bluetooth network, go to the Ethernet, FireWire, or Bluetooth pane, as appropriate, in the Network system preference, and choose Off in the Configure IPv4 pop-up menu.

Using Network Utility

Apple provides Network Utility to test your network status and Mac's network configuration. It's available in the Utilities folder; in the Finder, choose Go ➪ Utilities or press Shift+⌘+U to go to that folder. Network Utility has eight panes.

Info

Figure 23.5 shows the utility's Info pane, which shows the status of the Mac's network adapters: the IP address (the Internet Protocol-format address on the network), MAC address (the Media Access Control identifier that is unique to each device), information on the equivalent itself, and information on the recent data traffic through it.

You choose which network connection, called the *network interface*, to monitor using the pop-up menu. Most Macs have three built-in network interfaces: en0, the Ethernet jack; en1, the Wi-Fi radio; and fw0, the FireWire jack. If you install other network interfaces on your Mac, such as a 3G wireless broadband card, they show up as well.

FIGURE 23.5

Network Utility provides a suite of tools for checking the Mac's network connections, as well as other activity on the network.

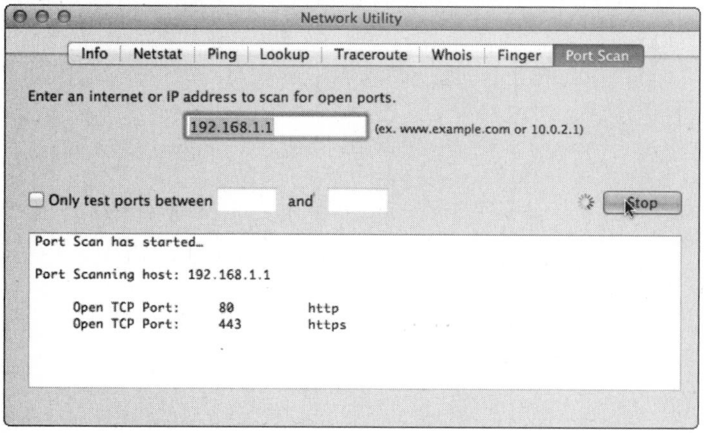

Netstat

This pane enables you to explore detailed network settings. Check one of the four options—the network routing table, protocol statistics, multi-cast information, or state of all socket connections—and click Netstat to get the results. Note that it can take the Mac several minutes to gather the results.

Ping

Use the Ping pane to see if a network device responds. It's the network version of poking someone to see if they're awake or alive. Enter the IP address or web address (URL), and click Ping. The pane shows whether the device responded to the ping.

Lookup

The Lookup pane asks a website or other network resource for information about itself. (You can choose what information you want by using the Select Information to Look Up pop-up menu.) Enter the IP address or URL, and click Lookup.

Traceroute

The Traceroute pane discovers all the servers that a connection goes through between your Mac and that server. When you enter an IP address or URL in your browser and click Trace, the Internet sends that request through a bunch of servers, each handing off the request to the next one available. (Some may be your own servers.) The response comes back the same way, often through a different route. You use Traceroute to look at these paths to see if any problematic servers are used, such as those that are delaying traffic.

Whois

The Whois database stores the ownership information for every web address. So if you want to know who owns a web domain or who is using a specific URL, enter it in this pane and click Whois. You should get a response listing the ownership information, including the domain registrar and the Web host used. If you don't get a response using the default whois. internic.net database, try some of the other databases listed in the pop-up menu or type one not listed that you prefer to use.

Finger

The Finger pane is where you can look up information about a specific user at a specific web address. Enter both the username and the web address, and click Finger. Note that many servers deny finger requests and respond with a "connection refused" message.

Port Scan

Use the Port Scan pane to see what services are available (open) at a specific URL or IP address. Enter the IP address or URL, and click Scan. For example, if you are having trouble transferring files via FTP or accessing an e-mail, you can scan the device's ports to see whether the relevant service is available. In the case of FTP, using Port Scan should show that the FTP is open on port 21. If it does not show up as open, you know that the FTP service is not enabled, and if it shows up on a different port, you know that it is configured in a non-standard manner and that you either need to adjust your access settings to it from the Mac or fix its settings at the server.

Summary

The Macintosh was the first computer to make networking easy, and today it provides the greatest amount of built-in networking support so Macs can easily join both Mac and Windows networks.

A network of computers and other devices typically is created by cabling the devices through a router or other central device, although wireless connections can be used instead of cables as well.

The Network system preference is where you configure a Mac to participate in a network, providing its unique ID (its IP address) and specifying other settings that help it access the Internet in addition to local servers, computers, and devices.

You can connect two Macs directly to each other to exchange files by using either a crossover Ethernet cable or a FireWire cable. In either case, you set a manual IP address for each Mac. You also can set a Mac to act as a wireless router so other Macs can connect to it wirelessly, and you can use Bluetooth to enable one Mac to connect to another wirelessly.

Before you can use the web to access content and services, you need to connect your Mac to the Internet. Typically, you connect to the Internet through a broadband Internet connection, such as through a DSL or cable modem, wireless router, or dial-up modem using a service from an ISP.

The Network system preference is also where you establish the settings that connect your Mac to the broadband Internet connection device, for access to the web. The Network system preference offers the Network Setup Assistant to help guide you through the setup for wired and wireless broadband connections, as well as for dial-up modem connections. You can also set up a secure connection that works through the INternet, called a VPN.

You also can connect to the Internet via cellular devices such as USB cellular modems, cellular/Wi-Fi interfaces such as the MiFi, and through a smartphone's wireless tethering capability (using Wi-Fi or Bluetooth, depending on the device). The setup differs from device to device, but often you can set them up in the Network system preference similar to setting up an external modem.

Mac OS X's Network Utility lets you test your network and examine its configuration.

Sharing Files and Other Resources

If you work with other people—and who doesn't?—you're going to share files and perhaps other resources. Sure, you can exchange files via e-mail, file servers (including Internet-based services as explained in Chapter 17), or various media such as CD-R (Compact Disc-Recordable) discs and flash drives. But Mac OS X also makes it easy to directly share files and other resources by providing you with access to other peoples' Macs and enabling them to access yours.

This direct sharing has been a hallmark of the Mac since shortly after the first Mac shipped. Since then, Apple has extended its capabilities so you can control other Macs and share a Mac's directly connected resources such as printers and Internet connections.

The key to direct sharing is to be able to access the Macs of others over the same local wired or wireless network or via the Internet (see Chapter 23). You also can set up sharing with Bluetooth devices by using the Bluetooth system preference, as Chapter 28 explains. If you've enabled this access, the actual sharing is easy. (See Chapter 18 for details on sharing files with Windows users.)

But be warned: Opening your Mac for sharing can make you a target for evildoers, so be sure to secure your Mac, as Chapter 26 explains.

IN THIS CHAPTER

Setting up sharing preferences

Providing files to and getting them from other users

Sending files to and receiving them from Bluetooth devices

Using AirDrop to exchange files

Observing and controlling other Macs

Accessing other Macs' DVD drives, printers, scanners, and Internet connections

Enabling File and Other Sharing

Even if your Mac is connected to a network or to the Internet, people can't share its files and resources unless you set up sharing. And anyone you want to connect to for sharing has to enable sharing on his or her Mac.

There is just one place to set up sharing: the Sharing system preference.

The Sharing system preference, shown in Figure 24.1, is where you do most of the setup work. Twelve types of sharing controls in the system preference appear in the list on the left: DVD or CD Sharing, Screen Sharing, File Sharing, Printer Sharing, Scanner Sharing, Web Sharing, Remote Login, Remote Management, Remote Apple Events, Xgrid Sharing, Internet Sharing, and Bluetooth Sharing.

FIGURE 24.1

The Sharing system preference's File Sharing pane

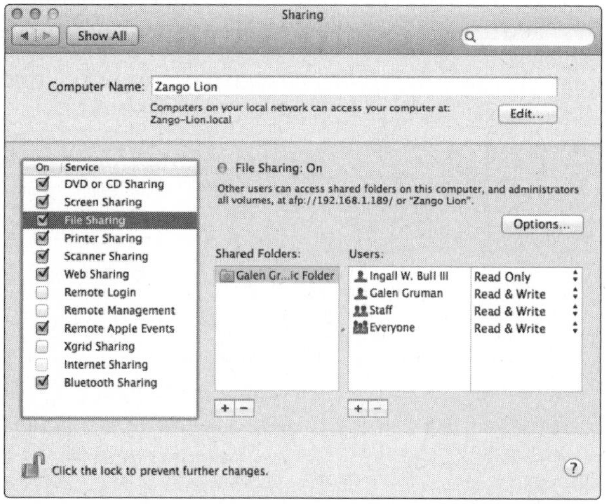

Here's what each pane configures, in order of how it appears in the Sharing system preference's list:

- **DVD or CD Sharing:** If selected, this option enables other users to access any DVDs or CDs mounted on your Mac. The only configuration setting is the Ask Me Before Allowing Others to Use my DVD Drive option.

- **Screen Sharing:** If selected, this option enables other users to see what's on your screen. You can choose to allow all users to see your screen or specify specific users, using the Allow Access For controls. The Computer Settings button, if clicked, shows a settings sheet with two additional options: one that lets anyone ask for permission to control (not simply observe) the screen and another that lets remote users connected via a VNC (virtual network computing) remote-control application control the screen if they type the password you specify here. Note that if Remote Management is enabled, it takes over screen sharing and disables the options in the Screen Sharing pane. Figure 24.2 shows the pane.

FIGURE 24.2

The Screen Sharing pane of the Sharing system preference

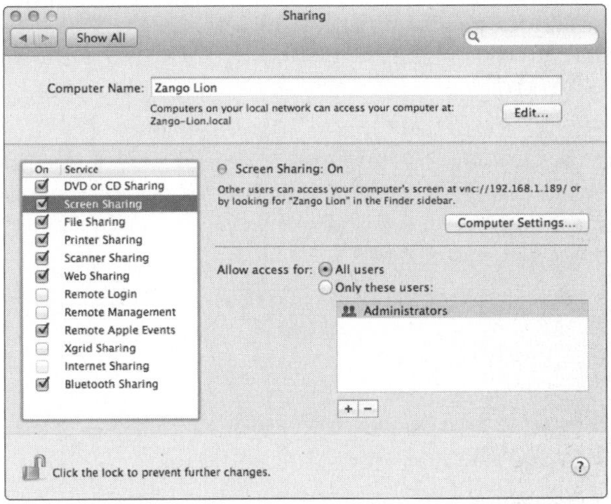

- **File Sharing:** If selected, this option enables people to share files with your Mac. You specify which folders to share in the Shared Folders window; click the + icon button to add a share folder, and click the – icon button to remove a selected share folder. You then specify in the Users window which users can share the selected share folder and the degree of permissible sharing—Read & Write, Read Only, and Write Only (Drop Box)—for that user. (You add and delete users by using the familiar + and – icon buttons.) Figure 24.1 shows the pane. Click the Options button to open a settings sheet to set up Windows file sharing via the Share Files and Folders Using SMB (Windows) option, described in Chapter 18. The Share File and Folders Using AFP option must be selected for other Macs to see your Mac on the network; it's thus selected by default. (AFP stands for Apple Filing Protocol, Apple's sharing technology.)

Tip

You also can enable file sharing for a disk or folder by selecting that item and pressing ⌘+I to open an Info window, as Chapter 3 explains. Select Shared Folder to add the disk or folder to the Shared Folders window in the File Sharing pane of the Sharing system preference. The Sharing system preference need not be active when you do this, but you will need to have it open at the File Sharing pane to change the sharing permissions for any disks or folders you make sharable via an Info window. ■

New Feature

Mac OS X Lion no longer lets you set your Mac up as an FTP (File Transfer Protocol) server, so the Share Files and Folders Using FTP option has been removed from the settings sheet in the File Sharing pane. ∎

- **Printer Sharing:** If selected, this option enables people to use printers attached to your Mac. This is a great way to share a non-networked printer with other users on your network. A list of available printers appears on the left of the pane. If you enabled sharing for a printer in the Print & Fax system preference, it will be selected here; otherwise, select it here to enable sharing. Select a shared printer and add or remove users from the window at right by using the familiar + and – icon buttons. You can give each user one of two permissions: Can Print and No Access. (Note that if you want to configure a printer, click the Open Print & Scan Preferences button as a shortcut to opening the Print & Scan system preference.)

- **Scanner Sharing:** If selected, this option enables people to use scanners attached to your Mac. Note that sharing is all or nothing: You can't specify access to just specific people or groups as you can with printer sharing. (Note that if you want to configure a scanner, click the Open Print & Scan Preferences button as a shortcut to opening the Print & Scan system preference.)

- **Web Sharing:** If selected, this option enables users on your network to see the web pages you place in the Sites folder in each user's Home folder, as well as the web pages you've stored in the /Library/WebServer/Documents folder. There are no configuration settings in the Web Sharing pane: It's simply on or off. (Chapter 25 explains web sharing in more detail.) The pane does show the URL for the website being served from your Mac.

- **Remote Login:** If selected, this option enables other users on your network to control your Mac by using the Terminal's ssh command (see Appendix D). You can select who those users are through the Allow Access For control.

- **Remote Management:** If selected, this option enables other users to take over your Mac by seeing your screen on theirs and then using their mice and keyboards to run your Mac remotely. You can select who those users are through the Allow Access For controls. For each user, you set exactly what they can control by clicking Options, which opens a settings sheet of options, as Figure 24.3 shows: Observe, Control, Show When Being Observed, Generate Reports, Open and Quit Applications, Change Settings, Delete and Replace Items, Start Text Chat or Send Messages, Restart and Shut Down, and Copy Items. The Computer Settings button, if clicked, shows a settings sheet with four additional options: one that lets anyone ask for permission to control (not simply observe) the screen; one that lets remote users connected via a VNC remote-control application control the screen if they type the password you specify here; one that puts a remote status indicator in your menu bar, so you get a visual indicator if someone is remotely managing your Mac; and a set of four text fields that lets you add descriptions about your computer that are included in any reports that are generated (typically something that your Mac administrator would set up).

Where are shared files kept?

When you give someone permission to put files in your Drop Box—by providing Write Only (Drop Box) file-sharing permission—just where are those files? They're in the Drop Box folder inside your Public folder, which is inside your Home folder. The path is /Users/*username*/Public/Drop Box.

So what is the Public folder for? Any files stored in the Public folder are accessible to any other user you've given Read Only or Read & Write file-sharing permission. Note that if any user on your Mac sets up file sharing, anyone with access to the Mac, whether a user logged into the Mac or a user who has file-sharing permissions to access the Mac over the network, can see the contents of *all* users' Public folders.

Note

People can use the Screen Sharing utility on their Macs to control or observe your Mac if Remote Management is enabled, as explained later in this chapter. For complete remote management of your Mac, such as to install software, do live troubleshooting, and generate reports on the Macs' activity, they must have the Apple Remote Desktop software, which is a separate purchase. ■

FIGURE 24.3

The options for remote-control sharing in the Sharing system preference's Remote Management pane

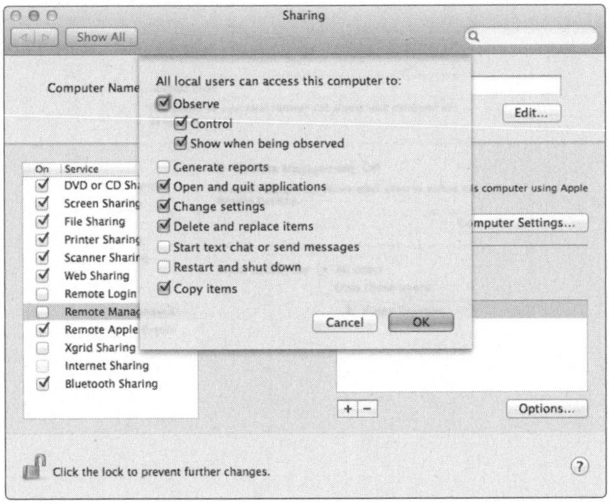

- **Remote Apple Events:** If selected, this option enables your Mac to accept commands and other information from other Macs, typically used for applications to collaborate with each other. You can select who those users are through the Allow Access For controls. (Note that this type of sharing is not common, so you should have a specific reason to turn it on.)

- **Xgrid Sharing:** If selected, this option enables your Mac to share its processing capabilities with other Macs in what is known as *grid computing*: Each Mac does a task—a part of the computation—and the results are then all combined, which helps speed up processing and takes advantage of the fact that most PCs are idle most of the time. In the Xgrid Sharing pane, use the Authentication Method pop-up menu to control access to your Mac via a password or single-sign-on certificate (or have no authorization). Click Configure to open a settings sheet where you set which controllers (systems that distribute the Xgrid tasks) your Mac should accept tasks from, as well as whether your Mac should accept a task at any time or only when it is idle.

- **Internet Sharing:** If selected, this option enables other users on the network to access the Internet through your Mac. Use the Share Your Connection From pop-up menu to determine which network connection your Mac must be using for its Internet connection to be shared: Wi-Fi, Ethernet, FireWire, Bluetooth, or any other connection available in the Network system preference (such as a USB 3G modem or MiFi device). Use the To Computers Using options to determine which network connections the other users' Macs must be using to connect to your Mac. Note that you can make your Mac act as a wireless router so other computers can connect directly to it even if there is no wireless network that you're all connected to. Selecting Wi-Fi Options opens a settings sheet where you set up the password these users must use to connect to your Mac wirelessly. (It's the same options you get in the Network system preference if you create an ad hoc network, as explained in Chapter 23.)

- **Bluetooth Sharing.** Select this option to enable file sharing with other Bluetooth-enabled devices. You control exactly what can be shared and with whom by using the several options in this pane. The When Receiving Items pop-up menu enables your Mac to accept and save files received, accept and open them, ask you what to do with them, and not accept (Never Allow) files. Select the Require Pairing option to force the other device to "pair" with your Mac, as explained in the Bluetooth system preference section later in this chapter. Use the Folder for Accepted Items pop-up menu to select where these received files are deposited. The When Other Devices Browse pop-up menu enables the Mac to automatically deny or allow—or ask you what to do—each time a Bluetooth device tries to browse your Mac's files to see what you have. You also can require pairing for browsing, as well as set up which other folder—just one, note—users can browse. If you want to set up your Bluetooth preferences, click Bluetooth Preferences to jump to the Bluetooth system preference. Figure 24.4 shows this pane.

FIGURE 24.4

The Bluetooth Sharing pane of the Sharing system preference

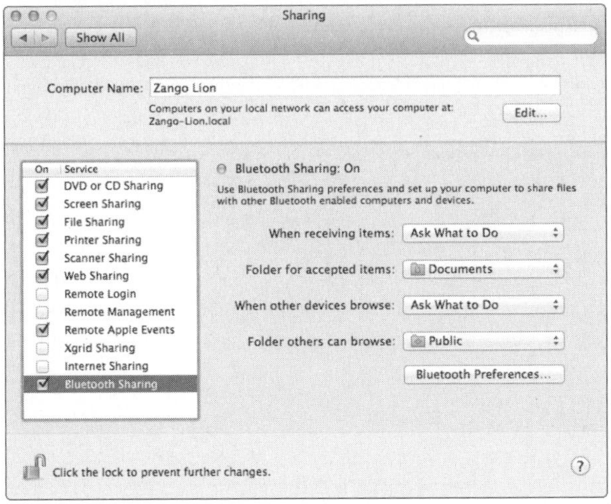

Accessing Files and Other Resources

With sharing enabled, you can now actually share stuff. Mac OS X makes it easy to do so.

Sharing files with other Macs

The most common type of sharing is the sharing of files with other Macs. If all is well, you'll see the other Macs in any Finder window in the Shared section of the Sidebar—whether they're connected over Ethernet, FireWire, Wi-Fi, or Bluetooth. Click the Mac's name and, if the Mac requires you to log in, click Connect As near the top right of the window and type your username and password, as Figure 24.5 shows.

If the shared Mac does not appear in the Finder window's Shared list, choose Go ➪ Connect to Server or press ⌘+K and click Browse to scan the network for shared Macs, then double-click them to get the login shown in Figure 24.6.

If the connection is successful, you'll see the other Mac's shared disks and folders as if they were any other folder on your Mac. The shared Mac also appears as a network volume icon on your desktop, so you can simply double-click it to open it while you remain connected.

FIGURE 24.5

Logging into a Mac that has enabled file sharing

FIGURE 24.6

Browsing for Macs on the network

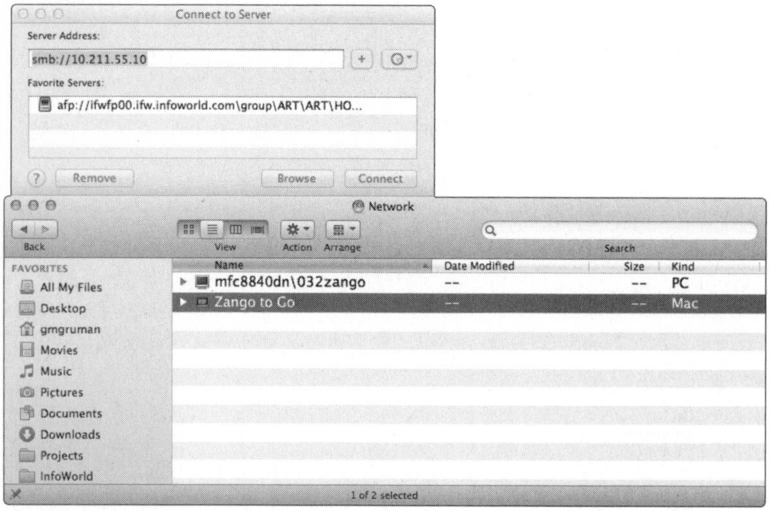

Note

When you open a disk or folder on your Mac that you've allowed to be shared with others, Mac OS X displays "Shared Folder" at the top of the window above the list of items in the disk or folder. That provides a handy reminder of what others have access to. ∎

Sharing files with Bluetooth

If you're sharing with other Macs via a Bluetooth connection, as explained in Chapter 23, those Macs appear in the Finder window's Shared list like any other Macs shared over the network. But if you're sharing files with a Bluetooth-connected device such as a smartphone (also explained in Chapter 23), you use a different method to share files.

If the Bluetooth icon is in the menu bar, choose Send File in its menu to select the files you want to transmit, then click Send to get the dialog box shown in Figure 24.7. You also can right-click or Control+click an item and choose Send File in the contextual menu. (Otherwise, enable this icon menu in the Bluetooth system preference. Or use the Bluetooth File Exchange utility.) Select the device you want to send the file to, then click Send to transmit the files. The file will be placed in whatever location that device has set up for receiving files.

FIGURE 24.7

Choosing a Bluetooth device to send a file to (left); getting permission from the recipient (center), and sending the file (right)

To get files from a Bluetooth device, choose Browse Device from the Bluetooth icon pop-up menu, choose the device, select from it the files you want, and click Get. (You also can click Send to choose files to send to the device.) You also can choose Browse Device from the Bluetooth icon pop-up menu in the menu bar. Figure 24.8 shows a device being browsed via Bluetooth.

Sharing files with AirDrop

Mac OS X Lion has a method similar to Bluetooth file sharing that lets Macs share files via Wi-Fi, if they're on the same network. The technology, called AirDrop, lets Mac OS X detect when another Mac is on the same network. If so, it adds the AirDrop item in the Finder window's Sidebar. Click AirDrop to search for those nearby Macs; they'll appear in the AirDrop Finder window. The people you want to share with also need to open AirDrop by clicking it on the Sidebar. All those who have an AirDrop Finder window open see each other's names and icons. Figure 24.9 shows an AirDrop Finder window.

You can then drag files onto a Mac user's icon or name. The person gets a dialog box asking whether to accept the file, and if he or she allows the file drop, the file is placed in the Downloads folder on his or her Mac.

FIGURE 24.8

Choosing a Bluetooth device to browse (left); viewing the folders made visible to that user (right)

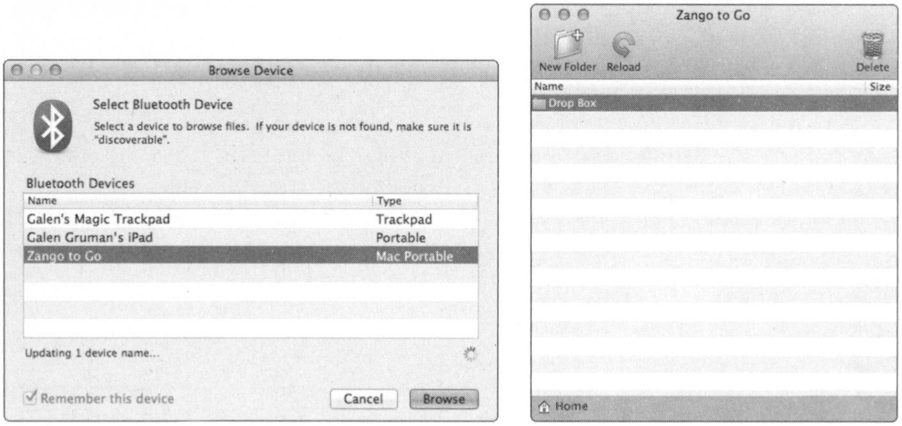

New Feature

AirDrop is new to Mac OS X Lion, and works only with other Mac OS X Lion computers. Note that it may not work on Macs built before 2009, as their Wi-Fi hardware typically does not support the peer-to-peer connection mode AirDrop requires. If your Mac doesn't support AirDrop, the AirDrop item does not appear in the Sidebar of your Finder windows. ■

FIGURE 24.9

The AirDrop Finder window. Any AirDrop-compatible Macs that are on the same Wi-Fi network appear in this window and can share files with each other.

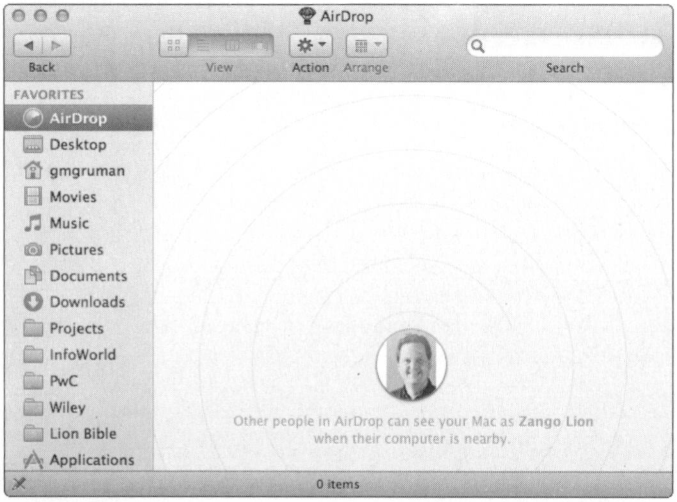

Sharing screens

When you connect to a Mac, as explained in the section "Sharing files with other Macs" earlier in this chapter, you have the option to share that Mac's screen by clicking Share Screen (see Figure 24.10) to launch the Screen Sharing utility. You may be asked for a password to connect, depending on the other user's settings in the Sharing system preference. (Likewise, Figure 24.10 shows a user seeking to share someone else's screen.)

FIGURE 24.10

Connecting to another computer to share its screen

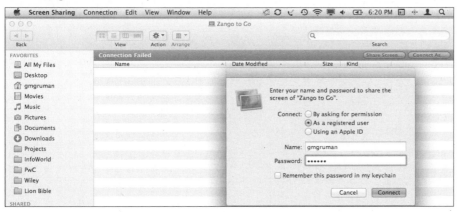

Once connected, you see the other user's screen and can switch between controlling the other Mac with your mouse or touchpad and keyboard—they now affect what's in the other user's screen—or observing the other Mac (such as for training or to troubleshoot a problem. Toggle between the two modes by choosing View ➪ Switch to Control Mode and View ➪ Switch to Observe Mode, or press Option+⌘+X to switch between them. (You can change that shortcut in the Preferences dialog box of the Screen Sharing utility; choose Screen Sharing ➪ Preferences or press ⌘+, [comma] to open it. Click in the Switch between Control and Observer field and type your preferred shortcut.)

Figure 24.11 shows a screen being shared. Figure 24.12 shows the icon pop-up menu (the icon of a two-footed monitor to the left of the Fax Modem icon pop-up menu) that appears in the menu bar of that other user's screen so he or she is aware of the sharing, can turn off the sharing from that icon pop-up menu, or change the sharing settings (in the Sharing system preference).

FIGURE 24.11

A screen-sharing session

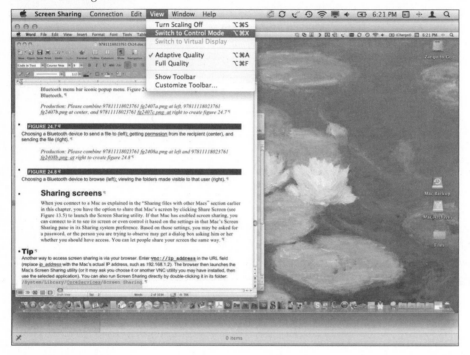

FIGURE 24.12

The person whose screen is being shared gets an icon menu (which looks like a two-footed monitor) in the menu bar, alerting him or her to the sharing, as well as providing controls over it.

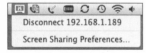

Tip

Another way to access screen sharing is via your browser. Type vnc://ip_address in the URL field (replace ip_ address with the Mac's actual IP address, such as 192.168.1.2). The browser then launches the Mac's Screen Sharing utility (or it may ask you to choose it or another VNC utility you may have installed, then use the application you choose). You also can run Screen Sharing directly by double-clicking it in its folder: /System/ Library/CoreServices/Screen Sharing. ∎

You also can change Screen Sharing's preferences by choosing Screen Sharing ⇨ Preferences or pressing ⌘+, (comma) when viewing someone else's screen. There are three sets of settings:

- **When Viewing a Computer with a Larger Screen:** You can choose to shrink the window to fit in your screen (the Scale to Fit Available Space option), or to scroll through the other Mac's screen (the Show Full Size option).

- **When Connecting to a Computer:** You can choose the initial state, either Always Attempt to Control If Possible or Initially Observe.

- **When Controlling a Mac:** You can choose Encrypt Passwords and Keystrokes Only (Faster) or Encrypt All Network Data (More Secure).

- **When Displaying Remote Screens:** You can choose Adapt Quality to Network Connections (Faster) or Show the Screen at Full Quality (More Detailed). You also can switch between these two modes during a screen-sharing session by choosing View Adaptive Quality or View ⇨ Full Quality.

- **Scroll the Screen:** The three options here control how the shared screen is scrolled (for when it does not fit in your screen): When the Cursor Reaches an Edge, Continuously with the Cursor, or Only When the Scroll Bars Are Adjusted. Note that the word *cursor* here really means pointer.

New Feature
The When Connecting to a Computer options and the Scroll the Screen options are new to Mac OS X Lion. ■

Sharing other resources

If you've enabled other types of sharing in the Sharing system preference, they're generally accessible as if they were local to your Mac using the same methods you would use for devices attached to your Mac:

- **CDs and DVDs:** Another Mac's shared DVD drive should appear in the Devices section in the sidebar of any Finder window as if it were a drive connected directly to your Mac.

- **Printers:** Another Mac's shared printer will display in the Default pane when you click the + icon button to add a printer in the Printers & Fax system preference (see Chapter 30).

- **Scanners:** Another Mac's shared scanner will appear as a device in the Image Capture utility on your Mac (see Chapters 14 and 30).

- **Internet:** Macs connected to your Mac via Ethernet, FireWire, Wi-Fi, or Bluetooth will have Internet access without having to do anything on their end. But your Mac may experience some slowdown if others use the Internet heavily through it.

- **Web:** Other Macs connected to your Mac can access the web pages in your Sites folder through their browser, as explained in Chapter 25.

Summary

If your Mac is accessible to other Macs via the local network, you can set it up to share files over Ethernet, FireWire, Wi-Fi, and Bluetooth connections. You can share files with other users over the same connections.

The new AirDrop feature lets Macs share folders without any setup, but it works only on recent Mac models running Mac OS X Lion on the same Wi-Fi network.

You also can share your DVD drive, connected printers, connected scanners, and Internet connections with users you provide sharing access to. Mac OS X also enables you to observe and control other Macs via its Screen Sharing utility.

Using Mac OS X as a Server

The very first version of Mac OS X released to the market was Mac OS X Server way back in January 1999 under the name Mac OS X Server 1.0—the first version for the desktop (Mac OS X 10.0 Cheetah) didn't come until March 2001.

So being a server to provision files and more to other computers has been in Mac OS X's DNA from the very beginning. In fact, it's been part of the Mac since the 1984 debut of the original Macintosh: Even that Mac came with a networking technology called AppleTalk that let Macs network with other Macs to share files and printers. That was revolutionary at the time, and it explains why networking and file sharing on other computers such as those running Windows remains an awkward process.

Mac OS X Lion has the same file-sharing capabilities as previous versions of Mac OS X, as Chapter 24 details. Like them, it also lets you use your Mac as a server for web pages, as this chapter covers.

But it's the server version of Mac OS X Lion—Mac OS X Lion Server—that you want for serious serving, such as of shared calendars, e-mail, wikis, files, and more to both Macs and PCs and even in some cases to iOS devices (iPhones, iPads, and iPod Touches). Plus they can back up their files to Mac OS X Server.

Mac OS X Lion Server is particularly well suited as a small-business server or as a departmental server because, after all, it is Mac OS X and has everything the regular Mac OS X does plus much easier versions of the server applications than you'll find in Windows or Linux.

IN THIS CHAPTER

Using Mac OS X as a web server

Touring Mac OS X Lion Server's Server application

Creating configuration profiles for Macs and iOS devices

Setting up the server itself with Server Admin

Adding and managing users with Workgroup Manager

Creating installation images with System Image Utility

Serving Web Pages from Mac OS X

Mac OS X comes with a built-in web server, the open-source Apache server software that the vast majority of websites also use, commercial or not. But you don't need to learn Apache to use it on the Mac; Mac OS X does the behind-the-scenes work for you. You also can use the desktop version of Mac OS X to serve such web pages—you don't need to install Mac OS X Server.

There are two kinds of websites you can host on your Mac: personal websites and a common website. Each user of your Mac can have his or her own personal website in the Home folder's Sites folder. There's also a common folder—`/Library/WebServer/Documents`—that you can use as a main website.

To make any or all of these websites available to others on your local network, put your website's files in the appropriate folders. Then turn on web sharing on your Mac by launching the Sharing system preference and selecting the Web Sharing option in the list of sharing services at left. If you click Web Sharing, the Web Sharing pane opens and displays the IP addresses your local network users will need to enter in their browsers to access your websites. (You can click the links in that pane to see the current web pages.)

Caution

If you have multiple users on your Mac, and one of them turns on web sharing within his or her account, web sharing is turned on for all accounts. ■

The common website's IP address (which users need to enter to access the site) is the same as for your Mac, followed by the folder indicator (/), such as `192.168.1.190/`. The personal website's IP addresses start with that main IP address and then add the username, such as `192.168.1.190/~galen/`. You don't have to have both a common and a personal website; Mac OS X simply lets you do both (actually, a common website and a personal website for each user account).

The web pages that Mac OS X can serve to others exist in the Sites folder in each user's Home folder. A placeholder `index.html` file is placed by Mac OS X in each Home folder. The `Library/WebServer/Documents/` folder also comes with a placeholder web page. Its name starts with `index.html` and adds a code for the language it's written in, such as `.en` for English, `.fr` for French, and `.pt` for Portuguese. (You may have just one such file, for your Mac's default language, or several, based on the languages enabled for the Mac.) To make the file accessible on the Internet, change its name (such as `index.html.en`) to simply `index.html`. Of course, the placeholder web page is not one you probably want to use as your home page, so you'll more likely end up placing your own web pages in this folder.

I don't recommend using a Mac running the desktop version of Mac OS X as a web server connected to the Internet—that can open you up to all sorts of hacking problems, as Chapter 26 explains. Plus, you need a continually available high-speed Internet connection to that Mac, which must be left on 24/7. You'll be hard pressed to find an Internet service provider (ISP) that offers such connections for home-based users. But if you want to have personal web pages at home or even within a department at work, Mac OS X can easily do the trick. For heavy-duty websites, use Mac OS X Server with a dedicated high-speed Internet connection, or use a web host or your Internet service provider to deliver the web pages to users.

The basics of web pages

Of course, you need web pages available in your site for people to see them. You can create the web pages in all sorts of applications: Microsoft Word and Apple Pages can save their files in HTML format, for example, and then there are professional website creation applications such as Adobe Dreamweaver (www.adobe.com) and Karelia Software's Sandvox (www.karelia.com).

The home page for a website should be named index.htm or index.html (it doesn't matter which). If a user types the URL without a page name, such as 192.168.1.190/~galen/, the Apache server delivers index.html or index.htm automatically if that page exists in the folder. If you don't use this filename, then the user must type the full URL to get to the page, such as 192.168.1.190/~galen/books.html.

Note

If you do host your own website from your Mac, it will need its own public IP (Internet Protocol) address, as Chapter 23 explains. And you'll need to register a domain with a domain registry service or with a DNS (Domain Name Service) provider that then maps to your public IP address so, for example, when a user types www.apple.com, he or she is sent to the correct IP address for the server hosting the site. An intranet site will need its own IP address as well, which you can set in the TCP/IP pane of the Network system preference, as Chapter 23 covers. ■

Using Mac OS X Lion Server

If you're a small business, Mac OS X Lion Server makes a great choice as a departmental server and—if your traffic volumes are modest and you have a secured, dedicated Internet connection—as a public web server or server for users who connect via the Internet. It's an even more obvious choice for use as an internal server.

New Feature

Mac OS X Server had been a separate, $499 product through the Snow Leopard version. But in Lion, it is a $50 add-on that you buy and download from the Mac App Store (see Chapter 9). Doing so simply downloads and installs the Server application and related server utilities. ■

Note

This chapter is not an exhaustive guide to Mac OS X Server, but instead a survey of its core capabilities. For the nitty-gritty detail a server administrator needs, please refer to Mac OS X Lion Server Bible by Richard Wentk or Mac OS X Lion Server For Dummies by John Rizzo, both from Wiley Publishing. Apple also provides setup documentation for the main Mac OS X Server services such as iCal and Mail that explain the Internet, network, and other technical connections that need to be in place; you can download the PDF guides files from http://www.apple.com/server/macosx/resources/documentation.html. ■

Setting Up Mac OS X Lion Server

When you upgrade a previous version of Mac OS X Server to Mac OS X Lion Server, the process is essentially the same as for Mac OS X (see Appendix A), except that you are asked for your organization name and administrator's e-mail address. The former is what users see when they connect to the server, and the latter is used to verify a server's authenticity when users first try to gain access.

During the upgrade installation, you are presented the Setting Up window. This window shows the status as Mac OS X Lion Server configures the various server applications.

If you install the Server application onto a Mac OS X Lion enviroment, you get the Welcome to Server window. Click Configure to convert your standard Mac OS X Lion environment to a Lion Server environment and to install and configure the core Server capabilities. This process can take several minutes.

Note
Mac OS X Server is Mac OS X, so everything else in this book applies to Mac OS X Server. ■

When you log in to Mac OS X Server, you should see the Server application (a globe icon) in the Dock, along with the usual Mac OS X applications. (If not, you can launch it from the Applications folder and add it to the Dock, as Chapter 2 explains.) The Server application is the control center for Mac OS X Lion Server, and the application you'll use most to manage server settings.

Mac OS X Lion Server also provides a set of server administration tools for more expert users; they reside in the Server folder in your Applications folder:

- Podcast Composer
- Server Admin
- Server Monitor
- System Image Utility
- Workgroup Manager
- Xgrid Admin
- Xsan Admin

New Feature
These tools are no longer installed on your Mac by default. To get them, launch the Server application and choose Tools ➪ Install Server Admin Tools to download and install them. (You can also download them from www.apple.com/support/downloads; search for Server Admin Tools to find the installation image.) Once installed, two of them—Server Admin and Workgroup Manager—also are available in the Server application's Tools menu, along with the Screen Sharing and Directory Utility tools that are installed with Lion Server. ■

Using the Server application

The way Mac OS X Lion Server works is through policies. You can set policies on the services and access for individual users and for groups of users, and those policies determine what each user can do.

For example, you might have a group called Sales for which you provide e-mail, iCal calendar, file sharing, and iChat message access, and for which you provide access configuration files for their iPhones, iPads, and iPod Touches to determine what they can and cannot do on those devices. You can also set up a company website that you make available to the Everyone group. You might also set up backup space on your server (or to storage devices attached to it) for each user to back up to via Time Machine, so all your backups are in one place. You might have a group called Developers for which you provide the same services that Sales gets but also can access a wiki server (for project information sharing).

Each group's policies determine what services it can use and what permissions it has for those services (for example, you may restrict members of the Sales group to being able to only download files from their file shares, not upload files to them).

New Feature

The Server application is new to Mac OS X Lion Server. In Mac OS X Snow Leopard, you configured services via the Server Preferences application. Wikis were handled as part of the Web service, not as a separate service. In the case of podcasts and wikis, you used the separate Podcast Composer application. ■

Mac server setup

The first thing to do in the Server application is set up the Mac server itself. The server (the Mac itself) is listed at the bottom of the initial window in the Sidebar under the Hardware label. Click it to open its management pane to the right. That pane has four subpanes:

- **Overview:** This subpane displays information on the Mac itself: its model, processor, serial number, total amount of attached storage, amount of RAM, startup disk name, Mac OS X Server version, and how long it's been running (servers are often kept on indefinitely so people have 24/7 access).

- **Settings:** This subpane lets you determine which services the server provides; select a service to enable it and deselect it to disable it.

  - **Allow Remote Login Using SSH:** This option lets another computer log in to the server over the network using a secure shell in Unix, which is handy when trying to manage a server in another location or if its Finder has stopped responding. Appendix D explains the concept of Unix shells.

  - **Enable Screen Sharing and Remote Management:** This option lets another user observe and/or manage your Mac server using the screen-sharing capabilities described in Chapter 24.

  - **Allow Remote Administration Using Server:** This option lets another Mac OS X Lion Server manage this server from its Server and Server Admin applications over the network. In some organizations, you may have multiple Mac servers, such as for different departments, and this option lets you manage them all over the network from any of the Mac OS X Lion Servers.

- **Dedicate System Resources to Server Services:** This option ensures that part of the Mac's memory and processing capability are reserved to run the server itself, so if you run regular Mac OS X applications on it, the server capabilities aren't slowed down.

- **Enable Apple Push Notifications:** This option lets your Mac server broadcast notifications to users, such as when they have new mail, a new software update, a new iOS configuration, and the like. The user sees either an alert window or an indicator in certain apps (such as the number-in-a-circle icon that the Mail application uses to show you have new unread messages). You need a certificate that establishes your identity to use this service; click the adjacent Edit button to set that up and manage it. (You can use your own or a corporate Apple ID as the basis of your certificate.)

- **SSL Certificate:** Several services require an SSL (Secure Socket Layer) certificate to encrypt their contents to ensure safe transmission over the Internet or network. Click Edit to manage those certificates for each of the services that require or prefer them, such as Address Book, iCal, iChat, Mail, and your website. Mac OS X Server creates a self-signed certificate automatically, but such certificates are deemed as untrusted by browsers and other applications, which validate a certificate against an independent certificate authority. You can get an SSL from such an authority, and to help you do that, Mac OS X Lion Server lets you save your self-signed certificate to get validated so you don't have to change certificates. Click Edit to the right of the SSL Certificate label, select a service using your self-signed certificate, then choose Generate Certificate Signing Request (CSR) from the Action icon pop-up menu (the gear icon). When you get the validated certificate, select the certificate the same way but choose Replace Certificate with Signed or Renewed Certificate. Certificate authorities include Comodo Group (`www.comodo.com`), Thawte (`www.thawte.com`), and VeriSign (`www.verisign.com`).

- **Network:** This subpane lets you change the Mac server's name on the network, both the name of the Mac itself (the Computer Name, which you can also change in the Sharing system preference as described in Chapter 24) and its server name (the Host Name). Click Edit adjacent to the option you want to change. This pane also displays the server's IP address on the local wired and Wi-Fi network; if a network is not configured, it shows that as well (configure the networks in the Network system preference, as Chapter 23 explains).

- **Storage:** This subpane shows all the attached storage devices and their contents, so you can determine access privileges for them all, as Figure 25.1 shows. Click a disk to select it; to select a folder, click the disclosure triangle to the left of the disk name and then click the desired folder. Then from the Action icon pop-up menu (the gear icon), choose Edit Permissions to change its permissions or choose Propagate Permissions to apply selected permissions to the disk's or folder's folders, subfolders, and files.

Tip

You can use the five buttons at the bottom of the Server application to be guided through common Mac OS X Server setup operations: Configure Network, Add Users, Review Certificates, Start Services, and Manage Devices. You can show or hide these buttons by clicking Next Steps. ■

FIGURE 25.1

The Storage subpane of the server settings pane

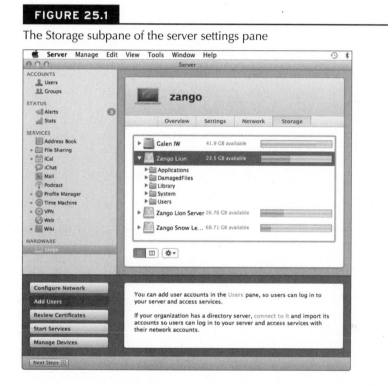

Setting up users and groups

You can't really apply policies or enable services until you have users and groups to apply them to or enable them for. Set up your users and groups in the Accounts section of the Server application's Sidebar. Click Users or press Shift+⌘+U to get a list of existing users, click Groups or press Shift+⌘+P to get a list of existing groups. Mac OS X Server has several users and groups predefined; the predefined users are the services themselves and the groups are predefined groups associated to specific services (that way, you can add your actual users to the appropriate groups without having to know what groups are needed in the first place).

Tip

To hide the display of those predefined service accounts, choose View ➪ View/Hide System Accounts or press Shift+⌘+−. ■

Mac OS X uses the Open Directory protocol for storing user and group information along with their policies. Open Directory can interact with the Active Directory protocol used by Microsoft Windows Server, so you can have the two servers integrate to apply policies across both Mac and Windows users. If your organization uses an Open Directory or Active Directory server, you can connect your Mac server to it by choosing Manage ➪ Connect to Directory. Doing so will populate the server with the users and groups defined there. You can also import user and group information from a compatible accounts file by choosing Manage ➪ Import Accounts from File.

You set up access to directory services by choosing Tools ➪ Directory Utility to open the Directory Utility (which is also available in regular Mac OS X for users via the Users & Groups system preference, as Chapter 27 explains). In it, you can:

- Choose what directory services protocols are enabled: Active Directory (Microsoft's service in Windows Server), LDAPv3 (the Lightweight Directory Access protocol version 3 used by several servers), and NIS (the Network Information Service available on Linux and Unix servers).

- Go to the Search Policy pane to specify where to search for user authentication information; options are Automatic, Local Directory (the default location on the Mac), and Custom Path, which if chosen displays the + icon button so you can add one or more authentication paths to search.

- Click the Edit icon button (the pencil icon) to edit the selected protocol's settings to communicate properly with the specified directory server on the network. In the Directory Utility, you can view and edit the specific services for the current user that a directory service manages by going to the Directory Editor pane.

To add a user or group yourself, click the + icon button at the bottom of the user or group list. To delete an existing user or group, select it and then click the – icon button. When adding a user, you provide the full name, account name (the short name), and password, and you can give that user administrator access to the Mac server if desired. The names and password should match what is set up on that user's own Mac.

When adding a group, you provide a full (descriptive) name and a group (short) name.

Note
Users and groups you add have a small globe icon appear at their lower-right corners in the user or group list. ■

To edit a user, select the account name and choose Edit User from the Action icon pop-up menu (the gear icon) or press ⌘+↓. In the pane that appears (see Figure 25.2), you can add the user to groups, delete the user from groups, change the username, and allow or disallow server administrator rights. Click the + icon button to add a group for the user to belong to. As you start typing (pressing the spacebar will do), the Browse option appears; click it to get a list of groups to choose from. As you type, any groups whose names include the text entered so far also appear, and you can choose any of them. You can also type the group name if you know it. Click Done when finished.

FIGURE 25.2

The pane when editing a user's settings in the Server application (left), and the pane when editing a group (right)

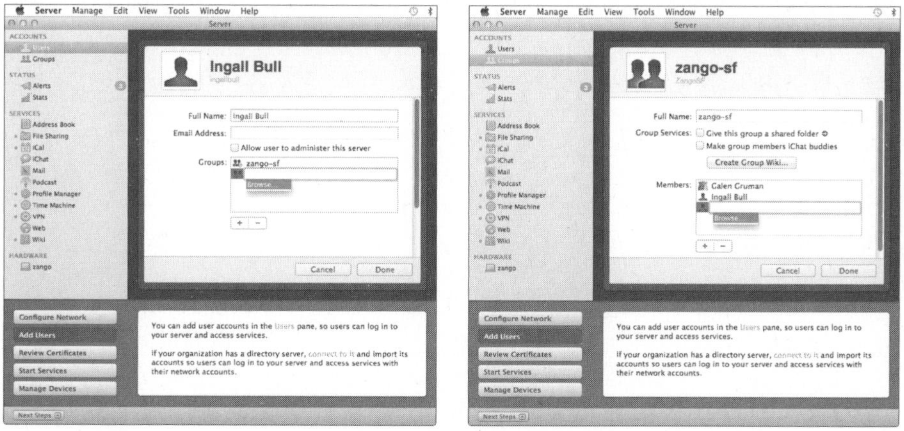

If you choose Edit Access to Services from the Action icon pop-up menu, the Server Access settings sheet appears, listing the services the user has available: Address Book, File Sharing, iCal Server, iChat Server, Mail Server, Podcast, Profile Manager, Time Machine, and VPN (for acting as a virtual private network server). (The list shows only services turned on in Mac OS X Server, as described later in this chapter.) Most of these services are enabled but grayed out, as they are available to all users with accounts in the Server application. Any that are optional (such as Time Machine) can be selected or deselected to add or remove that service for that user.

You also can manage a selected user's password. Choose Reset Password to change the user's network password, type the new password, and click OK.

If you choose Edit Global Password Policy, you can set the password rules for *all* non-administrative users—not just the selected user. In the settings sheet that appears, you can disable access on a specific date, after a specified number of days of access or after a specified number of days of inactivity, and/or after a specified number of failed login attempts. You also can set the rules for the user's network password, such as forcing it to not match the user's account name; to contain at least one letter, numeral, and/or special character, and/or to include both uppercase and lowercase letters; to be reset after the first login (you would do this when you issue a new password but want the user to come up with his or her own unique password for privacy reasons); to contain at least a specified number of characters; to differ from the last specified number of passwords used; and to be reset every specified number of months, weeks, or days. (These settings as a group are typically called *complex password requirements*.)

To edit a group, select the group name and click the Edit icon button (the pencil icon). As Figure 25.2 shows, in the resulting pane you can change the group name, give the group a shared folder, make the group members automatic iChat buddies, create a wiki for the group, and add members to the group (using the same process for adding users to a group when editing a user account).

Enabling and configuring services

The Server application lets you enable or disable the following services for users to access: Address Book, File Sharing, iCal, iChat, Mail, Podcast, Profile Manager, Time Machine, VPN, Web, and Wiki. They appear in the Services list in the Server application's Sidebar. If a green dot appears to the left of a service, it is enabled. To enable or disable a service, select it from the list, and in the pane that appears at right, slide the switch to On or Off, as desired.

In each service's pane, any configurable options also appear. Here are the options:

- **Address Book:** Select the Include Directory Contacts in Search to let users search the Mac OS X Server or other available directory (such as if Mac OS X Server is connected to an LDAP [Lightweight Directory Access Protocol] or Exchange Server) when looking for contact information, rather than just their own contacts list.

- **File Sharing:** Select disks and folders to share (these are called *share points* in Mac OS X Server), then edit their settings by clicking the Edit button (the pencil icon). You can specify which groups and users have access to that share point, as well as determine the file-sharing protocols they can use to access the share points: Apple Filing Protocol (AFP) for Mac users, Server Message Block (SMB) for Windows users, and WebDAV for iOS devices (iPhones, iPads, and iPod Touches). You also can allow guest (read-only) access and allow users to use the share point as their Home folder via AFP or SMB.

- **iCal:** Select the Allow Invitations Using Email Addresses so users can receive calendar invitations via e-mail. Click Edit to specify the e-mail address that sends the invitation, such as admin@*yourcompanyname*.com or calendar@*yourcompanyname*.com. You also can add locations and resources to iCal Server by clicking the + icon button; locations are physical locations such as meeting rooms that you allow people to schedule meetings in and resources are equipment such as projectors, cameras, and the like that you let people schedule the use of.

- **iChat:** You have two options here. Select the Enable Server-to-Server Federation option to let people add users managed through other servers onto their internal buddies list. Select the Archive All Chat Messages option to save all chat threads on the server (such as for compliance purposes).

- **Mail:** You can set up Mac OS X Server to provision e-mail to your company or family, acting as a mail server (it must be connected to the Internet to do this via a static IP address); set up your domain name by clicking the Edit button to the right of the Provide Mail For label. If you use an Internet service provider (ISP) or web host to handle your e-mail, select the Relay Outgoing Mail through ISP option to give Mac OS X Server its own e-mail account to send alerts and the like; click the Edit button to set up the outbound connection to your ISP or web host. If your Mac server is acting as the e-mail server, you can limit users to a specified amount of mail storage via the

Limit Mail to __ MB per User option and provide browser-based access to their e-mail (such as when they are not using their computer) via the Enable Webmail option. Click Edit Filtering Sessions to enable and adjust junk mail screening.

- **Podcast:** In this pane, you set who can access the podcasts made available via the Mac server (Anyone, Authenticated Users, and Podcast Owners) and set up who has administrative privileges (users and/or groups) to those podcasts.

- **Profile Manager:** In this pane, you can set up user profiles for Macs and iOS devices, which essentially configures what applications they can run, what security settings are enforced, and what resources they can access. Click Configure to set up Mac OS X Lion Server to manage profiles. Note that you need an SSL (Secure Sockets Layer) certificate to use Profile Manager; the section "Mac server setup" earlier in this chapter explains how to get one. (I cover Profile Manager in more detail later in this chapter.)

- **Time Machine:** In this pane, you set which disk is used for Time Machine backups stored on the server from users' Macs. Click Edit to get a list of attached storage devices, select the one you want, and click Use for Backup. I suggest you use a dedicated disk for your backups, not a disk used for other purposes as well.

- **VPN:** A virtual private network provides a secure connection between a user and a server, even across the public Internet. Often, a company uses a VPN to provide access to traveling employees to sensitive data stored on company servers. Use this pane to set up a VPN to the Mac server. You specify the shared secret (VPN password) and the IP address range for devices that must be accessed through the VPN, then click Save Configuration Profile to save the VPN information as a configuration file you can distribute to users through the Profile Manager; you also specify the IP address of the VPN server so users can access it from the Internet.

- **Web:** This pane lets you add websites served by the Mac server, both those available only on the network (an intranet site) and publicly via the Internet (an Internet website); the latter requires you have a dedicated connection to the Internet. Click the + icon button to add websites and specify what folder contains the HTML pages and related web page files. You also can restrict access to specific users and groups. Click the Edit button (the pencil icon) to change these settings after a website is enabled.

- **Wiki:** This pane lets you set who has permission to set up wikis (wikis are messaging boards often used by project teams to share status, queries, and information with the whole team as sort of a live log file). Your choices are All Users and Only Some Users; if you choose Only Some Users, a settings sheet appears in which you add the groups and users who may create wikis.

Monitoring server status

The Server application's Sidebar has a section called Status that has two options for monitoring the server itself:

- **Alerts:** Mac OS X Server lists any alerts, such as when settings have been changed here, so you can monitor what's been happening. You also can get more detail on a specific alert by selecting it and choosing View Alert from the Action icon pop-up menu (the gear icon) or pressing ⌘+↓, and you can have alerts e-mailed to addresses you specify by choosing Configure Email Addresses. To clear alerts you've read, choose Clear Alerts from the Action icon pop-up menu.

- **Stats:** You can generate charts of processor usage, memory usage, and network traffic for a period of time you specify.

Working with configuration profiles

In the Server application, the Profile Manager pane (see Figure 25.3) lets you issue invitations for Lion-based Macs and iOS devices to connect to your network. (Click Send to specify the e-mail addresses of people who should get those invitations.) But the real point of the Profile Manager is to control those connected Macs and iOS devices by installing configuration policies on them. That's why there's the Include Configuration for Services option to the left of the Send button; any configurations for the indicated services (shown as icons and usually including Address Book, iCal, iChat, and Mail, based on whatever services are active) are included with the invitation e-mail.

New Feature

The Profile Manager is new to Mac OS X Lion. But if you've used Apple's free iPhone Configuration Utility, you'll recognize the Profile Manager. Its capabilities are based on that utility but extend to create profiles for both Macs and iOS devices, not just iOS devices. (The Profile Manager essentially replaces the iPhone Configuration Utility.) ■

FIGURE 25.3

The Profile Manager pane in Server

There are two reasons to use configuration profiles:

- To prevent unwanted activities by users, usually for security and compliance reasons.
- To make it easy for users to set up their devices by using configuration profiles that do the settings for them.

These rationales are not mutually exclusive: You might want to restrict certain behaviors and make it easy to use other features.

The Profile Manager creates its default configuration profile for those services based on the policies you've set up in Server. Click the Edit button to generate that profile. Note that you need a validated certificate from a certificate authority, as explained earlier in this chapter, for mobile devices (iPhones, iPads, and iPod Touches) to be able to accept your configurations. Macs on your network can use the Mac server's self-signed certificate, though they will let their users know the certificate isn't trusted because no certificate authority has confirmed its authenticity.

Creating configuration profiles

The real action in profile creation and management happens outside of Server. Click Open Profile Manager to open the actual Profile Manager tool in Safari. You'll need to log in using your Mac OS X Lion Server username and password. Figure 25.4 shows the tool's Email pane.

Here, you set up profiles. Those profiles are of users, groups, and devices. The best approach is to set policies for groups, rather than individual users, because that way when users are added, they automatically get the profiles set for their groups.

Note

You also can set configuration profiles for individual users, devices (such as Macs shared by several people; for example, a conference room's Mac), and device groups (such as iPads shared by store clerks). Just select what you want to configure from the Sidebar—Devices, Device groups, Users, or Groups—and then select the user, device, or group in the adjacent pane, and go to the Policies pane in the rightmost pane. ■

First, select Groups from the Library section of the Sidebar, then select the group whose profile you want to set up in the middle pane. In the right pane are four subpanes: Profiles, Members, Activities, and About. You can add and delete members of the group in the Members pane—handy if you want to make a quick change without going back to the Server application—but the Profiles pane is where you do the configuration work itself.

To add or edit a profile, click Edit in the Profile pane; the button appears under the list of settings, of which there is just one (General) initially A settings sheet appears listing the configurable policies, which the Profile Manager calls *payloads*.

Select a payload and click Configure to set it up, as Figure 25.4 shows. Click Save when done, and configure all the other payloads you want set for this configuration profile. Leave a payload blank (don't configure it) to leave it unrestricted. Click OK when done configuring payloads.

FIGURE 25.4

The Profile Manager utility, displaying the Email configuration pane

The Profile Manager screen reappears, showing the configured payloads in the Profile pane. Be sure to click Save at the bottom of the right pane to save your changes (or Revert to cancel the changes).

Tip

When creating configuration profiles, I recommend that rather than try to have policies handle everything that you instead create multiple configuration profiles and then distribute to each group the one that applies to its members. (Macs and iOS devices can accept and install multiple configuration profiles, so a user can be part of several groups and get profiles for each.) That way, you can create configuration profiles that ease setup for common activities separately from those that restrict the behavior of specific users or groups. Doing so ultimately is easier to manage. ■

There are 26 payload panes representing 26 areas of configuration you can set per configuration profile. They are organized by the devices they can be installed on.

The first group of payload panes apply both to Macs and iOS devices:

- **General:** Here you set whether the configuration is automatically pushed via e-mail to the users who are associated to it or whether they need to download it manually from a web page. If you selected Manual Download, you also can set whether users can remove the configurations from their Mac or iOS device. If you require users to have a specific configuration, such as to limit access to meet compliance requirements, choose Never or With Authorization (they'll need an administrator password). If a configuration is meant to simplify user setup for optional activities, choose Always.

- **Passcode:** Here you set the password requirements for users to use their Mac or iOS devices. (This setting cannot be modified on the user device once installed, only through an updated configuration file.)

- **Email:** Here you can set up the basics of a user's e-mail account, such as the incoming and outgoing server settings that all users need to know for POP and IMAP servers (see Chapter 20).

- **Exchange:** Here you can set the basics of a user's Microsoft Exchange account setup (see Chapter 22).

- **LDAP:** Here you can set up the LDAP servers you want users to be able to access contact information from.

- **CardDAV:** Here you can set up access to shared Address Books or other contacts accessible via the CardDAV protocol.

- **CalDAV:** Here you can set up access to shared iCal calendars or other calendars accessible via the CalDAV protocol.

- **Network:** Here you can restrict the types of Wi-Fi and Ethernet networks the user can connect to, for both Mac OS X and iOS devices. For example, you can force a device to connect only to a specific Wi-Fi network (such as the one at home or at the office) or to not connect to "stealth" Wi-Fi networks (those not broadcasting their identity). You also can force the device to connect to networks via specified security protocols.

- **VPN:** Here you can set up the VPN settings, such as the shared secret that you don't want to unveil to users, for a device to use to gain access to your VPN account.

- **Certificate:** Here you can configure and install certificates on the user's Mac or iOS device so he or she has the appropriate credentials to access protected network and web resources.

- **SCEP:** Here you can configure Simple Certificate Enrollment Protocol certificates (used by Cisco Systems networks).

- **Web Clips:** Here you can configure and add web clips—widgets in Mac OS X and home screen links to web pages in iOS—that are preinstalled for the user.

The second group of payload panes applies to iOS devices only:

- **Restrictions:** Here you determine what iOS features are disabled, such as the camera, the ability to install apps, access to the iTunes Store, the use of JavaScript, the ability to join multiplayer games, and access to content beyond a specified maturity level. You also can require certain capabilities to be enabled, such as encrypted backups.

- **Subscribed Calendars:** Here you set up access to iCal calendars for users, so iCal accesses them automatically.

- **APN:** Here you can limit users to specific cellular networks, force a username to be used when trying to connect to cellular access points, force a specific password be used to connect to cellular access points, and set the proxy server and port.

The third group of payload panes applies to Macs only:

- **Restrictions:** Here you determine what Mac OS X features are disabled, restricted, or required, such as the ability to edit specific system preferences, the ability to install or run apps and widgets, and access to various types of media devices (internal disks, external disks, read-only optical discs, and recordable optical discs, and for allowed device types whether a password is required).

- **iChat:** Here you can set the instant messaging service to use as well as security settings.

- **Login Items:** Here you can set which applications, folders, file, and network volumes are connected when a user logs in, as well as whether users can override those login items or add their own login items.

- **Mobility:** Here you can set up and manage mobile accounts, meaning user accounts not tied to a specific Mac. For example, you might permit a user to use a personal Mac as well as a work Mac but make the personal Mac run a network copy of Mac OS X and access data and applications only from the network, then sync that information to his or her work Mac when that Mac is next used. Or you would allow a user to use any of several Macs, with the preferences and Home folder information kept synced among them because they are all tied to the same mobile account.

- **Dock:** Here you can set the Dock system preference for the user, the local preference settings. You also can set which applications, folders, and files display in the Dock, either instead of the user's choices or in addition to them.

- **Printing:** Here you can restrict or preconfigure users for certain printers, control whether they can print to additional printers, and force print jobs to include a footer you specify (such as "Company Confidential").

- **Parental Controls:** Here you set parental controls (see Chapter 27) over access to adult-oriented websites and what days and times kids can use the Mac.

- **Custom Settings:** Here you set which custom preference files to include. These are the com.*company.application* files you may have created in the iPhone Configuration Utility.

If you're configuring devices rather than groups or users, you have four additional options:

- **Directory:** Here you can set up the directory service you want Mac OS X users to have access to, such as for access to network resources (for example, an Open Directory server).

- **Login Window:** Here you can set a Mac OS X user's login options (see Chapter 27), including what scripts must run at login or logout and which users may log in to a specific Mac (useful when you have people logging in via the network or when a user brings a MacBook to a different office).

- **Software Update:** Here you can force a Mac OS X user to get Apple's software updates from a specific Mac OS X Lion Server rather than over the Internet from Apple so you can control whether and when updates are applied.

- **Energy Saver:** Here you set Mac OS X's Energy Saver system preference settings (see Chapter 28), such as how much inactivity causes the Mac to go to sleep.

As you update the various panes, you can see where you've set configurations under each pane's name: "Not Configured" means that pane has not been configured, so no configurations or restrictions are applied to the user, where as "*x* Payloads Configured" indicates how many payloads for that pane have been configured (*x* displays as the actual number of payloads).

Tip

If you open a configuration pane and click its Configure button, its default settings are automatically added to the configuration profile. If you decide not to apply that set of policies to this configuration profile, click the – icon button in the upper-right corner of the pane so none of these policies is applied to that configuration profile. If you see both + and – icon buttons, clicking + creates an additional payload (such as multiple e-mail accounts or multiple certificates). You can scroll through the payloads in the pane; click – at the upper right of a specific payload to remove it. ∎

Click Save to save your configuration profile; if you've not yet assigned that configuration to users or groups, you'll get an alert reminding you of that. (Click Revert to undo your changes since the last save.)

Note

Macs must run Mac OS X Lion to accept the configuration profile; Macs running earlier versions of Mac OS X cannot install these profiles. ∎

Managing users and devices via configuration profiles

Configuration profiles do no good until they are installed on users' Macs and iOS devices.

The configuration profile is e-mailed automatically when you save the configuration profile if you selected Automatic Push in the General pane for the configuration profile. (Thus, you need to have the e-mail address for each user in your Open Directory or other directory service, or set up via the Workgroup Manager.) The first time a user receives the configuration profile, he or she double-clicks the attached file to install it on a Mac or iOS device; any policies that don't apply to that device are ignored. A device already managed by the server will get the configuration profile installed automatically.

If you selected Manual Download in the General pane for the configuration profile, you can manually e-mail it to users or make it available as a link on a website that you direct users to. For example, you might have a company intranet with a welcome page on which you have a link to the company's standard configuration profile, and perhaps have specific welcome pages for different departments that have their additional configuration profiles available as links. (You'll likely want to have those welcome pages available only inside your network or on a password-protected or otherwise secure web page.)

Once a configuration profile has been installed, users see the Profiles system preference in the System section of the System Preferences application. If they open the system preference, they see a list of their profiles and can click any to see it details, as Figure 25.5 shows. Users also can install configuration profiles from the Profiles system preference by clicking the + icon button. They also can delete configuration profiles there, at least for those that the profile allows user deletion, by selecting a profile and clicking the – icon button.

On an iOS device, users see installed profiles in the General pane of the Settings app; if any profiles are installed, a Profile area displays near the bottom of the pane; tap it to see the installed profiles and, when permitted, delete them.

Managing devices directly

When you select a user, group, device, or device group, you can use the Action icon pop-up menu (the gear icon) below its details pane to manage that item immediately. Your options are to lock the device, clear its passcode (so no one can use the old passcode to log in), wipe the device's contents, or update the information on that device. The device can be a Mac or an iOS device, and if you select a group or device group, the action is applied to all members of that group.

FIGURE 25.5

Left: When a Mac OS X user has a configuration profile installed, the Profiles system preference appears in the System section of the System Preferences application. Right: The Profiles system preference showing the details of a configuration profile.

Using the Server Admin tool

Setting up a server involves more than setting up policies and services. That's where the Server Admin tool comes in. You can access it from Server by choosing Tools ⇨ Server Admin or by launching it from the Server folder in the Applications folder.

Server Admin's Sidebar lists any other available servers on the network plus the Mac server you're running it on (the local server). Click the disclosure triangle to the left of a server name to see what services are running; those with a green sphere icon are active. You can add a server, group, smart group, or service by clicking the + icon pop-up menu below the

Sidebar. A group is a collection of servers; just drag servers onto the group's name; a smart group is a collection of services, groups, and/or services that Mac OS X Lion automatically assembles and keeps updated based on rules you set.

Note

The services in Server Admin differ from those in the Server application. Those in the Server application are services that you make available to users; the services in Server Admin are ones the server itself uses, such as DNS, Firewall, NAT (network address translation), NetBoot (which lets users run Mac OS X from a server rather than from their own Macs, such as for contractors and guests), and Push Notification. However, both Server and Server Admin have Mail services; the Mail service in Server Admin is much more detailed and is the one you use to have a Mac server be the e-mail server for users and to define the Internet and other necessary configuration, whereas the Mail service in Server focuses on how a Mac server relays mail managed by an external e-mail server such as one provided by an ISP or web host. ■

New Feature

The Mac OS X Lion version of Server Admin has removed user-oriented services from the services that it manages. These services are now handled in the Server application. ■

Using the Server menu, you can stop and restart, add and remove servers, and export and import system administration preferences (so the settings from one Mac server's Admin Setup application can be applied to others).

You can configure a server by selecting it in the sidebar and using the panes that appear on the right side of the screen, as Figure 25.6 shows:

- **Overview:** This pane shows information about the Mac server's hardware, operating system, services, and status (connected users and uptime).

- **Logs:** This pane lets you view the log file for any of four areas using the pop-up menu at the bottom of the window: system, kernel, security, and Software Update.

- **Graphs:** This pane shows server activity graphically for either CPU usage or network traffic, as you choose in the pop-up menu at the bottom of the window. You also choose the timeframe for the report using the In the Past pop-up menu.

- **Server Updates:** This pane shows available Mac OS X Server updates available from Apple, as well as lets you check for such updates, ignore or install selected updates, and restart the server.

- **Access:** This pane has two subpanes: Services and Administrators. They work the same way: A list of services appears at the left side and a list of users and groups permitted to access the service appears at the right side. By default, the subpanes are set to apply the same permissions to all services, but you can change permissions for specific services by selecting the For Select Services Below option, selecting the specific service, and then changing the permissions for each user. For the Services subpane, by default all services are available to all users and groups, so it shows no users or groups. Click the + icon button to add users and groups if you want to change the services permissions for specific users or groups.

FIGURE 25.6

The Server Admin tool, showing the Settings pane for a selected server

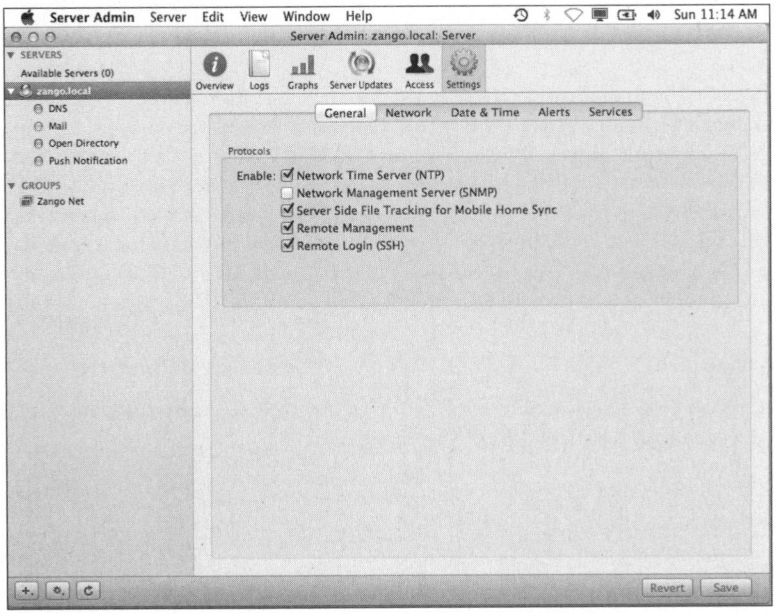

- **Settings:** This pane has five subpanes for configuring server behavior:
  - **General:** Here you enable or disable various protocols: Network Time Server, Network Management Server, Server Side File Tracking for Mobile Home Sync (used if mobile accounts are enabled, as described earlier in this chapter), Remote Management, and Remote Login via Unix's SSH secure shell.
  - **Network:** Here you can specify the computer name and local hostname, as well as see enabled network interfaces (such as Ethernet and Wi-Fi) and their IP address and DNS name.
  - **Date & Time:** Here you set the date and time that the server will use, or have it get the date automatically from Apple's Internet-based time server.
  - **Alerts:** Here you can specify that alerts are e-mailed (to whatever e-mail addresses are added via the + icon button) when a disk has less than a specified percentage of capacity left, when new server software updates are available, and/or a certificate is expired or near expiration.
  - **Services:** Here you can enable or disable the services available to the server.

Click Save to save your changes or Revert to undo them.

You configure services by selecting their name from the Server Admin application's sidebar then using the panes that appear specific to each service.

Note

A related utility is the Server Monitor tool, which you can launch from the Server folder in the Applications folder. With it, you can monitor the status of servers you add to its list, including memory, disks, power, network, and temperature. ■

Using the Workgroup Manager tool

With Mac OS X Server and the associated network and Internet connections all set up, you need one more piece of the puzzle handled: the users. To serve resources to users, the server has to know who the users are. If you use an Open Directory or Active Directory server elsewhere on the network, you connect Mac OS X Server to it (as explained earlier in this chapter) so it can import the user account information. But if you're using Mac OS X Server itself as the user account manager, you use Workgroup Manager to set up and manage that user directory.

You can open Workgroup Manager (shown in Figure 25.7) from the Server application by choosing Tools ➪ Workgroup Server or by launching it from the Server folder in the Applications folder. You see the directory of users in the Accounts pane, which you get by clicking the Accounts icon button in the toolbar, by choosing View ➪ Accounts, or pressing Shift+⌘+A.

Note the lock icon button at the far right of the Workgroup Manager under the toolbar. Click this button to lock or unlock the Workgroup Manager to disallow or allow changes.

FIGURE 25.7

The Workgroup Manager tool, showing the Basic subpane of the Accounts pane for a selected user

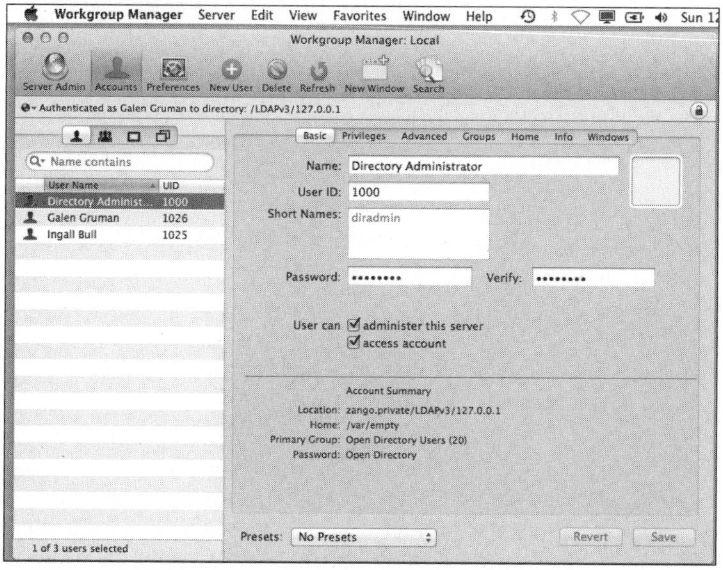

The accounts pane displays users, groups, computers, and computer groups separately. Use four icon buttons above the item list at the left side of the accounts pane to switch among them.

For each user, as Figure 25.7 shows, you use the Basic, Privileges, Advanced, Groups, Home, Info, and Windows subpanes to set the user's account ID, administrator privileges, group memberships, user information, and Home folder path (use the Home subpane for Mac users and the Windows subpane for Windows users). You also can select multiple users to apply common settings to them all. To add users, click the New User icon button in the toolbar, choose Server⇨New User, or press Shift+⌘+N. Note that you must be displaying the users list to get these options.

For each computer, you use the General subpane to set the device name and ID and the Network subpane to manage the computer's Ethernet ID and IP address. To add computers, click the New Device icon button in the toolbar, choose Server⇨New Computer, or press Shift+⌘+N. Note that you must be displaying the computers list to get these options.

For each group or computer group, you use the Basic, Members, and Group Folder subpanes to set the group account ID, its members, and shared folders for the group. To add groups, click the New User icon button in the toolbar, choose Server⇨New Group, or press Shift+⌘+N. Note that you must be displaying the groups list to get these options. Similarly, for computer groups, you must be displaying the computer groups list to add computer groups by clicking the New User icon button in the toolbar, choosing Server⇨New Group, or pressing Shift+⌘+N.

For selected users, groups, computers, and computer groups, you can set up their preferences for various aspects, such as Finder view and media access, by clicking the Preferences icon button in the toolbar, choosing View⇨Preferences, or pressing Shift+⌘+R. Figure 25.8 shows the options. These preferences are similar to the configuration policies described earlier in this chapter, except they apply only to network-connected Macs (as opposed to any Mac that installs a configuration profile from an e-mail or website link) and most can be set to be applied just once (such as for initial user setup) or kept applied (to ensure the Mac configuration remains consistent).

Click an icon for the desired preference to set it up, and click Done when you've completed that preference to return to the pane of preference options. Click Apply Now to apply the settings to the selected users, groups, or computers, or Revert to cancel the changes.

Using the System Image Utility tool

If you manage many Macs, especially in a larger organization, you may want to ensure that users, or groups of users, get consistent installations of Mac OS X and applications without having to go to each Mac and installing all the pieces manually. Or, if you have many guest users, such as contractors or shift workers who share the same Macs, you may want to set up Mac OS X and the appropriate applications on the network so these users boot from the network, not from their Mac's startup disks.

FIGURE 25.8

The Workgroup Manager tool, showing the Overview subpane of the Preferences pane for a selected group

Either way, you use System Image Utility found in the Server folder in the Applications folder. It has three image type options:

- **NetBoot Image:** Sets up the network-based startup images. These images appear in the Startup Disk system preference, so you can set a Mac to always boot from a specific network image. Users also can hold N as the Mac boots and then choose a network image from the screen that appears (make sure each image has a password so users can only launch their own network image). You might remove the internal startup disk from a Mac to prevent local boot, such as for Macs used by shift workers.

- **NetInstall Image:** Lets you create a preconfigured install image that users can then use to set up Mac OS X on their Macs rather than use the Mac App Store's installation disk image (see Appendix A). The image also can include applications these users should have in addition to Mac OS X and the applications that Apple provides with it.

- **NetRestore Image:** Lets you restore a user's Mac remotely over the network from a disk image created previously from the user's Mac.

To install a basic image, in the Sources list in System Image Utility's Sidebar, select a Mac OS X Lion startup disk attached to the Mac server from which to create the image. (To create a NetInstall image, you must have a Mac OS X Lion installation mounted, as you can create NetInstall images only from an installation image.) Then click Continue.

To install a customized workflow, select it from the Workflows section of the Sidebar, then click Run to use it. (If you modify it, you can save the changes over the existing workflow or save it as a new one.)

To create a custom workflow that sets specific options such as setting up the user account, accessing an installation source elsewhere on the network, or partitioning the startup disk, click Customize instead of Continue. Doing so creates an Automator workflow (see Chapter 13) to which you add the desired configuration options and define their settings. Click Save to save the workflow for later use and Run to execute it.

Summary

Mac OS X enables each user account to have its own personal website, plus you can set up a common website. The web pages and associated materials for personal websites are stored in each user's Sites folder, while the common website's files are stored at `/Library/WebServer/Documents`. Although technically the Mac can host websites accessible over the Internet, security and performance issues make this a less-than-ideal option. But within a network, for access by other users in your organization or home, the built-in web server capabilities can be useful.

Mac OS X Lion Server is now an inexpensive add-on to Mac OS X Lion. Its Server application and a suite of related server utilities let a Mac act as a server for file sharing, calendars, e-mail, wikis, podcasts, and more. The new ability to create configuration profiles via the Profile Manager lets you send both policy restrictions and predefined setup parameters for e-mail and other features to Macs and iOS devices such as iPhones, iPads, and iPod Touches.

Use the Server Admin application to set up the server itself, such as its networking protocols. The Server Monitor application lets you monitor the status of other Mac servers, all from a common console. Use Workgroup Manager to set up and manage the settings and (optionally) the default system preferences of users, groups, and computers. System Image Utility lets you create Mac OS X images so users can boot their Macs from the network as well as create installation images they can use to set up their Macs via the network.

Part VI

Securing Your Mac and Your Users

IN THIS PART

Chapter 26
Securing Your Mac

Chapter 27
Managing User Accounts

Securing Your Mac

It's a sad but true fact that there are people out there who steal or cause mischief. In the Internet Age, they now have incredible reach, able to damage thousands and even millions of computers by using all sorts of technology collectively known as *malware*: viruses, Trojan horses, worms, spyware, and more. Some of these folks even reach over the Internet or via other networks directly into your Mac to steal or damage data. And then there's the old-fashioned thief who simply steals your Mac, making all its private contents accessible—and some of that information could be valuable for identity thieves or business competitors.

Fortunately, there are many ways to protect your Mac. Mac OS X comes with some protection tools, and simply by setting various functions correctly you can secure many parts of your Mac as well. For those security areas not addressed within Mac OS X itself, there are applications available to protect you.

You should take security seriously, using the capabilities Apple provides in Mac OS X to keep your Mac safe. But don't panic: Macs are safer than Windows PCs, partly because Mac OS X is more secure and partly because all those evildoers are focused on Windows PCs, what 90 percent of the world's users work with, making themselves a big, juicy target. Macs continue to gain in popularity, but they remain a minority that the cyber thieves are so far content to ignore. On the other hand, Macs' higher sales value means they're more tempting for thieves looking for hardware to sell on the black market. Win some, lose some!

IN THIS CHAPTER

Understanding security threats

Securing Mac, data, and application access via passwords

Using the Keychain Access management utility

Protecting files with encryption

Safeguarding your location information

Protecting against network intrusions and Internet-based threats

Identifying the Four Key Vulnerabilities

So what are the areas of vulnerability? There are four key ones:

- **The Mac itself:** Someone could steal your Mac (or you might lose it and it is never returned by the person who finds it) to get a free or salable computer and any installed applications.

- **Your personal data stored on the Mac:** This includes your passwords, account log-ins, and so on. Given how many of us have iTunes accounts tied to our credit cards, there's more at stake than you might think.

- **Your business or other valuable data stored on the Mac:** This data could be of interest to an unethical competitor or acquaintance. It could include sales lists, financial records, draft contracts, legal records, medical records, music and video files, or love letters.

- **The Mac environment:** This refers to the Mac, Mac OS X, and your applications. These can be hijacked to turn your Mac into a "zombie PC" that generates spam and other malware unbeknown to you, damaging other computer users—particularly your friends, colleagues, and family members listed in your Address Book contacts. Or your Mac can simply be hijacked to steal its resources to help run something unbeknown to you, whether for good or ill.

A very determined thief can probably get past all these defenses, but very few thieves are that determined (unless you work for the CIA or a similar type of organization). The key is to *layer* your security defenses: If someone gets past one layer, there's another one to get past as well. This will dissuade most thieves and hackers, who will move on. (So even if they have your Mac, they'll end up just wiping its data and selling it to someone else on the black market, with your data no longer available. Just be sure you regularly back up your Mac's data, as Chapter 11 explains.)

So how do you layer your security? The best approach is to tackle it in the order the previous list of key vulnerabilities appear, as the next four sections explain.

Securing the Mac itself

Because your Mac is a physical thing, there's nothing that Mac OS X can do to prevent it from being lost or stolen. You need to guard it as you would any other valuable property.

An easy way to do so is by using a security cable that attaches to the security slot on most Macs or that loops through the handle on older desktop Macs. (Be sure to get the right one for your model!) Kensington (www.kensington.com) sells a variety of these.

If you own a MacBook or Mac Mini, putting it in a locked drawer when it's not in use is another easy way to secure it. And don't forget to lock away your backup disks when you're away.

Should these not work, or you lose the Mac when traveling, you can make the Mac less valuable to a thief by using password security to render the Mac inoperable to anyone who doesn't know the password, as described in the section "Using Password Protection" later in this chapter.

Tip
You may want to install the open source Prey (http://preyproject.com) software on your Mac, which lets you track its location, remotely lock access to it, send a "return to owner" message to it, and even wipe its data—the kind of functionality that Apple provides for its iPhone, iPad, and iPod Touch iOS devices. Prey is free for up to three computers. Software like Prey is no substitute for securing your Mac, but it might help if you lose the Mac while in transit. Apple's free iCloud service, when it goes live in fall 2011, will offer a similar Find My Mac service. iCloud will be available as an update to Mac OS X Lion and will be part of iOS 5. ∎

Securing your personal data

It's amazing how many accounts and passwords you use every day on your Mac. You likely have usernames and passwords for online banking, Wi-Fi access, online shopping, and downloading music, applications, and more from the iTunes Store and Mac App Store. Passwords are the first line of defense to securing your information, so it's critical that you ensure they are secure. Therefore, make sure you have passwords not only for your online accounts but also for your web browser (so someone can't just view your passwords in it), for your Mac (ditto), and for documents that contain sensitive personal data (you can password-protect Microsoft Office and PDF files, for example).

A password should not be something simple or obvious, such as your middle name, pet's name, birth date, or other such easily discovered information. But it does need to be something you'll remember, so it should be personal but not widely known. You can enhance the password by making it at least eight characters long (that makes it harder for password-generation utilities to come up with a matching password). A good technique is to substitute some letters with other characters to add an extra layer of challenge for password-guessers: You might replace O with 0, G with 6, L with 1, E with 3, and/or I with 1. (Just be consistent so *you* don't forget when to use the substituted character.)

Where possible, use one of three standard passwords to make it easy to remember what the password is likely to be. Too many passwords, and you'll forget. If you have just one and someone cracks it, all of your personal data can be compromised. You can use the Mac's Keychain Access utility to remember and retrieve passwords, as explained in the section "Using Password Protection" later in this chapter.

Securing your files

If someone does get into your Mac, your data files are there for the taking. Passwords can slow the person down, but if you have sensitive data, a determined thief—a business rival, a determined soon-to-be ex-spouse, a conniving roommate—can use a software program that bypasses the password security and accesses the files.

For data such as this, you can add a type of security called *encryption* that scrambles the file's contents in a way that only it can later unscramble. So even if someone gets the file, he or she can't make any sense of it, password-protected or not. As the section "Using Encryption" explains, Mac OS X comes with the FileVault feature (made even stronger in Mac OS X Lion), and there are third-party encryption tools that offer even better protection should you need it.

Securing your Mac environment

The final area of vulnerability is the Mac's environment: your network and Internet connections, as well as the disks used to bring data and software onto your Mac. A hacker can see your Mac on the network and tunnel through it to get to your Mac's data or even install malware. Virtually weekly news stories about a virus, worm, or Trojan horse threat appear in which a seemingly innocent download, web link, or e-mail attachment infects people's computers and steals their information, turns their computers into "zombies" that start infecting other people, or damages their data, applications, and even operating system. (That kind of attack is called *phishing*.)

These security holes are many, but you can close some of them off by using the Mac's network settings (such as the VPN capability described in Chapter 23) and built-in firewall, as well as anti-malware applications. Just be aware that hackers know about these technology-based protections, so they are turning more and more to fooling people into taking an unsafe action, such as by sending a message allegedly from a person or business you know with what appears to be a legitimate attachment or link. You have to make sure that the message is real: Look closely at its sender, URL, and/or file attachment name. The section "Plugging Security Holes" later in this chapter explains the various techniques you can use to protect yourself.

Using Password Protection

You can set passwords for your Mac in several places—keeping in line with the concept of layered security. The first place is for your user account, which is what sets up the first barrier for a data thief. You can then set passwords for other layers of your Mac's security barrier, from application access to file sharing privileges.

Setting the user account

When you set up your Mac, you set up a user account. And you were asked to give it a password, this password is required to log in to the Mac, as well as to install software and make other changes that could compromise Mac OS X.

Whether you established a password or not, take a minute and think whether the password is strong enough to protect your Mac's contents should it get lost or stolen. If not, change it. To do so, go to the Users & Groups system preference, select your account, and click Change Password. A settings sheet is displayed in which you type a new password (you have to type the old one as well, to prove to Mac OS X that you're the rightful owner and not a thief trying to lock out the owner), as Figure 26.1 shows. You also can type a password hint—just don't type one so obvious that someone can use it to figure out your password. (How can a person get to this point if he or she doesn't have your password to log on to the Mac in the first place? Easy: If you left the Mac running, he or she doesn't have to log in.)

New Feature

The Users & Groups system preference was called the Accounts system preference in previous versions of Mac OS X. Likewise, the Security & Privacy system preference was called the Security system preference. ∎

If you're not so good at inventing effective passwords, click the Password Assistant icon button (the key icon) to get the Password Assistant dialog box, also shown in Figure 26.1. Use the Type pop-up menu to choose a type of password—Memorable, Letters & Numbers, Numbers Only, Random, FIPS 181 Compliant, and Manual—and then pick an option from the Suggestion pop-up menu. Choose More Suggestions if you don't like the first batch of suggestions. The strength of the chosen password displays in the Quality meter. Use the Length slider to increase or decrease the number of characters in the password. If you choose Manual, you can type your own password and see how secure the Quality meter indicates it to be.

Note

The FIPS 181 Compliant option is designed to satisfy the Federal Information Protection Standard 181 used by government agencies and some businesses to produce secure, yet memorable, passwords. ∎

FIGURE 26.1

Use the Users & Groups system preference and, optionally, the Password Assistant, to set a secure password for your user accounts.

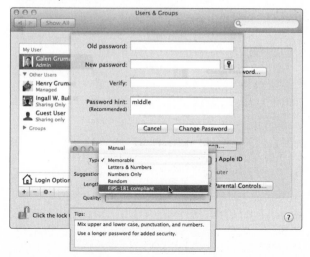

You can change the password for other users, if your account has administrator privileges, by selecting the account and clicking Reset Password. You also can give or remove these users' administrator privileges and set parental controls for them. Administrator privileges give the user wide access to your Mac's settings, including passwords, so don't give your kids, babysitter, or visitors such privileges. (Chapter 27 explains the parental control settings in detail; use them to restrict the activities that kids, babysitters, and guests have when using your Mac.) A user who has neither administrator privileges nor parental controls applied can change his or her password and access all of his or her files and applications, as well as files and applications made accessible to everyone, but that's it.

Note

Clicking Reset Password to change users' passwords does not change the password for their keychain, the file the Mac creates to store passwords for login. Keychains are covered later in this chapter. ■

You have one more option to think through in the Users & Groups system preference: Login Options. You can set an account to automatically log in. Note that doing so still requires that person to type a password, so it's fine to use this option if you use the Mac most of the time. If your Mac is shared among several people, choose Off in the Automatic Login pop-up menu. (Chapter 28 covers the Users & Groups system preference in more detail.)

With a password set for all the user accounts, passwords are required to log in to the Mac and to make system-level changes such as installing applications, enabling file sharing, and changing system preference.

Caution

If you forget your administrator password, and did not set Mac OS X Lion to accept your Apple ID and password as a substitute when you first installed it (see Appendix A) or later in the Users & Groups system preferences, you won't be able to administer your Mac. (If you don't have a non-administrator account, you may not be able to log in, and you won't be able to use any system preference that requires a password nor install any new software that requires a password for confirmation. And gone in Mac OS X Lion is the Reset Password utility to override the administrator password (the version from the Mac OS X Snow Leopard installation DVD does not work with Lion). ■

Enforcing password use

The next step is to make sure that passwords are required for sensitive operations, even after someone has logged in. After all, many people leave their Macs on when they're not using them, making them easy targets for someone who comes by when they're not around. You can require password use for several activities in the General pane of the Security & Privacy system preference, as shown in Figure 26.2.

The safest course is to make sure that all options are selected in the General pane. At a minimum, I recommend selecting Require Password and setting its pop-up menu to Immediately, so a password is needed as soon as the screen saver turns on. Just be sure to have the screen saver turn on after a relatively short time, such as five or 10 minutes, in the Screen Saver pane of the Desktop & Screen Saver system preference.

FIGURE 26.2

Use the General pane of the Security & Privacy system preference to determine when passwords are required by Mac OS X.

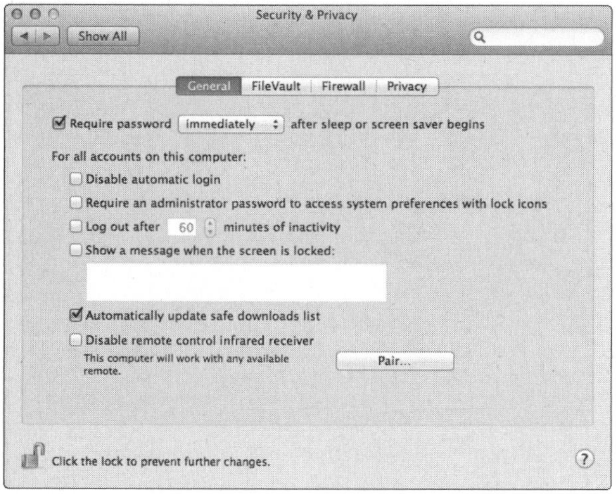

Selecting the Disable Automatic Login option overrides any automatic login set in the Users & Groups system preference, which is a way of discouraging another user with administrator privileges from automatically logging in, though because that person has admin privileges, he or she could simply deselect this option and turn automatic login back on. Still, it's a useful option to prevent those without admin privileges from automatically logging in.

Selecting the Require an Administrator Password to Access System Preference with Lock Icons option means that the Lock icon button (the brass padlock icon) at the bottom left of all system preferences that provide the lock is turned on, preventing the user from making any changes without supplying his or her password. This can be a pain when you're updating system Preferences, but as you typically don't do so often, it's a good idea to enable this setting. If you know you're going to update a lot of settings, turn off the lock setting temporarily, change the settings, and then turn it back on.

Tip

If you see an open lock on the bottom left of a system preference, it means anyone logged in can change its settings. Click the lock to require the user to enter his or her password to make changes. This is a good idea for a Mac left in a public space such as a family room or office, where strangers could have access to it. Two particularly sensitive system preferences—Security & Privacy and Users & Groups—are automatically locked by Mac OS X when you close the System Preferences application. The Date & Time, Energy Saver, Network, Parental Controls, Print & Scan, Sharing, Software Update, Startup Disk, and Time Machine system preferences remain unlocked until you lock them. The rest of the system preferences have no lock. ∎

Use the Show a Message When the Screen Is Locked option to display a message on the login screen, such as "Make sure no one is looking over your shoulder as you enter your password." (Chapter 1 explains the login process.)

Selecting the Log Out After __ Minutes of Inactivity option is more secure than requiring a password to wake a sleeping Mac. By logging out the user, all the applications that were running are also closed, so there's less chance that an attack via the network can succeed, as nothing is running to latch on to.

New Feature

The Show a Message When the Screen Is Locked option is new to Mac OS X Lion. Also, there's no longer the Use Secure Virtual Memory option in the General pane of the Security & Privacy system preference. That capability, which encrypts the scratch space that Mac OS X uses when you are working so a data thief can use it to find passwords or sensitive information, is now permanently turned on. ∎

Tip

If you want the contents of your Trash securely deleted when you empty the Trash, choose Finder ⇨ Secure Empty Trash. You can make secure deletion the default by choosing Finder ⇨ Preferences or pressing ⌘+, (comma) and selecting Empty Trash Securely in the Advanced pane of the Preferences dialog box. Secure-deleting the Trash eliminates another place where stray information can be uncovered by data thieves. ∎

Selecting the Disable Remote Control Infrared Receiver option means that someone can't control your Mac's iTunes or other media players via the remote control that comes with each Mac. Note that just not any remote control can access your Mac; you have to pair it first by clicking Pair and then pressing the remote control button to emit the infrared signal.

Preventing startup from other disks

One common way to get around having to know a login password is to attach an external disk to a Mac and then start from it. If that external disk's Mac OS X doesn't require a login password—or if it uses one the thief knows—then your startup disk's login password is useless.

Apple provides a way called a *firmware password* to tie your Mac's startup to a specific disk, one that requires a password to be able to choose a different startup disk. (After all, you may have a legitimate reason for choosing a different startup disk, such as to run the Recovery System or boot from the network for a contractor.)

You need an Intel-based Mac to tie Mac OS X to a specific default startup disk (Lion runs only on Intel-based Macs). Boot from the Recovery System (hold ⌘+R when you start up, as explained in Appendix A), choose the language you want the Recovery System to use (if asked), and when the Mac OS X Utilities dialog box appears, ignore its options and instead choose Utilities ⇨ Firmware Password Utility. In the dialog box that appears, click Change, select the Require Password option, and type the password to use. (You need to type it twice, to confirm you entered it correctly.) Click OK and restart the Mac.

The next time you try to start from a different disk—such as by holding Option, C, N, or T during startup to choose a disk, start from the DVD drive, start from a network volume, or start in Target Disk Mode, respectively—a lock icon appears onscreen with a text field underneath. You must type your firmware password and press Return or click the arrow icon to change the startup disk. Likewise, you won't be able to start up in the Recovery System by holding ⌘+R without knowing the firmware password.

Tip

Here's a way to really secure your Mac when you leave it, such as during vacation: Use Firmware Password Utility to tie startup to an external disk, and use a password that someone can't easily guess. Take the external startup disk with you, or leave it someplace else safe. Now someone who wants to access your Mac needs both that disk and your firmware password and is not likely to get access to either. ■

To disable this requirement, rerun Firmware Password Utility, deselect the Require Password option, click OK, and restart the Mac.

Setting passwords for applications

I strongly recommend you set passwords on applications, such as your browser, that provide access to personal and sensitive information, such as bank accounts—especially if you use their features to remember passwords and automatically enter them for you. Talk about a treasure trove for an identity thief! Here is how to require a password for common applications:

- **Apple Safari:** There is no way to require a password for Safari, but you can choose Safari ⇨ Private Browsing, which prevents Safari from storing any of your passwords, browser history, or download information, so a thief can't access them in the browser.

- **Mozilla Firefox:** Choose Firefox ⇨ Preferences or press ⌘+, (comma), go to the Security pane, and select Use a Master Password, type the password in the dialog box that appears, and click OK.

- **Opera:** Choose Opera ⇨ Preferences or press ⌘+, (comma), go to the Advanced pane, select Security from the list at left, click Set Master Password, type the password, click OK, select the Use Master Password to Protect Saved Passwords option. Then choose an option from the Ask for Password pop-up menu to specify when you want to be asked for a password to use Opera. Every Time Need is the most secure option, but Once per Session is fine if your Mac is not in a public location.

- **Google Chrome:** Like Safari, this browser has no ability to require a password to use it, but it does have the private browsing feature that stops it from storing personal data: Choose File ⇨ New Incognito Window or press Shift+⌘+N before browsing.

- **Mozilla Thunderbird:** Choose Thunderbird ⇨ Preferences, go to the Privacy pane and then to its Password subpane, and select Use a Master Password to Encrypt Stored Passwords. You can change the master password by clicking Change Master Password. You also can view or change saved passwords by clicking Edit Saved Passwords.

- **Microsoft Entourage:** With a document open, choose Entourage ⇨ Account Settings, double-click your user account, and go to the Account Settings pane. Either delete the password set in the Password text field or both type the password in the Password text field and select Save Password in My Mac OS Keychain so Keychain Access manages the password's accessibility.

- **Microsoft Outlook:** Choose Outlook ⇨ Preferences or press ⌘+, (comma) to open the Preferences dialog box, then click the Accounts icon to open the Accounts pane. Either delete the password set in the Password text field or both type the password in the Password text field and select Save Password in My Mac OS Keychain so Keychain Access manages the password's accessibility.

- **Microsoft Word:** With a document open, choose File ⇨ Save As and click Options, then type a password to open and/or modify the document (type the password if requested for confirmation). (There's also an option to remove personal information from the document when it's saved; this information comes from the User Information pane in Word's Preferences dialog box.) Click OK and then save the document.

- **Microsoft Excel:** With a document open, choose File ⇨ Save As and click Options, then go to the Security pane and type a password to open and/or modify the document (type the password if requested for confirmation). Click OK and then save the document.

- **Acrobat Professional:** With a document open, choose File ⇨ Properties and go to the Security pane. Choose Password Security from the Security Method pop-up menu, then complete the form of options for what you want protected. Click OK until you are returned to the document (type the password if requested for confirmation). When saved, the PDF file will have the security settings applied.

Note that there is no way to require a password to access Apple Mail e-mail accounts or Address Book contacts, nor is there a capability to require a password to open documents created in Apple iWork applications (Pages, Keynote, and Numbers) or in Microsoft PowerPoint. But a password is always required to purchase music, videos, and applications from the Apple iTunes Store and Mac App Store.

Tip
Using a utility such as 1Password (see Chapter 15) can secure all personal data such as credit card information that you have stored at the various websites you visit. ∎

Using Keychain Access

You may notice that Mac OS X sometimes asks you whether you want to save a password in a keychain; this prompt usually comes in the dialog box in which you are asked to type a password. When you say yes, the Mac stores the password and fills it in for you the next time that password is requested by Mac OS X or an application. (Note that when Keychain Access asks you for permission to share the stored password with the requesting application, you can choose to allow it just that once or always.)

Note

Not all applications use the keychain, so you can't count on it as the central storage for all your passwords. ■

This keychain-based autofill of passwords is very convenient, but can make your Mac less secure. The key to enjoying the convenience of Keychain Access and not compromising your security is to have a good password for your user account. That's because by default, Keychain Access adds those passwords to your login keychain—a keychain is a set of stored passwords, security certificates, and other credentials—and then asks for your login password any time a specific password is required.

In other words, it remembers your various passwords but needs you to remember just the master account password; when you tell it that, it tells the application the correct password for that application. So if your account password is weak, all your keychain-saved passwords are vulnerable.

Tip

If you want the login keychain password to differ from your account password, launch Keychain Access (it's in the Utilities folder in the Applications folder; press Shift+⌘+U in the Finder to open the Utilities folder quickly), select login in the Keychain list, and choose Edit ⇨ Change Password for Keychain "login", then type the new password. (You can change any selected keychain's password the same way.) ■

You can create separate keychains, not just use the login one established automatically when you create a user account. In the Keychain Access utility, choose File ⇨ New Keychain or press Option+⌘+N, give that keychain a name, and click Create. It's a very good idea to create a new keychain. Why? Because the login keychain is always open, making it less secure. A keychain you create is opened only when an application has stored a password in it, and then it closes after five minutes.

The trick is putting passwords in that new keychain. Whenever you are prompted to add a password to the keychain and answer yes, that password is placed in the login keychain, not in your other keychain. You have to manually move it in Keychain Access. Here's how:

1. **Display the password list for the login keychain by selecting login in the Keychains list and then its passwords by selecting Password in the Category list, both at the left side of the Keychain Access dialog box.**

2. **Drag the desired password from the central pane onto the desired keychain, as shown in Figure 26.3.**

3. **Type your account password (or login keychain password if different) to confirm that you want to move the password to the other keychain.**

Tip

You can use the same technique to move other credentials; choose the desired credential type in the Category list and then drag the actual credential from the central pane to the desired keychain. ■

FIGURE 26.3

Drag a password from the login keychain to move it to another keychain.

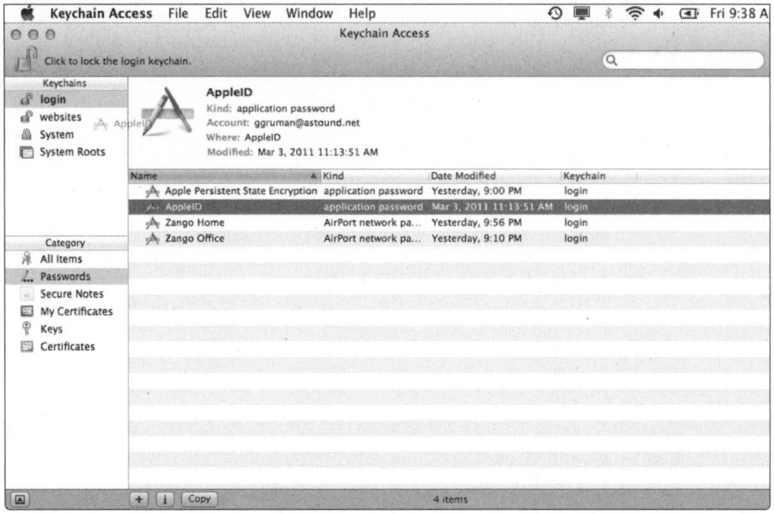

Note

Certificates are issued by websites to confirm their authenticity. Those in the My Certificates group are ones generated by the Mac such as for file sharing. Keys are used to access encrypted data. Secure Notes contains any text you want, so it is available for you later from the keychain, such as to store safe-deposit box combinations. ∎

You can control how a password is used. To do so, double-click the password and then go to the Access Control pane, shown in Figure 26.4. If any application should have access, select Allow All Applications to Access This Item. Otherwise, select Confirm Before Allowing Access. If you want to force the user to type the keychain password, also select Ask for Keychain Password. Select which applications may request the password by clicking the + icon button; any applications that have permission appear in the Name list. You can remove an application's permission to use the password by selecting it and clicking the – icon button. Click Save Changes when you're done.

You also can use Keychain Access to look up passwords you've forgotten. To do so, double-click the password and go to the Attributes pane (it should be open by default). Select the Show Password option. You will be asked for your account or keychain password once or twice; after you type the account or keychain password, the item's specific password appears in the Attributes pane.

Two other Keychain Access options are worth noting:

- In the General pane of the Preferences dialog box (choose Keychain Access ➪ Preferences or press ⌘+, [comma]), select Show Keychain Status in Menu Bar so an icon with the keychain's current status displays. A locked icon means the keychain is locked; an unlocked icon means it is not. You can manually lock or unlock a keychain from the menu bar or by choosing File ➪ Lock/Unlock Keychain "*keychainname*".

- If your keychain data gets corrupted, you can try to fix it by running Keychain First Aid. (Choose Keychain Access ➪ Keychain First Aid or press Option+⌘+A. You'll be asked for your password, and then can click Verify to see if the keychain has any issues, or click Repair to fix any issues.)

FIGURE 26.4

Use the Access Control pane to determine exactly what applications may access a stored password.

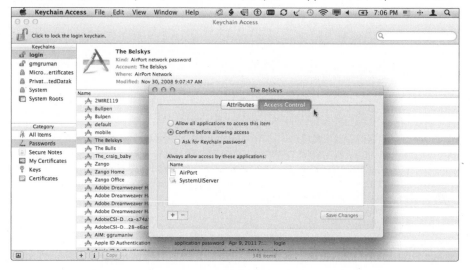

Using Encryption

Your Mac may contain files that you want to do more than password-protect due to their confidential or sensitive information. You've heard the stories about people losing thousands of financial records that were stored on a laptop that was lost. Had those laptops used encryption for those sensitive files, the risk of the loss would have been minuscule.

Mac OS X comes with an encryption utility called FileVault. You turn it on in the FileVault pane of the Security & Privacy system preference:

1. Click Turn On FileVault.

2. A settings sheet appears that requires each user with an account on the Mac to enter their password if they want to unlock the encrypted disk. Click Enable User to the right of each user that displays this button to enter their passwords. Then click Continue.

3. Another settings sheet appears that explains that Mac OS X creates a recovery key so you can access your Mac's encrypted startup disk should you ever forget your password. Click the disclosure triangle to the left of Show Recovery Key to see the automatically generated recovery key for your disk. Be sure to write it down and save it in a safe place. Then click Continue.

4. In the settings sheet that appears, you can select the Store the Recover Key with Apple option as an extra safety net to have Apple store your recovery key, which you can get from its website if you correctly answer the three questions you set up when enabling FileVault in this settings sheet. (Note that Apple won't guarantee access to your recovery from its website, so don't rely on only that option to find your recovery should you ever need it.) If you don't want Apple to store the recovery key, select Do Not Store the Recovery Key with Apple. Either way, click Continue.

5. In the settings sheet that appears, click Restart to begin the encryption, or click Cancel to not encrypt the disk.

After your Mac restarts, Mac OS X encrypts the startup disk. You can work with files and applications during that process—there's no wait for the encryption to be complete as there had been with previous Mac OS X versions of FileVault. But the encryption can take hours, so even though you can work while the encryption takes place, you should avoid restarting or shutting down the Mac until it's finished. (If you do restart or shut down, the encryption resumes when you start up again, but in the meantime, only some of your data is protected.) You can see the encryption status in the FileVault pane of the Security & Privacy system preference.

In that pane, you also can generate a new recovery key by clicking Change, such as if you lost the previous one or believe an unauthorized person gained access to it. You also can turn off encryption by clicking Turn Off Encryption. (You can also turn off encryption in Disk Utility, as described in Chapter 6.)

New Feature

Mac OS X Lion's FileVault is a major improvement from the FileVault capability of previous versions of Mac OS X. FileVault can now encrypt your whole startup disk—not just your Home folder as in previous versions. That brings its encryption to the standards required by government agencies and many large companies. And it can now be set to wipe your disks if someone tries to access your data without the correct credentials. Plus you can now encrypt your Time Machine backups, as Chapter 11 explains, and other disks by formatting them in Disk Utility, as Chapter 6 explains. ■

With FileVault on, Mac OS X automatically decrypts and encrypts files on your startup disk as you work with them, so long as you are logged in with the correct password. You'll likely notice that the Mac runs a bit slower because of that automatic encryption and decryption.

The FileVault capability in Mac OS X Lion encrypts only the contents of your startup disk; it does not encrypt files on attached storage media, such as external hard disks and USB thumb drives. But Mac OS X Lion does let you encrypt other disks: To encrypt attached storage media, you need to format them using one of the encrypted formatting options in Disk Utility, as Chapter 6 explains. You can also use a third-party tool such as PGP Software's PGP Whole Disk Encryption ($119; www.pgp.com).

Tip

If you want to encrypt an existing disk other than the startup disk but retain its contents, you either need to move its contents elsewhere temporarily so you can reformat the disk with encryption enabled, and then move back the data, or use a tool such as PGP Whole Disk Encryption to apply encryption to that existing disk. If you do use both Mac OS X's encryption on some disks and a third-party utility's on others, try to use the same passwords for both to make it easier to access their data. ∎

When you access an encrypted disk, such as an encrypted Time Machine backup disk or an encrypted external disk, Mac OS X Lion asks for the decryption password to open access to that disk's contents, as Figure 26.5 shows. Type it and click Unlock to access the disk's data, or click Cancel to ignore the disk (it does not display on the Mac). You can let the Mac automatically unlock the disk by selecting the Save Password in Keychain option before clicking Unlock.

Caution

You cannot access an encrypted disk's contents on Macs running earlier versions of Mac OS X—just Lion. ∎

FIGURE 26.5

The prompt you get when accessing an encrypted disk

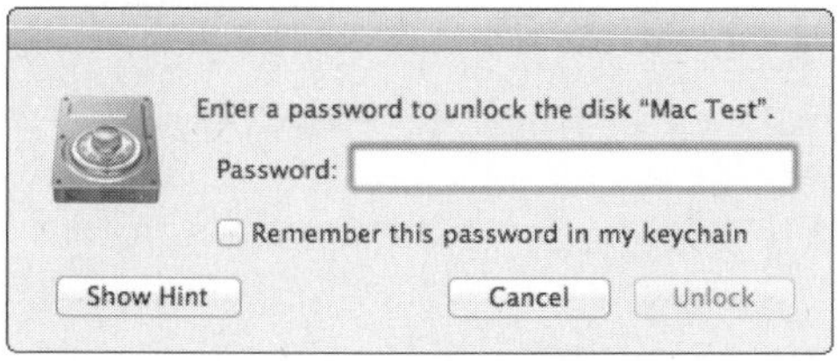

Protecting your Location Information

These days, more people use laptops than desktop computers. And Mac OS X can detect your current location by querying nearby Wi-Fi access points. That's great when you're traveling so your Mac displays the correct time zone, but it also opens up a new way to track your location. The rise of smartphones such as the iPhone and tablets such as the iPad has also created a whole new industry around location-based services, where apps and websites customize what they deliver based on your location, from showing local weather to sending you coupons for the nearby mall. So more and more applications and websites are starting to detect location information, not just for mobile devices but for computers.

Mac OS X Lion lets you manage whether applications can access your location information. The Privacy pane of the Security & Privacy system preference is where you can manage your location privacy and see what applications are checking your location. (If you use an iPhone, iPad, or iPod Touch, this capability will be familiar to you.)

New Feature

The Privacy pane and its location-information privacy controls are new to Mac OS X Lion. ∎

You can disable access to your location date by deselecting Enable Location Services. Note this also disables the ability in the Date & Time system preference to detect your current location to set the time zone automatically.

When an application tries to access your location information, it should ask your permission the first time using an alert box. In the Privacy pane of the Security & Privacy system preference, you see a list of all applications you've given permission, and you're able to deselect those you no longer want to access your location information. The next time they want to access your information, those deselected applications will ask you for permission again via an alert box. (Do note that system preferences such as Date & Time don't ask permission and do not show up in the Privacy pane's list of applications that access location information.)

Note

Any applications that have accessed your location information in the last 24 hours are marked with an arrow icon. ∎

Plugging Security Holes

The most popularized threat today is malware: viruses, Trojan horses, worms, spyware, and other threats typically delivered via the Internet. These can come into your Mac from web pages that run malicious code or have infected downloads, from e-mails that contain the same threats, or from hackers who find their way into your Mac through open ports on the network and on your broadband router (which connects you to the Internet).

There's little that Mac OS X can do about these threats, with one major exception: its internal firewall, which helps secure your network's connections from attacks. A minor exception is that Mac OS X does detect some types of phishing attacks—those that involve the installation of fake antivirus software, such as MacDefender—and provides a warning when you try to download the malware that the Safari browser has been fooled into presenting to you for download in a fake alert window. (I explain phishing in more detail later in this section.)

Protecting yourself from network attacks

If your Mac is exposed to the Internet, it could be a target for attack by a hacker. That's not too likely, as most Macs (and PCs) connect to the Internet through a router (such as a DSL or cable modem), and these routers should be set up to block traffic to non-standard network ports; to prevent *pinging* from outsiders (pinging is how hackers see what's on your side of the router); and to enable firewall, stateful packet, and endpoint filtering to detect and block threats. But if your router is not set up to keep hackers out of your internal network, you could be at risk.

Of course, anyone on your local network can access your Mac, especially if you've turned on file sharing, screen sharing, or other sharing functions covered in Chapter 24. Be sure that you don't provide more access than necessary with such functions; use the Mac's capability to restrict access to specified users and to require users to type valid passwords.

Mac OS X offers its own firewall to protect it from attacks via the network, which is helpful if you fear attacks from someone who's broken into your network or if your Internet router's security is questionable. To set it up, open the Security & Privacy system preference and go to the Firewall pane. First click Start to turn on the firewall, then click Advanced to open the settings sheet to specify what is blocked and what is allowed through the firewall, as shown in Figure 26.6.

In the settings sheet, you block all incoming connections by selecting the Block All Incoming Connections option; this blocks even connections permitted in the Sharing system preference. But the name is misleading; this option does not block the services that Apple considers essential: the DHCP (Dynamic Host Configuration Protocol) connection used to give your Mac an address on the network, the Bonjour service used to connect to network printers and similar devices, and the IPSec (Internet Protocol Security) service used to protect the data your Macs sends to the network.

You'll also notice in the settings sheet that any sharing services you enabled in the Sharing system preference, such as file sharing and screen sharing, are listed at the top with the indicator "Allow Incoming Connections." These can be disabled only in the Sharing system preference, not in the Security & Privacy system preference.

You can specify how to handle other connections, such as e-mail connections from a Microsoft Exchange Server, by adding them to the pane in the middle of the settings sheet. Click the + icon pop-up menu to add a service, choose the application that uses it (such as iCal or Microsoft Entourage) from the dialog box that appears, then set the permissions from the pop-up menu to the right of the application name. Your permissions choices for each application are Allow Incoming Connections and Block Incoming Connections.

The Automatically Allow Signed Software to Receive Incoming Connections option, if selected, can reduce the configuration effort for deciding what applications' incoming connections are permitted. This option lets applications that use a certificate accept connections even if not in the settings sheet's list. Such certificates are configured on the servers that handle the communications, typically by an IT department.

The Enable Stealth Mode option, if selected, essentially hides the Mac from applications that use the Internet Control Message Protocol (ICMP) to find computers, printers, and other devices on a network. This protocol is handy to help network administrators monitor their networks, but it also can be abused by hackers to find poorly protected computers.

FIGURE 26.6

The settings sheet for the Firewall pane of the Security & Privacy system preference

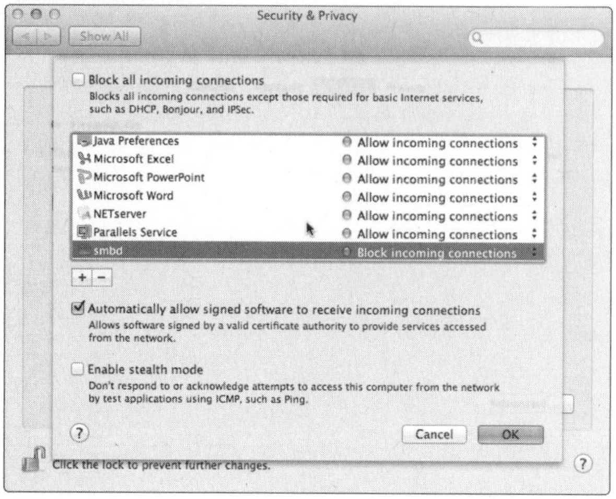

Note

Apple's approach to managing incoming connections is different than is typical for network administrators and Windows PC managers. They typically manage connections through network ports—addresses on a router that are usually assigned for specific connections. E-mail, for example, typically uses port 80. By shutting off ports whose associated service connections you don't want to allow in, you can block potential threats. But it requires knowing what each port is used for. By focusing on permissions for specific services and applications, Apple's firewall is easier for the average user to configure because it figures out what ports are affected. ∎

If you think your Mac might be vulnerable, you can use Network Utility to monitor its open ports, as Figure 26.7 shows. Launch Network Utility (it's in the Utilities folder in the Applications folder) and go to the Port Scan pane. Type your Mac's IP address (you can find this in the Network system preference; look for IP Address) to see what ports are open. You also can check your router by typing its IP address (also found in the Network system preference; look for Router). In fact, you can check for open ports for any computer, router, or website for which you have the IP address or URL. Your network administrator can tell you if any of the open ports are worrisome. (Chapter 23 explains Network Utility in more depth.)

If you seriously want to understand what's happening with your network ports, Network Utility isn't the right tool. You'll need a network monitoring utility for your Mac instead, such as NetMonitor ($10; http://homepage.mac.com/rominar/net.html) or Digital Sentry ($20; www.koingosw.com). If you're on a network, your network administrator will, or should, have the right tools to monitor security for the entire network, not just for your Mac.

Keeping Mac OS X up to date

Apple very nicely provides an automatic update feature that periodically checks for updates to Mac OS X and other Apple software, then downloads and installs that software. Not only do you get additional features from such updates, but you also get bug fixes and security patches that help protect your Mac from hackers and other ne'er-do-wells. You set the schedule for the automatic checking in the Software Update system preference, as described in Chapter 28. (The default schedule is weekly.)

Software Update runs automatically, but you also can make it look for updates whenever you want: Simply choose ⇨ Software Update and it looks for new updates.

When Software Update finds updates to install, it presents them in a list. It indicates any that require your Mac to restart. You can disable installation of any by deselecting the check box to the left of the update's description, or click Cancel to prevent the update from happening until the next check.

FIGURE 26.7

The Port Scan pane of Network Utility

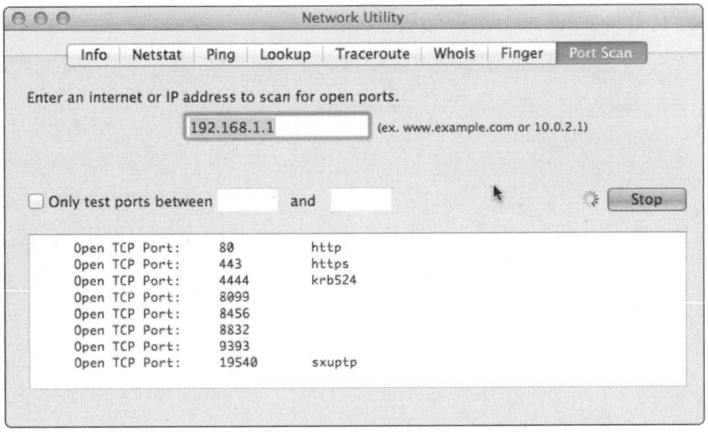

Protecting yourself from malware

To protect yourself from malware, the first line of defense is to be cautious in what you open on the web or in an e-mail. Never open an attachment or go to a website from a link in an e-mail whose sender you do not know. Your bank, credit card issuer, or mortgage holder will not send you an e-mail with a link to verify your account; the links are to a thief's website, which collects the account numbers from the unwary who naively enter it. If you think such an e-mail might be legitimate, open your web browser and type the web address you have on file or bookmarked, not the one that came in the e-mail. If there is a need to update your account, you'll be asked to do so when you log in to the account directly.

If you get a Valentine's e-mail from someone you don't know, or any message offering to share something interesting from a person you don't know, don't open it. The attachment is almost always malware. Yes, it's true that most malware is written for Windows PCs and won't work on your Mac, but there *is* some Mac malware, and there's no reason to think the Mac is somehow immune to attacks. It's *not*—it's just not the usual target. Note that if a friend's computer is infected, it may send you such links (it's been converted into a "zombie PC"); the hacker hopes you'll trust the friend's e-mail address and thus open the malware, in what's called a *phishing attack*. Ask yourself if your friend would really send such a message—most are written in broken or legalistic English, a sign of a foreign hacker, and few sound like the actual person you know.

Likewise, some websites present messages saying that they've detected a virus on your computer and ask you to click a link to remove it—these sites almost always actually install a virus or other piece of malware when you fall for their scam. Launch your own anti-virus software instead.

In some cases, you should consider buying anti-malware software, such as if you have children or parents who might be naive about where they go on the web and what e-mails they open. Intego's Internet Security Barrier X6 ($80 for two Macs, plus annual $30 renewal; www. intego.com) and Symantec's Norton Internet Security for Mac ($80, plus annual $30 renewal; www.symantec.com) both offer protection against viruses, worms, spyware, and Trojan horses—software that can take over your Mac, delete files, scan your contacts and send malware to them, and even record your passwords and account information and send it to the thieves who produced the malware. They also look for phishing attacks—those e-mails that have links to fake websites meant to steal your personal information—and other scams such as the e-mails falsely claiming to need your assistance to handle money on someone's behalf or the e-mails that ask you for money up front to process something (a pet adoption, a rent deposit, or account transfer are common ones) for someone without a local bank account in return for receiving your money back along with a fee "later."

E-mail programs—Apple Mail, Microsoft Entourage and Outlook, and Mozilla Thunderbird—all have junk settings that also try to detect scams and phishing expeditions. Be sure you turn the junk detection features on. And if you manage your own e-mail server (directly or through a web host), be sure to turn on its junk-mail detection features to reduce the amount of junk mail that actually makes it to your Mac. Ditto if you use an e-mail service such as Yahoo Mail or Google Gmail. Safari, Firefox, and other web browsers also try to detect phishing sites and warn you about suspect links.

Mac OS X also looks for malware behind the scenes, and will alert you if it detects what it suspects is a phishing, virus, or other malware attack when you download files. Mac OS X checks Apple's registry of suspect downloads daily unless you turn off that capability in the General pane of the Security & Privacy system preference by deselecting the Automatically Update Safe Downloads List option. (This capability was introduced in mid-2011 in a security update to Mac OS X Snow Leopard, so although it may appear to be a new Lion feature, it is not.)

All of these programs do their job, but they don't catch everything; human vigilance is still required.

New Feature

Mac OS X Lion takes a page from iOS and adds a capability called sandboxing that could make your Mac safer from malware and phishing attacks. In iOS, each app has its own reserved space (that's the sandbox) and keeps all its data in that space (that's why there is no file system on an iPhone, iPad, or iPod Touch), plus each app doesn't let other apps access its capabilities or data without explicit permission (that's why you have to use the Open In option in iOS to open data from another app). In Mac OS X, developers can use these same techniques to limit access to applications. For example, a contacts manager could be protected so e-mail programs couldn't access its entries, thwarting a usual phishing attack. But the key here is "could": developers have to actually implement sandboxing. Because you won't know whether the applications you use have such extra protection or not, follow the safety advice in this chapter anyhow. ∎

Summary

Your Mac could be vulnerable in any or all of four areas: It could be physically lost or stolen, its stored personal data such as account information and passwords could be compromised, your files with sensitive data could be accessed, and it could be breached by an outsider and infected with viruses or other malware.

Your first line of defense is to secure the Mac itself, such as by locking it when not in use. You can reduce the chances of someone who steals or finds your lost Mac gaining access to its files by setting a login password, or even by tying startup to a specific disk.

Passwords also should be set for individual applications where possible, as well as to open files with sensitive data, which some popular programs support. You also can set the Mac to require passwords to make several kinds of system-level changes, as well as restrict what guests and other users have access to on your Mac through a combination of passwords and user-access privileges set in the Sharing system preference.

Mac OS X can store passwords for many applications for you in what's called a keychain, so all you have to remember is your keychain password instead of all your separate application and web passwords. The Keychain Access utility lets you manage your passwords and other security credentials, as well as view them. Capabilities include choosing what passwords individual applications have access to and setting up separate keychains.

Mac OS X Lion's FileVault capability adds more protection to files stored on your startup disk, encrypting it so others can't access its data without a password or recovery key. You can also apply encryption to other disks by formatting them with encryption enabled in Disk Utility.

Other users also must be running Mac OS X Lion to access that encrypted disk. You can encrypt the backup file via Time Machine for both encrypted and unencrypted disks, but again will need the password or recovery key and a Mac running Mac OS X Lion to access to those backups.

Mac OS X offers a firewall capability to restrict access to the Mac's network connections to only approved services and applications. However, this should be used as an adjunct to, not a replacement for, the network's own firewall and other router-based security settings.

To protect yourself from malware such as viruses and spyware, you need to be careful as to what files you open and download, even if you are running anti-malware software.

CHAPTER

27

Managing User Accounts

T he Mac is a personal computer, so the idea of having, much less
managing, a user account on your Mac may seem like a bizarre
concept. After all, you're the user and it's your Mac, so why do
you need an account?

If you are truly the only user of the Mac, then the idea of an account can
seem unnecessary. Except that it isn't. And if more than one person uses
your Mac, you definitely need to set up and manage the accounts so each
user's data, applications, and so on are kept separate for privacy, security, and stability reasons.

First, assume you're truly the only user of the Mac. Why bother with a
user account? The basic reason is that your Mac has an account for you
whether you know it or not. And the benefit of managing that account is
to set up security, so if anyone else tries to use your Mac—particularly a
thief—he or she is blocked by the need to type a password to use that
Mac. Passwords are tied to user accounts, so you need the user account.
Plus, the user account is what Mac OS X uses to save some of your preferences, such as the login items (the applications and utilities that start
up automatically when your Mac starts up.)

Now look at why you might have multiple user accounts. In a business
setting, your IT department will need an account that enables it to
administer your Mac to keep the Mac updated and otherwise work on it
when you're not around. Plus, this account gives IT access to your Mac if
you leave the company, so IT can ready it for a new employee.

IN THIS CHAPTER

**Understanding why Mac OS X
supports multiple accounts**

**Adjusting the main user's
password and personal
settings**

**Specifying applications to start
automatically at login**

**Controlling startup options for
all users**

**Adding and configuring
additional users**

**Switching among user
accounts**

**Specifying, applying, and
monitoring parental controls**

In a home setting, chances are other family members—as well as guests such as the babysitter and your visiting friends—will want to use your Mac, at least occasionally. You don't really want them to have access to all your applications and data, do you? Or be able to install and remove applications, right? If you create user accounts for those other people, you can make it as if they have their own separate Mac, keeping your part of the Mac safe and secure.

Plus, you can apply parental controls to some of those accounts, so you can restrict your kids' activities, such as the hours they can use the Mac or the websites they can visit. Even if you don't let your kids use your Mac, you'll want to use the parental controls to control their Macs, essentially making you the IT administrator with full access from your user account on their Mac and limiting their access within their user accounts.

Cross-Reference

For more on Mac OS X's security controls, see Chapter 26. For details on file sharing, see Chapter 24. ■

Setting Up User Accounts

When you install Mac OS X—or first use it on a new Mac—a default user account is set up for you, giving you full rights to the Mac and to change other user's accounts—something called *administrator privileges*.

You can modify those default settings, as well as create new user accounts, in one place: the Users & Groups system preference. (Choose ■➪ System Preferences and click the Users & Groups icon [the two silhouettes] to open the Users & Groups system preference.) Figure 27.1 shows the initial pane in that system preference, the Password pane. At left is the list of user accounts, which initially shows your user account and the Guest user account. In the list of accounts, the currently logged-in account is at the top under the My User label, and other configured accounts are under the Other Users label.

New Feature

The Users & Groups system preference had been called the Accounts system preference in previous versions of Mac OS X. The system preference also now refers to accounts as users, not as accounts. ■

Note

If the Lock icon button (the bronze padlock icon) at the bottom left of the Users & Groups system preference is closed, you must unlock it to make most changes. Click it and type your password when requested, then press Return or click Unlock. The Lock icon button changes to an open lock, indicating that the system preference is unlocked. Click the Lock icon button again to lock it. ■

Adjusting personal settings

The Users & Groups system preference has three groups of settings related to your user account and how it functions:

FIGURE 27.1

The Password pane of the Users & Groups system preference is where you set basic user account settings.

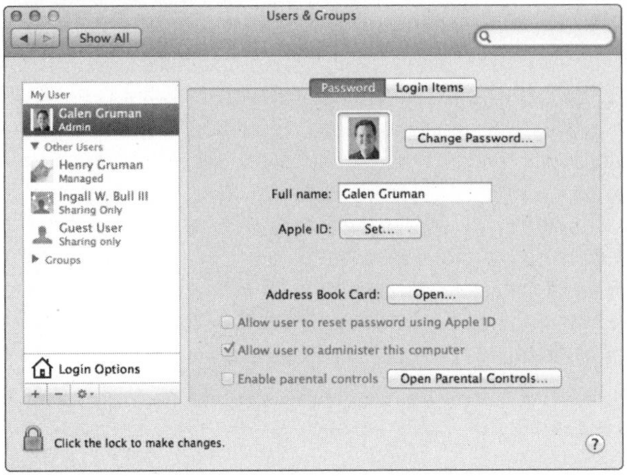

- The Password pane is where you set your password, select the picture used to identify your account, and set up other personal settings.

- The Login Options button at the bottom of the user accounts list in the Password pane opens a new, unnamed pane that enables you to determine how you log in to the Mac at startup.

- The Login Items pane is where you set which applications open when your Mac starts up.

Name, password, and related settings

The most commonly used settings are visible in the pane itself: controlling your name and password. Here are the key controls for setting these personal settings:

- **Full Name:** Type your username in the Full Name field; this is the name that shows up as your Mac's name when you log in. (Note that the name of your Mac on the network, such as if you enable file sharing, is set in the Sharing system preference, as Chapter 24 explains.)

- **Apple ID:** Type your Apple IDs (you can have several) by clicking the Set button (it becomes Change once you've added an ID). Your Apple ID is used in Apple's various online stores—the iTunes Store, iBookstore, Newsstand, iOS App Store, and the Mac App Store—to make purchases and to access your iCloud account (see Chapter 17).

New Feature
The Apple ID option replaces the MobileMe option in previous versions of Mac OS X, expanding its scope to store all your Apple IDs. ∎

- **Address Book Card:** Click Open to open the Address Book application (see Chapter 21) to set up your address book card, which can include your name, address, e-mail, and other information that you can have several Mac applications use, such as to share your electronic business card with other users.

- **Picture:** Click the picture to choose a different image to represent yourself from Apple's image library, or choose Edit Picture at the top of that library to open a settings sheet in which you can take a new picture by using a camera attached to the Mac (such as the iSight camera built into many Macs); click the camera icon button to take that photo. You can use an existing picture you have stored on your Mac by clicking Choose below the camera icon button and then navigating through your disks and folders to that desired picture. Or use the Recent Pictures pop-up menu to choose a picture previously used. Use the slider to zoom in or out of your chosen picture, and drag the picture within its preview rectangle to crop it to your liking. (*Crop* means to cut off one or more sides of an image.) Figure 27.2 shows a photo being cropped. Click Set when done.

- **Change Password:** Click Change Password to open a settings sheet where you can change your login password (or set one up if you don't have one). Chapter 23 covers the password options in detail.

Note

By default, the account that is set up when you install Mac OS X or that is set up for you on your new Mac, has administrator privileges. Thus, the Allow User to Administer This Computer option is already selected. It's also grayed out for the default user because at least one account has to have administrator privileges. ■

FIGURE 27.2

Crop the image you want to use to represent your user account by dragging it within the cropping box; use the slider to enlarge or reduce the image.

New Feature

As Appendix A explains, when you install Mac OS X Lion, you now have the option of having Lion accept your Apple ID and its password if you forget your administrator password. (Chapter 1 explains how to enter the Apple ID and password in the login window if you forget your password.) But note if you don't take that option and decide to enable the use of your Apple ID as a backup login, you can do so by selecting the Allow User to Reset Password Using Apple ID option in the Password pane of the Users & Groups system preference. ■

Login items

When you install some programs, they set themselves automatically to load when your Mac starts up (or restarts). Examples include iTunes, which loads a function to look for music CDs and iPods when inserted so it can open automatically when they are detected, and antivirus applications, which begin running immediately upon startup to catch possible threats to your Mac. But you also can set your user account so any application loads at startup; this way the apps you always use are ready to go after the Mac starts. For example, you might have your mail program set to launch at startup.

As Figure 27.3 shows, the Login Items pane displays all applications and utilities set to launch at startup, and it's where you add applications to the automatic startup list. The controls are simple:

FIGURE 27.3

The Login Items pane of the Users & Groups system preference

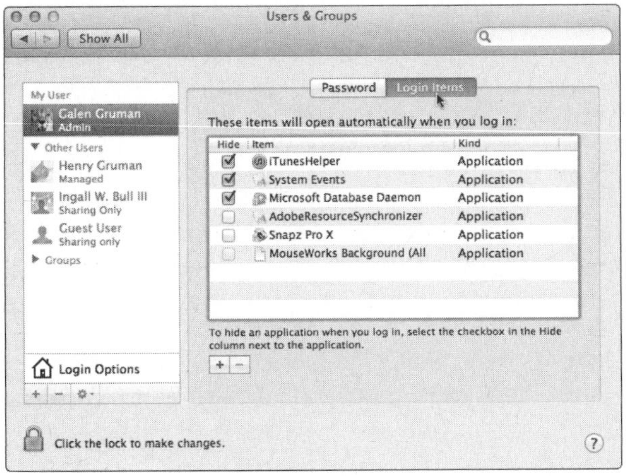

- **Add an item for automatic startup.** Click the + icon button, then locate the application or utility you want to launch automatically. (Chances are it will be in the Applications folder or the Utilities folder, both of which are covered in Chapter 14.)
- **Remove an item for automatic startup.** Select it in the list and click the − icon button.

- **Display an item after automatic startup.** Select the Hide check box to the left of the application name. (The Hide option is selected by default when you add applications to the automatic startup list.) The application will be visible onscreen after the Mac starts; for example, if you make Apple Mail a startup item, you see the window with your e-mail after startup.

- **Hide an item after automatic startup.** Deselect the Hide check box. It will run minimized, so its dialog boxes and so on will not display on-screen. You can display the application in full by clicking its icon on the Dock. (Chapter 2 covers the Dock in detail.)

That's it!

Login options

There's another set of personal settings for your account that you control by clicking Login Options at the bottom of the user accounts list. When you click Login Options, Mac OS X displays an untitled pane.

Note

The login options affect all user accounts on the Mac, which is why the Password and Login Options panes disappear when you change login options. ∎

Here you can set the Mac to automatically log in to a specific user account by choosing that account in the Automatic Login pop-up menu, rather than requiring the user to sign in each time you start up the Mac. Choose Off to require that a user be chosen at startup.

Note

The Automatic Login pop-up menu may be grayed out. If so, that means automatic login is disabled in the General pane of the Security & Privacy system preference, as Chapter 26 explains. ∎

Using the Display Login Window As options, you can control how the list of accounts appears when you start or restart the Mac. The List of Users option shows each username (and associated image), so a user clicks the desired name and then types the password for that user. The Name and Password option requires the users to type their usernames and passwords. This second option is more secure, as it forces users to remember their usernames (something a thief is not likely to know), not just their passwords, but because it requires them to remember their usernames, it can be a pain when users repeatedly forget their usernames.

Other options for the login screen are:

- **Show the Sleep and Shut Down Buttons.** If selected, this option controls whether these buttons, plus the Restart button, are displayed at the login screen at startup.

- **Show Input Menu in Login Window:** If selected, this option enables users to switch to a different language's keyboard from the login screen—great for a Mac that is used as a public terminal, such as a store or dorm rec room, or if you have family or perhaps an exchange student who speak languages other than English.

- **Show Password Hints:** If selected, this option shows the password hint for each account; you set that password hint in the Password pane when you set up the account's password.

- **Use VoiceOver in Login Window:** If selected, this option makes the Mac read aloud the options in the login screen for visually impaired users (see Chapter 8).

- **Show Fast User Switching Menu As:** If selected, this option adds an option to the menu bar that enables you to quickly log out of your current account and log in to another one. The best part is that the previous user's applications are not closed, so they continue to run while the user is logged out and thus can keep doing their work. There's a pop-up menu with this option that has three options to control what is displayed in the menu bar: Icon, which shows the icon of a person's head; Name, which shows the user account name (such as Galen Gruman); and Short Name (such as gmgruman), which shows the user's short name established when you first created the user account, as explained in the section "Managing additional user accounts" later in this chapter.

- **The Join button:** When you click this button (to the right of the Network Account Server label), you can set the directory services to use to determine who can log in to various services, applications, and databases on the network and what their settings are; this option enables a business to manage these settings from a central location. Clicking this button opens a settings sheet. Here, you choose a server from the Server pop-up menu or type a server name in the Server text field.

  Or click the Open Directory Utility button to open the Directory Utility. In it, you can:

  - In its Services pane, choose what directory services protocols are enabled: Active Directory (Microsoft's service in Windows Server), LDAPv3 (the Lightweight Directory Access Protocol version 3 used by several servers), and NIS (the Network Information Service available on Linux and Unix servers).

  - Also in the Services pane, click the Edit icon button (the pencil icon) to edit the selected protocol's settings to communicate properly with the specified directory server on the network.

  - Go to the Search Policy pane to specify where to search for user authentication information and for contacts lookup; options are Automatic, Local Directory (the default location on the Mac), and Custom Path, which if chosen displays the + icon button so you can add one or more authentication paths to search.

  - If you're an expert in directory services, you can go to the Directory Editor pane to view and modify the directory settings for user, protocols, services, and other functions.

- Click Apply to accept the changes made in the Directory Utility and return to the Users & Groups system preference.

New Feature

The NIS option replaces the BSD (Berkeley Standard Distribution, a form of Unix) option in previous versions of Mac OS X, expanding Unix server directory support beyond BSD versions. The Directory Editor pane and capability is new to Mac OS X Lion. ■

New Feature

Mac OS X Lion adds the Action icon pop-up menu (the gear icon) below the list of user accounts. (It displays only if you are logged in as an administrator.) It has one option: Set Master Password. Use this option to set a password that an administrator can use to access all user accounts, as well as to create new passwords to users who have forgotten their passwords. ■

Managing additional user accounts

As noted in this chapter's introduction, many Macs have—or should have—more than one user account set up.

In a business environment, the IT staff should have an administrator account on all Macs so staff members can manage them whether or not they know each user's password. And you might want to set up user accounts on Macs used by several people, such as contractors or employees who work in different shifts on the same Mac (for example, customer support staff or sales clerks).

In a home environment, even if you have several computers, you'll very likely want at least a guest account for babysitters and other visitors. You'll also want to have your own administrator-type account on your kids' Macs. And you likely want to set up accounts for individual family members on a Mac accessible to everyone, such as one in the family room or one you take on family vacations.

Adding accounts

To add user accounts to your Mac, click the + icon button at the bottom of the user accounts list on the left of the Password or Login Items pane in the Users & Groups system preference. The controls and options are nearly the same as described in the previous sections of this chapter. But there are a few differences and additions to note.

When you create an account, you fill out the unnamed pane, most of whose options match the options you see in the Password pane for an existing account. But some are unique to creating an account:

- **New Account pop-up menu:** This menu enables you to determine the type of account: Administrator, Standard, Managed with Parental Controls, Sharing Only, and Group. An administrator has full access to Mac OS X and can manage other users' accounts. A standard user can manage only his or her own account and access any information available to all users. An account with parental controls is restricted in what it can do, as explained in the section "Using Parental Controls" later in this chapter. A sharing-only account can only access files over the network if file sharing is enabled, as described in Chapter 24. A group is a way of giving multiple user accounts a common set of settings, as described in the section "Using account groups" later in this chapter.

Tip

You can change a user's account type to Administrator, Standard, or Managed with Parental Controls after you create the account. Just select or deselect the Allow User to Administer This Computer option in the Password pane to change the type to or from an Administrator type, and just select or deselect the Enable Parental Controls option to change the type to or from a Managed with Parental Controls type. An account that has both options deselected is a Standard type. ■

Note

You cannot change a Sharing Only account to a different type later, nor can you change one of the other account types to a Sharing Only account later. ■

- **Account Name:** This text field lets you set a short name (or nickname) for the user; this name is used as the name of the Home folder. (It had been called Short Name in previous versions of Mac OS X.)

Click Create User to create the new account.

Caution

If you create an account without providing a password, Mac OS X asks if you're sure you don't want a password set and lets you cancel the creation so you can type a password. Remember that any user account that has no password can be a conduit for a thief or hacker to access the Mac, as Chapter 26 explains. ■

Managing accounts

After you create a user account, you won't see the Password or Login Items panes. Instead, there's just the Users & Groups system preference window with the user accounts list and one pane with the user picture, Reset Password button, Full Name field, Set button (to type your Apple ID, such as used in iTunes), and—for the Administrator, Standard, and Managed with Parental Controls types only—the Allow User to Administer This Computer and Enable Parental Controls options.

You must start up or log in to the user accounts to modify their Address Book Card settings and to access the Password and Login Items panes.

Note

Multiple user accounts can have administrator privileges, giving them equal control over the Mac. ■

Deleting accounts

You can delete a user account by selecting it from the list and then clicking the – icon button. You are then asked what to do with the user's home folder and all the applications and files stored within it: Save them as a disk image file, move them to the Users folder's Deleted Users subfolder, or delete them.

A disk image compresses everything into one file that you then have to double-click to see the various individual files inside; it's handy when you want to move the files to an archive disk for storage. The Deleted Users subfolder makes all the files easily accessible but takes more room, so it's ideal if you think you'll need access to the various files for a while. Of course, you could also move this folder to an archive disk.

Using guest accounts

Mac OS X comes with the predefined guest account, called Guest User, that is meant for use by occasional users who you don't want to set up individual user accounts for. This is the perfect account for the babysitter, your visiting nephews and nieces, and your kids' after-school friends.

To enable the guest account, click Guest User in the accounts list and then select the Allow Guests to Log In to This Computer option. Note that a guest account does not require a password, so anyone can log in to it from your Mac's login screen. (But no one can log in to your Mac remotely over the network by using this account.) And note that when a guest user logs out (or restarts or shuts down the Mac), all the files in the guest account's Home folder are deleted.

You can further restrict what the guest account can do when logged in through these two options:

- **Enable Parental Controls:** Select this option to restrict when access is permitted, what applications and websites can be accessed, and so on, as described in the section "Using Parental Controls" later in this chapter. (You can click Open Parental Controls to open the Parental Controls system preference to specify those permissions.)

- **Allow Guests to Connect to Shared Folders:** Deselect this option so guests cannot access the files in the Users folder's Shared subfolder; that keeps these files accessible just to people who have individual user accounts.

Using account groups

As noted earlier in this chapter, you can create account groups. After creating a group, the label Groups appears in the user accounts list. Click the disclosure triangle to see the list of groups. Then select a group to add individual user accounts to it. You get a list of user accounts in the Membership area of the screen; simply select the users you want in that group (and deselect those you don't).

The reason to set up a group is to simplify file sharing. When you set up file sharing (see Chapter 24), you can give permission to specific groups to access various disks, folders, and files. It's easier to select a group when giving such permissions than to select every individual user who should have access. Plus, when you add and delete users from a group, the file-sharing permissions don't need to be changed to reflect the changes in users—whoever is a member of the group that has file-sharing permission has access to those shared resources only as long as he or she is a member of that group.

Switching among accounts

When you start up the Mac, you log in as a specific user. But restarting the Mac to switch users is time consuming, plus it closes applications you may want to keep running, such as e-mail or file downloading.

You could log in and out between users by choosing ⌁ Log Out *username* or pressing Shift+⌘+Q to log out the current user and then log in as a different user via the Mac's login screen. But, just as with restarting, this closes all active programs.

There's a faster way to switch users when you have several people using a Mac over a short period of time, such as during the course of an evening. When you do this *fast user switching*, all the accounts remain logged in as you switch to other users—and all applications remain running—but only one user is active at any time.

But you can fast-switch among accounts only if you selected the Show Fast User Switching Menu As option, as explained earlier in this chapter. When that option is selected, an icon or name appears in the menu bar that enables you to select a user to switch to, as Figure 27.4 shows. All logged-in users display a white check mark in an orange circle to the left of their names.

Logging in as a different user when fast user switching is enabled

Tip

If your Mac is logged in to a Standard or Managed with Parental Controls account, you can still make many administrator-only changes, such as adjusting system preferences where the Lock icon button displays the closed-padlock icon. Clicking the Lock icon button prompts the Mac to ask for an administrator's username and password. If you type such a username and password for an administrator user account set up on this Mac, you have full administrator privileges until you close the lock (which may happen automatically when you exit the system preference or utility or switch to something else). ■

Using Parental Controls

Kids, teenagers, and some adults tend to do dangerous or stupid things when using a computer. They might snoop in your personal or financial files. They might accidentally delete your work files. They might install applications—perhaps unwittingly from a website that promises games or other innocent-seeming downloads—that contain viruses, spyware, or other malware (see Chapter 26). They might go to websites that contain pornography, extreme violence, or other inappropriate material. Or they stay up all night playing games and surfing the web instead of sleeping or doing their homework. Or they spend their weekends online instead of visiting friends or participating in outdoor activities.

If you log in as an administrator, you can restrict the ability to do these unwanted things. You do so by using Mac OS X's parental controls.

The first step is to set these users' accounts as Managed with Parental Controls in the Users & Groups system preference. When you create a new account you want to manage by using parental controls, choose Managed with Parental Controls in the New Account pop-up menu. If you didn't do that, select the Enable Parental Controls option in the Password pane of the Users & Groups system preference for each user account you want to restrict, or select an account in the Parental Controls system preference and click Enable Parental Controls.

After you have set these user accounts to the Managed with Parental Controls type, you need to specify what the restrictions are. You do so in the Parental Controls system preference, as shown in Figure 27.5. The system preference opens automatically to the Apps pane. If the user of the managed account tries to access a prohibited service, he or she is asked to type an administrator's username and password—this is also how you can perform otherwise unpermitted actions when logged in to that user's account.

On the left of the Parental Controls system preference is a list of users who have either a Standard or Managed with Parental Controls account type. If you select the Guest Account or a Standard user account, the system preference asks you whether you want to turn on parental controls for that account, essentially converting it to a Managed with Parental Controls account type.

When you select a Managed with Parental Controls account, you have five panes that you can configure restrictions in: Apps, Web, People, Time Limits, and Other.

Note

When Mac OS X Snow Leopard debuted, its Parental Controls system preference had five panes: System, Content, Mail & iChat, Time Limits, and Logs. But Apple changed these through the Mac OS X 10.6.6 and 10.6.7 updates to Snow Leopard. So although some of this system preference's controls may appear to be changed or new to some Snow Leopard users, they were not introduced in Mac OS X Lion. ■

FIGURE 27.5

The Parental Controls system preference's Apps pane

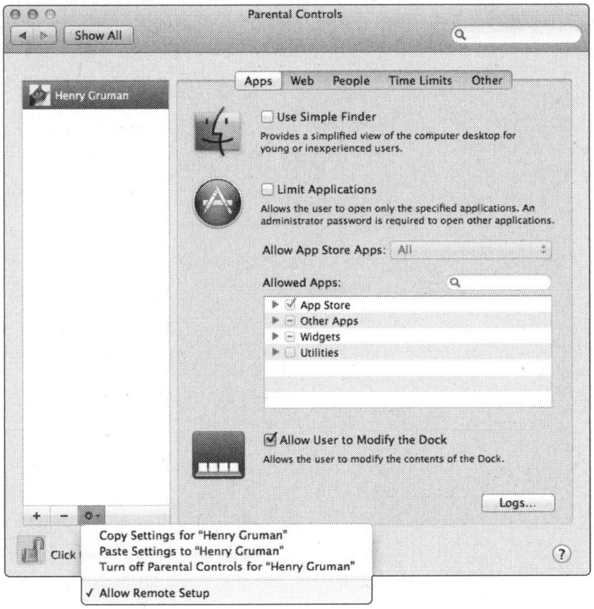

Apps pane

In the Parental Controls system preference's Apps pane, you set the following options:

- **Use Simple Finder:** If this is selected, it directs the Mac to use the Simple Finder, a stripped-down Finder version suited for smaller children. Figure 27.6 shows an example of the Simple Finder. Instead of showing users disks and folders, it simply provides three folders in the Dock—Applications, Documents, and Shared—from which users access applications and files. When opened, these folders have a simple, standard display, with none of the options that Finder windows typically have. Note that you can temporarily (until the next login) switch to the Full Finder by choosing Finder ⇨ Run Full Finder, but you will need an administrator username and password for Mac OS X to change the Finder view.

- **Limit Applications:** If this option is selected, Mac OS X restricts the user to the applications in the following list. The list has several pre-established categories: App Store, Widgets, Others Apps, and Utilities. (Other compatible applications, such as iWork, appear in the list if you have installed them.) You can enable and disable a group by selecting or deselecting the check box to the group's left. To enable or disable individual applications in a group, expand the group by clicking the disclosure triangle to the left of its name to get a list of all applications in it. Then select or dese-lect the applications as desired. (Note how the group's check box changes to – when it contains a mix of enabled and disabled applications. To quickly find a specific application, type some or all of its name in the search box above the right side of the applications list. You also can restrict the types of applications you can buy via the Mac App Store by choosing a rating level from the All App Store Apps pop-up menu (All means there are no restrictions).

- **Allow User to Modify the Dock:** If selected, the user can change what appears in the Dock in his or her account. (This option does not affect the Dock for other users.)

Note

The applications listed in the Apps pane come from two sources: applications installed in the main Applications folder (making them accessible to all users) and those in the user's own Applications folder. The main Applications folder is the one you see when you open the startup disk in a Finder window; the user's Application folder is in his or her Home folder. ∎

FIGURE 27.6

An example of Simple Finder, which provides a limited set of Mac OS X capabilities suited for small children and other inexperienced users

Tip

If you want to control access to the web, e-mail, and instant messaging, be sure to disable any web applications other than Safari, any e-mail applications other than Apple Mail, and any instant-messaging applications other than iChat. That's because Mac OS X has parental controls for web, e-mail, and instant messaging access only for these three Apple programs, which come with Mac OS X. ∎

Web pane

In the Web pane of the Parental Controls system preference, you have the following options:

- **Allow Unrestricted Access to Websites:** By selecting this option, you are letting the user access any site on the web—that is, imposing no restrictions.

- **Try to Limit Access to Adult Websites Automatically:** By selecting this option, you can set the Mac to automatically filter websites on which it detects inappropriate content. (Note that there's no guarantee that it will block all such sites, and it may also mistakenly block legitimate sites.) If you select this option and click Customize, you can add sites that you will always allow access to and those you will not allow access to, regardless of the Mac's own "judgment").

- **Allow Access to Only These Websites:** By selecting this option, you can restrict the account to specific websites that you specify. Click the + icon button and then type the URL for the approved site. (To make it easier to enter the URLs, I suggest you open a bookmark list in your browser or in TextEdit and copy and paste each URL in turn into the list). Mac OS X provides a starter list of sites that Apple suggests are suitable for children. You can remove any you don't approve of by selecting them one at a time and clicking the – icon button.

Caution

The Web pane's web filtering works only with Apple's Safari browser, so you should disallow access to other browsers in the Apps pane of the Parental Controls system preference. ∎

People pane

In the People pane, you can specify whether to limit the user's ability to exchange e-mail and instant-messaging chats with the addresses you specify. First, specify what you are limiting by selecting the Limit Mail and/or Limit iChat options at the top of the pane.

Click the + icon button to add a user, then use one of these two ways to add allowed users from the settings sheet that appears:

- Click the Expand icon button (the down-pointing triangle) to the right of the Last Name field to open the Address Book, and choose a user from it. Choosing a user adds his or her name to the First Name and Last Name fields (you can't type in them yourself when the Address Book is visible).

- Type the person's name in the First Name and Last Name fields and then his or her e-mail address or AIM handle in the Allowed Accounts field. Specify using the adjacent pop-up menu whether the address is an e-mail or AIM address. To add that person to your Address Book, select the Add Person to My Address Book option. Click the + icon button to the right of that pop-up menu to open a new row for a new address. (To delete one address for an approved person, select it and click the – icon button.)

Click Add when done.

New Feature

In Mac OS X Lion, you can no longer block a person's Jabber instant-messaging handle to restrict communications with him or her. ■

Note

You cannot modify an approved person's entry once added. Instead, you must delete it by selecting the person in the list and clicking the – icon button; then create a new entry for that person by clicking the + icon button and reentering all the information. ■

By typing an e-mail address in the Send Permissions Requests To text field, you tell Mac OS X to automatically send you an e-mail when this restricted user tries to contact someone not on the approved list.

Caution

The People pane's filtering works only with Apple's Mail and iChat programs, so you should disallow access to other e-mail and instant-messaging applications in the Apps pane of the Parental Controls system preference. ■

Time Limits pane

In the Time Limits pane, you can make sure your kids, or other users, aren't using the computer instead of sleeping or doing other activities. Figure 27.7 shows the options:

- **Weekday Time Limits:** In this section, select the Limit Computer Use To option to have Mac OS X stop this user account from working after the amount of time you specify in the adjacent slider is reached. Note that Mac OS X tracks the total time used each day, even if the user logs in and out throughout the day.

- **Weekend Time Limits:** In this section, select the Limit Computer Use To option to have Mac OS X stop this user account from working after the amount of time you specify in the adjacent slider is reached.

- **Bedtime:** In this section, select the School Nights option to set the times during which the Mac cannot be used (typically, when you want your child to be asleep) from Sunday night through Thursday night. Use the adjacent time fields to select the specific times. Select the Weekend option and its adjacent time fields to set when during Friday and Saturday nights that the Mac cannot be used.

FIGURE 27.7

The Time Limits pane of the Parental Controls system preference

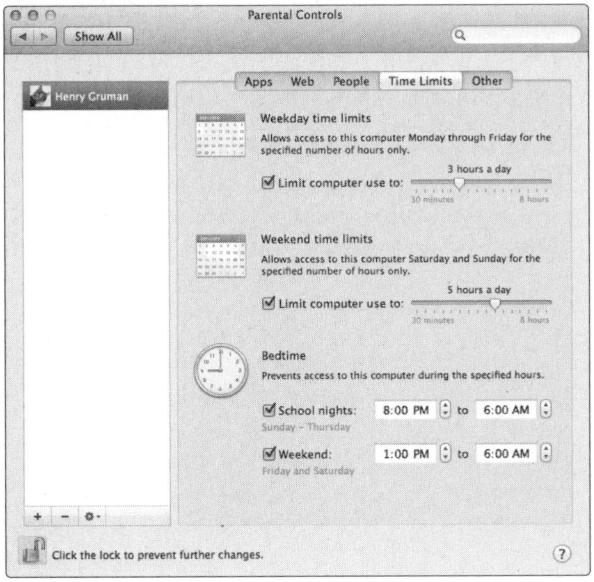

Note

The Bedtime settings can be used for any time periods you choose, not just nighttimes. So if you don't want your kids to use the computer during the days on weekends, you could restrict the times to, say, between 10 p.m. and 6 p.m., so the user could use the Mac only on weekend evenings. ■

Other pane

In the Other pane, you have four controls:

- **Hide Profanity in Dictionary:** If selected, profane ("dirty" or "swear") words are hidden in the information displayed in the Dictionary application (see Chapter 14).

- **Limit Printer Administration:** If selected, the user can't add or change printers (see Chapter 30).

- **Limit CD and DVD Burning:** If selected, the user can't create CDs or DVDs by using the Mac's optical drives (see Chapter 3).

- **Disable Changing the Password.** If selected, the user can't change his or her own password to log in. (You can always override the password if desired, as explained in Chapter 26.)

Getting activity logs

You can track the user's website, application, and chat activity by clicking the Logs button in the Apps, Web, or People panes. In the settings sheet that appears, select which of the four types of activities you want to see the logs for by selecting it in the Log Collections list: Websites Visited, Websites Blocked, Applications, and iChat. The details for that collection appear in the Logs pane. To get details on which type of activity—such as for each application—was used, expand the log by clicking the right-facing triangle icon.

Use the Show Activity For pop-up menu to control how much of the user's activity is displayed (the options are Today, One Week, One Month, Three Months, Six Months, One Year, and All). Use the Group By pop-up menu to choose how the activity is organized in the display, by date or—depending on what log is selected in the log list at left—application, contact, or website.

If you decide that an activity is inappropriate—for example, if the user is chatting too much—you select the item in the log and click Block to turn off access to the application, website, or contact used for that activity. If you want to see what that application's state is, such as to read e-mails in Mail or see what music and videos are in iTunes, select the application in the log and click Open to launch it.

Settings management

There are several options for managing parental control settings by using the accounts list at the left of the Parental Controls system preference.

If you are setting similar restrictions for multiple user accounts, select the first user account for which you have completed the settings, then click the gear-shaped icon pop-up menu and choose Copy Settings for "*username*". Then select the user account you want to copy these settings to, click the Action icon pop-up menu (the gear icon), and choose Paste Settings to "*username*".

You can set Mac OS X to let you manage parental controls remotely from another Mac that has access to this one over the network. To do so, select the Manage Parental Controls from Another Computer option. This option enables a parent to adjust parental controls or monitor activity from work while the child is home, for example, or check on the computer in a child's bedroom from her Mac in the family room. Those Macs appear in the list of accounts in your Parental Controls system preference.

This option is available in three locations:

- When you first open the Parental Controls system preference, before any user account is selected, the Manage Parental Controls from Another Computer option displays in the main pane. Select it.

- Select a Managed with Parental Controls user account, click the Action icon pop-up menu (the gear icon), and choose Allow Remote Setup.

- Select either the guest account or a Standard user account to see it. The main pane in the system preference will indicate that parental controls are not on for this account, and provide an option to turn it on. Don't do so, but do select the Manage Parental Controls from Another Computer option.

However you turn on this option, you're enabling the remote control for all Managed with Parental Control user accounts.

Finally, you can disable parental controls for a selected user account by clicking the Action icon pop-up menu (the gear icon) and choosing Turn Off Parental Controls for "*username*". (This is the same as deselecting the Enable Parental Controls option in the Password pane of the Users & Groups system preference.)

Summary

Mac OS X supports multiple user accounts. This enables businesses to give IT staff administrator privileges on all Macs, as well as enables parents to establish separate accounts for their kids, guests, and others at home. Each account can be given different privileges and access rights, controlling access to files, applications, and Internet services such as e-mail, web pages, and instant messaging.

The default user account has administrator privileges, giving it control over all other accounts. The default user should establish password protection on his or her account, as well as other users' accounts, to prevent misuse of the Mac by unauthorized users. Administrators also can set a master password that lets them reset users' passwords when users forget them and access accounts protected by disk encryption.

Users can adjust personal settings, such as the images used to represent them, as well as set up the applications that launch when they start or log in to their user accounts on the Mac.

User accounts can be one of several types, including Administrator, Standard, Managed with Parental Controls, and Sharing Only. The Mac's administrator—and there can be several—can change any other user's settings. A Standard user can manage only his or her account's settings. A Managed with Parental Control user's permissions are determined by an administrator using Mac OS X's parental controls. The special guest account, called Guest User, automatically deletes all files saved in that account when the user logs out, making it ideal for occasional users such as babysitters and your kids' friends; its privileges also can be restricted by using parental controls.

A Sharing Only user can connect only to file shares as determined through Mac OS X's file-sharing controls. You also can set up account groups, which makes file sharing easier to manage for all types of users.

There are several ways to switch among user accounts, including restarting the Mac into a different account, logging out of the current account and logging into a different account, and using the fast-switch capability to let a new user log in while keeping previously logged-in users' accounts active. In this third approach, applications continue to run for logged-out users.

The Parental Controls system preference enables administrators to restrict the applications that other accounts can use, as well as set time limits and restricted use hours for the Mac on a per-user basis. These controls also enable the administrator to decide how much control each account has over printers, the Dock, CD and DVD creation, and its own password.

The parental controls also can restrict access to specific websites or websites deemed inappropriate for children, as well as restrict who the user can correspond with via e-mail and instant messaging. But these three controls work only with Apple's Safari, Mail, and iChat applications, not with alternative products.

Administrators can monitor the activities of accounts to which parental controls have been applied, such as seeing the data and times for accessed applications, websites blocked, and logs of chat sessions. Administrators also can open applications used by the parentally controlled users to see their state, such as the e-mails sent and received and the music and video downloaded.

To ease the management of parental controls, administrators can apply settings from one user to other users, as well as allow access to the Mac's parental controls from a remote Mac. This enables a parent to adjust parental controls or monitor activity from work while the child is home, for example.

Part VII

Configuring Mac Preferences and Services

IN THIS PART

Chapter 28
Setting System Preferences

Chapter 29
Managing Fonts

Chapter 30
Printing, Faxing, and Scanning

CHAPTER 23

Setting System Preferences

The Mac is ready to run out of the box, but you need to adjust anything with as many capabilities as Mac OS X to the peculiarities of your equipment, software, environment, and, yes, personal preferences. You use the System Preferences application to do this customization work.

Mac OS X has as many as 32 system preferences you can adjust. And each system preference has multiple settings within it, so you can make hundreds of customization decisions. That's a bunch, and it attests to Mac OS X's flexibility, but don't worry about facing so many options. You can adjust system preferences at any time, choosing which you want to adjust—and leaving alone the ones you don't want change.

You can adjust several other Mac OS X preferences that are not found in the System Preferences application. You can adjust what displays in the Finder windows, as well as adjust the access permissions and other attributes of your Mac's disks, both of which are covered later in this chapter. You also can adjust the fonts available to your applications, as explained in Chapter 29, plus you can add and remove applications from the Dock, as explained in Chapter 2.

IN THIS CHAPTER

How to access system preferences

Setting personal preferences

Adjusting hardware preferences

Specifying Internet and wireless settings

Customizing system-level preferences

Adjusting System Preferences

To change system preferences, you open the System Preferences application by choosing System Preferences. You get the window shown in Figure 28.1. The 27 standard Mac OS X system preferences appear, as do any system preferences installed by any of your applications or hardware.

FIGURE 28.1

The System Preferences application window

For example, if your Mac has a configuration profile installed (see Chapter 25), the Profiles system preference appears. If you connect a pen-based tablet to your Mac, you see the Ink system preference. And if your Mac Pro has FibreChannel storage disks attached, you see the FibreChannel system preference. Ditto for the Xsan system preference if you use that storage networking technology. If you upgraded from Mac OS X Snow Leopard, you have the MobileMe system preference to manage that optional service, which Apple is discontinuing in June 2012.

New Feature

The Mail, Contacts & Calendars system preference and Profiles system preference are new to Mac OS X Lion. The Security system preference has been renamed Security & Privacy, the Print & Fax system preference has been renamed Print & Scan, the Exposé & Spaces system preference has been renamed Mission Control, and the Accounts system preference has been renamed Users & Groups. The Universal Access systems preference also has been moved from the System group to the Personal group. And the Internet & Network group has been renamed Internet & Wireless. ■

By default, the system preferences are organized by category: Personal, Hardware, Internet & Wireless, System, and Other. (Other is where your non-Apple system preferences are stored, and this category appears only if you have non-Apple system preferences installed.) To get an alphabetical arrangement of your system preferences, choose View ➪ Organize Alphabetically.

New Feature

You can hide individual system preferences to customize the appearance of the application, a new capability in Mac OS X Lion. To do so, choose View ➪ Customize. Check boxes appear at the lower right of each system preference icon; deselect those you don't want to appear. Click Done when you're finished. ■

When you are in a system preference, it may not be clear how to go back to the System Preferences application window. The easy way is to click the Show All button at the top of the window, or click the left-facing arrow icon button. (Those arrow buttons let you move backward or forward through the system preferences you've opened, like the Back and Forward buttons in a web browser.) You also can right-click or Control+click the System Preferences icon in the Dock to get a pop-up menu of all system preferences, or choose the desired system preference from the System Preference application's View menu; these two approaches are especially handy when the System Preferences application window is obscured onscreen by other windows.

You also can just start typing the function you are looking for in the Search box in the System Preferences application window; doing so highlights the system preferences most likely to have what you are looking for.

Tip

In each system preference's window, click the Help icon button (the ? icon) to get basic help on the system preference's settings. ■

Note

Many system preferences—Date & Time, Energy Saver, Network, Parental Controls, Print & Scan, Security & Privacy, Sharing, Software Update, Startup Disk, Time Machine, and Users & Groups—require that you provide your account login password to change them. If the Lock icon button (the bronze lock icon) at the system preference window's lower left is closed, click it; you're asked for your account password to allow changes to this system preference. The Lock icon button displays an opened lock, so you know you can make changes; click it again to require a password for further changes. ■

Personal preferences

The group of personal preferences focuses mainly on preferences about how you like to work, such as the language you use, what Finder features—such as hot corners and the screen saver—you want active, what the desktop background is, and so on. But the best way to distinguish personal preferences from the others is that these preferences are stored as part of a user's profile, so if you have set up your Mac for use by multiple users (what Mac OS X calls *accounts*, as explained in Chapter 27), each user can have separate personal preferences. The other preferences affect all users.

Desktop & Screen Saver

People love to show off pictures, so computer screens are often used as really big frames for doing so. Knowing this about people, Apple includes several dozen desktop backgrounds that give your Mac's screen a distinct look—and you can add your own images as well.

In the Desktop pane, shown in Figure 28.2, select from any of the images in the list at the left. The Desktop Pictures and Solid Colors folders provided by Apple have an assortment of backgrounds you can use. Just click the desired image within its folder.

New Feature

The selection of desktop background images in Mac OS X Lion is strongly reduced compared to previous versions. Now, there's just one folder of photos (Desktop Pictures), whose selection contains mainly new images, such as that of a galaxy, a lion, and several African-themed photos. Gone are the starfield images emblematic of Mac OS X Leopard and Snow Leopard, as well as the series of plant, abstract, and artwork images previously available. ∎

Or you can use your own images. To access images in the Pictures folder, click the disclosure triangle next to the Folders label in the Sidebar and then click Pictures. Add images from elsewhere on your Mac by clicking the + icon button below the list, and navigate to the desired image. If you select a folder that contains images, the folder is added to the Folders list, making all its images available. (Select an image or folder and click the – icon button to delete the image or folder from the list. Don't worry: The actual file or folder is not deleted from your Mac.)

Note

If you have iPhoto installed on your Mac, you also have iPhoto as an option in the image sources list. ∎

You should know about a few other options in the Desktop pane as well:

- **Change Picture:** If this option is selected, Mac OS X automatically replaces the desktop picture with the next one in the list. It cycles through every image available, based on the schedule you select in the Change Picture pop-up menu.

- **Random Order:** This option is available only if Change Picture is selected, and the pictures change in random order, not in the order they appear in the list at the left.

- **Translucent Menu Bar:** This option enables some of the desktop background to appear behind the Apple menu bar. This can be distracting if you have a dark image under that bar, so you may want to disable this option in that case.

You use the Screen Saver pane (refer to Figure 28.2) to set what happens to your screen display after the computer is idle. Screen savers began as a way to prevent *burn-in*: An image would etch itself into your screen after several hours, leaving a ghostly imprint over your display. A screen saver uses either a changing series of images, or a single image that moves across the screen, to prevent this. Burn-in was a hazard of early CRT monitors, but has not been an issue in years. Today, a screen saver is more a fashion statement and a way to let colleagues who come to your desk when you're not there know you've been away for a while.

You choose your desired screen saver image from the list at the left, which includes several images from Apple. Note that if you use the Shuffle option, you are presented a list of Apple-provided screen savers; select the ones you want Mac OS X to pull from as it shuffles the images. If you double-click an item in the list, you get various display options such as Cross-Fade between Slides, Message, and Delay; these options vary based on the type of screen saver selected. (You also can click the Options button instead to get these options.)

As with the Desktop pane, use the + and – icon buttons to add and delete sets of images from the list. You can bring in a folder of images, subscribe to an RSS feed, or go to an Apple website page that enables you to buy image sets.

FIGURE 28.2

The Desktop & Screen Saver system preference, with its Desktop pane (left) and its Screen Saver pane (right)

In the pane, you have several options for your screen saver:

- **Select the Use Random Screen Saver option to have Mac OS X choose images randomly from the image list.**

- **Select the Show with Clock option to have Mac OS X place a clock on the screen saver display.**

- **Use the Start Screen Saver sliders to select how long the system must be idle before the screen saver begins.** If this setting will start the screen saver after the Energy Saver system preference has put the monitor to sleep, Mac OS X displays a note to that effect under the slider, with a link that opens the Energy Saver system preference. If you don't adjust the Start Screen Saver slider and/or the Energy Saver system preference so the screen saver starts before the monitor is put to sleep, the screen saver simply doesn't turn on—the display sleep setting "wins" over the screen saver setting.

- **Click Hot Corners to associate a command with each of the four corners of the screen.** Then when you move the mouse all the way into that corner, that command executes. This feature is identical to the Hot Corners controls in the Mission Control system preference, so I cover these settings there.

- **Click the Options button to open a settings sheet of options specific to the selected screen saver.** These options vary widely, from setting the speed of an effect to choosing an RSS feed source. Note that some screen savers have no options, so the Options button is grayed out in these cases.

- **Choose from the three Display Style icon buttons to determine how the screen image displays.** (Note that these options are available only if you select a picture from the Screen Savers list.) Slideshow presents each image in the set in order. Collage creates a collage dynamically from the images. And Mosaic creates a grid of images from the set.

Click Test to see how your screen saver will display with the options you've selected.

Note

Hot corners—used in the Desktop & Screen Saver and Mission Control system preferences—were called active screen corners in previous versions of Mac OS X. ■

Note

The Screen Saver system preference does not reduce your display's power consumption when idle. Use the Energy Saver system preference to turn your monitor off while it is idle to reduce your power usage. ■

Dock

The Dock system preference, not surprisingly, controls the Dock (covered in Chapter 2) that provides quick access to applications. Its options are straightforward:

- **Use the Size slider to set the size of the Dock's icons.**
- **Select the Magnification option and then adjust its slider to make the Dock item that your mouse is hovering over larger (so you know your mouse is over it).**
- **Select the Left, Bottom, or Right option in the Position on Screen control to determine at which edge of the screen the Dock displays.**
- **Use the Minimize Window Using pop-up menu to determine how an open application's window shrinks into the Dock when you minimize it (by clicking the Close – icon button in the window's upper left).** Your choices are Scale Effect and Genie Effect; try each to see which effect you prefer.
- **Select Minimize Windows into Application Icon to have windows minimize into the related application icon on the Dock rather than into its own separate icon.**
- **Select Animate Opening Applications to make their Dock icons bounce as they are loading (so you know they are loading).**
- **Select Automatically Hide and Show the Dock to make the Dock disappear while you are not using it.** (To open it, move your mouse to the very edge of the screen where it displays, as you selected via the Position on Screen control.)
- **Select Show Indicator Lights for Open Applications to display a blue globe below running applications in the Dock, so you can easily tell they are running.**

New Feature

The Minimize Window into Application Icon option and the Show Indicator Lights for Open Applications option are new to Mac OS X Lion. (In previous versions of Mac OS X, the indicator light always displayed for open applications.) ■

General

Use this system preference to customize the appearance of the Finder and other windows. Figure 28.3 shows the General system preference. The options are largely self-explanatory, with options to change the color of buttons and highlighted text, to determine when scroll bars appear in windows and how scrolling behaves, to set the icon size for items in Finder windows' Sidebar, to determine how many recent applications and other items display in the Recent Items list (accessed by choosing ⟶ Recent Items), to determine whether to restore applications' windows after quitting and reopening the applications, and to manage how text is displayed on LCD monitors.

The General system preference

Note that the option chosen in the Appearance pop-up menu affect the color of windows' Close, Minimize, and Zoom buttons. If Appearance pop-up menu is set to Graphite, the buttons are all a medium gray. If the Appearance pop-up menu is set to Blue, the Close button is red, the Minimize button is yellow, and the Zoom button is green.

New Feature

The General system preference changes the options for scroll bars to reflect the new approach in Mac OS X Lion when you use gesture-savvy input devices such as the Magic Trackpad or Magic Mouse. When such devices are connected to your Mac, by default Mac OS X Lion hides scroll bars until it detects you are trying to move through a window, as Chapter 4 explains. ∎

New Feature

New to Lion's General system preference is the ability to specify the size of icons in the Sidebar. Also new is the Restore Windows When Quitting and Reopening Apps option. ∎

The Use LCD Font Smoothing When Available option really does make the text on an LCD monitor look nicer, so I recommend you keep that setting. Note that some applications, notably those from Adobe Systems, have their own font-smoothing options, but enabling both does no harm.

Language & Text

The Language & Text system preference deals primarily with language settings, but also deals with associated attributes such as calendars and currencies. As Figure 28.4 shows, it has four panes.

FIGURE 28.4

The Language & Text system preference, with its Language pane at upper left, Text pane at upper right, Formats pane at lower left, and Input Sources pane at lower right

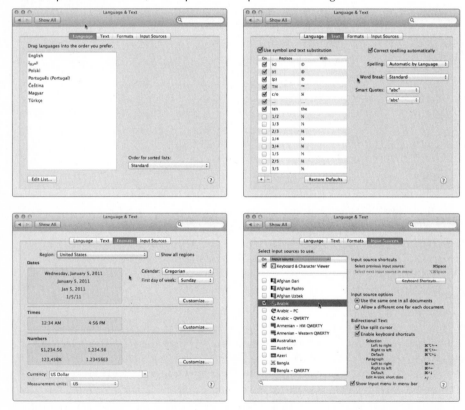

In the first pane, Language, you select the languages available to Mac OS X. At the left is a list of all available languages; drag a language to change the order in which it appears in the language lists Mac OS X may present to you in various settings. To edit what languages appear, click Edit List and in the settings sheet that appears, deselect any languages you don't want to appear, and select any languages you do want to appear.

At the right side of the pane is the Order for Sorted Lists pop-up menu. This menu enables you to choose the sort order—the alphabetization order or equivalent—for sorted lists.

In the second pane, Text, you control several aspects of text entry. Note that these features work only with applications designed to use them, including Apple's TextEdit, iWork suite (Pages, Numbers, and Keynote), iChat, and iMovie. But expect more applications to support these new features over time.

Using the Symbol and Text Substitution subpane, you can tell Mac OS X what text to automatically substitute with other text, such as automatically replacing (c) with ©. Be sure to select Use Symbol and Text Substitution to enable this substitution (it is selected by default).

Mac OS X comes with several substitutions predefined; those that are selected in the On column are active, meaning that when you type the text in the Replace column, Mac OS X automatically substitutes the text in the With column. You can add your own substitutions by clicking the + icon button at the bottom of the pane and entering the "before" and "after" text in the Replace and With columns, respectively. To delete a substitution, select it and click the – icon button. To disable but not delete a substitution, just deselect it. Click Restore Defaults to undo all changes you've made to the Symbol and Text Substitution pane and return to the Mac OS X defaults.

New Feature

The ability to turn substitution and spell-checking on or off is new to the Language & Text's Text pane in Mac OS X Lion. In previous versions of Mac OS X, they were always on. Also new is the ability to select Finnish and Hebrew in the Word break pop-up menu. ∎

On the right side of the pane are the rest of the text-control options:

- **Spelling:** This pop-up menu lets you override the spelling dictionary used by compatible applications. Be sure that the Correct Spelling Automatically option is selected for this feature to work (it is selected by default). The default option—Automatic by Language—uses the spelling dictionary for whatever language you have selected in the application for the text you are working on or, for applications that don't let you choose a working language, whatever language is at the top of the list in the Language pane of the Language & Text system preference. The Spelling pop-up menu lets you select a specific language and force the use of its spelling dictionary no matter what language you are working in.

- **Word Break:** This pop-up menu lets you select how Mac OS X determines where words break, so when you double-click text, it knows what to select. For most people, the default option of Standard should be kept. Four of the menu options—Finnish, Greek, Hebrew, and Japanese—are useful when you work primarily in another language despite what is set as your primary language in the Language pane. The other available option—English (United States, Computer)—modifies the normal English rules of using patterns of spaces and breaks (such as paragraph returns) to determine where words break to also handle some of the unique conventions in programming languages. For example, in a programming language, the text *aKey:aValue* is considered to be two words (*aKey* and *aValue*), with the colon indicating where the word break is. But in normal English, *aKey:aValue* is considered to be one word, so double-clicking it selects the entire string. Thus, a programmer would choose English (United States, Computer) as his or her Word Break option.

- **Smart Quotes:** These two pop-up menus let you choose what quotation marks are used when you type " and ' on the keyboard around words. In English, the standards are *"abc"* and *'abc,'* respectively, but this pop-up menu lets you choose the standards for other languages, such as *«abc»* and *‹abc›* used in continental French for quotations.

In the third pane, Formats, you choose the basic formats for dates, time, numbers, and money. When you choose your region or country from the Region pop-up menu, Mac OS X chooses the standards for that region or country. (By default, a list of common regions displays; select Show All Regions to see the complete list.)

You can override the defaults for your chosen region using the controls below the Region pop-up menu. For example, if you're in the United States where Sunday is the traditional start of the weekly calendar but prefer to have your calendar begin on Monday as the start of the workweek, choose Monday from the First Day of Week pop-up menu. You also can change the calendar used from the default Gregorian to Buddhist, Islamic, Japanese, or any of seven other calendars in use in the world. You can customize the calendar display, such as always abbreviating months' names, by clicking the Customize button. Customize buttons are available for time display (such as how to display a.m. and p.m.) and for numbers (such as whether thousands are separated by commas).

Two pop-up menus control the measurement systems for money (the Currency pop-up menu) and whether Mac OS X's default units are English, such as feet and pounds, or metric, such as meters and kilograms (the Measurement Units pop-up menu).

The fourth pane, Input Sources, tells Mac OS X what keyboards and equivalent input sources to use. Check the input sources for each language you use; note that some languages have different keyboard options and may have multiple versions to choose from. You can select as many input sources as you want.

Tip
Use the Search box to type part of a name to narrow the available options to those containing that text. ∎

Note that the language you chose as your primary language when you installed Mac OS X is automatically enabled and grayed out, so it is always active and cannot be turned off. If you select one or more additional input sources, the Input Source icon menu appears in the menu bar, displaying the flag of your primary input's country. This menu also includes an option to open the Language & Text system preference.

Note

If you have a gesture-capable touchpad, you get the Trackpad Handwriting option for the Simplified Chinese and Traditional Chinese languages, as the sidebar "Touch-based Chinese handwriting" in Chapter 29 explains. ■

Note the Keyboard & Character Viewer option at the top of the input sources list. It adds to the Input Source icon menu in the menu bar options to open the Character Viewer and Keyboard Viewer panels for access to special characters (see Chapter 29). It also adds a menu option to open the Keyboard system preference.

Note

If you select the Keyboard & Character Viewer option—but do not select additional input sources—the Input Source icon menu in the menu bar uses the Character Viewer icon (an asterisk in a box). ■

If you have a pen-based tablet attached to your Mac, you also have the Ink Server option at the top of the input sources list; you use the Ink Server input source for handwriting recognition in pen-based tablets. (If you have such a tablet connected to your Mac, you also have a system preference called Ink that enables you to configure the handwriting recognition.)

The Input Source Shortcuts section of the pane shows the keyboard shortcuts that let you navigate among language input sources: ⌘+spacebar to go to the next input source and Option+⌘+spacebar to go to the previous input source. If you have selected multiple language input sources, the Keyboard Shortcuts button becomes available so you can change these defaults; clicking it opens the Keyboard system preference's Keyboard Shortcuts pane.

Use the Input Source Options radio buttons to choose whether the current input source applies to all open documents or whether you want to assign different input sources to each document.

Finally, if you have selected both a left-to-right language (such as in Western languages like English and French) and a right-to-left language (such as Arabic, Hebrew, and Persian) as input sources, the Bidirectional Text section (refer to Figure 28.4) appears with these options:

- **Use Split Cursor:** This option for bidirectional text, if selected, displays a split cursor that indicates a boundary between text using left-to-right reading order and right-to-left order. When moving the cursor through documents that contain both left-to-right and right-to-left text, the cursor changes where the reading order changes, so you can choose which direction to go at the boundary.

- **Enable Keyboard Shortcuts:** This option for bidirectional text, if selected, enables shortcuts for moving within text selections and among paragraphs, as well as for editing the Arabic short date format. (The shortcuts are visible in Figure 28.4.)

Mission Control

This system preference determines how the Mission Control and related Exposé and Spaces capabilities work (see Chapter 2 for more details on using them). Figure 28.5 shows the system preference.

FIGURE 28.5

The Mission Control system preference

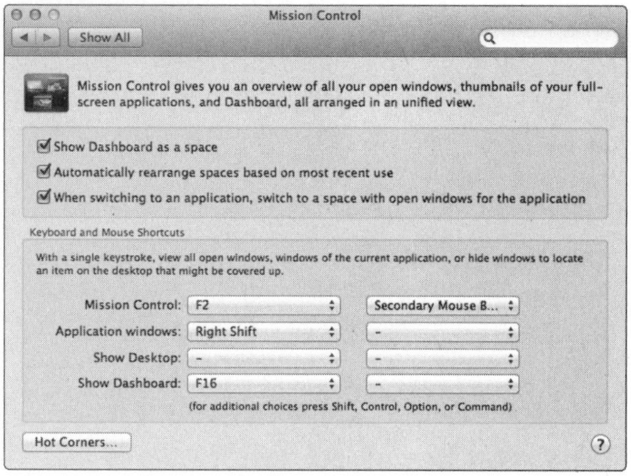

The first three options control the behavior of spaces:

- **Show Dashboard as a Space:** This option, if selected, treats the dashboard as a space, so you can navigate it as part of navigating spaces.

- **Automatically Rearrange Spaces Based on Most Recent Use:** If this option is selected, the spaces are reordered from left to right each time you log in based on how often you use each one, with the most recent being the leftmost. If you deselect this option (the default), spaces remain in the order they were created.

- **When Switching to an Application, Switch to a Space with Open Windows for the Application:** When you open an application from the Dock or Finder, this tells Mac OS X to open the space in which that application has open windows. The idea is that the space where an application has open windows is the one you are actively using.

New Feature

Spaces is now always on in Mac OS X Lion; you cannot turn it off as in previous versions of Mac OS X. Also gone from the Mission Control system preference are the Exposé and Spaces panes. Their features have been largely combined into one pane, and you now add spaces via Mission Control and assign applications via the Dock's application menus, as Chapter 2 explains. ∎

In the Keyboard and Mouse Shortcuts area, you set the keys and mouse button clicks that trigger the various Mission Control display options: Mission Control (this displays all open windows and spaces), application windows (the App Exposé capability), the desktop, and the Dashboard (see Chapter 14 for details on the Dashboard). For each option, the left pop-up menu sets the key, while the right pop-up menu sets the mouse click.

If any of your choices conflict with other key or mouse button assignments, a yellow warning icon (an exclamation point [!] in a triangle) appears next to the affected option.

Your final option is Hot Corners (which had been called Active Screen Corners in previous versions of Mac OS X). In the settings sheet that appears when you click Hot Corners, you set what action occurs when you place your mouse all the way in the selected corner. The pop-up menu for each corner is set to – by default, which means no action. For each corner, your options are Mission Control, Application Windows, Desktop, Dashboard, Launchpad, Start Screen Saver, Disable Screen Saver, and Put Display to Sleep.

New Feature
The ability to launch the Launchpad (covered in Chapter 2) is new to the hot corners options. Also, the Mission Control replaces the All Windows option in previous versions of Mac OS X. ∎

Tip
If you press and hold any combination of the modifier keys—⌘, Option, Shift, and Control—when selecting a menu option for a hot corner, that modifier key (or combination of modifier keys) must be pressed when clicking the corner to invoke the specified action. ∎

Security & Privacy
Use the Security & Privacy system preference to control access to your Mac and the data stored on it. The system preference has four panes: General, FileVault, Firewall, and Privacy. Chapter 26 explains how to use the Security system preference's settings.

New Feature
The FileVault capability in Mac OS X Lion's Security & Privacy system preference encrypts the entire startup disk, not just the Home folder encryption as in previous versions. Also new is the Privacy pane to control applications' access to your location information. ∎

Spotlight
As Chapter 5 details, Spotlight is the Mac's internal search function—that field in the upper-right of the Finder window preceded by a magnifying glass icon. The Mac searches its files for whatever text you type there. In the Spotlight system preference's Search Results pane, you select the types of files that you want Spotlight to search and deselect those you don't want it to search. You also can change the order in which Spotlight displays its search results by dragging the categories within the list; the order of the list is the order in which the results display in the Spotlight results.

The Privacy pane enables you to tell Spotlight what folders and disks not to search. Click the + icon button to add folders and disks; select a folder or disk from the list and click the – icon button to remove it from the Privacy list (and thus make it searchable).

Both the Search Results and Privacy panes also let you assign keyboard shortcuts to begin a Spotlight search and to open a Finder search window.

Universal Access

The Universal Access system preference helps users with various disabilities use the Mac. There are panes for visual appearance to help the visually impaired, for audio feedback to help the hearing-impaired, and for keyboard, mouse, and touchpad usage for the physically impaired. Chapter 8 covers each pane's settings in detail.

Hardware preferences

You can manage the Mac's hardware by using hardware system preferences. Note that three hardware system preferences—FibreChannel, Ink, and Xsan—appear only if you have the compatible hardware installed (a FibreChannel storage device on a Mac Pro or Xserve computer, a pen-based tablet, and an Xsan network storage system on a Mac Pro or Xserve, respectively).

CDs & DVDs

Use the CDs & DVDs system preference to set up the Mac's default behavior when you insert a CD or DVD into its drive. You can configure the default behavior for five conditions using the following pop-up menus:

- When You Insert a Blank CD
- When You Insert a Blank DVD
- When You Insert a Music CD
- When You Insert a Picture CD
- When You Insert a Video DVD

In each case, you have the following options:

- **Select the Ask Me What to Do menu option to have the Mac prompt you as to what to do when the condition occurs.** This option is available only for the When You Insert a Blank CD and When You Insert a Blank DVD menu options.
- **Select one of the preferred applications listed to handle the specific condition, such as choosing iTunes as the option for When You Insert a Music CD.** This way, iTunes automatically opens when you insert a music CD.
- **Assign your own application for the condition by choosing Open Other Application, which then enables you to navigate through the Applications folder to choose the default application for that condition.**

- **Have the Mac run a script, instead of an application, by choosing Run a Script.** This enables you to navigate through the Mac (it starts in the Public folder) to choose the default AppleScript for that condition.

- **Have the Mac do nothing by choosing Ignore.**

Displays

You use the Displays system preference to adjust how your monitors display their images. Figure 28.6 shows two of the system preference's panes: Display and Arrangements. A third pane, Color, lets you select and calibrate color profiles.

The panes vary if you have more than one monitor connected to your Mac; the Arrangements pane doesn't appear if you have just one monitor. And if you have multiple monitors, a separate Displays system preference window opens for each one, as Figure 28.6 shows. Whether you have one or more monitors attached, each Displays system preference shows the name of the monitor. (Color LCD is the name for a MacBook's built-in LCD screen.)

Note

If you have a MacBook with an external monitor connected, and you've closed the laptop lid, the built-in LCD screen turns itself off. In that case, when you open the Displays system preference, you don't see any controls for that LCD screen—Mac OS X essentially thinks it's disconnected. If you open the laptop lid, Mac OS X detects the built-in LCD screen and provides the controls for it in the Displays system preference. ■

FIGURE 28.6

The Displays system preference's Display pane with two monitors connected (left) and the Arrangement pane (right)

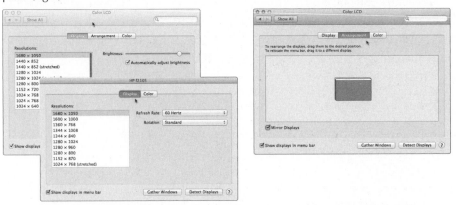

The Display pane enables you to set the resolution for the monitor's display by selecting one of the options in the Resolutions list at the left. The higher the resolution, the more information is crammed into the screen, which of course makes each element smaller. Typically, you should leave the resolution set to the default resolution because it usually provides the best balance between readability and workspace amount; Mac OS X automatically detects the default resolution when you first connect a monitor.

The Refresh Rate pop-up menu is a legacy control you can usually ignore. First, LCD monitors support only one refresh rate (60 hertz), so the control is irrelevant for any LCD monitors. Second, if you do have an old-style CRT monitor, chances are good that it runs at the maximum 75 hertz setting (which provides the most stable image) and can be left at that setting; only very old CRTs can't run at that rate. In the case of a Mac's built-in LCD screen, the Refresh Rate pop-up menu doesn't display.

Use the Rotation pop-up menu to rotate the entire screen display. You use this option rarely, such as when you want to physically turn a monitor so it's standing higher than wider and rotate the display accordingly, turn the display upside down so someone standing in front of you can read the display, or use the monitor with an old-style projector that inverts the displayed image. Note this option does not appear for a MacBook's built-in screen.

New Feature

Mac OS X Lion displays a new set of controls for a Mac's built-in monitor and some camera-equipped Apple displays, such as the Cinema Display series: the Brightness slider and the Automatically Adjust Brightness option. If selected, this option has Mac OS X detect the brightness of the light shining on the monitor and has the monitor adjust its brightness appropriately. Note that this can cause a strobe effect in some environments, such as where the light changes due to frequent shadows. ∎

If you have multiple monitors connected to your Mac (and turned on), a separate Displays window appears for each, with the name of the monitor in each window's title bar. Often, each monitor shows the Displays window for itself. If you want all the Displays windows to be brought together onto one monitor, go to the Displays window for the monitor you want them all to display on and click Gather Windows in its Display pane.

If you want to manage basic monitor settings without opening the Displays system preference, select the Show Displays in Menu Bar option; you see the Displays icon menu (a monitor icon) in the menu bar from which you can change screen resolution and open the Displays system preference. (The Number of Recent Items menu option enables you to choose how many recently used screen resolutions display in the selection list.)

Click Detect Displays if the Mac doesn't automatically recognize a monitor you've connected to it.

In the Arrangements pane, you tell the Mac how your multiple monitors are physically arranged, so it can arrange the display properly across them. The monitor with the white bar at the top is the "main" monitor, the one in which the menu bar, Dock, and System Preferences will appear; you can drag that to any monitor to make it the "main" monitor. You change monitor arrangements by dragging them around until their arrangement matches their physical arrangement on your desk or wall. You can arrange monitors side to side and/or top to bottom.

If you're not sure which monitor is which, click Detect Displays to have the Mac superimpose a number on each connected monitor, so you can see what order they are arranged in. This matters because the Mac has no idea what the physical arrangement of your monitors is, and it makes a guess on how they are arranged and then displays the screen across them. If it guesses wrong, you could move the mouse off the right side of one monitor only to see it appear on the monitor to its left, not the one to its right. (You rearrange the way the Mac tiles the screens in the Arrangements pane.)

If you want to mirror the displays, select the Mirror Displays option. You typically do this when you have connected a monitor for a presentation to others but still want to use your laptop's screen to run the presentation, or when you're using a MacBook "docked" with a monitor at your desk.

Note
If you use an Apple Cinema Display monitor, you get a unique pane—Options—in the Displays system preference. In the Options pane, you can turn off or on two buttons on these displays: the Power button and the Display Preferences button. ■

The other pane in the Displays system preference is the Color pane. Here you choose which color profile to use for the monitor, as well as view the profile settings. (You need to be a color expert to make any sense of those settings.) For the most accurate color display, be sure to use the color profile specific to your monitor; in some cases, you may need to install this profile from a CD or download a file provided by the manufacturer, while in other cases, Apple supplies the profile with Mac OS X.

Over time, monitors drift away from their profile's color settings, and what they display no longer precisely matches what the Mac "thinks" they are displaying based on their profiles. This is particularly true of old-style CRT monitors. There's another cause for such display drift: The lighting in your environment can wash out the colors you see, or having strongly colored walls can confuse your brain and distort the accuracy of the colors you see, even if the monitor is displaying them in a technically correct way. No matter what might be making what you see different than what the Mac "thinks" it's displaying, you can use the Display Calibrator Assistant utility to make what you see closer to what the Mac "thinks" you're seeing.

To do so, click Calibrate in the Displays system preference's Color pane. The Display Calibrator Assistant opens. Follow its instructions; when you're finished, the utility generates a new profile for your monitor that makes it display colors accurately in your specific environment. You might want to run this utility once a year or when you make significant changes to your workspace's lighting or color scheme. Figure 28.7 shows some of the adjustments the utility helps you detect and then make.

Energy Saver
Electronic equipment can suck down power, which is costly both in terms of money and environmental damage. The Energy Saver system preference, shown in Figure 28.8, enables you to reduce your energy usage. If you have a MacBook, you get two panes—Battery and Power Adapter—so you can set the energy usage settings independently, with settings for when you are plugged in and ones for when you are running on battery power. For desktop Macs, you get just one pane.

FIGURE 28.7

The Display Calibrator Assistant utility generates a color profile for use in the Displays system preference's Color pane that helps increase the color accuracy of your monitor. Shown here are two of the steps in that calibration process.

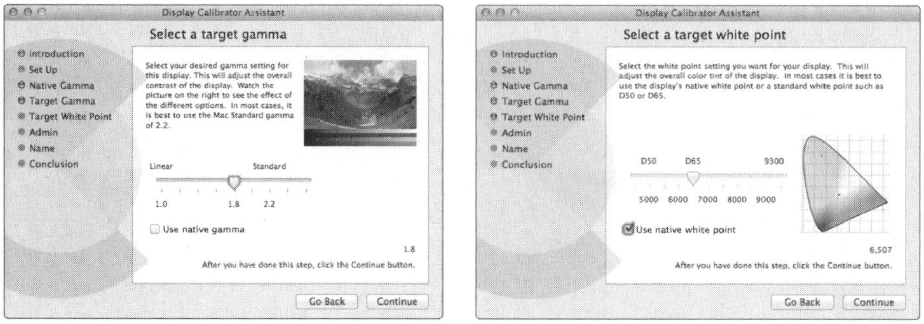

For desktop Macs and for the Power Adapter pane for MacBooks, you have the following options:

- **Use the Computer Sleep slider to determine how many minutes of inactivity put the entire Mac to sleep.**

- **Use the Display Sleep slider to determine how many minutes of inactivity puts the monitor—often the greatest user of power for computers—to sleep.** If you make this value larger than the Computer Sleep value, the Energy Saver panel automatically adjusts the Computer Sleep setting to match the Display Sleep setting.

- **Select the Put Hard Disk(s) to Sleep When Possible option to let the Mac save energy whenever it can when the disks are inactive.** Because disks can restart very quickly, selecting this option rarely makes your Mac feel sluggish.

- **Select the Wake for Ethernet Network Access option so your IT administrator or a network device can wake your Mac over the (wired) Ethernet network, such as to change settings or back up your files remotely.** (Activity on a Wi-Fi network will not wake the Mac.)

- **Select the Automatically Reduce Brightness Before Display Goes to Sleep option to have Mac OS X turn down the screen brightness when it has been idle for a while but before the Display Sleep idle time has been reached.** This saves power but makes the screen turn back on faster in that "twilight" idle time.

- **Select the Start Up Automatically after a Power Failure option if you want the Mac to restart if the power goes out.** You would choose this if you were running the Mac unattended, such as for use as a server.

- **Select the Restart Automatically If the Computer Freezes option if you want the Mac to restart if the Finder crashes.** You would choose this if you were running the Mac unattended, such as for use as a server.

If you don't like your settings and want to start over, or you are unsure what settings to use, click the Restore Defaults button to undo your settings changes and have Apple's recommended settings used instead.

New Feature

The Restart Automatically If the Computer Freezes option is new to Mac OS X Lion. ■

Note

One energy-saving option not available in the Energy Saver system preference is available in the Keyboard system preference's Keyboard pane: the ability to turn off the backlighting for the keyboard (on Macs that have such illumination). ■

On a MacBook, the Battery pane has the same options, with the following three exceptions:

- **It has no Wake for Ethernet Network Access option.** This is because you're not likely to be on the company network when running on battery power.

- **It has no Restart Automatically after a Power Failure option.** This is because the only power failure that would occur when running on battery power is that the battery runs out of power, in which case it can't restart the Mac.

- **It has an additional option: Slightly Dim the Display When Using This Power Source.** This option both saves power and gives you a visual cue when you are working on battery power (handy if the power cord has been pulled out and you don't realize it).

Caution

A MacBook switches automatically to its battery if the power goes out, which could drain the battery if the laptop is left unattended. ■

If you have a MacBook, the Energy Saver system preference also provides an option to display the battery status in the menu bar.

Typically, you would set the Computer Sleep and Display Sleep times to be smaller for the Battery pane's energy-saving savings to minimize unnecessary power usage.

The Energy Saver system preference offers one more control, and it is one that can help save energy but also provides convenience: the capability to schedule when the Mac turns on and off (or goes to sleep and wakes up). Click Schedule to get a settings sheet of options (refer to Figure 28.8). To set a startup or wakeup time, select Start Up or Wake, and then choose what days (Every Day, Weekdays, Weekends, or a specific day) and the time to start up or wake up. To turn off a Mac or put it to sleep at a scheduled time, select the option preceding the second row, and choose the desired action in the adjacent pop-up menu: Sleep, Shut Down, or Restart; set the days and times for the desired action as well. Click OK to save the schedule. To disable the schedule, deselect the options.

FIGURE 28.8

The scheduling options in the Energy Saver system preference

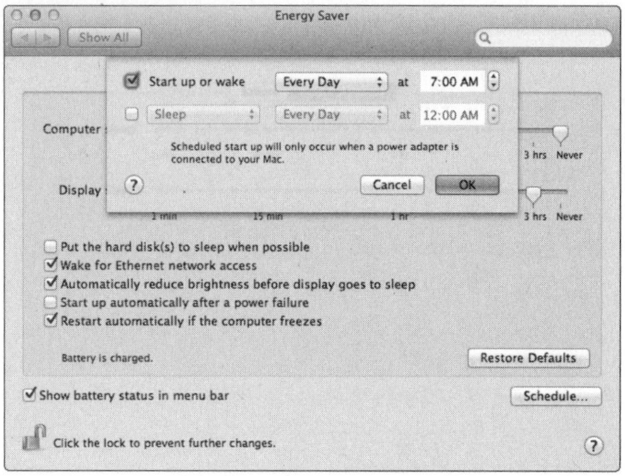

The capability to schedule the Mac's on/wake and off/sleep times can save energy by turning off computers that employees leave on when they go home. It also can have their—or your—Macs up and running when they—or you—arrive at the office (or while you are pouring your coffee at home or getting the kids ready for school). What you can't do is set a complex schedule, such as separate startup and shutdown times for weekdays and for weekends.

Note that the schedule takes effect only when the Mac is plugged in, not when it is running on battery power. Also note that if you are using the Mac past its off/sleep time, you get an alert and a chance to stop the Mac from being turned off or put to sleep.

FibreChannel

Available only if your Mac has FibreChannel drives attached (such as on a Mac Pro or the discontinued Apple Xserve), this system preference enables you to set the basic settings for your FibreChannel drives and the communication with a FibreChannel storage network, such as the connection setting (Automatic, Arbitrated Loop, or Point-to-Point).

Ink

If you connect a compatible pen-based tablet to your Mac, you should see the Ink system preference. It enables you to control pen input, such as whether to perform handwriting recognition and how to handle various pen strokes. The key control is Handwriting Recognition, which you can set to On or Off. The system preference itself has three panes:

- **General:** You use this pane to tell the Mac how closely spaced your handwriting is (to help it better decipher what you write), what language you are writing in, how to determine when you are switching from using the pen to write to using the pen as a mouse, and which fonts to use to display the converted handwriting.

- **Gestures:** You use this pane to set the special pen strokes used to indicate actions, such as cutting text, pasting text, entering a tab, or selecting all text.

- **Word List:** You use this pane to enter special words (such as technical terms) that Mac OS X would not find in its own handwriting-conversion dictionaries.

Note that not all applications support handwriting; those that do typically display an Ink toolbar that enables you to select special commands (such as clicking a button for the ⌘ key when using the pen) and perhaps require you to write your text in a specific area, reserving a separate area for the converted text for you to correct or accept.

Keyboard

It's easy to take the keyboard for granted, but when you look at the Keyboard system preference, you realize how much it actually does. This system preference has two panes: Keyboard and Keyboard Shortcuts.

In the Keyboard pane, shown in Figure 28.9, you likely want to set the Key Repeat Rate and the Delay Until Repeat rate sliders. When you hold a key, Mac OS X keeps "typing" that key for you. You set how many times per second it does so via the Key Repeat Rate, while you set how long it waits to begin repeating the key via Delay Until Repeat. If you tend to let your fingers linger on keys, you might want to move the Delay Until Repeat closer to the Long end of the slider to avoid inadvertent repeated keystrokes.

The Mac automatically assigns the function keys—such as F1 and F12, and thus sometimes called *F keys*—to specific actions, as Chapter 2 explains. (Some keyboards include symbols to indicate what those default actions are.) But you may want to save those function keys for other purposes—particularly if your Mac is acting as a terminal to a Windows, Unix, or other server that uses those F keys for other purposes. If you select the Use All F1, F2, etc. as Standard Function Keys option, the Mac does not do its normal actions when you press the function keys. (In that case, hold the Fn key when pressing those keys to get the default actions: For example, if F12 is the key for increasing the speaker volume on your keyboard, press Fn+F12 to increase the volume.)

If your Mac has automatic backlighting for its keyboard, turn that feature on by selecting the Illuminate Keyboard in Low Light Conditions option. To avoid wasting energy, use the slider below that option to tell the Mac how long to wait after the last keystroke to turn off that backlighting; it turns back on as soon as you begin typing again.

If the Show Keyboard & Character Viewers in Menu Bar is selected, you can access these two quick-access panels to special characters from the Input Sources icon menu in the menu bar. (These viewers are covered in the section on the Language & Text system preference in this chapter.)

Click the Modifier Keys button to open a settings sheet where you can change the behavior of the standard Mac modifier keys: Caps Lock, ⌘ (Command), Option, and Control. You can assign any of these four keys to any of those four purposes, as well as disable any of these keys by choosing No Action. Few people have a need to reassign these keys. If you have multiple keyboards, you can customize their modifier keys separately, by choosing a keyboard from Select Keyboard pop-up menu. (Laptop users are most likely to have multiple keyboards: the one embedded in the MacBook and an external keyboard kept on the desk.)

At the bottom of the Keyboard pane is the Set Up Bluetooth Keyboard button. Click this button to open a settings sheet from which Mac OS X scans for a Bluetooth keyboard. If it finds one, the keyboard's name appears in a list. Click Continue to establish a connection (called pairing) between the Mac and the keyboard.

FIGURE 28.9

The Keyboard pane (left) and the Keyboard Shortcuts pane (right) in the Keyboard system preference

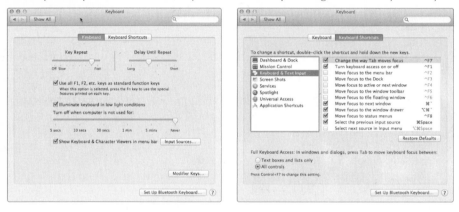

The second pane, Keyboard Shortcuts, enables you to turn on and off keyboard shortcuts used by Mac OS X, plus reassign existing shortcuts and create new ones. The left side of the pane has a list of shortcut types (refer to Figure 28.9): Dashboard & Dock, Mission Control, Keyboard & Text Input, Screen Shots, Services, Spotlight, Universal Access, and Application Shortcuts.

Note
One of the categories, Services, doesn't let you change shortcuts, but it lets you define what services appear in an application's Services submenu, as Chapter 12 explains. ∎

Select the desired group to get a list of its shortcuts in the right part of the pane. Then select the check box for a shortcut to turn it on; deselect it to turn off a shortcut. To change a shortcut, double-click the shortcut itself from the list, and type the new shortcut. A yellow exclamation-mark-in-a-triangle icon appears if the shortcut is used elsewhere so you know you have more than one menu item using the same shortcut. (You can restore the default shortcuts by clicking Restore Defaults.)

You also can add new shortcuts in this pane if you've selected Application Shortcuts:

1. **Click the + icon button to open a settings sheet where you specify the new shortcut.**

2. **Using the Application menu, choose the specific application for which the shortcut should be available, or choose All Applications.**

3. **In the Menu Title text field, enter the exact name of the menu option you want the shortcut to invoke.** For example, if you want to add a shortcut to Address Book's Delete Card menu option in its Edit menu, enter **Delete Card**.

4. **In the Keyboard Shortcut text field, enter the shortcut you want to assign to this menu option.**

5. **Click Add.**

Note that as you add shortcuts, they appear in the Applications set of shortcuts, which opens automatically as you enter a new shortcut. Any shortcuts available to all applications display under the All Applications heading, while shortcuts assigned to a specific application appear under that application's name. Use the disclosure triangle to open and close the shortcut lists under each header.

Also note that some applications don't support Mac OS X's capability to assign new shortcuts. Even if you add a shortcut for such applications in the Keyboard Shortcuts pane, they don't work. One way to tell if an application supports your new shortcut is to see if its menu displays the shortcut you added; if not, it likely doesn't support such shortcuts. (The reason also could be that you mistyped the menu option name.)

To delete a shortcut, select it and click the – icon button.

When you're working in dialog boxes and similar containers of controls, Mac OS X enables you to press Tab to move among text boxes and lists; you use the mouse to access other controls such as pop-up menus and check boxes. If you want to access all controls using just the keyboard, change the Full Keyboard Access setting to All Controls. (You also can press Control+F7 at any time to switch between the two tabbing approaches.)

Mouse

You use the Mouse system preference, shown in Figure 28.10, to set basic mouse behavior. Note that the system preference's options differ based on what type of mouse is attached to your Mac.

The two settings that most everyone should adjust to their personal preferences are Tracking Speed and Double-Click Speed, both of which provide sliders to adjust their speeds, plus. (These options are available no matter what type of mouse you're using, though the Double-Click Speed slider is found in the Mouse & Trackpad pane of the Universal Access system preference if you are using a gesture-savvy mouse, not in the Mouse system preference.)

Tracking is the speed at which the onscreen mouse pointer follows the movements of the actual mouse on your desk or other surface. The faster it is set, the farther across the screen the mouse pointer moves, which is great if you have little space on your work surface in which to move the actual mouse—but not so great if you need precise control such as when drawing. You should experiment with the settings to see what feels right most of the time.

Use the Double-Click Speed slider to set how quickly you must double-click a mouse button for the Mac to register it as a double-click action instead of as two separate clicks. Most people should leave this near the Fast side of the slider, but if you find yourself struggling to double-click fast enough, slow this setting down until it feels natural.

If you use a basic, single-button mouse with no scroll wheel or scroll ball or just a MacBook's built-in trackapd, the Mouse system preference has just two sliders: Tracking Speed and Double-Click Speed.

If you use a mouse with more than one button and/or a scroll wheel or slider, more options appear in the system preference, as Figure 28.10 shows.

For example, you may see the Move Content in the Direction of Finger Movement When Scrolling or Navigating option. When using a touchpad, you scroll your fingers up to move the content with a window up, but with a mouse's scroll wheel or scroll ball, you typically scroll down to move the scroll bar down, which moves the window's content up. In other words, the gesture and the mouse movement move in opposite directions to achieve the same result. But if the Move Content in the Direction of Finger Movement When Scrolling or Navigating option is selected, you can use the different (traditional) mouse and gesture directions to achieve the same result. If deselected (the default), you have to scroll the mouse wheel or ball up—not down—to move a window's content up. (Chapter 2 explains the gestures supported in Mac OS X Lion.)

Also, you may see the Scroll Speed slider to control the movement of the pointer based on the movement of the mouse's scroll wheel or scroll ball. You may see the Primary Mouse Button options (Left and Right) to determine which button pressed to indicate a click (the other— usually the right button—becomes the button for Control+clicking). And you may see the Zoom Using Scroll Wheel While Holding option that if selected uses the key chosen in the adjacent pop-up menu to zoom in or out from the current pointer position.

New Feature

If you use a gesture-savvy mouse such as the Apple Magic Mouse, the Double-Click Speed slider has moved to the Mouse & Trackpad pane of the Universal Access system preference (a copy of the Tracking Speed slider also resides in the pane). ∎

New Feature

Also new in Lion's version of the Mouse system preference are the Move Content in the Direction of Finger Movement When Scrolling or Navigating option for scrolling mice and both the Scroll Direction: Natural option and the division of the system preference into two panes (Point & Click and More Gestures) for gesture-savvy mice. ∎

For a gesture-savvy mouse, there are different options, as Figure 28.10 shows, available in two panes: Point & Click and More Gestures.

FIGURE 28.10

The Mouse system preference for a basic mouse (upper left), a two-button mouse with a scroll wheel (upper right), and a touchpad-equipped mouse (the two bottom images)

In the Point & Click pane, you have three options:

- **Scroll Direction: Natural:** If deselected, this option has the scroll gesture work like a normal mouse wheel scroll: scrolling up moves the contents down within the window. If this option is selected (the default), the scroll gesture has the window contents move with the direction of your fingers.

- **Secondary Click:** You can enable a Control+click (what the system preference calls a *secondary click* and most people call a *right-click*) with this option, as well as choose which side of the touchpad is tapped to get a Control+click using the pop-up menu beneath the option.

- **Smart Zoom:** If selected, this option enables a one-finger double-tap to zoom into (and then out of, if you double-tap again) the area you tap on.

In the More Gestures pane, you also have three options:

- **Swipe Between Pages:** If selected, this option lets you use gestures to move among pages or panes such as in a browser or in the System Preferences application. You choose the gesture using the pop-up menu beneath the option: Scroll Left or Right with One Finger, Swipe Left or Right with Two Fingers, and Swipe with One or Two Fingers.

- **Swipe Between Full-Screen Apps:** If selected, this option lets you use gestures to move among full-screen applications using a two-finger left or right swipe.

- **Mission Control:** If selected, this option opens and closes the Mission Control view (see Chapter 2) with a two-finger double-tap.

No matter what type of mouse you have attached to your Mac, the Mouse system preference has the Set Up Bluetooth Mouse button to let you install a Bluetooth mouse.

Note

If you're using a Bluetooth mouse, its battery status displays at the bottom left of the Mouse system preference. ■

Print & Scan

Use the Print & Scan system preference, shown in Figure 28.11, to add printers, scanners, and faxes to your Mac, as well as to set the default printer and paper size for all printers.

FIGURE 28.11

Left: The Print & Scan system preference with a printer selected. Upper right: The settings if a scanner is selected. Lower right: The settings if a fax modem is selected.

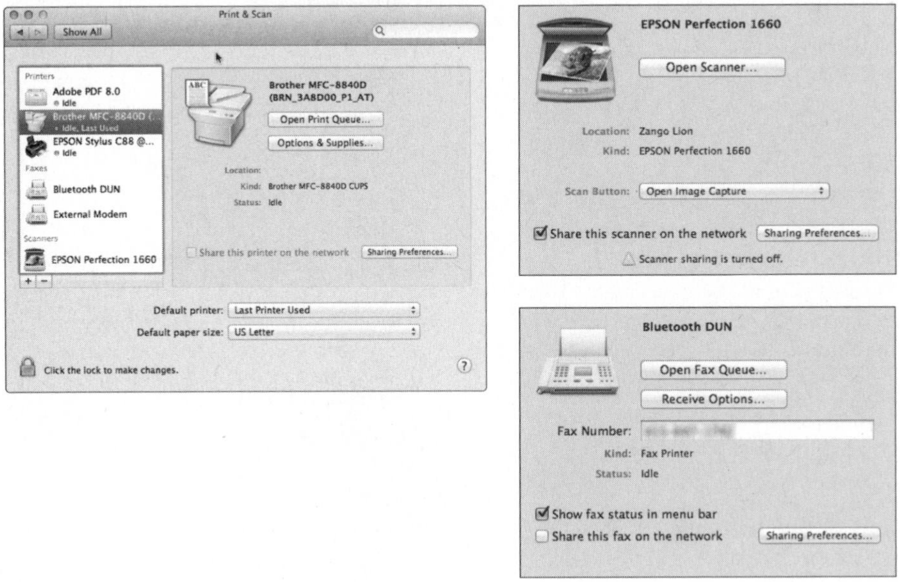

No matter what device is selected in its device list, there are two printing controls always available:

- The Default Printer pop-up menu tells Mac OS X what printer to use when you have several attached (directly or via the network) and you print directly through the shortcut ⌘+P or via a Print button, rather than use the Print dialog box in which you can choose a destination printer. Choose Last Printer Used to use whatever printer was last selected, or choose a specific printer in the pop-up menu.

- The Default paper Size pop-up menu tells Mac OS X what paper size to assume is in the printer when you print without using the Print dialog box. There are a range of North American and European paper sizes to choose from; the default is the norm for your country, such as US Letter in the U.S. and Canada.

Cross-Reference

Chapter 30 explains how to add printers, fax modems, and scanners to your Mac so they appear in the Print & Scan system preference. The rest of this section assumes you have these devices connected and visible in the Print & Scan system preference. ■

If a printer is selected in the list of devices, select the Share This Printer with Other Users on the Network option to make the selected printer available to other users, but note that when they print to shared printers through your Mac, your Mac may operate more slowly as it processes the print job. You can restrict which printers are available and who may access them by clicking Set Permissions, which opens the Sharing system preference described in Chapter 24. (The Set Permissions button appears only if you have selected Share This Printer with Other Users on the Network.)

If a fax modem is selected, you can select Share This Fax on the Network, and if a scanner is selected, you can select Share This Scanner on the network. In both cases, clicking Sharing Preferences opens the Sharing system preference so you can adjust the sharing settings, as Chapter 24 explains.

If a printer is selected and you click Options & Supplies, you get a dialog box with three panes. Its General pane enables you to change the printer name and add a location label (handy in an office where you might add a location label such as "5th Floor South"). Some printers have their own management utilities; if so, the Open Printer Utility button may appear in the General pane to give you access to that printer's own management tool. The Driver pane enables you to choose which printer driver to use for the printer (typically because the printer was installed without the right driver available or because you want to use an updated version of the driver). The Supply Level pane shows information on the paper and toner available, but only if the printer communicates that information to the Mac.

If a scanner is selected, you can click Open Scanner to begin scanning. You also may see the Scan Button pop-up menu, if the scanner supports this feature. It tells Mac OS X what application to open when someone begins scanning from the scanner; options include Preview (see Chapter 14), Image Capture (also see Chapter 14), and Other, which lets you pick another application.

If a fax modem is selected, you can click the Open Fax Queue button to see the received faxes stored on the Mac and Receive Options to specify if the fax modem answers calls automatically and, if so, after how many rings and whether to print or e-mail the received faxes automatically. You also set the fax number here, so any faxes you send are properly identified as the number they were sent from (a legal requirement in many countries). You also can select the Show Fax Status in Menu Bar option to have the Fax Status icon menu appear in the menu bar.

Sound

You use the Sound system preference to control the noises your Mac makes, as well as how it handles audio inputs and outputs. Figure 28.12 shows the Sound system preference. All three panes in the Sound system preference—Sound Effects, Output, and Input—have the Output Volume slider to control how loudly audio is played by the Mac (select the Mute option to turn off audio output altogether), as well as the Show Volume in Menu Bar option that, if selected, adds a slider to the menu bar that enables you to easily adjust output volume at any time.

FIGURE 28.12

The Sounds Effects pane (left) and Input pane (right) of the Sound system preference. (The Output pane, not shown, is very similar to the Input pane.)

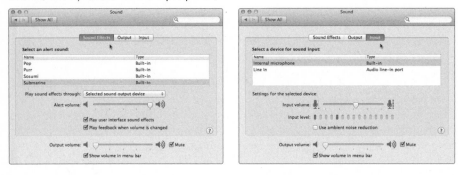

The Sound Effects pane controls the alert and other feedback sounds the Mac makes. In the Select an Alert Sound area, select the sounds you want the Mac to make when it displays alerts. (Double-click a sound to hear it; be sure the Mac's volume is loud enough for you to hear it.) Use the Alert Volume slider to set how loud the alert sound plays relative to the Mac's overall output volume (which you set in the Output Volume slider). Choose what device plays the alerts sound via the Play Sound Effects Through pop-up menu; choose Selected Sound Output Device to use whatever speaker is set in the Output pane, or Internal Speakers to force the alerts to play only through the internal speakers.

Tip

To add your own sounds to the list of alert sounds, add them to the `Library/Sounds` folder for the current user—not to the `Library` folder at the root or System levels. The sounds must be in Apple's AIFF format, a format that the Garage Band application supports. ∎

New Feature

The ability to control whether Front Row sound effects play is gone from the Sound system preference in Mac OS X Lion, as Mac OS X Lion no longer includes that application (see Chapter 16). ∎

You can control two settings related to sound effects generated by the Mac:

- **Play User Interface Sound Effects:** Select this option to have the Mac use its special sounds for key activities, such as emptying the trash or taking a screen shot, using the Grab utility (see Chapter 14).

- **Play Feedback When Volume Is Changed:** Select this option to have the Mac play a special sound when you increase or decrease the volume.

The Output pane lists all audio output devices available, such as speakers, headsets, and recording devices. Select a device from the list, and any controls appear below. Many devices offer the Balance slider, which enables you to adjust the balance between the right and left speakers.

You use the Input pane to control how the Mac receives and processes audio. Any connected audio inputs display in a list. Select the desired input to adjust its settings. In all cases, you see the Input Level indicator, which shows whether the input device is picking up any audio and, if so, at what volume (refer to Figure 28.12). Use this indicator to make sure the audio device is receiving audio correctly. Practically every input device also displays the Input Volume slider, which you adjust as needed to get the sound level high enough to be heard clearly, while not being so loud that it overloads the sound processor and creates distortion. Some devices offer the Ambient Noise Reduction option that, if selected, tries to remove background noise from what the Mac "hears."

Trackpad

The Trackpad system preference is similar to the Mouse system preference, with additional features specific to touchpads. The Tracking Speed, Double-Click Speed, and Scrolling Speed sliders, to those in the Mouse system preference (covered earlier in this chapter).

Likewise, the Move Content in the Direction of Finger Movement When Scrolling or Navigating option for non-gesture-savvy touchpads and the Scroll with Finger Direction option for gesture-savvy touchpads work identically to the same options in the Mouse system preference.

Figure 28.13 shows the Trackpad system preference. Note that the gestures displayed depend on what type of touchpad you have. The figure shows the controls for an Apple Magic Trackpad (which has the most supported gestures when this book went to press) and for a 2006 MacBook Pro (which has the fewest supported gestures) as examples of the range.

Use the Set Up Bluetooth Trackpad button to add an external touchpad such as the Apple Magic Trackpad to your Mac.

A basic touchpad-equipped Mac has the following options:

- **Use Two Fingers to Scroll:** If selected, you must use two fingers to scroll via the touchpad. This option prevents accidental scrolling if you have a finger resting on the touchpad and your finger drifts. If you select Two Fingers to Scroll, you also can enable horizontal scrolling (by selecting Allow Horizontal Scrolling) and set the scrolling speed via the Scrolling Speed slider.

- **Zoom While Holding:** If selected, this works the same as the Zoom Using Scroll Wheel While Holding option in the Mouse system preference.

- **Clicking:** If selected, you can tap the touchpad to act as a mouse click. Enabling this option also enables you to select Dragging, which enables you to double-tap the touchpad and then drag across the touchpad without lifting your finger to drag the current object. If you also select the Drag Lock option, you must tap the touchpad to stop dragging the object; otherwise, you just have to lift your finger off the touchpad. You would consider selecting Drag Lock if you have to drag items far beyond where your finger can move on the touchpad. In such a case, you would lift your finger off the touchpad and then put it down and drag more.

- **Tap Trackpad Using Two Fingers for Secondary Click:** If selected, you can use gestures to right-click or Control+click by putting both fingers on the touchpad and clicking the touchpad button.

- **Ignore Accidental Trackpad Input:** If selected, this option tells Mac OS X to ignore slight touches on the touchpad, under the assumption they were not intentional gestures.

FIGURE 28.13

The Trackpad system preference for the a basic touchpad (upper left) and its three panes for a gesture-savvy touchpad

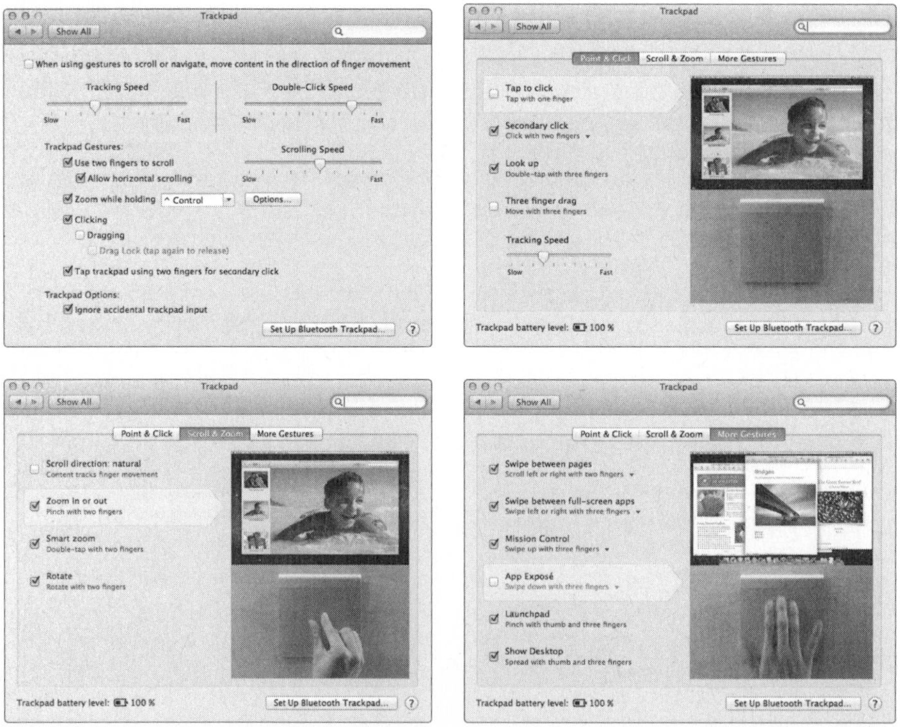

If your MacBook's touchpad supports three- and four-finger gestures or if you have a Magic Trackpad external touchpad, you have different options available in the Trackpad system preference's three panes.

New Feature

For gesture-savvy touchpads, the Double-Click Speed and Scrolling Speed sliders are available not in the Trackpad system preference but in the Mouse & Trackpad pane of the Universal Access system preference. ■

In the Point & Click pane, you have these options:

- **Tap to Click:** If selected, a single-finger tap acts like clicking a mouse or touchpad button.
- **Secondary Click:** If selected, this option detects the chosen gesture as a right-click or Control+click; In the pop-up menu beneath the option, choose from three gestures: Click or Tap with Two Fingers, Click in Bottom Right Corner, and Click in Bottom Right Corner. (The last two options refer to the corners of the touchpad, not the screen.)
- **Look Up:** If this option is selected, a two-finger double-tap uses Mac OS X's built-in dictionary to look up the definition for text that you double-tapped.
- **Three-Finger Drag:** If selected, dragging with three fingers moves the selected object.

In the Scroll & Zoom pane, you have these options (all selected by default):

- **Scroll Direction: Natural:** If selected, this option has the windows contents move in the same direction as your fingers when you scroll—the usual behavior for a gesture-based scroll. Deselect the option to have the scrolling work like that of a mouse's scroll wheel.
- **Zoom In or Out:** If selected, this option uses the two-finger pinch gesture (usually a thumb and a finger) to zoom in and the two-finger expand gesture to zoom out.
- **Smart Zoom:** If selected, this option enables a one-finger double-tap to zoom into the area you tap on. Repeating the gesture zooms out.
- **Rotate:** If selected, this option interprets a twist of two fingers as a rotate command; the rotation follows the direction of your finger twist.

In the More Gestures pane, you have these options:

- **Swipe Between Pages:** If selected, this option lets you use gestures to move among pages or panes such as in a browser or in the System Preferences application. You choose the gesture using the pop-up menu beneath the option: Scroll Left or Right with Two Fingers, Swipe Left or Right with Three Fingers, and Swipe with Two or Three Fingers.
- **Swipe Between Full-Screen Apps:** If selected, this option lets you use gestures to move among full-screen applications using one of the two options in the pop-up menu beneath the option: Swipe Left or Right with Three Fingers, or Swipe Left or Right with Four Fingers.

- **Mission Control:** If selected, this option opens and closes the Mission Control view of all open windows (see Chapter 2) with your choice (from the pop-up menu beneath) of a three-finger swipe up or a four-finger swipe up.

- **App Exposé:** If selected, this option opens and closes the App Exposé view of the current application's windows (see Chapter 2) with your choice (from the pop-up menu beneath) of a three-finger swipe down or a four-finger swipe down.

- **Launchpad:** If selected, this option interprets a four-finger pinch gesture (with a thumb on one side and three fingers on the other) as a command to display the Launchpad (see Chapter 14).

- **Show Desktop:** If selected, this option interprets a four-finger expand gesture (with a thumb on one side and three fingers on the other) as a command to display the desktop.

Note

If you're using a Bluetooth touchpad, its battery status displays at the bottom left of the Trackpad system preference. ■

Xsan

Available only if your Mac has network storage volumes attached (such as on a Mac Pro or the discontinued Apple Xserve) that are managed with Apple's Xsan software, this system preference enables you to set the basic settings for your network storage volumes.

Internet and wireless preferences

The Mac is a great control center for using Internet- and network-based services, and the five system preferences in this section are where you set up the Mac to work with the rest if the world.

Bluetooth

Bluetooth is a wireless data technology that enables devices to communicate over short distances, typically less than 15 feet. You see it mainly in hands-free headsets for cell phones, but Macs come with their own Bluetooth radio so you can wirelessly connect various devices, such as PDAs and smartphones for sharing information, headsets for use as a wireless headphone and microphone, wireless printers, GPS location devices, and wireless input devices such as mice, touchpads, and keyboards.

Cross-Reference

Chapter 24 covers the Bluetooth File Exchange utility that enables you to share files with Bluetooth devices. Later in this chapter, I cover the Sharing system preference in which you set up the Bluetooth file-sharing preferences. ■

Use the Bluetooth system preference to manage how Bluetooth devices connect to your Mac. Figure 28.14 shows the Bluetooth system preference with the detailed information for a configured device. For Bluetooth to work on your Mac, the On option must be selected in the Bluetooth system preference. Even then, nothing happens until you've paired the Mac with a compatible Bluetooth device.

Mac OS X's menu bar icons

Several system preferences install icons in your menu bar that provide shortcut access to various controls. The figure here shows the icon menus that various system preferences can install in the menu bar. Note that the Date & Time menu's icon can be any of three choices: the time, the day and time, or a clock icon. Also note the Input Source menu's icon displays as a flag if you have multiple languages selected as input sources in the Language & Text system preference, rather than displaying the Character Viewer icon as shown here.

From left to right, the icon menus are Screen Sharing, Universal Access, Fax Status, Modem Status, VPN Status, Time Machine, Wi-Fi, Displays, Speaker Volume, Battery Status, Date and Time, Character Viewer, Bluetooth, Users & Groups, and Spotlight. Note that the Modem Status menu's icon is also used for the WWAN Status icon menu, such as when you have a 3G modem installed (WWAN stands for *wireless wide area network*); if you have both a fax modem and a WWAN device active, they share the same icon menu.

To use one of these menu bar items, just click it and a pop-up menu of options appears. The system preferences offer an option to turn off or on the display of these menu bar icons; look for an option called Show *description* in Menu Bar in the relevant system preferences' panes. Selecting the option displays the icon menu in the menu bar, while deselecting it removes the icon menu.

Note that other applications may install their own icon menus in the menu bar;. But they may not have an easy way to remove them from the menu bar. Check the applications' Preferences dialog boxes, as well as the icon menus themselves for an option to turn off their display.

Tip

Be sure to select the Show Bluetooth Status in the Menu Bar option so you can tell at a glance whether Bluetooth is active on your Mac and whether devices are connected. In the menu bar, you see a stylized B icon menu that shows you what is connected, provides submenus of configuration options and battery status for each connected device, and enables you to turn Bluetooth on and off. If the icon is gray, Bluetooth is turned off; if it has a dashed line running through it, at least some devices are connected, and if it is solid black, then Bluetooth is on but nothing is connected through it. ■

Pairing means to establish a two-way connection, which you can do from either end of the connection. To have a device find your Mac and initiate pairing, your Mac must be *discoverable*, meaning it is broadcasting its name and availability. Select the Discoverable option in the Bluetooth system preference to make the Mac discoverable. More typically, though, you initiate the pairing from your Mac because you have the benefit of a screen, mouse or touchpad, and keyboard to manage the pairing process.

Caution

Turning on the Discoverable option can pose a security risk, because it allows other devices to find and connect to your Mac via Bluetooth. ■

FIGURE 28.14

The Bluetooth system preference showing detailed device information for a Magic Trackpad

To pair a device, make sure it is set up as discoverable, and click the + icon button in the Bluetooth system preference. The Mac searches for discoverable Bluetooth devices and lists those it finds in the Bluetooth Setup Assistant dialog box that appears; select the desired device and click Continue, following the instructions, which vary based on the device you're pairing. (If the device is not displayed, but you know its device ID, you can enter it manually by clicking Specify Device.) When you're finished, you are returned to the Bluetooth system preference, where your paired devices appear in the list at the left, as Figure 28.14 shows. (Click the – icon button to delete a Bluetooth device's connection to your Mac.)

Note

You can add a Bluetooth keyboard directly from the Keyboard system preference, a mouse from the Mouse system preference, and a touchpad from the Trackpad system preference using the Set Up Bluetooth devicename buttons that appear in each. ∎

You see device information, such as connection status, in the pane at the right. If a device has a Connected status of Not Connected, you must tell the device to connect to your Mac; not all devices do this automatically, and the method for initiating a connection varies from device to device, so check your device manual.

You manage a paired Bluetooth device by selecting it in the list at the left of the Bluetooth system preference and clicking the Action icon pop-up menu (the gear icon). The options in this menu vary based on the device's capabilities and its connection status. But at the very least you see a Show More Info option, which provides deep detail as to the device's abilities and status, and the Add to Favorites/Remove from Favorites option (depending on whether the device is a favorite, meaning it is automatically reconnected when the Mac starts up).

Other common options in the Action icon pop-up menu include Connect or Disconnect (depending on whether the device is currently connected), Rename (to give the device a friendlier name in this system preference and in the Bluetooth icon menu in the menu bar), Update Name, and Update Services. (The latter two options refresh the data read from the Bluetooth device, in case it has been upgraded.)

If you select Show More Info (so that a check mark appears to the left of the menu option), more details appear in the pane to the right of the device list for the selected device (refer to Figure 28.14). Two options are worth noting.

A Bluetooth modem, handheld device, or computer typically has the Action icon pop-up menu option of Edit Serial Ports to configure the connection with Bluetooth devices. (Be sure to read the device's manual to understand these settings before adjusting them.) Devices use two technical methods, called *serial ports*, to communicate—RS-232 and Modem—and you can select those here when you want to override the default connection settings established when you paired the device. Click the + icon button to add such serial port configurations, and adjust the options shown in the window. (Click the – icon button to delete a selected serial port configuration.) Click Apply to save the changes when you're finished.

A Bluetooth device that supports file sharing usually has the Send File and Browse Device options (see Chapter 24).

The Bluetooth system preference has two other sets of options of note:

- **Click Sharing Setup to turn on Bluetooth file sharing.** This opens the Sharing system preference covered later in this chapter.

- **Click Advanced to open a settings sheet in which to set up the basic behaviors for Bluetooth on your Mac (for all devices):**

  - Select the Open Bluetooth Setup Assistant at Startup If No Keyboard Is Detected option to have Mac OS X open the Bluetooth Setup Assistant when it can't find the wireless keyboard you previously set up. (This way you know something's wrong and can correct it immediately).

  - Select the Open Bluetooth Setup Assistant at Startup If No Mouse or Trackpad Is Detected option to have Mac OS X open the Bluetooth Setup Assistant when it can't find the wireless mouse or touchpad you previously set up.

  - Select the Allow Bluetooth Devices to Wake This Computer option to enable devices such as a keyboard and mouse to wake the Mac when it goes to sleep. Otherwise, you have to connect a wired device to wake the Mac up or open a MacBook to use its built-in keyboard or touchpad. If selected, this option does not let other devices, such as a PDA or headset, wake the Mac up.

  - Select the Reject Incoming Audio Requests option to have the Mac ignore when a Bluetooth headset or other audio device tries to connect to it. If you've set up your cell phone's Bluetooth headset to work with your Mac, you may want this option selected so the headset doesn't take over your Mac's audio when you didn't intend for it to do so (for example, just because it happens to be in your pocket).

  - Click the + icon button to add more serial ports for Bluetooth devices to use to connect to the Mac and specify whether they use the RS-232 or Modem connection protocols. You should add such serial ports to your Mac only if you have devices that require them. Select the On option for each serial port you want to make active, and select the Pair (key icon) option for each serial port that you want to require pairing for. To delete a serial port connection, select it and click the – icon button. (The default serial port is called Bluetooth-PDA-Sync, and it can't be deleted.)

Mail, Contacts & Calendars

When you add communications accounts—e-mail, chat, calendars, and the like—such as in Mail, iChat, and iCal, they are automatically added to the new Mail, Contacts & Calendars system preference, so you can manage them all in one place.

If you click an account, the right pane lists which applications it is used with: Address Book, iCal, iChat, and/or Mail, as Figure 28.15 shows. Select or deselect an application to control whether it can use that communications account. For accounts that use any of these applications you also can click Details to open a settings sheet to see the e-mail address and update the name and description for the account.

Tip

Double-click Mail, iChat, iCal, or Address Book in an account's right pane to open that application and its Preference dialog box's Accounts pane. ∎

If you click the Add Account item, at the bottom of the account list, you get a list of Internet services in the right pane. Click a service—iCloud, Microsoft Exchange, Gmail, Yahoo, AOL, or Other—to sign in and make the service available to your Mac's Apple applications. If you choose Other, a settings sheet opens with options to add a Mail account, an iChat account, a CalDAV account, a CardDAV account, an LDAP account, or a Mac OS X Server account. Choose the desired account type and click Create.

Delete an account by selecting it in the account list and then click the – icon button.

FIGURE 28.15

The Mail, Contacts & Calendars system preference for an account that can be accessed by multiple applications (left) and for an account that works with just e-mail (right)

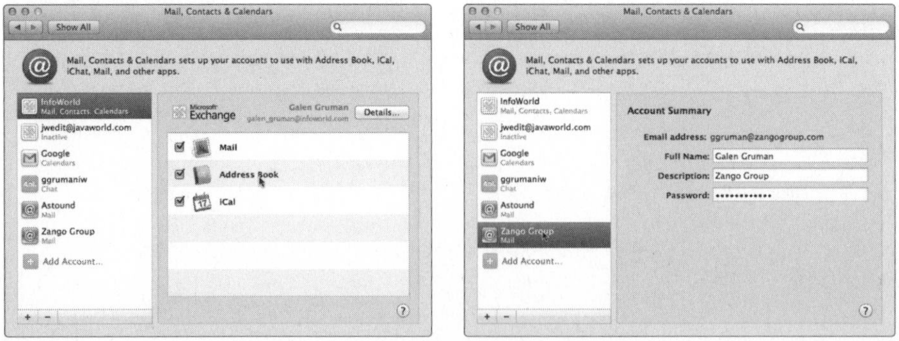

Cross-Reference

Chapter 20 covers Mail and iChat. Chapter 21 covers Address Book and iCal, including CardDAV, CalDAV, and LDAP accounts. Chapter 25 covers Mac OS X Server. ■

Network

To connect to the Internet or just other Macs and PCs, you need to be connected to a network. Use the Network system preference to manage your network settings. Most Macs have four separate network interfaces available, plus the ability to make dial-up connections to the Internet via a modem:

- **Ethernet:** This is the standard wired network connection, which uses a wider version of a phone connector called an RJ-45 jack. On the other end of the cable is typically a router, a box that manages all the traffic among the Macs and other devices such as PCs and printers. A special type of router—a DSL modem or a cable modem at home—also handles the connection between your network and the Internet. (Intermediary forms of routers are called *hubs* and *switches*.)

- **Wi-Fi:** This wireless networking technology known formally as IEEE 802.11a/b/g/n wireless is basically a wireless version of Ethernet that is meant for sending lots of data to a wireless router that can be as far as 300 feet away.

- **External Modem:** This appears only if you've added an external USB modem to your Mac at some point in the past. You enter the phone number and other connection settings for that modem to connect to your dial-up service.

- **Bluetooth:** This is a short-range type of wireless network, typically used when you want to make your cell phone act as a modem for your Mac. Note that the Mac also uses Bluetooth to have other devices connect to it, such as headsets and printers; the settings for those kinds of Bluetooth connections are covered in the Bluetooth system preference section earlier in this chapter.

- **FireWire:** This is a wired connection (formally called IEEE 1394) typically used for attaching disks and video equipment that also can be used to create a network across Macs and PCs when you don't have a regular network to plug them into.

You can think of a network interface as a door through which connections are made.

Cross-Reference

Chapter 23 covers how to set up and manage networking on your Mac, so look there for detailed explanations of what the various Network system preference settings do. It also explains all those networking acronyms. Also refer to Chapter 23's coverage of Network Utility, which can help you troubleshoot your network and its connections to the Internet. ■

Sharing

The Mac has long been a sharing-oriented computer, with the ability to share files, printers, and even access to the Internet with other Macs on your local network. Such sharing can be dangerous if it is not managed, especially now that people can come into your local network through the Internet and potentially access your computer without your knowledge. You use the Sharing system preference to control who gets access to what on your Mac, as Chapter 24 explains in detail.

System preferences

The last group of Apple-supplied system preferences controls the behavior of Mac OS X's user interface.

Date & Time

To make sure your Mac is set to the right date and time, and displays that information the way you prefer, use the Date & Time system preference.

You set the date and time in the Date & Time pane, shown in Figure 28.16. Normally, you just ensure that the Set Date and Time Automatically option is selected; if you're connected to the Internet, the Mac uses the selected time server in the adjacent pop-up menu to get the current date and time. But you can override these by deselecting the option and changing the date and time fields below, or using the calendar and clocks to change the date and time. To change the calendar system you use (such as to Islamic or Buddhist) or change how dates and times display, click Open Language & Text to jump to the Language & Text system preference (covered earlier in this chapter) and then go to its Formats pane.

Use the Time Zone pane to set your current time zone. You see a map of the world, where you can click your approximate location to get the current time zone. Then choose your specific location from the Closest City pop-up menu; this option ensures that any local time-zone rules are followed on your Mac. Or, to have Mac OS X set the time for you based on detecting your location, select the Set Time Zone Automatically Using Current Location option. (And if Mac OS X gets the time zone wrong, just deselect the option and manually choose your location.)

FIGURE 28.16

The Date & Time system preference's Date & Time pane (left) and Time Zone pane

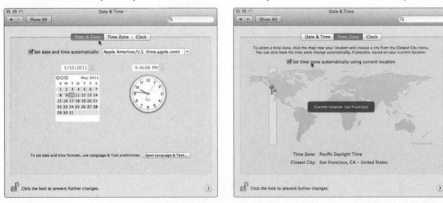

Note

The ability to have Mac OS X detect the current time zone depends on the Mac being able to connect to a network from which it can determine your approximate location and the Enable Location Services option being selected in the Privacy pane of the Security & Privacy system preference, covered in Chapter 26. ■

The Clock pane enables you to control whether and how the current date and time display in your Mac's menu bar. To display them, be sure that the Show Date and Time in Menu Bar option is selected. You can customize the display by selecting or deselecting the following options: Display the Time with Seconds, Flash the Time Separators (to make the colon flash), Use a 24-Hour Clock, Show AM/PM, Show Day of the Week, and Show Date. You also can select whether the time displays in Digital or Analog format. (The Digital format shows the time using numbers, such as 12:15, and the Analog format shows a small clock with hour and minute hands.)

You can set the Mac to announce the time out loud by selecting the Announce the Time option. Use the adjacent pop-up menu to select how often: On the Hour, On the Half Hour, or On the Quarter Hour. You also can choose which Mac voice to use by clicking Customize Voice.

Parental Controls

A Mac is a very powerful device, with access to the Internet and its riches and dangers, as well as access to applications, information, and media content that's not appropriate for everyone. Use Mac OS X's Parental Control system preference to help shield people—usually children—from sensitive applications and content on your Mac. Chapter 27 covers this system preference in detail.

Profiles

If your Mac has a configuration profile installed, the Profiles system preference appears. It lists all installed profiles so you can see their details. You can also add additional profiles from this system preference and delete profiles that don't prohibit user deletion. Chapter 25 covers configuration profiles and the Profiles system preference in more depth.

Software Update

It seems that software is never finished; it either has flaws ("bugs") that need to be fixed or new features that the whizzes at Apple and other companies keep inventing. These days, companies such as Apple periodically create updates to fix the bugs and add new features, which they then distribute over the Internet. In the Software Update system preference, you can set your Mac to get these updates automatically for Mac OS X and other Apple software on a schedule of your choosing.

Figure 28.17 shows the Software Update system preference's Scheduled Check pane, where you set the update parameters. By default, the Check for Updates option is selected, and the adjacent pop-up menu is set to Weekly, so the Mac checks once a week for any updates. Deselect the option to stop automatic checking, or change the pop-up menu to Daily or Monthly to change the frequency. Also by default, the Mac is set to download the updates automatically so they're ready to install. (Deselect the Download Updates Automatically option to prevent automatic downloading.) When Mac OS X downloads an update, it displays an alert asking you for permission to install it.

FIGURE 28.17

The Software Update system preference's Scheduled Check pane

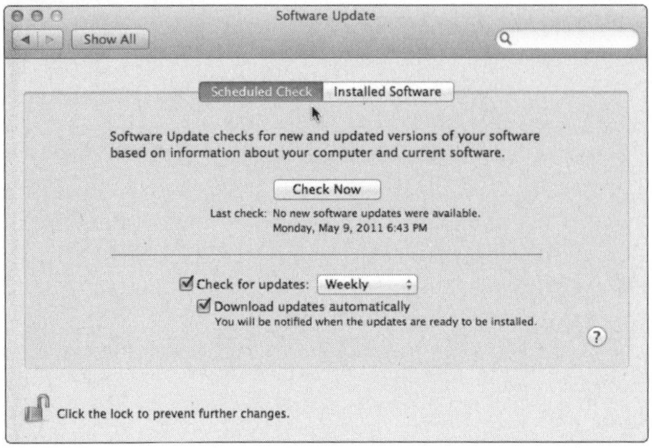

Tip

You can have Mac OS X check for updates at any time by clicking Check Now in the Scheduled Check pane. But it's easier to choose ➪ Software Update to do this. ∎

The Installed Software pane of the Software Update system preference shows a list of previously installed updates in case you want to verify that you have a specific update.

Speech

Your Mac can talk to you, and you use the Speech system preference to control when and how it talks to you. You also can talk to it using the Speech system preference to help it recognize your words. (See Chapter 8 for more details on Mac OS X's speech features as they apply to the visually impaired.)

You use the Speech Recognition pane to configure the Mac to hear and interpret what you say to it. Figure 28.18 shows the pane. To enable speech recognition, turn it on by selecting the On option for Speakable items.

Whether or not speech recognition is on, you can configure its settings in the Settings and Commands subpanes. First, look at the Settings subpane.

The Microphone pop-up menu enables you to select which microphone the Mac should use to interpret your speech. Most Macs have a built-in microphone, but you also could use an external microphone connected to the Line In jack or a wireless headset connected via Bluetooth (as explained in the Bluetooth system preference section earlier in this chapter). Whatever microphone you choose, help the Mac hear it correctly by clicking Calibrate. A dialog box appears after a few seconds that lists several phrases for you to speak so the Mac can make whatever adjustments are necessary in its processing of your voice to understand what you're saying.

FIGURE 28.18

The Speech system preference's Speech Recognition pane, with the Settings subpane visible (left) and the Text to Speech pane (right)

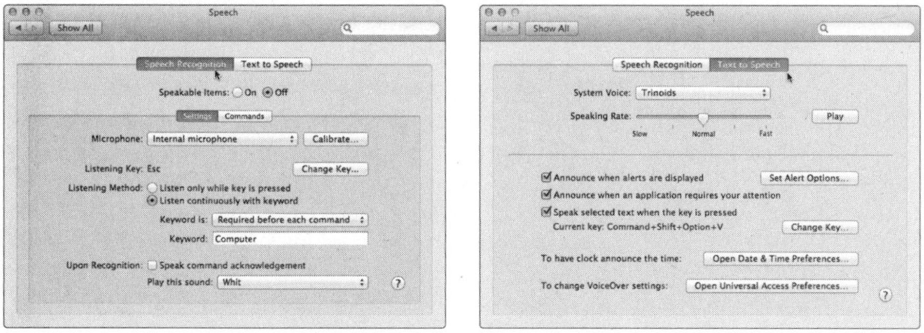

Several controls determine how the Mac listens to you:

- **Change Key:** Click this button to open a settings sheet in which you type in the key you want to use to turn the listening on and off. The default is Esc, so you would press Esc before speaking a command, and press Esc again when you're finished so the Mac doesn't try to interpret anything else it hears as a command.

- **The Listening Method options:** Use this set of options to choose how the Mac listens for commands. Select Listen Only When Key Is Pressed to use the shortcut set up via Change Key to toggle listening off and on. Select Listen Continuously with Keyword to tell the Mac to listen all the tine, and when it hears a keyword you specify, to begin interpreting what you say next as a command—just like how the *Star Trek* starship *U.S.S. Enterprise* crew would say "Computer" before asking the computer a question. Set the keyword in the Keyword field; note that longer words or phrases are best (such as "Computer Command" or "Listen Macintosh") because they are easier to detect and less likely to be something you'd say in another context. In the Keyword Is pop-up menu, you can require the Mac to hear that keyword before each and every command, to not require it at all, to require it if at least 15 seconds have elapsed from the last command, or to require it if at least 30 seconds have elapsed from the last command. Those last two options are helpful if you typically issue many commands in sequence because they require you to say the keyword just at the beginning of that sequence.

- **Speak Command Acknowledgment:** Select this option if you want the Mac to make a noise when it understands your command correctly, so you know it did understand you properly before moving on. Choose that confirmation sound using the Play This Sound pop-up menu.

You use the Commands subpane to tell the Mac what commands to listen for. Select as many of the commands sets that Apple provides for you as you want the Mac to do when you speak the commands: Address Book, Global Speakable Items (commands that all applications use), Application Specific Items (commands unique to it that the application supplies), Application Switching (commands to switch among applications, as well as launch and quit them), Front

Window (commands for names of interface elements such as buttons and check boxes in the active window of an application), and Menu Bar (commands for the menu bar items running on your Mac).

To see what the actual speakable commands are, click Open Speakable Items Folder to see all the speech command files.

Note

You can configure two of the standard commands sets using the Configure button: Address Book and Global Speakable Items. If Address Book is selected, you can select which names in your address book you want to be able to speak as part of your commands; a settings sheet with a list of entries appears when you click Configure. If Global Speakable Items is selected, you can tell the Mac to listen for variations of common commands—so it understands "What is the time?" and "Tell me the time" as the same thing—instead of listening only for the actual command as written in the menu or dialog box; deselect Speak Command Names Exactly as Written in the window that appears when you click Configure. ∎

Use the Text to Speech pane to control how the Mac talks to you; the pane is shown in Figure 28.18. Choose your preferred system voice using the System Voice pop-up menu and the rate at which the voice speaks using the Speaking Rate slider. You can hear how the voice and rate sound by clicking Play.

New Feature

Mac OS X Lion's list of voices has expanded considerably, to several dozen. Plus, voices are available for more than a dozen languages, so they speak more correctly for those languages than the previous English-oriented voices did. (Note that these foreign-language voices are often hard to understand when speaking English.) Choose Customize in the System Voices pop-up menu to see the list of these foreign voices, as well as a selection of novelty voices such as Zarvox and Deranged that used to appear in the Systems Voices pop-up menu. Most of these new voices are not automatically installed with Mac OS X Lion, so if you select any of them, you get a prompt asking if you want to download the voices over an Internet connection. ∎

You can set several alerts and announcements for the Mac to speak:

- **Announce When Alerts Are Displayed:** Select this option to have the Mac read any alerts that Mac OS X or your applications display. This can alert you to an issue if you're away from your computer. Click Set Alert Options to configure how the alerts are spoken; you can choose a different voice, set a delay of up to a minute for how long the alert is onscreen before the Mac speaks it, and choose (or create) an alert phrase, such as "Alert!," "Pardon Me!," or "Zoinks!" (You'd have to create that last one by choosing Edit Phrase List in the Phrase pop-up menu in the window that appears after you click Set Alert Options.)

- **Announce When an Application Requires Your Attention:** Select this option to have the Mac verbally tell you that an application needs you to respond. This is the verbal version of the dancing icon in the Dock, which also occurs when an application is waiting for you to fill in a dialog box or respond to some other prompt.

- **Speak Selected Text When the Key Is Pressed:** Select this option to have Mac OS X read aloud whatever text is selected when you press the shortcut. By default, that shortcut is Shift+Option+⌘+V, but you can change it by clicking the Change Key button and entering a new shortcut in the settings sheet that appears.

Tip

The key combination you set to read aloud selected text also stops the Mac—when you press it—from speaking any alert or other announcement that is in progress. So it acts as a "shush" shortcut, not just a "read this" shortcut. ■

- **Open Date & Time Preferences:** Click this button to jump to the Date & Time system preference, where you can set the Mac to announce the time every hour, half hour, or 15 minutes. (See the Date & Times system preference section earlier in this chapter.)

- **Open Universal Access Preferences:** Click this button to jump to the Universal Access system preference (covered later in this chapter), where you can turn on the VoiceOver utility that helps the visually impaired by reading the screen to them, as Chapter 6 explains.

Startup Disk

Most people have just one startup disk, but they still should know about the Startup Disk system preference, shown in Figure 28.19. For example, if you use Macs at your business and don't want to start from your internal disk (perhaps you're lending the Mac to a contractor)— or can't because it is damaged—you would click the Network Startup icon and then click Restart so your Mac can run remotely using a startup disk elsewhere on the network that your Mac administrator set up (Chapter 25 explains how to do so using Mac OS X Server).

FIGURE 28.19

The Startup Disk system preference

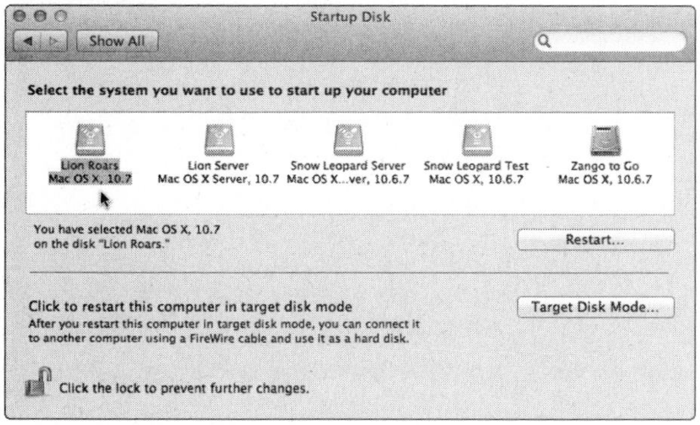

Or if you want to transfer lots of files to another Mac and you don't have a network connection that enables you to use file sharing, you can go to the Startup Disk system preference and click Target Disk mode, which makes the current Mac reboot so it appears to the other Mac as a hard disk. (The two need to be connected via a FireWire cable.)

If you have several startup disks, click the desired startup disk in the Startup Disk system preference. The next time you start the Mac, it uses that disk. (Click Restart to restart now.) This is a helpful option if you are testing applications or other configurations; you can set up Mac OS X on an external disk for such testing and start from that disk, while still having your regular startup disk untouched.

Tip

If you have multiple startup disks, or if you want to start up from the new Recovery System, you can choose which startup disk to use when you start up: Just hold Option as the Mac starts, and after a few seconds, you see icons for each available startup disk. Use the arrow keys or mouse to move to the one you want, and press Return or click the ↑ icon button that appears below the selected disk. ■

Time Machine

The Time Machine utility is an amazingly easy way to back up your Mac's files and restore them when needed. Chapter 11 explains how to use Time Machine and what its system preference settings are.

Users & Groups

You use the Users & Groups system preference to set up user accounts for your Mac. In many cases, there is only one user (you), but you might set up multiple accounts on the same Mac for different family members so each member has his or her own independent space for files and applications. In a work setting, you might have a separate account for an administrator on each Mac.

Chapter 27 explains the settings available in the Users & Groups system preference.

Summary

Mac OS X uses the System Preferences application to provide access to as many as 31 sets of controls for standard Mac functions, depending on your Mac's hardware. Three system preferences—FibreChannel, Ink, and Xsan—appear only if you have the appropriate hardware attached to your Mac. One—Profiles—appears only if configuration profiles have been installed in Mac OS X Lion. Another—MobileMe—appears if you upgraded from Mac OS X Snow Leopard.

You can view system preferences sorted alphabetically or by group. Using the View menu, you can switch to any system preference, or you can use the navigation buttons (Show All and the left-facing and right-facing triangles) in the System Preferences application window to move among system preferences. You also can hide individual system preference icons from the System Preferences application window by choosing View ⇨ Configure and deselecting specific system preferences.

By default, the System Preferences application groups system preferences into four categories: Personal, Hardware, Internet & Wireless, and System. A fifth category, Other, appears for any system preferences installed by non-Apple applications or devices.

Managing Fonts

When the Mac was introduced in 1984, two things set it apart from the PCs of the day. One was the use of a mouse-driven graphical user interface. The other was the use of fonts (also referred to as *typefaces*). Never before could you use typography in your documents, and the result was the desktop publishing revolution that ushered in the popularization of the media because anyone could produce good-quality publications. When the web rose in the late 1990s, fonts were part of the basic mix of its presentation capabilities.

So the Mac has a long history of being font oriented. Over the years, font technology has changed significantly, and the Mac OS has kept up with those changes. Mac OS X works with five kinds of font technologies, and it provides a management tool that enables you to control which fonts are active. (Because each font takes system memory, if you have a large font collection, you may not want them all loaded in memory at once.)

IN THIS CHAPTER

Defining what fonts are

Discovering where Mac OS X stores fonts

Understanding font formats

Using Font Book to add and manage fonts

Knowing when to use third-party font managers

Accessing special characters

Exactly What Is a Font?

Technically, what computer users call a *font* is what typographers call a *typeface*: a set of characters available in one or more related stylistic variations. For example, the font/typeface Arial has the styles Arial Regular, Arial Italic, Arial Bold, Arial Bold Italic, Arial Black, and Arial Black Italic. In typographic terminology, that collection is a typeface and each stylistic variation is a font. In computer terminology, that collection is a font or font family, and each stylistic variation is a style, typestyle, face, or typeface (depending on what program you're using). For consistency, this book uses the terms *font* for the set and *style* for the individual variations. Figure 29.1 shows a selection of fonts and their styles.

FIGURE 29.1

An assortment of fonts and their styles

American Typewriter Regular, Light, **Bold**, Condensed, Condensed Light, **Condensed Bold**

Arial Regular, *Italic*, **Bold**, ***Bold Italic***, **Black**

ITC Eras Book, Medium, **Demi**, Light, **Bold**, **Ultra**

Gill Sans Regular, *Italic*, **Bold**, ***Bold Italic***, Light, *Light Italic*

Helvetica, *Oblique*, **Bold**, ***Bold Oblique***

Hoefler Text Regular, *Italic*, **Black**, ***Black Italic***

Lucida Grande Regular, **Bold**

Marker Felt Thin, Wide

ITC Mendoza Roman Book, *Book Italic*, Medium, *Medium Italic*, **Bold**, ***Bold Italic***

Times New Roman Regular, *Italic*, **Bold**, ***Bold Italic***

Font Formats

Today, Mac OS X supports five font formats without the use of additional software: PostScript Type 1, PostScript Multiple Master, TrueType, OpenType, and dfont.

Note

Many fonts are available in several of these formats. Despite having the same name, they may not offer the same characters, especially foreign-language characters and special symbols. Also, font makers add new characters over time to their fonts, so an older version of a font may have fewer special characters than the newer version. In either case, you can have a compatibility issue if you share files with other people whose fonts may be a different version or a different format. ∎

When the Mac debuted in 1984, there was just one font format, a bitmap format of fixed sizes. (A *bitmap* is a series of dots, or pixels, that combine to form a shape.) Each font's styles were rendered for each size as a series of pixels. That meant you could get 9-, 10-, and 12-point text, but not 11- or 13-point. Because the professional typesetting industry also used photo-typesetting technology that rendered fonts at only specific sizes, that didn't feel like a limitation. But since then, the world of fonts has changed dramatically.

PostScript Type 1

The same year that the Mac debuted, so did a technology called PostScript, developed at Xerox by John Warnock and Chuck Geschke. They could not get Xerox to commercialize it, so they started their own company, Adobe Systems. Unlike the bitmap fonts of the original Mac OS, PostScript fonts were essentially mathematical equations that described fonts as a series of lines and curves (called *outline fonts*). A PostScript device could take those equations and, for any size, calculate the pixels needed to render it. That meant that font size was no longer set ahead of time but could be handled on the fly. In 1985, Apple saw the value of PostScript and adopted it in the Mac OS (then called the System) and in Apple's laser printers. That same year, a company called Aldus released PageMaker, the first desktop publishing program and one that used PostScript.

By 1986, the PostScript approach of outline fonts was the standard for professional-level desktop publishing. Mac OS X continues to support PostScript Type 1 fonts. Note that these fonts have two sets of files: printer files (the outlines) and screen files (bitmaps that Mac OS can use immediately to display text, rather than having to render the fonts at standard screen sizes, which can slow it down). Most PostScript fonts package these together in what are called suitcase files, but sometimes they are stored separately. The screen file has a short name such as `HelveBolIta`, while the printer file has a long name such as `Helvetica Bold Italic`. You need both files for Mac OS X to use the Type 1 font.

Tip

Because PostScript Type 1 has essentially been superseded by the OpenType format, you should favor buying OpenType versions of fonts instead of PostScript Type 1 fonts, and consider replacing your older Type 1 fonts as you can. ■

TrueType

Over the years, new font formats emerged. Microsoft and Apple felt Adobe was charging too much for PostScript technology, so they created a competing outline font standard called TrueType that they both used in their operating systems (Windows and Mac OS X, respectively). Mac OS X comes with more than a dozen TrueType fonts and uses TrueType as its primary font format.

Bitmap fonts

For the 1980s and early 1990s, bitmap fonts survived as well because the Mac OS continued to support its original bitmap format. Adobe supported the bitmap technology as well for non-Apple computers, so it offered both PostScript Type 1 outline fonts and PostScript Type 3 bitmap fonts. The Type 3 fonts didn't really get much adoption, and bitmap fonts in general are rarely used any more in any operating system. Today, Mac OS X does not support bitmap fonts.

Microsoft relied on TrueType fonts for its Internet Explorer browser—which quickly became the standard browser on most computers—making TrueType fonts the de facto web font standard. Mac OS X uses the same TrueType fonts as Microsoft does for web display compatibility: Arial, Courier New, Georgia, Tahoma, Times New Roman, Trebuchet, and Verdana.

Note that TrueType fonts come in two file formats: TrueType (file extension .ttf) and TrueType Collection (.ttc). A TrueType Collection file includes multiple styles in one file (such as Baskerville.ttc, which includes Regular, Italic, Bold, Bold Italic, Semibold, and Semibold Italic), while a "regular" TrueType file contains just one specific style (such as CorsivaBold.ttf containing just Corsiva Bold and Corsiva.ttf containing just Corsiva Regular).

PostScript Multiple Master

Adobe responded to the TrueType alliance with a "professional" variation of PostScript called Multiple Masters, where people used Adobe Type Manager software to create their own font variations. But few other programs provided support for Multiple Master fonts, and they have largely faded away. Even Adobe no longer produces new Multiple Master fonts.

However, today Mac OS X supports Multiple Master fonts (they all have "MM" in the filename), so you can use those that you have. But if you want to create your own variations, you'll need a font editor capable of doing so, such as FontLab Studio ($649; www.fontlab.com). You can tell there's not much demand for editing Multiple Master fonts given that FontLab Studio hasn't been updated since 2007.

OpenType

Adobe, Microsoft, and Apple stopped competing over font standards after a few years, instead jointly developing the OpenType format that the recent versions of Mac OS X and Windows support natively. OpenType typically has many more characters available—for languages such as Russian, Greek, Hebrew, Arabic, and Japanese, as well as many specialized symbols for everything from currency to scientific expressions—than either PostScript Type 1 or TrueType. (To be fair, TrueType fonts released in recent years have increased the number of characters available in response to what's available in OpenType fonts.)

Today, several of the fonts that come preinstalled in Mac OS X are OpenType fonts, such as Aquakana and Hiragino. (Both are Japanese-language fonts.)

dfont

Meanwhile, Apple developed a bitmap font format called the *dfont*, which it uses for its user interface, so it can guarantee that regardless of other font technologies active within Mac OS X, the menus, icon names, and so on will always display properly.

You can't buy dfont-format fonts, so the only reason to know they exist is so you know their purpose and don't mistakenly delete them.

Where Fonts Reside

Mac OS X stores fonts in several locations, which can be confusing. Here are the fonts locations and what is stored (or should be stored) in each:

- **/Library/Fonts:** This folder contains the fonts that come preinstalled with Mac OS X, as well as fonts installed by a user with administrator privileges for use by all users, whether through Apple's Font Book application (covered later in this chapter) or simply copied to that folder. The fonts installed here are available to all users.

- **/System/Library/Fonts:** This folder contains the essential fonts needed by Mac OS X. You should never add or delete fonts in this folder. The fonts here are available to all users.

- **/*username*/Library/Fonts:** This folder contains fonts available to just that user, typically installed by a user *with or without* administrator privileges.

- **/Network/Library/Fonts:** If you're running Mac OS X over a network, this folder contains the fonts that the network administrator has installed for all network users to have access to.

The simplest way to install fonts is to copy or move the files to the appropriate font folder. The safest way is to use the Font Book application that comes with Mac OS X, so you avoid the possibility of placing them in the wrong location or of deleting necessary files in those folders while you're there.

Managing Fonts in Font Book

To help you manage the fonts on your Mac, Apple provides the Font Book application. Why would you manage fonts? The key reason is that if you have lots of fonts, having them all loaded in memory can slow down your Mac's performance. Another reason is that if you have lots of fonts, you can be overwhelmed with font choices in your word-processing and page-layout software's font lists.

But Font Book also helps you deal with duplicate font files (which can confuse Mac OS X and applications) and corrupted font files (which can cause application and system crashes). Figure 29.2 shows Font Book, with a font highlighted that has a duplicate. Note how Font Book indicates problem fonts with a yellow triangle icon, as well as shows a detailed warning below its font preview window. (See the section on management options for fonts later in this chapter to learn how to deal with issues such as duplicate fonts.)

New Feature

Mac OS X Lion's Font Book removes the Action icon pop-up menu (the gear icon). Use the menu bar or contextual menu instead to access the controls that were offered via the Action icon pop-up menu in previous versions. ■

Automatic font monitoring

Font Book tracks the state of your fonts and can take action when fonts are added or deleted if you tell it to in its Preferences dialog box (choose Font Book⇨Preferences or press ⌘+, [comma]). Note that Font Book tracks this status even when it's not running.

The Font Book application, with a duplicate font highlighted

You have these options:

- **Default Install Location:** This pop-up menu determines which Fonts folder to add new fonts to. The options are User, which places them in /*username*/Library/ Fonts and makes then available only to the current user, and Computer, which places them in /Library/Fonts and makes them available to all users. Note that you must have administrator privileges (see Chapter 27) to choose Computer.

- **Resolve Duplicates by Moving Files to the Trash:** If selected, Font Book automatically puts duplicate font files in the Trash when you tell it to resolve duplicate fonts, as explained later in this chapter. If this option is deselected (the default), Font Book asks you what to do with the duplicate files.

- **Automatic Font Activation:** This option, which is selected by default, tells Font Book to automatically enable a font if you open a document that uses that font, even if you didn't previously enable it in Font Book. (But you must have installed the font via Font Book for it to be able to auto-activate it.) The Ask Me Before Activation suboption, which is not selected by default, tells Font Book to ask you whether to activate a disabled font when an application needs it.

- **Alert Me If System Fonts Change:** If selected (the default), Mac OS X alerts you when any of the system fonts—the master fonts stored in /System/Library/Fonts—are changed, meaning added, deleted, or replaced. You really should leave the system fonts alone to ensure proper display and operation of Mac OS X, so it's best to leave this option selected.

New Feature

In the Font Book Preferences dialog box, Mac OS X Lion has removed two controls (Validate Fonts Before Installing and Ask Me Before Activating), and added one controls (Resolve Duplicates by Moving Files to the Trash). Note that fonts are now validated automatically when added. ■

Adding fonts

As is typical in Font Book, there are several ways to add fonts:

- Choose File ⇨ Add Fonts.
- Press ⌘+O.
- Drag a font into the Font List (the center column).
- Click the second + icon button under the Font List, at the bottom of the window.
- Right-click or Control+click within the Font List and choose Add Fonts from the contextual menu.

For all the methods other than dragging the font files, navigate to the disk or folder that contains the fonts to be added, select those you want (you can select folders and individual font files), and click Open.

If you enabled font validation in the Preferences dialog box, Font Book checks the font file before adding it and alert you if there are any issues, as Figure 29.3 shows (there, the issue is that the font duplicates one already installed).

Previewing fonts

By default, Font Book shows you the alphabet in a pane on the right for whatever font is selected. You can change the size of this preview by selecting a font size from the Fit menu or using the slider at the far right.

To see all characters in the font, choose Preview ⇨ Repertoire or press ⌘+2. To see the alphabet and numerals, choose Preview ⇨ Sample or press ⌘+1. To see your custom text for the preview, choose Preview ⇨ Custom or press ⌘+3 and then type in the preview area whatever you want the preview to be.

FIGURE 29.3

The Font Validation dialog box that appears when Font Book detects a problem with a font being installed

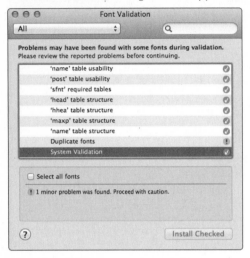

You can disable this preview window by choosing Preview ➪ Hide Preview or pressing Option+⌘+I. Re-enable it by choosing Preview ➪ Show Preview or pressing Option+⌘+I. And you can switch between that preview and the technical font details by choosing Preview ➪ Show/Hide Font Info or pressing ⌘+I. This information includes font format, languages supported, location on your Mac, and font file version.

Tip

If you right-click or Control+click a font in the Font List and choose Preview Font from the contextual menu, a separate preview window appears. It includes a pop-up menu that enables you to switch easily among the various styles available for that font. ■

New Feature

The Font Book application in Mac OS X Lion adds four icon buttons at the upper left of the dialog box, as shown in Figure 29.2. These icon buttons change the preview window, providing the same controls available in the Preview menu. From left to right, they are Sample, Repertoire, Custom, and Font Info. ■

Working with font collections

Font Book categorizes fonts several ways. In its leftmost column (labeled Collections), it displays groups of fonts. By default, Font Book displays several collections:

- **All Fonts:** This collection, if selected, displays all fonts available on the Mac in the Font list to its right.

- **Computer:** This group shows all fonts displayed in the `/Library/Fonts` and `/System/Library/Fonts` folders. Note this collection displays only if you have fonts installed in the current user's Fonts folder, so you can see which fonts are available to all users versus those available only to the current user.

- **User:** This collection displays all fonts installed in the current user's `Library/Fonts` folder. Note this collection displays only if you have fonts installed in the current user's Fonts folder.

- **English:** This collection displays all Roman-based fonts. (This option's name changes to your default language if you installed Mac OS X using a different default language.)

- **PDF:** This collection shows the basic fonts that PDF files need to have available: Courier, Helvetica, Times, Symbol, and Zapf Dingbats.

- **Standards:** This collection shows the fonts in your various Fonts folders. Note that this collection displays only if you've added fonts to Mac OS X.

New Feature

The Standards collection is new to Mac OS X Lion. If you choose File ➪ Restore Standard Fonts, Font Book removes all fonts from these folders that did not come with Mac OS X, placing them in a new folder named Fonts (Removed) in Library folder. This is a great tool to clean up Fonts folders that over time have become full of rarely used fonts; you can then add back those you actually use. ■

- **Fixed Width:** This collection shows all default fonts whose characters are equally wide, such as typewriter and old-style computer terminal fonts: Andale Mono, Courier, Courier New, and Monaco.

- **Fun:** This collection shows the default fonts that Apple characterizes as whimsical: American Typewriter, Herculanum, Marker Felt, Papyrus, and Zapfino.

- **Modern:** This collection shows the default fonts that Apple characterizes as modern-looking, meaning simple and clean in appearance: Futura, Gill Sans, Helvetica Neue, and Optima.

- **Traditional:** This collection shows the default fonts that Apple characterizes as traditional looking, meaning formal and old-fashioned: Baskerville, Big Caslon, Cochin, Copperplate, and Didot.

- **Web:** This collection shows the default fonts that are commonly used in web pages: Andale Mono, Arial, Arial Black, Brush Script MT, Comic Sans MS, Georgia, Impact, Monaco, Times New Roman, Trebuchet MS, Verdana, and Webdings.

- **Windows Office Compatible:** This collection shows the fonts installed with Microsoft Office. Note that this collection appears only if you have installed Office and its fonts.

A collection is more than a font grouping in Font Book. Other software—such as TextEdit and Apple's Pages—can display these collections in their font lists, making it easy for users to choose from a subset of fonts organized on the basis of visual style or project standards. In both TextEdit and Pages, choose Format ⇨ Fonts ⇨ Show Fonts, as Figure 29.4 shows, to display the *font panel*.

Tip

Users of collections-savvy applications such as TextEdit and Pages can add their own fonts to the font panel's Favorites collection by choosing Add to Favorites from the Action icon pop-up menu (the gear icon), as well as add their own collections by clicking the + icon button. ∎

In Font Book, you can create your own font collections in any of several ways: Choose File ⇨ New Collection, press ⌘+N, right-click or Control+click in the Collections list and choose New Collection, or click the + icon button under the Collections list. Now drag fonts from the Fonts list into the collection or library. You also could have selected the fonts first in the Fonts list and then created the new collection to add those fonts to it.

Another type of font grouping you can create is called a *library*. Its main difference from a collection is that it is not visible to programs such as TextEdit and Pages, so it's really meant for font management only within Font Book. To create a library, choose File ⇨ New Library, press Option+⌘+N, or right-click or Control+click in the Collections list and choose New Library.

FIGURE 29.4

Font collections defined in Font Book are available in some applications, such as Pages (shown here) and TextEdit.

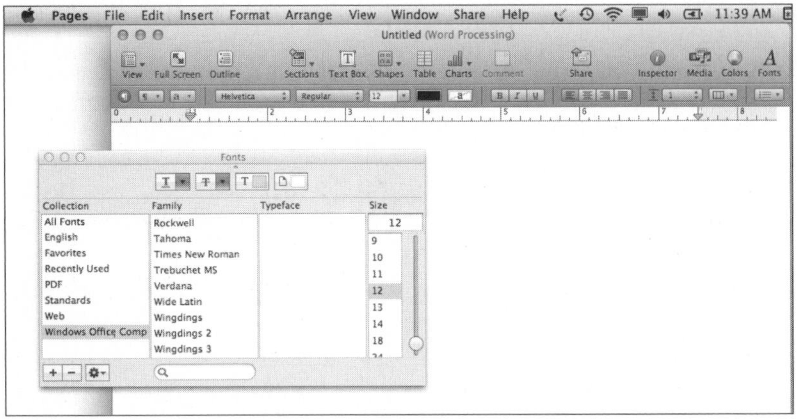

Managing fonts with other software

Although Mac OS X ships with Font Book for font management, other options available that do the same thing are available. But why even bother?

The most common reason is if you're working in a workgroup, where the fonts are centrally managed. Font Book doesn't support that multiuser scenario, whereas three other products do: Extensis's Universal Type Server (`www.extensis.com`), Inside Software's FontAgent Pro TeamServer (`www.insider software.com`), and Linotype's FontExplorerX Server (`www.fontexplorerx.com`).

You also might consider these vendors' font management tools for individuals—Extensis's Suitcase Fusion, Inside Software's FontAgent Pro, and Linotype's FontExplorerX Pro—to get a little more oomph in your Mac's font management. For example, they not only auto-activate fonts as needed, but also auto-deactivate them when you close an Adobe Creative Suite or QuarkXPress document that uses them (assuming no other open documents also use the temporarily enabled fonts). And they tend to offer more font preview options as well as font-repair capabilities.

Note
If you select your new collection or library, you'll see in the Fonts list only the fonts within it. So select a different collection or library, such as All, to see available fonts in the Fonts list and drag the desired ones into the new collection or library. ■

So what can you do with collections and libraries within Font Book? Turn on or off entire sets of fonts, controlling their availability to Mac OS X and to applications; validate fonts; and remove the files from Font Book and Mac OS X.

Managing fonts

There are several controls available via menus for managing fonts. Here are the management options available for any fonts or collections that are selected (remember that you can select multiple items by ⌘+clicking them):

- Choose Edit ➪ Disable "*fontname*" or press Shift+⌘+D to turn off the selected fonts or Edit ➪ Enable "*fontname*" to turn on the selected fonts. (This option is also available in the contextual menu.)

- Choose Edit ➪ Disable "*collectionname*" or press Shift+⌘+E to turn off a select collection's fonts or Edit ➪ Enable "*collectionname*" to turn on its fonts.

- Choose File ➪ Remove "*fontname*" Family to remove the selected font files from both Font Book and Mac OS X (the font files are placed into the Trash). (This option is also available in the contextual menu.)

- Choose File ➪ Export Fonts to copy the selected collection, library, fonts, or styles to a folder of your choice on the Mac.

- Choose File ➪ Print or press ⌘+P to print the selected collection, library, fonts, or styles so you have an easy reference.

- Choose File ➪ Show in Finder or press ⌘+R to open the folder that contains the selected file. (This option is also available in the contextual menu. But it is not available for collections or libraries through the File menu or the contextual menu.)

Tip

Another way to enable or disable fonts is to select the collection, library, fonts, or styles and then click the third icon at the bottom of the dialog box. If it displays as a selected check box, deselecting it turns off the grouping's fonts. If it displays as an empty check box, selecting it turns on the selected styles, fonts, collection, or library. ■

There are also general management options available to handle all fonts, not just those you have selected:

- Choose Edit ➪ Look for Duplicates or press ⌘+L to quickly find and select all duplicated fonts on your Mac. If Font Book finds any duplicates, a settings sheet appears with three buttons: Resolve Manually, Resolve Automatically, and Cancel. If you click Resolve Manually, the settings sheet show in Figure 29.5 appears. It shows the duplicate fonts. Select a font from the bottom of the settings sheet (the selected font has a gray background). To see where its font file is located, click Reveal in Finder. To use the selected font and deactivate the other copy, click Resolve This Duplicate. If the Resolve Duplicates by Moving Duplicate Font Files to the Trash option is selected, the deactivated font's file is also deleted. Use the Back and Forward icon buttons (the left- and right-facing triangle icons) to move among the detected duplicates. When you resolve the last duplicate (or click Cancel to leave the duplicates alone), the settings sheet closes.

- Choose Edit ➪ Special Characters or press Option+⌘+T to open the Character Viewer covered later in this chapter.

- Choose File ➪ Validate Fonts to see if the font files are corrupt. (This option is also available in the contextual menu.) When the Font Validation dialog box is open, you can choose File ➪ Save Report or press ⌘+S to save the validation's findings as a file. You also can choose File ➪ Print or press ⌘+P to print the findings. Figure 29.3 earlier in this chapter shows the dialog box that appears if errors are found.

- Choose File ➪ Validate File to check for corruption in a font file not installed in Font Book.

New Feature

Font Book in Mac OS X Lion changes how you resolve duplicate fonts. Gone is the Edit ➪ Resolve Duplicates menu option. Instead, you use the new settings sheet that appears after you choose Edit ➪ Look for Duplicates or press ⌘+L. ■

FIGURE 29.5

The settings sheet where you resolve duplicate fonts

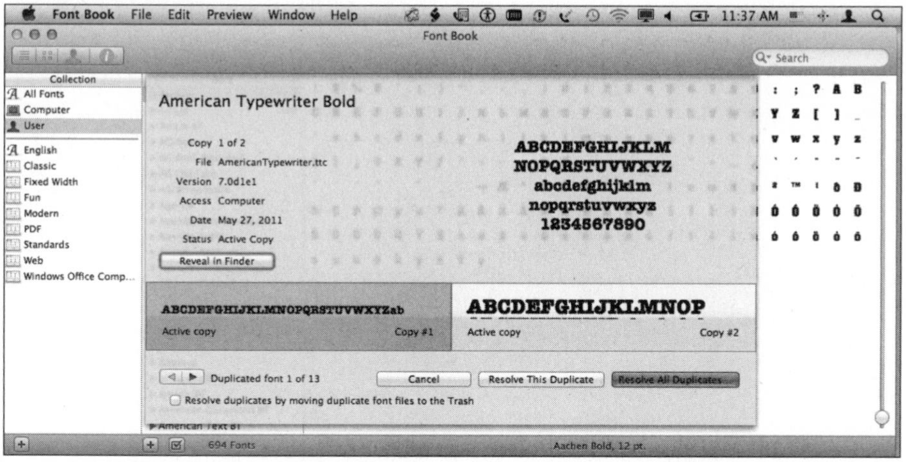

Finding fonts

You can search for fonts several ways in Font Book: Type a font name in the search box at the upper right of the Font Book application window, choose Edit⇨Find⇨Font Search, or press Option+⌘+F. (Those last two options simply highlight the search box so you can begin typing immediately.) Note that the search looks at whatever fonts are displayed in the Fonts list, so be sure to select All Fonts or other collection or library that is likely to contain your sought-after font.

Accessing Special Characters

With your fonts installed and enabled, they're ready for use in your applications. Applications designed to work with fonts will have controls that let you apply fonts to text, typically through the Edit menu, but perhaps also elsewhere, such as in style sheets. What may be less obvious is how to access the special characters available in many fonts, whether foreign-language characters or special symbols. After all, they don't show up on your keyboard.

Using keyboard shortcuts

Symbols are commonly used in all sorts of documents, from legal symbols to scientific ones. That's why most fonts have a selection of popular symbols built in that you can access via keyboard shortcuts. Table 29.1 shows the shortcuts for common symbols for Macintosh fonts, and Table 29.2 shows the shortcuts for foreign characters such as accented letters.

TABLE 29.1

Shortcuts for Common Symbols

Character	Mac OS X Shortcut	Character	Mac OS X Shortcut
Legal		**Mathematics**	
Copyright (©)	Option+G	Virgule (/ for building fractions)	Option+Shift+1
Registered trademark (®)	Option+R	Infinity (∞)	Option+5
Trademark (™)	Option+2	Division (÷)	Option+/
Paragraph (¶)	Option+7	Root (√)	Option+V
Section (§)	Option+6	Greater than or equal to (≥)	Option+>
Dagger (†)	Option+T	Less than or equal to (≤)	Option+<
Double dagger (‡)	Option+Shift+T	Inequality (≠)	Option+=
Currency		Rough equivalence (≈)	Option+X
Cent (¢)	Option+4	Plus or minus (±)	Option+Shift+=
Euro (€)	Option+Shift+2	Logical not (¬)	Option+L
Pound sterling (£)	Option+3	Per mil (‰)	Option+Shift+R
Yen (¥)	Option+Y	Degree (°)	Option+Shift+8
Punctuation		Function (ƒ)	Option+F
Bullet (•)	Option+8	Integral (∫)	Option+B
Ellipsis (…)	Option+; (semicolon)	Variation (∂)	Option+D
Em dash (—)	Option+Shift+– (hyphen)	Greek beta (ß)	Option+S
En dash (–)	Option+– (hyphen)	Greek mu (µ)	Option+M
Open double quote (")	Option+[	Greek Pi (Π)	Option+Shift+P
Closed double quote (")	Option+Shift+[	Greek pi (π)	Option+P
Open single quote (')	Option+]	Greek Sigma (Σ)	Option+W
Closed single quote or apostrophe (')	Option+Shift+]	Greek Omega (Ω)	Option+Z
Keyboard double quote (")	Control+'	**Miscellaneous**	
Keyboard single quote (')	Control+Shift+'	Apple logo ()	Option+Shift+K
		Open diamond (◊)	Option+Shift+V

TABLE 29.2

Shortcuts for Western European Accents and Foreign Characters

Character	Mac OS X Shortcut	Character	Mac OS X Shortcut
acute (´)*	Option+E *letter*	Í	Option+E I
breve (˘)	Option+B *letter***	í	Option+E i
cedilla (¸)*	***; see Ç and ç	Ì	Option+` I
circumflex (ˆ)*	Option+I *letter*, Option+6 *letter***	ì	Option+` i
double acute (˝)	Option+J *letter***	Ï	Option+U I
double grave (‶)	Shift+Option+Y *letter***	ï	Option+U i
grave (`)*	Option+` *letter*	Î	Option+I I
hacek (ˇ)	Option+V *letter***	î	Option+I i
macron (¯)	Option+A *letter***	Ñ	Option+N N
ogonek (˛)	Option+M *letter***	ñ	Option+N n
ring (°)	Option+K *letter***	Ó	Option+E O
strikethrough bar (ł, ɨ)	Option+L *letter***	ó	Option+E o
subscript dot (.)	Option+X *letter***	Ò	Option+` O
superscript dot (˙)	Option+W *letter***	ò	Option+` o
tilde (˜)*	Option+N *letter*	Ö	Option+U O
trema (¨)*	Option+U *letter*	ö	Option+U o
umlaut (¨)*	Option+U *letter*	Õ	Option+N O
Á	Option+E A	õ	Option+N o
á	Option+E a	Ô	Option+I O
À	Option+` A	ô	Option+I o
à	Option+` a	Ø	Option+Shift+O
Ä	Option+U A	ø	Option+O
ä	Option+U a	Œ	Option+Shift+Q
Ã	Option+N A	œ	Option+Q
ã	Option+N a	ß	Option+S
Â	Option+I A	∫	Option+B
â	Option+I a	Ú	Option+E U
Å	Option+Shift+A	ú	Option+E u
å	Option+A	Ù	Option+` U
Æ	Option+Shift+'	ù	Option+` u
æ	Option+'	Ü	Option+U U

continued

TABLE 29.2 *(continued)*

Character	Mac OS X Shortcut	Character	Mac OS X Shortcut
Ç	Option+Shift+C	ü	Option+U u
ç	Option+C	Û	Option+I U
É	Option+E E	û	Option+I u
é	Option+E e	Ÿ	Option+U Y
È	Option+` E	ÿ	Option+U y
è	Option+` e	Spanish open exclamation (¡)	Option+1
Ë	Option+U E	Spanish open question (¿)	Option+Shift+/
ë	Option+U e	French open double quote («)	Option+\
Ê	Option+I E	French close double quote (»)	Option+Shift+\
ê	Option+I e		

* Enter the shortcut for the accent and then type the letter to be accented. For example, to get é, type Option+E and then the letter *e*. (Apple calls these accent-generating key combinations *dead keys*.)

** The U.S. extended keyboard must be enabled for these accents to be available; do so in the Input Sources pane of the Language & Text system preference, as Chapter 28 explains.

*** To use the cedilla for characters other than ç and Ç, a language keyboard must be selected that supports the character, such as Turkish; do so in the Input Sources pane of the Language & Text system preference, as Chapter 28 explains.

Using other tools

Some applications come with tools to insert special characters not visible on the keyboard or accessible via keyboard shortcuts. For example, in Adobe InDesign, choose Type ⇨ Glyphs or press Option+Shift+F11. In Microsoft Word, choose Insert ⇨ Symbol. In Pages and in TextEdit, choose Edit ⇨ Special Characters.

But no matter which applications you use, you can always rely on the two built-in tools in Mac OS X: the Keyboard Viewer and Character Viewer. The Keyboard Viewer gives you a visual quick reference to keyboard shortcuts, while the Character Viewer enables you to access any character available on your Mac, even those that have no keyboard shortcuts.

Both are available under the Input Sources icon menu in the menu bar. Note that you might need to turn on the Input Source icon menu by choosing ⇨ System Preferences, and then going to the Input Sources pane of the Language & Text system preference. Select the Show Input Menu in Menu Bar option. Also be sure the On check box is selected for the Keyboard &

Character Viewer at the top of the Name list so the Keyboard Viewer and Character Viewer are available in the Input Sources icon menu. Note that if you select Keyboard & Character Viewer, the Show Input Menu in Menu Bar option is automatically selected. (Chapter 21 explains the Language & Text system preference in more detail.)

Touch-based Chinese handwriting

Mac OS X has a feature for users wanting to write the Chinese strokes called *trackpad handwriting*. This makes innovative use of the gesture-savvy touchpad found on newer MacBooks and the Apple Magic Trackpad to input the complex array of strokes used in Chinese logographs (more commonly called *ideograms* or *characters*). (Chapter 2 covers gestures in detail.)

To use trackpad handwriting, go to the Input Sources pane of the Language & Text system preference. In the list of input sources at left, select one or both of the Chinese languages: Simplified Chinese (used in mainland China) and Traditional Chinese (used in Taiwan). Each has several sub-options for different stroke styles, including the Trackpad Handwriting option, which if selected enables stroke entry on a gesture-savvy touchpad. (If you don't see the Trackpad Handwriting option, your Mac's touchpad does not support this feature.) The Show/Hide Trackpad Handwriting keyboard shortcut description also appears in the Input Source Shortcuts section at right.

When working in the Finder or other applications, press Control+Shift+spacebar to display the Trackpad Handwriting window; any characters you input are entered at the current text cursor location. The interface appears on the lower half of the desktop and in front of all other windows (including the active window), as the figure shows. You can type text in documents, filenames, or any other part of Mac OS X that would normally enter letters typed on the keyboard.

In the Trackpad Handwriting window, there are virtual buttons on the left and right side of the trackpad, and the touchpad's central area is where you draw character strokes using a single finger. As you draw, white strokes appear on-screen in the Trackpad Handwriting interface to match your movements. To the right of those strokes appear three possible ideogram matches, with the character at the top being the one that Mac OS X believes to be the closest match. To select a character, press the part of the touchpad that corresponds to its location on the Trackpad Handwriting window. On the left side of the Trackpad Handwriting window are three virtual buttons; from top to bottom, they are Delete, Space, and Return.

Note that you can still use the keyboard to type characters at the same time as using the Trackpad Handwriting window. But while the Trackpad Handwriting window is on-screen you cannot control the pointer. You toggle between using the Trackpad Handwriting window and using the pointer by pressing Control+Shift+spacebar.

After you open the Keyboard Viewer, just hold the modifier keys such as Option and ⌘ to see what characters are available for each key, as Figure 29.6 shows. Now just press the key that gets you the special character you want. Note that accent characters are highlighted in gold; if you type a letter after entering that accent, you get an accented letter, as Tables 29.1 and 29.2 explain.

FIGURE 29.6

Mac OS X's Keyboard Viewer

New Feature

Mac OS X Lion has greatly simplified the Character Viewer. ■

If you open the Character Viewer, shown in Figure 29.7, you get a window that has a series of icon buttons on the left side. Click a button to see the type of characters it represents, such as accented Roman or mathematical. You can select which types of characters are available, and thus what icons display, by choosing Customize List from the Action icon pop-up menu (the gear icon). Select the types of characters you want to be available in the Character Viewer and click Done to make the changes.

Double-click a character to insert it in your current document or text field. Hover the pointer over a character until the *i* icon appears; click it to open the details sheet for that character, as Figure 29.7 shows. Click Add to Favorites to add the character to your favorites list (Favorites is one of the icon buttons in the left side of the Character Viewer). Click the Close box to close the details sheet.

Tip

You also can use a utility like Ergonis's PopChar X utility (€30, www.ergonis.com) to find and insert special characters. ■

FIGURE 29.7

FIGURE 29.7

The Character Viewer (left) and the details sheet for a specific character (right)

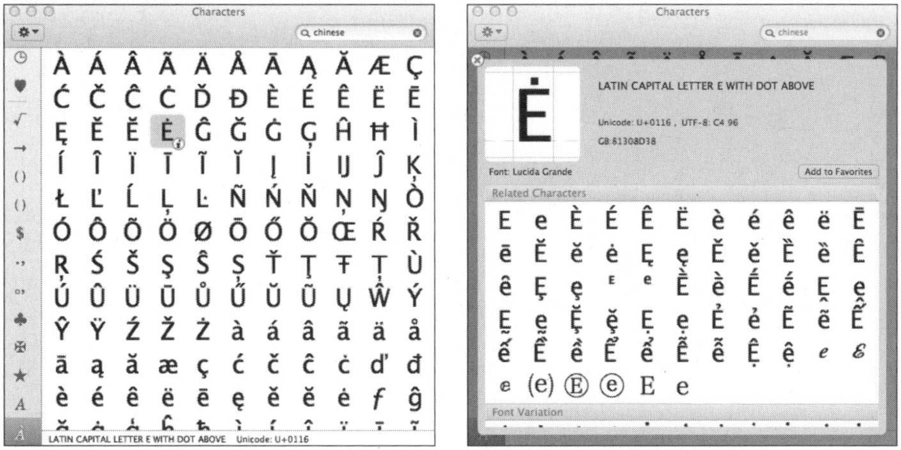

Summary

Mac OS X supports five font file formats: PostScript Type 1, PostScript Multiple Master, TrueType, OpenType, and dfont. TrueType and OpenType are the modern typographic standards, while the two PostScript formats are being phased out. The dfont format is internal to Mac OS X for use in menus and other user interface elements, so you cannot buy fonts in that format.

Fonts can be stored in any of several locations, with /*username*/Library/Fonts used for fonts available only to a specific user, /Library/Fonts for fonts available for all users, and /System/Library/Fonts for system-required fonts.

The Font Book application enables you to both install and manage fonts, such as detecting and resolving duplicate fonts, detecting corrupt font files, and creating groups of fonts for easy activation and deactivation. Some groups, called *collections*, are available to other applications such as TextEdit and iWork Pages to give users easily navigated font sets. Font Book also enables you to preview fonts, plus it can auto-activate fonts that aren't enabled but needed by a document.

You can buy font managers to use instead of Font Book, which makes sense if you are managing fonts across a workgroup of users or if you need some of their specialized capabilities such as font repair.

To use the special characters, called *glyphs*, in fonts, you can use several methods, including keyboard shortcuts, the Keyboard Viewer and Character Viewer utilities that come with Mac OS X, or a separately purchased utility such as Ergonis's PopChar X. The support for gesture-based Chinese handwriting via touchpads provides an additional input method for Chinese text.

CHAPTER

Printing, Faxing, and Scanning

I n an era of electronic documents, there's still a place for printed ones. When it's time to print a document, or send someone a fax copy, you need to ensure that your Mac is properly set up for the printers and fax modem you have.

Mac OS X manages printing, faxing, and scanning from the Print & Scan system preference, as described in Chapter 28. Any devices listed in the system preference are available for applications that print, fax, or scan.

You can have multiple printers, faxes, and scanners configured for your Mac. Sometimes you have multiple devices connected to your Mac, sometimes you use different printers, faxes, and/or scanners at different locations and want your Mac to be set up for them, and sometimes both situations apply. Your Mac will recognize a printer, fax, or scanner for which it's configured when that device becomes available, but it must be connected directly or via the network to be able to set it up in the first place.

IN THIS CHAPTER

Adding printers, scanners, and fax modems to your Mac

Configuring printers, fax modems, and scanners

Configuring settings in applications' Print dialog boxes

Setting print queue options for specific print jobs

Sending and receiving faxes

Using scanners

New Feature

The Print & Scan system preference had been called Print & Fax in previous versions of Mac OS X. ■

Setting Up Printers, Fax Modems, and Scanners

You can connect your printer, fax modem, and scanner to your Mac in any of several ways, depending on your device's capabilities. These include using USB, FireWire, wired network (Ethernet), wireless network (Wi-Fi), and Bluetooth wireless connections. If your device uses any of the wireless or Ethernet settings, refer to its manual to see how to set it up so your Mac can see it, such as specifying its IP address if it's an Ethernet or Wi-Fi device or making it discoverable if it's a Bluetooth device. Devices that connect directly to the Mac via a USB or FireWire cable usually need no special setup on the printer itself.

Your printer, fax modem, or scanner may have come with an installation CD or instructions for downloading its installation software from the web. In such cases, you typically need to run this software before the device is connected to copy the drivers the Mac needs to properly work it. But in some cases, you need to run this software *after* the device is connected. And in other cases, Mac OS X already has the drivers needed to use the device, so there's no need to run a setup program. Again, check your device's setup instructions.

Note

Mac OS X installs drivers for any printers, fax modems, and scanners used previously on that Mac (if you are upgrading from a previous version) or that it detects (if you are installing Mac OS X for the first time). That saves hard disk space. If you later add a printer and have an Internet connection, Mac OS X checks whether Apple has the appropriate drivers and downloads them for you over the Internet if it does. ∎

Just to confuse matters further, the setup programs of some printers, fax modems, and scanners handle the entire setup job for you, so when done you see the printer, fax modem, or scanner in the Print & Scan system preference. Others install just the driver and require you to complete the setup yourself, as outlined next.

Adding devices

After you know when (or even whether) to install device-specific software, you're ready to go. Connect your printer, fax modem, or scanner, open the Print & Scan system preference, and click the + icon pop-up menu at the bottom left of the window.

New Feature

In Mac OS X Lion, the + icon pop-up menu in the Print & Scan system preference replaces the + icon button in previous versions' Print & Fax system preference. ∎

Any network or Bluetooth devices—printers, fax modems, and scanners—that are available should display in the pop-up menu, as shown in Figure 30.1. To install a device connected via a USB or other cable directly to your Mac, choose Add Other Printer or Scanner to open the Add Printer dialog box, shown in Figure 30.2. You also use this dialog box to add network or Bluetooth devices that do not appear in the + icon pop-up menu.

Note

A locally attached fax device won't appear unless it is connected to a phone line. Likewise, a scanner must be powered on for it to appear in the Add Printer dialog box. ∎

Note

Mac OS X doesn't see the scanners and fax modems in multifunction printers as scanners and fax modems—it just sees the printer capabilities in such devices. Thus, you can't set Mac OS X to fax or scan from such devices via the Print & Scan system preference. But some devices may come with drivers, such as the Twain drivers for scanners, that let applications directly connect to the fax mode or scanner. Check with the multifunction device's manufacturer to see what support it offers for use with Mac applications. ∎

FIGURE 30.1

The Print & Scan system preference detect network printers, scanners, and fax modems to make them accessible to your Mac when you click the + icon pop-up menu.

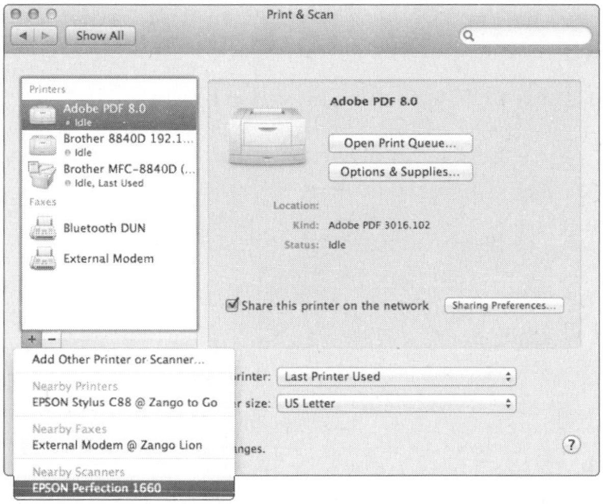

In the Default pane of the Add Printer dialog box, detected local and network printers and scanners appear. Fax modems appear in the separate Fax pane, but the controls are the same as for printers and scanners. Select a device and then use the appropriate options in the pane:

- You typically can edit its Name and Location information; the Location field is typically used in an office to say in what part of the building the printer is located.

- If your Mac has the correct driver, it displays in the Print Using pop-up menu. If you want to override that choice, or if no driver appears, choose Select Printer Software to choose a driver already installed on your Mac. A list then appears for you to choose from. If your Mac doesn't have the correct driver, choose Other to select it from a disk or folder on or attached to your Mac.

Note

The pop-up menu is Print Using and the menu option is Select Printer Software even when you have selected a scanner or fax modem. ∎

- Click Add when done.

Your printer, fax modem, or scanner is now ready.

When adding a locally attached printer, scanner, or fax modem, the Add Printer dialog box appears listing detected devices. At left is the Default pane for adding most printers and scanners, and at right is the IP pane for adding some network devices.

In some cases, network devices do not display in the + icon pop-up menu. But you can add them in the Add Printer dialog box, using either the IP pane or the Windows pane.

Use the IP pane for printers attached via an Ethernet or Wi-Fi network. Most such printers use the Internet Printing Protocol, so choose that from the Protocol pop-up menu. Exceptions include many Hewlett-Packard printers, which instead use HP JetDirect. The third protocol option, Line Printer Daemon, is no longer common. No matter what the protocol is, type the printer's IP address, as shown in Figure 30.2. Mac OS X will try to find the correct driver for it; change the setting in the Print Using pop-up menu if it can't find the right driver or chooses the wrong one. Change the Queue field only if your printer's documentation or network administrator tells you what the Queue information should be.

Use the Windows pane for printers attached via a local Windows share network if you are using one.

In either case, you can change the Name and Location fields to your liking. Click Add when done.

To delete a printer, scanner, or fax modem you no longer use, select it in the Print & Scan system preference, then click the – icon button below the device list.

Note

You can share a printer, scanner, or fax modem with other users on the network by enabling File Sharing (for printers and fax modems) or Scanner Sharing (for scanners) in the Sharing system preference, as Chapter 24 explains. A printer, scanner, or fax modem must not be powered down or asleep if you want it available to be shared. Your Mac also must be on and connected to the network for others to see the devices connected to it, though it's fine if your Mac is asleep. ■

Tip

A very easy way to print or fax a document is to drag the document onto the device's icon. You can place the device icon onto the desktop, in a Finder window, or on the Dock by dragging its icon from the Print & Scan system preference. To add the device icon to the Dock, you also can right-click or Control+click the icon when you are printing, faxing, or scanning and choose Keep in Dock from the contextual menu. Double-clicking the device icon opens its print or fax queue or, for a scanner, opens the scanner window. ■

Configuring printers

If you have multiple printers connected, choose which one you want to be the default printer by using the Default Printer pop-up menu. You also can set the default paper size by using the Default Paper Size pop-up menu. (Figure 30.1 earlier in this chapter shows the Print & Scan system preference options when a printer is selected.)

To make a printer available for use by other users on your local network, select it from the printer list and then select the Share This Printer with Other Users on This Network option. (You typically share local printers, such as those connected via a USB cable to one Mac; network printers are already shared with everyone on the network.) Note that your Mac must have Printer Sharing enabled in the Sharing system preference, as explained in Chapter 24. If Printer Sharing is not enabled, you'll see an alert in the Print & Scan system preference; click Sharing Preferences to jump to the Sharing system preference to turn Printer Sharing on, then select which printers to share. You can set separate controls for different users, with two options for each: Can Print and No Access.

Clicking the Options & Supplies button opens a dialog box that enables you to change Name and Location fields (in the General pane), change the printer driver (in the Driver pane), and check on ink or toner and paper supply levels (in the Supply Levels pane). The supply levels display only for printers that can communicate this information to the Mac. The General pane also may show an Open Printer Utility button for those printers that offer a utility to do things like clean their print heads and change the ink saturation.

Tip

Another way to manage your printers is via a web browser, if you have administrator privileges (which means you have an administrator account's username and password, as explained in Chapter 27). Type http://localhost:631/admin as the URL to get the Mac's Unix-based printer management tool. Click Manage Printers to configure your printers; the controls are essentially the same as in the Print & Scan system preference and in the print queue, though here they are all available in one place. ■

If you have multiple printers, such as in an office, you can help distribute the load by pooling them. Pooling treats multiple printers as if they were one printer, and the Mac automatically figures out which one to send a job to based on availability. To create a printer pool, select the printers in the Print & Scan system preference (click the first one, and ⌘+click the others). Now click Create Printer Pool and give that pool a name. If you select that pool's name in the Print dialog box's Printer pop-up menu, the Mac will automatically choose which printer to use.

The Open Print Queue button opens the queue of active print jobs, as described later in this chapter.

Configuring fax modems

Mac OS X offers fewer controls for configuring fax modems than it does for printers. You can't set one as the default if you have multiple fax modems, and you can't pool multiple fax modems.

What you can do, as Figure 30.3 shows, is:

- Click Receive Options to determine whether your fax modem answers incoming calls and under what conditions, as Figure 30.3 shows. In the settings sheet that appears, you can specify how many rings must occur before it answers the phone, whether and where to save received faxes as image files, whether and where to print received faxes, and whether and where to forward received faxes as image attachments via e-mail.

- In the Fax Number field, specify the fax number for the device, so faxes you send have the fax number printed at the top of each page, as is required by law in many countries.

FIGURE 30.3

Left: The settings for a selected fax modem in the Print & Scan system preference. Right: The settings sheet where you set receive options for a fax modem.

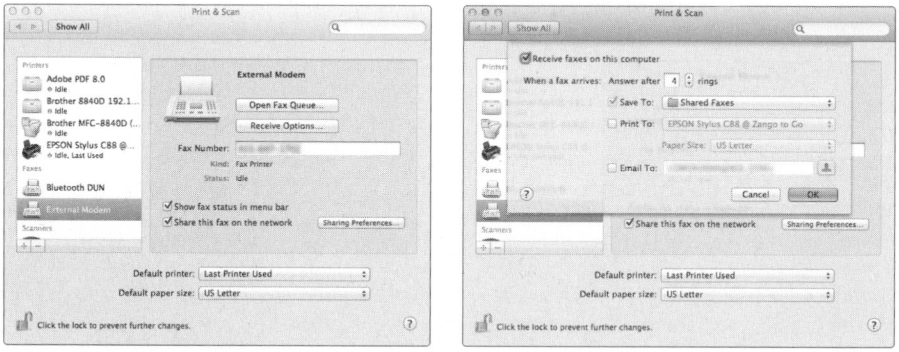

- Select the Fax Status in Menu Bar option to display the Fax Status icon menu in the menu bar, from which you can monitor the status of a fax being sent or received, open fax preferences (the Print & Scan system preference), and open the folder of received faxes.

- Select the Share This Fax on the Network option to let others use the fax modem over the network. If your Sharing system preference doesn't have printer sharing enabled, an alert appears below this option; click Sharing Preferences to configure printer (and this fax modem) sharing.

Click Open Fax Queue to open the queue of active fax jobs, as described later in this chapter.

Configuring scanners

Mac OS X also offers just a few configuration controls for scanners. Those options, shown in Figure 30.4, are:

FIGURE 30.4

The settings for a selected scanner in the Print & Scan system preference

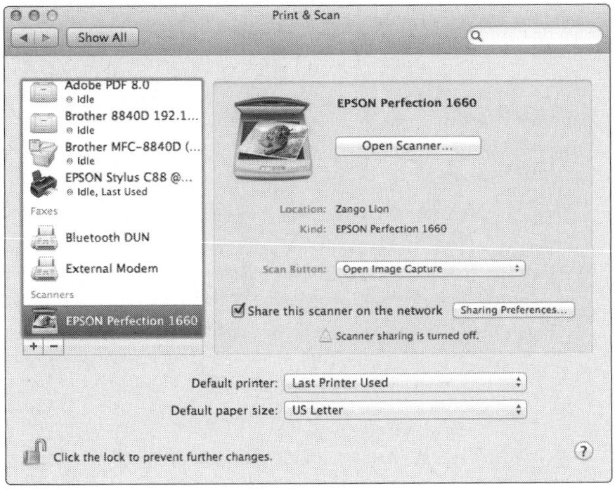

- In the Scan Button pop-up menu, choose what happens when someone presses the Scan or Start button on the scanner. The options are Open Scanner Window, covered later in this chapter; Open Preview, which scans the image and opens it the Preview application; Open Image Capture, which scans the image and opens it in the Image Capture application; Other, which lets you choose an application that the scanned image opens in or that controls the scanner; and No Application, which does nothing.

- Select the Share This Scanner on the Network option to let others use the scanner over the network. If your Sharing system preference doesn't have scanner sharing enabled, an alert appears below this option; click Sharing Preferences to configure scanner sharing.

The Open Scanner button opens controls for scanning an image, as described later in this chapter.

Printing

Using a printer is typically easy once it's set up on your Mac: Choose File ⇨ Print or press ⌘+P from the application you want to print from. Sometimes, the application may have a Print icon button as well in a toolbar. After you select any options for your print job and click Print, the Mac works with the printer behind the scenes so you can get back to work.

Using the Print dialog box

When you print, a Print dialog box, such as that the one shown in Figure 30.5, appears. The basic layout is the same for most applications, though you may see some slight layout and visual differences such as where the print preview displays (or if it does) and how preview pages are navigated.

The standard options include controls over which printer to use, how many pages to print, how many copies of those pages, and whether to print collated and/or two-sided pages. The pop-up menu at lower left lets you "print" the file to a PDF file or to a fax modem (if you have one installed), and sometimes do other actions such as Mail the file, as Figure 30.5 shows.

The Print dialog boxes in many applications can be expanded to show more controls, as shown in Figure 30.6. Apple's applications typically use the Show Detail button to display the expanded Print dialog box. Many other applications have an icon menu button of an upward-pointing triangle that you click to show the expanded Print dialog box.

In these expanded Print dialog boxes (and in some "regular" ones), the unnamed pop-up menu usually in the center right of the dialog box contains more controls, which when selected change the options in the bottom right of the dialog box. The common pop-up menu options are:

- **Layout:** Enables you to print multiple thumbnails (smaller versions of your pages) onto a single sheet of paper, add a border to your printed page, enable two-sided printing, and flip the page output.
- **Paper Handling:** Enables you to choose to print all pages, even pages, or odd pages; print front to back or back to front; and scale the page to fit the paper size.

- **Paper Feed:** Enables you to select which paper tray to use for the printing, including using a different tray for the first page (such as for stationery).

- **Cover Page:** Enables you to print a cover page before or after the document and even fill in a billing code.

- **Print Settings** or **Printer Features:** Enables you to set options specific to the current printer, such as choosing which version of PostScript to use or what image resolution to use.

Note

The unnamed pop-up menu may show more options than listed here. Most are installed by the printer driver to make its specific functionality available. And many applications add their own menu options for any special printing functions they offer. ■

FIGURE 30.5

An application's "regular" Print dialog box (in Pages, in this case)

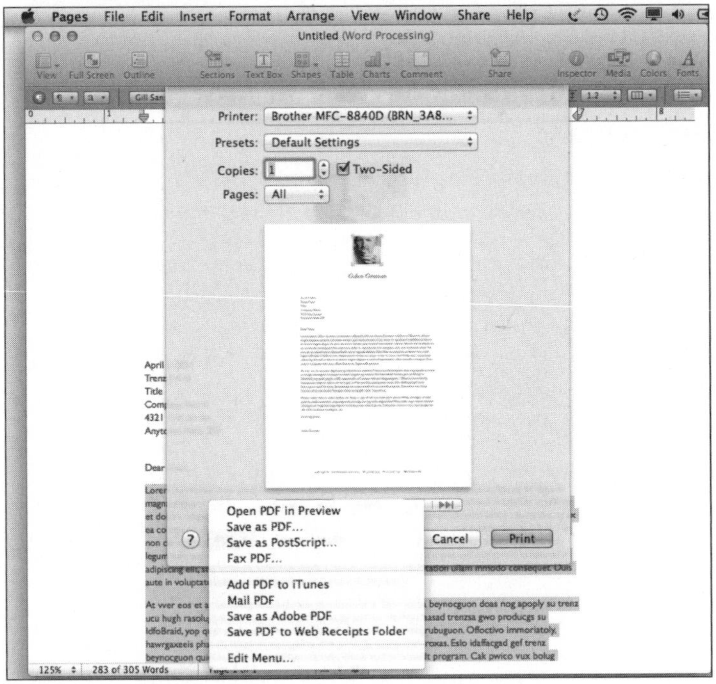

FIGURE 30.6

An application's expanded Print dialog box (in Pages, in this case)

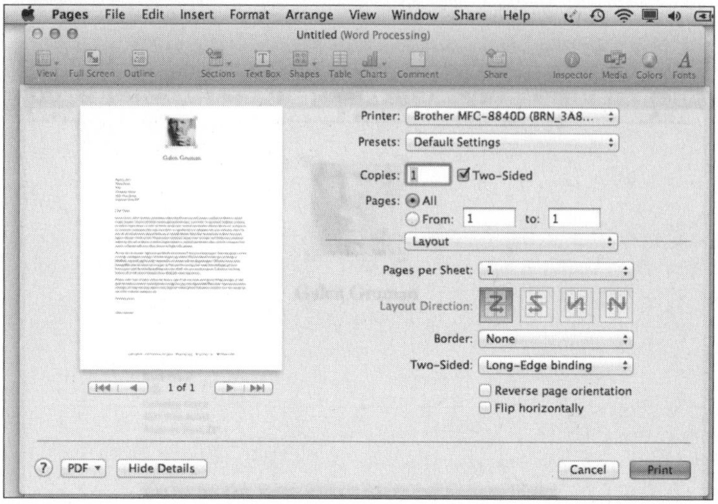

Managing the print queue

After you click Print, the Mac creates the necessary data for the printer, often storing that data on your hard disk until the printer can accept it, in a process called *spooling*.

While the Mac is spooling the print job, you have some control over it, such as pausing the job or canceling it. When you print, the printer's icon appears in the Dock; right-click or Control+click it to see the available options. The key ones are the printer name, Status (which shows the status of the current print job), Pause Printer, and Printer Setup. Choosing Pause Printer suspends printing; the option changes to Resume Printing. Choosing Printer Setup opens the General pane you get when clicking Options & Supplies in the Print & Scan system preference.

Choosing the printer name from the contextual menu—or simply clicking the printer icon in the Dock—opens the print queue shown in Figure 30.7. The print queue shows the status of all print jobs in process or waiting to be sent. You can select any print job listed and click Delete to end its output or Hold to pause it. Other print jobs are unaffected. Click Pause Printer to suspend all print jobs, even if none is currently in process; the button changes to Resume Printer when clicked.

The print queue also has several menu options that are useful. The Printer menu's options include Customize Toolbar (to change what buttons display), Make Default (to make the current printer the default one), Print Test Page, and Network Diagnostics. Some multifunction devices also may show the Open Scanner Utility option. The Jobs menu enables you to hold, delete, and get details on print jobs, which you also can do from the print queue's buttons; but it also has the very handy Show Completed Jobs and Show Everyone's Jobs that give you a complete printing history and a way to see where various print jobs came from, respectively.

Tip

After you print, the printer may stay in the Dock and its print queue remains open. If you don't want the print queue to remain open, right-click or Control+click the icon to get its contextual menu, then choose Auto Quit in that menu. If Auto Quit is checked, the print queue closes any print job that is done. The printer icon also removes itself from the Dock when the print job is complete. To keep the printer icon in the Dock permanently, choose Keep in Dock. ■

FIGURE 30.7

The print queue for a selected printer enables you to manage individual print jobs, as well as the printer itself.

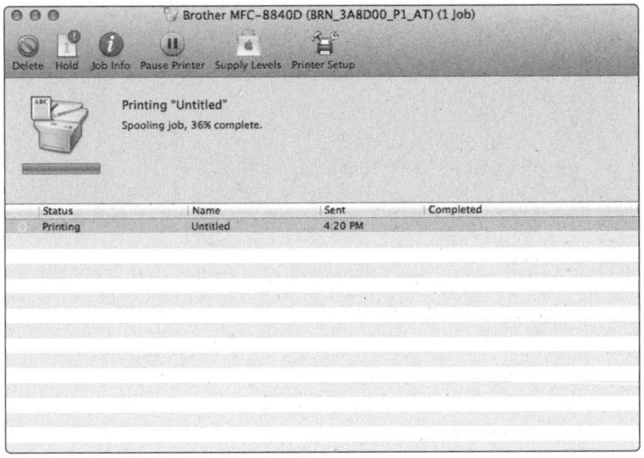

Faxing

With your fax modem set up, using it is easy: From any application that can print, choose File ➪ Print or press ⌘+P to display the Print dialog box. Choose the fax modem from the Printer pop-up menu, as shown in Figure 30.8, and fill in the fax information, such as fax number to send to and the information for the cover page in the bottom right of the Print dialog box. Click Fax when you're ready to send the fax.

Note

As with printers, fax modems appear in the Dock when you fax. You have the same controls with the fax icon as you do with a printer icon, such as viewing the fax queue. ■

FIGURE 30.8

The Print dialog box when you choose to fax a document rather than print it

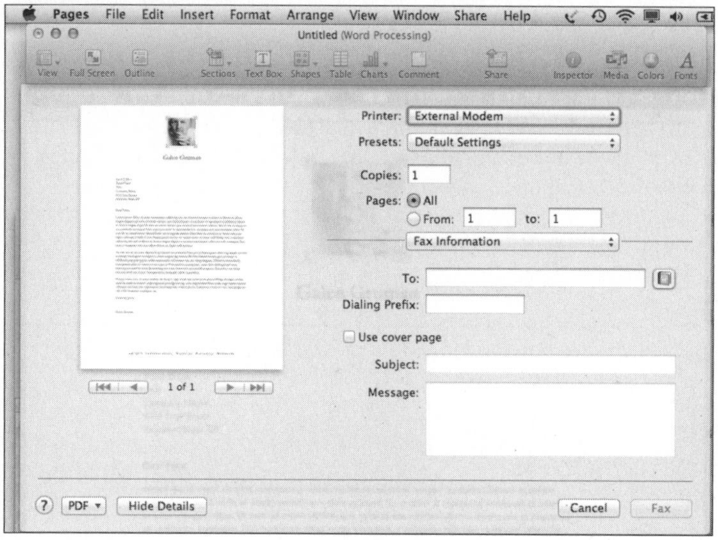

If you set your fax modem to receive faxes, you can open the folder of received faxes by choosing Open Received Faxes Folder in the Fax Status icon pop-up menu in the menu bar, or navigate to /Users/Shared/Faxes in the Finder.

Scanning

You can initiate a scan in several ways once a scanner is set up on your Mac:

- Click Open Scanner from the Print & Scan system preference to open the scan window, as shown in Figure 30.9. Choose the destination for the scan in the Scan To pop-up menu and click Scan to scan the image, or click Show Details to get more controls over the scan, as also shown in Figure 30.9.

- If the Scan Button control is available and set up for the scanner in the Print & Scan system preference, as described earlier in this chapter, press the scanner's Scan or Start button. The selected application will launch on your Mac and show the scanned images. If you assigned the Scan button, the options shown in Figure 30.9 appear. If you chose Preview or Image Capture, those applications open, providing the controls explained in Chapter 14.

- If you added the scanner icon to the Dock, the desktop, or a Finder window, double-click it (single-click in the Dock) to open the scan window shown in Figure 30.9.

Note

The options in the scan window will vary based on the capabilities of the scanner. ■

Applications can often control a scanner directly, so you can initiate a scan without switching to the scan window. For example, in Preview, choose File ⇨ Import from Scanner. In Image Capture, select the scanner from the device list to automatically launch the scan window. (Chapter 14 covers both applications.) Other applications, such as Adobe Photoshop, require a driver to be installed to work directly with scanners.

FIGURE 30.9

The scan window when first opened (left). Click Show Details to see the scanning controls and preview (right).

Summary

Mac OS X lets you connect one or more printers, fax modems (including fax machines), and scanners so you can print, fax, and scan documents. You typically can connect printers, fax modems, and scanners via USB, FireWire, Bluetooth, Ethernet, and Wi-Fi connections, though FireWire-capable devices are uncommon.

Mac OS X has drivers for some devices preinstalled and can download others from the Internet automatically to set them up for you. But you should run the setup utility if one comes with your device (on a disc or from the manufacturer's website).

Note that multifunction printers that have fax and/or scan capabilities require the manufacturer's drivers to be installed for your Mac to access those fax and scan features, even if the Mac has the drivers built in for the printer services. Also note that these devices typically appear only as printers in the Fax & Scan system preference, so you cannot manage them there or create shortcut icons to them as you can normally do with printers, fax modems, and scanners.

The Print & Scan system preference contains the management controls for printers, fax modems, and scanners. It also lets you access the print and fax queues that display the status of current jobs, as well as the scan window for scanners.

To use a printer, open the Print dialog box by choosing File ⇨ Print or pressing ⌘+P. You'll see a variety of configuration options, such as page side, duplexing, and quality level; these options vary from printer model to printer model. For faxing, you also use the Print dialog box, but choose the fax device from the Printer pop-up menu. The Print button then changes to Fax.

When you click Print to start the print job, the instructions that are destined for the printer are first spooled to a temporary file on your Mac then sent on to the printer. This lets you continue working on the document while it is printing. Because the Mac stores these print-job files, you can manage them by opening the print queue via printer icon in the Dock. You see a list of all open print jobs and their status; you can delete, reorder, pause, or resume each job. There's a similar queue for fax jobs.

Using a technique called *pooling*, the Mac can send print jobs to any available printer. The advantages are that jobs are sent first to idle devices, speeding output; the disadvantage (at least for printing) is you don't know which printer's output tray has your document.

When you scan via the scan window, you can choose what application to open the scanned image in, as well as display a variety of controls over the scan, such as the color depth. You also can initiate scans directly from applications such as Image Capture and Preview.

Part VIII

Appendixes

IN THIS PART

Appendix A
Installing Mac OS X 10.7 Lion

Appendix B
What's New in Mac OS X Lion

Appendix C
Mac OS X Lion's Key
Technologies

Appendix D
Commanding Unix

Installing Mac OS X 10.7 Lion

You can't, of course, use Mac OS X Lion until it's installed on your computer. If you've recently bought a brand-new Mac, it's likely that Mac OS X Lion is already installed, although you should still check to see if there have been any updates using the Software Update utility covered in Chapter 14.

However, you may already own a Mac with an earlier version of Mac OS X and want to upgrade to Lion. Or you may have no operating system at all on your Mac because of a hard disk crash and thus require a fresh install.

Upgrading or installing Mac OS X is a relatively easy process, and Apple has created a custom installer that leads you through the process step by step. But before you go about installing anything, you first need to ensure that your Mac can run Mac OS X Lion.

Mac OS X Lion is designed to take full advantage of the multi-core processors found in the latest generation of Intel computers. Because of this, you need to have a Mac with an Intel CPU. This includes all Mac Pro towers, all MacBook, MacBook Air, and MacBook Pro laptops, every iMac desktop released since January 2006, and every Mac Mini desktop released since March 2006. (You cannot run Mac OS X Lion on any PowerPC-based Mac.)

These are the official system requirements:

- Mac OS X Snow Leopard 10.6.8 or later; if you have an older Mac OS X version, you must upgrade to Snow Leopard 10.6.8 first.

- An Internet connection and the Apple ID associated to the Mac App Store.

IN THIS APPENDIX

Preparing a Mac for Mac OS X installation or upgrade

Installing or upgrading Mac OS X

Transferring data from a PC

Setting up a Mac after installation

Transferring applications and data from another Mac

Installing Java

Reinstalling Mac OS X in case of failure

- An Intel Core 2 Duo, Core i3, Core i5, Core i7, or Xeon processor.
- At least 2GB of RAM.
- A built-in display or display connected to an Apple-supplied video card supported by your computer.
- At least 8GB of disk space available for Mac OS X itself, or 12GB of disk space if you install the developer tools. You should also allow at least an extra 10GB for application installation, file saving, and free space for Mac OS X to move data around.

New Feature

Unlike previous versions of Mac OS X, Mac OS X Lion is not available on a DVD or other physical medium. It must be downloaded from the Mac App Store (see Chapter 9) and installed from its disk image. That installation image is saved to a hidden partition on the hard disk and can be accessed in the future by pressing and holding ⌘+R when booting your Mac to launch the Recovery System. You also can press and hold Option during startup, then select Recovery HD (which is the invisible partition) from the row of disks and press Return to launch the Recovery System. ∎

New Feature

Mac OS X Lion can be installed on virtual machines (VMs), such as those created by Parallels Desktop and VMware Fusion (see Chapter 18), a capability previously limited to Mac OS X Lion Server. The Lion license permits installation on two VMs per Mac in addition to directly on the Mac's physical disk. ∎

Preparing for Installation

After you have confirmed that your Mac computer meets the system requirements for Mac OS X Lion, you need to prepare your computer for the update.

The first step is to ensure that your computer's firmware is up to date. Firmware is a computer program that resides in the Mac's motherboard and controls it; as with application software, it can be updated with new instructions.

The easiest way to ensure that software and firmware are up to date is to use the built-in Software Update program. Choose ⌘↔ Software Update in the Finder. If any updates are available, they appear in the main window; click the Install button, and enter your administrator password. You also can download firmware updates from www.apple.com/support/downloads.

Caution

Do not interrupt a firmware upgrade; you could permanently damage your Mac by doing so. If you are installing a firmware update on a MacBook, make sure you connect it to a main power source so there's no chance of the battery dying mid-upgrade. ∎

Setting up a Mac for installation

It is likely that you are installing Mac OS X Lion on a hard disk (your startup disk) already containing a previous version of Mac OS X, replacing the existing Mac OS X with Mac OS X Lion. Doing so keeps all your settings and doesn't require reinstalling all your applications.

Note

You can install Mac OS X on disks other than your startup disk. Mac OS X lets you install it on multiple disks, which is handy if you're a developer or IT staffer testing different configurations. For more regular users, you might want to install Mac OS X on a portable disk so you can carry one environment between, say, your home and work Macs. ■

You also can install Mac OS X on an erased disk. Doing so makes sense if you've let your Mac's disk accumulate programs and files over the years that you never use (think of it as extreme spring cleaning). First, be sure to deactivate any software that ties itself to your Mac via activation, such as Adobe Creative Suite and QuarkXPress; otherwise, you lose that software license. Then download the Mac OS X Lion installer from the Mac App Store. Back up the disk or the files and applications you want to keep—including the Lion installer—to a bootable external disk. Boot from that external disk, use Disk Utility (see Chapter 6) to erase the original startup disk, and run the Lion installer from that external boot disk.

Note

If you erase an encrypted disk (see Chapter 26), the disk remains encrypted even after you erase it. (Disk Utility does let you set a new encryption password, though.) You need to know the encryption password to install Mac OS X on it. If you don't want the erased disk to be encrypted, select the disk in Disk Utility and choose File ⇨ Turn Off File Encryption. Then erase the disk. ■

Caution

I strongly recommend you copy the installer image to another bootable disk or have another Mac handy that you can re-download the installer image from should something go wrong with the installation; otherwise, you may have a damaged hard disk and no way to recover the installer. ■

Making a note of system settings

Before heading into the installation, I recommend that you make a note of your current networking and Internet preferences. If you are upgrading from a previous version of Mac OS X, these system preferences should be transferring from your old installation to the new Mac OS X Lion one. However, it is still prudent to make a note of them just in case they are not preserved.

To see these settings, choose ⌘ ⇨ System Preferences and click the Network icon button to open the Network system preference. Depending on your method of connecting to the Internet (most likely Ethernet or Wi-Fi), you may need to make a record of the settings in the Wi-Fi, TCP/IP, DNS, and Proxies panes. To see these panes, click the Advanced button. (See Chapter 23 for more on the Network system preference.)

Also make a note of any settings in the Sharing system preference (see Chapter 24), especially if you are using features such as remote login or Xgrid sharing, or if you have any custom file-sharing settings.

Backing up your data

I strongly advise that you back up your Mac's startup disk before beginning the upgrade. You can use this backup to restore your current operating system in the case of a mishap during installation. Even if the installation does not go awry, upgrading an operating system can result in applications compatibility issues. In these circumstances, many users revert to the previous operating system while waiting for the developer of any incompatible application to issue an update.

To back up your startup disk, you need a second hard disk. Those with Mac Pros can install an additional internal SATA disk or on an external disk. Those with iMacs, Mac Minis, or MacBooks need to use an external disk.

There are two ways to go about backing up your hard disk. The most common option is to use Apple's Time Machine backup utility. This is covered in detail in Chapter 11.

The second option is to create a complete clone of your hard disk using Disk Utility (see Chapter 6) or a program such as Bombich Software's Carbon Copy Cloner (www.bombich. com). In the event of an emergency, you can boot from this external clone of your hard disk (by pressing and holding the Option key during startup and selecting the cloned disk as the startup disk). If you used Disk Utility, you can clone the disk back to your startup disk after booting into the Recovery System (covered later in this appendix) or from the installation DVD. If you used a utility such as Carbon Copy Cloner, boot into the cloned disk and then run the utility to copy the complete hard disk from the cloned disk back to your startup disk.

Tip

If you back up your current Mac OS X startup disk and then reformat it before installing Mac OS X Lion on it, you can transfer your accounts, settings, and applications to the "fresh" Mac OS X disk from the backup by using the Migration Assistant, explained later in this appendix, once the installation of Lion is complete. ∎

Running the Mac OS X Installer

Now that you have prepared the hard disk, backed up your current version of Mac OS X, and made a record of your current system settings, it's finally time to begin installing Mac OS X Lion.

If you install Mac OS X Lion on a disk or partition that has a previous version of Mac OS X, the installer upgrades that previous version to Lion as well as upgrading any Mac OS X–provided applications (see Chapter 14), while retaining your other applications and documents. If install it on an empty (new or erased) disk or partition , you get just Mac OS X Lion and its included applications.

License agreement window

After you buy and download Mac OS X Lion, the installation image downloads to your Mac and, when complete, the Mac OS X Lion installer opens to the license agreement window. (If the installer does not open automatically, go to the Applications folder and double-click the Install Mac OS X application. Click the Continue button, and enter your administrator password.)

A settings sheet appears with the legal agreement, called a *license*, that you agree to abide by to use Mac OS X. Technically, you didn't buy Mac OS X, you licensed its use from Apple, and Apple's licensing terms restrict how you use it. You can't resell Mac OS X or give it away, for example. You can't install it on non-Apple computers. You can't reverse-engineer, modify, or otherwise access Apple's secrets stored in the operating system. You also agree that, basically, Apple's not responsible if something goes wrong and that Apple has the ability to detect some information about your Mac for use in refining future versions.

You also choose File ➪ Save Software License or press Shift+⌘+S to save a copy of the agreement, although if you are preparing to do a clean install, you should save it to an external storage device. You also can choose File ➪ Print Software License or press ⌘+P to print the license.

Click Agree to continue. A settings sheet may ask you to reconfirm your agreement.

Disk selector window

A window appears that usually shows your startup disk in the center. This also is one of your last chances to stop; choose Mac OS X Installer ➪ Quit Mac OS X Installation or press ⌘+Q to quit the installer.

If you want to install Mac OS X on it, click Install to install the standard Mac OS X on that disk.

Otherwise, click Show All Disks to see all the compatible disks attached to your Mac, and select the one on which you want to install Mac OS X. Note that any encrypted disks display an alert indicator (a ! in a yellow triangle) and the text "This disk is locked"; double-click an encrypted disk to get a dialog box in which you can enter the password that makes the disk available for installing Mac OS X.

New Feature

No longer available as an installation option is the Rosetta technology that let Mac OS X run applications designed only for PowerPC-based Macs. Such applications do not run in Mac OS X Lion, though the vast majority of them have already been updated to run on Intel-based Macs, either as universal binaries or "native" Intel applications. ■

Preparing to Install window

Once you begin the installation, the Preparing to Install window appears, showing a progress bar. During this step, the installer is creating the hidden Recovery HD partition that holds the Recovery System used both for this installation and later reinstallations, as described later in this appendix.

Stopping the Mac OS X installation

Until you click the Install button and get the install process underway, you can stop the installation at any time by choosing Mac OS X Installer ⇨ Quit Mac OS X Installation. If you do this, you are asked to confirm that you really intend to quit the installation; if you quit, the Mac restarts after asking you to select a startup disk. No matter what you select as the startup disk, you can change it by pressing and holding the Option key while your Mac boots up to select a different boot disk. You also can boot up to your original installation by pressing and holding the mouse or touchpad button during the boot process. (This automatically ejects the DVD.)

You also can quit the installation process while the installation is taking place by choosing Mac OS X Installer ⇨ Quit Mac OS X Installer. This isn't really advisable, though, because it leaves you without the operating system fully installed. If you select this option, you get a warning message and the options Restart, Don't Quit, or Select a Startup Disk.

Be warned: Do not quit the Mac OS X installation if you are performing a recovery operation. Doing so may cause your Mac to not be able to boot into any disk as it tries to find the disk you were recovering—a disk whose contents it made invisible when it started the recovery process and may have left invisible when you interrupted it.

If you want to cancel the installation, click Cancel to either quit from the installer or to choose a different disk to install Mac OS X Lion on.

Once the Recovery System is installed, you can click Restart or wait until the Mac reboots itself.

Installation progress window

A window appears showing the progress of your installation. When it's done, Mac OS X is installed on your disk. The process is largely automated and takes 30 to 45 minutes (depending on the speed of your system). There is little for you to do other than watch the progress bar, so now might be a good time to read up on what's new in Mac OS X Lion in Appendix B.

When the process is finished the Mac restarts itself.

After the installation process is complete, your Mac boots up. Owners of new Mac systems, and those that have just installed Mac OS X Lion on a blank or erased disk, get to watch a short and stylish welcome video.

Setting Up Your Mac

If you upgraded to Mac OS X Lion, you're ready to go—Lion uses your previous Mac OS X version's settings.

If you installed Mac OS X to a new disk or to an erased disk—in other words, you did not upgrade an earlier version of Mac OS X—Migration Assistant immediately launches after the Lion installation has completed.

Welcome window

Migration Assistant starts with the Welcome window, which asks you to select a country or region; English-language installations have six default regions: United States, Canada, United Kingdom, Australia, New Zealand, and Ireland. If you live outside of one of these areas, select the Show All check box to bring up a comprehensive list of countries.

If you wait for about 30 seconds, a note appears at the bottom of the screen. It informs you that you can enable VoiceOver speech system by pressing Esc. VoiceOver is part of Mac OS X's Universal Access settings, designed for people with different access requirements, such as the hearing impaired and the visually impaired. These technologies are covered in more depth in Chapter 6.

When you're ready, click Continue.

Select Your Keyboard window

This window enables you to choose a keyboard layout that matches your region. There is usually an option based on your region selection in the previous window; if this is the wrong area for your keyboard layout or if you want a different layout than the default for your region, select the Show All option and select the appropriate keyboard. Then press Continue.

Server settings window

If you are upgrading Mac OS X Server to Lion Server, you are then asked to provide the name of your organization, and provide the e-mail address for the network administrator. Press Continue to install or upgrade the server applications and configure them.

Transfer Information to This Mac window

This window is useful for users who have upgraded from another Mac system, those who are replacing a PC with a Mac, and those who have used Time Machine or a program such as Carbon Copy Cloner to back up their data. In this window, you can launch a program called Migration Assistant to transfer system information from one Mac to another or from a PC to the Mac. (The original backup source is unaffected by this transfer.)

To run Migration Assistant, choose any of the first three options when presented with the question "Would you like to transfer your information?" and click Continue:

- From Another Mac
- From a Windows PC

- From Time Machine or Other Disk
- Don't Transfer Now

Tip

You can run the Migration Assistant program at any time, not just during initial setup. You can find the Migration Assistant in the Utilities folder. ■

Caution

If you transfer applications that use activation, such as QuarkXPress and Adobe Creative Suite, be sure to deactivate them before transferring them. Otherwise, you may lose the license to use the application. These programs tie licenses to specific (activated) computers to prevent illegal copying, but if an activated copy is on a disk that is damaged or erased, the license tied to that disk is usually lost as well. ■

New Feature

Mac OS X Lion can import settings for e-mail, calendar, and contacts from Microsoft Windows PCs using the new Migration Assistant for Windows application, which helps those replacing a PC with a Mac. But it cannot transfer applications from Windows to Mac OS X. ■

Transferring information from another computer

The Select the Source window appears if you select From Another Mac or From a Windows PC. Make sure the other computer is on the same network as your new Mac. Run the Migration Assistant on that other Mac or PC. On the other Mac, select the To Another Mac option; on a PC, click Continue twice. The computers look for each other, and when they find each other, you see the old computer's name in the new Mac's Select the Source Window. Click Continue.

Note

To run Migration Assistant on the old Mac, no other applications may be running; you get a prompt to close them all if any are running. Also, you may have to update Migration Assistant on your Snow Leopard Mac to be able to use Migration Assistant to transfer files to your Lion Mac. If so, the Select the Source window indicates that on the Lion Mac. Run Software Update on the Snow Leopard Mac to get the updated Migration Assistant. ■

Note

To get Migration Assistant for Windows, go to www.apple.com and search for Migration Assistant Windows to download the utility on your PC. Your PC must have Apple's Bonjour networking enabled, which it should if you have iTunes installed (you can download Bonjour from www.apple.com). If your PC runs Windows XP, you may need to install Microsoft's .Net Framework 2.0 or later if it's not already installed. (Windows Update usually installs that update for you; you can get it at www.microsoft.com as well.) ■

You're then shown a passcode in the Select the Source window; make sure it matches the passcode shown in the other computer, and click Continue on the old Mac or PC. The Transfer Your Information window opens.

You now select what you want to transfer. On a Mac, these are your options:

- Users
- Applications
- Settings
- Other Files and Folders

By default, all four areas are checked, and performing this transfer recreates your original Mac's setup in the new operating system. Although you can select to transfer individual users' accounts, you cannot selectively choose what is transferred for each of the areas. (You cannot, for example, choose specific applications to transfer from your old installation to the new one; it's all or none.)

Note that the Select the Source window shows how much disk space you'll have left after the transfer. If the number is negative (highlighted in red), that means you don't have enough disk space to transfer everything you selected. You need to deselect some information. Unfortunately, you can't select which applications to install (they are likely to be the bulk of your transferred information) to reduce space used.

From a PC, you can import e-mail settings and messages from Microsoft Outlook (2003, 2007, or 2010 32-bit versions), Outlook Express, Windows Mail, or Windows Live Mail. For Outlook, Outlook Express, and Windows Mail, you can migrate only the currently logged-in user's data; if you have multiple user accounts on Windows, you need to run the transfer separately for each user, logging into each in turn. (In that case, you should log into the appropriate user account on the Mac for each user when transferring that user's e-mail account from the PC.)

Migration Assistant for Windows also transfers calendars from Microsoft Outlook as well as contacts from Outlook Express and Windows Contacts (the Contacts folder in your home folder on the PC). Note that any calendar event attachments are not copied to the Mac, and contact files that do not contain a first name, company name, or display name are not migrated.

Note

Purchases from the iTunes Store do not work on the new Mac until you authorize them in iTunes. (Chapter 16 covers iTune's authorization process.) For some media, such as apps, videos, and some music purchases, you can authorize only five computers at any one point, so you may need to deauthorize one Mac or PC before authorizing the new one. Therefore, be sure to deauthorize iTunes in the old computer before migrating your settings to the new Mac. ∎

Transferring information from another disk

The Select the Source window appears if you select From Time Machine or Other Disk. Any disks connected to your Mac via a USB, FireWire, or Thunderbolt cable display in the window. To see volumes on the network, click Select Network, sign into your Wi-Fi network if necessary, and click Continue. Any network volumes should then appear in the disk list.

Select the disk you want to transfer information from, and click Continue. The Transfer Your Information window appears with the same options as if you were using Migration Assistant (explained in the previous section): Users, Applications, Settings, and Other Files and Folders. Click Transfer to transfer the selected information.

Note that the Select the Source window shows how much disk space you'll have left after the transfer. If the number is negative (highlighted in red), that means you don't have enough disk space to transfer everything you selected. You need to deselect some information. Unfortunately, you can't select which applications to install (they are likely to be the bulk of your transferred information) to reduce space used.

Note
If you transfer information from a Mac or PC, Migration Assistant skips any of the remaining windows described in the rest of this section for which it got the necessary information. ■

Enter Your Apple ID window

If you have an Apple ID, such as to log into your iTunes account, enter it in this window. You also can enter your .Mac, MobileMe, or iCloud e-mail address if you have one (see Chapter 17). If you don't have an Apple ID or compatible address, leave the fields blank. Click Continue.

Registration Information window

The information you fill out in this page is sent automatically to Apple via the Internet. (If you want to get more information on why Apple is collecting your information and what it is used for, click the Privacy Policy button.) You cannot leave anything in this page blank, and there is no button option to skip registration. However, you can to skip registration by pressing ⌘+Q, then clicking Skip.

When you have filled out the registration information, click Continue; this takes you to the A Few More Questions window, which has two pull-down menus requesting information on where you primarily will be using this computer and what best describes what you do. Here you also find the Stay in Touch check box; selecting this option means Apple sends you e-mails regarding new products, software updates, and newsworthy information.

Create Your Computer Account window

Before you can start using your Mac, you need to create a user account. (Chapter 27 takes an in-depth look at user accounts.)

You need to enter a name and a short name. The name should be your full name, and the short name should be the name that Mac OS X knows you by (it's also the name for your Home folder). You also need to type a password and verify it by typing it in again. It is imperative that you pick a password that is memorable, because there is no way to retrieve a password that you have forgotten. Finally, you must enter a password hint to jog your memory.

You also have two options:

- Allow My Apple ID to Reset This User Password, which if selected means if you forget your password, you can use your Apple ID to change the user password to something new. (Clicking the ? icon button on the right side of the password field when logging in opens a pop-over with an option for resetting the password; that pop-over also shows your password hint.) You also can set this later in the Users & Groups system preference's Password pane, as Chapter 27 explains.
- Require Password When Logging In, which if selected means you are asked for your password each time you log in to the Mac, such as when you start or restart it.

When you're finished, click Continue.

Select a Picture for This Account window

This part of the setup process attaches a picture to your account. If your Mac has a built-in iSight camera, as most do (or if you have an iSight attached to your Mac), you can take a quick snapshot of yourself to attach to your account. Otherwise (or if you are a bit camera-shy), you can choose a picture from the picture library, which brings up 54 pictures provided by Apple. Before taking your photograph, keep in mind that the snapshot is used throughout Mac OS X and shared by programs such as Address Book, although you can easily change it at a later time.

Select Time Zone window

This window enables you to select a time zone for your Mac. You can use the map to click a geographic region, type the name of a nearby city, or select Set Time Zone Automatically Using Current Location. (Whatever option you choose also sets the date and time for you automatically.) After making your selection, click Continue.

Secure My Mac window

You can set Mac OS X to automatically encrypt all files on the startup disk, which secures them if someone else gets your Mac or its startup disk. Select the Turn On Encryption option, and enter a password that gives you access to the disk's contents. This password is critical to remember, because if you lose it, you lose access to your disk's contents. (Chapter 26 explains the new disk encryption capability in Mac OS X Lion and how to use it.) Click Continue when you're finished.

New Feature

The capability to encrypt your startup disk is new to Mac OS X Lion. ■

Don't Forget to Register window

If you skipped the registration process (by pressing ⌘+Q and selecting Skip on the registration page), this window appears, letting you know that you can register by double-clicking the Send Registration file in your Home folder. Click Continue.

Thank You window

Click Start Using Lion to complete the setup.

You get the login window if you installed Mac OS X Lion on an empty disk or partition; enter your password to log in.

If Mac OS X Lion detects any incompatible applications, it displays an alert dialog box informing you of that fact; any such applications are placed in a folder called Incompatible Apps. Also, if Mac OS X Lion detects other disks attached to your Mac, it displays an alert dialog box asking if you want to use one for Time Machine backups.

Installing the Java Runtime

When using a new Mac OS X installation, you're likely to get an alert dialog box at some point saying that a particular service or application needs Java and asking if you would like to download Java.

The Java runtime is a tool that runs applications written in Oracle's Java language on the Mac. (There are also runtimes for Windows and Linux.) Java is often used by web-based applications, because no matter what type of computer the user has, it can run.

New Feature

Mac OS X Lion no longer installs Java along with Mac OS X. The free Java runtime must now be installed independently, which assures you always have the latest version. The first time you run Mac OS X after you install or upgrade to Mac OS X Lion, the Software Update utility checks for the latest version of Java when you reboot after the installation and offers to install it for you. ■

Click Install Java to have Mac OS X look for the latest version of Java and install it on your Mac. You need an active Internet connection. If you click Not Now, you can run Software Update to install Java later.

Reinstalling or Recovering Mac OS X

Should your Mac's startup disk get damaged or corrupted, you can reinstall Mac OS X on it using several methods. Obviously, try repairing the disk first using Disk Utility, as Chapter 6 explains, because that could well solve the issue preventing you from starting up from that disk. (I suggest you keep the Mac OS X Snow Leopard installation DVD, if you have it, handy so you can use it to start up and run Disk Utility from a non-startup disk.)

Assuming you do need to reinstall Mac OS X, try the Recovery System in Mac OS X Lion. To run the Recovery System, restart the Mac and hold ⌘+R while restarting until the Mac OS X installation window appears. You also can get to it by holding Option during startup until the connected disks display; click Recovery HD or use the → or ← key to go to Recovery HD and then press Return. The Recovery System uses an invisible partition that Mac OS X Lion installed on your disk the first time you installed Mac OS X Lion.

New Feature
The Recovery System is new to Mac OS X Lion. ■

If you can't run the Recovery System and don't make a copy of the Mac OS X Lion installer disk image on a bootable disk, you can sign in to the App Store from another Mac, re-download the installer from the Purchases pane, connect your Mac to that other Mac via FireWire Target Disk Mode (see Chapter 1), and then re-install Lion from that other Mac onto yours.

When you boot from the Recovery System, you can run various utilities such as Disk Utility and Network Utility from the Utilities menu in the Install Mac OS X application.

Launching the Recovery System

When you launch the Recovery System, you may first get a window in which you select your language, then press the → button to continue. (If you accidentally choose the wrong language, you change it in the next screen by choosing File ⇨ Choose Language.)

After a few seconds, the Mac OS X Utilities screen appears, with four options: Restore from Time Machine Backup, Reinstall Mac OS X, Get Help Online, and Disk Utility. Select an option and click Continue to run it. Or, use the Utilities menu to access Firmware Password Utility (see Chapter 26), Network Utility (see Chapter 23), and Terminal (see Appendix D).

You also can quit the Recovery System and boot into another disk (if you have one) by choosing Mac OS X Utilities ⇨ Quit Mac OS X Utilities or pressing ⌘+Q.

Getting help online

If you want to go to Apple's support page by selecting the Get Help Online option, make sure your Mac is connected to a network; you can connect to a Wi-Fi network by using the Wi-Fi icon menu in the menu bar. Once you select Get Help Online and click Continue, the Safari browser launches and opens the Apple website. When you're done, choose Safari ⇨ Quit Safari or press ⌘+Q to return to the Recovery System's Mac OS X Utilities window.

Reinstalling Mac OS X

Reinstalling Mac OS X is similar to upgrading Mac OS X: The Recovery System replaces Mac OS X itself and the Apple-provided applications and utilities, but you other applications and documents are unaffected.

Caution

Do not interrupt a reinstallation operation. Doing so can make it impossible for your Mac to restart into any disk. That's because the Recovery System sets the startup disk to its invisible partition, which can become permanently invisible or corrupted if the reinstallation is interrupted— such as by shutting off the Mac midway through the process. Without access to that partition, the Recovery System has no disk to start from, and for some reason it often won't let you choose a different startup disk when it gets in that confused state. ∎

Restoring from Time Machine

Another, more drastic option is to run the Restore from Time Machine backup tool that appears in the Recovery System's main window and is available in the Utilities menu when you boot from the installation DVD. This replaces the entire contents of your disk with the last backup recorded in Time Machine. The advantage of using Time Machine rather than reinstalling the original Mac OS X is that the Time Machine backup includes any system updates you've applied since the original installation. The disadvantage is that any files not backed up since the Time Machine backup was made could be permanently lost.

Using Disk Utility

If the startup disk appears to be corrupt or damaged, try repairing it using Disk Utility and then reinstalling Mac OS X, as Chapter 6 explains. If the disk is unrecoverable, you may need to erase it using Disk Utility and reinstall Mac OS X. Doing so means you lose all your applications and data, unless the data were backed up and available to be restored via Time Machine or other utility.

You also could use Disk Utility to clone another disk or disk image to replace the contents of your current disk, as Chapter 6 explains. This is handy for installing a common set of applications to multiple users along with Mac OS X Lion, but it runs the risk of the various Macs all having the same account information on them, which can cause issues on the network.

What's New in Mac OS X Lion

I f you've just bought your first Mac, all of Mac OS X is new to you (and congratulations, by the way!). But chances are good that you've used Mac OS X before and are upgrading to Mac OS X Lion. This appendix puts in one place what's changed in Mac OS X Lion compared to Mac OS X Snow Leopard, the previous version. It helps you zero in on what's changed and refers you to the chapters that fill in all the details.

I've organized the summaries of what's new by category, so you can see what new features are related and are likely to affect specific activities.

Installing and Setting Up Mac OS X

Mac OS X Lion is no longer available on a DVD or other physical medium. It must be downloaded from the Mac App Store and installed from its disk image. That installation image is saved to a hidden partition on the hard disk and can be accessed in the future by pressing and holding ⌘+R when booting your Mac to launch the Recovery System. You can also press and hold Option during startup, then select Recovery HD (which is the invisible partition) from the row of disks and press Return to launch the Recovery System.

Mac OS X Lion no longer installs Java along with Mac OS X. The free Java runtime must now be installed independently, which assures you always have the latest version. If an application requires Java and the Java runtime is not installed on your Mac, Mac OS X Lion displays an alert dialog box from which you can download the current Java runtime.

IN THIS APPENDIX

Installation and setup

Startup and login

Finder navigation, menus, gestures, shortcuts, and Dock

Icons, files, and folders

Spotlight search

System preferences

The Help Center

Application capabilities and services

The general-purpose Mac OS X applications

Safari, QuickTime Player, Mail, Address Book, and iCal

Disk Utility and Time Machine

User accounts and parental controls

Security and privacy

Network setup and file sharing

Fonts and special characters

Printers, fax modems, and scanners

Speech and the VoiceOver Utility

Unix

Mac OS X Server

Mac OS X Lion can be installed on virtual machines (VMs) such as those created by Parallels Desktop and VMware Fusion (see Chapter 18), a capability previously limited to Mac OS X Lion Server. The Lion license permits installation on two VMs per Mac in addition to directly on the Mac's physical disk.

No longer an installation option is the Rosetta technology that let Mac OS X run applications designed only for PowerPC-based Macs. Such applications do not run in Mac OS X Lion, though the vast majority of them have already been updated to run on Intel-based Macs, either as universal binaries or "native" Intel applications.

The Migration Assistant can now import settings for e-mail, calendar, and contacts from Microsoft Windows PCs, which helps those replacing a PC with a Mac. But it cannot transfer applications from Windows to Mac OS X.

The Recovery System is new to Mac OS X Lion. When you install Mac OS X Lion, an invisible partition containing the Mac OS X installer is placed on your hard disk, so you can recover Mac OS X without needing the installation DVD. To run the Recovery System, restart the Mac and hold down ⌘+R while restarting until the Mac OS X installation window appears. You also can get to it by holding Option during startup until the connected disks display; click Recovery HD or use the → or ← key to go to Recovery HD and then press Return.

The Remote Install Mac OS X utility has been removed from Mac OS X Lion; the delivery of the Lion installer from the Mac App Store makes it unnecessary.

Starting Up and Logging In

When you shut down, restart, or log out of Mac OS X, the confirmation dialog box gives you the option to have windows reopen upon startup or login. Thus, you can begin where you left off, with the documents and applications opened where they had been when you shut down, restarted, or logged out.

The login window in Mac OS X Lion has been redesigned for a slicker look. But it works the same way as in previous versions of Mac OS X.

Clicking the ? icon button on the right side of the password field when logging in opens a pop-over that has an option for resetting the password using your Apple ID, if you enabled that capability during installation (see Appendix A) or in the Users & Groups system preference (see Chapter 27). That pop-over also shows your password hint, should you want to see it before it's automatically displayed after three failed login attempts.

Cross-Reference
Chapter 1 explains how to start, restart, shut down, and log in and out of your Mac. ∎

Using the Finder

By far, the most changes in Mac OS X Lion involve changes to the Finder, mainly in its navigation capabilities but also in Finder window, menu, Dock, and gesture functions.

Cross-Reference

Chapter 2 covers the Finder's menus, the Dock, Mission Control, Exposé, Spaces, and gesture capabilities. Chapter 3 explains the Finder window and its capabilities. Chapter 4 explains how to work with icons, files, folders, and disks. Chapter 5 explains how to work with the Spotlight search function. ■

Application and window navigation

Mission Control is new to Mac OS X Lion, providing an Exposé-like view of all running apps and their open windows, so you can navigate among them in one place. It also incorporates the Exposé and Spaces features.

As Spaces is now a feature within Mission Control, you add spaces there rather than in the Exposé & Spaces system preference (now called the Mission Control system preference), as in previous versions of Mac OS X. You no longer assign applications to spaces in the system preference; instead, you do so in the Dock's menu for each application.

Gestures

Spaces—the feature that lets you set shortcuts and hot corners to switch among different view modes—now lets you switch to the Dashboard (see Chapter 14) when using gestures.

Mac OS X Lion adds the four-finger pinch and spread gestures for viewing the Launchpad and desktop, the three-finger double-tap gesture for looking up text, and the two-finger double-tap for smart zooming; and Lion redefines the four-finger and three-finger swipe gestures to support the new Mission Control feature.

Finder menus

The File ➪ New Folder with Selection capability lets you create a folder containing the selected files and/or folders.

The App Store menu option in the menu is new to Mac OS X Lion, though the App Store was available to Snow Leopard users as part of a system update in late 2010. Gone from the menu is the Mac OS X Downloads menu option, which has been essentially replaced with the App Store menu.

The AirDrop, All My Files, Downloads, and Library options in the Go menu are new to Mac OS X Lion; they open the AirDrop file-sharing folder , the All My Files smart folder, the Downloads folder, and the Library folder, respectively.

The Clean Up By menu option is new to Mac OS X Lion's View menu; it lets you sort the icons by criteria such as name or date. Also new are the Date Last Opened and Date Added options in the View menu's Arrange By submenu. (These options affect the display in Finder windows.)

There's no longer an icon menu for Spaces in the menu bar when Spaces is enabled (as it always is in Mac OS X Lion); instead, use keyboard shortcuts to switch among them.

Shortcuts

The ⌘+/ shortcut for Show Status Bar in the Finder's View menu is new to Mac OS X Lion.

The shortcut for App Exposé view has changed in Mac OS X Lion to Control+↓, from the previous shortcut of F3. Press Control+↑ to go back to the regular view. If you're in the regular Finder view, press Control+↑ to go to the Mission Control view, and press Control+↓ to go back to the regular Finder view. You also can use gestures.

Likewise, the shortcut to open the Dashboard has changed to Control+←; it had been F4 in most Macs in earlier versions of Mac OS X. Press Control+→ to go back to the regular Finder view.

The Dock

In Mac OS X Lion's Dock, the Launchpad, App Store, and FaceTime icons are new. And there's no longer a Dashboard icon, iChat icon, Spaces icon, or Time Machine icon. The Dashboard, iChat, and Time Machine applications still exist; they're just no longer loaded into the Dock by default. Likewise, the Applications folder is no longer placed in the Dock by default (Apple would prefer you use Launchpad). The Spaces feature no longer exists as its own application but remains as part of the Mac OS X navigation capabilities via the Mission Control feature.

Mac OS X Lion no longer shows the App Exposé view of open application windows when you click and hold a Dock application icon; you now must choose Show All Windows from the contextual menu. This makes the behavior identical whether you use the right-click or Control+click technique or the click and hold technique to display the contextual menu.

Finder, application, and document windows

The changes in windows are fairly subtle, but they do change some of what you see onscreen and how you interact with windows.

The Sidebar

Mac OS X Lion has updated the look of Finder windows and its icons. The Sidebar icons, for example, have that precision-cut-aluminum feel that Apple's recent Macs favor, muting the colors of previous Mac OS X versions. Likewise, folders' corners are a tad sharper than before.

Mac OS X Lion has changed how you show and hide the Sidebar's sections. Previous versions used disclosure triangles to reveal and hide the sections' contents. Lion uses a subtler technique: Hover the pointer over the section name, and a button appears to its right. If the section's list is visible, the button is labeled Hide; if the section's list is hidden, the button says Show.

The All My Files item in Finder windows' Sidebar is new, showing all documents on your Mac in a sortable list. By default, new Finder windows display in this view; you can change this default in the Finder Preference's dialog box's New Finder Windows Show pop-up menu.

The AirDrop item in the Finder windows' Sidebar is also new, letting you share files with other Mac OS X Lion users on your network whose Macs support this feature (see Chapter 24).

The Favorites section in Mac OS X Lion Sidebar had been called Places in Mac OS X Snow Leopard and Leopard. Gone in Mac OS X Lion is the All item in the Finder window's Sidebar, in its Shared section. That item let you quickly browse your network connections. In Lion, you must use the Connect to Server dialog box's Browse button instead to find network connections not shown in the Sidebar (press ⌘+K to open that dialog box). Also gone from the Mac OS X Lion Sidebar is the Search For section, which had common Spotlight searches presented as links, such as Search For sections are Today, Yesterday, Past Week, All Images, All Movies, and All Documents. Instead, only searches you explicitly place in the Sidebar now display in it.

Finder windows

There are two new options for sorting the contents of a Finder window—Date Last Opened and Date Added—in the View menu's Arrange By submenu. These options also are available the View Options dialog box.

There's now a shortcut (⌘+/ shortcut) to show the status bar in a Finder window.

Gone in Mac OS X Lion is the handle at the bottom of each column for resizing column widths when working in column view. You now just drag the column boundary at any location.

The Apply to Subfolders option for the View Options settings is new to Mac OS X Lion. It applies your settings to all the folders within the current folder, saving you lots of effort if you want consistent view options within a folder hierarchy.

The pill-shaped icon button at the right side of the title bar in previous versions of Mac OS X no longer exists in Lion. It hid the toolbar on windows that had them. But you can still hide the toolbar portion of the title bar in Finder windows and in some application and document windows: Right-click or Control+click the title bar, and choose Hide Toolbar from the contextual menu. Repeat the action to show the toolbar.

Gone from the Customize Toolbar settings sheet for Finder windows are the Customize and Separator icons. New are the New Folder and the Labels buttons. And the default toolbar icon lineup has changed: In Mac OS X Leopard and Snow Leopard, the toolbar by default included the Quick Look icon but not the Arrange icon. Mac OS X Lion does not include by default Quick Look in its toolbar but does include Arrange. The Finder windows' toolbar uses new icons for many of the buttons, and the Customize Toolbar settings sheet arranges the buttons in two rows rather than three. (If you upgrade Leopard or Snow Leopard to Lion, the toolbar retains whatever icons, but using their new designs, you had in Leopard or Snow Leopard).

All windows

Mac OS X Lion changes how you scroll within a window when you use a gesture-savvy input device. By default, scroll bars no longer automatically appear in windows, displaying instead only when Lion detects you're navigating the window. (You can force the display of scroll bars in the General system preference.)

Also, the color of the scroll track and slider now depends on the color of the window: If the surrounding background is light, the track is light gray and the slider is dark gray. If the surrounding background is dark, the track is dark gray and the slider is light gray.

No matter what types of input devices you use, Mac OS X Lion also gets rid of the scroll arrow icons on the scroll tracks that you could click in previous Mac OS X versions to scroll through a window. There's no system preference option to bring these arrow icons back.

Mac OS X Lion now lets you resize windows by dragging on any corner or side; you're no longer limited to dragging the bottom-right corner as in previous versions. (This also means the three-line icon that previous versions of Mac OS X had on the bottom-right corner to indicate the drag handle is gone in Lion.) If a window is resizable by dragging its corner or side, the pointer changes from the standard arrowhead icon to a double-arrow icon as you hover on the corner or side.

Icons, files, and folders

You can select multiple files and folders and choose File ⇨ Group as Folder to create a new folder to place them in.

Mac OS X Lion adds a visual clue as you move or copy multiple items: A red circle displaying the number of items selected now appears below the pointer as you drag them.

The Keep Both Files button in the Copy dialog box when moving or copying items across disks or volumes is new to Mac OS X Lion. If you click Keep Both Files, Mac OS X appends a numeral to the end of its name: 1 for the first copy, 2 for the second, and so on.

The live icon previews for files have been enhanced in Mac OS X Lion to let you navigate through multi-page documents, not just videos and audio files.

Mac OS X Lion has enhanced the Quick Look window. The Zoom button and Open button are both new in the regular Quick Look window, which also now has an appearance more like regular windows than in previous versions of Mac OS X. And the full-screen view adds the Add to iPhoto button, so you can sync compatible files to your iPhone, iPad, or iPod Touch more easily.

Spotlight

The Show All in Finder option in the Spotlight results sheet is the new name for what had been called Show All in previous versions of Mac OS X.

Spotlight results in the Finder window can now be displayed in column view mode, unlike in previous versions of Mac OS X, as well as in the previously supported icon, list, and Cover Flow view modes.

When you enter a search term in the Search box, Spotlight displays a menu of likely search options, such as Kind or Sent By. Choose one of those to have the search automatically use that criterion rather than add the criterion manually.

If you want to get more details on a Spotlight menu bar result, hover the pointer over it for a few seconds. Using the Quick Look facility in Mac OS X (see Chapter 4), Spotlight displays a preview of the item in a pop-over to the left of the results sheet. (In some cases, it can't provide such previews, such as for applications and web searches.)

Using System Preferences

You can now hide individual system preferences to customize the appearance of the application. To do so, choose View ➪ Customize. Check boxes appear at the lower right of each system preference icon; deselect those you don't want to appear. Click Done when you're finished.

The Mail, Contacts & Calendars system preference and the Profiles system preference are new to Mac OS X Lion. The Appearance system preference has been renamed General, the Security system preference has been renamed Security & Privacy, the Print & Fax system preference has been renamed Print & Scan, the Exposé & Spaces system preference has been renamed Mission Control, and the Accounts system preference has been renamed Users & Groups. And the Internet & Network group has been renamed Internet & Wireless.

In the default arrangement of the System Preferences application, the Universal Access systems preference has been moved from the System group to the Personal group.

Hot corners—used in the Desktop & Screen Saver and Mission Control system preferences—had been called active screen corners in previous versions of Mac OS X.

Cross-Reference
Chapter 28 explains how to work with system preferences. ■

Desktop & Screen Saver

The selection of desktop background images in Mac OS X Lion is strongly reduced compared to previous versions. Now, there's just one folder of photos (Desktop Pictures), whose selection contains mainly new images, such as that of a galaxy, a lion, and several Africa-themed photos. Gone are the starfield images emblematic of Mac OS X Leopard and Snow Leopard, as well as the series of plant, abstract, and artwork images previously available.

Displays

In the Display pane, Mac OS X Lion displays a new set of controls for a Mac's built-in monitor and some camera-equipped Apple displays, such as the Cinema Display series: the Brightness slider and the Automatically Adjust Brightness option. If selected, this option has Mac OS X detect the brightness of the light shining on the monitor and has the monitor adjust its brightness appropriately. Note that this can cause a strobe effect in some environments, such as where the light changes due to frequent shadows.

Dock

In the Dock system preference, the Minimize Window into Application Icon option and the Show Indicator Lights for Open Applications option are new. (In previous versions of Mac OS X, the indicator light always displayed for open applications.)

Energy Saver

The Restart Automatically If the Computer Freezes option is new to Mac OS X Lion's Energy Saver system preference.

General

The General system preference (previously called the Appearance system preference) changes the options for scroll bars to reflect the new approach in Mac OS X Lion when you use gesture-based input devices such as the Magic Trackpad or Magic Mouse. When such devices are connected to your Mac, by default Mac OS X Lion hides scroll bars until it detects you are trying to move through a window, as Chapter 4 explains.

New to the General system preference is the Restore Windows When Quitting and Reopening Apps option. Also new is the ability to specify the size of icons in the Sidebar.

Language & Text

The ability to turn substitution and spell-checking on or off is new to the Language & Text's Text pane. In previous versions of Mac OS X, they were always on. Also new is the ability to select Finnish and Hebrew in the Word break pop-up menu.

Mail, Contacts & Calendar

The Mail, Contacts & Calendar system preference is new to Mac OS X Lion. It lets you set up and view the services such as e-mail, contacts, and calendars available to e-mail, chat, and other communications accounts. It also lets you change usernames and passwords for e-mail accounts.

Mission Control

The Exposé & Spaces system preference is now called Mission Control. It no longer has two panes (Exposé and Spaces), instead placing all controls in one pane. Gone are the controls for adding spaces and assigning applications to them; instead, you now add spaces via Mission Control and assign applications via the Dock's application menus, as Chapter 2 explains.

The ability to launch the Launchpad (covered in Chapter 2) is new to the system preference's Exposé hot corners options. Also, the Mission Control replaces the All Windows option in previous versions of Mac OS X.

Spaces is now always on in Mac OS X Lion; you cannot turn it off as in previous versions of Mac OS X.

Mouse and Trackpad

The option to set the content scrolling direction in the Mouse and Trackpad system preferences is new to Mac OS X Lion and reflects the greater integration of gesture support. When using a touchpad, you typically scroll your fingers up to move the content with a window up, but with a mouse's scroll wheel or scroll ball, you typically scroll down to move the scroll bar down, which moves the window's content up. In other words, the touchpad gesture and the mouse movement move in opposite directions to achieve the same result. If this option is selected, you can use the different (traditional) mouse and gesture directions to achieve the same result. (Chapter 2 explains the gestures supported in Mac OS X Lion.)

If the content scrolling direction option is deselected (the default) in the Mouse system preference, you have to scroll the mouse wheel or ball up—not down—to move a window's content up. In the Trackpad system preference, if this option is deselected (also the default), swiping two fingers up (the scrolling gesture) moves the window content up.

For gesture-savvy mice and touchpads, the controls over double-click and scrolling speed, scrolling behavior, and dragging behavior have been moved in Mac OS X Lion from the Mouse and Trackpad system preferences to the Universal Access system preference.

Profiles

The Profiles system preference is new to Mac OS X and displays only if one or more configuration profiles are installed (see Chapter 25).

Sound

The ability to control whether Front Row sound effects play is gone from the Sound system preference in Mac OS X Lion, as Mac OS X Lion no longer includes that application (see Chapter 16).

Time Machine

The Time Machine system preference now lets you encrypt backup disks.

The Time Machine system preference in Mac OS X Lion lets you manage the Auto Save option, as well as control its locked-document settings, as Chapter 10 explains—at least for documents from applications that support the Auto Save capability.

Using the Help System

Mac OS X Lion has significantly reworked the organization of the help system's contents. It's also given it the name Help Center. (You open the Help Center from the Finder or an application using the Help menu or clicking the ? icon button within applications and system preferences.)

At the bottom of the Help Center window are icon buttons to give you quick access to several of the Apple applications that come with Mac OS X. The See All Link opens a pane with help links not only to Apple applications but to third-party applications. It even has a handy Recent Applications section at the top under the assumption that any questions you have are likely about the applications you recently used.

Mac OS X Lion has expanded the number of sections for help on VoiceOver commands from six to nine; new ones are Web, Standard Gestures, and New and Changed Commands. VoiceOver is Mac OS X's facility for speaking screen contents and providing audio feedback on user actions to help the visually impaired.

Cross-Reference

Chapter 7 explains the Help Center. ■

Working with Applications and Documents

Although the Finder is the main application in Mac OS X, it's not the only one. Mac OS X provides several general-purpose applications, as well as under-the-hood core capabilities that applications use.

Application core capabilities

The Launchpad is new to Mac OS X Lion, providing a series of full-screen panes that list your applications, modeled on the home screens in iPhones, iPads, and iPod Touches. You can rearrange the applications in these panes and create folders of them.

There is no longer a touchpad gesture that opens the application switcher (the row of open applications you can access by pressing ⌘+Tab) in Mac OS X Lion. The four-finger horizontal swipe that had been used in Mac OS X Snow Leopard now moves you through spaces, as Chapter 2 explains.

Applications can now use a new user interface method called a pop-over, which Mac OS X Lion has adopted from the iOS used in Apple's mobile devices. A pop-over contains basic settings—as a small dialog box might—and pulls down from whatever you click to get it, much like a menu.

Applications can now run in full-screen mode, which hides the menu bar and anything else onscreen. To enter full-screen mode, choose View⇨ Enter Full Screen or click the Enter Full-Screen icon button at the top right of the application window. To get the menu bar back, just hover the pointer where the menu bar usually appears and click the Exit Full Screen icon button at the far right of the menu bar.

Mac OS X has borrowed a concept from iOS (Apple's mobile operating system) called sandboxing, which developers can use to restrict the interaction between their applications and other applications and/or the Finder. For example, an application might disable access to Address Book so it can't be used by a Trojan horse to steal your contacts, or an application might restrict copy and paste to just the Finder. (See Chapter 26.)

Cross-Reference
Chapter 9 explains the core elements for applications that Mac OS X provides. ■

Application document controls

Mac OS X Lion adds a capability called *Versions* that lets documents keep track of all the changes you make to them, so you can revert changes easily, even in files that get moved or sent to other people. If an application supports this capability, the Save menu option is named Save a Version.

Mac OS X Lion also adds a capability called *Auto Save* that saves changes to your document as you make them (in applications that implement this capability). That way, should your Mac freeze or lose its power, you haven't lost the changes you made since the last explicit save (when you choose File⇨ Save a Version or press ⌘+S). Note that the incremental changes saved since the last explicit save aren't available through the Versions feature's revert capability until you explicitly save the file.

The Auto Save feature also locks a file two weeks after it was last saved, so if you open the file to read it and accidentally save it, you get a dialog box that asks you to unlock the file first or to save the changes in a copy of the file—this lock is meant to prevent inadvertent changes to an old document. (You can change that lock period in the Time Machine system preference.) You also can immediately lock or unlock a document in a compatible application using the new menu to the right of a document's title.

Cross-Reference
Chapter 10 explains the core services for documents that Mac OS X provides. ■

Application helper services

New to Mac OS X Lion's services are the New Terminal at Folder, New Terminal Tab at Folder, and Encode Selected Video Files services in the Files and Folders group.

In the Messaging group, Mac OS X Lion has renamed the Send File service to New Email with Attachment, the Send Selection service to New Email with Selection, and the Send To service to New Email To Address.

New to Mac OS X Lion are the Open Man Page in Terminal and Search Man Pages in Terminal services in the Text group.

Cross-Reference
Chapter 12 explains how to use the Mac's services, which are a form of application helper. ■

Mac OS X's general-purpose applications

Mac OS X Lion no longer includes the iSync application that had synced contact and other data from some pre-iPhone–era cell phones, nor does it include the Front Row playback app meant to make a Mac display video like a TV; the full-screen mode in iTunes and QuickTime Player handles that need now.

The Exposé and Spaces utilities no longer appear in Mac OS X Lion's Utilities folder. They've been replaced with the Mission Control application in the Applications folder. (Chapter 2 covers Mission Control.) Now included with Mac OS X Lion is FaceTime (see Chapter 20), which Apple began including in new Macs sold in 2011 and charged $1 to download from the Mac App Store for older Macs. New to FaceTime in Mac OS X Lion is the iOS-style Preferences pane, which appears instead of the previous Preferences dialog box if you choose FaceTime ➪ Preferences or press ⌘+, (comma). In it, you can turn FaceTime on or off, set up or change your accounts, and specify the e-mail addresses where you can be reached for FaceTime sessions.

Widgets that are no longer included in the Dashboard are Business, Google, iTunes, and People.

The shortcut to open the Dashboard has changed to Control+← in Mac OS X Lion; it had been F4 in most Macs in earlier versions of Mac OS X.

The inclusion of the Oxford British English dictionary and thesaurus is new to Mac OS X Lion's Dictionary application.

Photo Booth now opens by default in full-screen mode, from which you can navigate the various effects using the navigation icons at the bottom of the screen. If you switch to regular view, the effects grid remains but the background changes. The Mac OS X Lion version of Photo Booth has a dozen or so fancy new distortion effects, which follow your face as you move within the picture frame. If you like an effect, double-click the photo to get a larger window, where you can adjust your pose and take the picture using the Camera icon. (You can switch back to the effects view by choosing View ➪ Show Effects or pressing ⌘+2.)

Preview

Preview's Go menu has renamed the Previous and Next options to the Up and Down options and added the Next Item and Previous Item options. Next Item and Previous Item move among pages, whereas Up and Down move among screens. Gone from the Preview toolbar are the Next Item and Previous Item icon buttons. The toolbar icons have also been redesigned.

Also new is the Enter Full Screen option in Preview's View menu.

In Mac OS X Lion, Preview moves several controls from the View ⇨ Sidebar submenu to the main View menu. Four—Content Only, Thumbnails, Tablet of Contents, and Contact Sheet—give you different ways to view multiple images or pages in files, such as in PDF files, for easier navigation. The PDF Display menu option and its submenu options have changed to the Page Display menu option and its submenu options; the new version extends the ability to display PDF files as single pages, a continuous roll of pages, or as facing pages to other document types. Gone from the View menu is the Automatically Resize menu option.

TextEdit and Preview now use the new Versions capability in Lion (see Chapter 10), so the File ⇨ Save menu option becomes File ⇨ Save a Version after the first time you save a document, and the File ⇨ Save As menu option has been replaced with the File ⇨ Duplicate menu option. The File ⇨ Revert to Saved menu option now lets you choose which version to revert to, rather than reverting to the last-saved version as in Mac OS X Snow Leopard and earlier. They also use the Auto Save capability that includes locking files after a specified period of nonuse or when a user explicitly locks a file, as Chapter 10 also explains.

System Information had been called System Profiler in previous versions of Mac OS X. Its About This Mac window in Mac OS X Lion has been enhanced to show more information about both Mac OS X and the Mac model you have, plus its new Display, Storage, Memory, Battery, Support, and Service icon buttons give you quick access to key information on your Mac, such as hard disk usage, battery charge level, and memory configuration.

Mac OS X Lion adds the Podcast Publisher application to the Utilities folder, which you can use to create podcasts and upload them to compatible servers, such as Mac OS X Server, or send them to others via e-mail. Lion retains the previous Mac OS X versions' Podcast Composer application, which lets you create podcasts but requires a connection to Mac OS X Server to work.

Cross-Reference
Chapter 14 details the built-in general-purpose applications in Mac OS X. ∎

Safari web browser

Mac OS X Lion includes the newest version of Safari: Safari 5.1. (Mac OS X Snow Leopard came with Safari 4 but later was updated to Safari 5.0.) Among the new version's new capabilities is support for full-screen mode.

Safari 5.1 also provides the Reading List pane, where you can add web pages that you want to read later. It's meant as a temporary placeholder for web pages, rather than as a permanent collection of easily accessible links (that's what bookmarks are designed for).

Also new is the Downloads icon button that appears to the right of the Search box in the Safari toolbar. The Downloads button shows an indicator of the download progress while you are downloading files. Click it to display a pop-over listing recent downloads; it works just like the Downloads dialog box accessed by choosing Window⇨Downloads. (Note that the shortcut Option+⌘+L no longer opens the Downloads dialog box; instead, it now opens the Reading List pane.)

If you access a website that uses certificate-based security, the name of the website or its company may appear in bold green text to the right of the URL field. Click it to see the contents of its security certificate. The Security icon button may also appear in the far right of the title bar, next to the Enter Full Screen icon button; the Security icon button also displays the certificate's contents.

The menu options for showing and hiding the Reader mode in Lion's version of Safari are now called Show Reader and Hide Reader. They had been Enter Reader and Exit Reader in previous versions of Safari.

Safari 5.1 changes the bookmarking process slightly. You now must choose the location via the unnamed pop-up menu before you can enter the bookmark's name; in previous versions of Safari, both the location pop-up menu and name field were immediately available. Also new is the addition of the Reading List and Top Sites options in the location pop-up menu.

Yahoo is now the default search engine in Safari 5.1, not Google.

The version of Safari that comes with Mac OS X Lion rearranges the Preferences dialog box's Security pane to split its options between that pane and the new Privacy pane, which also includes new controls on managing websites' access to your location. (Chapter 23 covers location security.)

Cross-Reference
Chapter 19 explains how to use Safari. ∎

Media playback applications

Mac OS X Lion does not come with the Front Row application for watching videos in full-screen mode. The application was used in previous versions of Mac OS X to make a computer monitor display movies like a TV. In Mac OS X Lion, you use the full-screen mode in iTunes or QuickTime Player for the same purpose. Choose View⇨Enter Full Screen, press ⌘+F, or click the Enter Full Screen icon button in the playback window's onscreen controls (the icon of two arrows pointing in opposite directions). Move the pointer while a video is playing in full-screen mode to display the onscreen controls, and click the icon button again or press ⌘+F to return to the regular window size.

New to QuickTime Player in Mac OS X Lion is the ability to export video to Vimeo, Flickr, Facebook, and Mail. Two of its iTunes export options also have been renamed to reflect Apple's current iOS device line-up (as reflected in the menu options iPod and iPhone, and iPad and iPhone 4).

The ability to buy e-books from the Mac's iTunes is new to iTunes 10.3, which was released in conjunction with Mac OS X Lion. Also new to iTunes 10.3 is support for the iCloud automatic updates service, so music, apps, and books bought on any Mac, PC, or iOS device linked to the same Apple ID are automatically available to all other devices linked to the same account.

Cross-Reference

Chapter 16 explains how to use QuickTime Player and Mac OS X's main media application, iTunes. ∎

Mail application

The Mail application changes the default view for mail messages, arranging the message preview as a window on the right side of the Mail Message Viewer rather than below the message list. The new Message Viewer layout allows for longer message lists and larger preview window sizes. But you can return to the old display by selecting the new Use Classic Layout option in the Viewing preferences pane.

Also new in the Preferences dialog box's Viewing pane for managing onscreen display are the Show To/Cc Label in the Message List option, the Show Contact Photos in the Message List option, the List Preview pop-up menu, and the set of options in the Viewing Conversations section.

The Fonts & Colors preferences pane in Mail's Preferences dialog box no longer offers the Mailbox Font option to change the appearance of the list of mailboxes in the Sidebar of the Message Viewer.

Mail in Mac OS X Lion enhances the message threading capability from previous versions and calls that enhanced approach *conversations*. It groups related messages into one list, so only the latest message appears in your message list, and opening it opens the content of all the related messages—if you are using the new columnar Message Viewer layout. (This feature is often called *message threading* in other e-mail applications, and it works similarly to how message threading works in iOS devices.) Previous versions of Mail could thread messages but not display all the messages' content in one place; the classic Message Viewer window shows threaded messages the same way as previous versions of Mail.

The Favorites bar is new to Mail in Mac OS X. In addition to the default folders placed in it, you can drag any mailbox folders from the Sidebar into it to get quick access to frequently used folders. Drag a folder out to remove it from the Favorites bar.

The Export Mailbox option had been named Archive Mailbox in previous versions of Mac OS X.

The Mail application no longer provides a disclosure triangle for attachments in the message header to let you preview the attachments' icons. Instead, use Quick Look to preview the attachments, use the Save pop-up menu to save them, or go to the bottom of the message to see the attachments' icons.

The version of Mail included with Mac OS X Lion changes the arrangement of icon buttons in the toolbar. It adds the Flag and Hide/Show Related Messages icon buttons, and removes the

To Do icon button. The to-do capability has been dropped from Mail, and the Hide/Show Related Messages icon button is the new name for the former Threads icon button. (Right-click or Control+click the toolbar and choose Customize Toolbar from the contextual menu to add or remove icon buttons from the Mail toolbar.)

When you use the toolbar's Search field, Mail 5.1 opens a results sheet that lists likely matches based on its index of your e-mails and contacts, organized by category such as recipient and subject.

Mail lets you flag messages by assigning one of seven colored flags to them. You decide what those colors mean to you; they simply act as visual labels. You can quickly apply a red flag to a message by pressing Shift+⌘+L. Flagging a message helps you find it later in your message list, plus you can quickly see all flagged messages by clicking the Flagged button below the toolbar (or choosing a specific mailbox from its pop-up menu). To remove a flag from a message, click the Unflag button in the toolbar (it displays only if you have selected a flagged message), or choose Message ➪ Flag ➪ Clear Flag.

In Mac OS X Lion's version of Mail, the Exchange mail account replaces what had been labeled Exchange 2007 in Mac OS X Snow Leopard. It's the same feature, but Apple removed the "2007" because it applies to both Exchange 2007 and Exchange 2010 servers.

The TLS Certificates pop-up menu is new to the Account Information subpane of the Accounts pane in Mail's Preferences dialog box. Use it to choose a Transport Layer Security certificate if required by your web host or ISP; Mac OS X provides a unique TLS certificate for each user account.

Mail now supports Exchange's Out of Office feature, so you can set up automatic replies to people who e-mail you that you are not checking your e-mail. To set up an out-of-the-office notice, right-click or Control+click your Exchange account in the Sidebar and choose Out of Office from the contextual menu. The Account Info dialog box appears, set to the Out of Office pane.

The Save as Draft icon button has been removed from the New Message dialog box's toolbar in Mac OS X Lion's version of Mail. It's also not available through the Customize Toolbar settings sheet.

Mail in Mac OS X Lion has dropped support for to-do items; you must use iCal to create and manage such reminders (see Chapter 21).

Cross-Reference

Chapter 20 explains how to use Mail, and Chapter 22 explains how to work with Microsoft Exchange servers. ■

Address Book application

Mac OS X Lion's Address Book application has undergone a significant overhaul in its appearance, now looking very much like the Address Book app on an iPad.

The new look for Address Book means it takes more work to get to groups of contacts; instead of being listed at the left side of the Address Book window, in Mac OS X Lion you now must choose View ➪ Groups, press ⌘+3, or click the Group icon (the red ribbon with two silhouettes) to see your various calendars and groups.

To send someone's contact information as a vCard mail attachment (which the recipient can open in Mail and have automatically added to their Address Book), click the Share button in a card you want to send. Mail opens with a new, blank message that has the vCard attached.

The Default Account pop-up menu has moved from the Accounts pane to the General pane in Address Book's Preferences dialog box. And the Font Size menu that had been in the General pane is gone.

Cross-Reference

Chapter 21 explains how to use Address Book. ■

iCal application

Mac OS X Lion changes how iCal appears, making it look and work more like the version of iCal on the iPad. As part of this change, the list of calendars that used to appear on the left side of the window must now be opened in a pop-over by clicking the Calendars button or choosing View ➪ Show Calendar List. Also gone is the Mini Calendar view that let you see your current month in a small window when in other calendar views, though the Week view in iCal now also shows the current month in a miniature calendar.

In some cases for invitations displayed in iCal, if the server supports this capability, when you enter a person's name in the Invitees field, a link appears below labeled Available Meeting Times. Click it to see when that person's schedule shows him or her to be available.

iCal no longer has the Notification pane to list all outstanding invitations. You have to look for them in your calendar or in the Invitations icon button.

In the General pane of the Preferences dialog box, you can now set a default calendar in which appointments are added. (You can always move an appointment while you are adding it or after you added it.)

Also in the Preference dialog box's General pane, the Show Event Times option now displays times in day and week views, not just month views. Gone is the Synchronize iCal with Other Computers and Devices Using MobileMe option.

Cross-Reference

Chapter 21 explains how to use iCal. ■

Working with Disks and Backups

Mac OS X Lion's Disk Utility drops two Mac OS Extended (also known as HFS+) format variants—the two non-journaled regular and case-sensitive formats. Journaling slows down disk access a bit to allow the indexing for recovery purposes, so previous Mac OS X versions offered non-journaled formatting to help out users with older, slower disks. But these days, all disks are fast enough to support journaling.

But Lion adds two Mac OS Extended formats: encrypted journaled and case-sensitive encrypted journaled. That way, you don't have to separately encrypt a new or reformatted partition.

Mac OS X Lion lets you turn off encryption on a disk in Disk Utility.

When you select a backup disk in Time Machine, you now have the option to encrypt it, so no one without the correct password can access its contents.

On MacBooks, Mac OS X Lion automatically saves a copy of recent changes to the startup, which helps Mac OS X recover files if your files hadn't yet been backed up (which could be days or weeks for a MacBook-toting traveler). No user action is required.

Cross-Reference

Chapter 6 explains Disk Utility. Chapter 11 explains how to use Time Machine in specific and how to back up your data in general. Chapter 26 explains disk encryption. ∎

Working with User Accounts and Parental Controls

The system preference you use to set up and manage user accounts is now called Users & Groups rather than Accounts, as in previous versions of Mac OS X.

When setting up user account information in the Users & Groups system preference, the Apple ID option replaces the MobileMe option, expanding its scope to store all your Apple IDs.

In the Directory Utility accessed via the Users & Groups system preference, the NIS option replaces the BSD (Berkeley Standard Distribution, a form of Unix) option in previous versions of Mac OS X, expanding Unix server directory support beyond BSD versions. The Directory Editor pane and capability is new to Mac OS X Lion.

In the Users & Groups system preference, Mac OS X Lion adds the Action icon pop-up menu (the gear icon) below the list of user accounts. (It displays only if you are logged in as an administrator.) It has one option: Set Master Password. Use this option to set a password that an administrator can use to access all user accounts, including those protected with encryption (see Chapter 26), as well as to create new passwords for users who have forgotten their passwords.

In Mac OS X Lion's Parental Controls system preference, you can no longer select a person's Jabber instant-messaging handle to restrict communications with him or her.

Cross-Reference
Chapter 27 explains how to set up and manage user accounts and parental controls. ∎

Securing Your Mac

The Security & Privacy system preference had been called the Security system preference.

The new Privacy pane of the Security & Privacy system preference is where you can manage your location privacy by turning on or off location sharing, as well as see what applications are checking your location.

There's no longer the Use Secure Virtual Memory option in the General pane of the Security & Privacy system preference. That capability, which encrypts the scratch space that Mac OS X uses when you are working, so a data thief can use it to find passwords or sensitive information, is now permanently turned on.

The Show a Message When the Screen Is Locked option in the Security & Privacy system preference's General pane is new to Mac OS X Lion. This displays a message on the login screen, such as "Make sure no one is looking over your shoulder as you enter your password."

In Mac OS X Lion, the FileVault capability of previous versions of Mac OS X has been changed to encrypt your whole startup disk—not just your Home folder. That brings its encryption to the standards required by government agencies and many large companies.

Disk encryption also is available in Time Machine when you set up a backup disk as Chapter 11 explains, in Disk Utility when you erase (format) a disk (you also can remove encryption from a disk here) as Chapter 6 explains, and when you install Mac OS X Lion as Appendix A explains.

Developers can restrict the interaction between their applications and other applications and/or the Finder to make them more secure using the new sandboxing feature in Mac OS X Lion. For example, an application might disable access to Address Book so it can't be used by a Trojan horse to steal your contacts, or an application might restrict copy and paste to just the Finder.

Cross-Reference

Chapter 26 explains Mac OS X's security capabilities. ■

Working with Networks

Mac OS X Lion uses the name Wi-Fi instead of AirPort to refer to wireless networks. Thus, what had been called the AirPort menu bar icon menu is now the Wi-Fi menu bar icon menu, and what had been called the AirPort pane in the Network system preference is now the Wi-Fi pane. (Wi-Fi is the name of the wireless standard used; AirPort is Apple's brand name for its Wi-Fi hardware.)

The Hardware pane shown after clicking Advanced in the Network system preference had been called the Ethernet pane in previous versions of Mac OS X.

Mac OS X Lion does not let you edit Wi-Fi settings such as password and security type for preferred networks, so the Edit icon button (the pencil icon) in previous versions of the Network system preference's Wi-Fi pane does not exist in Mac OS X Lion. To change a preferred network, you must delete it and add it back. But if the only change needed is to update the password, you get a prompt if the stored password doesn't match the required password, and you get a chance to enter it and save it for future use.

Also gone from the Wi-Fi pane is the Disconnect from Networks When Logging Out option; Wi-Fi connections are always disconnected when you log out from the Mac, not just when you shut down or restart the Mac.

Mac OS X Lion removes the ability to set up a Bluetooth personal area network (PAN) from the Network system preference. This is now handled in the Sharing system preference, as Chapter 24 explains.

AirDrop is new to Mac OS X Lion, and works only with other Mac OS X Lion computers. Note that it may not work on Macs built before 2009, as their Wi-Fi hardware may not support the peer-to-peer connection mode AirDrop requires. If your Mac doesn't support AirDrop, the AirDrop item simply does not appear in the Sidebar of your Finder windows.

In the Screen Sharing utility's Preferences dialog box, the When Connecting to a Computer options and the Scroll the Screen options are new to Mac OS X Lion. The When Connecting to a Computer option lets you choose the initial state, either Always Attempt to Control If Possible or Initially Observe. The three Scroll the Screen options control how the shared screen is scrolled (for when it does not fit in your screen): When the Cursor Reaches an Edge, Continuously with the Cursor, or Only When the Scroll Bars Are Adjusted. (Note that the word *cursor* here really means pointer.)

Cross-Reference

Chapter 23 covers networking in Mac OS X, and Chapter 24 explains file sharing. ■

Working with Fonts

Mac OS X Lion's Font Book removes the Action icon pop-up menu (the gear icon). Use the menu bar or contextual menu instead to access the controls that were offered via the Action icon pop-up menu in previous versions.

In the Font Book Preferences dialog box, Mac OS X Lion has removed two controls (Validate Fonts Before Installing and Ask Me Before Activating), and added one controls (Resolve Duplicates by Moving Files to the Trash). Note that fonts are now validated automatically when added.

The Font Book application in Mac OS X Lion adds four icon buttons at the upper left of the dialog box. These icon buttons change the preview window, providing the same controls available in the Preview menu. From left to right, they are Sample, Repertoire, Custom, and Font Info.

The Standards font collection is new to Mac OS X Lion's Font Book application. If you choose File ⇨ Restore Standard Fonts, Font Book removes all fonts from these folders that did not come with Mac OS X, placing them in a new folder named Fonts (Removed) in Library folder. This is a great tool to clean up Fonts folders that over time have gotten full of rarely used fonts; you can then add back those you actually use.

Font Book in Mac OS X Lion changes how you resolve duplicate fonts. Gone is the Edit ⇨ Resolve Duplicates menu option. Instead, you use the new settings sheet that appears after you choose Edit ⇨ Look for Duplicates or press ⌘+L.

Mac OS X Lion has greatly simplified the Character Viewer. You now get to the detailed controls by hovering the pointer over a character and clicking the *i* icon button that appears.

Cross-Reference
Chapter 29 explains how to install and manage fonts, as well as how to access special characters. ∎

Printing, Faxing, and Scanning

The Print & Scan system preference had been called Print & Fax in previous versions of Mac OS X.

In Mac OS X Lion, the + icon pop-up menu in the Print & Scan system preference replaces the + icon button in previous versions' Print & Fax system preference. Any network or Bluetooth devices—printers, fax modems, and scanners—that are available should now display in the pop-up menu. To install a device connected via a USB or other cable directly to your Mac, choose Add Other Printer or Scanner to open the Add Printer dialog box.

Cross-Reference

Chapter 30 covers the use of printers, fax modems, and scanners. ∎

Using Speech and the VoiceOver Utility

The voices that the Mac uses to speak to users have expanded greatly in Mac OS X Lion. There are now several dozen voices available, including many optimized for a variety of foreign languages. These voices are available in the Text to Speech pane of the Speech system preference by choosing Customize from the System Voice pop-up menu. Note that most of the new voices are not installed with Mac OS X Lion and instead are downloaded to your Mac over the Internet once you select them.

The Speech subpane in the VoiceOver Utility's Verbosity pane, which controls Mac OS X's assistive capabilities for the visually impaired, was named in General in previous versions of Mac OS X, and the Braille subpane is new to Mac OS X Lion.

The Use Phonetics option is new in the Verbosity pane's Speech subpane. It has Mac OS X speak words when it encounters individual letters, such as "a alpha" or "t tango" when, for example, it sees *a* or *t* alone.

The Enable Fast Searching option in the Navigation pane of the VoiceOver Utility is new. This option lets you move more quickly to other elements onscreen. In the adjacent pop-up menu, choose Left Command Key or Right Command Key to set which ⌘ key is used to invoke fast search. Then use that ⌘ key with the first letter of the desired control name to jump to it.

The Web pane in the VoiceOver Utility has been broken into three subpanes, the Enable Live Regions option is new, the option to have a verbal cue when a web page loads is new, and the list of Web Rotor options has been expanded.

The ability to choose a separate output device for VoiceOver audio is new.

The new Touch subpane in the VoiceOver Utility's Visuals pane has just one option, the Background Transparency slider, which you use to decrease or increase the opacity of the dimmed area around your touchpad pointer. Note that this subpane appears only if you have a gesture-savvy touchpad connected to your Mac.

The new Trackpad subpane in the VoiceOver Utility's Commanders pane controls how VoiceOver works with your touchpad. Note that this subpane appears only if you have a gesture-savvy touchpad connected to your Mac.

The new Quick Nav Commander in the VoiceOver Utility's Commanders pane works in much the same way as the NumPad Commander and Keyboard Commander, except it lets you assign commands to single characters as well as use the arrow and other navigation-oriented keys.

When setting keyboard shortcuts in the VoiceOver Utility's Keyboard subpane (in the Commanders pane), you can choose Both Option Keys, which means both Option keys must be pressed to invoke the VoiceOver keyboard shortcut.

The Show Eight-Dot Braille option and Display Alert Messages slider are new to the Layout subpane in the VoiceOver Utility's Braille pane. The eight-dot method allows for single-cell display of extended characters, whereas the traditional six-dot method does not. The Display Alert Messages slider controls how long alerts display on the Braille reader. Slide it all the way to the left to turn off the display of alerts.

The ability to set up separate activity settings in the VoiceOver Utility (in the Activities pane) is new to Mac OS X Lion. (Activities are basically groups of applications and functions that you use to have different VoiceOver behaviors based on the types of tasks you are doing.)

Cross-Reference

Chapter 8 explains the Speech system preference, the VoiceOver Utility, and Mac OS X's other assistive capabilities. ∎

Working with Unix

In Mac OS X Lion, you can set new windows and tabs to open with the same settings as the current one or with the default settings set in the Preferences dialog box.

Also in Terminal's Preferences dialog box, you can set the color for text in the Terminal windows and panes.

Cross-Reference

Appendix D describes the capabilities of the Terminal application and surveys the basic capabilities of the Unix language and X11 graphical user interface that Mac OS X supports. ∎

Using Mac OS X Server

Mac OS X Server is now a $50 add-on to Mac OS X Lion, and no longer a separate operating system product. You buy and download Server from the Mac App Store and install it on an existing Mac OS X Lion environment.

Mac OS X Lion Server adds the Server application to manage server settings and server applications. It replaces the Server Preferences application from previous versions and is meant to be the central management tool for Mac OS X Lion.

The server administration tools that reside in the Server folder inside the Applications folder—Podcast Composer, Server Admin, Server Monitor, System Image Utility, Workgroup Manager, Xgrid Admin, and Xsan Admin—are no longer installed on your Mac by default. To get them, launch the Server application and choose Tools ➪ Install Server Admin Tools to download and install them. (You also can download them from `www.apple.com/support/downloads`; search for Server Admin Tools to find the installation image.) Once installed, two of them—Server Admin and Workgroup Manager—also are available in the Server application's Tools menu, along with the Screen Sharing and Directory Utility tools that are installed with Lion Server.

Lion Server now guides you through configuring your Mac as a server. It also provides local and remote administration—for users and groups, push notifications, file sharing, calendaring, mail, contacts, chat, Time Machine, VPN, web, and wiki services—from a central console.

The new Profile Manager delivers profile-based setup and management for Mac OS X Lion as well as for iPhone, iPad, and iPod Touch iOS devices. It also integrates with your directory services and can deliver automatic over-the-air profile updates to devices using the Apple Push Notification service. Users can see, add, and, if permitted, delete their profiles in the Profiles system preference in Mac OS X or in the General pane of the Settings app in iOS.

The Wiki Server 3 has simplified file sharing and wiki page creation.

Lion Server provides wireless file sharing for iPads, using the WebDAV capability.

Cross-Reference

Chapter 25 explains how to use Mac OS X Server, as well as how to use the web server functions in the standard version of Mac OS X. ∎

Mac OS X Lion's Key Technologies

M ac OS X has an extremely slick interface, but underneath it is a world-class operating system based on open standards. Below the shiny exterior of the Mac OS X interface sits a rock-solid Unix-based operating system core called Darwin. (The "X" in Mac OS X refers to both Unix and the fact that it came after Mac OS 9.)

With its first, server-only version released in 1999 and its first desktop version in 2001, Mac OS X was designed from the ground up to replace the older, or "classic," Mac operating system that Apple had been using since the original Mac launched in 1984. Because it is based on Unix, Mac OS X provides an extremely stable environment for applications to run in. And because Unix is so Internet-centric, Mac OS X can be integrated into virtually any computing environment (although it is designed to work only on an Apple-branded computer).

Unix is widely used in servers and workstations managed by technical experts; this has given Unix a reputation for being a complex OS sitting in the domain of the technical elite. Mac users need not fear Mac OS X's Unix core because Apple has created a world-class GUI (graphical user interface); users need not be concerned with Unix's command-line interface.

Mac OS X merged Unix's reliability with Apple's famous ease of use, creating an operating system like no other. But Unix is still at the heart of Mac OS X, and those users who want to explore the underside of Mac OS X can do so using a program called Terminal (see Appendix D).

In the meantime, let's look more closely at all the parts that make up Mac OS X under the hood.

IN THIS APPENDIX

Understanding the technologies at the core of Mac OS X

Using the graphics and media technologies in Mac OS X

Knowing the application-supporting technologies in Mac OS X

Core Processing Technologies

At the root of it all, an operating system is based on what's called a *kernel*, the heart that lets it interact with all the hardware and with applications. Surrounding this kernel are other core technologies that work with the major subsystems, such as graphics and memory.

Darwin

Underneath Mac OS X sits Darwin 10.0, which is a result of a joint operation between the open-source community and Apple. Darwin is a complete open-source Posix (Portable Operating System Interface) operating system (based on Unix) released by Apple in 2000 and continuously developed alongside Mac OS X.

Darwin forms the base of Mac OS X and also the base of the iOS operating system used by the iPhone, iPad, iPod Touch, and Apple TV devices. It comprises code created by Apple, as well as code from NextStep, Free BSD (Berkeley Software Distribution), and other open-source software projects.

Darwin is released under the Apple Public Source License, which the Free Software Foundation approved as a free software license from Darwin 2.0. Thus, many independent projects modify or enhance Darwin.

XNU kernel

At the heart of Darwin lies the XNU (X Is Not Unix) kernel developed by NeXT (founded by Apple cofounder Steve Jobs), and later Apple (after Jobs returned there). The kernel is the central component of most computer operating systems and sits between the hardware and software components. It is responsible for managing system resources, especially memory, the CPU, and I/O (input/output) devices.

XNU combines the Mach microkernel developed by Carnegie Mellon University with BSD and a device driver framework called I/O Kit.

The XNU kernel is a complicated beast, but at its heart, the Mach microkernel handles threads and processing; BSD sits between the GUI and the kernel and handles users' IDs, permissions, and the network file system; the I/O Kit enables drivers to run from the user space instead of the kernel space, which ensures that the kernel does not crash if these drivers crash. If a kernel space driver crashes, it may cause a "kernel panic" that requires your Mac to be physically restarted.

Kernel panics are extremely rare in Mac OS X. When one occurs, the screen fades to a dark gray with white text, with the following message in several languages: "You need to restart your computer. Press the power button for several seconds or press the Restart button." Figure C.1 shows Mac OS X suffering from a kernel panic.

FIGURE C.1

The dreaded but very rare kernel panic crash. When it occurs, you need to physically restart your Mac.

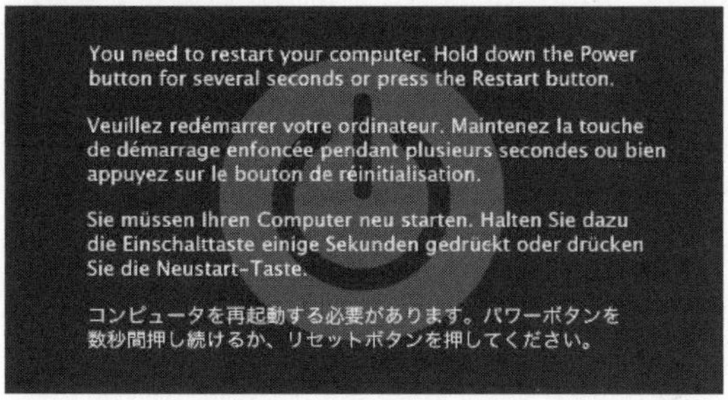

You need to restart your computer. Hold down the Power button for several seconds or press the Restart button.

Veuillez redémarrer votre ordinateur. Maintenez la touche de démarrage enfoncée pendant plusieurs secondes ou bien appuyez sur le bouton de réinitialisation.

Sie müssen Ihren Computer neu starten. Halten Sie dazu die Einschalttaste einige Sekunden gedrückt oder drücken Sie die Neustart-Taste.

コンピュータを再起動する必要があります。パワーボタンを数秒間押し続けるか、リセットボタンを押してください。

64-bit kernel

The journey from older 32-bit processors and applications to the 64-bit ones has been a long, but worthwhile, process. 32-bit processors are limited to 4GB of RAM, with 2GB application support—a figure that looks increasingly tame as computer technology marches onward.

The real advantage in offering 64-bit support is that it enables Mac OS X and applications to address more than 4GB of RAM; thus Mac OS X can support up to a theoretical 32TB (terabytes) of RAM. Although this amount sounds ridiculous today, it places Mac OS X in good stead for the future.

The underlying 64-bit support was first introduced in Mac OS X 10.3 Panther, which expanded a virtual address space in the kernel to 64 bits; this enabled a single non-GUI (graphical user interface) process to access the 8GB of memory that the Mac Pro of the time offered, but doing so required specialized programming.

Mac OS X 10.4 Tiger took the process further by enabling any non-GUI process that was coded for 64-bit to see a 64-bit address space (the idea being that a program could run a 64-bit task to do the 64-bit number crunching and report back to the 32-bit GUI); Mac OS X 10.5 Leopard introduced full 64-bit support for any GUI application to access 4TB of RAM. Mac OS X 10.6 Snow Leopard completed the journey by making the entire Mac OS X 64-bit.

Grand Central Dispatch

In recent years, the race for faster processors has switched from clock speeds to multiple cores; the now-standard multi-core processor essentially places multiple processors onto one chip, theoretically letting the processor do two, four, or eight times as much processing. But not all programmers know how to take full advantage of multi-core computing.

Grand Central Dispatch is designed to take advantage for these multi-core processors by making the entire Mac OS X "multi-core–aware" and optimizing it to allocate tasks (called *threads*) across multiple cores and multiple processors. It aims to make it easier for programmers to get the full performance from modern computers.

Symmetric multi-processing

Symmetric multi-processing (SMP) is the computing term for a multi-processor computer architecture where two or more processors can connect to a single shared main memory. In the case of multi-core processors, such as those used in Intel-based Macs, the SMP architecture treats individual cores as separate processors.

SMP technology takes advantage of multiple processors by assigning applications to specific processors or by splitting up parts of applications (known as *threads*) between multiple processors simultaneously. Mac OS X also is optimized to take advantage of a technique known as *optimized kernel resource locking*, which provides superior SMP performance by enabling multiple CPUs to access different portions of the kernel simultaneously.

Mac OS X 10.5 Leopard introduced multi-processor competency, with support for up to eight simultaneous cores (found in the dual quad-core Mac Pro). Grand Central Dispatch technology takes the Mac's SMP capability even further by implementing FreeBSD's ULE scheduler into Mac OS X (ULE is short for SCHED_ULE), which can set CPU affinity per processor, per thread, producing a great speed boost to multi-threaded applications.

Preemptive multi-tasking

Since Mac OS 7 (then called System 7), every Mac operating system has allowed more than one application to be open at the same time. This capability is known as *multi-tasking*. Before the introduction of Mac OS X, Macs used a technology known as *cooperative multi-tasking*, in which they would negotiate which applications got the Mac's resources and for how long before switching to the next application. (This switching among applications happened so quickly that, to a person, it appeared as if they were running simultaneously.) But for cooperative multi-tasking to work, tasks had to be programmed to yield when they did not require system resources—and not everyone played by the rules.

The first version of Mac OS X replaced this cooperative approach with *preemptive multi-tasking*, which enables privileged tasks or parts of the system to interrupt, and then later resume, other tasks. Thus, no task could hog all the resources. Preemptive multi-tasking is a more efficient method of task management, and it enables Mac OS X to remain responsive even during processor-intensive tasks.

OpenCL

OpenCL (Open Computing Language) joins OpenGL (Open Graphics Library) in enabling Mac OS X to take full advantage of the incredibly fast graphics cards and processors shipping with modern Macs. Whereas OpenGL (explained later in this appendix) is designed to harness the power of graphics cards to draw visual effects, OpenCL is designed to extend this power beyond graphics and provide parallel processing with your main CPU.

Protected memory and advanced memory management

Protected memory ensures that applications run inside their own memory spaces and prevents applications from going beyond memory that is allocated to them. Protected memory also ensures that if an application crashes, it can be terminated without harming other applications.

The physical RAM in your Mac is managed automatically by Mac OS X and is augmented with virtual memory dynamically as it is needed. (Virtual memory uses space on your hard disk in place of physical RAM.) This means that you no longer have to set allocated memory amounts manually to applications, as you did in the classic Mac OS. Advance memory management also alleviates the out-of-memory conditions that used to affect Mac users.

Graphics and Media Technologies

The visual muscle of Mac OS X is the stuff of legend. Apple's operating system is one of the most graphically powerful on earth. Mac OS X harnesses several of the best technologies around to achieve this visual prowess: Quartz, OpenGL, and QuickTime form the three pillars of Apple's graphical competence.

Over the last decade some of the greatest strides in hardware performance have come from increasingly powerful graphics cards. Apple has taken advantage of this with two software technologies: Core image and Core Animation. These technologies improve performance by reducing floating-point unit (FPU) utilization by offloading it to the graphics-processing unit (GPU).

Quartz

Quartz is a two-dimensional graphics-rendering system known as Quartz 2D and a composition engine that sends instructions to the graphics card called Quartz Compositor. Together they are generally called either Quartz or Core Graphics.

Key features of Quartz include built-in support for the Portable Document Format (PDF) created by Adobe Systems, plus on-the-fly rendering, compositing, and anti-aliasing. It supports multiple font formats, including TrueType, PostScript Type 1, and OpenType (see Chapter 29). Apple's ColorSync technology is also supported by Quartz to enable accurate color calibration in the print/graphics environment (see Chapter 28).

OpenGL

Open Graphics Library (OpenGL) began its life with graphics workstation maker Silicon Graphics in 1992 and is a cross-platform API (application programming interface) for applications that produce 2-D and 3-D graphics. It has more than 250 functions for creating 3-D scenes. It is widely used by applications that require intensive three-dimensional graphics—CAD/CAM (computer-aided design and computer-aided manufacturing), medical imaging, computer simulation, video games, and so on—and it is a direct competitor to Microsoft's DirectX technology. The capabilities of OpenGL have extended with each incarnation of Mac OS X and increasingly powerful graphics cards included in Macs. You can find a table of capabilities plus general information on OpenGL at `http://developer.apple.com/graphics imaging/opengl`.

QuickTime

QuickTime is a cross-platform (available for Mac OS X and Windows) media-authoring and distribution engine. It is used by applications to play and edit media files. (The current version is called QuickTime X.) It supports more than 50 video, audio, and still-image formats, including MOV, ACC, MP3, MPEG-1, JPEG, and TIFF. QuickTime has a plug-in architecture that enables developers to create additional components; these widen the range of media format types. QuickTime also supports video streaming, enabling viewers to watch video or listen to audio as it is streamed over the Internet.

Apple ships the QuickTime Player with Mac OS X to play or stream media (see Chapter 16). iTunes, iPhoto, and the Finder also use it.

Aqua

Aqua is the name of Mac OS X's GUI; it also refers to the primary visual theme of Mac OS X. As the name implies, it is based around water, with translucent and reflection effects. The Aqua interface also pays many visual nods to the Mac hardware: Mac OS X's original two-tone style of menu bars complemented the original Bondi Blue iMacs, whereas the metallic look used in today's Mac OS X ties closely to the aluminum used on most Macs.

Mac OS X Application Environments

Mac OS X has a distinguished history, and as such, Apple has had to build several application environments over time and include them with Mac OS X so it can run both modern software and legacy applications.

An application environment consists of various system resources, components, and services that enable an application to function. Mac OS X has numerous application environments, including Cocoa, Carbon, Java, AppleScript, and WebObjects, plus BSD and X11.

Cocoa

Cocoa is Mac OS X's native object-orientated application environment. Applications developed in Cocoa are designed exclusively for Mac OS X and do not run on any other operating system, including Mac OS 9 (discontinued a decade ago, so nearly extinct today).

The Cocoa programming environment automates many aspects of the application to comply with Apple's human interface standards; as such, Cocoa applications usually have a distinctive look in keeping with Mac OS X's Aqua interface. Common Cocoa applications include Mail, Safari, and Preview.

Cocoa applications take full advantage of some of the key Mac OS X features covered earlier in this appendix, including advanced memory management, preemptive multi-tasking, and symmetric multi-processing.

Carbon

Carbon is Mac OS X's second application environment, one that is quickly disappearing as Apple encourage developers to stop using this 15-year-old environment. The great advantage that Carbon offers is that developers can create applications that run both in "classic" versions of Mac OS (versions 8.1 and 9) and in Mac OS X. But because Mac OS X is now more than a decade old, there are very few applications in use that use Carbon.

When running in Mac OS X, Carbon applications take advantage of Mac OS X's modern feature set, including the Aqua interface. This can make it difficult to tell whether an application is written in Carbon or Cocoa. One disadvantage to Carbon applications is that they cannot use 64-bit processes in the GUI; it is impossible to compile 64-bit Carbon applications.

Tip

To tell whether an application is created with Cocoa or Carbon in Mac OS X, click the desktop to put an application window in the background, and then press ⌘ and try to resize the window. If it is a Cocoa application, it stays in the background, whereas a Carbon application pops to the foreground. ■

Frameworks

Mac OS X frameworks contain code that is dynamically loaded and shared by multiple applications. The presence of frameworks reduces the need for applications that share common code to each load an individual version of the code. Examples include media playback, opening and saving files, and rendering PDFs.

Mac OS X has two main frameworks: Foundation Kit (known simply as Foundation) and Application Kit (known as AppKit). Foundation is used for non-GUI functions, and AppKit is used for GUI functions.

New Feature

The new AV Foundation framework in Mac OS X Lion provides essential services for developers working with time-based audio-visual media. Through an Objective-C interface, developers can play, examine, and compose audio-visual media in their applications. An array of powerful classes also makes it simple to edit and encode media files. With AV Foundation, developers can create applications that capture audio and video from external devices and manipulate them in real time. ■

Understanding packages and bundles

Cocoa and Carbon applications in Mac OS X are often contained in *packages* (also known as *bundles*). These appear in the Finder (usually in the Applications folder) as a single icon, but they actually contain all the files and folders used by the application. So, instead of having to open an application's folder (as you must in Windows) to find the program itself, you just double-click the package and Mac OS X finds and loads the program for you.

You can see the contents of a package by right-clicking or Control+clicking the package and choosing Show Package Contents from the contextual menu.

Java

Java is a programming language originally developed by Sun Microsystems and now owned by Oracle. Mac OS X installs the current version of Java for you if an application needs it and updates it as needed via the Software Update utility.

New Feature

Java is no longer installed along with Mac OS X; instead, it is downloaded from the Internet after Mac OS X first runs, as Appendix A explains. ■

The advantage to developing in Java is that applications can run on any platform that contains a compatible Java virtual machine, such as Mac OS X, Windows, and Linux. Java development is increasingly rare, though, because it is generally considered to be more time-consuming to develop for than rival cross-platform environments; still, Java is commonly used in Web-based applications. Sun released most of Java to the open-source community in 2006.

Core Location

Core Location is a technology that uses known Wi-Fi hot spots to triangulate your current position. Mac OS X uses it to automatically determine your current time zone and adjusts the clock accordingly.

BSD and X11

BSD (Berkley Software Distribution) is a Unix application environment that usually deals with command-line executable shell scripts, command-line tools, and daemons (programs that run in the background). X11 extends the BSD environment by adding a set of interfaces for graphical applications, in effect enabling a GUI environment for BSD Unix applications.

Commanding Unix

W hy is there an appendix on using Unix in a book on Mac OS X? Because underneath Mac OS X is the Berkeley Software Distribution (BSD) version of Unix, which you can access through the Terminal application in the Utilities folder on your Mac. So Mac users also have the ability to use Unix. If you're a developer, that may thrill you.

If you're a "regular" user, you may want to stay far away. But even regular users can benefit from using Unix, because it gives you fast ways to do some file functions such as renaming that can be time-consuming when using a graphical user interface (GUI) such as the Finder. (You can automate some of these using the Automator tool, as Chapter 13 explains; you don't use Unix directly there, but it accesses these same Unix commands.)

I'm not going to teach you Unix in this appendix. After all, this is a book about Mac OS X. Plus there are plenty of good books on Unix that you can and should refer to, so you get the same level of depth on that operating system as this book gives you on Mac OS X. Here, I'll simply tour the Unix commands that regular Mac users are likely to use.

Note

Unix books from Wiley, the publisher of this book, include *Mac OS X Unix Toolbox* by Christopher Negus, *The Mac OS X Command Line: Unix Under the Hood* by Kirk McElhearn, *Beginning Unix* by Paul Love et al., and *Beginning Shell Scripting* by Eric Foster-Johnson et al. ∎

IN THIS APPENDIX

Using Terminal

Using the Unix shell

Using basic Unix commands

Working with X11

When you use Unix, you're leaving the GUI behind and returning to textual commands. If you're old enough to remember the PC's DOS, you know what I mean. If not, think of these textual commands as the same as writing a script in AppleScript Editor (see Chapter 13). It is the same thing, except you type in your commands live in Terminal, just as you use the pointer live in the Finder's GUI to get stuff done. You work in a simple screen where you type your commands and Unix provides its responses; this is called a *command-line interface* (CLI).

You can use Unix on the Mac in two ways: via the Terminal application or by booting only into Unix (to do so, press and hold ⌘+S during startup until you see the Unix command prompt) in what is called *single-user mode*.

Working with Terminal

The first step to getting started with the Unix CLI on Mac OS X is to launch Apple's Terminal application, which resides in the Utilities folder (press Shift+⌘+U to jump there in the Finder). Terminal can perform a variety of tasks, but its simplest function is accessing the Unix shell. When you launch Terminal, it appears as shown in Figure D.1.

FIGURE D.1

Mac OS X's Terminal application, with the tab bar shown. Left: The default session window or tab theme. Right: The Man Pages theme in a session tab divided into two panes.

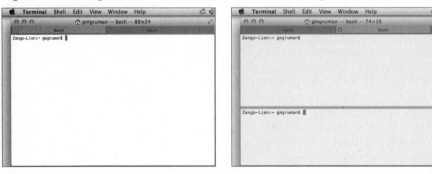

When you launch Terminal, you are looking at a working Bash shell's command prompt. (A shell is a variation of Unix's command language, which you can see by how the command prompt changes; you can think of it as a dialect.) You don't have to use Bash; Terminal supports several other shells, including tcsh. To change shells, open Terminal's Preferences dialog box (choose Terminal ➪ Preferences or press ⌘+, [comma]), go to the Startup pane, and in the Shell Opens With option, select Command (Complete Path) and enter your preferred shell path in the text field below (/bin/bash for Bash or /bin/tcsh for tcsh).

Some notes on using Terminal:

- Press ↑ to display the last command you entered, edit it if desired, and press Return to have the shell run it again. You can scroll up to any previous commands from the current session to rerun it or an edited version of it.

- You can drag files from the Finder into the shell rather than type their pathnames and filenames—it's an easy way to specify files in the command prompt.

- You can drag text clippings or text selections from Mac OS X applications that support drag-and-drop text into the command prompt to place that text there (again, so you don't have to retype it). You also can copy and paste text into the command prompt.

- To protect other applications on the Mac or the network from detecting the text you type into Terminal, choose Terminal ➪ Secure Keyboard Entry.

- You can save all the commands and responses into a text file for offline review and archiving from a Terminal session by choosing Shell ➪ Export Text As or pressing ⌘+S. You also can select text within the shell window using the mouse or touchpad and copy and paste it inside the window or elsewhere in Mac OS X using the standard Mac OS X commands (see Chapter 4).

- You also can print a window's or tab's contents by choosing Shell ➪ Print or pressing ⌘+P. To print just selected text in the window or tab, choose Shell ➪ Print Selection or press Option+⌘+P.

- You can add language encodings for languages other than the defaults for your Mac in the Preferences dialog box. Do so in the Encodings pane by selecting the desired languages. Note these encodings are available only in Terminal; to change Mac OS X's languages, use the Language & Text system preference as described in Chapter 28.

Multiple sessions

Much like the Safari web browser, Terminal enables you to open multiple session windows and tabbed panes (which it calls *tabs*) so that you can perform more than one task at a time. You open new windows and tabs via the Shell menu; each window or tab has an independent copy of the shell running in it; so, for example, you can copy a file while another is being used to create a document.

You can have multiple Terminal windows or tabs open at the same time; choose Shell ➪ New Window ➪ *theme*. Or press ⌘+N to open a new window using the Basic theme. For tabbed panes, choose Shell ➪ New Tab ➪ *theme*. Or press ⌘+T to open a new window using the Basic theme.

Being able to choose a specific theme is handy for distinguishing Terminal windows, so you can more easily keep track of what you are doing in each. Terminal's Preferences dialog box (choose Terminal ➪ Preferences or press ⌘+, [comma]) enables you to customize Terminal with themes or create your own themes by changing the color scheme, font, text size, cursor style, window size, and more using the controls in the Settings pane. For a faster but less customizable way to change Terminal's visual settings, choose Shell ➪ Show Inspector or press ⌘+I to open the Inspector panel, and then choose the desired appearance in the Settings pane.

Unix or UNIX?

Even though Unix is not an acronym (its name derives from the fact that it's the single-user, desktop and workstation version of the 1960s Bell Labs multi-user operating system Multics used in mainframes of the time), you often see it styled as UNIX. That's because in the 1940s through 1970s, when computers were incredibly expensive devices used only by a very small number of government agencies and large companies, scientists and engineers used all caps to refer to all computer systems and languages, as a way of indicating these were not human systems and languages. Thus, non-Unix languages such as Fortran and Basic were also styled as FORTRAN, COBOL, and BASIC, despite not being acronyms (they stand for Formula Translator, Common Business Language, and nothing, respectively).

Apple helped break that style with its Macintosh, which used both a natural name rather than some odd creation like Unix or Multics and capitalized it like any other name. Soon after, computer scientists began using human names and standard capitalization for new languages, such as Pascal, Smalltalk, Ada, and later Java. But many in the Unix community continue to use the old-fashioned all-caps style to refer to Unix and many Unix programs.

Ironically, many Unix users also refer to some facilities in all lowercase (such as the vi text editor), because of the convention of entering computer commands in all lowercase to save keystrokes in the typing-intensive world of early computer systems.

New Feature

In Mac OS X Lion, you can set new windows and tabs to open with the same settings as the current one or with the default settings set in the Preferences dialog box. ■

You can save a set of windows as a group that you can reopen all at once later: Choose Window ➪ Save Windows as a Group to create the group, and choose Window ➪ Open Window Group to open the group. Note that if you enable Use Window Group When Terminal Starts when creating a group, that group opens automatically when you launch Terminal.

You can have multiple Terminal sessions running in the same Terminal window or tab, so you can see the multiple sessions all at the same time. Choose Window ➪ Split Pane or press ⌘+D to open a new pane for a new session in the current Terminal window or tab. (You can open as many as you like.) To close a pane, be sure it is the active pane, and choose Windows ➪ Close Split Pane or press Shift+⌘+D.

By default, each tab has the name of the shell, which isn't very helpful in knowing what each is open for. You can change a tab's title by choosing Shell ➪ Edit Title or pressing Shift+⌘+I and entering a new title in the *second* text field in the Info pane of the Inspector panel that appears. (The first text field changes the title of the Terminal window itself.

The command prompt

In a session, you see a prompt at the beginning of each line. It indicates the name of the Mac and your location in the folder hierarchy. The Bash shell's command prompt looks like

Zango-Lion:~ gmgruman$ and the tcsh shell's command prompt looks like [Zango-Lion:~] gmgruman%.

In this example, zango is the name of the Mac given in the Sharing system preference (see Chapter 24), the ~ (tilde) signifies you're in the user's Home folder (/Users/gmgruman in this example). Finally, gmgruman indicates which user is logged in. If you go into the Documents folder, the prompt then looks like Zango-Lion:Documents gmgruman$ in Bash or [Zango-Lion:~/Documents] gmgruman% in tcsh.

Note that everything stayed the same except the tilde was replaced with Documents in Bash and /Documents in tcsh, indicating that you have moved from the Home folder to its Documents folder.

Tip

To quickly run a single Unix command without opening a new session, choose Shell ⇨ New Command or press Shift+⌘+N, and enter the command in the dialog box that appears, and click Run. ■

Remote access

Terminal is an ideal way to connect remotely to other Unix systems, including other Macs. You can access the remote-connection capabilities easily by choosing Shell ⇨ New Remote Connection. A dialog box opens with the various types of remote access services available. Click a service, and a list of nearby computers appears. Select a computer or enter a domain name or IP address for an unlisted computer in the field at the bottom of the dialog box. Either way, click Connect to start a session.

Usually, using the Secure Shell (SSH) service is best. This provides a shell environment like the one on the local system, except this shell is running on the remote system and any commands run in it are carried out on that remote system. It can be handy to access a Mac when Finder is not responding.

Tip

You can enable SSH on your Macs to make it simple to remotely access those Macs. To enable SSH on the Mac you want to be available for remote access, open the Sharing system preference and select the Remote Login option. (Most Linux PCs come with SSH enabled by default.) ■

The shell's special characters

The shell uses several special characters. For example, the asterisk (*) is used as s *wildcard*, meaning it can represent anything. For example, if you tell the shell to show files by the name of *, it shows all files; if you tell it to show files named *.doc, it shows all files with the file extension .doc.

The tilde (~) is useful when you're dealing with filenames. It represents the current user's Home folder, saving you the trouble of always typing something like /Users/jdoe.

Perhaps two of the handiest advanced symbols are the inequality symbols: < and >. When used in commands, the item on the side containing the point receives whatever is on the other side. For example, whatever is to the left of < receives from whatever is to the right of <, while whatever is to the right of > receives whatever is to the left of >. You often use these symbols to feed information from one program or device to another program or device.

Note

In Terminal, the caret (^) indicates the use of the Control key; for example, ^c means to press Control+C. Note that in Terminal's documentation and Preferences dialog box, the Control key is referred to as Ctrl, for consistency with the Windows, Linux, and Unix PC key of that name. ■

Much like other programs on a Mac, sometimes programs running in the shell go awry. When that happens, you can use Control+C to quit and Control+Z to force-quit the Unix program. Always try Control+C first because force-quitting could cause data loss.

The dollar sign ($) enables you to tap into *variables*, which hold information temporarily; referring to a variable's name is equivalent to referring to whatever value is currently stored in the variable. The shell provides many variables automatically (such as $PATH to indicate the current path and $HOME to indicate the home folder, which is usually the same as ~ but can be set to a different folder). You can create variables as well.

One of the most useful special characters in the repertoire is the backslash (\), called the *escape character*. The backslash usually influences how the shell processes the following letter. This is helpful, for example, if you want to use a dollar sign as a dollar sign and not as a symbol denoting a variable. For example, to type the phrase "I have $20.00" in the shell, you would enter **I have \$20.00**.

If you enter the phrase as I have $20.00, the shell interprets $2 as a variable and the phrase is interpreted as I have 0.00.

You can use the backslash to invoke other special characters. For example, if you want to create a variable with a carriage return in it, pressing Return does not work within a shell command, because the shell interprets a press of the Return key as an instruction to run the command, not as the Return character. But you can type \r to enter an actual carriage return in the text string. These sorts of symbols are especially useful when scripting the shell.

Scripting the shell

Scripting can be a huge timesaver if you use a set of commands over and over on a regular basis. Much of Mac OS X can be scripted (or otherwise automated) using AppleScript and Automator, as covered in Chapter 13. Scripting in the shell accomplishes a similar goal; shell scripts are relatively similar to batch scripts (.bat files) that longtime computer users will remember from Microsoft's MS-DOS.

At its simplest, a shell script is essentially a text document with one command on each line. When run, each line executes in turn. Although not required, shell scripts typically have the file extension .sh, as in myscript.sh.

Tip
You can use scripts written in other shells' commands or in other scripting languages, not just the commands included in your current shell. ∎

Using Basic Unix Commands

Most Unix commands observe a specific way of typing commands, known as a *command syntax*. Unix's command syntax typically involves typing a command (frequently a program name) followed by parameters that specify how that command should perform. These parameters are important because many Unix commands, unlike the GUI programs you use in Mac OS X, do not seek further user input after they have been launched. After typing a command, you must always press Return (often referred to as Enter in Unix help documents and labeled as such on PC keyboards) to issue the command, much as you would click OK to confirm your selections in a dialog box.

For example, to view files via the command line, type **ls** and press Return. (From this point I assume you know to press Return at the end of each command.) After doing so, you see a list of the files in the current folder.

However, if you want to see only Word documents, add a parameter to narrow the list results. For example, *.doc narrows the list to any filename (the * wildcard special character is explained earlier in this chapter) ending in .doc (the file extension for Word files): **ls *.doc**.

If you also want to display the results in a detailed list with information such as permissions and date, rather than multiple columns, you can add another parameter: **ls –l *.doc**. The –l is the parameter that says to show a detailed list.

Many commands can have dozens or even hundreds of different parameters and parameter combinations. Although some of these are shared from program to program, the combinations may be hard to figure out on your own. That's why you need to read documentation for a command to get the best use out of it.

Reading man pages

Man pages (short for *manual pages*) are brief documentation displayed in the shell on how to use a given command. They are particularly helpful in learning the syntax of the command in question. You access these man pages using the man command followed by the name of the program you want to learn about. For example, man ls displays the manual page for the ls command.

The typical man page is divided into several sections, as shown in Figure D.2. At the top is the header, which displays the name of the command and the section of the manual it is in. The header section is followed by a section that provides a short summary of the command, a synopsis of the parameters available for the command, and a description. Following a paragraph or two of explanation about the command is a typically exhaustive, or near exhaustive, list of parameters. An examples section often follows this. Finally, and sometimes most use-fully, is a See Also section, which can often point you in the direction of a related, and more appropriate, command for a given job.

A man page

Managing files and directories

No matter your level of expertise—or interest—in Unix, the commands to work with files and folders (what Unix calls *directories*) are ones you'll use often.

Moving about folders

When launching a new shell, you typically start in your Home folder, as explained earlier. You can see the full path to the open folder using the `pwd` command. This gives a response something like `/Users/gmgruman/Documents/Projects/Wiley`.

To change directories, use `cd`. Entering `cd` without any further parameters takes you back to the current user's Home folder. Add the pathname to go to a specific folder, such as `cd /usr/bin`. If you want to go into the Documents folder of the current user, it's easiest to use the tilde shorthand for the Home folder: `cd ~/Documents`, which is the same as typing `cd /Users/gmgruman/Documents`. You also can easily move up from a subfolder to its parent folder by typing the `cd ..` command.

Viewing a folder's contents

To see a listing of a folder's contents, use the `ls` (list) command. To view the contents of a different folder, add the pathname after the `ls` command; for example, `ls /usr/bin`. Entering the `ls` command by itself returns a multi-column list of all the files in the folder that are not hidden. Adding the `-a` parameter displays all files in the folder, including hidden files; for example, `ls -a`.

If you want to see basic information about the files along with the list—for example, the date modified and the file size (similar to what is shown in a Finder window's list view)—use the `ls -lh` instead.

Copying, moving, renaming, and deleting files and folders

The commands to move and copy files are `mv` and `cp`, respectively. In both cases, you enter the command, the filename (including its path if not in the current folder), and the path to where you want to move or copy the file. As always, you can use the wildcard (`*`) to specify multiple files that share all or part of a filename.

```
cp -r ~/Documents/Movies/* ~/Movies/
mv ~/Documents/Important\ Word\ Document.doc ~/Desktop/
```

The example `cp` command moves any files located in the first location, including folders, to the second location (the Movies folder in the user's Home folder).

The example `mv` command moves the file `Important Word Document.doc` from the user's Documents folder to the user's desktop. (The `\` preceding the spaces is an escape character, meaning to process the space as a space in the filename, not as a separator of shell commands and variables. I explained such special characters earlier in this appendix.)

If you move a folder, the `mv` command takes the folder and all its contents and relocates them to the new location; the command is the same as if you were working with a file. But if you try to copy a folder using `cp`, you get an error message. That's because to copy entire folders, you must add the `-r` parameter to the command; for example: `cp -r ~/Documents/Movies/* ~/Movies/`.

Note

Many Apple file types are not actually normal files at all, but folders with a special file extension on the end (such folders are called bundles or packages). Mac OS X applications (`.app`) and iMovie projects (`.rcproject`) are two examples. Although the Finder displays these packages as if they were a single file, Unix shells view them as folders with a collection of files in them. This means that to copy them, you need to use the `-r` flag, just like when copying other folders. ∎

The shell has no command to rename a file. Instead, you just move it, providing a new filename. That moves the old file into its new name. You can rename and move a file at the same time by specifying both the pathname and new filename. In the first example here, I'm renaming the file `Important Word Document.doc` to `Instructions.doc`, and in the second example, I'm also moving it to the desktop:

```
mv ~/Documents/Important\ Word\ Document.doc Instructions.doc
mv ~/Documents/Important\ Word\ Document.doc ~/Desktop/Instructions.
   doc
```

To delete a file, use the `rm` command; for example, `rm Instructions.doc` or `rm ~/Desktop/Instructions.doc`. As with copying, you need to add the `-r` parameter to delete folders; for example, `rm -r ~/Documents/Projects/Wiley`.

Caution

Unix doesn't have the same "are you sure?" features as Mac OS X, so you can easily rename, delete, or otherwise change critical system files and folders and have no way to confirm you meant to before the command is implemented. Deleted files also are not placed in the Trash when deleted via the shell. So be very careful. ■

Changing file and folder permissions

As Chapter 3 explains, you can change access permissions for files and folders using the Info window in Mac OS X. Normally, files and folders are readable and writable only by the user whose account they were created in and by the administrator. But you can set up groups of users (via the Sharing system preference, detailed in Chapter 24) and assign privileges to them and other individual users in the Unix shell as well, using the `chmod` command.

The `chmod` command can have as many as five parameters: the security group, the type of change (+ to add and – to remove), the permission you want to add or remove, and the file or folder you want to change the permission of. The four security groups are `u` for user, `g` for group, `o` for other, and `all` for everyone; these correspond to the four types of security groups shown in the Sharing system preference and Info window. The three permissions are `r` for read, `w` for write, and `x` for execute (such as for scripts and applications).

You can set multiple permissions at the same time by combining parameters and their options. For example, `chmod u-r ~/Desktop/Instructions.doc` removes the current user's permission to read the file `Instructions.doc` that's stored on the desktop. And `chmod go+rw ~/Documents/Projects/Wiley` lets any member of a group and anyone in the "others" category both read and write the contents of that folder.

Getting disk and file system statistics

Earlier in this appendix, I described the `ls` command to view a folder's contents. But the shell has other commands to get information on file and disks.

Use the `df -h` (disk and file) command to show all disks, discs, and network volumes connected to and mounted on your Mac, as well as how much space they have used and have available. (If you use just `df`, you get the usage information in bytes, not the more comprehensible kilobytes and megabytes that `df -h` provides.)

Each storage device in Unix is assigned a name, which is the name listed under the Filesystem column of the response to a df command. For example, the label /dev/disk0s3 indicates that the disk mounted as / is the system's primary hard disk (its startup disk) and that the partition mounted is number 3. If the disk had been partitioned with multiple partitions (for example, a second partition to run Windows in Boot Camp), there would be another disk labeled /dev/disk0s4.

Tip

The df command displays not just the mounted storage volumes but also some internal "volumes" that Mac OS X uses to refer to special folders and locations, such as /dev, /home, and /net. To remove these from the df results, use df -lg instead. ∎

If you want to know where the space is being used on disks and volumes, use the du –h (disk usage) command. It lists the folders in the current disk or folder and their usage information. (If you enter du instead of du –h, you get the size information in bytes rather than kilobytes and megabytes.)

Often, du provides way too much information. You can limit how deep in the folder hierarchy for which it displays usage information using the –d (depth) parameter. Follow this parameter with the number of folder levels to report on; for example, du – 1 – reports one level down, and du – 9 – reports all the way through nine levels down.

Logging in as a different user or as a superuser

When you open Terminal, you are automatically logged in with your Mac OS X user account. This enables you to view, edit, and delete the same files and run the same sorts of procedures you can do from Mac OS X as a normal, non-administrative user.

To log out of a shell session, just close the Terminal window (click the Close icon button for the window or choose Shell ⇨ Close Window) or close the individual tab, if you are using more than one pane (click the Close icon button on the pane's tab or choose Shell ⇨ Close Tab).

Note

If you have multiple tabs open, you can close the active one by pressing ⌘+W, and you can close the entire window (and all tab) by pressing Shift+⌘+W. If you have only one tab open, pressing ⌘+W closes the entire window. If you quit Terminal, all the tabs and windows close as well. ∎

Sometimes, however, you may want to work as a different user, such as if you are an IT support staffer working on an employee's Mac. If you set up the Macs appropriately for the workplace, the user doesn't have administrator privileges and instead logs in as a non-administrative user (see Chapter 27). But you'll probably need administrator privileges, and rather than restart the Mac in the administrator account, you can just give yourself administrator privileges in the shell session. You also might want to log in as a different user on a Mac that has multiple user accounts, so you can use Unix using your account even though the Mac is currently logged into someone else's account (whether or not either of you has administrator privileges).

To do so, just use the su command (it comes from *superuser*, though that term has a different meaning in Unix, as the next section explains) using another user's username as a parameter, followed by a space and a hyphen: su administrator –. (If the username includes spaces, put quotation marks around the username: su "Galen Gruman" –. You can avoid remembering to do that by using the account's short name, such as gmgruman.)

Log out back to the original account using the exit command.

Note

The hyphen in the su "Galen Gruman" – example tells su to launch the new shell just as if Galen himself had launched it. For most cases, this is the most useful procedure. However, you may want to act as another user but work with a file in the current folder. To do this, leave the hyphen off the command: su "Galen Gruman". Note that the hyphen-less command works only if the current directory is one that both the current user and the user account you are trying to log into have permission to view. ■

For most purposes, the ability to use su to assert someone else's privileges is fine; however, you occasionally may need system administrator access to perform commands. Traditionally, this access is permitted on Unix systems by logging into what is known as the *root* user, also known as the *superuser*. However, Mac OS X and some other recent Unix variants, such as Ubuntu Linux, have discarded the root user by default. In its place, if your Mac OS X user account has been made an administrator account (see Chapter 27), you can use the sudo command to achieve the same powers previously available to the separate superuser account. For example, if you want to view files belonging to another user account, you can type **sudo ls /Users/*otheruser***, replacing *otheruser* with the actual user account name. This sudo command prompts you for your account's password to ensure that you have permission to use it (a guest account would not, for example).

Tip

The Bash and tcsh shells can be run with the sudo command (sudo bash), which gives superuser privileges to everything done in that particular shell session. You also can use sudo su to run a true root user shell, rather than as a shell with root privileges; in that case, /var/root is set as your current Home folder. But be cautious: Leaving a root shell open allows anyone with access to your system to do virtually anything to it. ■

Tip

There is a 5-minute timeout when you use sudo, after which you must enter a password again to regain superuser privileges. You can avoid this password requirement if you use sudo bash or sudo su. ■

Using standard input, standard output, and pipes

Unix provides facilities to direct the input and output of information. By default, the standard input (called STDIN in Unix) is your keyboard and the standard output (called STDOUT) is your monitor. But you can change that, for example, to have the results of a command output to a text file or printer, or to have the contents of a database be the input to another database.

You use the inequality signs (< for input and > for output) described earlier in the section on special characters to direct that output. The information moves in the direction of the point, so < moves the input to the first location from the second (STDINPUT), and > moves the information from the first location to the second (STDOUTPUT)—it helps to think of < and > as directional arrows.

Note that using two inequality signs (<< or >>) appends the information to the input or output, whereas using one (< or >) creates or replaces the content in that input or output.

Here are some examples:

```
mail joan < recipes.txt
echo "Hello World" > hello.txt
du -h / >> directoryreport.txt
```

Sometimes, a command provides too much data to fit on screen. If you booted into Mac OS X, you can always scroll through the Terminal window to go through that information—that's one advantage of Terminal being a Mac OS X application rather than the complete environment as in a Linux PC. But because Unix was designed for non-graphical interfaces, it provides its own facility for managing the display of the data presented, called a *pipe*, that you access using the | special character. You need that if you booted the Mac into single-user mode and thus have only the Unix operating system running.

You may want to peruse the information immediately, but a command like du -h run in the main folder of a hard disk is too much to fit on the screen. This is where the shell's pipe character (|) can become very useful. The pipe character, like the inequality signs, enables you to manipulate interactions with a program's output. The simplest example is causing a program like du to pause its output every time it fills up the screen, so you can easily move up and down the results list at your leisure. For example, du -h / | less causes the shell to display the first screen of the du results; you need to scroll down using ↓ or Return to see the rest of the contents.

The down side of this method is that you have to finish scrolling down, which can take a long time using the ← or Return keys, before you can enter another command. To break that scrolling requirement, choose Shell ➪ Send Hard Reset or press Option+⌘+R.

Tip

If you want to search the output, when the output has appeared, you just type a forward slash (/) followed by the text you want to find. For example, typing /lion searches for lion in the output. ■

Using X11

Unix is a text-based operating system, but there is a graphical environment that can run in it. That GUI, called X Windowing System (or X11 for short), is provided with Mac OS X in the Utilities folder: Just double-click the X11 application to open the X1 window in its Terminal view, called Xterm. There, you can type the name of the X11 application you want to run using the standard pathnames and press Return to run the application, or you can run an application by choosing it from the Applications menu. (Choose Applications ➪ Customize to add applications to that list.)

X11 also loads automatically if you have downloaded an X11-based application onto your Mac and have launched that application. (You can put those applications in the Dock, create aliases to them, and otherwise manage their files like any Mac OS X application.) The Gimp image editor is an example of such an X11 application. Figure D.3 shows X11 running Gimp.

FIGURE D.3

X11 running the Gimp image editor

Glossary

AAC (Advanced Audio Coding)—A standard for creating digital music files. It's the default format for iTunes music and is higher in quality than the more commonly used MP3 format.

absolute pathname—A pathname that specifies the exact location of a single directory. An absolute pathname begins at the root directory, a slash (/), and traverses through the Unix file system, ending at the desired directory or file, and naming each directory that is passed through. Each directory that is passed through is named and separated by a slash. /Users/galen/Documents is the absolute pathname of the user Galen's Documents folder. Compare to *relative path*.

active application—The application visible in the foreground. If iTunes is the active application, its name is visible in bold in the menu bar, directly to the right of the (Apple) menu.

ActiveSync—Microsoft's technology to keep e-mail, contacts, and calendars continuously synchronized between its Exchange servers and computers using its Outlook and Entourage applications. Mac OS X (as well as iOS) includes ActiveSync, allowing Apple's Mail, iCal, and Address Book to synchronize automatically to Exchange servers as well.

adapter—A device that lets devices with different connector standards connect to each other.

admin—See *administrator account*.

administrator account—A type of Mac OS X user account that gives the user access to system-wide resources, including the abilities to modify system preferences, create and edit other user accounts, and install applications. When

Mac OS X is initially set up, the first user created is an administrator.

adopted ownership—When a Mac OS X user account is deleted, its contents can be transferred to an existing administrator account. The admin is said to be adopting ownership of the previous user's files.

Advanced Memory Management—A Mac OS X capability that automatically and dynamically assigns and handles the allocation of both physical RAM and virtual memory to applications and processes as needed.

AirDrop—The technology introduced in Mac OS X Lion that allows compatible Macs on the same network to see each other and allow users to place documents in each other's Documents folder without enabling file sharing.

AirPort Base Station—An Apple wireless router that connects 802.11-equipped (Wi-Fi) computers (Macintosh or otherwise) and other devices (such as printers and hard disks) to it, allowing them to connect to each other and to an Internet gateway. The Extreme and Express versions also can wirelessly share attached USB printers, while the Time Capsule model includes a disk for wireless data backup.

alias—Also known as a *shortcut*, an alias is a pointer file that can dynamically locate its target file or folder. (You would use it to place a pointer from, say, the desktop to a file buried deep in your Mac's folder hierarchy for easy access.) The pathway is not lost if either the original or the alias is moved to a different location on the same volume. Under the Mac file system, each file has a unique identifier, which can be traced even if the file has moved.

Glossary

anti-aliasing—A technique that causes text and graphics to appear smoother when displayed using the relatively low resolution of a computer screen. Shading and blending of otherwise jagged lines are used to fool the eye into seeing a cleaner image.

Apache—An open-source web server provided within every copy of Mac OS X and Mac OS X Server. Apache is the most widely used web server (powering more than two thirds of all websites) on the Internet. It runs on a variety of platforms, including Unix-based and Windows servers.

API—See *application programming interface*.

app—Short for *application*, this term usually refers to applications available on iOS and other mobile devices. However, Apple uses the same word in its Mac App Store to refer to traditional computer applications.

Apple Filing Protocol (AFP)— Mac OS X's built-in technology that lets Macs share files with each other over network connections.

** (Apple) menu**—Located at the top-left corner of the screen, this menu contains commands that affect the Mac as a whole, no matter what application you may be running at the time. Example functions include changing the settings of the Dock, updating Mac OS X, and shutting down the Mac.

AppleCare Knowledge Base—Located at www. apple.com/support, the Knowledge Base is Apple's official web-based library of articles and information pertaining to the usage and support of its products.

AppleScript—A Mac-only scripting language used for automating tasks and customizing application features, as well as creating stand-alone applets. The language is heavily English based (more so than most scripting languages), making it easy to learn and decipher.

AppleScript is included with every copy of Mac OS X. An application that lets you create AppleScripts for its functions is called *scriptable*.

applet—A mini-application program that is usually Java- or AppleScript-based. Java applets often are embedded within web pages (like an Internet search engine), and AppleScripts are often integrated within a larger application to perform a certain function; within Apple's DVD Player application, for example, you can use the Scripts menu to run an AppleScript that accesses a specific time within a movie.

application—A software program such as Adobe Photoshop, the Finder, iTunes, Microsoft Word, Safari, and TextEdit.

application programming interface (API)— The method by which an application or operating system makes its functions available for use by other applications and system components. For example, the QuickTime API would be called upon to add movie and sound features to an application.

Applications folder—The default location for all applications installed on the Mac. Applications do not have to be placed in this folder, but it is a good idea to keep them here, both so you can easily find them later and in case their software update features require them to be in that folder.

Aqua—Apple's name for the look and feel of the graphical user interface that distinguishes Mac OS X from competitors such as Microsoft Windows. The pulsating OK buttons, the photo-realistic icons, and the fancy Genie effect that occurs when a window is minimized to the Dock are all examples of Aqua.

archive—A single compressed file containing files and folders. These archives typically take less space, making them more efficient for e-mailing and backup storage. The StuffIt and Zip formats are common archive formats for the

Mac, with the Zip format supported natively in Mac OS X.

argument—A piece of information that is passed to a Unix command on the command line. Arguments are usually filenames or directory names. For example, in the command `% chown galen:staff/Users/galen/Documents`, the argument is the Documents folder's file path (`galen:staff/users/galen/`).

arrow keys—The four keys that move the pointer vertically or horizontally: ↑, ↓, →, and ←. PC users call them *cursor keys.*

ASCII (American Standard Code for Information Interchange)—The most basic character set used by almost all modern computers. ASCII uses the codes 0 through 127 to represent uppercase and lowercase letters, punctuation, space, and numbers. An enhanced ASCII version uses the codes 0 through 255 to support a wider variety of characters, but ASCII has largely been supplanted by Unicode and the ISO/IEC 10646 Universal Character Set (UCS) standards. Mac OS X uses both Unicode and UCS, both of which support the original ASCII codes as well.

authentication—The process of verifying that someone is, in actuality, who he or she claims to be. Under Mac OS X, when you type a correct password into the login screen, you are being authenticated before being allowed to log in to the system.

Auto Save—The capability introduced in Mac OS X Lion that applications can use to automatically save documents and to lock documents from accidental saves if they have not been edited in a user-specified period.

Automator—A Mac OS X utility used to create workflows that let you automate functions in Automator-compatible applications and then save those workflows for later reuse.

auto-scrolling—When you drag an item to the edge of a window, Mac OS X automatically scrolls the workspace for you, instead of requiring you to manually click the window's scroll arrows or drag the scroll bar first to reveal the off-window workspace.

AV Foundation—A new framework within Mac OS X's core that provides essential services for working with time-based audiovisual media. Through an Objective-C interface, developers can use AV Foundation to play, examine, and compose audiovisual media in their application, as well as to edit and encode media files, and capture audio and video from external devices and manipulate them. Also see *frameworks.*

background program—A program that, while running, is usually not visible to the Mac's user. Launch the Activity Monitor utility to see examples of this. The iChat Agent is one such example. This process runs in the background and can sign the user on to the instant messaging service even if the iChat application is not open yet.

backup—A copy of files and other data meant to help recover from data loss, which may occur due to hardware failure, corruption, viruses, natural disasters, theft, and human error. A backup can be as simple as a collection of files copied to a disk or CD, or a complete replica of your Mac's files and system preferences stored on a hard disk or network file server automatically by using a program such as Mac OS X's own Time Machine.

badge—An indicator (usually elliptical) that overlays an icon or other control. For example, when you drag items in the Finder, a badge with the number of items being dragged appears near the pointer.

binary—The number system that computers use, which is base two, unlike the number system humans use, which is base ten. Binary has two number choices: one or zero. A single binary digit is called a *bit.*

Glossary

binary file—A type of compressed and encoded file, usually containing the `.bin` file extension. MacBinary files are encoded so that the data contained in them can be stored on other operating systems (like Microsoft Windows) and transferred back and forth without issue. Mac OS X can decode these files; just double-click them.

BinHex—A method of encoding and compressing binary files for download and transfer. BinHex files have a `.hqx` file extension and are a common format in which to receive Macintosh software downloads. Mac OS X can decode these files; just double-click them.

bit—Stands for *binary digit*. A bit is the smallest unit of information storage, a one or a zero, a yes or a no, an on or an off, a true or a false.

bit depth—The number of bits of information that are required to represent the number of colors available on the screen. For example, a screen that can display thousands of colors is set at a bit depth of 16 bits (2^{16} supports up to 65,536 colors).

bitmap font—A font composed of pixels, rather than scalable outlines, and thus limited in the text sizes it supports. Bitmap fonts are all but extinct.

Bluetooth—A short-range wireless networking technology standard supported by most Macs, typically used to connect headphones, headsets, smartphones, and other devices to a Mac.

Blu-ray—A recent standard for high-capacity optical discs. It is not natively supported in Mac OS X, though programs such as Roxio's Toast enables Macs to write to (but not read) Blu-ray drives.

Bonjour—An Apple networking technology requiring no configuration. Connect and turn on the device, and your Mac can see it and use it. Because it is an Apple standard, non-Apple devices (as well as some fairly old Apple devices) may not offer support for the technology. Note that Apple provides Bonjour software for Microsoft's Windows operating system as well; the software is available at `http://support.apple.com/downloads/Bonjour_for_Windows`.

bookmark—A saved hyperlink in a web browser, which lets you click the link to get to its web page easily in the future. For example, when using Safari, if you want to save *Macworld*'s website (`www.macworld.com`) for future viewing, you can choose Bookmarks ➪ Add Bookmark to save the location, and then just click the bookmark in the future to get to the website, instead of retyping `www.macworld.com` each time.

boot—The act of powering on a Mac and having the operating system loaded and started. Also called *bootup* and *startup*.

Boot Camp—Apple's technology that enables Mac OS X to create a separate disk partition from which you can run Microsoft Windows on a Mac with an Intel-based processor. You can boot between Mac OS X and Windows, but not run both simultaneously under Boot Camp. Using a technology called virtual machines, applications such as EMC VMware Fusion and Parallels Desktop let you run both Mac OS X and Windows simultaneously.

bootup—See *boot*.

bridge—A piece of hardware used to move traffic between two different types of networks or networking hardware. An AirPort Base Station is a bridge when it routes information from a wired Ethernet network to its wireless one.

browser—See *web browser*.

BSD (Berkeley Software Distribution)—There are many different versions or "flavors" of Unix, including distributions called Linux, Solaris, and AIX. BSD is an umbrella term for the Unix flavor that has been released by the University of

California at Berkeley. Mac OS X is based on this version.

BSD subsystem—Together with the Mach kernel, the BSD subsystem makes up Apple's own flavor of Unix, called Darwin. On top of Darwin, Apple placed its proprietary frameworks (such as Carbon, Cocoa, and QuickTime) and its Aqua user interface, resulting in Mac OS X.

bug—An error in a piece of software (like a program) or hardware (like a printer) that causes an unwanted behavior, usually resulting in a malfunction. A well-known bug was the Y2K bug, which left many computers (Macs excluded) vulnerable to reverting to the year 1900 instead of the year 2000, due to the two-digit year limitation encoded in most software. Updates, or patches (also known as *bug fixes*), are usually released to repair bugs.

built-in memory—Apple's terminology for the RAM (random access memory) that is physically installed in the Mac.

bundle—Another term for *package*.

burn—When information is recorded onto a CD or DVD, the disc is said to be burned. The term stems from the way optical discs are recorded, which involves using a laser beam to heat a layer of photosensitive dye.

burn-in—1. A condition affecting CRT monitors in which a vestige of an unchanging screen image remains visible after the image changes and even after the computer has powered off. Today's computer screens are no longer susceptible to burn-in. 2. The process of letting a new or hardware-upgraded Mac run for at least several hours to make sure the system is functioning correctly.

button—A displayed control that, when clicked, causes an action to take place. (Apple's formal name for this control is *push button*.) A label on

the button indicates the action that the button performs. The label may be text or an icon. Buttons with text labels are generally rectangular with rounded ends. Buttons with icon labels may be any shape.

byte—One byte is comprised of eight bits. A byte is the smallest unit of storage that the Mac recognizes. Bytes are commonly measured by many thousands (kilobytes, or K), millions (megabytes, or MB), billions (gigabytes, or GB), and trillions (terabytes, or TB) at a time.

Carbon—Apple's technology that enables developers to create applications that run in both Mac OS 9 and Mac OS X, appearing to be "native" applications in both OSes. Given that Mac OS 9 was discontinued more than a decade ago, few developers still create Carbon applications.

CardBus—A compact form of the PCMCIA add-in card slot standard used for many years by Apple in its laptops. It has been replaced by the ExpressCard standard. See *ExpressCard* and *PCMCIA*.

case-sensitive—*Case-sensitive* means that it matters whether or not letters are capitalized. Passwords in Mac OS X are case-sensitive. In some instances, such as in the screen saver password window, the dialog box informs you if the Caps Lock key is pressed, alleviating the frustration of being sure you have the correct password but unknowingly having entered it in all caps.

character—A written representation of a letter, digit, or symbol. A single character could be the letter W or an exclamation point. Also called a *glyph*.

check box—A type of user-interface option that gives you the option of activating or deactivating a setting, offered by an application or within the operating system. A check box has three states: blank, checked, or dashed. A check indicates a setting is chosen; a blank means a setting has

Glossary

not been chosen; and, in the case where a check box has a disclosure triangle that reveals sub-check boxes, a dash is shown if some sub-check boxes are checked and others are not. Compare this option to the *radio button*.

Classic—The Mac OS 8 and Mac OS 9 operating systems' application environment. The term is used to refer to applications designed to run in these pre-Mac OS X applications. Mac OS X Lion does not support Classic applications, unlike pre-Snow Leopard versions of Mac OS X.

CLI—See *command-line interface.*

click—The quick pressing and release of a mouse button or touchpad button or the equivalent short tap gesture on a touchpad. A click is usually used to select an object or location.

click-through—The ability to interact directly with an item in an inactive window. For example, you can operate the Close, Minimize, and Zoom buttons in most inactive Aqua windows.

client—A program (or a computer running a program) that requests and receives information or services from a server.

clipping file—A file created by the Finder to hold material that has been dragged from a document to the desktop or a Finder window.

closed network—A Wi-Fi network that requires you to type its name to connect to it. Such a network does not display in Mac OS X's list of available networks and is meant to essentially be hidden from all but those who know the network exists. Also called an *invisible network.*

Cocoa—Applications that are specifically developed for Mac OS X. Cocoa applications are incompatible with older Macintosh operating systems, such as Mac OS 9. Cocoa applications take advantage of all Mac OS X's modern OS features, such as advanced memory, preemptive multi-tasking, multi-processing, and the Aqua interface.

codec (compressor-decompressor)—A tool (software, hardware, or both) that compresses data so it takes less space to store and decompresses compressed data back to its original form for playback or other use. Codecs are typically used for audio and video files.

collated—The process of printing multiple copies of a document so each copy has all its pages in the correct order.

color depth—See *bit depth.*

color picker—The panel in which you specify a custom color either by clicking within a color wheel or by clicking a color sample or other form of preselected color values.

ColorSync—Apple's technology to ensure accurate reproduction of color as graphics move from application to screen to printer.

column view—A view of files and folders in a Finder window in which each folder's contents is displayed in its own column, providing a horizontal hierarchy of your disk's contents.

⌘ (Command)—The key used to invoke Mac OS X and application functions from the keyboard. For example, ⌘+A is used to select all, while ⌘+Q is used to quit an application. It is often combined with other modifier keys such as Option, Shift, and Control.

command-line interface—A keyboard-only method of interacting with the operating system. The Mac uses the Terminal application to accept command lines.

comment—An AppleScript line or a Unix command line with a number sign or hash character (#), which in either case means that the line is descriptive and not a command to be performed.

compile—To convert the human-readable text of a programming language (such as C or any of its derivatives) into command codes that a Mac can execute. In AppleScript, compiling checks the script for nonconformance with AppleScript grammar, such as the use of a parenthesis.

compression algorithm—A method for compressing data so it fits in less space and can be transferred more quickly. Each compression algorithm generally works best with one type of data, such as photographs, video or motion pictures, and computer-generated animation. Three characteristics of a compression algorithm determine how effectively it compresses: compression ratio, fidelity to the original data, and speed.

compression ratio—Indicates the amount of compression and is calculated by the size of the original source data by the size of the compressed data. Larger compression ratios mean greater compression and generally (although not always) a loss of quality in the compressed data.

conditional—A programming command that evaluates a condition (stated as part of the conditional) to determine whether another command or set of commands should be performed. Also referred to as a *conditional statement*.

configuration profile—A group of settings that can restrict user access to specified applications and controls and to preconfigure security and other settings for users. Such profiles can be created in Mac OS X Server and distributed to Macs and iOS devices.

connector—The part of a cable, usually a plug, that connects into a device's jack.

contextual menu—A contextual menu lists commands relevant to an item that you right-click or Control+click.

Control—A modifier key on the Mac used both for application and system shortcuts and for opening contextual menus (when the Control key is held and the mouse or touchpad button is pressed). Applications' menus use the symbol ^ to indicate this key.

conversation—See *message threading*.

Core Location—A technology that uses known Wi-Fi hot spots to triangulate your current position. In Mac OS X, it is used to automatically determine your present time zone and adjusts the clock accordingly.

Cover Flow view—A view of files and folders in a Finder window in which files and folders are represented as a series of album-cover–like icons that you can "thumb through" using the → and ← keys. This view is based on the popular Cover Flow view in iTunes for visually finding music by album cover.

CPU (central processing unit)—The key component in a computer for processing the instructions that let the operating system, drivers, and applications operate. It is a silicon chip that contains millions of circuits.

CPU core—Modern CPUs contain several independent processing engines, called cores, that act as if they were separate CPUs. This multicore CPU approach allows more processing power to be delivered by computers, using less energy, costing less to produce, and taking less space than having multiple, separate CPUs.

crack—A means of circumventing a program's security.

crop markers—Small triangles that indicate the beginning and end of a selected part of a movie in iMovie HD.

crossover cable—A cable whose wires are reversed inside the plug at one end of the cable. Such a cable is required for most pre-2002 Macs to allow direct-connection networking.

cursor—1. A pointer, also called the I-beam pointer, that indicates the current position in text. 2. A name for the arrow keys (traditionally used by PC users).

Glossary

custom installation—The process by which you can selectively install Mac OS X packages' components.

daisy-chaining—The process of connecting one peripheral or network device to another device, linking them so they can share data. This is often done with Ethernet networking hubs to extend the size of an Ethernet network: One hub is connected to another to allow more connections in total than the first hub can support by itself. The same technique is used with FireWire and Thunderbolt devices to connect one to the next and eventually to a single Mac, which can then access them all.

Darwin—The core technologies underlying Mac OS X that Apple acquired from NeXT and then made available as open-source code for anyone to use. (The version used in Mac OS X and iOS is called Rhapsody.)

Dashboard—Mac OS X's window containing active widgets and the controls to activate and deactivate widgets.

dead keys—The keys that generate accented characters when typed in combination with the Option key and in proper sequence. For example, pressing Option+E and then typing **O** generates Ó on a U.S. keyboard.

desktop—The default screen in Mac OS X after you boot up, showing all connected disks and any folders or files you placed on the desktop. It is used both as the starting point for navigating your Mac's disks, folders, and files, as well as a convenient place to put frequently used files and folders or the aliases to them.

device—A piece of hardware attached to a computer, either internally or externally. Some examples include keyboards, scanners, and disks.

device driver—Software that controls a device, such as a printer or scanner. The driver contains data required to fully use the device.

DHCP (Dynamic Host Configuration Protocol)—A networking service in which a host device, such as a router, dynamically assigns network information (such as TCP/IP addresses) to client computers to grant them access to other network services.

dialog box—A movable window that displays options you can set or select; when open, a dialog box usually prevents you from accessing other controls in the application. A dialog box typically has a button for accepting the changes and another button for canceling the changes. Both buttons close the dialog box.

digital signature—Like its handwritten counterpart, a digital signature identifies the person who vouches for the accuracy and authenticity of the signed document. A digital signature typically involves a code appended to or included with the file that is verified against an independent database of authenticated codes on the Internet or network.

DIMM—A DIMM (dual in-line memory module) is a small circuit board containing memory of the format standard in desktop Macs. A SO-DIMM (Small Outline DIMM) is the laptop version.

directory—Another name for a folder.

Directory Services—Provides a consolidated user list that can be shared via multiple network services or servers for authentication. Directory Services do not provide the user list data itself but rather describe how they are set up and enable the communication of the data.

disc—An optical storage medium such as CD or DVD.

disclosure triangle—A user-interface control that regulates how much detail you see in a window. When the window is displaying minimal detail, clicking a disclosure triangle reveals additional detail and may automatically enlarge the window to accommodate it (this is called *expanding* the option). Clicking the same triangle again hides detail and may automatically shrink the window to fit (this is called *collapsing* the option).

disk—A magnetic or other non-optical storage medium such as a hard disk or solid-state drive.

disk cache—A technique for improving system performance by storing recently used information from disk in a dedicated part of memory. Accessing information in memory is faster than accessing information on disk.

disk image—A file that, when mounted using Disk Utility or a similar utility, appears on the desktop as if it were a removable disk.

display mirroring—See *video mirroring.*

DisplayPort—A recent standard for video-display connections that has become the standard on newer Macs.

DNS (Domain Name System)—A service that resolves domain names to IP addresses, and vice versa.

Dock—Mac OS X's quick-access bar for applications, as well as for access to the Trash, the Downloads folder, and open files.

domain name—The part of a URL that identifies the owner of an Internet location. A domain name has the form companyname.com, organization name.net, schoolname.edu, militaryunitname.mil, governmentagencyname.gov, and so on.

dongle—A hardware adapter or device that typically plugs into a jack and either sticks out from that jack or dangles from a short cord plugged into that jack.

double-click—Two clicks that occur very quickly together, used as a way to indicate an action for whatever is clicked, such as opening a file.

double-click speed—The rate at which you have to click the mouse or touchpad button so Mac OS X perceives two clicks in a row as a single event.

download—The process of receiving software or other files from another computer or server, whether over the Internet or a local network.

dpi (dots per inch)—A measure of how fine or coarse the dots are that make up a printed image. More dots per inch means smaller dots, and smaller dots mean finer (less coarse) printing.

drag—To move the pointer while holding down the mouse or touchpad button (or using the equivalent touchpad gesture); this moves, or drags, the selected object.

drag-and-drop editing—To copy or move selected text, graphics, or other material by dragging it to another place in the same window, a different window, or the desktop. Some applications do not support drag-and-drop editing.

drag-and-drop open—To drag a document onto a compatible application in the Finder or Dock; when you release the mouse or touchpad button, the application launches (if it's not already running) and opens the document.

drive—A hardware device that contains a storage medium, such as a hard disk, solid-state memory, or optical disc reader.

Drop Box—A shared folder located inside a user's Public folder in which other users may place items (when peer-to-peer file sharing is enabled), but only the folder's owner can see them.

drop-down menu—See *menu* and *pop-up menu*.

DSL (Digital Subscriber Line)—An Internet access service that uses standard telephone wiring. It typically is offered as an add-on to regular phone service, but also can be offered without phone service.

duplex—A method of automatically printing on both sides of the page.

DVI (Digital Video Interface)—The video-display connection standard used on many Macs. The DisplayPort technology has displaced DVI on newer Macs.

dynamic IP address—See *DHCP*.

dynamic RAM allocation—An operating system technology that allows Mac OS X to respond to an application's request for more or less memory as needed.

Easter egg—An undocumented "feature" usually hidden inside an application by a programmer without the publisher's knowledge. An Easter egg might be a hidden message or credits reel. You reveal it by performing secret combinations of keystrokes and clicks.

enclosing folder—The folder in which another file (or folder) exists.

encryption—The process of scrambling the data in a file or message so it cannot be understood by anyone without the correct decryption key. Mac OS X Lion offers the FileVault capability to encrypt its startup disks, Disk Utility can encrypt disks and partitions when it formats them, and the Time Machine utility can encrypt backup files.

Esc—A key, commonly spoken as "escape," that is usually used to stop an action, clear a field, or close a user-interface element. Note that its behavior depends on the application that is running when you press it.

escape character—A character used in programming languages and command-line interfaces to indicate that the next character is to be used literally, not interpreted as a wildcard or other special character. In Unix, a backslash (\) is used as the escape character, but some languages use other characters.

Ethernet—A high-speed standard for connecting computers and other devices in a wired network. Ethernet ports are built into most Macs, in many printers, and even in some disk drives.

event message—A means of interprocess communication. Applications can send event messages to one another. When an application receives an event message, it takes an action according to the content of the message. This action can be anything from executing a particular command to taking some data, working with it, and then returning a result to the program that sent the message.

Exchange—Microsoft's server software for managing e-mail, contacts, and calendars. This server software is typically used in businesses and is supported natively in Mac OS X.

ExFAT—The file system used on solid-state drives formatted in Windows.

expand—A touchpad gesture comprised of spreading fingers apart, usually used to zoom out (expand the view area).

Exposé—Apple's window management function, which is designed to afford users easy access to all open applications, windows, or the desktop.

ExpressCard—A connection standard for a hardware device that can be inserted into a slot in a laptop. The ExpressCard standard replaces the CardBus standard; CardBus devices cannot be used in an ExpressCard slot, or vice versa, without a special adapter.

extension—See *file extension.*

F keys—The keys at the top of most Mac keyboards labeled F1 through F12 (or F16 on extended keyboards); also called *function keys.* They are typically used to quickly change Mac settings, such as increasing the speaker volume or displaying the Dashboard. Applications may assign them different functions; when both Mac OS X and an application use an F key, holding Fn while pressing the F key usually invokes the application's assigned function instead of Mac OS X's.

file extension—The last part of a file's name, typically three or four letters, following a period. The extension helps to designate an item's file type.

file server—A computer running a program that makes files centrally available for other computers on a network.

file sharing—The technology that lets you share files with people whose computers are connected to yours in a network. Mac OS X uses Apple Filing Protocol but also supports Windows' SMB protocol for file sharing.

file system—A method of organizing data on a volume. Mac OS X uses either HFS+ or the UFS file system for its hard disks, either HFS+ or ExFAT for solid-state drives, UDF for DVDs, and either HFS or ISO 9660 for CD-ROMs.

file type—See *file extension*.

FileVault—The whole-disk encryption feature for startup disks in Mac OS X Lion. (See *encryption*.)

filter—1. A technique using user-defined rules to process messages in Mail, such as to delete unwanted messages automatically and place certain messages in specified folders automatically. 2. A technology that applies special effects to an image, such as a visual effect to a QuickTime movie.

Finder—The core system application that allows users to interact with the operating system, such as opening folders and navigating windows, using icons and input devices such as mice and touchpads.

firewall—A device or software that places a block between your Mac and other computers and devices in your local network or on the Internet. The firewall is meant to keep out unauthorized users and applications, and can be used to prevent local users from accessing unauthorized services or sharing unauthorized data with outsiders.

FireWire—Apple's name for the IEEE 1394 standard of device connections, typically used for external storage drives and video cameras. See *IEEE 1394*.

firmware—Low-level programming stored on a device that tells the hardware of a computer (or device) how to operate.

Fn—A key that is used as a modifier key, primarily with the F keys.

folder action—An AppleScript script attached to a folder so it can watch and respond to user interaction with that folder in the Finder.

font—A set of characters that have a common and consistent design, such as Helvetica Bold or Apple Gothic.

font family—A collection of differently styled variations (such as bold, italic, and plain) of a single font. Many fonts come in the four basic styles: plain, bold, italic, and bold italic. Some font families include many more styles, such as light, medium, black, and condensed.

Glossary

Fonts folder—Mac OS X has several Fonts folders, each of which can hold bitmap, PostScript Type 1, OpenType, and TrueType fonts. Fonts stored in `/System/Fonts` are available for Mac OS X, for all applications, and for all users; only fonts installed by Mac OS X should be kept here. Fonts stored in `/System/Library/Fonts` are also available for Mac OS X, all applications, and all users. Fonts stored in `/System/Users/username/Library/Fonts` are available only for Mac OS X and applications when that specific user account is active.

4G—Fourth-generation radio technology for data transfer that began to be deployed in 2010 in some areas, augmenting the 3G networks typically used for wireless data by iPhones, iPads, and other mobile devices. Types of 4G technologies include LTE and WiMax. Each carrier chooses which ones it supports. Also see *3G*.

fps (frames per second)—A measurement of how smoothly a motion picture plays. More frames per second means smoother playback. This measurement is used when discussing the frame rate of time-based media.

frame—One still image that is part of a series of still images, which, when shown in sequence, produce the illusion of movement.

frame rate—The number of frames displayed in one second. The TV frame rate is 30 fps in the United States and other countries that use the NTSC broadcasting standard and 25 fps in countries that use the PAL or SECAM standard. The standard movie frame rate is 24 fps. Also see *fps*.

frameworks—Mac OS X frameworks contain dynamically loading code that is shared between applications. Frameworks alleviate the need for applications that utilize identical code to load multiple iterations of the same code simultaneously.

freeware—Free software primarily distributed over the Internet and from person to person. Most freeware is still copyrighted by the person who created it. You can use it and give it to other people, but you can't sell it. Also see *shareware*.

FTP (File Transfer Protocol)—A data communications protocol that the Internet and other TCP/IP networks use to transfer files between computers.

FTP site—A collection of files on an FTP server available for downloading.

full motion—Video displayed at frame rates of 24 to 30 fps. The human eye perceives fairly smooth motion at frame rates of 12 to 18 fps. Also see *fps* and *frame rate*.

full-screen mode—The display of an application or video without the Finder's menu bar or windows. Typically, controls are hidden until you move the pointer or press a key; they then appear briefly unless used.

function keys—See *F keys*.

gamma—The relationship between the intensity of color and its luminance.

gamma correction—A method of compensating for the loss of detail that the human eye perceives in dark areas.

Genie effect—The visual effect used when minimizing or maximizing an application to or from the Dock, in which it appears to expand or shrink much like a genie going into or out of a bottle. Mac OS X also offers the Scale effect.

Genius—A technology used in iTunes that analyzes music for patterns to determine what other music is similar. It is meant to help create playlists of similar music and to provide suggestions of similar music users also may want to purchase when buying a specific song. Genius also is used in other Apple stores, such as the App Store, to make recommendations for similar products.

gestures—A user-interface technique in which you use one or more fingers' motion across a Mac's touchpad (typically available on MacBooks since 2008 and in the optional Apple Magic Trackpad for all Macs) or on an iPhone, iPad, or iPod Touch to control the device. Example gestures include pinching, expanding, swiping, rotating, tapping, and dragging. See *touchpad*.

glyph—A character in a font, such as a letter, punctuation, space, or symbol.

GPU (graphics processing unit)—A processing chip that can reside on a computer's motherboard or on its graphics card, designed to handle the delivery of video, such as in games and movies to the computer screen. Mac OS X's OpenCL technology lets it use the GPU for non-graphical operations when the GPU is not in use, speeding up application performance.

Grand Central Dispatch—The technology in Mac OS X that automatically divides up tasks within an application across each CPU core, allowing faster processing than in pre-Snow Leopard versions of Mac OS X.

group—A method of assigning privileges, such as access rights, to multiple users at once so they have identical levels of access and can all have their privileges changed simultaneously by changing just their group's settings.

guest—A network user who is not identified by a name and password.

guest account—The user account that you can set up for a Mac that provides limited access to the Mac's files and applications for guests, such as the babysitter or your kids' friends.

GUI (graphical user interface)—A means of interacting with and controlling a computer by manipulating graphical objects shown on the display, such as windows, menus, and icons. Also see *command-line interface*.

H.264—A video standard used by Apple to compress and play video. Also known as MPEG-4 Part 10 and MPEG-4 AVC. Also see *MPEG-4* and *codec*.

hack—1. A programming effort that accomplishes something resourceful or unconventional. 2. A disparaging term for a quick fix or for a poorly skilled technician.

hacker—1. A person who likes to tinker with computer technology and especially with computer software code. Some hackers create new software and enable existing hardware to do things unintended by the original manufacturer, but many hackers make unauthorized changes to existing software. 2. Someone who maliciously breaks into secure systems over the Internet or other network connection.

handler—A named set of AppleScript commands that you can execute by naming the handler elsewhere in the same script instead of repeating the entire set of commands several times in different parts of a script. This is also sometimes called a *subroutine*.

helper application—A program that handles a particular kind of media or other data encountered on the Internet. Examples include the Adobe Reader and Adobe Flash helper applications that let browsers open PDF files and play Flash files, respectively.

help tag—A short description of the object under the mouse pointer in a Mac OS X application. The description appears in a small yellow box near the object. These also are known as *Tool Tips* when used in panels and dialog boxes.

Glossary

HFS (Hierarchical File System)—A file format designed for hard disks and CD-ROMs, it is now used just for CD-ROM drives on Mac OS X. Also see *ISO 9660*.

HFS+ (Hierarchical File System Plus)—An extended file format designed for high-capacity hard disks, it is the standard format for disks in Mac OS X. In Mac OS X's Disk Utility, the HFS+ formatting is called Mac OS Extended.

Home folder—The folder in which users store all their personal files; each user account has its own Home folder, which is found in `/Users`. Mac OS X also preserves settings for the user in his or her Home folder's Library folder.

home page—The main page of a website, the one that appears when a web browser first opens a website if no specific page is indicated (such as `www.apple.com`).

home screen—The screens on iOS devices that display application icons. Mac OS X Lion offers a similar home screen view with its Launchpad capability.

hot spots—1. For networking, a hot spot is an area in a public place that has Wi-Fi wireless Internet access. 2. In the VoiceOver interface to help the visually impaired, hot spots are markers you insert in text by pressing Control+Option+Shift+*n*, where *n* is a numeral from 0 to 9. You jump to a hot spot by pressing Control+Option+*n*. 3. In QuickTime VR, hot spots are places in a panorama that you can click to go to another scene in the panorama or to a QuickTime VR object.

hover—To let the pointer stay in one place for several seconds. Doing so often displays the contents of a hot spot or causes the application to reveal information about whatever is beneath the pointer.

hub—On an Ethernet network, a device that passes signals from any device connected to one of the hub's RJ-45 ports to all other devices connected to the hub; these are rarely used in modern networks because they do not intelligently manage traffic as switches and routers do. *Hub* also can refer to a device that provides multiple USB or FireWire ports from a single connection.

HTML (Hypertext Markup Language)—The language used in creating web pages to control their appearance and functionality.

hyperlink—Text or graphics on a web page or in a document such as a PDF file or Word file that when clicked opens a new page or resource on the Internet or in a local network. Hyperlinked text is often underlined and displayed in blue, while hyperlinked graphics often have a blue border around them. Whether or not they have such highlighting, the mouse pointer changes from an arrow icon to a hand icon when it passes over the hyperlinked element. Often called simply *links*.

I-beam pointer—The pointer that appears when in text. It looks like a large, thin *I* character, thus its name. It's also called a *cursor*.

iCloud—A service for Mac OS X Lion and iOS 5 users that syncs data and applications among devices automatically and provides centralized backup for iTunes, iCal, Address Book, iWork, and other applications via the Internet. It replaced the MobileMe service in fall 2011.

icon—A small picture that represents an entity such as a program, document, folder, or disk. Icons are used in folders to represent file types and contents and in application user-interface elements such as buttons.

icon view—A view of files and folders in a Finder window in which each folder's contents is displayed as a grid of icons.

iDisk—A service within the discontinued MobileMe service that provided remote storage accessible via the Internet. Third-party services such as Box.net, Dropbox, Soonr, and SugarSync provide similar cloud storage capabilities as iDisk.

IEEE 1394—A standard for high-capacity device serial-bus connections, typically used for external hard disks and digital cameras. IEEE 1394a, known as FireWire 400, has two versions: the 8-pin version used by many Macs and the 6-pin version (which lacks the ability to transfer power to the device) that requires an adapter to be connected to a Mac. Beginning in 2008, Macs began shipping with the faster IEEE 1394b technology, known as FireWire 800.

IEEE 802.11a, 802.11b, 802.11g, 802.11n—A set of wireless networking standards that includes 802.11b (the oldest), which can deliver data as fast as 11 Mbps; 802.11a and 802.11g (the next oldest), both of which can run as fast as 54 Mbps; and 802.11n (the newest), which can run as fast as 108 Mbps. Apple's AirPort base stations use 802.11b technology, while its AirPort Extreme base stations use 802.11g or 802.11n technology, depending on when they were made. Each Mac model also supports a specific standard, depending on when it was made. Each standard supports all standards previous to it, so older equipment can always run on newer equipment; the sole exception is 802.11a, which uses different radio spectrum than the other standards and thus can work only with 802.11a-compatible equipment.

IEEE 802.1x—An authentication standard used in Ethernet and Wi-Fi networks to verify that a user's credentials have not been compromised during a login attempt.

iMac—Apple's line of all-in-one Macs.

IMAP (Internet Message Access Protocol)—A protocol for allowing access to e-mail servers, it is typically used by corporate e-mail servers such as Microsoft Exchange, IBM Lotus Notes, and Novell GroupWise to provide users access to e-mail when working outside the corporate networks.

inbound port mapping—A scheme for directing all requests coming into a local network from the Internet for a particular service, such as a web server, to a particular computer on the local network.

inherited permissions—Privileges that are inherited from a parent folder to child folders and all files within.

initialization—A process that creates a blank disk directory. The effect is the same as erasing the disk, even though it's only the directory of files that is deleted, not the files themselves. (Without the directory, Mac OS X and applications can't find those files, so they appear to be deleted as well.)

input method—The technical means for entering text characters and other glyphs. Usually, an input method refers to the keyboard arrangement for a specific language, but it also can refer to the gestures used on a touchpad to draw characters such as in Chinese.

insertion point—A blinking vertical bar in a text window or field that indicates where text is inserted when you start typing.

installation—The process of putting a new or updated version of software on your disk.

Internet—A global network that provides e-mail, web pages, news, file storage and retrieval, and other services and information.

Internet gateway—A device such as a router that enables all the computers on a local network to connect to the Internet, optionally sharing a single public IP address on the Internet.

Glossary

Internet service provider (ISP)—A company that gives you access to the Internet via a phone line, cable line, or other technology.

interpreted—The technique used by Unix shells and other scripting languages such as Perl to perform each command as it is encountered instead of converting all commands to machine instructions in advance.

interprocess communication—The technology that enables programs to send each other messages requesting action and receive the results of requested actions. Mac OS X has several forms of interprocess communication, one of which is Apple events, which is the basis of AppleScript.

invisible network—See *closed network*.

iOS—The operating system used by the iPhone, iPad, and iPod Touch. It and Mac OS X share the same core technologies.

IP address—In IPv4, a 32-bit binary number, such as 192.168.0.1, that uniquely identifies a computer or other device on a network that uses the Internet Protocol. IPv6 is the 128-bit successor.

iPad—Apple's tablet device that combines web, e-mail, contact management, media playback, gaming, and application launching.

iPhone—Apple's mobile device that combines phone, web, e-mail, contact management, media playback, gaming, and application launching. A version without the phone capabilities is called the iPod Touch.

iPod—Apple's line of music- and video-playing devices. A version called the iPod Touch is less a music and video player and more an iPhone without the phone.

ISO 9660—The International Standards Organization's formatting standard for CD-ROMs. Mac OS X can read and write the CDs in the ISO 9660 format, but its native CD format is HFS. (Windows PCs use ISO 9660 as their default CD format.) Also see *HFS*.

ISO/IEC 10646 Universal Character Set (UCS)—See *UCS*.

ISP—See *Internet service provider*.

iSync—Apple's discontinued technology to synchronize data across applications and devices, such as between a PDA (personal digital assistant) and iCal.

jack—The receptacle for a cable to plug into.

Java—A programming language developed by Sun Microsystems. Java is platform independent, allowing its applications to function within any platform as long as the Java virtual machine software is available and installed. (Mac OS X comes with a Java virtual machine preinstalled but asks users if they would like to download Java if an application uses it.)

JavaScript—A scripting language typically used by web pages to deliver functionality not supported by HTML.

kernel—The core of Mac OS X. The kernel provides services for all other elements of the operating system. Also see *Mach 3.0 Microkernel*.

kernel panic—When Mac OS X encounters a critical error it cannot recover from, it suspends all operations and displays a black screen telling you to power down the Mac and restart; this is called a kernel panic. (Windows users are no doubt familiar with the PC's equivalent, the Blue Screen of Death.)

kerning—Adjusting the space between specific pairs of letters so the spacing within the word looks consistent.

764

kext—The kernel extension files that some devices and applications install to access core Mac OS X capabilities. These files are typically hidden from users, but if they get corrupt or are installed on an incompatible Mac, an error message displays asking the user to take corrective action. They are typically found in the `/Library/Extensions` folder.

keychain—The technology that enables you to store passwords and passphrases for network connections, file servers, some types of secure websites, and encrypted files. The Keychain Access utility lets you manage the Mac OS X keychain.

label—A means of color-coding files, folders, and disks in the Finder. Each of the eight label types has its own color and title.

LAN (local area network)—See *local network.*

landscape—A page or image orientation that is wider than it is tall.

launch—The act of getting an application started.

Launchpad—The application launch window introduced in Mac OS X Lion, based on the home screen interface in iOS.

LDAP (Lightweight Directory Access Protocol)—A software protocol that enables the location of individuals, groups, and other resources such as files or devices on a network.

Library folder—A folder that contains resources and preferences for Mac OS X. Mac OS X has several Library folders: `/Library`, which is the core library used by Mac OS X and should not be altered; `/System/Library`, which holds additional features you or applications install meant for use by all user accounts; and `/Users/username/Library`, which holds additional features you or applications install for just that user account.

ligature—A glyph composed of two merged characters. For example, f and i can be merged to form the *fi* ligature.

link—See *hyperlink.*

list view—A view of files and folders in a Finder window in which each folder's contents are displayed as a list. Folders have a disclosure triangle that, when clicked, expands the list to include that folder's contents.

little arrows—The informal name for *stepper controls.*

localhost—The current Mac's generic network address (typically the same as the IP address 127.0.0.1), used when in Unix or in network testing utilities to indicate the current Mac no matter what IP or network address it may have been assigned by a router or other device (and thus useful when troubleshooting networking issues).

localization—The development of software whose dialog boxes, screens, menus, and other screen elements use the language spoken in the region in which the software is sold.

local network—A system of computers that are interconnected for sharing information and services and that are located in close proximity, such as in an office, home, school, or campus. Compare to *WAN.*

log in—The process of entering a username and password to begin a session with Mac OS X or another secured resource such as a network connection.

log out—A command to quit current user settings and return the Mac OS X system or other secured resource back to the login screen.

loop—To repeat a command, movie, song, or an entire playlist.

lossless—A type of compression algorithm that regenerates exactly the same data as the uncompressed original.

LPR (Line Print Remote) printer—A printer that contains a protocol that allows it to accept print jobs via TCP/IP.

.Mac—See *MobileMe*.

Mac Mini—Apple's line of small desktop computers that do not come with a built-in monitor.

Mac OS Extended—See *HFS+*.

Mac Pro—Apple's line of large, tower-style desktop Macs, typically used for high-end, performance-heavy tasks.

MacBinary—A scheme for encoding the special information in a pre-Mac OS X file into a file format appropriate for transmission over the Internet.

MacBook—Apple's name for its laptop computers. There are three lines: The MacBook, designed for home and "light" use; the MacBook Pro, designed for business and high-end use; and the MacBook Air, designed for extreme thinness and lightness.

Mach 3.0 Microkernel—Developed at Carnegie Mellon University, the Mach 3.0 Microkernel has a closely tied history to BSD (Berkeley Software Distribution) Unix. Mach gives Mac OS X the features of protected memory architecture, preemptive multi-tasking, and symmetric multi-processing.

mail account—The configuration settings that provide an e-mail client application, such as Apple's Mail, access to a specific user's e-mail from a server.

mailbox—In Apple's Mail, a collection of messages and folders that are typically associated to a specific mail account but also can include content from other mail accounts, such as when setting up a smart mailbox.

malware—Software that is intended to do harm. Common types include Trojan horses, viruses, and worms.

man pages—Documentation for some of the Unix commands (which are actually Unix programs) and other Unix components available through Mac OS X's Terminal application.

marquee—The rectangular selection area that appears when you hold and click the mouse or touchpad button and then drag the pointer. Release the mouse or touchpad button to complete the selection.

maximize—The act of expanding a dialog box or application window that has been collapsed to an icon in the Dock or to a title bar within the application window. Compare to *minimize*.

memory protection—An operating system technology that makes it impossible for one active application to read and write data from another active application's space in memory. Memory protection helps applications run with fewer crashes.

menu—A list of commands that is typically accessible from a drop-down menu, in which a clicked menu label causes the list of available commands to display below it, or from a pop-up menu, in which a click menu opens a menu that usually displays over the pop-up menu.

menu bar—The row at the top of the Mac OS X screen that begins with the menu, is followed by the current application's menus, and then provides icon menu items provided by Mac OS X and other applications. The and icon menu items are always available, while the application's menu items change based on which application is currently available.

message threading—The collection of related messages into one window, so the entire thread can be viewed at once. Apple's Mail calls these message threads *conversations*.

Microsoft ActiveSync—See *ActiveSync*.

Microsoft Exchange—See *Exchange*.

MIDI (Musical Instrument Digital Interface)—Developed in 1983 by several of the music industry's electronics manufacturers, MIDI is a data transmission protocol that permits devices to work together in a performance context. MIDI doesn't transfer music; it transfers information about the notes and their characteristics in a format that another MIDI device can reconstruct the music from.

minimize—The act of collapsing a dialog box or application window to an icon in the Dock or to a title bar within the application window. Compare to *maximize*.

Mission Control—The view introduced in Mac OS X Lion of all open applications and their open windows, so you can navigate among them easily.

MobileMe—An Apple service discontinued in June 2011 that provided users with e-mail accounts, Internet-based storage, the ability to share and synchronize calendars and address books data among several devices and users, and the ability to remotely control other Macs with a technology called *Back to My Mac*. The MobileMe service had previously been called .Mac. *See iCloud*.

modem—A device that connects a computer to the telephone system. It converts digital information from the sending computer into analog-format sounds for transmission over phone lines and converts sounds from phone lines to digital information for the receiving computer. (The term *modem* is a shortened form of modulator/

demodulator.) This term is also used informally for devices that connect computers using digital technologies (such as cable, DSL, and ISDN "modems") that perform no digital/analog conversion.

modem script—Software consisting of the modem commands necessary to start and stop a remote access connection for a particular type of modem.

modifier key—A key on the Mac's keyboard used to access an application shortcut, special character, or other special function; typically in combination with other keystrokes or mouse or touchpad button presses. The Mac's modifier keys are ⌘ (Command), Control, Fn, Option, and Shift.

motherboard—The main circuit board of a computer.

mount—To connect to and access the contents of a disk or other volume. Mounting of connected (and powered) internal and external disks (hard disk, DVD, CD, and so on) is automatic and occurs every time you start up the computer or connect such disks to the Mac.

MOV—Apple's QuickTime-based format for organizing, storing, and exchanging time-related data.

movie—Any time-related data, such as video, sound, animation, and graphs, that change over time.

MP3—A standard for digital music files that is widely used but provides lower quality than the AAC format used as the standard in iTunes.

MPEG-4 (MP4)—A standard for digital video files commonly used on the Mac, Windows, and the Internet.

multi-core CPU—See *CPU core*.

multimedia—A presentation combining text or graphics with video, animation, and/or sound, presented on a computer.

multi-tasking—The capability to have multiple programs open and executing concurrently.

multi-threading—An operating system technology that allows tasks in an application to share processor resources.

Multi-Touch trackpad—Apple's name for its MacBooks' gesture-compatible touchpad. See *gestures.*

navigate—To open disks and folders until you have opened the one that contains the item you need; to go from one web page to another.

network—A collection of interconnected, individually controlled computers, printers, and other devices, together with the hardware, software, and protocols used to connect them. A network lets connected devices exchange messages and other information.

network adapter—A device that provides a network port to devices that don't have one built in. One type, called a *network interface card* (NIC), inserts into a Mac's CardBus, ExpressCard, or PCI slot. Another type, called a *network adapter* or *dongle*, connects to a USB jack.

network administrator—Someone who sets up and maintains a centralized file server and/or other network services.

networking protocol—See *protocol.*

network interface card (NIC)—See *network adapter.*

network location—1. A specific arrangement of all the various Network system preference settings that can be put into effect all at once (for example, by choosing it from ⇨ Location). 2. The geographic location associated to a cellular radio or Wi-Fi access point used by Mac OS X to determine your current location, such as to automatically update the current time zone.

network name—See *SSID.*

network time servers—Computers on a network or the Internet that provide the current time of day.

newsgroup—A collection of people and messages on the Internet pertaining to that particular subject.

NFS (Network File System)—The Unix equivalent of personal file sharing. NFS allows users to view and store files on a remote computer.

object—A kind of information (such as words, paragraphs, audio, images, and characters) that an application knows how to work with. An application's AppleScript dictionary lists the kinds of objects it can work with under script control.

ODBC (Open Database Connectivity)—A standard used by Mac OS X to allow applications to connect to external databases.

OpenCL (Open Computing Language)—A technology in Mac OS X that lets applications use the Mac's GPU, when otherwise idle, to speed processing.

OpenGL (Open Graphics Library)—An industry standard for three-dimensional graphics rendering. It provides a standard graphics API by which software and hardware manufacturers can build 3-D applications and hardware across multiple platforms on a common standard.

open source—Typically refers to software developed as a public collaboration and made freely available.

OpenType—A standard for fonts that provides a very wide range of characters, including contextual variants. The OpenType standard is based on a hybrid of the PostScript Type 1 and TrueType font standards.

operating system—Software that controls the basic activities of a computer system. Also known as *system software.*

option—In panels, dialog boxes, and other user-interface elements, a selectable control to enable or disable a specific attribute or feature. The most common types of options are check boxes and radio buttons; other forms include sliders and stepper controls.

Option—A frequently used modifier key on the Mac, indicated in applications' menus by the symbol ⌥.

original item—A file, folder, or disk to which an alias points and which opens when you open its alias.

orphaned alias—An alias that has lost its link with its original item (and, therefore, Mac OS X cannot find it).

outline font—A font whose glyphs are outlined by curves and straight lines that can be smoothly enlarged or reduced to any size and then filled with fine dots during printing. Example outline font formats are PostScript Type 1, TrueType, and OpenType.

owner—The user who can assign access privileges to a file or folder.

package—A folder that the Finder displays as if it were a single application file. The Finder normally hides the files inside a package so users can't change them. A package is also a logical grouping of files that are related, such as all the items that make up fax software or all the parts of QuickTime. Sometimes referred to as a *bundle.*

palette—See *panel.*

pane—An Aqua GUI element comprised of separate screens within a single window. In many dialog boxes and panels, only one pane is visible at a time; you switch among them by using a button, pop-up menu, or tab. Panes may contain their own set of panes, called *subpanes.*

panel—An auxiliary window that contains controls or tools that displays information for an application; it usually floats above regular windows of the same application. Panels are also called *palettes.* Also see *dialog box*, *pop-over*, and *settings sheet.*

parental controls—A set of restrictions that can be applied to user accounts, such as to prevent children from accessing X-rated web pages or spending more than a specified number of hours per day using the Mac.

partition—1. An identifiable logical division of a hard disk. Sometimes referred to as a *volume.* 2. To divide a hard disk into several smaller volumes, each of which the computer treats as a separate disk.

passphrase—Like a password, but generally consisting of more than one word. (The larger a password or passphrase, the more difficult it is to guess or otherwise discover.)

password—A combination of letters and/or symbols that must be typed accurately to access information or services on the Internet or a local network.

path—A way of writing the location of a file or folder by specifying each folder that must be opened to get at the file. The outermost folder name is written and each folder name is followed by a slash (/). See also *absolute pathname* and *relative path.*

PCMCIA (Personal Computer Memory Card International Association)—In the small-factor version known as Cardbus, PCMCIA is a hardware interface typically found in laptops. Small credit-card-sized devices are easily installed and removed from the laptop to expand functionality. Also see *ExpressCard.*

Glossary

PDF (Portable Document Format)—A platform-independent file format developed by Adobe Systems. PDF files are often used in lieu of printed documents, as electronic transmission methods get more and more commonly accepted.

peer-to-peer file sharing—A technology for allowing computers to access files and folders located on other computers rather than on a central file server. Less powerful than server-client file sharing, it is cheaper and easier to configure.

peripheral—A device typically connected to a computer from the outside, as opposed to installed within it, such as printers, scanners, external storage drives, and digital cameras.

Perl—A scripting language typically used by web pages to deliver functionality not supported by HTML.

permissions—See *privileges*.

PHP—A scripting language typically used by web pages to deliver functionality not supported by HTML. It originally stood for Personal Home Page but now has no meaning.

pinch—A gesture in which you bring the fingers together, typically used to zoom in.

Ping—1. A support tool that can be used to verify and validate the connectivity status of IP-aware network devices. 2. Apple's social network for music aficionados, included in iTunes.

pipe—A means of directing the output of one Unix command to the input of the next Unix command. Expressed in a Unix command line with a vertical bar symbol (|).

pixel—Short for *picture element*, a pixel is the smallest dot that a display can show.

pixel depth—See *bit depth*.

playhead—A marker that tracks movie frames as they are shown, indicating the location of the current frame in relationship to the beginning and end of the movie.

playlist—A collection of songs arranged in a particular sequence.

plug—The end of a connector or cable that is inserted into a receptacle such as a jack.

plug-ins—Software that works with an application to extend its capabilities. For example, plug-ins for the Firefox browser application are available to integrate FTP services and to access related files used to create the page being viewed.

podcast—A set of audio files that is typically used to provide a series of episodes of a radio or other radio-like program. Podcasts are often delivered via iTunes, but also can be delivered as RSS feeds and from web pages.

pointer—The icon that indicates the current location onscreen for your mouse or touchpad; it usually appears as an arrowhead but can change shape to indicate the type of object beneath it.

pooling—A technique that lets the Mac choose from multiple printers or fax machines, to minimize send delays.

POP (point of presence)—A telephone number that gains access to the Internet through an Internet service provider.

POP (Post Office Protocol)—A standard for accessing e-mail from a server. It is the most common e-mail protocol in use, especially for consumer-grade e-mail accounts such as those provided by iCloud, Gmail, and Yahoo Mail. It is less adept at supporting multiple devices' access to the same e-mail account as the IMAP and Exchange protocols are.

pop-over—A user interface introduced in Mac OS X Lion and borrowed from iOS that acts like a panel but whose location is tied to a specific area of the screen (usually to the button that invokes it). A pop-over usually has very few controls in it, unlike a panel.

pop-up menu—See *menu*.

port—1. As referred to within the Network system preference, a port is some form of physical connection to a data network. 2. A synonym for a jack.

portrait—A page or image orientation that is taller than it is wide.

PostScript—Adobe's language for converting the mathematical equations used to represent text and shapes into the pixels and dots used, respectively, to display items on a monitor and to print items on a printer.

PostScript printers—Printers that interpret Adobe-developed PostScript language to create printed pages. Commonly used in environments where precise and accurate printing is a must.

PostScript Type 1 font—An outline font that conforms to the specifications of the PostScript page description language. PostScript fonts can be smoothly scaled to any size, rotated, and laid out along a curved path. Compare to *TrueType* and *OpenType*.

PPD (PostScript Printer Description)—A file that contains the optional features of a PostScript printer, such as its resolution and paper tray configuration.

PPP (Point-to-Point Protocol)—An industry standard for the communication between computing devices over dial-up connections.

PPPoE (Point-to-Point Protocol over Ethernet)—An implementation of PPP over Ethernet, used by Internet service providers that want to regulate access or meter usage of its subscribers, like DSL connections.

PRAM (parameter RAM)—A small amount of battery-powered memory that stores system settings, such as time and date.

preemptive multi-tasking—A technique that prioritizes processor tasks by order of importance. Preemptive multi-tasking allows the Mac to handle multiple tasks simultaneously. This method of managing processor tasks more efficiently allows the Mac to remain responsive, even during the most processor-intensive tasks.

primary script—The language script system used by system dialog boxes and menus. If you are working on a computer that is set up for English, Roman is your primary script; your secondary script can be any other installed language script, such as Japanese.

printer driver—Software that prepares pages for and communicates with a particular type of printer.

print job—A file of page descriptions that is sent to a particular type of printer. Also called a *print request* or *spool file*.

print request—See *print job*.

print server—A device or software that manages one or more shared printers on a network.

private IP address—An IP address for use on a local network. Compare to *public IP address*.

privileges—Privileges provide the control mechanism for regulating user access to files, folders, and applications within Mac OS X.

process—Programs or threads (tasks) within a program that are currently running on the computer.

Glossary

processor—See *CPU* and *GPU*.

program—A set of coded instructions directing a computer in performing a specific task. Also called an *application*.

program linking—The process of sharing programs by sending and receiving event messages across a network.

protected memory—This technique isolates applications in their individual memory workspaces. In the event of an application crash, the program can be terminated without having a negative effect on other running applications or requiring a restart of the computer.

protocol—A set of rules for the exchange of data between computer systems.

proxy icon—A little icon next to the title of a Finder window. It represents the folder whose contents currently appear in the window. You can drag the proxy icon to any folder, volume, or the Trash.

proxy server—A device that acts as an intermediary between a user's workstation and the Internet. When a request is made for Internet content, the request is passed along to the proxy server. The proxy server acts on behalf of the client and forwards the request on to the Internet. It then relays the retrieved response to the user.

public IP address—An IP address for use on the Internet. Compare to *private IP address*.

push button—Apple's formal name for a button.

Quartz—A powerful two-dimensional graphics rendering system used in Mac OS X. Quartz has built-in support for PDF, on-the-fly rendering, compositing, and anti-aliasing. It supports multiple font formats, including TrueType, Postscript Type 1, and OpenType. Quartz supports Apple's ColorSync color-management

technology, allowing for consistent and accurate color in the print/graphics environment.

Quick Look—Mac OS X's technology that lets you preview many types of files' contents from the Finder, rather than having to open them in an application to see their contents.

QuickTime—Apple's proprietary, cross-platform multimedia authoring and distribution engine. QuickTime is both a file format and a suite of applications. Mac OS X Snow Leopard and later use a performance-optimized version called QuickTime X.

radio buttons—A type of user-interface control in which you can select only one setting from a group. They work like the station presets on a car radio. Also see *option*.

RAID (redundant array of independent disks)—A set of standards for using multiple hard disks as if they were one disk. One type of RAID configuration creates an automatic backup of the primary disk, while others store data across multiple disks to reduce the impact of a hardware failure on any one disk.

RAM (random access memory)—1. The high-speed, quickly rewritable memory space available for use by a computer to load applications, data, and other active information. 2. A common label for the memory chips used to provide random access memory capabilities. On a Mac, the specific RAM chips are called *DIMMs* or *SO-DIMMs*, depending on the type of Mac you have.

RAM disk—Memory set aside to be used as if it were a very fast hard disk.

raster image—An image made of lines of discrete dots for the display screen or the printer. Compare to *vector image*.

Reader—1. Adobe's free application for reading PDF files. 2. The capability in Safari to display web pages stripped of menus, ads, and other distractions.

Reading List—The capability introduced in Safari 5.1 to save links to individual web pages for later reading separately from your bookmarks.

record—A structured collection of data in AppleScript (and in other programming languages), in which each data item has a name and a value.

Recovery System—A special bootup option that opens the recovery and reinstallation files that Mac OS X Lion places in a hidden location on your startup disk, in case your startup disk does not boot. Press and hold ⌘+R when starting up the Mac to enter the Recovery System.

regular expression—A shorthand method of expressing a string of characters or various permutations of a string of characters. Used in Unix command lines and often abbreviated as *regexp*.

relative path—A path that does not begin with a slash character and is therefore assumed to start in the current directory.

remote installation—The process of installing Mac OS X or an application onto a Mac from another Mac over a network. This is required for the MacBook Air, which has no DVD drive, but it also is useful for businesses that want to centrally manage software installation on all users' Macs from one master system.

Rendezvous—The original name for Apple's Bonjour technology.

repeat loop—An arrangement of AppleScript commands that begins with a Repeat command and ends with an End Repeat command. AppleScript executes the commands between the Repeat and End Repeat commands for the number of times specified in the Repeat command.

resolution—1. The horizontal and vertical pixel capacity of a display or printer, measured in pixels. 2. The number of pixels per inch for a display, scanner, or printer; a higher number means there is more data per square inch, resulting in a more accurate rendering. 3. The perceived smoothness of a displayed or printed image.

resolve an alias—What Mac OS X does to find the original item represented by an alias.

resources—Information such as text, menus, icons, pictures, and patterns used by Mac OS X, an application, and other software. Also refers to a computer's processing power, memory, and disk space.

Rhapsody—The core technologies underlying Mac OS X and iOS, derived from the OpenStep operating system (originally named NextStep) created in 1989 by NeXT, which Apple cofounder Steve Jobs had started and which Apple acquired in 1997 from NeXT when Jobs rejoined Apple to serve as its CEO.

right-click—Pressing the right mouse button on a multi-button mouse or on an Apple Magic Mouse that can detect which side of its single button you are pressing. Or using the equivalent gesture on a touchpad. In Mac OS X, right-clicking opens a contextual menu for whatever object is right-clicked, if one is available. With one-button mice that cannot detect right-clicks, you can Control+click the object instead to open its contextual menu.

rip—To convert tracks from audio CDs, typically into MP3 or AAC format, into files stored on a computer or other device.

RIP (raster image processor)—Software that translates PostScript code into an image made of rows of dots.

Glossary

ROM (read-only memory)—Non-editable information, typically located within a hardware device, usually used to provide specifications as to the device's behavior. Compare to *RAM*.

root—1. The name of the user account that has control over all folders and files on a computer, including the contents of the normally off-limits `/System` folder. 2. The top-level directory of a file system.

root level—The main level of a disk, which is what you see when you open the disk icon.

Rosetta—Apple's technology that enabled Intel CPU-based Macs to run applications designed for the PowerPC CPU that Apple had previously used. It is no longer available in Mac OS X Lion, so PowerPC-only applications do not run in Lion.

rotate—A gesture comprised of twisting fingers on the touchpad, usually used to rotate the current object.

router—A network device that manages the delivery of information among computers and between computers and the Internet and other network devices. Unlike a hub or bridge, a router sends information only to the intended recipient, instead of broadcasting information to all devices and letting them figure out if it was intended for them. That makes routers much more efficient for managing network traffic than bridges or hubs are. Also see *Internet gateway*.

Samba—An open-source version of Microsoft's SMB protocol for file sharing. Until Mac OS X Lion, Mac OS X used Samba to permit file sharing with Windows PCs.

sandboxing—The process of limiting applications' ability to interact with Mac OS X and other applications, so as to reduce the chances that malware can infect them. Also see *malware*.

Scale effect—The visual effect used when minimizing or maximizing an application to or from the Dock, in which it appears to expand or shrink in a rapid series of steps. Mac OS X also offers the *Genie effect*.

screen saver—Software that was originally designed to protect against monitor burn-in by showing a constantly changing image on the display while the computer is idle. Although modern monitors do not suffer from burn-in, screen savers remain popular as a way to personalize the computer or to indicate that the user has been away for some time.

script—1. A set of commands that a computer program can execute directly, often as an adjunct to an existing application, without having to be compiled into a separate software application. Example scripting languages include AppleScript, JavaScript, Perl, and PHP. 2. A collection of AppleScript commands that perform a specific task. 3. Short for language script system, which is software that defines a method of writing (vertical or horizontal, left to right or right to left). A language script also provides rules for text sorting, word breaking, and the formatting of dates, times, and numbers.

script applet—AppleScript scripts saved as applets (small applications).

script recording—A process in which AppleScript watches as you work with an application and automatically writes a corresponding script.

scriptable application—An application that can be controlled by AppleScript commands.

scripting additions—Plug-ins that add commands to the AppleScript language.

scroll—1. Moving the contents within a window, using the scroll bars in the window or by using the scroll wheel or scroll ball on a mouse to move the window's contents. 2. A gesture comprised of moving usually two fingers in an up, down, left, or right direction to move the contents within the current window in the same direction as the gesture.

scroll bar—The area in the scroll bar that contains the scroll track and scroll thumb and indicates the relative position of the current contents in the window to all the contents in the document.

scroll thumb—The slider-like element in the scroll track that you select and move with the mouse or touchpad to navigate the window's contents.

scroll track—The area in the scroll bar that you move the scroll thumb through to navigate the window.

scrolling list—This user-interface technique displays a list of values in a box with an adjacent scroll bar. Clicking a listed item selects it. You may be able to select multiple items by pressing Shift or ⌘ while clicking each desired one.

scrub—To move quickly forward or backward through a movie by dragging the playhead.

search path—An ordered search for resources within a Mac OS X system.

Secure FTP (SFTP)—A variant of the FTP protocol that encrypts the transmission to keep the information secure during transit. See *FTP*.

selection rectangle—A dotted-line box that you drag around items to select them all. Also called a *marquee*.

server—Software or a device that provides information or services to clients on demand.

service—Available from the Services submenu in the application menu, a service is a function,

typically for simple needs, that can be used in most applications. Services provided with Mac OS X include a translator between traditional and simplified Chinese, a screen-capture utility, and a tool to read aloud selected text. Applications may install their own services.

settings sheet—A user-interface element containing additional options that applies to and is attached to another window (usually to a dialog box), ensuring you won't lose track of which window the options apply to. Also called a *sheet*.

shared folder—The place where local user accounts can share files among themselves locally on the system.

shareware—Software distributed over the Internet and from person to person on a trial basis. You pay for it if you decide to keep using it. Also see *freeware*.

sheet— See *settings sheet*.

shell—Part of the Unix operating system that interprets command lines.

Shift—A frequently used modifier key on the Mac, indicated in applications' menus by the symbol ⇧. Its main use is to produce uppercase versions of letters.

Sidebar—The Sidebar is located at the left side of all Finder windows and contains shortcuts to mounted volumes and commonly used folders.

single-user mode—Entered during the system startup by pressing and holding ⌘+S during the boot process after the startup chime. Single-user mode goes straight to the command line, eliminating the GUI until a reboot occurs. This mode is typically used for troubleshooting.

sleep—A mode available in Mac OS X that does not power down the Mac but does suspend most operations to preserve power while keeping the

Mac ready to be reactivated quickly. It's used as an alternative to shutting down and restarting, both of which are more time consuming. Note that a sleeping laptop does use power, so eventually a laptop not connected to a power cord depletes its battery when in sleep mode.

slider—A displayed control consisting of a track that displays a range of values or magnitudes and the slider itself, also known as the *thumb*, which indicates the current setting. You can change the setting by dragging the slider's thumb.

slot—An opening in which you can insert a compatible device or disk. For example, laptops often have an ExpressCard slot in which to insert hardware devices, and most Macs have a slot in which you can insert a CD or DVD.

slow keys— A method in Mac OS X's Universal Access controls that helps those who accidentally press keys by requiring a key to be pressed for a short period, so Mac OS X can better differentiate between accidental and intentional keypresses.

smart folder—A folder whose contents are determined by setting up a series of rules in the Finder; these rules let you manage folders' contents automatically. The smart folder contains aliases to the original files and folders, so the original files and folders also are available in their normal locations.

smart mailbox—A mailbox created by setting up a series of rules in Apple's Mail; these rules let you manage e-mail automatically. The smart mailbox contains aliases to the original e-mails, so the original e-mails also are available in their normal mailboxes.

smart playlist—A playlist created by setting up a series of rules in iTunes; these rules let you manage music and other media files automatically, as well as transfer an ever-updating playlist to your iPod, iPad, or iPhone, such as music you've not heard recently. The smart playlist contains aliases to the original files, so the original files also are available in their normal playlists and albums.

smoothing—See *anti-aliasing*.

SMB (Server Message Block)—The Windows protocol used to enable peer-to-peer file sharing.

SMTP (Simple Mail Transfer Protocol)—A protocol typically used to send e-mail through a server to the recipient.

SO-DIMM—See *DIMM*.

software—One or more programs that consist of coded instructions that direct a computer in performing tasks. Also called *applications*, though *software* is a broader term that includes utilities, widgets, scripts, and all other forms of coded instructions.

soundtrack—The audible part of a movie.

space—A method to make only certain applications available, to help users organize their work and simplify what they see onscreen. The Spaces feature in Mac OS X lets you create multiple spaces that you can then switch among; each space displays windows for those apps assigned to it.

Spaces—The Mac OS X capability that creates and manages spaces.

splat—Unix jargon for the number-sign symbol (#).

spool file—See *print job*.

spooling—A printer-driver operation in which the driver saves page descriptions in a file (called a *spool file*) for later printing.

Spotlight—Mac OS X's technology for indexing and searching all contents available to the Finder. In Finder windows, the Spotlight technology lets you search by filename, file attributes, and file contents, using user-configurable queries.

SSD (solid-state drive)—A storage device that uses flash memory to hold data.

SSH (Secure Shell)—A protocol for securely accessing a remote computer.

SSID (Service Set Identifier)—The name that a wireless access point or router broadcasts to identify itself to Wi-Fi devices so they know it's available for making a connection to. Mac OS X calls this a *network name*.

SSL (Secure Socket Layer)—A technology that protects data over a network or Internet connection by encrypting the data. Some web pages use SSL to protect sensitive data in forms such as credit card numbers, and some e-mail servers use SSL to protect passwords and e-mail messages.

stack—A user-interface element in Mac OS X's Dock that presents the contents of the Downloads, Documents, and other folders as a stack of documents when you hover the pointer over it.

standard input—The source of Unix commands, which is the keyboard by default.

standard output—The destination for the result of Unix commands, which is the Terminal window by default.

startup—See *boot*.

startup disk—A disk that contains the software needed for the computer to begin operation.

static IP address—An IP address that doesn't change when you begin an Internet session or when your computer starts up.

stationery pad—A template document that contains preset formatting and contents; Mac OS X's Info window lets you convert any document into a stationery pad. Also called a *template*.

status bar—A strip in the bottom part of a Finder window that shows how much free space is available on the volume that contains the currently displayed folder.

stepper controls—Icon buttons that contain triangle-shaped arrows; these controls let you raise or lower a value incrementally. Clicking a stepper control or pressing the corresponding arrow key on the keyboard changes the value one increment at a time. Clicking and holding a stepper control or pressing and holding its corresponding arrow key on the keyboard continuously changes the value until it reaches the end of its range. These are informally called *little arrows*.

sticky keys—A method in Mac OS X's Universal Access controls that helps those with typing difficulties more easily enter multiple-key shortcuts.

streaming media—Movies, audio, and other time-oriented media files designed to be played over the Internet while they are downloading, as opposed to needing to be completely downloaded before they can be played.

stuffed file—A file (or group of files) that has been compressed in the StuffIt file format from Smith Micro. Also see *Zip file*.

submenu—A secondary menu that pops out from the side of another menu. A submenu appears when you click a menu item that has a right-facing triangle icon at its right side. Submenus are sometimes referred to as *hierarchical menus*.

subnet mask—A 32-bit binary number used to identify a segment of a network.

Glossary

subpane—See *pane.*

suite—1. In AppleScript, a group of related commands and other items. 2. A set of applications sold together, such as Apple's iWork and iLife suites, and Adobe Creative Suite.

SuperDrive—Apple's name for a recordable DVD drive. Different Mac models have different capabilities in their SuperDrives, such as support for dual-layer recording, based on the technology available when the specific Mac model was designed.

superuser—See *root.*

swipe—A gesture comprised of dragging one or more fingers quickly across the touchpad. Its function depends on the application.

switch—1. A central device on an Ethernet network that passes signals from any device connected to it to any other device connected to it. Also see *hub*, *Internet gateway*, and *router.* 2. Options you can specify as part of a Unix command.

symbolic link—A representative file that contains exact information as to where a file or folder resides.

symmetric multi-processing—The technology that allows the operating system to take advantage of two processors by assigning applications to a specific processor or by splitting an application's tasks among multiple processors simultaneously.

system administrator—A person who has the knowledge and authority to make changes to settings that affect the fundamental operation of a computer's operating system.

System folder—The folder that contains the essential components of Mac OS X.

system preference—A set of controls used to control the configuration and capabilities of a specific aspect of Mac OS X or the Mac hardware. Choose ⬛⇨ System Preferences to access the System Preferences application in which you set the individual system preferences.

system software—Software that controls the basic activities of a computer system. Also known as the operating system.

tabbed pane—The name for a pane that you access by clicking a tab-like label to expose its available controls. Also see *pane.*

tap—A gesture involving usually a quick press and release of a finger on the touchpad surface. Unlike a click, you do not actually push the touchpad surface down.

tasks—Functions executed by an application, script, or utility for a specific purpose, such as sending a file to the printer or opening a window.

TCP/IP (Transmission Control Protocol/ Internet Protocol)—The basic communication protocol of the Internet.

Telnet—An application that allows remote users to interact with Mac OS X's command line over TCP/IP, assuming they are authorized to do so.

template—The common name for what Mac OS X calls a *stationery pad.*

Terminal—An application that allows local users to interact with Mac OS X's Unix command line.

text behavior—The set of rules used in a particular language for alphabetizing, capitalizing, and distinguishing words.

thread—1. A string of messages about the same subject in a newsgroup or in an e-mail client. Also see *message threading.* 2. A single task being executed within an application; the term is typically used to indicate a task that can operate at the same time as other tasks.

3G—Indicates third-generation cellular communications technology, which is capable of providing web and e-mail access over a cellular network. Many standards qualify as 3G, including CDMA2000 1XRTT and EVDO, EDGE, and HSDPA, and each carrier chooses which ones it supports. See also *4G*.

thumb—The movable part of a slider control that indicates the current setting.

Thunderbolt—The Intel external bus technology introduced by Apple in some Macs in 2011 to provide up to 10 Gbps connections to storage media and display devices (such as monitors). A Thunderbolt jack is physically identical to a DisplayPort jack and can work with DisplayPort devices as well as Thunderbolt devices. Like FireWire, Thunderbolt devices can be daisy-chained so several devices can be connected to one Thunderbolt jack on the Mac.

Time Capsule—An Apple hardware device that acts as a Wi-Fi router and as a backup disk that multiple Macs can back up data to wirelessly.

Time Machine—An Apple utility included in Mac OS X that automates the backup of the Mac's applications and data and permits easy restoration of backed-up data in case of accidental deletion, file corruption, or other error.

title bar—The top row in a Finder window or document window that indicates the name of the folder or document, respectively.

Tool Tips—See *help tag*.

toolbar—The top area of a Finder window, directly below the title bar, that provides access to various options through the use of icon buttons and to the Spotlight search field. Many applications also use toolbars in their application windows.

touchpad—A device that detects the presence and motion of human fingers, and interprets those motions (called gestures) as commands such as zooming in or scrolling. Apple's MacBooks have built-in touchpads, and external touchpads are available to add gesture input to other Macs. Also see *trackpad*.

track—One channel of a movie, containing video, sound, closed-captioned text, MIDI data, time codes, or other time-related data.

tracking—The overall spacing among letters in an entire document or text selection. Text with loose tracking has extra space between the characters in words. Text with tight tracking has characters squeezed close together.

tracking speed—The rate at which the pointer moves as you drag the mouse or move your finger on the touchpad.

trackpad—A type of touchpad. Historically, a trackpad could detect only unidirectional gestures, such as taps, swipes, and scrolls, whereas the recent-generation touchpads allow for gestures that use multiple fingers and non-linear movements. Apple calls its touchpads *trackpads*.

trackpad handwriting—A technology in Mac OS X that enables you to enter Chinese characters by drawing them with your finger on a touchpad.

Trash—Mac OS X's folder for deleted items. It is accessible from the Dock, and you can drag items out of the Trash to undelete them. After the Trash is emptied, the items are no longer recoverable without special software.

translator—A program that translates your documents from one file format to another file format, such as a PICT graphic to a GIF graphic.

Glossary

Trojan horse—Destructive software that masquerades as something useful, such as a utility program or game. Compare to *virus* and *worm*; see also *malware*.

trough—See *scroll track*.

TrueType—The outline font technology built into Mac OS X (and Microsoft Windows). TrueType fonts can be smoothly scaled to any size onscreen or to any type of printer. Also see *PostScript Type 1 font* and *OpenType*.

Type 1 font— See *PostScript Type 1 font*.

UCS—Formally the ISO/IEC 10646 Universal Character Set standard, this joint standard from the International Standards Organization and the International Electrotechnical Commission defines how characters for any language are encoded and interpreted by operating systems and applications. Mac OS X uses this standard as well as the similar Unicode standard to provide access to fonts' characters.

UDF (Universal Disk Format)—The standard for formatting regular DVDs. Recordable CDs also can be formatted by using this standard. Also see *Blu-ray*.

UFS (Unix File System)—An alternative to the HFS+ file system format for Mac OS X.

Unicode—A standard for encoding characters in any language used by Mac OS X to access and render more than 100,000 characters from languages throughout the world. Unicode is similar to the UCS standard also supported by Mac OS X.

Universal Access—Apple's term for assistive technologies meant to help the hearing, visually, and physically impaired use the Mac.

universal binary—A format for Mac applications that lets them run on both PowerPC-based and Intel-based Macs natively.

Unix—A complex and powerful operating system whose TCP/IP networking protocol is the basis of the Internet. The name *Unix* is actually a pun: It was the single-user derivative of a multiuser, time-shared mainframe operating system at Bell Labs called Multics (the Multiplexed Information and Computing System). It was created so researchers could play space-war games on less-expensive computers instead of the mainframes they managed.

unmount—To remove a disk's icon from the desktop and make the disk's contents unavailable.

upload—The process of sending files from one computer to another computer.

URL (Uniform Resource Locator)—An Internet address. This can be the address of a web page, a file on an FTP site, or anything else that you can access on the Internet.

Usenet—A worldwide Internet bulletin board system that enables people to post messages and join discussions about subjects that interest them.

user—1. Someone who uses a computer. 2. Someone who can log in to your computer with a unique name and a password.

user account—The set of permissions that can be set up for each individual who uses a specific Mac. Each account can be configured differently, providing access to different folders and applications. Each user has a Home folder in which his or her applications and data are stored separately from that of other users.

user group—An organization that provides information and assistance to people who use computers. For the names and phone numbers of user groups near you, check Apple's web page (www.apple.com/usergroups/find.html).

user preferences—Unique settings where users configure the behavior and appearance of applications and system software.

username—A name that can be used to log in to a Mac OS X system, application, or network service.

Utilities folder—A folder within the Applications folder that contains the utilities that Apple includes with Mac OS X. You can store other companies' utilities here as well.

variable—A container for information in a script. You can place data in a variable and then use it elsewhere in the script.

vector image—A form of computer artwork comprised of lines and shapes, each defined by mathematical formulas. Unlike raster images, vector art can be resized to any dimension with no loss of quality, because it is not comprised of a finite amount of dots, but rather geometric lines and shapes. Also see *PostScript*.

verbose mode—Useful for troubleshooting, this bootup mode displays all system activity in text format during the boot process. Press and hold ⌘+V during bootup to get verbose mode.

version—A copy of a file that has changes from the previous edition.

Versions—The capability introduced in Mac OS X Lion that applications can use to save versions of file within their documents, not as separate files, so users can revert to a previous version easily if desired.

video mirroring—The duplication of one screen image on two displays connected to a computer.

virtual machine—A disk file that appears to be a functional computer when opened, complete with operating system, applications, and files.

A virtual machine is used to run Java programs on Macs, as well as to run Windows alongside Mac OS X by using the EMC VMware Fusion or Parallels Desktop applications.

virtual memory—Additional memory made available by Mac OS X treating part of a hard disk as if it were built-in memory.

virus—Software designed to spread itself by illicitly attaching copies of itself to legitimate software. Some viruses perform malicious actions, such as erasing your hard disk. Even seemingly innocuous viruses can interfere with the normal functioning of your Mac. Compare to *Trojan horse* and *worm;* see also *malware*.

VNC (virtual network computing)—A protocol used to allow one computer to remotely access and manage another over a network or the Internet. Mac OS X uses VNC in its screen-sharing capability.

VoiceOver—Apple's technology that reads text and user-interface elements to the visually impaired, to help them use the Mac.

volume—A network disk or file share that Mac OS X sees as if it were a locally attached disk. (Note some people use the word *volume* to refer to any disk or disk partition.) Also see *disk* and *partition*.

WAN (wide-area network)—A network composed of two or more LANs, a WAN is a network that is typically spread out over a large area.

web browser—A program that displays and interacts with web pages on the Internet.

web page—A basic unit that the web uses to display information (including text, pictures, animation, audio, and video clips). A web page also can contain hyperlinks to the same page or to other web pages (on the same or a different web server).

Glossary

web server—A computer or a program running on a computer that provides and delivers web pages and associated files to a web browser.

web spot—An Apple technology that automatically identifies sections of a web page, such as individual stories, to help the visually impaired navigate the page using the VoiceOver utility.

white point—A setting that determines whether colors look warm (reddish) or cool (bluish). Measured in degrees Kelvin, with warm white points having lower temperatures than cool white points.

white space—Any combination of blank spaces, tab characters, or line returns; in other words, characters that are blank.

widgets—Lightweight utilities that run in Mac OS X's Dashboard. Some come with Mac OS X and with various applications, but the Safari browser also can create widgets from snippets of web pages.

Wi-Fi—The computer industry's marketing name for the IEEE 802.11 family of wireless networking standards.

wildcard—A character that represents a range of characters in a regular expression. For example, an asterisk (*) stands for any individual character.

workflow—A series of steps that can be recorded and repeated by Mac OS X's Automator utility.

worm—A malicious file that replicates like a virus but without attaching itself to other software. It may be benign or malicious. Compare to *Trojan horse* and *virus;* see also *malware.*

WPA (Wi-Fi Protected Access)—A security standard meant to secure access to and transmit over Wi-Fi networks.

write-protect—The process of locking a disk so it cannot be erased, have its name changed, have files copied to it or duplicated from it, or have files or folders it contains moved to the desktop or Trash.

WWAN (wireless wide area network)—A cellular data technology such as LTE or WiMax. Also see *3G* and *4G.*

X11—The graphical user interface for BSD Unix applications running in Mac OS X.

Xgrid—A technology that enables your Mac to share its processing capabilities with other Macs, in what is known as *grid computing.*

XNU—At the heart of the Darwin operating system lies a XNU ("X is not Unix") kernel developed by NeXT, and later Apple.

Zip file—A file (or group of files) that has been compressed using Mac OS X's Archive command. Mac OS X opens Zip files when you double-click them. Windows and Unix systems create Zip files as well, using the WinZip and gzip applications, respectively.

Index

Special Characters and Numerics

 (Apple) menu
  defined, 750
  launching applications from, 192
  opening applications from, 212
  overview, 25–27
⌘ (Command) key, 15, 754
| (pipes), 746–747, 770
1Password utility, 330
3G
  defined, 779
  Internet connection devices, 517
  syncing through, 363
4G
  defined, 760
  Internet connection devices, 517
64-bit kernel, 729

A

AAC (Advanced Audio Coding)
  converting, 247, 333
  defined, 749
  quality of, 332
absolute pathname, 749
accepting invitations, iCal, 483–484
access points (switches), 504, 778
Account Info dialog box, Mail, 449–450
accounts. See also user accounts
  Address Book, 477
  iCal
    overview, 479–480
    setting preferences, 487
  Mail
    defined, 443
    deleting, 446
    importing existing, 427
    overview, 442–443
    setting preferences, 431–434
    setting up new, 424–427
    turning on/off, 446
  Microsoft Exchange, 493–495
Action icon pop-up menu, toolbar, Finder windows, 62, 64
active applications
  closing windows in, 82
  cycling through, 82, 197
  defined, 196–197, 749
  identifying, 196–197
  printing, 140
  quitting, 10, 206
active windows, 85–86
ActiveSync, 425, 489, 491, 493, 749
activity logs, 604
Activity Monitor utility, 207–209, 302–303
Acute Systems TransMac utility, 375
ad hoc (direct connection) networks, 504–505, 515–516
adapters
  defined, 749
  network, 521, 768
  USB-to-Ethernet, 310, 506
Add Printer dialog box, 674–676
Address Book application
  cards
    adding, 472–473
    editing, 472–473
    managing, 476
    personal, 590
  configuring in Server application, 548
  distribution lists, 475
  groups
    managing, 476
    overview, 473–474
  new features of, 718–719
  overview, 285–286, 471
  setting preferences
    accounts, 477
    general, 476–477
    phone numbers, 478
    templates, 477–478
    vCards, 478

Address Book application *(continued)*
    syncing, 358
    using with Microsoft Exchange
        setting up for Exchange 2000 and 2003, 497
        setting up for Exchange 2007, 496–497
Address Book application icon, 36
Address Book widget, 315
administrator accounts, 587, 590, 594–595, 597, 749
Adobe Acrobat Professional, 574
Adobe AIR, 329
Adobe Creative Suite, 191
Adobe Dreamweaver, 541
Adobe Reader, 773
adopted ownership, 749
Advanced Audio Coding. *See* AAC
Advanced Memory Management, 731, 733, 749
AFP (Apple Filing Protocol), 503, 750
`afp` prefix, 377
AirDrop
    defined, 749
    as new feature, 722
    sharing files via, 229, 533–534
AirPlay, 348
AirPort routers, 237, 512, 749
AirPort Utility
    overview, 302–303
    setting up Time Machine with Time Capsule device,
        240
AirPort Wi-Fi card, 31
aliases
    creating, 93
    defined, 749
    orphaned, 769
    resolving, 773
    status icons on, 87
American Standard Code for Information Interchange
        (ASCII), 299, 751
AND Boolean operator, 118, 141
Android devices, syncing, 497
Android utilities, 329
animating open applications in Dock, 45, 614
anti-aliasing, 731, 750
Apache web server, 540–541, 750
API (application programming interface), defined, 750
App Store
    installing applications from, 188–190
    overview, 286
    updating applications, 191
App Store application icon, 36–37

Apple (🍎) menu
    defined, 750
    launching applications from, 192
    opening applications from, 212
    overview, 25–27
Apple Developer Connection website, 264
Apple Filing Protocol (AFP), 503, 750
Apple ID, 589, 591, 699
Apple Mac OS X Support website, 145
Apple Manuals website, 145
Apple TV, 348
AppleCare Knowledge Base, 145, 750
AppleCare Service and Support website, 145
AppleScript
    accessing, 30
    application commands and objects, 260–261
    Automator
        backing up files, 234
        defined, 751
        overview, 276–278, 286
        recording actions, 279–280
        renaming multiple items, 94
    creating scripts, 258–260
    defined, 103, 750
    drag-and-drop script application
        extending script, 273–274
        overview, 271
        processing dropped files, 272–273
        repeat loops, 273
        retrieving dropped files, 271
    enabling Script menu, 274
    Finder utility
        breaking long statements, 268–269
        capitalization, 266
        conditional statements, 267–268
        ending use of application, 269
        file information, 266
        first statement, 264–265
        overview, 264
        parentheses, 266–267
        testing, 270
        variables, 265
        viewing results, 265
    folder actions
        attaching to folders, 103–104
        defined, 759
        editing, 105
        using, 105
    language of, 255–256

linking programs across networks
    allowing remote events, 274–275
    overview, 274
    scripting across networks, 275–276
messages and events, 254–255
modifying existing scripts, 269
overview, 253
saving scripts, 263–264
scripting additions, 256
scripting shell, 740–741
AppleScript Editor utility
    changing text formatting, 265
    dictionary window, 261–263
    overview, 256, 303
    script window, 257–258
    scriptable applications and environments, 257
AppleScript icon, menu bar, 30
applets, 308–309, 750
application access utilities, 329
application environments
    BSD, 594, 720, 734, 752–753
    Carbon, 233, 733
    Classic, 754
    Cocoa, 732–733, 754
    Core Location, 734, 755
    frameworks, 733–734, 760
    Java, 700, 734, 764
    security vulnerabilities, 566, 568
    X11 utility, 313, 734, 747–748, 782
application menu, 27–28
application programming interface (API), defined, 750
application switcher, 197–198, 712
application windows, defined, 82
applications (apps)
    controls, 199–204
    defined, 188, 283, 750
    full-screen mode, 204–205, 713, 716
    help resources, 142–143
    icons representing, 87
    installing
        from disc, 190–191
        downloaded, 190
        from Mac App Store, 188–190
    Launchpad, 193–196
    limiting with parental controls, 599–600
    multiple open
        background application alerts, 198–199
        overview, 196–197

reducing clutter with Hide command, 198
        switching among applications, 197–198
    new features of
        Address Book, 718–719
        core capabilities, 712–713
        document controls, 713
        general-purpose, 714
        helper services, 714
        iCal, 719
        Mail, 717–718
        playback, 716–717
        Safari web browser, 715–716
    opening, 192–193
    opening documents from, 213–214
    overview, 187–188
    passwords for, 573–574
    preinstalled, 284–302
    quitting
        from within application, 206
        from Dock, 206
        with Force Quit command, 207–209
        by logging out, 206–207
        overview, 10, 205
        by restarting, 206–207
        by shutting down, 206–207
    removing, 191–192
    syncing Macs and iOS devices via iCloud, 362–364
    updating, 191
    using Spotlight with
        contextual menu, 119–120
        supported applications, 120
Applications folder
    accessing, 188
    defined, 750
    launching applications from, 192
    overview, 105, 107
    preinstalled applications in, 284–302
apps. *See* applications
AppZapper, 192
Aqua, 732, 750
archives, defined, 750–751
arguments, defined, 751
Arrange icon pop-up menu, toolbar, Finder windows, 62
arrow keys (cursor keys), 751
ASCII (American Standard Code for Information
        Interchange), 299, 751
attachments, e-mail, 452–454, 459, 476
audio chatting, 465–467

Audio Hijack Pro utility, 324
audio management utilities, 324
Audio MIDI Setup utility, 303–304
Audio Recording dialog box, QuickTime Player, 352, 354
authentication, 427–428, 434, 544, 751
Auto Fill control, Safari, 411
Auto Save capability, 222, 227–228, 713, 751
automatic login
    disabling, 6
    overview, 5–6
Automator application
    backing up files, 234
    defined, 751
    overview, 276–278, 286
    recording actions, 279–280
    renaming multiple items, 94
auto-scrolling, 751
AV Foundation framework, 733, 751

B

Back icon button, toolbar, Finder windows, 61
Back to My Mac feature, iCloud, 366
background images, 21, 611–612
background programs, 751
backups
    defined, 751
    new features of, 720
    overview, 231
    preparing to install Mac OS X Lion, 692
    setting up
        choosing medium, 232–233
        overview, 231–232
        selecting software, 233–234
    Time Machine
        overview, 234–235
        restoring files, 241–244
        setting up, 236–239
        with Time Capsule, 240–241
        using external disks, 235–236
    wireless, 237
badges
    containing ! character inside triangle, 450
    containing ~ character, 446, 450
    containing numbers, 91, 454
    defined, 751
    red ellipse, 39, 91
battery power
    monitoring utilities, 324
    options for, 627–628

Battery Status icon, menu bar, 32
Berkeley Software Distribution (BSD), 594, 720, 734, 752–753
bidirectional text, 619
binary, defined, 751
binary files, defined, 752
BinHex (.hqx) files, 752
bit depth (color depth; pixel depth), 307, 686, 752
bitmap fonts, 654–656, 752
bits, defined, 752
BlackBerry devices, syncing, 497
BlackBerry utilities, 329
Bluetooth connections
    connecting Macs via, 516
    connecting to Internet via, 518
    defined, 752
    keyboards and mice, 385–386, 630, 642
    networking, 507, 645
    options for, 640–644
    setting up Macs for, 514
    sharing files via, 530–531, 533
Bluetooth File Exchange utility, 304–305
Bluetooth icon, menu bar, 32–33
Bluetooth system preference, 33, 640–644
Blu-ray discs, 289, 752. See also optical discs (CDs, DVDs, Blu-ray)
Bombich Software Carbon Copy Cloner, 234, 692
Bonjour chat, 464, 752
bookmarking
    defined, 752
    help entries in Help Center, 141–142
    Safari
        other browsers versus, 420
        overview, 399, 401–403
        preferences, 416
    syncing bookmarks, 359, 368
Boolean operators, 118–119, 140–141
Boot Camp
    defined, 752
    key assignments for Windows and Mac keyboards, 386
    setting up, 382–385
    using Windows via, 385–386
Boot Camp Assistant utility, 305
boot process. See startup (boot) process
BootP (Bootstrapping Protocol), 509
Box storage service, 211, 325–326, 369
breaking long scripting statements, 268–269
Bridge application, 213
bridges, defined, 752

brightness of monitor, 624, 626
British dictionaries, 288, 315–316
BSD (Berkeley Software Distribution), 594, 720, 734, 752–753
BSD subsystem, 753
buddies, iChat, 437
bugs, 647, 753
built-in memory, defined, 753
Bundle Contents button, AppleScript Editor, 258
bundles (packages), 258, 263–264, 734, 743, 769
Burn icon button, toolbar, Finder windows, 64
burn-in, 612, 753
burning to optical discs
    burn folders, creating, 124–125
    defined, 753
    Finder burn, 125
    finishing burn, 125–126
    limiting access with parental controls, 603
buttons (push buttons)
    defined, 202–203, 753, 772
    VoiceOver feature, 151–152
buying
    music, 336–338
    videos, 346
bytes, defined, 753

C

Calculator application, 286–287
Calculator widget, 315
CalDAV protocol, 479, 485, 488, 553, 644
CampTune utility, 384
Cancel button, defined, 202
caption panel, VoiceOver, 149–150, 178
Carbon, 733, 753
Carbon Copy Cloner, 234, 692
Carbonite, 233
CardBus standard, 753
CardDAV Address Book Server, 477
CardDAV protocol, 285, 477, 553, 644
cards, Address Book
    adding, 472–473
    editing, 472–473
    managing, 476
    personal, 590
    setting preferences, 478
case-sensitivity
    defined, 753
    journaling, 129–130, 720

passwords, 6
    in scripts, 266
CDs. See optical discs (CDs, DVDs, Blu-ray)
CDs & DVDs system preference, 622–623
cellular Internet connections, 518–519, 554
central processing units. See CPUs
Character Viewer mini-application, 32, 629, 668–672
characters, defined, 753
check boxes
    defined, 203, 753–754
    VoiceOver feature, 151–152
Chess application, 286–287
Chinese handwriting, 669
Chrome browser, 419–420, 573
Classic application environment, 754
Clear key, 16
CLI (command-line interface), 754
click gesture, 19
clicking
    defined, 754
    mouse options, 633
    overview, 17–18
    trackpad options, 639
click-through, 754
client applications, 490, 754
Clipboard
    effect of drag-and-drop editing, 221
    overview, 218–219
clipping files (clip editing), 221–222, 754
cloning disks, 239
Close button, 82–83
closed (invisible) networks, 754
closing
    documents, 228–229
    windows, 52, 82–83
cloud services
    backing up to, 233
    defined, 211
    iCloud service
        defined, 762
        overview, 331, 361–362, 497
        storage limit, 339
        syncing content and apps purchased from online stores, 362–364
        syncing documents and other information, 364–369
    Microsoft, 375
    overview, 369–370
Cnet Version Tracker website, 323

Index

Cocoa, 732–733, 754

CoconutBattery utility, 324

CoconutWiFi utility, 328

codecs, defined, 754

collating, 680, 754

color depth (bit depth), 307, 686, 752

color picker, 754

color profiles, 625

ColorSync Utility, 305–306, 754

column view
    defined, 754
    Finder windows, 69–70
    preview, 101

columns
    column view, 70
    list view, 68
    VoiceOver feature, 152

Command (⌘) key, 15, 754

command prompt, 738–739

command-line help, 144–145

command-line interface (CLI), 754

comments, defined, 754

communications utilities, 329

Comodo Group, 544

Compile button, AppleScript Editor, 258

compiling, 258, 754–755

composing e-mail messages
    addressing, 457
    controls, 459–460
    overview, 455–457
    setting preferences, 438–441
    text entry, 457–459

compressing files, 53, 96, 326, 381

compression algorithm, 755

compression ratio, 755

concatenated disk sets, 131, 135

conditional statements (conditionals), 267–268, 755

conferencing utilities, 325

configuration profiles
    creating, 551–555
    defined, 755
    managing users and devices via, 555–556
    overview, 550–551

Connect icon button, toolbar, Finder windows, 64

Connect to Server command, Finder contextual menu, 40

Connect to Server dialog box, 376

connectors, defined, 755

Console utility, 306

Contacts application, 113, 644

contents pane, Finder windows, 58

contextual menus
    defined, 22–23, 755
    overview, 34–35
    Spotlight, 119–120

Control key
    defined, 755
    overview, 15–16

conversations (message threads), 454–455, 717, 755, 767

converting
    audio files, 247, 333
    Chinese text, 249
    measurement units, 318–319
    Windows file formats, 372

cookies, 414

Copy command, 218–219

Copy dialog box, 91–92

copying
    disks, 128
    between documents, 220–221
    files and folders, 743–744
    items, 90–92

Core Location, 734, 755

core processing technologies
    64-bit kernel, 729
    Advanced Memory Management, 731, 733, 749
    Darwin, 728, 756
    Grand Central Dispatch, 729–730, 761
    OpenCL, 730–731, 768
    preemptive multi-tasking
        background application alerts, 198–199
        defined, 771
        overview, 196–197, 730
        reducing clutter with Hide command, 198
        switching among applications, 197–198
    protected memory, 731, 772
    symmetric multi-processing, 730, 778
    XNU kernel, 728–729, 782

Cover Flow view, 70–72, 755

CPU core, 755

CPUs (central processing units)
    defined, 755
    symmetric multi-processing, 730
    usage, 557

cracking, defined, 755

crop markers, 755

crossfading songs, 333

crossover cables, 506, 755
currency (money), 618, 666
cursor
    defined, 755
    sizing, 161
cursor keys (arrow keys), 751
custom installation, defined, 756
Customize Toolbar settings sheet, 62–64
Cut command, 218–219
cycling through
    active applications, 82, 197
    windows, 58

D

daisy-chaining, 756
Darwin, 728, 756
Dashboard application
    defined, 756
    overview, 287
    widgets, 313–315
Dashboard application icon, 37
data detectors
    Mail, 454
    TextEdit, 301
Date & Time system preference, 32, 646–647
Data Robotics Drobo device, 135
dead keys, 668, 756
declining invitations, iCal, 484
Delete icon button, toolbar, Finder windows, 64
Delete key, 15–16
deleting
    accounts from Mail, 446
    e-mail messages, 461
    files and folders, 743–744
    items, 92–93
    keyboard shortcuts, 631
    messages in Mail, 432–433, 448
    user accounts, 595–596
deselecting items, 88
desktop
    background images, 21, 611–612
    defined, 756
    overview, 13–14, 21–22
    view settings, 76–77
Desktop & Screen Saver system preference,
        22, 611–614, 709
Desktop folder, 107
Develop menu, Safari, 415

Development services, 247
device drivers, defined, 756
devices, defined, 756
Devices section, Sidebar, Finder windows, 65
dfont fonts, 656
DHCP (Dynamic Host Control Protocol), 509–510, 518,
        520, 581, 756
dialog boxes, 199–200, 756
dictation, 163
Dictionary application
    hiding profanity in, 603
    overview, 287–288
Dictionary widget, 315–316
dictionary window, AppleScript Editor
    displaying, 261–262
    overview, 262–263
Digital Sentry, 582
digital signatures, 756
Digital Subscriber Line (DSL), 509, 517–520, 758
Digital Video Interface (DVI), 758
DigitalColor Meter utility, 306
DIMM (dual in-line memory module), 756
direct connection (ad hoc) networks, 504–505, 515–516
directories, 81, 756
Directory Services, 546, 593, 726, 756
Directory Utility, 593, 720
disabled, access for
    Speech system preference, Speech Recognition pane
        adjusting settings, 164–165
        configuring, 163–164
        overview, 162–163
        Speech Commands window, 167–168
        Speech Feedback window, 166–167
        Text to Speech options, 168–171
        using microphone, 163
    Universal Access system preference
        Hearing pane, 156–157
        Keyboard pane, 157–159
        Mouse & Trackpad pane, 159–162
        overview, 147–148, 622
        Seeing pane, 148–156
    VoiceOver Utility
        Activities pane, 183–184
        Braille pane, 181–183
        Commanders pane, 179–181
        General pane, 171–172
        Navigation pane, 175
        Sound Settings pane, 177
        Speech pane, 174–175

disabled, access for *(continued)*
> Verbosity settings, 172–174
> Visuals pane, 177–179
> Web pane, 176–177

disclosure triangles, 203–204, 757

discs. *See* optical discs (CDs, DVDs, Blu-ray)

disk and file system statistics, 744–745

disk cache, 124, 757

disk icons, 86–88

disk images (. dmg files)
> creating, 128
> defined, 122, 757
> installing downloaded applications, 190
> starting up from, 4–5
> System Image Utility tool, 560–562

disk management utilities, 325–326

Disk Utility
> adding disks, 129–131
> checking disks, 127–128
> cloning disks, 239
> configuring RAID in, 135–136
> copying disks, 128
> fixing disks, 127–128
> formatting disks, 129–131, 374
> overview, 126–127, 307
> partitioning disks, 129–131
> recovering Mac OS X Lion, 702
> restoring disks, 128

disks
> accessing, 122–123
> defined, 81, 122, 757
> disconnecting from volumes, 123–124
> Disk Utility
> > adding disks, 129–131
> > checking disks, 127–128
> > cloning disks, 239
> > copying disks, 128
> > fixing disks, 127–128
> > formatting disks, 129–131, 374
> > overview, 126–127, 307
> > partitioning disks, 129–131
> > restoring disks, 128
> ejecting, 15–16, 53, 64, 123–124
> icons representing, 87
> new features of, 720
> overview, 121
> permissions, changing, 72–73

RAID
> overview, 131–133
> setting up, 133–136
> view settings, 77–79
> Windows, 374–375

DiskTracker utility, 325

display (video) mirroring, 781

Display Calibrator Assistant utility, 625–626

DisplayPort technology, 757

Displays icon, menu bar, 32

Displays system preference, 32, 623–625, 710

distribution lists, Address Book, 475

. dmg files. *See* disk images

DNS (Domain Name Service) servers, 509–511, 757

Dock
> animating open applications in, 45, 614
> application side of, 39–40
> automatically hiding, 44–45
> defined, 757
> files and windows side of, 40–42
> icons
> > adding, 37
> > moving, 38
> > overview, 36–37
> > removing, 37–39
> limiting changes to with parental controls, 600
> magnification, 43–44, 614
> minimizing windows in, 45–46
> opening applications from, 192–193, 212
> overview, 13–14, 35–37
> positioning, 44–45
> Profile Manager tool, 554
> quitting applications from, 206
> sizing, 43
> using Force Quit command from, 207
> VoiceOver feature, 151

Dock system preference
> customization options, 42–46
> overview, 614, 710
> Show Indicator Lights for Open Applications option, 39

document windows, defined, 82

documents
> closing, 228–229
> creating
> > from copy of another document, 216
> > overview, 216
> > with stationery pads, 217
> on Dock, working with, 41

editing
    clippings, 221–222
    Copy command, 218–219
    Cut command, 218–219
    drag and drop, 219–221
    overview, 217–218
    Paste command, 218–219
icons representing, 87
moving, 229
new features of
    controls, 713
    Preview, 715
opening
    from within applications, 213–214
    from Finder, 212–213
    with Open dialog box, 214–215
overview, 211–212
saving
    copies, 225
    older documents, 227–228
    overview, 222–223
    using Save As dialog box, 223–224
    Versions, 225–227
sharing, 229–230
syncing Macs and iOS devices via iCloud
    managing storage, 367
    services, 366–367
    setting up, 364–366
    on Windows PCs, 367–369
Documents folder, 107
Documents folder icon, 37
Documents to Go application, 369–370
Domain Name Service (DNS) servers, 509–511, 757
domain names, defined, 757
dongles, defined, 757
dots per inch (dpi), 289, 757
double-clicking
    defined, 757
    overview, 18
    speed of, 162, 631–632, 639, 757
double-tap gesture, 19
downloading
    applications, 190
    defined, 757
Downloads dialog box, Safari, 410, 413
Downloads folder, 107, 705
Downloads folder icon, 37
Downloads pop-over, Safari, 410–411

dpi (dots per inch), 289, 757
drafts, Mail, 430
drag gesture, 19
drag-and-drop editing
    defined, 757
    in documents, 219–220
    between documents, 220–221
drag-and-drop open
    defined, 757
    extending script, 273–274
    overview, 271
    processing dropped files, 272–273
    repeat loops, 273
    retrieving dropped files, 271
dragging
    defined, 757
    with mouse, 17
Dragon Dictate, 163
drag-select gesture, 19
drives, 122, 757
Drobo device, 135
Dropbox utility, 211, 229, 325–326, 369, 757–758
drop-down menus, 22–25, 758
DSL (Digital Subscriber Line), 509, 517–520, 758
dual in-line memory module (DIMM), 756
duplexing, 686, 758
DVD Player application, 288–290, 348–351
DVDs. *See* optical discs (CDs, DVDs, Blu-ray)
DVI (Digital Video Interface), 758
Dynamic Host Control Protocol (DHCP), 509–510, 518,
    520, 581, 756
dynamic RAM allocation, 758

E

Easter eggs, 42, 758
e-books, 361, 717
Edit menu, 29, 54
Eject icon button, toolbar, Finder windows, 64
Eject key, 15–16
ejecting disks, 15–16, 53, 64, 123–124
e-mail. *See also* Mail application
    attachments, 452–454, 459, 476
    limiting access with parental controls, 601–602
    Profile Manager tool, 553
    security, 583–585
    sending while away from home, 428–429
    sharing with Windows PCs via, 380–381

emoticons, 466

enclosing folders, 56, 119, 758

encryption
    of backups, 238
    defined, 758
    erasing encrypted disks, 130, 691
    formatting partitions, 129
    overview, 568, 577–579

End key, 16

Energy Saver system preference, 32, 555, 625–628, 710

Enter Full Screen button, 204–205

Enter key, 15–16

Entourage, 574

environments. *See* application environments

eppc prefix, 274

Ergonis PopChar X utility, 326, 670

Esc key, 16, 758

escape character, 740, 743, 758

ESPN widget, 316

Ethernet (RJ-45) ports, 506

Ethernet connections
    connecting Macs, 515
    defined, 758
    overview, 645
    setting up Macs for, 508–511

event messages, 254–255, 758

events
    AppleScript
        overview, 254–255
        remote, 274–275
        sharing, 530
    iCal
        creating, 481–482
        editing, 481–482

Excel, 574

Exchange. *See* Microsoft Exchange

ExFAT (FAT64) format, 123, 130, 374, 725, 758

Exit Full Screen button, 205

expand gesture, 20, 758

exporting
    audio files, 356
    screencast files, 355
    video files, 355

Exposé view (live previews)
    accessing, 45, 640
    defined, 758
    overview, 46–50
    preferences for, 620–621

ExpressCard standard, 759

extended keyboards, 15–16, 160, 180, 386, 668

Extensis Suitcase Fusion utility, 326

Extensis Universal Type Server, 663

external hard disks
    backing up to, 233, 237, 692
    installing, 135
    moving backup to bigger, 239
    starting up from, 4–5
    using Time Machine with, 235–236

F

F keys (function keys), 15, 17, 629, 759

FaceTime application, 290, 423, 468–470, 714

FaceTime application icon, 36–37

Fast User Switching, 33, 593, 597

FAT64 (ExFAT) format, 123, 130, 374, 725, 758

Favorites bar, Mail, 444, 446

Favorites section, Sidebar, Finder windows, 65

Fax icon, menu bar, 31

faxing
    adding devices, 674–677
    configuring fax modems, 678–679
    new features of, 723–724
    options for, 635–636
    overview, 673–674, 683–684
    sharing faxes, 677

Fetch utility, 329, 381

FibreChannel system preference, 628

file application owners, changing, 74, 212

file compression, 53, 96, 326, 381

file extensions
    changing file application owners, 74, 212
    defined, 759
    hiding/showing, 88, 373
    overview, 88
    Windows, 373–374
    writing scripts that recognize, 266

file icons, 86–88

file information, scripting to retrieve, 266

File menu, 28–29, 52–54

file servers
    defined, 759
    sharing through, 375

file sharing
    with AirDrop, 533–534
    with Bluetooth, 533
    defined, 759
    enabling, 526–531

with other Macs, 531–532
overview, 525–538
with Windows PCs
  connecting directly, 376–378
  letting Windows users connect directly to Macs, 378–380
  through servers, 375–376
  via e-mail, 380–381
  via FTP, 381
  via web services, 381
file specifications (file specs), 265
file synchronization utilities, 325–326
file systems
  defined, 759
  Spotlight, 110
  statistics, 744–745
File Transfer Protocol (FTP), 329, 381, 760
file types, finding, 269
filenames
  conventions for, 95
  Windows, 373–374
files
  binary, 752
  clipping, 221–222, 754
  compressing, 53, 96, 326, 381
  copying, 743–744
  deleting, 743–744
  exporting, 355–356
  icons representing, 87
  moving, 743–744
  permissions, 744
  permissions, changing, 72–73
  renaming, 743–744
  security vulnerabilities, 567–568
  special controls, 107–108
  stuffed, 777
Files and Folders services, 247
FileVault utility, 577–579, 621, 759
FileZilla utility, 329, 381
filters
  defined, 759
  image, 277–278
  Mail, 435–436, 441–443
Find banner, Safari, 411
Find My Mac feature, iCloud, 366–367
Finder
  behavior for files and folders
    disk, folder, and file permissions, 72–73
    file application owners, 74

defined, 759
desktop, 21–22
Dock
  adding icons to, 37
  animating open applications in, 45, 614
  application side of, 39–40
  automatically hiding, 44–45
  files and windows side of, 40–42
  magnification, 43–44, 614
  minimizing windows in, 45–46
  moving icons around, 38
  overview, 35–37
  positioning, 44–45
  removing icons from, 37–38
  sizing, 43
Exposé, 46–50
forced quitting, 40, 57
input devices
  keyboard, 15–17
  mouse, 17–18
  touchpad, 18–21
menus, 22–35, 51–58, 76–79
Mission Control, 46–50
new features of
  application navigation, 705
  Dock, 706
  files, 708
  Finder windows, 707
  folders, 708
  gestures, 705
  icons, 708
  keyboard shortcuts, 706
  menus, 705–706
  Sidebar, 706–707
  Spotlight, 708–709
  windows, 705, 708
opening documents from, 212–213
overview, 13–15, 51
preferences, 74–76
scripting utilities for
  breaking long statements, 268–269
  capitalization, 266
  conditional statements, 267–268
  ending use of application, 269
  file information, 266
  first statement, 264–265
  overview, 264
  parentheses, 266–267
  testing, 270

Index

Finder *(continued)*
    variables, 265
    viewing results, 265
  Simple Finder version, 599–600
  Spaces, 46–50
Finder application icon, 36
Finder menu, 51–52
Finder Preferences dialog box, 74
Finder windows
  defined, 82
  opening, 58–59
  opening applications from, 193, 212
  overview, 14
  Sidebar, 64–66
  title bar, 60–61
  toolbar, 61–64
  using Spotlight from, 115–118
  view modes
    choosing, 66
    column view, 69–70
    Cover Flow view, 70–72
    icon view, 66–67
    list view, 67–69
FIPS 181 compliance, 569
Firefox browser, 419–420, 573
firewalls, 580–582, 759
FireWire connections
  connecting Macs, 506, 515
  defined, 759
  networks, 645
  overview, 122
firmware
  defined, 759
  passwords, 4, 572–573
  upgrading, 690
Flexible Space control, toolbar, Finder windows, 64
Flight Tracker widget, 316
Flip4Mac utility, 327, 332, 372
floppy disks, 232
Fn key, 16, 759
folder actions
  attaching to folders, 103–104
  defined, 759
  editing, 105
  using, 105
Folder Actions Setup dialog box, 104–105
folder icons, 86–88
folder paths, 268, 769

folders
  copying, 743–744
  deleting, 743–744
  on Dock, working with, 41
  folder actions
    attaching to folders, 103–104
    defined, 759
    editing, 105
    using, 105
  icons representing, 87
  moving, 743–744
  permissions, 72–73, 744
  renaming, 743–744
  smart, 101–103, 776
  special
    Home folder, 106–107
    system folders, 105–106
  spring-loaded, 75, 90
  view settings, 77–79
  viewing contents of, 743
Font Book application
  adding fonts, 659
  automatic font monitoring, 658–659
  finding fonts, 665
  font collections, 660–663
  managing fonts, 663–665
  new features of, 723
  overview, 290, 657
  previewing fonts, 659–660
font families, 759
font management utilities, 326, 663
Font Validation dialog box, 659–660
FontAgent Pro utility, 326, 663
FontExplorerX Server, 326, 663
FontLab Studio, 656
fonts (typefaces)
  defined, 653–654, 759
  formats
    dfont, 656
    OpenType, 656
    overview, 654
    PostScript Multiple Master, 656
    PostScript Type 1, 655
    Safari, 414
    TrueType, 655–656
    using cross-platform, 374
  libraries of, 662
  locating, 657

Mail, 436
new features of, 723
special characters
accessing using Character Viewer, 668–672
accessing using keyboard shortcuts, 665–668
accessing using Keyboard Viewer, 668–671
Fonts folder, 658, 661, 723, 760
Force Quit Applications dialog box, 208
Force Quit command
from Activity Monitor, 207–209
from Dock, 207
Force Quit dialog box, 207
forced shutdowns
Finder, 40, 57
overview, 10
formatting disks, 129–131
Forward Delete key, 15–16
Forward icon button, toolbar, Finder windows, 62
forwarding e-mail messages, 460–461
4G
defined, 760
Internet connection devices, 517
four-finger pinch and spread gesture, 20–21
four-finger swipe gesture, 20–21, 197
fps (frames per second), 353, 760
frame rate, 355, 760
frames, defined, 760
frames per second (fps), 353, 760
frameworks, 733–734, 760
fraudulent sites, 413
freeware, 760
Front Row application, 347
FTP (File Transfer Protocol), 329, 381, 760
ftp prefix, 377
FTP sites, 381, 760
full motion, 760
full-screen mode
applications, 204–205, 713, 716
defined, 760
videos, 347, 350
function keys (F keys), 15, 17, 629, 759

G

gamma, defined, 760
gamma correction, 203, 760
General section, Info window, 98

General system preference, 614–616, 710
Genie effect, 46, 614, 760
Genius feature, 341–342, 760–761
gestures
appearance of scroll bars, 84
defined, 761
with gesture-savvy mouse, 633–634, 711
support for, 18–21
with trackpad, 637–639
Get Info icon button, toolbar, Finder windows, 64
glyphs, 668, 761
Go menu, 56–58
Go to Folder command, Finder contextual menu, 40
Google Chrome browser, 419–420, 573
Google Docs, 211
GPU (graphics processing unit), 731, 761
Grab utility, 307
grammar checker, 458
Grand Central Dispatch, 729–730, 761
Grapher utility, 308
graphical user interface (GUI), 21, 761
graphics and media technologies
Aqua, 732, 750
OpenGL, 731–732, 768
Quartz, 731, 772
QuickTime, 732, 772
graphics processing unit (GPU), 731, 761
grid computing, 530
groups
Address Book
managing, 476
overview, 473–474
defined, 761
Mail, 439
Server application, 545–548
smart
iCal, 474
VoiceOver feature, 152
user account, 594–595
GroupWise, 490, 497
guest accounts, 588, 594, 596, 761
guests
defined, 761
file sharing, 548
Home Sharing, 348
System Image Utility tool, 560
GUI (graphical user interface), 21, 761

Index

H

H.264 standard, 247, 761
hackers, 761. *See also* security
hacking, 761. *See also* security
handlers, 761
Help Center
    accessing, 30, 58
    browsing, 139–140
    navigating, 141–142
    new features of, 712
    overview, 137–139
    retrieving help from Internet, 143
    searching, 140–141
Help key, 16
Help menu, 30, 58
help resources
    application help, 142–143
    command-line help, 144–145
    Help Center
        accessing, 30, 58
        browsing, 139–140
        navigating, 141–142
        new features of, 712
        overview, 137–139
        retrieving help from Internet, 143
        searching, 140–141
    help tags, 137, 144, 761
    online recovery help, 701
    outside sources, 145–146
    overview, 137–146
    VoiceOver feature, 152–153
help tags, 137, 144, 761
helper applications, 761. *See also* services
HFS (Hierarchical File System), 123, 762
HFS+ (Hierarchical File System Plus; Mac OS Extended),
      129–130, 375, 720, 762
Hide command, 198
hiding
    application windows, 40
    Dock automatically, 44–45
    file extensions, 88, 373
    profanity in Dictionary application, 603
    Sidebar in Finder windows, 61
    system preferences, 610
    title bar in windows, 82
    toolbar in Finder windows, 61
Hierarchical File System (HFS), 123, 762

Hierarchical File System Plus (HFS+), 129–130, 375,
      720, 762
history, Safari browser, 402, 404–406, 413
Home folder, 106–107, 762
Home icon button, Safari, 396, 406
Home key, 16
home networks, 504–505
home pages, 406, 412, 541, 762
home screens, 762. *See also* Launchpad application
Home Sharing capability, 348
Hot Corners feature, 613–614, 621, 709
hot spots, 162, 762
hot swapping, 133
hovering, 762
.hqx (BinHex) files, 752
HTML (Hypertext Markup Language), 99, 299–300,
      411, 762
http prefix, 377
https prefix, 397
hubs, 504, 762
hyperlinks, 397–399, 762
Hypertext Markup Language (HTML), 99, 299–300,
      411, 762

I

iAntivirus utility, 330
I-beam pointer, 17, 762
IBM Lotus Notes, 490, 497
iBooks application, 361
iCal application
    accounts, 479–480
    events
        creating, 481–482
        editing, 481–482
    invitations, 430, 482–484
    navigating, 480–481
    new features of, 719
    overview, 290, 471, 478–479
    publishing calendars, 485–486
    setting preferences
        accounts, 487
        advanced, 487–488
        general, 486–487
    subscribing to calendars, 485–486, 553
    syncing, 358
    to-do items, 484–485

using with Microsoft Exchange
    setting up for Exchange 2000 or 2003, 495–496
    setting up for Exchange 2007 or 2010, 495
    using with Exchange 2007 or 2010, 496
iCal application icon, 36
iCal widget, 316
iChat application
    chatting, 465–466
    configuring in Server application, 548
    file sharing, 467–468
    limiting access with parental controls, 601–602
    options for, 644
    overview, 290–291, 423
    Profile Manager tool, 554
    screen sharing, 467–468
    setting up, 463–465
    using audio, 465–467
    using video, 465–467
iChat application icon, 37
iCloud service
    defined, 762
    overview, 331, 361–362, 497
    storage limit, 339
    syncing content and apps purchased from online
        stores, 362–364
    syncing documents and other information, 364–369
icon view, 66–67, 762
icons
    defined, 762
    desktop
        arrangement of, 21–22
        overview, 14
    disk, 86–88
    Dock
        adding, 37
        moving, 38
        overview, 36–37
        removing, 37–39
    document, 87
    emoticons, 466
    file, 86–88
    folder, 86–88
    proxy, 772
iDisk, 325, 369, 763
iDrive, 233
IEEE 802.1x, 510, 763
IEEE 802.11a/b/g/n, 517, 645, 763
IEEE 1394, 506, 645, 763
iLife suite, 188, 285
IM (instant messaging). *See* iChat application

iMacs, 763
Image Capture application, 291–292
IMAP (Internet Message Access Protocol), 425, 434,
    490, 763
importing
    existing e-mail accounts into Mail, 427
    images from cameras and scanners, 291–292
    music, 333, 335–336
    videos, 346
inactive windows, 85–86
inbound port mapping, 763
Info window
    changing file application owners, 74
    changing permissions, 72–73
    General section, 98
    icon, 97–98
    locking items, 97
    More Info section, 99
    Name & Extension section, 99
    opening, 111
    Preview section, 99
    Spotlight Comments section, 98
    summary, 97–98
inherited permissions, 763
initialization, 763
Ink system preference, 628–629
Input Language icon, menu bar, 32
input method, defined, 763
insertion point
    defined, 763
    moving, 96
Inside Software FontAgent Pro utility, 326, 663
installation DVDs, 690
installation packages (`.pkg` files), 190
installing
    applications
        from discs, 190–191
        downloaded, 190
        from Mac App Store, 188–190
    defined, 763
    external hard disks, 135
    Java runtime, 700
    Mac OS X Lion
        Migration Assistant, 694–700
        new features of, 703–704
        overview, 689–690
        preparing to, 690–692
        running installer, 692–694
        stopping installation, 694
    Recovery System, 693–694

Index

instant messaging (IM). *See* iChat application
Intego Internet Security Barrier X6, 584
Internet. *See also* networking
    connecting to
        Internet connection devices, 517–518
        manually, 518–519
        with Network Setup Assistant utility, 519–520
        overview, 516
    defined, 763
    disconnecting from, 520–521
Internet gateways, 763
Internet Message Access Protocol (IMAP), 425, 434,
    490, 763
Internet Protocol (IP) addresses. *See* IP addresses
Internet radio, 345
Internet Security Barrier X6, 584
Internet service providers. *See* ISPs
Internet services, 248
interpreting, defined, 764
interprocess communication, defined, 764
invisible (closed) networks, 754
invitations, iCal application, 430, 482–484
iOS devices (iPads, iPod Touches, iPhones)
    iOS, defined, 764
    iPads, defined, 764
    iPhones, defined, 764
    iPods, defined, 764
    syncing
        overview, 339–340
        via iCloud, 362–369
        via iTunes, 357–361
    using with Microsoft Exchange, 497–499
IP (Internet Protocol) addresses
    defined, 764
    finding computer's, 377
    overview, 511
    private, 511, 771
    public, 511, 772
    static, 520, 548, 777
iPads. *See* iOS devices (iPads, iPod Touches, iPhones)
iPartition utility, 384
iPhones. *See* iOS devices (iPads, iPod Touches, iPhones)
iPod Touches. *See* iOS devices (iPads, iPod Touches,
    iPhones)
Ipswitch WS_ FTP Pro utility, 381
iSight cameras, 293, 699
ISO 9660, 764
ISO/IEC 10646 Universal Character Set (UCS), 780

ISPs (Internet service providers)
    connection types, 519–520
    defined, 764
    junk mail headers set by, 435
    sending e-mail while traveling, 428–429
iSync application, 714, 764
item information
    Info window
        General section, 98
        icon, 97–98
        More Info section, 99
        Name & Extension section, 99
        Preview section, 99
        Spotlight Comments section, 98
        summary, 97–98
    Quick Look feature
        column view mode preview, 101
        live preview icons, 99–100
        Quick Look window, 100–101
        slideshow viewer, 101
iTunes application
    books, 717
    icon controls, 338
    Internet radio, 345
    music
        buying, 336–338
        importing, 335–336
        managing, 339–342
        overview, 332
        playing, 342–343
        setting preferences, 333–335
    overview, 292–293, 331–332
    podcasts, 343–345
    preferences dialog box
        Devices pane, 361
        General pane, 333
        Parental pane, 335
        Playback pane, 333–334, 345
        Sharing pane, 334–335
        Store pane, 362
    syncing Macs and iOS devices
        Apps pane, 359–360
        Books pane, 361
        Info pane, 358–359
        overview, 339–340, 357–358
        setting preferences, 361
    transferring purchases to new computer, 697
    updating, 332

videos
  buying, 346
  importing, 346
  managing, 346–347
  playing, 347
  setting preferences, 345–346
iTunes application icon, 36
iTunes Match service, 339
iWork suite
  full-screen mode, 204
  syncing documents, 364

J

Jabber, 290, 463, 602, 721
jacks, defined, 764
Japanese dictionaries, 288, 316
Java, 700, 734, 764
Java Preferences utility, 308–309
JavaScript, 372, 413, 553, 764
journaling, 129–130, 720
junk mail, 433, 435–436, 448, 461, 584

K

Karelia Software Sandvox, 541
Kensington security cables, 566
kernel, 728, 764
kernel panic, 728–729, 764
kerning, 764
kext, 765
Keyboard & Character Viewer icon, menu bar, 32
keyboard shortcuts
  accessing special characters, 665–668
  assigning new, 630–631
  bidirectional text, 619
  for common symbols, 665–668
  cut, copy and paste, 219
  deleting, 631
  turning on/off, 630
  using for menu options, 24
Keyboard system preference, 32, 250–251, 629–631
Keyboard Viewer mini-application, 32, 629, 668–671
keyboards
  Bluetooth connections, 385–386, 630, 642
  extended, 15–16, 160, 180, 386, 668
  overview, 15–17
  slow keys, 158, 159, 776
  sticky keys, 157–158, 777
  VoiceOver feature, 150–151

Keychain Access utility, 309–310, 574–577
keychain technology, 765

L

Label icon button, toolbar, Finder windows, 64
labels, 54, 74–75, 765
landscape orientation, 469, 765
Language & Text system preference, 32, 616–619, 710
LANs (local area networks), 504, 517, 520, 765
launching, 192–193, 765
Launchpad application
  accessing, 193, 640
  creating groups in, 195
  defined, 765
  launching applications from, 193
  navigating, 194–195
  overview, 193–196, 293
  rearranging applications within, 195–196
Launchpad application icon, 36–37
LCD Font Smoothing, 616
LDAP (Lightweight Directory Access Protocol), 438–439, 553, 765
Library folder, 105, 107, 765
ligatures, 765
Lightweight Directory Access Protocol (LDAP), 438–439, 553, 765
Line Print Remote (LPR) printers, 766
links, 397–399, 762
Linotype FontExplorerX Server, 326, 663
list views. See view modes
little arrows (stepper controls), 203–204, 765, 777
live preview icons, 99–100
live previews. See Exposé view
local area networks (LANs), 504, 517, 520, 765
local networks. See also networking
  chatting over, 463–465
  defined, 765
  setting up Macs for
    Bluetooth connections, 514
    Ethernet connections, 508–511
    overview, 507–508
    VPNs, 514–515
    Wi-Fi connections, 512–513
localhost, defined, 765
localization, defined, 765
location information security, 579–580
location services, 414

locking
documents, 227–228, 239
items, 96–97
logging in
automatically loading applications, 39, 591–594
defined, 765
as different user, 745–746
login window
icon buttons, 7
options, 6
new features of, 704
options, 592–594
overview, 5–6
password entry, 6–7
as superuser, 745–746
logging out
defined, 765
overview, 7–8
quitting applications by, 206–207
loops
defined, 765
playing music in, 343
playing video in, 353
repeat, 273, 773
lossless, 332, 766
LPR (Line Print Remote) printers, 766

M

Mac App Store
installing applications from, 188–190
overview, 286
updating applications, 191
Mac Life magazine and website, 146
Mac Mini, 766
Mac Mini Servers, 133
Mac OS Extended (HFS+), 129–130, 375, 720, 762
Mac OS X Lion
application environments, 732–734
installing
overview, 689–690
preparing for, 690–692
running installer, 692–694
stopping installation, 694
installing Java runtime, 700
Migration Assistant
Create Your Computer Account window, 698–699
Don't Forget to Register window, 700

Enter Your Apple ID window, 698
Registration Information window, 698
Secure My Mac window, 699
Select a Picture for This Account window, 699
Select Time Zone window, 699
Select Your Keyboard window, 695
server settings window, 695
Thank You window, 700
Transfer Information to This Mac window, 695–698
Welcome window, 694–695
new features of
applications, 712–719
backups, 720
disks, 720
documents, 712–719
faxing, 723–724
Finder, 705–709
fonts, 723
Help Center, 712
installing, 703–704
logging in, 704
Mac OS X Server, 726
networking, 722
Parental Controls, 720–721
printing, 723–724
scanning, 723–724
security, 721–722
setting up, 703–704
Speech system preference, 724–725
starting up, 704
System Preferences application, 709–712
Unix, 725
user accounts, 720–721
VoiceOver Utility, 724–725
Windows, 725
recovering
getting help online, 701
launching Recovery System, 701
overview, 700–701
from Time Machine, 702
using Disk Utility, 702
reinstalling, 702
serving web pages from, 540–541
technologies
core processing technologies, 728–731
graphics and media technologies, 731–732
overview, 727
updating, 583

Mac OS X Lion installer
  disk selector window, 693
  installation progress window, 694
  license agreement window, 693
  overview, 692
  Preparing to Install window, 693–694
Mac OS X Lion Server
  configuration profiles
    creating, 551–555
    managing users and devices via, 555–556
    overview, 550–551
  managing devices directly, 556
  new features of, 726
  overview, 539–562
  Server Admin tool, 556–559
  Server application
    enabling and configuring services, 548–549
    Mac server setup, 543–545
    monitoring status, 549–550
    overview, 543
    users and groups, 545–548
  setting up, 542
  System Image Utility tool, 560–562
  Workgroup Manager tool, 559–560
Mac Pro
  defined, 766
  installing internal hard disks on, 134
Mac User Group (MUG) Center, 145
Mac user groups, 145
MacBinary, 766
MacBooks, 766
MacDrive utility, 375
MacFixIt website, 146
Mach 3.0 Microkernel, 766
MacSpeech Scribe, 163
MacTalk user forum, 145
Macworld magazine and website, 146, 323
Magic Mouse, 18, 84, 632
Magic Trackpad, 18, 84
magnification, Dock, 43–44, 614
Mail, Contacts & Calendars system preference
  iCloud settings, 364, 366
  as new feature, 709–710
  overview, 644–645
Mail application
  accounts
    defined, 766
    importing existing, 427

    overview, 442–443
    setting up new, 424–427
    turning on and off, 446
  configuring in Server application, 548–549
  mailboxes
    defined, 443, 766
    maintaining, 448–450
    overview, 443–446
    smart, 446–448, 776
  messages
    deleting, 461
    forwarding, 460–461
    junking, 461
    moving, 461
    overview, 450
    reading, 451–455
    redirecting, 460–461
    replying, 460–461
    saving, 460
    sending, 460
    writing, 455–460
  monitoring activity, 450
  new features of, 717–718
  options for, 644
  overview, 293, 423
  preferences dialog box
    Accounts pane, 431–434
    Composing pane, 438–441
    Fonts & Colors pane, 436
    General pane, 430–431
    Junk Mail pane, 435–436
    overview, 427
    Rules pane, 441–442
    Viewing pane, 436–438
  priority indicators, 456, 460
  RSS feeds, 462
  setting preferences
    accounts, 431–434
    composing, 438–441
    fonts and colors, 436
    general, 430–431
    junk mail, 435–436
    overview, 427
    rules, 441–442
    viewing, 436–438
  syncing, 358
  using notes in, 462–463

using with Microsoft Exchange
    accounts, 493–495
    setting up for Exchange 2000 or 2003, 493
    setting up for Exchange 2007 or 2010, 491–493
Mail application icon, 36
mailboxes, Mail
  defined, 443, 766
  maintaining, 448–450
  overview, 443–446
  smart, 446–448, 776
malware, 565, 583–586, 766
man pages, 137, 144–145, 250, 741–742, 766
Mark/Space Missing Sync utility, 329
marquees (selection rectangles), 17, 766, 775
maximizing, 83, 766
media playback and delivery utilities, 327
MediaFour MacDrive utility, 375
memory protection, 766
menu bar
  defined, 766
  Finder
    arranging items on, 33
    icon menus, 641
    overview, 13–14, 22
    setting up Time Machine from, 236
    translucence of, 612
  icons
    AppleScript, 30
    Battery Status, 32
    Bluetooth, 32–33
    Displays, 32
    Fax, 31
    Input Language, 32
    Keyboard & Character Viewer, 32
    Modem, 31
    Spotlight, 33
    Time, 32
    Time Machine, 31
    Universal Access, 31
    User, 33
    Volume, 32
    VPN, 31
    Wi-Fi, 31
    WWAN, 31
  items
    Apple menu, 25–27
    application menu, 27–28
    Edit menu, 29

File menu, 28–29
Help menu, 30
Script menu, 30
View menu, 29
Window menu, 29–30
  using Spotlight from, 112–114
  VoiceOver feature, 151
menus
  Apple, 25–27, 192, 212, 274, 750
  application, 27–28
  contextual, 34–35
  defined, 766
  drop-down, 23–25
  Edit, 29, 54
  File, 28–29, 52–54
  Finder, 51–52
  Go, 56–58
  Help, 30, 58
  menu bar icons, 30–33
  overview, 22–23
  pop-up, 33–34
  Script, 30, 274
  symbols, 25
  using keyboard shortcuts for, 24
  View, 29, 54–56, 76–79
  Window, 29–30, 58
message threads (conversations), 454–455, 717, 755, 767
Message Viewer window, Mail, 443–445, 451
Messaging services, 248
metadata, 97, 111. *See also* Spotlight
microphones, 163–164, 648
Microsoft ActiveSync, 425, 489, 491, 493, 749
Microsoft Entourage, 574
Microsoft Excel, 574
Microsoft Exchange
  defined, 758
  overview, 489–491
  using Address Book with, 496–497
  using iCal with, 495–496
  using iOS devices with, 497–499
  using Mail with, 425, 491–495
Microsoft Office
  speed of, 372
  uninstalling, 191
Microsoft SharePoint, 375–376
Microsoft Windows integration
  disks and storage media, 374–375
  file extensions, 373–374

filenames, 373–374
new features of, 725
overview, 371–372
running Windows on Macs
    Boot Camp, 382–386
    overview, 381–382
    virtual machines, 387–392
sharing files
    connecting to PCs directly, 376–378
    letting Windows users connect directly to your
        Mac, 378–380
    through servers, 375–376
    via e-mail, FTP, and web services, 380–381
    via FTP, 380–381
    via web services, 380–381
Microsoft Windows Phone 7 devices, 497
Microsoft Windows Phone 7 utilities, 329
Microsoft Windows storage media, 374–375
Microsoft Word, 574
MIDI (Musical Instrument Digital Interface), 303–304, 767
Migration Assistant utility
    Create Your Computer Account window, 698–699
    Don't Forget to Register window, 700
    Enter Your Apple ID window, 698
    new features of, 704
    overview, 310–311
    Registration Information window, 698
    Secure My Mac window, 699
    Select a Picture for This Account window, 699
    Select Time Zone window, 699
    Select Your Keyboard window, 695
    server settings window, 695
    Thank You window, 700
    Transfer Information to This Mac window
        overview, 695–696
        transferring information from another computer,
            696–697
        transferring information from another disk,
            697–698
    Welcome window, 694–695
Minimize button, windows, 83
minimizing
    defined, 767
    Speech Feedback window, 167
    windows, 29–30, 45–46, 83, 614
Missing Sync utility, 329
Mission Control application
    accessing, 634, 640
    defined, 767

    as new feature, 705, 714
    overview, 46–50, 293
Mission Control system preference, 620–621, 711
MobileMe
    backing up to, 233
    defined, 767
    website, 211
Modem icon, menu bar, 31
modem script, 767
modems, 517, 645, 767
modifier keys, 15, 629–630, 767
money (currency), 618, 666
monitors
    brightness of, 624, 626
    multiple, 623–625
    preferences for, 623–624
    resolution, 32, 289, 623–624, 773
    rotating display, 624
More Info section, Info window, 99
motherboards, 690, 767
mounting disks, 127, 767
mouse
    gesture-savvy, 633–634, 711
    overview, 17–18
    tracking speed, 631–632, 779
mouse keys, 160–161
Mouse system preference, 631–634, 711
MOV (QuickTime movie) format, 112, 732, 767
Movie Recording dialog box, QuickTime Player, 352, 354
movies, 767. *See also* videos
Movies folder, 107
Movies widget, 316
moving
    among folders, 742
    backup to bigger external hard disks, 239
    Dock icons, 38
    document content with drag and drop
        in document, 219–220
        between documents, 220–221
    documents, 229
    e-mail messages, 433, 461
    files and folders, 743–744
    icons around Dock, 38
    insertion point, 96
    items, 90–92
Mozilla Firefox browser, 419–420, 573
Mozilla Thunderbird, 573
Mozy, 233
MP3 format, 332, 767

MPEG-4 (MP4) format, 332, 767
MUG (Mac User Group) Center, 145
multimedia, defined, 768
multiple open applications. *See* preemptive multi-tasking
multi-threading, 768
Multi-Touch trackpad, 768. *See also* trackpads (touchpads)
music
    AirPlay, 348
    Home Sharing capability, 348
    iTunes application
        buying music, 336–338
        Genius feature, 341–342
        importing music, 333, 335–336
        overview, 332
        parental settings, 335
        playing music, 333–334, 342–343
        playlists, 340–341
        radio, 345
        rating music, 342
        sharing music, 334–335
        syncing with iPods, iPads, and iPhones, 339–340
        view modes, 339
    QuickTime Player
        creating audio files, 354–355
        editing audio files, 354
        exporting audio files, 356
        playing audio files, 352–353
        playing media files, 343, 716
Music folder, 107
Musical Instrument Digital Interface (MIDI), 303–304, 767

N

Name & Extension section, Info window, 99
navigating, defined, 768
nested sub-menus, 23
NetMonitor, 582
network adapters, 521, 768
network administrators, defined, 768
Network File System (NFS), 768
network locations, 26, 768
Network Setup Assistant utility, 519–520
Network system preference, 31, 507–516, 518–521, 645, 722
network time servers, 558, 646, 768
Network Utility
    Finger pane, 523
    Info pane, 521–522
    Lookup pane, 522

    Netstat pane, 522
    overview, 311
    Ping pane, 522
    Port Scan pane, 523–524
    Traceroute pane, 522
    Whois pane, 523
networking
    connecting Macs directly
        Bluetooth connections, 516
        Ethernet connections, 515
        FireWire connections, 515
        Wi-Fi connections, 516
    linking programs across networks
        allowing remote events, 274–275
        overview, 274
        scripting, 275–276
    network, defined, 768
    network attacks, 580–583
    Network Utility
        Finger pane, 523
        Info pane, 521–522
        Lookup pane, 522
        Netstat pane, 522
        overview, 311
        Ping pane, 522
        Port Scan pane, 523–524
        Traceroute pane, 522
        Whois pane, 523
    new features of, 722
    overview, 503–524
    setting up Macs for
        Bluetooth connections, 514
        Ethernet connections, 508–511
        overview, 507–508
        VPNs, 514–515
        Wi-Fi connections, 512–513
    sharing connections, 530, 537
    technologies
        overview, 504–505
        wired connections, 506
        wireless connections, 506–507
newsgroups, 449, 490–491, 493–494, 768
Newsstand store, 362
NFS (Network File System), 768
NOT Boolean operator, 119, 141
notes
    syncing, 359
    using in iCal, 484
    using in Mail, 432, 440, 462–463

Novell GroupWise, 490, 497
NTFS for Mac OS X utility, 375, 384
Num Lock key, 15

O

objects, defined, 768
ODBC (Open Database Connectivity), 768
office networks, 504–505
Office suite
    speed of, 372
    uninstalling, 191
OK button, 202
1Password utility, 330
Open Application event, 254
Open Computing Language (OpenCL), 730–731, 768
Open Database Connectivity (ODBC), 768
Open dialog box, 213–215
Open Dictionary dialog box, 261
Open Directory protocol, 546
Open Documents event, 254
Open in Dashboard control, Safari, 411
open source, defined, 768
OpenCL (Open Computing Language), 730–731, 768
OpenGL (Open Graphics Library), 731–732, 768
opening
    applications, 192–193
    documents
        from within applications, 213–214
        from Finder, 212–213
        with Open dialog box, 214–215
OpenType fonts, 374, 656, 768
Opera browser, 419, 573
operating systems, defined, 769. *See also* iOS devices
        (iPads, iPod Touches, iPhones); Mac OS X Lion
optical discs (CDs, DVDs, Blu-ray)
    backing up to, 232
    Blu-ray, 289, 752
    burning to
        burn folders, creating, 124–125
        defined, 753
        Finder burn, 125
        finishing burn, 125–126
        limiting access with parental controls, 603
        playlists, 341
    CDs & DVDs system preference, 622–623
    defined, 757
    DVD Player application, 288–289, 348–351
    ejecting, 123–124

importing media from, 332–333, 335–336
installation DVD, 690
installing applications from, 190–191
sharing, 526, 537
starting up from, 4–5
OR Boolean operator, 119, 141
ordered lists, 203–204
original items, defined, 769
orphaned aliases, 769
Out of Office feature, Exchange, 494
outline fonts, 655, 769
OWA (Outlook Web Access), 425, 490
owners, defined, 769

P

packages (bundles), 258, 263–264, 734, 743, 769
Page Up/Page Down keys, 16
Pages application, 24
pairing Bluetooth devices, 514, 516, 530, 641–642
panels, 200–201, 769
panes (tabbed panes)
    defined, 769, 778
    overview, 201–202
    Safari, 407–409, 412, 416
Paragon Software NTFS for Mac OS X utility, 375, 384
Parallels Desktop utility, 305, 329, 381, 387–390
parameter RAM (PRAM), 771
parental controls
    for media content, 335
    defined, 769
    guest account, 596
    iTunes application, 335
    new features of, 720–721
    Profile Manager tool, 554
    user accounts managed with, 594–595, 597
Parental Controls system preference
    activity logs, 604
    Apps pane, 599–601
    Other pane, 603
    overview, 598–599, 647
    People pane, 601–602
    settings management, 604–606
    Time Limits pane, 602–603
    Web pane, 601
parentheses, in scripts, 266–267
partitioning disks, 129–131, 769
partitions, 122, 381–385, 769
passphrases, 769

Index

password hints, 7, 593
passwords
    administrator, 594
    for applications, 573–574
    defined, 769
    enforcing use of, 570–572
    firmware, 4, 572–573
    incorrect, 6–7
    Keychain Access, 309–310, 574–577
    limiting changes to with parental controls, 603
    logging in, 6–7
    Mail, 427–428
    1Password utility, 330
    preventing startup from other disks, 572–573
    Profile Manager tool, 553
    secure, 567
    Server application, 546
    Time Capsule device, 240
    user account, 568–570, 589–591, 698–699
Paste command, 218–219
Pasteboard, 29
path bar, Finder windows, 58
Path icon pop-up menu, toolbar, Finder windows, 64
paths
    folder, 268, 769
    relative, 773
    search, 775
PC Tools iAntivirus utility, 330
PCMCIA (Personal Computer Memory Card International Association), 769
PDF (Portable Document Format), 113, 770
peer-to-peer file sharing, 770
peer-to-peer networks, 503
peripherals, defined, 770
Perl, 770
permissions (privileges). *See also* user accounts
    changing, 72–73
    defined, 771
Personal Computer Memory Card International Association (PCMCIA), 769
phishing, 413, 568, 584
Photo Booth application, 293–295, 714
Photo Booth application icon, 36
Photo Stream service, iPhoto, 367–368
PHP, 770
pictures, user account, 590, 699
Pictures folder, 107

Pictures services
    Capture Full Screen, 248
    Capture Screen Using Timer, 248
    Capture Selection from Screen, 248
    Import Images, 248
    Set Desktop Picture, 248
pinch gesture, 20, 770
pinging, 581, 770
pipes (|), 746–747, 770
pixel depth (bit depth), 307, 686, 752
pixels, defined, 770
.pkg files (installation packages), 190
playback windows, 82
playhead, 770
playing
    music
        iTunes application, 333–334, 342–343
        QuickTime Player, 352–353
    videos
        iTunes application, 347
        QuickTime Player, 352–353
playlists, 340–341, 770, 776
Plex utility, 327–328
plug-ins, defined, 770
plugs, defined, 770
Podcast Capture utility, 311
Podcast Publisher utility, 311, 715
podcasts, 549, 770
point of presence (POP), 770
pointers
    defined, 770
    seeing, 161
Point-to-Point Protocol over Ethernet (PPPoE), 509, 771
Point-to-Point Protocol (PPP), 771
pooling printers, 678, 770
POP (point of presence), 770
POP (Post Office Protocol), 424–425, 770
PopChar X utility, 326, 670
pop-overs, 200–201, 770
pop-up blocker, Safari, 410
pop-up menus, 22, 33–34
Portable Document Format (PDF), 113, 770
portrait orientation, 469, 771
ports, defined, 771
Post Office Protocol (POP), 424–425, 770
PostScript, 771
PostScript Multiple Master fonts, 656

PostScript Printer Description (PPD), 771
PostScript printers, 771
PostScript Type 1 font, 374, 655, 771
PPD (PostScript Printer Description), 771
PPP (Point-to-Point Protocol), 771
PPPoE (Point-to-Point Protocol over Ethernet), 509, 771
PRAM (parameter RAM), 771
preemptive multi-tasking (multiple open applications)
    background application alerts, 198–199
    defined, 768, 771
    overview, 196–197, 730
    quitting, 206
    reducing clutter with Hide command, 198
    switching among applications, 197–198
preferred networks, 512
Preview application
    capturing images with, 296–297
    display options, 298
    editing images with, 297
    new features of, 715
    opening files with, 295–296
    overview, 295
    PDF files, 297–298
Preview application icon, 36
Preview section, Info window, 99
Prey software, 567
primary script, 771
Print & Scan system preference, 634–636, 674–680, 723
Print dialog box, 680–684
Print Documents event, 254
print jobs, defined, 771
print queues, 682–683
print servers, 771
printer drivers, 635, 677, 681, 771
printing
    adding printers, 674–677
    configuring printers, 677–678
    limiting access with parental controls, 603
    new features of, 723–724
    options for, 634–635
    overview, 673–674
    pooling printers, 678, 770
    print queue, 682–683
    Profile Manager tool, 554
    sharing printers, 528, 537, 635, 677
    using Print dialog box, 680–682
private IP addresses, 511, 771

privileges. *See* permissions; user accounts
processes
    defined, 771
    stopping, 302
Profile Manager tool, 550–555
Profiles system preference, 647, 711
program linking, 274, 772
programs, defined, 188, 772
protected memory, 731, 772
protocols, defined, 772
proxy icons, 772
proxy servers, 415, 464, 510, 554, 772
PTHPasteboard, 219
Public folder, 107
public IP addresses, 511, 772
publishing calendars, 485–486
push buttons. *See* buttons
push messaging, 434
push notifications, 544

Q

Quartz, 731, 772
Quick Look feature
    column view mode preview, 101
    defined, 772
    e-mail attachments, 453–454
    live preview icons, 99–100
    previewing items, 107
    Quick Look window, 100–101
    slideshow viewer, 101
    using with Cover Flow view, 72
Quick Look icon button, toolbar, Finder windows, 64
Quickoffice Pro application, 369–370
QuickTime, 732, 772
QuickTime movie (MOV) format, 112, 732, 767
QuickTime Player application
    creating media files, 354–355
    editing media files, 354
    exporting audio files, 356
    exporting video and screencast files, 355
    overview, 299, 351
    playing media files, 343, 352–353, 716
Quit Application event, 254
quitting applications
    from within application, 206
    from Dock, 206
    Force Quit command, 207–209

quitting applications *(continued)*
    by logging out, 206–207
    overview, 10, 205
    by restarting, 206–207
    by shutting down, 206–207

R

radio, 345
radio buttons, 202–203, 772
Radioshift utility, 324
RAID (redundant array of independent disks)
    configurations, 132–133
    defined, 772
    overview, 131–133
    setting up
        configuring in Disk Utility, 135–136
        external hard disks, installing, 135
        Mac Mini Servers, 133
        Mac Pro, 134
RAID Utility, 311
RAM (random access memory), 26, 543, 690, 729,
        731, 772
RAM disk, 772
raster image processor (RIP), 773
raster images, 772
rating music, 342
Reader mode, Safari, 399–400, 773
reading e-mail messages, 451–455
Reading List, Safari, 403–404, 773
read-only memory (ROM), 774
read-only status, 97
Really Simple Syndication (RSS) feeds, 402, 417–419, 462
RealVNC utility, 327
recently downloaded files, 410
Record button, AppleScript Editor, 258
records, defined, 773
recovering Mac OS X Lion
    getting help online, 701
    launching Recovery System, 701
    overview, 700–701
    from Time Machine, 702
    using Disk Utility, 702
Recovery System
    defined, 773
    installing, 693–694
    launching, 701
    as new feature, 703–704
    overview, 4, 701–702

redemption codes, 190
redirecting e-mail messages, 460–461
redundant array of independent disks. *See* RAID
refresh rate, 624
regular expressions, defined, 773
regular playlists, 340
reinstalling applications, 285
relative paths, 773
Reload the Current Page (Reload; Refresh) icon button,
        Safari, 396, 407
reminders (to-do items), iCal, 113, 484–485
remote access
    to parental controls, 604–605
    utilities for, 327
    via Terminal, 739
remote installation, 773
remote management, 528–529, 543–544
removing
    applications, 191–192
    buttons from login window, 7
    icons from Dock, 37–38
renaming
    files and folders, 743–744
    items, 93–96
Rendezvous, 773
repeat loops, 273, 773
repeat rate, keyboard, 629
repeating music, 343
repetitive strain injury (RSI), 163
replying to e-mail messages, 460–461
Report a Bug control, Safari, 411
resolution, 32, 289, 623–624, 773
resolving aliases, 773
resources, defined, 773
Restart button, 7
restarting Macs
    options for, 10, 626–627
    quitting applications by, 206–207
restoring disks, 128
restoring files with Time Machine
    overview, 241–243
    searching for changes, 243
    Time Machine browser
        exiting, 243–244
        using, 242–243
Retrospect utility, 233
Return key, 16
Rev disks, 232
Rhapsody, 773

right-click gesture, 19
right-clicking, 18, 773
RIP (raster image processor), 773
ripping, defined, 773
RJ-45 (Ethernet) ports, 506
Rogue Amoeba Audio Hijack Pro utility, 324
Rogue Amoeba Radioshift utility, 324
ROM (read-only memory), 774
root, defined, 774
root level, 105, 774
Rosetta technology, 693, 774
rotate gesture, 20, 774
rotating monitor display, 624
routers, 504, 774
rows, navigating with VoiceOver feature, 152
Roxio Retrospect utility, 233
Roxio Toast 11 Pro utility, 289, 327
Roxio Toast 11 Titanium utility, 327
RSI (repetitive strain injury), 163
RSS (Really Simple Syndication) feeds, 402, 417–419, 462
rules, Mail, 441–442, 461
Run button, AppleScript Editor, 258

S

Safari application icon, 36
Safari browser
    changing default search engine, 406
    controls
        interface, 410
        navigation buttons, 406–407
        overview, 396, 398
        sharing, 409–410
        specialty, 410–411
        tabbed panes, 407–409
        views, 409
        windows, 407–409
    navigating web with
        bookmarks, 399, 401–403
        history, 404–406
        hyperlinks, 397–399
        Reading List, 403–404
    new features of, 715–716
    overview, 299, 395–397
    passwords for, 573
    preferences dialog box
        accessing, 411
        Advanced pane, 415

        Appearance pane, 414–415
        AutoFill pane, 417
        Bookmarks pane, 416
        Extensions pane, 418
        General pane, 412–413
        Privacy pane, 414
        RSS pane, 417–418
        Security pane, 413
        Tabs pane, 416
    RSS, 418–419
    setting preferences, 411–418
Salling Media Sync utility, 329
Samba, 774
sandboxing, 585, 713, 774
Sandvox, 541
Save As dialog box, 222–224
saving
    documents
        copies, 225
        older, 227–228
        overview, 222–223
        using Save As dialog box, 223–224
        Versions capability, 225–227
    downloaded files, 413
    e-mail messages, 460
    scripts, 263–264
    web pages as files, 410
Scale effect, 46, 774
scanning
    adding scanners, 674–677
    configuring scanners, 679–680
    new features of, 723–724
    options for, 635
    overview, 673–674, 684–686
    sharing scanners, 528, 537, 677
SCEP (Simple Certificate Enrollment Protocol), 553
screen capture, 307, 327–328
Screen Recording dialog box, QuickTime Player, 355
screen savers, 612–614, 774
screen sharing, 467–468, 526–527, 529, 535–537, 722
screencast files, exporting, 355
script applets, 774
Script Debugger, 256
Script menu, 30, 274
script recording, 255, 774
script window, AppleScript Editor, 257–258
scriptable applications, 257, 774
scripting additions, 256, 774

Index

scripts. *See also* AppleScript
    defined, 255, 774
    modifying existing, 269
scroll bars
    defined, 775
    options for, 615
    windows, 83–85
scroll gesture, 19, 775
scroll thumb, 775
scroll track, 84, 706, 775
scrolling
    automatic, 751
    defined, 774–775
    with mouse, 711
    options for, 632–633
    with trackpad, 637, 639, 711
scrolling list, 775
scrubbing, 775
Search box
    Safari, 396, 406–407
    toolbar, Finder windows, 62
search engines, setting default, 406, 412
search path, 775
searching. *See also* Spotlight
    for changes in Time Machine, 243
    Help Center, 140–141
Searching services, 249
secondary clicks, 633, 638
Secure FTP (SFTP), 775
Secure Shell (SSH), 543, 558, 739, 777
Secure Socket Layer (SSL) authentication, 427–428, 434,
        544, 777
security
    encryption, 577–579
    iChat, 464
    location information, 579–580
    Mac OS X installation, 699
    malware, 583–586
    network attacks, 580–583
    new features of, 721–722
    overview, 565
    passwords
        for applications, 573–574
        enforcing use of, 570–572
        Keychain Access, 574–577
        preventing startup from other disks, 572–573
        user account, 568–570
    vulnerabilities
        environment, 568
        files, 567–568
        Macs, 566–567
        personal data, 567
Security & Privacy system preference,
        570–572, 621, 721
security cables, 566
security certificates, 397
Security icon button, Safari, 397, 399
security utilities, 329–330
selecting
    multiple items, 89–90
    single items, 88–89
selection rectangles (marquees), 17, 766, 775
Self-Monitoring Analysis and Reporting Technology
        (S.M.A.R.T.) information, 128
sending e-mail messages, 460
Server Admin tool, 556–559
Server application
    enabling and configuring services, 548–549
    groups, 545–548
    Mac server setup, 543–545
    monitoring status, 549–550
    overview, 541–543
    users, 545–548
Server Message Block (SMB) protocol, 376–379, 776
servers, defined, 775
Service Set Identifier (SSID), 512, 777
services
    availability of, 245–246
    changing preferences, 250–251
    defined, 284, 775
    Development, 247
    Files and Folders, 247
    Internet, 248
    Messaging, 248
    overview, 245–246
    Pictures, 248–249
    Searching, 249
    Text, 249–250
settings sheets, 62, 200–201, 775
SFTP (Secure FTP), 775
shared folders, 775
Shared section, Sidebar, Finder windows, 65
SharePoint, 375–376
shareware, 775

Index

sharing
- documents, 229–230
- faxes, 677
- files
  - with AirDrop, 533–534
  - with Bluetooth, 533
  - enabling, 526–531
  - with other Macs, 531–532
  - overview, 525–538
  - in Parallels Desktop utility, 387
- folders with guest account, 596
- music and videos, 334–335, 348, 360
- printers, 635, 677
- programs through events messages, 274–276
- scanners, 677
- screen sharing, 467–468, 526–527, 529, 535–537, 722
- via iChat, 467–468
- web pages, 409–410
- web sharing, 528, 537
- with Windows PCs
  - connecting directly, 376–378
  - letting Windows users connect directly to Macs, 378–380
  - overview, 371
  - through servers, 375–376
  - via e-mail, 380–381
  - via FTP, 381
  - via web services, 381

Sharing & Permissions section, Info window, 72–73
Sharing system preference, 525–531, 645–646
sharing-only user accounts, 594–595
shell, defined, 775
Shift key, 15, 775
showing
- application windows, 40
- file extensions, 88, 373
- Sidebar in Finder windows, 61
- system preferences, 610
- title bar in windows, 82
- toolbar in Finder windows, 61

shuffling music, 343
Shut Down button, 7
shutting down (turning off) Macs, 9–10, 206–207
Sidebar, Finder windows
- defined, 775
- hiding/showing, 61
- overview, 58, 64–66

signatures
- digital, 756
- e-mail, 440–441, 443, 459
Simple Certificate Enrollment Protocol (SCEP), 553
Simple Finder, 599–600
Simple Mail Transfer Protocol (SMTP), 426, 428, 776
single-user mode, 4, 775
Sites folder, 107, 540
64-bit kernel, 729
sizing
- cursor, 161
- Dock, 43
- windows, 85, 708
Ski Resort widget, 316–317
Skype utility, 329
Sleep button, 7
sleep mode
- defined, 775–776
- options for, 626–628
- overview, 8–9
- setting preferences for, 9
- waking up from, 4
sliders
- defined, 203–204, 776
- scroll bar, 84
- VoiceOver feature, 151–152
slideshow viewer, Quick Look facility, 101–102
slots, defined, 776
slow keys, 158, 159, 776
S.M.A.R.T. (Self-Monitoring Analysis and Reporting Technology) information, 128
smart folders, 101–103, 776
Smart FTP Home utility, 381
smart groups
- iCal, 474
- VoiceOver feature, 152
smart mailboxes, Mail, 446–448, 776
smart playlists, 341, 776
Smart Quotes feature, 618
smartphones, syncing, 497
SMB (Server Message Block) protocol, 376–379, 776
smb prefix, 376–377
Smith Micro StuffIt utility, 326, 750, 777
SMP (symmetric multi-processing), 730, 778
SMTP (Simple Mail Transfer Protocol), 426, 428, 776
Snapz Pro X utility, 327
software, defined, 188, 776

Index

Software Update system preference, 647–648
Software Update utility, 555, 583, 690
solid-state disks/drives (SSDs), 122, 374, 777
solutions, defined, 188
Soonr utility, 369–370
sorting
    e-mail messages, 451
    folder items, 42
    iCal reminders, 485
    window items, 55
Sound system preference, 32, 636–637, 711–712
soundtracks, 776
Space Flexible Space control, toolbar,
            Finder windows, 64
Spaces application
    defined, 776
    overview, 46–50
    preferences for, 620–621
Spaces application icon, 37
Spaces icon menu, 33
special characters
    accessing using Character Viewer, 668–672
    accessing using keyboard shortcuts, 665–668
    accessing using Keyboard Viewer, 668–671
    shell, 739–740
Speech Commands window
    active commands, 168
    overview, 167–168
Speech Feedback window
    controls, 166–167
    minimizing, 167
    overview, 166
speech recognition
    adjusting settings
        Calibrate button, 164–165
        Change Key button, 165
        Listening Method options, 165
        Microphone pop-up menu, 164
        Upon Recognition options, 165
    configuring, 163–164
    Speech Commands window
        active commands, 168
        overview, 167–168
    Speech Feedback window
        controls, 166–167
        minimizing, 167
        overview, 166

Text to Speech options
    Announce When Alerts Are Displayed option, 170
    Announce When Application Requires Your
            Attention option, 170
    Open Date & Time Preferences button, 171
    Open Universal Access Preferences button, 171
    overview, 168–169
    Speak Selected Text When Key Is Pressed
            option, 170
    using microphone, 163
Speech system preference
    new features of, 724–725
    overview, 648–651
    Speech Recognition pane
        adjusting settings, 164–165
        Calibrate button, 164–165
        Change Key button, 165
        configuring, 163–164
        Listening Method options, 165
        Microphone pop-up menu, 164
        overview, 162–164
        Speech Commands window, 167–168
        Speech Feedback window, 166–167
        Text to Speech options, 168–171
        Upon Recognition options, 165
        using microphone, 163
    Text to Speech pane
        Announce When Alerts Are Displayed option, 170
        Announce When Application Requires Your
                Attention option, 170
        Open Date & Time Preferences button, 171
        Open Universal Access Preferences button, 171
        overview, 168–169
        Speak Selected Text When Key Is Pressed
                option, 170
spell checker
    Mail, 438, 458–459
    options for, 617
splat, 776
split cursor, 619
spooling, 682–683, 776
Spotlight
    Boolean operators, 118–119
    creating smart folders, 102–103
    defined, 777
    function of, 110–112
    opening applications from, 193, 212

overview, 109–110
search results, 119
using
    with applications, 119–120
    from Finder windows, 115–118
    from menu bar, 112–114
    within Open dialog box, 215
    within Save As dialog box, 224
Spotlight Comments section, Info window, 98
Spotlight icon, menu bar, 33
Spotlight Store, 110
Spotlight system preference, 621–622
spring-loaded folders, 75, 90
SSDs (solid-state disks/drives), 122, 374, 777
SSH (Secure Shell), 543, 558, 739, 777
SSID (Service Set Identifier), 512, 777
SSL (Secure Socket Layer) authentication, 427–428, 434,
    544, 777
stacks, 41–42, 777
standard input (STDIN), 746–747, 777
standard output (STDOUT), 746–747, 777
standard user accounts, 594–595, 597
starting Macs, 3–4
startup (boot) process
    automatic startup list, 39, 591–592
    defined, 752
    new features of, 704
    overview, 3
    problems with, 4
Startup Disk system preference, 651–652
startup disks
    choosing, 4–5
    creating additional, 127
    defined, 777
    installing Mac OS X on, 691
    preventing startup from other disks, 572–573
    using Windows via Boot Camp, 385
static IP addresses, 520, 548, 777
status bar
    defined, 777
    Finder windows, 59
    windows, 85
stepper controls (little arrows), 203–204, 765, 777
Stickies application, 299
Stickies widget, 317
sticky keys, 157–158, 777
Stocks widget, 317

Stop button, AppleScript Editor, 258
streaming media, defined, 777
striping, 131, 135
stuffed files, 777
StuffIt utility, 326, 750, 777
style sheets, 415
submenus, 23–24, 777
subnet masks, 511, 777
subpanes, 201–202
subscribing to calendars, 485–486
subtitles, 346
SugarSync utility, 326, 369–370
Suitcase Fusion utility, 326
suites, defined, 778
SuperDrives, 5, 52–53, 122, 125, 778
SuperDuper, 234
superusers, 745–746
swipe gesture, 20, 778
switches (access points), 504, 778
switching
    among applications, 197–198
    among documents, 220–221
    among user accounts, 597
    Fast User Switching, 33, 593, 597
Symantec Norton Internet Security for Mac, 584
symbol and text substitution, 617
symbolic links, 778
symmetric multi-processing (SMP), 730, 778
synchronizing
    iTunes with iPods, iPads, and iPhones, 339–340
    Macs and iOS devices via cloud storage services,
        369–370
    Macs and iOS devices via iCloud
        content and apps purchased from online stores,
            362–364
        documents and other information, 364–369
        overview, 331, 339, 361–362
    Macs and iOS devices via iTunes on Mac
        Apps pane, 359–360
        Books pane, 361
        Info pane, 358–359
        overview, 357–358
        Preferences for iOS devices, 361
    Mail, 448
    overview, 357
    preventing, 340
system administrators, 778

Index

System folder, 105–106, 778
System Image Utility tool, 560–562
System Information utility, 311–312, 715
System Preferences application
    accessing, 5, 609, 611
    hardware preferences
        CDs & DVDs, 622–623
        Displays, 32, 623–625, 710
        Energy Saver, 32, 555, 625–628, 710
        FibreChannel, 628
        Ink, 628–629
        Keyboard, 32, 250–251, 629–631
        Mouse, 631–634, 711
        Print & Scan, 634–636, 674–680, 723
        Sound, 32, 636–637, 711–712
        Trackpad, 18–19, 637–640, 711
        Xsan, 640
    Internet and wireless preferences
        Bluetooth, 33, 640–644
        Mail, Contacts & Calendars, 364, 366, 644–645,
            709–710
        Network, 31, 507–516, 518–521, 645, 722
        Sharing, 525–531, 645–646
    overview, 299, 609–611, 709
    personal preferences
        Desktop & Screen Saver, 22, 611–614, 709
        Dock, 39, 42–46, 614, 710
        General, 614–616, 710
        Language & Text, 32, 616–619, 710
        Mission Control, 620–621, 711
        Security & Privacy, 570–572, 621, 721
        Spotlight, 621–622
        Universal Access, 31, 147–162, 622, 780
    system preferences
        Date & Time, 32, 646–647
        Parental Controls, 598–606, 647
        Profiles, 647, 711
        Software Update, 647–648
        Speech, 162–171, 648–651, 724–725
        Startup Disk, 651–652
        Time Machine, 228, 236–239, 652, 712
        Users & Groups, 33, 568–570, 588–594, 598–606,
            652, 720–721
System Preferences application icon, 37
System Profiler utility, 312
system requirements, 689–690
system software, defined, 778

T

Tab key, 16
tabbed panes. *See* panes
tabbed windows, 86
tablets
    handwriting recognition, 619
    options for, 628–629
    syncing, 497
tap gesture, 19, 778
tape drives, 232
tasks, defined, 778
TCP/IP (Transmission Control Protocol/Internet
    Protocol), 509, 778
TechTool Pro utility, 4, 326
Telestream Flip4Mac utility, 327, 332, 372
Telestream WMV Player Pro utility, 372
television, playing DVDs to, 289. *See also* videos
Telnet, 778
templates
    Address Book, 477–478
    defined, 778
    stationery pads
        creating, 217
        creating documents with, 217
        defined, 777
        saving, 224
Terminal utility
    command prompt, 738–739
    defined, 778
    man pages, 137, 144–145, 250, 741–742, 766
    multiple sessions, 737–738
    overview, 313, 736–737
    remote access, 739
    scripting shell, 740–741
    special characters, 739–740
text behavior, 778
text entry utilities, 330
text fields, VoiceOver, 152
Text services
    Add to iTunes as a Spoken Track, 249
    Convert Selected Simplified Chinese File, 249
    Convert Selected Simplified Chinese Text, 249
    Convert Selected Traditional Chinese File, 249
    Convert Selected Traditional Chinese Text, 249
    Create Collection from Text, 249
    Create Font Library from Text, 249
    Make New Sticky Note, 250

New TextEdit Window Containing Selection, 250
Open Man Page in Terminal, 250
Search Man Pages in Terminal, 250
Show Address in Google Maps, 250
Summarize, 250
TextEdit application, 299–301
TextExpander utility, 330
Thawte, 544
threads, defined, 778–779
3G
defined, 779
Internet connection devices, 517
syncing through, 363
three-finger double-tap gesture, 20–21
three-finger swipe gesture, 21
thumbs
scroll, 779
slider, 779
Thunderbird, 573
Thunderbolt connections, 122, 779
Tile Game widget, 318
Timbuktu Pro utility, 327
Time Capsule device, 237, 240–241, 779
Time icon, menu bar, 32
Time Machine application
accessing, 31
configuring in Server application, 549
defined, 779
overview, 231–235, 302
recovering Mac OS X Lion from, 702
restoring files
exiting Time Machine browser, 243–244
overview, 241–243
searching for changes, 243
using Time Machine browser, 242–243
setting up
choosing backup disk, 237–238
choosing exclusions and options, 238–239
configuring, 236–237
using external disks, 235–236
using with applications, 244
using with Time Capsule, 240–241
Time Machine application icon, 37
Time Machine Error dialog box, 238
Time Machine icon, menu bar, 31
Time Machine system preference, 228, 236–239, 652, 712
time zone, setting, 481, 487, 646–647, 699

title bar
defined, 779
Finder windows, 58, 60–61
windows, 82–83, 85–86
Toast 11 Pro utility, 289, 327
Toast 11 Titanium utility, 327
to-do items (reminders), iCal, 113, 484–485
toolbar
application, 199
defined, 779
Finder windows
customizing, 62–64
hiding/showing, 61
overview, 58
Safari, 408
tools, defined, 188
Top Sites view, Safari, 402–403, 405
touchpads. See trackpads
tracked changes capability, 227
tracking, 779
tracking speed, mouse, 631–632, 779
Trackpad system preference, 18–19, 637–640, 711
trackpads (touchpads)
behavior settings, 161–162
defined, 779
handwriting, 669, 779
overview, 18–21
tracks, defined, 779
Translation widget, 318
translators, 779
TransMac utility, 375
Transmission Control Protocol/Internet Protocol (TCP/IP), 509, 778
Transmit utility, 329
Trash folder
defined, 779
deleting items, 92–93
moving deleted e-mail messages to, 433
removing applications, 191–192
retrieving items from, 38
Trash folder icon, 37
Trojan horses, 329–330, 568, 584, 780
TrueType fonts, 374, 655–656, 780
turning off (shutting down) Macs, 9–10, 206–207
two-finger double-tap gesture, 20–21
two-finger scroll gesture, 20
typefaces. See fonts

U

UCS (Universal Character Set), 780
UDF (Universal Disk Format), 123, 780
UFS (Unix File System), 780
unavailable status, 97
Undo command, 92
Unicode, 780
Uniform Resource Locators (URLs), defined, 780
Unit Converter widget, 318–319
Universal Access icon, menu bar, 31
Universal Access system preference
    defined, 780
    Hearing pane, 156–157
    Keyboard pane
        slow keys, 159
        sticky keys, 157–158
    Mouse & Trackpad pane
        adjusting behavior, 161–162
        hot spots, 162
        mouse keys, 160–161
        overview, 159–160
        seeing pointer, 161
    overview, 31, 147–148, 622
    Seeing pane
        display options, 156
        VoiceOver, 148–153
        zoom options, 153–155
universal binary, 780
Universal Character Set (UCS), 780
Universal Disk Format (UDF), 123, 780
Universal Type Server, 663
Unix
    booting into, 4
    commands
        disk and file system statistics, 744–745
        file and directory management, 742–744
        file and folder permissions, 744
        logging in as different user or as superuser, 745–746
        man pages, 741–742
        overview, 741
        pipes, 746–747
        standard input and output, 583
    defined, 780
    overview, 725, 735–736, 738
    Terminal
        command prompt, 738–739
        multiple sessions, 737–738
        overview, 736–737
        remote access, 739
        scripting shell, 740–741
        special characters, 739–740
    X11 utility, 747–748
Unix File System (UFS), 780
unmounting disks, 127, 780
updating
    applications, 191
    Mac OS X, 583
    Software Update utility, 555, 583, 647–648, 690
upgrading firmware, 690
uploading, defined, 780
URLs (Uniform Resource Locators), defined, 780
USB connections
    backing up to external hard disks, 233
    overview, 122
USB-to-Ethernet adapters, 310, 506
Usenet, 780
user accounts
    adding, 594–595
    administrator accounts, 587, 590, 594–595, 597, 749
    defined, 5, 780
    deleting, 595–596
    groups, 596
    guest accounts, 596, 761
    logging in
        as different user, 745–746
        as superuser, 745–746
    login procedure, 5–7
    managing, 595
    new features of, 720–721
    overview, 587–588
    Parental Controls system preference
        activity logs, 604
        Apps pane, 599–601
        Other pane, 603
        overview, 598–599
        People pane, 601–602
        settings management, 604–606
        Time Limits pane, 602–603
        Web pane, 601
    passwords, 568–570
    personal settings
        login items, 591–592
        login options, 592–594
        password, 589–591
        username, 589–591
    switching among, 597
user groups, 145, 780

User icon, menu bar, 33
user preferences, 781. *See also* System Preferences
        application
usernames
    defined, 781
    incorrect, 6
    Mail, 427–428
    Time Capsule device, 240
    user accounts, 589–591
users
    defined, 780
    managing via configuration profiles, 555–556
    overview, 545–548
Users & Groups system preference
    Login Items pane, 589, 591–592
    Login Options button, 589, 592–594
    new features of, 720–721
    overview, 33, 568–570, 588, 652
    Parental Controls
        activity logs, 604
        Apps pane, 599–601
        Other pane, 603
        overview, 598–599
        People pane, 601–602
        settings management, 604–606
        Time Limits pane, 602–603
        Web pane, 601
    Password pane, 589–591
Users folder, 106
utilities
    defined, 188, 283
    extending Mac OS X with
        application access, 329
        audio management, 324
        battery monitoring, 324
        communications, 329
        conferencing, 325
        disk management, 325
        file synchronization, 325–326
        file transfer, 329
        font management, 326
        media playback and delivery, 327
        remote access, 327
        screen capture, 327–328
        security, 329–330
        text entry, 330
        Wi-Fi monitoring, 328
    overview, 323–324
    preinstalled, 302–313
    unnecessary, 326

Utilities folder
    accessing, 188, 194–195
    defined, 781
    preinstalled utilities in, 302–313

V

values, variable, 265
variables, 265, 781
vCards
    sending as e-mail attachments, 476
    setting preferences, 478
vector images, 781
verbose mode, 4, 781
Verbosity settings, VoiceOver Utility
    Announcements subpane, 173–174
    Braille subpane, 173
    Hints subpane, 174
    Speech subpane, 172–173
    Text subpane, 173
VeriSign, 544
Versions capability, 222, 225–227, 713, 715, 781
video (display) mirroring, 781
video chatting, 465–467
videoconferences, 325. *See also* FaceTime application
videos
    AirPlay, 348
    Apple TV, 348
    DVD Player, 348–351
    Home Sharing capability, 348
    iTunes application
        buying videos, 346
        importing videos, 346
        managing videos, 346–347
        playing videos, 347
        setting preferences, 345–346
    QuickTime Player
        creating video files, 354–355
        editing video files, 354
        exporting video and screencast files, 355
        playing video files, 352–353
View menu
    desktop view settings, 76–77
    folder and disk view settings, 77–79
    overview, 29, 54–56
view mode selectors, toolbar, Finder windows, 62
view modes (list views)
    defined, 62, 765
    Finder windows
        choosing, 66
        column view, 69–70

view modes (list views) *(continued)*
    Cover Flow view, 70–72
    icon view, 66–67
    list view, 67–69
    overview, 76–78
  iTunes application, 339, 346–347
  overview, 66
  selecting multiple items in, 89
virtual machines, 381, 387–392, 781
virtual memory, 572, 721, 731, 781
virtual network computing (VNC), 527–528, 536, 781
virtual private network (VPN) icon, menu bar, 31
virtual private networks (VPNs), 429, 490, 514–515, 549, 553
VirusBarrier utility, 330
viruses, 781
Visualizer, iTunes, 343
VMware Fusion utility, 305, 329, 381, 387–391
VNC (virtual network computing), 527–528, 536, 781
VoiceOver Utility
  Activities pane, 183–184
  Braille pane
    Displays subpane, 182–183
    Layout subpane, 182
    overview, 181
  buttons, 151–152
  check boxes, 151–152
  columns, 152
  Commanders pane
    Keyboard subpane, 180–181
    NumPad subpane, 180
    Quick Nav subpane, 181
    Trackpad subpane, 179–180
  defined, 781
  Dock, 151
  General pane
    Allow VoiceOver to Be Controlled with AppleScript option, 172
    Greeting options, 171–172
    portable preferences, 172
  help resources, 152–153
  keyboard commands, 150
  keyboard help, 150–151
  menu bar, 151
  Navigation pane, 175
  new features of, 724–725
  overview, 148–150, 313
  rows, 152
  sliders, 151–152

smart groups in web pages, 152
Sound Settings pane, 177
Speech pane
  Pronunciation subpane, 174–175
  Voices subpane, 174
text fields, 152
Verbosity settings
  Announcements subpane, 173–174
  Braille subpane, 173
  Hints subpane, 174
  Speech subpane, 172–173
  Text subpane, 173
Visuals pane
  Braille Panel subpane, 178
  Caption Panel subpane, 178
  Menus subpane, 178–179
  Touch subpane, 178
  VoiceOver cursor subpane, 177
Web pane
  Navigation subpane, 176
  Page Loading subpane, 176
  Web Rotor subpane, 176–177
volume control, 32, 157, 343, 636–637
Volume icon, menu bar, 32
volumes
  accessing, 122–123
  defined, 121, 781
  disconnecting disks from, 123–124
  virtual, 122
VPN (virtual private network) icon, menu bar, 31
VPNs (virtual private networks), 429, 490, 514–515, 549, 553

W

waking Macs up from Sleep mode, 9
WANs (wide-area networks), 517, 781
Weather widget, 318
web browsers. *See also* Safari browser
  defined, 781
  limiting access with parental controls, 601
  managing printers via, 677
  reasons for using other, 419–422
  setting default, 412
web clips, 319–321
Web Clips widget, 319, 553
web pages
  defined, 781
  overview, 541
  saving as files, 410

serving from Mac OS X, 540–541

smart groups in, 152

web servers, defined, 782

web sharing, 528, 537

web spots, 177, 782

WebDAV accounts, 290, 326, 369

white points, 782

white space, 782

wide-area networks (WANs), 517, 781

wide-area wireless network (WWAN) icon, menu bar, 31

wide-area wireless networks (WWANs), 31, 782

widgets

Adobe AIR, 329

defined, 283, 782

managing, 314–315

from other sources, 320–321

overview, 313–314

preinstalled, 315–320

Widgets widget, 319–320

Wi-Fi connections

connecting Macs directly, 516

defined, 645, 782

setting up Macs for, 512–513

Wi-Fi icon, menu bar, 31

Wi-Fi monitoring utilities, 328

Wi-Fi Protected Access (WPA), 782

wikis, 549

wildcards, 739, 741, 743, 782

Window menu, 29–30, 58

windows. *See also* Finder windows

active and inactive, 85–86

controls

scroll bar, 83–85

status bar, 85

title bar, 82–83

new features of

navigating, 705

sizing, 708

sizing, 85

switching between, 86

Windows integration. *See* Microsoft Windows integration

Windows Phone 7 devices, 497

Windows Phone 7 utilities, 329

Windows storage media, 374–375

wired connections, 506

wireless connections, 506–507

WMV Player Pro utility, 372

Word, 574

Word Break feature, 617–618

workflows, 274–279, 286, 782

Workgroup Manager tool, 559–561

World Clock widget, 320

worms, 584, 782

WPA (Wi-Fi Protected Access), 782

write-protect, 782

writing e-mail messages

addressing, 457

controls, 459–460

overview, 455–457

setting preferences, 438–441

text entry, 457–459

WS_ FTP Pro utility, 381

WWAN (wide-area wireless network) icon, menu bar, 31

WWANs (wide-area wireless networks), 31, 782

X

X11 utility, 313, 734, 747–748, 782

Xgrid, 530, 782

XNU kernel, 728–729, 782

Xsan system preference, 640

Y

Yuuguu utility, 325

Z

Zip disks, 232

Zip files

compressing items into, 96

defined, 782

extracting contents of, 96

installing downloaded applications, 190

utilities for, 326

Zoom button, windows, 83

zoom screen gesture, 20

zooming

with mouse, 633

Safari, 409

Seeing pane, Universal Access system preference

Maximum Zoom and Minimum Zoom sliders, 153

Show Preview Rectangle When Zoomed Out option, 154

Smooth Images option, 154–155

Use Scroll Wheel with Modifier Keys to Zoom option, 155

When Zoomed In, Screen Image Moves options, 155

Zoom Follows Keyboard Focus option, 155

with trackpad, 638–639

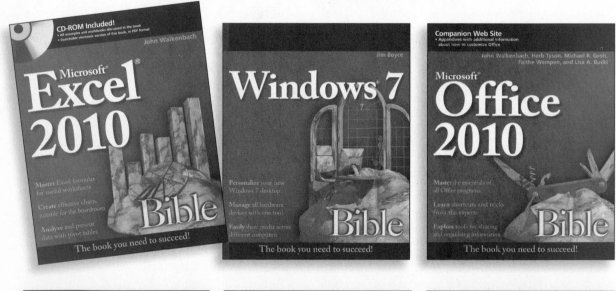